## Financial Accounting Standards Board (FASB) (1973 to pr...

### Statements of Financial Accounting Standards
**SFAS No.**

### Statements of Financial Accounting Concepts (SFAC)
**SFAC No.**

(There are over 40 FASB *Interpretations* of the above ARB and ATB *Bulletins*, APB *Opinions*, and FASB *Statements*.)

# Intermediate

# Accounting:

## Concepts,

## Methods, and

## Uses

**Third Edition**

**Sidney Davidson,** Ph.D., CPA
*University of Chicago*

**Clyde P. Stickney,** D.B.A., CPA
*Dartmouth College*

**Roman L. Weil,** Ph.D., CPA, CMA
*University of Chicago*

**The Dryden Press**
*Chicago · New York · Philadelphia*
*San Francisco · Montreal · Toronto*
*London · Sydney · Tokyo · Mexico City*
*Rio de Janeiro · Madrid*

Acquisitions Editor: James Walsh
Developmental Editor: Susan Layton
Project Editor: B. L. Weber
Production Manager: Mary Jarvis
Design Director: Alan Wendt
Cover Designers: Harry Voigt, William Seabright
Text Designer: Harry Voigt
Indexers: Shirley Moore, Naples Editing Service and Cherie Worman

Address orders to:
383 Madison Avenue
New York, New York 10071

Address editorial correspondence to:
One Salt Creek Lane
Hinsdale, Illinois 60521

Library of Congress Catalog Card Number: 80-65795
ISBN: 0-03-058916-9
Printed in the United States of America
 23 144 98765432

CBS College Publishing
The Dryden Press
Holt, Rinehart and Winston
Saunders College Publishing

## The Dryden Press
## Series in Accounting

Belkaoui
COST ACCOUNTING: A MULTIDIMENSIONAL EMPHASIS

Davidson/Stickney/Weil
FINANCIAL ACCOUNTING, 3rd edition

Davidson/Stickney/Weil
INTERMEDIATE ACCOUNTING, 3rd edition

Davidson/Schindler/Stickney/Weil
MANAGERIAL ACCOUNTING

Huefner/Largay
ADVANCED FINANCIAL ACCOUNTING

Mueller/Smith
ACCOUNTING: A BOOK OF READINGS

Person/Wolinsky
THE PERSON/WOLINSKY CPA EXAM SUPPLEMENT FOR:
    AUDITING/BUSINESS LAW/COST ACCOUNTING/FEDERAL
    INCOME TAX/FINANCIAL ACCOUNTING/INTERMEDIATE ACCOUNTING

Reynolds/Slavin/Sanders
ELEMENTARY ACCOUNTING, 2nd edition

Slavin/Reynolds/Sanders
FINANCIAL ACCOUNTING: A BASIC APPROACH

Titard
MANAGERIAL ACCOUNTING: AN INTRODUCTION

For our families

*Whatever be the detail with which you cram your students, the chance of their meeting in after life exactly that detail is almost infinitesimal; and if they do meet it, they will probably have forgotten what you taught them about it. The really useful training yields a comprehension of a few general principles with a thorough grounding in the way they apply to a variety of concrete details. In subsequent practice the students will have forgotten your particular details; but they will remember by an unconscious common sense how to apply principles to immediate circumstances.*

**Alfred North Whitehead**
The Aims of Education and Other Essays

# Preface

*Intermediate Accounting* covers standard topics, but differs from other textbooks in both approach and revision strategy.

## Approach

The subtitle should more appropriately read: *Economic Events, Accounting Concepts, Accounting Methods, and Uses*. This sequence summarizes our approach to the topics covered in this text.

For students to understand the accounting for an event, they must understand the event itself. That is, they must understand the economic reasons for and consequences of specific business transactions before they can grasp the logic behind the specific accounting procedures followed. For example, the accounting for leases is more easily understood if lease transactions are compared and contrasted with installment purchases and sales of assets. The measurement of pension cost becomes clearer when one understands how the benefit formula, actuarial assumptions, and funding pattern affect the total amount of cash that must be paid by the employer to the pension fund. The logic behind the detailed rules relating to the calculation of earnings per share is more easily understood if one grasps why dilution is of concern and how it can occur. This approach requires that more time be spent introducing the transaction. This is time well spent, however, when students can learn more quickly the specific accounting procedures followed and retain them.

Second, we place emphasis on the accounting concepts that link economic events with specific accounting methods or procedures. Given the numerous and seemingly diverse set of topics covered in intermediate accounting principles courses, students sometimes fail to see the common threads that underlie the various topics. These common threads are the underlying concepts of accounting. An understanding of these concepts not only helps students grasp current accounting rules but should equip them to adapt to changes in these rules as they occur in the future.

Two common conceptual themes run throughout this book. First, there is a link between the valuation of assets and liabilities on the balance sheet and the measurement of revenues and expenses on the income statement. Valuing assets such as land at historical cost means that changes in the market value of the land while it is held will not be recognized as income. On the other hand, valuing assets such as marketable securities and inventories at lower-of-cost or market means that decreases in market value are reflected in income while the assets are held. This linking of asset and liability valuation with income measurement permits students to understand more easily alternative accounting methods. For example, the differences between the percentage-of-completion and completed-contract methods for long-term contracts, the point-of-sale versus installment methods for sales made on a deferred payment basis, and the successful-efforts versus full-costing methods for natural resource activities are more easily understood if one considers the effects on both the balance sheet and the income statement.

A second common conceptual theme is that *total* revenues from an operating transaction equals cash in, *total* expenses equals cash out, *and* net income equals cash in minus cash out. Accrual accounting simply allocates these totals and net amounts to the accounting periods affected. Given the emphasis of current accounting practice on the accrual rather than the cash basis of accounting, students often lose sight of the fact that inflows and outflows of cash dictate the *amount* of revenues, expenses, and net income. Accrual accounting merely dictates its *timing* of recognition. Thus, the total effect on net income of a lease over its life is identical regardless of whether the operating or capital lease method is used. Only the timing of expense recognition differs. Likewise, the total amount of pension cost to be recognized as an expense by the employer over the life of a pension plan is equal to the cash paid to the pension fund. Accounting procedures dictate how this total amount is allocated to various periods as an expense.

While we feel it is important that students understand the economics behind various business transactions and grasp underlying accounting concepts, this book gives equal emphasis to accounting methods and procedures. One does not thoroughly understand a business transaction and its related accounting concepts until one can construct the journal entry for recording it and analyze its effects on the financial statements. Consequently, this book is filled with analyses of business transactions and the required journal entries.

While we do not slight the *how,* neither do we paraphrase large portions of APB *Opinions* and FASB *Statements.* We attempt to equip students to read the original pronouncements for themselves. The serious accounting student will want to have his or her own copy of the *Current Pronouncements.*

Finally, we relate the accounting measurements made with the disclosure of these measurements in the financial statements. Accountants have been criticized for placing too much emphasis on the accounting procedures and not enough on the *communication* of these measurements to the users of financial statements. Appendix A presents a detailed set of financial statements and notes for International Corporation. These financial statements are adapted from the actual financial statements of Westinghouse Corporation. As particular topics are covered throughout the book, the relevant aspects of the financial statements and notes from Appendix A are integrated into the discussion.

Various textbooks place varying degrees of emphasis on economic transactions, concepts, methods, and uses. The manner in which we balance and integrate these four dimensions is based on our experience in teaching the intermediate principles course. As with our students, however, we continue to learn and to adapt and welcome your comments and suggestions regarding this balance.

## Revision Strategy

When the first edition of Intermediate Accounting was published in 1980, we indicated that the book would be revised annually. The intention was to provide the most up-to-date book possible each year. The current edition is the third such annual edition.

It has become clear, however, that the pace of new pronouncements in any particular year may not justify the costs of a new edition. These costs include not only production costs but costs borne by instructors in updating their courses. Consequently, the revision cycle in future years will be related more directly to the pace of new pronouncements. In some years, this will mean an annual edition, but in other cases the revisions will be less frequent.

## Major Changes in This Edition

**1.** Chapter 7 incorporates the provisions on sales returns from *Statement No. 48.*

**2.** Chapter 9 discusses LIFO conformity and the new Insilco decision.

**3.** Chapter 10 presents an expanded numerical illustration of conventional, FIFO, LIFO, and dollar-value LIFO retail inventory methods.

**4.** Chapter 12 has been substantially revised to incorporate changes in tax depreciation brought about by the Economic Recovery Tax Act of 1981. The new Accelerated Cost Recovery System is described and illustrated and contrasted with depreciation computed for financial reporting.

**5.** Chapter 20 is on income taxes and likewise it has been substantially revised to incorporate changes brought about by the Economic Recovery Tax Act of 1981. The impact of the Act on the measurement of deferred taxes and investment credits is considered. New material has been added on accounting for the purchase and sale of tax benefits.

**6.** Less important SEC and FASB pronouncements have also been integrated where appropriate. In addition, questions and problems from recent CPA examinations have been added.

## A Closer Look

In the event that you have not previously used *Intermediate Accounting,* we would like to point out several unique aspects of the book.

**1.** Chapter 4 presents an early introduction to the statement of changes in financial position. The discussion is kept at a basic level so that students can grasp the general relationship between income flows and cash flows. Then, as various topics are discussed in succeeding chapters, the funds-flow effects are also considered. Chapter 24 presents a synthesis of the statement of changes in financial position.

**2.** Chapter 5 presents the general principles of asset valuation and income measurement. Various asset valuation methods are discussed and the implications for income measurement illustrated. These general principles underlie the specific accounting procedures discussed in Chapters 6–14.

**3.** Chapters 7 and 8 present an integrated discussion of revenue recognition, emphasizing the conditions when revenue is recognized prior to sale, at the time of sale, and subsequent to the time of sale. By placing the material on revenue recognition in one place, rather than scattering it throughout the book, the student can more easily grasp the common underlying principles.

**4.** Chapter 9 and 10 link together quantity-based and dollar-value LIFO. It is shown that the two methods are identical except for the "unit" that gets counted. Likewise, Chapter 10 links the gross profit and retail methods for inventory, showing their common theme.

**5.** Chapter 15 presents a discussion of the principles of liability valuation and income measurement, analogous to Chapter 5 for assets. These general principles underlie the specific procedures discussed in Chapters 16–20.

**6.** Chapter 18 compares and contrasts a lease with an installment purchase of an asset to motivate understanding of the operating and capital lease methods. It also shows why lease accounting problems have been difficult to resolve by extending Chapter 15's discussion of accounting for executory contracts.

**7.** Chapter 19 is on pensions and distinguishes the roles of the employer (plan sponsor) and the pension fund. The manner in which the benefit formula, actuarial assumptions, and funding pattern affect the total amount of cash required to be paid by the employer to the fund is distinguished from the accounting recognition of that total as pension expense over the life of the pension plan.

**8.** Chapter 23 presents a discussion of accounting changes showing that the effects of such changes could be reflected retroactively, currently, or prospectively. Arguments for each of these three are given, and actual practice is fitted into the framework.

**9.** Each chapter contains questions, exercises, and problems. These vary in difficulty from questions merely requiring reference to the text for an answer to complex CPA problems. The quantity and variety of such questions, exercises, and problems should permit the instructor to design a course for the particular type of students encountered. Note should be made of the short mind-expanding cases based on AICPA *Technical Practice Aids*. These cases illustrate the judgments required of professional accountants. See, for example, questions 8.20, 10.7, 10.9, 20.5, and 20.29.

## Instructional Aids

An instructor's manual is provided to users of *Intermediate Accounting*. The first section of the instructor's manual contains a suggested course outline, a list of check figures for various exercises and problems in the text, and a set of notes and comments for each chapter. The notes and comments include, by chapter, a list of learning objectives, comments about the structuring of class sessions for coverage of the chapter, and detailed class teaching notes. Also included is a set of estimated times and principal learning objectives for each question, short cases, exercise, and problem. The second section of the instructor's manual contains suggested solutions to all assignment material. These suggested solutions have been constructed so that supporting computations are clearly shown.

A set of Transparency Masters is available to users of *Intermediate Accounting*. Masters are provided for important exhibits and figures in the text as well as solutions to numerous exercises and problems at the end of each chapter.

A Test Bank, prepared by Professor Albert W. Wright of California State University, Northridge, is also available; it contains over 1,000 objective and problem-type questions.

Student supplements to *Intermediate Accounting* include a Study Guide, also prepared by Professor Albert W. Wright, and a booklet containing multiple choice CPA Examination questions. More detailed descriptions of these items appear in the **To The Student** section of the preface.

## To The Student

Though *Intermediate Accounting* is virtually self-contained, four supplements are available to aid your study of the text in particular and accounting in general:

**1. Study Guide.** Professor Albert W. Wright of California State University, Northridge, has prepared a comprehensive Study Guide to accompany *Intermediate Accounting*. The Study Guide provides a chapter-by-chapter review of key accounting concepts, principles, and procedures as well as a comprehensive self-test for each chapter to reinforce students' understanding. By taking each chapter's self-test in the Study Guide, you can get immediate feedback on your understanding of the text material. Ask your instructor or your bookstore to order copies from the publisher, The Dryden Press.

**2.** *CPA Examination Questions*. This supplement, prepared by Samuel Person and Daniel Wolinsky, contains multiple-choice questions from the most recent CPA Examinations, which have been reorganized into chapters corresponding to those in *Intermediate Accounting*. Ask your instructor or bookstore to order copies from the publisher, The Dryden Press.

**3. Accounting: The Language of Business.** This paperbook presents a 60-page glossary of accounting terms as well as several annotated financial statements of real companies (General Electric and Penn Central) similar in style to Appendix A but more detailed. You or your bookstore can order copies from the publisher: Thomas Horton & Daughters, 26662 S. Newtown Drive, Sun Lake, Arizona 85224.

**4. Financial Accounting Standards: Original Pronouncements and Accounting: Current Text.** The original pronouncements of the Committee on Accounting Procedure, the Accounting Principles Board, and the Financial Accounting Standards Board are annually compiled into paperback books published for the Financial Accounting Standards Board and the AICPA by Commerce Clearing House. The first of these books is organized by pronouncement, while the second is organized by subject matter and includes an index. You need not own both books, and your instructor may prefer that you use one rather than the other; find out before you buy. Because *Intermediate Accounting* does not attempt to cover esoteric detail, the serious student will want to own a copy of the original rules and learn how to use it. Both practicing accountants and financial analysts should be comfortable with the form in which original pronouncements are published and should know how to use them. Your bookstore can order copies from the publisher: Commerce Clearing House.

# Acknowledgments

Many people helped put this book together. They know who they are, and they know we know who they are. Thanks.

Steven A. Allen
Gary C. Biddle
Melanie Brennan
Andrew Butula
Gregory Collins
Joseph J. Cramer, Jr.
Sylvia Dobray
Gere Dominiak
Robert K. Eskew
Flora Foss
Willis Greer
Paul Guttmann
Leon Hanouille
Barbara Haskell
Vivian Hopkins
Carol Inberg
Monroe Ingberman
Mary Jarvis
James A. Largay III

Susan Layton
Richard Leftwich
Robert Libby
A. M. Massa
Shirley Moore
Leonard Morrissey
Richard Murdock
Sandra Myers
John A. Nikander
Hugo Nurnberg
Norman Orrell
Steven L. Ostlund
Sidney Paul
Beverly Peavler
Jane Perkins
D. D. Ray
Blaine A. Ritts
Jordan Roderick
Raymonde Rousselot

Brother Cornelius Russell
Katherine Schipper
Lisa Skelton
Suzanne Sweet
Carl Texter
Arthur L. Thomas
Richard L. Townsend
George Ulseth
Harry Voigt
James Walsh

Brian Link Weber
Alan Wendt
Robert Wennagel
Elizabeth Widdicombe
Gerald F. Wiles
Cherie Worman
Albert W. Wright
Katherine Xenophon-Rybowiak
Miriam Zales

Throughout the writing of this book, we often referred to other popular intermediate accounting texts. We have learned from them. We hope we have improved on them. Whether we have or not, we gratefully acknowledge our debt to these other books.

S.D.
C.P.S.
R.L.W.

# Contents

Chapter 4     *Review of the Accounting Process:
Statement of Changes in Financial Position*

Chapter 8      *Revenue Recognition and Receivables: At Times Other Than Time of Sale*

Chapter 9      *Inventories and Cost of Goods Sold: The Basic Concepts*

Chapter 10    *Inventories and Cost of Goods Sold: Uses and Methods*

*Chapter 13*          ***Amortization of Natural Resources and Intangibles***

## Part Three    Liability Recognition and Related Expenses

Chapter 26     *Accounting for Changing Prices*

## Part Six — Appendices and Tables

*Part One*
## Review of Basic Financial Accounting Concepts and Principles

# Chapter 1
# *Objectives and Environment of Financial Reporting*

1.1 You are about to begin a study of intermediate and advanced financial accounting principles. The material to be covered comprises a large part of the work of the professional accountant. In the course of this study you will learn the technical principles and procedures of financial accounting and you will begin to develop the judgmental skills necessary to apply them in professional practice.

1.2 Before you become immersed in the study of "generally accepted accounting principles," it is appropriate to consider first some broader questions about the objectives and environment of financial reporting. What purposes are served by financial accounting reports? Should the private sector or the public sector, or both, be responsible for establishing accounting principles? Should the accounting principles established be those most consistent with some comprehensive theoretical framework, or merely those acceptable to the largest number of financial statement preparers and users? As will soon become evident, there are no definitive answers to these questions. An understanding of the issues involved will permit you, however, to appreciate the current environment of financial reporting.

## Resource Allocation Decisions and Accounting Information

1.3 You will recall from elementary economics courses that the central economic problem is allocating limited resources among competing, alternative uses. Individuals must decide whether their earnings should be used to purchase consumer goods and services or should be invested in a savings account, stocks, bonds, or real estate. Business firms must decide whether to invest their resources in inventory, plant and equipment, employee training, advertising, research and development, or other alternatives. Governments must decide whether resources should be allocated to defense, highway construction, welfare, space programs, and so on.

1.4 In each of these cases, the decision is made in terms of the *return* anticipated from each alternative and the *risk* associated with that return. Owners of wealth are generally risk averse. That is, they demand a higher return for accepting greater risks. One can place funds in a savings account and be virtually certain of earning 5.5 percent interest each year. Alternatively, one can acquire shares of common stock of General Motors

Corporation. The return from this investment is comprised of dividends plus changes in the market price of the shares while they are held. Future dividends and market price changes are likely to be affected by general economic conditions, such as the level of employment, inflation, and interest rates; industry conditions, such as availability of labor and raw materials; and specific firm factors, such as managerial skills, investment and financing policies, and so on. It is clear that the return anticipated from investing in General Motors Corporation is more uncertain, or risky, than the return from investing in a savings account. In order to induce individuals to invest in shares of common stock, the expected return must be larger than 5.5 percent of the initial investment to compensate for the additional risk involved.

1.5    Different business firms seeking capital offer different levels of return and risk.* The principal role of financial accounting and reporting is offering information to investors and lenders that is useful in assessing returns and risks associated with investment alternatives. The specific ways in which financial statement information is used in assessing return and risk are discussed throughout this book, particularly in the chapter on financial statement analysis. The important point at this stage of the discussion is to understand the general role of accounting information in resource allocation decisions.

## Qualitative Attributes of Accounting Information

1.6    There is little disagreement that accounting information should be useful to decision makers. But what are the characteristics of "useful" accounting information? Throughout this text we consider various procedures for measuring and reporting the effects of a given event or transaction. It will be helpful if we are armed with some standards or criteria for choosing among alternative methods. Six qualitative characteristics of useful accounting information have been suggested by the Financial Accounting Standards Board: (1) relevance to decisions, (2) reliability, (3) consistency and comparability, (4) efficiency, (5) materiality, and (6) understandability.†

## Relevance to Decisions

To be useful, financial statements should provide information that is helpful in answering questions the decision maker faces in making investment decisions. As discussed in the previous section, investment decisions are based on assessments of expected return and risk. It is desirable, therefore, that financial statements provide information useful for confirming prior expectations about return and risk and for forming expectations about future rates of return and risk. To be relevant to a decision, information must be available on a sufficiently timely basis to influence the decision    1.7

There are several practical problems in using relevance as a basis for selecting from among alternative sets of information. One difficulty is determining the types of information needed by various users. The information required by bankers or security analysts is not necessarily the same as that required by small investors. A second difficulty comes in deciding whose needs should count most. Disclosure of information on the profitability of a firm's product lines may be helpful to investors, but at the same time it might reveal information so useful to its competitors that current shareholders would be hurt.    1.8

## Reliability

Reliability relates to the confidence that can be placed in financial statement information. A particular measurement (for example, de-    1.9

---

*Modern financial theory makes a distinction between systematic (market-wide) and nonsystematic (firm-specific) risks. At this stage in our discussion, we make no distinction between these two types of risk.

†Financial Accounting Standards Board, *Statement of Financial Accounting Concepts No. 2.,* "Qualitative Characteristics of Accounting Information" (May 1980).

preciation expense) may be highly relevant to the decision maker but not very reliable because of estimates required in the measurement process. Likewise, a particular measurement may be highly reliable (for example, average shoe size of top executives) but not relevant to a decision. For a measure to be reliable, there must be agreement between the measure and the attribute measured, verifiability, and neutrality.

1.10 **Agreement between Measure and Attribute Measured** Accounting involves the identification of relevant attributes (for example, financial position), the measurement of those attributes (for example, assets, liabilities), and the reporting of the results of the measurements made (as, for example, in a balance sheet). The measures used should accurately represent the attributes being measured. For example, does the practice of recording only those assets acquired through arm's-length transactions result in an accurate measure of the financial resources of a firm? Does the practice of recording only those liabilities for which benefits have been received result in an accurate measure of creditors' claims on the financial resources of a firm? In a sense the measure used takes the place of, or becomes a surrogate for, the attribute being measured. Unless the measure accurately describes the desired attribute, the resulting measurements will not be reliable indicators of the object or item being measured.

1.11 **Verifiability** A second element of reliability is verifiability. Reliability concerns the confidence that can be placed in financial statement information. The level of confidence can be increased if the financial statements have been subject to audit by an independent accountant. An audit may be helpful in reducing bias that the managers of a firm, in their own interests, might have injected into the report. An audit also serves as a check on clerical processing errors that might have occurred.

1.12 **Neutrality** A third element of reliability is neutrality. Neutrality refers to freedom from

bias on the part of accounting standard-setting bodies with respect to the interest of a particular group or individual or to a particular predetermined result. For example, companies involved in leasing buildings and equipment have argued before standard-setting bodies that long-term leases should not be shown on the financial statements as liabilities. If companies involved in leasing were required to show such leases as liabilities, it is argued, they would purchase buildings and equipment rather than lease them, and the leasing industry would be hurt. In deciding the appropriate accounting treatment of long-term leases, standard-setting bodies, according to the neutrality criterion, should be concerned with the relevance and reliability of the resulting information and not with the effect of its standards on any particular industry, group, or individuals.

1.13 Whether standard-setting bodies can or should be neutral with respect to the effects of standards set on particular groups or individuals remains controversial. It has been argued that these bodies must consider the social and economic consequences of their standards if they are to survive as viable standard-setting agencies. Otherwise, the government or some other institution will impose a political resolution to the reporting issue under consideration.*

## Consistency and Comparability

1.14 Information about a firm gains in usefulness if it can be compared with similar information about the same firm in other periods of time and with similar information of other firms. A particular firm may change its methods of accounting over time. During the mid-1970s, many firms switched from a first-in, first-out (FIFO) to a last-in, first-out (LIFO) cost-flow assumption for inventories. The time-series trends in inventories, assets, cost of goods sold, and net income for these firms were based on amounts that were not strictly

---

*For an expanded discussion of this view, see Stephen A. Zeff, "On the Rise of 'Economic Consequences' ": *Journal of Accountancy* 146 (December 1978): 56–63.

comparable because of the change in method. The requirement that independent accountants qualify their opinions for changes in accounting methods is an effort to inform the reader of the financial statements that a firm has not consistently used the same methods of accounting over time.

1.15 Interfirm comparability of information may be affected by the use of different accounting methods. Firms have flexibility in choosing among alternative accounting principles in the case of inventories and cost of goods sold, depreciable assets and depreciation expense, and other areas. Two firms with identical physical inventories or plant assets may report different amounts for these items depending on the inventory cost-flow assumption and depreciation method used. The financial statements of the two firms will therefore not be comparable.

1.16 Another factor affecting interfirm comparability is the requirement that all firms use the same method of accounting in particular circumstances even though their economic situations differ. For example, Financial Accounting Standards Board *Statement No. 2* (October 1974) requires all firms to treat research and development expenditures as an expense in the period in which the costs are incurred. The measurement of the assets of a firm heavily engaged in research will not be comparable with that of a firm that conducts little or no research.

## Efficiency

1.17 When the benefits of information to users exceed the cost of providing it, the information-generating process is said to be *efficient*. In recent years, the Financial Accounting Standards Board, the Securities and Exchange Commission, the New York Stock Exchange, and other agencies have been requiring the disclosure of more and more financial statement data. In most cases, the benefit/cost relationship is not analyzed carefully. This is caused partly by the difficulty of measuring the benefits of additional information. Will the disclosure of sales and earnings by segments of a business result in a better allocation of capital among firms? If so, how do we measure these benefits? Failure to assess the benefit/cost trade-off adequately is also caused by the fact that the cost of generating the information is seldom borne by the agency requiring its disclosure and only occasionally by the individuals using the information. Despite difficulties in measurement, some consideration should be given to the benefit/cost trade-off in decisions to require additional or alternative accounting measurements and disclosures.

## Materiality

1.18 The amount of financial information about a firm that might be disclosed is enormous. In assessing the benefit/cost trade-off, consideration should be given to whether the information is likely to have a significant, or material, impact on decisions. Materiality must be judged not only by the magnitude of a particular item but with regard to the nature of the item and its role in a particular decision. The Financial Accounting Standards Board has been unable to formulate any general standards for assessing materiality. Instead, the Board has prescribed specific materiality criteria in particular standards as it has deemed appropriate.

## Understandability

1.19 A sixth qualitative attribute of accounting information is understandability. This attribute is concerned with the manner in which the measurements made are reported, or disclosed, in the financial statements.

1.20 An important difficulty in applying this criterion is deciding what level of sophistication is to be assumed of the financial statement user. Should the financial statements be made understandable to security analysts, bankers, and similar individuals? Or should they also be made understandable to the "unsophisticated user" with limited knowledge and resources? The growing complexity of business activities and related accounting measurements are making it extremely difficult for financial statements to convey information that is understood by the unsophisticated user.

*Figure 1.1*
**Qualitative Characteristics of Accounting Information**

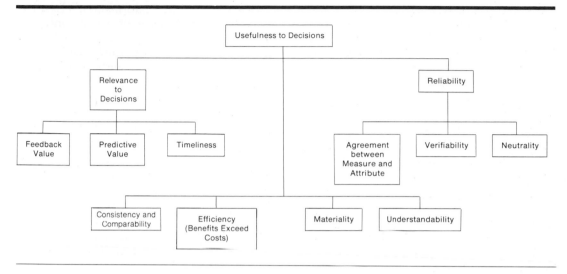

## Conflicts among Qualitative Attributes

1.21　In selecting either the foregoing set or some other set of criteria for evaluating the usefulness of accounting information, conflicts among the criteria will inevitably arise. For example, financial statement users might feel that the most relevant valuation basis for land, buildings, and equipment is the current selling price of each asset. If there is no ready second-hand market, however, current selling prices for used, specialized assets may be difficult to determine and verify. Trade-offs between relevancy and reliability are therefore required. Similar trade-offs are likely to be necessary between relevance and understandability in designing a single set of general-purpose financial statements that are to serve a wide variety of users' information needs.

## Summary of Qualitative Attributes

1.22　The six qualitative attributes of accounting information discussed in this section (summarized in Figure 1.1), are merely possibilities. To a large extent, they represent the at-tributes suggested by the Financial Accounting Standards Board and by independent researchers over the past several years. Up to this time, however, they have not been rigorously applied by rule-making bodies in specifying acceptable methods of accounting. They have been viewed merely as desirable attributes that, in a normative sense, accounting information should possess.

## Standard-Setting Process— Why and by Whom

1.23　The methods of accounting that business firms are permitted to use in preparing their financial statements for investors and other external parties are referred to as "generally accepted accounting principles." For the most part, these principles are established by professional accounting and official governmental bodies. Two questions frequently raised are the following: Should the establishment of acceptable accounting principles be regulated or left for the free-market system to decide; and, second, if a regulatory system is preferred, how should the responsibility be split between the private and the public sectors?

## Free-Market Approach

1.24 Advocates of a free-market approach to establishing acceptable methods of accounting and reporting argue that accounting information may be viewed as an economic good much the same as other goods and services. There is a demand for information on the part of current and prospective shareholders and creditors. There is a supply of information coming from firms in the form of financial statements, press releases, interviews, and similar means. Information about the financial affairs of business firms is also provided by security analysts and firms such as Standard & Poor's and Moody's. As with any economic good, an equilibrium price can be established for accounting information. Suppose now that investors are willing to pay for a new type of accounting information that is not currently provided. Either a supplier of the information will come forward to sell it, or potential users of the information will feel that the required price is so high that the cost of information exceeds its expected benefit. The free-market system operating in this way, it is argued, could be used as the mechanism for establishing the types of information reported, the recipients of the information, and the accounting principles used.

## Regulatory Approach

1.25 Advocates of a regulatory approach argue that accounting information differs from other economic goods and that a free-market system, as described above, would not work. In a free-market system, price determines who gets private economic goods. Price, however, cannot serve the allocative function with respect to accounting information because such information is often a "public good." Once a firm publishes accounting information, it becomes freely available to everyone. Those willing to pay for information about a company cannot easily exclude those who have not paid from using the information. Economists refer to this phenomenon as the "free-rider" problem. The users of the information do not bear the cost of providing it. Because users do not bear the cost, they will simply ask for more and more information. The free-market approach will not necessarily reach the socially optimal equilibrium position where the benefits of the information exactly equal its cost.

1.26 Advocates of a regulatory approach also argue that individuals, particularly those with limited knowledge about accounting and limited resources to acquire it, do not possess sufficient market power to elicit the kind of information they need for their decisions. A regulatory agency is therefore necessary to protect their interests.

1.27 There are of course counterarguments offered. Accounting information is a free good because regulatory agencies (for example, the Securities and Exchange Commission) require the public disclosure of certain information. If public disclosure were not required, access to the information could be limited to those willing to pay the market price for it.

1.28 Our current reporting system is probably best characterized as regulatory rather than free market. However, there is a role being played by the market system. Publicly available information is often not in the form that is needed by certain users. They are willing to pay others (for example, security analysts, Standard & Poor's) to make the necessary aggregations and transformations of publicly available information to put it in more useful form.

1.29 Although our current financial accounting and reporting system is primarily a regulated one, we are still left with the question as to whether the private or the public sector should have the regulatory authority.

**Private-Sector Regulation** Advocates of a private-sector approach generally cite expertise and acceptability in support of their position. It is argued that practicing accountants, because of their day-to-day experiences, are more familiar than individuals in

*Figure 1.2*
**Deductive and Inductive Processes**

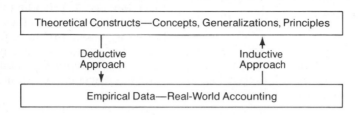

the public sector with the significance of various accounting problems and the feasibility of alternative solutions. They also possess the necessary technical knowledge to develop and implement alternative measurement and disclosure systems. Because of this greater expertise, pronouncements are more likely to be acceptable to practicing accountants, business firms, and financial statement users.

1.31 **Public-Sector Regulation** Advocates of a public-sector approach generally cite legality and objectivity in support of their position. Pronouncements of Congress or one of its agencies are more easily enforceable by law and compliance can thereby more easily be made mandatory. In addition, it is suggested that the public sector is more likely to be insulated from private pressures (for example, practicing accountants, business firms, statement users) and can therefore be more objective in setting accounting principles.

1.32 There are, of course, counterarguments to each of these statements. The public versus private sector issue is part of a broader question regarding the appropriate role of the government in a market-oriented economy. Individual value judgments are required in addressing this broader question, and none are offered here.*

---

*For an expanded discussion of the issues considered in this section, see J. W. Buckley and J. F. Weston, eds., *Regulation and the Accounting Profession* (Belmont, Calif.: Lifetime Learning Publications, 1980).

## Standard-Setting Process— How

The establishment of accounting standards, or principles, might be carried out through either a deductive or an inductive process. In a deductive process, the movement is from generalizations to particulars. We begin with a set of given assumptions or generalizations and then determine which of several alternative accounting principles under consideration is most logically consistent with the given assumptions or generalizations. In an inductive process, the movement is from particulars to generalizations. We begin with a set of empirical observations about the accounting principles actually used or preferred and then infer which principles should be required. Figure 1.2 summarizes these two processes.

### Deductive Approaches

Several deductive approaches to standard setting are discussed below. These deductive approaches are **(1)** axiomatic, **(2)** decision model, and **(3)** financial reporting objectives. These approaches differ primarily with respect to the nature of the initial assumptions or generalizations.

**Axiomatic** Under an axiomatic approach, a theoretical structure of accounting definitions, assumptions, and concepts is established. For example, part of such an axiomatic structure might be as follows:

1.33

1.34

1.35

**Definition:** Asset—a resource with future service potential.

**Assumption:** Objectivity—financial statement users prefer accounting reports that minimize subjective determinations and are subject to audit by independent accountants.

**Concept:** Accounting asset—resources are recognized as accounting assets if they result from a past exchange and their future benefits can be measured with reasonable precision.

Now assume that a standard-setting body must decide whether assets such as inventory, plant, and equipment should be stated at acquisition cost, current replacement cost, or current selling price. Acquisition cost amounts are most logically consistent with the axiomatic structure outlined above because of their greater objectivity and would, therefore, be the valuation method selected.

1.36 The principal benefit of an axiomatic approach is the greater internal consistency of the accounting standards that is likely to result. If each new accounting issue is decided using the same theoretical structure, pronouncements are less likely to be contradictory.

1.37 There are several drawbacks to an axiomatic approach. First, it is difficult to obtain a consensus on the content of the axiomatic structure. Various writers have suggested alternative structures,* and it has not been possible to develop a single structure acceptable to professional accountants, business firms, and financial statement users. A second difficulty is developing an axiomatic structure sufficiently precise that accounting principles under consideration can be either clearly accepted or rejected. For example, current replacement cost or current selling prices for inventory items may be just as consistent with the above axiomatic structure as acquisition cost amounts if there are active markets for the inventory items.

**Decision Model** The decision-model approach begins with the premise that accounting information, to be useful, must satisfy the information needs of financial statement users. The approach is operationalized by studying the manner in which resource allocation decisions are made, developing a model of that decision process, and then determining the type of information needed as an input to the decision model. Standard-setting bodies would then select the accounting principles that conform most closely to the information needs of those decision models.† We discussed earlier that resource allocation decisions are based on assessments of expected return and risk. An extensive study of the manner in which these assessments are made should produce a decision model from which accounting principles could be deductively derived. 1.38

1.39 The principal benefit of the decision-model approach is its emphasis on the use rather than the generation of accounting information. There is an important drawback, however. There are a large number of uses and users of accounting reports and it would be difficult to develop a single model, or even a relatively few decision models, that could be used in setting accounting principles.

**Financial Reporting Objectives** A third deductive approach is to establish a set of financial reporting objectives that would serve as a type of "constitution" for the establishment of accounting principles. These objectives would be broad statements about the purposes of accounting and the general types of information needed by statement users. 1.40

1.41 For example, a set of financial reporting objectives might be as follows:

---

*For example, see Maurice Moonitz, "The Basic Postulates of Accounting," *Accounting Research Study No. 1,* (New York: AICPA, 1961); Raymond J. Chambers, *Accounting, Evaluation and Economic Behavior* (Englewood Cliffs, N.J.: Prentice-Hall, 1966).

†For an expanded discussion of this approach, see *A Statement of Basic Accounting Theory* (Evanston, Ill.: American Accounting Association, 1966).

**1.** Financial reporting should provide useful information for assessing expected return and risks of investment alternatives.

**2.** Financial reporting should provide information on the resources of a firm and the claims on those resources.

**3.** Financial reporting should provide information on the efficiency and effectiveness with which management has used and is likely to use resources committed to the firm.

1.42 As indicated by the foregoing, financial statement objectives tend to be broad generalizations. In order to use such objectives in setting accounting principles, they must be translated into more specific definitions, concepts, and guidelines.

1.43 The Financial Accounting Standards Board has issued a set of financial reporting objectives* that are to serve as a basis for establishing accounting principles. These financial reporting objectives are discussed more fully later in this chapter. It is as yet too early to determine if the financial reporting objectives approach will be any more successful in the standard-setting process than the other deductive approaches tried previously.

### Inductive Approaches

1.44 Two inductive approaches to setting accounting principles are discussed next: (1) synthesis of current practices and (2) political.

1.45 **Synthesis of Current Practices** This approach is based on the premise that acceptable accounting principles should be those used most often by business firms in preparing their accounting reports. Such principles have stood the test of time with respect to their feasibility. The role of the standard-setting body is to monitor reporting prac-

tices and attempt to capture in their pronouncements changes in accounting measurements and disclosures.†

1.46 The concern for feasibility, or practicability, in this approach is commendable. However, it can be seriously criticized from several standpoints. First, little guidance is provided to firms when new reporting issues emerge. Second, firms have a natural incentive to report as favorable an image as possible, independent of whether the accounting principles used portray economic reality or satisfy information needs of users.

1.47 **Political** A second inductive approach is to view the standard-setting process as a political process. Various preparer and user groups express opinions on the accounting principles they feel should be followed. The standard-setting body evaluates the merits of various positions, implicitly considering the relative power of the various groups, and then issues a pronouncement on the accounting principles that will be permitted.

### Current Standard-Setting Approach

1.48 Seldom has the standard-setting process followed any one of these approaches to the exclusion of the others. In most cases a combination of approaches is employed. The current standard-setting process is perhaps best described as a combination of the financial reporting objectives and political approaches. This will become apparent as we consider more fully the development of accounting standards in the next section.

## Standard-Setting Process— As It Is

1.49 Frequent references are made throughout this book to "generally accepted accounting

---

*Financial Accounting Standards Board, *Statement of Financial Accounting Concepts No. 1,* "Objectives of Financial Reporting by Business Enterprises," (November 1978).

†This was a common approach to developing accounting principles several decades ago. See, for example, A. C. Littleton, *Structure of Accounting Theory* (Evanston, Ill.: American Accounting Association, 1953); George O. May, *Financial Accounting: A Distillation of Experience* (New York: Macmillan, 1943).

principles,'' or GAAP. These ''principles'' are a combination of definitions, concepts, methods, and procedures used by business firms in preparing their financial statements. In this section, we consider the need for, and nature of, these principles and the process through which they are developed. The terms accounting *principles* and *standards* are used interchangeably in this discussion.

## Need for Accounting Standards

1.50 The number of users and uses of financial accounting reports is large. Consider, for example, the banker contemplating a six-month loan to a firm, an investor planning to purchase or sell a firm's bonds, preferred stock, or common stock, a merger analyst contemplating the acquisition of another firm, or a governmental agency considering antitrust action. In addition, there are a variety of accounting methods and procedures that a firm could conceivably use in preparing its financial statements. If each firm developed its own accounting methods and designed its accounting reports to satisfy each of the various users of its financial statements, the cost of processing and communicating accounting information would be enormous. Instead, a single set of general-purpose financial statements is prepared in an effort to satisfy the information needs of the various user groups. To enhance the understandability and comparability of these statements, a set of accounting principles generally acceptable to both statement preparers and users and promulgated by standard-setting bodies such as the Financial Accounting Standards Board is used.

## Nature of Accounting Standards

1.51 The nature of accounting principles may perhaps be best understood by contrasting them with principles in physics and mathematics. In physics and other natural sciences, a principle is a description, derived by repeated experimentation and testing, of the relationship between two physical objects or events. The criterion for evaluating a principle in physics is the degree to which the predictions indicated by the principle correspond with physically observed phenomena. In mathematics, a principle is a description, based on logical reasoning, of the relationship between sets of mathematical symbols. The criterion for evaluating a principle in mathematics is the internal consistency of the principle with the accepted set of definitions and axioms. Accounting principles are a description of the manner in which particular transactions and events are measured and then reported in a set of financial statements. Unlike those in the physical sciences, principles in accounting do not naturally exist awaiting discovery. Unlike mathematics, accounting has no structure of definitions and concepts that can be rigorously and unambiguously used in developing accounting principles. Accounting principles are judged on their general acceptability to preparers and users of financial statements. As we discuss in the next section, accounting principles are developed largely as a result of a political process in which the various interested parties exert their influence on the policy-formulation process.

## Development of Accounting Standards

During the last few decades, several inductive and deductive approaches to developing accounting standards have been used by accounting policy makers. The current standard-setting process is a combination of the financial reporting objectives (deductive) and political (inductive) approaches. 1.52

**Emphasis on Financial Reporting Objectives** The Financial Accounting Standards Board has established a set of financial reporting objectives that serves as a basis for the setting of ''generally accepted accounting principles.'' The list of objectives begins with broad statements about the purposes served by financial reporting and then sets out more specific types of information to be provided in financial accounting reports. The objectives are summarized below. 1.53

1. Financial reporting should provide information that is useful to present and potential investors and creditors and other users in making

rational investment, credit and similar decisions. The information should be comprehensible to those who have a reasonable understanding of business and economic activities and are willing to study the information with reasonable diligence.

2. Financial reporting should provide information to help present and potential investors and creditors and other users in assessing the amounts, timing, and uncertainty of prospective cash receipts from dividends or interest and from the proceeds from the sale, redemption, or maturity of securities or loans. The prospects for those cash receipts are affected by an enterprise's ability to generate enough cash to meet its obligations when due and its other cash operating needs, to reinvest in operations and to pay cash dividends and may also be affected by perceptions of investors and creditors generally about that ability, which affect market prices of the enterprise's securities.

3. Financial reporting should provide information about the economic resources of an enterprise, the claims on those resources (obligations of the enterprise to transfer resources to other entities and owners' equity), and the effects of transactions, events and claims on those resources.

4. Financial reporting should provide information about an enterprise's financial performance during a period. . . . The primary focus of financial reporting is information about an enterprise's performance provided by measures of earnings and its components.

5. Financial reporting should provide information about how an enterprise obtains and spends cash, about its borrowing and repayment of borrowing, about its capital transactions, including cash dividends and other distributions of enterprise resources to owners, and about other factors that may affect an enterprise's liquidity and solvency.

6. Financial reporting should provide information about how management of an enterprise has discharged its stewardship responsibility to owners (stockholders) for the use of enterprise resources entrusted to it. Management of an enterprise is periodically accountable to the owners not only for the custody and safekeeping of enterprise resources but also for their efficient and profitable use and for protecting them to the extent possible from unfavorable economic impacts

of factors in the economy such as inflation or deflation and technological and social changes.

7. Financial reporting should include explanations and interpretations to help users understand financial information provided.*

Financial reporting should provide information to help present and potential investors assess the amount and timing of future cash flows to them from business enterprises (expected return) and the uncertainty of those cash flows (risk). This reporting objective is accomplished by providing information about (1) an enterprise's economic resources and claims on those resources, (2) an enterprise's financial performance during a period, and (3) an enterprise's sources and uses of cash. The three principal financial statements currently prepared (balance sheet, income statement, and statement of changes in financial position) are the mechanisms used to satisfy these reporting objectives. Information should also be provided to indicate how effectively management has used resources entrusted to it. There is currently no separate report on stewardship provided by business firms. Assessments of stewardship must be made by comparing a specific enterprise's performance and financial position with some standard or basis of comparison (for example, a minimum rate of return on common shareholders' equity of 12 percent). Financial reporting should also include explanatory or interpretative comments if they aid users in understanding the financial information provided.  1.54

These financial reporting objectives provide focus to the financial reporting process. They are too broad, however, to be used directly in the setting of accounting standards. First, a set of definitions, concepts, and broad principles must be established (discussed in Chapter 2). Then a set of acceptable valuation and measurement methods must be specified (discussed in Chapters 5 and 15). This theoretical structure, referred to as a *conceptual framework* and promul-  1.55

---

*Financial Accounting Standards Board, *Statement of Financial Accounting Concepts No. 1,* "Objectives of Financial Reporting by Business Enterprises," (November 1978).

gated in the form of *Statements of Financial Accounting Concepts,* then provides a more complete basis for setting accounting standards (discussed in the remainder of the book).

1.56 **Recognition of Political Nature of Standard-Setting Process** The establishment of a set of financial reporting objectives and related definitions, concepts, and broad principles discussed in the preceding section is an effort to provide a systematic basis for setting accounting standards. There is a recognition, however, that the standard-setting process is largely a political one. Various persons or groups exert their power in the decision process that yields generally accepted accounting principles.

1.57 An example of the manner in which the political process functions in developing generally accepted accounting principles is described by Horngren.* The accounting principle of concern in his discussion is the valuation of marketable securities using current market prices. You may not be able to follow all of the technical aspects of the example, but you should be able to observe the workings of the political process.

The heart of the issue concerning marketable securities deals with when portfolio gains and losses should be recognized. There is a variety of views ranging from predominant present practice (whereby only realized gains and losses are included in income) to some version of spreading (whereby all gains and losses from changes in market prices are included in income but on some three- to ten-year moving-average, long-term yield basis) to a flow-through approach (whereby all gains and losses are included in income as the prices of marketable securities fluctuate from quarter to quarter).

Another set of issues concerns whether portfolio losses or gains belong in an income statement in the first place. Instead, some accountants believe that a two-statement approach is needed. If adopted, a separate statement of realized and unrealized gains would be used.

---

*Charles T. Horngren, "The Marketing of Accounting Standards," *Journal of Accountancy,* 136 (October 1973): pp. 61–66.

An intensive study of this topic was begun in September 1968. Heavy interaction persisted between the APB and all interested parties, particularly representatives of the insurance industry, whose income statements would be dramatically affected by any new accounting standards. In May 1971, there was a two-day public hearing on the issues.

After about three years of spasmodic deliberations, the APB was ready to issue an exposure draft of an Opinion. The Board had narrowed its preferences to two methods using one income statement: either flow-through or spreading. In September 1971, the Board approved a draft favoring flow-through. The draft was to be "mini-exposed" to the SEC, the insurance industry and others who had been actively involved. The intention of the Board was to have full public exposure of the Opinion after the October APB meeting.

The insurance companies were bitterly opposed to flow-through. They blitzkrieged Washington. The SEC, armed with its own preferences and buttressed by industry reactions, informed the APB that it could not support flow-through. At this point, flow-through was a dead duck because higher management (the SEC) had, in effect, overruled the APB.

At its October meeting, the APB again discussed the topic. Because flow-through was no longer an acceptable alternative, the Board changed its preferences to either spreading or a two-statement approach. The Board voted in favor of a two-statement approach, although strong voices were raised in support of spreading. In November, these alternatives were explored with the SEC and the insurance industry. At its December meeting, the Board was informed that the fire and casualty companies had also strongly objected to the spreading method. One potent spokesman for the SEC found some merit in the spreading method, but he informed the Board that the SEC would not impose it or any solution on an industry that was adamantly opposed to it. So spreading was dead.

The Board then discussed two alternatives: (1) some version of a two-statement method and (2) a modification of predominant current practice whereby all companies in all industries would show marketable securities at market value in the balance sheet, unrealized gains and losses in stockholders' equity, and only realized gains and losses in the income statement. However, the fire and casualty companies also vigorously opposed the two-statement method.

Note how the feasible alternatives changed in response to the likelihood of acceptability. The constraints became more binding as the months wore on:

1. September—flow through or spreading.
2. October—spreading or two-statement.
3. December—two-statement or slight modification of status quo.

Discussions of various versions of the December alternatives were renewed in early 1972. But the Board could not resolve the issues and the SEC was noncommittal on anything except "no flow-through." During the course of the discussions, the top managements of 15 or 20 large insurance companies met together about the issue more than once and also with the SEC commissioners at least once.

The marketable securities scenario was concluded by an APB report to the SEC in March 1972 that summarized the APB deliberations and the alternatives. However, the report offered no preferred solution.

1.58 Some of the more important participating groups in the current standard-setting process are described next.

1.59 **Congress and the SEC** In the Securities Act of 1933 and the Securities and Exchange Act of 1934, Congress accepted the ultimate legal authority for prescribing the methods of accounting used in preparing financial statements for shareholders of publicly held corporations. Congress has delegated its authority to the Securities and Exchange Commission (SEC), an agency of the federal government. Although the SEC has legal authority to prescribe accounting principles, since 1938 it has delegated most of the responsibility for doing so to the accounting profession.* In most cases, the SEC serves

as an advisor or consultant on proposed accounting standards. In a few instances, the SEC has effectively exerted its legal authority by disagreeing with positions taken within the accounting profession.

1.60 In recent years, the pronouncements of the SEC have been concerned primarily with format and disclosure in the financial statements. The SEC requires that certain financial statement information be included in the annual report to shareholders. This annual report to shareholders, along with certain supplementary information, must then be included in the annual report submitted to the SEC (known as the *10–K report*).†

1.61 Among the publications of the SEC are the following:

*Regulation S-X:* A document pertaining to the form and content of financial statements required to be filed with the SEC.

*Accounting Series Releases:* A series of opinions on accounting principles that together with Regulation S-X are the primary statements on the form and content of financial statements filed with the Commission.

*Staff Accounting Bulletins:* A series of reports, prepared in a question-and-answer format, that discuss certain reporting issues in greater depth than provided in *Regulation S-X* or the *Accounting Series Releases*.

1.62 **Financial Accounting Standards Board** Since 1973, the Financial Accounting Standards Board (FASB) has been the principal agency outside the federal government responsible for developing accounting principles. The current functioning of the FASB may be better understood if we consider briefly the evolutionary development that led to its creation.

1.63 *Historical Perspective* Practicing accountants, through their professional associations, have been involved in the development of accounting principles for the past five decades. The American Institute of Certified Public Accountants, or AICPA, is the

---

*In *Accounting Series Release No. 4* (1938), the SEC implicitly encouraged the profession to develop authoritative support for particular accounting principles. The SEC formally affirmed its delegation of responsibility by recognizing the authoritative nature of the pronouncements of the Financial Accounting Standards Board in *Accounting Series Release No. 150* (December 1973).

---

†*Accounting Series Releases No. 279, 280, and 281*, Securities and Exchange Commission (1980).

principal organization of practicing accountants. Officially appointed committees or boards within the AICPA had the responsibility for specifying acceptable accounting methods between 1938 and 1973.

1.64    Between 1938 and 1959, the Committee on Accounting Procedure issued *Accounting Research Bulletins* on various topics. In all, 51 *Bulletins* were issued, on topics such as inventory pricing, depreciation, long-term contracts, consolidated financial statements, and others. The topics tended to be considered individually by the Committee, with relatively little regard for the internal consistency of the various *Bulletins*. The pronouncements tended to reflect the best judgments of the Committee members based on their professional experience. By the late 1950s, it became apparent that the topic-by-topic approach in which the professional judgments of an ever-changing Committee were expressed was resulting in a complicated set of sometimes contradictory accounting principles.

1.65    The Accounting Principles Board (APB) was created in 1959 to overcome some of these weaknesses of the Committee on Accounting Procedure. The APB, according to its initial charter, was to differ in two important respects from the Committee on Accounting Procedure. First, it was to establish a comprehensive structure of accounting theory, beginning with a set of basic postulates, followed by a set of broad principles, and ending with a set of rules to guide the application of the principles in specific situations. Second, the process of developing this theoretical structure was to be based on a comprehensive research program.

1.66    Between 1959 and 1973, the APB issued 31 *Opinions* on various accounting problems. These pronouncements established accounting principles in a broad range of areas, including earnings per share, corporate acquisitions, accounting for intercorporate investments, and others. The APB also issued four *Statements*. These *Statements* recommended, but did not require, the disclosure of certain supplemental information. To provide a basis for the deliberations of the APB, a series of 15 *Accounting Research Studies* were published on particular topics.

Although the initial objective of the APB   1.67
to develop a comprehensive structure of accounting theory based on sound background research was laudatory, it soon became apparent that this Board could not function any more effectively than its predecessor in developing accounting principles. All of the members of the APB were CPAs, and most were partners with national and international public accounting firms. The number of members varied from 18 to 21 over the APB's life. It is not surprising that this large body, comprised of individuals working part-time as Board members and having loyalties to major clients, would have difficulty agreeing on controversial issues. As had occurred previously, each topic tended to be considered independently. The results of prior research, even when conducted, tended to be given little consideration, whereas practical expediency appears to have been given substantial weight.

*Structure of FASB* In 1971, a committee,   1.68
known as the Study Group on the Establishment of Accounting Principles, was established within the accounting profession to study the process of developing accounting principles. The recommendations of this committee were implemented with the creation of the Financial Accounting Foundation, the Financial Accounting Standards Board (FASB), and the Financial Accounting Standards Advisory Council.

The Financial Accounting Foundation is   1.69
composed of trustees appointed by various accounting organizations. Its responsibilities include raising funds to support the FASB, appointing members to the FASB, appointing members to the FASB Advisory Council, and periodically reviewing the basic process of standard setting.

The Financial Accounting Standards   1.70
Board has responsibility for setting accounting standards. The FASB differs structurally from the APB in two important respects. First, there are seven members of the FASB. They serve on a full-time basis and must sever all relations with their previous employers. This severance of relations increases the independence of Board members, and reduces chances for undue influ-

ence by their previous employers. Second, the FASB may have as members individuals with backgrounds in corporate controllership, academia, government services, and financial markets as well as former practicing CPAs. When originally organized, there was a requirement that there be four practicing CPAs on the Board, but that requirement was dropped in 1977. Thus, a range of viewpoints is brought into the standard-setting process.

1.71    The Financial Accounting Standards Advisory Council is composed of approximately 35 members; it advises the FASB on establishing priorities for topics to be considered and reacts to proposed standards. The Council serves merely in an advisory capacity to the FASB.

1.72  *Standard Setting under the FASB*  The process of setting accounting principles under the FASB has two noteworthy attributes. First, the FASB follows a rather complex due-process procedure in its deliberations. The process generally followed is summarized as follows.

**1.**  A reporting issue is identified and placed on the Board's agenda.

**2.**  The technical staff of the FASB, in consultation with a group of knowledgeable persons in the accounting and business community (formed in a "task force"), prepares a *Discussion Memorandum* (DM) on the reporting issue. The DM is intended to be an impartial discussion of the principal questions to be considered by the Board.

**3.**  The DM is "exposed" to the public for a period of at least 60 days.

**4.**  A public hearing on the contents of the DM is held. Individuals and organizations have an opportunity at this point to comment on the questions raised or on questions not raised and to indicate support for particular positions.

**5.**  The FASB, after considering the oral and written comments received, prepares an Exposure Draft of a Proposed Statement of Financial Accounting Standards. The Exposure Draft takes a definitive position on the major issues under consideration.

**6.**  The Exposure Draft is "exposed" to the public for a period of at least 30 days.

**7.**  A second public hearing is usually held. The comments this time are directed at the content of the Proposed Standard.

**8.**  After additional consideration of the comments received, the Board either **(a)** adopts the Proposed Standard as an official Statement of Financial Accounting Standard, **(b)** revises the Proposed Standard before making it official, in some cases allowing additional opportunities for public comment (in effect, returning to step **6**), **(c)** delays issuance of an official Standard but keeps the issue on its active agenda, or **(d)** decides not to issue an official Standard and takes the issue off of its agenda.

The Board's due-process procedure recognizes that the standard-setting process is a political one and that all constituents must be given ample opportunity to have their say about the final decision. It also recognizes that accounting standards are judged according to their acceptability to several groups. By involving the various preparer and user groups in the deliberation process, it is hoped that these groups will be able to make more informed recommendations and be more tolerant of viewpoints that differ from their own.    1.73

A second attribute of the standard-setting process under the FASB is that an effort is made to relate specific accounting Standards to more general-purpose financial statement objectives. This approach is in response to the criticisms directed at the FASB's predecessors of following a topic-by-topic approach. Unless the Board's pronouncements are integrated with some underlying set of objectives or purposes of financial statements, the possibility exists that the pronouncements will become internally inconsistent. It is too early as yet to determine if the FASB will be any more successful in relating its pronouncements to a set of objectives for financial statements than was the APB in relating its pronouncements to an underlying theoretical structure of axioms and general principles.    1.74

1.75 **Other Participants in the Standard-Setting Process** The SEC and the FASB are the primary standard-setting bodies. Several groups and organizations, however, play an important role in influencing the standards established.

1.76 *Accounting Profession* The accounting profession is composed of practicing accountants, financial managers, controllers, academicians, and others. Each of these groups has its own professional organization or association (American Institute of Certified Public Accountants, National Association of Accountants, Financial Executives Institute, American Accounting Association). These professional organizations, through either their committees or members, often express positions on proposed accounting principles.

1.77 The *American Institute of Certified Public Accountants* (AICPA) is the national organization of certified public accountants. Its publications and committees have been influential in the development of accounting principles and practices. Prior to 1973, its influence was exerted through the Committee on Accounting Procedure (1938–1959) and the APB (1959–1973). When the FASB was established in 1973 as an organization independent of the AICPA, two committees were set up within the Institute to participate in the standard-setting process. The Accounting Standards Executive Committee (AcSEC) issues *Statements of Position* on matters not dealt with by the FASB. These *Statements* are authoritative pronouncements but are not binding on AICPA members in the way that FASB *Statements* are binding.* The Auditing Standards Executive Committee (AudSEC) was established

to develop standards and guidelines for the auditing activity and to oversee the enforcement of professional ethics. The AICPA also issues Industry Accounting Guides and Industry Audit Guides on certain topics not previously considered or under active consideration by the FASB. These pronouncements constitute "generally accepted accounting principles" on the topics that have been considered. Among the topics covered in prior pronouncements have been accounting for land-development companies, colleges and universities, and franchisors. Among the Institute's publications are the following:

*Journal of Accountancy:* A monthly periodical containing articles, pronouncements, and sections of direct interest to practicing members of the profession.

*Accounting Trends and Techniques:* An annual publication presenting a survey of the accounting and reporting practices of 600 large industrial and commercial corporations. It presents statistical tabulations on specific practices, terminology, and disclosures together with illustrations taken from individual annual reports.

*Accountants' Index:* A series published each quarter (with annual summaries) in which the literature pertaining to accounting for the period covered is indexed. The index service is also obtainable through an on-line computer system.

The AICPA also coordinates the National 1.78 Automated Accounting Research System (NAARS). Subscribers to this system can access, through an on-line computer system, illustrations of a wide variety of accounting and reporting problems excerpted from corporate annual reports.

The *American Accounting Association* is 1.79 primarily an organization for accountants in academic work, but it is open to all who are interested in accounting. It participates in the development of generally accepted accounting principles and practice, and it promotes the academic phases of accounting theory, research, and instruction. Among its influential publications are the following:

---

*Rule 203 of the Code of Professional Ethics of the AICPA provides that: "A member shall not express an opinion that financial statements are presented in conformity with generally accepted accounting principles if such statements contain any departure from an accounting principle promulgated by the body designated by Council to establish such principles. . . ." Council of the AICPA has designated the FASB, and its predecessor bodies (APB and CAP), as the body to promulgate principles.

*The Accounting Review:* A quarterly periodical containing articles and sections covering a broad span of subjects related to accounting practice, research, and instruction for purposes of both external and internal reporting.

*Accounting and Reporting Standards for Corporate Financial Statements:* A comprehensive presentation of accounting principles for external reporting purposes. The principles enumerated indicate the direction toward which the Association feels accounting and reporting should be moving rather than necessarily a reflection of currently accepted accounting principles.

*A Statement of Basic Accounting Theory:* An integrated statement that seeks to identify the field of accounting, to establish standards by which accounting information can be judged, to point out possible improvements in accounting practice, and to present a useful framework for scholars who wish to extend the uses of accounting.

*Statement on Accounting Theory and Theory Acceptance:* A description of the process through which accounting theory is developed and validated. Whereas the two preceding publications focus on the content of accounting principles and theories, this publication is more concerned with the process of developing the principles and theories.

*Studies in Accounting Research:* A series of research studies on specific theoretical and current topics carried out by members of the American Accounting Association. Among the topics of recent studies have been the theory of accounting measurement, the allocation problem in financial accounting, and alternative income theories.

1.80    The *National Association of Accountants* is a national society generally open to all engaged in activities closely associated with managerial accounting. Among its publications are the following:

*Management Accounting:* A monthly periodical.

*Research Series:* A series of monographs on subjects of internal and external accounting.

*Accounting Practice Reports:* A series of summaries of surveys on current practice in a limited area of accounting.

The *Financial Executives Institute* is an    1.81 organization of financial executives of large businesses, such as chief accountants, controllers, treasurers, and financial vice-presidents. Among its publications are the *Financial Executive,* a monthly periodical, and a number of studies on problems confronting accounting and financial management.

Income tax legislation and administration    1.82 have had a substantial impact on the standards of accounting and reporting. Although the income tax requirements in themselves do not establish principles and practices for general external reporting, their influence on choice of acceptable procedures is substantial. At the federal level, in addition to the *Internal Revenue Code* passed by the Congress, there are the *Regulations* and *Rulings* of the Internal Revenue Service, and the opinions of the U.S. Tax Court.

**Financial Statement Users** The FASB    1.83 seeks representation from those doing security analysis and thus some representation from user interests. Professional organizations of financial statement users, such as the Financial Analysts Federation and the Investment Bankers Association, frequently comment on proposed accounting principles to the FASB and SEC. Any individual user of financial statements can, of course, comment on existing or proposed accounting principles to the FASB, SEC, or a member of Congress.

**Summary** In this section, we have described the major forces influencing the development of accounting standards. Figure    1.84 1.3 summarizes the standard-setting process. The SEC and the FASB are partners in the process. The SEC has the legal authority to prescribe accounting standards. Officially, the SEC has delegated most of the responsibility for doing so to the FASB. The relative role of each of these two entities in standard setting, however, is continually in a state of flux. On certain issues, particularly those relating to disclosure, the SEC estab-

*Figure 1.3*
**Participants in the Standard-Setting Process**

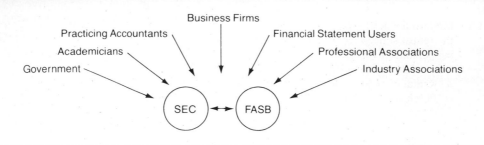

lishes reporting standards. On others, particularly those relating to measurement, the FASB sets accounting standards. Each of these entities must react to pressures brought upon it by Congress, practicing accountants, business firms, and others. As with any political process, there are shifts in power over time among the various participants and thus changes in the relative influence of each group. The SEC and the FASB must continually assess the economic logic behind positions expressed and ensure that various pronouncements are internally consistent with each other.

## Questions

1.1    Review the meaning of the following concepts or terms discussed in this chapter.
  a. Expected return and risk.
  b. Relevance to decisions.
  c. Reliability.
  d. Neutrality.
  e. Comparability.
  f. Efficiency.
  g. Materiality.
  h. Understandability.
  i. Generally accepted accounting principles (GAAP).
  j. Deductive and inductive approaches to developing accounting principles.
  k. Securities and Exchange Commission.
  l. *Accounting Series Releases.*
  m. *Staff Accounting Bulletins.*
  n. Financial Accounting Standards Board.
  o. Committee on Accounting Procedure.
  p. *Accounting Research Bulletins.*
  q. Accounting Principles Board.
  r. *APB Opinion.*
  s. *APB Statement.*
  t. *Accounting Research Study.*
  u. *Discussion Memorandum.*
  v. *Statement of Financial Accounting Concepts*
  w. *Statement of Financial Accounting Standards.*
  x. Accounting Standards Executive Committee.
  y. Auditing Standards Executive Committee.
  z. Industry Accounting Guides.

1.2    Review the meaning of the following concepts or terms discussed in this chapter.
  a. *Journal of Accountancy.*
  b. *Accounting Trends and Techniques.*
  c. *Accountants' Index.*

    **d.** National Automated Accounting Research System.
    **e.** American Accounting Association.
    **f.** *The Accounting Review*.
    **g.** National Association of Accountants.
    **h.** Financial Executives Institute.

**1.3**    Modern financial theory suggests that investment alternatives should be assessed in terms of the return anticipated and the risk or uncertainty associated with that return. For the following personal investments, indicate how the anticipated return might be measured, and suggest some of the factors affecting the risk or uncertainty of that return.
    **a.** Rental of an apartment under a three-year rental agreement.
    **b.** Purchase of an automobile for cash.
    **c.** Purchase of a house under a 20-year mortgage agreement.

**1.4**    Six qualitative attributes of accounting information were discussed in this chapter: relevance to decisions, reliability, comparability, efficiency, materiality, and understandability. Refer to the report of the independent accountant accompanying the financial statements of International Corporation presented in Appendix A at the back of the book.
    **a.** What qualitative attributes of accounting information are suggested or implied in the independent accountant's report?
    **b.** In what respects is your response to part **a** similar to and different from the six qualitative attributes discussed in the chapter?

**1.5**    A financial analyst has suggested that management's forecasts of future quarterly and annual earnings be included in a firm's annual report each period. It has been further suggested that the independent accountant become involved in some way in checking or attesting to these forecasts. Evaluate these proposals, using the six qualitative attributes of accounting information discussed in the chapter.

**1.6**    A noted accountant once stated: "We achieve less and less comparability in financial statements as we obtain greater and greater uniformity in generally accepted accounting principles." Do you agree? Why or why not?

**1.7**    Lack of comparability can occur in the financial statements of a single firm over several accounting periods or in the financial statements of several firms for a single accounting period. Explain.

**1.8**    "A firm's internal auditors can accomplish many of the same objectives as a firm's independent, or external, auditors." Do you agree? Why or why not?

**1.9**    It has been suggested that data on backlog orders (that is, customer orders placed but not yet filled) be presented in corporate financial statements. How might you study the expected benefits and costs of providing customer backlog data?

**1.10**    What is the meaning of the statement: "Accounting information is a public good"? What changes in the structure of financial reporting would be necessary to make accounting information a private, or economic, good?

**1.11**    "The unsophisticated investor has little knowledge of accounting principles and procedures and limited power to acquire the kinds of information needed for investment decisions. Governmental regulation of the type of information presented in corporate annual reports is therefore necessary to protect the unsophisticated investor.'' Assume that you and a colleague have been asked to debate this statement. Prepare a list of the principal issues involved (without arguing either for or against the statement).

**1.12** Distinguish between the deductive and inductive approaches to developing accounting principles.

**1.13** ''Accounting principles must be developed using *both* deductive and inductive approaches.'' Explain.

**1.14** Based on your background in introductory accounting courses, list what you feel are the five most basic axioms or postulates of financial accounting. Using your list of axioms or postulates, determine which one of the following pairs of items is most logically consistent with your axiomatic structure.
**a.** Cash basis or accrual basis of accounting.
**b.** Acquisition cost or current replacement cost valuations for inventory and depreciable assets.

**1.15** Refer to the tentative set of financial statement objectives proposed by the FASB listed in paragraph 1.53 in the text. Using the objectives, determine which one of the following pairs of items is most logically consistent with these objectives.
**a.** Cash basis or accrual basis of accounting.
**b.** Acquisition cost or current replacement cost valuations for inventory and depreciable assets.

**1.16** List the major advantages and disadvantages of inductive approaches to developing accounting principles.

**1.17** Generally accepted accounting principles are the methods of accounting used by business firms in preparing their financial statements. A principle in physics, such as the law of gravity, serves as a basis for developing theories and explaining the relationships among physical objects. In what ways are generally accepted accounting principles similar to and different from principles in physics?

**1.18** Distinguish between measurement and disclosure.

**1.19** ''The approach to developing accounting standards of the Committee on Accounting Procedure was largely inductive, whereas the approach of the Accounting Principles Board was largely deductive.'' Do you agree? Why or why not?

**1.20** Distinguish between *APB Opinions* and *APB Statements*.

**1.21** Distinguish between *Accounting Research Bulletins* and *Accounting Research Studies*.

**1.22** In what respects can the current structure of the FASB be traced to weaknesses in the structure of the Committee on Accounting Procedure and the APB?

**1.23** Compare and contrast *Accounting Research Bulletins, APB Opinions,* and *FASB Statements of Financial Accounting Standards*.

**1.24** What are the advantages and disadvantages of the due-process procedure following by the FASB in setting accounting standards?

**1.25**  Distinguish between "Statements of Position" of the Accounting Standards Executive Committee and Industry Accounting Guides.

**1.26**  (Adapted from CMA Examination.) A press release announcing the appointment of the trustees of the new Financial Accounting Foundation stated the Financial Accounting Standards Board (to be appointed by the trustees) "will become the established authority for setting accounting principles under which corporations report to the shareholders and others" (AICPA news release, July 20, 1972).
a. No mention is made of the SEC in the press release. What role does the SEC play in setting accounting principles?
b. How have accounting principles been set in the past 10 years? In your answer identify the body performing this function, the sponsoring organization, and the method by which the body arrives at its decision.
c. What methods have management and management accountants had to influence the development of accounting principles in the past 10 years?

**1.27**  (Adapted from CMA Examination.) Some accountants have said that politicization in the development and acceptance of generally accepted accounting principles (that is, standard setting) is taking place. Some use the term "politicization" in a narrow sense to mean the influence by governmental agencies, particularly the Securities and Exchange Commission, on the development of generally accepted accounting principles. Others use it more broadly to mean the compromising that takes place in bodies responsible for developing generally accepted accounting principles because of the influence and pressure of interested groups (SEC, American Accounting Association, businesses through their various organizations, National Association of Accountants, financial analysts, bankers, lawyers, and so on).
a. The Committee on Accounting Procedures of the AICPA was established in the mid- to late 1930s and functioned until 1959, at which time the Accounting Principles Board came into existence. In 1973, the Financial Accounting Standards Board was formed and the APB went out of existence. Do the reasons these groups were formed, their methods of operation while in existence, and the reason for the demise of the first two indicate an increasing politicization (as the term is used in the broad sense) of accounting standard setting? Explain your answer by indicating how the CAP, the APB, and the FASB operated or expect to operate. Cite specific developments that tend to support your answer.
b. What arguments can be raised to support the "politicization" of accounting standard setting?
c. What arguments can be raised against the "politicization" of accounting standard setting?

**1.28**  On January 1 of the current year, First National Bank loaned $100,000 to McGann Corporation. The loan as well as interest at 15 percent is repayable one year later (maturity value equal to $115,000).

On the day after the bank made the loan, a fire destroyed virtually all of the plant facilities of McGann Corporation. The loss was not insured. McGann Corporation informed First National Bank that it would be unable to repay the loan at the end of the year. It asked the bank to postpone the repayment date so the company would have time to get back on its feet.

At this point the bank considered its options. It could wait until the end of the current year, when the loan is due. When repayment is not made, the bank could force the firm into bankruptcy. After lengthy court proceedings, the bank estimated that it would probably realize only about 20 percent of the amount loaned (that is, $20,000). Alternatively, it could give the company additional time before the loan becomes due. If the company is able to survive, the bank may be able to recoup a larger proportion of the loan than the 20 percent expected if bankruptcy occurs.

The bank agreed to postpone the repayment to the end of the fifth year after the loan was made (that is, a four-year postponement relative to the original maturity date). The maturity amount will still be $115,000 ($100,000 principal plus $15,000 interest).

This debt restructuring might conceivably be accounted for by the bank in one of the following three ways:

1. Find the present value of $115,000 discounted back five years at 15 percent. Write down the loan to this present value amount and recognize a loss immediately. Interest revenue each year will be computed using the 15 percent rate.

2. Find the present value of $115,000 discounted back five years at a discount rate higher than 15 percent to compensate for the increased riskiness of McGann Corporation. Write down the loan to this present value amount and recognize a loss immediately. Interest revenue each year will be computed using the higher rate selected.

3. Find the interest rate that will discount $115,000 back five years so that its present value equals $100,000. Use this interest rate to recognize interest revenue over the life of the loan.

   a. Which of these three approaches best reflects the economic reality of this debt restructuring? Explain.
   b. Which approach do you think would be most favored by the bank?
   c. Which approach do you think would be most favored by the bank's independent accountant?
   d. A pronouncement by the Financial Accounting Standards Board requires that the third approach be followed in this case. Attempt to reconcile this position with your responses to a., b., and c. above.

# Chapter 2
## Form and Content of Principal Financial Statements

2.1 Three principal financial statements are generally included in corporate annual reports to shareholders and in filings with the Securities and Exchange Commission: a balance sheet, an income statement, and a statement of changes in financial position. In this chapter we review the form and content of each of these financial statements. The procedures for preparing them are discussed in Chapters 3 and 4. The discussion in Chapters 2, 3, and 4 focuses on financial statements as they are currently prepared. In later chapters, current measurement and reporting practices are subjected to a more thorough evaluation.

2.2 In addition to the financial statements presented in this chapter, a complete set of financial statements and notes for International Corporation is presented in Appendix A at the back of the book. You may find it helpful to refer to these financial statements as you read this chapter.

### The Balance Sheet: Measuring Financial Position

2.3 The balance sheet, or statement of financial position, presents a snapshot of the assets of a firm and claims on those assets (liabilities and owners' equity) as of a specific moment in time. Exhibit 2.1 presents a comparative balance sheet for Precision Products Com-

pany as of December 31, 1980 and 1981. The balance sheet derives its name from the fact that it shows the following balance, or equality:

$$\text{Assets} = \text{Liabilities} + \text{Owners' Equity.}$$

That is, a firm's assets are in balance with, or equal to, the claims on those assets by creditors and owners. The balance sheet views assets from two angles: a listing of the specific forms in which they are held (for example, cash, inventory, equipment) and a listing of the persons or interests that have claims on them (for example, suppliers, employees, governments, shareholders). The concepts and conventions underlying the balance sheet can be best understood by addressing the following questions:

1. Which resources of a firm are recognized as assets?

2. What valuations are placed on these assets?

3. How are assets classified, or grouped, within the balance sheet?

4. Which claims against a firm's assets are recognized as liabilities?

5. What valuations are placed on these liabilities?

6. How are liabilities classified within the balance sheet?

*Exhibit 2.1*
**Precision Products Company**
**Consolidated Balance Sheet**

| ASSETS | 12/31/1981 | 12/31/1980 |
|---|---|---|
| Current Assets | | |
| Cash | $ 72,000 | $ 69,000 |
| Marketable Securities | 93,000 | 94,000 |
| Notes Receivable | 20,000 | 10,000 |
| Accounts Receivable | 405,000 | 382,000 |
| Less: Allowance for Uncollectible Accounts | (41,000) | (35,000) |
| Raw Materials Inventory | 176,000 | 189,000 |
| Work-in-Process Inventory | 462,000 | 456,000 |
| Finished Goods Inventory | 643,000 | 605,000 |
| Prepaid Insurance | 5,000 | 6,000 |
| Prepaid Rent | 9,000 | 9,000 |
| Total Current Assets | $1,844,000 | $1,785,000 |
| Investments | | |
| Investment in Bonds of A Co. | $ 95,000 | $ 95,000 |
| Investment in Common Stock of B Co. | 217,000 | 217,000 |
| Total Investments | $ 312,000 | $ 312,000 |
| Property, Plant, and Equipment | | |
| Land | $ 145,000 | $ 135,000 |
| Building | 1,965,000 | 1,843,000 |
| Less: Accumulated Depreciation | (546,000) | (466,000) |
| Machinery and Equipment | 1,343,000 | 943,000 |
| Less: Accumulated Depreciation | (580,000) | (445,000) |
| Total Property, Plant, and Equipment | $2,327,000 | $2,010,000 |
| Intangibles | | |
| Goodwill | $ 55,000 | $ 60,000 |
| Organization Costs | 25,000 | 25,000 |
| Total Intangibles | $ 80,000 | $ 85,000 |
| Total Assets | $4,563,000 | $4,192,000 |

**7.** What valuation is placed on the owners' equity in a firm, and how is the owners' equity disclosed?

## Asset Recognition

2.4 Assets are resources that have the potential for providing a firm with future economic benefits. In short, *an asset is a future benefit*. To be recognized as an asset, a resource (other than cash) must have four characteristics:

**1.** The resource must, singly or in combination with other resources, contribute directly or indirectly to future net cash inflows (or to obviating future net cash outflows).

**2.** The enterprise must be able to obtain the benefit from the resource and control the access of others to it.

**3.** The transaction or event giving rise to the enterprise's claim to or control of the benefit must already have occurred.

**4.** The future benefit must be quantifiable or measurable in units of money.*

**Example 1** Precision Products Company 2.5 sold merchandise and received a note from a customer, who agreed to pay $1,000 within 3 months. This note receivable is an asset of Precision Products Company, because a

---

*Financial Accounting Standards Board, *Statement of Financial Accounting Concepts No. 3* (December 1980), pars. 17 and 20.

*Exhibit 2.1 continued*

| LIABILITIES AND SHAREHOLDERS' EQUITY | 12/31/1981 | 12/31/1980 |
|---|---|---|
| **Current Liabilities** | | |
| Notes Payable | $ 100,000 | $ 100,000 |
| Accounts Payable | 711,000 | 706,000 |
| Wages Payable | 102,000 | 98,000 |
| Income Taxes Payable | 62,000 | 55,000 |
| Estimated Liability for Warranties | 97,000 | 96,000 |
| Rental Fees Received in Advance | 13,000 | 16,000 |
| Total Current Liabilities | $1,085,000 | $1,071,000 |
| **Long-Term Debt** | | |
| Mortgage Payable | $ 112,000 | $ 122,000 |
| Bonds Payable | 500,000 | 500,000 |
| Less: Discount on Bonds Payable | (15,000) | (16,000) |
| Total Long-Term Debt | $ 597,000 | $ 606,000 |
| Total Liabilities | $1,682,000 | $1,677,000 |
| **Shareholders' Equity** | | |
| Convertible Preferred Stock ($100 par, 6% cumulative dividends): Par Value | $ 200,000 | $ 200,000 |
| Common Stock ($1 par value, 1,500,000 shares authorized; 1980: | | |
| 1,000,000 outstanding; 1981: 1,100,000 outstanding): Par Value | 1,100,000 | 1,000,000 |
| Capital Contributed in Excess of Par Value | 496,000 | 465,000 |
| Retained Earnings | 1,228,000 | 1,015,000 |
| Total | $3,024,000 | $2,680,000 |
| Less Cost of Treasury Stock | (143,000) | (165,000) |
| Total Shareholders' Equity | $2,881,000 | $2,515,000 |
| Total Liabilities and Shareholders' Equity | $4,563,000 | $4,192,000 |

right has been established to receive a definite amount of cash in the future as a result of the previous sale of merchandise.

2.6 **Example 2** Precision Products Company acquired manufacturing equipment costing $200,000 and agreed to pay the seller over a period of 2 years. After the final payment, legal title to the equipment will be transferred to Precision Products Company. The equipment is Precision's asset, even though Precision Products Company does not possess legal title, because it has obtained the rights and responsibilities of ownership and can sustain those rights as long as the payments are made on schedule.

2.7 **Example 3** Precision Products Company plans to acquire a fleet of new trucks next year to replace those wearing out. These new trucks are not now assets, because no exchange has taken place between Precision Products Company and a supplier and, therefore, no right to the future use of the trucks has been established.

2.8 **Example 4** Precision Products Company has developed a good reputation with its employees, customers, and citizens of the community. This good reputation is expected to provide benefits to the firm in its future business activities. A good reputation, however, is generally *not* recognized as an asset. Although Precision Products Company has made various expenditures in the past to develop the reputation, the future benefits are considered to be too difficult to quantify with a sufficient degree of precision to warrant recognition as an asset.

2.9 Most of the difficulties in deciding which items to recognize as assets are related to unexecuted or partially executed contracts. In Example 3, suppose that Precision Products Company entered into a contract with a local truck dealer to acquire the trucks next year at a cash price of $50,000. Precision has acquired rights to future benefits, but the contract has not been executed. Unexecuted contracts of this nature are generally not recognized as assets in accounting. Precision will recognize an asset for the trucks when they are received next year.

2.10    To take the illustration one step further, assume that Precision Products Company advances the truck dealer $10,000 of the purchase price upon signing the contract. Precision has acquired rights to future benefits and has exchanged cash. Current accounting practice would treat the $10,000 advance as a deposit on the purchase of equipment and report it as an asset under a title such as Advances to Suppliers. The trucks would not be shown as assets at this time, however, because Precision is not yet deemed to have received sufficient future rights to justify their inclusion in the balance sheet. Similar asset-recognition questions arise when a firm leases buildings and equipment under long-term leases or manufactures custom-design products for particular customers. These issues are discussed more fully in later chapters.

## Asset Valuation

2.11    The financial statements currently prepared by publicly held firms are based primarily on one of two valuation methods—one for monetary assets and one for nonmonetary assets.

2.12    *Monetary assets,* such as cash and accounts receivable, are generally shown on the balance sheet at their current cash, or cash-equivalent, values. Cash is stated at the amount of cash on hand or in the bank. Accounts receivable from customers are stated at the amount of cash expected to be collected in the future. If the period of time until a receivable is to be collected spans more than 1 year, then the expected future cash receipt is discounted to a present value. Most accounts receivable, however, are collected within 1 to 3 months. The amount of future cash flows is approximately equal to the present value of these flows, and the discounting process is ignored.

2.13    *Nonmonetary assets,* such as merchandise inventory, land, buildings, and equip-

ment, are stated at acquisition cost, in some cases adjusted downward for depreciation reflecting the services of the assets that have been consumed.

2.14    The acquisition cost of an asset may include more than its invoice price. Cost includes all expenditures made or obligations incurred in order to prepare the asset for its intended use. Transportation cost, costs of installation, handling charges, and any other necessary and reasonable costs incurred in connection with the asset up to the time it is put into service should be considered as part of the total cost assigned to the asset. For example, the cost of an item of equipment might be calculated as follows:

| | |
|---|---:|
| Invoice Price of Equipment .............. | $8,000 |
| Less: 2% Discount for Prompt Cash Payment ........................... | 160 |
| Net Invoice Price ........................ | $7,840 |
| Transportation Cost ..................... | 232 |
| Installation Costs ....................... | 694 |
| Total Cost of Equipment ................ | $8,766 |

The acquisition cost of this equipment to be recorded in the accounting records is $8,766.

2.15    Instead of disbursing cash or incurring a liability, other forms of consideration (for example, common stock, merchandise inventory, land) may be given in acquiring an asset. In these cases, acquisition cost is measured by the market value of the consideration given or the market value of the asset received, depending on which market value is more readily determinable.

**Foundations for Acquisition Cost**  Accounting's use of acquisition-cost valuations for nonmonetary assets rests on three important concepts or conventions. First, a firm is assumed to be a *going concern.* That is, it is assumed that the firm will remain in operation long enough for all of its current plans to be carried out. Any increases in the market prices of assets held will be realized in the normal course of business by way of higher prices for the firm's products. Current selling prices of the individual assets are therefore assumed to be largely unimportant. Second, acquisition-cost valuations

2.16

are considered to be more objective than those obtained from using other valuation methods. *Objectivity* in accounting refers to the ability of several independent measurers to come to the same conclusion about the valuation of an asset. It is relatively easy to obtain consensus on what constitutes the acquisition cost of an asset. Differences among measurers can arise in determining an asset's current replacement cost, current selling price, or present value of future cash flows. A reasonable degree of consensus is necessary if financial statements are to be subject to audits by independent accountants. Third, acquisition cost generally provides more conservative valuations of assets (and measures of earnings) relative to the other valuation methods. Many accountants feel that the possibility of misleading financial statement users will be minimized when assets are stated at lower rather than higher amounts. Thus, *conservatism* has evolved as a convention to justify acquisition-cost valuations.

## Asset Classification

2.17 The classification of assets within the balance sheet varies widely in published annual reports. The principal asset categories are described below.

2.18 **Current Assets** The term *current assets* "is used to designate cash and other assets or resources commonly identified as those that are reasonably expected to be realized in cash or sold or consumed during the normal operating cycle of the business."* The operating cycle for most businesses involves the following steps:

**1.** Acquisition of merchandise inventory for cash or on account.

**2.** Sale of merchandise for cash or on account.

**3.** Collection of cash from credit customers.

**4.** Payment of cash for operating expenses and purchases of merchandise on account.

---

*Accounting Research Bulletin No. 43*, AICPA (1953), chap. 3A.

For most businesses, this operating cycle 2.19 occurs several times each year. By convention, current assets generally represent those resources that will be realized in cash or sold or consumed within 1 year of the date of the balance sheet. Included in current assets are cash; marketable securities held as short-term investments; accounts and notes receivable net of allowance for uncollectible accounts; inventories of merchandise, raw materials, supplies, work in process, and finished goods; and prepaid operating costs. Prepaid costs, or prepayments, are current assets to the extent that if they were not paid in advance, then current assets would be required to be used to acquire them within the next operating cycle.

**Investments** The section of the balance 2.20 sheet labeled "Investments" includes primarily the investments in securities of other firms where the purpose of the investment is long term in nature. For example, shares of common stock of a supplier might be purchased to help assure continued availability of raw materials. Or shares of common stock of a firm in another area of business activity might be acquired to permit the acquiring firm to diversify its operations. When one corporation (the parent) owns more than 50 percent of the voting stock in another corporation (the subsidiary), consolidated financial statements are usually prepared. That is, the specific assets, liabilities, revenues, and expenses of the subsidiary are merged, or consolidated, with those of the parent corporation. When consolidated financial statements are prepared, the account Investment in Subsidiary is eliminated as part of the consolidation process. Intercorporate investments in securities shown in the Investments section of the balance sheet are therefore investments in firms whose financial statements have not been consolidated with the parent or investor firm.

The holders of a firm's long-term bonds 2.21 may require that cash be set aside periodically so that sufficient funds will be available to retire, or redeem, the bonds at maturity. The funds are typically given to a trustee, such as a bank or insurance company, which invests the funds received. Funds set aside for this purpose are shown in a Sinking Fund account and classified under Investments on the balance sheet.

2.22 **Property, Plant, and Equipment** Property, plant, and equipment (sometimes called *plant assets* or *fixed assets*) includes the tangible, long-lived assets used in a firm's operations over a period of years and generally not acquired for resale. This category includes land, buildings, machinery, automobiles, furniture, fixtures, computers, and other equipment. The amount shown on the balance sheet for each of these items (except land) is acquisition cost less accumulated depreciation. Land is presented at acquisition cost.

2.23 **Intangible Assets** Intangible assets include such items as patents, trademarks, franchises, and goodwill. The expenditures made by the firm in *developing* intangible assets are usually not recognized as assets, because of the difficulty of determining the existence and amount of future benefits. Intangible assets *purchased* from other firms are recognized as assets, however, because an exchange between independent entities has taken place and evidence is thereby provided as to the existence and amount of future benefits.

## Liability Recognition

2.24 A liability represents an obligation of a firm to make payment of a reasonably definite amount at a reasonably definite future time for benefits or services received currently or in the past. To be recognized as a liability, an obligation must have four characteristics:

**1.** The obligation must involve a probable future sacrifice of resources—a future transfer of cash, goods, or services (or a foregoing of a future cash receipt).

**2.** The obligation must be one of the specific enterprise.

**3.** The transaction or event giving rise to the enterprise's obligation must already have occurred.

**4.** The amount of the obligation and the time of its settlement must be measurable with reasonable accuracy.*

**Example 1** Precision Products Company 2.25 purchased merchandise inventory and agreed to pay the supplier $5,000 within 30 days. This obligation is a liability, because Precision Products Company has received the goods and must pay a definite amount at a reasonably definite future time.

**Example 2** Precision Products Company 2.26 borrowed $2,000,000 by issuing long-term bonds. Annual interest payments of 8 percent must be made on December 31 of each year, and the $2,000,000 principal must be repaid in 20 years. This obligation is also a liability, because Precision Products Company has received the cash and must repay the debt in definite amounts at definite future times.

**Example 3** Precision Products Company 2.27 provides a 3-year warranty on its products. The obligation to maintain the products under warranty plans creates a liability. The selling price for its products implicitly includes a charge for future warranty services. As customers pay the selling price, Precision Products Company receives a benefit (that is, the cash received). Past experience provides a basis for estimating the proportion of customers who will seek services under the warranty agreement and the expected cost of providing warranty services. Thus, the amount of the obligation can be estimated with a reasonable degree of accuracy, and it is shown as a liability.

**Example 4** Precision Products Company 2.28 rents excess office space to other firms. The rent for each calendar year is received during November of the preceding year. The receipt of each year's rent creates a liability

---

*Financial Accounting Standards Board, op. cit., pars. 17 and 29.

that will be satisfied by providing rental services.

2.29 **Example 5** Precision Products Company has signed an agreement with its employees' labor union, promising to increase wages 6 percent and to provide for medical and life insurance. This agreement does not immediately give rise to a liability, because services have not yet been received from employees that would require any payments for wages and insurance. As labor services are received, a liability will arise.

2.30 The most troublesome questions of liability recognition relate to unexecuted contracts. The labor union agreement in Example 5 is an unexecuted contract. Other examples include leases, pension agreements, and purchase-order commitments. Whether or not unexecuted contracts should be recognized as liabilities has been and continues to be controversial.

## Liability Valuation

2.31 Most liabilities are monetary in nature. Those due within 1 year or less are stated at the amount of cash expected to be paid to discharge the obligation. If the payment dates extend more than 1 year into the future (for example, as in the case of the bonds in Example 2 above), the liability is stated at the present value of the future cash outflows.

2.32 A liability that is discharged by delivering goods or rendering services, rather than by paying cash, is nonmonetary. For example, magazine publishers typically collect cash for subscriptions, promising delivery of magazines over many months. Cash is received currently, whereas the obligation under the subscription is discharged by delivering magazines in the future. Theaters and football teams receive cash for season tickets and in return incur an obligation to admit the ticket holder to future performances. Landlords receive cash in advance and are obligated to let the tenant use the property. Such nonmonetary obligations are included among liabilities. They are stated, however, at the amount of cash received rather than at the expected cost of publishing the magazines or of providing the theatrical or sporting entertainment. The title frequently used for liabilities of this type is Advances from Customers.

## Liability Classification

2.33 Liabilities in the balance sheet are typically classified in one of the following categories.

2.34 **Current Liabilities** The term *current liabilities* "is used principally to designate obligations whose liquidation is reasonably expected to require the use of existing resources properly classified as current assets, or the creation of other current liabilities."* Included in this category are liabilities to merchandise suppliers, employees, and governmental units. Notes and bonds payable are also included to the extent that they will require the use of current assets within a relatively short period of time, typically during the next 12 months.

2.35 **Long-Term Debt** Obligations having due dates, or maturities, more than 1 year after the balance sheet date are generally classified as long-term debt. Included are bonds, mortgages, and similar debts, as well as some obligations under long-term leases.

2.36 **Other Long-Term Liabilities** Obligations not properly considered as current liabilities or long-term debt are classified as *other long-term liabilities,* or *indeterminate-term liabilities.* Included are such items as deferred income taxes and some deferred pension obligations.

## Owners' Equity Valuation and Disclosure

2.37 The owners' equity, or interest, in a firm is a residual interest.† That is, the owners

---

*Accounting Research Bulletin No. 43,* op cit.

†Although owners' equity is equal to assets minus liabilities, accounting provides an independent method for calculating its amount. This method is presented in the next chapter.

have a claim on all assets not required to meet the claims of creditors. The valuation of the assets and liabilities included in the balance sheet therefore determines the valuation of total owners' equity.

2.38 The remaining question concerns the manner of disclosing this total owners' equity. A distinction is typically drawn between contributed capital and earnings retained by a firm. In preparing the balance sheet for a corporation, the amounts contributed directly by shareholders for an interest in the firm (that is, capital stock) are separated from the subsequent earnings realized by the firm in excess of dividends declared (that is, retained earnings).

2.39 In addition, the amount received from shareholders is usually further disaggregated into the *par* or *stated value* of the shares and *amounts contributed in excess of par value or stated value*. The par or stated value of a share of stock is a somewhat arbitrary amount assigned to comply with corporation laws of each state. As a result, the distinction between par or stated value and amounts contributed in excess of par or stated value is of questionable informational value but is typically shown nonetheless.

### Balance Sheet Account Titles

2.40 Appendix 2.1 at the end of the chapter shows balance sheet account titles that are commonly used. The descriptions given for each account should help in understanding various assets, liabilities, and owners' equities as well as in selecting appropriate terms for solving problems.

## The Income Statement: Measuring Earnings Performance

2.41 The second principal financial statement is the income statement. Exhibit 2.2 presents an income statement for Precision Products Company for the year ended December 31, 1981. Most published income statements are presented in comparative form for the most recent 3 years. The income statement provides a measure of the operating performance of a firm for some particular period of time. Net income is equal to revenues and gains minus expenses and losses. Revenues measure the inflow of net assets (assets less liabilities) from selling goods and providing services. Expenses measure the outflow of net assets that are used up, or consumed, in the process of generating revenues. As a measure of operating performance, revenues reflect the services rendered by the firm and expenses indicate the related efforts required or expended.

Gains and losses arise from transactions 2.42 that are only peripherally related to a firm's primary operating activities. In contrast with revenues and expenses, gains and losses are "net" rather than "gross" concepts. For example, the difference between the selling price and the book, or recorded, value of an item of equipment sold is reported in the income statement as a gain (if positive) or a loss (if negative). The difference between the cash expenditure required to pay off a liability and the book, or recorded, value of the liability is reported on the income statement as a gain (if negative) or a loss (if positive).

### Periodic Performance Measurement

The income statement is a report on earnings 2.43 performance over a specified period of time. Years ago, the length of this period varied substantially among firms. Income statements were prepared at the completion of some activity, such as after the round-trip voyage of a ship between England and the colonies or at the completion of a construction project.

The earnings activities of most modern 2.44 firms are not so easily separated into distinguishable projects. Instead, the income-generating activity is carried on continually. For example, a plant is acquired and used in manufacturing products for a period of 40 years or more. Delivery equipment is purchased and used in transporting merchandise to customers for 5, 6, or more years. If the preparation of the income statement

*Exhibit 2.2*
**Precision Products Company**
**Consolidated Income Statement**
**for the Year Ended**
**December 31, 1981**

Income from Continuing Operations:
  Revenues:
    Sales ................................................................. $2,201,000
    Less: Sales Contra, Estimated Uncollectibles ............................. (35,000)
    Net Sales ............................................................ $2,166,000
    Interest, Dividends, Rents, and Royalties ............................... 230,000
    Gain on Sale of Equipment ............................................. 4,000
      Total Revenues ..................................................... $2,400,000

  Expenses:
    Cost of Goods Sold ................................................... $1,182,000
    Selling .............................................................. 463,000
    Administrative ....................................................... 126,000
    Interest ............................................................. 40,000
    Income Taxes ......................................................... 263,000
      Total Expenses ..................................................... 2,074,000
    Income from Continuing Operations .................................... $  326,000

Income, Gains, and Losses from Discontinued Operations (Net of Income Tax
  Effects):
  Net Income of a Segment during the Year Prior to the Date When Decision Was
    Made to Dispose of Segment (Net of Income Taxes of $58,000) ........... $   63,000
  Estimated Loss from Sale of Segment Including Operating Losses of $18,000
    during the Phase-out Period (Net of Income Tax Savings of $38,000) ........... (44,000)
      Total from Discontinued Operations ................................. 19,000
Income before Extraordinary Items ........................................ $  345,000

Extraordinary Gains and Losses (Net of Income Tax Effects):
  Loss from Expropriation of Plant Assets in Canada (Net of Income Tax Savings
    of $45,000) ......................................................... $  (60,000)
  Loss of Merchandise Inventories in Illinois due to Hurricane (Net of Income
    Tax Savings of $57,000) ............................................. (30,000)
      Total Extraordinary Losses ......................................... (90,000)

Income Effect of Change in Accounting Principles (Net of Income Tax Effects):
  Cumulative Difference in Prior Years' Earnings due to a Change from the Double-Declining-Balance
    Method to the Straight-Line Method of Depreciation on Equipment (Net of Income
    Taxes of $44,000) ................................................... 48,000
Net Income to Shareholders ............................................... $  303,000

| Earnings per Share: | **Primary** | **Fully Diluted** |
|---|---|---|
| Continuing Operations | $.33 | $.31 |
| Discontinued Operations | .02 | .02 |
| Extraordinary Items | (.09) | (.09) |
| Change in Accounting Principle | .05 | .05 |
| Total Earnings per Common Share | $.31 | $.29 |

were postponed until all earnings activities were completed, the report might never be prepared and, in any case, would be too late to help a reader appraise performance and make decisions. An accounting period of uniform length is used to facilitate timely comparisons and analyses across firms. An accounting period of *1 year* underlies the principal financial statements distributed to shareholders and potential investors. In order to provide even more timely information, most publicly held firms also report earnings data for interim periods within the regular annual accounting period. These interim reports generally cover 3-month periods, or "quarters."

## The Accounting Basis for Recognizing Revenues and Expenses

2.45 When one measures earnings performance for the accounting period, some activities will have been started and completed within the period. For example, during a particular accounting period, merchandise might be purchased from a supplier, sold to a customer on account, and the account collected in cash. Few difficulties are encountered in measuring performance in these cases. The difference between the cash received from customers and the cash disbursed to acquire, sell, and deliver the merchandise represents earnings from this series of transactions.

2.46 Many earnings activities, however, are started in one accounting period and completed in another. Buildings and equipment are acquired in one period but used over a period of several years. Merchandise is sometimes purchased in one accounting period and sold during the next period, whereas cash is collected from customers during a third period. A significant problem in measuring performance for specific accounting periods concerns the determination of the amount of revenues and expenses to be recognized from earnings activities that are in process as of the beginning of the period or are incomplete as of the end of the period. Two approaches to measuring earn-

ings performance are ( 1) the cash basis of accounting, and (2) the accrual basis of accounting.

**Cash Basis of Accounting** Under the *cash* 2.47 *basis of accounting,* revenues from selling goods and providing services are recognized in the period when cash is received from customers. Expenses are typically reported in the period in which expenditures are made for merchandise, salaries, insurance, taxes, and similar items. To illustrate the determination of net income under the cash basis of accounting, consider the following example.

John and Kathy Williams open a hardware 2.48 store on January 1, 1981. They contribute $10,000 cash and borrow $6,000 from a local bank. The loan is repayable on June 30, 1981, with interest charged at the rate of 10 percent per year. A store building is rented on January 1, and 2 months' rent of $2,000 is paid in advance. The premium of $1,200 for property and liability insurance coverage for the year ending December 31, 1981, is paid on January 1. During January, merchandise costing $20,000 is acquired, of which $13,000 is purchased for cash and $7,000 is purchased on account. Sales to customers during January total $25,000, of which $17,000 is sold for cash and $8,000 is sold on account. The acquisition cost of merchandise sold during January is $16,000, whereas various employees are paid $2,500 in salaries.

Exhibit 2.3 presents an income statement 2.49 for Williams' Hardware Store for the month of January 1981 under the cash basis of accounting. Sales revenue of $17,000 reflects the portion of the total sales of $25,000 made during January that was collected in cash. Although merchandise costing $20,000 was acquired during January, only $13,000 cash was disbursed to suppliers, and this amount is therefore recognized as an expense of the period. Expenses recognized for salaries, rent, and insurance reflect the amounts of cash disbursements during January for these services, without regard to whether or not the services were fully consumed by the end of January. The net loss for January under the cash basis of accounting is $1,700.

As a basis for measuring performance for 2.50

*Exhibit 2.3*

**Williams' Hardware Store
Income Statement
for the Month of January 1981
(Cash Basis of Accounting)**

| | | |
|---|---:|---:|
| Cash Receipts from Sales of Merchandise ............. | | $17,000 |
| *Less Cash Expenditures for Merchandise and Services:* | | |
| Merchandise ............... | $13,000 | |
| Salaries ................... | 2,500 | |
| Rental .................... | 2,000 | |
| Insurance ................. | 1,200 | |
| Total Cash Expenditures .. | | 18,700 |
| Net Loss ................. | | ($1,700) |

a particular accounting period (for example, January 1981 for Williams' Hardware Store), the cash basis of accounting is subject to two important and somewhat related criticisms. First, revenues are not matched adequately with the cost of the efforts required in generating the revenues. Performance of one period therefore gets mingled with the performance of preceding and succeeding periods. The store rental payment of $2,000 provides rental services for both January and February, but under the cash basis, the full amount is recognized as an expense during January. Likewise, the annual insurance premium provides coverage for the full year, whereas under the cash basis of accounting, none of this insurance cost will be recognized as an expense during the months of February through December.

2.51  The longer the period over which future benefits are received, the more serious is this criticism of the cash basis of accounting. Consider, for example, the investments of a capital-intensive firm in buildings and equipment that might be used for 10, 20, or more years. The length of time between the purchase of these assets and the collection of cash for goods produced and sold can span many years.

2.52  A second, and probably less serious, criticism of the cash basis of accounting is that it postpones unnecessarily the time when revenue is recognized. In most cases, the sale (delivery) of goods or rendering of services is the critical event in generating revenue. The collection of cash is relatively routine, or at least highly predictable. In these cases, recognizing revenue at the time of cash collection may result in reporting the effects of earnings activities one or more periods after the critical revenue-generating activity has occurred. For example, sales to customers during January by Williams' Hardware Store totaled $25,000. Under the cash basis of accounting, $8,000 of this amount will not be recognized until February or later, when the cash is collected. If the credit standings of customers have been checked prior to making sales on account, it is highly probable that cash will be collected, and there is little reason to postpone recognition of the revenue.

2.53  The cash basis of accounting is used principally by lawyers, accountants, and other professional people who do not maintain inventories of goods for sale, have relatively small investments in multiperiod assets, such as buildings and equipment, and who tend to collect cash from their clients soon after services are rendered. Some firms use a *modified cash basis of accounting,* under which the costs of buildings, equipment, and similar items are treated as assets when purchased. A portion of the acquisition cost is then recognized as an expense when services of these assets are consumed. Except for the treatment of these long-lived assets, revenues are recognized at the time cash is received and expenses are reported when cash disbursements are made. Some physicians and dentists with relatively heavy investments in equipment use the modified cash basis of accounting.

2.54  Most individuals use the cash basis of accounting for the purpose of computing personal income and personal income taxes. Where inventories are an important factor in generating revenues, such as for a manufacturing or merchandising firm, the Internal Revenue Code prohibits a firm from using the cash basis of accounting in its income tax returns.

*Exhibit 2.4*
**Williams' Hardware Store**
**Income Statement**
**for the Month of January 1981**
**(Accrual Basis of Accounting)**

| | | |
|---|---:|---:|
| Sales Revenue .............. | | $25,000 |
| *Less Expenses:* | | |
| Cost of Merchandise Sold  ... | $16,000 | |
| Salaries Expense  ........... | 2,500 | |
| Rent Expense  .............. | 1,000 | |
| Insurance Expense  .......... | 100 | |
| Interest Expense  ............ | 50 | |
| Total Expenses  ........... | | 19,650 |
| Net Income .................. | | $ 5,350 |

2.55 **Accrual Basis of Accounting** Under the *accrual* basis of accounting, revenue is recognized when some critical event or transaction occurs that is related to the earnings process. In most cases, this critical event is the sale (delivery) of goods or the rendering of services. The nature and significance of this critical event are discussed later in the chapter. Under the accrual basis of accounting, costs incurred are reported as expenses in the period when the revenues to which they relate are recognized. Thus, an attempt is made to *match* expenses with associated revenues. When particular types of costs incurred cannot be closely identified with specific revenue streams, they are treated as expenses of the period in which services of an asset are consumed or future benefits of an asset disappear.

2.56 Exhibit 2.4 presents an income statement for Williams' Hardware Store for January 1981 using the accrual basis of accounting. The entire $25,000 of sales during January is recognized as revenue even though cash in that amount has not yet been received. Because of the high probability that outstanding accounts receivable will be collected, the critical revenue-generating event is the sale of the goods rather than the collection of cash from customers. The acquisition cost of the merchandise sold during January is $16,000. Recognizing this amount as cost of

goods sold expense leads to an appropriate matching of sales revenue and merchandise expense in the income statement. Of the advance rental payment of $2,000, only $1,000 applies to the cost of services consumed during January. The remaining rental of $1,000 applies to the month of February. Likewise, only $100 of the $1,200 insurance premium represents coverage for January. The remaining $1,100 of the insurance premium provides coverage for February through December and will be recognized as an expense during those months. The interest expense of $50 represents 1 month's interest on the $6,000 bank loan at an annual rate of 10 percent $(= \$6,000 \times .10 \times \frac{1}{12})$. Although the interest will not be paid until the loan becomes due on June 30, 1981, the firm benefited from having the funds available for its use during January and an appropriate portion of the total interest cost on the loan should be recognized as a January expense. The salaries, rental, insurance, and interest expenses, unlike the cost of merchandise sold, cannot be associated directly with revenues recognized during the period. These costs are therefore reported as expenses of January.

2.57 The accrual basis of accounting provides a better measure of earnings performance for Williams' Hardware Store for the month of January than does the cash basis, both because revenues are measured more accurately and because expenses are associated more closely with reported revenues. Likewise, the accrual basis will provide a superior measure of performance for future periods, because activities of those periods will be charged with their share of the costs of rental, insurance, and other services to be consumed.

2.58 Several important questions regarding the recognition of revenues and expenses have not yet been considered:

**1.** When, or at what point(s), within the earnings process is revenue recognized (that is, what is the nature of the critical revenue-generating event)?

**2.** How do we measure or determine the amount of revenue to be recognized?

**3.** When, or at what point(s), within the earnings process are expenses reported (that is, what is the nature of the matching convention)?

**4.** How do we measure or determine the amount of expenses to be reported?

We consider the principles employed in measuring revenues and expenses in the next two sections.

## Revenue Recognition and Measurement Principles

2.59   In reporting revenue, we are concerned with *when* it arises (a timing question) and *how much* is recognized (a measurement question).

2.60   **Timing of Revenue Recognition** The earnings process for the acquisition and sale of merchandise might be depicted as shown in Figure 2.1. Revenue could conceivably be recognized at the time of purchase, sale, or cash collection, at some point(s) between these events, or even continuously. To answer the timing question, we must have a set of criteria for revenue recognition.

2.61   *Criteria for Revenue Recognition* The criteria currently required to be met before revenue is recognized are as follows:

**1.** All, or a substantial portion, of the services to be provided have been performed.

**2.** Cash, receivables, or some other asset susceptible to objective measurement has been received.

Chapter 8 discusses in detail the various methods of revenue recognition introduced here.

*Recognition at the Point of Sale* For the vast majority of firms involved in selling goods and services, revenue is recognized at the time of sale (delivery). This method of recognizing revenues is called the *completed-sale,* or in some contexts the *completed-contract,* method of revenue recognition. The goods have been transferred to the buyer or the services have been performed. Future services, such as for warranties, are likely to be insignificant, or if significant, can be estimated with reasonable precision. An exchange between an independent buyer and seller has occurred that provides an objective measure of the amount of revenue. If the sale is made on account, past experience and an assessment of customers' credit standings provide a basis for predicting the amount of cash that will be collected. The sale of the goods or services is therefore the critical revenue-generating event. Under the accrual basis of accounting, revenue is typically recognized at the time of sale.   2.62

*Recognition at the Time of Production* On some long-term construction projects, the buyer and the seller agree in advance on the contract price and the timing of cash payments. Revenue from these long-term contracts is often recognized during the period of production. The earnings process for a particular long-term construction project may span several years. If the firm waited until the project was completed to recognize revenue, the efforts and accomplishments of   2.63

---

## Figure 2.1
**Earnings Process for the Acquisition and Sale of Merchandise**

| Purchase of Merchandise | Sale of Merchandise | Collection of Cash |

several accounting periods would be recognized in the one period when the contract was completed. This approach would give an unsatisfactory measure of performance for each period during the contract. In these cases, some firms use the *percentage-of-completion method* of recognizing revenue. A portion of the total contract price, based on the degree of completion of the work, is recognized as revenue each period. This proportion is determined using either engineers' estimates of the degree of completion or the ratio of costs incurred to date to the total expected costs for the contract.

2.64 Although future services required on these long-term construction contracts can be substantial at any given time, the costs to be incurred in providing these services can often be estimated with reasonable precision. The existence of a contract indicates that a buyer has been obtained and a price for the construction services has been set. Cash is usually collected from the buyer as construction progresses or the assessment of the customer's credit standing leads to a reasonable expectation that the contract price will be received in cash after construction is completed. Construction activities are therefore the critical revenue-generating events. The actual schedule of cash collections is *not* significant for the revenue-recognition process when the percentage-of-completion method is used.

2.65 Some firms involved with construction contracts postpone the recognition of revenue until the construction project and the sale are completed. This method is the same as the completed-sale basis, but is often referred to as the *completed-contract method* of recognizing revenue. In some cases, the completed-contract method is used because the contracts are of such short duration (such as 3 or 6 months) that earnings reported with the percentage-of-completion method and the completed-contract method are not significantly different. In these cases, the completed-contract method is used because it is generally easier to implement. Some firms use the completed-contract method in situations when a specific buyer has not been obtained during the periods

while construction is progressing, as is sometimes the case in constructing residential housing. In these cases, future selling efforts are required and substantial uncertainty may exist regarding the contract price ultimately to be established and the amount of cash to be received.

The primary reason for a contractor's not 2.66 using the percentage-of-completion method when a contract exists is the uncertainty of total costs to be incurred in carrying out the project. If total costs cannot be reasonably estimated, the percentage of total costs incurred by a given date also cannot be estimated, and the percentage of services already rendered (revenue) cannot be determined.

*Recognition at the Point of Cash Collection* 2.67 Occasionally, estimating the amount of cash or other assets that will be received from customers is extremely difficult. Therefore, an objective measure of the services rendered and the benefits to be received cannot be made at the time of sale. Under these circumstances, revenue is recognized at the times cash is collected.

This basis of revenue recognition is some- 2.68 times used by land-development companies. These companies typically sell undeveloped land and promise to develop it over several future years. The buyer makes a nominal down payment and agrees to pay the remainder of the purchase price in installments over 10, 20, or more years. In these cases, future development of the land is a significant aspect of the earnings process. Also, substantial uncertainty often exists as to the ultimate collectibility of the installment notes, particularly those not due until several years in the future. The critical revenue-generating event in this case is the collection of cash. When revenue is recognized as the periodic cash collections are received and costs incurred in generating the revenue are matched with the revenue, the firm is using either the *cost-recovery-first method* or the *installment method* of accounting. The cost-recovery-first method and the installment method are similar to the cash basis of accounting, because revenue is recognized as cash is received. The cost-recovery-first and installment methods, however, are accrual methods of accounting, because an effort is made to match expenses with associated revenues.

2.69    For most sales of goods and services, past experience and an assessment of customers' credit standings provide a sufficient basis for predicting the amount of cash to be received. The cost-recovery-first and installment methods are therefore not used in these situations, and revenue is recognized at the time of sale.

2.70    *Recognition between Purchase and Sale* The period between the acquisition or production and the sale of merchandise and other salable goods is referred to as a *holding period*. The current market prices of these assets could change during this holding period. Such changes are described as *unrealized holding gains and losses,* because a transaction or exchange has not taken place.

2.71    Unrealized holding gains could be recognized as they occur. Accountants typically wait, however, until the asset is sold or exchanged before recognizing the gain. At that time, an inflow of net assets subject to objective measurement is presumed to have taken place. Because the accountant assumes that the firm is a going concern, the unrealized gain will be recognized as revenue in a future period in the ordinary course of business. Thus, the recognition of revenue and the valuation of assets are closely associated. Nonmonetary assets are typically stated at acquisition cost until sold. At the time of sale, an inflow of net assets occurs (for example, cash, accounts receivable), and revenue reflecting the previously unreported unrealized gain is recognized. This treatment of unrealized holding gains has the effect of shifting income from periods when the asset is held and the market price increases to the later period of sale. The longer the holding period (as, for example, land used for several decades), the more is income likely to be shifted forward in time by the process of requiring an arm's-length transaction before recognizing the gain.

2.72    Current accounting practices do not always treat unrealized holding losses in the same way as unrealized holding gains. Inventory is an example. If the current market prices of inventory items decrease below the acquisition cost during the holding period, the asset is usually written down and the unrealized loss is recognized. This treatment of losses rests on the convention that earnings should be reported conservatively. Considering the estimates and predictions required in measuring revenues and expenses, some accountants feel it is desirable to provide a conservative measure of earnings so that statement users will not be misled into thinking the firm is doing better than it really is.

2.73    The inconsistent treatment of unrealized gains and unrealized losses does not seem warranted. The arguments used against recognizing unrealized gains apply equally well to unrealized losses. If gains cannot be determined objectively prior to sale, then how can losses be measured prior to sale? If losses can be measured objectively prior to sale, then why cannot gains? We consider the accounting treatment of unrealized holding gains and losses further in Chapters 5, 9, and 26.

**Measurement of Revenue** The amount of revenue recognized is generally measured by the cash or cash-equivalent value of other assets received from customers. As a starting point, this amount is the agreed-upon price between buyer and seller at the time of sale. Some adjustments to this amount may be necessary, however, if revenue is recognized in a period prior to the collection of cash. 2.74

*Uncollectible Accounts* If some of the cash for a period's sales is not expected to be collected, the amount of revenue recognized for that period must be adjusted for estimated uncollectible accounts arising from those sales. Logic suggests that this adjustment of revenue should occur in the period when revenue is recognized and not in a later period when specific customers' accounts are declared to be uncollectible. If the adjustment is postponed, reported income of subsequent periods will be affected by earlier 2.75

decisions to extend credit to customers. Thus, the performance of the firm for both the period of sale and the period when the account is judged uncollectible will be measured inaccurately. Income in the period of sale is overstated. Income in the period when the uncollectible becomes apparent is understated. The two errors cancel each other out; but here, as elsewhere, two wrongs do not make a right.

2.76 *Delayed Payments* If the period between the sale of the goods or services and the time of cash collection extends over several years, it is likely that the selling price includes an interest charge for the loan conveying the right to delay payment. Under the accrual basis of accounting, this interest element should be recognized as interest revenue during the periods between sale and collection when the loan is outstanding. To recognize all potential revenue entirely in the period of sale would be to recognize too soon the return for services rendered over time in lending money. Thus, when cash collection is to be delayed, the measure of current revenue should be the selling price reduced to account for the interest element applicable to future periods. Only the *present value* of the amount to be received should be recognized as revenue during the period of sale. For most accounts receivable, the period between sale and collection spans only 2 to 3 months. The interest element is likely to be relatively insignificant in these cases. As a result, in accounting practice no reduction for interest on delayed payments is made for receivables to be collected within 1 year or less. This procedure is a practical expedient rather than a strict following of the underlying accounting theory.

## Expense Recognition and Measurement Principles

2.77 Analogous to the questions raised regarding revenue recognition, we are confronted with the questions of *when* expenses are recognized and at *what amount* they are stated.

**Timing of Expense Recognition** Recall 2.78 that assets represent resources providing future benefits to the firm. *Expenses* are a measurement of the assets consumed in generating revenue. Assets may be referred to as *unexpired* (or *deferred*) *costs* and expenses as *expired costs* or "gone assets." Our attention focuses on the question of when the asset expiration takes place. The critical question is "When have asset benefits expired—leaving the balance sheet—and become expenses—entering the income statement as reductions in owners' equity?" Thus:

*Balance Sheet*      *Income Statement*
Assets or Unexpired Costs → Expenses or Expired Costs

*Expense Recognition Criteria* The criteria 2.79 currently employed by accountants in making the timing decision may be summarized as follows:

**1.** Asset expirations, or expenses, directly associated with particular types of revenue are recognized as expenses in the period in which the revenues are recognized. This treatment is called the *matching convention,* because cost expirations are matched with revenues.

**2.** Asset expirations, or expenses, not directly or easily associated with revenues are treated as expenses of the period in which services are consumed in operations.

*Product or Production Costs* The cost of 2.80 goods or merchandise sold is perhaps the easiest expense to associate with revenue. At the time of sale, the asset physically changes hands. Revenue is recognized, and the cost of the merchandise transferred is treated as an expense.

A *merchandising firm* purchases inven- 2.81 tory and later sells it without changing its physical form. The inventory is shown as an asset stated at acquisition cost on the balance sheet. Later, when the inventory is sold, the same amount of acquisition cost is shown as an expense (cost of goods sold) on the income statement.

2.82    A *manufacturing firm,* on the other hand, incurs various costs in changing the physical form of the goods it produces. These costs are typically of three types: **(1)** direct material, **(2)** direct labor, and **(3)** manufacturing overhead (sometimes called indirect manufacturing costs). Direct material and direct labor costs can be associated directly with particular products manufactured. Manufacturing overhead includes a mixture of costs that provide a firm with a capacity to produce. Examples of manufacturing overhead costs are expenditures for utilities, property taxes, and insurance on the factory, as well as depreciation on manufacturing plant and equipment. The services of each of these items are used, or consumed, during the period while the firm is creating new assets, the inventory of goods being worked on or held for sale. Benefits from direct material, direct labor, and manufacturing overhead are, in a sense, transferred to, or become embodied in, the asset represented by units of inventory. Because the inventory items are assets until sales are made to customers, the various direct material, direct labor, and manufacturing overhead costs incurred in producing the goods are treated as unexpired costs and included in the valuation of the inventory. Such costs, which are assets transformed from one form to another, are called *product costs.* Product costs are assets; they become expenses only when the goods in which they are embodied are sold.

2.83    *Selling Costs* In most cases, the costs incurred in selling, or marketing, a firm's products relate to the units sold during the period. For example, salaries and commissions of the sales staff, sales literature used, and most advertising costs are incurred in generating revenue currently. Because these selling costs are associated with the revenues of the period, they are reported as expenses in the period when the services provided by these costs are consumed. It can be argued that some selling costs, such as advertising and other sales promotion, provide future-period benefits for a firm and should continue to be treated as assets. However, distinguishing what portion of the cost relates to the current period to be recognized as an expense and what portion relates to future periods to be treated as an asset can be extremely difficult. Therefore, accountants typically treat selling and other marketing activity costs as expenses of the period when the services are used. These selling costs are treated as *period expenses* rather than as assets, even though they may enhance the future marketability of a firm's products.

*Administrative Costs* The costs incurred in   2.84 administering, or directing, the activities of the firm cannot be closely associated with units produced and sold and are, therefore, like selling costs, treated as period expenses. Examples include the president's salary, accounting and data-processing costs, and the costs of conducting various supportive activities such as legal services and corporate planning.

**Measurement of Expenses** Expenses are   2.85 costs expired, or assets consumed, during the period. The amount of an expense is therefore the amount of the expired asset. Thus, the basis for expense measurement is the same as for asset valuation. Because assets are stated primarily at acquisition cost on the balance sheet, expenses are measured primarily by the acquisition cost of assets.

## Format and Classification within the Income Statement

The income statement might contain some   2.86 or all of the following sections or categories, depending on the nature of the firm's income for the period:

1.  Income from continuing operations,

2.  Income, gains, and losses from discontinued operations,

3.  Extraordinary gains and losses, and

4.  Adjustments for changes in accounting principles.

The great majority of income statements include only the first section. The other sections are added if necessary.*

**2.87**   **Income from Continuing Operations** Revenues, gains, expenses, and losses from the continuing areas of business activity of a firm are presented in the first section of the income statement. The income taxes attributable to this income are also included. A heading such as "Income from Continuing Operations" is used if there are other sections in the income statement.

**2.88**   **Income, Gains, and Losses from Discontinued Operations** If a firm sells a major line or segment of its business during the year or contemplates its sale within a short time after the end of the accounting period, Accounting Principles Board *Opinion No. 30* requires that any income, gains, and losses (net of income tax effects) related to that segment be disclosed separately from ordinary, continuing operations in a section of the income statement entitled "Income, Gains, and Losses from Discontinued Operations."† This section follows the section presenting income from continuing operations. The separate disclosure of income

from discontinued operations is intended to alert the reader to the fact that this source of income should not be considered in an ongoing assessment of a firm's profitability.

Two dates are important in measuring the income effects of discontinued operations. The *measurement date* is the date on which a firm commits itself to a formal plan to dispose of a segment. The *disposal date* is the date of closing the sale, if the segment is to be sold, or the date operations cease, if the segment is to be abandoned.   **2.89**

Net income of the segment prior to the measurement date should be reported as a separate item in the "Discontinued Operations" section of the income statement. Exhibit 2.2 indicates that the segment disposed of during the year generated income, net of income taxes, of $63,000 prior to the date when a decision was made to dispose of the segment.   **2.90**

At the measurement date, an estimate is made of the gain or loss expected to be realized on the sale or abandonment of the segment. An estimate is also made of the net income or net loss expected to be generated by the segment between the measurement date and the disposal date. The estimated gain or loss on disposal and the estimated net income or net loss are then netted. If the net amount is a loss, it is recognized in the year that includes the measurement date. If the net amount is a gain, it is recognized only when the income or gain is realized.‡ These provisions of APB *Opinion No. 30* rest on the convention of recognizing losses as soon as they become evident but postponing the recognition of gains until they are realized.   **2.91**

Exhibit 2.2 indicates that a loss on the sale of the segment was anticipated. In addition, it was expected that operations would produce a loss of $18,000 during the phase-out period. These estimated losses are recognized in the year that includes the measurement date. If actual losses, either from operations or from disposal of the segment, turn out to be different from those anticipated, their income effect is reported in the   **2.92**

*Historically, controversy has existed concerning whether unusual, nonrecurring types of income should be included in the income statement for the period (referred to as the *clean surplus theory*) or whether they should be charged or credited directly to Retained Earnings (referred to as the *current operating performance theory).* Advocates of the clean surplus theory argued that income items, even though unusual and nonrecurring, were nonetheless income items and should therefore appear in the income statement. Advocates of the current operating performance theory argued that predictions of future income would be enhanced if the current period's income statement included only those types of income that were expected to continue in the future. Accounting Principles Board *Opinion No. 30* takes a compromise position by requiring that all income items appear in the income statement, but the items must be classified as to their continuing, discontinuing, or extraordinary nature.

†Accounting Principles Board, *Accounting Principles Board Opinion No. 30* (1973).

‡Ibid., par. 15.

year of disposal in the "Discontinued Operations" section of the income statement.

2.93  **Extraordinary Gains and Losses** Extraordinary gains and losses (net of their income tax effects) are also presented in a separate section of the income statement. For an item to be classified as *extraordinary,* it must generally meet all three of the following criteria:

1. Unusual in nature,
2. Infrequent in occurrence, and
3. Material in amount.*

These criteria are applied as they relate to a specific firm and similar firms in the same industry, taking into consideration the environment in which the entities operate. Thus, an item might be extraordinary for some firms and ordinary for others. Examples of items likely to be extraordinary for most firms are losses from hurricanes and tornadoes, and expropriation or confiscation of assets by certain foreign governments. Precision Products Company shows losses for both of these items in its income statement in Exhibit 2.2. Since 1973, when Accounting Principles Board *Opinion No. 30* was issued, extraordinary items are seldom seen in published annual reports except for gain or loss on bond retirements and the benefits of tax-loss carryforwards.

2.94  **Adjustments for Accounting Changes** As a part of the process of measuring and reporting financial statement data, four types of accounting changes might occur:†

1. Change in accounting estimate,
2. Change in accounting principle,
3. Change in reporting entity, and
4. Correction of error in prior years' financial statements.

---

*Accounting Principles Board, *Accounting Principles Board Opinion No. 30* (1973); Financial Accounting Standards Board, *Statement of Financial Accounting Standards No. 4* (1975).

†Accounting Principles Board, *Accounting Principles Board Opinion No. 20* (1971).

Each of these accounting changes is discussed briefly here. They are considered more fully in Chapter 23.

*Change in Accounting Estimate* The peri-  2.95 odic measurement of earnings and financial position requires that numerous estimates be made (for example, estimated rate of uncollectibles on accounts receivable, estimated salvage value and useful life on depreciable assets, estimated liability under warranty plans). As new information becomes available, original estimates may be altered. New technology might lessen the useful life of depreciable assets. Improved quality control might reduce the claim rate on warranties.

No attempt is made to correct the financial statements of prior years when a change  2.96 in an accounting estimate takes place.** Instead, the effect of the change is spread over the current and future years' financial statements. For example, assume that a machine was acquired 4 years ago for $10,000. The machine originally had an estimated useful life of 10 years and zero salvage value. Straight-line depreciation of $1,000 per year was recognized during the first 4 years. At the beginning of the fifth year, the total estimated life was revised downward from 10 to 8 years because the rate of technical obsolescence was greater than originally anticipated. APB *Opinion No. 20* requires that the book value at the beginning of the fifth year of $6,000 (= $10,000 − $4,000) be depreciated over the *remaining* useful life (that is, 4 years). Thus, the asset will be depreciated at the rate of $1,000 per year during years 1 to 4 and at the rate of $1,500 per year during years 5 to 8.

Unless the effect of a change in account-  2.97 ing estimate is material in amount, it is seldom disclosed separately in the financial statements.

*Change in Accounting Principle* Firms some-  2.98 times change their methods of accounting.

---

**Ibid., par. 31.

For example, a firm might change from using a first-in, first-out (FIFO) cost-flow assumption for inventories to weighted-average cost-flow assumption. Or a firm may change its depreciation method from the double-declining-balance method to the straight-line method.

2.99 Although there are several exceptions, most changes in accounting principles are accounted for as follows:*

**1.** Financial statements for prior periods included for comparative purposes are presented as previously reported.

**2.** The cumulative effect of changing to a new accounting principle on the amount of retained earnings at the beginning of the period in which the change is made is included in net income of the period of the change.

2.100 Precision Products Company changed from the double-declining-balance to the straight-line method of depreciation during 1981. The difference between the depreciation actually taken under the double-declining-balance method and the depreciation that would have been taken under the straight-line method for all prior years until January 1, 1981, is shown, net of income tax effects, in a separate section of the income statement in Exhibit 2.2. Depreciation expense for 1981 is included in cost of goods sold, selling, and administrative expenses, as appropriate, using the straight-line method. Thus, the effect of the change in accounting principle on prior years' net income is included in a separate section of the income statement of the year of the change.

2.101 *Change in Reporting Entity* The reporting entity may change from one period to the next as a result of a change in the specific subsidiaries comprising the group for which consolidated or combined financial statements are prepared. In cases where the current reporting entity differs from the entity as previously reported, APB *Opinion No. 30*† requires that the financial statements of all prior periods be restated to reflect financial information for the new reporting entity.

*Correction of Errors in Prior Years' Financial Statements* Errors in prior years' financial statements may result from mathematical mistakes, mistakes in the application of accounting principles, or oversight or misuse of facts that existed at the time the financial statements were prepared. Errors are corrected by restating the financial statements of prior years to eliminate the effects of the errors.** 2.102

To summarize, the effects of errors and the effect of changes in the reporting entity are changed retroactively. Effects of changes in accounting principle are generally made currently. The effect of changes in accounting estimates are made during the current and future periods. The rationale for these varying treatments of accounting changes is discussed in Chapter 23. 2.103

**Earnings per Share** Earnings-per-share data must be shown in the body of the income statement of a publicly held company in order to receive an accountant's unqualified opinion.‡ Earnings per common share is conventionally calculated by dividing net income minus preferred stock dividends by the average number of outstanding common shares during the accounting period. For example, assume that a firm had net income of $500,000 during the year 1981. Dividends declared and paid on outstanding preferred stock were $100,000. The average number of shares of outstanding common stock during 1981 was 1,000,000 shares. Earnings per common share would be $.40 [= ($500,000 − $100,000)/1,000,000]. 2.104

If a firm has securities outstanding that can be converted into or exchanged for common stock, it may be required to present two sets of earnings-per-share amounts: *primary earnings per share* and *fully diluted earnings per share*. For example, some firms issue convertible bonds or convertible preferred 2.105

*Ibid., par. 19. See paragraph 23.87 in Chapter 23 for exceptions.

†Ibid., par. 34.

**Ibid., par. 36.

‡Accounting Principles Board, *Accounting Principles Board Opinion No. 15* (May 1969).

stock that can be exchanged directly for shares of common stock. Also, many firms have employee stock option plans under which shares of the company's common stock may be acquired by employees under special arrangements. If these convertible securities were converted or stock options were exercised and additional shares of common stock were issued, the amount conventionally shown as earnings per share would probably decrease, or become *diluted*. When a firm has outstanding securities that, if exchanged for shares of common stock, would decrease earnings per share by 3 percent or more, a dual presentation of primary and fully diluted earnings per share is required.*

2.106    Precision Products Company shows both primary and fully diluted earnings per-share amounts in its income statement in Exhibit 2.2. The dilution is probably attributable to the convertible preferred stock, although there may also be stock options outstanding. Earnings-per-share calculations are discussed more fully in Chapter 22.

# The Statement of Changes in Financial Position: Measuring Funds Flows

2.107    The third principal financial statement is the statement of changes in financial position. Exhibit 2.5 presents the statement of changes in financial position for Precision Products Company for 1981. This statement explains the inflows (sources) and outflows (uses) of funds during a period. "Funds" are usually defined as working capital (current assets minus current liabilities). Some firms use a more restrictive definition of funds, such as cash only, cash and marketable securities, or cash, marketable securities, and accounts receivable net of current liabilities. The statement also discloses other significant changes in financial position, even though the transactions or events do not affect working capital directly. For example, during the year Precision Products Company

issued shares of its common stock in exchange for a building. Included among the sources of working capital in Exhibit 2.5 is "Common Stock Issued in Exchange for Building" in the amount of $122,000. Among the uses of working capital is "Building Acquired by Issuing Common Stock" in the amount of $122,000. Even though this transaction did not affect working capital directly, it is included in the statement so that changes in the structure of Precision's assets and equities can be analyzed.

## Rationale for the Statement of Changes in Financial Position

2.108    Precision Products Company was formed in January 1976. During its first 3 years of operations, net income increased steadily, from $10,000 in 1976 to $130,000 in 1978. During this time, however, the firm had increasing difficulty paying its bills as they became due.

2.109    This experience of Precision Products Company is not unusual. Many firms, particularly those experiencing rapid growth, discover that their cash position is deteriorating despite an excellent earnings record. The statement of changes in financial position provides information that is useful in assessing changes in a firm's liquidity by reporting on the flows of funds into and out of a business.

**Income Flows and Cash Flows**   The revenues and expenses reported in the income statement differ from the cash receipts and disbursements during a period for two reasons:

**1.** The accrual basis of accounting is used in determining net income, so that the recognition of income does not necessarily coincide with the receipt of cash from customers, and the recognition of expenses does not necessarily coincide with the disbursement of cash to suppliers, employees, and other creditors.

**2.** The firm has cash receipts and disbursements not directly related to the process of generating earnings, such as from issuing

2.110

---

*Ibid., par. 15.

*Exhibit 2.5*
**Precision Products Company**
**Consolidated Statement of Changes in**
**Financial Position**
**for the Year Ended December 31, 1981**

**SECTION I. SOURCES AND USES OF WORKING CAPITAL**

Sources of Working Capital:

A. From Operations:

| | | | |
|---|---|---|---|
| Income from Continuing Operations | | $326,000 | |
| Add Back Expenses and Losses Not Using Working Capital: | | | |
| Depreciation of Plant and Equipment | | 285,000 | |
| Amortization of Intangibles | | 5,000 | |
| Amortization of Bond Discount | | 1,000 | |
| Subtract Revenues and Gains Not Providing Working Capital from Operations: | | | |
| Gain on Sale of Equipment | | (4,000) | |
| Working Capital Provided by Continuing Operations | | | $613,000 |
| Income from Discontinued Operations | | $ 19,000 | |
| Add Back Expenses and Losses from Discontinued Operations Not Using | | | |
| Working Capital | | 54,000 | |
| Working Capital Provided by Discontinued Operations | | | 73,000 |
| Extraordinary Losses | | $ (90,000) | |
| Add Back Loss from Expropriation of Plant Assets Not Using Working Capital | | 60,000 | |
| Working Capital Used for Extraordinary Items | | | (30,000) |
| Cumulative Effect of Accounting Change on Prior Years' Earnings | | $ 48,000 | |
| Subtract Increase in Earnings Not Providing Working Capital | | (48,000) | — |
| Total from Operations and Extraordinary Items | | | $656,000 |

B. Proceeds from Issuing Noncurrent Debt and Capital Stock:

| | | | |
|---|---|---|---|
| Treasury Stock Sold | | $ 53,000 | |
| Common Stock Issued in Exchange for Building | | 122,000 | |
| Total from Issuing Noncurrent Debt and Capital Stock | | | 175,000 |

C. Proceeds from Disposition of Noncurrent Assets:

| | | | |
|---|---|---|---|
| Sale of Segment | | $ 9,000 | |
| Sale of Equipment | | 7,000 | |
| Total from Selling Noncurrent Assets | | | 16,000 |
| Total Sources of Working Capital | | | $847,000 |

Uses for Working Capital:

A. For Distributions to Owners:

| | | | |
|---|---|---|---|
| Cash Dividends on Preferred Stock | | $ 12,000 | |
| Cash Dividends on Common Stock | | 78,000 | |
| Total for Distributions to Owners | | | $ 90,000 |

B. For Retiring Noncurrent Debt or Acquiring Capital Stock:

| | | | |
|---|---|---|---|
| Mortgage Principal Payments | | $ 10,000 | |
| Treasury Stock Acquired | | 22,000 | |
| Total for Retiring Noncurrent Debt or Acquiring Capital Stock | | | 32,000 |

C. For Acquiring Noncurrent Assets:

| | | | |
|---|---|---|---|
| Land | | $ 10,000 | |
| Machinery and Equipment | | 548,000 | |
| Building Acquired by Issuing Common Stock | | 122,000 | |
| Total for Acquiring Noncurrent Assets | | | 680,000 |
| Total Uses of Working Capital | | | $802,000 |
| Increase (Decrease) in Working Capital for the Year | | | $ 45,000 |

*Exhibit 2.5 continued*

**SECTION II. ANALYSIS OF CHANGES IN WORKING CAPITAL ACCOUNTS**

Current Asset Increases (Decreases):

| | |
|---|---:|
| Cash | $  3,000 |
| Marketable Securities | (1,000) |
| Accounts and Notes Receivable (Net of Allowance for Uncollectible Accounts) | 27,000 |
| Raw Materials Inventory | (13,000) |
| Work-in-Process Inventory | 6,000 |
| Finished Goods Inventory | 38,000 |
| Prepaid Insurance | (1,000) |
| Prepaid Rent | — |
| Net Increase (Decrease) in Current Asset Items | $ 59,000 |

Current Liability Increases (Decreases):

| | |
|---|---:|
| Notes Payable | $  — |
| Accounts Payable | 5,000 |
| Wages Payable | 4,000 |
| Income Taxes Payable | 7,000 |
| Estimated Liability for Warranties | 1,000 |
| Rental Fees Received in Advance | (3,000) |
| Net Increase (Decrease) in Current Liability Items | $ 14,000 |
| Net Increase (Decrease) in Working Capital for the Year | $ 45,000 |

capital stock or bonds, paying dividends, or purchasing buildings and equipment.

2.111   In Exhibit 2.4, we observed that Williams' Hardware Store had net income of $5,350 during its first month of operations. Net Income was calculated using the accrual basis of accounting. Exhibit 2.3, however, showed that operations resulted in a net decrease in cash of $1,700. Cash receipts from customers were less than sales revenue, and cash expenditures to suppliers, insurance companies, and others were different from the amounts of expenses recognized. The cash position of Williams' Hardware Store improved during the month, however, because of nonoperating sources of cash, primarily in the form of a bank loan and capital contributions by owners.

2.112   **Cash Flows and Working Capital Flows**
The statement of changes in financial position reports on the flows of funds into and out of a firm during a period of time. In the previous section, funds were viewed as cash. The term "funds," however, is a general one, which can have different meanings

depending on the circumstances. Consider the following two questions, which the management of a firm might raise:

1. Does the firm have sufficient funds to acquire new machinery immediately?

2. Will the firm have sufficient funds to acquire new equipment within the next 6 months?

In answering the first question, management is likely to consider the amount of cash on hand and in its bank account. It would also consider if the equipment could be acquired on account from one of its regular suppliers. In answering the second question, management would, in addition, consider if the firm had marketable securities or other assets that could be sold for cash during the next 6 months. It should be clear, however, that *time is the important factor* in answering the questions about available funds. When the time horizon is short, the meaning of funds must be more restrictive than when the time horizon is longer.

2.113   The statements of changes in financial position of most publicly held firms use a definition of funds broader than cash. In most

---

*Figure 2.2*
**Sources and Uses of Working Capital**

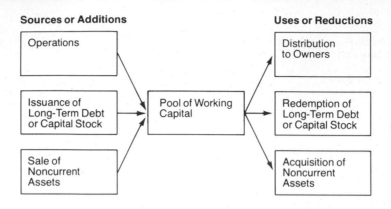

---

published annual reports, the statement explains the change in the net current asset position, or *working capital,* of the firm. That is, funds are defined as the difference between current assets (cash, readily marketable securities, accounts receivable, inventories, and current prepayments) and current liabilities (accounts payable, salaries payable, and other short-term obligations). Current assets are those assets that are either cash or are expected to be turned into cash, or sold, or consumed within the operating cycle, usually 1 year. Current liabilities are obligations expected to be discharged or paid within approximately 1 year. Thus, the amount of working capital at a particular time represents the excess of cash and near-cash assets over near-term claims on these liquid assets. This broader definition of funds is considered by many to provide more useful information to investors and other users of a firm's financial statements than does the more restrictive definition of funds as cash alone. Still, some analysts find cash to be a useful definition of funds.

## Content of the Statement of Changes in Financial Position

2.114   The statement of changes in financial position presents information on the sources (increases) and uses (decreases) of working capital during a period. The major sources and uses are depicted graphically in Figure 2.2 and are described below.

**1.** *Sources—operations.* The excess of revenues increasing working capital over expenses using working capital is the most important source of funds. When assessed over several years, working capital from operations indicates the extent to which the operating or earnings activities have generated more working capital than is used up. The excess from operations can then be used for dividends, acquisition of buildings and equipment, or repayment of long-term debt if necessary.

**2.** *Sources—issuance of long-term or capital stock.* In the long run, a firm must generate most of its funds from operating activities. Potential shareholders are not willing to invest in unprofitable firms. Neither are banks willing to lend large amounts of funds to firms that do not generate profits. A potentially profitable firm finds that it can raise funds by issuing shares to owners or by borrowing. The amount of funds that can be generated by issuing stock or by borrowing is limited, however, by the degree of the firm's past success and the marketplace's assessment of the firm's prospects.

**3.** *Sources—sale of noncurrent assets.* The sale of buildings, equipment, and other noncurrent assets results in an increase in working capital. These sales generally cannot be viewed as a major source of financing for an ongoing firm, because the amounts received from the sales are not likely to be sufficient to replace the assets sold.

**4.** *Uses—distributions to owners.* Dividends are generally a recurring use of working capital, because most publicly held firms are reluctant to omit the payment of dividends, even during a year of poor earnings performance.

**5.** *Uses—redemption of long-term debt or capital stock.* In most instances, publicly held firms redeem or pay long-term debt at maturity with the proceeds of another bond issue. Thus, these redemptions often have little effect on the *net* change in working capital. Some firms also occasionally reacquire or redeem their own capital stock for various reasons.

**6.** *Uses—acquisition of noncurrent assets.* The acquisition of noncurrent assets such as buildings and equipment usually represents an important use of working capital. These assets must be replaced as they wear out, and additional noncurrent assets must be acquired if a firm is to grow.

## Classification within the Statement of Changes in Financial Position

2.115 The statement of changes in financial position contains two sections. The first section lists the sources and uses of working capital for the period. The items in this first section might be classified as being related to:

1. Earnings activities,
2. Distributions to the firm's owners,
3. Financing activities, and
4. Investing activities.

The first item in the statement reports the amount of working capital provided (or used) by operations. This item indicates whether the earnings activities of the firm (that is, acquiring and selling goods or services) have resulted in an increase or decrease in working capital. Working capital provided by operations is the primary source of capital for dividends. Frequently, expansion of the firm's activities is financed with working capital provided by operations. Working capital provided (or used) by operations is therefore an important indicator of the firm's financial health, particularly when working capital flows are assessed over several years.

2.116 The derivation of the amount of working capital provided (or used) by operations is typically shown in the statement by beginning with the amount of net income for the period and adjusting net income for expenses not using working capital and revenues not providing working capital. The amount of working capital provided or used by operations might better be disclosed by listing revenues that provide working capital and then subtracting only those expenses that use working capital. The end result is the same under both methods of presentation. The first procedure leads some statement readers to the mistaken conclusion that depreciation is a source of working capital.

2.117 The sources and uses of working capital from financing activities include the issuance and redemption of common or preferred stock or long-term bonds. The sources and uses of working capital from investing activities include the purchase and sale of land, buildings, equipment, and other noncurrent assets. The declaration of dividends is a use of working capital.

2.118 Whereas the first section of the statement of changes in financial position presents the sources and uses of working capital, the second section summarizes the change in each of the working capital accounts. A firm might have a significant increase in working capital for a period (that is, sources exceed uses). However, if most of the increase results from an increase in inventories, the firm may not necessarily be more liquid. The second section of the statement of changes in financial position indicates the manner in which the increase (or decrease) in working capital for the period affected the individual working capital accounts.

## Relationship between the Principal Financial Statements

2.119  The preceding sections have considered the form and content of the three principal financial statements. The relationship among these statements might be depicted as follows:

2.120  The balance sheet reports the assets, liabilities, and owners' equity of a firm *at a specific moment in time*. This financial statement, therefore, reports *levels,* or *stocks*. The income statement and statement of changes in financial position, in contrast, report *flows*. That is, they report changes in amounts *over a period of time*. The income statement reports on the inflows of net assets in the form of revenues and the outflows of net assets in the form of expenses. The statement of changes in financial position reports on the inflows and outflows of funds. Funds flows are related either to operations, distributions to owners, financing activities, or investing activities.

2.121   The three principal financial statements articulate with each other. That is, the amounts reported in the income statement and statement of changes in financial position (financial statements reporting flow amounts) must tie in, or reconcile, with the amounts reported in the balance sheet at the beginning and end of the period (financial statement reporting levels, or stock amounts). Articulated financial statements provide a double-check feature inherent in a double-entry accounting system. They also reflect essential interrelationships of an enterprise's resources and its earnings, financing, and investing activities.

## Other Items in Annual Reports

2.122  The information presented in the three principal financial statements is condensed. For example, the amount shown for long-term debt may be comprised of 20 or more individual debt issues with varying interest rates and maturity dates. The amount shown as income tax expense may differ from an amount indicated by the statutory tax rate because of investment credits, capital gains, or other provisions. To supplement the information presented in the three principal financial statements, various explanatory notes and supporting schedules are used.

### Notes to the Financial Statements

2.123  Every set of published financial statements is supplemented by explanatory notes. These notes are an integral part of the statements. One of the notes typically lists the major accounting methods used in preparing the financial statements (for example, timing of revenue recognition, inventory cost-flow assumption, depreciation method). The first note to the financial statements of International Corporation in Appendix A illustrates this disclosure of accounting methods. The notes also elaborate on items presented in the financial statements. For example, note 16 lists the various debt issues included under "Debentures and Other Debt" on the balance sheet. Note 5 provides detailed information on income tax expense, explaining why it differs from an amount calculated by using the statutory tax rate. The notes to the financial statements tend to be factual rather than interpretative.

### Reconciliation of Retained Earnings

2.124  The beginning and ending balances in retained earnings must be reconciled in the financial statements. The reconciliation can appear either in a separate statement or as the lower section in a combined statement of income and retained earnings. In most instances, net income and dividends are the only reconciling items.

2.125    Occasionally an adjustment or correction

of prior years' income statements will appear as an addition to or a subtraction from the beginning balance in retained earnings. Examples might include corrections of errors in prior years' financial statements and retroactive restatements for certain changes in accounting principles or procedures.

2.126   The reconciliation of retained earnings for International Corporation is shown at the bottom of the income statement in Exhibit A.1 in Appendix A at the back of the book.

## Statement of Changes in Contributed Capital

2.127   As with retained earnings, a reconciliation of changes in the capital stock and additional paid-in capital accounts must be presented. This reconciliation includes the effects of financing by issuing capital stock, conversion of debt or preferred shares into common shares, issue of shares to employees under stock option plans, issue of shares to shareholders as a stock dividend, and reacquisitions of the firm's shares on the market and held as treasury shares. In Appendix A, note 18 to International Corporation's financial statements presents the statement of changes in contributed capital.

## Auditor's Opinion

2.128   An important section of the annual report to the shareholders is the opinion of the independent certified public accountant on the financial statements, supporting schedules, and notes. Exhibit 2.6 illustrates an auditor's opinion for International Corporation.

2.129   The opinion usually follows a standard format and contains two paragraphs—a *scope* paragraph and an *opinion* paragraph. The scope paragraph indicates the financial presentations covered by the opinion and affirms that auditing standards and practices generally accepted by the accounting profession have been adhered to unless otherwise noted and described. Exceptions to the statement that the auditor's "examination was made in accordance with generally ac-

cepted auditing standards" are seldom, if ever, seen in published annual reports. There are occasional references to the auditor's having relied on financial statements examined by other auditors, particularly for subsidiaries or for data from prior periods.

2.130   The opinion expressed by the auditor in the second paragraph is the heart of the independent auditor's report. The opinion may be *unqualified* or *qualified*. The great majority of opinions are unqualified; that is, there are no exceptions or qualifications to the auditor's opinion that the statements "present fairly the financial position . . . and the results of operations and the changes in financial position . . . in conformity with generally accepted accounting principles applied on a consistent basis."

2.131   Qualifications to the opinion result primar-

---

*Exhibit 2.6*
**Example of Auditor's Opinion**

---

**Report of Independent Accountants to the Board of Directors and Shareholders of International Corporation**

We have examined the statement of financial position of International Corporation and consolidated subsidiaries as of December 31, 1981 and 1980, and the related statements of income and retained earnings and changes in financial position for the years ended December 31, 1981, 1980, and 1979. Our examination was made in accordance with generally accepted auditing standards, and accordingly included such tests of the accounting records and such other auditing procedures as we considered necessary in the circumstances.

In our opinion, the aforementioned financial statements present fairly the financial position of International Corporation and consolidated subsidiaries at December 31, 1981 and 1980, and the results of their operations and the changes in their financial position for the years ended December 31, 1981, 1980, and 1979, in conformity with generally accepted accounting principles applied on a consistent basis.

*Stuckey Wells + Co.*

1101 E. 58th Street
Chicago, Illinois 60637

February 11, 1982

---

ily from material uncertainties regarding valuation or realization of assets, outstanding litigation or tax liabilities, or accounting inconsistencies between periods caused by changes in the application of accounting principles. An opinion qualified as to fair presentation is usually noted by the phrase *subject to;* an opinion qualified as to consistency in application of accounting principles is usually noted by *except for,* with an indication of the auditor's approval of the change.

2.132    A qualification so material that the auditor feels an opinion cannot be expressed as to the fairness of the financial statements as a whole must result in either a *disclaimer of opinion* or an *adverse opinion.* Adverse opinions and disclaimers of opinion are extremely rare in published reports.

## Summary of Current Accounting Theory

Accounting theory consists of a set of assumptions, concepts, broad principles, and modifying conventions that provides the rationale, or support, for the specific accounting procedures used in preparing financial statements. Exhibit 2.7 summarizes the current body of accounting theory. Standard-setting bodies, such as the FASB and APB, have been concerned primarily with establishing acceptable accounting procedures. In establishing these procedures, these bodies have relied on the set of assumptions, concepts, basic principles, and modifying conventions that comprise accounting theory. The body of accounting theory summarized in Exhibit 2.7 has not been officially prom- 2.133

*Exhibit 2.7.*
**Current Theoretical Structure
of Financial Reporting**

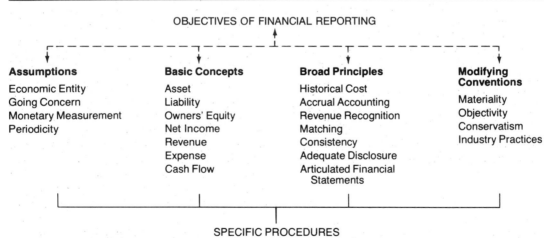

ulgated by any standard-setting body. Instead it has evolved over time as an *implicit* part of the standard-setting process. Although this theoretical structure can, in general, be related to the objectives of financial reporting discussed in Chapter 1, no rigorous effort has yet been made by standard-setting bodies to interrelate the two.* Thus, the objectives of financial reporting and the theoretical structure should be viewed as general guidelines for setting accounting standards and procedures instead of an axiomatic structure for logically deducing them.

2.134     In this section we summarize briefly each of the elements of the theoretical structure outlined in Exhibit 2.7. Most of these elements have been discussed in this chapter.

## Assumptions

2.135   Four basic assumptions of current financial reporting are economic entity, going concern, monetary measurement, and periodicity.

2.136   **Economic Entity** One assumption of accounting is that financial statements are prepared for an identifiable economic entity. Under a free-market economic system, resources are committed to various units of activity, or entities (business firms, industry associations, and so on). These entities then use the resources received to generate a return for the providers of capital. Financial statements provide information for assessing the accountability of these entities for the resources received.

2.137     Most problems of identifying the economic entity are caused by differences between the economic entity and the legal entity. In accounting we attempt to emphasize substance over form; that is, we focus on the unit, or entity, engaged in a common economic, or business, activity even though it may not be viewed as a separate legal entity.

2.138   *Example 1* Joan Webster operates a hardware store in her neighborhood as a sole proprietorship. According to the laws of most states, Webster's business assets and personal assets are mingled. That is, suppliers of merchandise to the hardware store can obtain payment for their claims from some or all of her personal assets if business assets are insufficient. Even so, the entity in accounting is the hardware store alone, because this is the organizational unit carrying on the business activity.

2.139   *Example 2* Roger Green and Bill White own and manage an apartment complex, called the Leisure Living Apartments, as a partnership. Under the laws of most states, their personal assets as well as the business assets are subject to the claims of creditors. Even so, the accounting entity is the apartment complex alone, because this is the organizational unit carrying on the business activity.

2.140   *Example 3* The Domestic Corporation operates through its subsidiaries in 23 states. Each subsidiary is organized as a separate legal corporation under the laws of the state in which it is located. The accounting entity is a combination (or consolidation) of Domestic Corporation and all of its 23 subsidiary corporations, because these legally separate units operate as a single economic entity. For purposes of internal performance evaluation by management, however, Domestic Corporation might treat each subsidiary as a separate reporting entity. Thus, we see that the scope of the economic entity can be related to the purpose to be served by the financial statements.

2.141     The entity for which a set of financial statements has been prepared can be determined from the heading of each statement. For the three examples above, the headings might read: Webster's Hardware Store, Leisure Living Apartments, and Domestic Corporation and Consolidated Subsidiaries.

2.142   **Going Concern** The economic entity is assumed to have an indefinite life. That is, the firm is expected to continue operating with the resources received at least long enough for current expectations and plans to be carried out and for the reasonably foreseeable future period after that.

---

*Recent efforts by the FASB to develop a conceptual framework for financial reporting are aimed at such an integration.

2.143   The going-concern assumption has been used to justify historical cost valuation for assets instead of some type of current value (current replacement cost, current selling price). It is argued that assessments of an entity's accountability will be made on a continuing basis over time as the resources are used in generating income. Any differences between historical cost and current values of assets will manifest themselves in net income. Short-run measures of the current, or liquidation, values of assets are therefore of little importance.*

2.144   **Monetary Measurement** Economic entities carry out a diverse set of activities in raising and using capital. Labor services transform raw materials into finished products. The sales staff sells the products. An administrative support structure assists in the production and selling efforts. Accounting requires some common denominator to express these diverse activities in a meaningful form. That common denominator is monetary measurement. Accounting measures transactions and events in terms of their monetary amount and aggregates the resulting monetary measures into a set of financial statements.

2.145   In parallel, accounting assumes that the monetary measuring unit is stable over time. In this way, monetary measurements made several years ago are assumed to be of the same underlying dimension as monetary measurements made currently. Aggregations of the various monetary measurements can thereby be made more meaningfully.

2.146   The assumption of a stable monetary measuring unit has been violated, particularly in recent years, with continuing inflation.

---

*The issues involved in selecting a valuation basis for assets are too complex to be discussed adequately in this chapter. The critical question is "accountability for what?" Conventional financial statements assume accountability for the historical dollar amount of resources committed to the entity. It can be argued that the entity should also be held accountable for the current dollar equivalent of the historical cost amount or the current value of the assets used (see discussion in Chapter 26).

The dollar has a substantially different amount of purchasing power today than it did 5 or 10 years ago. Monetary measurements made over time using the dollar as the measuring unit therefore do not have the same underlying dimension. Chapter 26 discusses techniques for stabilizing the measuring unit.

**Periodicity** Given the going-concern assumption, there is no automatic terminal date to an entity's existence and, therefore, no preestablished time for reporting on accountability for resources received. Providers of capital must assess accountability on an ongoing basis and, therefore, require periodic financial statements.   2.147

By convention, an accounting period of 1 year underlies the principal financial statements distributed to shareholders and potential investors. Most firms prepare their annual reports using the calendar year as the accounting period. A growing but still relatively small number of firms, however, use a *natural business year*. The use of a natural business year is an attempt to measure performance at a time when most earnings activities have been substantially concluded. The ending date of a natural business year varies from one firm to another. For example, J. C. Penney uses a natural business year ending on January 31, which comes after completion of the Christmas shopping season and before the start of the Easter season. American Motors uses a year ending September 30, the end of its model year. A. C. Nielsen (producers of television ratings and other surveys) uses a year ending August 31, just prior to the beginning of the new television season.   2.148

Most publicly held firms also issue quarterly financial statements to provide users with even more timely information.   2.149

## Basic Concepts

The basic concepts of financial accounting, discussed earlier in the chapter and summarized briefly below, are definitional in nature.   2.150

2.151   **Asset** A resource that has the potential for providing an entity with future economic services or benefits. The resources that are recognized as assets have the following characteristics:

**1.** The resource must, singly or in combination with other resources, contribute directly or indirectly to future net cash inflows (or to obviating future net cash outflows).

**2.** The enterprise must be able to obtain the benefit from the resource and control the access of others to it.

**3.** The transaction or event giving rise to the enterprise's claim to or control of the benefit must already have occurred.

**4.** The future benefit must be quantifiable or measurable in units of money.*

2.152   **Liability** An obligation of an entity to transfer economic resources to other entities in the future. Obligations that are recognized as liabilities have the following four characteristics:

**1.** The obligation must involve a probable future sacrifice of resources—a future transfer of cash, goods, or services (or a forgoing of a future cash receipt).

**2.** The obligation must be one of the specific enterprise.

**3.** The transaction or event giving rise to the enterprise's obligation must already have occurred.

**4.** The amount of the obligation and the time of its settlement must be measurable with reasonable accuracy.†

2.153   **Owners' Equity** The residual interest in, or claim on, the assets of an entity by the entity's owners. Owners' equity is equal to assets minus liabilities. It is also equal to capital contributions of owners plus the accumulated earnings of the entity in excess of dividends declared.

*Financial Accounting Standards Board, *Statement of Financial Accounting Concepts No. 3* (1980), pars. 17 and 20.

†Ibid., pars. 17 and 29.

**Net Income** Net income for a period is the   2.154
excess of revenues and gains over expenses and losses.

**Revenue** Revenue is a measure of the net   2.155
assets (assets less liabilities) received from selling goods or providing services.

**Expense** Expense is a measure of the net as-   2.156
sets (assets less liabilities) used up, or consumed, in the process of generating revenue.

**Cash Flow** The inflows of cash from cus-   2.157
tomers, creditors, and owners in excess of the outflows of cash to suppliers, employees, other creditors, and owners. Over long-enough time periods, income equals cash inflows less cash outflows. Cash flows differ from revenues and expenses whenever **(1)** revenues are recognized at a time different from the time when cash is received and expenses are recognized at a time different from the time when cash is disbursed and **(2)** there are cash flows not directly related to the earnings process, such as from borrowing or capital contributions by owners.

## Broad Principles

Seven broad principles of financial account-   2.158
ing are historical cost, accrual accounting, revenue recognition, matching, consistency, adequate disclosure, and articulated financial statements.

**Historical Cost** Nonmonetary assets are   2.159
initially recorded at their historical, or acquisition, cost amount. Acquisition cost is equal to the amount of cash given or the cash-equivalent value of other consideration exchanged. Included in acquisition cost are all expenditures made to prepare the asset for its intended use. In addition to the invoice price of the asset, acquisition cost might include freight charges, insurance and taxes, installation costs, and others.

Nonmonetary assets are stated at acquisi-   2.160
tion cost until all or a portion of their service potential has been consumed. At this time, all or a portion of the acquisition cost becomes an expense. In the case of most in-

ventory items, the asset stated at acquisition cost becomes an expense when the inventory items are sold. In the case of depreciable assets, the acquisition cost becomes an expense piecemeal over the assets' lives (in the case of depreciable assets used in selling and administrative activities) or as products manufactured with the depreciable assets are sold (in the case of depreciable assets used in manufacturing).

2.161 **Accrual Accounting** Net income, or earnings, is calculated using the accrual basis of accounting. Under the accrual basis, revenue is recognized at a time in the earnings process when some critical event takes place (see discussion of revenue recognition below) and expenses are recognized so as to match expenses as closely as possible with revenue. The accrual basis of accounting is to be distinguished from the cash basis of accounting, where revenue is recognized when cash is received and expenses are recognized when cash expenditures are made.

2.162 **Revenue Recognition** Revenue is recognized at a point in the earnings process when (1) all, or a substantial portion, of the services to be provided have been performed, and (2) cash, receivables, or some other asset susceptible to objective measurement has been received. In most cases, revenue is recognized at the time of sale.

2.163 **Matching** Asset expirations, or expenses, directly associated with particular types of revenue are recognized as expenses in the period in which the revenues are recognized. That is, cost expirations are matched with revenues. Asset expirations, or expenses, not directly or easily associated with revenues are treated as expenses of the period in which services are consumed in operations. That is, cost expirations are matched with, or allocated to, the period of benefit.

2.164 **Consistency** The particular set of accounting principles and procedures selected by an entity should be used consistently over time. In this way, more meaningful interperiod comparisons can be made. When an entity changes its accounting principles or procedures, the effect of the change must be clearly disclosed in the financial statements. In addition, the opinion of the independent accountant must be qualified (consistency exception) for the year of the change.

**Adequate Disclosure** The disclosure of information in the financial statements is presumed to be sufficiently adequate so that an intelligent reader can make an informed judgment or decision. There are three questions relating to this adequate disclosure principle.    2.165

First, what level of sophistication should be assumed of the financial statement reader? Should disclosures be aimed at the level of the credit or security analyst or at the level of a relatively uninformed investor? The FASB has stated that financial information "should be comprehensible to those who have a reasonable understanding of business and economic activities and are willing to study the information with reasonable diligence."*    2.166

Second, how can the concept of adequate disclosure be made operational? In past years, the accounting profession and the courts interpreted adequate disclosure to mean that the disclosures were sufficient so as not to mislead the statement reader. Recent thinking has been shifting this concept from one of "not misleading" to one of being informative. For example, until recently firms seldom disclosed the amounts of payments made to foreign officials to obtain business in a particular country. Failure to make such disclosures was not considered to mislead readers, because such payments were common practice among firms doing business abroad. Recent thinking is that disclosure of such information is necessary to inform statement readers of the extent to which such payments are made.    2.167

Third, at what point is excessive disclosure a concern? The FASB and the SEC have been requiring the disclosure of increasing amounts of information in recent    2.168

---

*Financial Accounting Standards Board, *Statement of Financial Accounting Concepts No. 1* (1978), par. 34.

years. It is possible that the financial reporting process has become so complex that statement readers cannot process and understand all of the information reported. It is also possible that the benefits of some of the disclosures do not exceed the cost of generating the information.

2.169   **Articulated Financial Statements** Various items in the financial statements (for example, revenues) should tie in, or be reconcilable, with related items in other financial statements (for example, increases in cash or accounts receivable). Articulated financial statements provide an internal check on the double-entry recording process and relate an enterprise's resources to its earnings, financing, and investing activities.

## Modifying Conventions

2.170   Four conventions that modify accounting principles and practices are materiality, objectivity, conservatism, and industry practices.

2.171   **Materiality** The materiality convention makes operational the principle of adequate disclosure. A particular disclosure (whether quantitative or descriptive) is material if it is likely to affect a decision made by a user of the financial statements. The materiality convention would be used in responding to questions such as the following. Should payments made to foreign officials to obtain business in a particular country be set out separately or included in "selling and administrative expenses"?* Should a loss on the sale of a major asset be set out separately or included in "other expenses"? Should restrictions on the use of assets imposed by creditors be disclosed? Should operating losses of certain segments of the firm be disclosed or aggregated with profits of other segments?

2.172   The materiality convention, though applied often in preparing financial statements, is difficult to define explicitly. Materiality judgments form an important part of the work of the independent accountant. The FASB currently has the concept of materiality under study.

**Objectivity** The process of measuring and reporting the financial effects of a firm's activities requires numerous estimates and judgments. For example, over what period will the benefits of an asset be received? What is the pattern of the future benefits? These estimates and judgments inject uncertainty into the measurement and reporting process. The judgments of individuals can vary in response to the questions with the resultant effects on the financial statements.   2.173

To help reduce subjective bias in financial reporting, the objectivity convention has been developed. When there is extreme uncertainty in the measurement process, there is a tendency to say that the measurement method that is most objective (least subjective) should be followed. Objectivity has been used to justify historical cost valuations, rather than current cost valuations, for assets. It has also been used implicitly by the FASB in requiring that research and development costs be treated as an expense in the period when expenditures are made because of the subjectivity involved in deciding if there are future benefits and, if so, over what period the benefits will be received.   2.174

**Conservatism** A third modifying convention is conservatism. When there are two or more equally objective methods of accounting, it is suggested that the method resulting in the most conservative measure of earnings should be used. Given the uncertainties in the measurement process, it is argued that it is best not to present an overly optimistic picture of performance that might mislead readers.   2.175

Conservatism is a two-edged sword, however. Some readers might be misled by the conservatively stated amounts. For example, management of a firm might be fired because owners felt that performance had been   2.176

---

*The Congress and the SEC have concluded that any payment to a foreign official to secure business is, by definition, material. See the Foreign Corrupt Practices Act and various SEC rulings on its implications.

unsatisfactory, when earnings reported on a less conservative basis would not have led to such action. Also, conservatively reported amounts for a particular year will result in amounts with just the opposite effects in later years. For example, the double-declining-balance depreciation method results in the largest depreciation expense and usually the smallest earnings during the first few years of an individual asset's life but the smallest depreciation charges and the largest earnings during the last few years of its life.

2.177 **Industry Practices** Certain industries follow particular accounting principles and procedures that differ from those followed by most other firms. For example, investments in securities by insurance companies are generally stated at current market values instead of lower of acquisition cost or market value. Inventories of meat packing houses and grain products firms are likewise typically stated at current market value. Care must be exercised by the independent accountant and financial statement user to assess if these departures from conventional principles and procedures are justifiable.

## Appendix 2.1: Balance Sheet Account Titles

2.178 The following list shows balance sheet account titles that are commonly used. The descriptions should help in understanding the nature of various assets, liabilities, and owners' equities as well as in selecting appropriate terms for solving problems. Alternative account titles can be easily devised. The list is not intended to exhaust all the account titles used in this book or appearing in the financial statements of publicly held firms.

### Assets

2.179 *Cash on Hand* Coins and currency, and such items as bank checks and money orders. The latter items are merely claims against individuals or institutions, but by custom are called "cash."

*Cash in Bank* Strictly speaking, merely a claim against the bank for the amount deposited. Cash in bank consists of demand deposits, against which checks can be drawn, and time deposits, usually savings accounts and certificates of deposit. In published statements, the two items of Cash on Hand and Cash in Bank usually are combined under the title Cash.

*Marketable Securities* Government bonds or stocks and bonds of corporations. The word *marketable* implies that they can be bought and sold readily through a security exchange such as the New York Stock Exchange.

*Accounts Receivable* Amounts due from customers of a business from the sale of goods or services. The collection of cash occurs some time after the sale. These accounts are also known as "charge accounts" or "open accounts." An alternative title is Customers' Accounts. The general term Accounts Receivable is used in financial statements to describe the figure representing the total amount receivable but, of course, the firm keeps a separate record for each customer.

*Allowance for Uncollectible Accounts* The estimated amount of accounts receivable that is not expected to be collected. The balance in the Allowance account is subtracted from the balance in the Accounts Receivable account on the balance sheet to show the net amount of accounts receivable expected to be collected in cash. Because the balance in the Allowance account is subtracted from the balance in another account, it is referred to as a *contra account*.

*Notes Receivable* Amounts due from customers or from others to whom loans have been made or credit extended, when the claim has been put into writing in the form of a promissory note.

*Interest Receivable* Interest on assets such as promissory notes or bonds that has accrued, or come into existence, through the passing of time but that has not been collected as of the date of the balance sheet.

*Merchandise Inventory* Goods on hand that have been purchased for resale, such as canned goods on the shelves of a grocery store or suits on the racks of a clothing store.

This item is frequently shown simply as Merchandise.

*Finished Goods Inventory* Completed but unsold manufactured products.

*Work-in-Process Inventory* Partially completed manufactured products.

*Raw Materials Inventory* Unused materials from which manufactured products are to be made. Sometimes combined with supplies under the title Stores.

*Supplies Inventory* Lubricants, cleaning rags, abrasives, and other incidental materials used in manufacturing operations. Stationery, computer cards, pens, and other office supplies. Bags, twine, boxes, and other store supplies. Gasoline, oil, spare parts, and other delivery supplies. Alternative titles, such as Factory Supplies, Office Supplies, Store Supplies, and Delivery Supplies, could be used.

*Prepaid Insurance* Insurance premiums paid for future coverage. An alternative title is Unexpired Insurance.

*Prepaid Rent* Rent paid in advance of future use of land, buildings, or equipment.

*Advances to Suppliers* The general name used to indicate payments made in advance for goods to be received at a later date. If no cash is paid by a firm when it places an order, then no asset is recognized.

*Investments* The cost of bonds or shares of stock in other companies, where the firm's purpose is to hold the bonds or shares for relatively long periods of time.

*Land* Land occupied by buildings or used in operations.

*Buildings* Factory buildings, store buildings, garages, warehouses, and so forth.

*Machinery and Equipment* Lathes, ovens, tools, boilers, computers, motors, bins, cranes, conveyors, and so forth.

*Furniture and Fixtures* Desks, tables, chairs, counters, showcases, scales, and other such store and office equipment. Other titles, such as Office Furniture and Fixtures and Store Furniture and Fixtures, could be used.

*Office Machines* Typewriters, adding machines, bookkeeping equipment, calculators, and so forth. Sometimes combined with Furniture and Fixtures.

*Automobiles* Delivery trucks, sales staff's cars, and so forth.

*Accumulated Depreciation* This account shows the cumulative amount of the cost of long-term assets (such as buildings and machinery) that has been allocated to prior periods as depreciation in measuring net income or to the costs of production. The amount in this account is subtracted from the acquisition cost of the long-term asset to which it relates in determining the *net book value* of assets to be shown in the balance sheet. Thus, accumulated depreciation is a contra account.

*Organization Costs* Amounts paid for legal and incorporation fees, for printing the certificates for shares of stock, and for accounting and any other costs incurred in organizing the business so it can begin to function. This asset is seen most commonly on the balance sheets of corporations.

*Patents* A right granted for up to 17 years by the federal government to exclude others from manufacturing, using, or selling a certain process or device. Under current generally accepted accounting principles, research and development costs must be treated as an expense in the year incurred rather than being recognized as an asset with future benefits.* (This treatment seems to us to be at odds with good accounting theory.) As a result, a firm that develops technology will not normally show it as an asset. On the other hand, a firm that purchases a patent from another firm or from an individual will recognize the patent as an asset. This inconsistent treatment of internally developed and externally purchased patents is discussed more fully in Chapter 13.

*Goodwill* An amount paid by one firm in acquiring another business enterprise that is greater than the sum of the values assignable to other assets. A good reputation and other desirable attributes are generally not recognized as assets by the firm that creates or develops them. However, when one firm acquires another firm, these desirable attributes are indirectly recognized as assets, be-

---

*Financial Accounting Standards Board, *Statement of Financial Accounting Standards No. 2* (1974).

cause they are a factor in determining the valuation of goodwill.

## Liabilities

2.180 *Accounts Payable* Amounts owed for goods or services acquired under an informal credit agreement. These accounts are usually payable within 1 or 2 months. The same items appear as Accounts Receivable on the creditor's books.

*Notes Payable* The face amount of promissory notes given in connection with loans from the bank or the purchase of goods or services. The same items appear as Notes Receivable on the creditors' books.

*Payroll Taxes Payable* Amounts withheld from wages and salaries of employees for federal and state payroll taxes and the employer's share of such taxes.

*Withheld Income Taxes* Amounts withheld from wages and salaries of employees for income taxes that have not yet been remitted to the taxing authority. This is a tentative income tax on the earnings of employees, and the employer acts merely as a tax-collecting agent for the federal and state governments. A few cities also levy income taxes, which the employer must withhold from wages.

*Interest Payable* Interest on obligations that has accrued or accumulated with the passage of time but that has not been paid as of the date of the balance sheet. The liability for interest is customarily shown separately from the face amount of the obligation.

*Income Taxes Payable* The estimated liability for income taxes, accumulated and unpaid, based on the taxable income of the business from the beginning of the taxable year to the date of the balance sheet. Because sole proprietorships and partnerships do not pay federal income taxes directly, this term will appear only on the books of a corporation or other taxable entity.

*Advances from Customers* The general name used to indicate payments received in advance for goods to be delivered or services to be furnished to customers in the future. If no cash is received when a customer places an order, then no liability is shown.

*Rent Received in Advance* An example of a nonmonetary liability. The business owns a building that it rents to a tenant. The tenant has prepaid the rental charge for several months in advance. The amount applicable to future months cannot be considered a component of income until the rent is earned as service is rendered with the passage of time. Meanwhile the advance payment results in a liability payable in services (that is, in the use of the building). On the records of the tenant the same amount would appear as an asset, Prepaid Rent.

*Mortgage Payable* Long-term promissory notes that have been given greater protection by the pledge of specific pieces of property as security for their payment. If the loan or interest is not paid according to the agreement, the property can be sold for the benefit of the creditor.

*Bonds Payable* Face amount borrowed by the business for a relatively long period of time under a formal written contract or indenture. The loan is usually obtained from a number of lenders, each of whom receives one or more bond certificates as written evidence of his or her share of the loan.

*Discount or Premium on Bonds Payable* The difference between the face value of bonds and their initial issue price is shown in the Discount on Bonds Payable account (if the difference is positive) or the Premium on Bonds Payable account (if the difference is negative). The discount or premium is amortized over the life of the bonds as an adjustment to interest expense. The Discount on Bonds Payable account is a contra account to Bonds Payable. The Premium on Bonds Payable account is an *adjunct account* to Bonds Payable because the balance in this account is added to the balance in the Bonds Payable account on the balance sheet.

*Debenture Bonds* The most common type of bond, except in the railroad and public utility industries. This type of bond carries no specific security or collateral; instead it is issued on the basis of the general credit of the business. If other bonds have a prior claim on the assets of the business, then the debenture is called *subordinated*.

*Convertible Bonds* A bond that the holder can *convert* into, or "trade in" for, shares of common stock. The number of shares to be received when the bond is converted into stock, the dates when conversion can occur, and other details are specified in the bond indenture.

*Capitalized Lease Obligations* The present value of future commitments for cash payments to be made in return for the right to use property owned by someone else.

*Deferred Income Taxes* Certain income tax payments are delayed beyond the current accounting period. This item, which appears on the balance sheet of most U.S. corporations, is discussed in Chapter 20.

## Owners' Equity

2.181 *Common Stock* Amounts received for the par or stated value of a firm's principal class of voting stock.

*Preferred Stock* Amounts received for the par value of a class of a firm's stock that has some preference relative to the common stock. This preference is usually with respect to dividends and to assets in the event the corporation is liquidated. Sometimes preferred stock is convertible into common stock.

*Capital Contributed in Excess of Par or Stated Value* Amounts received from the issuance of common or preferred stock in excess of such shares' par value or stated value. This account is also referred to as Additional Paid-in Capital or sometimes as Premium on Preferred (or Common) Stock.

*Stock Warrants* The amount in this account represents the amount the firm received for issuing certificates that permit the holders to purchase shares of stock at a specified price. The rights contained in stock warrants are usually exercisable for only a limited period.

*Retained Earnings* An account reflecting the increase in net assets since the business was organized as a result of generating earnings in excess of dividend declarations. When dividends are declared, net assets are distributed, and retained earnings are reduced by an equal amount.

*Treasury Shares* This account shows the cost of shares of stock originally issued but subsequently reacquired by the corporation. Treasury shares are not entitled to dividends and are not considered to be "outstanding" shares. The cost of treasury shares is almost always shown on the balance sheet as a deduction from the total of the other shareholders' equity accounts. Accounting for treasury shares is discussed in Chapter 21.

2.182 A balance sheet that includes many of the accounts described in this section is presented in Appendix A, Exhibit A.2, for International Corporation.

## Questions and Short Cases

2.1 Review the meaning of the following concepts or terms discussed in this chapter.

a. Asset.
b. Liability.
c. Owners' equity.
d. Going-concern assumption.
e. Objectivity.
f. Conservatism.
g. Current assets.
h. Investments.
i. Property, plant, and equipment.
j. Intangible assets.
k. Monetary asset or liability.

l. Nonmonetary asset or liability.
m. Current liability.
n. Long-term debt.
o. Net income.
p. Revenue.
q. Expense.
r. Cash basis of accounting.
s. Accrual basis of accounting.
t. Product cost.
u. Period expense.

v. Income from continuing operations.
w. Income, gains, and losses from discontinued operations.
x. Extraordinary gains and losses.
y. Change in accounting estimate.
z. Change in accounting principle.

2.2   Review the meaning of the following concepts or terms discussed in this chapter.

    **a.** Change in reporting entity.

    **b.** Correction of error in prior years' financial statements.

    **c.** Earnings per share (primary and fully diluted).

    **d.** Funds flow.

    **e.** Income flows versus cash flows.

    **f.** Cash flows versus working capital flows.

    **g.** Working capital provided by operations.

    **h.** Stock versus flow.

    **i.** Scope and opinion paragraphs in auditor's opinion.

    **j.** "Subject to" and "except for" opinions.

    **k.** Economic entity.

    **l.** Monetary measurement.

    **m.** Periodicity.

    **n.** Historical cost.

    **o.** Matching.

    **p.** Adequate disclosure.

    **q.** Materiality.

    **r.** Industry practices.

2.3   Relate the concepts of stock and flow to your personal checking account.

2.4   Distinguish between revenue and cash receipts from customers.

2.5   Distinguish between cash expenditures to suppliers and employees and expenses.

2.6   "All assets eventually become expenses." Do you agree? Why or why not?

2.7   Distinguish between the following four elements of accounting theory: assumptions, concepts, broad principles, modifying conventions.

2.8   If the going-concern assumption were not made, what difference might it make in the amount at which the following items would be shown in the financial statements?

    **a.** Accounts Receivable.

    **b.** Prepaid Rent.

    **c.** Inventories.

    **d.** Land.

2.9   Financial statements are based on the assumption that the monetary measuring unit is stable over time. For which items in the balance sheet, income statement, and statement of changes in financial position is this assumption most severely violated?

2.10   The president of a company stated: "The current value of this company is a good deal larger than the amount you accountants show as assets on the balance sheet." What do you think the president had in mind when making this statement?

2.11   What relationship do you see between the periodicity assumption and the accrual basis of accounting?

2.12   Conservatism is viewed as a modifying convention in accounting. Indicate who might be hurt by conservatively stated accounting reports.

2.13   A firm sold a tract of land during the year at a gain. In its financial statements, the firm included this gain in Other Income. The independent accountant must assess whether this method of presentation is appropriate or whether the gain should be disclosed separately, either in the income statement or in the notes to the financial statements. How do you think an independent accountant makes such a judgment?

2.14   "The objectivity convention largely eliminates the need for judgments by the independent accountant." Do you agree? Why or why not?

**2.15**   Under what circumstances are qualified opinions expressed on a set of financial statements?

**2.16**   If an item is important enough to warrant disclosure in a note to the financial statements, why is it not disclosed in the body of the statements?

**2.17**   New terminology continues to replace certain old terminology in accounting reports. For each of the following items of old terminology, suggest reasons why the terms have been or are being replaced by the terms shown in parentheses.
   **a.** Prepaid Expenses (by Prepaid Insurance, Prepaid Rent).
   **b.** Reserve for Depreciation (by Accumulated Depreciation).
   **c.** Unearned Revenue (by Advances from Customers).
   **d.** Capital Surplus (by Additional Paid-in Capital).
   **e.** Earned Surplus (by Retained Earnings).
   **f.** Net Worth (by Shareholders' Equity).

**2.18**   Explain the difference, if any, between the items referred to by the following pairs of terms.
   **a.** Qualified opinion and unqualified opinion.
   **b.** "Subject to" opinion and "except for" opinion.
   **c.** Statement of financial position and statement of changes in financial position.
   **d.** Income from continuing operations and income from discontinued operations.
   **e.** Primary earnings per share and fully diluted earnings per share.
   **f.** Income from continuing operations and working capital provided by continuing operations.
   **g.** Statement of changes in financial position and funds statement.
   **h.** Working capital provided by operations and cash flow provided by operations.

**2.19**   Beaumont Chemical Company produces an extensive line of chemical products. Its production methods are such that pollutants are continually emitted into the air. Using the theoretical structure summarized in Exhibit 2.7, discuss the asset valuation and income measurement issues in each of the following independent situations.
   **a.** Beaumont has decided not to install emission-control equipment in order to bring pollutant levels down to legally prescribed maximums. Instead, it merely pays fines as they are imposed
   **b.** Beaumont has installed emission-control equipment that will reduce pollutant levels to prescribed maximums. The equipment has a 5-year estimated life.
   **c.** Beaumont has installed emission-control equipment that will reduce pollutant levels below the prescribed maximums. As before, the equipment has a 5-year estimated life.
   **d.** Same as part **c**, except that the reduction of pollutants below maximum levels creates for Beaumont a pollution emission right. This right can be sold to other firms whose pollutant levels are in excess of the maximum. Buyers of this right can avoid fines if their actual level of emissions minus the amounts attributable to the emission right do not exceed the legal maximums. These rights lapse if they are not sold each year. Beaumont did not sell its emission rights during the current year.
   **e.** Same as part **d**, except the rights can be accumulated for 3 years. Beaumont did not sell its emission rights during the current year.
   **f.** Same as part **d**, except that Beaumont sold emission rights during the current year that were created last year.

**2.20**   Indicate whether or not each of the following items would be recognized as assets by a firm according to current generally accepted accounting principles.
   **a.** The cash received from a customer for services to be provided in a future accounting period.

b. A contract signed by a customer to purchase $10,000 of merchandise next year.

c. A reputation for quality products.

d. A patent on a new invention developed by a firm.

e. A good credit standing.

f. A delivery truck.

g. A degree in engineering from a reputable university, awarded to the firm's chief executive.

h. The right to insurance coverage for the coming year. The 1-year premium for the period has already been paid.

i. The right to warranty services on the delivery truck in part **f**. The warranty period runs for 3 more years.

2.21 Indicate whether or not each of the following events immediately gives rise to an asset. If an asset is recognized, state an account title and amount.

a. An investment of $9,000 is made in a government bond. The bond will have a maturity value of $10,000 in 10 years.

b. An order for $900 of merchandise is received from a customer.

c. Merchandise inventory with a list price of $500 is purchased. Payment is made immediately in order to secure a 2-percent discount for prompt payment.

d. Notice has been received from a manufacturer that materials billed at $6,000, with payment due within 30 days, have been shipped by freight. The seller retains title to the materials until they are received by the buyer.

e. A contract is signed for the construction of a specially designed piece of machinery. The terms are $6,000 down upon signing the contract and the balance of $9,000 upon delivery of the equipment. The purchaser gives a check for $6,000. Consider this question from the standpoint of the purchaser.

f. A check for $800 is sent to a landlord for 2 months' rent in advance (consider from the standpoint of the tenant, often called the *lessee*).

g. A check for $2,000 is written to obtain an option to purchase a tract of land. The price of the land is $22,500. Consider from the standpoint of the person writing the check.

h. Bonds with a face value of $100,000 are purchased for $97,000. The bonds mature in 25 years. Interest is payable by the issuer of the bonds at the rate of 8 percent annually.

2.22 Indicate whether or not each of the following events immediately gives rise to the recognition of an asset. If an asset is recognized, state an account title and amount.

a. Raw materials with an invoice price of $7,200 are purchased on account from Williams Wholesalers.

b. Defective raw material purchased in part **a** for $200 is returned to Williams Wholesalers.

c. The bill of Williams Wholesalers (see parts **a** and **b**) is paid promptly. A discount of 2 percent offered by the seller for prompt payment is taken. Discounts are treated as a reduction in the cost of raw materials.

d. A machine is purchased for $16,000 cash.

e. The cost of transporting the new machine in part **d** to the plant site is paid in cash, $450.

f. Material and labor costs incurred in installing the machine in part **d** total $400 and are paid in cash.

2.23 In each of the following transactions, give the title(s) and amount(s) of the asset(s) that would appear on the balance sheet.

a. A firm purchases a delivery truck with a list price of $12,000. The dealer allows a discount of $650 from the list price for payment in cash. Dealer preparation charges on the truck amount to an extra $250. The dealer collects a 5-percent sales tax on the price paid for the truck and preparation charges. In addition, the dealer collects a $65 fee to be remitted to the state for this year's license plates and $500 for a 1-year insurance policy provided by the dealer's insurance agency. The firm pays a body shop $60 for painting the firm's name on the truck.

b. A firm acquires a building that has been appraised at $1,000,000 by a certified real estate appraiser. The firm pays for the building by giving up shares in the General Electric Company at a time when equivalent shares traded on the New York Stock Exchange for $1,050,000.

c. A firm acquires a building that has been appraised at $1,000,000 by a certified real estate appraiser. The firm pays for the building by giving up shares in Small Timers, Inc., whose shares are traded only on the Cincinnati Stock Exchange. The last transaction in shares of Small Timers, Inc., occurred 4 days prior to this asset swap. Using the prices of the most recent trades, the shares of stock of Small Timers, Inc., given in exchange for the building have a market value of $1,050,000.

**2.24**  Give an illustration, other than those in the text, of each of the following:

a. A situation in which property is not shown as an asset on the balance sheet of the firm that has possession of the property.

b. A situation in which property is shown as an asset on the balance sheet of a firm even though the firm does not have legal title to the property.

**2.25**  Indicate whether or not each of the following items is recognized as a liability by a firm according to current generally accepted accounting principles.

a. Unpaid wages of employees.

b. A tenant's obligation to maintain a rented office building in good repair.

c. The amount payable by a firm for a newspaper advertisement that has appeared but for which payment is not due for 30 days.

d. An employee who is the incompetent brother-in-law of the firm's president.

e. The reputation for not paying bills promptly.

f. The outstanding common stock of a corporation.

g. An obligation to deliver merchandise to a customer next year for which cash has been received.

h. An obligation to provide rental services to a tenant who has paid 3 months' rent in advance.

**2.26**  Indicate whether or not each of the following events immediately gives rise to the recognition of a liability. If a liability is recognized, state an account title and amount.

a. A landscaper agrees to improve land owned by the company. The agreed price for the work is $525. Consider from the standpoint of the company.

b. Additional common stock with a par value of $60,000 is issued for $62,500.

c. A check for $44 is received by the publisher for a 2-year future subscription to a magazine.

d. A construction company agrees to build a bridge for $2,000,000. A down payment of $200,000 is received upon signing the contract, and the remainder is due when the bridge is completed.

e. During the last pay period, employees earned wages amounting to $24,500 that they have not been paid. The employer is also liable for payroll taxes of 8 percent of the wages earned.

f. A landlord receives $900 for 3 months' rent in advance.

g. A 60-day, 8-percent loan for $10,000 is obtained at a bank.

h. A firm signs a contract to purchase at least $6,000 worth of merchandise during the next 3 months.

2.27 Some of the assets of one firm correspond to the liabilities of another firm. For example, an account receivable on the seller's balance sheet would be an account payable on the buyer's balance sheet. For each of the following items, indicate whether it is an asset or a liability and give the corresponding account title on the balance sheet of the other party to the transaction.

a. Advances by Customers.
b. Bonds Payable.
c. Cash in Bank.
d. Interest Receivable.
e. Prepaid Insurance.
f. Rental Fees Received in Advance.

2.28 Indicate the amount of revenue, if any, in each of the following transactions, assuming the accrual basis of accounting is used.

a. Goods that cost $800 are sold for $900 cash.
b. Goods that cost $800 are sold on account for $900.
c. Goods that cost $800 are sold on account for $800.
d. Goods that cost $850 are sold for $800 cash.
e. Cash of $900 is received from customers to apply to their accounts.
f. A deposit of $900 is received on a $20,000 order for goods.
g. Bonds are issued for $30,000 cash.
h. Shares of common stock are issued for $30,000 cash.

2.29 Under the accrual basis of accounting, cash receipts and disbursements may precede, coincide with, or follow the period in which revenues and expenses are recognized. Give an example of each of the following:

a. A cash receipt that precedes the period in which revenue is recognized.
b. A cash receipt that coincides with the period in which revenue is recognized.
c. A cash receipt that follows the period in which revenue is recognized.
d. A cash disbursement that precedes the period in which expense is recognized.
e. A cash disbursement that coincides with the period in which expense is recognized.
f. A cash disbursement that follows the period in which expense is recognized.

2.30 Assume that the accrual basis of accounting is used and that revenue is recognized at the time the goods are sold or services are rendered. How much revenue is recognized during the month of May in each of the following transactions?

a. Collection of cash from customers during May for merchandise sold and delivered in April, $6,200.
b. Sales of merchandise during May for cash, $4,600.
c. Sales of merchandise during May to customers to be collected in June, $6,400.
d. A store building is rented to a toy shop for $600 a month, effective May 1. A check for $1,800 for 3 months' rent is received on May 1.
e. Data in part d, except that collection is received from the tenant in June.

2.31 Assume that the accrual basis of accounting is used and that revenue is recognized at the time goods are sold or services are rendered. Indicate the amount of expense recognized during March, if any, in each of the following situations.

a. Rent is paid on March 1, $2,800, for the 2 months starting at that time.
b. An advance on the April salary is paid to an employee on March 28, $200.
c. Property taxes on a store building for the year of $3,600 were paid in January.
d. An employee earned $800 of commissions during March, but has not yet been paid.
e. The cost of equipment purchased on March 26, to be put into operation on April 1, is $6,000.

   f. $800 of supplies were purchased during March. On March 1, supplies were on hand that cost $500. At March 31, supplies that cost $300 were still on hand.
   g. Data of part **f**, except that $200 of supplies were on hand at March 1.
   h. At March 1, the balance in the Prepaid Insurance account was $4,800. The insurance policy had 6 months to run at that time.

**2.32** Indicate which of the following transactions involve the immediate recognition of revenue under the accrual basis of accounting.
   a. The delivery of an issue of a magazine to subscribers.
   b. The sale of an automobile by an automobile agency.
   c. A collection of cash from accounts receivable debtors.
   d. The borrowing of money at a bank.
   e. The sale of merchandise on account.
   f. The collection of cash by a barber for a haircut.
   g. The rendering of dry-cleaning services on account.
   h. The issue of shares of preferred stock.
   i. The sale of tickets by a symphony box office for a concert to be given in 2 weeks.
   j. Same as part **i**, except that sale was made by Ticketron, a ticket broker.

**2.33** In which of the following situations should there be an immediate recognition of revenue under the accrual basis of accounting?
   a. The shipment of goods that have been paid for in advance.
   b. The receipt of an order for a carload of merchandise.
   c. The interest earned on a savings account between interest payment dates.
   d. The issue of additional shares of common stock for cash.
   e. The completion of production of a batch of shoes by a shoe factory.
   f. The deduction of union dues from an employee's paycheck (from the standpoint of the employer).
   g. Transaction **f** from the standpoint of the union when the dues are received from the employer.
   h. The sale of a season ticket to a future series of concerts.

**2.34** Assume that the accrual basis of accounting is used and that revenue is recognized at the time goods are sold or services are rendered. Indicate the amount of revenue or expense recognized during November in each of the following situations.
   a. A bank loaned a customer $20,000 on June 1. The loan was repaid on November 30 with interest at the rate of 8 percent per year. Consider from the standpoint of the bank.
   b. Same as part **a** except the loan is repayable on February 28 of next year.
   c. Marketable securities costing $5,500 plus broker's commission of $90 are purchased on November 10.
   d. A cashier leaves town with $4,000 of the firm's money during November. The loss is covered by insurance (consider from the standpoint of the firm).
   e. An insurance company received insurance premiums of $8,400 during November for 24 months' coverage beginning November 1.

**2.35** Indicate the amount of revenue recognized, if any, from each of the following related events assuming that the accrual basis of accounting is used.
   a. Purchase orders are received from regular customers for $6,000 of merchandise. A 2-percent discount is allowed, and generally taken, for prompt payment.
   b. The customers' orders are filled and shipped by way of the company's trucking division.

    c. Invoices totaling $6,000 are sent to the customers.

    d. The merchandise is received by customers in the correct quantities and according to specifications.

    e. Checks in the amount of $5,880 (= .98 × $6,000) are received from customers in payment of the merchandise.

    f. On reinspection several days later, merchandise with a gross invoice price of $400 is found to be defective by customers and returned for appropriate credit.

**2.36** Give the amount of expense recognized, if any, from each of the following related events, assuming that the accrual basis of accounting is used.

    a. The purchasing department notifies the stockroom that the supply of 1/2-inch plywood has reached the minimum point and should be reordered.

    b. A purchase order is sent to Central Lumber Company for $9,000 of the material.

    c. An acknowledgment of the order is received. It indicates that delivery will be made in 15 days but that the price has been raised to $9,400.

    d. The shipment of plywood arrives and is checked by the receiving department. The correct quantity has been delivered.

    e. The purchase invoice arrives. The amount of $9,400 is subject to a 2-percent discount if paid within 10 days.

    f. On reinspection, plywood with a gross invoice price of $200 is found to be defective and returned to the supplier.

    g. The balance of the amount due the Central Lumber Company is paid in time to obtain the discount.

    h. The plywood is sold to customers for $11,000.

**2.37** Indicate whether labor wages and salaries for each of the following types are (1) product costs or (2) period expenses:

    a. Cutting-machine operators.

    b. Delivery labor.

    c. Factory janitors.

    d. Factory payroll clerks.

    e. Factory superintendent.

    f. General office secretaries.

    g. Guards at factory gate.

    h. Inspectors in factory.

    i. Maintenance workers who service factory machinery.

    j. Night watch force at the factory.

    k. General office clerks.

    l. Operator of a lift truck in the shipping room.

    m. President of the firm.

    n. Sales manager.

    o. Shipping room workers.

    p. Sweepers who clean retail store.

    q. Traveling salespersons.

**2.38** Indicate whether costs for each of the following types of materials and supplies are (1) product costs or (2) period expenses:

    a. Cleaning lubricants for factory machines.

    b. Paper for central office computer.

    c. Glue used in assembling products.

    d. Supplies used by factory janitor.

    e. Gasoline used by salespersons.

    f. Sales promotion pamphlets distributed.

    g. Materials used in training production workers.

**2.39** Indicate whether each of the following costs is (1) a period expense, (2) a product cost, or (3) some balance sheet account other than those for product costs:

    a. Office supplies used.

    b. Salary of factory supervisor.

c. Purchase of a fire insurance policy on the store building for the 3-year period beginning next month.

d. Expiration of 1 month's protection of the insurance in part c.

e. Property taxes for the current year on the factory building.

f. Wages of truck drivers who deliver finished goods to customers.

g. Wages of factory workers who install a new machine.

h. Wages of mechanics who repair and service factory machines.

i. Salary of the president of the company.

j. Depreciation of office equipment.

k. Factory supplies used.

**2.40**  Accounts might be classified in the balance sheet and income statement in one of the following categories:

(1) Current assets.

(2) Investments.

(3) Fixed assets.

(4) Intangibles.

(5) Current liabilities.

(6) Long-term liabilities.

(7) Shareholders' equity.

(8) Income statement items.

(9) Items excluded from the balance sheet and income statement under present generally accepted accounting principles.

Various accounts that might be presented in the financial statements are listed below. Using the numbers above, indicate the appropriate classification of each of the following accounts. Use an X before the number if the account is a contra account. For example, Allowance for Uncollectible Accounts is X-1. State any assumptions that you feel are necessary.

a. Accounts Payable.

b. Accounts Receivable.

c. Accumulated Depreciation.

d. Advances by Customers.

e. Advances to Suppliers.

f. Advertising Expenses.

g. Allowance for Uncollectibles.

h. Building.

i. Cash.

j. Certificate of Deposit.

k. Common Stock.

l. Current Maturities of Bonds Payable (to be paid from general cash account).

m. Current Maturities of Bonds Payable (to be paid from cash in bond sinking fund).

n. Customers' Deposits.

o. Deposits on Equipment Purchases.

p. Depreciation Expense.

q. Dividends Payable.

r. Estimated Liabilities under Warranty Contracts.

s. Finished Goods Inventory.

t. Furniture and Fixtures.

u. Gain on Sale of Equipment.

v. General and Administrative Expenses.

w. Goodwill.

**2.41**  Refer to the instructions accompanying the preceding questions. Indicate the appropriate classification of each of the following accounts.

a. Income Taxes Withheld.

b. Interest Expense.

c. Interest Payable.

d. Interest Receivable.

e. Investment in General Motors Stock.

f. U.S. Treasury Notes.

g. Investment in Unconsolidated Subsidiary.

h. Land.

i. Machinery.

j. Marketable Securities.

k. Merchandise Inventory.

l. Mortgage Payable (noncurrent).

m. Notes Payable (due in 3 months).

n. Notes Receivable (due in 6 months).

o. Patents.

p. Plant.

q. Preferred Stock.

r. Prepaid Insurance.

s. Raw Materials Inventory.

t. Rental Revenue.

u. Retained Earnings.

     v. Sales Discounts and Allowances.     x. Unexpired Insurance.
     w. Tools and Dies.     y. Work in Process.

**2.42** The results of various transactions and events are classified within the income statement in one of the following three sections: **(1)** income from continuing operations, **(2)** income, gains, and losses from discontinued operations, and **(3)** extraordinary items. Using the appropriate number, identify the classification of each of the following transactions or events. State any assumptions you feel are necessary.
a. Depreciation expense for the year on a company automobile used by its president.
b. Uninsured loss of a factory complex in Maine as a result of a hurricane.
c. Gain from the sale of marketable securities.
d. Loss from the sale of a delivery truck.
e. Loss from the sale of a division that conducted all of the firm's research activities.
f. Earnings during the year up to the time of sale of the division in part **e.**
g. Loss in excess of insurance proceeds on an automobile destroyed during an accident.
h. Loss of plant, equipment, and inventory held in a South American country when confiscated by the government of that country.

 **2.43** Adjustments for accounting changes may be treated in one of the following ways:
**(1)** The change is treated as an adjustment of the financial statements as prepared and presented in prior periods.
**(2)** The cumulative effects of the change on all prior years' financial statements is included in the calculation of net income for the period of the change but disclosed separately.
**(3)** The effect of the change is included in net income for the current and future period and not necessarily disclosed separately.

Using the numbers above, indicate the treatment of each of the following terms.
a. A change from the sum-of-the-years'-digits method to the straight-line method of depreciation on all equipment.
b. Correction of an overstatement of inventory at the end of the previous period as a result of counting twice several pages of the inventory summary.
c. An adjustment in the allowance for uncollectible accounts after an aging of the accounts revealed that the previous period's provision had been too large.
d. An increase in the annual depreciation rate for certain machinery because new technology had hastened the rate of obsolescence.
e. Correction of depreciation expense for prior years because salvage value was improperly treated in calculating depreciation under the double-declining-balance method.

**2.44** Transactions affecting the statement of changes in financial position might be classified in one of the following categories:
**(1)** Source of working capital (net)—operations.
**(2)** Source of working capital—increase in financing.
**(3)** Source of working capital—sale of noncurrent assets.
**(4)** Use of working capital—distributions to owners.
**(5)** Use of working capital—reduction in old financing.
**(6)** Use of working capital—acquisition of noncurrent assets.
**(7)** None of the above.

Using the numbers above, indicate the classifications of each of the following transactions in a statement of changes in financial position using working capital as the definition of "funds."

If the transaction would not be classified in one of these categories, state the reason. Ignore income tax effects.

a. Shares of a firm's own stock are reacquired on the open market.

b. Merchandise is sold to customers on account.

c. Cash is collected from customers who purchased merchandise on account in part **b**.

d. A dividend is declared by the board of directors. The dividend will be paid early in the next accounting period.

e. A patent is acquired from its inventor for cash.

f. A building is acquired. The firm signs a note that requires payment of 10 percent of the purchase price each year.

g. Preferred stock is issued for cash.

h. A tract of land is exchanged for equipment.

i. Salaries of employees for the period are paid in cash.

j. Merchandise is purchased from suppliers on account.

k. Payment is made to the supplier in part **j**.

l. A machine is sold for an amount equal to its book value.

m. Depreciation expense is recognized for the period.

**2.45**   Comment on any unusual features of the following balance sheet of the Western Sales Corporation (see following page).

**Western Sales Corporation
Balance Sheet
for the Year Ended
December 31, 1981**

### ASSETS

Current Assets:

| | | |
|---|---:|---:|
| Cash and Certificates of Deposit | $ 86,500 | |
| Accounts Receivable—Net | 193,600 | |
| Merchandise Inventory | 322,900 | $ 603,000 |

Investments (substantially at cost):

| | | |
|---|---:|---:|
| Investment in U.S. Treasury Notes | $ 60,000 | |
| Investment in Eastern Sales Corp. | 196,500 | 256,500 |

Fixed Assets (at cost):

| | | |
|---|---:|---:|
| Land | $225,000 | |
| Buildings and Equipment—Net | 842,600 | 1,067,600 |

Intangibles and Deferred Charges:

| | | |
|---|---:|---:|
| Prepaid Insurance | $ 1,200 | |
| Prepaid Rent | 1,500 | |
| Goodwill | 2 | 2,702 |
| Total Assets | | $1,929,802 |

### LIABILITIES AND SHAREHOLDERS' EQUITY

Current Liabilities:

| | | |
|---|---:|---:|
| Accounts Payable | $225,300 | |
| Accrued Expenses | 10,900 | |
| Income Taxes Payable | 89,200 | $ 325,400 |

Long-Term Liabilities:

| | | |
|---|---:|---:|
| Bonds Payable | $500,000 | |
| Pensions Payable | 40,600 | |
| Contingent Liability | 100,000 | 640,600 |

Shareholders' Equity:

| | | |
|---|---:|---:|
| Common Stock—$10 par value, 50,000 shares issued and outstanding | $625,000 | |
| Earned Surplus | 338,802 | 963,802 |
| Total Liabilities and Shareholders' Equity | | $1,929,802 |

2.46   Comment on any unusual features of the following income statement of Nordic Enterprises, Inc.

### Nordic Enterprises, Inc.
### Income Statement
### December 31, 1981

| | | |
|---|---:|---:|
| Revenues and Gains: | | |
| Sales Revenue | $1,964,800 | |
| Rental Revenue | 366,900 | |
| Interest Revenue | 4,600 | |
| Gain on Sale of Equipment | 2,500 | |
| Gain on Sale of Subsidiary | 643,200 | $2,982,000 |
| | | |
| Expenses and Losses: | | |
| Cost of Goods Sold | $1,432,900 | |
| Depreciation Expense | 226,800 | |
| Salaries Expense | 296,900 | |
| Interest Expense | 6,600 | |
| Loss of Plant due to Fire | 368,800 | |
| Income Tax Expense | 200,000 | |
| Dividends Expense | 100,000 | 2,632,000 |
| Net Income | | $  350,000 |

2.47   (Adapted from CPA Examination.) The statement of sources and uses of funds of The D. Sweeney Corporation as prepared by the corporation's accountants is shown below.

### The D. Sweeney Corporation
### Statement of Sources and Uses of Funds
### for the Year Ended December 31, 1981

| | |
|---|---:|
| Sources of Funds: | |
| Net Income | $ 52,000 |
| Depreciation and Depletion | 59,000 |
| Increase in Long-Term Debt | 178,000 |
| Common Stock Issued under Employee Option Plan | 5,000 |
| Total Sources | $294,000 |
| | |
| Uses of Funds: | |
| Cash Dividends | $ 33,000 |
| Expenditures for Plant | 202,000 |
| Investments and Other Uses | 9,000 |
| Total Uses | $244,000 |
| Increase in Funds for Year | |
| Sources Minus Uses | $ 50,000 |
| Analysis of Changes in Funds: | |
| Increase in Cash | $ 53,000 |
| Increase in Receivables and Inventories | 5,000 |
| Less: Increase in Current Liabilities | (8,000) |
| Increase in Funds for Year | $ 50,000 |

The following additional information is available on The D. Sweeney Corporation for the year ending December 31, 1981.

(1) Depreciation Expense ............................................. $ 58,000
  Depletion Expense ................................................ 1,000
                                                                     $ 59,000

(2) Increase in Long-Term Debt ..................................... $600,000
  Retirement of Debt .............................................. 422,000
    Net Increase .................................................. $178,000

(3) Expenditures for Plant ......................................... $222,000
  Proceeds from Retirement of Plant (Book Value $16,000) .......... 20,000
    Net Expenditures .............................................. $202,000

(4) On July 1, 1981, when its market price was $5 per share, 16,000 shares of Sweeney Corporation common stock were issued in exchange for 4,000 shares of preferred stock.

(5) The income statement for the year contains the following lines.
  Extraordinary Items:
    Loss on Expropriation of Plant in South America .................... $10,000
      Less: Applicable Taxes ........................................ 4,000
      Total Extraordinary Loss ...................................... $ 6,000

a. Identify the weaknesses in the form and format of The D. Sweeney Corporation's statement of sources and uses of funds.

b. For each of the five items of additional information for the statement of sources and uses of funds, indicate the preferable treatment, if any, and explain why the suggested treatment is preferable.

## Problems and Exercises

2.48 Wilson Corporation acquired a machine on January 1, 1979 for $200,000. At the date of acquisition, the machine had an estimated useful life of 10 years and no salvage value. The machine is being depreciated on a straight-line basis. On January 1, 1981, it is decided that the machine's total estimated useful life should be 12 years instead of 10 years. Assuming that this change in useful life is to be recognized, compute the amount of depreciation expense on this machine for 1981.

2.49 Dominick Corporation reported net income as follows: year 1: $15,000; year 2: $25,000; year 3: $40,000. Its net income for year 4 has been calculated to be $60,000. However, before the financial statements for year 4 are finalized, Dominick Corporation discovers that its depreciation expense on a particular machine has been overstated as follows: year 1: $2,500; year 2: $2,000; year 3: $1,500; year 4: $1,000. Assume an income tax rate of 40 percent. Calculate the revised amount of net income for year 4.

2.50 Page Corporation began operations in year 1. It reported net income as follows: year 1: $500,000; year 2: $640,000; year 3: $760,000. Its net income for year 4 is calculated to be $900,000. However, before the financial statements for year 4 are finalized, it decides to change from the sum-of-the-years'-digits method to the straight-line method for year 4. Depreciation expense under the straight-line method would have been less than the amounts under the sum-of-the-years'-digits method as follows: year 1: $40,000; year 2: $45,000; year 3: $60,000; year 4: $75,000. Assume an income tax rate of 40 percent. Calculate the revised amount of net income for year 4.

2.51 Compute the missing balance sheet amounts in each of the four independent cases below. Items marked "?" should be calculated.

| | a | b | c | d |
|---|---|---|---|---|
| Noncurrent Assets | $600,000 | $3,000,000 | $400,000 | ? |
| Shareholders' Equity | ? | 1,850,000 | 430,000 | $ 400,000 |
| Total Assets | ? | ? | 600,000 | ? |
| Current Liabilities | 400,000 | 500,000 | ?* | ?** |
| Current Assets | 450,000 | ? | ?* | ?** |
| Noncurrent Liabilities | 200,000 | ? | ? | 500,000 |
| Total Liabilities and Shareholders' Equity | ? | 3,400,000 | ? | 1,000,000 |

*Working capital = current assets − current liabilities = $60,000.
**Working capital = current assets − current liabilities = $80,000.

2.52 Compute the missing amount affecting retained earnings for the year 1981 in each of the independent cases below.

| | a | b | c | d | e |
|---|---|---|---|---|---|
| Retained Earnings, December 31, 1980 | $400,000 | ? | $840,000 | $60,000 | $60,000 |
| Net Income | 60,000 | $300,000 | 260,000 | ? | (40,000)* |
| Dividends Declared and Paid | 10,000 | 40,000 | ? | 50,000 | ? |
| Retained Earnings December 31, 1981 | ? | 600,000 | 940,000 | 80,000 | 10,000 |

*Net loss.

2.53 Compute the change in working capital for 1981 in each of the independent cases below.

| | a | b | c | d |
|---|---|---|---|---|
| Noncurrent Assets: | | | | |
| January 1, 1981 | $140,000 | $ 800,000 | $500,000 | $800,000 |
| December 31, 1981 | 200,000 | 1,000,000 | 600,000 | 700,000 |
| Noncurrent Liabilities: | | | | |
| January 1, 1981 | 140,000 | 400,000 | 200,000 | 400,000 |
| December 31, 1981 | 160,000 | 500,000 | 500,000 | 360,000 |
| Shareholders' Equity: | | | | |
| January 1, 1981 | 80,000 | 320,000 | 200,000 | 400,000 |
| December 31, 1981 | 80,000 | 400,000 | 250,000 | 480,000 |

2.54 P. Williamson opened a clothing store on January 1, 1981. Williamson invested $8,000 and borrowed $9,000 from the local bank. The loan is repayable on June 30, 1981, with interest at the rate of 8 percent per year.

Williamson rented a building on January 1, and paid 2 months' rent in advance in the amount of $1,200. Property and liability insurance coverage for the year ending December 31, 1981, was paid on January 1 in the amount of $720.

Williamson purchased $20,000 of merchandise inventory on account on January 2 and paid $8,000 of this amount on January 25. The cost of merchandise on hand on January 31 was $11,000.

During January, cash sales to customers totaled $9,000 and sales on account totaled $3,000. Of the sales on account, $1,000 were collected as of January 31.

Other costs incurred and paid in cash during January were as follows: utilities, $400; salaries, $450; taxes, $250.

**a.** Prepare an income statement for January, assuming that Williamson uses the accrual basis of accounting with revenue recognized at the time goods are sold (delivered).

**b.** Prepare an income statement for January, assuming that Williamson uses the cash basis of accounting.

**c.** Which basis of accounting do you feel provides a better indication of the operating performance of the clothing store during January? Why?

**2.55** Computer Consultants, Inc., opened a consulting business on July 1, 1981. Dorothy Bowen and Tom Green each contributed $6,000 cash for shares of the firm's common stock. The corporation borrowed $6,000 from a local bank on August 1, 1981. The loan is repayable on July 31, 1982, with interest at the rate of 10 percent per year.

Office space was rented on August 1, with 2 months' rent paid in advance. The remaining monthly rental fees of $650 per month were made on the first of each month beginning October 1. Office equipment with a 3-year life was purchased for cash on August 1 for $3,600.

Consulting services rendered for clients between August 1 and December 31, 1981, were billed at $14,000. Of this amount, $9,000 was collected by year-end.

Other costs incurred and paid in cash by the end of the year were as follows: utilities, $450; salary of secretary, $5,800; supplies used, $350. Unpaid bills at year-end are as follows: utilities, $60; salary of secretary, $800; supplies used, $80.

**a.** Prepare an income statement for the 5 months ended December 31, 1981, assuming that the corporation uses the accrual basis of accounting, with revenue recognized at the time services are rendered.

**b.** Prepare an income statement for the 5 months ended December 31, 1981, assuming that the corporation uses the cash basis of accounting.

**c.** Which basis of accounting do you feel provides a better indication of operating performance of the consulting firm for the period? Why?

**2.56** (Adapted from CPA Examination.) The Century Company, a diversified manufacturing company, had four separate operating divisions engaged in the manufacture of products in each of the following areas: food products, health aids, textiles, and office equipment.

Financial data for the two years ended December 31, 1981 and 1980, are presented below:

| | Net Sales | | Cost of Sales | | Operating Expenses | |
| --- | --- | --- | --- | --- | --- | --- |
| | 1981 | 1980 | 1981 | 1980 | 1981 | 1980 |
| Food Products .. | $3,500,000 | $3,000,000 | $2,400,000 | $1,800,000 | $ 550,000 | $ 275,000 |
| Health Aids ...... | 2,000,000 | 1,270,000 | 1,100,000 | 700,000 | 300,000 | 125,000 |
| Textiles ......... | 1,580,000 | 1,400,000 | 500,000 | 900,000 | 200,000 | 150,000 |
| Office Equipment . | 920,000 | 1,330,000 | 800,000 | 1,000,000 | 650,000 | 750,000 |
| | $8,000,000 | $7,000,000 | $4,800,000 | $4,400,000 | $1,700,000 | $1,300,000 |

On January 1, 1981, Century adopted a plan to sell the assets and product line of the office equipment division and expected to realize a gain on this disposal. On September 1, 1981, the division's assets and product line were sold for $2,100,000 cash resulting in a gain of $640,000 (exclusive of operations during the phase-out period).

The company's textiles division had six manufacturing plants, which produced a variety of textile products. In April 1981, the company sold one of these plants and realized a gain of $130,000. After the sale, the operations at the plant that was sold were transferred to the remaining five textile plants, which the company continued to operate.

In August 1981, the main warehouse of the food products division, located on the banks of the Bayer River, was flooded when the river overflowed. The resulting damage of $420,000 is not included in the financial data given above. Historical records indicate that the Bayer River normally overflows every 4 to 5 years, causing flood damage to adjacent property.

For the 2 years ended December 31, 1981 and 1980, the company had interest revenue earned on investments of $70,000 and $40,000, respectively.

For the 2 years ended December 31, 1981 and 1980, the company's net income was $960,000 and $670,000, respectively.

The provision for income tax expense for each of the two years should be computed at a rate of 50 percent.

Prepare in proper form a comparative statement of income of the Century Company for the two years ended December 31, 1981, and December 31, 1980. Footnotes are not required.

**2.57**  The following data are taken from the accounting records of the Oak Merchandising Company as of December 31, 1980 and 1981, before financial statements are prepared. The amounts shown represent the balances in the various accounts on the dates indicated.

| Oak Merchandising Company—Account Balances | December 31, 1980 | | December 31, 1981 | |
|---|---|---|---|---|
| Accounts Payable | | $   97,320 | | $   98,715 |
| Accounts Receivable—Net | $  580,335 | | $  617,530 | |
| Accrued Liabilities and Withholdings Payable | | 74,800 | | 76,700 |
| Additional Paid-In Capital | | 700,000 | | 700,000 |
| Administrative Expense | 449,160 | | 447,260 | |
| Bonds Payable (6%) | | 300,000 | | 300,000 |
| Cash | 114,080 | | 149,485 | |
| Common Stock | | 100,000 | | 100,000 |
| Cost of Goods Sold | 3,207,840 | | 3,220,390 | |
| Depreciation Expense | 45,710 | | 48,825 | |
| Dividends Declared on Common Shares— Cash | 50,000 | | 68,750 | |
| Dividends Declared on Preferred Shares— Cash | 6,000 | | 6,000 | |
| Dividends Payable | | — | | 13,750 |
| Federal and State Income Tax Expense | 104,975 | | 122,675 | |
| Federal and State Income Taxes Payable | | 104,975 | | 111,675 |
| Interest Expense on Notes | 2,900 | | 3,100 | |
| Interest Expense on Bonds | 20,000 | | 20,000 | |
| Interest and Dividend Revenue | | 16,010 | | 18,070 |
| Inventories | 616,120 | | 633,690 | |
| Investments in Subsidiaries | 162,000 | | 162,000 | |
| Notes Payable | | 51,500 | | 53,400 |
| Notes Receivable | 65,600 | | 68,400 | |
| Plant and Equipment—Net | 391,880 | | 407,885 | |
| Preferred Stock | | 100,000 | | 100,000 |
| Prepaid Insurance | 8,240 | | 7,640 | |
| Retained Earnings (January 1) | | 333,425 | | 409,660 |
| Royalties Revenue | | 37,020 | | 44,285 |
| Sales | | 4,552,320 | | 4,613,605 |
| Selling Expenses | 642,530 | | 656,230 | |
| | $6,467,370 | $6,467,370 | $6,639,860 | $6,639,860 |

Additional data:

(1) Preferred shares: 6 percent, cumulative, $100 par value, 2,000 shares authorized.

(2) Common shares: $1 par value, 150,000 shares authorized.

**a.** Prepare a well-organized comparative statement of income and retained earnings for 1981.

**b.** Prepare a well-organized comparative balance sheet for December 31, 1980 and 1981.

2.58 The accounting records of the Wilcox Manufacturing Company at December 31, 1981, before the financial statements are prepared show the following balances in various accounts:

## Wilcox Manufacturing Company

| | | |
|---|--:|--:|
| Accounts Payable | | $ 91,000 |
| Accounts Receivable | $ 262,000 | |
| Accumulated Depreciation—Buildings | | 24,000 |
| Accumulated Depreciation—Machinery and Equipment | | 72,000 |
| Administrative Expenses | 340,000 | |
| Advances from Customers on Special Orders | | 6,900 |
| Allowance for Uncollectible Accounts | | 7,000 |
| Buildings | 110,000 | |
| Cash in Bank | 13,500 | |
| Cash on Hand | 850 | |
| Common Stock | | 350,000 |
| Cost of Goods Sold | 1,467,500 | |
| Dividend Revenue | | 5,700 |
| Dividends Declared on Common Stock | 17,500 | |
| Dividends Declared on Preferred Stock | 12,000 | |
| Dividends Payable | | 14,750 |
| Factory Supplies Inventory | 2,800 | |
| Federal Income Tax Expense | 41,200 | |
| Federal Income Taxes Payable | | 41,200 |
| Finished Goods Inventory | 91,000 | |
| First Mortgage Bonds Payable (10%) | | 52,500 |
| Interest Expense on Bonds | 4,500 | |
| Interest Expense on Notes | 1,680 | |
| Interest Payable | | 2,600 |
| Interest Receivable | 100 | |
| Interest Revenue on Notes | | 220 |
| Investment in Subsidiary | 117,500 | |
| Land | 24,000 | |
| Machinery and Equipment | 260,000 | |
| Notes Payable (short-term) | | 26,600 |
| Notes Receivable | 19,000 | |
| Patents | 25,000 | |
| Payroll Taxes Payable | | 11,700 |
| Preferred Stock | | 200,000 |
| Prepaid Insurance | 1,400 | |
| Raw Materials Inventory | 84,000 | |
| Retained Earnings (January 1) | | 177,940 |
| Royalty Revenue | | 5,000 |
| Sales | | 2,460,000 |
| Sales Discounts | 49,000 | |
| Sales Returns and Allowances | 35,000 | |
| Selling Expenses | 480,000 | |
| Withheld Income Taxes Payable | | 15,420 |
| Work-in-Process Inventory | 105,000 | |
| | $3,564,530 | $3,564,530 |

Additional data:

Preferred stock: 6-percent, cumulative, par value $100 per share, authorized $500,000, callable at 110, preference in case of involuntary dissolution at $105 per share and accrued dividends.

Common stock: No par, authorized 50,000 shares, outstanding 35,000 shares.

**a.** Prepare a well-organized statement of income and retained earnings for 1981.
**b.** Prepare a well-organized balance sheet for December 31, 1981.

2.59 The accounting records of the National Sales Company at December 31, 1981, before the financial statements are prepared show the following balances in various accounts:

### National Sales Company

| | | |
|---|---:|---:|
| Accounts Payable | | $ 75,000 |
| Accounts Receivable | $ 73,750 | |
| Accumulated Depreciation—Building | | 40,000 |
| Accumulated Depreciation—Equipment | | 95,000 |
| Administration Expenses | 178,600 | |
| Advances by Customers | | 1,250 |
| Allowance for Uncollectible Accounts | | 6,500 |
| Building | 90,000 | |
| Cash in Bank | 60,800 | |
| Cash on Hand | 1,200 | |
| Common Stock | | 200,000 |
| Cost of Goods Sold | 984,000 | |
| Dividends Declared on Common Stock | 20,000 | |
| Dividends Declared on Preferred Stock | 6,000 | |
| Equipment | 240,000 | |
| Federal Income Tax | 31,420 | |
| Federal Income Taxes Payable | | 31,420 |
| Interest and Dividend Revenue | | 5,100 |
| Interest Expense | 4,200 | |
| Interest and Dividends Receivable | 1,250 | |
| Interest Payable | | 300 |
| Investment in Stock of Interstate Stores, Inc. | 61,000 | |
| Land | 15,000 | |
| Marketable Securities | 18,000 | |
| Merchandise Inventory | 135,000 | |
| Notes Payable (current) | | 30,000 |
| Note Payable to Insurance Company (8%; due 1/1/1987) | | 50,000 |
| Notes Receivable | 15,000 | |
| Payroll Taxes Payable | | 660 |
| Preferred Stock | | 100,000 |
| Prepaid Insurance | 2,100 | |
| Prepaid Rent | 3,000 | |
| Retained Earnings (January 1) | | 70,210 |
| Sales | | 1,462,000 |
| Selling Expenses | 226,300 | |
| Supplies Inventory | 5,400 | |
| Wages Payable | | 3,600 |
| Withheld Income Taxes Payable | | 980 |
| | $2,172,020 | $2,172,020 |

Additional data:

Preferred stock: 6-percent, cumulative, $100 par value, preference in involuntary liquidation of $110 per share, 1,000 shares authorized and issued.

Common stock: no par, 30,000 shares authorized; 20,000 shares issued and outstanding.

**a.** Prepare a well-organized statement of income and retained earnings for 1981.

**b.** Prepare a well-organized balance sheet for December 31, 1981.

**2.60** The accounting records of Stewart Corporation reveal the following information concerning income items for 1981 before considering any income tax effects.

### Revenues and Gains

| | |
|---|---|
| Sales | $500,000 |
| Gain on Sale of Equipment | 20,000 |
| Interest Revenue | 5,000 |
| Gain on Disposal of Tire Division | 90,000 |

### Expenses and Losses

| | |
|---|---|
| Cost of Goods Sold | 350,000 |
| Selling and Administrative Expenses | 75,000 |
| Interest Expense | 15,000 |
| Loss from Tornado in Florida | 40,000 |
| Loss from Operations of Tire Division Prior to Decision to Dispose of Segment | 10,000 |
| Loss from Operations of Tire Division Subsequent to Decision to Dispose of Segment | 25,000 |

Appropriate income tax rates are as follows:

| | |
|---|---|
| Gain on Sale of Equipment | 30% |
| Gain on Disposal of Tire Division | 35% |
| Loss from Tornado in Florida | 28% |
| All Other Income and Expenses | 46% |

The decision to dispose of the tire division was made February 15, 1981. The segment was sold on August 18, 1981. Prepare an income statement for Stewart Corporation for 1981.

# Chapter 3
# *Review of the Accounting Process: Balance Sheet and Income Statement*

3.1 The financial statements of a business firm, discussed in Chapter 2, are the end products of a firm's accounting system. Before the financial statements can be prepared, the financial effects of various transactions and events must first be measured, classified, and recorded in the accounting system and the results periodically summarized for presentation in the financial statements. Chapters 3 and 4 review the accounting process that generates the three principal financial statements. This chapter considers the procedures for preparing the balance sheet and the income statement. Chapter 4 focuses on the statement of changes in financial position.

## The Accounting Process

3.2 The accounting process involves four principal steps:

**1.** Identification of accounting events.

**2.** Measurement of relevant attributes of these events.

**3.** Recording of measured attributes in the accounting system.

**4.** Periodic preparation of the financial statements.

Each of these steps is discussed below. Figure 3.1 depicts the accounting process graphically.

## Identification of Accounting Events

3.3 Numerous events and transactions occur regularly in the life of a business firm. Many of these events involve exchanges with entities external to the firm. Raw materials are purchased from suppliers for use in production. Automobiles are purchased from dealers for use by the sales staff. Finished products are sold to customers. Cash is collected from customers and disbursed to suppliers, employees, and governmental agencies. Other events affect the financial position of the firm but do not involve external exchanges. The firm's marketing staff might develop a new promotional campaign that is expected to increase future sales. The firm's engineering staff might develop a more efficient method of manufacturing the firm's products. Competitors might introduce new products that could erode the firm's market share. Congress might alter the statutory income tax rate, thereby increasing the firm's future income taxes. Which of these events are recognized as accounting events and recorded in the firm's accounting system?

*Figure 3.1*
**Summary of the Accounting and
Reporting Process**

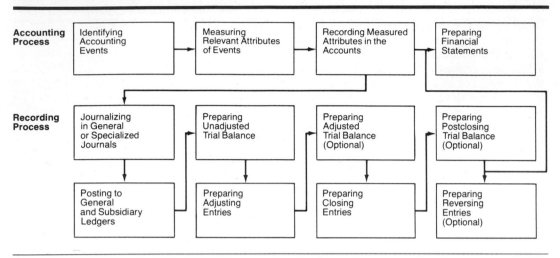

3.4 In general, events are recognized as accounting events only if they **(1)** have already occurred, **(2)** affect the financial position of individual business entities, and **(3)** can be measured in monetary terms with a reasonable degree of precision.*

3.5 **Example 1** The purchase of raw materials, equipment, and other assets, the sale of finished products to customers, the collection of cash from customers, and the disbursement of cash to suppliers, employees, and governmental agencies are all recognized as accounting events. In each case, an exchange with an entity or individual external to the firm has occurred. The arm's-length negotiations that take place in such exchanges provide a price, or amount, for quantifying the impact of the transaction on the financial position of the firm.

3.6 **Example 2** The use of depreciable assets, the transfer of raw materials to the factory, and the transfer of completed products to

*Financial Accounting Standards Board, *Statement of Financial Accounting Concepts No. 1* (1978), pars. 17–21.

the finished goods storeroom are also accounting events. When these events occur, they affect the asset structure of the firm (that is, the portion of total assets in raw materials, work-in-process, and finished goods inventories, depreciable assets, and other assets). The measurement of the impact of these events on the financial position of the firm could be based on the increase (in the case of inventory transfers) or decrease (in the case of depreciable assets) in the market value of the assets involved. Under current generally acceptable accounting principles, however, measurement of changes in the market value of such assets is not considered to be sufficiently objective for quantifying the events. As a consequence, the events are quantified using the initial acquisition cost of the depreciable assets, raw materials, factory labor services, and so on.

**Example 3** A firm has signed a contract to 3.7 pay for the construction of a new plant, which is to be completed in 3 years. The firm has also contracted with certain customers to provide specified amounts of merchandise over the next 2 years. *Signing* such contracts is generally not recognized as an accounting event. Although an exchange of promises has taken place, all of the performance under the contracts will occur in the future.

3.8 **Example 4** The development of a new promotional campaign by a firm's marketing staff or the development of a more efficient production process by a firm's engineering staff would not be recognized as accounting events. Such developments are events that have already taken place. However, their impact on the financial position of the firm will be felt in the future through increased revenues or reduced expenses. The measurement of the impact cannot be currently quantified in a sufficiently objective manner to warrant recognition as an accounting event.

3.9 **Example 5** The introduction of new products by competitors and the increase in corporate income tax rates on future earnings are likewise not recognized as accounting events. Their impact will be felt in the future and cannot be currently quantified with a reasonable degree of precision.

3.10 Many current reporting issues involve questions of recognizing accounting events. Does the adoption of a pension plan in which a firm counts the services of employees prior to adoption of the plan constitute an accounting event? Does the change in price, or market value, of land held by a firm constitute an accounting event? The difficulties encountered by standard-setting bodies in responding to these and similar questions suggest that the criteria for defining an accounting event are not precise rules. They are general guidelines that require judgment in their application.

## Measurement of Relevant Attributes

3.11 Once an accounting event has been identified, the impact of the event on the financial position of the firm must be measured. This measurement process involves two steps: **(1)** specifying the attribute to be measured, and **(2)** measuring the attribute. Under generally accepted accounting principles, the attribute measured is normally the economic benefit or sacrifice of the accounting event to the firm at the time it occurred. This benefit or sacrifice is quantified using the *historical exchange price*. The purchase of raw materials is measured using the cash consideration given to acquire the raw materials. The acquisition of equipment is measured using the cash or market value of other consideration given in exchange. The transfer of finished products from the production floor to the finished goods storeroom is measured using the historical exchange price paid for raw materials, labor services, and other factors of production.

3.12 Use of the historical economic benefit or sacrifice as the attribute measured and the historical exchange price as the measure of that attribute is consistent with the three criteria for an accounting event: An event has already occurred, and the impact of the event on the financial position of a firm can be measured with a reasonable degree of precision. There is considerable controversy, however, as to the relevance of historical benefits and sacrifices and historical exchange prices to users of financial statements. It has been argued that the performance of a firm is more accurately evaluated using current benefit and sacrifice and current exchange, or market, prices. We consider these questions more fully in later chapters.

3.13 Accounting events, once they have been measured, are expressed in terms of their dual impact on the financial position of a firm. Most accounting events involve exchanges with entities external to the firm. Such exchanges have two effects on financial position: **(1)** an outflow—what is given up in the exchange, and **(2)** an inflow—what is received in the exchange. The accounting system recognizes this dual impact of the exchange. For example, a firm gives up cash or other consideration in exchange for raw materials, depreciable assets, labor services, and so on. A firm borrowing from a bank receives cash in exchange for a promise to repay the loan with interest at a later time.

*Exhibit 3.1*
**Illustration of Dual Effects
of Transactions on
Balance Sheet Equation**

| Transaction | Assets = | | Equities | | |
| --- | --- | --- | --- | --- | --- |
| | Assets | = | Liabilities | + | Share-holders' Equity |
| (1) 20,000 shares of $10 par value common stock are issued for $200,000 cash. (Increase in both an asset and an equity.) | +$200,000 | | 0 | + | $200,000 |
| Subtotal ...................................... | $200,000 | = | 0 | + | $200,000 |
| (2) Equipment costing $75,000 is purchased for cash. (Increase in one asset and decrease in another asset.) | − 75,000 + 75,000 | | | | |
| Subtotal ...................................... | $200,000 | = | 0 | + | $200,000 |
| (3) Merchandise inventory costing $20,000 is purchased from a supplier on account. (Increase in both an asset and an equity.) | + 20,000 | | +$20,000 | | |
| Subtotal ...................................... | $220,000 | = | $20,000 | + | $200,000 |
| (4) Merchandise inventory costing $12,000 is sold to customers for $18,000. (Increase in both an asset and an equity; decrease in both an asset and an equity.) | + 18,000 − 12,000 | | | + | 18,000 − 12,000 |
| Subtotal ...................................... | $226,000 | = | $20,000 | + | $206,000 |
| (5) The supplier in (3) is paid $10,000 of the amount due. (Decrease in both an asset and an equity.) | − 10,000 | | − 10,000 | | |
| Subtotal ...................................... | $216,000 | = | $10,000 | + | $206,000 |
| (6) The supplier in (3) accepts 500 shares of common stock at par value in settlement of $5,000 of the amount owed. (Increase in one equity and decrease in another equity.) | | | − 5,000 | + | 5,000 |
| Total ......................................... | $216,000 | = | $ 5,000 | + | $211,000 |

## Recording of Measured Attributes

3.14 The dual effects of accounting events are recorded in the firm's accounting system so that the accounting equation (assets equal equities) is continually maintained. An accounting event will have one of the following four effects or some combination of these effects:

1. It increases both an asset and an equity.

2. It decreases both an asset and an equity.

3. It increases one asset and decreases another asset.

4. It increases one equity and decreases another equity.

3.15 To illustrate the dual effects of transactions on the balance sheet equation, con-sider the selected events shown in Exhibit 3.1. We could prepare a balance sheet and income statement using information from the preceding analysis. Total assets are $216,000. We could retrace the effects of each transaction on total assets to ascertain what portion of the $216,000 represents cash, merchandise inventory, and equipment. Likewise, we could trace the effects of each transaction on total liabilities and owners' equity to ascertain which liability and owners' equity amounts comprise the $216,000 total. Even a few transactions during the accounting period make this approach to preparing financial statements cumbersome. Considering the thousands of transactions during the accounting period for most firms, some more practical approach to accumulating amounts for the financial statements is necessary. To accumulate the changes that take place in each financial statement item, we use a device known as an *account*.

3.16    The requirement for a satisfactory account is simple. Because each financial statement item that changes can only increase or decrease, all an account need do is to provide for accumulating the increases and decreases that have taken place during the period. Any balance carried forward from the previous period is added to the total increases; the total decreases are deducted, and the result is the amount of the ending balance in the account for the current period.

3.17    The account may take many possible forms, and several are commonly used in accounting practice. Perhaps the most useful form of the account for textbooks, problems, and examinations is the skeleton account, usually called the *T-account*. This form of the account is not used in actual practice, except perhaps for memorandums or preliminary analyses. However, it satisfies the requirement of an account and it is easy to use. As the name indicates, the T-account is shaped like the letter T and consists of a horizontal line bisected by a vertical line. (See figure below.) The name or title of the account is written on the horizontal line. One side of the space formed by the vertical line is used to record increases in the item and the other side to record the decreases. Spaces for dates and other information can, of course, be provided.

**Account Title**

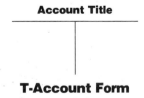

**T-Account Form**

The form that the account takes in actual records depends on the type of accounting system being used. In manual systems the account may take the form of a single "ledger" sheet with columns for recording increases and decreases; in punched-card systems the account may take the form of a group of cards; in computer systems it may be a group of similarly coded items on a tape. Whatever its form, an account contains space for recording increases and decreases in the account that result from accounting events during the period.

3.18    Given the two-sided account, we must choose which side will be used to record increases and which, decreases. By long-standing custom, the following rules are used:

**1.** Increases in assets are entered on the left side and decreases in assets on the right side.

**2.** Increases in liabilities are entered on the right side and decreases in liabilities on the left side.

**3.** Increases in owners' equity (including revenues) are entered on the right side and decreases in owners' equity (including expenses) on the left side.

This custom has an element of logic. A common form of balance sheet shows assets on the left and liabilities and owners' equity on the right. Following this example, asset balances should appear on the left side of accounts; equity balances should appear on the right. But asset balances will appear on the left only if asset increases are recorded on the left side of the account. Similarly, right-hand equity balances can be produced only by recording equity increases on the right. When each transaction is properly analyzed into its dual effects on the accounting equation, and when the above three rules for recording the transaction are followed, then every transaction results in equal amounts in entries on the left- and right-hand sides of various accounts.

3.19    Two terms may now be added to our vocabulary, *debit* (Dr.) and *credit* (Cr.). These terms have an interesting history, but today they should be thought of merely as convenient abbreviations. *Debit* is an abbreviation for "record an entry on the left side of an account" when used as a verb and is an abbreviation for "an entry on the left side of an account" when used as a noun or adjective. *Credit* is an abbreviation for "record an entry on the right side of an account" when used as a verb and is an abbreviation for "an entry on the right side of an account" when used as a noun or adjective. These terms have no other meaning in accounting. More convenient abbreviations than *debit* and *credit* certainly seem possible, but these have become part of the accounting language through centuries of use and are not likely to be displaced. Often, however, the word *charge* is used instead of *debit,* both as a noun and as a verb.

3.20 In terms of balance sheet accounts, a debit or charge indicates **(1)** an increase in an asset, **(2)** a decrease in a liability, or **(3)** a decrease in an owners' equity item. A credit indicates **(1)** a decrease in an asset, **(2)** an increase in a liability, or **(3)** an increase in an owners' equity item. In terms of income statement (owners' equity) accounts, a debit indicates **(1)** a decrease in a revenue, or **(2)** an increase in an expense. A credit indicates **(1)** an increase in a revenue, or **(2)** a decrease in an expense.

3.21 In order to maintain the equality of the balance sheet equation, the amounts debited to various accounts for each accounting event must equal the amounts credited to various accounts. Likewise, the sum of balances in accounts with debit balances at the end of each period must equal the sum of balances in accounts with credit balances. The conventional use of the account form and the terms debit and credit can be summarized as follows:

**Asset Accounts** =

| Beginning Balance Increases (Dr.) | Decreases (Cr.) |
| --- | --- |
| Ending Balance | |

**Liability Accounts** +

| Decreases (Dr.) | Beginning Balance Increases (Cr.) |
| --- | --- |
| | Ending Balance |

**Owners' Equity Accounts**

| Decreases (Dr.) | Beginning Balance Increases (Cr.) |
| --- | --- |
| | Ending Balance |

**Expense Accounts**

| Increases (Dr.) | Decreases (Cr.) |
| --- | --- |

**Revenue Accounts**

| Decreases (Dr.) | Increases (Cr.) |
| --- | --- |

## Preparation of Financial Statements

3.22 The final step in the accounting process is preparing the financial statements. Data on individual accounting events are recorded in the accounts as they occur. These data are periodically aggregated and summarized and provide the basis for preparing the financial statements.

## Overview of the Recording Process

3.23 The remainder of this chapter describes and illustrates more fully the third step in the accounting process—the recording of the dual effects of accounting events in the accounts and the subsequent procedures for preparing the financial statements. The accounting system designed around the double-entry recording procedure generally involves the following operations:

**1.** Entering the results of each accounting event in the *general journal* (or a specialized journal), a process called *journalizing*.

**2.** Posting the journal entries from the general (or specialized) journal to the accounts in the *general ledger*.

**3.** Preparing an *unadjusted trial balance* of the accounts in the general ledger.

**4.** Making *adjusting journal entries* to accounts listed in the unadjusted trial balance and posting them to the appropriate general ledger accounts.

**5.** Preparing an adjusted, preclosing trial balance (optional).

**6.** Making *closing journal entries* to revenue and expense accounts in the adjusted trial balance and posting them to appropriate general ledger accounts.

**7.** Preparing a postclosing trial balance (optional).

**8.** Making *reversing journal entries* to general ledger accounts after adjusting and closing journal entries have been posted (optional).

3.24   These steps were summarized graphically in Figure 3.1 and are discussed more fully below.

### Journalizing

3.25   Each accounting event is initially recorded in the general journal in the form of a *journal entry*. The standard journal entry format is as follows:

```
Date                      Amount
Account Debited  .............. Debited
     Account Credited  ..........      Amount
                                       Credited
Explanation of transaction or
event being journalized.
```

The *general journal* is merely a book or other device containing a listing of journal entries. The general journal is often referred to as the "book of original entry," because

accounting events initially enter the accounting system through it.

In addition to the general journal, most    3.26
firms also maintain *specialized journals*. These journals are used instead of the general journal to record transactions that occur regularly. For example, a Cash Receipts Journal might be used to record all transactions in which cash is received. The amounts shown each week or month in the Cash Receipts Journal are totaled and the resulting sum is posted on the debit side of the general ledger account for Cash. The general journal is then used to record all transactions that are not recorded in either the Cash Receipts Journal or some other specialized journal. Specialized journals might be used for cash disbursements, sales, purchases, or accounts payable. Appendix 3.1 at the end of this chapter discusses specialized journals more fully.

### Posting

At periodic intervals (for example, weekly    3.27
or monthly), the accounting events journalized in either the general journal or a specialized journal are entered, or posted, to the individual accounts in the general ledger. Whereas the general and specialized journals accumulate data for each accounting event, the general ledger accumulates data according to the effect of accounting events on particular accounts. The general ledger is often a book with a separate page for each account. The "pages" in a general ledger may be referenced by an access number in a computer's memory bank. The T-account, described earlier, serves as a useful surrogate for a general ledger account.

Firms may also maintain subsidiary ledg-    3.28
ers for particular accounts in the general ledger. For example, a subsidiary ledger for accounts receivable would contain a listing of the amounts due from each of the firm's customers. The sum of the amounts in the accounts-receivable subsidiary ledger should equal the amount shown for Accounts Receivable in the general ledger. In this case, the general ledger account would

be a "controlling account" for the detailed amounts in the subsidiary ledger. Subsidiary ledgers are also discussed in Appendix 3.1.

## Preparing the Unadjusted Trial Balance

3.29 A trial balance is a listing of each of the accounts in the general ledger with its balance at a particular time. All accounts with debit balances (normally assets, expenses, and dividend declarations) are listed and summed. All accounts with credit balances (normally liabilities, capital stock, retained earnings, and revenues) are listed and summed. If the double-entry recording process has been carried out properly and there have been no errors in transferring amounts from the general journal to the general ledger, then the total amount in accounts with debit balances should be equal to the total amount in accounts with credit balances. If the trial balance is out of balance, it is necessary to retrace the steps followed in processing the accounting data to find the source of the error. A trial balance prepared at the end of a period before any end-of-period adjusting entries are made is called an *unadjusted trial balance*.

## Adjusting Entries

3.30 The entries made during the period in the general journal result primarily from transactions between the firm and outsiders (for example, suppliers, employees, and customers). Other events occur, however, for which no specific transaction signals the need for a journal entry, but which must be considered in measuring net income for the period and financial position at the end of the period. For example, buildings and equipment are continually used in the process of generating revenues. Because the services of these assets are consumed during the period, a portion of their acquisition cost must be recognized as a period expense or a product cost. Similarly, insurance coverage expires continually throughout the year. Because the services of the asset, Prepaid Insurance, are gradually consumed, a portion of the asset must be recognized as a period expense or a product cost.

Other kinds of events occur that affect the 3.31 revenues and expenses of the period but for which a transaction with an outsider will not occur until a subsequent period. For example, salaries and wages are earned by administrative employees during the last several days of an accounting period, but they will not be paid until the following accounting period. Such salaries and wages, although payable in the next accounting period, are expenses of the current period under the accrual basis of accounting. Similarly, interest accrues continually on a firm's notes receivable or payable. Interest will be collected or paid in a subsequent period, but a portion of the interest must be recognized as revenue or expense in the current period.

Adjusting entries are prepared at the end 3.32 of an accounting period. These entries alter the balances in general ledger accounts in order that revenues and expenses are properly measured for the period and that the amounts in balance sheet accounts at the end of the period are correctly stated. Adjusting entries are typically entered in the general journal and then posted to the appropriate general ledger accounts.

A second trial balance might be prepared 3.33 of the general ledger accounts after adjusting entries have been made. Such a trial balance is referred to as an *adjusted* or *preclosing trial balance*.

## Closing Entries

Revenue and expense amounts could be re- 3.34 corded directly in the Retained Earnings account. For example, the sale of merchandise on account results in an increase in assets (accounts receivable) and retained earnings (sales revenue) and a decrease in assets (merchandise inventory) and retained earnings (cost of goods sold). Measurement of the *amount* of net income would be relatively simple if revenues and expenses were recorded directly in the Retained Earnings account. Net income would be determined from the following equation:

$$\begin{array}{c}\text{Net}\\\text{Income}\end{array} = \begin{array}{c}\text{Retained}\\\text{Earnings}\\\text{End of}\\\text{Period}\end{array} - \begin{array}{c}\text{Retained}\\\text{Earnings}\\\text{Beginning}\\\text{of Period}\end{array} + \text{Dividends.}$$

3.35   In preparing an income statement, however, we are interested in the components of net income: the sources of revenue and the types of expenses. Such information aids users in evaluating a firm's profitability over time. To facilitate the preparation of the income statement, individual revenue and expense accounts are maintained during the accounting period. These accounts begin the accounting period with a zero balance. During the period, revenues and expenses are recorded in the accounts as they arise. At the end of the period, the balance in each revenue and expense account represents the cumulative revenues and expenses *for the period*. These amounts are reported in the income statement, which shows the net income of the period.

3.36   Because revenues and expenses are basically components of retained earnings, the balance in each revenue and expense account is transferred at the end of the period to the Retained Earnings account. Each revenue and expense account will then have a zero balance after the transfer. Retained Earnings will be increased (or decreased) by the amount of net income (or net loss) for the period.

3.37   The end result of maintaining separate revenue and expense accounts during the period and transferring their balances to the Retained Earnings account at the end of the period is the same as if revenues and expenses were initially recorded directly in the Retained Earnings account. The purpose of using separate revenue and expense accounts is to facilitate the preparation of the income statement in which specific types of revenues and expenses are disclosed. Once this purpose has been served, the usefulness of separate revenue and expense accounts *for a given accounting period* has ended. Having been reduced to a zero balance at the end of the accounting period, these accounts begin the following accounting period with a zero balance and are therefore ready for entry of the revenue and expense amounts of the following period.

3.38   The process of transferring the balances in revenue and expense accounts to retained earnings is referred to as the *closing process,* because each revenue and expense account is closed, or reduced to a zero balance. Because revenue and expense accounts accumulate amounts for only a single accounting period, they are called *temporary accounts*. On the other hand, the accounts on the balance sheet reflect the cumulative changes in each account from the time the firm was first organized, and are not closed each period. The balances in these accounts at the end of one period are carried over as the beginning balances of the following period. Balance sheet accounts are called *permanent accounts*.

3.39   The closing entry for income statement accounts with debit balances (usually expenses) is

| | | |
|---|---|---|
| Retained Earnings | | X |
|   Income Statement Accounts with Debit | | |
|     Balances | | X |

3.40   The closing entry for income statement accounts with credit balances (usually revenues) is

| | | |
|---|---|---|
| Income Statement Accounts with Credit | | |
|   Balances | | X |
|     Retained Earnings | | X |

3.41   An alternative closing procedure uses an "Income Summary" account. Individual revenue and expense accounts are first closed to the Income Summary account. The income statement is prepared using information on individual revenues and expenses in the Income Summary account. The balance in the Income Summary account, representing net income for the period, is then closed to Retained Earnings. The end result of both closing procedures is the same.

3.42   Closing entries are usually entered in the general journal and then posted to appropriate accounts in the general ledger. A trial balance of the general ledger accounts after closing entries have been posted is called a *postclosing trial balance*. This trial balance will show zero balances in all revenue and expense accounts.

## Reversing Entries

3.43 Some firms follow a procedure of making reversing entries on the *first day of a new accounting period*. These entries are made to simplify the recording process during the new accounting period. For purposes of completeness, we briefly describe and illustrate reversing entries here.

3.44 First, examine the problem that reversing entries are designed to solve. Suppose that salaries are paid every other Friday, with paychecks compensating employees for the two weeks just ended. Suppose, further, that total salaries accrue at the rate of $5,000 per 5-day work week. The bookkeeper is accustomed to making the following entry every other Friday:

(1)

| | | |
|---|---|---|
| Salary Expense | 10,000 | |
| Cash | | 10,000 |

To record salary expense and salary payments.

3.45 If paychecks are delivered to employees on Friday, December 26, then the adjusting entry made on December 31 (or, perhaps, later) to record accrued salaries for December 29, 30, and 31 would be

(2)

| | | |
|---|---|---|
| Salary Expense | 3,000 | |
| Salaries Payable | | 3,000 |

To charge operations of the current year with all salaries accrued as of December 31.

The Salary Expense account would be closed as part of the December 31 closing entries. On the next payday, January 9, the salary entry would have to be

(3)

| | | |
|---|---|---|
| Salary Expense | 7,000 | |
| Salaries Payable | 3,000 | |
| Cash | | 10,000 |

To record salaries split between expense of the current year and liability carried over from the preceding year.

To make this entry (3), the bookkeeper must look back into the records to see how much of the debit is to Salaries Payable accrued from the previous year so that total debits are properly split between this year's expense and the accrued liability carried over from last year. Notice that this entry forces the bookkeeper both (a) to refer to balances in old accounts and (b) to make an entry different from the one customarily made, entry (1).

3.46 The reversing entry, made just after the books have been closed for the preceding year, makes the salary entry for January 9, the same as that made on all other Friday paydays. The entry, made on January 2, merely *reverses* the adjusting entry (2):

(4)

| | | |
|---|---|---|
| Salaries Payable | 3,000 | |
| Salary Expense | | 3,000 |

To reverse the adjusting entry.

This entry results in a zero balance in the Salaries Payable account and a *credit* balance in the Salary Expense account. If entry (4) is made on January 2, then the entry on January 9 will be the customary entry (1). Entries (4) and (1) together have exactly the same effect as entry (3).

3.47 The following entries summarize the journal entries to record salaries, both with and without reversing entries.

| | (a) Using Reversing Entries | | (b) Not Using Reversing Entries | |
|---|---|---|---|---|
| 12/31 | | | | |
| Salary Expense | 3,000 | | 3,000 | |
| Salaries Payable | | 3,000 | | 3,000 |
| Adjusting entry to recognize accrued salaries. | | | | |
| 12/31 | | | | |
| Income Summary | 261,000 | | 261,000 | |
| Salary Expense | | 261,000 | | 261,000 |
| Closing entry. Amount is assumed. | | | | |
| (Financial statements are prepared.) | | | | |
| 1/2 | | | | |
| Salaries Payable | 3,000 | | — | |
| Salary Expense | | 3,000 | | — |
| To reverse the adjusting entry of December 31. | | | | |

1/9

| | | |
|---|---|---|
| Salary Expense ....... | 10,000 | 7,000 |
| Salaries Payable ...... | — | 3,000 |
|    Cash in Bank ..... | 10,000 | 10,000 |

To record payment of salaries.

3.48 The procedure followed when reversing entries are used can be outlined as follows:

**1.** The required adjustment is made at the end of an accounting period.

**2.** The closing entry is made as usual.

**3.** As of the first day of the following period, an entry is made reversing the adjusting entry.

**4.** When a payment is made, the entry is made as though no adjusting entry had been recorded.

3.49 Deciding whether or not to use reversing entries is a case where cost-benefit analysis of record keeping procedures is required. With computer-based data-processing systems, reversing entries can be easily made on the first day of each new accounting period. The choice of whether or not to reverse has no effect, of course, on the financial statements. Reversing entries are not considered further in this text and are not required in any of the problems at the end of each chapter.

## Illustration of the Accounting Process for a Merchandising Firm

3.50 Wilson's Shoe Store, Inc., has been in business since 1978. Exhibit 3.2 shows a trial balance taken from its general ledger accounts on January 1, 1981, the first day of an accounting period. To facilitate understanding, in this illustration the asset accounts are designated (A), the liability accounts (L), and the owners' equity accounts (OE). Trial balances do not usually contain such designations.

3.51 Note that the revenue and expense accounts are not included in this trial balance; they have zero balances at the beginning of an accounting period. Two of the accounts

*Exhibit 3.2*
**Wilson's Shoe Store, Inc.**
**Trial Balance**
**January 1, 1981**

| | Accounts with Debit Balances | Accounts with Credit Balances |
|---|---|---|
| Cash (A) ........... | $ 60,000 | |
| Accounts Receivable (A) .... | 140,000 | |
| Allowance for Uncollectible Accounts (XA) .... | | $ 14,000 |
| Merchandise Inventory (A) ..... | 350,000 | |
| Land (A) ........... | 200,000 | |
| Building and Equipment (A) ... | 1,050,000 | |
| Accumulated Depreciation (XA) . | | 170,000 |
| Accounts Payable (L) ...... | | 270,000 |
| Bonds Payable (L) .. | | 200,000 |
| Common Stock (OE) . | | 500,000 |
| Additional Paid-in Capital (OE) ...... | | 400,000 |
| Retained Earnings (OF) .... | | 246,000 |
| Total ........... | $1,800,000 | $1,800,000 |

in the trial balance, Allowance for Uncollectible Accounts and Accumulated Depreciation, are *contra accounts*. A contra account accumulates amounts that are subtracted from the amount in another account. Allowance for Uncollectible Accounts is a contra account to Accounts Receivable. Accumulated Depreciation is a contra account to Buildings and Equipment. The nature and use of these contra accounts are discussed later in this illustration. An asset contra account is designated XA in the trial balance.

### Journalizing

3.52 The transactions of Wilson's Shoe Store during 1981 and the appropriate journal entries at the time of the transactions follow.

3.53 (1) Merchandise costing $710,000 is purchased on account.

Merchandise Inventory (A) ....... 710,000
   Accounts Payable (L) ........ 710,000

3.54 (2) Sales during the year are $1,250,000, of which $450,000 are for cash and the remainder are on account.

Cash (A) ..................... 450,000
Accounts Receivable (A) ....... 800,000
   Sales Revenue (OE) ....... 1,250,000

3.55 (3) The cost of merchandise sold during 1981 is $780,000.

Cost of Goods Sold (OE) ........ 780,000
   Merchandise Inventory (A) ... 780,000

3.56 (4) Salaries of $220,000 are paid in cash during the year.

Salaries Expense (OE) ........... 220,000
   Cash (A) ................... 220,000

3.57 (5) Customers' accounts of $650,000 are collected.

Cash (A) ...................... 650,000
   Accounts Receivable (A) ..... 650,000

3.58 (6) Payments of $540,000 are made to merchandise suppliers for purchases on account.

Accounts Payable (L) ........... 540,000
   Cash (A) ................... 540,000

3.59 (7) A premium of $3,000 is paid on January 1, 1981, for a 3-year property and liability insurance policy.

Prepaid Insurance (A) ........... 3,000
   Cash (A) ................... 3,000

The debit in this entry, made on January 1, 1981, is to an asset account, because the insurance provides 3 years of coverage beginning on that date. The entry to reduce the Prepaid Insurance account and to record the insurance expense for 1981 is one of the adjusting entries made at the end of the accounting period.

3.60 (8) Warehouse space not needed in the company's operations is rented out for 1 year beginning December 1, 1981. The annual rental of $1,200 is received at that time.

Cash (A) ....................... 1,200
Rental Fees Received in
   Advance (L) .............. 1,200

3.61 (9) Annual interest on the long-term bonds outstanding at the rate of 8 percent is paid on December 31, 1981.

Interest Expense (OE) ............ 16,000
   Cash (A) ................... 16,000

3.62 (10) A 90-day note was received from a customer on December 1, 1981. The note replaced the customer's open account receivable balance of $10,000 arising from an earlier sale. The note bears interest at the rate of 9 percent per year.

Notes Receivable (A) ........... 10,000
   Accounts Receivable (A) ..... 10,000

3.63 (11) The board of directors declared a cash dividend of $30,000 on December 28, 1981. The dividend is to be paid on January 20, 1982.

Retained Earnings (OE) .......... 30,000
   Dividends Payable (L) ........ 30,000

## Posting

3.64 The entries in the general journal are posted to the appropriate general ledger accounts. In this illustration, the posting operation takes place on December 31, 1981. The T-accounts in Exhibit 3.3 show the opening balances from the trial balance in Exhibit 3.2 and the effects of transactions (1) through (11).

*Exhibit 3.3*
**Wilson's Shoe Store, Inc.**
**T-Accounts Showing Beginning and**
**Ending Balances and Transactions**
**during 1981**

| Cash (A) | | | |
|---|---|---|---|
| Bal. 1/1 | 60,000 | | |
| (2) | 450,000 | 220,000 | (4) |
| (5) | 650,000 | 540,000 | (6) |
| (8) | 1,200 | 3,000 | (7) |
| | | 16,000 | (9) |
| Bal. 12/31 | 382,200 | | |

| Accounts Receivable (A) | | | |
|---|---|---|---|
| Bal. 1/1 | 140,000 | | |
| (2) | 800,000 | 650,000 | (5) |
| | | 10,000 | (10) |
| Bal. 12/31 | 280,000 | | |

| Allowance for Uncollectible Accounts (XA) | |
|---|---|
| | 14,000 Bal. 1/1 |
| | 14,000 Bal. 12/31 |

| Notes Receivable (A) | | |
|---|---|---|
| Bal. 1/1 | 0 | |
| (10) | 10,000 | |
| Bal. 12/31 | 10,000 | |

| Merchandise Inventory (A) | | | |
|---|---|---|---|
| Bal. 1/1 | 350,000 | | |
| (1) | 710,000 | 780,000 | (3) |
| Bal. 12/31 | 280,000 | | |

| Prepaid Insurance (A) | | |
|---|---|---|
| Bal. 1/1 | 0 | |
| (7) | 3,000 | |
| Bal. 12/31 | 3,000 | |

| Land (A) | | |
|---|---|---|
| Bal. 1/1 | 200,000 | |
| Bal. 12/31 | 200,000 | |

| Building and Equipment (A) | | |
|---|---|---|
| Bal. 1/1 | 1,050,000 | |
| Bal. 12/31 | 1,050,000 | |

| Accumulated Depreciation (XA) | |
|---|---|
| | 170,000 Bal. 1/1 |
| | 170,000 Bal. 12/31 |

| Accounts Payable (L) | | | |
|---|---|---|---|
| | | 270,000 | Bal. 1/1 |
| (6) | 540,000 | 710,000 | (1) |
| | | 440,000 | Bal. 12/31 |

| Dividends Payable (L) | | |
|---|---|---|
| | 0 | Bal. 1/1 |
| | 30,000 | (11) |
| | 30,000 | Bal. 12/31 |

| Rental Fees Received in Advance (L) | | |
|---|---|---|
| | 0 | Bal. 1/1 |
| | 1,200 | (8) |
| | 1,200 | Bal. 12/31 |

| Bonds Payable (L) | |
|---|---|
| | 200,000 Bal. 1/1 |
| | 200,000 Bal. 12/31 |

| Common Stock (OE) | |
|---|---|
| | 500,000 Bal. 1/1 |
| | 500,000 Bal. 12/31 |

| Additional Paid-in Capital (OE) | |
|---|---|
| | 400,000 Bal. 1/1 |
| | 400,000 Bal. 12/31 |

| Retained Earnings (OE) | | | |
|---|---|---|---|
| (11) | 30,000 | 246,000 | Bal. 1/1 |
| | | 216,000 | Bal. 12/31 |

| Sales Revenue (OE) | | |
|---|---|---|
| | 0 | Bal. 1/1 |
| | 1,250,000 | (2) |
| | 1,250,000 | Bal. 12/31 |

| Cost of Goods Sold (OE) | | |
|---|---|---|
| Bal. 1/1 | 0 | |
| (3) | 780,000 | |
| Bal. 12/31 | 780,000 | |

| Salaries Expense (OE) | | |
|---|---|---|
| Bal. 1/1 | 0 | |
| (4) | 220,000 | |
| Bal. 12/31 | 220,000 | |

| Interest Expense (OE) | | |
|---|---|---|
| Bal. 1/1 | 0 | |
| (9) | 16,000 | |
| Bal. 12/31 | 16,000 | |

*Exhibit 3.4*
**Wilson's Shoe Store, Inc.**
**Unadjusted Trial Balance**
**December 31, 1981**

| | Accounts with Debit Balances | Accounts with Credit Balances |
|---|---|---|
| Cash (A) ............ | $ 382,200 | |
| Accounts Receivable (A) ..... | 280,000 | |
| Allowance for Uncollectible Accounts (XA) ..... | | $ 14,000 |
| Notes Receivable (A) . | 10,000 | |
| Merchandise Inventory (A) ....... | 280,000 | |
| Prepaid Insurance (A) . | 3,000 | |
| Land (A) ............ | 200,000 | |
| Building and Equipment (A) ..... | 1,050,000 | |
| Accumulated Depreciation (XA) .. | | 170,000 |
| Accounts Payable (L) . | | 440,000 |
| Dividends Payable (L) . | | 30,000 |
| Rental Fees Received in Advance (L) ..... | | 1,200 |
| Bonds Payable (L) .... | | 200,000 |
| Common Stock (OE) .. | | 500,000 |
| Additional Paid-in Capital (OE) ....... | | 400,000 |
| Retained Earnings (OE) ...... | | 216,000 |
| Sales Revenue (OE) ... | | 1,250,000 |
| Cost of Goods Sold (OE) .......... | 780,000 | |
| Salaries Expense (OE) . | 220,000 | |
| Interest Expense (OE) . | 16,000 | |
| Totals ............ | $3,221,200 | $3,221,200 |

## Preparing the Unadjusted Trial Balance

3.65    Exhibit 3.4 shows the unadjusted trial balance of Wilson's Shoe Store as of December 31, 1981. The amounts in the unadjusted trial balance are taken directly from the ending balances in the T-accounts shown in Exhibit 3.3.

## Preparing Adjusting Entries

Adjusting entries must be made at the end of    3.66
1981 to alter the balances in the general ledger accounts in order to recognize all revenues and expenses for the proper reporting of net income and financial position. Several examples of adjusting entries are illustrated for Wilson's Shoe Store in the following sections.

**Recognition of Accrued Revenues and Re-**    3.67
**ceivables** Revenue is earned as services are rendered. For example, rent is earned as a tenant uses the property. Interest, a "rent" for the use of money, is earned as time passes on a loan. It is usually not convenient, however, to record these amounts as they accrue day by day. At the end of the accounting period, there may be some situations in which revenue has been earned but for which no entry has been made, either because cash has not been received or the time has not arrived for a formal invoice to be sent to the customer. A claim has come into existence that, although it may not be due immediately, should appear on the balance sheet as an asset and be reflected in the revenues of the period. The purpose of the adjusting entry for interest eventually receivable by the lender is to recognize on the balance sheet the right to receive cash in an amount equal to the interest already earned and to recognize the same amount as revenue on the income statement for the period.

Wilson's Shoe Store received a 90-day    3.68
note from a customer on December 1, 1981. At year-end, the note is included as an asset on the trial balance. Interest earned during December, however, is not reflected in the unadjusted trial balance. The note earns interest at the rate of 9 percent per year. By convention in business practice, interest rates stated on loans are almost always stated as annual interest rates. Also, by convention, a year equal to 360 days is usually assumed to simplify the calculation of interest earned. Interest of $75 is earned by Wilson's Shoe Store, Inc., during December. This amount is equal to the $10,000 principal

times the 9 percent annual interest rate times the elapsed 30 days divided by 360 days ($75 = $10,000 × .09 × 30/360). The adjusting entry to recognize the asset, Interest Receivable, and the interest earned, is

(12)
Interest Receivable (A) .................... 75
    Interest Revenue (OE) ................. 75

**3.69 Recognition of Accrued Expenses and Payables** As various services are received, their cost should be reflected in the financial statements, whether or not payment has been made or an invoice received. Here, also, it is frequently not convenient to record these amounts day by day. It is likely that some adjustment of expenses and liabilities will be necessary at the end of the accounting period.

3.70  Salaries and wages earned during the last several days of the accounting period that will not be paid until the following accounting period illustrate this type of adjustment. According to payroll records, employees of Wilson's Shoe Store earned salaries of $12,000 during the last several days of 1981 that were not recorded at year-end. The adjusting entry is

(13)
Salaries Expense (OE) ............. 12,000
    Salaries Payable (L) .......... 12,000

Other examples of this type of adjusting entry include costs incurred for utilities, taxes, and interest.

**3.71 Allocation of Prepaid Operating Costs** Another type of adjustment arises because assets are acquired for use in the operations of the firm but are not completely used during the accounting period in which they are acquired. For example, Wilson's Shoe Store paid $3,000 on January 1, 1981, for a 3-year insurance policy. During 1981, one-third of the coverage expired, so $1,000 of the premium should be reflected as insurance expense. The balance sheet on December 31, 1981, should show $2,000 of prepaid insurance among the assets, because only this portion of the premium is a future benefit—

the asset of insurance coverage to be received over the next 2 years.

3.72  The nature of the adjusting entry to record an asset expiration as an expense depends on the recording of the original payment. If the payment resulted in a debit to an asset account, the adjusting entry must reduce the asset and increase the expense for the services used up during the accounting period. Wilson's Shoe Store recorded the payment of the insurance premium on January 1, 1981, as follows:

(7)
Prepaid Insurance (A) ............... 3,000
    Cash (A) ....................... 3,000

The adjusting entry is, therefore:

(14)
Insurance Expense (OE) ............. 1,000
    Prepaid Insurance (A) .......... 1,000

Insurance expense for 1981 is $1,000, and prepaid insurance in the amount of $2,000 is shown as an asset on the balance sheet on December 31, 1981.

3.73  Instead of debiting an asset account at the time the premium is paid, some firms debit an expense account. For example, Wilson's Shoe Store might have recorded the original premium payment as follows:

(7a)
Insurance Expense (OE) ............. 3,000
    Cash (A) ....................... 3,000

Because many operating costs become expenses in the period in which the expenditure is made (for example, monthly rent, office supplies), this second procedure for recording expenditures during the year sometimes reduces the number of adjusting entries that must be made at year-end. In the situation with the insurance policy, however, not all of the $3,000 premium paid is an expense of 1981. If the original journal entry had been (7a), the adjusting entry would then be

(14a)
Prepaid Insurance (A) ............... 2,000
    Insurance Expense (OE) ......... 2,000

After the original entry in (7a) and the adjusting entry in (14a), insurance expense for 1981 is reflected in the accounts at $1,000, and prepaid insurance at $2,000. The *end result* of these two approaches to recording the original payment of the premium is the same. The *adjusting entries,* however, are quite different.

3.74 **Recognition of Depreciation** When assets such as buildings, machinery, furniture, and trucks are purchased, their acquisition cost is debited to appropriate asset accounts. Although these assets may provide services for a number of years, eventually their future benefits will expire. Therefore, the portion of an asset's cost that will expire is spread systematically over its estimated useful life. The charge made to the current operations for the portion of the cost of such assets consumed during the current period is called *depreciation* expense. Depreciation involves nothing new in principle; it is identical with the procedure for prepaid operating costs presented previously. For example, the cost of a building is a prepayment for a series of future services, and depreciation allocates the cost of the services to the periods in which services are received and used.

3.75 Various accounting methods are used in allocating the acquisition cost of long-lived assets to the periods of benefit. One widely used method is the *straight-line method.* Under this procedure, an equal portion of the acquisition cost less estimated salvage value is allocated to each period of the asset's estimated useful life. The depreciation charge for each period is determined as follows:

$$\frac{\text{Acquisition} - \begin{array}{c}\text{Estimated}\\\text{Salvage}\\\text{Cost} \quad \text{Value}\end{array}}{\begin{array}{c}\text{Estimated Useful}\\\text{Life in Periods}\end{array}} = \begin{array}{c}\text{Depreciation}\\\text{Charge for}\\\text{Each Period}\end{array}$$

Internal records indicate that the Building and Equipment account of Wilson's Shoe Store is composed of a store building with an acquisition cost of $800,000 and a group of items of equipment with an acquisition cost of $250,000. At the time the building was acquired, it had an estimated 40-year useful life and a zero salvage value. Depreciation expense for each year of the building's life is calculated to be

$$\frac{\$800,000 - \$0}{40 \text{ years}} = \$20,000 \text{ per year.}$$

At the time the equipment was acquired, it 3.76 had an estimated useful life of 6 years and an estimated salvage value of $10,000. Annual depreciation is, therefore,

$$\frac{\$250,000 - \$10,000}{6 \text{ years}} = \$40,000 \text{ per year.}$$

The adjusting entry to record depreciation of $60,000 (= $20,000 + $40,000) for 1981 is

(15)

| | | |
|---|---|---|
| Depreciation Expense (OE) | ........ 60,000 | |
| Accumulated | | |
| Depreciation (XA) | ........... | 60,000 |

The credit in entry (15) could have been made directly to the Building and Equipment account, because the credit records the portion of the asset's cost which has expired, or become an expense, during 1981. The same end result is achieved by crediting the Accumulated Depreciation account, a contra-asset account, and then deducting the balance in this account from the acquisition cost of the assets in the Building and Equipment account on the balance sheet. Using the contra account enables the financial statements to show both the acquisition cost of the assets in use and the portion of that amount that has previously been recognized as an expense. Showing both acquisition cost and accumulated depreciation amounts separately provides a rough indication of the relative age of the firm's long-lived assets.*

Note that the Depreciation Expense ac- 3.77 count includes only depreciation for the current accounting period, whereas the Accu-

---

*Consider an asset costing $10,000 with accumulated depreciation of $4,000 and straight-line depreciation of $1,000 per year. We can estimate that the asset is 4 years old (= $4,000 accumulated depreciation/$1,000 depreciation per year).

mulated Depreciation account reflects the cumulative depreciation charges on the present assets since acquisition. The Accumulated Depreciation account is sometimes referred to as Allowance for Depreciation.

3.78 **Valuation of Accounts Receivable** When sales are made to customers on account, it is usually expected that some of the accounts will not be collected. In Chapter 2, we indicated that the primary objective in accounting for uncollectible accounts is to ensure that sales revenue of the period reflects only the amount of cash expected to be collected. That is, adjustments for anticipated uncollectible accounts should be charged against sales revenue *in the period of the sale.* The principal accounting problem here arises from the fact that individual accounts may not be judged uncollectible until some time after the period of sale. An estimate of the probable amount of uncollectible accounts must therefore be made in the period of sale.

3.79 Based on past experience, Wilson's Shoe Store estimates that 2 percent of sales on account during the year will ultimately become uncollectible. Because sales on account during 1981 were $800,000, the adjusting entry to provide for estimated uncollectible accounts of $16,000 (= .02 × $800,000) is

(16)
Sales Contra, Estimated
  Uncollectibles (OE)  ....  .,,.,.  16,000
    Allowance for Uncollectible
      Accounts (XA) ..............       16,000

The debit entry is to an income statement account. Because revenue should be stated at the amount expected to be collected in cash, the amount in this account is preferably deducted from sales revenue on the income statement as a contra account. Many firms, however, debit an expense account, such as Bad Debt Expense or Uncollectible Accounts Expense, which is included in the expense section rather than the revenue section of the income statement. The effect on net income is the same in either case.

3.80 The credit entry to recognize estimated uncollectible accounts is to a balance sheet account that is shown as a contra to Ac-

counts Receivable. The net amount, accounts receivable less estimated uncollectibles, indicates the amount of cash expected to be collected from customers. Using the contra account permits the disclosure of the total receivables outstanding as well as the estimated amount that will be collected.

At periodic intervals, individual customers' accounts are reviewed to assess their collectibility. Accounts deemed to be uncollectible are eliminated or "written off." Wilson's Shoe Store determined on December 31, 1981, that specific customers' accounts totaling $15,000 would never be collected. The adjusting entry to write off these individual accounts is

3.81

(17)
Allowance for Uncollectible
  Accounts (XA) ..................  15,000
    Accounts Receivable (A) .......       15,000

Note that net income is not affected by the write-off of the specific customers' accounts. Net income is affected in the period of sale when a provision is made for uncollectible accounts [for example, entry (16) and similar entries made in prior years]. When the $15,000 of specific customers' accounts is written off at the end of 1981, there is no additional effect on net income. Also note that the amount, accounts receivable less estimated uncollectibles, on the balance sheet is not affected by the write-off, because both the asset and contra asset are reduced by an equal amount.

**Valuation of Liabilities** When cash is received from customers before merchandise is sold or services are rendered, the cash receipt creates a liability. For example, Wilson's Shoe Store received $1,200 on December 1, 1981, as 1 year's rent on warehouse space. When the cash was received, the liability account, Rental Fees Received in Advance, was credited. One month's rent has been earned as of December 31, 1981. The adjusting entry is

3.82

(18)
Rental Fees Received in Advance (L)  .....  100
    Rent Revenue (OE)  ..................       100

The remaining $1,100 of the advance rental is yet to be earned and is carried on the December 31, 1981, balance sheet as a liability.

3.83 **Correction of Errors** Various errors and omissions may be discovered at the end of the accounting period as the process of checking, reviewing, and auditing is carried out. For example, the sales for 1 month during the year might have been recorded as $38,700 instead of $37,800. Or the sale to a specific customer might not have been recorded. Entries must be made at the end of the accounting period to correct for these errors. There were no such errors in the accounts of Wilson's Shoe Store.

3.84 **Trial Balance after Adjusting Entries** The adjusting entries are posted or entered in the general ledger in the same manner as entries made during the year. A trial balance of the general ledger accounts after adjusting entries are made could be prepared. Exhibit 3.5 presents the trial balance data before and after adjusting entries for Wilson's Shoe Store. The exhibit indicates the effect of the adjustment process on the various accounts. The number in parentheses identifies the debit and credit components of each adjusting entry.

## Preparing Closing Entries

3.85 Each temporary revenue and expense account of Wilson's Shoe Store could be closed by a separate entry. Some recording time is saved, however, by closing all revenue and expense accounts in a single entry as follows:

```
(19)
Sales Revenue (OE)  . . . . . . . . .  1,250,000
Interest Revenue (OE)  . . . . . . . .       75
Rent Revenue (OE)  . . . . . . . . . .      100
     Cost of Goods Sold (OE) . .            780,000
     Salaries Expense (OE)  . . . .         232,000
     Interest Expense (OE)  . . . . .        16,000
     Insurance Expense (OE)  . . .            1,000
     Depreciation Expense (OE) .             60,000
     Sales Contra, Estimated
        Uncollectibles(OE) . . . . . . .     16,000
     Retained Earnings (OE)  . . .          145,175
```

The amount credited to Retained Earnings is the difference between the amounts debited to revenue accounts and the amounts credited to expense and sales adjustments accounts. This amount is the net income for the period.*

As discussed earlier, an alternative clos- 3.86 ing procedure uses a temporary "Income Summary" account. For example, the entry to close the Sales Revenue account under this alternative procedure is

```
(19a)
Sales Revenue (OE)  . . . . . . . . . .  1,250,000
     Income Summary (OE)  . . .              1,250,000
```

The entry to close the Cost of Goods Sold account is

```
(19b)
Income Summary (OE)  . . . . . . .   780,000
     Cost of Goods Sold (OE) . .             780,000
```

Similar closing entries are made for the other revenue and expense accounts. The Income Summary account will have a credit balance of $145,175 after all revenue and expense accounts have been closed. The balance in the Income Summary account is then transferred to Retained Earnings:

```
(19c)
Income Summary (OE)  . . . . . . .   145,175
     Retained Earnings (OE) . . .            145,175
```

The end result of both closing procedures is the same. Revenue and expense accounts, as well as the Income Summary account if one is used, have zero balances after closing entries, and the Retained Earnings account is increased by the net income for the period of $145,175. Exhibit 3.6 shows the Income Summary account for Wilson's Shoe Store after all revenue and expense accounts have been closed at the end of the period.

---

*The amount credited to Retained Earnings in the closing entry is called a *plug*. When making some journal entries in accounting, often all debits are known, as are all but one of the credits (or vice versa). Because the double-entry recording procedure requires equal debits and credits, the unknown quantity can be found by subtracting the sum of the known credits from the sum of all debits (or vice versa). This process is known as *plugging*.

*Exhibit 3.5*
**Wilson's Shoe Store, Inc. Trial Balance
before and after Adjusting Entries[a]
December 31, 1981**

| Accounts | Unadjusted Trial Balance | | Adjusting Entries | | Adjusted Trial Balance | |
|---|---|---|---|---|---|---|
| | **Debit** | **Credit** | **Debit** | **Credit** | **Debit** | **Credit** |
| Cash (A) .................. | $ 382,200 | | | | $ 382,200 | |
| Accounts Receivable (A) ...... | 280,000 | | | $ 15,000 (17) | 265,000 | |
| Allowance for Uncollectible | | | | | | |
| Accounts (XA) ............. | | $ 14,000 | $ 15,000 (17) | 16,000 (16) | | $ 15,000 |
| Notes Receivable (A) ........ | 10,000 | | | | 10,000 | |
| Interest Receivable (A) ........ | | | 75 (12) | | 75 | |
| Merchandise Inventory (A) .... | 280,000 | | | | 280,000 | |
| Prepaid Insurance (A) ........ | 3,000 | | | 1,000 (14) | 2,000 | |
| Land (A) ................... | 200,000 | | | | 200,000 | |
| Building and Equipment (A) ... | 1,050,000 | | | | 1,050,000 | |
| Accumulated | | | | | | |
| Depreciation (XA) .......... | | 170,000 | | 60,000 (15) | | 230,000 |
| Accounts Payable (L) ........ | | 440,000 | | | | 440,000 |
| Salaries Payable (L) .......... | | | | 12,000 (13) | | 12,000 |
| Dividends Payable (L) ........ | | 30,000 | | | | 30,000 |
| Rental Fees Received in | | | | | | |
| Advance (L) .............. | | 1,200 | 100 (18) | | | 1,100 |
| Bonds Payable (L) ........... | | 200,000 | | | | 200,000 |
| Common Stock (OE) ........ | | 500,000 | | | | 500,000 |
| Additional Paid-in | | | | | | |
| Capital (OE) ............... | | 400,000 | | | | 400,000 |
| Retained Earnings (OE) ....... | | 216,000[b] | | | | 216,000 |
| Sales Revenue (OE) ......... | | 1,250,000 | | | | 1,250,000 |
| Interest Revenue (OE)   ...... | | | | 75 (12) | | 75 |
| Rent Revenue (OE) .......... | | | | 100 (18) | | 100 |
| Cost of Goods Sold (OE) ..... | 780,000 | | | | 780,000 | |
| Salaries Expense (OE) ....... | 220,000 | | 12,000 (13) | | 232,000 | |
| Interest Expense (OE) ........ | 16,000 | | | | 16,000 | |
| Insurance Expense (OE) ...... | | | 1,000 (14) | | 1,000 | |
| Depreciation Expense (OE)  ... | | | 60,000 (15) | | 60,000 | |
| Sales Contra, Estimated | | | | | | |
| Uncollectibles (OE) ........ | | | 16,000 (16) | | 16,000 | |
| Totals ................. | $3,221,200 | $3,221,200 | $104,175 | $104,175 | $3,294,275 | $3,294,275 |

[a]This convenient tabular form is often called a *work sheet*. Most work sheets are more elaborate than this one, but their purpose is the same—to display data in a form for easy computations and financial statement preparation. The typical work sheet would not show just two final columns called Adjusted Trial Balance, but would show four columns: Income Statement Debit and Credit, and Balance Sheet Debit and Credit. The horizontal sum of the amounts in an income account is shown in the appropriate debit or credit income statement column of the work sheet. The horizontal sum of the amounts in a balance sheet account is shown in the appropriate debit or credit balance sheet column of the work sheet. Work sheets are discussed more fully in Appendix 3.2.

[b]$246,000 balance in Retained Earnings at the beginning of the year less $30,000 dividends declared during the year which was debited to the Retained Earnings account.

## Exhibit 3.6
### Illustration of Income Summary Account for Wilson's Shoe Store, Inc.

| Income Summary Account (OE) | | | | Retained Earnings (OE) | |
|---|---|---|---|---|---|
| Cost of Goods Sold | 780,000 | 1,250,000 Sales Revenue | | 246,000 Beginning Balance | |
| Salaries Expense | 232,000 | 75 Interest Revenue | | | |
| Interest Expense | 16,000 | 100 Rent Revenue | Dividends 30,000 | 145,175 Net Income ← | |
| Insurance Expense | 1,000 | 1,250,175 | | | |
| Depreciation Expense | 60,000 | | | 361,175 Ending Balance | |
| Sales Contra, Estimated Uncollectibles | 16,000 | | | | |
| To Close Income Summary Account | 145,175 | | | | |
| | 1,250,175 | | | | |

3.87 A postclosing trial balance could now be prepared. This trial balance would be similar (but with different amounts) to the trial balance in Exhibit 3.2.

## Exhibit 3.7
### Wilson's Shoe Store, Inc. Income Statement for the Year Ending December 31, 1981

**Revenues:**

| | | |
|---|---|---|
| Sales Revenue | | $1,250,000 |
| Less Sales Contra, Estimated Uncollectibles | | 16,000 |
| Net Sales Revenue | | $1,234,000 |
| Interest Revenue | | 75 |
| Rent Revenue | | 100 |
| Total Revenues | | $1,234,175 |

**Less Expenses:**

| | | |
|---|---|---|
| Cost of Goods Sold | $ 780,000 | |
| Salaries Expense | 232,000 | |
| Interest Expense | 16,000 | |
| Insurance Expense | 1,000 | |
| Depreciation Expense | 60,000 | |
| Total Expenses | | 1,089,000 |
| **Net Income** | | $ 145,175 |

## Financial Statement Preparation

3.88 The income statement, balance sheet, and any desired supporting schedules can be prepared from information in the adjusted trial balance. The income statement of Wilson's Shoe Store for 1981 is presented in Exhibit 3.7. Exhibit 3.8 presents an analysis of changes in retained earnings. Exhibit 3.9 presents the comparative balance sheets for December 31, 1980 and 1981.

## Exhibit 3.8
### Wilson's Shoe Store, Inc. Analysis of Changes in Retained Earnings for the Year Ending December 31, 1981

| | | |
|---|---|---|
| Retained Earnings, December 31, 1980 | | $246,000 |
| Net Income | $145,175 | |
| Less Dividends | 30,000 | |
| Increase in Retained Earnings | | 115,175 |
| Retained Earnings, December 31, 1981 | | $361,175 |

*Exhibit 3.9*
**Wilson's Shoe Store, Inc.**
**Comparative Balance Sheet**
**December 31, 1980 and 1981**

| ASSETS | | December 31, 1980 | | December 31, 1981 |
|---|---|---|---|---|
| **Current Assets:** | | | | |
| Cash | | | $ 60,000 | $ 382,200 |
| Accounts Receivable | $ 140,000 | | $ 265,000 | |
| Less Allowance for Uncollectible Accounts | 14,000 | | 15,000 | |
| Accounts Receivable—net | | | 126,000 | 250,000 |
| Notes Receivable | | | — | 10,000 |
| Interest Receivable | | | — | 75 |
| Merchandise Inventory | | | 350,000 | 280,000 |
| Prepaid Insurance | | | — | 2,000 |
| Total Current Assets | | | $ 536,000 | $ 924,275 |
| **Property, Plant, and Equipment:** | | | | |
| Land | | | $ 200,000 | $ 200,000 |
| Building and Equipment—at acquisition cost | $1,050,000 | | $1,050,000 | |
| Less: Accumulated Depreciation | 170,000 | | 230,000 | |
| Building and Equipment—net | | | 880,000 | 820,000 |
| Total Property, Plant, and Equipment | | | $1,080,000 | $1,020,000 |
| **Total Assets** | | | $1,616,000 | $1,944,275 |

| LIABILITIES AND SHAREHOLDERS' EQUITY | December 31, 1980 | December 31, 1981 |
|---|---|---|
| **Current Liabilities:** | | |
| Accounts Payable | $ 270,000 | $ 440,000 |
| Salaries Payable | — | 12,000 |
| Dividends Payable | — | 30,000 |
| Rental Fees Received In Advance | — | 1,100 |
| Total Current Liabilities | $ 270,000 | $ 483,100 |
| **Long-Term Debt:** | | |
| Bonds Payable | 200,000 | 200,000 |
| Total Liabilities | $ 470,000 | $ 683,100 |
| **Shareholders' Equity:** | | |
| Common Stock—at par value | $ 500,000 | $ 500,000 |
| Additional Paid-in Capital | 400,000 | 400,000 |
| Retained Earnings | 246,000 | 361,175 |
| Total Shareholders' Equity | $1,146,000 | $1,261,175 |
| **Total Liabilities and Shareholders' Equity** | $1,616,000 | $1,944,275 |

## Summary

3.89  Many of the controversial issues in financial reporting involve the first two steps in the accounting process: the identification of accounting events and the measurement of the relevant attributes of these events. In cases where official rule-making bodies have not issued reporting standards on a particular topic, practicing accountants must make professional judgments in dealing with these event recognition and measurement issues. Their judgments are based on the general criteria for event recognition (past event affecting the financial position of a business firm, the impact of which can be measured in monetary terms with reasonable precision), and measurement (use of historical exchange price to measure historical benefit and sacrifice, duality convention) established by the Financial Accounting Standards Board.

3.90    Once the first two steps in the accounting process have been completed, the third step (recording of measured accounting events) is relatively routine. The accounting system must be designed to ensure that accounting events are properly recorded initially and that they are subsequently processed through the accounting system in such a way that net income for the period and financial position at the end of the period are properly measured.

## Appendix 3.1: Accounting Journals and Ledgers

3.91  This appendix describes and illustrates some of the more common types of journals and ledgers used in accounting systems.

### Journals

3.92  The *journal* presents a chronological record of accounting events. *Journalizing* consists of analyzing the accounting events into the proper debits and credits and recording the results of the analysis in a journal. The journal contains accounting information classi-

fied by accounting event. Further, each accounting event is analyzed and recorded completely before the next one is entered. The journal is the first place in which a complete formal record of the accounting event is made. It is thus sometimes called *the book of original entry.* By recording all information relating to each accounting event in one place, the journal provides a chronological history, or running record, of the various events and transactions of the firm. The number of transactions, even in a small business, is so large that errors are bound to occur. It would be almost impossible to locate errors if a record such as the journal were not kept. Each journal entry can be checked independently for equal debits and credits, and postings in the ledger accounts can be traced back to the journal to determine the origin, authorization, and analysis of each transaction.

The journal may take three possible forms: 3.93 (1) two-column journal, (2) multicolumn journal, or (3) specialized journal.

**The Two-Column Journal Form** The most 3.94 common journal form is the two-column form presented in Exhibit 3.10. Essentials of the two-column form are a pair of columns to record the debits and credits and a place to indicate the names of the accounts affected by the transaction. As posting is done, there will be entered in the reference (Ref.) column the number, or page, of the account to which the amount has been posted, or, perhaps, a check mark to indi-

*Exhibit 3.10*
**Two-Column Journal Form**

| Date | | | Accounts and Explanation | Ref. | Debit | Credit |
|---|---|---|---|---|---|---|
| 9 | 1 | | Cash | √ | 1 5 0 0 0 | |
| | | | Accounts Receivable | √ | | 1 5 0 0 0 |
| | | | Collection from R. Wood on account. | | | |
| | | | | | | |
| | | | | | | |

cate that the posting has been done. A transaction involving the receipt of $150.00 from R. Wood as payment on an account receivable is shown in Exhibit 3.10 in the two-column journal.

3.95    The two-column journal form is the one commonly used for the general journal of a firm.

3.96    **Multicolumn Journal** The process of posting, or transferring, figures from the journal to the general ledger accounts is laborious and monotonous. When the two-column journal form is used, each journal debit and credit must be copied into the general ledger individually. In practice this simple two-column form is usually replaced by a more elaborate journal or journals. One labor-saving device is to expand the journal into a multicolumn record. The *multicolumn* journal provides several debit and several credit columns to replace the two-column form. This subdivision permits separate columns to be reserved for the entering of debits or credits in accounts, such as Cash and Sales for a merchandising firm, that are used often. A simple multicolumn journal form is shown in Exhibit 3.11. The transaction involving the receipt of cash from R. Wood on account is entered in the multicolumn journal.

3.97    Designing a multicolumn journal requires selecting the accounts to be allocated special columns. Columns should be provided for the debits or credits, or both, of those accounts that are used most frequently. In practice it may not be easy to discover which will be used most often. If the business has been in operation for some time, the past transactions can be studied and a tabulation made of the number of entries to each side of each account. If there is no experience to use as a guide, an attempt is made to anticipate the types of transactions that will occur most frequently and a tentative set of column headings is selected. In any case, the column headings may have to be changed from time to time so that the multicolumn format may be used efficiently. When only one multicolumn journal is used, two columns must always be reserved to record the debits and credits to the accounts for which specialized columns are not provided. The multicolumn journal is composed of two segments: **(1)** specialized columns for frequent items and **(2)** an attached two-column journal form to provide for all other items.

3.98    The principal advantage of using specialized columns is the savings in posting time. The posting of a column total to the general ledger takes the place of the posting of each of the individual items that appear in the column. Specialized columns also facilitate the process of journalizing, because most bookkeepers find it easier to analyze transactions when the commonly used accounts are spread across a columnar sheet. Each entry also takes less vertical space, and more entries can therefore be made on a journal page.

3.99    **Specialized Journals** The advantages of specialization can be extended further by replacing the multicolumn journal by a group

*Exhibit 3.11*
**Multicolumn Journal**

| Date | | Explanation | Cash | | Merchandise Sales | | Other Accounts | | | |
|---|---|---|---|---|---|---|---|---|---|---|
| | | | Debit | Credit | Debit | Credit | Debit | Credit | Ref. | Account Title |
| 9 | 1 | Collection from R. Wood on account | 150.00 | | | | | 150.00 | | Accounts Receivable |

*Exhibit 3.12*
**Cash Receipts Journal**

CASH RECEIPTS JOURNAL                                                                 Page 46

| Date | | Explanation | Cash Dr. | Accounts Receivable Cr. | Sales Cr. | Other Cr. | Account Title |
|---|---|---|---|---|---|---|---|
| 9 | 1 | Collection from R. Wood on Account | 150.00 | 150.00 | | | |
| 9 | 5 | Sale of Merchandise to Customers | 250.00 | | 250.00 | | |
| 9 | 12 | Collection from J. Smith on Account | 75.00 | 75.00 | | | |
| 9 | 19 | Receipt of Dividend from Ford Motor Company | 120.00 | | | 120.00 | Dividend Revenue |
| 9 | 25 | Sales of Merchandise to Customers | 400.00 | | 400.00 | | |
| | | | √995.00 | √225.00 | √650.00 | √120.00 | |

of specialized journals. There is no standard set of journals suitable for all firms. However, in most concerns four specialized journals are likely to be used in addition to the general journal: cash receipts; cash disbursements; revenue recognition (particularly sales); and acquisition of goods and services (particularly purchases of merchandise and raw materials). The size of the firm and the nature of its operations will, of course, affect the number and types of specialized journals employed. A cash receipts journal and a cash disbursements journal are described briefly below.

*Cash Receipts Journal* A cash receipts journal provides a chronological listing of all transactions involving the receipt of cash. Exhibit 3.12 shows an example of a cash receipts journal. Each transaction is entered in

3.100

*Exhibit 3.13*
**Cash Disbursements Journal**

CASH DISBURSEMENTS JOURNAL                                                                 Page 64

| Date | | Check Number | Payee | Cash Cr. | Accounts Payable Dr. | Selling and Administrative Expense Dr. | Other Dr. | Account Title |
|---|---|---|---|---|---|---|---|---|
| 9 | 4 | 246 | G. Winkle | 80.00 | | 80.00 | | |
| 9 | 7 | 247 | Stephens Wholesale | 163.00 | 163.00 | | | |
| 9 | 16 | 248 | Harris Insurance | 96.00 | | | 96.00 | Prepaid Insurance |
| 9 | 22 | 249 | City of Norwich | 62.00 | 62.00 | | | |
| 9 | 28 | 250 | Burkett Supply | 105.00 | | 105.00 | | |
| | | | | √506.00 | √225.00 | √185.00 | √96.00 | |

*Exhibit 3.14*
**Ledger Form**

CASH

| Date | | Explanation | Ref. | Dr. | Date | | Explanation | Ref. | Cr. |
|---|---|---|---|---|---|---|---|---|---|
| 9 | 1 | Balance | | 634.00 | | | | | |
| 9 | 30 | Cash Receipts Journal | 46 | 995.00 | 9 | 30 | Cash Disbursements Journal | 64 | 506.00 |
| 9 | 30 | Balance | | 1,123.00 | | | | | |

the Cash Receipts Dr. column. An entry is also made in either the Accounts Receivable Cr., Sales Cr., or Other Cr. column. At periodic intervals, such as weekly or monthly, the total amount in each column is posted to the appropriate general ledger accounts. For example, at the end of September, $995.00 would be debited to the Cash account in the general ledger. Likewise, $225.00 would be credited to the Accounts Receivable account in the general ledger. (A checkmark indicates that an amount has been posted.)

3.101 *Cash Disbursements Journal* A cash disbursements journal contains a sequential listing of all cash disbursements made. If all disbursements are made by check, a desirable procedure for control purposes, the cash disbursements journal will list each check written (credits to the Cash account) and the appropriate account debited. Exhibit 3.13 presents a typical cash disbursements journal. Each disbursement is entered in the Cash Cr. column. An entry is also made in either the Accounts Payable Dr., Selling and Administrative Expense Dr., or Other Dr. column. At periodic intervals, the total amount in the Cash Cr. column ($506.00) is posted to the credit side of the general ledger account for Cash. Similar entries are made on the debit sides of the other general ledger accounts.

## Ledgers

3.102 A group of accounts arranged in orderly fashion is known as a *ledger*. The account is the unit of classification within the ledger for accumulating information. There are few essential requirements for the form of a ledger account. Space should be provided for the following data: account title; date of transaction; debit and credit amounts; and a reference to trace the posting to its source in a journal. Space for other explanatory data may sometimes be useful. The standard ledger form presented in Exhibit 3.14 provides space for an explanation of each entry. A separate column is sometimes added to show the balance of the account.

Note that the debit to the Cash account in 3.103 the ledger is equal to the total cash receipts for September taken from the Cash Receipts Journal in Exhibit 3.12. Likewise, the credit to the Cash account is equal to the total cash disbursements for September listed in the Cash Disbursements Journal. The reference (Ref.) is to the appropriate page in these two specialized journals.

All firms maintain a general ledger. There 3.104 is usually one ledger sheet for each balance sheet and income statement account. Some firms also maintain subsidiary ledgers. Subsidiary ledgers contain a listing of individual items that comprise the total in a general ledger account. A subsidiary accounts receivable ledger would contain a listing of the individual customers' accounts and amounts due. The sum of the amounts in the subsidiary ledger should equal the total in the general ledger account. The amounts shown in the two ledgers are reconciled periodically, and any differences are investigated and cor-

*Exhibit 3.16*
**Wilson's Shoe Store, Inc.**
**Work Sheet**
**Year Ended December 31, 1981**

| Accounts | Unadjusted Trial Balance | | Adjusting Entries | | Adjusted Trial Balance | | Income Statement | | Balance Sheet | |
|---|---|---|---|---|---|---|---|---|---|---|
| | Debit | Credit | Debit | Credit | Debit | Credit | Debit | Credit | Debit | Credit |
| Cash (A) | $ 382,200 | | | | $ 382,200 | | | | $ 382,200 | |
| Accounts Receivable (A) | 280,000 | | | $ 15,000 (17) | 265,000 | | | | 265,000 | |
| Allowance for Uncollectible Accounts (XA) | | $ 14,000 | $ 15,000 (17) | 16,000 (16) | | $ 15,000 | | | | $ 15,000 |
| Notes Receivable (A) | 10,000 | | | | 10,000 | | | | 10,000 | |
| Interest Receivable (A) | | | 75 (12) | | 75 | | | | 75 | |
| Merchandise Inventory (A) | 280,000 | | | | 280,000 | | | | 280,000 | |
| Prepaid Insurance (A) | 3,000 | | | 1,000 (14) | 2,000 | | | | 2,000 | |
| Land (A) | 200,000 | | | | 200,000 | | | | 200,000 | |
| Building and Equipment (A) | 1,050,000 | | | | 1,050,000 | | | | 1,050,000 | |
| Accumulated Depreciation (XA) | | 170,000 | | 60,000 (15) | | 230,000 | | | | 230,000 |
| Accounts Payable (L) | | 440,000 | | | | 440,000 | | | | 440,000 |
| Salaries Payable (L) | | | | 12,000 (13) | | 12,000 | | | | 12,000 |
| Dividends Payable (L) | | 30,000 | | | | 30,000 | | | | 30,000 |
| Rental Fees Received in Advance (L) | | 1,200 | 100 (18) | | | 1,100 | | | | 1,100 |
| Bonds Payable (L) | | 200,000 | | | | 200,000 | | | | 200,000 |
| Common Stock (OE) | | 500,000 | | | | 500,000 | | | | 500,000 |
| Additional Paid-in Capital (OE) | | 400,000 | | | | 400,000 | | | | 400,000 |
| Retained Earnings (OE) | | 216,000 | | | | 216,000 | | | | 216,000 |
| Sales Revenue (OE) | | 1,250,000 | | | | 1,250,000 | | $1,250,000 | | |
| Interest Revenue (OE) | | | | 75 (12) | | 75 | | 75 | | |
| Rent Revenue (OE) | | | | 100 (18) | | 100 | | 100 | | |
| Cost of Goods Sold (OE) | 780,000 | | | | 780,000 | | $ 780,000 | | | |
| Salaries Expense (OE) | 220,000 | | 12,000 (13) | | 232,000 | | 232,000 | | | |
| Interest Expense (OE) | 16,000 | | | | 16,000 | | 16,000 | | | |
| Insurance Expense (OE) | | | 1,000 (14) | | 1,000 | | 1,000 | | | |
| Depreciation Expense (OE) | | | 60,000 (15) | | 60,000 | | 60,000 | | | |
| Sales Contra, Estimated Uncollectibles (OE) | | | 16,000 (16) | | 16,000 | | 16,000 | | | |
| Subtotals | $3,221,200 | $3,221,200 | $104,175 | $104,175 | $3,294,275 | $3,294,275 | $1,105,000 | $1,250,175 | $2,189,275 | 145,175 |
| Net Income for the Year | | | | | | | 145,175 | | | 145,175 |
| Totals | | | | | | | $1,250,175 | $1,250,175 | $2,189,275 | $2,189,275 |

*Exhibit 3.15*
### Examples of Controlling Accounts

| General Ledger Controlling Account | Type of Subsidiary Record |
|---|---|
| Accounts Receivable | Individual customers' ledger accounts, or a file of uncollected sales invoices. |
| Accounts Payable | Individual ledger accounts, or a file of unpaid purchase invoices. |
| Capital Stock | A record of the stock certificates and number of shares held by each shareholder. |
| Notes Receivable | A file of uncollected notes receivable, or a "register" or book in which the notes are listed. |
| Raw Material on Hand | Separate record card for each item of material used in manufacturing. |
| Equipment | Separate record card for each item of equipment. This is often known as a plant ledger. |
| Land | Separate record cards showing description and cost of each parcel of land owned. |

rected. When such a system of internal checks between the general ledger and subsidiary ledgers is used, the general ledger accounts are referred to as "controlling accounts." Exhibit 3.15 lists some common controlling accounts. Note that the subsidiary record is not always a group of ledger accounts in the standard ledger form. It may be a group of specially designed forms.

# Appendix 3.2: Preparation of a Work Sheet

3.105  To facilitate the preparation of the income statement and balance sheet at the end of an accounting period, a work sheet is often used. Exhibit 3.16 presents an example of a work sheet. This work sheet contains pairs of debit and credit columns for:

1. Unadjusted trial balance.
2. Adjusting entries.
3. Adjusted trial balance.
4. Income statement.
5. Balance sheet.

All of the required procedures at the end of an accounting period can be conveniently summarized in the work sheet, facilitating the preparation of the financial statements. A work sheet does not eliminate any of the usual end-of-period procedures. Adjusting and closing entries must still be made, entered in the general journal, and posted to the appropriate general ledger accounts. The work sheet is simply a mechanism for aggregating all of the data from these end-of-period procedures and organizing it in a useful form for preparing the financial statements.

## Illustration of Work Sheet Preparation

3.106  The data presented in the chapter for Wilson's Shoe Store, Inc., is used to illustrate the preparation of a work sheet.

3.107  **Unadjusted Trial Balance** The first two columns contain the account balances taken from the general ledger at the end of the period before adjusting entries have been made. The debit and credit columns are summed to ensure that the trial balance is in balance.

3.108  **Adjusting Entries** The adjusting entries made at the end of the accounting period are entered in the next two columns. Note that the debits and credits for each entry are cross-referenced in the adjusting entries columns. The numbers used for cross-referencing in this case refer to the numbered journal entries in the chapter. Letters are often used as cross-references instead of numbers to avoid the possibility of confusing the amount of the adjusting entry with its cross-reference.

3.109 **Adjusted Trial Balance** The amounts in the adjusted trial balance columns are the sum or net amounts for each account in the first four columns. Adjusted trial balance columns are not essential in a work sheet, but they do facilitate the completion of the income statement and balance sheet columns.

3.110 **Income Statement** The amount in each income statement account in the adjusted trial balance is extended to the appropriate debit or credit column in the income statement section of the work sheet. A subtotal of the total debits (expenses and revenue contras) and the total credits (revenues) is then calculated. The difference between these two subtotals is net income or net loss for the period. For Wilson's Shoe Store, revenues exceeds expenses and revenue contra by $145,175. This amount is entered in the debit column in the income statement section to equate the two income statement columns. The amount is also entered in the credit column in the balance sheet section. The placement of the net income amount in these two columns is analogous to the entry to close revenue and expense accounts to retained earnings (see entries 19 and 19c in paragraphs 3.85 and 3.86). The credit in the balance sheet column is to "net income for the year" instead of retained earnings. Retained earnings at the end of the year must be calculated from the work sheet ($361,175 = $216,000 + $145,175).

3.111 **Balance Sheet** The final step is to extend the amounts for each balance sheet account from the adjusted trial balance to the appropriate debit and credit columns in the balance sheet section of the work sheet. An equality between the debit and credit columns serves as a check on the work sheet preparation procedures.

## Alternative Work Sheet Formats

3.112 The particular columns used in a work sheet depend on a firm's accounting system and the financial statements and schedules to be prepared. Two alternative work sheet formats are discussed briefly below.

3.113 **Combined Income and Retained Earnings Columns** Some firms prepare a combined statement of income and retained earnings. The seventh and eighth columns in the work sheet in Exhibit 3.16 can be altered to include information for both of these statements. Exhibit 3.17 contains a partial work sheet to illustrate the procedure. Recall from the text that dividends declared and paid during 1981 were $30,000. For purposes of this illustration, it is assumed that a Dividends Declared account was debited when the dividend was declared instead of Retained Earnings. Thus, the balance in the Retained Earnings account on the trial balance at the end of 1981 is its balance as of January 1, 1981.

3.114 The revenues, expenses, and revenue contra accounts are extended from the adjusted trial balance columns to the income and retained earnings statement columns in Exhibit 3.17 precisely the same as was done in Exhibit 3.16. The difference between the subtotals of the two columns of $145,175 is net income for the year. This amount is again entered in the debit column to equate the two columns. Instead of being entered as a credit in the balance sheet columns, as was done in Exhibit 3.16, the amount is entered as a credit in the income and retained earnings columns. The retained earnings amount on the adjusted trial balance, assuming dividend declarations are debited to a Dividends Declared account, is the balance on January 1, 1981, of $246,000. This amount is entered in the credit column. The dividends declared are entered in the debit column. A second subtotal is now taken. The difference between the column totals of $361,175 is the balance in the retained earnings at the end of the year. This amount is entered in the debit column of the income and retained earnings statement section to equate the two columns. It is also entered in the credit column in the balance sheet section. The principal difference between the work sheets in Exhibits 3.16 and 3.17 is that the ending balance in Retained Earnings is calculated ex-

*Exhibit 3.17*
**Wilson's Shoe Store, Inc.**
**Partial Work Sheet**
**Year Ended December 31, 1981**

| Account | Income and Retained Earnings | | Balance Sheet | |
|---|---|---|---|---|
| | Debit | Credit | Debit | Credit |
| Sales Revenue (OE) .............................. | | $1,250,000 | | |
| Interest Revenue (OE) ............................ | | 75 | | |
| Rent Revenue (OE) ............................... | | 100 | | |
| Cost of Goods Sold (OE) ......................... | $ 780,000 | | | |
| Salaries Expense (OE) ........................... | 232,000 | | | |
| Interest Expense (OE) ........................... | 16,000 | | | |
| Insurance Expense (OE) .......................... | 1,000 | | | |
| Depreciation Expense (OE) ....................... | 60,000 | | | |
| Sales Contra, Estimated Uncollectibles (OE) ........... | 16,000 | | | |
| Subtotal ...................................... | $1,105,000 | $1,250,175 | | |
| Net Income for the Year ........................ | 145,175 | | | |
| Total ........................................ | $1,250,175 | $1,250,175 | | |
| Retained Earnings (Beginning of Year) ............... | | 246,000 | | |
| Net Income for the Year ......................... | | 145,175 | | |
| Dividends Declared ............................. | 30,000 | | | |
| Subtotal ...................................... | $1,280,175 | $1,641,350 | | |
| Retained Earnings (End of Year) .................... | 361,175 | | | $361,175 |
| Total ........................................ | $1,641,350 | $1,641,350 | | |

plicitly in Exhibit 3.17 but must be calculated separately in Exhibit 3.16.

3.115 **Merchandise Accounts in the Work Sheet** The illustration in the text implicitly assumed that Wilson's Shoe Store used a perpetual inventory system. Purchases of inventory items were debited to the Merchandise Inventory account. At the time of sale, the cost of the merchandise sold was credited to the Merchandise Inventory account and debited to Cost of Goods Sold. Chapter 9 points out that many firms use a periodic inventory system. In a periodic system, purchases of merchandise inventory are usually debited to a Purchases account. Freight-in, returns, discounts, and allowances on items purchased are debited or credited as appropriate to separate accounts. Under a periodic system, the balance in the Merchandise Inventory account at any time *during* an accounting period is its balance as of the beginning of the period. No entry is made in the Merchandise Inventory account as items are either purchased

or sold. At periodic intervals, usually quarterly or annually, inventory is counted to determine the amount of inventory still on hand. Any difference between the beginning inventory plus net purchases and the amount still on hand (ending inventory) is assumed to have been sold.

To illustrate the preparation of a work 3.116 sheet when a periodic inventory system is in use, assume that the following data are obtained for Wilson's Shoe Store for 1981:

| | | |
|---|---|---|
| Beginning Inventory, January 1, 1981 ...... | | $350,000 |
| Plus: Purchases ...... | $730,000 | |
| Freight-in ....... | 10,000 | |
| Less: Returns ........ | (5,000) | |
| Discounts ...... | (20,000) | |
| Allowances ..... | (5,000) | |
| Net Purchases ......... | | $710,000 |
| Goods Available for Sale ............. | | $1,060,000 |
| Less Ending Inventory, December 31, 1981 ... | | (280,000) |
| Cost of Goods Sold ..... | | $780,000 |

*Exhibit 3.18*
**Wilson's Shoe Store, Inc.**
**Partial Work Sheet**
**Year Ended December 31, 1981**

| Account | Adjusted Trial Balance | | Income Statement | | Balance Sheet | |
|---|---|---|---|---|---|---|
| | **Debit** | **Credit** | **Debit** | **Credit** | **Debit** | **Credit** |
| Merchandise Inventory ................... | $350,000 | | $350,000 | $280,000 | $280,000 | |
| Purchases .......................... | 730,000 | | 730,000 | | | |
| Freight-in ........................... | 10,000 | | 10,000 | | | |
| Returns ............................ | | $ 5,000 | | 5,000 | | |
| Discounts .......................... | | 20,000 | | 20,000 | | |
| Allowances ......................... | | 5,000 | | 5,000 | | |

3.117  Exhibit 3.18 presents a partial work sheet for Wilson's Shoe Store assuming that a periodic inventory system is used. The amount in the Merchandise Inventory account in the adjusted trial balance at the beginning of the year is entered in the debit column in the income statement section of the work sheet. The amounts in the Purchases, Freight-in, Returns, Discounts, and Allowances accounts are likewise entered in their appropriate debit or credit columns. The amount in the ending inventory of $280,000, as determined by physical count, is entered in the credit column in the income statement section and the debit column in the balance sheet section. The total of the amounts in the debit column in the income statement section of $1,090,000 (= $350,000 + $730,000 + $10,000) exceeds the total of the amounts in the credit column of $310,000 (= $280,000 + $5,000 + $20,000 + $5,000) by $780,000. This is the Cost of Goods Sold for the period. The work sheet will not show a separate line for Cost of Goods Sold. Its amount is calculated implicitly when the income statement columns are summed.

## Questions

**3.1** Review the meaning of the following concepts or terms discussed in this chapter.
- a. Accounting process.
- b. Accounting event.
- c. Historical economic sacrifice or benefit.
- d. Historical exchange price.
- e. Current economic sacrifice or benefit.
- f. Current exchange price.
- g. Dual effects of accounting events.
- h. Debit and credit recording conventions.
- i. Recording process.
- j. Journalizing.
- k. General journal.
- l. Specialized journal.
- m. Journal entry.
- n. Posting.
- o. General ledger.
- p. Subsidiary ledger.
- q. Unadjusted trial balance.
- r. Adjusting entries.
- s. Adjusted preclosing trial balance.
- t. Closing entries.
- u. Postclosing trial balance.
- v. Reversing entries.

**3.2** "The terms 'accounting event' and 'external exchange' are synonymous." Do you agree? Why or why not?

**3.3**  In what sense might the transfer of raw materials from the raw materials storeroom to the production floor be considered an exchange? In what sense might using up the service potential of a depreciable asset be considered an exchange?

**3.4**  Using the criteria listed in the text, discuss whether each of the following should be considered an accounting event.
  **a.** The president of a company suffers a heart attack.
  **b.** A company issues options, or rights, to employees to purchase shares of the company's stock at any time in the next 2 years for 80 percent of its market value at the time of the purchase.
  **c.** A company receives an order from a customer for $1,000 of merchandise to be delivered next month.
  **d.** Refer to part **c.** Assume that a $400 partial payment is received with the order.
  **e.** A company is sued by a customer who was allegedly injured last year from using one of the company's products.

**3.5**  Using the criteria listed in the text, discuss whether each of the following should be considered an accounting event.
  **a.** A company signs an agreement with a local bank to repay a personal loan made to the company's president in the event that the president is unable to repay the loan when it is due.
  **b.** A company maintains checking accounts in several foreign banks for use in paying foreign suppliers. The exchange rate between the U.S. dollar and the foreign currency in which the checking accounts are denominated has just changed materially.
  **c.** A trade association, as a result of a consumer testing program, has selected the company's television sets as having the best picture in the industry.
  **d.** The employees of a company have gone on strike. The strike is expected to be lengthy.
  **e.** The Internal Revenue Service has notified the company that, based on its examination, an additional $250,000 of taxes are due on prior years' incomes.

**3.6**  **a.** Your performance in this course will be graded by your professor. What attributes of your performance might be measured by the professor in assigning a final grade?
  **b.** The performance of a business firm is likewise evaluated periodically. What attributes of a firm's performance could be conceivably measured?
  **c.** Under generally accepted accounting principles, what attributes of a firm's performance are currently measured?

**3.7**  Accounting events have a dual impact on the financial position of a firm: an outflow—what is given up—and an inflow—what is received. Identify the outflow and inflow in each of the following accounting events.
  **a.** A firm acquires a tract of land and signs a note promising to pay for the land over the next 10 years.
  **b.** A firm issues a check for $120 for telephone service for last month.
  **c.** The New Orleans plant of a company is destroyed by a hurricane. The plant is fully insured.
  **d.** Same as part **c,** but the plant is not insured.
  **e.** A dividend is declared by a company's board of directors. The dividend is payable next year.

**3.8**  "Revenue and expense accounts are useful accounting devices, but they could be dispensed with." Explain.

**3.9**   **a.** Before the books have been closed, what types of accounts will normally have debit balances? Credit balances?

   **b.** After the books have been closed, what types of accounts will normally have debit balances? Credit balances?

**3.10**   "Owners' equity accounts are increased with credit entries and decreased with debit entries." Can you think of exceptions to this statement?

**3.11**   "Adjusting entries always involve an entry to at least one balance sheet account and at least one income statement account." Do you agree?

**3.12**   Distinguish among adjusting entries, closing entries, and reversing entries.

**3.13**   Distinguish among unadjusted trial balance, adjusted preclosing trial balance, and postclosing trial balance.

**3.14**   "The total of the debit column in a postclosing trial balance at the end of the period will equal total assets on the end-of-the-period balance sheet." Do you agree? Why or why not?

**3.15**   In the business world many transactions are routine and repetitive. Because accounting records business transactions, many accounting entries are also routine and repetitive. Because of the double-entry system and its often desirable redundancy, knowing one-half of an entry permits a reasoned guess about the other half. The items below give the account name for one-half of an entry. Indicate your best guess as to the name of the account of the *routine* other half of the entry. Also indicate whether the other account is increased or decreased by the transaction.

   **a.** Debit: Cost of Goods Sold.
   **b.** Debit: Accounts Receivable.
   **c.** Credit: Accounts Receivable.
   **d.** Debit: Accounts Payable.
   **e.** Credit: Accounts Payable.

   **f.** Credit: Accumulated Depreciation.
   **g.** Credit: Prepaid Insurance.
   **h.** Debit: Property Taxes Payable.
   **i.** Debit: Merchandise Inventory.

**3.16**   The particular time when various events and transactions are recorded in the accounts is often a matter of clerical efficiency. For each of the items below, describe the likely entry during each month and the adjusting entry at the end of each month, assuming that financial statements are prepared monthly.

   **a.** The rental on buildings and equipment of $600 is paid in advance at the beginning of each month.
   **b.** Property taxes for the calendar year of $3,600 are paid on July 1.
   **c.** Selling and office supplies, $375, are purchased once each month but used each day in small amounts.
   **d.** A firm rents out excess office space at the rate of $500 a month, payable in advance for each calendar quarter of the year.

**3.17**   Give an example of each of the following types of adjusting entries other than the example used for Wilson's Shoe Store in the text.

   **a.** Recognition of accrued revenues and receivables.
   **b.** Recognition of accrued expenses and payables.
   **c.** Allocation of prepaid operating costs.
   **d.** Valuation of accounts receivable.
   **e.** Valuation of liabilities.

**3.18**   a. What advantage is there to using multicolumn journals instead of two-column journals?
   b. What advantage is there to using specialized journals instead of multicolumn journals?
   c. What advantage is there to using subsidiary ledgers in conjunction with a general ledger?

**3.19**   Why should formal financial statements be prepared when a work sheet containing all of the income statement and balance sheet data has been completed?

**3.20**   Indicate whether each of the following statements is true or false.
   F  a. Posting is the process of recording entries in a journal.
   F  b. A general journal is not needed when specialized journals are used.
   F  c. The balances in individual subsidiary ledger accounts are not included in the general ledger trial balance.
   F  d. A controlling account is a group of subsidiary ledger accounts that are kept in detail outside of the general ledger.
   F  e. A specialized journal must have an equal number of debit and credit columns.
   T  f. A sales journal would not normally have an Other Accounts Cr. column.
   T  g. A general journal must have at least one column for debits and at least another column for credits.
   F  h. The use of subsidiary ledgers facilitates the taking of a trial balance.
   F  i. When a controlling account is credited, one of the subsidiary ledger accounts is debited.
   T  j. There is usually more detail about an individual transaction in the general journal than in the general ledger.

## Problems and Exercises

**3.21**   The Merchandise Supply Company received a $3,000, 3-month, 12-percent promissory note, dated December 1, 1981, from Virdon Stores to apply on its account.
   a. Give the journal entry for the receipt of the note on December 1, 1981.
   b. Give any required adjusting and closing entries on December 31, 1981, assuming that the accounting period is the calendar year.
   c. Give the journal entry that would be made, assuming that the note was paid in full at maturity.

**3.22**   The Missouri Realty Company rents office space to Speciality Sales Company at the rate of $500 per month. Collection has been made for rental through January 31, 1981.
   The following transactions occurred on the dates indicated:

(1) February 2, 1981: Collection, $500.
(2) April 1, 1981: Collection, $1,000.
(3) June 1, 1981: Collection, $1,500.

Present dated journal entries for the above transactions and for adjustments and closing from February 2 to June 30, inclusive, as they relate to Missouri Realty Company, assuming that the company closes its books monthly.

**3.23**   For the selected transactions of Covington Company listed below, present journal entries, including adjusting and closing entries, from January 15, 1981, through July 1, 1981. Assume that only the notes indicated were outstanding during the period. The accounting period is 1 month.

(1) The company issued a $1,000, 2-month, 12-percent promissory note on January 15, 1981, in lieu of payment on an account due that date to White Wholesale Company.

(2) The note and interest were paid at maturity.

(3) The company issued a $2,000, 3-month, 12-percent promissory note to the White Wholesale Company on the date of purchase of merchandise, April 1, 1981.

(4) The note and interest are paid at maturity.

**3.24** On February 1, 1981, the Landon Manufacturing Company paid $2,400 rental on a machine for the 6-month period February 1, 1981, to July 31, 1981. No additional rentals were paid during this period. The rented machine was returned to its owner on July 31. Present dated journal entries, including adjusting and closing entries, assuming that:

**a.** The accounting period is 1 month.

**b.** The accounting period is the calendar quarter (March 31, and so on).

**3.25** On January 1, 1981, the Office Supplies account of the Drexel Company had a balance of $1,200. During the next 3 months, supplies were acquired, on account, in the amount of $6,000. On March 31, 1981, a physical inventory was taken and supplies costing $1,500 were found to be on hand. The accounting period is the calendar quarter ending March 31.

Prepare journal entries to record the above acquisition as well as adjusting and closing entries, assuming that:

**a.** An asset account is debited at the time of acquisition of supplies.

**b.** An expense account is debited at the time of acquisition of supplies.

**3.26** The trial balance of the Wagner Company at the end of 1981, its first year of operations, includes $18,000 of outstanding customers' accounts. An analysis reveals that 90 percent of the total credit sales of the year has been collected and that no accounts have been charged off as uncollectible.

The auditor estimated that 1 percent of the total credit sales will become uncollectible.

On December 31, 1981, it was concluded that the account of H. J. Williams, who had owed a balance of $200 for 6 months, was uncollectible and should be written off at that time.

Present dated journal entries to record the following:

**a.** Adjustment for estimated uncollectible accounts on December 31, 1981.

**b.** Write-off of the H. J. Williams account on December 31, 1981.

**c.** Any required closing entry on December 31, 1981, the end of Wagner Company's accounting period.

**3.27** The subsidiary plant assets ledger of A. C. Adams Company reveals that the following assets were in use throughout the quarter ending March 31, 1981.

| Asset | Cost | Estimated Life | Estimated Salvage Value |
|---|---|---|---|
| Building | $166,000 | 40 years | $6,000 |
| Office Fixtures | 1,200 | 10 years | 160 |
| Calculators | 1,760 | 8 years | 160 |
| Typewriters | 600 | 6 years | 120 |
| Delivery Truck | 8,000 | 4 years | 1,120 |

**a.** Present adjusting journal entries on March 31, 1981, assuming that the straight-line depreciation method is used and that no depreciation has been recorded since December 31, 1980. The A. C. Adams Company uses an Accumulated Depreciation account.

**b.** Give any required closing entries on March 31, 1981, assuming that this is the end of an accounting period.

**3.28** In recording the adjusting entries of the Hammond Sales Company, Inc., at the end of 1981, the following adjustments were omitted:

(1) Depreciation on the delivery truck of $1,500.
(2) Insurance expired on the delivery truck of $300.
(3) Interest accrued on notes payable of $75.
(4) Interest accrued on notes receivable of $165.

Indicate the effect (exclusive of income tax implications) of these omissions on the following items in the financial statements prepared on December 31, 1981.

|  |  |
|---|---|
| **a.** Current assets. | **d.** Selling expenses. |
| **b.** Noncurrent assets. | **e.** Net income. |
| **c.** Current liabilities. | **f.** Retained earnings. |

 **3.29** Present journal entries for each of the following separate sets of data, ignoring closing entries.

**a.** On January 15, 1981, a $2,000, 2-month, 12-percent note was received by the company. Present adjusting entries at the end of each month and the entry for collection at maturity.

**b.** The company uses one Merchandise Inventory account to record the beginning inventory and purchases during the period. The balance in this account on December 31, 1981, was $480,000. The inventory of merchandise on hand at that time was $70,000. Present the adjusting entry.

**c.** The company rents out part of its building for office space at the rate of $500 a month, payable in advance for each calendar quarter of the year. The first quarter's rental was received on February 1, 1981. Present adjusting and collection entries for the first quarter. Assume that the books are closed monthly.

**d.** The company leases branch office space at $1,000 a month. Payment is made by the company on the first of each 6-month period. Payment of $6,000 was made July 1, 1981. Present payment and adjusting entries through August 31, 1981. Assume that the books are closed monthly.

**e.** The balance of the Prepaid Insurance account on October 1, 1981, was $200. On December 1, 1981, the company renewed its only insurance policy for another 3 years beginning on that date by payment of $3,960. Present journal entries for renewal and adjusting entries through December 31, 1981. Assume that the books are closed quarterly.

**f.** The Office Supplies on Hand account had a balance of $300 on December 1, 1981. Purchases of supplies in the amount of $380 were recorded in the Office Supplies Expense account during the month. The inventory of office supplies on December 31, 1981, was $290. Present any necessary adjusting entry at December 31, 1981.

**g.** An office building was constructed at a cost of $250,000. It was estimated that it would have a useful life of 50 years from the date of occupancy, October 31, 1981, and a residual value of $10,000. Present the adjusting entry for the depreciation of the building in 1981. Assume that the books are closed annually at December 31.

**h.** Experience indicates that 1 percent of the accounts arising from sales on account will not be collected. Sales on account during 1981 were $180,000. A list of uncollectible accounts totaling $400 as of December 31, 1981, was compiled. Present journal entries for the annual provision for uncollectible accounts and the write-off of specific customers' accounts as of December 31, 1981. The books are closed annually.

**3.30** Give the journal entry to record each of the transactions below as well as any necessary adjusting entries on December 31, 1981, assuming that the accounting period is the calendar year and the books are closed on December 31.

a. Morrissey's Department Store had sales of $400,000 during 1981: $250,000 were for cash, and $150,000 were on account. Accounts totaling $120,000 were collected. Past experience indicates that 2 percent of sales on account will probably become uncollectible. Specific accounts totaling $2,500 were determined to be uncollectible during the year.

b. Harrison's Supply Company received a 90-day note from a customer on December 1, 1981. The note in the face amount of $2,000 replaced an open account receivable of the same amount. The note is due with interest at 8 percent per year on March 1, 1982.

c. Thompson's Wholesale Company purchased a 3-year insurance policy on September 1, 1981, paying the 3-year premium of $10,800 in advance.

d. William's Products Company acquired a truck on July 1, 1981, for $10,000 cash. The truck is expected to have a $2,000 salvage value and a 4-year life.

e. Greer Electronics Company acquired an automobile on September 1, 1980, for $6,000 cash. The automobile is expected to have $1,200 salvage value and a 4-year life.

f. Devine Company rented out excess office space for the 3-month period beginning December 15, 1981. The first month's rent of $7,200 was received on this date.

g. Prentice Products Corporation began business on November 1, 1981. It acquired office supplies costing $6,000 on account. Of this amount, $5,000 was paid by year-end. A physical inventory indicates office supplies costing $2,500 were on hand on December 31, 1981.

**3.31** The following trial balance is taken from the books of the Burton Shoe Stores, Inc., at April 30, 1981. The books were closed on March 31, 1981.

| | | |
|---|---:|---:|
| Accounts Payable | | $ 9,000 |
| Accounts Receivable | $ 30,000 | |
| Accumulated Depreciation | | 12,000 |
| Allowance for Uncollectible Accounts | | 3,000 |
| Capital Stock | | 90,000 |
| Cash | 5,600 | |
| Cost of Goods Sold | 74,500 | |
| Customers' Deposits | | 200 |
| Furniture and Fixtures | 20,000 | |
| Income Tax Expense | — | |
| Income Tax Payable | | 1,800 |
| Interest Expense on Notes | — | |
| Interest Payable | | 600 |
| Interest Receivable | 50 | |
| Interest Revenue | | 10 |
| Merchandise Inventory | 88,500 | |
| Notes Payable | | 20,000 |
| Notes Receivable | 5,000 | |
| Payroll Taxes Payable | | 162 |
| Prepaid Insurance | 3,550 | |
| Prepaid Rent | 200 | |
| Rent Payable | | — |
| Retained Earnings | | 10,803 |
| Sales | | 88,000 |
| Sales Contra, Estimated Uncollectibles | — | |
| Selling and Administrative Expenses | 9,000 | |
| Withheld Income Taxes Payable | | 825 |
| | $236,400 | $236,400 |

Additional data:

(1) The Customers' Deposits account is intended to represent deposits that have been received from customers on orders not yet delivered. A review of the outstanding balance

reveals that one such order in the amount of $75 has been delivered and charged to accounts receivable. Also, it has discovered that a deposit of $35 on April 10 was recorded as a sale, although the goods have not been delivered as yet.

(2) The $5,000 note receivable is dated February 1, 1981, and is due August 1, 1981. It bears interest at 6 percent per annum. A 2-month, 6-percent note for $4,000 was collected with interest on April 15. The collection was recorded properly.

(3) The insurance premiums are $2,700 per annum. No entries have been made in the Prepaid Insurance account during April.

(4) At April 1, 1981, rent had been prepaid to April 15, 1981. No rent payment was made during the month, although rental services were received throughout the month.

(5) Depreciation of 12 percent of cost per annum is to be charged on the furniture and fixtures.

(6) The $20,000 of notes payable represents a single note which bears interest at 9 percent per annum. The note is dated December 1, 1980, and is due June 1, 1982. Interest is to be paid on June 1 and December 1 of each year.

(7) It is estimated that 1½ percent of the charge sales of the month will prove to be uncollectible. Total charge sales, after giving effect to the correction of (1), were $70,400.

(8) The employer's share of payroll taxes on wages earned by employees during the month is $374. No credit entries were made to the Payroll Taxes Payable account during the month.

(9) Assume that taxable income is the same as net income reported on the financial statements. Use a tax rate of 40 percent.

Present adjusting journal entries as of April 30, 1981. Use only accounts listed in trial balance.

3.32    The trial balance of The North Sales Company as of March 31, 1981, appears below. The accounting period covers 3 months of operations.

| | | |
|---|---:|---:|
| Accounts Payable | | $ 11,528 |
| Accounts Receivable | $ 30,000 | |
| Accumulated Depreciation | | 10,000 |
| Advances by Customers | — | — |
| Allowance for Uncollectible Accounts | | 400 |
| Capital Stock | | 50,000 |
| Cash | 8,725 | |
| Cost of Goods Sold | — | — |
| Dividends Declared | 2,000 | |
| Furniture and Fixtures | 20,000 | |
| Income Tax Expense | — | — |
| Income Tax Payable | — | — |
| Interest Expense | 40 | |
| Interest Receivable | — | — |
| Interest Revenue | | 50 |
| Interest Payable | | 30 |
| Merchandise Inventory | 35,000 | |
| Notes Payable | | 5,400 |
| Notes Receivable | 4,000 | |
| Payroll Taxes Payable | | — |
| Prepaid Insurance | 480 | |
| Purchases | 60,000 | |
| Retained Earnings | | 15,160 |
| Sales | | 82,672 |
| Sales Contra, Estimated Uncollectibles | — | |
| Selling and Administrative Expense | 15,295 | |
| Store Supplies on Hand | 150 | |
| Withheld Income Tax Payable | | 450 |
| | $175,690 | $175,690 |

Additional data:

(1) A statement is received from the bank after the trial balance was taken. A comparison of the statement and accompanying documents with the accounting records indicates that:

The bank has deducted $3 for collection and exchange fees that have not been entered on the books.

A check in the amount of $89 in payment of an advertising invoice of that amount had been recorded in the company records as $98.

(2) The furniture and fixtures are depreciated at the rate of 3 percent per quarter.

(3) The total of the estimated uncollectibles to arise from sales of the quarter is 1½ percent of the total sales.

(4) The inventory of merchandise on March 31 is $34,600.

(5) The insurance premiums are $960 a year payable in advance. No entries have been made in the Prepaid Insurance account during the quarter.

(6) The employer's share of payroll taxes on employees' wages earned during the quarter is $500, of which $332 has been recognized previously at times of payment.

(7) The note receivable is a 3-month, 12-percent note dated January 15, 1981.

(8) The notes payable consist of two notes as follows:

A $3,000, 6-month, 12-percent note dated December 1, 1980.

A $2,400, 3-month, 10-percent note dated January 15, 1981.

(9) Inventory of store supplies on hand at March 31, 1981, is $190.

(10)A review of the Accounts Receivable Subsidiary Ledger reveals that one account with a $120 balance is deemed to be uncollectible. One account has a credit balance of $280.

(11)Federal income tax for the quarter is estimated to be $1,440.

Prepare adjusting journal entries as of March 31, 1981. Use only the accounts listed in the trial balance.

**3.33** The following unadjusted trial balance is taken from the books of the Kathleen Clothing Company at July 31, 1981. The company closes its books monthly.

Additional Data:

(1) Depreciation on equipment is to be calculated at 20 percent of cost per year (assume zero salvage value).

(2) Depreciation on furniture and fixtures is to be calculated at 15 percent of cost per year (assume zero salvage value).

(3) The leasehold represents long-term rent paid in advance by Kathleen. The monthly rental charge is $400.

(4) One invoice of $340 for the purchase of merchandise from the Peoria Company on account was recorded during the month as $430. The account has not yet been paid.

(5) Commissions unpaid at July 31, 1981, are $380. All salaries have been paid. The balance in the Salaries and Commissions Payable account represents the amount of commissions unpaid at July 1.

(6) Merchandise with a sales price of $250 was recently delivered to a customer, and charged to Accounts Receivable, although the customer had paid $250 in advance.

(7) The estimated uncollectible account rate is 1 percent of the charge sales of the month. Charge sales were 80 percent of the sales of the month.

(8) An analysis of outstanding customers' accounts indicates that two accounts totaling $240 should be written off as uncollectible.

(9) The balance in the Prepaid Insurance account relates to a 3-year policy that went into effect on January 1, 1981.

| | | |
|---|---:|---:|
| Accounts Payable | | $ 12,695 |
| Accounts Receivable | $ 18,000 | |
| Accumulated Depreciation | | 8,240 |
| Advances by Customers | | 540 |
| Allowance for Uncollectible Accounts | | 1,200 |
| Capital Stock | | 40,000 |
| Cash | 9,000 | |
| Equipment | 2,640 | |
| Depreciation Expense | — | — |
| Dividends Payable | — | — |
| Furniture and Fixtures | 12,000 | |
| Income Tax Expense | — | — |
| Income Tax Payable | | 3,500 |
| Insurance Expense | — | |
| Leasehold | 10,800 | |
| Merchandise Cost of Goods Sold | — | — |
| Merchandise Inventory | 49,500 | |
| Miscellaneous Expenses | 188 | |
| Prepaid Insurance | 450 | |
| Rent Expense | — | — |
| Retained Earnings | | 13,068 |
| Salaries and Commissions Expense | 2,020 | |
| Salaries and Commissions Payable | | 500 |
| Sales | | 25,000 |
| Sales Contra, Estimated Uncollectibles | — | — |
| Supplies Inventory | 145 | |
| | $104,743 | $104,743 |

(10) A dividend of $2,000 was declared on July 31, 1981.
(11) The inventory of merchandise on July 31, 1981, was $30,500.
(12) Income tax expense for the month is estimated to be $1,280.

Present adjusting journal entries at July 31, 1981. Use only the accounts listed in the trial balance.

3.34 The balance sheet accounts of Blake's Radio Shop at July 1, 1981, are as follows:

| | | |
|---|---:|---:|
| Cash | $1,720 | |
| Repair Parts Inventory | 600 | |
| Office Supplies Inventory | 80 | |
| Equipment | 2,000 | |
| Accumulated Depreciation | | $ 200 |
| Accounts Payable | | 2,200 |
| Brenda Blake, Capital | | 2,000 |
| | $4,400 | $4,400 |

A summary of the transactions for July is as follows:
(1) Performed repair services, for which $800 in cash was received immediately.
(2) Performed additional repair work, $300, and sent bills to customers for this amount.
(3) Paid creditors, $500.
(4) Took out insurance on equipment on July 1, and issued a check to cover 1 year's premium of $84. Debit should be to Prepaid Insurance.

(5) Paid $50 for a series of advertisements that appeared in the local newspaper during July.

(6) Issued check for $120 for rent of shop space for July.

(7) Paid telephone bill for the month, $30.

(8) Collected $150 of the amount charged to customers in item (2).

(9) The insurance expired during July is calculated at $7.

(10) Cost of repair parts used during the month, $130.

(11) Cost of office supplies used during July, $30.

(12) Depreciation of equipment for the month is $24.

a. Open T-accounts and insert the July 1 balances. Record the transactions for the month in the T-accounts, opening additional T-accounts for individual revenue and expense accounts as needed.

b. Prepare an adjusted, preclosing trial balance at July 31, 1981.

c. Enter closing entries in the T-accounts using an Income Summary account.

d. Prepare an income statement for the month of July and a balance sheet as of July 31, 1981.

3.35  The trial balance of Safety Cleaners and Dyers at the end of February 1981 is shown below. The books have not been closed since December 31, 1980.

| | | |
|---|---:|---:|
| Cash | $ 3,560 | |
| Accounts Receivable | 15,200 | |
| Supplies Inventory | 4,800 | |
| Prepaid Insurance | 1,040 | |
| Equipment | 65,000 | |
| Accumulated Depreciation | | $ 10,600 |
| Accounts Payable | | 6,980 |
| P. O. Grey, Capital | | 60,000 |
| Sales | | 46,060 |
| Salaries and Wages Expense | 26,600 | |
| Cost of Outside Work | 2,040 | |
| Advertising Expense | 900 | |
| Rent Expense | 1,200 | |
| Power, Gas, and Water Expense | 880 | |
| Supplies Used | — | |
| Depreciation Expense | — | |
| Miscellaneous Expense | 2,420 | |
| | $123,640 | $123,640 |

A summary of the transactions for the month of March 1981 is as follows:

(1) Sales: For cash, $24,000: on account, $15,800.

(2) Collections on account, $20,000.

(3) Purchases of outside work (cleaning done by wholesale cleaners), $1,800, on account.

(4) Purchases of supplies, on account, $3,800.

(5) Payments on account, $5,000.

(6) March rent paid, $1,000.

(7) Supplies used (for the quarter), $6,340.

(8) Depreciation (for the quarter), $3,420.

(9) March salaries and wages of $21,120 are paid.

(10) Bills received but not recorded or paid by the end of the month: advertising, $400: power, gas, and water, $580.

(11) Insurance expired (for the quarter), $600.

a. Open T-accounts and enter the trial balance amounts.
b. Record the transactions for the month of March in the T-accounts, opening additional T-accounts as needed. Cross-number the entries.
c. Enter closing entries in the T-accounts using an Income Summary account.
d. Prepare an adjusted, preclosing trial balance at March 31, 1981, an income statement for the 3 months ending March 31, 1981, and a balance sheet as of March 31, 1981.

**3.36**   The trial balance of the Handy Harriet's Hardware Store on September 30, 1981, is as follows:

| | | |
|---|---:|---:|
| Cash | $ 86,500 | |
| Accounts Receivable | 54,500 | |
| Merchandise Inventory | 136,300 | |
| Prepaid Insurance | 800 | |
| Equipment | 420,000 | |
| Allowance for Uncollectible Accounts | | $   6,500 |
| Accumulated Depreciation | | 166,000 |
| Accounts Payable | | 66,300 |
| Note Payable | | 10,000 |
| Salaries Payable | | 2,500 |
| Capital Stock | | 300,000 |
| Retained Earnings | | 146,800 |
| Total | $698,100 | $698,100 |

Transactions during October and additional information are as follows:
(1) Sales, all on account, total $150,000.
(2) Merchandise inventory purchased on account from various suppliers is $88,400.
(3) Rent for the month of October of $22,000 is paid.
(4) Salaries paid to employees during October are $38,700.
(5) Accounts receivable of $63,800 are collected.
(6) Accounts payable of $73,200 are paid.
(7) Miscellaneous expenses of $8,200 are paid in cash.
(8) The premium on a 1-year insurance policy was paid on June 1, 1981.
(9) Equipment is depreciated over a 10-year life. Estimated salvage value of the equipment is considered to be negligible.
(10) Employee salaries earned during the last two days of October but not paid are $4,300.
(11) Based on past experience, the firm estimates that 1 percent of all sales on account will become uncollectible.
(12) Specific customers' accounts of $3,800 are determined to be uncollectible.
(13) The note payable is a 90-day, 12-percent note issued on September 30, 1981.
(14) Merchandise inventory on hand on October 31, 1981, totals $151,500.

a. Prepare general journal entries to reflect the transactions and other events during October. Indicate whether each entry records a transaction during the month (**T**) or is an adjusting entry at the end of the month (**A**).
b. Set up T-accounts and enter the opening balances in the accounts on September 30, 1981. Record the entries from part **a** in the T-accounts, creating additional accounts as required.
c. Prepare an adjusted, preclosing trial balance as of October 31, 1981.
d. Prepare an income statement for the month of October.
e. Enter the appropriate closing entries at the end of October in the T-accounts, assuming that the books are closed each month. Use an Income Summary account.
f. Prepare a balance sheet as of October 31, 1981.

**3.37**  Refer to Problem **3.31**. Prepare a 10-column work sheet for Burton Shoe Stores, Inc., using the following column headings: Unadjusted Trial Balance: Debit and Credit; Adjusting Entries: Debit and Credit; Adjusted Trial Balance: Debit and Credit; Income Statement: Debit and Credit; Balance Sheet: Debit and Credit.

**3.38**  Refer to Problem **3.32**. Prepare a 10-column work sheet for the North Sales Company using the following column headings: Unadjusted Trial Balance: Debit and Credit; Adjusting Entries: Debit and Credit; Adjusted Trial Balance: Debit and Credit; Statement of Income and Retained Earnings: Debit and Credit; Balance Sheet: Debit and Credit.

**3.39**  Refer to Problem **3.33**. Prepare a 10-column work sheet for Kathleen Clothing Company using the following headings: Unadjusted Trial Balance: Debit and Credit; Adjusting Entries: Debit and Credit; Adjusted Trial Balance: Debit and Credit; Income Statement: Debit and Credit; Balance Sheet: Debit and Credit.

**3.40**  The trial balance of the general ledger of the Renuit Shop, Inc., on July 1, 1981, is as follows:

| | | |
|---|---:|---:|
| Cash | $ 700 | |
| Supplies Inventory | 425 | |
| Tools | 2,000 | |
| Accumulated Depreciation | | $ 800 |
| Accounts Payable | | 625[a] |
| Common Stock | | 500 |
| Retained Earnings | | 1,200 |
| Repair Service Revenue | | — |
| Cost of Repair Supplies Used | — | |
| Salary Expense | — | |
| Utilities Expense | — | |
| Depreciation Expense | — | |
| Total | $3,125 | $3,125 |

[a]Amount is payable to Handicraft Supply Company.

The transactions during July are as follows:

(1) Cash is received on July 3 for repair work done, $360.
(2) Supplies are purchased on account from Handicraft Supply Company on July 10, $185.
(3) Cash payments are made on July 31 as follows: salaries, $125; utilities, $13; Handicraft Supply Company on account, $725.
(4) Cash is received for repair work done on July 31, $310.
(5) Depreciation on tools for the month is $55.
(6) The cost of supplies used during the month is $255.

  a. Open T-accounts for the accounts listed in the trial balance on July 1, 1981, and enter the opening balances.
  b. Construct a six-column journal with the following column headings: Cash, Debit and Credit; Revenue for Repair Services, Credit; Supplies, Debit; Other Accounts, Debit and Credit. Also include columns for Date, Explanations, and Other Accounts Titles.
  c. Enter transactions (1) through (4) in the six-column journal.
  d. Post amounts from the six-column journal to the appropriate T-accounts.
  e. Prepare an unadjusted trial balance.
  f. Prepare a two-column general journal. Enter the adjusting entries for items (5) and (6) on July 31, 1981.

g. Post the adjusting entries to the T-accounts.

h. Prepare an adjusted trial balance.

i. Enter the closing entries on July 31, 1981, in the general journal and then post them to the general ledger accounts.

j. Prepare a postclosing trial balance.

**3.41**  The most common transactions of the Beal Antique Shop, Inc., are as follows:

Sales for cash and on account
Payments for purchases of merchandise by cash and by check
Collections of cash from customers
Payments of operating expenses by cash and by check
Deposits in the bank

Subsidiary ledgers are used for customers' accounts and operating expense accounts. A direct posting procedure is not to be used.

The following are the transactions for July 15–31:

| | |
|---|---|
| July 15 | Cash sales, $200. |
| 16 | Sale, on account, L. C. Jones, $80; cash sales, $60. |
| 17 | $500 of common stock is issued for cash. |
| 18 | Deposit in bank, $750. |
| 18 | Cash sales, $250. |
| 20 | Collection from a customer, A. C. Hines, $75. |
| 21 | Sale, on account, A. O. Brown, $85. |
| 22 | Store fixtures are purchased for $800 from the Office Supply Company. A check (No. 550) is issued, $200; the balance is covered by an installment contract. |
| 23 | Merchandise is purchased for $650 from the East Antique Company. Check (No. 551) is issued in full payment. |
| 25 | Cash sales, $200. |
| 25 | Deposit in bank, $525. |
| 25 | Collection from a customer, M. A. Cross, $90. |
| 27 | A note payable is issued to the bank, $1,000. The proceeds are added by the bank to the firm's account. |
| 28 | Sale, on account, W. I. Snow, $95; cash sales, $60. |
| 29 | A telephone bill is received from the Bell Telephone Company. Check (No. 552) is issued, $12. |
| 30 | Merchandise is acquired from the Specialty Furniture Company, $550. Check (No. 553) is issued in payment of the accompanying invoice. |
| 31 | The clerk is paid for the second half of the month. Check (No. 554) is issued for earnings of $300, less deductions of 6 percent for payroll taxes and $45 for income tax. |

a. Prepare an 11-column journal with the following column headings: Cash on Hand (Dr. and Cr.); Cash in Bank (Dr. and Cr.); Accounts Receivable (Dr. and Cr.); Merchandise Inventory (Dr.); Selling and Administrative Expenses (Dr.); Sales (Cr.); Other Accounts (Dr. and Cr.). Also include columns for Date, Explanations, and Other Accounts Titles.

b. Enter each of the transactions during July in the 11-column journal.

**3.42**  E. S. Brady and R. E. Brady own and operate Brady Business Services, Inc., providing mimeographing and public stenographic services. At September 30, 1981, the trial balance of the general ledger and the schedules of the subsidiary ledgers are as follows:

---

### General Ledger

| | | |
|---|---:|---:|
| Cash on Hand | $ 500 | |
| Cash in Bank | 5,000 | |
| Accounts Receivable | 9,500 | |
| Supplies on Hand | 3,300 | |
| Prepaid Insurance | 960 | |
| Office Equipment | 19,500 | |
| Accumulated Depreciation | | $ 7,200 |
| Accounts Payable | | 4,900 |
| Equipment Contract Payable | | 3,000 |
| Capital Stock | | 10,000 |
| Retained Earnings | | 13,660 |
| Total | $38,760 | $38,760 |

### Accounts Receivable

| | |
|---|---:|
| Baum & Co. | $ 1,220 |
| Clark's Market | 300 |
| David Bros. | — |
| Forest Stores | 1,800 |
| H. B. Gross | 590 |
| Moll & Co. | 750 |
| Ohio Realty | — |
| Porter and Sons | 290 |
| A. B. Reck | 1,450 |
| Standard Service | 3,100 |
| Total | $ 9,500 |

### Accounts Payable

| | |
|---|---:|
| Burton, Inc. | $ 250 |
| City Supply Co. | 2,360 |
| Mears & Co. | 450 |
| P. A. Page, Inc. | 1,080 |
| Snell Bros. | 760 |
| Total | $ 4,900 |

---

The following transactions took place during the month of October:

October 1   Received $450 in cash for secretarial work completed and delivered today.

1   Completed and delivered mimeograph work for Moll & Company and invoiced them for $510.

2   Issued check (No. 100) for $600 to K. M. Bear for rent for the month of October. (Checks are issued in serial number order.)

3   Received check for $1,800 from Forest Stores in payment of their account balance.

3   Deposited $2,250 in the bank.

6   Issued checks (Nos. 101–104) in payment of September 30 balances to Burton, Inc., City Supply Company, P. A. Page, Inc., and Snell Brothers.

6   Acquired on account paper and other mimeograph supplies from City Supply Company, $1,050.

7   Cash receipts for the day were $330 for stenographic service and $1,250 for mimeograph work.

7   Deposited $1,580 in the bank.

8   Received the following invoices: Mears & Company, $100, for repairs to office equipment; Burton, Inc., $480, for office supplies; P. A. Page, Inc., $250 for mimeograph supplies.

10   Received checks from the following customers for the September 30 balances: Baum & Company, Clark's Market, Moll & Company, Porter and Sons, and Standard Service.

| | |
|---|---|
| 10 | Deposited $5,660 in the bank. |
| 10 | Issued check (No. 105) for $150 for advertising invoice received from the *Daily Register*. |
| 13 | Issued check (106) for $1,500 to Hall Office Equipment, Inc., for monthly payment on the equipment purchase contract. |
| 13 | Completed and delivered the following mimeograph jobs and invoiced the customers: Ohio Realty, $460; Davis Brothers, $200; Standard Service, $930. |
| 14 | Receipts for the day for stenographic work, $620. |
| 14 | Deposited $620 in the bank. |
| 15 | Issued check (No. 107) for $90 to Blott Typewriter Services for repairs on machines. |
| 16 | Received a check for $550 from S. V. Smith for mimeograph work completed and delivered today. |
| 17 | Receipts for the day: stenographic services, $100; mimeograph work, $850. |
| 17 | Deposited $1,500 in the bank. |
| 17 | Issued checks (Nos. 108–109) to Mears & Company and P. A. Page, Inc., for invoices of October 8. |
| 20 | Issued check (No. 110) to City Supply Company for invoice of October 6. |
| 20 | Purchased the following operating supplies on account: City Supply Company, $1,500; Snell Brothers, $950. |
| 20 | Issued check (No. 111) to a customer, S. V. Smith, as an adjustment reducing the amount he had paid for mimeograph work, $50 (adjustment due to error in calculating the charge on October 16). |
| 21 | Received a check from H. B. Gross for $590 in payment of September 30 balance. |
| 21 | Other cash receipts for the day: stenographic services, $440; mimeograph work, $460. |
| 21 | Deposited $1,490 in the bank. |
| 23 | Issued check (No. 112) for $450 to Mears & Company. |
| 24 | Billed the following customers for mimeograph work completed and delivered: Clark's Market, $210; Forest Stores, $445; Moll & Company, $1,070. |
| 24 | Issued a check (No. 113) for $500 as a dividend. |
| 27 | Cash receipts for the day: stenographic services, $270; mimeograph work; $1,500. |
| 27 | Deposited $1,770 in the bank. |
| 29 | Issued a credit memo to Moll & Company for $100 as an adjustment on invoice of October 24 (incorrect rate used). |
| 30 | Issued check (No. 114) to Southwestern Telephone Company for telephone bill for the month, $120. |
| 31 | Paid $50 out of cash on hand for machinery repair. |
| 31 | Cash receipts for the day: mimeograph work, $435. |
| 31 | Issued checks (Nos. 115–116) for October salaries: E. S Brady, $2,750; R. E. Brady, $2,500. |
| 31 | Deposited $385 in the bank. |

**a.** Open T-accounts for each of the general ledger accounts and insert the September 30 balances.

**b.** Record the October transactions in a 12-column journal. The amount-column headings in the journal are as follows: Cash on Hand, Dr. and Cr.; Cash in Bank, Dr. and Cr.; Accounts Receivable, Dr. and Cr.; Accounts Payable, Dr. and Cr.; Supplies on Hand, Dr.; Sales Revenue, Cr.; Other Accounts, Dr. and Cr. There should also be columns for Date, Explanation, and Other Accounts Titles.

**c.** Post the transactions during October from the journal to the general ledger T-accounts.

**d.** Prepare an unadjusted trial balance of the general ledger accounts as of October 31.

**3.43** This problem is a continuation of Problem **3.42**. Additional information as of October 31, 1981, follows:

**(1)** Ending inventory of supplies amounts to $4,750.

**(2)** The insurance policy acquired on October 1, 1980, runs for 3 years.

(3) Office equipment was acquired on September 30, 1979, at a cost of $19,500. It was estimated that the salvage value of the equipment at the estimated retirement date, September 30, 1984, would be $1,500.

(4) Income tax expense is estimated to be $600.

    **a.** Construct a two-column general journal. Prepare any adjusting entries required on October 31, 1981, and enter them in the general journal.

    **b.** Post the adjusting entries to the general ledger T-accounts.

    **c.** Prepare an adjusted preclosing trial balance.

    **d.** Prepare the closing entries for the revenue and expense accounts, enter them in the general journal, and post them to the general ledger T-accounts.

    **e.** Prepare a postclosing trial balance.

**3.44** This problem is a continuation of Problems **3.42** and **3.43**.

    **a.** Prepare a 10-column work sheet with the following column headings: Unadjusted Trial Balance (Dr. and Cr.); Adjusting Entries (Dr. and Cr.); Adjusted Trial Balance (Dr. and Cr.); Income Statement (Dr. and Cr.); Balance Sheet (Dr. and Cr.)

    **b.** Prepare an income statement for the month of October and a balance sheet for October 31, 1981, for Brady Business Services, Inc.

**3.45** Referring to Problem **3.42**, prepare the following specialized journals:

    (1) Cash receipts and disbursements journal with the following columns: Date; Cash on Hand, Dr. and Cr.; Cash in Bank, Dr.; Accounts Receivable, Cr. (amount, name of customer); Sales Revenue, Cr.; Other Accounts, Dr. (amount, account title, explanation).

    (2) Check register with the following columns: Date, Payee; Check Number; Cash in Bank, Cr.; Accounts Payable, Dr.; Other Accounts, Dr. (amount, reference, account title, explanation).

    (3) Revenue journal for use where credit is extended, with the following columns: Date; Name of customer; Reference; a single column for Accounts Receivable, Dr.; and Sales Revenue, Cr.

    (4) Invoice register with the following columns: Date; Name of Creditor; Accounts Payable, Cr.; Supplies on Hand, Dr.; Other Accounts, Dr. (amount, account title, explanation).

Record the transactions during October in the appropriate journal.

**3.46** Refer to Problem **3.42**. Prepare the subsidiary ledgers for Accounts Receivable and Accounts Payable as of October 31, 1981, using the format shown in Problem **3.42**.

# Chapter 4
## Review of the Accounting Process: Statement of Changes in Financial Position

4.1 The statement of changes in financial position reports the flow of funds into and out of a business during an accounting period. "Funds" are usually defined as current assets minus current liabilities, or working capital. Some firms define funds as cash only, or cash plus marketable securities, or cash plus marketable securities minus current liabilities.* Funds typically come from three sources: **(1)** operations, **(2)** increases in external financing (debt or equity issues), and **(3)** disposition of noncurrent assets. Funds are generally used for **(1)** operations, **(2)** distributions to owners, **(3)** decreases in external financing, and **(4)** acquisition of noncurrent assets. Published statements of changes in financial position group all operating sources and operating uses of funds together and show the *net* amount of funds provided from or used in operations. Figure 4.1 summarizes the various sources and uses of funds.

4.2 In this chapter, we review the accounting procedures for preparing the statement of changes in financial position. Most accounting systems are designed primarily to accumulate information for the preparation of the income statement and the balance sheet. Individual asset, liability, owners' equity, revenue, and expense accounts are maintained so that earnings for the period and financial position at the end of the period can be computed. Accounting systems are generally not designed to accumulate information in a form that can be used directly in preparing the statement of changes in financial position. Two reasons for this situation can be suggested. First, income statements and balance sheets have been prepared and published for decades, whereas the statement of changes in financial position has been a required statement only since 1971.† The redesign of complex accounting systems is a costly process, so that changes tend to evolve slowly. Second, and perhaps more important, information necessary for the preparation of the statement of changes in financial position can generally be obtained directly from the income statement and comparative balance sheets. It is not necessary to redesign the accounting system when the needed information can be obtained as ancillary output of the existing system.

4.3 The statement of changes in financial position for most firms is prepared at the end of the accounting period after the income statement and balance sheet have been pre-

---

*The Financial Accounting Standards Board is currently reconsidering the topic of accounting for the flow of funds and the appropriate definition of "funds." A new reporting standard is expected in 1983.

†Accounting Principles Board, *Accounting Principles Board Opinion No. 19* (March 1971).

**Figure 4.1**
**Sources and Uses of Working Capital**

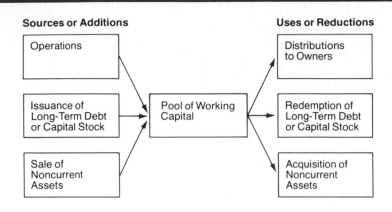

pared. The procedure for preparing the statement of changes in financial position discussed in this chapter follows the same process. The first illustration assumes that funds are defined as working capital. The second illustration defines funds as cash. Because the approach is basically the same in both cases, the preparation of the statement using other definitions of funds is a straight-forward extension of the procedures illustrated.

4.4    To help understand the procedures for preparing the statement, it will be useful to begin by examining the effect of various transactions on working capital.

## Analysis of the Effects of Transactions on Working Capital

### Algebraic Formulation

4.5  The effects of various transactions on working capital might be seen by reexamining the accounting equation. In doing so, we use the following notation:

CA represents current assets.

CL represents current liabilities.

NCA represents noncurrent assets.

NCL represents noncurrent liabilities.

OE represents owners' equity.

$\Delta$ represents the change in an item, whether positive (an increase) or negative (a decrease), from the beginning of a period to the end of the period.

The accounting equation states that

$$\text{Assets} = \text{Liabilities} + \text{Owners' Equity.}$$
$$CA + NCA = CL + NCL + OE.$$

Furthermore, this equation must be true for balance sheets constructed at both the start of the period and the end of the period. If the start-of-the-period and end-of-the-period balance sheets maintain the accounting equation, then the following equation must also be valid:

$$\Delta CA + \Delta NCA = \Delta CL + \Delta NCL + \Delta OE.$$

Rearranging terms in this equation, we get the working capital equation:

$$\Delta CA - \Delta CL = \Delta NCL + \Delta OE - \Delta NCA.$$

Working capital is equal to current assets minus current liabilities, so the left-hand side of the above equation represents the net change in working capital. The right-hand side of the equation, reflecting changes in all *nonworking* capital accounts, must also be equal *in amount* to the net change in working capital. The equation states that increases in working capital (left-hand side) are equal to, or caused by, the increase in noncurrent liabilities plus the increase in owners' equity less the increase in noncurrent assets (right-hand side). Next, we illustrate how the changes in the noncurrent accounts on the right-hand side bring about the change in working capital on the left-hand side.

## Illustration of Transactions Analysis

4.6 We can analyze some typical transactions to demonstrate how the equation is maintained and how working capital is affected.

4.7 Assume that the following events occur during 1981 for the Abbott Corporation:*

1. Merchandise costing $70,000 is acquired on account.

2. Merchandise costing $60,000 is sold to customers on account for $125,000.

3. Salaries of $19,000 are paid in cash.

4. Other expenses of $13,000 are paid in cash.

5. Cash collections of customers' accounts total $90,000.

6. Cash payments to suppliers of merchandise total $50,000.

7. Salaries earned but not paid as of December 31, 1981, are accrued, $1,000.

8. Other expenses not paid as of December 31, 1981, are accrued, $2,000.

9. Depreciation for 1981 is recorded, $10,000.

10. Long-term debt is issued for cash, $100,000.

---

*To simplify this illustration, we have not provided information on the amounts in balance sheet accounts on January 1, 1981. As will become evident later in the chapter, however, some cash receipts and disbursements represent settlements of beginning-of-the-period receivables and payables.

11. Dividends of $10,000 are declared and paid.

12. Equipment costing $125,000 is acquired for cash.

The effects of these transactions on the working capital equation,

$$\Delta CA - \Delta CL = \Delta NCL + \Delta OE - \Delta NCA,$$

are analyzed in Exhibit 4.1. Working capital decreased by $5,000 during 1981. Both sides of the equation show this net change. The net change in working capital during a period (left-hand side of the equation) can therefore be explained, or analyzed, by focusing on the changes in nonworking capital accounts (right-hand side of the equation). For Abbott Corporation, the net decrease in working capital of $5,000 is explained as follows:

| | |
|---|---|
| Increases in Working Capital: | |
| From Operations ................... | $ 30,000 |
| From Issuing Long-Term Debt ....... | 100,000 |
| Total Increases ................. | $130,000 |
| Decreases in Working Capital: | |
| For Dividends ..................... | $ 10,000 |
| For Acquisition of Equipment ....... | 125,000 |
| Total Decreases ................. | $135,000 |
| Net Decrease in Working Capital ..... | $ 5,000 |

Note several aspects of the transactions 4.8 analysis in Exhibit 4.1. First, the recording of depreciation for the period does not affect working capital. A noncurrent asset is decreased and owners' equity is decreased. No working capital accounts are affected. (Working capital was reduced in the period when the noncurrent asset was acquired.) Second, some transactions during the year have no net effect on working capital, because they merely result in transfers among working capital accounts. Several examples are the purchase of merchandise on account, the collection of accounts receivable, and the payment of accounts payable. These transactions, therefore, do not explain the *change* in working capital during the period.

Exhibit 4.1

**Analysis of the Effects of Abbott Corporation's Transactions during 1981 on Working Capital and Nonworking Capital Accounts**

| Transactions | Effect on Working Capital Equation | | | | | | | | |
| --- | --- | --- | --- | --- | --- | --- | --- | --- | --- |
| | Working Capital Changes | | | = | ΔNCL | + | Nonworking Capital Changes | | |
| | ΔCA | – | ΔCL | = | | + | ΔOE | – | ΔNCA |
| (1) Merchandise costing $70,000 is acquired on account, increasing a current asset and a current liability | $ 70,000 | – | $70,000 | = | 0 | + | 0 | – | 0 |
| (2) Merchandise costing $60,000 is sold to customers on account for $125,000, increasing the current asset, accounts receivable, by $125,000, decreasing the current asset, inventory, by $60,000, and increasing owners' equity by $65,000 | $125,000 (–$ 60,000) | – | 0 | = | 0 | + | $65,000 | – | 0 |
| (3) Salaries of $19,000 are paid in cash, decreasing a current asset and owners' equity | (–$ 19,000) | – | 0 | = | 0 | + | (–$19,000) | – | 0 |
| (4) Other expenses of $13,000 are paid in cash, decreasing a current asset and owners' equity | (–$ 13,000) | – | 0 | = | 0 | + | (–$13,000) | – | 0 |
| (5) Cash collections of customers' accounts total $90,000, increasing the current asset, cash, and decreasing the current asset, accounts receivable | $ 90,000 (–$ 90,000) | – | 0 | = | 0 | + | 0 | – | 0 |
| (6) Cash payments to suppliers of merchandise total $50,000, decreasing a current asset and a current liability | (–$ 50,000) | – | (–$50,000) | = | 0 | + | 0 | – | 0 |
| (7) Salaries of $1,000 earned but not paid as of December 31, 1981, are accrued, increasing a current liability and decreasing owners' equity | 0 | – | $ 1,000 | = | 0 | + | (–$ 1,000) | – | 0 |
| (8) Other expenses of $2,000 not paid as of December 31, 1981, are accrued, increasing a current liability and decreasing owners' equity | 0 | – | $ 2,000 | = | 0 | + | (–$ 2,000) | – | 0 |
| (9) Depreciation for 1981 of $10,000 is recorded, decreasing owners' equity and noncurrent assets | 0 | – | 0 | = | 0 | + | (–$10,000) | – | (–$ 10,000) |
| Total from Operations | ($ 53,000) | – | $23,000 | = | 0 | + | $20,000 | – | (–$ 10,000) |
| (10) Long-term debt is issued for cash, $100,000, increasing a current asset and a noncurrent liability | $100,000 | – | 0 | = | $100,000 | + | 0 | – | 0 |
| (11) Dividends of $10,000 are declared and paid, decreasing a current asset and owners' equity | (–$ 10,000) | – | 0 | = | 0 | + | (–$10,000) | – | 0 |
| (12) Equipment costing $125,000 is acquired for cash, decreasing a current asset and increasing noncurrent assets | (–$125,000) | – | 0 | = | 0 | + | 0 | – | $125,000 |
| Totals | $ 18,000 | – | $23,000 | = | $100,000 | + | $10,000 | – | $115,000 |
| Net Change in Working Capital and Nonworking Capital | –$ 5,000 | | | = | | | –$ 5,000 | | |

4.9    The information necessary to prepare the statement of changes in financial position can be generated, or developed, using the transactions analysis approach illustrated in Exhibit 4.1. This approach quickly becomes cumbersome, however, as the number of transactions increases. In addition, there are numerous transactions during the year that have no net effect on working capital (for example, collection of accounts receivable, payment of accounts payable). These transactions can effectively be ignored in explaining the change in working capital. In the next section, we describe a procedure for preparing the statement of changes in financial position that uses the T-account discussed in the previous chapter and information from the income statement and balance sheet for the period.

## Preparation of the Statement of Changes in Financial Position: Funds Defined as Working Capital

4.10    In this section, we present a step-by-step procedure for preparing the statement of changes in financial position. We then illustrate this procedure using the transactions of Abbott Corporation for 1981.

### The Procedure and an Illustration

4.11    **Step 1** Obtain balance sheets for the beginning and end of the period covered by the statement of changes in financial position. The comparative balance sheets of Abbott Corporation for December 31, 1980 and 1981, are presented in Exhibit 4.2. Properly prepared balance sheets classify both assets and equities as either current or noncurrent. The distinction between current and noncurrent items is essential to the preparation of the statement of changes in financial position when funds are defined as working capital.

4.12    **Step 2** Prepare a "T-account" *work sheet*. Recall from Chapter 3 that a work sheet is merely a mechanism for summarizing data to simplify the preparation of a financial statement. In preparing a T-account work sheet, first prepare a master T-account titled "Working Capital." This account is merely an aggregation of the individual current asset and current liability accounts into a single summary account. An example of this master T-account is shown in the top portion of Exhibit 4.3. Note that this T-account has sections labeled "From Operations" and "Other (Nonoperating)" sources and uses. Transactions affecting working capital during the period are classified under one of these headings to aid in the preparation of the statement of changes in financial position. This procedure is explained later in this section. The beginning and ending amounts of working capital are then entered in the master T-account. The beginning and ending amounts of working capital for Abbott Corporation are $45,000 (= $90,000 − $45,000) and $40,000 (= $108,000 − $68,000), respectively. The check marks indicate that the figures are balances. The number at the top of the T-account is the opening balance; the one at the bottom is the closing balance. Note that the master T-account, Working Capital, is another means of expressing the left-hand side of the working capital equation in Exhibit 4.1.

4.13    After the master T-account for Working Capital has been prepared (as at the top of Exhibit 4.3), the work sheet is completed by preparing T-accounts for *each* noncurrent asset and noncurrent equity account. Enter the beginning and ending balances in each account for the period as given in Exhibit 4.2. The lower portion of Exhibit 4.3 shows the T-accounts for each noncurrent asset and noncurrent equity. Note that these individual T-accounts are another means of expressing the right-hand side of the working capital equation in Exhibit 4.1.

4.14    The T-account work sheet for Abbott Corporation after completion of step **2** is shown in Exhibit 4.3.

4.15    **Step 3** Explain the change in the master working capital account between the beginning and end of the period by explaining or

*Exhibit 4.2*
**Abbott Corporation**
**Comparative Balance Sheets for**
**December 31, 1980 and 1981**

| ASSETS | December 31, 1980 | December 31, 1981 |
|---|---|---|
| **Current Assets** | | |
| Cash | $ 30,000 | $ 3,000 |
| Accounts Receivable | 20,000 | 55,000 |
| Merchandise Inventory | 40,000 | 50,000 |
| Total Current Assets | $ 90,000 | $108,000 |
| **Noncurrent Assets** | | |
| Buildings and Equipment (Cost) | $100,000 | $225,000 |
| Accumulated Depreciation | (30,000) | (40,000) |
| Total Noncurrent Assets | $ 70,000 | $185,000 |
| Total Assets | $160,000 | $293,000 |
| **EQUITIES** | | |
| **Current Liabilities** | | |
| Accounts Payable—Merchandise Suppliers | $ 30,000 | $ 50,000 |
| Accounts Payable—Other Suppliers | 10,000 | 12,000 |
| Salaries Payable | 5,000 | 6,000 |
| Total Current Liabilities | $ 45,000 | $ 68,000 |
| **Noncurrent Liabilities** | | |
| Bonds Payable | $ 0 | $100,000 |
| **Owners' Equity** | | |
| Capital Stock | $100,000 | $100,000 |
| Retained Earnings | 15,000 | 25,000 |
| Total Owners' Equity | $115,000 | $125,000 |
| Total Equities | $160,000 | $293,000 |

accounting for the change in the balance of each nonworking capital account during the period. This step is accomplished by *reconstructing the entries originally recorded in the accounts during the period*. The reconstructed entries are written in the appropriate T-accounts. You will see that once the net change in each of the nonworking capital accounts has been accounted for, sufficient information will have been generated to account for the net change in working capital. That is, if you have explained the changes in the right-hand side of the working capital equation, you will also have explained the causes of the changes in working capital itself on the left-hand side.

The process of reconstructing the transactions during the year is usually easiest if supplementary information is accounted for first. Assume that the following information is obtained concerning the Abbott Corporation for 1981:

**1.** Net income is $20,000.

**2.** Depreciation expense is $10,000.

**3.** Dividends declared and paid total $10,000.

The analytical entry to record the information concerning net income is

4.16

Exhibit 4.3
**T-Account Work Sheet for
Abbott Corporation**

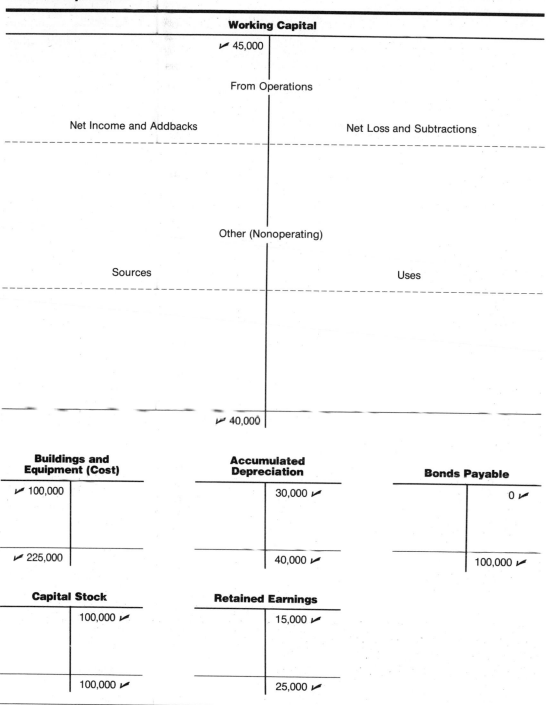

(1)

```
Working Capital (Operations— Net
    Income) ....................... 20,000
        Retained Earnings ............        20,000
Entry recorded in T-account work
sheet.
```

To understand this entry, review the process of recording revenues and expenses and the closing entries for those temporary accounts from Chapter 3. All of the journal entries that together record the process of earning $20,000 net income are equivalent to the following single journal entry:

```
Net Assets (= All Assets – All
    Liabilities) ..................... 20,000
        Retained Earnings ............        20,000
Summary entry equivalent to record-
ing earnings of $20,000.
```

In the analytical entry (1) above, the debit results in showing a provisional increase in working capital from operations in an amount equal to net income for the period. In the summary journal entry, we debit Net Assets. The initial assumption at this stage of preparing the statement of changes in financial position is that all of the net assets generated by the earnings process were *current* net assets (or working capital).

4.17    Some portion of the items recognized as expenses and deducted in determining net income does not, however, decrease working capital. The portion of the expenses that does not affect working capital is added to the provisional increase in working capital to calculate the net amount of working capital from operations. Such an adjustment for an expense not using working capital is illustrated for depreciation expense in entry (2).

(2)

```
Working Capital (Operations—
    Depreciation Expense Addback) .. 10,000
        Accumulated Depreciation .....        10,000
Entry recorded in T-account work
sheet.
```

Because depreciation expense was deducted in calculating net income but did not reduce working capital, the amount of depreciation expense must be added back to net income in determining the amount of working capital provided by operations. The results of entries (1) and (2) might be summarized as follows:

```
Working Capital (Operations— Net
    Income and Addbacks) .......... 30,000
        Retained Earnings ...........        20,000
        Accumulated Depreciation .....        10,000
```

This combined entry shows that the operating activities of Abbott Corporation resulted in a $30,000 increase in working capital during 1981. That is, revenues increasing working capital exceeded expenses using working capital (total expenses less depreciation expense) by $30,000.

4.18    The supplementary information concerning dividends declared and paid of $10,000 is recorded as follows:

(3)

```
Retained Earnings ................ 10,000
    Working Capital (Other Uses—
        Dividends) .................        10,000
Entry recorded in T-account work
sheet.
```

4.19    Once the supplementary information has been reflected in the T-accounts, it is necessary to make inferences about the reasons for the remaining changes in the nonworking capital accounts. (If the statement of changes in financial position were being prepared for an actual firm, such inferences might not be necessary, because sufficient information regarding the change in each account is likely to be available from the firm's accounting records.) The Buildings and Equipment (Cost) account shows a net increase of $125,000 (= $225,000 – $100,000). Because we have no other information, we must assume or deduce that buildings and equipment costing $125,000 were acquired during the year. The analytical entry is

(4)

```
Buildings and Equipment (Cost) .. 125,000
    Working Capital (Other
        Uses—Acquisitions of
        Buildings and Equipment) .        125,000
Entry recorded in T-account work
sheet.
```

4.20    The Bonds Payable account increased $100,000 during 1981. Because we have no other information, we must assume or deduce that long-term bonds were issued during the year. The analytical entry is

(5)
Working Capital (Other Sources—
    Long-Term Bond Issue)  . . . . . . . 100,000
        Bonds Payable  . . . . . . . . . . . .          100,000
Entry recorded in T-account work
sheet.

4.21    Exhibit 4.4 presents the T-account work sheet for Abbott Corporation for 1981 after analytical entry (5). All changes in the non-working capital T-accounts have been explained. If the work has been done correctly, the change in the Working Capital account has also been explained by the entries in the master Working Capital account.

4.22    Exhibit 4.4 shows the sum of the debit entries in the Working Capital account to be $130,000, whereas the sum of the credit entries is $135,000. There is an excess of credits over debits in the account of $5,000, which accounts for the decrease in working capital from $45,000 to $40,000 during the year.

4.23    We can see in Exhibit 4.4 that operations provided working capital of $30,000 (−$20,000 + $10,000), whereas new bond issues provided $100,000 of working capital. Working capital of $135,000 was used: $10,000 for dividends and $125,000 for new buildings and equipment.

4.24    **Step 4** The final step is the preparation of the formal statement of changes in financial position. The statement for Abbott Corporation is shown in Exhibit 4.5. Section I presents the sources and uses of working capital. This section of the statement is prepared directly from information in the master Working Capital account. Section II of the Statement of Changes in Financial Position analyzes the changes in the individual current asset and current liability accounts. That is, the manner in which the net change in working capital (explained in Section I of the statement) affects the various working capital accounts is analyzed in Section II.

The information needed for preparing Section II is obtained from the comparative balance sheets in Exhibit 4.2.

4.25    The information in Section II of the statement is necessary for a complete assessment of a firm's liquidity and changes in the structure of its assets and equities. The net change explained in Section I can result from the offsetting of much larger increases and decreases in individual current asset and current liability accounts. For example, cash decreased by $27,000, whereas accounts receivable increased by $35,000 during the year. Together, this represents an increase of $8,000 in the firm's most liquid assets. However, most of the increased liquidity does not reflect cash immediately available to pay liabilities or to make purchases. Instead, cash must first be collected from customers. Financial statement readers interested in assessing changes in the structure of the firm's working capital would find the information in Section II of the statement of changes in financial position to be useful.

## Extension of the Illustration

4.26    The illustration for Abbott Corporation is simpler than the typical published statement of changes in financial position in at least four respects:

1. There are only a few balance sheet accounts whose changes are to be explained.

2. Several types of more complex transactions that affect the sources of working capital from operations are not involved.

3. Each transaction recorded in step 3 involves only one debit and one credit.

4. Each explanation of a change in a non-working capital account involves only one transaction, except for the Retained Earnings account.

Most of the complications that arise in preparing the statement of changes in financial position arise from accounting events that are not discussed until later chapters. As we discuss these transactions, we shall illustrate their effects on the statement of changes in

*Exhibit 4.4*
**T-Account Work Sheet for
Abbott Corporation**

**Working Capital**

|  |  |
|---|---|
| ✔ 45,000 |  |

From Operations

| Net Income and Addbacks | | Net Loss and Subtractions |
|---|---|---|
| Net Income | (1) 20,000 | |
| Depreciation Expense | (2) 10,000 | |

Other (Nonoperating)

| Sources | | | Uses |
|---|---|---|---|
| Long-Term Bonds Issued | (5) 100,000 | 10,000 (3) | Dividends Declared and Paid |
| | | 125,000 (4) | Buildings and Equipment Acquired |

|  |  |
|---|---|
| ✔ 40,000 |  |

| **Buildings and Equipment (Cost)** | |
|---|---|
| ✔ 100,000 | |
| (4) 125,000 | |
| ✔ 225,000 | |

| **Accumulated Depreciation** | |
|---|---|
| | 30,000 ✔ |
| | 10,000 (2) |
| | 40,000 ✔ |

| **Bonds Payable** | |
|---|---|
| | 0 ✔ |
| | 100,000 (5) |
| | 100,000 ✔ |

| **Capital Stock** | |
|---|---|
| | 100,000 ✔ |
| | 100,000 ✔ |

| **Retained Earnings** | |
|---|---|
| | 15,000 ✔ |
| (3) 10,000 | 20,000 (1) |
| | 25,000 ✔ |

*Exhibit 4.5*
**Abbott Corporation**
**Statement of Changes in**
**Financial Position**
**for the Year 1981**

### SECTION I. SOURCES AND USES OF WORKING CAPITAL

**Sources of Working Capital**

Operations

| | | |
|---|---:|---:|
| Net Income | $ 20,000 | |
| Add Back Expenses Not Using Working Capital: Depreciation | 10,000 | |
| Total Sources from Operations | | $ 30,000 |
| Proceeds from Long-Term Bonds Issued | | 100,000 |
| Total Sources of Working Capital | | $130,000 |

**Uses of Working Capital**

| | |
|---|---:|
| Dividends | $ 10,000 |
| Acquisition of Buildings and Equipment | 125,000 |
| Total Uses of Working Capital | $135,000 |
| Net Decrease in Working Capital during the Year (Sources Minus Uses) | $  5,000 |

### SECTION II. ANALYSIS OF CHANGES IN WORKING CAPITAL ACCOUNTS

**Current Asset Item Increases (Decreases)**

| | | |
|---|---:|---:|
| Cash | $(27,000) | |
| Accounts Receivable | 35,000 | |
| Merchandise Inventory | 10,000 | |
| Net Increase (Decrease) in Current Asset Items | | $ 18,000 |

**Current Liability Increases (Decreases)**

| | | |
|---|---:|---:|
| Accounts Payable—Merchandise Suppliers | $ 20,000 | |
| Accounts Payable—Other Suppliers | 2,000 | |
| Salaries Payable | 1,000 | |
| Net Increase (Decrease) in Current Liability Items | | 23,000 |
| Net Decrease in Working Capital during the Year (Net Increase in Current Liability Items Minus Net Increase in Current Asset Items) | | $  5,000 |

financial position. We can illustrate now one complication caused by a supplementary disclosure. Suppose that the firm sold some of its buildings and equipment during the year at their book value; the cash proceeds from disposition are equal to acquisition cost less accumulated depreciation of the assets. With this assumption, there will be no gain or loss on disposition.

4.27   Let us reconsider Abbott Corporation with the following information. Abbott Corporation sold some equipment during 1981. This equipment cost $10,000 and was sold

for $3,000 at a time when accumulated depreciation on the equipment sold was $7,000. The actual entry made during the year to record the sale of the equipment was as follows:

| | |
|---|---:|
| Cash | 3,000 |
| Accumulated Depreciation | 7,000 |
|     Buildings and Equipment | |
|       (Cost) | 10,000 |

Journal entry for sale of equipment.

Assume that the comparative balance sheets   4.28
as shown in Exhibit 4.2 are correct and thus

that the net decrease in working capital for 1981 is still $5,000. The entries in the T-accounts must be altered to reflect this new information. The following entry in the T-accounts is required to recognize the effect of the sale of equipment:

(1a)
Working Capital (Other Sources—
   Proceeds from Sale of Equipment) . 3,000
Accumulated Depreciation .......... 7,000
     Buildings and Equipment (Cost) .      10,000
Entry recorded in T-account work
sheet.

The debit to Working Capital (Other Sources—Proceeds from Sale of Equipment) shows the proceeds of the sale.

4.29    As a result of entry (1a), the T-accounts for Buildings and Equipment (Cost) and Accumulated Depreciation would appear as follows:

| Buildings and Equipment (Cost) | | Accumulated Depreciation | |
|---|---|---|---|
| ✓ 100,000 | | | 30,000 ✓ |
| | 10,000 (1a) | (1a) 7,000 | |
| ✓ 225,000 | | | 40,000 ✓ |

When it comes time to explain the change in the account, Buildings and Equipment (Cost), the T-account indicates that there is an increase of $125,000 and a credit entry (1a) of $10,000 to recognize the sale of equipment. The net increase in the Buildings and Equipment (Cost) account can only be accounted for, given the decrease already entered, by assuming that new buildings and equipment have been acquired during the period for $135,000.

4.30    The reconstructed entry to complete the explanation of the change in this account would be as follows:

(4a)
Buildings and Equipment (Cost) .. 135,000
   Working Capital (Other
     Uses—Acquisition of
     Buildings and Equipment) .      135,000
Entry recorded in T-account work
sheet.

Likewise, when the change in the T-account for Accumulated Depreciation is explained, there is a net credit change of $10,000 and a debit entry (1a) of $7,000 to recognize the sale. Thus, the depreciation charge for 1981 must have been $17,000. The reconstructed entry to complete the explanation of the change in the Accumulated Depreciation account would be as follows:

(2a)
Working Capital (Operations—
   Depreciation Expense Addback) .. 17,000
     Accumulated Depreciation .....      17,000
Entry recorded in T-account work
sheet.

A revised T-account work sheet for Abbott Corporation incorporating the new information on the sale of equipment is presented in Exhibit 4.6.

## Preparation of the Statement of Changes in Financial Position: Funds Defined as Cash

### Algebraic Formulation

4.31    The effect of various transactions on cash can be seen by reexamining the accounting equation. Recall that the change in working capital was defined earlier as follows:

$$\Delta CA - \Delta CL = \Delta NCL + \Delta OE - \Delta NCA.$$

We can expand this equation by classifying changes in current assets into (1) changes in cash and (2) changes in current assets other than cash. The above equation can be rewritten:

$$\Delta Cash + \Delta CA \text{ (Other than Cash)} - \Delta CL = \Delta NCL + \Delta OE - \Delta NCA.$$

Rearranging:

$$\Delta Cash = \Delta CL + \Delta NCL + \Delta OE - \Delta CA \text{ (Other than Cash)} - \Delta NCA.$$

*Exhibit 4.6*
**Revised T-Account Work Sheet
for Abbott Corporation**

### Working Capital

✔ 45,000

### From Operations

| Net Income and Addbacks | | Net Loss and Subtractions |
|---|---|---|
| Net Income | (1)  20,000 | |
| Depreciation Expense | (2a)  17,000 | |

### Other (Nonoperating)

| Sources | | | | Uses |
|---|---|---|---|---|
| Sale of Equipment | (1a)    3,000 | 10,000 (3) | | Dividends Declared and Paid |
| Long-Term Bonds Issued | (5)  100,000 | 135,000 (4a) | | Buildings and Equipment Acquired |

✔ 40,000

| **Buildings and Equipment (Cost)** | | **Accumulated Depreciation** | | **Bonds Payable** | |
|---|---|---|---|---|---|
| ✔ 100,000 | | | 30,000 ✔ | | 0 ✔ |
| (4a) 135,000 | 10,000 (1a) | (1a) 7,000 | 17,000 (2a) | | 100,000 (5) |
| ✔ 225,000 | | | 40,000 ✔ | | 100,000 ✔ |

| **Capital Stock** | | **Retained Earnings** | |
|---|---|---|---|
| | 100,000 ✔ | | 15,000 ✔ |
| | | (3) 10,000 | 20,000 (1) |
| | 100,000 ✔ | | 25,000 ✔ |

4.32 The left-hand side of the equation, representing the change in cash during a period, must be equal *in amount* to the changes in all noncash accounts. Thus, by analyzing and explaining all changes in noncash accounts during a period, we shall have developed the information necessary to explain the change in cash.

## The Procedure and an Illustration

4.33 We illustrate the construction of a statement of changes in financial position with cash as the definition of funds for the Abbott Corporation for 1981. The steps outlined below parallel those described for a working capital definition of funds.

4.34 **Step 1** Obtain balance sheets for the beginning and end of the period. The comparative balance sheets of Abbott Corporation for December 31, 1980 and 1981, are presented in Exhibit 4.2.

4.35 **Step 2** Prepare a T-account work sheet. First prepare a master account titled Cash. This account will show the change in cash for the period; and after the work sheet is complete, it will show the causes of that change in cash. The master account will show sections ''From Operations'' and ''Other (Nonoperating)'' to separate the two kinds of transactions affecting cash. The master T-account for Cash is another way of expressing the left-hand side of the above equation.

4.36 After the master T-account for Cash has been prepared (as at the top of Exhibit 4.7), the work sheet is completed by preparing T-accounts for *each noncash account*. These accounts are shown at the bottom of Exhibit 4.7 for the Abbott Corporation. The beginning and ending balances in the accounts for the period are entered in each of the separate T-accounts. The T-account work sheet for Abbott Corporation after completion of step 2 is shown in Exhibit 4.7.

4.37 **Step 3** Explain the change in the master Cash account by explaining the changes in the noncash accounts. This step is accomplished by reconstructing on the work sheet the entries originally recorded in the accounts during the period. The reconstructed entries are written in the appropriate T-accounts. Once the net change in each of the noncash accounts has been explained, then sufficient information will have been generated to explain the net change in cash. We start with the supplementary information, which, for the Abbott Corporation for 1981, is

1. Net income is $20,000.

2. Depreciation expense is $10,000.

3. Dividends declared and paid total $10,000.

4.38 The analytical entry to record the information concerning net income is

(1)

Cash (Operations—Net Income) .... 20,000
    Retained Earnings ........... 20,000
Entry recorded in T-account work sheet.

The reason for this entry is the same as that given under entry (1) in the working capital section. Operations are assumed to lead to a provisional increase in cash in an amount equal to net income for the period. This amount must then be adjusted for revenues and expenses not affecting cash.

4.39 The supplementary information about depreciation is recorded in entry (2):

(2)

Cash (Operations—Depreciation
   Expense Addback) .............. 10,000
    Accumulated Depreciation ..... 10,000
Entry recorded in T-account work sheet.

Depreciation is an expense that did not use cash and is therefore added back to net income.

4.40 The supplementary information concerning dividends declared and paid of $10,000 is recorded as follows:

(3)

Retained Earnings ................ 10,000
    Cash (Other Uses—Dividends) . 10,000
Entry recorded in T-account work sheet.

*Exhibit 4.7*
**T-Account Work Sheet for
Abbott Corporation
(Using Cash as Funds)**

**Cash**

| | |
|---|---|
| ✓ 30,000 | |

*From Operations*

| | |
|---|---|
| Net Income and Additions | Net Loss and Subtractions |

*Other (Nonoperating)*

| | |
|---|---|
| Sources | Uses |

| | |
|---|---|
| ✓ 3,000 | |

| **Accounts Receivable** | | **Merchandise Inventory** | | **Buildings and Equipment (Cost)** | |
|---|---|---|---|---|---|
| ✓ 20,000 | | ✓ 40,000 | | ✓ 100,000 | |
| ✓ 55,000 | | ✓ 50,000 | | ✓ 225,000 | |

| **Accumulated Depreciation** | | **Accounts Payable— Merchandise Suppliers** | | **Accounts Payable— Other Suppliers** | |
|---|---|---|---|---|---|
| | 30,000 ✓ | | 30,000 ✓ | | 10,000 ✓ |
| | 40,000 ✓ | | 50,000 ✓ | | 12,000 ✓ |

| **Salaries Payable** | | **Bonds Payable** | | **Retained Earnings** | |
|---|---|---|---|---|---|
| | 5,000 ✓ | | 0 ✓ | | 15,000 ✓ |
| | 6,000 ✓ | | 100,000 ✓ | | 25,000 ✓ |

Next, we explain the changes in the noncash accounts in order of their appearance on the work sheet.

4.41　　The Accounts Receivable account shows an increase of $35,000. The analytical entry to record this assumed information in the work sheet is

(4)

Accounts Receivable　.............　35,000
　　Cash (Operations—
　　　Subtractions)　..............　　　　35,000
Entry recorded in T-account work sheet.

The operations of the period led to increased sales. Not all of these sales resulted in an increase in cash. Some of the increase in sales resulted in an increase in Accounts Receivable. Here, we are defining funds as Cash only; thus not all sales increased funds. Because we start the statement of changes in financial position with Net Income, in deriving the amount of Cash from Operations we must subtract *that portion of revenues not producing cash,* such as the increase in Accounts Receivable.

4.42　　The next noncash account showing a change is that for Merchandise Inventory. That account shows an increase during the year of $10,000. As the operations of the firm have expanded, so has the amount carried in inventory. The analytical entry in the work sheet to explain the change in Merchandise Inventory is

(5)

Merchandise Inventory　............　10,000
　　Cash (Operations—
　　　Subtractions)　..............　　　　10,000
Entry recorded in T-account work sheet.

Abbott Corporation found it necessary to increase the amount of inventory carried to make possible increased future sales. An increase in inventory is ordinarily an operating use of cash. Because we start the statement of changes in financial position with net income, in deriving cash from operations we must subtract from net income the incremental investment in inventories during the year.

The next noncash account showing a 4.43 change is that for Buildings and Equipment (Cost). The entry here and the reason for it are essentially the same as in the earlier example [see entry (4) in the working capital illustration].

(6)

Buildings and Equipment (Cost)　..　125,000
　　Cash (Other Uses—Acquisitions
　　　of Buildings and Equipment)　.　　　　125,000
Entry recorded in T-account work sheet.

Acquisition of buildings and equipment is a nonoperating use of cash.

The next noncash account showing a 4.44 change is that for Accounts Payable—Merchandise Suppliers. As the amounts carried in inventory have increased, so has the amount owed to suppliers of inventory. The analytical entry to explain the increase in the amount of Accounts Payable—Merchandise Suppliers is

(7)

Cash (Operations—Net Income and
　　Additions)　.....................　20,000
　　Accounts Payable—
　　　Merchandise Suppliers　......　　　　20,000
Entry recorded in T-account work sheet.

Ordinarily, one thinks of using cash to acquire inventory. Suppliers who allow a firm to pay later for goods and services received now are effectively supplying a firm with cash. Thus an increase in the amount of accounts payable for inventory results from a transaction where inventory increased but cash did not decrease, which is equivalent to saying that an increase in payables is a source of cash, even if only a temporary one. The increase in cash resulting from increased payables for inventory is an operating source of funds.

The next noncash account showing a 4.45 change is Accounts Payable—Other Suppliers. As the scope of operations has increased, so has the amount owed to others. The analytical entry to explain the increase in the amount of Accounts Payable—Other Suppliers is

(8)

Cash (Operations—Net Income and
   Additions) ....................... 2,000
      Accounts Payable—Other
         Suppliers .....................         2,000
Entry recorded in T-account work sheet.

The reasoning behind this entry is the same as for entry (7), just above. Creditors who permit a firm to owe them more are effectively a source of cash.

4.46    The same reasoning applies to a firm's employees who are owed an increased amount of Salaries Payable, the next noncash account showing a change. The analytical entry to record the increase in Salaries Payable is

(9)

Cash (Operations—Net Income and
   Additions) ....................... 1,000
      Salaries Payable ................         1,000
Entry recorded in T-account work sheet.

Employees who do not demand immediate payment for salaries earned have provided their employer with cash, at least temporarily.

4.47    The final noncash account showing a change not yet explained is Bonds Payable. It shows a net increase of $100,000 for the year. The analytical entry in the T-account work sheet to explain the change in bonds payable is

(10)

Cash (Other Sources—Long-Term
   Bond Issue) ................. 100,000
      Bonds Payable .............         100,000

4.48    The explanation of this entry is the same as for entry (5) in the working capital illustration.

Exhibit 4.8 presents the T-account work sheet for a cash-only definition of funds for Abbott Corporation for 1981. All changes in the noncash T-accounts have been explained with the 10 entries. If the work is correct, the causes of the change in the Cash account have been presented in the entries in the master Cash account.

4.49    **Step 4** The final step is the preparation of a formal statement of changes in financial po-

sition. The statement for Abbott Corporation using cash as the definition of funds is presented in Exhibit 4.9. It is prepared directly from the information provided in the master T-account for Cash in the completed work sheet.

## Funds Defined as All Financial Resources

Accounting Principles Board *Opinion No.*   4.50
*19* requires that published statements of changes in financial position use "all financial resources" as the definition of funds. To understand the rationale for this broad definition of funds, consider the following transactions.

**1.** A building is acquired by assuming a long-term mortgage on the property.

**2.** Capital stock is issued in exchange for land.

**3.** Convertible bonds or convertible preferred stocks are converted into, or exchanged for, common stock.

Each of these transactions affects the asset   4.51
and/or equity structure of the firm. There is no effect, however, on either working capital or cash. If funds were defined as either working capital or cash, these transactions would not normally be disclosed. APB *Opinion No. 19* requires that transactions of this nature be disclosed as both a source and a use of funds in equal dollar amounts *regardless of the definition of funds otherwise used in the statement.* Disclosure of these transactions follows a *dual transaction assumption.* Each transaction is assumed to occur in two steps and to flow through the Cash account as an intermediate step. Thus, cash is received upon assumption of a long-term mortgage and the cash is then used to acquire the building. Common stock is issued for cash and the proceeds used to redeem convertible bonds or convertible preferred stock. In Chapter 2, Exhibit 2.5 illustrates the required disclosures for transactions of this nature.

Note that the transactions of concern are   4.52

*Exhibit 4.8*
**T-Account Work Sheet for**
**Abbott Corporation**
**(Using Cash as Funds)**

### Cash

✓ 30,000

#### From Operations

| Net Income and Additions | | | | | Net Loss and Subtractions |
|---|---|---|---|---|---|
| Net Income | (1) | 20,000 | 35,000 | (4) | Increased Accounts Receivable |
| Depreciation Expense | (2) | 10,000 | 10,000 | (5) | Increased Merchandise Inventory |
| Increased Accounts Payable to Merchandise Suppliers | (7) | 20,000 | | | |
| Increased Accounts Payable to Other Suppliers | (8) | 2,000 | | | |
| Increased Salaries Payable | (9) | 1,000 | | | |

#### Other (Nonoperating)

| Sources | | | | | Uses |
|---|---|---|---|---|---|
| Long-Term Bonds Issued | (10) | 100,000 | 10,000 | (3) | Dividends Declared and Paid |
| | | | 125,000 | (6) | Buildings and Equipment Acquired |

✓ 3,000

| **Accounts Receivable** | |
|---|---|
| ✓ 20,000 | |
| (4) 35,000 | |
| ✓ 55,000 | |

| **Merchandise Inventory** | |
|---|---|
| ✓ 40,000 | |
| (5) 10,000 | |
| ✓ 50,000 | |

| **Buildings and Equipment (Cost)** | |
|---|---|
| ✓ 100,000 | |
| (6) 125,000 | |
| ✓ 225,000 | |

| **Accumulated Depreciation** | |
|---|---|
| | 30,000 ✓ |
| | 10,000 (2) |
| | 40,000 ✓ |

| **Accounts Payable— Merchandise Suppliers** | |
|---|---|
| | 30,000 ✓ |
| | 20,000 (7) |
| | 50,000 ✓ |

| **Accounts Payable— Other Suppliers** | |
|---|---|
| | 10,000 ✓ |
| | 2,000 (8) |
| | 12,000 ✓ |

| **Salaries Payable** | |
|---|---|
| | 5,000 ✓ |
| | 1,000 (9) |
| | 6,000 ✓ |

| **Bonds Payable** | |
|---|---|
| | 0 ✓ |
| | 100,000 (10) |
| | 100,000 ✓ |

| **Retained Earnings** | |
|---|---|
| | 15,000 ✓ |
| (3) 10,000 | 20,000 (1) |
| | 25,000 ✓ |

*Exhibit 4.9*
**Abbott Corporation**
**Statement of Changes in**
**Financial Position**
**Cash Definition of Funds**
**for the Year 1981**

**Sources of Cash**
*Operations:*

| | | |
|---|---|---|
| Net Income ................................................. | $20,000 | |
| Additions: | | |
| Depreciation Expense Not Using Cash ................................... | 10,000 | |
| Increased Accounts Payable | | |
| To Suppliers of Merchandise ......................................... | 20,000 | |
| To Other Suppliers ................................................. | 2,000 | |
| Increased Salaries Payable .......................................... | 1,000 | |
| Subtractions: | | |
| Increased Accounts Receivable ...................................... | (35,000) | |
| Increased Merchandise Inventory ....................................... | (10,000) | |
| Total Sources from Operations ............................................. | | $ 8,000 |
| *Nonoperating Sources:* | | |
| Proceeds of Long-Term Bond Issue ...................................... | | 100,000 |
| Total Sources of Cash .................................................. | | $108,000 |

**Uses of Cash**

| | | |
|---|---|---|
| Dividends .......................................... | | $ 10,000 |
| Acquisition of Buildings and Equipment ..................................... | | 125,000 |
| Total Nonoperating Uses of Cash ............................................. | | $135,000 |
| Net (Decrease) in Cash for Year: Sources − Uses ........................... | | ($ 27,000) |
| Net (Decrease) in Cash Account for Year: From Balance Sheet ........................................................... | | ($ 27,000) |

those involving only nonworking capital accounts. In preparing a T-account work sheet, these transactions should be recorded in the work sheet following a dual transaction assumption. When the actual statement is prepared, these transactions are then shown as sources and uses of funds (Working Capital, Cash, or Other accounts). Thus, use of the all-financial-resources definition of funds simply means that transactions involving only nonworking capital accounts are disclosed along with those affecting the primary definition of funds.

## Summary

4.53 The preparation of the statement of changes in financial position takes place at the end of an accounting period. Four essential steps are involved:

1. Select a definition of funds.

2. Determine the change in the account or accounts that are included in the definition of funds.

3. Determine the change in all other balance accounts other than those in step 2.

4. Reconstruct the transactions that occurred during the period that explain the changes in the nonfund accounts in step 3.

As a result of explaining the changes in nonfund accounts, the change in the fund account(s) in step 2 will also be explained. A formal statement of changes in financial position can then be prepared from the analysis in step 4.

## Appendix 4.1: Columnar Work Sheet for Preparation of the Statement of Changes in Financial Position

4.54 The procedure for preparing the statement of changes in financial position discussed in the text uses a T-account work sheet. In this appendix, we illustrate the preparation of the statement using a columnar work sheet. We demonstrate the preparation of a columnar work sheet using both working capital and cash as the definition of funds. Data for Abbott Corporation for 1981 are used in the illustrations.

### Work Sheet Format

4.55 Refer to Exhibit 4.10, where a columnar work sheet is presented. The rows of the work sheet are arranged in two major sections: (1) account changes and (2) analysis of changes in accounts. The account changes section lists first the account or group of accounts used as the definition of funds. Exhibit 4.10 is the form of work sheet used when funds are defined as working capital. Next are listed all remaining balance sheet accounts (nonworking capital accounts in this case).

4.56 The second section lists the major sources and uses of working capital. Recall that funds are provided by (1) operations, (2) additional external financing, and (3) sale of noncurrent assets. Funds are used for (1) distributions to owners, (2) reduction in external financing, and (3) acquisition of noncurrent assets. These six categories are listed in the "Analysis of Changes in Accounts" section of the work sheet.

4.57 The columns of the work sheet are arranged in two major sections: (1) changes to be explained, and (2) changes explained. Each section has columns labeled "Debit" and "Credit." The first two columns list the amount and the debit or credit nature of the change in each account or group of accounts listed under account changes. The net change in all working capital accounts is entered as a single amount (debit change if

working capital increased during the period: credit change if working capital decreased). The changes in the nonworking capital accounts during the period are entered next. The total amount of debit changes should equal the total amount of credit changes.

4.58 Most of the time required in preparing a columnar work sheet goes into completing the third and fourth columns. These columns serve two functions: (1) to explain the changes in all nonworking capital accounts, and (2) to provide detailed information explaining the change in working capital.

4.59 Portions of each of the columns in the work sheet are shaded to indicate that amounts are not entered in these sections. Once you become familiar with the format of the work sheet, it will not be necessary to shade the various sections each time a problem is worked.

### Preparation of Work Sheet: Working Capital Definition of Funds

4.60 The steps in completing the work sheet are described and illustrated below. Data for Abbott Corporation for 1981 as presented in the text are used in the illustrations.

4.61 **1.** Enter the net change in each balance sheet account or group of accounts in the "Changes to Be Explained" columns. Exhibit 4.2 lists the amounts in each balance sheet account of Abbott Corporation at the beginning and end of 1981. The net changes in these accounts are calculated and entered in the first two columns of Exhibit 4.11. Working capital was $45,000 (= $90,000 − $45,000) at the beginning of the year and $40,000 (= $108,000 − $68,000) at the end of the year. This change represents a decrease, or credit change, in working capital of $5,000. The debit change of $125,000 is equal to the sum of the credit changes of $125,000.

**2.** Prepare work sheet entries that explain the changes in each nonworking capital account. Each of these entries will generally also involve a debit or credit in the "Analysis of Changes in Accounts" section of the work sheet. These entries are merely reconstruc-

*Exhibit 4.10*
**Columnar Work Sheet Format**

| | Changes to Be Explained | | Changes Explained | |
|---|---|---|---|---|
| | **Debit** | **Credit** | **Debit** | **Credit** |
| **Account Changes** | | | | |
| Working Capital . . . . . . . . . . . . . . . . . . . . | | | ///// | ///// |
| **Nonworking, Capital Accounts** | | | | |
| Buildings and Equipment . . . . . . . . . . . . . | | | | |
| Accumulated Depreciation . . . . . . . . . . . | | | | |
| Bonds Payable . . . . . . . . . . . . . . . . . . . . . | | | | |
| Capital Stock . . . . . . . . . . . . . . . . . . . . . . | | | | |
| Retained Earnings . . . . . . . . . . . . . . . . . | | | | |
| **Analysis of Changes in Accounts:** | | | | |
| **Sources** | | | | |
| (1) Operations | ///// | ///// | | ///// |
| Addbacks . . . . . . . . . . . . . . . . . . . . . . | | | | |
| Depreciation . . . . . . . . . . . . . . . . . | | | | |
| Other . . . . . . . . . . . . . . . . . . . . . . . . | | | | |
| Subtractions . . . . . . . . . . . . . . . . . . . . | | | ///// | |
| (2) External Financing | | | | ///// |
| Bonds . . . . . . . . . . . . . . . . . . . . . . . . | | | | |
| Stocks . . . . . . . . . . . . . . . . . . . . . . . | | | | |
| (3) Sale of Noncurrent Assets | | | | |
| Land . . . . . . . . . . . . . . . . . . . . . . . . | | | | |
| Buildings and Equipment . . . . . . . . . . . | | | | |
| **Uses** | | | | |
| (1) Distribution to Owners . . . . . . . . . . . . . . . | | | ///// | |
| (2) Reduction in Financing | | | | |
| Bonds . . . . . . . . . . . . . . . . . . . . . . . . | | | | |
| Stocks . . . . . . . . . . . . . . . . . . . . . . . | | | | |
| (3) Acquisition of Noncurrent Assets | | | | |
| Land . . . . . . . . . . . . . . . . . . . . . . . . | | | | |
| Buildings and Equipment . . . . . . . . . . . | | | | |
| Total . . . . . . . . . . . . . . . . . . . . . . | | | | |

4.62    tions of entries *originally made during the period and recorded in the accounts.* The process of reconstructing transactions during the period is generally easiest if additional information is accounted for first.

The following information is obtained for Abbott Corporation for 1981:

1. Net income is $20,000.
2. Depreciation expense is $10,000.
3. Dividends declared and paid total $10,000.

4.63    The analytical entry to record the information concerning net income is

*Exhibit 4.11*
**Abbott Corporation Work Sheet – Funds
Defined as Working Capital
for the Year Ended December 31, 1981**

| | Changes to Be Explained | | Changes Explained | |
|---|---|---|---|---|
| | Debit | Credit | Debit | Credit |
| **Account Changes** | | | | |
| Working Capital . . . . . . . . . . . . . . . . . . . . | | 5,000 | | |
| | | | | |
| **Nonworking, Capital Accounts** | | | | |
| Buildings and Equipment . . . . . . . . . . . . . | 125,000 | | 125,000 (4) | |
| Accumulated Depreciation . . . . . . . . . . . . | | 10,000 | | 10,000 (2) |
| Bonds Payable . . . . . . . . . . . . . . . . . . . . | | 100,000 | | 100,000 (5) |
| Capital Stock . . . . . . . . . . . . . . . . . . . . . . | — | — | | |
| Retained Earnings . . . . . . . . . . . . . . . . . . | | 10,000 | 10,000 (3) | 20,000 (1) |
| | | | | |
| **Analysis of Changes in Accounts:** | | | | |
| **Sources** | | | | |
| (1) Operations | | | | |
| Net Income . . . . . . . . . . . . . . . . . . . . . . | | | 20,000 (1) | |
| Addbacks | | | | |
| Depreciation . . . . . . . . . . . . . . . . . . . . | | | 10,000 (2) | |
| Other . . . . . . . . . . . . . . . . . . . . . . . . . . | | | | |
| Subtractions | | | | |
| | | | | |
| (2) External Financing | | | | |
| Bonds . . . . . . . . . . . . . . . . . . . . . . . . . | | | 100,000 (5) | |
| Stocks . . . . . . . . . . . . . . . . . . . . . . . . . | | | | |
| | | | | |
| (3) Sale of Noncurrent Assets | | | | |
| Land . . . . . . . . . . . . . . . . . . . . . . . . . . | | | | |
| Buildings and Equipment . . . . . . . . . . . | | | | |
| | | | | |
| **Uses** | | | | |
| (1) Distribution to Owners . . . . . . . . . . . . . . . | | | | 10,000 (3) |
| | | | | |
| (2) Reduction in Financing | | | | |
| Bonds . . . . . . . . . . . . . . . . . . . . . . . . . | | | | |
| Stocks . . . . . . . . . . . . . . . . . . . . . . . . . | | | | |
| | | | | |
| (3) Acquisition of Noncurrent Assets | | | | |
| Land . . . . . . . . . . . . . . . . . . . . . . . . . . | | | | |
| Buildings and Equipment . . . . . . . . . . . | | | | 125,000 (4) |
| Total . . . . . . . . . . . . . . . . . . . . . . . . . . . . | 125,000 | 125,000 | 265,000 | 265,000 |

(1)
| Sources: Operations (Net | | |
|---|---|---|
| Income) . . . . . . . . . . . . . . . . . . . . . . . | 20,000 | |
| Retained Earnings . . . . . . . . . . . | | 20,000 |

Income is presumed to provisionally increase working capital by an amount equal to net income for the period. Some revenues do not provide working capital and some expenses do not use working capital. Adjustments to net income are therefore required.

The only required adjustment in this case is for depreciation. The analytical entry is

4.64

(2)

| | | |
|---|---|---|
| Sources: Operations (Addback) ..... | 10,000 | |
| Accumulated Depreciation ..... | | 10,000 |

4.65   The entry to recognize the declaration and payment of dividends is

(3)

| | | |
|---|---|---|
| Retained Earnings ................ | 10,000 | |
| Uses: Distributions to Owners .... | | 10,000 |

4.66   Once all of the additional information has been entered in the work sheet columns, it is necessary to make inferences about any remaining unexplained changes in nonworking capital accounts. Buildings and Equipment increased by $125,000 during the year. Without information to the contrary, we must assume that buildings and equipment were acquired during the year. The analytical entry is

(4)

| | | |
|---|---|---|
| Buildings and Equipment ........ | 125,000 | |
| Uses: Acquisition of Noncurrent Assets .................... | | 125,000 |

4.67   The Bonds Payable account increased by $100,000 during the year, suggesting the following entry:

(5)

| | | |
|---|---|---|
| Sources: External Financing ..... | 100,000 | |
| Bonds Payable ............. | | 100,000 |

4.68   All of the changes in the nonworking capital accounts have now been explained. If the work has been done correctly, the net change in working capital should also have been explained in the lower portion of columns three and four. We see:

| | |
|---|---|
| Sources: | |
| Operations ($20,000 + $10,000) ...... | $ 30,000 |
| External Financing (Bonds) ........ | 100,000 |
| Total Sources ................. | $130,000 |
| Uses: | |
| Dividends ...................... | $ 10,000 |
| Acquisition of Noncurrent Assets (Buildings and Equipment) ........ | 125,000 |
| Total Uses .................... | $135,000 |
| Net Decrease in Working Capital ...... | $ 5,000 |

4.69   A formal statement of changes in financial position can now be prepared using the information in the lower portion of the third and fourth columns of the work sheet.

## Preparation of Work Sheet: Cash as Definition of Funds

4.70   Exhibit 4.12 presents a completed work sheet for Abbott Corporation for 1981, using cash as the definition of funds. The general format of this work sheet and the procedures for completing it are similar to those illustrated in Exhibit 4.11, where funds were defined as working capital.

4.71   The principal format differences are in the items included in the "Account Changes" and "Analysis of Changes in Accounts" sections. The account changes in Exhibit 4.12 are separated into two groups: (1) cash and (2) noncash accounts. The adjustments to net income include not only additions and subtractions for items such as depreciation but additions for credit changes in working capital accounts other than cash and subtractions for debit changes in working capital accounts other than cash. We explain these additions and subtractions more fully below.

4.72   The procedures for completing the work sheet are as follows:

1. Enter the net change in each balance sheet account in the "Changes to Be Explained" section. The sum of the debit changes ($170,000) must equal the sum of the credit changes ($170,000).
2. Prepare work sheet entries that explain the change in each noncash account. The first three entries are as follows:

(1)

| | | |
|---|---|---|
| Sources: Operations (Net Income) .. | 20,000 | |
| Retained Earnings ............ | | 20,000 |

(2)

| | | |
|---|---|---|
| Sources: Operations (Addbacks) .... | 10,000 | |
| Accumulated Depreciation ..... | | 10,000 |

(3)

| | | |
|---|---|---|
| Retained Earnings ................ | 10,000 | |
| Uses: Distributions to Owners ................. | | 10,000 |

4.73   Next we make inferences about changes in the remaining accounts. Accounts Receiv-

*Exhibit 4.12*
**Abbott Corporation Work Sheet—
Funds Defined as Cash for the Year
Ended December 31, 1981**

| | Changes to Be Explained | | Changes Explained | |
|---|---|---|---|---|
| | Debit | Credit | Debit | Credit |
| **Account Changes** | | | | |
| Cash ............................ | | 27,000 | | |
| | | | | |
| **Noncash Accounts** | | | | |
| Accounts Receivable ................ | 35,000 | | 35,000 (4) | |
| Merchandise Inventory .............. | 10,000 | | 10,000 (5) | |
| Buildings and Equipment ............. | 125,000 | | 125,000 (6) | |
| Accumulated Depreciation ........... | | 10,000 | | 10,000 (2) |
| Accounts Payable—Merchandise ...... | | 20,000 | | 20,000 (7) |
| Accounts Payable—Other ............ | | 2,000 | | 2,000 (8) |
| Salaries Payable .................... | | 1,000 | | 1,000 (9) |
| Bonds Payable .................... | | 100,000 | | 100,000 (10) |
| Capital Stock ....................... | | — | | |
| Retained Earnings .................. | | 10,000 | 10,000 (3) | 20,000 (1) |
| | | | | |
| **Analysis of Changes in Accounts:** | | | | |
| **Sources** | | | | |
| (1) Operations | | | | |
| Net Income ........................ | | | 20,000 (1) | |
| Addbacks | | | | |
| Depreciation ..................... | | | 10,000 (2) | |
| Credit Change in Working Capital | | | | |
| Accounts (Other Than Cash) ..... | | | | |
| Accounts Payable—Merchandise ... | | | 20,000 (7) | |
| Accounts Payable—Other ......... | | | 2,000 (8) | |
| Salaries Payable ................. | | | 1,000 (9) | |
| Subtractions | | | | |
| Debit Changes in Working Capital | | | | |
| Accounts (Other Than Cash) ..... | | | | |
| Accounts Receivable .............. | | | | 35,000 (4) |
| Merchandise Inventory ............ | | | | 10,000 (5) |
| | | | | |
| (2) External Financing | | | | |
| Bonds ........................... | | | 100,000 (10) | |
| | | | | |
| (3) Sale of Noncurrent Assets ............. | | | | |
| | | | | |
| **Uses** | | | | |
| (4) Distribution to Owners ................ | | | | 10,000 (3) |
| | | | | |
| (5) Reduction in Financing ............... | | | | |
| | | | | |
| (6) Acquisition of Noncurrent Assets | | | | |
| Buildings and Equipment ............ | | | | 125,000 (6) |
| | | | | |
| Total .......................... | 170,000 | 170,000 | 333,000 | 333,000 |

able increased by $35,000. That is, increases in accounts receivable from sales on account exceeded cash collections from customers by $35,000. Because we wish to determine the amount of cash provided by operations, we must subtract this $35,000 from net income (that is, revenues included in the calculation of net income exceeded cash collections from customers by $35,000). The analytical entry is

(4)

```
Accounts Receivable  .............. 35,000
    Source: Operations
       (Subtractions)  ...............        35,000
```

4.74  Similarly, purchases of merchandise exceeded the cost of merchandise sold by $10,000 during the year. This $10,000 must be subtracted from net income because cash expenditures for merchandise exceeded the amount subtracted as cost of goods sold in determining net income. The analytical entry is

(5)

```
Merchandise Inventory  ........... 10,000
       Source: Operations
          (Subtractions)  .............        10,000
```

4.75  The analytical entry to account for the increase in buildings and equipment is the same as before:

(6)

```
Buildings and Equipment  ....,... 125,000
       Uses: Acquisition of
          Noncurrent Assets  ........        125,000
```

4.76  Accounts payable to merchandise suppliers increased by $20,000. Purchases of merchandise exceeded cash payments to suppliers by $20,000. Thus, $20,000 must be added to net income to calculate the impact of operations on cash. The analytical entry is

(7)

```
Sources: Operations (Addbacks) .... 20,000
    Accounts Payable—
       Merchandise Suppliers  ......        20,000
```

Similar reasoning applies to the next two entries:

(8)

```
Sources: Operations (Addbacks)  ...... 2,000
    Accounts Payable: Other  .........        2,000
```

(9)

```
Sources: Operations (Addbacks)  ...... 1,000
    Salaries Payable  ................        1,000
```

4.77  The analytical entry to account for the change in Bonds Payable is the same as before:

(10)

```
Sources: External Financing  ..... 100,000
    Bonds Payable  ............        100,000
```

4.78  All of the changes in noncash accounts have now been explained. The change in cash has likewise been explained as shown below:

| | | |
|---|---:|---:|
| Sources: | | |
| Operations ($20,000 + $10,000 + | | |
| $20,000 + $2,000 + $1,000 − | | |
| $35,000 − $10,000)  ............... | $  8,000 | |
| External Financing—Bonds  ......... | 100,000 | |
|    Total Sources  ............... | | $108,000 |
| Uses: | | |
| Dividends  ...................... | $ 10,000 | |
| Acquisition of Noncurrent Assets: | | |
|   Buildings and Equipment  ......... | 125,000 | |
|    Total Uses  .................... | | $135,000 |
| Net Decrease in Cash  ............... | | $ 27,000 |

4.79  A formal statement of changes in financial position using cash as a definition of funds can now be prepared.

## Questions and Short Cases

**4.1**  Review the meaning of the following concepts or terms discussed in this chapter.

a. Funds flow.
b. Funds defined as working capital.
c. Funds defined as cash.
d. Funds defined as all financial resources.
e. T-account work sheet.
f. Reconstruction of entries originally made during the period.
g. Working capital provided by operations.
h. Cash flow provided by operations.
i. Dual transactions assumption.
j. Columnar work sheet.

4.2 "Time is the critical variable when deciding on the appropriate definition of funds." Explain.

4.3 The text states: "Most accounting systems are designed primarily to accumulate information for the preparation of the income statement and the balance sheet." How might an accounting system be designed so that information for the statement of changes in financial position (using working capital as the definition of funds) could be obtained directly from the accounting system?

4.4 Suggest several reasons why the statement of changes in financial position has been required by generally accepted accounting principles for a shorter period than have been the income statement and the balance sheet.

4.5 Indicate the relationship implied in each of the following equations:
   a. $CA + NCA = CL + NCL + OE$.
   b. $\Delta Cash = \Delta CL + \Delta NCL + \Delta OE - \Delta CA$ (Other Than Cash) $- \Delta NCA$.
   c. $CA - CL = NCL + OE - NCA$.
   d. $CA + NCA - CL - NCL = OE$.
   e. $\Delta CA - \Delta CL = \Delta NCL + \Delta OE - \Delta NCA$.

4.6 A student asked: "Why do I need to make inferences about reasons for changes in balance sheet accounts in preparing the T-account work sheet? If I were preparing a statement of changes in financial position for an actual firm, I would simply look at the general ledger accounts to determine the transactions that caused the change in each account." How would you respond to this student?

4.7 Why is it necessary to prepare a formal statement of changes in financial position even when the T-account work sheet has been correctly prepared and adequately labeled?

4.8 "Whenever a particular balance sheet account has the same beginning and ending balance, it can be omitted from the T-account work sheet." Do you agree? Why or why not?

4.9 The comparative balance sheet of Pratt Corporation showed the following:

| | |
|---|---|
| Property, Plant, and Equipment (Net): | |
| December 31, 1980 | $600,000 |
| December 31, 1981 | $650,000 |
| Mortgage Payable on Property, Plant, and Equipment: | |
| December 31, 1980 | $400,000 |
| December 31, 1981 | $450,000 |

The firm's accountant made the following analytical entry in the T-account work sheet at the end of 1981:

| | | |
|---|---|---|
| Property, Plant, and Equipment | 50,000 | |
| Bonds Payable | | 50,000 |

Is this entry likely to be correct? Why or why not?

4.10 A condensed statement of changes in financial position for Wilson Corporation is shown here:

**Wilson Company**
**Statement of Changes in**
**Financial Position for a Year**

**Part I:**

| | | |
|---|---|---:|
| Sources: | Operations | $250,000 |
| | Issue of Bonds | 50,000 |
| | Sale of Equipment | 10,000 |
| | Total | $310,000 |
| Uses: | Dividends | $ 50,000 |
| | Acquisition of Equipment | 160,000 |
| | Total | $210,000 |
| Increase in Working Capital | | $100,000 |

**Part II:**

Analysis of Changes in Working Capital Accounts:

| | |
|---|---:|
| Cash | $ 40,000 |
| Accounts Receivable | 160,000 |
| Merchandise Inventories | 110,000 |
| Bank Loan Payable | (100,000) |
| Accounts Payable | (45,000) |
| Taxes Payable | (40,000) |
| Dividends Payable | (25,000) |
| Increase in Working Capital | $100,000 |

What additional insights are provided in Part II of the condensed statement about the change in working capital that cannot be obtained in Part I?

4.11 Chapter 3 indicates that the amortization of a prepayment (rent, insurance) is the same in principle as the depreciation of buildings and equipment. Why is the amortization of prepaid insurance treated differently in the statement of changes in financial position from the depreciation of equipment?

4.12 "It is not necessary to prepare a T-account work sheet when funds are defined as cash. We can simply prepare a statement of cash receipts and expenditures directly from the general ledger account for Cash." Do you agree? Why or why not?

4.13 Indicate whether each of the following statements is true or false. When converting "net income" to cash flow provided by operations:
T a. Depreciation expense is added.
T b. An increase in accounts receivable is subtracted.
F c. A decrease in merchandise inventories is subtracted.
T d. An increase in accounts payable is added.
F e. A decrease in salaries payable is added.
F f. An increase in bonds payable is added.
T g. An increase in the allowance for uncollectible accounts is added.

4.14 A firm uses working capital as its definition of funds. In order to comply with Accounting Principles Board *Opinion No. 19*, a dual transactions assumption must be made for certain transactions. These transactions must then be disclosed separately as both a source and a use of funds of equal amount in the statement of changes in financial position. Which of the following transactions would be disclosed separately following a dual transactions assumption?

a. Common stock is issued in acquiring a tract of land.

b. Equipment is acquired on account (payable next month).

c. Common stock is issued to the company's president in exchange for services received.

d. Bonds payable coming due within the next year are reclassified from the "noncurrent" to the "current" liability section of the balance sheet.

e. A tract of unused land owned by a company is exchanged for equipment needed in production.

4.15 Exhibit 4.13 shows a simplified statement of changes in financial position for a period. Nine of the lines in the statement are numbered (1)–(9). Other lines are various subtotals and grand totals; these are to be ignored in the remainder of the question. Assume that the accounting cycle is complete for the period and that all of the financial statements have been prepared. Then it is discovered that a transaction has been overlooked. That transaction is recorded in the accounts and all of the financial statements are corrected. For each of the following transactions or adjusting entries, indicate which of the numbered lines of the funds statement is affected.

*Exhibit 4.13*
**Simplified Funds Statement**
**for a Period**
**(Questions 4.15, 4.16, and 4.17)**

**Sources of Funds**
*From Operations:*

| | |
|---|---|
| Net Income | (1) |
| Additions for Expenses Not Using Funds | + (2) |
| Subtractions for Revenues Not Producing Funds | − (3) |
| Total Funds Provided by Operations | S1 |

*Other Sources:*

| | |
|---|---|
| Issues of Long-Term Debt and Owners' Equity | (4) |
| Proceeds from Dispositions of Noncurrent Assets | (5) |
| Total Other Sources of Funds | S2 |
| Total Sources of Funds | S1 + S2 |

**Uses of Funds**

| | |
|---|---|
| Distributions to Owners (Dividends) | (6) |
| Acquisition of Noncurrent Assets | (7) |
| Retirement of Noncurrent Debt and Equity Securities | (8) |
| Total Uses of Funds | S3 |
| Sources of Funds Minus Uses of Funds = Change in Funds for Year, (S1 + S2 − S3) | T |

**Analysis of Changes in Funds Accounts**

| | |
|---|---|
| Change in Funds Accounts | (9) |
| Increases in Funds Minus Decreases in Funds = Changes in Funds for Year, (9) = (S1 + S2 − S3) | T |

Define funds as working capital. If net income, line (1), is affected, be sure to indicate whether it decreases or increases. Ignore income tax effects.
a. Depreciation expense on cash register.
b. Purchase of machinery for cash.
c. Declaration of a cash dividend on common stock: the dividend has not been paid at the close of the fiscal year.
d. Issue of preferred stock for cash.
e. Issue of common stock for cash.
f. Proceeds of sale of common stock investment, a noncurrent asset, for cash. The investment was sold for book value.
g. Merchandise Inventory is sold for a price in excess of cost, but payment is received in the form of a long-term note receivable.

4.16 Refer to the instructions in the preceding question. Repeat those instructions for the following transactions.
a. Amortization of patent, treated as a period expense.
b. Amortization of patent, charged to production activities (product cost).
c. Acquisition of a factory site by issue of capital stock.
d. Purchase of inventory on account.
e. Uninsured fire loss of merchandise inventory.
f. Collection of an account receivable.
g. Issue of bonds for cash.

4.17 Refer to Exhibit 4.13 and to the instructions in Question 4.15. Now define funds as cash only. Expand the meanings of lines (2) and (3) of Exhibit 4.13 as follows:

**Line (2):** Additions for Expenses and Losses Not Using Cash, for Decreases in Current Asset Accounts Other Than Cash, and for Increases in Current Liabilities.
**Line (3):** Subtractions for Revenues and Gains Not Producing Cash, for Increases in Current Asset Accounts Other Than Cash, and for Decreases in Current Liabilities.

Analyze the effects of the transactions on the funds statement for the period.
a. Use transactions a–g of Question 4.15.
b. Use transactions a–g of Question 4.16.

4.18 (Adapted from CPA Examination.) The statement of changes in financial position is normally a required basic financial statement for each period for which an earnings statement is presented. The reporting entity has flexibility in form, content, and terminology of this statement to meet the objectives of differing circumstances. For example, the concept of "funds" may be interpreted to mean, among other things, cash or working capital. However, the statement should be prepared based on the "all financial resources" concept.
a. What is the "all financial resources" concept?
b. What are two types of financial transactions that would be disclosed under the "all financial resources" concept that would not be disclosed without this concept?
c. What effect, if any, would each of the following five items have on the preparation of a statement of changes in financial position prepared in accordance with generally accepted accounting principles using the cash concept of funds?
(1) Accounts receivable—trade.
(2) Inventory.
(3) Depreciation.

(4) Issuance of long-term debt in payment for a building.

(5) Payoff of current portion of debt.

4.19 The purpose of this problem is to convince you that depreciation expense uses no funds and that depreciation is not a source of funds. To carry out this exercise, get one writing pen, a dollar's worth of change, and a piece of paper. Put 40 cents, the writing pen, and the piece of paper on the other side of the desk and put 60 cents on your side of the desk.

(1) Your balance sheet now looks like the one shown below.

---

### My Balance Sheet as of Now (Question 4.19)

| Assets | | Equities | |
|---|---|---|---|
| Cash ............................. | $0.60 | Contributed Capital ................ | $0.60 |

---

(2) You are about to acquire a *noncurrent* asset, one long-lived writing pen. The pen costs 40 cents.

(3) Acquire the pen by exchanging 40 cents for the pen that is now across the desk. Record the following journal entry:

| | | |
|---|---|---|
| Noncurrent Assets ..................................................... | 0.40 | |
| Cash ........................................................ | | 0.40 |

(4) Acquire the piece of paper, a current asset item, by trading 5 cents for the paper that is now across the desk. Record the following journal entry:

| | | |
|---|---|---|
| Current Asset—Paper Inventory ............................... | 0.05 | |
| Cash ........................................................ | | 0.05 |

(5) Sign your name on the piece of paper you now have with the pen you acquired. (No journal entry is required.)

(6) Because of a sudden surge in your popularity, your autograph has become valuable. Sell your autograph to the other side of the table for 80 cents. Record the following journal entry:

| | | |
|---|---|---|
| Cash ........................................................ | 0.80 | |
| Sales .......................................................... | | 0.80 |

(7) The accounting period is over. Record an adjusting entry to recognize 10 cents depreciation for the period on the writing pen:

| | | |
|---|---|---|
| Depreciation on Noncurrent Assets ............................................... | 0.10 | |
| Accumulated Depreciation on Noncurrent Assets ............................. | | 0.10 |

(8) Depreciation on Noncurrent Assets is, in this case, a cost of work-in-process inventory that is to be counted as part of Cost of Goods Sold. Record the following journal entry to measure Cost of Goods Sold:

| | | |
|---|---|---|
| Cost of Goods Sold ........................................................ | 0.15 | |
| Depreciation on Noncurrent Assets ........................................ | | 0.10 |
| Current Asset—Paper Inventory ............................................ | | 0.05 |

(9) Close all temporary accounts with the following entry:

| | | |
|---|---|---|
| Sales | ............ | 0.80 |
| Cost of Goods Sold | .......... | 0.15 |
| Retained Earnings | .......... | 0.65 |

**a.** Ignore income taxes. Prepare an income statement for the period just ended and a balance sheet as of the end of the period.

**b.** Prepare a statement of changes in financial position for the period just ended. Start with net income and adjustments thereto.

*Note:* Observe that depreciation used no funds not otherwise counted in the nonoperating sources and uses. Funds were provided by selling one autograph. Notice that your funds on hand at the end of the period do not depend on the amount of depreciation on the pen for the period. If this is not clear, repeat parts **a** and **b** assuming depreciation of $0.30 or $0.00 in step **(7)**.

## Problems and Exercises

**4.20**    The comparative balance sheet of Hunt Corporation shows the following:

| | |
|---|---|
| Equipment (Net of Accumulated Depreciation): | |
| December 31, 1980 | $280,000 |
| December 31, 1981 | 500,000 |

The income statement indicated that depreciation expense on equipment was $50,000 for the year. A machine costing $140,000 was sold for its book value of $30,000.

**a.** Prepare an analysis explaining the change in "Equipment (Net of Accumulated Depreciation)" during 1981.

**b.** Indicate how each of the transactions identified in the analysis in **a** would be disclosed in the statement of changes in financial position for the year using working capital as the definition of funds.

**4.21**    The comparative balance sheet of the Kanodia Company showed a balance in the Buildings and Equipment account at December 31, 1981, of $24,600,000; at December 31, 1980, the balance was $24,000,000. The Accumulated Depreciation account showed a balance of $8,600,000 at December 31, 1981, and $7,600,000 at December 31, 1980. The statement of changes in financial position reports that expenditures for buildings and equipment for the year totaled $1,300,000. The income statement indicates a depreciation charge of $1,200,000 for the year and a gain of $53,000 from the disposition of buildings and equipment in the determination of the net income.

Compute the acquisition cost and accumulated depreciation of the buildings and equipment retired during the year and the proceeds from their disposition.

**4.22**    The comparative balance sheet of Clipper Corporation revealed the following:

| | December 31, 1980 | December 31, 1981 |
|---|---|---|
| Convertible Preferred Stock | $100,000 | $ 80,000 |
| Common Stock | 500,000 | 578,000 |
| Additional Paid-in Capital | 300,000 | 329,000 |
| Retained Earnings | 450,000 | 480,000 |

The following additional information is obtained:

(1) Net income for the year was $60,000.

(2) Dividends of $10,000 were declared and paid.

(3) Common stock with a par value of $50,000 was issued for $75,000 cash.

(4) Common stock with a par value of $1,000 was issued to the company's president in place of $1,500 cash compensation. Salary expense was debited.

(5) Common stock with a par value of $7,000 was issued in exchange for a piece of equipment. The equipment could have been purchased for $10,500 cash.

(6) A long-pending lawsuit against the company was finally settled during the year for $20,000.

a. Prepare an analysis that explains the change in each of the four owners' equity accounts.

b. Indicate how each of the transactions identified in **a** would be disclosed in a statement of changes in financial position for the period using working capital as the definition of funds.

**4.23**   The account Bonds and Mortgage Payable increased from $630,000 at the beginning of 1981 to $710,000 at the end of 1981. The following additional information is obtained:

(1) Bonds in the principal amount of $150,000 were issued during the year on the open market for $150,000.

(2) The proceeds of the bonds issued in (1) were partially used to repurchase bonds having a principal amount and a book value of $130,000. No gain or loss was realized on the repurchase.

(3) Equipment costing $100,000 was acquired during the year, with a mortgage assumed for part of the purchase price.

a. Prepare an analysis that explains the change in Bonds Payable during 1981.

b. Indicate how each of the transactions identified in part **a** would be disclosed in a statement of changes in financial position for 1981.

**4.24**   The following items were found in the financial statements of Henson Corporation for the year:

| | |
|---|---:|
| Sales | $360,000 |
| Depreciation Expense | 180,000 |
| Income Taxes | 40,000 |
| Other Expenses | 80,000 |
| Common Stock Issued during the Year | 70,000 |

Compute the amount of working capital provided by operations for the year.

**4.25**   Refer to Problem **4.24** for Henson Corporation. Assume the following changes in working capital accounts other than cash:

| | |
|---|---:|
| Accounts Receivable | $90,000 Increase |
| Merchandise Inventories | 60,000 Increase |
| Prepayments | 10,000 Decrease |
| Accounts Payable | 60,000 Increase |
| Taxes Payable | 15,000 Decrease |

Compute the amount of cash provided by operations.

**4.26**  The income statement of Jensen Corporation for 1981 is shown here:

| | |
|---|---:|
| **Continuing Operations:** | |
| Sales | $ 740,000 |
| Cost of Goods Sold | (320,000) |
| Depreciation Expense | (80,000) |
| Selling Expense | (60,000) |
| Administrative Expenses | (50,000) |
| Income Tax Expense | (70,000) |
| Total from Continuing Operations | $ 160,000 |
| **Extraordinary Items:** | |
| Loss from Expropriation of Plant and Equipment in Chile | $ (80,000) |
| Uninsured Loss of Inventory due to Hurricane | (20,000) |
| Total from Extraordinary Items | $(100,000) |
| Net Income | $  60,000 |

The current asset and current liability sections of the comparative balance sheet were composed of the following:

| | December 31, 1980 | December 31, 1981 |
|---|---:|---:|
| Cash | $  140,000 | $  160,000 |
| Accounts Receivable | 1,265,000 | 1,349,000 |
| Merchandise Inventory | 846,500 | 901,600 |
| Accounts Payable | 1,439,300 | 1,562,900 |

**a.** Compute the amount of working capital provided by operations.
**b.** Compute the amount of cash provided by operations.

**4.27**  Condensed financial statement data for the Calhoun Company are shown in Exhibits 4.14 and 4.15.

Supplementary Information: Equipment costing $7,000 and with $6,000 of accumulated depreciation was sold for $1,000.
**a.** Prepare a T account work sheet for the statement of changes in financial position for the year 1981. Use a working capital definition of funds.
**b.** Prepare a statement of changes in financial position for the year 1981. Use a working capital definition of funds.

**4.28**  Refer to Problem **4.27** concerning Calhoun Company. Work parts **a** and **b**, defining funds as cash.

**4.29**  Condensed financial statement data for the Hill Company for the year are shown in Exhibits 4.16 and 4.17. Expenditures on new Plant and Equipment for the year amounted to $233,000. Old Plant and Equipment that had cost $108,000 were sold during the year. It was sold for cash at book value.
**a.** Prepare an income statement (including a reconciliation of retained earnings) for the year.
**b.** Prepare a statement of changes in financial position for the Hill Company for the year defining funds as working capital. Support the statement of changes in financial position with a T-account work sheet.

*Exhibit 4.14*
**Calhoun Company**
**Comparative Balance Sheets**
**(Problems 4.27 and 4.28)**

| | January 1, 1981 | December 31, 1981 |
|---|---|---|
| **ASSETS** | | |
| Cash | $ 13,000 | $ 16,000 |
| Accounts Receivable | 46,000 | 50,000 |
| Inventory | 72,000 | 71,000 |
| Land | 11,000 | 11,000 |
| Buildings and Equipment (Cost) | 300,000 | 313,000 |
| Less Accumulated Depreciation | (160,000) | (167,000) |
| Total Assets | $282,000 | $294,000 |
| **LIABILITIES AND SHAREHOLDERS' EQUITY** | | |
| Accounts Payable | $ 55,000 | $ 39,000 |
| Notes Payable (Current) | 15,000 | 13,000 |
| Mortgage Payable | 30,000 | 30,000 |
| Common Stock | 110,000 | 115,000 |
| Retained Earnings | 72,000 | 97,000 |
| Total Liabilities and Shareholders' Equity | $282,000 | $294,000 |

*Exhibit 4.15*
**Calhoun Company**
**Statement of Income**
**and Retained Earnings**
**for the Year 1981**
**(Problems 4.27 and 4.28)**

| | | |
|---|---|---|
| Revenues | | $160,000 |
| Expenses: | | |
| Cost of Goods Sold | $80,000 | |
| Wages and Salaries | 15,000 | |
| Depreciation | 13,000 | |
| Income Taxes | 7,000 | |
| Total | | 115,000 |
| Net Income | | $ 45,000 |
| Dividends on Common Stock | | 20,000 |
| Addition to Retained Earnings for Year | | $ 25,000 |
| Retained Earnings, January 1, 1981 | | 72,000 |
| Retained Earnings, December 31, 1981 | | $ 97,000 |

**4.30**   Refer to Problem **4.29** for Hill Company. Work parts **a** and **b** defining funds as cash.

**4.31**   Condensed financial statement data of the Sunder Company for the years ending December 31, 1980, 1981, and 1982 are presented in Exhibits 4.18 and 4.19. The original cost of the noncurrent assets sold during 1981 was $216,000. These assets were sold for cash at their net book value. Prepare a statement of changes in financial position for the year 1981 with *funds* defined as working capital. Support the statement with a T-account work sheet.

**Exhibit 4.16**
**Hill Company**
**Postclosing Trial Balance**
**Comparative Data**
**(Problems 4.29 and 4.30)**

|  | January 1 | December 31 |
|---|---|---|
| **Debits:** | | |
| Cash | $ 52,000 | $ 48,000 |
| Accounts Receivable | 163,000 | 191,000 |
| Plant and Equipment (Cost) | 1,693,000 | 1,818,000 |
| | $1,908,000 | $2,057,000 |
| **Credits:** | | |
| Accounts Payable | $ 76,000 | $ 83,000 |
| Accumulated Depreciation | 506,000 | 564,000 |
| Long-Term Debt | 220,000 | 310,000 |
| Capital Stock | 601,000 | 611,000 |
| Retained Earnings | 505,000 | 489,000 |
| | $1,908,000 | $2,057,000 |

**Exhibit 4.17**
**Hill Company**
**Income and Retained Earnings**
**Statement Data**
**(Problems 4.29 and 4.30)**

| | |
|---|---|
| Sales | $1,326,000 |
| Cost of Goods Sold (Excluding Depreciation) | 923,000 |
| Selling and Administrative Expenses | 243,000 |
| Depreciation Expense | 130,000 |
| Interest Expense | 20,000 |
| Other Expenses | 26,000 |

*Exhibit 4.18*
**Sunder Company**
**Postclosing Trial Balance**
**Comparative Data**
**(Problems 4.31 and 4.32)**

| | 12/31/1980 | 12/31/1981 | 12/31/1982 |
|---|---|---|---|
| **Debits:** | | | |
| Current Assets | $ 580,000 | $ 644,000 | $ 684,000 |
| Noncurrent Assets | 3,232,000 | 3,358,000 | 3,750,000 |
| Total Debits | $3,812,000 | $4,002,000 | $4,434,000 |
| **Credits:** | | | |
| Current Liabilities | $ 162,000 | $ 160,000 | $ 166,000 |
| Accumulated Depreciation | 1,394,000 | 1,440,000 | 1,490,000 |
| Long-Term Debt | 212,000 | 180,000 | 270,000 |
| Capital Stock | 754,000 | 846,000 | 1,028,000 |
| Retained Earnings | 1,290,000 | 1,376,000 | 1,480,000 |
| Total Credits | $3,812,000 | $4,002,000 | $4,434,000 |

*Exhibit 4.19*
**Sunder Company**
**Income and Retained Earnings**
**Statement Data**
**(Problems 4.31 and 4.32)**

| | 1981 | 1982 |
|---|---|---|
| Sales | $1,820,000 | $1,940,000 |
| Interest and Other Revenue | 10,000 | 14,000 |
| Cost of Goods Sold (Excluding Depreciation) | 740,000 | 826,000 |
| Selling and Administrative Expenses | 640,000 | 602,000 |
| Depreciation | 174,000 | 196,000 |
| Federal Income Taxes | 110,000 | 132,000 |
| Dividends Declared | 80,000 | 94,000 |

4.32 Refer to the data in Problem **4.31** for Sunder Company. Prepare a T-account work sheet and a statement of changes in financial position for 1982 using working capital as the definition of funds. Noncurrent assets were sold at their book value. Expenditures on new noncurrent assets totaled $636,000 during 1982.

4.33 Financial statement data for the Current Products Company for the years ending December 31, 1980, and December 31, 1981, are presented in Exhibit 4.20.

Exhibit 4.20
**Current Products Company**
**Comparative Balance Sheets**
**(Problems 4.33 and 4.34)**

|  | 12/31/80 | 12/31/81 |
|---|---|---|
| **ASSETS** | | |
| **Current Assets** | | |
| Cash | $ 175,000 | $ 192,000 |
| Accounts Receivable | 248,000 | 359,000 |
| Inventory | 465,000 | 683,000 |
| Total Current Assets | $ 888,000 | $1,234,000 |
| **Noncurrent Assets** | | |
| Land | $ 126,000 | $ 138,000 |
| Buildings and Machinery | 3,746,000 | 3,885,000 |
| Less Accumulated Depreciation | (916,000) | (1,131,000) |
| Total Noncurrent Assets | $2,956,000 | $2,892,000 |
| **Total Assets** | $3,844,000 | $4,126,000 |
| **LIABILITIES AND SHAREHOLDERS' EQUITY** | | |
| **Current Liabilities** | | |
| Accounts Payable | $ 156,000 | $ 259,000 |
| Taxes Payable | 149,000 | 124,000 |
| Other Short-Term Payables | 325,000 | 417,000 |
| Total Current Liabilities | $ 630,000 | $ 800,000 |
| **Noncurrent Liabilities** | | |
| Bonds Payable | 842,000 | 825,000 |
| Total Liabilities | $1,472,000 | $1,625,000 |
| **Shareholders' Equity** | | |
| Common Stock | $ 846,000 | $ 863,000 |
| Retained Earnings | 1,526,000 | 1,638,000 |
| Total Shareholders' Equity | $2,372,000 | $2,501,000 |
| **Total Liabilities and Shareholders' Equity** | $3,844,000 | $4,126,000 |

Additional Information:
(1) Net income for the year was $186,000: dividends declared and paid were $74,000.
(2) Depreciation expense for the year was $246,000 on buildings and machinery.
(3) Machinery originally costing $61,000 and with accumulated depreciation of $31,000 was sold for $30,000.

Prepare a statement of changes in financial position for the Current Products Company for 1981 with funds defined as working capital. Support the statement with a T-account work sheet.

**4.34** Refer to Problem **4.33** for Current Products Company. Work the problem using cash as the definition of funds.

4.35   Condensed financial statement data for General Electronics Corporation for 1981 are presented in Exhibit 4.21.

---

*Exhibit 4.21*
**General Electronics Corporation**
**Comparative Balance Sheets**
**(Problem 4.35)**

| | 12/31/80 | 12/31/81 |
|---|---|---|
| **ASSETS** | | |
| Current Assets | $262,230 | $302,060 |
| Noncurrent Assets (at Cost) | 483,550 | 511,470 |
| Accumulated Depreciation | (167,230) | (185,710) |
| Total Assets | $578,550 | $627,820 |
| **LIABILITIES AND SHAREHOLDERS' EQUITY** | | |
| Current Liabilities | $ 87,810 | $103,690 |
| Bonds Payable | 97,610 | 84,390 |
| Total Liabilities | $185,420 | $188,080 |
| Common Stock | $150,000 | $150,500 |
| Additional Paid-in Capital | 6,870 | 6,930 |
| Retained Earnings | 236,260 | 282,310 |
| Total Shareholders' Equity | $393,130 | $439,740 |
| Total Liabilities and Shareholders' Equity | $578,550 | $627,820 |

---

Additional information:
(1) During 1981, noncurrent assets originally costing $50,040 were sold for their book value of $6,150.
(2) During 1981, net income was $117,330 and dividends were $71,280.
(3) During 1981, bonds were redeemed for their book value.

From the above information, prepare a statement of changes in financial position for 1981. Support the statement with a T-account work sheet.

4.36   The Quinta Company presents the accompanying postclosing trial balance (Exhibit 4.22) and statement of changes in financial position (Exhibit 4.23) for the year 1981.

Investments, buildings and equipment, and land were sold for cash at their net book value. The accumulated depreciation of the equipment sold was $20,000. Current liabilities were $75,000 at the start of the year and $125,000 at the end of the year.

Prepare a balance sheet for the beginning of the year, January 1, 1981.

*Exhibit 4.22*
**Quinta Company**
**Postclosing Trial Balance**
**December 31, 1981**
**(Problem 4.36)**

**Debit Balances:**

| | |
|---|---|
| Working Capital (= Current Assets – Current Liabilities) | $200,000 |
| Land | 40,000 |
| Buildings and Equipment | 500,000 |
| Investments (Noncurrent) | 100,000 |
| Total Debits | $840,000 |

**Credit Balances:**

| | |
|---|---|
| Accumulated Depreciation | $200,000 |
| Bonds Payable | 100,000 |
| Common Stock | 200,000 |
| Retained Earnings | 340,000 |
| Total Credits | $840,000 |

4.37 Refer to Problem **4.27** for Calhoun Company. Prepare a columnar work sheet for the preparation of a statement of changes in financial position for 1981 using the format discussed in Appendix 4.1. Define funds as working capital.

4.38 Refer to Problem **4.27** for Calhoun Company. Prepare a columnar work sheet for the preparation of a statement of changes in financial position for 1981 using the format discussed in Appendix 4.1. Define funds as cash.

4.39 Refer to Problem **4.33** for Current Products Company. Prepare a columnar work sheet for the preparation of a statement of changes in financial position for 1981 using the format discussed in Appendix 4.1. Define funds as working capital.

4.40 Refer to Problem **4.33** for Current Products Company. Prepare a columnar work sheet for the preparation of a statement of changes in financial position for 1981 using the format discussed in Appendix 4.1. Define funds as cash.

*Exhibit 4.23*
**Quinta Company**
**Statement of Changes in**
**Financial Position**
**For the Year 1981**
**(Problem 4.36)**

**SOURCES OF WORKING CAPITAL**

**A. From Operations**

| | |
|---|---:|
| Net Income | $200,000 |
| Addback for Depreciation Expense Not Using Working Capital | 60,000 |
| Total Sources from Operations | $260,000 |

**B. Proceeds from Issues of Securities and Debt**

| | | |
|---|---:|---:|
| Capital Stock Issue | $60,000 | |
| Bond Issue | 40,000 | |
| Total Proceeds | | 100,000 |

**C. Proceeds of Disposition of Noncurrent Assets**

| | | |
|---|---:|---:|
| Sale of Investments | $40,000 | |
| Sale of Buildings and Equipment | 15,000 | |
| Sale of Land | 10,000 | |
| Total Proceeds | | 65,000 |
| **Total Sources of Working Capital** | | $425,000 |

**USES OF WORKING CAPITAL**

| | |
|---|---:|
| **A.** Dividends | $200,000 |
| **B.** Acquisition of Buildings and Equipment | 130,000 |
| **Total Uses of Working Capital** | $330,000 |

**Increase in Working Capital during the Year**

| | |
|---|---:|
| (Sources Minus Uses) | $ 95,000 |

**Net Increase in Working Capital Items**

| | |
|---|---:|
| (Net Current Asset Item Increases Minus Net Current Liability Item Increases) | $ 95,000 |

# Part Two
## *Asset Valuation and Income Measurement*

# Chapter 5
## Asset Valuation and Income Measurement: Underlying Concepts

5.1 In Chapters 6 through 14, we study the specific "generally accepted accounting principles" applicable to each major type of asset (that is, cash, receivables, inventories, and so on). These chapters discuss the valuation of various assets and the impact of these valuations on the measurement of net income. As Chapter 2 points out, historical, or acquisition, cost valuations dominate the balance sheet and the income statement. In several instances, however, some form of current or present valuation basis is used. The general discussion of asset valuation and income measurement concepts presented in this chapter provides the conceptual base for understanding the specific accounting principles and procedures discussed in the next nine chapters.

## Relationship between Asset Valuation and Income Measurement

5.2 Assets are resources that have the potential for providing future benefits, or services, to a firm. To be recognized as an asset, these future benefits, or services, must be measurable in a reasonably objective manner. The process of applying a quantitative amount to this future service potential is referred to as *asset valuation.*

5.3 Revenues are a measure of the inflow of net assets (increase in cash, receivables, or decrease in liabilities) from selling goods and providing services. Expenses are a measure of the net assets used up, or consumed, in the process of generating revenues. The process of applying a quantitative amount to revenues and expenses is referred to as *income measurement.*

5.4 Asset valuation and income measurement are closely related. Assume, for example, that a firm sold merchandise on account for $100. The merchandise had originally cost the firm $60. The journal entries to record the sale are as follows:

Accounts Receivable ..................... 100
    Sales Revenue ..................... 100

Cost of Goods Sold ..................... 60
    Merchandise Inventory .............. 60

5.5 The amount receivable from customers quantifies the amount of revenue recognized. The acquisition cost of the merchandise inventory sold quantifies the amount of expense recognized as cost of goods sold.

5.6 The relationship between asset valuation and income measurement can be seen algebraically. The balance sheet balances at both the beginning and the end of the period. If the amount for each balance sheet component at the beginning of a period is subtracted from the corresponding amount at the end of the period, we get the *change* in each component during the period as follows:

$$
\begin{array}{l}
\begin{bmatrix}
\text{Assets at} \\ \text{End of} \\ \text{Period}
\end{bmatrix}
=
\begin{bmatrix}
\text{Liabilities} \\ \text{at End of} \\ \text{Period}
\end{bmatrix}
+
\begin{bmatrix}
\text{Contributed} \\ \text{Capital at} \\ \text{End of} \\ \text{Period}
\end{bmatrix}
+
\begin{bmatrix}
\text{Retained} \\ \text{Earnings} \\ \text{at End of} \\ \text{Period}
\end{bmatrix} \\[2em]
\begin{bmatrix}
\text{Assets at} \\ \text{Beginning} \\ \text{of Period}
\end{bmatrix}
=
\begin{bmatrix}
\text{Liabilities} \\ \text{at Beginning} \\ \text{of Period}
\end{bmatrix}
+
\begin{bmatrix}
\text{Contributed} \\ \text{Capital at} \\ \text{Beginning} \\ \text{of Period}
\end{bmatrix}
+
\begin{bmatrix}
\text{Retained} \\ \text{Earnings at} \\ \text{Beginning} \\ \text{of} \\ \text{Period}
\end{bmatrix}
\end{array}
$$

$$
\begin{bmatrix}
\text{Change} \\ \text{in} \\ \text{Assets}
\end{bmatrix}
=
\begin{bmatrix}
\text{Change} \\ \text{in} \\ \text{Liabilities}
\end{bmatrix}
+
\begin{bmatrix}
\text{Change in} \\ \text{Contributed} \\ \text{Capital}
\end{bmatrix}
+
\begin{bmatrix}
\text{Change in} \\ \text{Retained} \\ \text{Earnings}
\end{bmatrix}
$$

The change in retained earnings is usually equal to net income minus dividends. Thus:

$$
\begin{bmatrix}
\text{Change} \\ \text{in} \\ \text{Assets}
\end{bmatrix}
=
\begin{bmatrix}
\text{Change} \\ \text{in} \\ \text{Liabilities}
\end{bmatrix}
+
\begin{bmatrix}
\text{Change in} \\ \text{Contributed} \\ \text{Capital}
\end{bmatrix}
+
\begin{bmatrix}
\text{Net} \\ \text{Income}
\end{bmatrix}
-
\text{Dividends}
$$

Rearranging:

$$
\begin{bmatrix}
\text{Net} \\ \text{Income}
\end{bmatrix}
=
\begin{bmatrix}
\text{Change in} \\ \text{Assets}
\end{bmatrix}
-
\begin{bmatrix}
\text{Change in} \\ \text{Liabilities}
\end{bmatrix}
-
\begin{bmatrix}
\text{Change in} \\ \text{Contributed} \\ \text{Capital}
\end{bmatrix}
+
\text{Dividends}
$$

In the preceding example, assets increased, or changed, by $40 (= $100 − $60), and net income in an equal amount was recognized. We assume in this example, however, that accounts receivable are valued at the amount of cash expected to be collected from customers and that merchandise inventory sold is valued at its acquisition cost. Suppose instead that the merchandise had been valued on the balance sheet at the current cost of replacing it. If, while the merchandise was held, the cost of replacing it increased from $60 to $75, the following journal entry would be made to revalue the inventory:

| | | |
|---|---|---|
| Merchandise Inventory ................... | 15 | |
|     Holding Gain ........................ | | 15 |

The holding gain would be recognized as an element of net income during the period(s) while the inventory was held and its replacement cost increased.

5.7    Assume now that the inventory, recorded on the books at its current replacement cost of $75, is sold for $100. The following journal entries would be made to record the sale:

| | | |
|---|---|---|
| Accounts Receivable .................... | 100 | |
|     Sales Revenue ..................... | | 100 |
| Cost of Goods Sold .................... | 75 | |
|     Merchandise Inventory .............. | | 75 |

Total net income from the acquisition, holding, and sale of the merchandise inventory is $40 [= ($100 − $75) + $15], the same amount as in the case where historical cost valuations are used. The timing of the income recognition and the valuation of the inventory on the balance sheet differ, however, between the two valuation bases.

5.8    The valuation basis for assets can have an important effect on the amount at which assets are reported on the balance sheet and on the amount and pattern of income reported for the accounting periods. In the next section, we consider several asset valuation bases and the related effect of each basis on income measurement.

## Asset Valuation Bases

5.9    A business firm deals in two principal markets: input markets and output markets. It purchases raw materials, labor services, production facilities, and so on from suppliers, employees, governmental units, and others. These goods and services provide the inputs for the firm's operations. After transforming or combining these inputs in some desired manner, the firm sells its finished products or services to customers, who form its output market. A principal aim of business activity is to sell the goods or services in the output market for a larger amount than was required to obtain the various inputs. Asset valuations might be based on either input market values or output market values.

5.10    In addition, because prices change over time, the input or output market values might be based on past prices, current prices, or expected future prices. A combination of these two markets and three time dimensions provides several possible asset valuation bases. Exhibit 5.1 summarizes these bases, which are discussed more fully below.

*Exhibit 5.1*
**Asset Valuation Bases**

| Market | Time Dimension | | |
|--------|------|---------|--------|
|        | **Past** | **Current** | **Future** |
| Input  | Acquisition, or Historical, Cost | Current Entry Value | — |
| Output | — | Current Exit Value | Present Value of Future Cash Flows |

## Acquisition, or Historical, Cost

5.11   The acquisition, or historical, cost of an asset is the amount of cash payment (or cash-equivalent value of other forms of payment) made by a firm in acquiring an asset in its input market. This amount is usually objectively determinable by referring to the contracts, invoices, and canceled checks underlying the transaction, or exchange. Because a firm is not compelled to acquire a given asset, it must expect the future benefits from that asset to be at least as large as its acquisition cost. Acquisition cost, then, is the lower limit on the amount that a firm considers the future benefits of an asset to be worth at the time of acquisition.

5.12   The valuation of assets at acquisition cost generally implies that revenues are not recognized until assets are sold or exchanged in the firm's output market. At this time, an exchange occurs between the firm and its customers that provides a new basis of valuation for the asset received (that is, cash or accounts receivable). Assets that are normally sold (for example, merchandise inventory) are stated on the balance sheet at acquisition cost until the time of sale. At the time of sale, the acquisition cost of the asset is recognized as an expense. Assets whose services are normally consumed in operations instead of sold (for example, depreciable assets) are stated on the balance sheet at acquisition cost until consumption of their service potential takes place. At this time, the acquisition cost of the assets' services is either recognized as an expense (depreciation on selling and administrative facilities) or is included in the valuation of products manufactured (depreciation on manufacturing facilities). When acquisition cost valuations are used, therefore, the principal accounting events recognized are external exchanges in either a firm's input markets or its output markets.

5.13   **Example 1** Assume that Miller Corporation purchased for cash 200 units of merchandise on January 1, 1981, at a unit price of $60 each. Half of the units were sold for cash on July 1, 1981, for $75 each. The other half of the units were kept in inventory for the remainder of 1981. The accounting period is the calendar year. Under the acquisition-cost valuation basis, the only accounting events recognized are the two exchanges: one in the input market and one in the output market. The journal entries to record these events are as follows:

Jan. 1, 1981

| | | |
|---|---|---|
| Merchandise Inventory | 12,000 | |
| Cash | | 12,000 |

To record the acquisition of 200 inventory items at $60 each.

July 1, 1981

| | | |
|---|---|---|
| Cash | 7,500 | |
| Sales Revenue | | 7,500 |

To record the sale of 100 inventory items at a price of $75 each.

July 1, 1981

| | | |
|---|---|---|
| Cost of Goods Sold | 6,000 | |
| Merchandise Inventory | | 6,000 |

To record an expense for the cost of inventory items sold.

5.14   Net income for 1981 is $1,500 (= $7,500 − $6,000). This amount represents the difference between the assets received in the output market and the assets given up in the input market when the items sold were originally acquired. Net income will be a positive amount whenever current selling prices exceed the acquisition cost of goods or services sold (including the cost of services needed to make the sale). Acquisition cost valuations, therefore, provide measures of accountability, or stewardship, for the amount of resources originally given up in input markets.

5.15 Acquisition cost valuations dominate the balance sheet under current generally accepted accounting principles. Acquisition costs are generally used for inventories, prepayments, investments in securities, land, depreciable assets, and purchased intangibles.

5.16 Compared to other valuation bases discussed in this chapter, acquisition cost valuations are relatively objective. Several independent accountants looking at the documents underlying the purchase of inventory items would probably agree on the acquisition cost amount. Acquisition cost valuations have several important weaknesses, however. Changes in the prices of assets while they are held are not recognized as accounting events. Yet these changes in prices affect the ongoing profitability of the firm. The balance sheet amounts for assets will also be out of date, thereby misstating the current financial position of the firm. In addition, the amounts reported for certain expenses (cost of goods sold, depreciation) will reflect these out-of-date valuations. In the determination of net income, revenues based on current prices will be matched with expenses based on older acquisition cost prices. The next two valuation bases discussed overcome these weaknesses.

## Current Entry Value

5.17 The amount a firm would have to pay currently in its input market to acquire an asset that it holds is referred to as the asset's *current entry value* (that is, the amount required to "enter" into ownership of the asset).*

---

*Current entry value can be defined in different ways. *Current reproduction cost* is the cost of replacing the identical assets owned by a firm. The reproduction cost of a 30-year-old steel mill is the current cost of acquiring or constructing a steel mill with identical physical and operating characteristics. *Current replacement cost* is the cost of replacing the service po-

**Calculation of Current Entry Value** In 5.18 calculating the current entry value of various assets, several sources of price data might be used. For merchandise inventory, suppliers' catalogs could be consulted. For manufacturing firms with work-in-process and finished goods inventories, the various factor inputs into production must be identified and the current cost of acquiring each factor must be found. There is likely to be greater difficulty establishing the current input cost of manufacturing overhead components than of direct material and direct labor because of the numerous indirect cost elements involved in the determination.

The current entry value of depreciable as-  5.19 sets is usually more difficult to compute. If there are established second-hand markets, as is often the case for automobiles, furniture, and standardized equipment, the current entry value can easily be found. For specially designed equipment and buildings, however, the current entry value must be estimated using specific price indexes or real estate appraisals. The calculation of the current entry value of depreciable assets requires that the operating capabilities of each asset be defined and then a new asset with similar capabilities be identified. The current cost of the new asset must then be adjusted downward to reflect the inferior condition of the asset owned.

---

tential of assets owned. The replacement cost of a 30-year-old steel mill that produces 100,000 tons of steel per year is the current cost of acquiring a new steel mill with the same output, or productive, capability. The current cost of a new steel mill would be adjusted downward to reflect the used condition of the asset owned.

If a new steel mill were acquired currently, it is likely that the new steel mill would operate more efficiently (that is, use less material, labor, or other factor inputs per ton of processed steel) than the 30-year-old steel mill. The reduced operating costs that would be realized if a new steel mill were acquired are referred to as *cost savings*. The replacement cost of the new asset should be adjusted downward for the cost savings. See paragraph 180, Financial Accounting Standards Board *Statement No. 33*. That statement requires the supplemental disclosure of certain assets and expenses stated at "current cost."

**5.20 Effect on Asset Values and Net Income** Under a current entry value system, assets are revalued whenever entry values change. When entry values increase, the assets are revalued upward and a *holding gain* is recognized. When entry values decrease, the assets are revalued downward and a *holding loss* is recognized.

5.21 Net income under a current entry value system is composed of two elements: **(1)** holding gains and losses that occur while assets are held during an accounting period, and **(2)** an operating margin recognized at the time assets are sold equal to the difference between the selling price of goods or services sold and the current entry value of the goods or services. Thus, both exchanges in the firm's input and output markets as well as changes in entry values are recognized as accounting events.

5.22 **Example 2** Refer to Example 1. Assume that the current entry value of the inventory items was $65 on July 1, 1981, and $68 on December 31, 1981. The journal entries made under a current entry value cost system would be as follows:

Jan. 1, 1981
Merchandise Inventory ........... 12,000
   Cash ..................... 12,000
To record the acquisition of 200 units of inventory at a unit price of $60.

July 1, 1981
Merchandise Inventory ........... 500
   Holding Gain ................ 500
To recognize a holding gain on the 100 units of inventory sold whose entry value increased from $60 to $65 per unit.

This gain is sometimes referred to as a realized holding gain, because the inventory items have been sold. An unrealized holding gain could also be recognized on July 1, 1981, on the 100 units still in inventory. However, because the accounting period is the calendar year, the recognition of holding gains and losses on assets still held is more easily recorded at the end of the accounting period.

July 1, 1981
Cash ............................. 7,500
   Sales Revenue ................ 7,500
To record the sale of 100 units at $75 each.

July 1, 1981
Cost of Goods Sold ................ 6,500
   Merchandise Inventory .......... 6,500
To record the cost of inventory items sold at their current entry value of $65 each.

Dec. 31, 1981
Merchandise Inventory .............. 800
   Holding Gain ................... 800
To recognize the holding gain on 100 units of inventory whose entry value increased from $60 at acquisition to $68 per unit at the end of the period. This gain is sometimes referred to as an unrealized holding gain.

5.23 Net income on a current entry value basis is composed of two elements: **(1)** an operating margin of $1,000, equal to the excess of the selling price (= $7,500) over the current cost of replacing the items sold (= $6,500), and **(2)** holding gains of $1,300 (= $500 + $800) on inventory items while they were held.

5.24 The operating margin is a measure of the firm's ability to set prices sufficiently high to cover the current costs of replacing items sold or services used. If selling prices are not high enough to provide funds for replacing items sold or operating capacity used, then the level of operating capacity may deteriorate. Thus, the operating margin can be used to assess management's accountability, or stewardship, for the maintenance of operating capacity.

5.25 The holding gain (or loss) is a measure of the firm's success in acquiring and holding inventory. Many observers attach less importance to holding gains than to operating margins. They point out that if a firm is to maintain its operating capacity, assets sold must be replaced at the current higher costs. Holding gains do not, it is argued, increase the value of a firm. Opponents point out, however, that a firm which purchases assets early in anticipation of increased acquisition costs and recognizes holding gains will be better off than a firm which delays purchases and therefore has to pay the higher acquisition costs.

5.26 **Current Entry Values and Generally Accepted Accounting Principles** As indicated in the preceding section, acquisition cost valuations dominate the balance sheet. Current entry valuations are sometimes used, however. They enter into the determination of "market" under the lower-of-cost-or-market valuation for inventories. Current entry value amounts are also used to value assets donated to a firm, as when a governmental unit donates land or buildings to a firm as an inducement to locate in a particular area.

5.27    The rapid, and continuing, rise in prices experienced during the last decade has led standard-setting bodies to require disclosure of current entry value data as supplemental information to the conventional financial statements based on acquisition costs. *Statement No. 33* of the FASB requires the disclosure in the annual report to shareholders of the current cost of inventories, depreciable assets, cost of goods sold, and depreciation expense as well as certain other current cost data.

5.28 **Evaluation of Current Entry Values** The major strength of using current entry values is that it provides a measure of a firm's ability to maintain its current operating capacity level. Also, assets are stated on the balance sheet at current costs, rather than out-of-date acquisition costs. The major criticism of using current entry values is the subjectivity involved in determining asset values. Several accountants attempting to determine the current entry value of a specific asset could arrive at widely different amounts.

## Current Exit Value

5.29 Instead of using current entry values, assets might be stated at the amount at which they could currently be sold after deducting any selling costs (the so-called *current exit value, net realizable value,* or *net liquidation value*). In calculating current exit values, it is usually assumed that the assets would be sold in an orderly fashion, instead of through a forced sale at some "distress" price.

**Calculating Current Selling Price** The 5.30 current exit value of assets such as marketable securities and merchandise or finished goods inventories, for which active markets exist, is relatively easy to determine. Likewise, the current exit value for some fixed assets is easily determinable if active markets exist for used machinery or fixtures of the type being valued. Real estate agents might be consulted in determining the current exit value of land and buildings. For partially completed inventory items and specially designed equipment, no second-hand markets exist. Calculating exit values for such items is difficult.

**Effect on Asset Values and Net Income** 5.31 When current exit values are used, assets are *initially* recorded at the amount at which they could be sold, instead of the amount the firm paid to acquire the assets. In perfectly efficient markets, the entry value of an asset should be approximately equal to its exit value at the time of acquisition. For example, the current cost of acquiring common stock of a publicly held corporation should be approximately the same amount (except for brokerage commissions) as the net amount that would be received if the common stock were being sold.

Any change in an asset's exit value while 5.32 it is held is recognized as a change in the valuation of the asset and as income. For example, changes in the exit value of inventory items while they are being manufactured would be recognized as income as production takes place and value is being added. Changes in the exit value of timber while it is growing would likewise be reflected in the valuation of the timber and in the amount of income recognized each period.

The sale of an asset does not give rise to 5.33 income when assets are stated at exit values. The sale merely requires that an entry be made reducing the item sold (merchandise inventory) and increasing the asset received (cash or accounts receivable). Because the item sold is already stated at the amount to be received, no additional income is recognized from the exchange.

5.34 Net income under both an acquisition cost system and a current exit value system will be equal to the difference between the selling price of an item and its acquisition cost. Under an acquisition cost system, all of this income is recognized in the period when an item is sold. That is, output values are substituted for input values only at the time of sale. Under a current exit value system, income is recognized in the period when the asset is acquired and each subsequent period as selling prices change. That is, output values are substituted for input values at the time of acquisition and during each subsequent period.

5.35 The method of asset valuation chosen affects the *timing* of income recognition, but not the total *amount* of income recognized. Throughout the study of accounting, the reader should remember that the methods of accounting for various transactions affect the timing of income but not the total amount. Over long-enough time periods, income is equal to cash in less cash out.

5.36 **Example 3** Refer to Example 1. Assume that the selling price for the inventory items was $62 on January 1, 1981, $75 on July 1, 1981, and $85 on December 31, 1981. The journal entries made under a current exit value system are as follows:

Jan. 1, 1981
Merchandise Inventory ............ 12,400
    Cash ....................... 12,000
    Gain from Acquisition of
        Inventory ................... 400
To record the acquisition of 200 units of inventory for $60 each and to recognize as a gain the difference between current exit value (selling price) of $62 and acquisition cost of $60.

July 1, 1981
Merchandise Inventory ............ 1,300
    Gain from Increase in Net Selling Price ................... 1,300
To revalue the 100 units sold to their

current exit value [(100 × $75) − (100 × $62)] and recognize a gain.

July 1, 1981
Cash ......................... 7,500
    Merchandise Inventory ........ 7,500
To record the sale of inventory.

Dec. 31, 1981
Merchandise Inventory ............ 2,300
    Gain from Increase in Net
        Selling Price ................ 2,300
To revalue merchandise inventory to its current exit value [(100 units × $85) − (100 units × $62)] and recognize a gain.

Net income is composed of an initial gain of $400 at the time of acquisition and additional gains of $3,600 (= $1,300 + $2,300) when selling prices increased during the year.

5.37 The preceding example is overly simple in that the firm was assumed to have only two assets, cash and merchandise inventory. It is more likely that other assets, such as buildings, equipment, and investments in securities, would be held. Because a firm acquires these assets for use, rather than for future sale, the entry value and the exit value *at the time of acquisition* for most such assets should be approximately the same. As these assets are used or held over time, however, the amount at which they could be sold will change. The security investments may increase or decrease in selling price depending on general economic conditions, industry factors, and performance of the particular firm whose securities are held. Selling prices of buildings and equipment will likely change over time as prices increase and as the service potential of these assets is used up. Net income under a current exit value system will include gains and losses on these assets while they are held.

5.38 The two distinguishing characteristics of using current exit values are (1) assets are continually revalued to current exit values each period, and (2) all gains and losses are recognized prior to the time assets are sold.

5.39 **Current Exit Values and Generally Accepted Accounting Principles** In the conventional financial statements based primarily on acquisition cost amounts, current exit values are used infrequently. As Chapter 9 points out, the net selling price of inventory items is used as the upper limit for "market" in determining lower-of-cost-or-market values. Net selling prices are also used in applying the lower-of-cost-or-market valuation method to marketable securities (current asset) and investments in securities (noncurrent asset). Firms involved in growing agricultural products or mining gold sometimes value their inventories at net selling prices, thereby recognizing income prior to the time of sale. When nonmonetary assets are exchanged for other nonmonetary assets (for example, land given in exchange for equipment), the equipment is recorded at the current market value, or selling price, of the land given in exchange.

5.40 **Evaluation of Current Selling Prices** Use of current exit values provides a measure of the firm's ability to maintain the exit, or liquidation, value of its assets. A positive net income amount will be reported only when the exit value of a firm's net assets (assets minus liabilities) increases during a period. Also, assets are stated on the balance sheet at amounts reflecting current selling prices, instead of out-of-date acquisition prices.

5.41 The current exit valuation basis is subject to the same criticisms as using current entry values. The valuations tend to be more subjective than those using acquisition cost, and therefore more difficult to audit. The use of current exit values is subject to several additional criticisms, however. One criticism attacks the rationale for using exit prices. It is argued that assets are acquired so that they can be used in operations. In many cases, selling the assets is not even considered as an alternative. Yet management's performance is judged on an earnings measure that includes changes in exit values. A second and somewhat related criticism is that there may be some specially designed assets that have zero or relatively small selling prices (value in exchange) because of the lack of interested buyers or because the assets are so integrated into permanent structures that removal costs would be very high. These assets may have a significant *value in use,* however, to the firm. Under a current exit value valuation system, such assets would be stated at zero or very small amounts. A substantial loss might have to be recognized upon acquisition of such specialized assets.

## Present Value of Future Cash Flows

5.42 An asset is a resource that provides future benefits. This benefit is the ability of an asset either to generate future net cash receipts or to reduce future cash expenditures. For example, accounts receivable from customers lead directly to future cash receipts. Merchandise inventory can be sold for cash or promises to pay cash. Equipment can be used to manufacture products that can then be sold for cash. A building that is owned reduces future cash outflows for rental payments. Because these cash flows represent the future services, or benefits, of assets, they could be used in the valuation of assets. Because cash can be invested to yield interest revenue over time, today's value of a stream of future cash flows, called its "present value," is worth less than the sum of the cash amounts to be received or saved over time. The balance sheet is prepared as of a current date. If future cash flows are used in the valuation of assets, then the future cash flows must be discounted to find their present value as of the balance sheet date. Appendix B at the back of the book discusses the discounting methodology.

**Calculating the Present Values of Future Cash Flows** To calculate the present value of the future cash flows from an asset, three types of information are required: **(1)** the amount of each future cash flow, **(2)** the timing of each future cash flow, and **(3)** an appropriate discounting rate. For example, assume that half of the inventory items acquired by Miller Corporation in Example 1 were expected to be sold for $7,500 cash (= 100 units × $75) on July 1, 1981, and the other half were expected to be sold for 5.43

$7,500 cash on July 1, 1982. The discount rate is assumed to be 8 percent per year, compounded semiannually, or 4 percent per 6-month period. The present value of these two cash flows on January 1, 1981, is

$7,500 × .96154 (See Appendix B,
   Table 2, 1 period, 4 percent) ........ $ 7,211.55
$7,500 × .88900 (See Appendix B,
   Table 2, 3 periods, 4 percent) ........   6,667.50
     Total ......................... $13,879.05

The first $7,500 cash flow is discounted for one 6-month period at 4 percent. The second cash flow is discounted for one and one-half years at the 4-percent semiannual rate (three 6-month periods).

5.44    Calculating the present value of individual assets entails several problems. One is the uncertainty of the amounts and timing of future cash flows. The amounts and timing can be affected by the introduction of new products by competitors, the rate of inflation, and other factors. A second problem is allocating the cash receipts from selling a single item of inventory to all of the assets involved in its production and distribution (for example, equipment, buildings, sales staff's automobiles). A third problem is selecting the appropriate rate to be used in discounting the future cash flows back to the present. Is the interest rate at which the firm could borrow the appropriate one? Or is the rate at which the firm could invest excess cash the one that should be used? Or is the appropriate rate the firm's overall cost of capital?

5.45 **Effect on Asset Values and Net Income**
When the asset valuation system is based on the present value of future cash flows, assets are *initially* recorded at the present value of the future cash flows expected to be generated by the assets. Any difference between this initial present value amount and the acquisition cost of the asset is recognized as income. In this respect, asset valuation systems based on current exit values and present values of future cash flows are similar. They differ only with respect to the *amount* of income initially recognized. As assets are held over time, the remaining time until cash flows are to be received gets smaller and smaller. The present value of these cash flows, therefore, gets larger and larger. Assets are restated upward over time to reflect this increasing present value. When the cash flows are actually received, the asset will be stated in an amount equal to the cash received. The periodic upward restatement in value represents the interest revenue accruing with the passage of time. Restatement is also required if the estimates of the amount or timing of future cash flows change.

5.46    Net income under a present-value-of-cash-flows system is composed of three elements: **(1)** the initial gain caused by the difference between the present value of the future cash flows and the acquisition cost of an asset, **(2)** interest revenue as the asset is held over time and the future cash flows become nearer, and **(3)** gains and losses due either to changes in the estimated amounts or timing of future cash flows or to changes in the discount rate used.

5.47 **Example 4** Continuing the example for Miller Corporation, we assumed that, on January 1, 1981, half of the 200 inventory items purchased were expected to be sold for $75 cash each on July 1, 1981, and the other half were expected to be sold for $75 cash each on July 1, 1982. Assuming a discount rate of 8 percent compounded semiannually, we demonstrated earlier that the present value of the cash flows on the date of acquisition was $13,879.05. The journal entries made under a present value system are as follows:

Jan. 1, 1981
Merchandise Inventory ....... 13,879.05
   Cash ..................           12,000.00
   Gain from Acquisition of
     Inventory .............          1,879.05
To record the acquisition of inventory at the present value of expected future cash flows and to recognize as a gain the difference between the present value of future cash flows and the acquisition cost.

July 1, 1981

| | | |
|---|---|---|
| Merchandise Inventory ....... | 288.45 | |
|    Interest Revenue ........ | | 288.45 |

To recognize interest revenue for 6 months at 4 percent on the valuation of the items sold ($288.45 = .04 × $7,211.55).

July 1, 1981

| | | |
|---|---|---|
| Cash ..................... | 7,500.00 | |
|    Merchandise Inventory ... | | 7,500.00 |

To record the sale of merchandise ($7,500.00 = $7,211.55 + $288.45).

Interest revenue could also be recognized on the increase in present value from January 1 to June 30 on the 100 units not sold. Continuing our earlier assumption that the accounting period is the calendar year, however, the recognition of interest revenue on these units is postponed until adjusting entries are made on December 31, 1981. The adjusting entry is

Dec. 31, 1981

| | | |
|---|---|---|
| Merchandise Inventory .......... | 544.07 | |
|    Interest Revenue ............. | | 544.07 |

To recognize interest revenue for 1981 at 8 percent compounded semiannually:

| | | |
|---|---|---|
| .04 × $6,667.50 ............... | $266.70 | |
| .04 × ($6,667.50 + $266.70) ..... | 277.37 | |
|    Total ..................... | $544.07 | |

The 100 units in inventory are now stated at $7,211.57 (= $6,667.50 + $544.07). This is the present value on December 31, 1981, of the $7,500 to be received on July 1, 1982, when the items are sold. Information available on December 31, 1981, however, indicates that the selling price has increased from $75 to $85 per unit. The valuation of the inventory must be increased to reflect this increase in future cash flows:

Dec. 31, 1981

| | | |
|---|---|---|
| Merchandise Inventory ......... | 961.52 | |
|    Gain from Increase in Selling | | |
|      Prices ................. | | 961.52 |

To revalue the inventory for the increase in present value of future cash flow arising from an increase in selling price from $75 to $85 and to recognize the resulting gain.

Net Present Value:

| | | |
|---|---|---|
|   $8,500.00 × .96154 ......... | $8,173.09 | |
| Present Value | | |
|   Recorded ................. | 7,211.57 | |
|   Increase in Present Value ... | $ 961.52 | |

Net income for 1981 is composed of (1) a gain of $1,879.05 at the time of acquisition, (2) interest revenue of $832.52 (= $288.45 + $544.07), and (3) a gain of $961.52 arising from an increase in selling price. Net income under a current exit value system, as discussed in the previous section, recognizes all of the difference between the initially expected selling price and the acquisition cost as income at the time of acquisition. Net income under a present-value-of-cash-flows system allocates a portion of this difference to future periods as interest revenue to reflect the interest element implicit in the selling price. 5.48

**Present-Value Valuation Basis and Generally Accepted Accounting Principles** A monetary asset is a claim to a fixed amount of cash collectible at some time in the future. Monetary assets include cash, accounts receivable, notes receivable, leases receivable, investments in bonds, and similar items. Generally accepted accounting principles require that monetary assets with payments extending more than 1 year into the future be stated at the present value of the future cash flows discounted at the market rate of interest appropriate to the obligation at the time it was acquired (referred to as the *historical market rate*).* Any changes in market interest rates after the asset is acquired are not considered in the valuation of monetary assets. (Changes in market interest rates will cause the market value of the obligation to increase or decrease. Under the acquisition, or historical, cost basis of accounting, these changes in market value are usually not recognized.) Short-term monetary assets, such as most receivables from customers, are stated at the amount actually 5.49

---

*Accounting Principles Board, *Opinion No. 21* (1971).

receivable. The remaining time until such receivables are collected is usually sufficiently short so that the present value of the amount receivable and the amount receivable at maturity are not materially different. The discounting process for short-term monetary assets is therefore ignored.

5.50     The accounting for long-term monetary assets is conceptually the same for any sort of item: single-payment note receivable, multi-payment note receivable, lease receivable, investment in bonds, or whatever. The seemingly different account titles used for these various items obscure the common underlying theme for their accounting. This section states the underlying theme and briefly illustrates it. Discussion in later chapters of specific long-term monetary assets is unified by the common theme presented here.

5.51     A clear understanding of the accounting for long-term monetary assets requires some familiarity with compound interest concepts and methods, as presented in Appendix B of this book. The reader is urged to review the materials there to confirm understanding or to study them with some care if this is a first exposure. One cannot master accounting principles beyond an elementary level without a working knowledge of compound interest.

5.52     Exhibit 5.2 illustrates the accounting for five types of monetary assets. Each of these assets involves the receipt of all promised amounts of cash within the first 2 years after the monetary asset is acquired. The market interest rate at the time each monetary asset was acquired is 10 percent per year.

5.53   *Single-Payment, Noninterest-Bearing Note Receivable of $1,000 Due 2 Years from Today*   A firm sold a tract of land costing $600. It received a note from the buyer with a face amount of $1,000 due 2 years from today. This note is called "noninterest-bearing" because there are no periodic payments made between the date the note came into being and the date when it is due. There is also no explicit interest rate stated on the note. The market place, however, implicitly charges this borrower 10 percent per year. The present value of the note on the day received is $826.45. This is the present value of $1,000 discounted for 2 years at 10 percent per year. The note is recorded at its present value and a gain of $226.45 is recognized on the sale of the land. At the end of the first year, interest revenue is recognized equal to the recorded amount of the note at the beginning of the year times the historical market interest rate of 10 percent. Interest revenue for the first year is $82.64 (= .10 × $826.45). This amount also increases the recorded value of the note. At the end of the first year, the note is stated at $909.09. This amount is equal to the amount initially recorded of $826.45 plus interest recognized for the first year of $82.64. The recorded amount of $909.09 is also equal to the present value of the $1,000.00 maturity value discounted for 1 year at 10 percent ($909.09 = $1,000.00 × .90909). During the second year, interest revenue at 10 percent is recognized based on the recorded amount of the liability at the beginning of the second year ($90.91 = .10 × $909.09). This amount is added to the recorded amount of the note. On December 31 of the second year, the note has a recorded value of $1,000.00 (= $826.45 + $82.64 + $90.91). The $1,000.00 face amount of the note is then collected.

*Annual Coupon Bond with 10-Percent Coupons and $1,000 Face Amount*   5.54   In the second example, a firm acquires a bond with a $1,000 face, or maturity, value. This bond pays interest at the rate of 10 percent per year on the face value. The market rate of interest at the time the bond is acquired is also 10 percent. The present value of the future interest and principal payments discounted at the 10 percent market rate is $1,000.00. When a bond has coupon payments equal to the market rate of interest, the bond will have a market value equal to its face value. Interest revenue for the first year is again 10 percent times the recorded amount of the bond at the beginning of the year. The recorded value of the bond is increased in the amount of the interest recognized. It is immediately decreased, however, for the cash received. The accounting in the second year follows a similar procedure.

*Exhibit 5.2*
## Accounting for Long-Term Monetary Assets Based on the Present Value of Future Cash Flows

|  | Single-Payment Note of $1,000.00 Maturing in Two Years | | | Two-Year Annual Coupon Bond—10%  ($100) Coupons | | |
|---|---|---|---|---|---|---|
|  | Amount | Dr. | Cr. | Amount | Dr. | Cr. |
| 1. Compute Present Value of Future Contractual Payments Using Historical Interest Rate on Day Monetary Asset Is First Acquired. Rate is 10.0%. Payment to Be Received |  |  |  |  |  |  |
| (a)  1 Year Hence | $    0.00 |  |  | $  100.00 |  |  |
| (b)  2 Years Hence | 1,000.00 |  |  | 1,100.00 |  |  |
| Multiply Payments to Be Received by Present Value Factors (Table 2) |  |  |  |  |  |  |
| .90909 × (a) | 0 |  |  | 90.91 |  |  |
| .82645 × (b) | 826.45 |  |  | 909.09 |  |  |
| (c)  Total Present Value | $  826.45 |  |  | $1,000.00 |  |  |
| 2. Record Initial Asset and Cash or Other Assets Given Up from Step 1. |  |  |  |  |  |  |
| Dr. Monetary Asset |  | 826.45 |  |  | 1,000.00 |  |
| Cr. Cash or Other Assets |  |  | 600.00 |  |  | 1,000.00 |
| Gain on Sale |  |  | 226.45 |  |  |  |
| 3. First Recording (Payment Date or End of Period): End of First Year |  |  |  |  |  |  |
| (a)  Compute Interest Revenue as Monetary Asset × Historical Interest Rate. |  |  |  |  |  |  |
| Amount on Line 1 (c) × 0.10 | 82.64 |  |  | 100.00 |  |  |
| (b)  Record Interest Revenue |  |  |  |  |  |  |
| Dr. Monetary Asset |  | 82.64 |  |  | 100.00 |  |
| Cr. Interest Revenue |  |  | 82.64 |  |  | 100.00 |
| (c)  Record Cash Received (If Any) |  |  |  |  |  |  |
| Dr. Cash |  | — |  |  | 100.00 |  |
| Cr. Monetary Asset |  |  | — |  |  | 100.00 |
| (d)  Compute Book Value of Monetary Asset |  |  |  |  |  |  |
| Beginning Balance | 826.45 |  |  | 1,000.00 |  |  |
| Add Interest Revenue | 82.64 |  |  | 100.00 |  |  |
| Subtotal | 909.09 |  |  | 1,100.00 |  |  |
| Subtract Cash Received (If Any) | — |  |  | (100.00) |  |  |
| = Ending Balance | $  909.09 |  |  | $1,000.00 |  |  |
| 4. Second Recording: End of Second Year |  |  |  |  |  |  |
| (a)  Compute Interest Revenue as Monetary Asset × Historical Interest Rate |  |  |  |  |  |  |
| Ending Balance on Line 3(d) × .10 | $    90.91 |  |  | $  100.00 |  |  |
| (b)  Record Interest Revenue |  |  |  |  |  |  |
| Dr. Monetary Asset |  | 90.91 |  |  | 100.00 |  |
| Cr. Interest Revenue |  |  | 90.91 |  |  | 100.00 |
| (c)  Record Cash Received (If Any) |  |  |  |  |  |  |
| Dr. Cash |  | 1,000.00 |  |  | 1,100.00 |  |
| Cr. Monetary Asset |  |  | 1,000.00 |  |  | 1,100.00 |
| (d)  Compute Book Value of Monetary Asset |  |  |  |  |  |  |
| Beginning Balance | 909.09 |  |  | 1,000.00 |  |  |
| Add Interest Revenue | 90.91 |  |  | 100.00 |  |  |
| Subtotal | 1,000.00 |  |  | 1,100.00 |  |  |
| Subtract Cash Received (If Any) | (1,000.00) |  |  | (1,100.00) |  |  |
| = Ending Balance | $      0 |  |  | $      0 |  |  |

| Two-Year Annual Coupon Bond—8% ($80) Coupons | | | Two-Year Annual Coupon Bond—12% ($120) Coupons | | | Level-Payment Note Annual Payments of $576.19 | | |
|---|---|---|---|---|---|---|---|---|
| Amount | Dr. | Cr. | Amount | Dr. | Cr. | Amount | Dr. | Cr. |
| $ 80.00 | | | $ 120.00 | | | $ 576.19 | | |
| 1,080.00 | | | 1,120.00 | | | 576.19 | | |
| | | | | | | | | |
| 72.73 | | | 109.09 | | | 523.81 | | |
| 892.57 | | | 925.62 | | | 476.19 | | |
| $ 965.30 | | | $1,034.71 | | | $1,000.00 | | |
| | | | | | | | | |
| | 965.30 | | | 1,034.71 | | | 1,000.00 | |
| | | 965.30 | | | 1,034.71 | | | 700.00 |
| | | | | | | | | 300.00 |
| | | | | | | | | |
| 96.53 | | | 103.47 | | | 100.00 | | |
| | 96.53 | | | 103.47 | | | 100.00 | |
| | | 96.53 | | | 103.47 | | | 100.00 |
| | 80.00 | | | 120.00 | | | 576.19 | |
| | | 80.00 | | | 120.00 | | | 576.19 |
| 965.30 | | | 1,034.71 | | | 1,000.00 | | |
| 96.53 | | | 103.47 | | | 100.00 | | |
| 1,061.83 | | | 1,138.18 | | | 1,100.00 | | |
| (80.00) | | | (120.00) | | | (576.19) | | |
| $ 981.83 | | | $1,018.18 | | | $ 523.81 | | |
| | | | | | | | | |
| $ 98.18 | | | $ 101.82 | | | $ 52.38 | | |
| | 98.18 | | | 101.82 | | | 52.38 | |
| | | 98.18 | | | 101.82 | | | 52.38 |
| | 1,080.00 | | | 1,120.00 | | | 576.19 | |
| | | 1,080.00 | | | 1,120.00 | | | 576.19 |
| 981.83 | | | 1,018.18 | | | 523.81 | | |
| 98.18 | | | 101.82 | | | 52.38 | | |
| 1,080.01 | | | 1,120.00 | | | 576.19 | | |
| (1,080.00) | | | (1,120.00) | | | (576.19) | | |
| $ 0* | | | $ 0 | | | $ 0 | | |

*Rounding Error of $0.01.

5.55 *Annual Coupon Bond with 8-Percent Coupons and $1,000 Face Amount* Unlike the previous case, this bond pays interest of only $80 (= .08 × $1,000) each year. The maturity value is again $1,000. If the market interest rate for this bond is 10 percent, it will have a present value of $965.30. This amount is equal to the present value of $80 discounted for 1 year and $1,080 (= $80 + $1,000) discounted for 2 years. The bond is recorded at its present value of $965.30. Interest revenue for the first year of $96.53 is equal to 10 percent times the recorded amount of the bond at the beginning of the year ($965.30). This amount is again added to the recorded amount of the note. The $80 coupon payment then reduces the recorded value. Observe that interest revenue for the first year is not equal to the coupon payment received, as in the previous case. The note has a recorded value at the end of the first year of $981.83. Interest revenue for the second year is $98.18 (= .10 × $981.83). This amount increases the recorded amount of the note to $1,080.01. The cash payment received at maturity reduces this book value to zero (except for a rounding error of $.01).

5.56 *Annual Coupon Bond with 12-Percent Coupons and $1,000 Face Amount* This case is just the opposite of the preceding one. The coupon rate of 12 percent exceeds the market interest rate of 10 percent. The present value of the $120 interest payments and the $1,000 maturity value discounted at the market interest rate of 10 percent is $1,034.71. Interest revenue of $103.47 (= .10 × $1,034.71) for the first year is less than the coupon payment received of $120.00 and the recorded amount of the note decreases, net, by $16.53 (= $120.00 − $103.47). Likewise, the interest revenue for the second year of $101.82 is less than the $120.00 coupon payment. The recorded amount of the note at the time of maturity is equal to the last cash payment received.

5.57 *Level-Payment Note with Payments of $576.19* A firm sold for $1,000.00 a tract of land costing $700.00. The buyer signed a note agreeing to pay $576.19 at the end of each of the next 2 years. The market interest rate is again 10 percent. The present value of the two $576.19 payments as of the beginning of the first year is $1,000.00. Interest revenue for the first year is $100.00 (= .10 × $1,000.00). The difference between the $576.19 payment received and the $100.00 interest revenue reduces the recorded value of the note. The accounting for the note in the second year follows the same procedures. Such level payments are often used for mortgages and leases.

*The Common Theme* The steps in accounting for long-term monetary assets using the present-value-of-future-cash-flows valuation method are summarized as follows: 5.58

1. Compute the initial present value amount based on the future cash flows and the market rate of interest at the time of acquisition. In some cases, both the initial present value amount and the market interest rate will be known. Sometimes the present value amount will be known and the market interest rate must be inferred. Sometimes, as Exhibit 5.2 illustrates, the market interest rate is known and the present value must be calculated.

   **a.** To compute the initial present value amount, given the contractual payments and the market interest rate, multiply each of the contractual payments by the present value factor (as from Table 2 at the back of the book) for a single payment of $1 to be received in the future.

   **b.** To compute the market interest rate, given the initial present value and the series of contractual payments, find the *internal rate of return* that will discount the series of contractual payments back to their present value. Appendix B illustrates the calculation of the internal rate of return.

2. Record a journal entry debiting the monetary asset and crediting the asset given up (cash, land, and so on) or the equity created

(sales revenue). In Exhibit 5.2, we use the generic term "Monetary Asset" in the journal entry, although in practice more descriptive titles are used. Record gain or loss as appropriate.

**3.** At a contractual payment date or at the end of an accounting period, whichever occurs first, compute interest revenue as the recorded amount of the monetary asset at the beginning of the period times the market interest rate at the time the monetary asset was initially received. Debit the computed amount to the monetary asset, increasing its recorded value, and credit interest revenue.

If a cash payment is received, debit cash and credit the monetary asset, reducing its recorded value. The recorded value is equal to the beginning balance plus interest revenue less cash payments received, if any.

Exhibit 5.2 does not directly indicate this fact, but if you were to return to step **1** at this point and compute the present value of the remaining contractual payments using the historical market interest rate (10 percent in the examples), then that present value equals the recorded value computed after step **3.**

**4.** At each payment date and at each period-end closing date, repeat step **3.** Eventually, when the final payment is made (as illustrated at the bottom of Exhibit 5.2), the entire amount of the monetary asset would have been collected. The remaining amount of the monetary asset is zero.

5.59 As Chapter 15 demonstrates, the accounting for long-term monetary liabilities is the mirror image of that used for long-term monetary assets illustrated in Exhibit 5.2. Where the lender or investor debits a monetary asset, the borrower credits a monetary liability; where the lender or investor credits interest revenue, the borrower debits interest expense. The amounts involved, however, are exactly the same.

5.60 **Evaluation of Present-Value-of-Future-Cash-Flows Valuation System** The present-value approach provides asset valuations that most closely approximate what

economists refer to as the *value in use* of assets. The system has an element of logic in that the valuation method attempts to capture the characteristic that makes a particular resource an asset—the ability to generate future cash flows. Whenever the timing and amount of future cash flows from an asset are not established in a contract or other agreement, there may be substantial difficulties in estimating the cash flow amounts necessary to calculate present values. The present-value method is used primarily for long-term monetary assets where the pattern of future cash flows is established at the time of sale.

## Summary of Valuation Methods

Exhibit 5.3 summarizes the four valuation methods discussed in this chapter. Keep in mind that the asset valuation basis affects the timing of income, but not its total amount. Income over long-enough time periods is cash in less cash out.

5.61

## Valuation Bases under Generally Accepted Accounting Principles

An accounting system could be designed in which all assets are valued using only one of the valuation methods discussed in this chapter. Generally accepted accounting principles, however, use all four valuation methods. In Chapters 6 through 14, we study the specific valuation method(s) used for each asset. To provide a bridge between the general discussion of valuation methods discussed in this chapter and the more specific discussion of asset valuations and income measurement in the next nine chapters, a summary of valuation methods for various assets is presented next.

5.62

**Cash** Cash is stated at its face, or current exchange, value.

5.63

---

*Exhibit 5.3*
### Summary of Asset Valuation Methods

| Valuation Method | Asset Valuation | Income Recognition | Strengths | Weaknesses |
|---|---|---|---|---|
| Acquisition Cost | Assets are stated at acquisition (past input) cost until they are either disposed of in an external exchange or their services are consumed in operations. | Revenues based on current output prices are matched against expenses based on acquisition cost when assets are disposed of or assets' services are consumed. Income measures accountability for historical dollars expended. | Acquisition cost values are relatively objective. | Ignores changes in input prices<br><br>Balance sheet values for assets are out of date.<br><br>Net income is based on matching current output prices against past input prices. |
| Current Entry Value | Assets are stated at current entry value. | Revenues based on current exit prices are matched against expenses based on current entry values when assets are disposed of. Also, changes in the entry value of assets while they are held are recognized as holding gains or losses. Income measures accountability for maintaining current operating capacity. | Balance sheet values for assets reflect current entry values.<br><br>The operating margin (revenues minus expenses based on current entry values) provides information on a firm's ability to maintain its operating capacity. Also, income is based on matching of current input and output prices. | Current entry value amounts are often difficult to determine, particularly for specialized assets. |

---

5.64 **Marketable Securities** A portfolio of marketable securities is stated at the lower of acquisition cost or current market value. Market value is the amount the firm would receive currently if it sold the securities (that is, current exit value). This amount should be approximately the same as the amount it would have to pay to acquire the securities (that is, current entry cost).

5.65 **Accounts and Notes Receivable** Trade receivables, those normally collected within a few months, are stated at the amount of cash expected to be collected. Theoretically, these receivables should be stated at the present value of the future cash flows. However, the discounting process is ignored because the amounts ultimately collectible and the present value of those amounts are not materially different. Long-term receivables are stated at the present value of the future cash flows.

**Inventories** Inventories are generally 5.66

EXHIBIT 5.3 (continued)
**Summary of Asset Valuation Methods**

| Valuation Method | Asset Valuation | Income Recognition | Strengths | Weaknesses |
|---|---|---|---|---|
| Current Exit Value | Assets are stated at current exit value. | Income is recognized **(1)** whenever assets are acquired for an amount smaller than that for which they could currently be sold and **(2)** whenever the current exit value of an asset changes while it is held. Income measures accountability for maintaining the liquidation value of a firm's assets. | Balance sheet values for assets reflect current exit values. | Exit values for specialized assets may be difficult to determine.<br><br>Exit values may be minimal even though assets have substantial value in use.<br><br>Management is evaluated on its ability to maintain liquidation values of assets even though assets were acquired for use rather than for sale. |
| Present Value of Future Cash Flows | Assets are stated at the present value of expected future cash flows attributable to the assets. | Income is recognized **(1)** whenever assets are acquired for a smaller amount than the present value of the expected future cash flows, **(2)** as the assets are held over time and interest revenue accrues, and **(3)** whenever the present value amount changes due to changes either in the amount or timing of cash flow or in the discount rate. | Balance sheet values reflect the present value of the cash flows that provide an asset with service potential. | The amount and timing of future cash flows are often difficult to predict.<br><br>The attribution of future cash flows to particular assets is often difficult to make.<br><br>The discount rate to be used is controversial. |

stated at the lower of acquisition cost or market. "Market" is usually equal to the current entry value of the inventory items. (As discussed in Chapter 9, the calculation of "market" may be more complex.) The Financial Accounting Standards Board requires supplemental disclosure of inventories and cost of goods sold based on current entry values (discussed further in Chapters 9 and 26).

5.67   **Prepayments** Prepayments are stated at the acquisition cost of the services (insurance, rent, and so on) to be received in future periods.

**Investments** Investments in bonds are initially stated at their acquisition cost. This amount is equal to the present value of the future cash flows (periodic interest plus repayment of principal) discounted at the market rate of interest appropriate for the bonds at the date of acquisition. The initial present value amount will usually differ from the   5.68

amount of cash to be received in the future. The amount at which the bonds are stated on the balance sheet is restated periodically to reflect the changing present value of the remaining cash flows.

5.69    Investments in stocks are also stated initially at their acquisition cost. The valuation method subsequent to acquisition depends on the percentage of stock owned. As discussed in Chapter 14, the lower-of-acquisition-cost-or-market valuation method is used if less than 20 percent of another company's stock is owned. As with marketable securities, "market" is equal to the amount that would be received if the securities were sold. If the ownership percentage is greater than or equal to 20 percent, the equity method must be used. As will be seen later, the equity method reflects a combination of the four valuation methods discussed in this chapter.

5.70    **Land** Land is stated at its acquisition cost.

5.71    **Buildings, Equipment, and Other Depreciable Assets** Depreciable assets are initially recorded at acquisition cost. As the services of these assets are consumed, a portion of the acquisition cost is recognized as an expense. Thus, the valuation method might be described as adjusted acquisition cost. The Financial Accounting Standards Board requires the supplemental disclosure of depreciable assets and depreciation expense based on current entry values (discussed further in Chapters 11, 12, and 26).

**Patents, Goodwill, and Other Purchased Intangibles** Intangible assets acquired in external exchanges are initially recorded at acquisition cost. A portion of the acquisition cost is then recognized as an expense each period. Thus, the valuation method might also be described as adjusted acquisition cost. Expenditures made by a firm to develop intangibles internally are usually immediately recognized as expenses, so asset valuation questions do not arise. 5.72

## Questions

5.1    Review the meaning of the following concepts or terms discussed in this chapter.
a. Asset valuation.
b. Income measurement.
c. Input market.
d. Output market.
e. Acquisition, or historical, cost.
f. Current entry value.
g. Operating margin.
h. Realized holding gain or loss.
i. Unrealized holding gain or loss.
j. Current exit value.
k. Value in exchange.
l. Value in use.
m. Present value of future cash flows.
n. Historical market interest rate.

5.2    "During the 1920s and 1930s, the emphasis in accounting was on the balance sheet and asset valuation. Since that time, the emphasis has shifted to the income statement and income measurement." Comment on this statement in light of the discussion in the chapter.

5.3    List the events recognized as accounting events under each of the following valuation bases:
a. Acquisition cost.
b. Current entry value.
c. Current exit value.
d. Present value of future cash flows.

5.4    One of the objectives of financial reporting included in FASB *Statement of Financial Accounting Concepts No. 1* is the following:

Financial reporting should provide information about how management of an enterprise has discharged its stewardship responsibility to owners (stockholders) for the use of enterprise resources entrusted to it. Management of an enterprise is periodically accountable to the owners not only for the custody and safekeeping of enterprise resources but also for their efficient and profitable use and for protecting them to the extent possible from unfavorable economic impacts of factors in the economy such as inflation or deflation and technological and social changes.

For each of the valuation bases listed below, indicate the nature of the stewardship responsibility reported on in light of the financial reporting objective quoted above:

a. Acquisition cost.

b. Current entry value.

c. Current exit value.

d. Present value of future cash flows.

5.5   Indicate the valuation basis (or bases) being described in each of the following cases:

a. Assets are stated at their past entry value until they are either sold or consumed in operations.

b. If there are no changes in acquisition cost and selling prices between the time an inventory item is purchased and the time it is sold, this valuation basis results in reporting all of the income from the purchase and sale transaction at the time the inventory is acquired.

c. Refer to part b. This valuation basis results in reporting the income from the purchase and sale transaction partially at the time the inventory is acquired and partially during the periods while the inventory item is held.

d. Refer to part b. This valuation basis results in the largest valuation of the inventory item on the balance sheet at the time of acquisition.

e. Even if there are no changes in acquisition (replacement) costs or selling prices during the entire current period while an inventory item is held, this valuation basis results in the reporting of income from the holding activity.

f. If there *are* changes in acquisition (replacement) cost and selling price between the time an inventory item is purchased and the time it is sold, this valuation basis results in reporting all of the income from the purchase and sale transaction at the time the inventory is sold.

g. Refer to part f. This valuation basis results in reporting the income from the purchase and sale transaction partially during the periods while the inventory item is held and partially at the time the inventory is sold.

h. Refer to part f. This valuation basis results in the smallest valuation of the inventory item on the balance sheet just prior to sale (assume a period of inflation).

5.6   Distinguish between the following pairs of terms:

a. Historical entry value and current entry value.

b. Current entry value and current exit value.

c. Current exit value and future exit value.

d. Realized holding gain and unrealized holding gain.

e. Operating margin and net income under a current entry value valuation basis.

f. Holding gains under a current entry value valuation basis and interest revenue under a present-value-of-future-cash-flows valuation basis.

g. Gain from acquisition of inventory under a current exit value and a present-value-of-future-cash-flows valuation basis.

h. Value in use and value in exchange.

i. Historical market interest rate versus current market interest rate.

# Problems and Exercises

5.7   Bell Corporation acquired for cash 300 units of inventory on January 2, 1981, for $30 each. At the time of acquisition, Bell Corporation anticipated that 200 of the units would be sold for cash on July 1, 1981, and the remaining 100 units would be sold for cash on December 31, 1981. The following costs and prices were expected to be in effect on various dates:

| Date | Entry Value | Exit Value |
| --- | --- | --- |
| January 2, 1981 | $30 | $32 |
| July 1, 1981 | 35 | 38 |
| December 31, 1981 | 38 | 41 |

The accounting period of Bell Corporation is the calendar year. The interest rate to be used in discounting is 10 percent.

**a.** Assuming that entry and exit values changed precisely as expected, give the journal entries relating to the purchase, holding, and sale of the inventory items using **(1)** acquisition costs, **(2)** current entry values, **(3)** current exit values, and **(4)** present values of future cash flows.

**b.** Prepare a multicolumn income statement for Bell Corporation for 1981, with a separate column for each of the asset valuation bases in **a.**

**5.8** Refer to the example in the chapter in which 200 units of inventory were acquired on January 1, 1981. On July 1, 1981, 100 of these units were sold for $75 each. The remaining 100 units were sold on July 1, 1982, for $85 each. Assume that all information regarding current entry, exit, and present values given in the chapter still apply. Prepare comparative income statements for each of the four valuation bases illustrated in the chapter, showing separately the amounts for 1981 and for 1982. The current entry value at the time of sale of the 100 inventory items sold on July 1, 1982, was $7,400.

**5.9** Madison Corporation acquired for cash 600 units of inventory on January 1, 1981, for $15 each. At the time of acquisition, Madison Corporation anticipated that 300 of the units would be sold for cash on July 1, 1981, and the remaining 300 units would be sold for cash on July 1, 1982. The following costs and prices were expected to prevail on various dates:

| Date | Entry Value | Exit Value |
| --- | --- | --- |
| January 1, 1981 | $15 | $16 |
| July 1, 1981 | 18 | 20 |
| December 31, 1981 | 22 | 26 |
| July 1, 1982 | 25 | 30 |

The accounting period of Madison Corporation is the calendar year. The interest rate to be used for discounting is 8 percent compounded semiannually.

**a.** Assuming that entry and exit values changed precisely as expected, determine the amount of income for 1981 and for 1982 using **(1)** acquisition costs, **(2)** current entry values, **(3)** current exit values, and **(4)** present values of future cash flows.

**b.** Give the journal entries to record the transactions and events relating to the purchase, holding, and sale of these inventory items using **(1)** acquisition costs, **(2)** current entry values, **(3)** current exit values, and **(4)** present values of future cash flows.

**5.10** A firm acquired an item of inventory on January 1, 1981, for $10. The item was sold on December 31, 1982, for $21. The following costs and prices were expected to prevail on various dates:

| Date | Entry Value | Exit Value |
| --- | --- | --- |
| January 2, 1981 | $10 | $11 |
| December 31, 1981 | 13 | 15 |
| December 31, 1982 | 17 | 21 |

The accounting period is the calendar year. The interest rate used for discounting is 10 percent compounded semiannually.

Construct four identical graphs, placing "Asset Valuation" on the vertical axis and "Time" on the horizontal axis. Label the four graphs "Acquisition Cost," "Current Entry Value," "Current Exit Value," and "Present Value of Future Cash Flows," respectively. Plot the change in valuation of the inventory during the 2-year period under each of the four valuation methods.

5.11   (Based on a presentation by George Staubus to the Financial Accounting Standards Board.) Figure 5.1 shows the valuation of an item of inventory over a 2-year period using acquisition costs, current entry values, current exit values, and present values of future cash flows. Changes in entry values and exit values occurred during the two periods precisely as anticipated. The item was sold during period 2. Using the letters shown on the graph, indicate the measurement of each of the following:
   a. Gross profit (= sales − cost of goods sold) based on acquisition costs.
   b. Unrealized holding gain or loss during period 1 using current entry values.
   c. Operating margin during period 2 using current entry values.
   d. Realized holding gain or loss during period 2 using current entry values.
   e. Unrealized holding gain or loss during period 2 using current entry values.
   f. Gain from acquisition using current exit values.
   g. Gain from increase in selling price during period 1 using current exit values.
   h. Gain from increase in selling price during period 2 using current exit values.
   i. Gain from acquisition during period 1 using present values of future cash flows.
   j. Interest revenue during period 1 using present values of future cash flows.
   k. Interest revenue during period 2 using present values of future cash flows.

## Figure 5.1
### Valuation of Merchandise Inventory

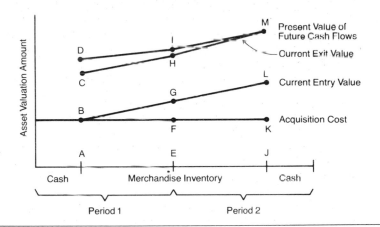

5.12   (Based on a presentation by George Staubus to the Financial Accounting Standards Board.) Figure 5.2 shows the valuation of an item of manufactured inventory over a 2-year period using acquisition costs, current entry values, current exit values, and present values of future cash flows. Changes in entry values and exit values during the 2-year period occurred precisely as anticipated. The item was sold during period 2. Using the letters shown on the graph, indicate the measurement of each of the following:

**a.** Gross profit (= sales − cost of goods sold) based on acquisition costs.
**b.** Unrealized holding gain or loss during period 1 using current entry values.
**c.** Operating margin during period 2 using current entry values.
**d.** Realized holding gain or loss during period 2 using current entry values.
**e.** Unrealized holding gain or loss during period 2 using current entry values.
**f.** Gain from acquisition using current exit values.
**g.** Gain from increase in selling price during period 1 using current exit values.
**h.** Gain from increase in selling price during period 2 using current exit values.
**i.** Gain from acquisition during period 1 using present values of future cash flows.
**j.** Interest revenue during period 1 using present values of future cash flows.
**k.** Interest revenue during period 2 using present values of future cash flows.

*Figure 5.2*
**Valuation of Manufactured Inventory**

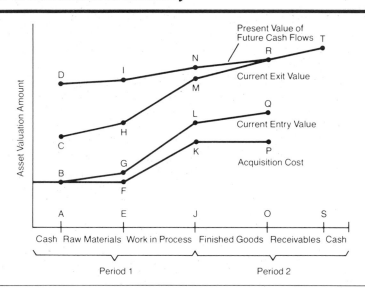

**5.13** The conventional accounting model based on acquisition costs rests on three important concepts:

**1.** Accounting Event—Events and transactions are recognized as accounting events and recorded in the accounts if they have already occurred, affect the financial position of individual enterprises, and can be measured with a reasonable degree of precision.

**2.** Asset—A resource that **(i)** singly or in combination with other resources contributes directly or indirectly to future cash flows, the benefit of which must **(ii)** arise from a transaction or event that has already occurred, **(iii)** accrue to the benefit of an individual enterprise, and **(iv)** be quantifiable or measurable in units of money.

**3.** Expense—A measure of the acquisition cost of goods or services that are either consumed in generating revenues during the current period or that cannot be carried forward as an asset to future periods because any future benefits are not measurable with a reasonable degree of precision.

Indicate whether or not each of the following items gives rise to an accounting event at the time it occurs. If so, indicate whether an asset or an expense is recognized at the time the accounting event occurs.

a. A firm places an order for a special machine costing $10,000. The machine, when received, will be used in manufacturing activities.

b. Notice is received from the manufacturer in part **a** that a $2,000 deposit on the machine is required. A check for $2,000 is issued immediately.

c. The machine in part **a** is received. Installation costs incurred on the machine total $800.

d. The machine acquired in part **c** has a 5-year life, zero estimated salvage value, and is depreciated using the straight-line method. During its first year, the machine is used in producing 4,000 units of product. Of the units manufactured, 1,000 remain unsold at the end of the first year.

e. The remaining 1,000 units in part **d** are sold during the second year of the machine's life.

f. Because of a new fire code, a department store must install additional fire escapes on a building leased from its owner. The fire escapes are acquired for $28,000 cash on January 1. The lease has 7 years to run as of January 1. The straight-line depreciation method will be used.

g. A company manufactures aircraft. During the current year, all sales were made to the government under defense contracts. The company spent $400,000 on institutional advertising to keep its name before the business community. It expects to resume sales of small jet planes to corporate buyers in 2 years.

h. A customer was injured while shopping in the firm's department store. The customer immediately sued the firm for $1,000,000, claiming gross negligence on the part of the department store.

i. Refer to part **h**. A court found the firm guilty and ordered that it pay the customer damages of $600,000. The damages were paid and a claim for the full amount paid is immediately made to the firm's insurance company.

j. Refer to part **i**. A check for $550,000 is received from the insurance company in full settlement of the insurance claim.

k. A company runs a large laboratory that has, over the years, found marketable ideas and products worth tens of millions of dollars. On average, the successful products have a life of 10 years. Expenditures on the laboratory during the current year were $1,500,000.

l. A firm received an offer of $40,000 to purchase a tract of land owned by the firm. The land was acquired several years ago for $15,000.

**5.14** Indicate whether or not each of the following events immediately gives rise to an asset. Assuming that the acquisition cost valuation method is used, state the account title and amount.

a. An investment of $7,600 is made in a corporate bond. The bond will have a maturity value of $10,000 in 4 years.

b. An order for $1,200 of merchandise is received from a customer.

c. Merchandise inventory costing $20,000 is acquired, with payment being made in time to secure a 2-percent discount for prompt payment.

d. A contract is signed for the construction of a specially designed piece of equipment. The terms of the contract are $10,000 down upon signing the contract and the balance of $20,000 due upon delivery of the equipment. Consider this question from the standpoint of the purchaser.

    **e.** A check for $1,500 is sent to an insurance company for insurance protection beginning next year. Consider this question from the standpoint of the company purchasing the insurance protection.

    **f.** A check is written for $1,000 to obtain an option to purchase a tract of land. The price of the land is $40,000. Consider this question from the standpoint of the firm writing the check.

**5.15** Give the amount of expense recognized, if any, from each of the following related events, assuming that the acquisition cost valuation basis and the accrual basis of accounting are used.

    **a.** The purchasing department notifies the stockroom that the supply of 1/2-inch plywood has reached the minimum point and should be reordered.

    **b.** A purchase order is sent to Central Lumber Company for $8,000 of the material.

    **c.** An acknowledgment of the order is received. It indicates that delivery will be made in 15 days but that the price has been raised to $8,400.

    **d.** The shipment of plywood arrives and is checked by the receiving department. The correct quantity has been delivered.

    **e.** The purchase invoice arrives. The amount of $8,400 is subject to a 2-percent discount if paid within 10 days.

    **f.** Upon reinspection, plywood with a gross invoice price of $100 is found to be defective and returned to the supplier.

    **g.** The balance of the amount due the Central Lumber Company is paid in time to obtain the discount.

    **h.** The plywood is sold to customers for $10,000.

**5.16** Assuming that the acquisition cost valuation basis is used and that revenue is recognized at the time goods are sold or services are rendered using the accrual basis of accounting, indicate the amount of expense recognized during March, if any, in each of the following situations:

    **a.** Rent of $1,800 is paid on March 1 for the 2 months starting at that time.

    **b.** An advance of $100 on the April salary is paid to an employee on March 28.

    **c.** Property taxes on a store building for the year of $2,400 were paid in January.

    **d.** An employee earned $900 of commissions during March, but has not yet been paid.

    **e.** The cost of equipment purchased on March 26, to be put into operation on April 1, is $5,000.

    **f.** $800 of supplies were purchased during March. On March 1, supplies were on hand that cost $400. At March 31, supplies that cost $300 were still on hand.

    **g.** Data of part **f**, except that $200 of supplies were on hand at March 1.

    **h.** At March 1, the balance in the Prepaid Insurance account was $4,800. The insurance policy had 12 months to run at that time.

**5.17** Assuming that the acquisition cost valuation basis is used, indicate whether each of the following costs are **(1)** period expenses, **(2)** product costs, or **(3)** some balance sheet account other than those for product costs.

    **a.** Office supplies used.

    **b.** Salary of factory supervisor.

    **c.** Purchase of a fire insurance policy on the store building for the 3-year period beginning next month.

    **d.** Expiration of 1 month's protection of the insurance in part **c**.

    **e.** Property taxes for the current year on the factory building.

    **f.** Wages of truck drivers who deliver finished goods to customers.

**g.** Wages of factory workers who install a new machine.
**h.** Wages of mechanics who repair and service factory machines.
**i.** Salary of the president of the company.
**j.** Depreciation of office equipment.
**k.** Factory supplies used.

**5.18**   Generally accepted accounting principles require that long-term monetary assets be stated at the present value of the future cash flows discounted at the market rate of interest appropriate to a particular monetary asset at the time the monetary asset was acquired. Give the journal entries during 1981 and 1982 for each of the following monetary assets acquired on January 2, 1981. The accounting period is the calendar year.

**a.** Single-payment, noninterest-bearing note of $5,000 maturing on December 31, 1982. The appropriate market rate of interest is 8 percent. The note was received from a customer who purchased a tract of land that had a cost to the seller of $3,000.

**b.** Level payment note with payments of $3,000 on December 31 of each of the years of 1981 through 1983. The interest rate appropriate to the note is 7 percent. The note was received from a customer who purchased a tract of land that had a cost to the seller of $8,000.

**c.** Annual coupon bond with 10-percent coupons ($1,000 total) and $10,000 face amount. The bond pays interest on December 31 of each year and matures on December 31, 1985. The market rate of interest appropriate to the bond is 8 percent. The bond was acquired for cash.

**5.19**   Give the journal entries during 1981 and 1982 for each of the following monetary assets acquired on January 2, 1981. The accounting period is the calendar year.

**a.** Single-payment, noninterest-bearing note of $10,000 maturing on December 31, 1983. The appropriate market rate of interest is 12 percent. The note was received from a customer who purchased a tract of land that had a cost to the seller of $6,000.

**b.** Annual coupon bond with 10-percent coupon ($1,000 total) payments and $10,000 face value. The bond pays interest on December 31 of each year and matures on December 31, 1982. The market rate of interest appropriate to the bond is 12 percent. The bond was acquired for cash.

**c.** Level payment note with payments of $2,000 on December 31 of each of the years 1981 through 1984. The interest rate appropriate to the note is 10 percent. The note was received from a customer who purchased a tract of land that had a cost to the seller of $5,000.

# Chapter 6
# *Cash and Marketable Securities*

6.1 This chapter discusses certain liquid, cash-like, or "quick" assets. Liquidity is essential for business operations. An insolvent company, one that cannot pay its bills and meet its commitments as they mature, will not survive no matter how large its owners' equity. Most companies going into bankruptcy have positive owners' equity on their balance sheets at the time of bankruptcy. One of the largest bankruptcies in history occurred in 1970 when the Penn Central Transportation Company was placed into bankruptcy by its parent holding company, the Penn Central Company. At that time, Penn Central Transportation Company had almost $2 billion of shareholders' equity, including some $500 million of retained earnings. Nevertheless, the company became insolvent because it could not meet "only" a few hundred million dollars in current obligations due at that time.

6.2 Moneylike assets are an important determinant of a firm's liquidity. Cash, marketable securities, accounts receivable, and notes receivable are the principal liquid assets of a business. In previous chapters, we have seen that these assets are *generally* stated at their current cash, or cash-equivalent, values on the balance sheet. This chapter explores in greater depth various inclusion and valuation questions for cash and marketable securities. The next chapter treats accounts and notes receivable.

## Cash

6.3 Cash is the most liquid asset. It is also the most vulnerable because of its susceptibility to theft or embezzlement. In this section, we consider cash inclusions and valuation as well as cash management and control.

### Cash Inclusions and Valuation

6.4 To be included in "Cash" on the balance sheet, items should be freely available for use as a medium of exchange. Included in this category is cash on hand in the form of coins, currency, travelers' checks, and undeposited checks. Cash on hand may be in petty cash or change funds (discussed later). Also included in "Cash" is cash in the bank in the form of demand deposits and savings accounts. Although there are generally certain restrictions on the immediate withdrawal of funds from savings accounts, they are usually considered to be sufficiently available for use as a medium of exchange to be included in "Cash." Rather than show each of the cash items separately on the balance sheet, most firms combine them into a single cash account. Separate accounts should be maintained internally in the ledger for each of the cash items.

6.5 *Accounting Series Release No. 148\** of the Securities and Exchange Commission presents a comprehensive discussion of the various items that may require separate disclosure as part of cash. The items discussed there include cash on hand, unrestricted demand deposits, restricted deposits held as compensating balances, time deposits, certificates of deposit, funds subject to repayment on call, special-purpose funds, funds held in cash accounts for ordinary operating purposes, balances kept in the bank as a form of payment to the bank for various nonlending services, and unused lines of credit. The following discussion reports some of the highlights of *Accounting Series Release No. 148*. Exhibit 6.6 at the end of this chapter illustrates many of these points.

6.6 **Foreign Currency** Foreign currency is included in "Cash" unless there are severe restrictions on a firm's ability to use the currency. For example, foreign currency held by a division located in a country that significantly restricts the outflow of capital would probably not be included in "Cash."

6.7 **Compensating Balances** A compensating balance generally takes the form of a minimum checking account balance that must be maintained in connection with a borrowing arrangement with a bank. For example, a firm might borrow $5 million from a bank and agree to maintain a 10-percent (= $500,000) compensating balance in an interest-free checking account. This arrangement results in a reduction of the amount effectively borrowed and an increase in the interest rate effectively paid by the borrower. Unless compensating balances are adequately disclosed, incorrect assessments of a firm's liquidity can occur.

---

\**Accounting Series Release No. 148*, "Amendments to Regulations S-X and Related Interpretations and Guidelines Regarding the Disclosure of Compensating Balances and Short-Term Borrowing Arrangements," SEC (1973). These rules tend to be followed in reports to shareholders as well as to the SEC.

6.8 Compensating balances are frequently excluded from the Cash account and shown in a separate account. Reports submitted to the Securities and Exchange Commission must separate cash generally available for the payment of corporate debts from cash held in compensating balance deposits whose use is contractually restricted by short-term borrowing agreements. These compensating balance amounts are included among current assets. Exhibit 6.6, appearing later in this chapter, illustrates the required disclosures. Similar compensating balances required by long-term borrowing arrangements should be included under noncurrent assets, preferably Investments. In cases where compensating balance arrangements exist but the firm is not legally precluded from using the cash, the nature of the arrangements and the amounts involved should be disclosed in notes to the financial statements.

6.9 **Special-Purpose Funds** Cash may be deposited in a special bank account and earmarked for a specific purpose. Sometimes management voluntarily sets aside cash to be used for new acquisitions of plant and machinery. Or the firm may set aside cash for the retirement of outstanding bonds in a *bond sinking fund*. Usually, the bond sinking fund will not be under the control of the firm, but under the control of a trustee as specified in the bond contract. Cash that is earmarked, either voluntarily or by contract, for the acquisition of long-term assets or the retirement of long-term debt is not shown as part of Cash in the balance sheet. Indeed, such funds are not even shown as current assets but usually appear instead in the Investments section of the balance sheet. Chapter 14 discusses such funds in more detail.

6.10 **Time Deposits and Certificates of Deposit** If a firm decides that it will not require the use of funds for some length of time, it may place its funds in a time deposit, or it may purchase a *certificate of deposit* from a bank. A time deposit is known in lay language as a "savings account." The bank pays interest on funds left in time deposits; the funds may be somewhat more difficult to use than funds in demand deposits. A certificate of deposit is like a time deposit except that the firm putting its funds into such a certificate promises not to withdraw the funds for a specified period while the bank promises to pay a higher interest rate than it does on time deposits. In an emergency, the firm can cash in the certificate before maturity, but it must pay a penalty for the privilege. The rules for prematurely cashing in certificates of deposit are, by current law, always enforced. These certificates should therefore be shown on the balance sheet on a line labeled Certificates of Deposit, separate from Cash, but this is not always done in practice.

6.11    Once a determination is made as to which items are to be included in "Cash," there are few valuation problems. Cash is normally stated at its face amount. Foreign currency must be translated to its U.S. dollar-equivalent amount using the exchange rate in effect on the date of the balance sheet.

6.12    **Unused Lines of Credit** Firms will often arrange with a bank for the bank to lend funds when the firm asks. The bank promises to lend funds under prearranged conditions at the firm's request. The firm may pay the bank a fee, such as one-half of one percent per year, for amounts made available under lines of credit but that the firm has not used. Such payments are classified as Interest Expense on the firm's income statement. Unused lines of credit are a form of liquidity about which investors may wish to know, and SEC *ASR No. 148* requires that they be disclosed in notes to the financial statements. Lines of credit are sometimes extended by lenders subject to conditions that the potential borrower maintain certain standards of creditworthiness. A line of credit subject to maintenance of creditworthiness does not, therefore, guarantee liquidity. *ASR No. 148* requires that lines of credit should contain a statement of the conditions under which the credit may be withdrawn.

## Cash Management

6.13    The management of cash involves two primary considerations. First, management must establish a system of internal controls to ensure that cash is properly safeguarded from theft or embezzlement. Typical internal control procedures include the separation of duties of individuals handling various cash receipt and disbursement tasks, the immediate depositing of cash receipts, the disbursement of cash only by authorized checks, and the regular preparation of bank account reconciliations.

6.14    Management is also concerned that cash balances be regulated in such a way that neither too much nor too little cash is available at any time. Cash on hand or in checking accounts generally does not earn interest. In fact, during inflationary periods, idle cash loses purchasing power and therefore decreases in real value. A firm does not want to maintain excessive cash balances. On the other hand, a firm does not want to find itself so short of cash that it is unable to meet its obligations as they become due or unable to take advantage of cash discounts.

6.15    One effective tool in cash management is the preparation of a weekly or monthly budget of cash receipts and disbursements. Such a budget will indicate both the time and amount when excess cash will be available for investment or when additional borrowing will become necessary.

## Controlling Cash

6.16    The system for controlling cash receipts should be designed to ensure that all money collected for a firm ends up in the firm's treasury. In most businesses, collections are received primarily through the mail in the form of bank checks, or in currency and coins from cash sales. The need to control the collection of currency and coins is obvious. All collections for cash sales should be recorded promptly, either in a cash register or some other device that both records the receipt and locks in the amount of the collection. Other kinds of collections are more susceptible to being mishandled because they occur less frequently. These include receipts from the sale of assets not normally intended to be sold, receipts from dividends and interest on investments, collections on notes receivable, proceeds of bank loans, and proceeds of stock or bond issues.

6.17 One possible way to provide effective control of cash receipts, once their collection is recorded, would be to maintain duplicate sets of records, each under separate supervision. But doing so would be expensive. The business need not undertake this expensive control device, however, if it **(1)** designs its cash-handling techniques so that the monthly statement received from its bank effectively serves as a duplicate record and **(2)** separates the functions of cash handling and record keeping. To use the bank statement as an effective cash-controlling device requires prompt depositing of all receipts and making all disbursements by check.

6.18 **Cash on Hand—Change Funds** Wherever cash in the form of currency and coins is received directly from customers, as in retail stores and theaters or by delivery truck drivers, a supply of currency and coins must be available for making change. It is possible to record such cash in an account such as Undeposited Cash or Cash on Hand separate from Cash in Bank. Controlling currency and coins used for making change is simpler, however, when specific accounts are opened for this purpose. Such accounts will show the amount that should be available for making change; periodic review of the actual amount of cash in change funds is then straightforward. Only in this section of this chapter do we draw a distinction between Cash on Hand and Cash in Bank. In the rest of the book, the context makes clear the account to which "Cash" refers. Usually, "Cash" means "Cash in Bank."

6.19 The entry to establish a change fund of $500 would be

Change Fund .......................... 500
    Cash in Bank ..................... 500

A check is drawn payable to "Cash," the actual currency and coins are obtained by "cashing" the check at the bank, and the money is then made available to the cashiers. The total change fund might be divided into five $100 funds, each one being assigned

to a cash register or to a delivery truck driver. During a day's operations, the currency and coins in the change fund are merged with the cash receipts. At the end of the day, the total amount of cash should equal the day's receipts plus the change fund. When the day's receipts are deposited, the change fund will remain to start the next day's activities.

6.20 Once a change fund has been established, no further entries are made in the Change Fund account unless the amount of the fund is to be increased or decreased.

6.21 **Cash on Hand—Petty Cash Funds** A petty cash ("imprest") fund provides for cash disbursements that are too small to merit the more detailed treatment required for drawing a bank check. Such a fund is also convenient for making payments more promptly than is possible under the more formal system. Although the amounts involved are usually small, proper safeguards should be established to prevent minor thefts, which could easily evolve into major losses. A signed receipt and an explanation should be required for each payment from the fund so that the sum of the actual cash and the signed receipts can be periodically checked against the total amount of the fund.

6.22 Establishing a petty cash fund is similar to setting up a change fund. If a fund of $100 is to be provided, the entry is

Petty Cash Fund ...................... 100
    Cash in Bank ..................... 100

The check is made payable to "Cash"; when the check is cashed, the money is placed in a special box, drawer, or cash register for safekeeping.

6.23 When a payment is made from the fund, a signed receipt is obtained indicating the nature of the payment, but no entries are made in the accounts at that time. At periodic intervals, the payments made from the fund are analyzed, a check is drawn for the total amount disbursed to replenish the fund, and the expenditures are charged to the appropriate accounts. The check is cashed, the money is placed in the special box or drawer, and the receipts are filed for future reference and audit. For example, suppose that $94 has been disbursed from the $100 fund and that an analysis of the signed receipts gives the following distribution of the expenditures:

| Item | Amount |
|---|---|
| Advances to Employees .............. | $40 |
| Advertising Expense ................ | 8 |
| Miscellaneous Selling Expenses ....... | 17 |
| Office Supplies Purchased and Used .. | 28 |
| Miscellaneous General and Administrative Expenses .......... | 1 |
| | $94 |

Suppose, further, that an actual count of cash shows only $4 in the fund. The $2 loss (= $100 − $94 − $4) is charged to Cash Over and Short or some other expense account. The amount in Cash Over and Short at the end of an accounting period is included in (or, if a credit balance, deducted from) Miscellaneous General and Administrative Expenses. The payments are charged to the proper accounts, replenishment of the fund is authorized, and a check for $96 is cashed to restore the balance of the fund to $100. The entry would be

| | | |
|---|---|---|
| Advances to Employees .............. | 40 | |
| Advertising Expense ................ | 8 | |
| Miscellaneous Selling Expenses ....... | 17 | |
| Office Supplies Used .... | 28 | |
| Miscellaneous General and Administrative Expenses (= $1 + $2).. | 3 | |
| Cash in Bank .................... | | 96 |

6.24 In those cases in which the fund is not replenished at the end of the accounting period, the disbursements from the fund must be recorded before the financial statements are prepared. An adjusting entry debiting the appropriate accounts and crediting the account Petty Cash Fund would then be necessary.

6.25 The Petty Cash Fund account usually does not receive any further entries once the fund has been established. Exceptions are made when the amount of the fund is to be altered or when an adjustment must be made at the end of the accounting period because a check has not yet been drawn to restore the cash in the fund to the original balance.

**Cash on Hand** If a firm follows the desirable 6.26 plan of depositing all receipts intact, disbursements will be made only from checking accounts or from petty cash funds. Any cash on hand will represent cash received since the last deposit, which usually will have been made the previous business day. A daily record of cash on hand is usually necessary. Information regarding cash receipts is received daily from various cashiers and drivers. The cash received usually accompanies the report; it is counted, the report is audited, and a summary is prepared for the business as a whole.

Suppose that the daily cash report showed 6.27 the following items: cash on hand, morning—$120; cash sales—$347; collections on accounts receivable (separate list of customers and amounts attached)—$1,524; deposited in bank—$1,871; and cash on hand, night—$120.

The information in the daily cash report 6.28 would be used in preparing the following journal entry:

| | | |
|---|---|---|
| Cash in Bank ...................... | 1,871 | |
| Sales .......................... | | 347 |
| Accounts Receivable ............. | | 1,524 |

Cash registers facilitate the accumulation of 6.29 cash data. There are many types, but the usual cash register is a combination of a cash drawer and several adding machines. The transactions are entered by hand. Then they are recorded and accumulated in one of the adding machines so that at the end of the day the totals are available for each of several divisions of the day's activities—the total cash sales (sometimes classified according to products or departments), total collections on account, and total sales of each salesperson.

**Cash in Bank—Deposits** A deposit ticket 6.30 provides the information for preparing the journal entry to record the deposit of cash funds in the checking account. The deposit ticket should be prepared in duplicate; the bank keeps the original and the firm keeps the duplicate. The duplicate is often initialed by the bank teller and used as a receipt for the deposit of the funds. The total on the deposit ticket is entered in a journal as a debit to Cash in Bank and a credit to Cash on Hand.

6.31 **Cash in Bank—Issuance of Checks** The information for the entry to record checks drawn in payment of bills comes from an approved check requisition for the disbursement. The customary entry will be a debit to Accounts Payable and a credit to Cash in Bank.

6.32 **Control of Disbursements by Check** All cash payments except for those of small amounts from the petty cash fund should be made by check. The firm can thereby restrict the authority for payments to a few employees. Often, firms provide further control by requiring that all checks be signed by two employees. Another control device is the use of a Cash Disbursements Journal or Check Register in which all checks issued are recorded. Using such a journal provides control because a single person, who is not allowed to authorize payments or to sign checks, is responsible for recording all payments.

6.33 In any case, control over disbursements should ensure that:

**1.** Disbursements are made only by authorized persons.

**2.** Adequate records support each disbursement. Such records attest that the disbursement was for goods and services procured by proper authority and actually received by the business. The records attest that payment has been made in accordance with the purchase contract.

**3.** The transaction is entered properly in the formal accounting records.

### The Bank Statement

6.34 Once each month the bank sends a statement together with the canceled checks that have been paid and deducted from the depositor's account and memorandums of any other additions or deductions that have been made by the bank. When the bank statement is received, it should be compared promptly with the record of deposits, checks drawn, and other bank items on the records of the firm.

The balance shown on the bank statement 6.35 will rarely correspond to the balance of the Cash in Bank account. The two basic causes of the difference are time lapses and errors. In the normal course of business activities, some items will have been recorded by either the bank or the firm without having reached the recording point on the other set of records, hence a *time lapse* difference. Causes of such differences include: checks outstanding (that is, checks recorded by the drawing firm but not yet received by the bank on which they were drawn), deposits mailed just before the bank statement date that do not appear on the bank statement, and transactions (such as service charges and collections of notes or drafts) that have not been recorded on the firm's books. The other basic difference is caused by errors in record keeping by either the firm or the bank. The process of comparing the bank statement with the books is known as *reconciling* the bank account, and the schedule prepared to demonstrate the results of the comparing is called a *bank reconciliation*. Exhibits 6.1, 6.2, and 6.3 show typical reconciliation schedules. The preparation of a bank reconciliation schedule is explained below.

**Forms of Bank Reconciliation** A bank rec- 6.36 onciliation explains the differences between the amount of cash the bank says the company has on deposit and the amount indicated on the company's books. Several forms of bank reconciliation are common. We do not explain them all, but the student who understands the purpose of the reconciliation and the causes of differences between book and bank balances of cash will be able to understand virtually any presentation. The most useful form of bank reconciliation for preparing accounting statements

*Exhibit 6.1*
**(Reconciliation of Bank and Book**
**Balances to Correct Balance)**
**Young Spring Company**
**Bank Reconciliation—**
**Citizens National Bank**
**April 1, 1981**

| | | |
|---|---:|---:|
| Balance Shown on Bank Statement, April 1 .................................................. | | $2,323.36 |
| Deposits of March 30 and 31, Not Yet Recorded by Bank ................................ | | 643.16 |
| Check of Young Wire Co. Deducted by Bank in Error .................................... | | 10.00 |
| | | $2,976.52 |
| Outstanding Checks: | | |
| #367 ................................................................... | $ 69.67 | |
| #470 ................................................................... | 142.53 | |
| #471 ................................................................... | 131.26 | |
| #472 ................................................................... | 131.44 | |
| #474 ................................................................... | 243.55 | |
| #475 ................................................................... | 305.52 | |
| Less Total Outstanding Checks ...................................................... | | (1,023.97) |
| **Adjusted Bank Balance**[a] .......................................................... | | $1,952.55 |
| Balance Shown on Books, April 1 ..................................................... | | $1,453.55 |
| Items Unrecorded on Books: | | |
| Collection of Note of J. T. Munn— | | |
| Face Amount of Note ................................................. | $500.00 | |
| Less Collection Charge ................................................ | (5.00) | 495.00 |
| Less Bank Service Charge for March ................................................. | | (14.00) |
| Adjusted Book Balance before Correction of Errors ................................. | | $1,934.55 |
| Check #467 for $168.81 Was Entered in the Check Register as $186.81. It Was Issued in March | | |
| to Pay a Previously Recorded Bill ................................................ | | 18.00 |
| **Adjusted Book Balance**[a] .......................................................... | | $1,952.55 |

[a]This is the amount that would be shown in the Cash in Bank account if a balance
sheet were prepared as of April 1, 1981.

takes as its goal the derivation of the "correct" amount of cash to be shown if a balance sheet were to be prepared on the reconciliation date. Both the book amount of cash and the bank amount of cash are adjusted to account for time lapses and errors. This form of reconciliation is sometimes called a "Reconciliation of Bank and Book Balances to Correct Balance." Exhibit 6.1 illustrates such a reconciliation.

6.37     Another form of reconciliation sometimes used starts with the bank balance and shows adjustments to derive the amounts shown on the books. Exhibit 6.2 illustrates this form, which is sometimes called "Reconciliation of Bank and Book Balances" or, simply, "Bank to Books."

6.38     We prefer the form illustrated in Exhibit 6.1 because it derives an amount for cash to be shown in the balance sheet and shows in the bottom section all of the events and transactions requiring adjusting entries (which we show below).

6.39     Finally, Exhibit 6.3 illustrates the "four-column bank reconciliation" or "proof of cash" used by some auditors. The four-column format presents four reconciliations at once:

1. Reconciliation of the beginning-of-period

## Exhibit 6.2
### (Reconciliation of Bank and Book Balances; Bank to Books)
### Young Spring Company
### Bank Reconciliation—
### Citizens National Bank
### April 1, 1981

| | | |
|---|---:|---:|
| Balance Shown on Bank Statement April 1, 1981 ..................... | | $2,323.36 |
| Add: | | |
| Bank Service Charge for March .... | | 14.00 |
| Deposits of March 30 and 31 Not Yet Recorded by Bank .............. | | 643.16 |
| Check of Young Wire Company Deducted by Bank in Error ....... | | 10.00 |
| | | $2,990.52 |
| Subtract: | | |
| Outstanding Checks | | |
| #367 ................ | $ 69.67 | |
| #470 ................ | 142.53 | |
| #471 ................ | 131.26 | |
| #472 ................ | 131.44 | |
| #474 ................ | 243.55 | |
| #475 ................ | 305.52 | |
| Total Outstanding ...... | | (1,023.97) |
| Collection of Note of J. T. Munn— | | |
| Face Amount of Note ... | $500.00 | |
| Less Collection Charge . | (5.00) | |
| Net Collection .......... | | (495.00) |
| Check #467 for $168.81 Was Entered in the Check Register as $186.81. It Was Issued in March to Pay a Previously Recorded Bill ........... | | (18.00) |
| Balance Shown in Books, April 1 ..... | | $1,453.55 |

bank and book balances to the "correct" amount.

2. Reconciliation of receipts during the period shown on the bank statement and on the books to the correct amount.

3. Reconciliation of disbursements during the period shown on the bank statement and on the books to the correct amount.

4. Reconciliation of the end-of-period bank and book balances to the "correct" amount.

In this text, unless a statement is made to

the contrary, the term *bank reconciliation* means reconciliation of bank and book balances to the correct balance as in Exhibit 6.1.

**Preparing the Bank Reconciliation Schedule** The purpose of the bank reconciliation is to explain the difference between the book balance of Cash in Bank and the bank's statement of the firm's cash on deposit and to indicate the required adjustments of the firm's accounts. If the bank statement is used as a control device, the bank reconciliation is the final step in the monthly procedure for controlling cash receipts and disbursements. The bank reconciliation provides a convenient summary of the adjusting entries that must be made by the firm to account for previous errors in recording cash-related transactions or for cash transactions that have not yet been recorded. 6.40

The preparer of the bank reconciliation should have the following items: the bank statement with canceled checks and other memoranda that accompany it, the reconciliation schedule for the preceding month, the journal containing all entries for deposits of cash into the bank, the Cash account from the general ledger, and any other journals (Cash Receipts Journal, Cash Disbursements Journal, Accounts Payable Journal) that contain entries in the Cash account. 6.41

Preparing the bank reconciliation schedule typically involves the following steps. 6.42

1. Enter at the top of the reconciliation schedule the balance as shown on the bank statement.

2. Enter next any deposits that have not been recorded on the bank statement. Such items usually occur because the bank has prepared the statement before the deposits for the last day or two have been recorded. If there are any time or date breaks in the list of deposits for the period, the bank should be notified promptly.

3. Enter any other adjustments of the bank's balance such as errors in recording canceled checks or deposits, or the return of checks belonging to some other customer of

*Exhibit 6.3*
**(Four-Column Bank Reconciliation)**
**Young Spring Company**
**Proof of Cash – Citizens National Bank**
**Month of March 1981**

| | Balance March 1[a] | + Receipts | Month of March[a] − Disbursements | = Balance April 1[b] |
|---|---|---|---|---|
| Shown on Bank Statement ................. | $2,346.78 | $22,456.39 | $22,479.81 | $2,323.36 |
| Deposits in Transit | | | | |
| On March 1 ........................... | 690.11 | (690.11) | | |
| On April 1 ........................... | | 643.16 | | 643.16 |
| Outstanding Checks | | | | |
| On March 1 ........................... | (1,010.66) | | (1,010.66) | |
| On April 1 ........................... | | | 1,023.97 | (1,023.97) |
| Check Deducted by Bank in Error ........... | — | | (10.00) | 10.00 |
| Adjusted Bank Balance[c] ................... | $2,026.23 | $22,409.44 | $22,483.12 | $1,952.55 |
| | | | | |
| Shown on Books ................. ....,.... | $2,026.23 | $21,914.44 | $22,487.12 | $1,453.55 |
| Collection of Note (Net) ................... | | 495.00 | | 495.00 |
| Unrecorded Service Charge for March ....... | | | 14.00 | (14.00) |
| Correction of Error in Recording | | | | |
| Check in Books ....................... | | | (18.00) | 18.00 |
| Adjusted Book Balance[c] ................... | $2,026.23 | $22,409.44 | $22,483.12 | $1,952.55 |

[a]Balance at March 1 and data for month have not been presented previously in this chapter.
[b]Data for April 1 are identical with those in Exhibit 6.1.
[c]These amounts for Cash would be shown on balance sheets for March 1 and April 1.

the bank. Errors on bank statements are infrequent.

**4.** Obtain a total.

**5.** List the outstanding checks. A list should be prepared, beginning with the checks still outstanding from the previous period and continuing with the outstanding checks that were drawn during the current period.

**6.** Deduct the sum of the outstanding checks from the total obtained in step **4.** The balance is the adjusted bank balance—the balance that would be shown on the bank statement if all deposits had been entered, all checks written had been returned, and no errors had been made; it is the final figure for this first section of the statement.

6.43   These steps will frequently conclude the reconciliation because this balance should correspond to the balance of the Cash in Bank account as of the bank statement date when there are no unrecorded transactions or errors. If these two amounts are not equal at this point, the following steps must be taken and shown in a second section of the reconciliation schedule.

**7.** Enter the Cash in Bank account balance as shown on the books as of the bank statement date.

**8.** Add or deduct any errors or omissions that have been disclosed in the process of reviewing the items returned by the bank. These will include such items as errors in recording deposits or checks, unnumbered checks that have not been entered in the check register, and service charges and collection fees deducted by the bank.

**9.** The net result is the adjusted book balance, and it must correspond to the adjusted bank balance derived in the first section. If it does not, the search must be continued for other items that have been overlooked.

6.44 **Adjusting Entries from Bank Reconciliation Schedule** The bank reconciliation schedule shows two distinct kinds of differences:

**1.** Differences between the balance shown on the bank statement and the adjusted bank balance.

**2.** Differences between the account balance in the firm's books and the adjusted book balance.

Only the second type of difference requires entries on the firm's books. Any deposits not recorded by the bank will presumably have been recorded by the time the reconciliation is prepared and, in any event, represent funds that the depositor may assume are in the bank and available for disbursement by check.

6.45 Entries must be made for all of the differences between the firm's account balance on the books and the adjusted book balance, because they represent errors or omissions that must be corrected. The reconciliations illustrated in Exhibits 6.1–6.3 require adjustments for bank service charges, for the collection of a note*, and for the check whose amount was incorrectly recorded.† The entries would be as follows:

| | | |
|---|---:|---:|
| Bank Service Charge Expense | 14 | |
| Cash in Bank | | 14 |
| Service charges for month of March. | | |

| | | |
|---|---:|---:|
| Cash in Bank | 495 | |
| Collection Expense | 5 | |
| Note Receivable, J. T. Munn | | 500 |
| Note collected by bank. | | |

---

*The reader may be unfamiliar with the transaction leading to the collection of the note. The firm holds a note receivable signed by J. T. Munn. The note is now due for payment. The firm presents the note to the bank and asks the bank to contact Munn and to attempt to collect the amount owed, including interest. The bank collects the amount due, $500 in this case, and keeps $5 as a fee for its services. It deposits the remaining $495 in the firm's checking account. The example here omits the complication caused by the likely accrual of interest since the last adjusting entry and the recording of interest revenue. The example assumes that interest revenue has previously been recorded and debited to the note receivable account.

†The bank must, of course, correct any error on its books when the mistake is called to its attention. We do not show the entry on the bank's books to correct its error reported in the reconciliation in Exhibit 6.1.

| | | |
|---|---:|---:|
| Cash in Bank | 18 | |
| Accounts Payable | | 18 |
| To correct entry of check #467. | | |

6.46 **Special Bank Accounts** Although a business may have several regular checking accounts, the accounting problems for each one are identical to those for a single account. Special accounts are often used, however, to serve particular payment needs, and they involve some variations in accounting technique. For example, a special payroll bank account may be used. The usual procedure is as follows. When the payroll is prepared, one check is drawn on a regular bank account for the total amount due the employees and is deposited in the special payroll account in the bank. The related entries would be

| | | |
|---|---:|---:|
| Salary Expense | 47,500 | |
| Salaries Payable | | 47,500 |
| To recognize salaries of pay period just ended. | | |

| | | |
|---|---:|---:|
| Salaries Payable | 47,500 | |
| Cash in Bank | | 47,500 |
| Check drawn for payment of all salaries. Check is to be deposited in special bank account. | | |

From the point of view of the firm and its Cash in Bank account, the $47,500 is no longer cash, but has been disbursed. Checks are drawn on the special bank account for the amount due each employee, using a separate series of numbers and checks.

6.47 Sometimes a certain sum is kept on deposit in the payroll bank account over and above the amount required for payrolls in order to provide for advances or to avoid service charges. In this case, a Payroll Cash account must be established by the firm with the extra deposit operating as a "revolving fund," much like a petty cash fund.

6.48 Special bank accounts are also used for dividend payments and, occasionally, for other purposes. The use of a special bank account:

**1.** Simplifies the accounting records for the regular checking accounts.

**2.** Permits, for special purposes, the use of

different signatures which are often printed by check-writing machines.

**3.** Facilitates the preparation of the bank reconciliation through the separation of large groups of similar transactions, each one of which can be identified and verified by itself.

6.49   The special bank account permits many like transactions to be accounted for in a single transaction in the primary Cash in Bank account.

6.50   *Special-Purpose Bank Accounts and Special-Purpose Funds* The reader should understand the difference between a special-purpose bank account and a special-purpose fund. A special-purpose *bank account,* such as the one described above for payroll disbursements, merely segregates part of the cash in bank for convenience in disbursements and record keeping. The amounts in special-purpose *funds* are generally not part of cash; most often, special-purpose funds are not even held in the form of cash, but in the form of interest-earning investments such as commercial paper or U.S. Treasury bills and notes. Special-purpose funds are amounts earmarked for uses such as repaying bonds when they come due ("bond sinking fund") or paying for a new plant ("plant fund"). Special-purpose funds are usually classified among "Investments" on the balance sheet. See Chapter 14.

6.51   **Summary of the Accounting for Cash** Management is always concerned about getting the best and safest use of its resources. The most versatile resource, cash, is also the most vulnerable. An effective internal-control system is essential to the proper management of cash. One way to provide control is to maintain duplicate and independent records of cash flows, but this is not necessary if a firm uses the monthly bank statement as a duplicate record. Using the bank statement as an effective control device requires depositing receipts daily and making all disbursements by check or through petty cash funds. By this means the bank recon-

ciliation serves as a control device because the bank record will reflect the cash inflows and outflows of the enterprise.

# Marketable Securities

A business may find itself with more cash   6.52 than it needs for current and near-term business purposes. Rather than allow cash to remain unproductive, the business may invest some of its currently excess cash in income-yielding securities, such as U.S. government bonds or stocks or bonds of other companies. Such uses of liquid assets are known as investments in *marketable securities* or *temporary investments* and are alternatives to putting cash in savings accounts or certificates of deposit. In this section, we consider the classification and valuation of the current asset "marketable securities." Chapter 14 discusses several kinds of securities and the accounting for them as long-term investments.

## Classification of Marketable Securities

Securities are classified as "marketable securities" and shown among current assets as long as they can be readily converted into cash *and* management intends to do so when it needs cash. Securities that do not meet both of these criteria are included under Investments on the balance sheet.

**Example 1** Wilson Manufacturing Corpora-   6.54 tion invested $150,000 of temporarily excess funds in U.S. Treasury notes. The notes mature in 3 months. This investment is properly classified among "marketable securities," because the notes can be sold at any time and even if not sold, the cash will be collected within 3 months.

**Example 2** Suppose that Wilson Manufac-   6.55 turing Corporation in Example 1 above had acquired 20-year bonds of American Telephone & Telegraph Company instead of the U.S. Treasury notes. Its intent in acquiring the bonds was the same as before, the investment of temporarily excess cash.* These bonds would likewise be classified as ''marketable securities,'' because they are traded in an established marketplace.

6.56 **Example 3** Webster Corporation acquired 10 percent of the outstanding shares of Haskell Corporation on the open market for $10,000,000. Webster Corporation plans to hold these shares as a long-term investment. Even though the shares of Haskell Corporation are readily marketable, they would not be classified as ''marketable securities,'' because Webster Corporation does not intend to turn the securities into cash within a reasonably short period. These securities would be classified under Investments on the balance sheet.

6.57 In published financial statements, all securities properly classified as ''marketable securities'' are grouped together and shown on a single line on the balance sheet. As we shall see below, however, a distinction is made for accounting purposes between *marketable debt securities* and *marketable equity securities*.

## Valuation of Marketable Securities

6.58 Marketable securities, like other assets, are initially recorded at acquisition cost. Acquisition cost includes the purchase price plus any commissions, taxes, and other costs incurred to acquire the securities. For example, if marketable securities are acquired for $10,000 and $200 is paid in commissions and taxes, the entry is

| | | |
|---|---|---|
| Marketable Securities | 10,200 | |
| Cash | | 10,200 |

6.59 Dividends on marketable securities are recognized when declared. Interest is recognized when earned. Assuming that $125 of dividends were declared and $150 of interest was earned on the marketable securities

above and these amounts were immediately received in cash, the entry is

| | | |
|---|---|---|
| Cash | 275 | |
| Dividend Revenue | | 125 |
| Interest Revenue | | 150 |

6.60 There is nothing unusual about the valuation of marketable securities at date of acquisition or the recording of dividends and interest. The valuation of marketable securities after acquisition may, however, depart from strict historical cost accounting.

6.61 **Marketable Equity Securities** Financial Accounting Standards Board *Statement of Financial Accounting Standards No. 12* (1975) requires that the *portfolio* of marketable equity securities (that is, common stock, preferred stock, stock options, and warrants classified as current assets) be stated at the lower of acquisition cost or market at the end of each period.† (A similar, but somewhat different, procedure is prescribed for equity securities classified as noncurrent assets. Chapter 14 describes that procedure.) Under the *lower-of-cost-or-market method,* decreases in the market value of a portfolio of marketable equity securities are recognized as holding losses each period as the decreases occur even though a market transaction or exchange has not taken place. The credit to reduce the carrying amount of the current asset Marketable (Equity) Securities is made to an account contra to Marketable (Equity) Securities usually called the Allowance for Excess of Cost of Marketable Securities over Market Value. Using a separate contra account enables the simultaneous identification of both the acquisition cost and the amount of decline, if any, in the market value of the portfolio. Separate identification of the cost and current market value, when below cost, are required because any sub-

---

*Corporate finance texts discuss the wisdom, or lack thereof, of investing for short time periods in long-term bonds whose market values can fluctuate as interest rates fluctuate.

---

†''Market value,'' as defined by FASB *Statement No. 12,* is the quoted market price for both buyers and sellers excluding brokerage commissions, taxes, and similar costs. Thus, it may be thought of as either a current entry or current exit value, exclusive of transactions costs.

sequent increase in the market value of the portfolio up to the original acquisition cost is recognized as a holding gain. The portfolio must never be stated at an amount greater than the original acquisition cost; that is, the allowance account can never have a debit balance. The footnote to paragraph 6.75 in the section on disclosure requirements discusses the FASB's choice of applying the lower-of-cost-or-market valuation rule to the entire portfolio, rather than security by security. The procedures for applying the lower-of-cost-or-market method are illustrated next.

6.62 **Example 4** Nurnberg Company acquired marketable equity securities during 1977 and 1978 as shown in Exhibit 6.4.* The entry to record the acquisitions of securities of A Company and B Company during 1977 is

```
Marketable Securities  .............  30,000
    Cash  .......................          30,000
```

6.63 *Unrealized Holding Loss* At the end of 1977, the portfolio of marketable equity securities (that is, the securities of A Company and B Company) had an aggregate acquisition cost of $30,000 (= $10,000 + $20,000) and an aggregate market value of $29,000 (= $11,000 + $18,000). A write-down of $1,000 is required to recognize the unrealized holding loss

```
Unrealized Holding Loss on Valuation
    of Marketable Securities  ...........  1,000
      Allowance for Excess of Cost of
        Marketable Securities over
          Market Value .................          1,000
```
Entry to adjust credit balance in allowance account to $1,000.

The loss account appears in the income statement for 1977 among the expenses. The allowance account is shown as a contra account to marketable securities on the balance sheet at the end of 1977. See Exhibit 6.5 for illustrations of the required disclosures.

___

*This example covers several years. It is likely that companies owning these securities for several years would classify them as investments. Then the accounting would be as explained in Chapter 14.

The entry to record the acquisitions during 1978 is — 6.64

```
Marketable Securities  ............  70,000
    Cash  ......................          70,000
```

At the end of 1978, the portfolio of marketable equity securities has an aggregate acquisition cost of $100,000 (= $10,000 + $20,000 + $30,000 + $40,000) and an aggregate market value of $97,000 (= $13,000 + $17,000 + $26,000 + $41,000). The unrealized holding loss is now $3,000 (= $100,000 − $97,000). The allowance account before adjustment has a balance carried over from 1977 of $1,000. Thus, an additional write-down of $2,000 is required at the end of 1978. — 6.65

```
Unrealized Holding Loss on Valuation
    of Marketable Securities  ..........  2,000
      Allowance for Excess of Cost of
        Marketable Securities over
          Market Value .................          2,000
```
Aggregate decline below cost is $3,000. Adjustment of $2,000 is needed to increase credit balance in allowance account from $1,000 to $3,000. Loss for year is $2,000.

The portfolio of marketable securities would be shown on the December 31, 1978, balance sheet at its market value of $97,000 (= $100,000 acquisition cost less $3,000 allowance). Income for 1978 is reduced by $2,000.

*Recovery of Unrealized Holding Loss* Taking the example one step further, assume that there were no acquisitions or dispositions of marketable equity securities during 1979 and that the market value of the portfolio at the end of 1979 was $102,000. The valuation of the portfolio of securities is increased but not to an amount greater than original acquisition cost. The entry is — 6.66

```
Allowance for Excess of Cost of
    Marketable Securities over Market
      Value  ...........................  3,000
        Recovery of Unrealized Holding
          Loss on Valuation of Marketable
            Securities ....................          3,000
```
To increase valuation of marketable securities to acquisition cost.

The debit entry above brings the balance in the allowance account to zero. The Recovery of Unrealized Holding Loss on Valuation of Marketable Securities account is included in the income statement for 1979 as a revenue, or gain. See Exhibit 6.5 for illustrative disclosures.

*Realized Gain or Loss through Sale* When 6.67 an individual marketable equity security is

---

## Exhibit 6.4
### Data for Illustration of Accounting for Marketable Securities

| Security | Date Acquired | Acquisition Cost | Market Value 12/31/1977 | 12/31/1978 | 12/31/1979 | 12/31/1980 | 12/31/1981 |
|---|---|---|---|---|---|---|---|
| A Company | 11/1/1977 | $10,000 | $11,000 | $13,000 | $ 14,000 | $12,000 | $10,000 |
| B Company | 12/1/1977 | 20,000 | 18,000 | 17,000 | 18,000 | —a | — |
| C Company | 2/1/1978 | 30,000 | — | 26,000 | 33,000 | 34,000 | —b |
| D Company | 4/1/1978 | 40,000 | — | 41,000 | 37,000 | 30,000 | 35,000 |
| | | | $29,000 | $97,000 | $102,000 | $76,000 | $45,000 |

aHoldings of B Company sold during 1980 for $18,500.

bHoldings of C Company sold during 1981 for $32,000.

---

## Exhibit 6.5
### Items in Income Statement and Balance Sheet of Nurnberg Company Illustrating Transactions in Marketable Securities

| | 1977 | 1978 | 1979 | 1980 | 1981 |
|---|---|---|---|---|---|
| **Excerpts from Income Statement for Year** | | | | | |
| Other Items (Assumed) before Taxes .......... | $200,000 | $200,000 | $200,000 | $200,000 | $200,000 |
| Realized Gain (Loss) on Sale of Marketable Securities ..................... | — | — | — | (1,500) | 2,000 |
| Unrealized Holding Loss on Valuation of Marketable Securities .................... | (1,000) | (2,000) | — | (4,000) | (1,000) |
| Recovery of Unrealized Holding Loss on Valuation of Marketable Securities ....... | — | — | 3,000 | — | — |
| Income before Taxes ...................... | $199,000 | $198,000 | $203,000 | $194,500 | $201,000 |
| **Balance Sheet Items at Year-End** | | | | | |
| Marketable Securities at Cost .............. | $ 30,000 | $100,000 | $100,000 | $ 80,000 | $ 50,000 |
| Less Allowance for Excess of Cost of Marketable Securities over Market Value .... | (1,000) | (3,000) | — | (4,000) | (5,000) |
| Marketable Securities at Lower of Cost or Marketa ................................ | $ 29,000 | $ 97,000 | $100,000 | $ 76,000 | $ 45,000 |

aNotes to the financial statements must disclose separately the unrealized gains on all securities with gains and the unrealized losses on securities with losses. These disclosures are discussed in more detail later in the chapter and are illustrated in the exhibit for the Caral Company. Consider, for example, the second column shown here and the underlying data reported in the preceding exhibit. Unrealized gains on securities with gains (A Company and D Company) total $4,000, while unrealized losses on securities with losses (B Company and C Company) total $7,000 [=($20,000 − $17,000) + ($30,000 − $26,000)]. Both the amounts of the unrealized gains of $4,000 and the unrealized losses of $7,000 appear in notes, while the net loss of $3,000 (= $7,000 − $4,000) appears in the allowance account for the year. For the third year shown here, the notes disclose that the aggregate market value of the securities exceeds their cost by $2,000.

sold, the realized gain or loss is the difference between the selling price and the acquisition cost of the individual security, regardless of the related balance in the allowance account.* For example, assume that the securities of B Company were sold during 1980 for $18,500. The entry to record the sales during 1980 is

Cash ......................... 18,500
Realized Holding Loss on Sale of
    Marketable Securities ...........  1,500
        Marketable Securities .........        20,000
To recognize realized holding loss of
$1,500 (= $20,000 original cost −
$18,500 proceeds of sale).

The realized holding loss would be deducted in calculating net income for 1980.

6.68    Because the lower-of-cost-or-market method is applied to the entire portfolio, rather than security by security, the amount of the decline in market value below cost is not recorded separately for each security. (In many cases, gains on some securities offset losses on others.)

6.69    The aggregate acquisition cost of the portfolio at the end of 1980 is now $80,000 (= $10,000 + $30,000 + $40,000). The aggregate market value of the portfolio at the end of 1980 is $76,000 (= $12,000 + $34,000 + $30,000). Thus, the allowance account should have a $4,000 balance. Because the allowance account has a zero balance carried over from 1979, the following entry is necessary at the end of 1980 to bring the allowance account to $4,000:

Unrealized Holding Loss on Valuation
    of Marketable Securities ........... 4,000
        Allowance for Excess of Cost of
        Marketable Securities over
        Market Value ................        4,000
To bring credit balance in allowance account to $4,000. Loss for the year is $4,000.

The securities are shown at $76,000 on the December 31, 1980, balance sheet in Exhibit

*Because the current buying and selling price will be the same, the "operating margin" as defined in Chapter 5 is zero. All gains or losses realized are therefore holding gains or losses.

6.5. Income for 1980 is reduced by $4,000 as well as by the realized loss of $1,500.

*Realized Gain and Unrealized Loss*  The    6.70 data for 1981 illustrate the simultaneous realization of a gain on sale of one security, and further unrealized holding losses on securities still held. Holdings of C Company that had cost $30,000 are sold for $32,000. The journal entry is

Cash ......................... 32,000
    Marketable Securities .........        30,000
    Realized Holding Gain on Sale
        of Marketable Securities .....        2,000
Sale of holding of C Company for
$2,000 more than original cost.

Securities held at the end of 1981 have an aggregate cost of $50,000 (= $10,000 + $40,000) and an aggregate market value of $45,000 (= $10,000 + $35,000). Thus, the balance in the allowance account must be $5,000. The journal entry is

Unrealized Holding Loss on Valuation
    of Marketable Securities ........... 1,000
        Allowance for Excess of Cost of
        Marketable Securities over
        Market Value ................        1,000
Adjustment of balance in allowance account from $4,000 to $5,000.

Income for 1981 is increased by the realized gain of $2,000 and reduced by the unrealized holding loss of $1,000. See Exhibit 6.5.

We have not illustrated in the example the    6.71 simultaneous occurrence of a realized gain (or loss) on securities sold and recovery of an unrealized holding loss on securities still held, but these events can occur together.

*Transfer of Securities between Current and    6.72 Noncurrent Portfolios*  The same holding of securities may be classified either as a current asset, Marketable Securities, or as a noncurrent asset, Investments, depending on the intentions of the owning company. Whenever a security is transferred from the current asset portfolio to the noncurrent asset portfolio or vice versa and the market price of the security is less than cost on the date of transfer, FASB *Statement No. 12* requires that the transaction be treated as though the security were sold for cash on that date and repurchased at the same price. Thus, the transfer between portfolios effectively establishes a realized loss and a new cost basis. Assume, for example, equity securities had been purchased for $10,000 and held as a noncurrent investment while the market price declined to $8,000. The investment has been accounted for using the lower-of-cost-or-market basis by a slightly different method—explained in Chapter 14—from that used for current assets. If the firm decides to reclassify the investment as a current asset, the following entry would be made:

Realized Holding Loss on
   Reclassification of Marketable
   Security as a Current Asset ....... 2,000
Marketable Securities (Current Asset) . 8,000
      Investments (Noncurrent Asset) ..     10,000

The loss appears on the income statement for the year; the cost basis of the current asset is $8,000; subsequent increases in market value, even to $10,000, are not recognized in the accounts.

6.73 **Order of Procedures for Lower-of-Cost-or-Market Method** Students often find the treatment of the various events relating to marketable securities confusing: the recording of realized gains or losses (through sale, reclassification from current to noncurrent or vice versa), the recording of unrealized losses, the recovery of unrealized losses, and the valuation of the allowance account. Confusion will be minimized and the final answer more likely to be correct if the transactions are analyzed and recorded in the following order:

1. Record any realized gains or losses from sales and reclassifications for the period just ending.

2. Compare the market value of the portfolio at the end of the period with its cost to ascertain the required credit balance in the allowance account (= cost less market value if cost exceeds market value, and zero otherwise).

3. Prepare a journal entry to adjust the al-

lowance account from its current zero or credit balance to its required credit or zero balance.
   **a.** If the adjustment requires a credit to the allowance account, then the debit is to the Unrealized Holding Loss account, which appears on the income statement.
   **b.** If the adjustment requires a debit to the allowance account, the credit is to the Recovery of Unrealized Holding Loss account, which appears on the income statement.

**Deferred Income Taxes** Only realized gains 6.74 and losses are subject to taxation. Unrealized losses (and later recoveries, if they occur) recognized for book purposes do not appear on the tax return. Timing differences, as discussed in Chapter 20, therefore arise.

**Disclosure Requirements** The acquisition 6.75 cost and market value of the equity securities in the portfolio at the end of the period must be reported. To make the required adjusting entry, these two amounts must be compared with the acquisition cost and market value of the equity securities in the portfolio at the start of the period, even though the individual equity securities in the portfolio may have changed drastically during the period. The notes to the financial statements must include the following disclosures relating to marketable equity securities:

1. Aggregate cost and aggregate market value of the portfolio at each balance sheet date.

2. The gross unrealized holding gain on all securities with gains at the most recent balance sheet date.

3. The gross unrealized holding loss on all securities with losses at the most recent balance sheet date.*

---

*The FASB reports in paragraph 31 of *Statement No. 12* that it chose to apply the lower-of-cost-or-market valuation basis to the entire portfolio, rather than the more conservative approach of applying it individually, because most firms look on their portfolio as a "collective asset." To decide whether or not such a view is theoretically defensible requires an understanding of modern portfolio theory, which is beyond the scope of this book. (We think it is defensible.) The

**4.** The unrealized holding gain or loss (that is, the change in the allowance account) included in net income each period.

**5.** The realized holding gain or loss included in net income each period.

**6.** Any significant changes in the net unrealized holding gain or loss or the net realized holding gain or loss after the most recent balance sheet date but prior to the issuance of the financial statements.

6.76    **Exempt Industries** FASB *Statement No. 12* does not apply to nonprofit organizations, mutual life insurance companies, and employee benefit plans, but it does apply to mutual savings banks and other profit-seeking mutual enterprises. In addition, companies in industries with specialized industry accounting practices for marketable securities, such as investment companies, broker-dealers, stock life insurance companies, and casualty insurance companies, may continue to follow the specialized accounting practices, which typically involve carrying marketable securities at market and reflecting unrealized gains or losses in the owners' equity section of the balance sheet.

6.77    **Marketable Debt Securities** FASB *Statement No. 12* addressed only marketable equity securities. The accounting for marketable debt securities follows *Accounting Research Bulletin No. 43* (Chapter 3A), which prescribes acquisition cost as the val-

uation method except "where market value is less than cost by a substantial amount and it is evident that the decline in market value is not due to a mere temporary condition, the amount to be included as a current asset should not exceed the market value."*

6.78    As a practical matter, many firms have adopted the lower-of-cost-or-market method for marketable debt securities during the past decade. The issuance of FASB *Statement No. 12* has made this practice even more acceptable. The lower-of-cost-or-market method is usually applied to the portfolio of marketable debt securities separately from the portfolio of marketable equity securities.

**Evaluation of Lower of Cost or Market**    6.79
The lower-of-cost-or-market valuation method provides only a partial solution to accounting for marketable securities. Since at least 1939, accounting theorists have argued that marketable securities should be shown at market value, whether greater or less than cost. Their very marketability makes valuing them on a current basis reasonably objective. The market value of the securities is the most relevant value for assessing a firm's liquidity. The FASB has taken the position, however, that permitting the write-up of marketable securities to an amount greater than acquisition cost would be a departure from historical cost accounting, a move that the FASB does not feel is appropriate yet. The case for market values for marketable securities is so strong that upward revaluations from acquisition cost may soon become part of generally accepted accounting principles. Keep in mind that the total gain (or loss) on the holding of a security is the difference between the cash received on disposal less the original cash cost; over long enough time periods, income equals cash-in less cash-out. The write-downs and write-ups, if any, merely allocate that income to the various accounting periods between the date of purchase and of sale as market conditions change.

---

FASB defended its choice of the whole-portfolio application in part as follows. *Statement No. 12* requires the parenthetic or footnote disclosure of the gross unrealized holding gain on all securities on which there are gains separately from the disclosure of the gross unrealized holding loss on all securities with losses. From these two disclosures, the reader can ascertain the extent to which the balance sheet valuation results from offsetting gains on some securities against losses on others. (If the lower-of-cost-or-market valuation basis were applied security by security, rather than to the entire portfolio, the net balance sheet amount would always be equal to or lower than the amount currently reported. The general rule is that in applying the lower-of-cost-or-market basis security by security, the net balance sheet amount would be the original cost of all securities less the amount of gross losses on securities where there are losses. One of the chapter-end problems explores this phenomenon.)

---

*Paragraph 14.49 of Chapter 14 and its footnote discuss the lack of guidance for deciding when a decline is "not due to a mere temporary condition."

*Exhibit 6.6*
**Detailed Illustration of Current**
**Assets on the Balance Sheet**
**Caral Company**
**Balance Sheet (Excerpts)**
**June 30, 1981 and 1980**

|  | June 30, 1981 | | June 30, 1980 | |
|---|---|---|---|---|
| **Current Assets** | | | | |
| Cash in Change and Petty Cash Funds | | $ 1,000 | | $ 800 |
| Cash in Bank | | 13,000 | | 11,000 |
| Cash Held as Compensating Balances | | 1,500 | | 1,500 |
| Certificates of Deposit | | 8,000 | | 7,500 |
| Marketable Securities Acquisition Cost | $30,000 | | $25,000 | |
| Less: Allowance for Excess of Cost of Marketable Securities over Market Value (On June 30, 1980, market value of $31,000 exceeds cost) | (3,000) | | — | |
| Marketable Securities at Lower of Cost or Market (See Note A) | | 27,000 | | 25,000 |
| Interest and Dividends Receivable | | 500 | | 400 |
| Accounts Receivable[a] | | 54,500 | | 53,700 |
| Merchandise Inventory[a] | | 72,000 | | 67,000 |
| Prepayments | | 4,800 | | 4,300 |
| Total Current Assets | | $182,300 | | $171,200 |

**Note A.** Gross unrealized holding gains and gross unrealized holding losses on Marketable Securities are as follows:[b]

|  | June 30, 1981 | June 30, 1980 |
|---|---|---|
| Gross Unrealized Holding Gains | $7,000 | $7,000 |
| Gross Unrealized Holding Losses | (10,000) | (1,000) |
| Net Unrealized Holding Gain (Loss) | ($3,000) | $6,000 |

[a]Additional, required disclosures for these items omitted here. See Chapters 7 and 9.

[b]Some income statement details are omitted here.

## Summary

6.80 This chapter has examined the accounting for cash and marketable securities. These assets are generally stated on the balance sheet at their current cash-equivalent value. Balance sheet classifications for these assets should indicate any restrictions on the use of these resources. Exhibit 6.6 illustrates disclosure of the current assets of the Caral Company, including some accounts discussed in later chapters. Most published balance sheets would not include so much detail as is shown here for the purposes of illustration. An immaterial account balance is, in practice, combined with another suitable account's balance.

## Questions and Short Cases

6.1 Review the meaning of the following concepts or terms discussed in this chapter.
   a. Liquidity.
   b. Insolvent.
   c. Change fund.
   d. Petty cash (imprest) fund.
   e. Demand deposits.
   f. Certificate of deposit.

g. Foreign currency.
h. Compensating balance.
i. Marketable securities.
j. Investments (noncurrent).
k. Marketable debt securities.
l. Marketable equity securities.
m. Lower of cost or market.

n. Unrealized holding loss on marketable securities.
o. Recovery of unrealized holding loss on marketable securities.
p. Realized holding gain or loss on marketable securities.

6.2   What evidence of cash control have you observed in a cafeteria? A department store? A theater? A gasoline service station?

6.3   The Tastee Delight ice cream stores prominently advertise on signs in the stores that the customer's purchase is free if the clerk does not present a receipt. Oakland's Original hot dog stand says that the customer's purchase is free if the cash register receipt contains a red star. What cash-control purposes do such policies serve?

6.4   Current assets are defined as those assets that are expected to be turned into cash, sold, or consumed during the next operating cycle. Cash is not always classified as a current asset, however. Explain.

6.5   Indicate whether or not each of the following items should be included in "Cash" on the balance sheet. If not, indicate how the item should be reported.
a. Cash that has been collected from customers and is awaiting deposit in the firm's checking account.
b. Cash left in cash registers each day to serve as a change fund.
c. Cash set aside in a special savings account to accumulate funds to replace equipment as it wears out. The firm is not legally obligated to use the funds for this purpose.
d. Cash set aside in a special savings account to accumulate funds to retire debt as it becomes due. The firm is legally obligated to use the funds for this purpose.
e. A postdated check received from a customer. The check is dated 60 days after the date of the balance sheet and cannot be cashed until the date written on the check.
f. A money order received from a customer.
g. Postage stamps.
h. Cash in a petty cash fund that is used for small miscellaneous expenditures, such as freight.
i. Cash in a checking account that must be maintained at a certain minimum level in accordance with a written loan agreement for a 6-month loan.

6.6   Would application of the lower-of-cost-or-market valuation method to the portfolio of marketable equity securities or to each marketable equity security individually result in the more conservative asset values and net income amounts?

6.7   Indicate the classification of the following securities in the balance sheet of Bower Corporation on December 31. Bower Corporation ordinarily holds bonds and notes until maturity.
a. U.S. Treasury Bills, acquired on October 15 of this year and maturing on April 15 of next year.
b. Shares of common stock of Home Savings and Loan Association held as an investment. Bower Corporation maintains savings accounts and certificates of deposit in Home Savings and Loan Association.
c. Shares of Brazil Coffee Corporation, a major supplier of raw materials for Bower Corporation's products. The shares are held to guarantee supplies of raw materials from Brazil Coffee Corporation.

    d. Shares of Overland Transportation Company. The shares were originally acquired as a temporary investment of excess cash. Overland Transportation Company has been so profitable that Bower Corporation plans to increase its ownership percentage, eventually obtaining 51 percent of the outstanding shares.

    e. American Telephone and Telegraph Company bonds that will mature in 10 years. The bonds were acquired with a cash advance from a customer on a contract for the manufacture of machinery.

**6.8** Douglas Corporation borrowed $1,000,000 from State National Bank on July 1, agreeing to repay the loan a year later. The bank charges Douglas Corporation interest at its prime lending rate, currently 15 percent. The principal and all interest on the loan are payable at maturity. Douglas Corporation must maintain a $100,000 compensating balance in an interest-free checking account at a State National Bank during the term of the loan.

    a. What is the effective annual interest rate that Douglas Corporation is paying on this loan?

    b. What message to Douglas Corporation is implicit in State National Bank's requirement that a compensating balance be maintained?

**6.9** (Adapted from AICPA *Technical Practice Aids.*) Truitt Textile Company purchased a series of commodity options entitling it to a delivery of cotton at a fixed price. Since the time the options were acquired, cotton has increased in price so much that a huge profit will be realized when the options are sold or when the cotton is accepted on delivery and resold. The expected profit on the cotton transactions is larger than the average annual net income over the last five years. When the profit is realized, how should it be reported?

**6.10** Suppliers and employees who do not demand immediate cash payments for their goods and services are effectively supplying a firm with cash, at least temporarily. In parallel, when a firm does not demand immediate payment for sales, but instead accepts an increased amount of accounts receivable, it is in effect using its own liquidity to supply cash to customers. Other things being equal, a firm would like to restrict severely the amount of cash loaned interest-free to customers (through accounts receivable) and increase without limit the amount of cash borrowed interest-free from suppliers and employees (through accounts and wages payable).

    Shown in Exhibit 6.7 are excerpts from the financial statements of Safeway Stores and Sears, Roebuck & Company for 3 years. Both of these companies are retailers—Safeway carries out most of its operations in grocery stores where most sales are for cash, whereas most of Sears' sales are credit sales in department stores. Some of Sears' credit sales, those for which payment is to be made more than 1 month or so after the sale, carry explicit interest charges to the customer. On the remainder of Sears' credit sales, there are no interest charges.

    Analyze the data given here to determine which company seems to be more successful in financing its operations with noninterest-bearing capital. Which company seems to be doing better over the 3 years reported on here? On what analysis do you base your answer? Is there such a thing as an interest-free loan? Explain.

**6.11** Refer to the financial statements for International Corporation in Appendix A at the back of the book.

    a. The consolidated balance sheet shows that cash increased from $98.9 million to $118.0 million during the year 1981, an increase of $19.1 million. Prepare an analysis that explains this change; indicate (1) the amount of cash obtained from operations, issuing bonds and stock, and other sources and (2) the amount of cash used for dividends, acquisition of

*Exhibit 6.7*
**Excerpts from the Financial
Statements of
Safeway Stores and
Sears, Roebuck & Company**

| | Dollar Amounts in Millions | | |
|---|---|---|---|
| | Year 1 | Year 2 | Year 3 |
| | Safeway Stores | | |
| Noninterest-Bearing Accounts Receivable ................. | $ 29 | $ 33 | $ 40 |
| Noninterest-Bearing Accounts Payable ................... | 530 | 525 | 636 |
| Total Equities ........................................ | 1,490 | 1,575 | 1,709 |
| Sales ................................................ | 8,185 | 9,717 | 10,443 |
| Net Income ......................................... | 79 | 149 | 106 |
| | Sears, Roebuck & Company | | |
| Noninterest-Bearing Accounts Receivable ................. | $ 230 | $ 222 | $ 227 |
| Total Accounts Receivable ............................ | 4,979 | 5,201 | 5,672 |
| Noninterest-Bearing Accounts Payable ................... | 843 | 1,120 | 991 |
| Total Equities ....................................... | 11,339 | 11,577 | 12,711 |
| Sales ................................................ | 13,101 | 13,640 | 14,950 |
| Net Income ......................................... | 511 | 523 | 695 |

property, plant and equipment, and other uses. (Hint: You may want to review the relevant procedures in Chapter 4.)

b. Prepare an analysis that explains the change in the Marketable Securities account of International Corporation between the beginning and end of 1981.

6.12 Marketable securities costing $1,000,000 are sold to another company. Consideration received from the other company is in the form of promises to pay $110,000 per year for ten years, or $1,100,000 in total. Does this transaction imply a likely gain or loss on sale of the marketable securities?

6.13 Indicate the treatment of each of the following independent events or transactions relating to marketable securities held as current assets.

a. A marketable equity security is transferred from the current asset portfolio to the noncurrent asset portfolio of investments at a time when the market value exceeds cost.

b. Same as in part a, but on the date of transfer, the market value is less than cost.

c. A portfolio of marketable debt securities, held as current assets, has market value less than cost at the end of the period when they were first acquired.

d. The portfolio in the preceding part has a market value greater than cost at the end of the second period, the one following acquisition.

## Problems and Exercises

6.14 Calculate the amount to be shown as "Cash" on the balance sheet as of December 31 for Stupp Transportation Company. Use the following information:

a. Coins, currency, and checks received from customers on December 31 but not yet deposited, $5,300.

b. Amount in a petty cash fund maintained for making small miscellaneous cash expenditures. The fund normally has a balance of $100, but expenditures of $14 were made on December 31.

c. The firm's postage meter was "filled" on December 31 and contains $500 of postage.

d. The books indicate that the balance in the firm's checking account on December 31 is $45,800. When the bank statement is received on January 10 of the next year, it is learned that one customer's check for $800, which was deposited on December 28, was returned to Stupp because the customer's account had insufficient funds. In addition, the bank collected during December a note receivable from one of Stupp's customers and added the amount to Stupp's bank account. The note had a face value of $200 and interest of $20.

e. Certificate of deposit for a face value of $10,000. The certificate was acquired on July 1 of this year and matures on June 30 next year. Simple interest of 8 percent per year accumulates on the certificate and is payable at maturity with the principal.

f. British sterling currency, £10,000. The exchange rate on December 31 is $2.00 per pound sterling.

**6.15** Prepare appropriate journal entries to record the following events. If a journal entry is not required, state the reason.

a. A petty cash fund of $500 is established on July 1 by drawing a check on the firm's regular checking account.

b. Disbursements from the petty cash fund from July 1 to July 7 are as follows: supplies, $146; postage, $85; freight, $36.

c. Disbursements from the petty cash fund from July 8 to July 15 are as follows: supplies, $67; freight, $24; travel advance, $100.

d. A check of the petty cash fund on July 15 reveals $40 in cash and receipts for the items in parts **b** and **c**.

e. On July 16, a check for $460 is drawn on the firm's regular checking account to replenish the petty cash fund.

**6.16** Prepare journal entries to record the following independent events.

a. Cash register tapes indicate that sales of $24,635 were made today. Cash in this amount is collected from the cash register drawers and deposited in the bank.

b. A petty cash fund for $100 is established by drawing a check on the regular checking account.

c. A firm borrows $10,000 from its bank. The loan agreement requires the firm to maintain a compensating balance of $1,000 in an interest-free account with the bank.

d. The payroll for the month of July totals $68,000. Checks drawn on the firm's special payroll account totaling $68,000 are issued to employees. A single check for this amount is drawn on the firm's regular checking account and deposited in the payroll account.

e. A count of a petty cash fund that began the period with $300 reveals receipts as follows: supplies, $146; postage, $45; travel advance, $40. Cash in the amount of $70 is also found in the fund. A check for $230 is written to replenish the fund.

f. The bank statement received indicates the following: service charge, $12; note from customer collected by the bank and added to account balance, $110 ($100 face plus $10 interest); the firm's check, correctly written and recorded in the books in the amount of $479, is charged against the firm's account for $497.

g. A check for $10,000 is drawn on the firm's regular checking account and deposited with a local bank serving as trustee under a bond sinking fund arrangement.

h. A certificate of deposit in the amount of $20,000 is acquired using funds in a time deposit (savings) account.

6.17    Refer to the Simplified Funds Statement for a Period in Exhibit 4.13. Nine of the lines in the statement are numbered. Line (2) should be expanded to say "Additions for Expenses, Losses, and Other Charges against Income Not Using Funds" and line (3) should be expanded to say "Subtractions for Revenues, Gains, and Other Credits to Income Not Producing Funds from Operations." Ignore the unnumbered lines in responding to the questions below.

Assume that the accounting cycle is complete for the period and that all of the financial statements have been prepared. Then it is discovered that a transaction has been overlooked. That transaction is recorded in the accounts and all of the financial statements are corrected. Define *funds* as *working capital*. For each of the following transactions or events, indicate which of the numbered lines of the funds statement is affected and by how much. Ignore income tax effects.

a. A firm owns marketable securities. Dividends of $10,000 are declared on the shares owned.

b. The portfolio of marketable securities has a market value of $50,000 less than their net amount shown on the balance sheet at the end of the previous accounting period. An entry is made changing the allowance account contra to marketable securities.

c. The market value of the same portfolio of marketable securities referred to in part **b** has increased $20,000 by the end of the next period. An entry is made changing the allowance account for marketable securities.

6.18    Elliott Company started business in 1978. The aggregate cost and aggregate market value of the portfolio of marketable equity securities of Elliott Corporation at various dates are shown below:

| Date | Aggregate Cost | Aggregate Market Value |
|---|---|---|
| December 31, 1978 | $150,000 | $140,000 |
| December 31, 1979 | 160,000 | 154,000 |
| December 31, 1980 | 170,000 | 175,000 |
| December 31, 1981 | 180,000 | 178,000 |

Give the journal entry required at the end of each year, assuming that the accounting period is the calendar year.

6.19    Data concerning marketable equity securities from the balance sheet and notes of Myers Company for 4 years are shown in Exhibit 6.8. Recall that balance sheet amounts result from applying the lower-of-cost-or-market rule to the entire portfolio rather than security by security.

a. What would the balance sheet amount be for each of the 4 years if the lower-of-cost-or-market rule were applied security by security rather than to the entire portfolio? If you cannot deduce this amount for any year, explain why.

b. State a rule for deducing from the disclosures required by the FASB the security-by-security result of applying a lower-of-cost-or-market valuation.

---

*Exhibit 6.8*
**Myers Company**
**Data on Marketable Securities**

| | Year 1 | Year 2 | Year 3 | Year 4 |
|---|---|---|---|---|
| **From Balance Sheet** | | | | |
| Marketable Securities at Cost .................... | $10,000 | $10,000 | $8,000 | $8,000 |
| Allowance for Excess of Cost of Marketable | | | | |
|   Securities over Market Value ................... | (2,000) | (2,000) | — | — |
| Market Securities at Lower of Cost or Market ...... | $ 8,000 | $ 8,000 | $8,000 | $8,000 |
| **From Notes** | | | | |
| Gross Unrealized Holding Gains on Securities | | | | |
|   Where Market Exceeds Cost .................... | $ 0 | $ 1,000 | $3,000 | $3,000 |
| Gross Unrealized Holding Losses on Securities | | | | |
|   Where Cost Exceeds Market .................... | $ 2,000 | $ 3,000 | $ 0 | $2,000 |

---

**6.20** Give the likely transaction or event that would result in making each of the following independent journal entries.

**a.** Marketable Securities ................................................ 10,000
      Cash ......................................................... 10,000

**b.** Unrealized Holding Loss on Valuation of Marketable Equity Securities ......... 4,000
      Allowance for Excess of Cost of Marketable Equity Securities over Market
        Value ...................................................... 4,000

**c.** Cash ......................................................... 1,200
      Loss on Sale of Marketable Securities .................................. 200
      Marketable Securities ..................................... 1,400

**d.** Allowance for Excess of Cost of Marketable Securities over Market Value ..... 1,000
      Recovery of Unrealized Holding Loss on Valuation of Marketable Equity
      Securities .................................................. 1,000

**6.21** **a.** Arrange the following data related to the Wendal Company in bank reconciliation form.

| | |
|---|---|
| Adjusted Bank Balance ................................................. | $6,853 |
| Adjusted Book Balance ................................................. | 6,853 |
| Balance per Bank Statement, October 31 ........................................ | 7,941 |
| Balance per Books, October 31 ....................................... | 6,075 |
| Error in Deposit of October 28; $457 Deposit Entered on Books as $475 ............ | 18 |
| Outstanding Checks ...................................................... | 1,233 |
| Payroll Account Check Deducted from This Account in Error by the Bank .......... | 145 |
| Proceeds on Note of W. Y. Jones, Taken by the Bank for Collection, Less Collection | |
|   Fee of $4 ............................................................... | 796 |

**b.** Present journal entries on the books of the Wendal Company to record the adjustments indicated in the bank reconciliation schedule.

**6.22** **a.** Prepare a bank reconciliation schedule at July 31 for the Home Appliance Company from the following information:

| | |
|---|---:|
| Balance per Bank Statement, July 29 | $1,240 |
| Balance per Ledger, July 31 | 714 |
| Deposit of July 30 Not Recorded by Bank | 280 |
| Debit Memo—Service Charges | 8 |
| Credit Memo—Collection of Note by Bank | 300 |

An analysis of the canceled checks returned with the bank statement reveals the following:
Check #901 for purchase of supplies was drawn for $58 but was recorded as $85.
The manager wrote a check for traveling expenses of $95 while out of town. The check was not recorded. The following checks are outstanding:

| | |
|---|---:|
| #650 | $120 |
| #721 | 162 |
| #728 | 300 |
| | $582 |

**b.** Journalize the adjusting entries required by the information revealed in the bank reconciliation schedule.

**6.23**  Refer to the data in Problem **6.22** for the Home Appliance Company. Prepare a bank reconciliation using the bank-to-book format.

**6.24**  Refer to the data in Problem **6.22** and the additional data given here. Prepare a bank reconciliation using four-column proof of cash format.

| | |
|---|---:|
| Balance per Bank Statement, June 30 | $ 1,400 |
| Balance per Ledger, June 30 | 1,170 |
| Cash Receipts for Month of July | 12,650 |
| Disbursements from Cash Account for Month of July | 13,106 |
| Deposits in Transit June 30, Recorded by Bank in July | 330 |
| Checks Outstanding on June 30, Clearing Bank in July | 560 |
| Checks Clearing Bank in July, Including the Amount, $560, Described Above | 13,160 |

**6.25**  On May 31, the books of the Locus Land Company show a debit balance in the Cash in Bank account of $4,799. The bank statement at that date shows a balance of $6,066. The deposit of May 31 of $205 is not included in the bank statement. Notice of collections made by the bank on mortgages of the company in the amount of $243, including interest of $8, and of bank service charges of $6, have not previously been received. Outstanding checks at May 31 total $1,235.
**a.** Prepare a bank reconciliation for the Locus Land Company at May 31.
**b.** Journalize the entries required upon preparation of the bank reconciliation schedule.

**6.26**  The following items are taken from the April 30 bank reconciliation schedule of the Porter Company. Present a journal entry required on the books of the company for each item: indicate if no adjustment is required.
(1) Outstanding checks total $1,650.
(2) A check drawn as $196 for office supplies was recorded in the appropriate journal as $169.
(3) Included among the checks returned by the bank was one for $150 drawn by the Paula Company and charged to this company in error.

(4) The April 3 deposit of $420 was not included on the bank statement.

(5) A debit memorandum in the amount of $10 was included for service charges for April.

(6) The bank collected a note of $1,750, including $50 interest, for the company.

(7) Checks for traveling expenses of $250 had not been entered in the journal.

(8) A check was written and recorded on April 29 for the regular monthly salary of an office employee who had resigned on March 31. The check has been voided, but an entry to record the voiding has not been made. The monthly salary was $600; deductions of 8 percent for FICA taxes and $120 for withheld income taxes were made from the amount due the employee.

6.27    The bank reconciliation of the Clark Company at March 31 was as follows:

| | |
|---|---:|
| Balance per Bank Statement, March 31 | $3,850 |
| Unrecorded Deposit | 475 |
| | $4,325 |
| Outstanding Checks | 820 |
| Adjusted Bank Balance, March 31 | $3,505 |

The bank statement, returned checks, and other documents received from the bank at the end of April provide the following information:

| | |
|---|---:|
| Balance, April 29 | $3,685 |
| Deposit of March 31 | 475 |
| Deposits of April 1–29, Including a Credit Memo for Collection of a Note, $808 | 16,160 |
| Canceled Checks Issued prior to April 1 | 600 |
| Canceled Checks Issued during April | 16,200 |

The Cash in Bank account of the Clark Company for the month of April shows deposits of $16,190 and checks drawn of $17,015. The credit memo has not yet been recorded on the books of the company; it represents the collection of a note with $800 face value on which $5 interest had been accrued as of March 31.

a. Prepare a bank reconciliation for the Clark Company at April 30.

b. Present journal entries for any adjustments of the company's books resulting from the information found in the bank reconciliation.

6.28    Information relating to the marketable equity securities of Mizal Corporation is summarized in Exhibit 6.9.

*Exhibit 6.9*
**Mizal Corporation**
**Marketable Equity Securities**

| Security | Date Acquired | Acquisition Cost | Date Sold | Selling Price | Market Value Dec. 31, 1980 | Market Value Dec. 31, 1981 |
|---|---|---|---|---|---|---|
| A | 1/ 5/1980 | $40,000 | 11/5/1981 | $43,000 | $41,000 | — |
| B | 6/12/1980 | 85,000 | — | — | 80,000 | $82,000 |
| C | 2/22/1981 | 48,000 | — | — | — | 46,000 |
| D | 3/25/1981 | 25,000 | 11/5/1981 | 23,000 | — | — |
| E | 4/25/1981 | 36,000 | — | — | — | 36,000 |

a. Give all journal entries relating to these marketable equity securities during 1980 and 1981, assuming that the calendar year is the accounting period.

b. Indicate the manner in which marketable securities would be presented in the balance sheet and related notes on December 31, 1980.

c. Indicate the manner in which marketable securities would be presented in the balance sheet and related notes on December 31, 1981.

6.29 Information relating to the marketable equity securities of Shelby Corporation is summarized in Exhibit 6.10.

---

*Exhibit 6.10*
**Shelby Corporation**
**Marketable Equity Securities**

| Security | Date Acquired | Acquisition Cost | Date Sold | Selling Price | Market Value Dec. 31, 1980 | Market Value Dec. 31, 1981 |
|---|---|---|---|---|---|---|
| W | 10/15/1980 | $142,000 | 2/15/1981 | $136,000 | $140,000 | — |
| X | 12/28/1980 | 56,000 | 11/28/1981 | 59,000 | 56,000 | — |
| Y | 2/15/1981 | 136,000 | — | — | — | $139,000 |
| Z | 11/28/1981 | 59,000 | — | — | — | 58,000 |

---

a. Give all journal entries relating to these marketable equity securities during 1980 and 1981, assuming that the calendar year is the accounting period.

b. Indicate the manner in which marketable securities would be presented in the balance sheet and related notes on December 31, 1980.

c. Indicate the manner in which marketable securities would be presented in the balance sheet and related notes on December 31, 1981.

6.30 Information relating to the marketable equity securities of TSS Company is shown in Exhibit 6.11.

---

*Exhibit 6.11*
**TSS Company**
**Marketable Equity Securities**

| Security | Date Acquired | Acquisition Cost | Date Sold | Selling Price | Market Value Dec. 31, 1980 | Market Value Dec. 31, 1981 |
|---|---|---|---|---|---|---|
| H | 4/26/1980 | $18,000 | 2/9/1981 | $15,000 | $16,000 | — |
| I | 5/25/1980 | 25,000 | 8/10/1981 | 26,000 | 24,000 | — |
| J | 11/24/1980 | 12,000 | — | — | 14,000 | $15,000 |
| K | 2/26/1981 | 34,000 | — | — | — | 33,500 |
| L | 12/17/1981 | 8,000 | — | — | — | 7,800 |

---

a. Compute the realized and the unrealized holding gain or loss for 1980, in accordance with FASB *Statement No. 12*.

b. Compute the realized and the unrealized holding gain or loss for 1981, in accordance with FASB *Statement No. 12*.

c. Repeat parts **a** and **b** but assume that lower-of-cost-or-market is applied for each security rather than the portfolio of securities. Base gains and losses on sale of each marketable security on its lower-of-cost-or-market book value.

d. Does application of lower-of-cost-or-market at the level of the portfolio or at the level of individual securities result in the more conservative asset values and measures of earnings?

6.31  On July 5, the Jozsi Company received its monthly statement together with canceled checks and other documents from the Westmoreland Bank. The following information is available from the statement and accompanying documents:

(1) Balance, May 31: $1,325,670.
(2) Deposits: No. 106, $89,980; No. 107, $95,450; Nos. 108–127, $1,912,540.
(3) Credit Memo: Deposit of May 23, previously erroneously added to the account of the Jazz Products Company, $20,330.
(4) Debit Memo: Service charges for June, $130.
(5) Checks canceled during June:

| No. 521 | $103,950 | No. 607 | $ 91,080 | No. 616 | $60,400 |
|---|---|---|---|---|---|
| 524 | 91,030 | 608 | 106,310 | 617 | 74,710 |
| 525 | 102,020 | 609 | 45,420 | 619 | 71,350 |
| 526 | 32,560 | 610 | 37,870 | 620 | 39,460 |
| 601 | 80,740 | 611 | 67,640 | 621 | 96,060 |
| 602 | 83,660 | 612 | 80,130 | 622 | 65,460 |
| 603 | 86,020 | 613 | 102,020 | 623 | 67,820 |
| 604 | 88,970 | 614 | 66,770 | 723 | 32,920 |
| 606 | 87,030 | 615 | 47,250 | | |

(6) Balance, June 30: $1,533,010.

A review of the records of the Jozsi Company indicates the following information relative to the checking account in the Westmoreland Bank:

(1) Balance, May 31: $998,020.
(2) Deposits: Nos. 107–126, $1,907,000; No. 127, $100,990; No. 128, $93,060.
(3) Checks issued during June:

| No. 601 | $ 80,740 | No. 610 | $ 37,870 | No. 619 | $71,350 |
|---|---|---|---|---|---|
| 602 | 83,660 | 611 | 67,640 | 620 | 39,460 |
| 603 | 86,020 | 612 | 80,130 | 621 | 96,060 |
| 604 | 88,970 | 613 | 102,020 | 622 | 65,460 |
| 605 | 81,050 | 614 | 66,770 | 623 | 67,820 |
| 606 | 87,030 | 615 | 47,250 | 624 | 62,510 |
| 607 | 91,080 | 616 | 60,400 | 625 | 60,430 |
| 608 | 103,610 | 617 | 74,710 | 626 | 64,450 |
| 609 | 45,420 | 618 | 93,210 | 627 | 73,840 |

(4) Balance, June 30: $1,117,930.
(5) The reconciliation of May 31 indicated the following: Outstanding checks as follows: No. 521, $103,950; No. 522, $42,340; No. 523, $66,060; No. 524, $91,030; No. 525, $102,020; No. 526, $32,560.
Deposit in transit: No. 106, $89,980.
Deposit erroneously credited to Jazz Products company: $20,330.
(6) Check No. 723 was issued by the Jazz Products Company.
(7) Any other errors indicated by a difference between the bank records and the company records are found to be errors by the company.

a. Prepare a statement reconciling the difference between the balance on the bank statement and the cash balance in the books as of May 31.

b. Prepare a bank reconciliation statement as of June 30. Use the format of Exhibit 6.1.

c. Present the journal entries which must be made on books of the Jozsi Company, as indicated in the reconciliation statement as of June 30.

6.32   The bank reconciliation of the commercial account of the Parrot Company at February 28 is as follows:

---

**Parrot Company**
**Lindell Bank—Commercial Account**
**Bank Reconciliation**
**February 28**

| | | |
|---|---:|---:|
| Balance per Bank Statement, February 28 | | $520,950 |
| Unrecorded Deposit of February 28 | | 63,640 |
| Payroll Check No. 822 deducted from this account in error | | 4,960 |
| | | $589,550 |
| Less Outstanding Checks: | | |
| No. 109 | $ 4,000 | |
| 214 | 70,020 | |
| 215 | 41,060 | |
| 216 | 6,030 | |
| 218 | 68,040 | |
| 220 | 39,990 | |
| Total Outstanding Checks | | 229,140 |
| Adjusted Bank Balance, February 28 | | $360,410 |
| Balance per Books, February 28 | | $358,680 |
| Error in Deposit of February 25; $57,360 entered as $53,760 | | 3,600 |
| Exchange and Collection Fees | $ 70 | |
| Error in Check No. 209; $14,210 entered as $12,410 | 1,800 | (1,870) |
| Adjusted Book Balance, February 28 | | $360,410 |

---

The cash account during the month of March records the following disbursements by check:

| No. 301 | $202,020 | No. 008 | $133,050 | No. 315 | $ 7,220 |
|---|---|---|---|---|---|
| 302 | 15,440 | 309 | 62,690 | 316 | 143,210 |
| 303 | 23,535 | 310 | 42,470 | 317 | 45,680 |
| 304 | 101,010 | 311 | 36,780 | 318 | 118,560 |
| 305 | 22,220 | 312 | 100,040 | 319 | 50,000 |
| 306 | 44,660 | 313 | 23,450 | 320 | 12,570 |
| 307 | 7,770 | 314 | 66,030 | 321 | 32,030 |
| | | | | Total | $1,290,435 |

The deposits journalized during the month of March are:

| Mar. 1 | $55,220 | Mar. 11 | $ 97,150 | Mar. 23 | $ 61,310 |
|---|---|---|---|---|---|
| 2 | 57,660 | 14 | 60,540 | 24 | 73,890 |
| 3 | 61,530 | 15 | 54,680 | 25 | 98,440 |
| 4 | 99,980 | 16 | 52,830 | 28 | 60,930 |
| 7 | 51,340 | 17 | 67,960 | 29 | 54,120 |
| 8 | 58,290 | 18 | 102,720 | 30 | 56,750 |
| 9 | 56,310 | 21 | 59,250 | 31 | 58,510 |
| 10 | 63,470 | 22 | 50,670 | | $1,513,550 |

The bank account in the ledger appears as follows:

**Commercial Account—Cash in Bank**

| March 1 | Balance | √ | 360,410 | March 15 | GJ | 5,500 |
|---|---|---|---|---|---|---|
| 31 | | CR | 1,513,550 | 31 | CR | 1,290,435 |

General journal entries affecting the bank account made during the month of March were:

March 15
Cash on Hand ............................................................... 5,500
    Cash in Bank ............................................................ 5,500
Check of A. B. Pitney returned by bank subsequent to deposit—insufficient funds. To be redeposited.

Checks and other memoranda returned by the bank with the statement of March 31, after sorting into serial number order:

| No. 214 | $ 70,020 | No. 304 | $101,010 | No. 314 | $ 66,030 |
|---|---|---|---|---|---|
| 215 | 41,060 | 305 | 22,220 | 316 | 143,210 |
| 216 | 6,030 | 306 | 44,660 | 318 | 118,560 |
| 218 | 68,040 | 308 | 130,350 | 319 | 50,000 |
| 301 | 202,020 | 309 | 62,690 | 320 | 12,570 |
| 302 | 15,440 | 311 | 36,780 | | |
| 303 | 23,535 | 312 | 100,040 | | |

Debit memo—$5,500: Check of A. B. Pitney returned because of insufficient funds.
Credit memo—$40,300: Collection of note of $40,000 plus interest of $400 less fee of $100.
    (Interest of $300 was accrued as of February 28).
Credit memo—$4,960: Payroll check deducted in error in February. See February 28 bank reconciliation.

Deposits shown on bank statement for March:

| | | |
|---|---|---|
| $63,640 | $ 63,470 | $61,310 |
| 4,960 CM | 97,150 | 40,300 CM |
| 55,220 | 60,540 | 73,890 |
| 57,660 | 54,680 | 98,440 |
| 61,530 | 52,830 | 60,930 |
| 99,980 | 67,960 | 54,120 |
| 51,340 | 102,720 | 56,750 |
| 58,290 | 59,250 | |
| 56,310 | 50,670 | |

CM = credit memorandum.

Balance shown on bank statement for March 31 is $765,125.

a. Present journal entries which must be made on the books of the Parrot Company following the preparation of the bank reconciliation at February 28.
b. Prepare a reconciliation statement at March 31. Use the format of Exhibit 6.1. Assume that any error detected was made by the company rather than the bank.
c. Present the journal entries which must be made on the books of the Parrot Company as indicated by the reconciliation statement of March 31.

# Chapter 7
# *Revenue Recognition and Receivables: Time of Sale*

7.1 The recognition of revenue from the sale of goods or services involves a *timing* question—when it is recognized—and a *measurement* question—how much is recognized. As Chapter 2 pointed out, revenue is usually recognized at the time goods are sold or services are rendered. The amount of revenue recognized is equal to the cash expected to be collected. Revenue may, however, be recognized either earlier or later than the time of sale. This chapter and the next discuss the accounting principles applicable to the recognition of revenue and the measurement of related receivables.

## Revenue Recognition at Time of Sale: General Principles

7.2 Revenue is recognized when (1) all, or a substantial portion, of the services to be provided have been performed, and (2) cash, a receivable, or some other asset susceptible to reasonably precise measurement has been received. For the vast majority of firms involved in selling goods and services, these criteria for revenue recognition are met at the time of sale (delivery). The goods have been transferred to a buyer or the services have been performed. Future services, such as for warranties, are likely to be insignificant, or if significant, can be estimated with

reasonable precision. The negotiations between the buyer and seller have resulted in an agreed-upon exchange price. This exchange price serves as the basis for initially measuring the amount of revenue to be recognized. Adjustments to this exchange price amount are usually necessary, however, to recognize the fact that cash in the full amount of the exchange price will not be collected. Adjustments may be necessary for discounts, returns, allowances, uncollectible accounts, and other items. The objective is to recognize revenue in the period of sale and report related receivables in an amount equal to the cash expected to be collected.

## Measurement of Revenue and Accounts Receivable

7.3 The sale of certain goods and services, such as retail food items, theatrical performances, and public transportation, are usually made for cash. Most sales of goods and services, however, are made on *open account*. Under an open account arrangement, the buyer agrees to abide by the general credit terms of the seller. The arrangement may require full payment within 30 days from the date of sale, or a certain percentage may be due each month (that is, the receivable is payable in installments). A formal note or contract is not usually prepared for sales on open account (although a sales slip might be signed by the customer acknowledging receipt of the merchandise or services).

7.4    Receivables relating to sales on open account are initially recorded at the exchange price. Adjustments to the exchange price may be made for trade and quantity discounts, cash discounts, delayed payments, returns and allowances, and uncollectible accounts. These adjustments could theoretically be made either (1) at the time of sale, (2) at the end of the period during which the sale takes place, or (3) during some future period when discounts are taken, merchandise is returned, or accounts are written off as uncollectible. Recognition of sales and receivables adjustments during the period of the sale (alternatives 1 and 2) results in a proper matching of the revenue adjustments with related revenues and a proper measurement of accounts receivable at the end of the period. Recognition of such adjustments in a subsequent period (alternative 3) when discounts are actually taken, merchandise is returned, or uncollectible accounts are written off will result in an improper matching of one period's sales adjustments with another period's sales. The cost of a system for making adjustments in the period of sale (alternatives 1 and 2), instead of in a later period, may outweigh the benefits of precise matching.

7.5    The adjustments for discounts, returns, allowances, and uncollectible accounts could be made by debiting Sales Revenue and crediting Accounts Receivable. The amount in the Sales Revenue account would be gross sales revenue reduced by total sales adjustments. The balance in the Accounts Receivable account would be the gross amounts receivable reduced by accounts receivable adjustments. By using this procedure, however, information about the separate effects of discounts, returns, allowances and uncollectible accounts would be lost. Such information can be useful to management, investors, and others in evaluating the selling and credit-granting activities of a firm. Therefore, sales and receivable adjustments are usually recorded in contra accounts. Contra sales adjustment accounts (for example, Sales Contra, Cash Discounts; Sales Contra,

Returns and Allowances; Sales Contra, Estimated Uncollectibles) have debit balances and are subtracted from Sales Revenue in the income statement. Contra accounts receivable accounts (Allowance for Sales Discounts, Allowance for Sales Returns and Allowances, Allowance for Uncollectible Accounts) have credit balances and are subtracted from Accounts Receivable in the balance sheet.

## Trade and Quantity Discounts

Firms sometimes grant *trade discounts* to certain types of customers. A retail hardware store, for example, may permit electricians and plumbers to purchase merchandise for their business use at less than the stated retail price. A building supply firm may permit construction companies to purchase building materials for a certain percentage less than the retail price.    7.6

*Quantity discounts* are offered when the quantity of goods purchased exceeds certain prescribed levels. For example, the regular price might be reduced 1 percent for each 1,000 units purchased, with a maximum reduction of 10 percent. The amount of quantity discounts permitted is constrained by the Robinson-Patman Act, which requires that all like customers be treated alike.    7.7

Trade and quantity discounts are viewed as adjustments of the *list price* to arrive at the agreed-upon exchange price. Because the sale of goods or services is initially recorded at the exchange price, no separate accounting treatment is required. (A firm may wish, however, to maintain records internally of the amount of trade and quantity discounts granted in order to evaluate the desirability of continuing the discount arrangement.)    7.8

## Cash Discounts

Cash discounts are offered to customers as an inducement to make prompt payments. The cash discount in effect represents an interest allowance if amounts are paid promptly. Cash discounts can be justified on the grounds that cash is received more    7.9

quickly and bookkeeping and collection costs are reduced.

7.10    The principal theoretical issue is whether cash discounts should be deducted from revenue at the time revenue is recognized, at the time of collection, or at some time in between. Three methods of accounting for cash discounts are **(1)** the gross price method, **(2)** the allowance method, and **(3)** the net price method.

7.11    **Gross Price Method** The simplest and most commonly used method of accounting for cash discounts is to record sales at the gross sales price and then to record discounts actually taken as a reduction in revenue at the time of collection. Assuming that a 2-percent discount is available, typical entries under the gross price method are as follows:

```
Accounts Receivable ................... 100
    Sales Revenue ...................       100
To record sale at gross sales price.

Cash .............................. 98
Sales Contra, Cash Discounts ...........  2
    Accounts Receivable ..............       100
To record collection and discount taken.
```

Sales Contra, Cash Discounts is a revenue contra account to be subtracted from Sales Revenue in computing net revenue.

7.12    If all discounts are taken in the same period as the sale to which they relate, the gross price method provides an accurate measurement of revenues for the period and receivables at the end of the period. Revenues are stated at the net amount of cash collected or to be collected and receivables are stated at the amount of cash expected to be collected in future periods.

7.13    If all cash discounts are not taken in the period of sale, the gross price method does not measure revenues and receivables accurately. Cash discounts taken early in the next period on the sales of the current period will be reported as reductions of the next period's sales. An improper matching of sales revenue and cash discounts will result. Also, the amount shown as accounts receivable at the end of the current period will overstate the amount of cash expected to be collected. To overcome these objections to the gross

price method, either the allowance method or the net price method may be used.

**Allowance Method** Under the allowance   7.14
method, sales are recorded initially at the gross invoice price. At the end of each period (monthly, quarterly), an estimate is made of the amount of cash discounts expected to be taken on that period's sales. The estimate is based largely on past experience and is often expressed as a percentage of sales on account for the period. The amount of estimated discounts is debited to Sales Contra, Cash Discounts, a revenue contra account, and credited to Allowance for Cash Discounts, an account contra to Accounts Receivable on the balance sheet. When cash discounts are actually taken, the Allowance for Cash Discounts account is debited.

To illustrate the mechanics of the allow-   7.15
ance method, assume that a new firm is organized on January 1, 1981, to sell hardware products. Selling terms are 2/10, net 30 (2 percent reduction from the billed, or invoiced, amount will be granted if payment is made within 10 days, or the full amount must be paid within 30 days). The experience of other companies indicates that three-fourths of the customers will take advantage of cash discounts available to them.

During January, sales, all on account,   7.16
amounted to $100,000. Journal entries would be made during January with the following combined effect:

```
Accounts Receivable ............ 100,000
    Sales Revenue ..............          100,000
To record sales.
```

Collections during January amounted to $80,000, on which cash discounts of $1,350 were taken:

```
Cash ......................... 78,650
Allowance for Cash Discounts ....  1,350
    Accounts Receivable ........          80,000
To record cash collections and dis-
counts taken.
```

At the end of January, an entry is made to record the estimated amount of cash discounts that will be taken on January sales (that is, actually taken in January and expected to be taken in future periods). The estimated amount is $1,500 (= .75 × $100,000 × .02).

| Sales Contra, Cash Discounts .... | 1,500 | |
| Allowance for Cash Discounts . | | 1,500 |

The balance in the Allowance for Cash Discounts Account is now $150 (= $1,500 − $1,350). This represents the estimated amount of cash discounts that will be taken in February on the $20,000 of accounts outstanding on January 31, 1981. Note that the discount period (10 days) will probably have lapsed on a large portion of this $20,000 of receivables. Of the portion on which the discount period has not lapsed (that is, receivables arising from sales during the last 9 days of January), it is estimated that cash discounts of $150 will be taken.

7.17    Periodically, usually once a year, the balance in the Allowance for Cash Discounts account should be compared with the total amount of discounts available by an examination of each account. If the balance seems to be too large or too small, the estimation rate used in future periods must be adjusted. This adjustment is viewed as a change in an accounting estimate for which retroactive correction is not permitted.*

7.18    **Net Price Method** A third method of accounting for cash discounts is to record sales at the net sales price (net of cash discounts allowed) and to recognize lapsed discounts as additional revenue when discounts are not taken. The journal entries under the net price method for a $100 sale with terms of 2/10, net 30, and paid within 10 days are as follows:

| Accounts Receivable ..................... | 98 | |
| Sales Revenue ...................... | | 98 |
| To record sales at net sales price. | | |

| Cash ................................... | 98 | |
| Accounts Receivable .................. | | 98 |
| To record collection within the discount period. | | |

_____

*Accounting Principles Board, *Opinion No. 20* (July 1971). Chapter 23 discusses in detail the rationale and procedure for the ''prospective-only'' treatment of changes in estimates.

If the account is not paid within 10 days, the following entry is required when the gross amount is received:

| Cash .................................. | 100 | |
| Accounts Receivable ................. | | 98 |
| Cash Discounts Lapsed .............. | | 2 |
| To record collection after the discount period has lapsed. | | |

The Cash Discounts Lapsed account is a revenue account on the income statement.

The net price method would appear to 7.19 have the greatest theoretical support. Revenues and receivables are initially recorded at the current cash equivalent amount (that is, net of cash discounts available). Any additional amount received is properly viewed as a financing charge—an amount earned for extending credit—rather than a payment for the goods or services transferred. Treatment under the net price method is consistent with the treatment of a sale for which no cash discount is allowed but a specific interest charge is made for late payment (discussed in the next section).

The net price method has its greatest 7.20 justification when there is a strong likelihood that all, or almost all, cash discounts will be taken, as is likely.† If a substantial portion of cash discounts will not be taken, the amount of Accounts Receivable on the balance sheet at the end of each period under the net price method will be understated by the amount of lapsed discounts likely to be collected on these accounts next period.

Accounting for cash discounts illustrates 7.21 the kinds of trade-offs often made in accounting practice between theoretical soundness and cost/benefit assessments. The net price method has the strongest theoretical support. This method, however, is considered to involve more record-keeping costs than the gross price method. Because the effects of the various methods on income statements and balance sheet amounts are usually not materially different, the gross price method is most commonly used.

_____

†See Question **QB.6** in Appendix B.

## Finance Charges

7.22  In contrast to cash discounts allowed for prompt payments, finance charges may be assessed on accounts receivable if they are not paid by a certain time. For example, no finance charge will be assessed if an account is paid within 30 days, but a finance charge of $1^1/_2$ percent per month will be assessed on receivables outstanding for more than 30 days.

7.23  Receivables on which finance charges may be assessed are properly recorded at the agreed-upon exchange price at the time of sale. Later, when finance charges accrue on an outstanding accounts receivable, an entry is made debiting Accounts Receivable and crediting Finance Revenue or Interest Revenue.

7.24  If a credit arrangement makes no explicit provision for interest (either through a cash discount or finance charge arrangement), then ideally the account receivable should initially be recorded at the present value of the future cash flows using an interest rate appropriate for the risk level of the customer. The difference between this present-value amount and the amount of cash ultimately collected should be recognized as interest revenue during the period(s) while the receivable is outstanding. Because these two amounts are usually not materially different, implicit interest on open accounts receivable collected within approximately 1 year after sale is ignored. The question of the recognition of interest arises more frequently in the context of notes receivable. Notes receivable are discussed later in this chapter.

## Sales Returns

7.25  Some firms permit customers wide latitude in returning goods that have been purchased. This is common in the book publishing business, and a similar right of return exists in record and other club programs. A question arises as to whether revenue should be recognized at the time of the initial sale or whether revenue recognition should be postponed until the time when goods may no longer be returned.

When sales returns are material, FASB   7.26 *Statement No. 48* permits the recognition of revenue at the time of the initial sale only when six conditions are met, the most important of which are that the selling price be substantially fixed or determinable at the date of sale and that the amount of future returns be reasonably estimable.* If these conditions are met and revenue is recognized at the time of sale, the selling firm is required to provide for estimated returns in the year of sale using the allowance method.† The *amount* for this provision is the difference between the initial selling price of merchandise expected to be returned and the cost of the merchandise. To illustrate, assume that merchandise costing $80,000 is sold on account for $100,000. Past experience indicates that 20 percent of this merchandise is likely to be returned. The following entries would be made in the year of sale:

| | | |
|---|---|---|
| Accounts Receivable | 100,000 | |
|     Sales Revenue | | 100,000 |
| Cost of Goods Sold | 80,000 | |
|     Merchandise Inventory | | 80,000 |
| Sales Contra, Sales Returns | 20,000 | |
|     Cost of Goods Sold | | 16,000 |
|     Allowance for Sales Returns | | 4,000 |

To provide for estimated sales returns.

Note that both sales (through the sales contra account) and cost of goods sold are reduced in this case. Assume now that merchandise with an intitial selling price of $5,000 is returned before the customer has paid for the goods. The entry would be:

| | | |
|---|---|---|
| Merchandise Inventory | 4,000 | |
| Allowance for Sales Returns | 1,000 | |
|     Accounts Receivable | | 5,000 |

When the amount of sales returns is not material, the allowance method illustrated above need not be used. Instead, the difference between the selling price of the returned goods and their cost (or net realizable value, if lower than cost) is charged to Sales

---

*Financial Accounting Standards Board, *Statement No. 48* (June 1981), para. 6.
†*Ibid.*, para. 7.

Contra, Sales Returns in the year of the return.

## Sales Allowances

7.27 A *sales allowance* is a price reduction granted to a customer, usually after the goods have been purchased and found to be damaged or defective. As in the case when sales returns are not material, an entry is made debiting a revenue contra account, Sales Contra, Sales Allowance, and crediting either Cash or Accounts Receivable. A combined account, Sales Contra, Sales Returns and Allowances, is sometimes used.

## Uncollectible Accounts

7.28 Whenever credit is extended to customers, there will almost certainly be some accounts that will never be collected. The uncollectible amount will vary among different types of businesses both as to its relative significance and as to its regularity. There are two methods of accounting for uncollectible accounts: **(1)** the direct charge-off method and **(2)** the allowance method.

7.29 **Direct Charge-Off Method** The direct charge-off method recognizes losses from uncollectible accounts in the period in which a specific customer's account is determined to be uncollectible. The method is sometimes called the ''direct write-off method.'' For example, if it is decided that the account receivable of John Sutherland for $180 has become uncollectible, the following entry would be made:

```
Bad Debt Expense ..................... 180
    Accounts Receivable ...............    180
To record loss from an uncollectible cus-
tomer's account.
```

7.30 When the direct charge-off method is used, it is common for the debit account to be labeled bad debt expense, because accounts written off do not necessarily arise from sales of this period. When the allowance method (discussed next) is used, the debit clearly relates to this period's sales and it is appropriate to label the debit as a sales adjustment rather than an expense. The expense title is sometimes used under the allowance method, however.

7.31 The direct charge-off method has three important shortcomings. First, the loss from uncollectible accounts is usually not recognized in the period in which the sale occurs and revenue is recognized. Too much income is recognized in the period of sale and too little in the period of write-off. Second, the amount of losses from uncollectible accounts recognized in any period is susceptible to intentional misrepresentation, because it is difficult to determine conclusively when a particular account becomes uncollectible. The direct charge-off method is not appropriate when such losses are significant in amount, occur frequently, and are reasonably predictable, as in retail stores. Third, accounts receivable on the balance sheet do not reflect the amount of cash expected to be collected.

7.32 **Allowance Method** An alternative procedure is the allowance method. The allowance method for uncollectible accounts is similar to the allowance method discussed earlier for cash discounts. To illustrate, assume that 2 percent of credit sales made during the current period will probably never be collected. If sales on account are $70,000, the following adjusting entry would be made at the end of the period:

```
Sales Contra, Estimated Uncollectibles .  1,400
    Allowance for Uncollectible
        Accounts ....................      1,400
To record estimate of uncollectible ac-
counts arising from credit sales for the
current period (.02 × $70,000).
```

The debit account, Sales Contra, Estimated Uncollectibles, is a contra account to Sales Revenue. The credit account, Allowance for Uncollectible Accounts, is a contra account to Accounts Receivable.

7.33 When a particular customer's account is judged to be uncollectible, it is written off against the allowance account. The write-off of the account of John Sutherland for $180 would be as follows:

```
Allowance for Uncollectible Accounts  .... 180
    Accounts Receivable ...............      180
To write off customer's account.
```

7.34 The allowance method overcomes all of the deficiencies of the direct charge-off method. The reduction of revenue for uncollectibles is recognized in the same period as the related sale. Also, there is no effect on income in the period of the write-off. The current asset, Accounts Receivable, and the contra current asset, Allowance for Uncollectible Accounts, are both reduced. The income effect occurs in the period of sale, and the exact moment of charge-off does not affect income, total current assets, or total assets.

7.35 **Rationale for the Revenue Contra Presentation** In practice, many firms do not treat the adjustment for estimated uncollectibles as a reduction in revenue. Instead the adjustment is treated as an administrative or selling expense, reported in the income statement as Bad Debt Expense. Net income for the period is the same whether the uncollectibles charge is treated as a revenue contra or as an expense provided that the same method for estimating the *amount* of uncollectibles is used.

7.36    We prefer to treat the adjustment for estimated uncollectibles as a reduction in revenue, not as an expense. To justify this preference, we ask, "What is the optimal amount of uncollectible accounts for a firm?" For most firms, the optimal amount of uncollectibles is not zero. If a firm is to have no uncollectible accounts, it must screen credit customers carefully, which is costly. Furthermore, the firm would deny credit to many customers who would pay their bills even though they could not pass a stringent credit check. Some of the customers who are denied credit will take their business elsewhere and sales will be lost. So long as the revenue collected from credit sales to a given class of customers exceeds the cost of goods sold and the selling expenses to that class of customers, the firm will be better off selling to that class rather than losing the sales. The rational firm should prefer granting credit to a class of customers who have a high probability of paying their bills, rather than losing their business, even though there may be some uncollectible accounts.

7.37    For example, if gross margin—selling price less cost of goods sold—on new credit sales is 20 percent of credit sales, then a firm could afford uncollectible accounts of up to 20 percent of new credit sales and still show increased net income, so long as selling and administrative expenses remain constant.

7.38    An expense is a "gone asset." Accounts that prove uncollectible are not assets, because the rational firm made credit sales expecting that a small percentage of those sales would never be collected. Hence, the amount of uncollectibles was never an asset or revenue in the first place. Thus we reach the conclusion that the amount of the uncollectible accounts should be treated as an adjustment in determining revenue, not as a "gone asset" or expense.

7.39    We do not suggest, of course, that a firm grant credit indiscriminately or ignore collection efforts for uncollected accounts receivable. We do suggest that a cost/benefit analysis of credit policy will probably dictate a strategy that results in some amount of uncollectible accounts, an amount that is reasonably predictable before any sales are made.

**Estimating the Amount of Uncollectible Accounts** Three methods are commonly used for estimating the amount of uncollectible accounts. The *percentage-of-sales method* applies an appropriate percentage to the credit sales during a period (the method illustrated above). It seems reasonable to assume that the amount of uncollectible accounts will vary with the volume of credit business. The percentage to be used can be determined by a study of the experience of the business or of similar businesses. The rates found in use generally range between $1/4$ percent and 2 percent of credit sales. If cash sales occur in a relatively constant proportion to credit sales, the percentage, proportionately reduced, can be applied to total sales for the period. The total sales amount may be more readily available than that for sales on account. Because the estimated uncollectible amount is merely added to the account, Allowance for Uncollectible Accounts, it is possible that over time the balance in the allowance account will be either too large or too small to absorb actual write-offs. The reasonableness of the balance in the allowance account should be checked periodically and the estimating percentage used in future periods adjusted if necessary.

7.41    A second procedure is the *percentage-of-receivables method*. This method rests on the presumption that a certain proportion of accounts receivable at the end of each period will become uncollectible. The *balance in the allowance account* is adjusted to this desired ending balance. For example, assume that 6 percent of accounts receivable at any time will not be collected. At the end of an accounting period, before adjusting entries are made but after specific uncollectible accounts have been written off, the accounting records show Accounts Receivable with a balance of $30,000 and Allowance for Uncollectible Accounts with a balance of $500. The desired ending balance in Allowance for Uncollectible Accounts is $1,800 (= .06 × $30,000). To bring the balance in the allowance account up to $1,800, the following entry must be made:

Sales Contra, Estimated Uncollectibles . 1,300
   Allowance for Uncollectible
     Accounts ................... 1,300
To adjust the balance in the allowance
account to $1,800 (= $500 + $1,300).

Theoretically, the $1,800 balance in the allowance account contains two parts: **(1)** a provision of $500 charged against earnings in prior periods on accounts still outstanding at the end of the current period, and **(2)** a provision of $1,300 charged against earnings of the current period on accounts arising from sales this period that have not yet been collected. Because the uncollectible accounts percentage is applied to total accounts receivable at the end of the period, not just those arising from the current period's sales, the provision of $1,300 in the entry above might be thought of as a combined entry: a provision for estimated uncollectibles arising from the current period's sales plus or minus an adjustment to the amount in the allowance account for deficient or excessive provisions relating to receivables still outstanding from prior periods' sales. The logic behind the percentage-of-receivables method is more difficult to follow than that of the percentage-of-sales method. The two methods should result, however, in approximately the same provision for uncollectible accounts each period and balance in the allowance account at the end of the period.

7.42    A third method of calculating the provision for uncollectible accounts is the *aging-of-accounts-receivable method*. This method is similar to the percentage-of-receivables method except that the procedure for computing the desired ending balance in the allowance account is more detailed. To apply the aging method, an aging schedule for accounts receivable is prepared. Such an aging schedule is shown in Exhibit 7.1. Accounts are classified into various categories depending on their collection status. The nature of the business and its credit terms will determine the specific classes used. The presumption is that the balance in the Allowance for Uncollectible Accounts should be large enough to cover substantially all accounts receivable past due for more than some specified period of time (for example,

*Exhibit 7.1*
**Illustration of Aging Accounts Receivable**

| Classification of Accounts | Amount | Estimated Uncollectible Percentage[a] | Estimated Uncollectible Amount |
|---|---|---|---|
| Not Yet Due .......................................... | $24,200 | 0.5% | $ 121 |
| 1–30 Days Past Due ............................... | 3,000 | 6.0 | 180 |
| 31–60 Days Past Due ............................. | 1,200 | 25.0 | 300 |
| 61–180 Days Past Due ............................ | 1,000 | 50.0 | 500 |
| More Than 180 Days Past Due ......................... | 600 | 95.0 | 570 |
|    Total ......................................... | $30,000 | | $1,671 |

[a]Amounts assumed for purposes of illustration.

6 months) and smaller proportions of more recent accounts. The analysis indicates that a balance of $1,671 is needed in the allowance account at the end of the current period. If we assume the balance in the allowance account before the adjustment is $500, then the adjusting entry is

Sales Contra, Estimated Uncollectibles .  1,171
    Allowance for Uncollectible
       Accounts  ....................        1,171
To adjust the balance in the allowance account to $1,671 (= $500 + $1,171).

Even when the percentage-of-sales or percentage-of-receivables methods are used, aging the accounts should be done periodically as an occasional check on the accuracy of the percentages being used. If the aging analysis shows that the balance in the allowance account is too large or too small, the apparent error should be corrected currently and the percentage used for future periods raised or lowered accordingly. 7.43

**Illustration of Allowance Method** Exhibit 7.2 illustrates the operation of the allowance 7.44

---

*Exhibit 7.2*
### Review of the Allowance Method of Accounting for Uncollectible Accounts

---

**Transactions in the First Period:**
(1) Sales are $800,000.
(2) Cash of $737,000 is collected from customers in payment of their accounts.
(3) At the end of the first period, it is estimated that uncollectibles will be 2% of sales; .02 × $800,000 = $16,000.
(4) Specific accounts totaling $6,000 are written off as uncollectible.
(5) The revenue, revenue contra, and other temporary accounts are closed.

**Transactions in the Second Period:**
(6) Sales are $1,000,000.
(7) Specific accounts totaling $17,000 are written off during the period as information on their uncollectibility becomes known. The debit balance of $7,000 will remain in the Allowance account until the adjusting entry is made at the end of the period; see (9).
(8) Cash of $973,000 is collected from customers in payment of their accounts.
(9) An aging of the accounts receivable, as in Exhibit 7.1, shows that the amount in the Allowance account should be $12,000. The amount of the adjustment is $19,000. It is determined as the difference between the desired $12,000 credit balance and the current $7,000 debit balance in the Allowance account.
(10) The revenue, revenue contra, and other temporary accounts are closed.

| Cash | | Accounts Receivable | | Allowance for Uncollectible Accounts | |
|---|---|---|---|---|---|
| | | (1)  800,000 | | | 16,000 (3) |
| (2)  737,000 | | | 737,000 (2) | | |
| | | | 6,000 (4) | (4)  6,000 | |
| Bal.  ? | | Bal.  57,000 | | | 10,000  Bal. |
| | | (6) 1,000,000 | | | |
| | | | 17,000 (7) | (7) 17,000 | |
| (8)  973,000 | | | 973,000 (8) | | |
| | | | | | 19,000 (9) |
| Bal.  ? | | Bal.  67,000 | | | 12,000  Bal. |

| Sales Contra, Estimated Uncollectibles | | Sales Revenue | |
|---|---|---|---|
| (3)  16,000 | | | 800,000 (1) |
| | Closed (5) | (5)  Closed | |
| (9)  19,000 | | | 1,000,000 (6) |
| | Closed (10) | (10)  Closed | |

method for uncollectibles over two periods. In the first period the percentage of sales method is used. In the second period the aging method is used. Normally, a firm would use the same method in all periods.

7.45 **Collection of Accounts Written Off** Even though a specific customer's account is written off, collection efforts will normally continue. Occasionally, accounts previously written off will be collected. Assuming that the allowance method is being used and an account for $60 previously written off is now collected, two journal entries are made. The first entry simply reverses the original entry for the write-off:

Accounts Receivable ..................... 60
    Allowance for Uncollectible Accounts ...   60
To reverse journal entry made previously to write off a customer's account.

The second entry records the receipt of cash on the customer's open account:

Cash .................................. 60
    Accounts Receivable ..................   60
To record the collection of cash on an open account.

These entries rest on the presumption that the account should not have been written off to begin with. If the percentage-of-receivables or aging method of estimating uncollectible accounts has been used, the balance in the allowance account may be overstated as a result of reversing the original write-off entry. This overstatement is corrected by making a smaller provision than would otherwise be made at the end of the current period. For example, the aging schedule in Exhibit 7.1 indicates that the balance in the allowance account at the end of the current period should be $1,671. The balance in the allowance account at the end of the period after recording the collection of the account previously written off is $560. A provision for uncollectible accounts of $1,111 (= $1,671 − $560) instead of $1,171 (= $1,671 − $500) needs to be made.

## Measurement of Revenues and Notes Receivable

7.46 Instead of using an open account credit arrangement, goods and services may be sold using a *promissory note*. Promissory notes may also be received in "settlement" of an open accounts receivable. A promissory note is a written contract in which one person, known as the *maker*, promises to pay another person, known as the *payee*, a definite sum of money. The money may be payable on demand or, as is more common, at a definite future date. A note may or may not provide explicitly for the payment of interest in addition to the principal amount.

7.47 The theoretically preferable method of accounting for notes is as follows:

**1.** At the time goods or services are sold, notes received from customers should be recorded at the present value of the future cash flows. The difference between the present value of the note received and the cost of the goods or services sold is recognized as the profit or income from the sale.

**2.** During each accounting period between the time of sale and final collection of the note, interest revenue should be recognized using the effective-interest method.

The amount of interest revenue each period is equal to the historical interest rate used in discounting multiplied times the book (present) value of the note at the beginning of the period. Any difference between the cash received during the period and the interest revenue recognized represents a repayment of principal.

7.48 By following this procedure, income over the life of the note will have two components: **(1)** a profit from the sales transaction equal to the difference between the cash-equivalent price at the time of sale (that is, the present value of future cash flows) and the cost of the good or service sold, and **(2)** interest revenue from extending credit to customers over the term of the note. The note will continually be stated on the balance sheet at the present value of the remaining cash flows.

7.49 Under current generally accepted accounting principles,* this theoretically preferable method is followed only for long-term notes (that is, those due more than 1 year after the time of sale). Short-term trade

---

*Accounting Principles Board, *Opinion No. 21* (August 1971).

notes are usually accounted for at face value. The accounting for various kinds of notes is discussed in the sections that follow.

## Short-Term Trade Notes

7.50  Accounting Principles Board *Opinion No. 21,* which requires that notes receivable be stated at the present value of future cash flows, specifically excludes from its provisions "receivables and payables arising from transactions with customers in the normal course of business which are due in customary trade terms not exceeding approximately one year."* The exclusion of short-term trade notes from the provisions of APB *Opinion No. 21* is due to the immaterial difference usually found between the amounts ultimately collectible and the present value of those amounts. The accounting for short-term interest-bearing and short-term noninterest-bearing notes is somewhat different.

7.51  **Short-Term Interest-Bearing Notes** Interest-bearing notes indicate a face amount together with explicit interest at a stated rate for such time as is stated in the note. For example, the basic elements of such a note dated July 1 might read: "Sixty days after date, the Suren Company promises to pay to the order of the Mullen Company thirty thousand dollars with interest from date at the rate of twelve percent per annum."

7.52  *Interest Calculations* The general formula for the calculation of interest for periods shorter than 1 year is

Base (Principal or Face) × Interest Rate × Time Period
= Interest.

The interest rate is almost always stated as an annual rate. This annual rate must be reexpressed as an appropriate rate for the time period of the note. If the time period is 6 months on a note with a 12-percent annual interest rate, then interest of 6 percent of the principal will be recognized during the term of the note. If the time period is 3 months on a 12-percent note, then interest of 3 percent of the principal will be recognized.

—————
*Ibid.

7.53  Interest calculations can be complicated by the odd number of days in a year and the variations in the number of days in a month. The interest at the rate of 12 percent per year on a $30,000 note for 60 days is $591.78 (= $30,000 × .12 × 60/365) if an exact computation is made. For many purposes, especially the calculation of accruals, a satisfactory approximation of the correct interest can be obtained by assuming that the year has 360 days and that each month is one-twelfth of a year. Thus, 30 days is the equivalent of 1 month, and 60 days is the equivalent of 2 months, or one-sixth of a year. Under this procedure, interest at 12 percent on a $30,000, 60-day note is $600.00 (= $30,000 × .12 × 60/360).

7.54  The types of transactions related to an interest-bearing note receivable are: receipt of note; interest recognition at an interim date; and collection, renewal, or dishonor at maturity date.

7.55  *Receipt of Note and Collection at Maturity* Short-term trade notes are usually received from customers in connection with sales or in settlement of an open account receivable. Assume that on July 1 the Mullen Company sold merchandise costing $24,000 to the Suren Company for $30,000. The Suren Company signed a $30,000 promissory note, promising to pay the $30,000 plus interest at 12 percent per year 60 days after the date of sale. The entries to record the sale and the receipt of the note are as follows:

```
July 1
Notes Receivable  .................  30,000
    Sales Revenue  ...............         30,000

Cost of Goods Sold  .............  24,000
    Merchandise Inventory  ........        24,000
```

7.56  Assuming that the accounting period of the Mullen Company is the calendar year, the entry upon collection at maturity is

```
Aug. 30
Cash  ..........................  30,600
    Notes Receivable  ............         30,000
    Interest Revenue  ............            600
```

7.57  Assuming the accounting period of the Mullen Company is one month, the interest revenue recognized at the interim date, July 31, is $300 (= $30,000 × .12 × 30/360). The entry is

July 31
Interest Receivable .................... 300
    Interest Revenue .................. 300

The entry upon collection at maturity is then

Aug. 30
Cash .......................... 30,600
    Notes Receivable ............. 30,000
    Interest Receivable ............ 300
    Interest Revenue .............. 300

7.58 The holder of the note need not have received it on the day the note was originally drawn. If the 60-day note received on July 1 from the Suren Company had been drawn on June 15, with other data being the same, the entry upon receipt would have been

July 1
Notes Receivable ................. 30,000
Interest Receivable ............... 150
    Sales Revenue ............... 30,000
    Interest Revenue .............. 150
Valuation at face value plus accrued
interest (= $30,000 × .12 × 15/360).

Cost of Goods Sold .............. 24,000
    Merchandise Inventory ........ 24,000

The entry upon collection at maturity on August 14 (15 days in June, 31 in July, and 14 in August), assuming that the accounting period is the calendar year, is

Cash .......................... 30,600
    Notes Receivable ............. 30,000
    Interest Receivable ............ 150
    Interest Revenue .............. 450

7.59 *Alternatives to Collection at Maturity* On the maturity date of a note, the person who holds the note must present it to the maker for payment. The note may be collected, as illustrated above, renewed, partially collected with renewal of the balance, or dishonored by the maker.

7.60 *Renewal* It is not unusual for a holder of a note to extend the time of payment by accepting a new note for one reaching the maturity date. The applicable interest might be collected; if so, the face value would remain the same as the original note. Assume collection of interest only at August 30 and renewal of the first note issued by the Suren

Company for another 30 days. If Mullen Company keeps its accounts on a calendar-year basis, Mullen's entries at maturity would be

Aug. 30
Cash .......................... 600
    Interest Revenue .............. 600

Aug. 30
Notes Receivable (due September
  29) .......................... 30,000
    Notes Receivable (due August
    30) ...................... 30,000
Renewal of note.

The last entry should be made, even though there is no net effect on the Notes Receivable account, in order that the accounting records will indicate the renewal of the note.

*Partial Renewal* If the interest of $600 and a 7.61 partial payment on principal of $10,000 had been collected and there had been a partial renewal of the note, the entry at maturity would be

Aug. 30
Cash .......................... 10,600
Notes Receivable (due September
  29) .......................... 20,000
    Notes Receivable (due August
    30) ...................... 30,000
    Interest Revenue .............. 600

*Dishonored Notes* If the maker does not pay 7.62 at maturity, the note has been *dishonored*. If there is no renewal and it is felt that the maker will eventually pay the note, no entry is necessary, although on the balance sheet the overdue note will be listed separately. Another possibility is to debit the amount due to an accounts receivable account on the ground that an overdue note has lost part of its status as a negotiable instrument and really represents only an ordinary claim against the maker. If the Suren Company note is dishonored at maturity, the entry, assuming an annual closing, is

Aug. 30
Accounts Receivable .............. 30,600
    Notes Receivable ............. 30,000
    Interest Revenue .............. 600
Note of Suren Company due but not
paid. It is believed that payment will
ultimately be received.

If the note is thought to be uncollectible, it might be written off as a loss:

Aug. 30
Loss on Uncollectible Notes    ....... 30,000
    Notes Receivable    ............    30,000
Note of Suren Company due but not
paid. It is believed that the amount
due is uncollectible, as the Suren
Company is now in bankruptcy.

Had interest been recognized previously, the loss amount would be increased accordingly. If an allowance method were used (as discussed earlier in this chapter for accounts receivable), the debit would be to the Allowance for Uncollectible Accounts and Notes account.

7.63    **Short-Term Noninterest-Bearing Notes**
Noninterest-bearing notes indicate a face amount that is also the maturity value. For example, the basic elements of such a note might read: "Sixty days after date (July 1), the Butler Company promises to pay to the order of the Dryer Company the amount of $30,000." Thus, no explicit rate of interest is given. However, the value of the note prior to maturity will be less than the maturity value of $30,000, the difference being the implicit interest that theoretically should be recognized. For example, if the credit standing of the Butler Company would permit it to borrow at 12 percent per year, then the present value of the note on July 1 is $29,412 (= maturity value of $30,000 times the present value factor for one period at 2 percent = $30,000 × .98039). The note would be recorded at $29,412 and the $588 difference between the present value and the maturity value recognized as interest revenue over the 60-day period. Because the present value and maturity value of most short-term noninterest-bearing notes are not materially different, generally accepted accounting principles do not require that such notes be recorded at their present value. The note, assuming that it was received for the sale of merchandise costing $24,000, would be recorded as follows:

July 1
Notes Receivable    ................ 30,000
    Sales Revenue    ................    30,000

Costs of Goods Sold    ............. 24,000
    Merchandise Inventory    ........    24,000

The entry at maturity would be

Aug. 30
Cash    .......................... 30,000
    Notes Receivable    .............    30,000

This accounting procedure for short-term, noninterest-bearing notes results in recognition of all of the income at the time of sale ($6,000 = $30,000 − $24,000) and none during later periods as interest revenue.

## Long-Term Trade Notes

7.64    Certain products, particularly large-dollar-value items such as construction equipment, are often sold under long-term credit arrangements. The seller usually receives a note from the buyer specifying the terms of payment. The note may or may not be interest bearing. The item sold often serves as collateral until the note is paid.

7.65    **Long-Term Interest-Bearing Trade Notes**
Long-term interest-bearing notes are initially recorded at the present value of the future cash flows to be received. As long as the interest rate specified on the note represents a reasonable borrowing rate for the particular customer, given the term of the note, creditworthiness of the borrower, and similar factors, then the present value of the note will equal its face value. For example, assume that Haskins Company sells a tract of land costing $80,000 to Anderson Company on December 31, 1981, for $100,000. Anderson Company signs a note agreeing to pay the $100,000 selling price plus interest at a rate of 8 percent per year on the unpaid balance. Equal payments of $38,803 are to be made at the end of each of the next 3 years. Assuming that 8 percent is a reasonable borrowing rate for Anderson Company, the present value of the note on the date of sale is calculated as follows:

**Present Value of Cash Payments at 8%:**

| | | |
|---|---|---|
| End of Year 1: $38,803 × .92593 ..... | | $ 35,929 |
| End of Year 2: $38,803 × .85734 ..... | | 33,267 |
| End of Year 3: $38,803 × .79383 ..... | | 30,804 |
| Total: $38,803 × 2.57710 ..... | | $100,000 |

*Exhibit 7.3*
**Amortization Schedule for a
$100,000, 8· Interest-Bearing Note
Payable in Three Installments
of $38,803 per Year**

| Period | Receivable at Beginning of Period | Interest Revenue | Cash Received | Payment of Principal | Receivable at End of Period |
|---|---|---|---|---|---|
| 1981 ....................... | — | — | — | — | $100,000 |
| 1982 ....................... | $100,000 | $ 8,000 | $ 38,803 | $ 30,803 | 69,197 |
| 1983 ....................... | 69,197 | 5,536 | 38,803 | 33,267 | 35,930 |
| 1984 ....................... | 35,930 | 2,873 | 38,803 | 35,930 | — |
| Total .................... | | $16,409 | $116,409 | $100,000 | |

7.66 The journal entry to record the sale is

Dec. 31, 1981
Notes Receivable ................ 100,000
    Land ...................... 80,000
    Gain on Sale of Land ......... 20,000
To record the receipt of a $100,000,
8-percent, interest-bearing note having a present value of $100,000
when discounted at 8 percent, the
transfer of land, and the recognition
of a gain on sale.

7.67 The cash payments received each period will
represent interest revenue plus payment of a
portion of the face value of the note. Exhibit
7.3 presents the amortization schedule for
this note. During the first year, interest revenue of $8,000 (= .08 × $100,000) will be
recognized. The journal entry is

Dec. 31, 1982
Cash ........................... 38,803
    Interest Revenue .............. 8,000
    Note Receivable .............. 30,803
To record first payment of note and to
recognize interest revenue.

On January 1, 1983, the note will have a
present value and book value of $69,197 (=
$100,000 − $30,803). Interest revenue for
1983 is $5,536 (= .08 × $69,197). The entry to
record the second cash payment is

Dec. 31, 1983
Cash .......................... 38,803
    Interest Revenue .............. 5,536
    Note Receivable .............. 33,267
To record second payment of note
and to recognize interest revenue.

The entry at the end of 1984 is 7.68

Dec. 31, 1984
Cash ........................... 38,803
    Interest Revenue .............. 2,873
    Note Receivable .............. 35,930
To record third payment of note and
to recognize interest revenue.

The interest rate stated on the note occa- 7.69
sionally may not represent a reasonable rate
of interest for the particular borrower, given
the specific characteristics of the note and
the creditworthiness of the borrower. In
these cases, Accounting Principles Board
*Opinion No. 21* requires that a more reasonable rate be determined and that this rate
be used to calculate the present value of
the future cash flows on the date the note
is received. The mechanics of accounting
for interest-bearing notes when the stated
interest rate is considered to be unreasonable is similar to the accounting for noninterest-bearing notes, which is discussed
next. Refer to the first and third illustrations in Exhibit 5.2.

**Long-Term Noninterest-Bearing Trade** 7.70
**Notes** As with similar short-term notes,
long-term noninterest-bearing notes have a
maturity value equal to their face value.
Implicit in the amount received at maturity
is a charge for interest, representing the
cost to the borrower and return to the
lender from delaying payment. APB *Opinion No. 21* requires that the interest implicit
in the note be recognized as interest revenue

by the lender over the term of the note. To accomplish this, the note must be initially recorded at the present value of the future cash flow(s) using the implicit rate of interest. The preferable methods of determining this initial present value amount are as follows:

1. If calculable, the established exchange price (which, presumably, is the same as the price for a cash sale) of property, goods, or services acquired or sold in consideration of a note may be used to establish the present value of the note.

2. When the notes are traded in an open market, the market rate of interest and market value of the note may be used as evidence of the present value.

7.71 If neither of these two methods can be followed, then the appropriate interest rate must be estimated, or *imputed*. The imputation takes into consideration the term of the note, the credit standing of the issuer, restrictive covenants, collateral, and, if appropriate, the tax consequences to the buyer and seller.

7.72   To illustrate, assume that Brooks Manufacturing Corporation sold a crane costing $65,000 to Carlson Company on December 31, 1981. Carlson Company paid $20,000 immediately and signed a note agreeing to pay $60,500 two years after the date of sale. Based on transactions with similar customers, the selling price for this crane when customers pay the entire price immediately is $70,000. With a $20,000 down payment, the present value of the $60,500 note must be $50,000 on December 31, 1981. The difference between the present value of the note of $50,000 and its $60,500 maturity value represents implicit interest. To calculate the implicit interest rate, we must find the rate that will discount $60,500 back 2 years so that it has a present value of $50,000. The implicit rate is 10 percent per year (that is, $60,500 × .82645 = $50,000; see Appendix Table 2).*

---

*Algebraically, solve for $r$ such that $50,000(1 + r)^2 =$ $60,500$.

The entry to record the sale of the crane   7.73 on December 31, 1981, might be as follows:

Dec. 31, 1981
Cash ............................ 20,000
Notes Receivable ................. 50,000
    Equipment (Crane) ............        65,000
    Gain on Sale of Equipment ....        5,000
To record sale of crane and receipt of
noninterest-bearing note at an implicit interest rate of 10 percent.

The Notes Receivable account is stated at the present value of the future cash flow (that is, $60,500 due 2 years after the date of sale discounted at 10 percent).

An alternative entry that results in pre-   7.74 cisely the same balance sheet and income statement amounts, and the one implicitly preferred by APB *Opinion No. 21,* is

Dec. 31, 1981
Cash ............................ 20,000
Notes Receivable .................. 60,500
    Discount on Notes Receivable ..        10,500
    Equipment (Crane) ............        65,000
    Gain on Sale of Equipment ....        5,000

The face amount of the note ($60,500) is recorded in the Notes Receivable account. The interest implicit in the note is recorded in a contra account to Notes Receivable. A balance sheet on December 31, 1981, would show the following:

Notes Receivable ...................... $60,500
Less Discount on Notes Receivable       (10,500)
Notes Receivable (Net) ...............   $50,000

This presentation informs the user of the financial statements as to the amount of cash that will be received in 2 years as well as the present value of that amount. When the note is recorded in a single Notes Receivable Account (net), this potentially valuable source of information for predicting future cash flows is lost. The illustrations of long-term notes throughout the remainder of this book use the contra account for Notes Receivable to record the interest on the note. Exhibit 5.2 illustrates the underlying principles of accounting for long-term notes.

To continue this example, the following   7.75 entry would be made on December 31, 1982, if Brooks Corporation closed its books once each year:

Dec. 31, 1982
Discount on Notes Receivable ........ 5,000
    Interest Revenue ............... 5,000
To recognize interest revenue for 1982 at the rate of 10 percent of the book (present) value at the beginning of the year of $50,000.

After this entry, the Discount on Notes Receivable account will have a remaining balance of $5,500. The note will be shown on the December 31, 1982, balance sheet at $55,000 (= $60,500 − $5,500). This amount is equal to the present value on December 31, 1982, of the $60,500 face value to be received one year later.

7.76    The entries on December 31, 1983, will be

Dec. 31, 1983
Discount on Notes Receivable ...... 5,500
    Interest Revenue ............. 5,500
To recognize interest revenue for 1983 at the rate of 10 percent of the book (present) value at the beginning of the year of $55,000.

Dec. 31, 1983
Cash .......................... 60,500
    Notes Receivable .............. 60,500
To record payment of note.

7.77  **Summary of Accounting for Long-Term Notes** To summarize, the accounting for long-term trade notes results in recognizing income in two portions: **(1)** a gain from the sales transaction equal to the difference between the present value of the note (and other consideration) received and the cost of the goods or services sold, and **(2)** interest revenue over the term of the note as the return for permitting customers to delay payment. In the case of interest-bearing notes, the face value and the present value will usually be the same. For noninterest-bearing notes, the face value of the note will exceed its present value. The interest, or discount, element in the note must be computed and recorded in a contra account to Notes Receivable, entitled Discount on Notes Receivable. The amount in the contra account is amortized over the life of the note as in-

terest revenue is recognized. The effective-interest method of amortization is used in most cases. Under the effective-interest method, a constant *rate* of interest is recognized on the amount of the note outstanding at the beginning of each period. If the results are not materially different, the straight-line amortization method (total discount divided by number of periods until note is due) can also be used. Exhibit 5.2 illustrates the effective-interest method.

## Receivables and Cash Generation

A firm may sometimes find itself temporarily  7.78 short of cash and unable to obtain financing from its usual sources. In such instances, accounts and notes receivable can be used to obtain financing. Accounts receivable may be assigned, pledged, or factored to a bank or finance company. Notes receivable may be sold or discounted at a bank. The accounting for each of these types of transactions is discussed below.

## Assigning Accounts Receivable

As a means of obtaining a loan from a bank  7.79 or finance company, a firm may *assign* its accounts receivable. The borrowing firm typically maintains physical control of accounts receivable, collects amounts remitted by customers, and then forwards the proceeds to the lending institution. The lending institution will require that the amount of accounts receivable assigned be greater than the principal amount of the loan to cover interest and allow for uncollectible accounts. The lending institution may require the substitution of new accounts if certain accounts become uncollectible.

To illustrate the accounting for assigned  7.80 accounts receivable, assume that on July 1, Wilson Company borrows $20,000 from its bank on a 6-month loan carrying interest at a rate of 1 percent per month on the unpaid balance of the loan. Wilson Company assigns $25,000 of its accounts receivable. The journal entries to record these events are as follows:

July 1
Cash ......................... 20,000
    Note Payable ................     20,000
To record loan from bank.

July 1
Accounts Receivable Assigned ..... 25,000
    Accounts Receivable ..........     25,000
To record assignment of Accounts Receivable.

If a balance sheet were prepared on July 1, the following disclosure of assigned accounts receivable would be made:

**Current Assets**
Accounts Receivable Assigned .... $25,000
Less Note Payable .............. (20,000)
    Equity in Assigned Accounts  .    $5,000

The note payable can be offset against assigned accounts receivable because collections will be specifically used to repay the loan. Assigned accounts receivable are disclosed separately from accounts receivable that have not been assigned to indicate that the collection of assigned receivables will not increase the liquid resources available to pay general trade creditors. Disclosure is often made in notes instead of in the body of the balance sheet as illustrated above.

7.81    Assume now that on July 31 Wilson Company collects $5,000 of assigned accounts receivable and immediately remits the amount collected to the lending bank. If Wilson Company closes its books monthly, the following entries will be made on July 31:

July 31
Cash ........................... 5,000
    Accounts Receivable Assigned ....     5,000
To record collection of assigned accounts receivable.

July 31
Interest Expense .................... 200
Note Payable ...................... 4,800
    Cash .........................     5,000
To recognize interest expense (at 1 percent of the $20,000 unpaid balance during July) and the repayment of the principal of the loan.

In more typical situations, collections from customers and remittances to the bank take place continually throughout the month. The calculation of the unpaid balance on which interest is assessed is somewhat more complicated than in this case.

## Pledging Accounts Receivable

Accounts receivable may also be *pledged* as security for a loan. Under a pledging arrangement, the borrowing firm repays the loan from its general cash account. It is not required, as with assigned accounts receivable, to transfer collections from customers directly to the lending institution. If the borrowing firm is unable to make payments when due, the lending institution has the right to seize the accounts receivable and sell them in settlement of the loan.   7.82

Formal recognition of the pledging arrangement is typically not made in the accounting records. Instead, notes to the financial statements will indicate that a portion of the accounts receivable has been pledged as collateral for a loan and may not be available for the payment of general (unsecured) creditors.   7.83

## Factoring Accounts Receivable

Firms experiencing severe financial difficulties may *factor*, or sell, their accounts receivable to obtain needed cash. No loan is created in this case. Instead, the accounts receivable are physically transferred to a bank or finance company and the borrowing firm relinquishes all rights to future collections.   7.84

The factoring of accounts receivable is recorded the same as the sale of any other asset. Cash is debited for the amount received, Accounts Receivable is credited for the book value of the receivables, and any difference is recognized as a gain or loss. Because banks and finance companies require a return from their purchase of accounts receivable, they will not pay the full face amount for receivables purchased. As a result, selling firms will usually recognize a   7.85

loss or expense when accounts receivable are factored.

7.86 To illustrate, assume that Oxford Corporation's records reveal the following on September 1:

| | |
|---|---:|
| Accounts Receivable (Gross) ......... | $200,000 |
| Less Allowance for Uncollectible Accounts ......................... | (10,000) |
| Accounts Receivable (Net) ........... | $190,000 |

Oxford Corporation factors these receivables to the Westside Finance Company and receives $160,000. The entry is

Sept 1
| | | |
|---|---:|---:|
| Cash .......................... | 160,000 | |
| Allowance for Uncollectible Accounts ..................... | 10,000 | |
| Loss from Factoring Accounts Receivable .................. | 30,000 | |
| Accounts Receivable ........ | | 200,000 |

To record sale of accounts receivable.

7.87 Separate disclosure of factored accounts receivable in the financial statements is not required, because the receivables are no longer on the books. Most firms are reluctant to factor their receivables because it often indicates to customers that the firm is experiencing financial difficulties. Customers may also be confused or annoyed at having to make remittances to the bank or finance company instead of the original selling firm. Factoring is a common practice in certain industries, however, even where firms are not experiencing financial difficulties. The textile industry is an example.

## Transferring Notes Receivable

7.88 Notes receivable from customers may likewise be used by a firm to obtain cash from a bank or finance company. A note may be transferred "without recourse." This procedure is equivalent to the sale of the note because the transferrer has no liability if the maker fails to pay at maturity. The entry to record transfer, or sale, of notes without recourse is similar to that when accounts receivable are sold. Cash is debited for the proceeds, the note and any related accrued interest accounts are credited, and the difference is recognized as a gain or loss.

7.89 More commonly, customers' notes are transferred "with recourse." The transferrer remains contingently liable in the event the maker fails to pay at maturity. Contingent liabilities are not shown among liabilities in the balance sheet. Instead, footnote disclosure of the potential obligation is made.

7.90 To illustrate the accounting for a note transferred with recourse, assume that Harris Company sells goods to Stephen's Company on July 1 for $30,000. Stephen's Company signs a note agreeing to pay $30,000 plus interest at an annual rate of 12 percent on August 30, 60 days later. On August 5, Harris transfers this note with recourse to State Bank. The bank will determine the amount of cash it will pay for the note by subtracting a "discount" from the amount it will receive at maturity (face amount of $30,000 plus interest at 12 percent for 60 days). This discount is the bank's return from purchasing the note. Assume that the bank requires a return of 10 percent per year on funds invested. The calculation of the amount the bank will pay for the note is as follows:

1. The maturity value of the note is calculated:

| | |
|---|---:|
| Face value ......................... | $30,000.00 |
| Interest to maturity ($30,000 × .12 × 60/360) ......................... | 600.00 |
| Maturity value ..................... | $30,600.00 |

2. The amount of the bank's discount is calculated by applying the discount rate to the maturity value *for the period of time the bank's funds are invested:*

| | |
|---|---:|
| Discount on $30,600 for 25 days at 10 percent ($30,600 × .10 × 25/360) ... | $ 212.50 |

3. The amount paid for the note is the difference between the maturity value and the discount:

| | |
|---|---|
| Maturity value ..................... | $30,600.00 |
| Discount ......................... | 212.50 |
| Proceeds ........................ | $30,387.50 |

7.91 The entries on Harris Company's books relating to the note, assuming that the books are closed monthly, are as follows:

**July 1**

| | | |
|---|---|---|
| Note Receivable ............ | 30,000.00 | |
| Sales Revenue ........... | | 30,000.00 |

To record note received from Stephen's Company.

**July 31**

| | | |
|---|---|---|
| Interest Receivable ........... | 300.00 | |
| Interest Revenue ......... | | 300.00 |

To record interest for July at 12 percent per year ($30,000 × .12 × 30/360).

**Aug. 5**

| | | |
|---|---|---|
| Interest Receivable ........... | 50.00 | |
| Interest Revenue ......... | | 50.00 |

To record interest for 5 days in August ($30,000 × .12 × 5/360).

**Aug. 5**

| | | |
|---|---|---|
| Cash ..................... | 30,387.50 | |
| Interest Receivable ....... | | 350.00 |
| Notes Receivable | | |
| Discounted ............ | | 30,000.00 |
| Interest Revenue ......... | | 37.50 |

To record cash received and to recognize interest revenue for the difference between the proceeds and the book value of the note and related interest.

7.92 The second entry on August 5 requires elaboration. The difference between the cash proceeds and the book value of the note (face amount of $30,000 plus accrued interest of $350) is in the nature of a gain or loss from the transfer. The difference arises because the interest rate on the note (12 percent in this example) differs from the interest rate used by the bank in discounting (10 percent). Harris Company benefits from this interest rate differential by receiving more than $30,000 plus interest at 12 percent while it held the note (July 1 to August 5). If the bank required a return greater than 12 per-

cent, the proceeds from the transfer would be less than the book value (face amount plus accrued interest) and a loss, or interest expense, would be recognized.

Observe that the account Notes Receivable Discounted is credited instead of Notes Receivable.* Because the transfer is made with recourse, Harris Company remains contingently liable on the note. This contingent liability is usually disclosed in a note, and the amount of Notes Receivable shown on the balance sheet is the net amount of notes after deducting discounted notes. An alternative method of disclosure is to treat the Notes Receivable Discounted account as a contra account to Notes Receivable. For example, if Harris Company had received $100,000 of notes from various customers on July 1 and later discounted the $30,000 note from Stephen's Company, the balance sheet would show:

7.93

**Current Assets**

| | | |
|---|---|---|
| Notes Receivable ......... | $100,000 | |
| Less Notes Receivable | | |
| Discounted ............ | (30,000) | |
| Notes Receivable (Net) . | | $70,000 |

The amount in the Notes Receivable Discounted account is more a symbol than a measure of the contingent liability, for if a note has to be made good, the amount that must be paid includes interest and penalty fees in addition to the face value. Usually, however, the aggregate credit balance in the account is more than the probable liability,

7.94

---

*The distinction between "Notes Receivable Discounted" and "Discount on Notes Receivable" may be confusing. The account, Discount on Notes Receivable, described earlier in this chapter, refers to the amount that must be subtracted from the face amount of a note to obtain its present value. The account, Notes Receivable Discounted, described above, refers to the notes that have been transferred before their maturity date to another holder in return for cash. Test your understanding of these terms by describing the events and transactions that would lead to a description of a Note Receivable for $10,000 with a Discount on Note Receivable of $350 being discounted for $9,650, or for $9,800, or for $9,500. (See Question Q7.30.)

because most notes are paid by their makers when they come due.

## Summary

7.95   Revenue from the sale of most goods and services is recognized at the time of sale. At this time, an exchange between the buyer and the seller has taken place at an agreed-upon exchange price. An assessment of the buyer's credit standing permits a reasonable estimate of the amount of cash that will be collected.

7.96   The amount of revenue ultimately recognized is generally not the agreed-upon exchange price. If cash in the full amount of the exchange price is not expected to be collected because of cash discounts, sales returns, uncollectible accounts, and similar factors, then the amount of revenue recognized must be reduced accordingly. These revenue reductions should preferably be recognized in the same period in which the related revenue is recognized in order to achieve a proper matching.

If notes are received in a sales transaction, 7.97 the accounting depends on the type and term of the note received. Short-term interest and noninterest-bearing notes are recorded at their face value. Long-term interest and noninterest-bearing notes are stated at the present value of the future cash flows discounted at a rate of interest appropriate to the borrower (customer) at the time the note is received. If the stated interest rate in an interest-bearing note is not considered a reasonable rate for the particular borrower, an appropriate interest rate must be imputed, given the amount and term of the note, creditworthiness of the borrower, and similar factors. Similar imputations of interest are required for long-term noninterest-bearing notes.

## Questions and Short Cases

7.1   Review the meaning of the following concepts or terms discussed in this chapter.

a. List price.
b. Exchange price.
c. Trade discount.
d. Quantity discount.
e. Gross price method for cash discounts.
f. Allowance method for cash discounts.
g. Net price method for cash discounts.
h. Sales return.
i. Sales allowance.
j. Direct charge-off method for uncollectible accounts.
k. Allowance method for uncollectible accounts.
l. Percentage-of-sales method of estimating uncollectible accounts.
m. Percentage-of-receivables method of estimating uncollectible accounts.
n. Aging-of-receivables method of estimating uncollectible accounts.
o. Promissory note.
p. Interest-bearing note.
q. Noninterest-bearing note.
r. Simple interest.
s. Compound interest.
t. Imputed interest.
u. Assigning accounts receivable.
v. Pledging accounts receivable.
w. Factoring accounts receivable.
x. Discounting notes receivable.
y. With recourse.
z. Without recourse.

7.2   If the objective in measuring revenue is to report the amount of cash to be collected, why not wait until cash is actually received from customers and thereby eliminate uncertainty as to the proper amount of revenue?

**7.3**   Sales and accounts receivable adjustments can be accounted for **(1)** at the time of sale, **(2)** at the end of the period in which the sale is made, or **(3)** during some future period when discounts are taken, merchandise is returned, or accounts are written off as uncollectible. Indicate which of the three approaches is apparently being followed in each of the independent cases below:

    **a.** When a customer's account is collected within the discount period, a debit entry is made to the Allowance for Cash Discounts account.

    **b.** When a customer's account is collected within the discount period, a debit entry is made to the Sales Contra, Cash Discounts account.

    **c.** When a customer returns merchandise, a debit entry is made in the Sales Contra, Sales Returns account.

    **d.** When a customer returns merchandise, a debit entry is made to the Allowance for Sales Returns account.

    **e.** When a specific customer's account is written off as uncollectible, a debit entry is made to Bad Debt Expense.

    **f.** When a specific customer's account is written off as uncollectible, a debit entry is made to the Allowance for Uncollectible Accounts account.

**7.4**   How does the accounting for trade discounts differ from the accounting for cash discounts?

**7.5**   How is the accounting for cash discounts similar to and different from the accounting for finance charges?

**7.6**   Three methods of accounting for cash discounts are **(1)** the gross price method, **(2)** the allowance method, and **(3)** the net price method. Which method is being described in each of the following independent cases?

    **a.** This method results in recognizing the smallest amount of sales revenue at the time of sale.

    **b.** These two methods result in recognizing the same amount of sales revenue at the time of sale.

    **c.** This method results in reporting the largest amount for accounts receivable in the balance sheet.

    **d.** This method results in reporting the smallest amount for accounts receivable in the balance sheet.

    **e.** This method requires that an adjusting entry be made at the end of the accounting period.

    **f.** This method results in reporting the largest *cumulative* amount of revenue over several periods of increasing sales.

    **g.** This method results in reporting the smallest *cumulative* amount of revenue over several periods of increasing sales.

**7.7**   Describe the relative strengths and weaknesses of the gross price method versus the net price method of accounting for cash discounts. In what ways are the weaknesses of the above methods overcome by the allowance method?

**7.8**   Columbus Record Club offers a "record of the month" to club members. Members not returning a card listing the record of the month by a prescribed date are sent the record. Approximately 30 percent of the members receiving these records return them to Columbus. Describe what you feel is an appropriate method of accounting for these sales returns.

7.9 The customary method of accounting for sales returns results in adequate reporting for the returned sales when the goods are returned in the same period in which they are sold. If the goods are returned in a period subsequent to that of the sale, distortion of the reported revenue figures results. Explain how sales returns may produce each of the described effects.

7.10 Two methods of accounting for uncollectible accounts are (1) the direct charge-off method, and (2) the allowance method. Which method is being described in each of the following independent cases?
   a. This method results in the largest *cumulative* amount of income over several periods of increasing sales.
   b. This method results in the largest amount of current assets on the balance sheet.
   c. This method results in a debit to a balance sheet account when a specific customer's account is written off as uncollectible.
   d. This method results in a reduction in current assets when a specific customer's account is written off as uncollectible.

7.11 a. An old wisdom in tennis holds that if your first serves are always good, then you are not hitting them hard enough. An analogous statement in business might be that if you have no uncollectible accounts, then you probably are not selling enough on credit. Comment on the validity of this statement.
   b. When are more uncollectible accounts better than fewer uncollectible accounts?

7.12 Under what circumstances will the Allowance for Uncollectible Accounts have a debit balance during the accounting period? The balance sheet figure for the Allowance for Uncollectible Accounts at the end of the period should never show a debit balance. Why?

7.13 "The allowance method lacks the objectivity of the direct charge-off method." Comment.

7.14 Describe the relative strengths and weaknesses of the direct charge-off versus the allowance method of accounting for uncollectible accounts.

7.15 Some accountants classify the periodic provision for estimated uncollectible accounts as an operating expense, whereas others classify it as a contra-revenue. Discuss the reasoning behind each of these approaches.

7.16 How does the percentage-of-sales method of estimating the amount of uncollectible accounts differ from the percentage-of-receivables method? How does the percentage-of-receivables method differ from the aging-of-receivables method?

7.17 Give the journal entries to record recoveries of accounts previously written off (a) if the allowance method is used, (b) if the direct charge-off method is used.

7.18 A particular company has been making its annual provision for uncollectible accounts based on 4 percent of credit sales. An aging of the accounts reveals that the balance in the allowance account at the end of the current year is too large by a material amount. What adjustment, if any, should be made? Explain.

7.19 Is there any advantage for a firm selling goods and services to use a promissory note credit arrangement instead of an open account credit arrangement? Are there disadvantages?

**7.20**   For what types of notes will the face value and the present value of the note likely be the same? For what types of notes will the face value and the maturity value of the note be the same?

**7.21**   "Income over the life of a note arising from a sales transaction will have two components: **(1)** a profit from the sales transaction, and **(2)** interest revenue from extending credit to customers over the term of the note."

Explain whether or not this statement is correct under current generally accepted accounting principles for each of the following types of notes:

**a.** Short-term interest-bearing notes.
**b.** Short-term noninterest-bearing notes.
**c.** Long-term interest-bearing notes.
**d.** Long-term noninterest-bearing notes.

**7.22**   Compare and contrast the accounting for short-term and long-term interest-bearing notes.

**7.23**   Compare and contrast the accounting for short-term and long-term noninterest-bearing notes.

**7.24**   Define *imputed interest* rate. Under what conditions is it necessary to impute an interest rate in accounting for notes?

**7.25**   The discount element in a long-term noninterest-bearing note is credited to Discount on Notes Receivable, an account contra to Notes Receivable. What is the rationale for using a contra account instead of simply reducing the book value of Notes Receivable directly?

**7.26**   The Weaver Company received a 5-year noninterest-bearing note on March 3, 1980, in exchange for property sold to the Dickerson Company. There was no established exchange price for this property, and the note has no ready market. The prevailing rate of interest on notes of this type was 10 percent on March 3, 1980, 10.2 percent on December 31, 1980, 10.3 percent on March 3, 1981, and 10.5 percent on December 31, 1981. What interest rate should be used to calculate interest revenue from this transaction for the year ended December 31, 1980? for the year ended December 31, 1981?

**7.27**   To obtain cash prior to the time that accounts receivable are collected, the accounts receivable can be **(1)** assigned, **(2)** pledged, or **(3)** factored with a financial institution. Indicate which arrangement is being described in each of the following cases:

**a.** Accounts receivable are sold to a financial institution; the financial institution collects amounts due directly from customers.
**b.** The company collects amounts due from customers but immediately remits the funds to the financial institution.
**c.** The company collects amounts due from customers but is not required to remit the funds collected to the financial institution.
**d.** At the time accounts receivable are initially used to obtain financing, the net effect on current assets is an increase equal to the cash received from the financial institution.
**e.** At the time accounts receivable are initially used to obtain financing, the net effect on current assets is a decrease equal to the difference between the cash received and the book value of the accounts receivable used to obtain funds.
**f.** Under this arrangement, the accounts receivable involved in the financing remain on the books but are reclassified in an account separate from other accounts receivable.

g. Under this arrangement, the accounts receivable involved in the financing remain on the books and are not reclassified to an account separate from other accounts receivable.

h. Under this arrangement, the accounts receivable involved in the financing are removed from the books.

7.28 Is the discounting of notes without recourse most similar to (a) assigning, (b) pledging, or (c) factoring accounts receivable? Explain.

7.29 The following disclosure appears in a firm's balance sheet:

| | | |
|---|---|---|
| Notes Receivable | $100,000 | |
| Less Discount on Notes Receivable | (10,000) | |
| Net | $ 90,000 | |
| Less Notes Receivable Discounted | (20,000) | |
| Net Notes Receivable | | $70,000 |

Describe the transactions and events that would lead to the disclosures made above.

7.30 Describe the events and transactions that would lead to a description of a Note Receivable for $10,000 with a Discount on Note Receivable of $350 being discounted for each of the following amounts. Consider each of these parts independently of the others.
a. $9,500.
b. $9,800.
c. $9,650.

## Problems and Exercises

7.31 The following are selected transactions of Singleton's Department Store.
(1) Merchandise costing $16,000 is sold on account to customers on December 23, 1981, at a gross invoice price of $20,000. Terms are 2/10, net 30.
(2) Customers purchasing goods in (1) at a gross invoice price of $12,000 pay on December 31, 1981, and take advantage of the cash discount.
(3) Customers purchasing goods in (1) at a gross invoice price of $3,000 pay on January 2, 1982, and take advantage of the cash discount.
(4) Customers purchasing goods in (1) at a gross invoice price of $4,000 pay on January 10, 1982.
a. Give the journal entries that would be made for each of these four events under the gross price method.
b. Give the journal entries that would be made for each of these four events under the net price method.
c. Assume that 80 percent of the customers normally pay within the discount period. Give the journal entries that would be made under the allowance method.

7.32 The following are related transactions of Lewis Hardware Store.
(1) Merchandise costing $28,000 is sold on account to Robertson Construction Company on March 15, 1981. The merchandise has a list price of $40,000, but a 10-percent trade discount is granted. Terms of sale are 2/10, net 30, based on the exchange price.
(2) Merchandise sold in (1) with an original list price of $10,000 is collected on March 20 in time for the customer to take advantage of the cash discount.

(3) Merchandise sold in (1) with an original list price of $30,000 is collected on March 30 after the cash discount period has lapsed.
   a. Give the journal entries to record these transactions under the gross price method.
   b. Give the journal entries to record these transactions under the net price method.

7.33   a. Heritage Carpet Store offers credit terms of 2/10, net 30, to its customers. On April 21 it sold carpets to a customer on account for $6,000. The customer paid for the carpets on May 20. Give the journal entries to record these transactions under the net price method.
   b. Tradition Carpet Store charges interest on unpaid customers' accounts at the rate of 2.04 percent per month. On April 21 it sold carpets to a customer on account for $5,880. The customer paid for the carpets plus accrued interest on May 20. Give the journal entries to record these transactions, assuming that the books are closed on December 31 of each year.

7.34   Sales on account of Davis Department Store, Inc., during 1981, its first year of operations, totaled $400,000. Collections from customers on these credit sales totaled $250,000. It is estimated that 2 percent of credit sales will become uncollectible. During 1981, $3,000 of specific customers' accounts were written off as uncollectible.
   During 1982, credit sales to customers totaled $500,000 and cash collections from customers on credit sales totaled $360,000. Specific customers' accounts totaling $6,500 were written off as uncollectible during 1982.
   a. Give the journal entries to record these events during 1981 and 1982 using the direct charge-off method.
   b. Give the journal entries to record these events during 1981 and 1982 using the allowance method.
   c. Will the direct charge-off method or the allowance method result in a larger net income for 1981? For 1982?
   d. Will the direct charge-off method or the allowance method result in larger total assets on December 31, 1981? On December 31, 1982?

7.35   The sales, all on account, of the Wilcox Company in 1981, its first year of operations, were $1,000,000. Collections totaled $850,000. On December 31, 1981, it was estimated that 1.5 percent of all sales would probably become uncollectible. During the year, specific accounts in the amount of $5,000 were written off.
   The company's *unadjusted* trial balance (but after all *non*adjusting entries were made) on December 31, 1982, included the following accounts and balances:

| | |
|---|---|
| Accounts Receivable (Dr.) | $90,000 |
| Allowance for Uncollectible Accounts (Dr.) | 6,000 |
| Sales Contra, Estimated Uncollectibles | — |
| Sales Revenue (Cr.) | $1,200,000 |

It was concluded that the estimated uncollectible rate of 1.5 percent of all sales should be applied to 1982 operations.
   Present journal entries for the following:
   a. Transactions and adjustments of 1981 related to sales and customers' accounts.
   b. Transactions for 1982 resulting in the above unadjusted trial balance amounts.
   c. Adjustment for estimated uncollectibles for 1982.

7.36   The amounts in certain accounts on January 1, 1981, and before adjusting and closing entries on December 31, 1981, are shown below:

|  | Jan. 1, 1981 | Dec. 31, 1981 |
|---|---|---|
| Accounts Receivable ..................................... | $800,000 Dr. | $960,000 Dr. |
| Allowance for Uncollectible Accounts .................... | 60,000 Cr. | 40,000 Dr. |
| Sales Contra, Estimated Uncollectibles ................... | 0 | 0 |
| Sales ................................................... | 0 | 4,000,000 Cr. |

During 1981, 90 percent of sales were on account. It was estimated that 3 percent of credit sales would become uncollectible. During 1981, one account for $3,000 was collected, although it had been written off as uncollectible during 1980.

**a.** Give the journal entries made during 1981 that explain the changes in the four accounts as listed above.

**b.** Give any adjusting entries required on December 31, 1981.

**7.37** The unadjusted trial balance of Williams Company on December 31, 1981, shows the following:

|  | Dr. | Cr. |
|---|---|---|
| Sales ......................................................... |  | $1,000,000 |
| Sales Returns ................................................. | $ 4,000 |  |
| Allowance for Uncollectible Accounts ............................ | 8,000 |  |
| Sales Contra, Estimated Uncollectibles ........................... | — |  |
| Accounts Receivable ............................................ | 250,000 |  |

Give the adjusting entry to provide for estimated uncollectible accounts for 1981 under each of the following approaches:

**a.** The percentage-of-sales method is used; the uncollectible rate is 2 percent of sales (net of returns).

**b.** The percentage-of-receivables method is used; the uncollectible rate is 4 percent of accounts receivable.

**c.** The aging-of-receivables method is used; the balance needed in the allowance account on December 31, 1981, is $11,000.

**7.38** The following data apply to the first two years of operations of Wilson Company during 1981 and 1982:

|  | 1981 | 1982 |
|---|---|---|
| Sales on Account ................................................. | $400,000 | $600,000 |
| Collections from Customers on Account ........................... | 298,000 | 456,400 |
| Write-Off of Customers' Accounts .................................. | 2,000 | 3,600 |

**a.** Assume that Wilson Company uses the percentage-of-sales method of estimating uncollectible accounts. Give the journal entries to provide for estimated uncollectibles at the end of 1981 and 1982, using 2 percent of sales as the estimation rate.

**b.** Assume instead that Wilson Company uses the percentage-of-receivables method of estimating uncollectible accounts. Give the journal entries to provide for estimated uncollectibles at the end of 1981 and 1982, using 6 percent of the balance in accounts receivable as the estimation rate.

**7.39** Shad Company's accounts receivable on December 31, 1981, show the following balances by ages:

| Age of Accounts | Balance Receivable |
|---|---|
| 0–30 Days ....................................................... | $400,000 |
| 31–60 Days ..................................................... | 150,000 |
| 61–120 Days .................................................... | 60,000 |
| More Than 120 Days ......................................... | 30,000 |

The credit balance in Allowance for Uncollectible Accounts before adjusting entries is $10,550 on December 31, 1981. Shad Company bases its provision for estimated uncollectibles on the aging-of-receivables method. Past experience indicates that the following percentages are appropriate: 0–30 days, .5 of 1 percent; 31–60 days, 1 percent; 61–120 days, 10 percent; more than 120 days, 60 percent.

Give the journal entry to provide for estimated uncollectibles on December 31, 1981. Be sure to show the calculation of the appropriate provision.

7.40   The data in the following schedule pertain to the first 8 years of the Gordon Company's credit sales and experience with uncollectible accounts:

| Year | Credit Sales | Related Uncollectible Accounts | Year | Credit Sales | Related Uncollectible Accounts |
|---|---|---|---|---|---|
| 1 ............ | $100,000 | $2,550 | 5 ............ | $250,000 | $3,000 |
| 2 ............ | 150,000 | 3,225 | 6 ............ | 275,000 | 2,700 |
| 3 ............ | 200,000 | 3,725 | 7 ............ | 280,000 | 2,875 |
| 4 ............ | 225,000 | 4,000 | 8 ............ | 290,000 | 2,925 |

Gordon Company has not previously used an Allowance for Uncollectible Accounts but has merely charged accounts written off directly to Uncollectible Accounts Expense.

What percentage of credit sales for a year would you recommend that Gordon Company charge to the sales adjustment account if one were to be set up at the end of year 8?

7.41   a. The Feldman Company has a gross margin on credit sales of 30 percent. That is, cost of goods sold on account is 70 percent of sales on account. Uncollectible accounts amount to 2 percent of credit sales. If credit is extended to a new class of customers, credit sales will increase by $10,000, 8 percent of the new credit sales will be uncollectible, and selling expenses will increase by $1,000. Will Feldman Company be better or worse off if it extends credit to the new class of customers and by how much?

b. How would your answer to part **a** differ if $2,000 of the $10,000 increase in credit sales would have been made anyway as sales for cash? (Assume that the uncollectible amount on new credit sales is $800.)

c. The Norman Company has credit sales of $100,000, a gross margin on those sales of 25 percent, and 3 percent of the credit sales are uncollectible. If credit is extended to a new class of customers, sales will increase by $40,000, selling expenses will increase by $1,500, and uncollectibles will be 5 percent of *all* credit sales. Verify that Norman Company will be $4,500 better off if it extends credit to the new customers. What percentage of the new credit sales are uncollectible?

7.42   Calculate simple interest on a base of $6,000 for the following intervals and rates, using a 360-day year:

a. 60 days at 12 percent.

b. 60 days at 8 percent.

c. 90 days at 9 percent.

d. 60 days at 16 percent.

    **e.** 15 days at 16 percent.          **g.** 5 months, 15 days at 12 percent.
    **f.** 6 months at 9 percent.           **h.** 4 months, 12 days at 9 percent.

**7.43** The Berlin Company sold merchandise costing $1,800 to Kamex Company for $2,400. The Kamex Company issued a promissory note, dated November 15, 1980, which bears interest at 12 percent and matures on March 15, 1981. The note is paid at maturity. Give the journal entries on the books of Berlin Company over the life of the note, assuming that the books are closed annually on December 31.

**7.44** The Martin Company sold merchandise costing $1,800 to Wood Company on November 15, 1980. The Wood Company issued a noninterest-bearing promissory note with a face value of $2,496 and a maturity date of March 15, 1981. Wood Company could borrow funds at its bank on November 15, 1980, at 12 percent interest per year.
    **a.** Assuming that the theoretically preferable effective-interest method of accounting for long-term notes is used, give the journal entries on the books of Martin Company over the life of the note assuming that the books are closed annually on December 31.
    **b.** Repeat step **a,** but give the journal entries required under current generally accepted accounting principles where implicit interest is ignored.

**7.45** On May 20, the Muriel Company received a note from B. M. Maxwell to be applied on account. The note is dated April 20, and is due October 20. The face value of the note is $900; it bears interest at 8 percent per year; the maker is B. F. McGrath. Maxwell is given credit for the face value of the note plus 1 month's accrued interest. The note is paid by the maker at maturity. Present journal entries on the books of Muriel Company for the note. The Muriel Company closes its books annually on June 30.

**7.46** The Cook Company sold merchandise costing $5,000 to J. K. Carlton for $6,000 on November 1, 1980. Carlton signed a promissory note, bearing interest at 10 percent per year and maturing on May 1, 1981. Cook Company closes its books on June 30 and December 31 of each year. The note was paid at maturity.
    **a.** Give the journal entries made by Cook Company over the term of the note.
    **b.** Give the journal entries made by Cook Company over the term of the note, assuming that the note is renewed at maturity on May 1, 1981, for another 3 months. At the time of renewal, the maker pays the interest accrued to May 1, 1981. The new note is paid at maturity on August 1, 1981.
    **c.** Give the journal entries made by Cook Company over the term of the note, assuming that $4,000 of the face value is renewed at maturity on May 1, 1981, for another 3 months. At the time of renewal, the maker pays the $2,000 principal plus all interest accrued to May 1, 1981. The new note is paid at maturity on August 1, 1981.
    **d.** Give the journal entries made by Cook Company over the term of the note, assuming that it is dishonored at maturity on May 1, 1981, and there is no hope of recovery. Cook Company does not use the allowance method for uncollectible notes.

**7.47** Cox Auto Corporation sold a fleet of trucks costing $75,000 to FOB Corporation on January 1, 1981. FOB Corporation paid $10,000 down and signed a noninterest-bearing promissory note for the remainder of the purchase price. The note has a face value of $102,883.80 and is payable in installments of $34,294.60 at the end of 1981, 1982, and 1983. The established exchange price based on a 100-percent cash transaction for this fleet of trucks is $100,000.
    **a.** Demonstrate that the interest rate implicit in the note is 7 percent per year.
    **b.** Prepare an amortization schedule similar to that in Exhibit 7.3 for the note, assuming that 7 percent is an appropriate interest rate for this note.

**c.** Give the journal entries on the books of Cox Auto Corporation over the life of the note, assuming that the books are closed annually on December 31.

**7.48** Standard Manufacturing Company sold an electrical generator costing $9,000,000 to Chicago General Hospital for $10,000,000 on January 1, 1981. Chicago General paid $2,000,000 and signed an $8,000,000 promissory note for the balance of the purchase price. The note is payable at the rate of $2,000,000 per year on December 31 of each of the next 4 years, with the first payment due on December 31, 1981. In addition, interest payments at the rate of 8 percent per year on the unpaid balance must be made on December 31 of each year.
 **a.** Prepare an amortization schedule for the $8,000,000 note similar to that shown in Exhibit 7.3, assuming that 8 percent is an appropriate interest rate for this note.
 **b.** Demonstrate that the present value of the future cash payments on the note on January 1, 1981, is $8,000,000.
 **c.** Give the journal entries on Standard's books on January 1, 1981, and at the end of 1981 through 1984, assuming that the books are closed annually on December 31.

**7.49** BBM Corporation manufactures and sells computers. On January 1, 1981, it sold a computer costing $450,000 to Sawyer Corporation for $500,000. Sawyer Corporation signed a $500,000 promissory note, agreeing to repay the note plus interest at 10 percent in three equal installments of $201,057.
 **a.** Demonstrate that the present value of the future cash flows on January 1, 1981, is $500,000 (the actual amount, unrounded, is $499,998.60), assuming that 10 percent is an appropriate interest rate for this note.
 **b.** Prepare an amortization schedule for the $500,000 note similar to that shown in Exhibit 7.3.
 **c.** Give the journal entries on BBM Corporation's books on January 1, 1981, and at the end of 1981, 1982, and 1983, assuming that the books are closed on December 31 of each year.

**7.50** **a.** Record the following events in journal entry form:
 **(1)** On April 1, 1981, Hanover Company borrows $50,000 from its bank on a 6-month loan carrying interest at the rate of 1 percent per month on the unpaid balance at the beginning of the month. To secure payment, Hanover Company assigns $60,000 of its accounts receivable.
 **(2)** Collections from customers during April total $12,000, and this amount is remitted to the bank on April 30.
 **(3)** Collections from customers during May total $15,000, and this amount is remitted to the bank on May 31.
 **b.** Illustrate the required disclosure in the balance sheet on May 31, the end of Hanover Company's fiscal year.

**7.51** The accounts receivable accounts of Norwich Company on October 1, 1981, are as follows:

| | |
|---|---:|
| Accounts Receivable ............................................... | $80,000 |
| Less Allowance for Uncollectible Accounts ............................ | (3,000) |
| Accounts Receivable—Net .......................................... | $77,000 |

Give the journal entries to record each of the following transactions and events.
 **(1)** On October 1, 1981, Norwich Company borrows $40,000 from its bank, signing a note agreeing to repay the loan with interest at a rate of 1 percent per month on the unpaid balance. The note is due on February 1, 1982. To secure the loan, Norwich Company assigns $50,000 of accounts receivable.
 **(2)** Collections from customers during October total $16,000, of which $10,000 relates to assigned accounts receivable. A check for $10,000 is issued to the bank on October 31.

(3) Collections from customers during November total $14,000, of which $8,000 relates to assigned accounts receivable. A check for $8,000 is issued to the bank on November 30.

(4) On November 30, 1981, accounts totaling $900 are written off as uncollectible. Of this amount, $600 relates to accounts that were assigned to the bank. The bank requires that these uncollectible accounts be replaced by other accounts receivable.

**7.52**   Refer to the data for Norwich Company in Problem **7.51**. To secure the $40,000 loan from the bank, the company pledges $50,000 of its accounts receivable on October 1, 1981. The note is repayable to the bank on February 1, 1982. Give any required journal entries on October 1, 1981.

**7.53**   Refer to the data for Norwich Company in Problem **7.51**. Norwich Company factors $50,000 of its accounts receivable to obtain the needed $40,000. Of the balance in the Allowance for Uncollectible Accounts, $1,875 is an appropriate portion applicable to the accounts factored. Give any required journal entries on October 1, 1981.

**7.54**   On November 1, the Atlantic Supply Company received a note from one of its customers to apply on its open account receivable. The 9-month, 9-percent note for $8,000, issued November 1, is valued at its face amount.

On January 31 of the next year, the Atlantic Supply Company endorses the note and transfers it with recourse to City National Bank. The Company's checking account at this bank is increased for the proceeds, $8,100.

Later, on August 8, the Atlantic Supply Company is notified by the bank that the note was collected from the customer at maturity.

Atlantic Supply Company closes its books annually on December 31.

Present dated journal entries on the books of Atlantic Supply Company relating to this note.

**7.55**   The Marans Corporation receives a 3-month, 10-percent note for $4,800 from the Hoffman Company, on account, on June 1, 1981. The Marans Corporation discounts the note with recourse at the bank on July 1, at a discount rate of 10 percent. The note is paid at maturity by the Hoffman Company.

   **a.** Present dated journal entries for the Marans Corporation related to the note, assuming that the books are closed monthly.

   **b.** Present the entry on July 1, if the note were discounted at 5 percent.

   **c.** Present the entry on July 1, if the note were discounted at 15 percent.

**7.56**   On May 10 the Zami Supply Company receives a note from one of its customers, Loriz Builders, Inc., to apply on its account. The 6-month, 12-percent note for $6,600, issued on May 10, is valued at its face amount.

On July 25 the Zami Supply Company endorses the note and transfers it with recourse to the Cobb Steel Products Company to settle an account payable. The note is valued at its face amount plus accrued interest.

On November 12 the Zami Supply Company is notified that the note was paid at maturity.

   **a.** Present dated entries on the books for the Zami Supply Company, assuming that it closes its books quarterly on March 31, June 30, and so on.

   **b.** Present dated entries on the books of the Cobb Steel Products Company, assuming that it closes its books quarterly on March 31, June 30, and so on.

**7.57**   Prepare dated journal entries for the following transactions of the Ducrest Company. The Ducrest Company closes its books annually on June 30.

(1) On June 10, 1981, the company receives a note from the Young Company to apply on its open account. The $9,000, 90-day, 8-percent note was issued by W. T. Williams on May 1. The company accepts the note at face value plus accrued interest.

(2) The interest adjustment at the end of the period is recorded.

(3) The note is discounted with recourse at the Westmoreland Bank at an 8-percent rate on July 5.

(4) On August 1, notice is received from the bank that the Young-Williams note has been collected at maturity.

**7.58**   Record each of the following transactions or events of Melton Corporation in journal entry form. The books are closed monthly.

(1) Jan. 1981: Sales to customers totaled $400,000 of which $320,000 was on account. Cash collections from credit customers totaled $135,000.

(2) Jan. 31, 1981: Melton Corporation estimates that 1 percent of goods sold will be returned and 2 percent of credit sales will become uncollectible. Melton Corporation uses the allowance method for sales returns and for uncollectible accounts.

(3) Feb. 10, 1981: Customers' accounts totaling $12,000 are written off as uncollectible.

(4) Feb. 15, 1981: The account of H. Arrend for $1,000 is past due. H. Arrend signs a promissory note for $1,000. The note is payable with interest at 10 percent on May 15, 1981.

(5) Feb. 15, 1981: Customers return goods originally sold on account for $250. The accounts have not yet been collected.

(6) Feb. 20, 1981: Melton Corporation borrows $60,000 from its bank. The note carries an interest rate of 1 percent of the unpaid balance per month. To secure the loan, Melton Corporation assigns $65,000 of its accounts receivable.

(7) Feb. 20, 1981: The note of H. Arrend is discounted with the bank with recourse. The bank discounted the note at 12 percent.

(8) Feb. 1981: Sales to customers totaled $420,000, of which $300,000 was on account. Cash collections from credit customers totaled $155,000. Of this amount, $1,200 was from customers whose accounts had previously been written off. $15,000 of the amounts collected was from customers whose accounts had been assigned to the bank on February 20.

(9) Feb. 28, 1981: A check is issued to the bank for $15,000 in connection with assigned accounts receivable.

**7.59**   Record each of the following transactions or events of Kessinger Corporation during October in journal entry form. The books are closed monthly.

(1) During October, 1981, goods costing $8,000 were sold to customers on account for $10,000. Terms of sales were 2/10, net 30. The gross price method of accounting for cash discounts is used.

(2) Cash collections during October from credit customers totaled $6,000, of which $4,900 was net of cash discounts taken. The remaining $1,100 collected was from customers who paid after the discount period had lapsed.

(3) On October 10, a note was received from B. Williams in the face amount of $500 in settlement of an open account receivable. The note bears interest at the rate of 10 percent per year and is due on January 10, 1982.

(4) On October 15, a tract of land costing $10,000 is sold to Maher Corporation. Maher Corporation signs a $25,000 noninterest-bearing promissory note due on April 15 of next year. The land has a market value of $24,250.

(5) On October 15, a second tract of land costing $40,000 is sold to Sundem Corporation.

Sundem Corporation signs a $66,550 noninterest-bearing promissory note due on October 15 three years hence. The land has a market value of $50,000.

(6) On October 20, the note of B. Williams is discounted with recourse to City National Bank. The bank discounted the note at 8 percent.

(7) On October 25, a note was received from R. Santo in the face amount of $600 in settlement of an open account receivable. The note was issued by J. Huntly on September 25, bears interest at 12 percent, and is due on November 25 of this year. R. Santo was given credit for the face amount of the note plus accrued interest.

(8) All necessary adjusting entries are made on October 31.

7.60 (Adapted from CPA Examination.) You are examining Braun Corporation's financial statements for the year ended December 31, 1981. Your analysis of the 1981 entries in the Trade Notes Receivable account is shown in Exhibit 7.4.

The following information is available:

(1) Balances at January 1, 1981, were a debit of $1,400 in the Interest Receivable account and a credit of $400 in the Unearned Interest Revenue account. The $118,000 debit balance in the Trade Notes Receivable account consisted of the following three notes:

| | |
|---|---|
| Allen note dated 8/31/1981 payable in annual installments of $10,000 principal plus accrued interest at 6% at each August 31 | $70,000 |
| Bailey note discounted to Braun at 6% on 11/1/1980 due 11/1/81 | 8,000 |
| Charnes note for $40,000 plus 6% interest dated 12/31/1980 due on 9/1/81 | 40,000 |

(2) No entries were made during 1981 to the Interest Receivable account or the Unearned Interest Revenue account; and only one entry, for a credit of $1,200 on December 31, appeared in the Interest Revenue account.

(3) All notes were from trade customers unless otherwise indicated.

(4) Debits and credits offsetting Trade Notes Receivable debit and credit entries were correctly recorded unless the facts indicate otherwise.

Prepare a work sheet to adjust each entry to correct or properly reclassify it, if necessary. Enter your adjustments in the proper columns to correspond with the date of each entry. Do not combine related entries for different dates. Your completed work sheet will provide the basis for one compound journal entry to correct all entries to Trade Notes Receivable and related accounts for 1981. Formal journal entries are not required. In addition to the information shown in the above analysis, the following column headings are suggested for your worksheet:

| | | | Adjustment or Reclassification Required | | |
|---|---|---|---|---|---|
| | | | | **Other Accounts** | |
| **Trade Notes Receivable** | **Trade Accounts Receivable** | **Interest Revenue** | **Account Title** | **Amount** | |
| **Debit (Credit)** | **Debit (Credit)** | **Debit (Credit)** | | **Debit** | **Credit** |

7.61 (Adapted from CPA Examination) On January 1 of the current year, the Pitt Company sold a patent to Chatham, Inc., which had a net carrying value on Pitt's books of $10,000. Chatham gave Pitt an $80,000 noninterest bearing note payable in five equal installments of $16,000, with the first payment due one year after the sale. There was no established exchange price for the patent, and the note had no ready market. The prevailing rate of interest for a note of this type on the date of the sale was 12 percent.

Calculate the amount of income or loss before income taxes (rounded to the nearest dollar) that Pitt should record for the first two years of the note based on the above facts.

*Exhibit 7.4*
**Braun Corporation**
**Analysis of Trade Notes Receivable**
**for the Year Ended December 31, 1981**

| Date 1981 | | Folio | Trade Notes Receivable Debit | Trade Notes Receivable Credit |
|---|---|---|---|---|
| Jan. 1 | Balance forward .................................. | | $118,000 | |
| Feb. 29 | Received $25,000, 6% note due 10/29/1981 from Daley, whose trade account was past due .............. | MEMO | | |
| Feb. 29 | Discounted with recourse Daley note at 6% ........ | CR | | $ 24,960 |
| Mar. 29 | Received noninterest-bearing demand note from Edge, the Corporation's treasurer for a loan ...... | CD | 6,200 | |
| Aug. 30 | Received principal and interest due from Allen and, in accordance with agreement, 2 principal payments in advance .................................... | CR | | 34,200 |
| Sept. 4 | Paid protest fee on note dishonored by Charnes | CD | 5 | |
| Nov. 1 | Received check dated 2/1/82 in settlement of Bailey note. The check was included in cash on hand 12/31/81 ...................................... | CR | | 8,120 |
| Nov. 4 | Paid protest fee and maturity value of Daley note to bank. Note discounted 2/29/81 was dishonored . | CD | 26,031 | |
| Dec. 27 | Accepted furniture and fixtures with a fair market value of $24,000 in full settlement from Daley ..... | GJ | | 24,000 |
| Dec. 31 | Received check dated 1/3/82 from Edge in payment of 3/29/81 note. (The check was included in petty cash until 1/2/82 when it was returned to Edge in exchange for a new demand note of the same amount.) ...................................... | CR | | 6,200 |
| Dec. 31 | Received principal and interest on Charnes note .... | CR | | 42,437 |
| Dec. 31 | Accrued interest on Allen note ................... | GJ | 1,200 | |
| | Totals ...................................... | | $151,436 | $139,917 |

7.62   (Adapted from CPA Examination) The Maple Corporation sells farm machinery on the installment plan. On July 1 of the current year, Maple entered into an installment sale contract with Agriculture, Inc., for an eight-year period. Equal annual payments under the installment sale are $100,000 and are due on July 1, with the first payment due and made on the date of the sale.

Additional information is as follows:

1. The amount that would be realized on an outright sale of similar farm machinery is $556,376.
2. The cost of the farm machinery sold to Agriculture is $417,000.
3. The finance charges related to the installment period are $243,624 based on a stated interest rate of 12 percent, which is appropriate.
4. Circumstances are such that the collection of the installments due under the contract is reasonably assured.

Calculate the income or loss before income taxes that Maple should record for the year of the sale, which ends on December 31, as a result of the above transaction.

# Chapter 8
## Revenue Recognition and Receivables: At Times Other Than Time of Sale

8.1 As discussed in Chapter 7, revenue from the sale of most goods and services is recognized at the time of sale. Under certain circumstances, however, revenue may be recognized either earlier or later than the time of sale. In this chapter, we explore revenue recognition in greater depth, focusing primarily on departures from the sales basis of revenue recognition.

### Revenue Recognition: General Principles

8.2 Figure 8.1 depicts graphically the earnings process for a typical good or service. Initially, production facilities and raw materials are acquired. These assets are combined with labor services during the period of production in manufacturing a product. The product is then sold. Because most goods and services are sold on credit, some time normally elapses between sale and collection of cash from customers.

8.3 Revenue could conceivably be recognized at any of the five times listed in Figure 8.1. The criteria currently required to be met before revenue is recognized are as follows:

1. All, or a significant portion, of the services to be provided have been performed.

2. Cash, a receivable, or some other asset susceptible to reasonably precise measurement has been received.

### Figure 8.1
#### Earnings Process for Good or Service

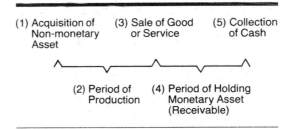

(1) Acquisition of Non-monetary Asset    (3) Sale of Good or Service    (5) Collection of Cash

(2) Period of Production    (4) Period of Holding Monetary Asset (Receivable)

8.4     In most cases, these criteria are met at the time of sale. A customer has been identified, an exchange price has been agreed to, the good or service has been delivered, and cash or a claim to cash has been received.

8.5     To justify recognizing revenue earlier than the time of sale, the following conditions must generally be met:

**1.** A specific customer has been identified and an exchange price agreed upon; in most cases, a formal contract has been signed.

**2.** A significant portion of the services to be performed have been performed, and the expected costs of future services can be estimated with reasonable accuracy.

**3.** An assessment of the customer's credit standing permits a reasonably accurate estimate of the amount of cash that will be collected.

These conditions may be met for certain long-term contracts and special-order merchandise.

8.6     To justify postponing the recognition of revenue until after the time of sale, at least one of the following conditions must generally be present:

**1.** Extreme uncertainty exists regarding the amount of cash that will be collected from customers, either because of the customer's financial condition or because of contingencies in the sales agreement. (Note that the concern here is not with the possibility that the uncollectible rate will be high. The concern is with whether the rate—high or low—can be estimated with reasonable precision. In statistical terms, the concern is with the standard deviation around the mean rather than with the mean itself.)

**2.** Future services to be provided are substantial, and their costs cannot be estimated with reasonable precision.

These conditions may be present in sales of real estate or franchises.

8.7     In the sections that follow, application of these criteria and conditions to revenue recognition is discussed for several types of businesses.

# Recognition during the Period of Production

## Long-Term Construction Contracts

On many long-term construction projects, the buyer and seller agree in advance on the contract price. In agreeing to the contract price, the construction company must have some reasonable basis for estimating the cost to be incurred under the contract so as to assure a satisfactory return. In agreeing to perform the contract work, the construction company must feel that the probability of collecting the contract price from the buyer is sufficiently high to warrant the investment of capital and labor services. Under these conditions, the criteria for revenue recognition are met prior to completion of the contract. Recognition of revenue during the period of production, or construction, is therefore justified in most cases.    8.8

**Percentage-of-Completion Method** The *percentage-of-completion method* is the accounting procedure used to recognize revenue during the period of production. A portion of the total contract price, based on the degree of completion of the work, is recognized as revenue each period. This proportion is determined using either engineers' or architects' estimates of the degree of completion, or the ratio of costs incurred to date to total expected costs for the contract, or sometimes a combination of the two. A portion of the estimated total contract costs is likewise recognized as an expense in each period to be matched against revenues. Thus the percentage-of-completion method is an accrual basis of accounting, because expenses are matched with revenues. The percentage-of-completion method is more accurately described as an *income,* rather than a revenue, recognition method, because the degree of completion determines both the amount of revenues and the amount of expenses recognized.    8.9

Most long-term construction contracts provide for periodic payments by the buyer as construction takes place. Although the collection of cash during the period of con-    8.10

struction helps confirm the construction company's probability assessments that the full contract price will ultimately be collected, the actual schedule of cash collections is not significant for the income-recognition process under the percentage-of-completion method. For example, a particular contract may provide for all of the contract price to be paid when the contract is completed. As long as the construction company can accurately assess the probability that the contract price will ultimately be received in cash, use of the percentage-of-completion method is still justified. Construction activity, not the collection of cash, is the critical income-generating event under the percentage-of-completion method.

8.11   **Completed-Contract Method** Some firms involved in construction projects postpone the recognition of income until the construction has been completed. This method is similar to revenue recognition at the time of sale, but in this context is referred to as the *completed-contract method*. In some cases, the completed-contract method is used because the contracts are of such short duration (such as 3 or 6 months) that earnings reported with the percentage-of-completion method and the completed-contract method are not materially different. In these cases, the completed-contract method is used because it is easier to implement. Some firms use the completed-contract method when a specific buyer has not been obtained while construction is progressing, as is sometimes the case in constructing residential housing. In these cases, future selling efforts are required and substantial uncertainty may exist regarding the selling price ultimately to be established and the amount of cash to be received. Perhaps the most important reason why some firms use the completed-contract method is the extreme difficulty sometimes encountered in obtaining reasonably accurate estimates of the total costs to be incurred on contracts extending over several years.

8.12   **Selection of Income-Recognition Method on Long-Term Contracts** *Statement of Po-*

sition *No. 81-1,* which is currently the official pronouncement on long-term contracts, states that the percentage-of-completion method is preferable when estimates of the cost to complete and extent of progress toward completion of long-term contracts are reasonably dependable.* The percentage-of-completion method is preferred because **(1)** income during each period of the contract will reflect the results of construction activity during the period (in contrast to the completed-contract method, where no income is recognized during the periods prior to completion while construction activity is taking place), and **(2)** the current status of uncompleted contracts will be reported more accurately, because current estimates of costs to complete and measures of the degree of completion will be reflected in the financial statement amounts (in contrast to the completed-contract method, where only the actual costs incurred are normally reported). The principal disadvantage of the percentage-of-completion method is that it must rely on estimates of the degree of completion and the future costs to be incurred in currently accruing income, both of which are subject to uncertainties. These uncertainties are removed if income recognition is postponed until the construction project is completed. *SOP No. 81-1* states that when lack of dependable estimates or inherent hazards cause forecasts to be doubtful, the completed-contract method is preferable.†

**Illustration of the Percentage-of-Completion Method** The mechanics of the percentage-of-completion method can be summarized as follows:   8.13

   **1.** Actual construction costs incurred are accumulated in a Construction in Process account, much the same as manufacturing costs are accumulated in a Work-in-Process Inventory account.

---

*Statement of Position No. 81-1,* "Accounting for Performance of Construction-Type and Certain Production-Type Contracts." AICPA (July 1981).
†Ibid.

**2.** As customers are billed for amounts periodically due on construction contracts, Accounts Receivable is debited and an account contra to the Construction in Process account, entitled Billings on Contracts in Process, is credited.

**3.** When cash payments are received from customers, Cash is debited and Accounts Receivable is credited.

**4.** At the end of each period, the degree of completion of the construction work is calculated using either engineers' or architects' estimates or the ratio of costs incurred to date to total expected costs. This degree-of-completion percentage is multiplied by the total expected income, or profit, from the contract (that is, contract price less total estimated costs). This calculation gives the *cumulative* amount of income that should be recognized during all periods since construction activity began. To determine the amount to be recognized during the current period, the amount actually recognized in prior periods is subtracted from the cumulative amount that should be recognized as of this stage of completion. The difference is the income to be recognized in the period. This amount is debited to the Construction in Process account and credited to an income statement account, such as Income from Long-Term Contracts.

**5.** When the contract is completed and the customer has been fully billed, the amount in the Construction in Process account (actual total costs incurred plus cumulative income recognized) should be equal to the amount in the account, Billings on Contracts in Process (contract price). The construction project is removed from the books by debiting Billings on Contracts in Process and crediting Construction in Process.

8.14 To illustrate the mechanics of the percentage-of-completion method, assume that Acme Construction Company contracted on May 15, 1981, to build a bridge for a city for $4,500,000. Acme estimated that the cost of constructing the bridge would be $3,600,000. Actual costs coincided with expectations and were incurred as follows: 1981: $1,200,000; 1982: $2,000,000; 1983: $400,000. The contract provided that the city be billed as follows: 1981: $1,000,000; 1982: $1,500,000; 1983: $2,000,000. Billings and payments were made on schedule. The bridge was completed and approved in 1983.

8.15 The estimated income from the contract is $900,000 (= $4,500,000 − $3,600,000). We shall assume that the degree of completion is based on the ratio of actual costs incurred to date divided by expected total costs. During 1981, $1,200,000 of the total $3,600,000 costs were incurred. Therefore, $1,200,000/$3,600,000, or 33.3 percent of the $900,000 income (= $300,000) is recognized. During 1982, an additional $2,000,000 of costs were incurred. The calculation of income recognized for 1982 is as follows:

$$\begin{aligned}\text{Percentage-of-Completion} &= \frac{\text{Cost Incurred to Date}}{\text{Total Estimated Costs}} \\ &= \frac{\$1,200,000 + \$2,000,000}{\$3,600,000} = 88.9\%.\end{aligned}$$

Cumulative Income to Be Recognized:

| | |
|---|---:|
| .889 × $900,000 .................... | $800,000 |
| Income Recognized During 1981 ....... | (300,000) |
| Income to Be Recognized During 1982 .. | $500,000 |

During 1983, the remaining $100,000 of the total $900,000 is recognized.

8.16 Exhibit 8.1 shows the journal entries under the percentage-of-completion method for the 3 years of the contract. Note that billing customers and receiving cash from customers do not affect the computation of income.

8.17 On the balance sheet for December 31, 1981, current assets would show the following:

**Current Assets**

| | |
|---|---:|
| Construction in Process ............. | $1,500,000 |
| Less Billings on Contracts in Process .. | (1,000,000) |
| Excess of Construction in Process over Billings .......................... | $ 500,000 |

## Exhibit 8.1
### Journal Entries and T-Accounts for the Percentage-of-Completion Method

| | 1981 | | 1982 | | 1983 | |
|---|---|---|---|---|---|---|
| 1. To record construction costs incurred: | | | | | | |
| Construction in Process ............ | 1,200,000 | | 2,000,000 | | 400,000 | |
| Cash, Accounts Payable, etc. ..... | | 1,200,000 | | 2,000,000 | | 400,000 |
| 2. To record billings to customer: | | | | | | |
| Accounts Receivable .............. | 1,000,000 | | 1,500,000 | | 2,000,000 | |
| Billings on Contracts in Process .. | | 1,000,000 | | 1,500,000 | | 2,000,000 |
| 3. To record cash collections: | | | | | | |
| Cash .......................... | 1,000,000 | | 1,500,000 | | 2,000,000 | |
| Accounts Receivable ............ | | 1,000,000 | | 1,500,000 | | 2,000,000 |
| 4. To record periodic income recognized: | | | | | | |
| Construction in Process ........... | 300,000 | | 500,000 | | 100,000 | |
| Income from Long-Term Contracts . | | 300,000 | | 500,000 | | 100,000 |
| 5. To record final approval and acceptance: | | | | | | |
| Billings on Contracts in Process .... | — | | — | | 4,500,000 | |
| Construction in Process .......... | — | | — | | | 4,500,000 |

| (A) Cash or Other Accounts | |
|---|---|
| (3) 1,000,000 | 1,200,000 (1) |
| (3) 1,500,000 | 2,000,000 (1) |
| (3) 2,000,000 | 400,000 (1) |

| (A) Construction in Process | |
|---|---|
| (1) 1,200,000 (4) 300,000 | |
| √ 1,500,000 (1) 2,000,000 (4) 500,000 | |
| √ 4,000,000 (1) 400,000 (4) 100,000 | 4,500,000 (5) |
| √ 0 | |

| (A) Accounts Receivable | |
|---|---|
| (2) 1,000,000 | 1,000,000 (3) |
| (2) 1,500,000 | 1,500,000 (3) |
| (2) 2,000,000 | 2,000,000 (3) |

| (XA) Billings on Contracts in Process | |
|---|---|
| | 1,000,000 (2) |
| | 1,000,000 √ 1,500,000 (2) |
| | 2,500,000 √ 2,000,000 (2) |
| (5) 4,500,000 | |
| | 0 √ |

| (OE) Income from Long-Term Contracts | |
|---|---|
| | 300,000 (4) |
| | 500,000 (4) |
| | 100,000 (4) |

If the balance in the Billings on Contracts in Process account on some contracts exceeds the balance in the Construction in Process account, the net amount for these contracts is reported among current liabilities under a title such as Excess of Billings over Construction in Process. Construction contract accounts are included among current assets and current liabilities, even though they may not be completed within one year, because the operating cycle for a construction company is likely to be longer than 1 year.

8.18    The SEC requires certain disclosures of long-term contract information in both the annual report to shareholders and the 10–K report submitted to the SEC. With respect to long-term contract receivables, the SEC requires disclosure of (1) amounts expected to be collected after 1 year, (2) amounts billed that contain retainage provisions, (3) amounts subject to uncertainty concerning collection. With respect to long-term contract inventories (shown on the balance sheet), the SEC requires disclosure of (1) the portion of total inventory cost relating to long-term contracts, (2) the valuation method used for long-term contracts, (3) the types of cost items included in the long-term contract inventories, particularly the treatment of deferred costs (for example, initial tooling costs), and general and administrative costs. Also shown must be the amount of billings netted against the inventory account.*

8.19    **Illustration of the Completed-Contract Method** The mechanics of applying the completed-contract method for the Acme Construction Company example considered earlier are illustrated in Exhibit 8.2. Note the following:

**1.** Actual costs incurred are debited to the Construction in Process account under both the percentage-of-completion and completed-contract methods.

**2.** Billings of customers and collections from customers are treated identically under both income-recognition methods.

_____

*Accounting Series Release No. 164, SEC (1974); Accounting Series Release No. 280, SEC (1980).

**3.** Under the completed-contract method, all of the $900,000 income, or profit, from the contract is recognized in 1983, the year of completion. The amount of income is the difference between the actual cost incurred as shown in the Construction in Process account and the contract price as shown in the Billings on Contracts in Process account.

**4.** If while construction is taking place it appears that a contract, when completed, will result in a net loss, all of the loss is recognized in the period in which the loss becomes evident, even though the contract has not been completed.

**Effect of Percentage-of-Completion and Completed-Contract Methods on Financial Statements** Income under the percentage-of-completion method is recognized earlier and more smoothly than under the completed-contract method. One cannot generalize, however, as to which method results in reporting the largest income for any particular year. This determination depends on the number and profitability of projects completed during the year. Current assets and total assets under the percentage-of-completion will be larger than under the completed-contract method in an amount equal to income recognized previously on uncompleted contracts under the percentage-of-completion method.    8.20

**Complexities in Applying the Percentage-of-Completion Method** The illustration for Acme Construction Company was simplified in order to demonstrate the basic mechanics of the percentage-of-completion method. Several complexities that may be encountered are discussed briefly below.    8.21

_Changes in Estimated Costs_ The amount of costs actually incurred on a contract may turn out to be either more or less than originally anticipated. If this occurs, estimates of total income, or profit, from the contract will be incorrect. The question arises as to whether prior years' financial statements should be corrected to reflect the revised cost information or whether a "catch-up" correction should be reflected in the current    8.22

*Exhibit 8.2*
**Journal Entries and T-Accounts for
the Completed-Contract Method**

|  | 1981 |  | 1982 |  | 1983 |  |
|---|---|---|---|---|---|---|
| 1. To record construction costs incurred: |  |  |  |  |  |  |
|    Construction in Process | 1,200,000 |  | 2,000,000 |  | 400,000 |  |
|      Cash, Accounts Payable, etc. |  | 1,200,000 |  | 2,000,000 |  | 400,000 |
| 2. To record billings to customers: |  |  |  |  |  |  |
|    Accounts Receivable | 1,000,000 |  | 1,500,000 |  | 2,000,000 |  |
|      Billings on Contracts in Process |  | 1,000,000 |  | 1,500,000 |  | 2,000,000 |
| 3. To record cash collections: |  |  |  |  |  |  |
|    Cash | 1,000,000 |  | 1,500,000 |  | 2,000,000 |  |
|      Accounts Receivable |  | 1,000,000 |  | 1,500,000 |  | 2,000,000 |
| 4. To record periodic income recognized: | NOT APPLICABLE TO COMPLETED-CONTRACT METHOD |  |  |  |  |  |
| 5. To record final approval and |  |  |  |  |  |  |
|   acceptance of contract and income: |  |  |  |  |  |  |
|    Billings on Contracts in Process | — |  | — |  | 4,500,000 |  |
|     Construction in Process |  | — |  | — |  | 3,600,000 |
|     Income from Long-Term Contracts |  | — |  | — |  | 900,000 |

| **(A) Cash or Other Accounts** | |
|---|---|
| (3) 1,000,000 | 1,200,000 (1) |
| (3) 1,500,000 | 2,000,000 (1) |
| (3) 2,000,000 | 400,000 (1) |

| **(A) Construction in Process** | |
|---|---|
| (1) 1,200,000 | |
| (4) — | |
| √ 1,200,000 | |
| (1) 2,000,000 | |
| (4) — | |
| √ 3,200,000 | |
| (1) 400,000 | |
| (4) — | 3,600,000 (5) |
| √ 0 | |

| **(A) Accounts Receivable** | |
|---|---|
| (2) 1,000,000 | 1,000,000 (3) |
| (2) 1,500,000 | 1,500,000 (3) |
| (2) 2,000,000 | 2,000,000 (3) |

| **(XA) Billings on Contracts in Process** | |
|---|---|
| | 1,000,000 (2) |
| | 1,000,000 √ |
| | 1,500,000 (2) |
| | 2,500,000 √ |
| | 2,000,000 (2) |
| (5) 4,500,000 | |
| | 0 √ |

| **(OE) Income from Long-Term Contracts** | |
|---|---|
| | — (4) |
| | — (4) |
| | — (4) |
| | 900,000 (5) |

year's financial statements. Accounting Principles Board *Opinion No. 20* treats revisions in estimated costs and profits under long-term contracts as a *change in accounting estimate*. Such changes cannot be cor-

rected retroactively. They must be corrected in the current period.*

---

*Accounting Principles Board, *Opinion No. 20*, AICPA (1971).

8.23    To illustrate, assume that through the end of 1981 the information discussed earlier regarding the Acme Construction Company contract remained the same. Actual costs of $1,200,000 out of a total estimated cost of $3,600,000 were incurred. One-third of the $900,000 expected income was recognized during 1981. Now suppose that during 1982 $2,200,000 of costs were incurred, instead of $2,000,000. Costs for 1983 are expected to be $500,000 instead of $400,000. The total estimated costs now appear to be $3,900,000 (= $1,200,000 + $2,200,000 + $500,000). Estimated total income from the contract is now $600,000 (= $4,500,000 − $3,900,000). The calculation of income for 1982 is as follows:

$$\frac{\text{Percentage-of-Completion}}{} = \frac{\text{Cost Incurred to Date}}{\text{Total Estimated Costs}} = \frac{\$3,400,000}{\$3,900,000}$$

$$= 87.2\%.$$

| Cumulative Income to Be | |
| --- | --- |
| Recognized: .872 × $600,000 ........ | $523,200 |
| Income Recognized during 1981 ........ | (300,000) |
| Income to Be Recognized during 1982 .. | $223,200 |

8.24  If revised cost estimates indicate that a loss on the contract is probable, then all of the loss is recognized immediately under the percentage-of-completion method, the same as under the completed-contract method.* An entry is made debiting an income statement account such as Estimated Losses on Uncompleted Contracts and crediting Construction in Process.

8.25  *Acquisition of Construction Materials in Advance of Their Use* Construction materials may be purchased several weeks or months before they are actually used in construction. Such purchases may be made to ensure availability of the materials or in anticipation of price increases. Theoretically, such costs should not be considered "actual costs incurred" for purposes of calculating the percentage-of-completion ratio until the materials have been physically used in production. As a practical matter, only when such costs

*Accounting Research Bulletin No. 45, AICPA (1955), pars. 6 and 11.

are significant and can be easily identified are they omitted from the percentage-of-completion ratio.

*Subcontractors' Costs* On most construction   8.26 projects, the primary contractor (Acme Construction Company) will hire other contractors or individuals to perform part of the construction work. This process is called *subcontracting*. The subcontractor may have important technical skills not possessed by the primary contractor, or certain components, such as heating and air conditioning ducts, may be manufactured more efficiently by subcontractors at other locations. The primary contractor may advance the subcontractor significant portions of the subcontract price while work is being performed. Such advances should not be considered part of "actual costs incurred" for purposes of calculating the percentage-of-completion ratio. Inclusion would overstate the degree of completion and thereby the income from the contract each period prior to completion. When significant subcontracting work is being performed on a contract, the accountant and independent auditor should ascertain if the amount shown as subcontracting cost reasonably reflects the amount of subcontract work completed.

## Special-Order Merchandise

Products may be manufactured to meet the   8.27 particular specifications of a buyer. Some products, such as personalized stationery, T-shirts, or similar items, have relatively short production periods and are produced under a signed purchase-order arrangement. Other products, such as nuclear reactors, airplanes, or heavy equipment, may require much longer production periods and be produced under a formal contract arrangement. Revenues from products in the first category are generally recognized at the time of sale or delivery to the customer. Although the conditions for earlier revenue recognition are probably met, the benefits of added precision in measuring revenues are not usually worth the record-keeping costs. On the other hand, revenues and expenses from products in the second category are often recognized using the percentage-of-completion method. As long as the conditions discussed earlier for use of the percentage-of-completion method are met, recognition of income during the period of production is justified.

### Products Requiring Aging

8.28  There are certain products for which aging constitutes a significant part of the production process. Wines and fine whiskeys are manufactured and then aged in barrels for 3 to 8 years or more. Tobacco is harvested and set to age for several years. Seedlings are planted in forests and permitted to grow for 20 or 30 years before being cut as timber. Livestock may be purchased and permitted to graze for 2 or 3 years before being brought to market.

8.29  As time passes, the economic value of these products increases. In some contexts, this increase in value is referred to as *accretion*. Should this increase in value be recognized as revenue as the aging takes place? Most accountants would probably argue that there is too much uncertainty regarding the exchange price ultimately to be realized to warrant recognition of revenue during the aging process. The exchange price will be affected by the quality of the finished product, supply and demand conditions in the market at the completion of aging, and similar factors.

8.30  Suppose, however, that the firm manufacturing one of these products (for example, the fine whiskey) contracts with a buyer to supply a particular quantity at a specified price when the aging is complete. In this case, it can be argued that the criteria for revenue recognition have been met at the time aging begins. A customer has been identified, an exchange price has been agreed upon, and future aging costs can be estimated with reasonable accuracy. Even in this case, most accountants would take a conservative viewpoint and postpone revenue recognition until the time of sale. Fires, storms, or other events might occur that would prevent completion of aging and preclude delivery under the contract. If revenue is not recognized as aging occurs, all costs incurred should be added to product cost and not charged to expense currently.

## Recognition at the Time of Cash Collection

8.31  Occasionally, estimating the amount of cash that will be collected from customers is extremely difficult. This may be due to the fact that the schedule of cash collections extends 10, 20, or more years, as in many real estate sales. Or sales may be made to a new class of customers or to customers in questionable financial condition for which reasonably reliable evidence for assessing potential collectibility is not available.

8.32  When there is great uncertainty about cash collections, either the *cost-recovery-first method* or the *installment method* should be used. Under the cost-recovery-first method, costs incurred in generating revenues are matched dollar for dollar with cash receipts until all such costs are recovered. Only when cumulative cash receipts exceed total costs will profit (that is, revenue without any matching expenses) be shown in the financial statements. The cost-recovery-first method is used only rarely for financial reporting purposes and is not allowed for income tax reporting.

8.33  Under the installment method, income, or gross margin, from the sale of goods or services (that is, selling price less cost of goods sold) is recognized as proportionate parts of the sales price are collected in cash. Thus, if 30 percent of the sales price is collected in cash, then 30 percent of the gross margin from the sale is recognized as income. The installment method is similar to the cash basis of accounting in that the collection of cash triggers the recognition of income. The installment method is an accrual basis of income, however, because expenses are matched with revenues.

8.34  In cases where there is extreme uncertainty regarding the collectibility of cash, we feel that the cost-recovery-first method is preferable to the installment method. The extreme uncertainty regarding the amount of cash to be collected is the justification for recognizing income later than the time of sale. Yet estimates of the amount of cash that will be collected are necessary if the installment method is to be used (gross margin = sales − cost of goods sold). If the level of uncertainty regarding the collectibility of cash is considered too high for recognition of revenue at the time of sale, then it should similarly be considered too high in most cases for use of the installment method. The cost-recovery-first method does not rely on an estimate of the amount of cash to be collected.

8.35 For most sales of goods and services, even those that provide for extended payment schedules, past experience and an assessment of customers' credit standings provide a sufficient basis for predicting the amount of cash to be received. Under these circumstances, the installment method is not permitted for financial reporting purposes.* The installment method is sometimes used for sales of real estate and franchises. In addition, the installment method is widely used for income tax purposes even when it is not permitted for financial reporting purposes. In the following sections we discuss the applicability of the installment method to sales of merchandise and of real estate and illustrate the mechanics of the installment method.

## Installment Sales: Merchandise

8.36 Retail stores commonly sell merchandise under installment payment plans. The application of the installment method of income recognition for these sales involves the following steps:

1. Merchandise sold on an installment basis is recorded similarly to any credit sale. Installment Accounts Receivable is debited and Installment Sales Revenue is credited. Also, Cost of Installment Sales is debited and Merchandise Inventory is credited. A separate Installment Accounts Receivable account is maintained for each period's sales so that subsequent collections can be identi-

*Accounting Principles Board, *Opinion No. 10* (1966), par. 12, footnote 8.

fied correctly as coming from a particular period's sales.

2. Cash collections from customers are recorded by debiting Cash and crediting the appropriate period's Installment Accounts Receivable account.

3. At the end of each period, the following entry is made:

```
Installment Sales Revenue  ..................  X
    Cost of Installment Sales  ..............     X
    Deferred Gross Margin  .................     X
```

This entry closes out the Installment Sales Revenue and Cost of Installment Sales accounts and establishes a Deferred Gross Margin account. The amount in the Deferred Gross Margin account represents the total income that will be recognized in the current and future periods as cash collections relating to those sales are received from customers. The Deferred Gross Margin account is shown as a contra account to the corresponding year's Installment Accounts Receivable account. Because revenue is not recognized at the time of sale under the installment method, consistency requires that the receivables be stated in terms of product costs and not selling prices. By subtracting the amount of the Deferred Gross Profit from the Installment Accounts Receivable, the net receivable is stated at an amount equal to the acquisition cost of the merchandise sold.

4. At the end of each period, the gross margin percentage *for the period* is calculated by dividing the amount of deferred gross margin by the amount of installment sales revenue. An entry is then made to recognize as income a portion of the deferred gross margin from current and prior years' installment sales. The appropriate gross margin percentages are multiplied by the cash collections made during the current period relating to current and prior years' installment sales. An entry such as the following is made:

```
Deferred Gross Margin (Current Year)  ........  X
Deferred Gross Margin (Last Year)  ...........  X
Deferred Gross Margin (Second Preceding
    Year)  ...................................  X
    Realized Gross Margin on Installment
        Sales  .............................     X
```

*Exhibit 8.3*
**Data for Illustration of the
Installment Method**

|  | **1981** | **1982** | **1983** |
|---|---|---|---|
| Installment Sales | $100,000 | $120,000 | $150,000 |
| Cost of Installment Sales | (80,000) | (90,000) | (115,500) |
| Gross Margin | $ 20,000 | $ 30,000 | $ 34,500 |
| Gross Margin Percentage | 20% | 25% | 23% |
| Selling and Administrative Expenses | $ 10,000 | $ 12,000 | $ 15,000 |
| Cash Collections: |  |  |  |
| 1981 Sales | 60,000 | 20,000 | 10,000 |
| 1982 Sales |  | 80,000 | 25,000 |
| 1983 Sales |  |  | 100,000 |

8.37    To illustrate the mechanics of the installment method, assume the data shown in Exhibit 8.3.

8.38    Exhibit 8.4 presents the journal entries that would be made in applying the installment method during the years 1981, 1982, and 1983. Note the following:

**1.** Separate installment accounts receivable and deferred gross margin accounts are maintained for each year's sales.

**2.** Selling and administrative costs are treated as period expenses in the year incurred. Under the installment method, no effort is generally made to defer these expenses and match them with the recognition of gross margin relating to that period's sales. This treatment of selling and administrative expenses is usually justified on the grounds of lack of materiality and ease of record keeping but is probably not theoretically supportable.

**3.** Cash collections are identified as coming from a particular year's sales, with the appropriate Installment Accounts Receivable account being credited.

**4.** The portion of the deferred gross margin recognized in each year is calculated as follows:

**For the Year 1981**
Collections from 1981
  Sales × 1981 Gross
  Margin Percentage   = $ 60,000 × .20 = $12,000

**For the Year 1982**
Collections from 1981
  Sales × 1981 Gross
  Margin Percentage   = $ 20,000 × .20 = $ 4,000
Collections from 1982
  Sales × 1982 Gross
  Margin Percentage   = $ 80,000 × .25 =  20,000
  Total  ...........  $24,000

**For the Year 1983**
Collections from 1981
  Sales × 1981 Gross
  Margin Percentage   = $ 10,000 × .20 = $ 2,000
Collections from 1982
  Sales × 1982 Gross
  Margin Percentage   = $ 25,000 × .25 =   6,250
Collections from 1983
  Sales × 1983 Gross
  Margin Percentage   = $100,000 × .23 =  23,000
  Total  ...........  $31,250

**Complexities in Applying the Installment Method** Several complexities often encountered in applying the installment method are discussed briefly below.     8.39

*Uncollectible Accounts* The accounting for uncollectible installment receivables differs in two important respects from most other trade receivables. First, the *amount* of the loss from an uncollectible account is usually not as large as the unpaid balance in the account. The seller generally has the right to repossess the merchandise if the buyer fails to make payment when due. The repos-     8.40

*Exhibit 8.4*
**Journal Entries to Apply the Installment Method**

| | 1981 | | 1982 | | 1983 | |
|---|---|---|---|---|---|---|
| 1. Installment Accounts Receivable—1981 ........ | 100,000 | | — | | — | |
| Installment Accounts Receivable—1982 ........ | — | | 120,000 | | — | |
| Installment Accounts Receivable—1983 ........ | — | | — | | 150,000 | |
| Installment Sales Revenue ............... | | 100,000 | | 120,000 | | 150,000 |
| | | | | | | |
| 2. Cost of Installment Sales .................... | 80,000 | | 90,000 | | 115,500 | |
| Merchandise Inventory ................... | | 80,000 | | 90,000 | | 115,500 |
| | | | | | | |
| 3. Selling and Administrative Expenses ........... | 10,000 | | 12,000 | | 15,000 | |
| Cash, Other Accounts .................... | | 10,000 | | 12,000 | | 15,000 |
| | | | | | | |
| 4. Cash ....................................... | 60,000 | | 100,000 | | 135,000 | |
| Installment Accounts Receivable—1981 .... | | 60,000 | | 20,000 | | 10,000 |
| Installment Accounts Receivable—1982 .... | | — | | 80,000 | | 25,000 |
| Installment Accounts Receivable—1983 .... | | — | | — | | 100,000 |
| | | | | | | |
| 5. Installment Sales Revenue .................... | 100,000 | | 120,000 | | 150,000 | |
| Cost of Installment Sales ................. | | 80,000 | | 90,000 | | 115,500 |
| Deferred Gross Margin—1981 ............. | | 20,000 | | — | | — |
| Deferred Gross Margin—1982 ............. | | — | | 30,000 | | — |
| Deferred Gross Margin—1983 ............. | | — | | — | | 34,500 |
| | | | | | | |
| 6. Deferred Gross Margin—1981 ................. | 12,000 | | 4,000 | | 2,000 | |
| Deferred Gross Margin—1982 ................. | — | | 20,000 | | 6,250 | |
| Deferred Gross Margin—1983 ................. | — | | — | | 23,000 | |
| Realized Gross Margin on Installment Sales . | | 12,000 | | 24,000 | | 31,250 |

sessed merchandise can be resold, thereby reducing the loss. Second, the *provision* for estimated losses on uncollectible accounts from a particular period's installment sales should, at least theoretically, be charged against earnings of the current and future periods in order to obtain a proper matching with realized gross margin. That is, the estimated losses from sales made during 1981 should be charged against earnings during 1981, 1982, and subsequent years as the receivables are collected and gross margin is recognized. This proper matching can be accomplished by making the usual entry under the allowance method for uncollectible accounts.

Sales Contra, Estimated Uncollectibles ... X
   Allowance for Uncollectible Accounts .    X

Then the amount in the Sales Contra, Estimated Uncollectibles account is treated as part of the journal entry to compute the deferred gross margin on that particular period's sales, as shown:

Installment Sales Revenue ............... X
   Cost of Installment Sales ............    X
   Sales Contra, Estimated
      Uncollectibles ....................    X
   Deferred Gross Margin ..............    X

The amount of deferred gross margin in the entry above is decreased as a result of including the provision for estimated uncollectibles as a negative element in its computation. As portions of the deferred gross margin are realized in the current and future periods, corresponding portions of the estimated losses from uncollectible accounts will implicitly be recognized.

8.41    As a practical matter, the amount in the Sales Contra, Estimated Uncollectibles account is usually charged against income in the year the sales are made, as is done for selling and administrative expenses. That is:

```
Income Summary  .....................   X
    Selling and Administrative Expenses  .      X
    Sales Contra, Estimated Uncollectibles .      X
```

The amount of deferred gross margin is larger in this case than in the more theoretically sound procedure described above. The larger deferred gross margin, which will be realized in current and future periods, occurs because all of the provision for estimated uncollectibles is recognized in computing net income in the period of sale.

8.42    When the allowance method is used, the difference between the market value of repossessed merchandise and the amount remaining in the Installment Accounts Receivable and Deferred Gross Margin accounts relating to the uncollectible account will be charged against the allowance account in the year of repossession. For example, assume that merchandise is sold during 1981 under an installment arrangement for $1,000. The gross margin percentage on sales during 1981 is 20 percent. The total gross margin is therefore $200 (= .20 × $1,000). During 1981 the customer pays $300, and $60 (= .20 × $300) of the deferred gross margin is recognized as income. During 1982, the customer defaults and the merchandise is repossessed. The market value of the repossessed merchandise is determined to be $500. The journal entry under the allowance method is

```
Merchandise Inventory  .................   500
Deferred Gross Margin—1981 ($200 −
    $60)  .................................   140
Allowance for Uncollectible Accounts  ....    60
    Installment Accounts Receivable—
        1981 ($1,000 − $300)  .............      700
To record repossessed merchandise and to
write off the receivable.
```

If the direct charge-off method had been used, the debit for $60 would have been to Loss from Uncollectible Accounts or Bad Debt Expense.*

*Interest on Installment Receivables* On most    8.43 installment sales of merchandise, interest is charged on the unpaid balance in the installment account. Each payment received is considered partially a payment of interest and partially a payment of the amount in the installment receivables account.

To illustrate, assume that merchandise is    8.44 sold at the beginning of 1981 for $4,000. The gross margin percentage during 1981 is 20 percent, so the total deferred gross margin at the time of sale is $800. The installment plan provides for interest at the rate of 10 percent per year on the unpaid balance. All payments are made at the end of each year. The top panel of Exhibit 8.5 shows the installment payment schedule for this sale. The payment each year is $1,608.46 (that is, the present value of an annuity of $1,608.46 per year for 3 years at 10 percent is $4,000). Over the 3 years, the payments represent a decreasing amount for interest and an increasing amount as payment of the $4,000 sales price. The lower panel of Exhibit 8.5 shows the computation of the realized gross margin for each of the 3 years. Note that the calculation of the realized gross margin is based, not on the total payment of $1,608.46 each year, but on the portion that represents a payment of the principal amount borrowed, or the selling price.

## Installment Sales: Real Estate

Real estate sales are often characterized by    8.45 relatively small down payments (10 to 20 percent) and extended payment periods (20 years or more). If the buyer defaults on payments due, the seller's only recourse in most cases is to repossess the property. The seller generally cannot sue to obtain payment from

---

*We believe that the direct charge-off method is preferable to the allowance method for uncollectible installment receivables. The installment method rather than the sales basis of income recognition is used because estimating the amount of uncollectibles is difficult; yet, such estimates are required in the application of the allowance method.

*Exhibit 8.5*
**Installment Payment Schedule and
Computation of Realized Gross Margin
for a $4,000 Sale and 20
Percent Rate of Gross Margin**

| | | Installment Payment Schedule | | |
|---|---|---|---|---|
| **Date** | **Cash (Debit)** | **Interest Revenue (Credit)** | **Installment Receivable (Credit)** | **Unpaid Balance** |
| 1/01/81 .......... | — | — | — | $4,000.00 |
| 12/31/81 .......... | $1,608.46 | $400.00 | $1,208.46 | 2,791.54 |
| 12/31/82 .......... | 1,608.46 | 279.15 | 1,329.31 | 1,462.23 |
| 12/31/83 .......... | 1,608.46 | 146.23 | 1,462.23 | 0 |
| Total .......... | $4,825.38 | $825.38 | $4,000.00 | |

| | Computation of Realized Gross Margin | | |
|---|---|---|---|
| **Year** | **Installment Payment of Principal** | **Gross Margin Percentage** | **Realized Gross Margin** |
| 1981 ............. | $1,208.46 | .20 | $241.69 |
| 1982 ............. | 1,329.31 | .20 | 265.86 |
| 1983 ............. | 1,462.23 | .20 | 292.45 |
| Total ............. | $4,000.00 | | $800.00 |

other assets of the buyer. In some cases, the seller performs substantial services after the sale takes place, such as arranging financing, managing, developing, or constructing the property, or guaranteeing a return to the buyer. For many real estate transactions, the criteria for revenue recognition may not be met at the time of sale. All, or a substantial portion, of the services to be provided may not be performed until some time after the sale, and it may be difficult to estimate the amount of costs to be incurred. In addition, at the time of sale it may be difficult to obtain a reasonably accurate estimate of the amount of cash ultimately to be received from the buyer. Postponement of revenue recognition on real estate sales until cash is received may therefore be appropriate.

8.46 The AICPA has established guidelines to be followed in determining whether revenue and profits on sales of real estate should be recognized at the time of sale or at a later date when cash is received. The latter approach requires the use of either the cost-re-

covery-first or installment method. To recognize revenue and profit at the time of sale:*

**1.** A buyer's initial investment and continuing investment should both be adequate to demonstrate a commitment to pay for the property.

**2.** The seller's continuing interest and involvement in the real estate transaction should be limited to that of a secured creditor.

Determining if these conditions are met requires the exercise of professional judgment in specific situations. In general, the first criterion is met if two conditions are satisfied: **(1)** The down payment is at least 25 percent of the sales value of the property, *and* **(2)** the payment each year is at least equal to the level annual payment needed to pay the remainder of the purchase price, including interest, over a period not exceeding 20 years. The second

---

*Accounting for Profit Recognition on Sales of Real Estate, AICPA (1973).

condition requires that the seller not be obligated to perform substantial services after the sale (such as those listed above).† If only one of these conditions is met, then the transaction will probably not qualify for revenue recognition at the time of sale.

8.47   To illustrate the application of these criteria to a real estate transaction, assume that on January 1, 1981, Diversified Industries sold land costing $80,000 to Williams Corporation for $100,000. Williams Corporation made a $15,000 down payment and signed a note agreeing to pay the remaining $85,000 in annual payments of $9,364 at the end of each of the next 25 years. This transaction does not qualify for revenue recognition at the time of sale. The down payment is less than 25 percent, and the period for repaying the remaining indebtedness exceeds 20 years.

8.48   The installment method would be used in this case. The note has a net present value of $85,000 (= $100,000 − $15,000). With payments of $9,364 per year, this implies an interest rate of 10 percent (that is, the present value of an annuity of $9,364 per year for 25 years at a discount rate of 10 percent is $85,000). The entry on January 1, 1981, to record the sale is:

Jan. 1, 1981
Cash ........................... 15,000
Note Receivable ($9,364 × 25) .... 234,100
    Discount on Note Receivable     149,100
    Land ............     80,000
    Deferred Gross Margin ......     20,000
To record sale of land for $100,000
consisting of $15,000 cash and a
note having a present value of
$85,000 (= $234,100 − $149,100).

The full amount receivable of $234,100 is recorded in the Note Receivable account and the discount, or interest, element is recorded in the Discount on Note Receivable account. The difference between the sales price of $100,000 and the cost of $80,000 is the gross margin from the sale. If this gross margin were recognized at the time of sale, the credit entry would be to a Gain on Sale of Land account. Because the installment method will be used, however, the credit is

—————
†Ibid.

to the Deferred Gross Margin account. The gross margin percentage is 20 percent.

8.49   On January 1, 1981, $15,000 of the $100,000 selling price is received as a down payment. The following entry must therefore be made to recognize a portion of the deferred gross margin:

Jan. 1, 1981
Deferred Gross Margin .............. 3,000
    Realized Gross Margin on
        Installment Sale ..............     3,000
To recognize gross margin realized
(= .20 × $15,000).

8.50   The first installment payment is received on December 31, 1981, and the following entries are made:

Dec. 31, 1981
Cash ............................. 9,364
    Note Receivable ................     9,364
To record installment payment.

Dec. 31, 1981
Discount on Note Receivable ......... 8,500
    Interest Revenue ...............     8,500
To record interest revenue for 1981
(= .10 × $85,000).

As is common with real estate loans, most of the early payments represent interest. Only $864 (= $9,364 − $8,500) represents a payment of a portion of the $85,000 principal amount. The following entry must also be made to recognize a portion of the deferred gross margin:

Dec. 31, 1981
Deferred Gross Margin .................. 173
    Realized Gross Margin on Installment
      Sale ...........................     173
To recognize gross margin realized (= .20
× $864).

Note that, as before, the amount of gross margin realized is based on the portion of the cash received that represents payment of principal.

8.51   The upper panel of Exhibit 8.6 summarizes the effects of the above journal entries on the appropriate T-accounts. The lower portion of Exhibit 8.6 shows the disclosure of information relating to this installment sale in the financial statements for 1981. The income statement includes two kinds of rev-

*Exhibit 8.6*
**T-Account Summary and Financial
Statement Disclosures of the
Installment Method for a
Real Estate Sale**

| Cash | | Note Receivable | | Discount on Note Receivable | |
|---|---|---|---|---|---|
| (1) 15,000 | | (1) 234,100 | 9,364 (3) | (4) 8,500 | 149,100 (1) |
| (3) 9,364 | | | | | |
| | | Bal. 224,736 | | | 140,600 Bal. |

| Deferred Gross Margin | | Land | | Interest Revenue | |
|---|---|---|---|---|---|
| (2) 3,000 | 20,000 (1) | | 80,000 (1) | | 8,500 (4) |
| (5) 173 | | | | | |
| | 16,827 Bal. | | | | 8,500 Bal. |

| Realized Gross Margin on Installment Sales | |
|---|---|
| | 3,000 (2) |
| | 173 (5) |
| | 3,173 Bal. |

### INCOME STATEMENT FOR 1981

**Revenues:**

| | |
|---|---|
| Sales (noninstallment sales; amount is assumed) | $200,000 |
| Realized Gross Margin on Installment Sales | 3,173 |
| Interest | 8,500 |
| Total Revenues | $211,673 |

### BALANCE SHEET ON DECEMBER 31, 1981

**Investments:**

| | | |
|---|---|---|
| Note Receivable | $224,736 | |
| Less Discount on Note Receivable | (140,600) | |
| Less Deferred Gross Margin | (16,827) | |
| Total | | $ 67,309 |

enues: **(1)** realized gross margin from the sale of the real estate, recognized as cash payments are received using the installment method, and **(2)** interest revenue from extending credit to the buyer using the effective-interest method. The note receivable from the buyer will either be a "current asset" or an "investment," depending on whether or not real estate sales are a common means of generating income for Diversified Industries. Because the note of Williams Corporation, the buyer, is the only note listed in the balance sheet, sales of real estate are probably not a primary means of generating profit. The note is, therefore, listed among "Investments." If the seller were a finance or insurance company that often finances real estate sales, the receivable would probably be classified as a current asset.

## Installment Sales: Other

8.52 There are several other types of sales for which the installment method may be appropriate. One example is retail sales of undeveloped real estate. Such sales differ from those discussed in the previous section primarily with respect to volume, size of down payment, and provision for customer re-funds. The usual pattern is as follows:

**1.** A large tract of undeveloped land is purchased and then subdivided into numerous residential housing lots.

**2.** The lots are sold to customers, usually with low down payments and limited checking of credit standings.

**3.** The seller promises to develop the land, so that at some future date (5, 10, or more years hence), it will be ready for housing construction.

**4.** The buyer promises to make periodic payments on the indebtedness. Payments made up to a certain period (usually around 1 year) may be refunded if the customer wishes to cancel the sales agreement.

8.53   In many cases, neither of the criteria for revenue recognition is met for retail land sales. Substantial future performance is required of the seller to develop the land. Also, difficulties often exist in estimating the amount of cash that will be received from customers. Either the installment, cost-recovery-first, or deposit method should be used.*

8.54   A second area where the installment method is often used is the sale of franchises. Sales of franchises have become common in the restaurant, motel, auto rental, and other businesses. The sale of a franchise is generally composed of three elements: **(1)** a right given to the buyer (franchisee) to sell the seller's (franchisor) products and use the franchisor's name in a particular locality for a given period of time, **(2)** a promise by the franchisor to assist the franchisee in locating land, constructing facilities, training employees, and performing other services necessary to begin business, and **(3)** the sale of merchandise (food, supplies) and services (advertising, record keeping) on an ongoing basis. An initial *franchise fee* is charged for the first two elements of the franchise sale. A periodic fee is charged for merchandise and services sold over time.

There is little question that the periodic   8.55
fee should be recognized as revenue in the period in which the merchandise and services are sold. The troublesome revenue-recognition issues relate to the initial franchise fee. Substantial services often must be performed prior to the opening of a franchise business. Also, the lack of business experience of many franchisees and the competitive market conditions encountered in franchise businesses lead to a high failure rate. Because the initial franchisee fee is usually paid in installments over 10 years or more, estimating the amount of cash ultimately to be collected can be difficult.

The FASB has ruled that the initial fran-   8.56
chise fee should not be recognized as revenue until the franchisor has substantially performed the services required to be performed and collection of the fee is reasonably assured.† Professional judgment is required to ascertain when these conditions are met. For example, assume that Pickin Chicken Delight, Inc., sold a franchise to Charles Sanders for $40,000. Sanders paid $5,000 and agreed to pay the remaining $35,000 in 10 installments of $3,500 each. Sanders' credit rating is such that he could borrow at 10 percent. The present value of the debt is $21,506 (= $3,500 × 6.14457). The entry made to record the initial franchise fee under various assumptions is as follows:

**1.** Only minimal services are required of the franchisor, there is no provision for refund of the initial franchise fee paid, and the franchisee has extensive business experience and is in sound financial condition.

| | | |
|---|---|---|
| Cash . . . . . . . . . . . . . . . . . . . . . . . . . . | 5,000 | |
| Note Receivable . . . . . . . . . . . . . . . . . . | 35,000 | |
| Discount on Note Receivable ($35,000 − $21,506) . . . . . . . . | | 13,494 |
| Franchise Fee Revenue . . . . . . . . | | 26,506 |

To record sale of franchise and recognize initial franchise fee revenue.

---

*The deposit method treats the receipt of cash at the time the sales agreement is signed as a deposit on a future sale. The amount is included among liabilities until sufficient performance under the sales agreement (for example, receipt of a substantial portion of the purchase price in cash or development of the land as required) justifies use of the installment method or the cost-recovery-first method. See *Accounting for Retail Land Sales,* AICPA (1973).

†Financial Accounting Standards Board, *Statement No. 45* (1981).

**2.** The franchisor is required to provide assistance in the design, construction, and opening of the business, and any portions of the initial franchise paid can be refunded prior to opening. No significant services are required of the franchisor after opening. The franchisee's business experience and financial condition are as given in the first example.

| | | |
|---|---|---|
| Cash ........................... | 5,000 | |
| Note Receivable ................. | 35,000 | |
|    Discount on Note Receivable | | |
|      ($35,000 − $21,506) ........ | | 13,494 |
|    Deferred Franchise Fee ........ | | 26,506 |

To record sale of franchise and to defer recognition of franchise fee as revenue until opening.

**3.** Same as **2** except that any portion of the initial franchise fee paid need not be refunded if the franchised business fails to open. The franchisee has no business background and is in questionable financial condition.

| | | |
|---|---|---|
| Cash ........................... | 5,000 | |
| Note Receivable ................. | 35,000 | |
|    Discount on Note Receivable | | |
|      ($35,000 − $21,506) ........ | | 13,494 |
|    Deferred Franchise Fee ........ | | 26,506 |

To record sale of franchise and to defer recognition of franchise fee until cash is received.

| | | |
|---|---|---|
| Deferred Franchise Fee ............ | 5,000 | |
|    Franchise Fee Revenue ........ | | 5,000 |

To record franchise fee revenue using the installment method (note that all of the first payment is for principal; no interest has yet accrued).

8.57 A wide variety of revenue-recognition methods are found in practice for the initial franchise fee, depending on the responsibilities of the franchisor and the credit standing of the franchisee.

## Consignment Sales

8.58 Some manufacturers ship their products to dealers on consignment. Under such arrangements, the manufacturer retains title to the merchandise. The dealer accepts the merchandise and promises due diligence in caring for and selling the merchandise to customers. Cash received from customers is remitted to the manufacturer (consignor) after the dealer (consignee) deducts a sales commission. A modified version of the sales basis of revenue recognition is used for consignment sales.

8.59 To illustrate, assume that Standard Products Company, a manufacturer, ships 300,000 units of product to dealers on consignment. The units cost $6 each to produce and sell for $10 each. Standard pays shipping costs of $120,000 in transporting the merchandise to dealers. During the year, dealers sell 250,000 of the units. After deducting a dealer commission of 10 percent, the remainder of the amount received from customers is remitted to Standard. Exhibit 8.7 presents the journal entries on Standard's books and the dealers' books for these consignment transactions. Note the following:

**1.** At the time of shipment, the consignor transfers the cost of the merchandise from one inventory account (Finished Goods Inventory) to another inventory account (Finished Goods on Consignment). The merchandise is not recorded as an asset on the consignee's books. The merchandise is the legal property of the consignor. The consignee merely holds the merchandise for the benefit of the consignor, much the same as the owner of a parking garage holds parked automobiles for the benefit of their owners.

**2.** The sale of the merchandise by the consignee creates a liability to the consignor for the selling price less commissions and expenses incurred. The consignor may be notified of the sales as they occur. More commonly, notification occurs at the time cash is remitted, because this generally follows soon after the sale.

## Summary Illustration of Income-Recognition Methods

8.60 As a summary of the material covered in the last two chapters, Exhibit 8.8 presents a comprehensive illustration of income recognition. The illustration relates to a contract for the construction of a bridge for $6 million. The expected and actual pattern of cash

*Exhibit 8.7*
**Journal Entries for Consignment Sales**

| Consignor (Standard Products Company) | Consignee (Dealers) |
|---|---|

1. Shipment of 300,000 units costing $6 each out on consignment to dealers.

    Finished Goods on
      Consignment  . . . . . . . . . .  1,800,000
        Finished Goods
          Inventory  . . . . . . . . . .     1,800,000

                      NO ENTRY

2. Payment of shipping charges for goods on consignment.

    Finished Goods on
      Consignment  . . . . . . . . . .    120,000
        Cash  . . . . . . . . . . . . . . . .      120,000

                      NO ENTRY

3. Sale of 250,000 units of consigned goods for $10 each.

    PROBABLY NO ENTRY

Cash  . . . . . . . . . . . . . . . . . . . . .  2,500,000
    Consignment Liability  . . . .     2,250,000
    Commission Revenue   . . .       250,000

4. Notification of consignor that sales have been made and remittance of sales price less 10 percent commission.

    Cash  . . . . . . . . . . . . . . . . . . . .  2,250,000
      Consignment Sales
        Revenue  . . . . . . . . . . .      2,250,000
    Cost of Consignment Goods
      Sold  . . . . . . . . . . . . . . . . .  1,600,000
        Finished Goods on
        Consignment
        [250,000/300,000 ×
        ($1,800,000 +
        $120,000)]  . . . . . . . . .        1,600,000

Consignment Liability  . . . . . . .  2,250,000
    Cash  . . . . . . . . . . . . . . . . . .     2,250,000

---

receipts and disbursements under the contract is as follows:

| Year | Expected and Actual Cash Receipts | Expected and Actual Cash Expenditures |
|---|---|---|
| 1977 . . . . . . . . | $  500,000 | $  800,000 |
| 1978 . . . . . . . . | 500,000 | 2,000,000 |
| 1979 . . . . . . . . | 1,000,000 | 2,000,000 |
| 1980 . . . . . . . . | 2,000,000 | — |
| 1981 . . . . . . . . | 2,000,000 | — |
| Total . . . . . . | $6,000,000 | $4,800,000 |

The bridge was completed in 1979. Exhibit 8.8 indicates the revenues, expenses, and income recognized each period under the contract using the cash method, the percentage-of-completion method, the completed-contract (completed-sale) method, the installment method, and the cost-recovery-first method. Not all five methods of income

recognition could be justified for financial reporting, nor could they all be used on the tax return in this case. They are presented merely for illustrative purposes. Note that the total revenues, expenses, and income recognized for the 5 years are the same for all methods. In historical cost accounting over long enough time periods, income is equal to cash inflows less cash outflows. There is, however, a significant difference in the patterns of annual income, depending on the accounting method used.

## Disclosure of Revenues and Receivables

Exhibit 8.9 presents an income statement for 1981 and Exhibit 8.10 presents a partial bal-

*Exhibit 8.8*
**Comprehensive Illustration of Revenue and Expense Recognition (All Dollar Amounts in Thousands)**

| Year | Cash Basis of Accounting[a] | | |
|------|---------|---------|---------|
|      | **Revenue** | **Expense** | **Income** |
| 1977 | $ 500 | $ 800 | $ (300) |
| 1978 | 500 | 2,000 | (1,500) |
| 1979 | 1,000 | 2,000 | (1,000) |
| 1980 | 2,000 | — | 2,000 |
| 1981 | 2,000 | — | 2,000 |
| Total | $6,000 | $4,800 | $1,200 |

| Year | Percentage-of-Completion Method | | | Completed-Contract Method | | |
|------|---------|---------|---------|---------|---------|---------|
|      | **Revenue** | **Expense** | **Income** | **Revenue** | **Expense** | **Income** |
| 1977 | $1,000[d] | $ 800 | $ 200 | $ — | $ — | $ — |
| 1978 | 2,500[e] | 2,000 | 500 | — | — | — |
| 1979 | 2,500[f] | 2,000 | 500 | 6,000 | 4,800 | 1,200 |
| 1980 | — | — | — | — | — | — |
| 1981 | — | — | — | — | — | — |
| Total | $6,000 | $4,800 | $1,200 | $6,000 | $4,800 | $1,200 |

| Year | Installment Method[b] | | | Cost-Recovery-First Method[c] | | |
|------|---------|---------|---------|---------|---------|---------|
|      | **Revenue** | **Expense** | **Income** | **Revenue** | **Expense** | **Income** |
| 1977 | $ 500 | $ 400[g] | $ 100 | $ 500 | $ 500 | $ 0 |
| 1978 | 500 | 400[g] | 100 | 500 | 500 | 0 |
| 1979 | 1,000 | 800[h] | 200 | 1,000 | 1,000 | 0 |
| 1980 | 2,000 | 1,600[i] | 400 | 2,000 | 2,000 | 0 |
| 1981 | 2,000 | 1,600[i] | 400 | 2,000 | 800 | 1,200 |
| Total | $6,000 | $4,800 | $1,200 | $6,000 | $4,800 | $1,200 |

[a]The cash basis is not allowed for tax or financial reporting if inventories are a material factor in generating income.

[b]The installment method is allowed for financial reporting only if extreme uncertainty exists as to the amount of cash to be collected from customers. Its use for tax purposes is not affected by the collectibility of cash.

[c]The cost-recovery-first method is allowed for financial reporting only if extreme uncertainty exists as to the amount of cash to be collected from customers. It is not permitted for tax purposes.

[d]$800/$4,800 × $6,000.

[e]($2,800/$4,800 × $6,000) − $1,000.

[f]($4,800/$4,800 × $6,000) − $3,500.

[g]$500/$6,000 × $4,800.

[h]$1,000/$6,000 × $4,800.

[i]$2,000/$6,000 × $4,800.

ance sheet and notes for Caral Corporation for December 31, 1981. These exhibits indicate the typical disclosures for many of the revenue and receivables topics discussed in Chapters 7 and 8. Note that receivables due from officers, employees, or affiliated companies must be shown separately from accounts and notes receivable from customers.* The financial statements of International Corporation in Appendix A also illustrate the disclosure of receivables.

*Accounting Research Bulletin No. 43, AICPA (1953), chap. 1A, par. 5.

## Exhibit 8.9
**Caral Corporation**
**Income Statement**
**for the Year Ended**
**December 31, 1981**

Revenues:

| | | |
|---|---:|---:|
| Sales—Gross (Note 1) ... | $5,000,000 | |
| Less: Cash Discounts | | |
|     Taken ......... | (45,000) | |
|     Sales Returns and | | |
|       Allowances ...... | (16,000) | |
|     Estimated | | |
|       Uncollectibles ... | (80,000) | |
| Net Sales .............. | | $4,859,000 |
| Realized Gross Margin | | |
|   on Installment Sales | | |
|   (Note 2) ............. | | 24,000 |
| Income from Long-Term | | |
|   Contracts (Note 4) ..... | | 540,000 |
| Interest Revenue: | | |
|   Trade Receivables ..... | $ 160,000 | |
|   Customers' Notes ..... | 3,500 | |
|   Installment Receivables . | 80,000 | |
|     Total Interest ........ | | 243,500 |
| Total Revenues ........ | | $5,666,500 |

Expenses:

| | | |
|---|---:|---:|
| Cost of Goods Sold ...... | | $3,460,000 |
| Selling and Administrative | | |
|   Expenses ............. | | 840,000 |
| Income Taxes .......... | | 800,000 |
|   Total Expenses ...... | | $5,100,000 |
| Net Income .............. | | $ 566,500 |

## Exhibit 8.10
**Caral Corporation**
**Partial Balance Sheet**
**December 31, 1981**

### CURRENT ASSETS

| | | |
|---|---:|---:|
| Cash .................... | | $ 410,000 |
| Accounts Receivable— | | |
|   Trade (Gross) (Note 1) ... | $1,430,000 | |
| Less: Allowance for Sales | | |
|     Returns and | | |
|     Allowances ........ | (10,000) | |
|   Allowance for | | |
|     Uncollectible | | |
|     Accounts .......... | (40,000) | |
| Accounts Receivable— | | |
|   Trade (Net) ............. | | 1,380,000 |
| Accounts Receivable— | | |
|   Construction Contracts .. | | 560,000 |
| Installment Notes Receivable | | |
|   (Gross) (Note 2) ......... | $ 830,000 | |
| Less: Discount on Note | | |
|     Receivable ........ | (260,000) | |
|     Deferred Gross | | |
|     Margin ............ | (76,000) | |
| Installment Notes Receivable | | |
|   (Net) .................. | | 494,000 |
| Notes Receivable (Net) | | |
|   (Note 3) ................ | | 35,000 |
| Receivables from Officers .. | | 50,000 |
| Construction in Process in | | |
|   Excess of Related Billings | | |
|   (Note 4) ................ | | 240,000 |
| Merchandise Inventories: | | |
|   On Hand ......... .... | $ 860,000 | |
|   On Consignment ........ | 45,000 | |
| Total Inventories .......... | | 905,000 |
| Land Held for Resale ...... | | 45,000 |
| Total Current Assets ....... | | $4,119,000 |

**Notes to Financial Statements of Caral Corporation**

**Note 1.** Revenue from the sale of merchandise is recognized at the time of sale. An immaterial amount of revenue from consignment sales is included in sales revenue. Cash discounts are accounted for using the gross price method. Sales returns, allowances, and uncollectible accounts are accounted for using the allowance method.

**Note 2.** A wholly owned real estate subsidiary sells undeveloped land to customers. Income from such sales is accounted for using the installment method.

**Note 3.** Customers' notes of $25,000 were discounted with recourse at local banks. The Company remains contingently liable to the banks in the event that the notes are not paid by customers at maturity.

**Note 4.** Income from the construction of special-order equipment is recognized using the percentage-of-completion method. Construction in process includes costs of $4,630,000 and accumulated profit of $870,000 in excess of related billings of $5,260,000.

## Questions and Short Cases

**8.1**  Review the meaning of the following concepts or terms discussed in this chapter.

    **a.** Criteria for revenue recognition.

    **b.** Conditions for recognizing revenue prior to the time of sale.

    **c.** Conditions for recognizing revenue after the time of sale.

    **d.** Percentage-of-completion method.

    **e.** Completed-contract method.

    **f.** Accretion.

    **g.** Cost-recovery-first method.

    **h.** Installment method.

    **i.** Gross margin.

    **j.** Deferred Gross Margin account.

    **k.** Realized Gross Margin account.

    **l.** Initial franchise fee.

    **m.** Consignment sales.

**8.2**  Distinguish between the two terms in each of the following independent cases:

    **a.** Revenue and income.

    **b.** Construction in Process and Work-in-Process accounts.

    **c.** Construction in Process and Billings on Contracts in Process accounts.

    **d.** Deferred Gross Margin and Realized Gross Margin accounts.

**8.3**  Under what circumstances should the percentage-of-completion method be used for long-term contracts? Under what circumstances should the completed-contract method be used?

**8.4**  "The percentage-of-completion method should be used for long-term contracts instead of the completed-contract method whenever possible." Do you agree? Why or why not?

**8.5**  Under the percentage-of-completion method, income (profit) is recognized piecemeal over the life of the contract. However, if a loss is expected, the entire loss is recognized immediately. What is the reason for this inconsistency?

**8.6**  Some material costs and subcontract costs are excluded from total costs incurred during the early stages of contract work in computing the degree of completion. Why are these costs excluded? What account is debited when these costs are incurred?

**8.7**  "Our company uses the percentage-of-completion method of accounting for long-term contracts. If management wants to know the average degree of completion of all long-term contracts, we can simply divide the balance in the Construction in Process account by the aggregate contract price of all contracts in process." Comment. Would your response be any different if the completed-contract method were being used?

**8.8**  Changes in accounting estimates are corrected currently and prospectively instead of retroactively under generally accepted accounting principles. Computationally, how are changes in cost estimates for long-term contracts under the percentage-of-completion method accounted for "currently and prospectively"?

**8.9**  Many retailers sell merchandise on an installment basis but are not permitted to recognize income for financial reporting purposes using the installment method. What is the justification for this seeming inconsistency?

**8.10**  Distinguish between the accounting for uncollectible accounts under the installment method and the completed-sale basis of revenue (income) recognition. Assume in both cases that the allowance method is used.

**8.11**  A company sold a machine during the year, receiving from the customer cash plus a noninterest-bearing note payable in five installments. Because the customer has a high credit rating, the gain from the sale of the machine cannot be recognized using the installment method. The interest on the note, however, can be recognized under the installment method. Do you agree? Why or why not?

**8.12**  How does the accounting for sales of developed real estate, such as buildings, differ from retail sales of undeveloped land?

**8.13**  What is the justification for postponing the recognition of revenue from consignment sales until the goods are sold by the consignee?

**8.14**  (Adapted from CPA Examination.) The December 31, 1981, balance sheet of Esther Corporation contains the following current assets:

| | |
|---|---:|
| Cash | $ 80,000 |
| Accounts Receivable | 50,000 |
| Inventories | 70,000 |
| Total | $200,000 |

An examination of the accounts reveals that accounts receivable are composed of the following items:

| **Accounts Receivable** | |
|---|---:|
| Customers' Accounts | $40,750 |
| Employees' Accounts— Current | 2,000 |
| Equity in $10,000 of Uncollected Accounts Assigned under Guaranty | 4,000 |
| Selling Price of Merchandise Sent by Esther on Consignment at 125% of Cost and Not Sold by Consignee | 6,250 |
| Allowance for Uncollectible Accounts | (3,000) |
| Total | $50,000 |

Indicate any changes you feel should be made in either the amounts reported or the methods of disclosure used for each of the items included in accounts receivable.

**8.15**  Discuss when revenue is likely to be recognized by firms in each of the following types of businesses:
a. A shoe store.
b. A ship-building firm constructing an aircraft carrier under a government contract.
c. A real estate developer selling lots on long-term contracts with small down payments.
d. A clothing manufacturer.
e. A citrus-growing firm.
f. A producer of television movies, where the rights to the movies for the first 3 years are sold to a television network and all rights thereafter revert to the producer.
g. A residential real estate developer who constructs only "speculative" houses and then later sells the houses to buyers.
h. A producer of fine whiskey that is aged from 6 to 12 years before sale.
i. A savings and loan association lending money for home mortgages.
j. A travel agency.
k. A printer who prints only custom-order stationery.
l. A seller of trading stamps to food stores redeemable by food store customers for various household products.

    **m.** A wholesale food distributor.

    **n.** A livestock rancher.

    **o.** A shipping company that loads cargo in one accounting period, carries cargo across the ocean in a second accounting period, and unloads the cargo in a third period. The shipping is all done under contract, and cash collection of shipping charges is relatively certain.

**8.16** (Adapted from AICPA *Technical Practice Aids*.) Monroe Cleaning Company sells long-term service contracts to clean office buildings. To new potential customers it offers the first year's services for free—giving a 3-year contract for the price of 2.

    How should the receipts for 2 years' services and the costs of providing 3 years' services be accounted for as revenues and expenses?

**8.17** (Adapted from AICPA *Technical Practice Aids*.) Hughes Fast Foods has a 1-cent sale each week. For example, a sale might offer two cheeseburgers for the price of one ($0.75) plus 1 cent. The company records the following entry for each such sale:

| | | |
|---|---|---|
| Cash ................................................................... | 0.76 | |
| Advertising Expense ................................................. | 0.74 | |
|     Sales Revenue ..................................................... | | 1.50 |

The company does this so that revenues and associated cost of goods sold are not distorted by the sale. Comment on this accounting.

**8.18** (Adapted from AICPA *Technical Practice Aids*.) Strong Company is a dealer in heavy equipment. It records all sales net of trade-ins. For example, assume that an item with a list price of $20,000 which would be sold for $18,000 cash is sold for $14,000 cash and used equipment taken in trade. Strong Company records revenue of $14,000. Comment on this procedure.

**8.19** (Adapted from AICPA *Technical Practice Aids*.) Dickens Recording Company sells station identification and jingles on tape to local radio and television stations. As partial payment for its services, Dickens receives broadcast time, which it resells.

    Should Dickens Recording Company recognize revenue when it receives the credit, when it is sold to others, when it is used by others, or when others pay for their time?

**8.20** (Adapted from AICPA *Technical Practice Aids*.) Kessler Funeral Home sells "pre-need" funeral plans. The customer pays a fixed fee, substantially less than the current price of a funeral. The fee is placed in a trust fund with a local bank. The fee must remain in the bank until the funeral is performed. Kessler may withdraw the income from the trust fund as it is earned. Kessler incurs certain expenses at the time of sale but none thereafter until the funeral is performed. What accounting seems appropriate for the fees received from customers, for trust income, for selling costs, and for funeral costs?

**8.21** (Adapted from AICPA *Technical Practice Aids*.) Dittman Stores sells groceries. It built an addition to its building to house a liquor store, which it rents to an independent liquor dealer. The dealer pays rent to Dittman Stores. Dittman wants reliable data on the dollar sales per square foot on the premises. Therefore, it records all of its own sales and the liquor sales in revenue accounts, subtracts all its own cost of goods sold and an amount for cost of liquor sold equal to the difference between liquor revenue and net rentals from the liquor store. The net margin from liquor sales is thus equal to net rent collected. Comment on this practice.

**8.22** (Adapted from AICPA *Technical Practice Aids*.) Bell Federal Savings & Loan lends money to homeowners through mortgages. In addition to charging interest, for example, of 12 percent of the outstanding loan, it charges 2 percent of the amount borrowed as "points." Cash in the amount of the nominal proceeds of the loan less the 2-percent fee is given to the borrower at the time of the loan. How should the 2 percent of loan proceeds be treated in the accounting for revenue from mortgages?

**8.23** (Adapted from AICPA *Technical Practice Aids.*) Kintzele Company prints booklets and other materials (such as "Sunday supplements" in local newspapers) under contract. New contracts are signed for each job, which typically takes no more than 2 or 3 weeks to complete. When an accounting period ends and part of an order is complete, the company recognizes revenue in the amount of the unit selling price per booklet multiplied by the number of booklets completed. It debits Unbilled Receivables. Comment on this procedure.

**8.24** (Adapted from AICPA *Technical Practice Aids.*) Harmelink Company runs resident homes for the aged. It sells equipment to its residents at retail value. A resident who leaves during the first year may return the item and receive a 75-percent refund of sales price. One who leaves during the second year may return the item for a 50-percent refund. If the resident stays longer than 2 years or dies at any time before 2 years have passed, there is no right of return. How should revenue be recognized for these sales?

**8.25** (Adapted from AICPA *Technical Practice Aids.*) Abendroth Company sold the service division of its company to Garrison Company. As part of the sale, Abendroth agreed not to compete with Garrison Company for 3 years. In addition to the payment for the division, Garrison agreed to make three separate annual payments for the noncompetition agreement.
  **a.** How should Abendroth Company account for the three collections received because it agreed not to compete?
  **b.** Assume, now, that the payments for agreeing not to compete are not spread over time, but are remitted with other proceeds at the time Garrison pays Abendroth.

**8.26** The general principles of revenue recognition discussed in Chapters 7 and 8 can be applied to various types of business. Recent FASB exposure drafts and Statements have been concerned with revenue recognition and the treatment of costs in different segments of the entertainment industry, including motion picture films, broadcasting, cable television, and records and music. Using the information presented below about each industry, discuss when revenue should be recognized in each case. Also consider when costs should be treated as expenses.
  **a.** Firms producing motion pictures initially incur a cost for the right to make a book, stage play, or other work into a motion picture. Costs are also incurred to produce the motion picture. In many cases, advertising costs will be incurred to promote the film nationally. Once completed, the rights to display the film will be sold, or licensed, to theaters on the basis of either a percentage of box office receipts or for a flat fee. Rights for certain films may also be sold to television networks on a fixed fee basis. In these arrangements, the network has the right to telecast the movie as often as it wishes during some specified period of time.
  **b.** Firms involved in broadcasting incur two general types of costs for their programs: (1) amounts paid to networks for the right to be a network affiliate and use network programs, and (2) amounts paid to the producers of specific programs (see **a** above) for the right to broadcast programs during specific periods of time.
  **c.** Cable television companies initially incur costs in constructing the cable television facilities. During the period of construction, costs are also typically incurred in obtaining subscribers and establishing programming. Once the facility is ready for broadcasting, subscribers will be hooked up to the system. During the first few years while the system is in

operation, the number of subscribers usually grows slowly. This slow growth rate occurs primarily because of constraints on the number of geographical areas that have been pre-wired and the number of subscribers that can physically be hooked up each day.

  d. Firms involved in producing records and music usually pay an artist (composer, singer, musician) for the right to use the artist's work. Amounts paid initially are usually charged against future royalties otherwise payable to the artist. The producing firm then sells the records and music over some agreed-upon period of time.

8.27   (Adapted from CPA Examination.) Southern Fried Shrimp sells franchises to independent operators throughout the southeastern part of the United States. The contract with the franchisee includes the following provisions:

  The franchisee is charged an initial fee of $25,000. Of this amount, $5,000 is payable when the agreement is signed and a series of five $4,000 payments are due at the end of each of the succeeding 5 years.

  All of the initial franchise fee collected by Southern Fried Shrimp is to be refunded and the remaining obligation canceled if, for any reason, the franchisee fails to open the franchise.

  In return for the initial franchise fee Southern Fried Shrimp agrees to **(1)** assist the franchisee in selecting the location for the business, **(2)** negotiate the lease for the land, **(3)** obtain financing and assist with building design, **(4)** supervise construction, **(5)** establish accounting and tax records, and **(6)** provide expert advice over a 5-year period relating to such matters as employee and management training, quality control, and promotion.

  In addition to the initial franchise fee, the franchisee is required to pay to Southern Fried Shrimp a monthly fee of 2 percent of sales for menu planning, recipe innovations, and the privilege of purchasing ingredients from Southern Fried Shrimp at or below prevailing market prices.

Management of Southern Fried Shrimp estimates that the value of the services rendered to the franchisee at the time the contract is signed amounts to at least $5,000. All franchisees to date have opened their locations at the scheduled time, and none has defaulted on any of the notes receivable.

  The credit ratings of all franchisees would entitle them to borrow at the current interest rate of 10 percent.

  When should revenue be recognized? Discuss this question of revenue recognition for both the initial franchise fee and the additional monthly fee of 2 percent of sales and give illustrative entries for both types of revenue.

## Problems and Exercises

8.28   (Adapted from CPA Examination.) In 1981, Long Corporation began construction work under a 3-year contract. The contract price is $800,000. Long Corporation uses the percentage-of-completion method for financial reporting purposes. The income to be recognized each year is based on the proportion of costs incurred to date to the total estimated costs of completing the contract. The financial statement presentations relating to this contract at December 31, 1981, are shown here.

**Long Corporation**

**BALANCE SHEET**

| | | |
|---|---:|---:|
| Accounts Receivable—Construction Contract Billings ........................ | | $15,000 |
| Construction in Process .................................................. | $50,000 | |
| Less Contract Billings ..................................................... | (47,000) | |
| Cost and Income of Uncompleted Contracts in Excess of Billings ................ | | 3,000 |

**INCOME STATEMENT**

| | |
|---|---:|
| Income (before Tax) on Long-Term Contract .................................. | 10,000 |

**a.** Determine the amount of cash collected during 1981 on this contract.

**b.** Determine the initial estimated total income before tax on this contract.

**8.29** Wyman Construction Company signed a contract on July 1, 1981, agreeing to build a warehouse for Patton Corporation at a contract price of $10,000,000. Wyman Construction Company estimated that construction costs would be as follows: 1981, $2,500,000; 1982, $4,000,000; 1983, $1,500,000. The contract provided that Patton Corporation would make payments on December 31 of each year as follows: 1981, $2,000,000; 1982, $5,000,000; 1983, $3,000,000. The contract was completed and accepted on December 31, 1983.

   **a.** Compute the amount of income Wyman Construction Company would recognize each year under the completed-contract method, assuming that actual costs and cash collections coincided with expectations.

   **b.** Compute the amount of income Wyman Construction Company would recognize each year under the percentage-of-completion method, assuming that actual costs and cash collections coincided with expectations. The percentage of completion is based on the ratio of actual costs incurred to date divided by total estimated costs.

   **c.** Give the journal entries for 1981, 1982, and 1983 under the completed-contract method.

   **d.** Give the journal entries for 1981, 1982, and 1983 under the percentage-of-completion method.

   **e.** Illustrate the disclosure of information relating to this contract in the balance sheet at the end of 1981, 1982, and 1983 under the completed-contract and the percentage-of-completion methods.

**8.30** Refer to the preceding problem. For each of the following independent changes, or new items of information, determine the amount of income that would be reported in 1981, 1982, and 1983 under the completed-contract and the percentage-of-completion methods.

   **a.** Of the $2,500,000 total costs incurred during 1981, it is determined that $1,200,000 represents the cost of construction materials purchased in 1981 but actually used in construction during 1982. Similarly, $700,000 of the $4,000,000 costs incurred in 1982 represent the cost of construction materials purchased in 1982 but actually used in 1983.

   **b.** Of the $2,500,000 total costs incurred during 1981, $1,000,000 represents payments to subcontractors for elevators, air conditioning ducts, and other items. The total subcontract price for these items is $1,000,000. It is determined that as of December 31, 1981, the manufacture of these subcontract items is 20 percent complete. The items are completed and delivered in 1982.

   **c.** Actual costs incurred during 1981 totaled $2,500,000, as originally expected. However, increases in labor and material costs during 1982 resulted in an increase of $500,000 in costs for 1982 beyond those originally anticipated. Costs for 1983 were expected to increase $200,000 beyond original estimates.

   **d.** Actual costs incurred during 1981 totaled $2,500,000, as originally expected. However, increases in labor and material costs during 1982 resulted in an increase of $1,200,000 in costs for 1982 beyond those originally anticipated. Costs for 1983 were expected to increase $1,000,000 beyond original estimates.

8.31 Lynn Corporation signed a contract on July 1, 1981, agreeing to build a baseball stadium for Entertainment Facilities, Inc. The contract price of $25,000,000 was billable and payable on December 31 of each year as follows: 1981, $5,000,000; 1982, $10,000,000; 1983, $8,000,000. A final payment of $2,000,000 was due upon completion and final acceptance of the stadium. Lynn Corporation anticipated the following construction costs: 1981, $4,000,000; 1982, $11,000,000; 1983, $5,000,000. Actual costs were incurred and progress payments were made as originally anticipated. The stadium was completed on December 28, 1983, but final approval and acceptance did not occur until January 15, 1984. Architects' estimates of the degree of completion as of December 31 of each year were as follows: 1981, 30 percent; 1982, 57 percent; 1983, 100 percent.

a. Compute the amount of income recognized during each of the years 1981 through 1984 under the percentage-of-completion method, assuming that the degree of completion is based on using the ratio of costs incurred to date divided by total expected costs.

b. Repeat step a but assume that the degree of completion is based on using architects' estimates of the degree of completion.

c. Assume the same information as above except that actual costs incurred in 1982 were $12,000,000 and were expected to be $5,400,000 in 1983. Repeat steps a and b.

8.32 On January 1, 1981, the Drew Construction Company entered into a contract for the construction of a dam at a price of $30,000,000. The contract provided for the payment to Drew Construction Company of $9,000,000 on December 31, 1981, and December 31, 1982, with the remainder being paid when the dam was completed. Drew Construction Company expected to complete the project by June 30, 1983. When the contract was signed, Drew Construction Company estimated the total construction costs to be the following:

| | |
|---|---|
| Materials | $10,000,000 |
| Labor (3,000,000 Hours at $3.00) | 9,000,000 |
| Administration and Supervision, Maintenance, and Other Overhead | 6,000,000 |

By the end of 1981, approximately 1,000,000 labor hours were completed at the expected rate. Drew Construction Company determined that $3,500,000 of material and $2,000,000 in overhead were charged to production during the year. Company engineers estimated that the project was 30 percent complete. During the year, Drew Construction Company negotiated a labor contract with its workers that was expected to add 10¢ to the hourly labor rate effective January 1, 1982. It was likewise believed that the total material costs would be $300,000 greater than expected. Overhead was expected to remain substantially as predicted.

At the end of 1982, it was determined that 1,300,000 labor hours had been spent on the project during the year, $3,995,000 in material was used, and $2,600,000 in overhead was charged to construction in 1982. Engineers estimated that the project was now 75 percent complete. On December 31, 1982, it was expected that total labor hours needed to complete the dam would exceed original estimates by 50,000 hours, but the overhead estimate was approximately $55,000 too large. No further revision in the material estimate was made at this time.

The dam was completed on August 1, 1983. A total of 760,000 labor hours were used during the year; material costs and overhead charged to construction amounted to $2,825,000 and $1,340,000, respectively. Drew Construction Company received all payments when due under the contract.

a. Compute the amount of income recognized from this project under the percentage-of-completion method for 1981, 1982, and 1983, based on information and cost expectations on December 31 of each respective year:

1. Under the assumption that the completion percentage is based on the ratio of costs incurred to total anticipated costs.
2. Under the assumption that the completion percentage is based on engineering estimates.

**b.** Give the journal entries that would be made by Drew Construction Company over the construction period, using both assumptions **(1)** and **(2)** above.

**8.33**  (Adapted from CPA Examination.) The Board of Directors of DeWitt Construction Company is meeting to choose between the completed-contract method and the percentage-of-completion method of accounting for long-term contracts for reporting in the Company's financial statements. You have been engaged to assist DeWitt's controller in the preparation of a presentation to be given at the Board meeting. The controller provides you with the following information:

1. DeWitt commenced doing business on January 1, 1981.
2. Construction activities for the year ended December 31, 1981, were as follows:

| Project | Total Contract Price | Billings through December 31, 1981 | Cash Collections through December 31, 1981 |
|---------|---------|---------|---------|
| A | $   520,000 | $   350,000 | $   310,000 |
| B | 670,000 | 210,000 | 210,000 |
| C | 475,000 | 475,000 | 395,000 |
| D | 200,000 | 70,000 | 50,000 |
| E | 460,000 | 400,000 | 400,000 |
| | $2,325,000 | $1,505,000 | $1,365,000 |

| Project | Contract Costs Incurred through December 31, 1981 | Estimated Additional Costs to Complete Contracts |
|---------|---------|---------|
| A | $   424,000 | $106,000 |
| B | 126,000 | 504,000 |
| C | 315,000 | — |
| D | 112,750 | 92,250 |
| E | 370,000 | 30,000 |
| | $1,347,750 | $732,250 |

3. All contracts are with different customers.
4. Any work remaining to be done on the contracts is expected to be completed in 1982.

**a.** Prepare a schedule by project computing the amount of income (or loss) before selling, general, and administrative expenses for the year ended December 31, 1981, that would be reported under:

1. The completed-contract method.
2. The percentage-of-completion method (based on estimated costs).

**b.** Following is a balance sheet that compares balances resulting from the use of the two methods of accounting for long-term contracts. For each numbered blank space on the statement, supply the correct balance [indicating dr. (cr.) as appropriate]. Disregard income taxes.

*DeWitt Construction Company*
*Balance Sheet*
*December 31, 1981*

| ASSETS | Completed-Contract Method | Percentage-of-Completion Method |
|---|---|---|
| Cash | $ xxxx | $ xxxx |
| Accounts (Contracts) Receivable | (1) | (4) |
| Cost of Uncompleted Contracts in Excess of Billings | (2) | — |
| Costs and Estimated Earnings in Excess of Billings on Uncompleted Contracts | — | (5) |
| Property, Plant, and Equipment, Net | xxxx | xxxx |
| Other Assets | xxxx | xxxx |
| | $ xxxx | $ xxxx |
| **LIABILITIES AND SHAREHOLDERS' EQUITY** | | |
| Accounts Payable and Accrued Liabilities | $ xxxx | $ xxxx |
| Billings on Uncompleted Contracts in Excess of Costs | (3) | — |
| Billings in Excess of Costs and Estimated Earnings on Uncompleted Contracts | — | (6) |
| Notes Payable | xxxx | xxxx |
| Common Stock | xxxx | xxxx |
| Retained Earnings | xxxx | xxxx |
| | $ xxxx | $ xxxx |

**8.34** The following information relates to the installment sales activity of Westside Stores, Inc., for 1981, its first year of operations:

| | |
|---|---|
| Installment Sales during 1981 | $600,000 |
| Cost of Goods Sold on Installment Basis | 510,000 |
| Collections from Customers | 280,000 |
| Unpaid Balances on Merchandise Repossessed | 15,000 |
| Market Value of Repossessed Merchandise | 9,000 |

Westside Stores, Inc., uses 4 percent of the *cost of goods sold* on an installment basis as the rate for estimated uncollectible accounts. The allowance method is used for uncollectible accounts. The periodic provision for estimated uncollectibles is treated as a period expense.

Prepare journal entries to record the above data, including any required adjusting entries on December 31, 1981, assuming that income is recognized as cash is collected using the installment method. Ignore interest revenue on outstanding installment receivables.

**8.35** The following information relates to the installment sales activity of Dollar Mart Department Store.

| | 1981 | 1982 | 1983 |
|---|---|---|---|
| Installment Sales | $60,000 | $130,000 | $250,000 |
| Cost of Installment Sales | 45,600 | 96,200 | 192,500 |
| Selling and Administrative Expenses | 8,500 | 15,400 | 29,600 |
| Cash Collections: | | | |
| 1981 Sales | 28,000 | 18,000 | 8,000 |
| 1982 Sales | — | 65,000 | 47,000 |
| 1983 Sales | — | — | 132,000 |

Ignore interest revenue on outstanding installment receivables in all parts of this problem.

a. Compute the amount of income before income taxes recognized during 1981, 1982, and 1983, if revenue is recognized at the time of sale.

b. Compute the amount of income before income taxes recognized during 1981, 1982, and 1983, if revenue is recognized at the time of cash collection using the installment method.

c. Give the journal entries for each of the 3 years, assuming that revenue is recognized at the time of sale. Also show any necessary adjusting and closing entries at the end of each year.

d. Give the journal entries for each of the 3 years, assuming that revenue is recognized at the time of cash collection using the installment method. Also show any necessary adjusting and closing entries at the end of each year.

e. Illustrate the disclosure of information relating to these installment sales in the balance sheet at the end of 1981, 1982, and 1983, assuming that revenue is recognized (1) at the time of sale, and (2) at the time of cash collection, using the installment method.

f. Which of these two revenue (income)-recognition methods resulted in the larger cumulative income over the 3-year period for Dollar Mart Department Store? Will this same relationship hold for most firms selling on an installment basis? Why or why not?

g. Which of these two revenue (income)-recognition methods resulted in the larger amount of current assets at the end of each year for Dollar Mart Department Store? Will this same relationship hold for most firms selling on an installment basis? Why or why not?

8.36 May Department Store sells merchandise on an installment basis. It uses 3 percent of the *cost of installment sales* as the rate for estimated uncollectible accounts, with the provision for uncollectibles charged against earnings in the year of sale. Ignore interest revenue on outstanding installment receivables in all parts of this problem. Installment sales activity during 1981, 1982, and 1983 follows:

|  | 1981 | 1982 | 1983 |
|---|---|---|---|
| Installment Sales | $85,000 | $89,000 | $96,000 |
| Cost of Installment Sales | 74,800 | 76,540 | 78,720 |
| Selling and Administrative Expenses | 4,000 | 4,800 | 6,500 |
| Cash Collections: |  |  |  |
|    1981 Sales | 34,000 | 32,000 | 11,000 |
|    1982 Sales |  | 35,500 | 29,600 |
|    1983 Sales | — | — | 39,700 |
| Unpaid Balance in Accounts Written Off: |  |  |  |
|    1981 Sales | 1,000 | 3,000 | 2,500 |
|    1982 Sales | — | 800 | 3,400 |
|    1983 Sales | — | — | 1,300 |

a. Compute the amount of income before income taxes for 1981, 1982, and 1983, assuming that May Department Store recognizes income at the time of cash collection using the installment method and uses the allowance method to account for uncollectible accounts. The installment sales arrangement of May Department Store does not permit it to repossess merchandise sold if the customer fails to pay amounts due.

b. Give the journal entries to record the installment sales transactions of May Department Store for 1981, 1982, and 1983. Be sure to give any required adjusting and closing entries at the end of each year.

8.37 (Adapted from CPA Examination.) The Dahlia Company has two divisions, the Tulip Division, which started operating in 1979, and the Birch Division, which started operating in 1980. The Tulip Division constructs waste water treatment plants for small communities throughout the United States. The Birch Division manufactures and sells computers.

All except two of the long-term contracts of the Tulip Division are appropriately accounted for under the percentage-of-completion method. Two contracts are accounted for under the completed-contract method because of the lack of dependable estimates of the costs of these contracts as they progress.

The aggregate contract price of long-term contracts recorded under the percentage-of-completion method was $6,000,000 on December 31, 1981. Costs incurred on these contracts were $1,500,000 in 1980 and $3,000,000 in 1981. Estimated additional costs of $1,000,000 are required to complete these contracts. Income of $160,000 from these long-term contracts was recognized during 1980. A total of $4,800,000 has been billed, of which $4,600,000 has been collected. No long-term contracts recorded under the percentage-of-completion method were completed in 1981.

The two long-term contracts recorded under the completed-contract method were started in 1980. One is a $5,000,000 contract. Costs incurred were $1,400,000 in 1980 and $1,600,000 in 1981. A total of $3,100,000 has been billed, and $2,800,000 has been collected. Although it is difficult to estimate the additional costs required to complete this contract, indications are that this contract will prove to be profitable.

The second contract is for $4,000,000. Costs incurred were $1,200,000 in 1980 and $2,600,000 in 1981. A total of $3,300,000 has been billed and $2,900,000 collected. Although it is difficult to estimate the additional costs required to complete the contract, indications are that there will be a loss of approximately $550,000.

On January 1, 1981, the Birch Division entered into an installment sales contract for the sale of a computer to Grove Company. Equal annual payments under the installment sale of $1,000,000 are required on January 1, 1981, and continuing through January 1, 1987. The cash selling price for the computer (that is, the amount that would be realized on outright sale) is $5,355,260. The cost of manufacturing the computer is $4,284,000. Circumstances are such that the collection of the installment contract is reasonably assured. The first installment payment was received on January 1, 1981. The sale to Grove Company was the only sale of the Birch Division during 1981.

Selling and administrative expenses, exclusive of amounts specified earlier, were $600,000 in 1981. Other income exclusive of amounts specified earlier was $50,000 in 1981.

Prepare an income statement for Dahlia Company for the year ended December 31, 1981, stopping at income (loss) before income taxes. Show supporting schedules and computations.

8.38 Mason Corporation sold a machine to financially troubled Seaver Company on January 1, 1981. The machine cost Mason Corporation $15,000 to manufacture. Seaver Company paid $4,000 immediately and signed a $16,000 promissory note for the remainder of the purchase price. The note is due in installments of $4,000 on December 31 of each of the years 1981 to 1984. In addition, Seaver Company must pay interest each year at the rate of 12 percent of the unpaid balance of the note at the beginning of the year. Machines of the type sold to Seaver Company generally sell for $20,000. Because of the uncertain financial position of Seaver Company, Mason Corporation properly decided to recognize income from the sale of the machine using the installment method.

The installment payment due on December 31, 1981, including interest, was received by Mason Corporation and properly recorded. On January 5, 1982, Seaver Company filed for bankruptcy. The machine was immediately repossessed by Mason Corporation. The market value of the machine at this time was $11,000.

**a.** Give the journal entries on Mason Corporation's books to record the transactions relating to this sale from January 1, 1981, to January 5, 1982.

**b.** What would your journal entry be on January 5, 1982, if the machine had a market value of $8,000 at the time of repossession?

**8.39**  Refer to the data for Cox Auto Corporation in Problem **7.47**. Assume that income from the sale of trucks is recognized as cash is received, using the installment method. Determine the amount of revenue (income) that Cox Auto Corporation would report from the transaction with FOB Corporation during 1981, 1982, and 1983.

**8.40**  Refer to the data for Standard Manufacturing Company in Problem **7.48**. Assume that income from the sale of the electrical generator is recognized as cash is received, using the installment method. Determine the amount of revenue (income) that Standard Manufacturing Company would report from the transaction with Chicago General Hospital during 1981, 1982, 1983, and 1984.

**8.41**  Refer to the data for BBM Corporation in Problem **7.49**. Assume that income from the sale of computers is recognized as cash is received, using the installment method. Determine the amount of revenue (income) that BBM Corporation would report from the transaction with Sawyer Corporation during 1981, 1982, and 1983.

**8.42**  McGee Corporation sold land and a special purpose building with a combined book value of $220,000 to Steele Corporation for $400,000 on January 1, 1981. There is no active market for land and a building of this type. The credit condition of Steele Corporation is such that it could borrow funds currently at 10 percent. Indicate the appropriate method of accounting for this real estate transaction under each of the following independent cases.
a.  Steele Corporation made a $100,000 down payment and agreed to pay the remaining $300,000 in equal annual installments of $39,442.13 on December 31 of each year until the note, including interest, is fully paid.
b.  Steele Corporation made a $120,000 down payment and agreed to pay the remaining $280,000 in equal annual installments of $31,163.96 on December 31 of each year until the note, including interest, is fully paid.
c.  Steele Corporation made an $80,000 down payment and agreed to pay the remaining $320,000 in equal annual installments of $42,071.61 on December 31 of each year until the note, including interest, is fully paid.

**8.43**  Vermont Specialty Products Company sells merchandise on a consignment basis through two dealers. Vermont Specialty Products Company allows the dealers a 20 percent commission on goods sold and reimburses the dealers for freight costs incurred. Selling prices are set by Vermont Specialty Products Company at 40 percent above manufacturing cost. The following information relates to consignment sales activity during 1981.

|  | Dealer A | Dealer B |
|---|---|---|
| Manufacturing Cost of Goods Shipped Out on Consignment | $12,000 | $25,000 |
| Freight Cost Incurred and Paid by Dealer | 1,500 | 2,100 |
| Selling Price of Merchandise Sold by Dealer | 11,000 | 18,000 |

The dealers transmitted the required amounts to Vermont Specialty Products Company during 1981, after deducting commissions and freight costs incurred.

   Give the journal entries on the books of Vermont Specialty Products Company relating to consignment sales activity during 1981.

**8.44**  Marcel Manufacturing Company shipped 500 units to dealers on consignment during 1981. The units cost $12 each to produce and sell at retail for $15 each. Dealers are allowed a 10 percent commission on units sold. Dealers sold 300 units during 1981. Marcel Manufacturing Company made the following journal entries on its books during 1981:

---

(1) Consignment Accounts Receivable ......................................... 7,500
    Consignment Sales Revenue .......................................... 7,500
    To record the shipment of 500 units to dealers at retail price of $15 each.

(2) Consignment Cost of Goods Sold ......................................... 6,000
    Finished Goods Inventory ............................................ 6,000
    To record cost of 500 units shipped out on consignment.

(3) Cash ......................................................... 4,050
    Consignment Accounts Receivable .................................... 4,050
    To record cash received from consignees.

---

Give any adjusting entries that you feel should be made at the end of 1981.

8.45  The Humbolt Electric Company received a contract late in 1981 to build a small electricity-generating unit. The contract price was $700,000 and it was estimated that total costs would be $600,000. Estimated and actual construction time was 15 months, and it was agreed that payments would be made by the purchaser as follows:

| | |
|---|---:|
| March 31, 1982 | $ 70,000 |
| June 30, 1982 | 105,000 |
| September 30, 1982 | 203,000 |
| December 31, 1982 | 161,000 |
| March 31, 1983 | 161,000 |
| | $700,000 |

Estimated and actual costs of construction incurred by the Humbolt Electric Company were as follows:

| | |
|---|---:|
| January 1–March 31, 1982 | $120,000 |
| April 1–June 30, 1982 | 120,000 |
| July 1–September 30, 1982 | 180,000 |
| October 1–December 31, 1982 | 120,000 |
| January 1–March 31, 1983 | 60,000 |
| | $600,000 |

The Humbolt Electric Company prepares financial statements quarterly at March 31, June 30, and so forth.

Compute the amount of revenue, expense, and net income for each quarter under each of the following methods of revenue recognition:

a. Production (percentage-of-completion) method.
b. Sales (completed-contract) method.
c. Cash collection (installment) method.
d. Cash collection (cost-recovery-first) method.
e. Which method do you feel provides the best measure of Humbolt's performance under this contract? Why?
f. Under what circumstances would the methods not selected in part e provide a better measure of performance?

8.46  The Webster Corporation produces a single product at a cost of $5 each, all of which is paid in cash when the unit is produced. The selling cost consists of a sales commission of $3 a unit and is paid in cash at the time of shipment. The selling price is $10 a unit; all sales are made on account. No uncollectible accounts are expected, and no costs are incurred at the time of collection.

During 1981, the firm produced 200,000 units, shipped 150,000 units, and collected $1 million from customers. During 1982, the firm produced 125,000 units, shipped 160,000 units, and collected $2 million from customers.

Compute the amount of net income for 1981 and 1982:

a. If revenue and expense are recognized at the time of production.

b. If revenue and expense are recognized at the time of shipment.

c. If revenue and expense are recognized at the time of cash collection.

d. A firm experiencing growth in its sales volume will often produce more units during a particular period than it sells. In this way, inventories can be built up in anticipation of an even larger sales volume during the next period. Under these circumstances, will recognition of revenue and expense at the time of production, shipment, or cash collection generally result in the largest reported net income for the period? Explain.

e. A firm experiencing decreases in its sales volume will often produce fewer units during a period than it sells in an effort to reduce the amount of inventory on hand for next period. Under these circumstances, will recognition of revenue and expense at the time of production, shipment, or cash collection generally result in the largest reported net income for a period? Explain.

8.47  The Linda Company begins business on January 1, 1981. Activities of the company for the first two years are summarized below.

| | 1981 | 1982 |
|---|---|---|
| Sales, All on Account | $200,000 | $300,000 |
| Collections from Customers | | |
|    On 1981 Sales | 90,000 | 110,000 |
|    On 1982 Sales | | 120,000 |
| Purchases of Merchandise | 180,000 | 240,000 |
| Inventory of Merchandise at 12/31 | 60,000 | 114,000 |
| All Expenses Other Than Merchandise, Paid in Cash | 32,000 | 44,000 |

Ignore interest revenue on outstanding receivables.

a. Prepare income statements for 1981 and 1982, assuming the company uses the accrual method of accounting.

b. Prepare income statements for 1981 and 1982, assuming the company uses the installment method of accounting.

8.48  (Adapted from CPA Examination.) Curtiss Construction Company, Inc., entered into a firm fixed-price contract with Axelrod Associates on July 1, Year 1, to construct a four-story office building. At that time, Curtiss estimated that it would take between two and three years to complete the project. The total contract price for construction of the building is $4,000,000. Curtiss appropriately accounts for this contract under the completed-contract method in its financial statements and for income tax reporting. The building was deemed substantially completed on December 31, Year 3. Delivery was made to the customer on January 2, Year 4. Estimated percentage of completion, accumulated contract costs incurred, estimated costs to complete the contract, and accumulated billings to Axelrod under the contract were as follows:

|  | At December Year 1 | At December Year 2 | At December Year 3 |
|---|---|---|---|
| Percentage of completion ..................... | 10% | 60% | 100% |
| Contract costs incurred ....................... | $ 350,000 | $2,500,000 | $4,250,000 |
| Estimated costs to complete the contract ........ | $3,150,000 | $1,700,000 | — |
| Billings to Axelrod ............................ | $ 720,000 | $2,160,000 | $3,600,000 |

a. Prepare schedules to compute profit or loss to be recognized as a result of this contract for the years ended December 31, Year 1, Year 2, and Year 3. Ignore income taxes.

b. Prepare schedules to compute the amount to be shown as "cost of uncompleted contract in excess of related billings" or "billings on uncompleted contract in excess of related costs" at December 31, Year 1, Year 2 and Year 3. Ignore income taxes.

8.49 (Adapted from CPA Examination.) On April 1, Year 1, Butler, Inc., entered into a cost-plus-fixed-fee contract to construct an electric generator for Dalton Corporation. Under such a contract, the contractor is reimbursed for all costs incurred plus a fixed fee that is independent of the costs incurred. At the contract date, Butler estimated that it would take two years to complete the project at a cost of $2,000,000. The fixed fee stipulated in the contract is $300,000. Butler appropriately accounts for this contract under the percentage-of-completion method. During Year 1 Butler incurred costs of $700,000 related to the project, and the estimated cost at December 31, Year 1, to complete the contract is $1,400,000. Dalton was billed $500,000 under the contract.

Compute the amount of gross profit to be recognized by Butler under the contract for the year ended December 31, Year 1.

# Chapter 9
# Inventories and Cost of Goods Sold: The Basic Concepts

9.1 In the last decade, many major U.S. corporations changed their method of accounting for inventories and cost of goods sold. As a result of the change in methods, these corporations reported net income that was smaller by hundreds of millions of dollars than would have been reported without the change. Paradoxically, perhaps, these firms were actually better off as a result of the change. This chapter shows how a firm can be better off reporting smaller, rather than larger, net income. We introduce the choices that any firm must make in accounting for inventories and show how the decisions made can affect reported expenses and net income for the period. The choices made in accounting for inventories can make two companies that are basically alike appear to be quite different. The next chapter treats some more advanced issues of valuing inventories and computing cost of goods sold.

## Inventory Terminology

9.2 The term *inventory*, as used in accounting and in this chapter, means a stock of goods or other items owned by a firm and held for sale or use in ordinary business operations. Tools, for example, are inventory in the hands of a tool manufacturer or hardware store, but not in the hands of a carpenter.

Marketable securities are inventory in the hands of a securities broker or dealer, but not in the hands of a manufacturer.

9.3 Goods held for sale by a retail or wholesale business are referred to as *merchandise* or *merchandise inventory;* goods held for sale by a manufacturing concern are referred to as *finished goods.* The inventories of manufacturing firms also include *work in process* (partially completed products in the factory) and *raw materials* (materials being stored which will become part of goods to be produced). Exhibit 9.6, presented later in the chapter, illustrates the various inventory accounts used in manufacturing. Supplies that will be consumed in administrative, selling, and manufacturing operations are also frequently included in inventories on the balance sheet.

9.4 The term *inventory* is sometimes used as a verb. To "inventory" a stock of goods means to prepare a list of the items on hand at some specified date, to assign a unit price to each item, and to calculate the total cost of the goods.

## Significance of Accounting for Inventories

9.5 One major objective of financial accounting is to measure periodic income. The role of accounting for inventories in measuring income is the assignment of cost to various accounting periods as expenses. The total cost of goods available for sale or use during a period must be allocated between the current period's usage (cost of goods sold, an expense) and the amounts carried forward to future periods (the end-of-period inventory, an asset).

9.6    One equation applies to all inventory situations and facilitates our discussion of accounting for inventory. In the following equation, all quantities are measured in physical units.

$$\underbrace{\text{Beginning Inventory} + \text{Additions}}_{\substack{\text{Goods Available for} \\ \text{Use or Sale}}} - \text{Withdrawals} = \text{Ending Inventory.}$$

If we begin a period with 1,000 lb of salt (beginning inventory) and if we purchase (add) 1,500 lb during the period, then there are 2,500 (= 1,000 + 1,500) lb available for use. If we use (withdraw) 1,300 lb during the period, then there should be 1,200 lb of salt left at the end of the period (ending inventory). For accounting purposes, the inventory equation can be rewritten as

$$\underbrace{\text{Beginning Inventory} + \text{Additions}}_{\substack{\text{Goods Available for} \\ \text{Use or Sale}}} - \underset{\text{Inventory}}{\text{Ending}} = \text{Withdrawals.}$$

If we begin the period with 1,000 lb of salt, if we purchase 1,500 lb of salt, and if we observe 1,200 lb of salt on hand at the end of the period, then we know that 1,300 (= 1,000 + 1,500 − 1,200) lb of salt were used, or otherwise withdrawn from inventory, during the period. The sum of Beginning Inventory plus Additions is usually called "Goods Available for Use or Sale." In this example, there are 2,500 lb of salt available for use or sale.

9.7    If accounting were concerned merely with keeping a record of physical quantities, there would be few problems in accounting for inventories. But, of course, accounting reports are stated in dollar amounts, not physical quantities. If all prices remained constant, inventory accounting problems would be minor, because all items would be valued at the same per-unit cost. Any variation in values of inventories would be attributable solely to changes in quantities. The major problems in inventory accounting arise from fluctuations over time in the unit acquisition costs of inventory items.

9.8    Consider the inventory of goods for sale in a merchandising firm. The inventory equation can be written as follows, with all quantities measured in dollars of cost:

$$\underset{\text{Inventory}}{\text{Beginning}} + \underset{\text{Purchases}}{\text{Net}} - \underset{\text{Goods Sold}}{\text{Cost of}} = \underset{\text{Inventory.}}{\text{Ending}}$$

Rearranging terms, the equation becomes

$$\underset{\text{Inventory}}{\text{Beginning}} + \underset{\text{Purchases}}{\text{Net}} - \underset{\text{Inventory}}{\text{Ending}} = \underset{\text{Goods Sold.}}{\text{Cost of}}$$

The valuation for the ending inventory will appear on the balance sheet as the asset Merchandise Inventory; the amount of Cost of Goods Sold will appear on the income statement as an expense of generating the sales revenue.

9.9    To illustrate, suppose that a merchandising firm (appliance store) had a beginning inventory of one toaster, "toaster 1," which cost $25. Suppose, further, that two toasters are purchased during the period, toaster 2 for $29 and toaster 3 for $30, and that one toaster is sold for $55. The three toasters are exactly alike in all physical respects; only their costs differ. Assume that there is no way to know which toaster was sold.

9.10    If financial statements are prepared with amounts measured in dollar terms, then some assumption must be made about which toaster was sold. The total cost of the three toasters available for sale is $84 (= $25 + $29 + $30), and the average cost of the toasters is $28 (= $84/3). There are at least four assumptions that can be made in applying the inventory equation to determine the Cost of Goods Sold expense for the income statement and the ending inventory for the balance sheet. These assumptions are shown in Exhibit 9.1. As the inventory equation and the toaster example both show, the higher the Cost of Goods Sold, the lower must be the Ending Inventory. The choice of which

*Exhibit 9.1*
**Assumptions for Inventory Illustrations**

| Assumed Item Sold | Cost of Goods Available for Sale (Beginning Inventory plus Purchases)[a] = | Cost of Goods Sold (for Income Statement) + | Ending Inventory (for Balance Sheet) |
|---|---|---|---|
| Toaster 1 .................................. | $84 | $25 | $59 |
| Toaster 2 .................................. | 84 | 29 | 55 |
| Toaster 3 .................................. | 84 | 30 | 54 |
| "Average" Toaster .......................... | 84 | 28 | 56 |

[a]Cost of goods available for sale = Cost of (toaster 1 + toaster 2 + toaster 3) = ($25 + $29 + $30) = $84.

particular pair of numbers to use—one for the income statement and one for the balance sheet—is determined by the *cost-flow assumption*. Making a cost-flow assumption is a major problem in accounting for inventories.

## Problems of Inventory Accounting

9.11 Discussion of inventory accounting can be conveniently split into consideration of individual problems, considered more or less separately. The remainder of this chapter discusses five such problems:

**1.** Periodic and perpetual methods of keeping track of items in inventory.

**2.** Valuation basis for items in inventory.

**3.** Costs included in acquisition cost.

**4.** Items included in inventory.

**5.** Cost-flow assumptions for the movement of goods and prices into and out of inventory.

The next chapter treats some more complex aspects of these inventory problems. The income tax laws affect some of the firm's choices in accounting for inventories. We discuss the impact of income taxes at the appropriate places.

## Inventory Methods

9.12 There are two principal methods of determining the physical quantity and dollar amount of an inventory. One is known as the *periodic* inventory method and the other as the *perpetual* inventory method. The periodic method is less expensive to use than the perpetual method, but the perpetual method provides useful information about thefts and other losses of inventory that are not provided by the periodic method.

## Periodic Inventory Method

The periodic inventory method calculates   9.13 the ending inventory figure by taking a physical count of units on hand at the end of an accounting period and multiplying the quantity on hand by the cost per unit.* Then the inventory equation calculates the withdrawals that represent the cost-of-goods-sold expense. The following form of the inventory equation computes the cost of goods sold under the periodic method:

$$\underbrace{\begin{matrix} \text{Beginning} \\ \text{Inventory} \\ \text{(known)} \end{matrix} + \begin{matrix} \text{Purchases} \\ \text{(known)} \end{matrix}}_{\substack{\text{Goods Available} \\ \text{for Use or Sale}}} - \begin{matrix} \text{Ending} \\ \text{Inventory} \\ \text{(counted)} \end{matrix} = \begin{matrix} \text{Cost of} \\ \text{Goods Sold.} \\ \text{(solved for)} \end{matrix}$$

When the periodic method is used, no en-   9.14 try is made for withdrawals (cost of goods sold) until the end of the accounting period when the time comes to compute ending inventory and the cost of goods sold. To illus-

*In many companies, inventory controls are sufficiently good that sampling methods, rather than exhaustive counts, can be used. See *Statement on Auditing Standards No. 1*, AICPA (1978), sec. 331.11.

trate the application of the periodic method, assume that sales during the year amounted to $123,500. The entries made to record sales during the year would have the combined effect of the following entry:

```
Cash and Accounts Receivable ... 123,500
    Sales ......................        123,500
Sales recorded for the entire year
have this effect.
```

At the end of the year, a physical count is taken, an inventory valuation is made, and the cost of the withdrawals is determined from the inventory equation. For example,

```
Cost of Merchandise Inventory,
    January 1 ........................  $ 10,000
Plus Merchandise Purchased (Net)
    During the Year ...................  100,000
Cost of Goods Available for Sale During
    the Year .........................  $110,000
Less Cost of Merchandise Inventory,
    December 31 .....................    (15,000)
Cost of Goods Sold During the Year  ..  $ 95,000
```

We assume that all purchases have been debited to the Merchandise Inventory account.* The cost-of-goods-sold expense is recognized in a single entry:

```
Cost of Goods Sold ............... 95,000
    Merchandise Inventory ........        95,000
Cost of Goods Sold recognized under
the periodic inventory method.
```

9.15 The principal disadvantage of the periodic inventory method is the assumption that all goods not accounted for by the physical inventory count have been sold or used. Any "shrinkages" (the general name for losses from such causes as breakage, theft, evaporation, and waste) are buried in the cost of goods sold. Thus, no information is generated to aid in controlling the amount of shrinkage. Furthermore, physically counting the inventory at the end of the accounting period can seriously interfere with normal business operations for several days. Some firms using the periodic inventory method even close down and engage practically the entire staff on the physical count and measurement of the items on hand. Preparing income statements more frequently than once a year is expensive when the inventory figures are obtained only by physically counting inventories.

**Estimating Inventory Values When the** 9.16
**Periodic Method Is Used** To count every item in inventory is costly. Firms try to do it as seldom as possible, consistent with requirements of generally accepted accounting principles and proper inventory control. When the periodic inventory method is used and financial statements are to be prepared, say, at the end of a month or quarter, reasonably good estimates of ending inventory and cost-of-goods-sold amounts can often be obtained with the *gross margin method* and various *retail methods*. The next chapter discusses details of these methods.

## Perpetual Inventory Method

The *perpetual* (or *continuous*) inventory 9.17 method records the cost of withdrawals at the time that items are taken from inventory. The perpetual inventory method calculates the cost of withdrawals by a constant tracing of costs removed from inventory. Such entries as the following may be made from day to day:

```
Accounts Receivable ................. 900
    Sales ..........................        900
Cost of Goods Sold ................. 546
    Merchandise Inventory ...........        546
To record the cost of goods withdrawn
from inventory and sold for $900.
```

The balance in the Merchandise Inventory account when postings for a period have been completed is the cost of the goods still on hand. Statements can be prepared without carrying out a physical count of inventory. The perpetual inventory method uses the following form of the inventory equation

---

*Seldom would a company using a periodic inventory method directly debit the cost of purchases to the Inventory account. Instead, it would debit a temporary inventory adjunct account, Purchases, which is later closed to the Inventory account. Later in this chapter, we discuss the use of the Purchases account.

to compute what should be in the ending inventory after each acquisition or withdrawal:

Beginning + Purchases − Withdrawals = Ending
Inventory    (known)      (recorded)    Inventory.
(known)                                 (solved for)

        Goods Available
        for Use or Sale

9.18 Using a perpetual inventory system does not eliminate the need to take a physical inventory in which the items of inventory on hand are counted and valued. A physical count and valuation must be done to check the accuracy of the book figures and to gauge the loss from shrinkages. The loss is the difference between the amounts in the Inventory account and the cost of the goods physically on hand. The loss would be recorded as follows, assuming a book balance for inventory of $10,000 and a valuation based on a physical count of $9,600:

Cost of Goods Sold (or Loss) . . . . . . . . . . . 400
    Merchandise Inventory . . . . . . . . . . . . . .    400

The credit reduces the book amount of inventory from its recorded amount, $10,000, to the correct amount, $9,600. The debit can be made either to the usual Cost of Goods Sold account or to a loss account, such as Loss from Inventory Shrinkages.

9.19 Some businesses using the perpetual method make a complete physical check at the end of the accounting period, in the same way as when the periodic inventory method is used. A more effective procedure is available. Rather than taking the inventory of all items at one time, the count may be staggered throughout the period. For example, a college bookstore may check actual physical amounts of textbooks and inventory account amounts at the end of the school year, whereas the comparison for sunglasses might be done in November. All items should be counted at least once during every year, but not all items need be counted at the same time. The count of a particular item should be scheduled for a time when the stock on hand is near its low point for the year. Where stockouts are costly, as in some manufacturing operations, counts are often made on the production line to maintain cost-effective control of inventory levels.

## Choosing between Periodic and Perpetual Inventory Methods

The perpetual method helps maintain up-to-date information on quantities actually on hand. Thus, its use is justified when being "out of stock" may lead to costly consequences, such as customer dissatisfaction or the need to shut down production lines. In such cases, the perpetual inventory system might keep track of the physical quantities of inventory but not the dollar amounts. Further, controlling losses is easier under a perpetual system because inventory records continuously indicate the goods that should be on hand. The periodic inventory method usually costs less to administer than the perpetual inventory method, but it provides no data on losses, shrinkages, and deterioration.   9.20

As with other choices that have to be made in accounting, the costs of any system have to be compared with its benefits. The periodic inventory method is likely to be cost-effective when being out of stock will not be extremely costly, when there is a large volume of items with a small value per unit, or when items are hard to steal or pilfer. Perpetual methods are cost-effective when there is a small volume of high-value items or when running out of stock is costly.   9.21

As the cost of record keeping with computers declines, the cost of perpetual systems declines. Their use, therefore, has increased over time.   9.22

## Bases of Inventory Valuation

The basis of valuation for inventories significantly affects both net income and the amount at which inventories are shown on the balance sheet. At least five bases of valuation are used for one purpose or another. The most common ones, discussed below, are acquisition cost, current cost as measured either by replacement cost or net re-   9.23

alizable value, lower of (acquisition) cost or market, and standard cost. Some of the following is review of fundamentals discussed in Chapter 5. Generally accepted accounting principles require the use of the lower-of-cost-or-market basis for most purposes.

## Acquisition Cost Basis

9.24 When the acquisition cost basis is used, units in inventory are carried at their historical cost until sold. In accounting, the terms *acquisition cost* and *historical cost* are used to mean the same thing.

9.25 Use of historical or acquisition costs in accounting implies the use of the *realization convention:* Increases (or decreases) in the market value of individual assets, including items of inventory, are not recognized as holding gains (or losses) until those assets are sold. Thus, when the acquisition cost basis is used for items in inventory, only sales transactions affect income. Any changes in the value of inventory items occurring between the time of acquisition and the time of sale are not recognized. The figure shown on the balance sheet for inventory will be more or less out of date depending on how much prices have changed since the items were acquired. The longer the time elapsed since acquisition, the more likely is the current value of the inventory to differ from its acquisition cost.

## Current Cost Bases

9.26 When a current cost basis is used, units in inventory are stated at a current market price. Two current-value bases are discussed below: current entry value, often called *replacement cost;* and current exit value, often called *net realizable value*.

9.27 When inventories are stated at current cost, gains and losses from changes in prices of inventory items are recognized during the holding period that elapses between acquisition (or production) and the time of sale.

9.28 Whereas an acquisition cost basis for inventory shows objective, verifiable information that may be out of date, a current cost basis shows current information that can be more useful but the amount shown may be more difficult to ascertain and to audit.

**Replacement Cost** The replacement cost of 9.29 an inventory item at a given time is the amount the firm would have to pay to acquire the item at that time. In computing replacement cost, one assumes that a fair market (or arm's-length) transaction between a willing buyer and a willing seller takes place. One also assumes that the inventory is bought in the customary fashion in the customary quantities. Replacement cost does not imply the forced purchase of inventory by a frantic buyer from a hoarding seller (which probably implies a premium price) or purchases of abnormally large quantities (which often can be bought at a lower-than-normal price) or purchases of abnormally small quantities (which usually cost more per unit to acquire).

**Net Realizable Value** The amount that a 9.30 firm could realize as a willing seller (not a "distressed seller") in an arm's-length transaction with a willing buyer in the ordinary course of business is *net realizable value,* an exit value. Because not all items of inventory are in a form ready for sale (there may be partially complete inventory in a manufacturing firm, for example) and because a sales commission and other selling costs must often be incurred in ordinary sales transactions, net realizable value is defined as the estimated final selling price of the inventory less any estimated costs necessary to make the item ready for sale and to sell it. To take several examples, agricultural products and precious metals on hand at the close of an accounting period are often stated at net realizable value. It may be easier to estimate a market price less selling costs than it is to determine the historical cost of a bushel of apples that has been harvested from an orchard.

## Lower-of-Cost-or-Market Basis

The lower-of-cost-or-market valuation basis 9.31 is the lesser of the two amounts: acquisition cost or "market value." Market value is generally replacement cost, but its definition in this context is somewhat more complex, as discussed below.

9.32 A decline of $5,000 in the market value of inventory might be recognized with the following entry:

Loss from Decline in Value of Inventory . 5,000
    Inventory ...................... 5,000

The credit is made directly to the Inventory account, not to a contra account as is done for marketable securities (and explained in Chapter 6), because subsequent recoveries in market value are not generally recorded as gains. When a periodic inventory system is used, the above entry is not recorded explicitly, but the loss is reflected in a higher cost of goods sold. Consider, for example, the following periodic calculation of cost of goods sold when beginning inventory is $12,000, purchases are $100,000, and ending inventory has a cost of $15,000 but a market value of $10,000.

|  | Cost Basis | Lower-of-Cost-or-Market Basis |
|---|---|---|
| Beginning Inventory .. | $ 12,000 | $ 12,000 |
| Purchases ... | 100,000 | 100,000 |
| Goods Available for Sale ....... | $112,000 | $112,000 |
| Less: Ending Inventory .. | (15,000) | (10,000) |
| Cost of Goods Sold ...... | $ 97,000 | $102,000 |

Note that cost of goods sold is $5,000 larger under the lower-of-cost-or-market basis than under the acquisition cost basis. The loss of $5,000 does not appear separately, but income is $5,000 smaller than when the acquisition cost basis is used. If the amount of the writedown to market is so large that the reader of the statements will be misled without separate disclosure of the decline in market value, then the writedown should be explicitly reported in the income statement. The writedown can be shown as an adjustment to cost of goods sold or as a loss, sep-arately reported as part of operating activities.

Generally accepted accounting principles justify the need for the lower-of-cost-or-market valuation basis as follows:*   9.33

A departure from the cost basis of pricing the inventory is required when the utility of the goods is no longer as great as its cost. Where there is evidence that the utility of goods, in their disposal in the ordinary course of business, will be less than cost, whether due to physical deterioration, obsolescence, changes in price levels, or other causes, the difference should be recognized as a loss of the current period. This is generally accomplished by stating such goods at a lower level commonly designated as market.

The lower-of-cost-or-market basis for inventory valuation is thought to be a "conservative" policy because **(1)** losses from decreases in market value are recognized before goods are sold, but gains from increases in market value are never recorded before a sale takes place and **(2)** inventory figures on the balance sheet are never greater, but may be less, than acquisition cost. That is, *holding losses* are reported currently, whereas *holding gains* are not reported until the goods are sold.   9.34

An examination of the effects of using the lower-of-cost-or-market basis over a series of accounting periods shows why the "conservatism" argument is questionable. Over long enough time periods, income equals cash in less cash out. For any one unit, there is only one total gain or loss figure—the difference between its selling price and its acquisition cost; the valuation rule merely determines how this amount of gain or loss is to be spread over the accounting periods between acquisition and final disposition. When the lower-of-cost-or-market basis is used, the net income of the present period may be "conservatively" lower than if the acquisition cost basis were used, but if so, the net income of a later period, when the unit is sold, will be "unconservatively" higher.   9.35

_____

*Accounting Research Bulletin No. 43, AICPA (1953), chap. 4, statement 5.

9.36 **Applying the Lower-of-Cost-or-Market Inventory Basis** Implementing the lower-of-cost-or-market basis for inventory valuation is more complicated than its name implies.* Acquisition cost and market value for each item must be found.

9.37 Lower of cost or market rests on an assumed relationship between a company's selling prices and its replacement costs. Usually a relationship does exist, and a decline in replacement costs will be followed by a decline in selling prices. A decline in replacement costs, therefore, is accepted as tentative evidence of a loss in the utility of inventory.

9.38 *Market* usually means replacement cost in the market in which a company buys, but there may be exceptions to this meaning when the assumed relationship between selling prices and replacement costs does not exist. For example, selling prices may decline relatively less than a decline in replacement costs, or selling prices may decline more sharply than replacement costs. To meet these situations, there are two exceptions to the usual meaning of market as current replacement cost.†

9.39 The first exception is that market should not exceed net realizable value. This establishes an upper limit on the amount carried forward in inventory. *Net realizable value* is defined as *estimated selling price in the ordinary course of business less reasonably predictable costs of completion and disposal.* Because of the effect of style changes on probable selling prices, obsolescence while in storage, or other factors, the future utility of some goods in inventory may not be appropriately measured by either original cost or current replacement cost. For example, assume that a manufacturer's inventory contains 500 items produced at a cost of $34 each. The manufacturer states that recent reductions in material prices would cut production cost to approximately $32 per unit. However, net realizable value is only $25 per unit because a competitor has just

introduced a new competing product selling at a much lower price. These goods would be written down to $25 per unit, their estimated net realizable value. The resulting inventory value would then be called *market*. Note that in this case anticipated prices in the market in which a company sells, not replacement costs in the market in which it buys, are used in applying the lower-of-cost-or-market rule.

9.40 The second exception is that market should not be less than net realizable value reduced by an allowance for an approximately normal profit margin.** This establishes a lower limit on the amount carried forward in inventory. This exception would apply when a reduction in replacement costs is expected to have only limited effect, or no effect, on selling prices. For example, assume that goods which cost $60 to buy or produce can now be replaced for $50. Assume also that the original selling price of $100 for these goods will still be realized. The incurred cost of $60, not the current replacement cost of $50, is properly carried forward in inventory because the utility of the goods has not been impaired by the reduction in current replacement cost. If it is believed these items will be sold at $95 and not at their original price of $100, a writedown of inventory from $60 to $55 is appropriate to provide for a "normal profit margin" of $40 when the goods are sold. Although the actual current market price is $50, the reduced inventory value of $55 would be termed market under lower of cost or market. In this second exception to the general rule that market means replacement cost, anticipated prices in the market in which a company sells are used in applying lower of cost or market.

9.41 When goods are written down below cost

---

*The methods described next are taken from *ARB No. 43,* chap. 4, statement 6.

†Professor Leonard E. Morrissey first brought the following explanations to our attention.

**Although the accounting pronouncements do not define "normal profit margin," there is nothing mysterious about the concept. Most businesses usually establish a selling price that has a relatively constant ratio to cost for similar kinds of goods. The percentage by which selling price generally exceeds cost is used to compute the normal profit margin. See the discussion in paragraph 10.24 of Chapter 10 on the foundations of the gross margin and retail inventory methods for more on this point and some examples.

Exhibit 9.2
**Lower of Cost or Market Illustrated
for Four Items
Normal Profit Is $9 per Unit**

| | Item 1 | Item 2 | Item 3 | Item 4 |
|---|---|---|---|---|
| **Calculation of Market Value** | | | | |
| (a) Replacement Cost | $92 | $96 | $92 | $85 |
| (b) Net Realizable Value | 95 | 95 | 95 | 95 |
| (c) Net Realizable Value Less Normal Profit Margin [= (b) − $9] | 86 | 86 | 86 | 86 |
| (d) Market = Midvalue [ (a), (b), (c)] | 92 | 95 | 92 | 86 |
| **Calculation of Lower of Cost or Market** | | | | |
| (e) Acquisition Cost | 90 | 97 | 96 | 90 |
| (f) Market [= (d)] | 92 | 95 | 92 | 86 |
| (g) Lower of Cost or Market = Minimum [(e), (f)] | 90 | 95 | 92 | 86 |

to market, this reduced amount is considered as cost in later fiscal periods. Thus, in subsequent inventories, any of these goods still on hand are not adjusted upward to their original cost even though market returns to the level from which the goods were written down.

9.42    Thus, the market value of an item used in the computation cannot exceed its net realizable value. Also, the market value of an item used in the computation cannot be *less than the net realizable value minus the normal profit* ordinarily realized on disposition of completed items of the type. The two exceptions to defining market value as replacement cost result in "market" being defined as the middle value (second largest or second smallest) of these three amounts: replacement cost, net realizable value, and net realizable value less a normal profit margin.

9.43    These results can be summarized by noting that

$$\text{Market Value} = \begin{array}{l}\text{Midvalue of (Replacement} \\ \text{Cost, Net Realizable Value,} \\ \text{Net Realizable Value Less} \\ \text{Normal Profit Margin).}\end{array}$$

$$\begin{array}{l}\text{Lower-of-Cost-or-} \\ \text{Market Valuation}\end{array} = \begin{array}{l}\text{Minimum (Acquisition Cost,} \\ \text{Market Value).}\end{array}$$

Exhibit 9.2 illustrates the calculation of the lower of cost or market valuation for four items. Notice that each of the four possible outcomes occurs once in computing lower of cost or market. Item 1 uses acquisition cost; item 2 uses net realizable value; item 3 uses replacement cost; and item 4 uses net realizable value less normal profit.

Another complication in using lower of cost or market is that the valuation can be applied to individual items, to classes of items, or to the entire inventory. If the valuations differ, the lowest inventory valuation will result from applying the rule item by item, and the highest from applying the rule to the entire inventory. Generally accepted accounting principles allow any of the three methods. (Contrast this with use of the lower-of-cost-or-market basis for marketable securities, where it must be applied to the entire portfolio. See Chapter 6.) Income tax regulations require that if lower of cost or market is used, then it must be applied on an item-by-item basis for tax reporting. Here, accounting for tax purposes need not be the same as for financial reporting. Exhibit 9.3 illustrates how the valuations differ as the rule is applied to items, to classes, and to the entire inventory.

9.44

**Summary** The lower-of-cost-or-market valuation basis has received wide acceptance in principle, but its practical use is probably less than the attention that it has received. The use of the lower-of-cost-or-market basis requires the calculation of both acquisition cost and "market" information for all items

9.45

*Exhibit 9.3*
**Illustration of
Lower-of-Cost-or-Market Basis
Applied to Units, to Classes,
and to the Entire Inventory**

| | | | | | | | Lower of Cost or Market Applied | | |
| | Per Unit | | | For All Units | | Item by Item | To Inventory Classes | To Total Inventory |
| Item | Quantity | Cost | Market[a] | Cost | Market[a] | | | |
| --- | --- | --- | --- | --- | --- | --- | --- | --- |
| Class I | | | | | | | | |
| A ........ | 20 | $ 20 | $ 18 | $ 400 | $ 360 | $ 360 | | |
| B ........ | 25 | 100 | 110 | 2,500 | 2,750 | 2,500 | | |
| Class Total ............... | | | | $2,900 | $3,100 | | $2,900 | |
| Class II | | | | | | | | |
| C ........ | 80 | $ 6 | $ 5 | $ 480 | $ 400 | 400 | | |
| D ........ | 60 | 12 | 10 | 720 | 600 | 600 | | |
| Class Total ............... | | | | $1,200 | $1,000 | | 1,000 | |
| Grand Total ............... | | | | $4,100 | $4,100 | | | |
| Ending Inventory at Lower of Cost or Market .......... | | | | | | $3,860 | $3,900 | $4,100 |

[a]Compiled as in Exhibit 9.2.

in inventory. It is difficult to gather the necessary information on replacement cost, net realizable values, and normal profit margins for each of the many items in an inventory. It is also difficult to calculate the market value of work in process and finished goods on the basis of present material prices, present labor rates, and present prices for each of the other costs of production operation. We think that the basis is often not used because of immateriality coupled with large record keeping costs. It is almost certainly used for valuable items and for other items where the decrease in price has been significant.

## Standard Costs

9.46    Standard cost is a predetermined estimate of what items of manufactured inventory *should* cost. Studies of past and estimated future cost data provide the basis for standard costs. Standard cost systems are frequently used by manufacturing firms for internal performance measurement and control. These are discussed in managerial and cost accounting texts. Standard cost is also used occasionally as the valuation basis for preparing financial statements when stan-

dard cost does not materially differ from actual cost. Units in inventory may be valued at standard cost, especially in the preparation of monthly or quarterly statements. If so, any excess of actual cost over standard cost (called an *unfavorable variance*) is usually debited to cost of goods sold or to other expenses of the period. If actual cost is less than standard cost, the favorable variance is usually credited to cost of goods sold.

## Generally Accepted Accounting Basis for Inventory Valuation

Generally, accounting uses a historical cost basis. Because the "market value" of inventory items can be significantly less than acquisition cost, either because of price changes for this kind of inventory generally or because of physical deterioration of the particular items in an inventory, generally accepted accounting principles require* the use of lower of cost or market. This is the same thing as saying that "market values" must be used in some cases. Computing market value requires both replacement cost

9.47

---

*ARB No. 43*, chap. 4, statements 5 and 6.

and net realizable value amounts. Thus, generally accepted accounting principles for inventory valuation and measurement of cost of goods sold require a combination of three valuation bases: acquisition cost, replacement cost, and net realizable value.

9.48 The FASB requires disclosure by large firms of the current cost of beginning inventory, ending inventory, and cost of goods sold in notes to the financial statements,* even though the financial statements are based on lower-of-cost-or-market values.

## Acquisition of Inventory

### Purchased Inventories

9.49 All costs incurred in connection with acquiring goods and preparing them for sale should enter into the acquisition cost valuation of the goods. For a merchandising firm, such costs should include purchasing, transportation, receiving, unpacking, inspecting, and shelving costs as well as that portion of bookkeeping and office costs that relate to the recording of purchases.

9.50 Because the amounts involved are often relatively small, and because it is difficult to assign a definite dollar amount for many of these costs to specific purchases, the tendency in practice is to restrict the actual additions to a few significant items that can easily be identified with particular goods, such as transportation costs. The costs of operating a purchasing department, the salaries and expenses of buyers, the costs of the receiving and warehousing departments, and the costs of handling and shelving are usually treated as expenses of the period in which they are incurred, although they are logically part of the total cost of merchandise made ready for sale.

9.51 **The Purchase Transaction** The procedures for recording purchases of merchandise, raw materials, and supplies vary a great deal from one business to another. Purchase

---

*Financial Accounting Standards Board, *Statement of Financial Accounting Standards No. 33* (1979).

transactions culminate when the goods are received and inspected and the purchase is entered into the records. From the legal point of view, purchases should be recorded in the formal accounting records when title to the goods passes. The question of when title passes is often a technical, legal matter, and the precise answer depends on a consideration of all of the circumstances of the transaction. As a convenience, the accountant usually recognizes purchases only after both the invoice and the goods are received and inspected. Adjustments may be made at the end of the accounting period to reflect the legal formalities for goods in transit that belong to the purchaser.

**Merchandise Purchases Account** During 9.52 the accounting period, acquisitions of merchandise can be debited either to the appropriate inventory account, such as Merchandise Inventory, or to a Merchandise Purchases account. (The shorter title Purchases is used in practice, but the full title is used here to avoid ambiguity.) The Merchandise Purchases account is a temporary, asset adjunct account. That is, the balance in Merchandise Purchases is closed at the end of each accounting period to the appropriate inventory account and does not appear in the balance sheet. The typical entry to record a specific purchase of merchandise is

Merchandise Purchases ............. 350
    Accounts Payable (or Cash) ........ 350
To record purchase of merchandise.

At the end of the period, the closing entry, assuming that merchandise costing $1,675 was purchased during the period, is

Merchandise Inventory .............. 1,675
    Merchandise Purchases .......... 1,675
To close purchases account to the inventory account.

The special account to record purchases is used to give more complete information about purchase transactions during the period than is provided when all purchases are debited directly to the Merchandise (or Raw Materials) Inventory accounts.

## Merchandise Purchases Adjustments

9.53 The invoice price of goods purchased will seldom measure the total acquisition cost correctly. Additional costs may be incurred in transporting and handling the goods, and deductions may be required for cash discounts, goods returned, and other allowances or adjustments of the invoice price. All of these adjustments could be handled through the one Merchandise Purchases account. Frequently, however, a number of contra and adjunct accounts are used for these adjustments so that a more complete analysis of the cost of purchases is available. Purchase Discounts, Freight-in, Purchase Returns, and Purchase Allowances are used to provide the needed detail. The accounting for purchase adjustments closely (but not exactly) parallels the accounting for sales adjustments discussed in Chapter 7.

## Merchandise Purchases Discounts

9.54 The largest adjustment to the invoice price of merchandise purchases is likely to be that for purchase discounts. Sellers often offer a discount from the invoice price for prompt payment. For example, the terms of sale "2/10, net/30" mean that a 2-percent discount from invoice price is offered if payment is made within 10 days and the full invoice price is due in any case within 30 days.* The amount of discounts taken during a period is sometimes shown as a special or "other" revenue item on the income statement. Some supporters of this treatment argue (incorrectly, we think) that the discounts represent interest earned on cash and so should be viewed as a revenue item.

9.55 A more appropriate interpretation, however, is to treat purchase discounts as a reduction in the purchase price. Purchases have a cash price, and if payment is delayed there is an additional charge for the right to delay payment and for the other additional services the seller is compelled to render. To view purchase discounts as revenue to the purchaser would indicate that revenue may be earned simply by buying goods and paying for them with cash within a specified time even though the goods have not been sold to others. It seems more reasonable to treat discounts as a reduction in the cost of merchandise purchased and thereby to defer their effect on net income until the goods have been sold.

9.56 Some accountants who recognize the logic of treating purchase discounts as a reduction in price nevertheless suggest that purchase discounts should be treated as "other" revenue for reasons of expediency. These accountants would treat discounts on major purchases, such as equipment, as reductions in the purchase price. They would not, however, deduct purchase discounts from the gross price of merchandise when the amounts involved are too small to justify the additional record-keeping effort. There is merit in the view that precision in accounting may cost more than the benefits received from greater accuracy. Whenever the amounts involved are not material or significant, the most convenient, rather than the logically correct, procedure may be satisfactory because the effects on net income are approximately the same.

9.57 Purchase discounts are often a material item; for some firms, the total of purchase discounts has been greater than net income. In this day of inexpensive computing, there should be little inconvenience or extra cost incurred in treating purchase discounts as a reduction in purchase price rather than as "other" revenue.

## Recording Purchase Discounts

9.58 Two alternatives for treating discounts on merchandise purchases are often used in practice: (1) Recognize the amount of discounts taken on payments made during the period, without regard to the period of purchase (gross price method); or (2) deduct all discounts made available from the gross pur-

---

*Question **QB.6** at the end of Appendix B attempts to help you understand that the interest rate implied in these terms of sales is about *45 percent per year*. That is, a purchaser who does not take such a discount is borrowing money at an interest rate of about 45 percent per year. Most purchasers find it advantageous to take such discounts and to borrow elsewhere at lower rates.

Exhibit 9.4
**Gross Price Method**

| | (1) Discount Taken | (2) Discount Not Taken |
|---|---|---|
| Purchases ..................... | 1,000 | 1,000 |
| Accounts Payable .......... | 1,000 | 1,000 |
| To record purchase. | | |
| Accounts Payable ............... | 1,000 | 1,000 |
| Cash ..................... | 980 | 1,000 |
| Purchase Discounts Taken ... | 20 | — |
| To record payment. | | |

Exhibit 9.5
**Net Price Method**

| | (1) Discount Taken | (2) Discount Not Taken |
|---|---|---|
| Purchases ..................... | 980 | 980 |
| Accounts Payable .......... | 980 | 980 |
| To record purchase. | | |
| Accounts Payable ............... | 980 | 980 |
| Purchase Discounts Lost ......... | — | 20 |
| Cash ..................... | 980 | 1,000 |
| To record payment. | | |

chase invoice prices at the time of purchase (net price method).

9.59   **Alternative 1: Gross Price Method** The gross price method of accounting for purchases records invoices at the gross price and accumulates the amount of discounts taken on payments made. Suppose that goods with a gross invoice price of $1,000 are purchased, 2/10, net/30. The entries to record the purchase and the payment (1) under the assumption that the payment is made in time to take the discount, and (2) under the assumption that the payment is too late to take advantage of the discount, are shown in Exhibit 9.4.

9.60   The balance in the Purchase Discounts Taken account is deducted from the balance in the Purchases account in calculating net purchases for a period. Such a deduction merely approximates the results achieved by treating purchase discounts as a reduction in purchase price at the time of purchase. It is only an approximation because the total adjustment includes discounts taken on payments made this period, without regard to the period of purchase.

9.61   An accurate adjustment would require eliminating the discounts taken related to purchases of previous periods while including the amount of discounts available at the end of the accounting period that are expected to be taken during the following period. This refinement in the treatment of purchase discounts, which follows a procedure analogous to the *allowance method* for cash

discounts discussed in Chapter 7, is seldom employed in practice.

9.62   **Alternative 2: Net Price Method** In recording purchases, the purchase discount is deducted from the gross purchase price immediately upon receipt of the invoice, and the net invoice price is used in the entries. The example used previously of a $1,000 invoice price for goods subject to a 2-percent cash discount would be recorded under the net price method as shown in Exhibit 9.5. Accounts remaining unpaid at the end of an accounting period on which the discount period has lapsed should be adjusted to their gross price amount by debiting Purchase Discounts Lost, and crediting Accounts Payable. The balance in the Purchase Discounts Lost account could be added to the cost of the merchandise purchased and, therefore, viewed as an additional component of goods available for sale. We believe, however, that discounts lost should be shown as a financial or general operating expense rather than as an addition to the cost of purchases, because lost discounts may indicate an inefficient office force or inadequate financing.* In this text, we treat purchase discounts lost as an expense unless an explicit contrary statement is made.

---

*Note that purchase discounts lost are treated as part of the cost of inventory under the gross price method, but as a financial or operating expense under the net price method. Information on discounts lost is not available under the gross price method.

## Other Purchase Adjustments

9.63    Several other adjustments to the cost of inventory merit discussion. These include freight, returns, allowances, and problems caused by goods in transit and consignment arrangements.

9.64    **Freight-in on Purchases** Transportation costs for purchased inventories are often material in amount, and management wishes separate reports on such costs. Consequently, these amounts are often accumulated in a separate account, Freight-in or Transportation on Purchases, which is an adjunct to the Purchases account. The entry to record $780 for shipping costs on merchandise or raw materials could be

Freight-in . . . . . . . . . . . . . . . . . . . . . . . . . . . . 780
   Accounts Payable  . . . . . . . . . . . . . . . . .     780

The Freight-in account is closed at the same time as the Purchases account to the Inventory account. When a separate Freight-in account is not used, freight costs are debited to Purchases or to Inventory.

9.65    **Purchase Returns** When goods are returned to the supplier, the purchaser requests a credit from the seller that can be applied against any unpaid bills or against future purchases. As long as the amount of the credit can be ascertained at the time of the return, efficient procedure records the return as soon as it is made as follows:

Accounts Payable (name of seller)  . . . . 3,450
   Purchase Returns (or Inventory) . . .      3,450

The credit is to an account contra to Purchases, called Purchase Returns. This account is used only when a Purchases account is used and is closed to Inventory at the same time the Purchases account is closed.

9.66    **Purchase Allowances** Occasionally, the seller ships faulty goods. On discovery of this fact, the purchaser does not always return the goods actually received. Instead, the purchaser negotiates with the seller a reduction in the purchase price from the amount originally agreed upon. Such a reduction is called a purchase *allowance*. If the amounts of allowances are material in a given business, these amounts can be accumulated in a separate account, contra to the Purchase account. Otherwise, the amounts are credited directly to Inventory. If, for example, goods with a net price of $13,500 are found to be defective and a reduced price of $11,750 is negotiated, the entries would be

Purchases (or Inventory)  . . . . . . . . . . . 13,500
   Accounts Payable (to seller)  . . . .          13,500
To record initial purchase and receipt
of goods.

Accounts Payable (to seller)  . . . . . . . .  1,750
   Purchase Allowances (or
      Inventory)  . . . . . . . . . . . . . . . . . .          1,750
To record reduction in agreed price to
$11,750.

The Purchase Allowances account is used only when a Purchases account is used. As such, the Purchase Allowances account is contra to an adjunct account; it is a "contra adjunct" account.

**Goods in Transit** The accountant usually    9.67
treats goods as being in the purchaser's inventory when they are in the purchaser's possession. Technically, however, goods should be counted in the purchaser's inventory only when legal title passes from the seller to the purchaser. When a balance sheet is prepared for a given time, the auditor must be careful to include only goods for which title has passed. Sometimes title to goods has passed even though the goods have not been received by the purchaser. Under other arrangements, goods physically in the purchaser's possession may not be included in the purchaser's inventory because the purchase agreement states that title passes only when the goods have been judged satisfactory by the purchaser.

Nearly all business arrangements for the    9.68
purchase of inventory specify an F.O.B. (free-on-board) point at which title passes from seller to purchaser. Goods might be purchased, for example, F.O.B. the purchaser's warehouse or F.O.B. the seller's shipping department or F.O.B. the time when the seller delivers the goods to the carrier. At the time the goods reach the F.O.B.

point, legal title passes. Once goods pass the F.O.B. point, the costs of insurance and the risks of loss belong to the purchaser. Customarily, whether the buyer or the seller pays the shipping charges is related to the F.O.B. point (for example, the buyer pays shipping charges when the F.O.B. point is the shipping point).

9.69    **Purchase Commitments When Market Declines below Cost** Businesses often find it useful to order goods well in advance of expected delivery and to agree to a price for those goods. This can lead to another departure from the cost basis to lower of cost or market. Because prices do not always change uniformly over time, businesses occasionally find themselves "locked in" to purchase commitments at prices higher than current prices. The generally accepted accounting principle of conservatism requires the firm to record the loss on purchase commitments when market prices decline substantially below a contracted price.* For example, suppose that a firm contracts to buy timber for delivery next year for $600,000. So long as the price for that amount of timber remains at $600,000 or more, no accounting recognition of the event is made, although footnote disclosure is appropriate if the market price rises substantially above $600,000. If, on the other hand, the market price of that timber declines, say, to $500,000, the firm records the loss as follows:

| | | |
|---|---:|---:|
| Loss on Purchase Commitments | 100,000 | |
| Estimated Liability for Purchase Costs in Excess of Market Value | | 100,000 |
| To record loss on purchase commitments. | | |

The Loss account appears on the income statement for the period and is closed to Retained Earnings. When the items are delivered, the following entry is made:

| | | |
|---|---:|---:|
| Inventory | 500,000 | |
| Estimated Liability for Purchase Costs in Excess of Market Value | 100,000 | |
| Accounts Payable | | 600,000 |

_____
*Accounting Research Bulletin No. 43, AICPA (1953), chap. 4, statement 10.

The inventory is recorded at an amount below cost. The amount is the same as would have been recorded if the loss on purchase commitment had not been recorded, but the inventory had been entered on the books for $600,000 and the amount written down to $500,000 on the lower-of-cost-or-market basis.

Chapter 16 treats some of the details of accounting for the Estimated Liability account.    9.70

**Consignment Arrangements** Under a consignment arrangement, a manufacturer or distributor (called the "consignor") places goods in the hands of a seller, such as a retail store (called the "consignee"), who attempts to sell the goods to third parties, such as consumers. Legally, the goods remain the property of the consignor until they are sold to a consumer. Then, the consignee collects the equivalent of a sales commission and pays the remainder of the sales proceeds to the consignor.    9.71

Chapter 7 pointed out that goods on consignment are inventory of the consignor, not of the consignee. The amounts shown by the consignor include, of course, freight, insurance, and other costs incurred to place the goods on the premises of the consignee.†    9.72

_____
†Sometimes goods are consigned by a manufacturer merely as a form of collateral or protection for a credit agreement. Generally, a manufacturer does not have the specific right to have the goods returned. In the case of bankruptcy without a consignment arrangement, the manufacturer becomes one of the unsecured creditors of the retailer. The manufacturer can "sell" to a retailer with a consignment agreement being used to safeguard the position of the seller, who can then recover the specific goods in case the retailer is unable to pay. The purchaser informally agrees to pay for the goods within a specified period of time, even though the goods have not been sold to a consumer. The consignment provides better protection to the manufacturer. Under these conditions, subject to the usual accounting treatment for expected uncollectibles, it would be proper for the manufacturer to count the goods as sold when they are delivered to the retailer and to exclude the goods from the manufacturer's inventory. The goods should appear in the retailer's inventory accounts.

*Exhibit 9.6*
**Flow of Manufacturing Costs through the Accounts**

**Balance Sheet**

**Income Statement**

**Raw Materials Inventory**

| Cost of Raw Materials Purchased | Cost of Raw Materials Used in Manufacturing → |
|---|---|

**Cash or Wages Payable**

| | Direct Labor Costs Incurred in Manufacturing → |
|---|---|

**Cash, Accumulated Depreciation, Other Accounts**

| | Overhead Costs Incurred in Manufacturing → |
|---|---|

**Work-in-Process Inventory**

| → Cost of Raw Materials Used in Manufacturing | Manufacturing Cost of Units Completed and Transferred to Storeroom |
|---|---|
| → Direct Labor Costs Incurred in Manufacturing | |
| → Overhead Costs Incurred in Manufacturing | |

**Finished Goods Inventory**

| → Manufacturing Cost of Units Transferred from Factory | Manufacturing Cost of Units Sold → |
|---|---|

**Cost of Goods Sold**

| Manufacturing Cost of Units Sold | |
|---|---|

Exhibit 9.7
**Treatment of Various Costs
Incurred by a Manufacturing Firm**

| Cost Item | Product Cost (Asset) | Period Expense Selling | Period Expense Administrative |
|---|---|---|---|
| **I. Salaries** | | | |
| A. President of Company[a] | X | X | X |
| B. Vice-President for Sales | | X | |
| C. Vice-President for Manufacturing | X | | |
| D. Production Supervisor | X | | |
| E. Sales Staff | | X | |
| F. Accountant (General Office)[a] | X | X | X |
| **II. Materials and Supplies** | | | |
| A. Raw Materials Purchased for Future Productive Use | X | | |
| B. Raw Materials Used in the Factory | X | | |
| C. Sales Pamphlets Distributed | | X | |
| D. Data-Processing Supplies Used | | | X |
| E. Cleaning Supplies Used in Factory | X | | |
| **III. Other** | | | |
| A. Insurance on Factory Building | X | | |
| B. Insurance on Sales Staff's Automobiles | | X | |
| C. Insurance on Office Building | | | X |
| D. Depreciation on Factory Equipment | X | | |
| E. Depreciation on General Office Data-Processing Equipment | | | X |
| F. Maintenance of Sales Staff's Automobiles | | X | |

[a]Should in principle be allocated between product cost and period expense in proportion to time spent on these functions. In practice this allocation is seldom done because it is immaterial; the item is usually treated entirely as a period expense.

## Manufactured Inventories

9.73 Amounts for manufactured inventories include raw material costs and all other costs incurred in changing the physical form of the raw materials into finished goods. Manufactured inventories typically include three types of costs: (1) direct material, (2) direct labor, and (3) manufacturing overhead (sometimes called "indirect manufacturing costs"). Costs included in manufactured inventories are called *product costs,* in contrast to period expenses.

9.74 Exhibit 9.6 shows how product costs flow through the accounts. Exhibit 9.7 shows how various costs are classified as product costs or period expenses in a manufacturing firm.

9.75 Separate inventory accounts are used for items at various stages of completion. The Raw Materials Inventory account includes the cost of raw materials purchased but not yet transferred to production. The balance in the Raw Materials Inventory account indicates the cost of raw materials on hand in the raw materials storeroom or warehouse. When raw materials are issued to producing departments, the cost of the materials is transferred from the Raw Materials Inventory account to the Work-in-Process Inventory account. The Work-in-Process Inventory account accumulates the costs incurred in producing units during the period. The Work-in-Process Inventory account is debited for the cost of raw materials transferred from the raw materials storeroom, the cost of direct labor services used, and the manufacturing overhead costs incurred (for example, factory utilities, taxes, insurance, and depreciation). The Work-in-Process Inventory account is credited for the total manufacturing cost of units completed in the factory and transferred to the finished goods storeroom. The Finished Goods Inventory account includes the total manufacturing cost of units completed but not yet sold. At the time of sale, the cost of units sold is transferred from the Finished Goods Inventory account to the Cost of Goods Sold account.

## The Cost Inclusion Question: Absorption versus Direct Costing

9.76 A cost inclusion question arises with respect to fixed manufacturing costs. Costs such as direct materials, direct labor, supplies, and similar costs vary in total with the number of units produced. Other costs, such as property taxes, insurance, and depreciation, tend to be fixed for a period regardless of the number of units produced. Two viewpoints exist as to the treatment of fixed manufacturing costs.

9.77 **Absorption Costing** One viewpoint, referred to as *absorption costing,* holds that both variable and fixed manufacturing costs should be treated as product costs. Fixed manufacturing costs generally provide a firm with a capacity to produce during a period, and variable manufacturing costs are incurred to carry out the actual production during the period. To manufacture products requires both kinds of cost incurrence, and both should be included in product costs.

9.78 **Direct Costing** The other viewpoint, referred to as *variable,* or *direct, costing* holds that only variable manufacturing costs should be treated as product costs. Fixed manufacturing costs should be treated as expenses of the period in which the costs are incurred.

9.79 A strong case can be made for variable, or direct, costing on theoretical grounds. One accounting principle is that of matching revenues and expenses. An expense is an expired asset, a "gone asset." The matching principle requires that asset expirations be recorded as expenses in the same period as the revenue generated by the asset is recognized.

9.80 Why is the salary of a sales manager (or depreciation on a store building) treated in total as a period expense rather than being allocated to individual sales as they occur? Once the firm decides to be, and to remain, in a line of business, it will need a sales manager (and a store). The sales manager's salary will have to be paid month after month. Paying the sales manager's salary this month does not remove the need to pay it next month. Depreciating the store building this month does not preclude depreciation next month. There will be no reduction in next month's costs as a result of incurring the cost for the sales manager or store depreciation this month. Thus, paying the salary or charging depreciation this month does not provide a future benefit. Costs that will have to be incurred next period are not reduced because of costs incurred this period. Such costs are sometimes called *unavoidable.*

9.81 If the salary of the sales manager were not treated as an expense, an expired asset, then it would have to be treated as an asset. An asset is a future benefit. The sales manager's salary is not generally thought to provide a future benefit. Almost all of the benefit occurs during the current month when the manager is working on this month's sales. Thus, virtually all accountants agree that the cost represented by the sales manager's salary is an expense of the period incurred. It does not provide a future benefit, and therefore cannot be an asset. It is an expired asset or expense. The same is true of depreciation on the store building.

9.82 Similarly, fixed manufacturing costs are unavoidable. They provide the capacity to produce this period and are not saved if for some reason, such as a shut-down of the production line, no product is manufactured. Consider the rent on a factory. A company is obligated to pay that rent whether or not its factory is used to produce anything. Factory rent is a cost of being a going concern. On the other hand, when raw materials are put into production today, the need to use other raw materials later for the same product is avoided. Raw materials costs are avoidable because incurring those costs now precludes incurring them later. As such, raw materials are properly a product cost.

9.83 Under absorption costing, unavoidable costs such as factory rent are part of the cost of inventory produced. If rent for the month is $5,000 and 1,000 parts are produced, then each part will carry $5 (= $5,000/1,000 units) of costs for rent; but if 2,000 units are produced, then each part will probably carry $2.50 (= $5,000/2,000 units) of costs for rent. Under absorption costing, we have the puzzling phenomenon that the cost of each unit produced can depend on the total number of units produced. If management wants to know what is happening to costs of units produced in the short run, it will probably prefer to know the incremental costs of production—direct labor, direct materials, and variable overhead. In direct costing, only the variable costs of production are included as product costs. All fixed costs are treated as period expenses.

9.84 All costs are variable if the time horizon is long enough. Leases need not be renewed, salaried workers can be fired or not replaced as they retire, equipment need not be replaced, and so on. But management is concerned with assessing performance over shorter time horizons. Direct costing often provides information that is more useful to management in the short run.

9.85 The basic question asked of each cost incurred in direct costing is, "Does incurring this cost today (or this period) keep us from having to incur that cost tomorrow (or in the future)?" If the answer is *yes*, then the cost in question is an incremental cost and is included in product cost. If the answer is *no,* then direct costing treats the cost in question as an expense of the period. Because raw materials used today in producing a unit eliminate the need to use raw materials tomorrow for that unit, raw materials are incremental product costs under direct costing. But factory rent must be paid whether or not any product is made, so direct costing treats factory rent as a period expense rather than as a product cost. Many factory overhead costs—salaries of factory supervisors and guards, depreciation, and property taxes, for example —will not be less next period for having been incurred this period. These costs are therefore period expenses in direct costing.

**Generally Accepted Accounting Principles** Although we believe that direct costing is theoretically preferable and provides better measures of operating performance, only absorption costing is permitted by generally accepted accounting principles and by the Internal Revenue Service. All references to inventory valuation in Chapters 9 and 10 are therefore based on absorption costing.

9.86

## Cost-Flow Assumptions

### Specific Identification and the Need for a Cost-Flow Assumption

If the individual units of an item can be physically identified as coming from a specific purchase, then there is no special problem in ascertaining the acquisition cost of the units withdrawn from inventory and the cost of the units still on hand. The cost can be marked on the unit or on its container, or the unit can be traced back to its purchase invoice or cost record. The inventory and cost of goods sold of an automobile dealer or of a dealer in fine diamonds or fur coats would probably be computed using specific identification of costs.

9.87

In most cases, however, new items are mixed with old units on shelves, in bins, or in other ways, and physical identification is impossible or impracticable. Moreover, it may be desirable (for reasons to be discussed in this section) to assume that cost flows differ from physical flows of goods.

9.88

The inventory *valuation* problem arises because there are *two* unknowns in the inventory equation:

9.89

| Beginning Inventory (known) | + | Net Purchases (known) | − | Cost of Goods Sold (unknown) | = | Ending Inventory. (unknown) |
|---|---|---|---|---|---|---|

The values of the beginning inventory and net purchases are known; the values of the cost of goods sold and of ending inventory are not known. The question is whether to value the units in ending inventory using the most recent costs, the oldest costs, the average cost, or some other alternative. Of course, the question could have been put in terms of valuing the cost of goods sold, for once we place a value on one unknown quantity, the inventory equation automatically determines the value of the other. The relation between the two unknowns, Cost of Goods Sold and Ending Inventory, in the inventory equation for historical costs is such that the higher the value assigned to one of them, the lower must be the value assigned to the other. Their sum must always equal the cost of goods available for use or sale.

9.90 When prices are changing, no historical cost-based accounting method for valuing both ending inventory and cost of goods sold allows the accountant to show current values on both the income statement and the balance sheet. For example, in a period of rising prices, if current, higher acquisition prices are used in measuring cost of goods sold shown on the income statement, then older, lower acquisition prices must be used in valuing the ending inventory shown on the balance sheet. As long as cost of goods sold and ending inventory are based on acquisition costs, financial statements can present current values in the income statement or the balance sheet, but not in both. Of course, combinations of current and out-of-date information can be shown in both statements.

9.91 If more than one purchase is made of the same item at different prices, and specific identification is not feasible or possible, then some assumption must be made as to the flow of costs in order to estimate the acquisition cost applicable to the units remaining in the inventory. One of three cost-flow assumptions is typically used for this purpose. These cost-flow assumptions are:

1. First-in, first-out (FIFO).
2. Last-in, first-out (LIFO).
3. Weighted average.

The demonstrations of each of these methods that follow are based on the toaster data introduced earlier in the chapter and repeated at the top of Exhibit 9.8. The example of the three toasters illustrates most of the important points about the cost-flow assumption required in accounting for inventories and cost of goods sold. Appendix 9.1 of this chapter presents a more computationally complex illustration, but it contains no new concepts.

## First-In, First-Out

9.92 The first-in, first-out cost-flow assumption, abbreviated FIFO, assigns the cost of the earliest units acquired to the withdrawals and the cost of the most recent acquisitions to the ending inventory. The cost flow assumes that the oldest materials and goods are used first. This cost-flow assumption conforms to good business practice in managing physical flows, especially in the case of items that deteriorate or become obsolete. Column (1) of Exhibit 9.8 illustrates FIFO. Toaster 1 is assumed to be sold, whereas toasters 2 and 3 are assumed to remain in inventory. The designation FIFO refers to the cost flow of units sold. A parallel description for ending inventory is last-in, still-here, or LISH.

## Last-In, First-Out

9.93 The last-in, first-out cost-flow assumption, abbreviated LIFO, assigns the cost of the latest units acquired to the withdrawals and the cost of the oldest units to the ending inventory. Some theorists argue that LIFO matches current costs to current revenues and therefore that LIFO better measures income. Column (3) of Exhibit 9.8 illustrates LIFO. The $30 cost of toaster 3 is assumed to leave, whereas the costs of toasters 1 and 2 are assumed to remain in inventory. The designation of LIFO refers to the cost flow for units sold. A parallel description for ending inventory is first-in, still-here, or FISH.

9.94 LIFO has attracted increasing attention since 1939 when it first became acceptable for income tax reporting. In a period of consistently rising prices, LIFO results in a higher cost of goods sold, a lower reported

*Exhibit 9.8*
**Comparison of Cost-Flow Assumptions**
**Historical Cost Basis**

### ASSUMED DATA

| | |
|---|---|
| Beginning Inventory: Toaster 1 Cost .................. | $25 |
| Purchases: Toaster 2 Cost ................. | 29 |
| Toaster 3 Cost ................. | 30 |
| Cost of Goods Available for Sale ..................... | $84 |
| Sales: One Toaster for ............................. | $55 |

### FINANCIAL STATEMENTS

| | Cost-Flow Assumption | | |
|---|---|---|---|
| | FIFO (1) | Weighted Average (2) | LIFO (3) |
| Sales ........................................................ | $55 | $55 | $55 |
| Cost of Goods Sold ......................................... | 25[a] | 28[b] | 30[c] |
| Gross Margin on Sales ..................................... | $30 | $27 | $25 |
| Ending Inventory ............................................ | $59[d] | $56[e] | $54[f] |
| Increase in Inventory for Period (= Ending Inventory − Beginning Inventory of $25) ................... | $34 | $31 | $29 |

[a]Toaster 1 cost $25.
[b]Average toaster costs $28 (= $84/3).
[c]Toaster 3 cost $30.
[d]Toasters 2 and 3 cost $29 + $30 = $59.
[e]2 Average toasters cost 2 × $28 = $56.
[f]Toasters 1 and 2 cost $25 + $29 = $54.

periodic income, and lower current income taxes than either FIFO or weighted-average cost-flow assumptions.

9.95 LIFO cannot usually be justified in terms of physical flows but is used because it produces a cost-of-goods-sold figure that is based on more up-to-date prices. In a period of rising prices, LIFO's higher (than FIFO's) cost-of-goods-sold figure reduces reported income and income taxes.

### Weighted Average

9.96 Under the weighted-average cost-flow assumption, the average of the costs of all goods available for sale (or use) during the month, including the cost applicable to the beginning inventory, must be calculated.*

---

*This description is technically correct only when a periodic inventory method is used. The appendix to this chapter describes the procedures for applying the weighted-average method in a perpetual inventory system.

The weighted-average cost is applied to the units on hand at the end of the month. Column (2) of Exhibit 9.8 illustrates the weighted-average cost-flow assumption. The weighted-average cost of toasters available for sale during the period is $28 [= $\frac{1}{3}$ × ($25 + $29 + $30)]. Cost of Goods Sold is thus $28 and ending inventory is $56 (= 2 × $28).

### Comparison of Cost-Flow Assumptions

9.97 FIFO results in balance sheet figures that are closest to current cost, because the latest purchases dominate the ending inventory valuation. The cost-of-goods-sold expense tends to be out of date, however, because it assumes that the earlier prices of the beginning inventory and the earliest purchases are charged to expense. When prices change, FIFO usually leads to the highest reported net income of the three methods when prices are rising and the smallest when prices are falling.

**Exhibit 9.9**
**Age of Information about Inventory Items**

| Cost-Flow Assumption | Income Statement | Balance Sheet | Inventory-on-Hand Assumption |
| --- | --- | --- | --- |
| FIFO ..................... | Old Prices | Current Prices ............. | LISH |
| LIFO ..................... | Current Prices | Very[a] Old Prices ........... | FISH |

[a]The oldest prices on the FIFO income statement are just over 1 year old in nearly all cases and the *average* price on the FIFO income statement (for a year) is slightly more than $1/2$ year old. The larger the rate of inventory turnover, the closer the average age on the income statement is to $1/2$ year. LIFO balance sheet items are generally much older than the FIFO income statement items, with some costs from the 1940s in many cases.

9.98    Because LIFO ending inventory contains costs of items acquired many years previously, LIFO produces balance sheet figures usually far removed from current costs. LIFO's cost-of-goods-sold figure closely approximates current costs. Exhibit 9.9 summarizes the differences between FIFO and LIFO. Of the cost-flow assumptions, LIFO usually implies the smallest net income when prices are rising (highest cost of goods sold), and the largest when prices are falling (lowest cost of goods sold). Also, LIFO results in the least fluctuation in reported income over the business cycle in businesses where selling prices tend to change as current prices of inventory items change.

9.99    The weighted-average cost-flow assumption falls between the other two in its effect both on the balance sheet and the income statement. It is, however, much more like FIFO than like LIFO in its effects on the financial statements. When inventory turns over rapidly, the weighted-average inventory values are almost as close to present prices as FIFO. Weighted averages reflect all of the prices during the period in proportion to the quantities purchased at those prices as well as beginning inventory costs carried over from the previous period.

## A Closer Look at LIFO

9.100    As we discussed above, LIFO usually presents a cost-of-goods-sold figure that is closely related to current costs. It also generally has the practical advantage of deferring income taxes.

9.101    In the last decade many firms, such as Du Pont, General Motors, Eastman Kodak, and Sears Roebuck, have switched from FIFO to LIFO. Given the rapid rate of price increases over the past decade, the switch from FIFO to LIFO has resulted in substantially lower cash payments for income taxes. For example, when Du Pont and General Motors switched from FIFO to LIFO, they each lowered current income taxes by about $150 million.*

9.102    LIFO usually leads, however, to a balance sheet figure for inventory so far removed from current values as possibly to delude and confuse readers of financial statements. For example, consider the current ratio (= current assets/current liabilities). The current ratio is often used by readers of financial statements to assess the liquidity of a company. If LIFO is used in periods of rising prices while inventory quantities are increasing, the amount of inventory included in the numerator will be much smaller than if the inventory were valued at current prices. Hence, the unwary reader may underestimate the liquidity of a company that uses a LIFO cost-flow assumption. Similarly, the calculation of inventory turnover (= cost of goods sold/average inventory during the period) can be drastically affected by using LIFO. When a company uses LIFO, the SEC requires that it disclose in notes the current value of beginning and ending inventory. These disclosures are illustrated in Appen-

*Thus, the apparent "paradox" in the introduction to this chapter is explained.

dix A at the back of the book for the International Corporation. See Note 9 in Appendix Exhibit A.4 and Exhibit 25.7.

9.103 A second criticism of LIFO relates to dipping into old LIFO layers. A major objective of using LIFO is to reduce current taxes in periods of rising prices and rising inventory quantities. Usually LIFO produces this result. If inventory quantities decline, however, the opposite effect can occur in the year of the decline, because older, lower costs per unit leave the balance sheet and are charged to expense.

9.104 For example, if under LIFO a firm must for some reason reduce end-of-period physical inventory quantities below what they were at the beginning of the period, then cost of goods sold will be based on the current period's purchases plus a portion of the older and lower costs in the beginning inventory. Such a firm will have larger reported income and income taxes in that period than if the firm had been able to maintain its ending inventory at beginning-of-period levels.

9.105 **Example** Assume that LIFO inventory at the beginning of 1981 consists of 46 units with a total cost of $342, as shown in Exhibit 9.10. Assume that the cost at the end of 1981

**Exhibit 9.10**
**Data for Illustration of LIFO Dips**

| **LIFO Layers** | | | |
|---|---|---|---|
| **Number of Units** | **Year Purchased** | **Cost per Unit** | **Total Cost** |
| 10 | 1977 | $ 5 | $ 50 |
| 11 | 1978 | 6 | 66 |
| 12 | 1979 | 8 | 96 |
| 13 | 1980 | 10 | 130 |
| 46 | | | $342 |

is $12 per unit. If 1981 ending inventory is more than 46 units, then the cost of goods sold will be roughly $12 per unit. If, however, the 1981 ending inventory drops to 10 units, then all the 36 units purchased in 1978 through 1980 will also enter cost of goods sold. These 36 units cost $292 (= $66 + $96 + $130), but the current cost of comparable units is $432 (= 36 units × $12 per unit).

Cost of goods sold will be $140 (= $432 − $292) smaller because of the "dip into old LIFO layers" of inventory. Income before taxes will be $140 larger than if inventory quantities had not declined from 46 to 10 units.

9.106 **Example** In reality, many LIFO firms have inventory layers built up since the 1940s, and the costs of the early units are often as little as 10 percent of the current cost. For these firms, a dip into old layers will substantially increase income. A footnote from a recent annual report of the U.S. Steel Corporation illustrates this phenomenon:

Because of the continuing high demand throughout the year, inventories of many steel-making materials and steel products were unavoidably reduced and could not be replaced during the year. Under the LIFO system of accounting, used for many years by U.S. Steel, the net effect of all the inventory changes [reductions] was to increase income for the year by about $16 million.

9.107 Finally, if matching physical flows with cost flows is considered important, then LIFO is unsatisfactory because it assumes an order of consumption that is not likely to conform to reality or to good business practice. Oldest materials are rarely sold or used last.

**LIFO's Effects on Purchasing Behavior** 9.108 Consider the quandary faced by a purchasing manager of a LIFO firm nearing the end of a year when the quantity sold for the year has exceeded the quantity purchased for the year. If the year ends with sales greater than purchases, the firm will dip into old LIFO layers and will have to pay increased taxes. Assume that the purchasing manager thinks current prices for the goods are abnormally high and prefers to delay purchasing until prices drop, presumably in the next period. Waiting implies, however, dips into old LIFO layers this period and higher taxes. Buying now may entail higher inventory and carrying costs. One disadvantage of LIFO is that it can induce behavior on the part of a firm attempting to manage its LIFO layers and cost of goods sold that would be unwise in the absence of tax effects. Some criticize

LIFO because it gives management the opportunity to manipulate income: Under LIFO, end-of-year purchases, which can be manipulated, affect net income for the year.

9.109    Others dislike LIFO because it eventually leads to balance sheet amounts that reflect very old purchase prices. Nevertheless, prices are likely to increase in the future rather than to decrease. Thus, most company managements will probably best serve their shareholders by using a LIFO cost-flow assumption in order to save income taxes.

## Income Tax Considerations

9.110    The differences between LIFO and FIFO cost-flow assumptions can lead to substantial differences in reported income. Similarly, the choices made on tax returns can lead to substantial differences in taxable income and, hence, in income tax payments. Other things being equal, the rational manager prefers lower taxes to higher taxes and would probably choose those accounting methods for tax purposes that minimize current taxes. Accounting choices for financial reporting and for tax returns can usually be made independently of one another, but generally not with respect to inventory-flow assumptions as discussed next.

9.111    **Conformity of Cost-Flow Assumptions** In only one major area in accounting has the Internal Revenue Service required firms to use the same method for financial reporting as for tax returns. When the LIFO flow assumption is elected for tax returns, the IRS requires that it must also be used in financial reports to owners. Once a firm has chosen to adopt LIFO for tax reporting, it must request permission from the IRS to change back to FIFO or weighted average, and may incur a tax liability if it does so. A 1981 court decision in the case of Insilco Corporation versus the IRS calls this so-called "LIFO conformity rule" of the IRS into question.*

---

*Insilco, the parent company, owns 100 percent of the shares of various subsidiaries which Insilco consolidates in reporting to Insilco shareholders. (See Chapter 14 for a discussion of consolidation.) Each subsid-

Moreover, certain members of Congress question the advisability of a conformity rule of this sort: there are no such comparable rules for the myriad other accounting principles where the firm can use one accounting method on the tax return and another in the financial statements (giving rise to timing differences, discussed in Chapter 20). Within the near future, the LIFO conformity rule may disappear, but at the time this book goes to press the IRS still enforces it, so the discussion, illustrations, and problems in this book assume it.

9.112    **Valuation Basis and Cost-Flow Assumption** The Internal Revenue Service does not permit the lower-of-cost-or-market valuation basis to be used with a LIFO cost-flow assumption. Consider the effect of allowing LIFO with lower of cost or market. When prices are rising, the LIFO cost-flow assumption results in a lower ending inventory amount and lower reported income than does FIFO. When prices are falling, the lower-of-LIFO-cost-or-market basis leads to an ending inventory amount approximately equal to that of the lower-of-FIFO-cost-or-market basis. The Internal Revenue Service is unwilling to allow a cost-flow assumption that, when compared to FIFO, results in lower taxable income when prices are rising and no higher taxable income when prices are falling. If LIFO coupled with the lower-of-cost-or-market basis were allowed, it would result in a guarantee of no worse tax position (falling prices) and the hope of a better tax position (rising prices) when compared to FIFO used with lower of cost or market. If a firm selects the LIFO cost-flow assumption for income tax purposes, there-

---

iary prepared its tax returns using LIFO and used LIFO in its financial statements reported to its single shareholder, the parent company Insilco. The parent company, however, used a FIFO cost flow assumption for the inventories of the subsidiaries in preparing consolidated financial statements which were sent to shareholders and other members of the investing public. Thus, claimed Insilco, it obeyed the law. While the IRS claimed that Insilco violated the intention of the law, the court agreed with Insilco. The IRS has indicated that it is awaiting another case (where all the issues are clearer than they apparently were in Insilco) before pressing the matter further.

9.113 fore, it must use the acquisition-cost basis of inventory valuation on its tax return.

Generally accepted accounting principles require the use of lower of cost or market when market is materially lower than cost, even when LIFO is used.

9.114 If a firm chooses the FIFO or average cost-flow assumption for income tax purposes, it can use either the acquisition cost or lower-of-acquisition-cost-or-market valuation basis on the tax return. These firms should select the lower-of-cost-or-market basis because it results in the immediate recognition of a loss whenever market prices at the end of the year are less than acquisition cost.

9.115 **Switching to LIFO** The preceding discussion of LIFO assumes that the firm has been using LIFO all along. The Internal Revenue Service rules for using LIFO tax reporting may require an adjusting entry when a firm switches to LIFO. Firms not using LIFO often use a lower-of-cost-or-market basis along with a FIFO or weighted-average cost flow assumption. The Internal Revenue Service does not allow LIFO to be used with a lower-of-cost-or-market basis for the reasons stated above. When a firm switches to LIFO, it must convert its beginning inventory valuations for the first LIFO period to a cost basis.

9.116 The cost of inventory at the beginning of the period is computed from recent invoices. This beginning inventory value is generally approximately the same as what it would be under FIFO cost-flow assumption. An entry is made, if necessary, to adjust the book value of inventory to the cost basis, at least for tax purposes. Assume that the cost of inventory based on the most recent purchase prices is $100,000 but that the book value of beginning inventory, formerly based on lower-of-cost-or-market (FIFO), is $80,000. The required entry is

| | | |
|---|---|---|
| Inventory | 20,000 | |
| Gain on Changing Inventory | | |
| Basis to Cost | | 20,000 |

To convert inventory to cost basis
from lower-of-cost-or-market basis.

The gain would be part of net income for the period of the LIFO switch but is shown separately in the income statement as "Cumulative Effect of Changes in Accounting Principles." See the discussion in Chapter 23.

9.117 Although most companies switch to LIFO to reduce reported income and to reduce taxes, switching to LIFO will result in higher taxable income in the year of the switch if the gain resulting from restating inventory to the cost basis from lower-of-cost-or-market more than offsets LIFO's higher cost of goods sold for the period of the switch.

## Identifying Operating Margin and Holding Gains

9.118 The reported net income under FIFO is generally larger than under LIFO during periods of rising prices. This higher reported net income is caused by the reporting of a larger *realized holding gain* under FIFO than under LIFO. The significance of holding gains in the calculation of net income under FIFO and LIFO is illustrated in this section. The conventionally reported gross margin (Sales − Cost of Goods Sold) can be split into (1) an operating margin and (2) a realized holding gain. In addition, there is usually an unrealized holding gain that is not currently included in income, but is disclosed in notes to the financial statements.

9.119 The difference between the selling price of an item and its replacement cost at the time of sale is called an *operating margin*. This operating margin gives some indication of the relative advantage that a particular firm has in the market for its goods, such as a reputation for quality or service. The difference between the current replacement cost of an item and its acquisition cost is called a *holding gain* (or *loss*). The holding gain (or loss) reflects the change in cost of an item during the period while the inventory item is held.

9.120 To illustrate the calculation of the operating margin and holding gain, consider the example of the toasters discussed in this chapter. The acquisition cost of the three items available for sale during the period is $84. Assume that one toaster is sold for $55. The replacement cost of the toaster at the time it was sold is assumed to be $32. The current replacement cost at the end of the month for each item in ending inventory is $35. The top portion of Exhibit 9.11 illustrates the separation of the conventionally reported gross margin into the operating margin and the realized holding gain.

9.121 The operating margin is the difference between the $55 selling price and the $32 replacement cost at the time of sale. The total operating margin of $23 is the same under both the FIFO and LIFO cost-flow assumptions. The *realized holding gain* is the difference between cost of goods sold based on replacement cost and cost of goods sold based on acquisition cost. The realized holding gain under FIFO is larger than under LIFO, because the earlier purchases at lower costs are charged to cost of goods sold under FIFO. This larger realized holding gain under FIFO is the principal reason why net income under FIFO is typically larger than under LIFO during periods of rising prices. In conventional financial statements,

the realized holding gain is *not* disclosed separately, as it is in Exhibit 9.11. Sometimes the realized holding gain on inventory is called *inventory profit*.

The calculation of an unrealized holding 9.122 gain on units in ending inventory is also shown in Exhibit 9.11. The *unrealized holding gain* is the difference between the current replacement cost of the ending inventory and its acquisition cost. When there is a beginning inventory containing an unrealized holding gain, the computation is slightly more complex; see Appendix 9.2 to this chapter for an illustration.) This unrealized holding gain on ending inventory is not reported in the income statement as presently prepared. The unrealized holding gain under LIFO is larger than under FIFO, because earlier purchases with lower costs are assumed to remain in ending inventory under LIFO. The sum of the operating margin plus all holding gains (both realized and unrealized) is the same under FIFO and LIFO. Most of the holding gain under FIFO is rec-

---

## Exhibit 9.11
### Reporting of Operating Margins and Holding Gains for Toasters Periodic Inventory Method

| | Cost-Flow Assumption | |
|---|---|---|
| | FIFO | LIFO |
| Sales Revenue | $55 | $55 |
| Less Replacement Cost of Goods Sold | 32 | 32 |
| Operating Margin on Sales | $23 | $23 |
| Realized Holding Gain on Toasters: | | |
| Replacement Cost (at Time of Sale) of Goods Sold | $32 | $32 |
| Less Acquisition Cost of Goods Sold (FIFO—Toaster 1; LIFO—Toaster 3) | 25 | 30 |
| Realized Holding Gain on Toasters | 7 | 2 |
| Conventionally Reported Gross Margin[a] | $30 | $25 |
| Unrealized Holding Gain: | | |
| Replacement Cost of Ending Inventory (2 × $35) | $70 | $70 |
| Less Acquisition Cost of Ending Inventory (FIFO—Toasters 2 & 3; LIFO—Toasters 1 & 2) | 59 | 54 |
| Unrealized Holding Gain on Toasters | 11 | 16 |
| Economic Profit on Sales and Holding Inventory of Toasters (Not Reported in Financial Statements) | $41 | $41 |

[a]Note that Exhibit 9.8 stops here.

ognized in determining net income each period, whereas most of the holding gain under LIFO is not currently recognized in the income statement. Instead, under LIFO the unrealized holding gain remains unreported, so long as the older acquisition costs are shown on the balance sheet as ending inventory.

9.123    The total increase in wealth for a period includes both realized and unrealized holding gains. That total increase, $41 in the example, is independent of the cost-flow assumption, but is not reported in financial statements under currently accepted accounting principles.

9.124    The FASB requires disclosure of the realized and unrealized holding gains on inventory (and plant) under certain conditions.* See the discussion in Chapter 26.

## Current Cost Basis Removes the Need for a Cost-Flow Assumption

9.125    The preceding sections illustrate the difficulty in constructing useful financial statements in historical cost accounting for inventory in times of changing prices. If a FIFO cost-flow assumption is used, then the income statement reports out-of-date cost of goods sold. If a LIFO cost-flow assumption is used, then the balance sheet reports out-of-date ending inventory. (See Exhibit 9.9.)

9.126    If a current cost basis for inventory is used, then up-to-date information can be shown on both statements. Using a current cost basis eliminates the realization convention in accounting and requires the accountant to make estimates of current costs. Some accountants think that the benefits of current data outweigh the costs of having less auditable numbers.

9.127    Exhibit 9.12 illustrates how the toaster example looks when both cost of goods sold and ending inventory are valued at replacement cost.

9.128    The first income figure, $23, is labeled *Op-

---

*Financial Accounting Standards Board, *Statement of Financial Accounting Standards No. 33* (1979).

*erating Margin.* This figure shows selling price less replacement cost of goods sold at the time of sale. This number has significance for companies operating in unregulated environments. The significance can perhaps be understood by considering the following assertion. If the toaster retailer pays out more than $23 in taxes and dividends, then there will be insufficient funds retained in the firm for it to replace inventory and to allow it to continue in business carrying out the same operations next period as it did this period. On the date of sale, a new toaster costs $32; the historical cost of the toaster sold, whether $25 or $30 or whatever number in between, is irrelevant to understanding the current economic conditions facing the retailer.

The second income item shown in Exhibit   9.129
9.12 is called *Holding Gains.* Holding gains of $18 occurred during the period on the toasters held in inventory. At the time of sale, the replacement cost of toasters had increased to $32. Thus, the holding gain on three toasters, on the date of sale of one of them, was $12 [= 3 × $32 − ($25 + $29 + $30)]. By the end of the accounting period there was another $6 [= 2($35 − $32)] holding gain on the two toasters still held in inventory as the replacement cost increased to $35.

The $41 income figure shown after the in-   9.130
clusion of holding gains is thought to be significant by some accountants. It represents the increase in wealth of the firm without regard to the realization convention. To the economist, income is the change in wealth during the period. The economist thinks it unimportant that a part of the gain has not been realized in an arm's-length transaction. So long as a firm's wealth has increased (through holding gains), then that firm is better off at the end of the period than at the start, and the firm has had income. To the economist and some accountants, income should be measured whether or not it has been realized in arm's-length transactions. Economic income, including all holding gains, is $41 in the example.

In recent years, generally accepted ac-   9.131
counting principles have required major cor-

---

*Exhibit 9.12*
**Using Replacement Cost Data to**
**Analyze Components of Income**

---

**ASSUMED DATA**

| | | |
|---|---|---:|
| Beginning Inventory: Toaster 1 Cost ......... | | $25 |
| Purchases: | Toaster 2 Cost ......... | 29 |
| | Toaster 3 Cost ......... | 30 |
| Historical Cost of Goods Available for Sale ... | | $84 |
| Sales: One Toaster for ..................... | | $55 |
| Replacement Cost of Toasters: | | |
| On Date of Sale ........................... | | $32 |
| At End of Period ......................... | | $35 |

---

**INCOME STATEMENT**

| | |
|---|---:|
| Sales ........................................................................ | $55 |
| Replacement Cost of Goods Sold .............................................. | 32 |
| Operating Margin ............................................................ | $23 |
| Holding Gains for Year[a] (see calculation below) ........................... | 18 |
| Economic Income ............................................................. | $41 |

**Calculation of Holding Gains for Year:**

| | |
|---|---:|
| Replacement Cost at Time of Sale[a] ................................. | $ 32 |
| Replacement Cost of Ending Inventory (2 × $35) ...................... | 70 |
| Total Replacement Cost ............................................. | $102 |
| Historical Cost of Goods Available for Sale ........................ | 84 |
| Total Holding Gains for Year ................................... | $ 18 |

---

[a]To give some recognition to the realization convention, the total holding gain might be divided into realized and unrealized portions. To do so requires knowing the acquisition cost of the toaster sold and that requires a cost-flow assumption. As Exhibit 9.11 indicates, if a LIFO assumption is made, then the realized holding gain is $2 and the realized income of $25 could be shown intermediate between the operating margin of $23 and the economic income of $41. See Appendix 9.2 for a more realistic illustration.

---

porations to disclose the current cost of goods sold computed at the time of sale and the current cost of ending inventory.* With such information, it is possible to measure operating margin and holding gains and to assess the economic performance of business firms. Chapter 26 discusses current costs more fully.

## Summary

9.132 Inventory measurements affect both the cost-of-goods-sold expense on the income statement for the period and the amount

---

*Ibid.

shown for the asset, inventory, on the balance sheet at the end of the period. The sum of the two must be equal to the beginning inventory plus the cost of purchases, at least in accounting based on acquisition costs and market transactions. The allocation between expense and asset depends on four factors:

1. The inventory method used.

2. The valuation basis used.

3. The types of manufacturing and other costs included in inventory.

4. The cost-flow assumption used.

The first factor involves a choice between periodic and perpetual inventory methods. The second factor involves a choice among the acquisition-cost basis, the lower-of-cost-or-market basis, or some current cost basis. Lower of cost or market is most often used. The third factor involves consideration of absorption and direct costing. Only absorption costing is permitted under generally accepted accounting principles. The fourth factor concerns a choice among the FIFO, LIFO, and weighted-average cost-flow assumptions. When a current cost basis is used, there is no need to use a cost-flow assumption, except to separate realized from unrealized holding gains.

# Appendix 9.1: Illustration of Calculations of Inventories and Cost of Goods Sold

9.133   The chapter describes and illustrates inventory accounting problems in the context of the simplistic toaster example where three items are available for sale and one is sold. In spite of its simplicity, that example captures nearly all of the important concepts in accounting for inventories and cost of goods sold. This appendix illustrates a more real-istic situation where additional complexities of calculation are considered.

The illustration in this appendix combines   9.134 various combinations of periodic and perpetual methods with FIFO, weighted-average, and LIFO cost-flow assumptions. Exhibit 9.13 contains the data for additions to, and withdrawals from, the inventory of item X during June that are used in the illustrations.

## First In, First Out

When a FIFO cost-flow assumption is used,   9.135 the unit prices to be applied to quantities on hand are usually calculated by working backward through the purchases until a sufficient quantity is accumulated to cover the inventory at the end of the month. If a physical count reveals that there are 115 units on hand at June 30, the prices paid for the most recently acquired 115 units comprise the ending FIFO inventory. The most recent purchase is the one of June 12, which accounts for 100 units at a cost of $125.00. The next most recent purchase is that of June 7. The remaining 15 units of inventory are priced at the $1.10 unit price of that purchase transaction, or $16.50. The total val-

*Exhibit 9.13*
**Data for Illustration of Inventory Calculations**

| | Units | Unit Cost | Total Cost |
|---|---|---|---|
| **Item X** | | | |
| Beginning Inventory, June 1[a] | 100 | $1.00 | $100 |
| Purchases, June 7 | 300 | 1.10 | 330 |
| Purchases, June 12 | 100 | 1.25 | 125 |
| Total Available for Sale | 500 | | $555 |
| Withdrawals, June 5 | 25 | | ? |
| Withdrawals, June 10 | 10 | | ? |
| Withdrawals, June 15 | 200 | | ? |
| Withdrawals, June 25 | 150 | | ? |
| Total Withdrawals during June | 385 | | ? |
| Ending Inventory, June 30 | 115 | | ? |
| Replacement Cost per Unit, June 30 | | $1.35 | |

[a]The example contains one simplifying assumption. Beginning inventory is shown as having the same opening valuation, $100, under all cost-flow assumptions. If costs had varied in the past, then the opening unit costs would have differed for each of the cost-flow assumptions.

uation of the inventory is, then, $141.50 as shown in Exhibit 9.14.

9.136    Under FIFO, perpetual and periodic inventory systems lead to identical cost-of-goods-sold and ending inventory amounts.

## Last In, First Out

9.137    **LIFO, Periodic** When the periodic inventory method is used with LIFO, the value of ending inventory is calculated by starting with the beginning inventory and then working forward through the purchases until sufficient units have been priced to cover the ending inventory. In the illustration, a physical count reveals that there are 115 units on hand at June 30. Thus, the prices paid for the oldest 115 units comprise the ending LIFO inventory. The oldest units on hand are those in the beginning inventory of June 1, which accounts for 100 units at a total cost of $100.00. The next oldest purchase is that of June 7. The remaining 15 units in ending inventory are priced at the $1.10 unit price of that transaction. The total value of ending inventory, assuming LIFO, is $116.50 as shown in Exhibit 9.15.

9.138    The type of calculation shown in Exhibit 9.15 is realistic only when the quantity on

---

**Exhibit 9.14**
**Ending Inventory and Cost-of-Goods-Sold Calculation Adopting the Periodic Inventory Method and a FIFO Cost-Flow Assumption**

**Item X**

| | |
|---|---:|
| 100 units @ $1.25 (from June 12 Purchase) | $125.00 |
| 15 units @ $1.10 (from June 7 Purchase) | 16.50 |
| Ending Inventory, June 30 | $141.50 |
| | |
| Cost of Goods Available for Sale | $555.00 |
| Less Ending Inventory | 141.50 |
| Cost of Goods Sold | $413.50 |

---

**Exhibit 9.15**
**Ending Inventory and Cost-of-Goods-Sold Calculation Adopting the Periodic Inventory Method and a LIFO Cost-Flow Assumption**

**Item X**

| | |
|---|---:|
| 100 units @ $1.00 (from Beginning Inventory) | $100.00 |
| 15 units @ $1.10 (from First Purchase, June 7) | 16.50 |
| Ending Inventory at Cost | $116.50 |
| | |
| Cost of Goods Available for Sale | $555.00 |
| Less Ending Inventory | 116.50 |
| Cost of Goods Sold | $438.50 |

hand never drops below the number of units in the beginning inventory, 100 units in the illustration. This would not be known unless perpetual inventory records were kept. This doubtful assumption weakens the logic of LIFO when a periodic inventory system is used. On the other hand, when a periodic inventory system is used, LIFO usually requires less pricing of inventory items at the end of the period: Because the quantity in the ending inventory is apt to be somewhat larger than the quantity in the beginning inventory, only the increase in units need be priced. (This increase in physical quantities

with its own set of prices is often called a *LIFO inventory layer.*)

**LIFO, Perpetual** When LIFO is used with a   9.139
perpetual inventory method, the balance carried forward after each addition to or withdrawal from inventory must be analyzed to reflect the costs applicable to the unused items. LIFO requires that the most recent costs be applied to withdrawals until the corresponding quantities have been absorbed and the balance on hand reflects the earliest purchase prices. Exhibit 9.16 illustrates the operation of LIFO with a perpetual inven-

*Exhibit 9.16*
**Ending Inventory and
Cost-of-Goods-Sold Calculation
Adopting the
Perpetual Inventory Method and a
LIFO Cost-Flow Assumption**

**Item X**

| Date | Received | | | Issued | | | Balance | | |
|------|-------|------|--------|-------|------|--------|-------|------|---------|
| | **Units** | **Cost** | **Amount** | **Units** | **Cost** | **Amount** | **Units** | **Cost** | **Amount** |
| 6/1 | | | | | | | 100 | $1.00 | $100.00 |
| 6/5 | | | | 25 | $1.00 | $ 25.00 | 75 | 1.00 | 75.00 |
| 6/7 | 300 | $1.10 | $330.00 | | | | { 75 | 1.00 | 75.00 |
| | | | | | | | { 300 | 1.10 | 330.00 |
| 6/10 | | | | 10 | 1.10 | 11.00 | { 75 | 1.00 | 75.00 |
| | | | | | | | { 290 | 1.10 | 319.00 |
| 6/12 | 100 | 1.25 | 125.00 | | | | { 75 | 1.00 | 75.00 |
| | | | | | | | { 290 | 1.10 | 319.00 |
| | | | | | | | { 100 | 1.25 | 125.00 |
| 6/15 | | | | 100 | 1.25 | 125.00 | { 75 | 1.00 | 75.00 |
| | | | | 100 | 1.10 | 110.00 | { 190 | 1.10 | 209.00 |
| 6/25 | | | | 150 | 1.10 | 165.00 | { 75 | 1.00 | 75.00 |
| Cost of Goods Sold | | | | | | $436.00 | { 40 | 1.10 | 44.00 |

**Ending Inventory Computation**

| | |
|---|---|
| 75 units @ $1.00 | $ 75.00 |
| 40 units @ $1.10 | 44.00 |
| Ending Inventory | $119.00 |

**Alternative Cost-of-Goods-Sold Computation**

| | |
|---|---|
| Cost of Goods Available for Sale | $555.00 |
| Less Ending Inventory | 119.00 |
| Cost of Goods Sold | $436.00 |

tory method. If prices are steadily increasing, then the cost of goods sold under LIFO with a perpetual method will never exceed, and will usually be less than, the cost of goods sold under LIFO with a periodic method. The two figures will be equal only when all additions during the period occur before any withdrawals. Most firms who use LIFO do so to save taxes. Because most of these firms do not acquire all of their additions during a period before making any withdrawals, few firms use a LIFO, perpetual combination.

## Weighted Average

9.140  **Weighted Average, Periodic** Exhibit 9.17 illustrates the weighted-average cost-flow assumption used with a periodic method. The weighted-average cost-flow assumption is physically appropriate for liquids and not unreasonable for other types of products where distinguishing different lots is difficult. The result shown in Exhibit 9.17 is correct, strictly speaking, only if no units were used or sold until after the firm made the last purchase that enters the computations of the weighted average. Seldom do all additions to inventory precede any withdrawals and, therefore, the logic of the method is somewhat weakened.

9.141  **Weighted Average, Perpetual** The weighted-average cost-flow assumption is often the easiest to apply with a perpetual inventory system, especially when the number of purchases is less than the number of withdrawals. The technique requires the calculation of a new average unit cost after each purchase, and this unit-cost figure is used to price all withdrawals until the next purchase is made. Hence, this method is often called the *moving-average method* when it is used with a perpetual inventory system. The illustration in Exhibit 9.18 indicates how the moving-average method operates with the use of perpetual inventory records. The inventory at the end of the month is valued at the last amount shown on the perpetual in-

*Exhibit 9.17*
**Ending Inventory and Cost-of-Goods-Sold Calculation Adopting the Periodic Inventory Method and a Weighted-Average Cost-Flow Assumption**

**Item X**

| | |
|---|---:|
| 6/1  100 units @ $1.00 ............... | $100.00 |
| 6/7  300 units @ $1.10 ............... | 330.00 |
| 6/12 100 units @ $1.25 ............... | 125.00 |
| 500 units @ $1.11 (= $555/500) .... | $555.00 |
| Ending Inventory (115 Units @ $1.11) ... | $127.65 |
| Cost of Goods Available for Sale ....... | $555.00 |
| Less Ending Inventory ............... | 127.65 |
| Cost of Goods Sold  ................. | $427.35 |

ventory form, $128.39. The unit price of $1.1166 is used only for determining the amount of subsequent withdrawals. The ending inventory of $128.39 is calculated as $295.88 less $167.49 (= 150 × $1.1166), not as 115 × $1.1166.

## Operating Margin and Holding Gains

9.142  Exhibit 9.19 illustrates identification of operating margin and holding gains for the inventory of item X. We have assumed that the 385 items withdrawn were all sold for a price of $1.50 each. In computing the replacement cost of goods sold, we use as a unit price for all goods sold on a given date the acquisition cost per unit at the most recent purchase date.

9.143  The calculation of the operating margin and holding gain in this more realistic example follows the same procedure used in the simpler toaster example. The acquisition cost of the 500 items available for sale during the period is $555. If 385 units were sold for, say, $1.50 each, the total revenue would be $577.50. The replacement cost of the items at the time they were sold can be determined from information in Exhibit 9.13 to be $473.50 [=(25 × $1.00) + (10 × $1.10) + (350 × $1.25)]. The operating margin is

*Exhibit 9.18*
**Ending Inventory and
Cost-of-Goods Sold Calculation
Adopting the
Perpetual Inventory Method and a
Moving-Average Cost-Flow Assumption**

**Item X**

| Date | Received Units | Received Cost | Received Amount | Issued Units | Issued Cost | Issued Amount | Balance Units | Balance Cost | Balance Amount |
|------|------|------|--------|------|------|--------|------|------|--------|
| 6/1  |      |        |          |     |        |          | 100 | $1.00  | $100.00 |
| 6/5  |      |        |          | 25  | $1.00  | $ 25.00  | 75  | 1.00   | 75.00   |
| 6/7  | 300  | $1.10  | $330.00  |     |        |          | 375 | 1.08   | 405.00  |
| 6/10 |      |        |          | 10  | 1.08   | 10.80    | 365 | 1.08   | 394.20  |
| 6/12 | 100  | 1.25   | 125.00   |     |        |          | 465 | 1.1166 | 519.20  |
| 6/15 |      |        |          | 200 | 1.1166 | 223.32   | 265 | 1.1166 | 295.88  |
| 6/25 |      |        |          | 150 | 1.1166 | 167.49   | 115 | 1.1166 | 128.39  |
| Cost of Goods Sold |  |  |  |  |  | $426.61 |  |  |  |

**Alternative Cost-of-Goods-Sold Computation**

| | |
|---|---|
| Cost of Goods Available for Sale | $555.00 |
| Less Ending Inventory | 128.39 |
| Cost of Goods Sold | $426.61 |

*Exhibit 9.19*
**Reporting of Operating Margins
and Holding Gains for Item X**

| | Cost-Flow Assumption FIFO | | Cost-Flow Assumption LIFO | |
|---|---|---|---|---|
| **Periodic Inventory Method** | | | | |
| Sales Revenue from Item X (385 × $1.50) | $577.50 | | $577.50 | |
| Less Replacement Cost of Goods Sold [(25 × $1.00) + (10 × $1.10) + (350 × $1.25)] | 473.50 | | 473.50 | |
| Operating Margin on Sales of Item X | | $104.00 | | $104.00 |
| Realized Holding Gain on Item X: | | | | |
| Replacement Cost of Goods Sold | $473.50 | | $473.50 | |
| Less Acquisition Cost of Goods Sold (FIFO—Exhibit 9.14; LIFO—Exhibit 9.15) | 413.50 | | 438.50 | |
| Realized Holding Gain on Item X | | 60.00 | | 35.00 |
| Conventionally Reported Gross Margin[a] | | $164.00 | | $139.00 |
| Unrealized Holding Gain on Item X: | | | | |
| Replacement Cost of Ending Inventory (115 × $1.35) | $155.25 | | $155.25 | |
| Less Acquisition Cost of Ending Inventory (FIFO—Exhibit 9.14; LIFO—Exhibit 9.15) | 141.50 | | 116.50 | |
| Unrealized Holding Gain on Item X | | 13.75 | | 38.75 |
| Economic Profit on Sales and Holding Inventory of Item X | | $177.75 | | $177.75 |

[a]Historical cost income statements usually omit information shown below this point.

$104.00 (= $577.50 − $473.50). The current replacement cost at the end of the month of the 115 units in ending inventory is $1.35 each, or a total of $155.25 (= 115 × $1.35). Thus the replacement cost of the goods sold plus the replacement cost of ending inventory is $628.75 (= $473.50 + $155.25). Total holding gain is $73.75 (= $628.75 − $555.00) and economic income is $177.75 (= $104.00 + $73.75).

9.144　The top portion of Exhibit 9.19 illustrates the separation of the conventionally reported gross margin into the operating margin and the realized holding gain. The lower portion of the exhibit shows unrealized holding gains. See also Appendix 9.2.

## Appendix 9.2: Calculation of Holding Gains When There is a Beginning Inventory

The illustrations in the text and in the preceding appendix are simplified because there are no holding gains in the beginning inventory. In practice, there will be a beginning inventory containing an unrealized holding gain. To derive the unrealized holding gain during a period, the unrealized holding gain in beginning inventory must be subtracted from the unrealized holding gain in ending inventory. Exhibit 9.20 illustrates the calculation.

*Exhibit 9.20*
**Calculating Holding Gains When There Is a Beginning Inventory**

|  | (Historical) Acquisition Cost Assuming FIFO | Current Cost |
|---|---|---|
| **Assumed Data** | | |
| Inventory, January 1 | $ 900 | $1,100 |
| Inventory, December 31 | 1,160 | 1,550 |
| Cost of Goods Sold for the Year | 4,740 | 4,850 |
| Sales for the Year $5,200 | | |
| **Income Statement for the Year** | | |
| Sales | $5,200 | $5,200 |
| Cost of Goods Sold | 4,740 | 4,850 |
| (1) Income from Continuing Operations | | $ 350 |
| Realized Holding Gains | | 110[a] |
| (2) Realized Income = Conventional Net Income (under FIFO) | $ 460 | $ 460 |
| Unrealized Holding Gain | | 190[b] |
| (3) Comprehensive Income | | $ 650 |

[a]Realized holding gain during a period is current cost of goods sold less historical cost of goods sold; for the year the realized holding gain under FIFO is $110 = $4,850 − $4,740. Some refer to this as "inventory profit."

[b]The total unrealized holding gain at any time is current cost of inventory on hand at that time less historical cost of that inventory. The unrealized holding gain during a period is unrealized holding gain at the end of the period less the unrealized holding gain at the beginning of the period. Unrealized holding gain prior to the year is $200 = $1,100 − $900. Unrealized holding gain during the year = ($1,550 − $1,160) − ($1,100 − $900) = $390 − $200 = $190.

## Questions and Short Cases

**9.1**  Review the meaning of the following concepts or terms discussed in this chapter.

**a.** Inventory (both as a noun and as a verb).
**b.** Inventory equation.
**c.** Purchases.
**d.** Purchase returns.
**e.** Purchase discounts.
**f.** Shrinkages.
**g.** Periodic inventory method.

**h.** Perpetual inventory method.
**i.** Acquisition cost basis.
**j.** Replacement cost.
**k.** Net realizable value.
**l.** Lower-of-cost-or-market basis.
**m.** Standard cost.

**n.** Absorption costing versus direct costing.
**o.** Cost-flow assumption.
**p.** FIFO.
**q.** LIFO.
**r.** Weighted average.
**s.** Realized holding gain.
**t.** Unrealized holding gain.

**9.2**  Goods that cost $800 are sold for $1,000 cash. Present the normal journal entries at the time of the sale:
**a.** When a periodic inventory method is used.
**b.** When a perpetual inventory method is used.

**9.3**  Which of the two inventory methods, periodic or perpetual, would you expect to find used in each of the following situations?
**a.** Greeting card department of a retail store.
**b.** Fur coat department of a retail store.
**c.** Supplies storeroom for an automated production line.
**d.** Automobile dealership.
**e.** Wholesale dealer in bulk salad oil.
**f.** Grocery store.
**g.** College bookstore.
**h.** Diamond ring department of a jewelry store.
**i.** Ballpoint pen department of a jewelry store.

**9.4**  Under what circumstances would the perpetual and periodic inventory methods both yield the same inventory amount if the weighted-average flow assumption were used?

**9.5**  Where on the balance sheet would you report the following items?
**a.** Merchandise received from a customer for rework.
**b.** Allowance reducing inventory cost to market.
**c.** Unsold goods at consignee's warehouse.
**d.** Goods out on approval to customers.
**e.** Materials received on consignment.

**9.6**  Compare and contrast the Merchandise Inventory account of a retail firm with the Finished Goods Inventory account of a manufacturing firm.

**9.7**  Under absorption costing, net income can increase although sales remain constant, whereas under direct costing income would not increase. How does this happen?

**9.8**  "Specific identification is an inferior method of assigning costs to inventories and to cost of goods sold because it enables management manipulation." Explain.

9.9    Indicate the treatment of each of the items below in the financial statements prepared at the end of an accounting period. The disposition is one of the following:

(1) Item appears on the balance sheet.
(2) Item is closed to a balance sheet account.
(3) Item appears on the income statement.
(4) Some other.

a. Raw Materials Inventory.
b. Purchase Discounts Lost.
c. Goods in transit that were shipped F.O.B. destination. (Answer from the seller's viewpoint.)
d. Purchase Returns.
e. Loss from Decline in Market Value of Inventory.
f. Purchase Discounts Taken.
g. Freight-in.
h. Work-in-Process Inventory.

9.10    Under what conditions should merchandise in transit be included in inventory?

9.11    The Lorim Company owned merchandise costing $430 that was shipped to its consignee's warehouse immediately following its arrival at Lorim. No accounting entry was made. The amount was omitted from the purchase figure for the year as well as from the ending inventory. How is net income for the year affected by this omission? The Company's financial position? Should materiality be considered to determine if an adjustment need be made?

9.12    The accounts listed below might appear in the records of a retail store. Their use is never required, but accounts such as these are often a convenience. From the name of the account and your understanding of the accounting for purchases and sales, indicate:
(1) Whether the account is a permanent account (to appear as such on the balance sheet) or a temporary account (to be closed at the end of the accounting period).
(2) The normal balance, debit or credit, in the account. If the account is a temporary one, give the normal balance prior to closing.
(3) If the account is a temporary one, give the kind of account it is closed to—balance sheet asset, balance sheet liability, balance sheet owners' equity through a revenue account, or balance sheet owners' equity through an expense (or revenue contra) account.

a. Merchandise Purchases.
b. Merchandise Purchase Allowances.
c. Merchandise Purchase Returns.
d. Allowance for Purchase Discounts.
e. Sales Tax on Purchases.
f. Freight-in on Purchases.
g. Sales Allowances.
h. Allowance for Sales Discounts.
i. Federal Excise Taxes Payable on Sales.
j. Purchase Discounts.
k. Purchase Discounts Taken.
l. Purchase Discounts Lost.

9.13    The cost of goods sold under a FIFO, perpetual system is the same as cost of goods sold under a FIFO, periodic system. The cost of goods sold under a LIFO, perpetual system generally differs from cost of goods sold under a LIFO, periodic system. Explain why LIFO differs from FIFO in this regard and describe the relation between the two cost of goods sold amounts under LIFO.

9.14    What is meant by the phrase "liquidation of a LIFO layer"? Why is this a concern for LIFO, but not for FIFO?

9.15    Summarize the differences in the application of LIFO for income tax purposes and for financial reporting purposes under generally accepted accounting principles.

**9.16**   A noted accountant once claimed that firms which use a LIFO cost-flow assumption will find that historical cost of goods sold is *greater than* replacement cost of goods sold computed as of the time of sale. Under what circumstances is this assertion likely to be true? (Hint: Compare the effects of periodic and perpetual methods on LIFO cost of goods sold.) Do you agree that the assertion is likely to be true?

**9.17**   a. During a period of rising prices, will the FIFO or LIFO cost-flow assumption result in the higher ending inventory amount? The lower inventory amount? Assume no changes in physical quantities between the beginning and end of the period.
   b. Which cost-flow assumption will result in the higher ending inventory amount during a period of declining prices? The lower inventory amount?

**9.18**   a. During a period of rising prices, will the FIFO or LIFO cost-flow assumption result in the higher cost of goods sold? The lower cost of goods sold? Assume no changes in physical quantities between the beginning and end of the period.
   b. Which cost-flow assumption, LIFO or FIFO, will result in the higher cost of goods sold during a period of declining prices? The lower cost of goods sold?

**9.19**   Listed below are a series of statements about a cost-flow assumption. Indicate the cost-flow assumption (LIFO, FIFO, weighted average) for which the statement is most descriptive. Assume a period of rising prices.
   a. Results in balance sheet amounts closely reflecting current replacement costs.
   b. Matches current costs with current revenues.
   c. Provides balance sheet amounts closely approximating the amounts under FIFO.
   d. LISH inventory-flow assumption.
   e. Tends to provide smoother income over the business cycle.
   f. Acceptable for income tax purposes only if it is also used for financial reporting purposes.
   g. Follows the physical flow of most goods.
   h. Results in balance sheet amounts reflecting very old costs.
   i. Requires the recomputation of unit cost as items are purchased and sold.
   j. FISH inventory-flow assumption.
   k. Results in highest net income when prices are rising.
   l. Matches old costs with current revenues.

**9.20**   (Adapted from CPA Examination.) Retail, Inc., sells normal brand name household products both from its own store and on consignment through The Mall Space Company.
   a. Should Retail, Inc., include in its inventory normal brand name goods purchased from its suppliers but not yet received if the terms of purchase are FOB shipping point (manufacturer's plant)? Why?
   b. Should Retail, Inc., include freight-in expenditures as an inventoriable cost? Why?
   c. Retail, Inc., purchased cooking utensils for sale in the ordinary course of business three times during the current year, each time at a higher price than the previous purchase. What would have been the effect on ending inventory and cost of goods sold had Retail, Inc., used the weighted-average cost method instead of the FIFO method?
   d. What are the products on consignment and how should they be presented on the balance sheets of Retail, Inc., and the Mall Space Company?

**9.21**   When there is a rapid inventory turnover, which cost-flow assumption produces almost the same results as FIFO?

**9.22**   (Adapted from AICPA *Technical Practice Aids*.) A firm operates an aircraft repair shop certified by the Federal Aviation Administration. In addition to an inventory of new parts, purchased from suppliers, the firm salvages and rebuilds other parts. Once these parts are rebuilt and certified by the FAA, they are functionally equivalent to new parts. The firm mixes the old parts with the new ones, uses them interchangeably, and sells them for the same prices as new parts.

The firm records all additions to the parts inventory account, whether new or used, at factory list price for new parts. Assume that during the current year parts available for sale cost $60,000, but have a factory list price of $100,000. List price of ending inventory amounts to $25,000.

How should the firm account for its inventories of new and used parts?

9.23   The LIFO Company and the FIFO Company both manufacture paper and cardboard products. Prices of timber, paper pulp, and finished paper products have generally increased by about 5 percent per year through the *start of this year*. Inventory data for the beginning and end of the year are shown below.

|  | January 1 | December 31 |
|---|---|---|
| LIFO Company Inventory (Last-In, First-Out) ................... | $19,695,000 | $15,870,000 |
| FIFO Company Inventory (First-In, First-Out, Lower of Cost or Market) .............................................. | 46,284,000 | 38,250,000 |

Income statements for the two companies for the year ending December 31 are as follows:

|  | LIFO Company | FIFO Company |
|---|---|---|
| Sales ........................................... | $57,000,000 | $129,000,000 |
| Expenses: |  |  |
| Cost of Goods Sold ............................... | $44,580,000 | $108,000,000 |
| Depreciation ..................................... | 5,400,000 | 12,000,000 |
| General Expenses .................................. | 2,220,000 | 5,400,000 |
| Income Taxes (40% of Pretax Income) ................ | 1,920,000 | 1,440,000 |
| Total Expenses ............................... | $54,120,000 | $126,840,000 |
| Net Income ...................................... | $ 2,880,000 | $ 2,160,000 |

a. Assuming that the prices for timber, paper pulp, and finished paper remained unchanged during the year, how would the two companies' respective inventory valuation methods affect the interpretation of their financial statements for the year?
b. How would the answer to part **a** differ if prices at the end of the year had been lower than at the beginning of the year?
c. How would the answer to part **a** differ if prices at the end of the year had been higher than at the beginning of the year?

9.24   Data for Companies A, B, and C, shown in Exhibit 9.21, are taken from the annual reports of three actual companies in the same industry for a recent year. One of these companies uses a LIFO cost-flow assumption for 100 percent of its inventories, another uses LIFO for about 60 percent of its inventories, and the other uses LIFO for about 45 percent of its inventories. From these data and the lessons of this chapter, answer the following questions, making explicit the reasoning used in each case.
a. From the cost-of-goods-sold data alone, which of the companies appears to be the 100-percent LIFO company? The 60-percent LIFO company? The 45-percent LIFO company?
b. From the ending-inventory data alone, which of the companies appears to be the 100-

Exhibit 9.21
**Data for Analysis of
LIFO and FIFO
Effects on Financial Statements**

| | Dollar Amounts in Millions | | | | |
|---|---|---|---|---|---|
| | | | Company | | |
| | **A** | **B** | **C** | **D** | **E** |
| Sales Revenue ................. | $14,950 | $10,445 | $5,152 | $15,697 | $5,042 |
| Cost of Goods Sold:[a] | | | | | |
| Historical Cost Basis ............ | 13,497 | 8,318 | 3,638 | 10,852 | 3,720 |
| Replacement Cost Basis ......... | 13,432 | 8,322 | 3,675 | 11,110 | 3,720 |
| Net Income ..................... | 695 | 106 | 108 | 931 | 383 |
| Ending Inventory: | | | | | |
| Historical Cost Basis ............ | 2,215 | 756 | 1,026 | 2,265 | 1,245 |
| Replacement Cost Basis ......... | 2,303 | 875 | 1,056 | 3,540 | 2,169 |
| Ratio of Net Income | | | | | |
| to Revenue ................... | 4.6% | 1.0% | 2.1% | 5.9% | 7.6% |

[a]Excludes depreciation charges.

percent LIFO company? The 60-percent LIFO company? The 45-percent LIFO company?

c. From your answers to parts **a** and **b,** draw a conclusion as to which of the companies appears to be which.

d. Note that Company A earned net income equal to 4.6 percent of sales, whereas Company B earned net income equal to 1.0 percent of sales. Can you conclude that Company A is more profitable than Company B? Why or why not?

e. Although all three of these companies are in the same industry, the nature of the goods sold and the operations of two of the companies are somewhat different from the nature of the goods sold and the operations of the third. Which of the three appears to be the one that is different from the other two?

9.25   (This question should not be attempted until the preceding question has been read ) Data for Company D and Company E shown in Exhibit 9.21 are taken from the annual reports of two actual companies for a recent year. One of these companies uses a LIFO cost-flow assumption for all of its inventories, whereas the other uses LIFO for only a portion. From these data and the lessons of this chapter, answer the following questions, making explicit the reasoning you used.

a. Which of the two companies is more likely to be the 100-percent LIFO company?

b. Data for Companies A, B, and C are also shown in Exhibit 9.20. These three companies are in an industry much different from the industries that include Company D and Company E. Which of the two industries is more likely to be related to retailing and which is more likely to be related to manufacturing?

# Problems and Exercises

9.26   The Raffel Manufacturing Company is computing the value of its inventory on December 31. For each of the items listed below, state the unit value that should be employed for inventory pricing purposes, using lower of cost or market.

| Item | Acquisition Cost | Replacement Cost | Selling Price | Estimated Cost to Complete and Sell | Normal Profit Margin |
|---|---|---|---|---|---|
| A .............. | $ 50 | $ 52 | $ 56 | $17 | $14 |
| B .............. | 40 | 36 | 44 | 6 | 2 |
| C .............. | 109 | 105 | 110 | 6 | 4 |
| D .............. | 6 | 7 | 9 | 2 | 1 |
| E .............. | 90 | 84 | 94 | 4 | 3 |

**9.27**  Several items have been omitted from the following income statement data. Fill in the missing amounts.

| | Year 1 | Year 2 | Year 3 |
|---|---|---|---|
| Sales ...................................................... | $600 | $720 | $ ? |
| Sales Returns ............................................ | ? | 30 | 20 |
| Net Sales ................................................. | ? | ? | 795 |
| Beginning Inventory ..................................... | ? | 20 | ? |
| Ending Inventory ........................................ | 20 | 55 | 70 |
| Purchases ................................................ | 255 | ? | 410 |
| Purchases Returns and Allowances ........................ | 5 | 10 | 15 |
| Freight-in ................................................ | 10 | 15 | 20 |
| Cost of Goods Sold ...................................... | 270 | 350 | ? |
| Gross Margin on Sales .................................... | 305 | ? | 395 |

**9.28**  Indicate the effect on Working Capital Provided by Operations of the following independent transactions. Include the effects of income taxes assuming that the tax rate is 40 percent of pretax income and that the accounting methods used on the tax return are the same as on the financial statements.
**a.** A firm using the lower-of-cost-or-market basis for inventories writes ending inventory down by $50,000.
**b.** A firm has been using FIFO. It switches to LIFO during the current year and finds that the cost of goods sold is $100,000 larger than it would have been under FIFO.

**9.29**  On December 30, 1980, merchandise amounting to $750 was received by the Perrin Company and was counted in its December 31 listing of all inventory items on hand. The invoice was not received until January 4, 1981, when the acquisition was recorded as a 1981 acquisition. The acquisition should have been recorded for 1980. Assume that the error was not discovered by the firm when the invoice was received and that Perrin Company uses the periodic inventory method. Indicate that effect (overstatement, understatement, none) on each of the following amounts.
**a.** Inventory, 12/31/80.
**b.** Inventory, 12/31/81.
**c.** Cost of goods sold, 1980.
**d.** Cost of goods sold, 1981.
**e.** Net income, 1980.
**f.** Net income, 1981.
**g.** Accounts payable, 12/31/80.
**h.** Accounts payable, 12/31/81.
**i.** Retained earnings, 12/31/81.

**9.30**  At the close of business, an examination of the detailed records of the Burns Company reveals the following items included in the regular inventory account. Which items should be included in the regular inventory account and at what amounts? If further data are needed to respond, specify the data requirements.

| Item | Cost |
|---|---|
| **a.** Ordered and in receiving department, invoice not received (goods shipped F.O.B. shipping point) .......................................... | $ 500 |
| **b.** Currently used in window display ........................................... | 22,000 |
| **c.** Included in warehouse count, but specifically segregated for shipment to a customer, F.O.B. customer's warehouse .......................... | 200 |
| **d.** In receiving department, returned by customer without explanation .............. | 40 |
| **e.** In shipping department, invoice not mailed .................................... | 100 |
| **f.** In shipping department, invoice mailed ....................................... | 50 |
| **g.** In receiving department, refused by us because of damage ..................... | 80 |
| **h.** Shipped today F.O.B. destination, invoice mailed ............................. | 200 |
| **i.** Shipped today F.O.B. shipping point, invoice mailed ........................... | 70 |
| **j.** In warehouse, damaged, not returnable ...................................... | 300 |
| **k.** Invoice received for goods ordered F.O.B. carrier, goods shipped but not received (we pay freight) ...................................... | 75 |

**9.31** Prepare a journal form with two pairs of columns, one headed Net Price Method and the other headed Gross Price Method. Using this journal form, show summary entries for the following events in the history of Evans and Foster, furniture manufacturers. Separate purchase accounts are used by the company.

(1) During the first year of operations, materials with a gross invoice price of $60,000 are purchased. All invoices are subject to a 2-percent cash discount if paid within 10 days.

(2) Payments to creditors during the year amount to $53,000, settling $54,000 of accounts payable at gross prices.

(3) Of the $6,000, gross, in unpaid accounts at the end of the year, the discount period has expired on one invoice amounting to $400. It is expected that all other discounts will be taken. This expectation is reflected in the year-end adjustment.

(4) During the first few days of the next period, all invoices are paid in accordance with expectations.

**9.32** The Beamer Company makes the following transactions at, or shortly after the close of its business year. Its business year ends December 31, and it uses the periodic inventory system. Review these transactions and make any correcting entries required before the financial statements for the year can be prepared. Should the inventory of $12,470 found by physical count be adjusted? Prepare any necessary entries and state the correct inventory at December 31. Assume that the books have not yet been closed and that separate purchase accounts are used.

(1) An invoice for $230, terms F.O.B. shipping point, was received and recorded January 1. The receiving report indicates that the goods were received December 29.

(2) An invoice for $750, terms F.O.B. shipping point, was received and recorded December 26. The receiving report indicates that the shipment was received December 27 in acceptable condition.

(3) An invoice for $465, terms F.O.B. destination, was received and recorded December 29. The attached receiving report indicates that the materials were received January 3.

(4) An invoice for $800, terms F.O.B. shipping point, was received December 20, but never recorded. The receiving report indicates that the goods were received December 23. The report bears a notation: "Wrong style #—returned for credit, December 24."

(5) An invoice for $330, terms F.O.B. shipping point, was received and recorded January 1. Although the invoice shows that the merchandise was shipped December 28, the receiving report indicated receipt of goods on January 3.

9.33 Bashkar Food Company contracted to purchase substantial quantities of wheat and corn, its two basic raw materials, for delivery in the next accounting period. The contract price of the wheat ordered is $100,000 and of the corn is $110,000. By the end of the current accounting period, the price of wheat had declined so that the same quantities could now be ordered for $80,000, but the price of corn had increased so that the same quantities would cost $115,000.

    a. Prepare a journal entry for the end of the period recognizing the loss on purchase commitments. Treat the two contracts separately.

    b. Prepare a journal entry for the end of the period recognizing the loss on purchase commitments. Treat the two contracts as one commitment, offsetting gain against loss.

    c. The chapter does not indicate which of the two treatments above generally accepted accounting principles prefer. Which do you prefer and why?

    d. Search other accounting reference sources to see if you can find any guidance as to which of the treatments is preferred by others.

9.34 The following are selected transactions of the Wearever Shoe Store.

    (1) A shipment of shoes is received from the Standard Shoe Company, $2,100. Terms 2/30, n/60.

    (2) Part of the shipment of (1) is returned. The gross price of the returned goods is $200, and a credit memorandum for this amount is received from the Standard Shoe Company.

    (3) The invoice of the Standard Shoe Company is paid in time to take the discount.

    a. Give entries on the books of the Wearever Shoe Store, assuming that the net price method is used.

    b. Give entries on the books of the Wearever Shoe Store, assuming that the gross price method is used.

9.35 The following applies to the operations of the Karot Corporation for the year:

| | |
|---|---:|
| Raw Materials Inventory, January 1 | $ 2,000 |
| Work in Process Inventory, January 1 | 4,000 |
| Finished Goods Inventory, January 1 | 5,000 |
| Raw Materials Purchased | 6,600 |
| Direct Labor Cost Incurred | 7,600 |
| Manufacturing Overhead Cost Incurred | 6,000 |
| Sales | 20,000 |
| Administrative Expense | 5,000 |

Given the following ending inventory amounts, compute the amount of income before taxes for the year.

| | |
|---|---:|
| Raw Materials Inventory, December 31 | $2,600 |
| Goods in Process Inventory, December 31 | 3,600 |
| Finished Goods Inventory, December 31 | 4,000 |

9.36 Plymouth Company began business on January 1, Year 1. The information concerning merchandise inventories, purchases, and sales for the first three years of operations is as follows:

| | Year 1 | Year 2 | Year 3 |
|---|---:|---:|---:|
| Sales | $600,000 | $660,000 | $900,000 |
| Purchases | 560,000 | 520,000 | 700,000 |
| Inventories, December 31: | | | |
|   At Cost | 160,000 | 190,000 | 190,000 |
|   At Market | 150,000 | 160,000 | 200,000 |

a. Compute the gross margin on sales (sales minus cost of goods sold) for each year, using the lower-of-cost-or-market basis in valuing inventories.

b. Compute the gross margin on sales (sales minus cost of goods sold) for each year, using the acquisition-cost basis in valuing inventories.

c. Indicate your conclusion whether the lower-of-cost-or-market basis of valuing inventories is "conservative" in all situations where it is applied.

9.37  (Adapted from CPA Examination.) The Frate Company was formed on December 1. The following information is available from Frate's inventory records for Product Ply:

|  | **Units** | **Unit Cost** |
| --- | --- | --- |
| January 1 | | |
| (Beginning Inventory) | 800 | $ 9.00 |
| Purchases: | | |
| January 5 | 1,500 | $10.00 |
| January 25 | 1,200 | $10.50 |
| February 16 | 600 | $11.00 |
| March 26 | 900 | $11.50 |

A physical inventory on March 31 shows 1,600 units on hand.

Compute the ending inventory at March 31 using each of the following inventory cost flow assumptions.

a. FIFO
b. LIFO
c. Weighted average.

9.38  The inventory footnote to the 1981 annual report of the Cheral Company reads in part as follows:

Because of continuing high demand throughout the year, inventories were unavoidably reduced and could not be replaced. Under the LIFO system of accounting, used for many years by Cheral Company, the net effect of all the inventory changes was to increase pretax income by $60,000 over what it would have been had inventories been maintained at their physical levels at the start of the year.

The price of Cheral Company's merchandise purchases was $22 per unit during 1981 after having risen steadily for many years. Cheral Company uses a periodic inventory method. Cheral Company's inventory positions at the beginning and end of the year are summarized below:

| **Date** | **Physical Count of Inventory** | **LIFO Cost of Inventory** |
| --- | --- | --- |
| January 1, 1981 | 30,000 units | ? |
| December 31, 1981 | 20,000 units | $260,000 |

a. What was the average cost per unit of the 10,000 units removed from the January 1, 1981, LIFO inventory?

b. What was the January 1, 1981, LIFO cost of inventory?

9.39  The Wendeth Company purchases mercury and sells it to domestic industrial corporations. Its records reveal the following beginning inventory and monthly purchases:

| | | |
|---|---|---|
| February 1, Inventory ............................................... | 500 lb | $2,000 |
| February 6, Purchased ............................................. | 1500 lb | 6,750 |
| February 17, Purchased ........................................... | 1750 lb | 8,750 |
| February 27, Purchased ........................................... | 1500 lb | 8,250 |

The inventory at February 28 is 1900 lb. Assume a periodic inventory method. Compute the cost of the inventory on February 28 under each of the following cost-flow assumptions: **a.** FIFO. **b.** Weighted average. **c.** LIFO.

**9.40** The following information concerning an item of raw materials is available:

| | |
|---|---|
| Nov. 2 Inventory .................................................... | 4,000 lb @ $5 |
| 9 Issued ........................................................ | 3,000 lb |
| 16 Purchased ................................................... | 7,000 lb @ $6 |
| 23 Issued ...................................................... | 3,000 lb |
| 30 Issued ...................................................... | 3,000 lb |

Compute the cost of goods sold and the cost of ending inventory on November 30 for each of the following combinations of inventory systems and cost-flow assumptions.
**a.** Periodic FIFO.      **d.** Perpetual FIFO.
**b.** Periodic weighted average.      **e.** Perpetual weighted average.
**c.** Periodic LIFO.      **f.** Perpetual LIFO.

**9.41** The Nopat Department Store records inventory information separately for each product it carries. The following transactions for product Y occurred during July.

| | |
|---|---|
| July 1, Beginning Inventory ...................................... | 200 units at $4 |
| July 10, Purchased ............................................... | 400 units at $2 |
| July 20, Purchased ............................................... | 300 units at $1 |
| July 6, Sold .................................................... | 100 units at $6 |
| July 21, Sold ................................................... | 300 units at $4 |
| July 24, Sold ................................................... | 100 units at $3 |

**a.** Assume a periodic inventory method. Compute the cost of goods sold and ending inventory using first a LIFO cost-flow assumption, then a FIFO cost-flow assumption.
**b.** Assume a perpetual inventory method and costs are computed at the time of each withdrawal. Compute the value of the ending inventory under a LIFO cost-flow assumption.
**c.** Assume a perpetual inventory method. What is the gross profit if inventory is valued using a FIFO cost-flow assumption?
**d.** Why does LIFO usually produce a lower gross margin than FIFO?

**9.42** The Harrison Corporation was organized and began retailing operations on January 1, 1980. Purchases of merchandise inventory during 1980 and 1981 were as follows:

| | Quantity Purchased | Unit Price | Acquisition Cost |
|---|---|---|---|
| 1/10/80 ........................................... | 100,000 | $.10 | $10,000 |
| 6/30/80 ........................................... | 40,000 | .15 | 6,000 |
| 10/20/80 .......................................... | 20,000 | .16 | 3,200 |
| Total 1980 ...................................... | 160,000 | | $19,200 |
| 2/18/81 ........................................... | 30,000 | $.18 | $ 5,400 |
| 7/15/81 ........................................... | 10,000 | .20 | 2,000 |
| 12/15/81 .......................................... | 50,000 | .22 | 11,000 |
| Total 1981 ...................................... | 90,000 | | $18,400 |

The number of units sold during 1980 and 1981 was 90,000 units and 110,000 units, respectively. Harrison Corporation uses a periodic inventory method.

a. Compute the cost of goods sold during 1980 under the FIFO cost-flow assumption.

b. Compute the cost of goods sold during 1980 under the LIFO cost-flow assumption.

c. Compute the cost of goods sold during 1980 under the weighted-average cost-flow assumption.

d. Compute the cost of goods sold during 1981 under the FIFO cost-flow assumption.

e. Compute the cost of goods sold during 1981 under the LIFO cost-flow assumption.

f. Compute the cost of goods sold during 1981 under the weighted-average cost-flow assumption.

g. For the 2 years 1980 and 1981 taken as a whole, will FIFO or LIFO result in reporting the larger net income? What is the difference in net income for the 2-year period under FIFO as compared to LIFO? Assume an income tax rate of 40 percent for both years.

h. Which method, LIFO or FIFO, should Harrison Corporation probably prefer and why?

9.43    (This problem should not be attempted until the preceding problem has been done.) Assume the same data for the Harrison Corporation as given in the previous problem. In addition, assume the following:

| | |
|---|---:|
| Selling Price per Unit: | |
| 1980 | $.25 |
| 1981 | .30 |
| Average Current Replacement Cost: | |
| 1980 | $.15 |
| 1981 | .20 |
| Current Replacement Cost: | |
| December 31, 1980 | $.17 |
| December 31, 1981 | .22 |

a. Prepare an analysis similar to that in Exhibit 9.11 for 1980, identifying operating margins, realized holding gains and losses, and unrealized holding gains and losses for the FIFO, LIFO, and weighted-average cost-flow assumptions.

b. Repeat part a for 1981. The economic profit for 1981 should equal $13,700.

c. Demonstrate that over the 2-year period, the economic profits of Harrison Corporation are independent of the cost-flow assumption.

9.44    Sales of Mimlor Company each year are 400 units at $10 each. Sales are made evenly during the year. Mimlor Company had a beginning inventory on January 1, year 1, of 120 units valued at $600. The comptroller of the Mimlor Company is currently using a FIFO cost-flow assumption. Assume that the cost of purchases on July 1 of a given year represents the average replacement cost of goods sold at the time the goods were sold during that year.

a. Compute Cost of Goods Sold assuming FIFO, LIFO, and current replacement cost. Reconcile the three different amounts by showing holding gains. Replacement cost at year-end was $9. Purchases made during year 1 were as follows:

| | |
|---|---:|
| March 1 | 100 units @ $6 |
| July 1 | 160 units @ $7 |
| October 1 | 100 units @ $8 |

b. Compute Cost of Goods Sold and holding gains for year 3 assuming FIFO, LIFO, and current replacement cost. Use the following data. Inventory on hand January 1, year 3:

100 units valued at $800 under both FIFO and LIFO. Replacement cost at year-end was $4. Purchases made during year 3 were as follows:

| | |
|---|---|
| March 1 | 160 units @ $7 |
| July 1 | 100 units @ $6 |
| October 1 | 120 units @ $5 |

**9.45** The Shiney Silver Company is a dealer in refined silver. Shiney Silver buys silver in large lots on the London Silver Exchange and sells silver to small users. On January 1, Shiney temporarily had no silver in inventory. During the year, Shiney bought a total of 20,000 ingots of silver at various prices, averaging $130 per ingot, and sold 12,000 ingots of silver at an average price of $150 per ingot.

On December 31, Shiney had 8,000 ingots of silver in inventory. On that date the price of silver on the London Exchange was $135 per ingot, but the Shiney management believed it could buy only 4,000 ingots at that price and would have to pay $138 per ingot for any silver above 4,000 ingots. On the other hand, if purchases were spread over a 3-month period, Shiney could buy up to 10,000 ingots at the $135 price.

Shiney estimated it could liquidate its entire inventory for $140 per ingot immediately, but during the normal course of business it could sell the inventory for $155 per ingot. The cost to prepare, sell, and deliver the silver is $2 per ingot. Shiney has fixed administrative costs of $5,000 per year.

Compute the inventory value, cost of sales, and net income for Shiney Silver for the year under each of the following valuation bases:
a. Lower of cost or market.
b. Net realizable value.
c. Replacement cost.

**9.46** On January 1, the merchandise inventory of Revsine Retail Store consisted of 1,000 units acquired for $450 each. During the year, 2,500 additional units were acquired at a price of $600 each while 2,300 units were sold for $800 each. The replacement cost of these units at the time they were sold averaged $600 during the year. The replacement cost of units on December 31 was $700 per unit.
a. Calculate cost of goods sold under both FIFO and LIFO cost-flow assumptions assuming no difference in the valuation of beginning inventory.
b. Prepare partial statements of income showing gross margin on sales as revenues less cost of goods sold with both FIFO and LIFO cost-flow assumptions.
c. Prepare partial income statements separating the gross margin on sales into operating margins and realized holding gains under both FIFO and LIFO.
d. Append to the bottom of the statements prepared in part c a statement showing the amount of unrealized holding gains and the total of realized income plus unrealized holding gains.
e. If you did the steps correctly, the totals in part d are the same for both FIFO and LIFO. Is this equality a coincidence? Why or why not?

**9.47** This problem tries to make clear the difference between the impact on financial statements of the choice between a FIFO and a LIFO flow assumption. Take 12 pieces of paper and mark each one with a number between 1 and 12 inclusive. Sort the pieces of paper into a pile with the numbers in consecutive order facing up, so that number 1 is on top and number 12 is on bottom. These 12 pieces of paper are to represent 12 identical units of merchandise purchased at prices increasing from $1 to $12. Assume that four of the units are purchased each period for three periods, that three units are sold each period, and that the periodic inventory method is used.

a. Compute the cost of goods sold and ending inventory amounts for each of the three periods under a FIFO flow assumption.

b. Compute the cost-of-goods-sold and ending inventory amounts for each of the three periods under a LIFO flow assumption.

c. Re-sort the 12 pieces of paper into decreasing order to represent declining prices for successive purchases. Compute the cost-of-goods-sold and ending inventory amounts for each of the three periods under a FIFO flow assumption.

d. Repeat part **c** using a LIFO flow assumption.

e. If you are not convinced that the following are all true statements, then repeat parts **a–d** until you are.

(1) In periods of rising prices and increasing physical inventories, FIFO implies higher reported income than does LIFO.

(2) In periods of declining prices and increasing physical inventories, LIFO implies higher reported income than does FIFO.

(3) Under FIFO, current prices are reported on the balance sheet and old prices are reported on the income statement.

(4) Under LIFO, current prices are reported on the income statement and very old prices are reported on the balance sheet.

(5) The difference between FIFO and LIFO balance sheet amounts for inventory at the end of each period after the first one is larger than the differences between FIFO and LIFO reported net income for each period after the first one.

f. Assume that in period 4, only one unit (number 13) is purchased for $13, but three are sold. What additional "truth" can you deduce from comparing LIFO and FIFO cost of goods sold when physical quantities are declining?

g. The LIFO portion of Figure 9.1 represents a periodic inventory method. In this part of the question, assume that in each period the first item is acquired before any sales occur.

---

*Figure 9.1*
**To Aid in Understanding
Problem 9.47**

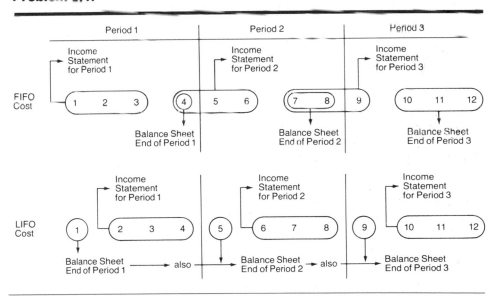

Then one item is sold; then the two items are purchased; then one more item is sold; then the last purchase is made and the last sale occurs. (If P represents purchase and S represents sale, the events are PSPPSPS.) Draw a figure similar to that in Figure 9.1 to represent a LIFO cost-flow assumption coupled with a perpetual inventory system. Convince yourself that in times of rising prices the LIFO cost-of-goods-sold figure with a periodic method exceeds LIFO cost of goods sold computed under a perpetual method.

9.48 The purpose of this problem is to help you explore the relationship between replacement cost of goods sold and historical LIFO cost of goods sold. The text makes several points in this regard:

(1) LIFO cost of goods sold is generally larger in a periodic system than in a perpetual system.

(2) LIFO cost of goods sold for most companies is insignificantly different from replacement cost of goods sold using replacement costs as of the time of sale.

(3) Historical LIFO cost of goods sold in a periodic inventory system is likely to be larger (although not significantly) than the replacement cost of goods sold using replacement cost at the time of sale.

The accompanying data are hypothetical. They are constructed from ratios of an actual retailing firm selling grocery products. Sales revenue for the year is $2,820,000. All expenses (including income taxes) other than cost of goods sold are $144,000 for the year. Exhibit 9.22 shows cost of goods available for sale.

*Exhibit 9.22*
**Data for Problem 9.48**

| | Replacement Cost of Goods Measured at | |
| --- | --- | --- |
| | Sales Dates (Mid-Month) | Purchases Dates (End of Month) |
| December 1980 | — | $ 300,000 |
| January 1981 | $ 201,000 | 202,000 |
| February 1981 | 203,000 | 204,000 |
| March 1981 | 205,000 | 206,000 |
| April 1981 | 207,000 | 208,000 |
| May 1981 | 209,000 | 210,000 |
| June 1981 | 211,000 | 212,000 |
| July 1981 | 213,000 | 214,000 |
| August 1981 | 215,000 | 216,000 |
| September 1981 | 217,000 | 218,000 |
| October 1981 | 219,000 | 220,000 |
| November 1981 | 221,000 | 222,000 |
| December 1981 | 223,000 | 224,000 |
| Replacement Cost of Goods Sold at Times of Sale | $2,544,000 | |
| Cost of Goods Available for Sale | | $2,856,000 |

The costs of the grocery items for this company increase during the year at a steady rate of about 1 percent per month. The company starts the year with an inventory equal to 1½ months' sales. These items were acquired at the end of December 1980 for $300,000. At the end of each month during 1981, the firm is assumed to acquire inventory in physical quantities equal to the next month's sales requirements. We assume that all sales occur at mid-month during each month and that all purchases occur at the end of a month to be sold during the next month. (These artificial assumptions capture the reality of a firm acquiring inventory on average $1/2$ month before it is sold and inventory turnover rate of about eight times per year.) Identical physical quantities are purchased and sold each month.

Exhibit 9.22 shows the actual cost of the items purchased at the end of each month and the replacement cost of those items if they had been acquired at mid-month.

At the end of the year, ending physical inventory is equal in amount to $1^{1}/2$ months' sales, which is the same as the physical quantity on hand at the start of the year.

a. Compute LIFO historical cost of goods sold and net income for 1981 using a periodic inventory method.

b. Compute LIFO historical cost of goods sold and net income for 1981 using a perpetual inventory method.

c. Compute net income for 1981 using replacement cost of goods sold at the time of sale.

d. What is the percentage difference between the largest and smallest cost-of-goods-sold figures computed in the preceding three parts?

e. What is the percentage error in using LIFO cost of goods sold to approximate replacement cost of goods sold? (Compute percentage errors for both LIFO periodic and LIFO perpetual calculations.)

f. Would you expect that most companies who use LIFO for tax purposes do so with a periodic inventory method or with a perpetual inventory method? Why?

9.49   (Adapted from CPA Examination.) The Topanga Manufacturing Company manufactures two products: Mult and Tran. At December 31, 1980, Topanga used the first-in, first-out (FIFO) cost-flow assumption. Effective January 1, 1981, Topanga changed to the last-in, first-out (LIFO) cost-flow assumption. The cumulative effect of this change is not determinable and, as a result, the ending inventory of 1980, for which FIFO was used, is also the beginning inventory for 1981 for LIFO. Any layers added during 1981 should be costed by reference to the first acquisitions of 1981. A periodic inventory system is used.

Information shown here was available from Topanga's inventory records for the two most recent years.

## Topanga Manufacturing Company

|  | Mult | | Tran | |
|---|---|---|---|---|
|  | Units | Unit Cost | Units | Unit Cost |
| **1980 Purchases:** | | | | |
| January 7 | 5,000 | $4.00 | 22,000 | $2.00 |
| April 16 | 12,000 | 4.50 | | |
| November 8 | 17,000 | 5.00 | 18,500 | 2.50 |
| December 13 | 10,000 | 6.00 | | |
| **1981 Purchases:** | | | | |
| February 11 | 3,000 | 7.00 | 23,000 | 3.00 |
| May 20 | 8,000 | 7.50 | | |
| October 15 | 20,000 | 8.00 | | |
| December 23 | | | 15,500 | 3.50 |
| **Units on Hand:** | | | | |
| December 31, 1980 | 15,000 | | 14,500 | |
| December 31, 1981 | 16,000 | | 13,000 | |

Compute the effect on income before income taxes for the year ended December 31, 1981, resulting from the change from the FIFO to the LIFO inventory method.

9.50   (Adapted from CPA Examination) Leininger Wholesale Company has been growing rapidly, but its accounting records have not been maintained properly. You were recently employed to correct the accounting records to assist in the preparation of the financial statements for the fiscal year ended January 31, 1981. One of the accounts you have been analyzing is entitled "Merchandise." That account in summary form follows. Numbers in parentheses following each entry correspond to related numbered explanations and additional information that you have accumulated during your analysis.

| Merchandise | | | |
|---|---|---|---|
| Balance, February 1, 1980 | (1) | Merchandise Sold | (5) |
| Purchases | (2) | Consigned Merchandise | (6) |
| Freight-in | (3) | | |
| Insurance | (4) | | |
| Freight-out on Consigned Merchandise | (7) | | |
| Freight-out on Merchandise Sold | (8) | | |

### Explanations and Additional Information

(1) You have satisfied yourself that the February 1, 1980, inventory balance represents the approximate cost of the few units in inventory at the beginning of the year. Leininger uses a FIFO cost-flow assumption.

(2) The merchandise purchased was recorded in the account at the vendors' catalog list price, which is the price appearing on the face of each vendor's invoice. All purchased merchandise is subject to a trade discount of 20 percent. These discounts have been accounted for as revenue when the merchandise was paid for.

All merchandise purchased was also subject to cash terms of 2/15, n/30. During the fiscal year Leininger recorded $3,500 in cash discounts as revenue when the merchandise was paid for. Some cash discounts were lost because payment was made after the discount period ended. All purchases of merchandise were paid for in the fiscal year in which they were recorded as purchased.

(3) All merchandise is purchased F.O.B. vendors' business locations. The freight-in amount is the cost of transporting the merchandise from the vendors' business locations to Leininger.

(4) The insurance charge is for an all-perils policy to cover merchandise in transit to Leininger from vendors.

(5) The credit to this account for merchandise sold represents the vendors' catalog list price of merchandise sold plus the cost of the beginning inventory; the debit of the entry was made to the Cost of Goods Sold account.

(6) Consigned merchandise represents goods that were shipped to Lee Company during December 1980, priced at the vendors' catalog list price. The offsetting debit was made to accounts receivable when the merchandise was shipped to Lee. Leininger does not account for consigned goods and consignment profits separately; therefore, it commingles all consignment inventories, costs, expenses, and revenues with those from nonconsigned goods.

On February 5, 1981, Leininger received a payment from Lee for one-third of the consigned merchandise, the quantity that was sold through January 31, 1981. The payment was recorded as a reduction in accounts receivable. Lee sold the merchandise at the agreed price, deducted its 16-percent sales commission and 4-percent advertising allowance, and remitted the difference. The remaining two-thirds of the consigned merchandise was unsold and held by Lee on January 31, 1981.

(7) The freight-out on consigned goods is the cost of trucking the consigned goods to Lee from Leininger.

(8) Freight-out on merchandise sold is the amount paid trucking companies to deliver merchandise sold to Leininger's customers.

Consider each of the eight numbered items independently and explain specifically how and why each item should have (if correctly accounted for) affected the amount of cost of goods sold to be included in Leininger's earnings statement, and the amount of any other account to be included in Leininger's January 31, 1981, financial statements. Organize your answer in the following format:

| Item Number | How and Why the Amount of Cost of Goods Sold Should Have Been Affected | How and Why the Amount of Any Other Account Should Have Been Affected |
|---|---|---|

9.51 (Adapted from CPA Examination.) The president of Knight Coat Company has retained you to assist in analyzing the content and pricing of the Company's inventories at December 31. Below is the information collected.

(1) Controlling accounts are maintained in the general ledger for manufacturing overhead, selling expenses, and general and administrative expenses. Detail ledgers support each controlling account and are balanced monthly. Analysis of detail charges revealed account classification errors resulting in a need to decrease manufacturing overhead by $300,000 and increase selling expenses by $85,000 and general and administrative expenses by $215,000.

(2) Overhead is charged to work-in-process monthly, crediting applied manufacturing overhead, based on direct labor cost at an expected rate of 47.5 percent. The balances before adjustment of manufacturing overhead and applied manufacturing overhead at December 31 were $1,000,000 and $950,000, respectively. Direct labor charges for the year were $2,000,000.

(3) All inventory on hand at the end of last year has been sold.

(4) Inventories are priced on a FIFO, lower-of-cost-or-market basis. Complete physical inventories were taken on December 31 and priced on a FIFO basis. The inventory accounts have been adjusted to the physical quantities and prices at December 31. No test has been made comparing inventory cost to market. Details of the inventory accounts as adjusted at December 31 follow:

| | Material | Direct Labor | Applied Overhead | Total |
|---|---|---|---|---|
| Raw Materials | $395,000 | $ — | $ — | $395,000 |
| Work in Process | 425,000 | 80,000 | 38,000 | 543,000 |
| Finished Goods | 315,000 | 60,000 | 28,500 | 403,500 |

(5) While reviewing the inventory pricing, the following was discovered:
(i) Knight received raw materials costing $12,000 five days after the beginning of the next year. The goods had been shipped December 12, at which time title passed to Knight. The invoice was recorded in December, but the goods were not counted in the December 31 physical inventory.
(ii) Invoices for $25,000 of raw materials physically counted at December 31 were not recorded until January of the next year.

(6) A comparison of inventory cost with market revealed finished goods inventory with material and direct labor costs of $100,000 and $22,000, respectively, had a replacement cost of $122,000 at December 31. Sales value of this inventory is $150,000. Selling costs are 20

percent of the selling price, and the normal profit margin is 10 percent of the selling price.
The books have not been closed. Prepare necessary adjusting journal entries, complete with explanations. Schedules supporting calculations should be in good form and either be included as part of the journal entry explanation or properly cross-referenced to the appropriate journal entry.

**9.52** (This problem should not be assigned to those who have not yet studied cost accounting, particularly standard cost systems.) Consider the operations of the SC-AC-DC Company for the year. Selling price is $100 per unit. Costs and operating data are listed below.

| | |
|---|---:|
| Standard Variable Costs per Unit: | |
| Materials and Labor ................................................. | $45 |
| Factory Overhead ................................................. | 10 |
| Total ......................................................... | $55 |
| | |
| Fixed Costs (Budgeted and Actual): | |
| Production ................................................. | $250,000 |
| Selling and Administrative ............................................. | 100,000 |
| Total ......................................................... | $350,000 |
| | |
| Operating Data: | |
| Plant Capacity ................................................. | 10,000 units |
| Sales ............................................................ | 9,500 units |
| Production ......................................................... | 9,000 units |

Total variances from standard costs for material, labor, and variable overhead were $4,500 unfavorable [(U) or Dr.] for the year. Standard variable costs per unit and total fixed costs remained the same over the last two periods. There were no variances from standard cost last period.

Under absorption costing, overhead is applied at rates based on 100 percent of capacity. All variances and underabsorbed overhead are charged to Cost of Goods Sold for the year.

**a.** Prepare tabular calculations of income for the SC-AC-DC Company for the year on (1) an absorption cost basis and (2) a direct costing basis.

**b.** Indicate how the two schedules in part **a** can be reconciled.

**c.** How would the income figures for part **a** have differed if production had been 9,500 units and sales 9,000 units?

10.1 Chapter 9 introduced the basic concepts of accounting for inventories and cost of goods sold. There we discussed the important problems of inventory valuation methods, acquisition cost inclusions, and cost-flow assumptions. This chapter explores in greater depth the accounting for inventories and cost of goods sold. We consider the application of LIFO in real-world settings and the use of various techniques for estimating inventory and cost of goods sold.

## Using LIFO in the Real World: Dollar-Value LIFO

10.2 Up to now, in describing LIFO we have assumed that the accountant keeps track of physical units. (Recall the discussion of toasters in Chapter 9 and of item X in Appendix 9.1.) When LIFO was first allowed for tax reporting, it was indeed applicable only to like physical units, such as tons of steel or board feet of lumber. The accountants at R. H. Macy & Company (the department store chain) wanted the tax-saving benefits of LIFO for their company. They devised a method of using LIFO for items that are not physically identical units, such as dresses or suits that change in style from year to year. This method is known as the *dollar-value LIFO* method and is illustrated in this section.

## Reasons for Dollar-Value LIFO

10.3 LIFO reduces income and saves taxes whenever prices are rising and inventories are not decreasing. If inventories decline in a given year, some of the original tax savings are paid in increased taxes that year.* To the extent that inventories decline, LIFO is less useful in saving or deferring income taxes. Consider using LIFO in a retail store that carries thousands of different items, most of which change in style from year to year. If LIFO were applied to each kind of dress, for example, it would not defer taxes because the inventory of dresses of a given style starts at zero and then declines to zero by the end of the season. Even if all dresses acquired in a given season are grouped together in one inventory class (or "inventory pool") and even if the amount of dresses on hand each selling season grows over time, the items in inventory at the end of one season are not on hand at the end of the next season. LIFO applied to physical units would not save taxes for a manufacturer or

---

*Strictly speaking, LIFO *defers* rather than *saves* taxes. But the deferral can be for such a long period that the present value of the eventual payments is near zero, and so it is correct to think of LIFO as saving taxes. In any case, LIFO saves dollars because the present value of taxes paid later is smaller than the present value of taxes paid earlier.

*Exhibit 10.1*
**Illustration of LIFO Computations
Using Physical Units – Steel Company**

Cost of sales equals cost of purchases for all years between base (first) year and tenth year. Only in base year and tenth year do purchases exceed sales; an inventory of 100,000 units is accumulated in base year.

|  |  | **Base (First) Year** | **Tenth Year** |
|---|---|---|---|
| Current Cost of Ending Inventory of Specialty Steel .................. | (1) | $100,000 | $216,000 |
| Price per Pound of Specialty Steel ... | (2) | $1.00 | $1.80 |
| Ending Inventory Expressed in Common Units: Number of Pounds of Steel on Hand = (1)/(2) ......... | (3) | 100,000 lb | 120,000 lb |
| LIFO Layers of Ending Inventory Expressed in Comparable (Physical) Units ........................ |  | 100,000 lb (from base year) | 20,000 lb (from tenth year) 100,000 lb (from base year) |
| [Total Agrees with Line (3)] ....... | (4) | 100,000 lb | 120,000 lb |
| LIFO Layers of Ending Inventory Expressed in Dollars of Cost of Year of Acquisition .............. | (5) | 100,000 lb × $1.00 = $100,000 | 20,000 lb × 1.80 = $ 36,000 100,000 lb × 1.00 = 100,000 |
| Cost of Ending Inventory for Balance Sheet .......................... | (6) | $100,000 | $136,000 |

Note: In practice, line (1) would be computed from lines (2) and (3).

retailer of dresses (or any other goods where styles change, such as automobiles or home appliances), because inventories physically grouped by style are close to zero at the end of each season; such inventories cannot grow over time.

10.4    Thus, if LIFO is to be used for style goods while saving taxes, it cannot be applied to physical units. To apply an inventory method requires counting something. Whereas we have been thinking of counting inventories in physical units of goods, the dollar-value method counts *dollars of a fixed purchasing power invested in goods*. So long as the dollar amount invested in individual classes or pools of inventory is growing, LIFO will not lose its usefulness merely because the physical goods in the inventory pool are changing. Dollar-value LIFO solves the problem caused by style goods.

10.5    Dollar-value LIFO serves another purpose. Assume that there is no problem with style goods. When inventory pools are narrowly defined to include only nearly identical goods, the quantities of some items may decrease while overall quantities are in-

creasing. For example, the inventory of 4'-by-8' sheets of 3/4" plywood is more likely to decrease than is the overall amount of plywood. Whenever the total amount of an inventory pool declines under LIFO, some tax benefits will be lost. The dollar-value method, based on dollars rather than physical units, allows inventory items to be grouped into broad pools (for example, a pool for plywood, generally, rather than a pool for each size) with different physical characteristics. Large inventory pools have two benefits: **(1)** dips into old LIFO layers become less likely,* and **(2)** record-keeping costs for inventory pools are reduced.

## How Dollar-Value LIFO Works

Exhibits 10.1 and 10.2 illustrate how dollar-   10.6 value LIFO works by showing its similarity to physical-unit LIFO. Exhibit 10.1 shows physical-unit LIFO and Exhibit 10.2 shows dollar-value LIFO, but the assumptions and

---

*Decreases in some items are more likely to be offset by increases in others.

*Exhibit 10.2*
**Illustration of LIFO Computations**
**Using Dollar-Value Units – Fashion**
**Goods Company**

Cost of sales equals cost of purchases for all years between base (first) year and tenth year. Only in base year and tenth year do purchases exceed sales; an inventory of 100,000 units is accumulated in base year.

|  |  | **Base (First) Year** | **Tenth Year** |
|---|---|---|---|
| Current Cost of Ending Inventory of Fashion Goods ............... | (1) | $100,000 | $216,000 |
| Price Index for Fashion Goods .... | (2) | 1.000 | 1.800 |
| Ending Inventory Expressed in Common Units: Cost of Current Year Inventory Stated in Base-Year Dollars = (1)/(2) ........... | (3) | C$100,000[a] | C$120,000[a] |
| LIFO Layers of Ending Inventory Expressed in Comparable (Base-Year Dollars) Units ............. | | C$100,000   (from base year) | C$ 20,000 (from tenth year) C$100,000 (from base year) |
| [Total Agrees with Line (3)] ..... | (4) | C$100,000[a] | C$120,000[a] |
| LIFO Layers of Ending Inventory Expressed in Dollars of Cost of Year of Acquisition ............. | (5) | C$100,000 × 1.000 = $100,000 | C$ 20,000 × 1.800 = $ 36,000 C$100,000 × 1.000 =   100,000 |
| Cost of Ending Inventory for Balance Sheet ................ | (6) | $100,000 | $136,000 |

[a]In practice, the amounts on lines (3) and (4) would be preceded with a conventional $ sign. We show the sign C$ before the amounts to make clear that these are comparable units. See the discussion of constant-dollar accounting in Chapter 26, where the notation is explained in detail.

numbers in the exhibits are the same. They apply to a situation, artificially simplified, in which the following assumptions have been made:

**1.** At the end of the first year, inventory on hand costs $100,000.

**2.** Sales equal purchases for the next 9 years.

**3.** Physical inventory increases during the tenth year.

**4.** Prices of the items in inventory grow at the rate of about 6 percent per year, so that by the end of the tenth year, prices are 80 percent higher (= $1.06^{10} - 1$) than at the beginning of the first year.

The critical assumptions for the illustration are that physical inventories increase between the first and tenth periods and that the prices of the items in inventory change. If there were no physical increase in inven-

tory, there would be no problem. If the prices did not change, the problem would be too simple. (It is *not* important that the two periods are 10 years apart or that prices increased rather than decreased.)

**Physical-Unit LIFO** Consider first Exhibit 10.1. The current cost of ending inventory of specialty steel appears on line (1), price per pound of specialty steel appears on line (2), and the number of physical units (pounds) of specialty steel appears on line (3). Ordinarily, one would count inventory to find out the number of pounds, line (3), and multiply that number by the price per pound, line (2), to get the number shown on line (1). The order shown here is chosen specifically to parallel the order for data encountered in the dollar-value method.

Line (3) states the inventory in common units that can be compared from one year to the other. The common units are physical

10.7

10.8

units—pounds. Line (4) "layers" the common units by year of acquisition. Reading across line (4) shows that year 10's inventory consists of 100,000 lb from the first (or base) year, and 20,000 lb from the tenth year. Then, line (5) converts the layers of common physical units into dollars of historical cost. Line (6) accumulates the sum of the dollars of cost. Lines (3) and (4) convert the $216,000 amount from line (1), the current value of the inventory, into layers of cost under the LIFO (or FISH: first-in, still-here) principle. It is not true that year 10's physical inventory actually consists of

100,000 lb carried over from the first, base, year. LIFO merely assumes that of the 120,000 lb currently on hand, 100,000 lb will be assigned base-year costs. Exhibit 10.3 depicts the process of constructing layers and assigning costs to them.

**Dollar-Value LIFO** Now consider Exhibit 10.9
10.2. The current cost of ending inventory of fashion goods (dresses, say) appears on line (1). A price index for these fashion goods appears on line (2). Whereas in the physical-units method we know the price of the physical units, in the dollar-value method we use

*Exhibit 10.3*
**LIFO Layers in Common Units and Nominal Dollars**

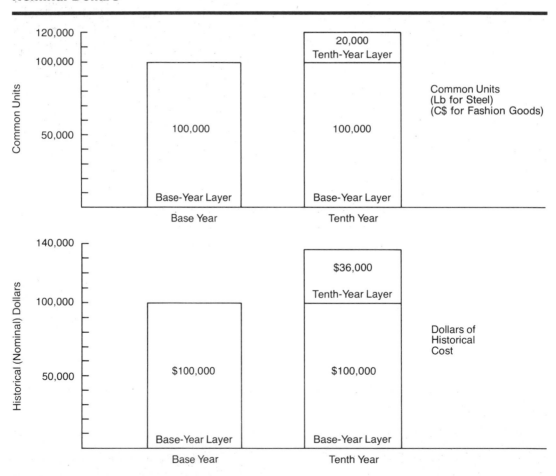

a price index for the types of goods in the inventory pool. A price index is a series of numbers, one per period. The number for a given period tells the average price during the period of a commodity or group of commodities relative to the price in a base period. If the price index in period 1 is 1.000 (or 1.400) and in period 10 is 1.800 (or 2.520), then we know that prices are 80 percent higher [= (1.800/1.000) − 1 = (2.520/1.400) − 1] in the tenth period than in the first.*

10.10    The amounts on line (3) result from dividing the amounts on line (1) by the amounts on line (2), just as in Exhibit 10.1. Line (3) states the inventory in common units comparable one year to the other. The common units are dollars of fixed purchasing power. If you are unaccustomed to thinking in terms of dollars of constant purchasing power, then interpreting the amounts on line (3) may be difficult. You can interpret the amounts this way: If you had an amount of money on hand in the *base* year equal to the amount shown on line (3), you could buy the physical quantity of inventory that was actually purchased by the amounts shown on line (1). Thus $120,000 on hand in the base year would buy a certain amount of inventory, say 120,000 lb at $1.00/lb. If prices have increased by 80 percent since the base year (to 180 percent of base-year levels), then that same physical quantity of inventory would cost $216,000 (= 1.80 × $120,000) in the tenth year.

10.11    The notation on line (3), "C$120,000," purposefully differs from the more common notation "$120,000." You should be aware that these are units of constant, base-year, purchasing power, not current dollars of year-10 purchasing power. The notation "C$" is used because of the FASB's use of that notation in its pronouncements on con-

stant dollar accounting, which is explained in Chapter 26. The symbol "C$" means "constant dollars" and serves exactly the same role in Exhibit 10.2 that the symbol "lb" serves in Exhibit 10.1.

Just as in the physical-units case, the pur-    10.12 pose of line (3) is to state the inventory in common units. In this case, the common units are dollars of base-year purchasing power. Line (4), just as in Exhibit 10.1, layers the *common units* by year of acquisition. Reading across line (4) shows that year 10's inventory of C$120,000 consists of C$100,000 from the base year and C$20,000 from the tenth year. Line (5) converts the layers of common units into dollars of cost.† Line (6) sums the dollars of cost. It is not true that the inventory was $5/6$ (= 100,000/120,000) acquired in the base year and $1/6$ acquired in the current year. LIFO cost flow merely assumes that $5/6$ of the amount physically on hand is assigned costs of the base year and $1/6$ of the amount is assigned costs of the tenth year.

Exhibit 10.3 illustrates the process of con-    10.13 structing LIFO layers of common units and of assigning historical costs to those layers.

## Procedures for Dollar-Value LIFO

The dollar-value LIFO method computes    10.14 the cost of ending inventory. The cost of beginning inventory is known from information generated at the end of the preceding accounting period. The cost of purchases is known, as usual. The inventory equation provides the cost of goods sold.

The dollar-value LIFO ending inventory    10.15 is found in six steps, corresponding to the six numbered lines of Exhibits 10.1 and 10.2. Exhibit 10.4 gives a more realistic example with the same six steps.

1. Compute the current cost of ending in-

---

*Many companies use price indexes supplied by the U.S. Bureau of Labor Statistics for dollar-value LIFO. The source of the price index need not concern us here. Keep in mind only that the price index traces the average prices over time of a type of good similar to those in the inventory pool. If you are unfamiliar with price indexes, their construction, and use, you might find helpful the discussion of general price indexes in Chapter 26.

---

†Some readers will readily see that the notation "C$20,000 × 1.800 = $36,000" on line (5) actually means "C$20,000 × 1.800 $ per C$ = $36,000." The $36,000 is a figure in nominal (tenth-year) dollars resulting from multiplying an amount expressed in base-year dollars times an index number that represents nominal dollars per base-year dollar.

*Exhibit 10.4*
**Illustration of Dollar-Value LIFO
Inventory Valuation**

Price Index for December 31 of Base Year = 1.000
Inventory Value at 12/31 of Base Year at Base Year Prices = $100,000 = C$100,000

| | First Year | Second Year | Third Year | Fourth Year | Fifth Year |
|---|---|---|---|---|---|
| (1) End-of-Year Inventory at Current Prices ........ | $120,000 | $90,000 | $110,000 | $100,000 | $120,000 |
| (2) Current Cost Price Index for End of Year ....... | 1.100 | 1.200 | 1.150 | 1.250 | 1.200 |
| (3) End-of-Year Inventory at Base-Year Prices [= (1)/(2)] ............ | C$109,091 | C$75,000 | C$95,652 | C$80,000 | C$100,000 |
| (4) LIFO Inventory Layers at Base-Year Prices: | | | | | |
| a. From Base-Year Stock ........... | C$100,000 | C$75,000 | C$75,000 | C$75,000 | C$75,000 |
| b. From First Year .... | 9,091 | 0 | 0 | 0 | 0 |
| c. From Second Year | — | 0 | 0 | 0 | 0 |
| d. From Third Year ... | — | — | 20,652 | 5,000 | 5,000 |
| e. From Fourth Year .. | — | — | — | 0 | 0 |
| f. From Fifth Year .... [Sum of Lines (4a) through (4f) = Line (3)] | — | — | — | — | 20,000 |
| (5) LIFO Inventory Layers at Cost in Year of Acquisition: | | | | | |
| a. From Base-Year Stock = (4a) × 1.000 ........... | $100,000 | $ 75,000 | $ 75,000 | $ 75,000 | $ 75,000 |
| b. From First-Year Stock = (4b) × 1.100 ........... | 10,000 | 0 | 0 | 0 | 0 |
| c. From Second-Year Stock = (4c) × 1.200 ........... | — | 0 | 0 | 0 | 0 |
| d. From Third-Year Stock = (4d) × 1.150 ........... | — | — | 23,750 | 5,750 | 5,750 |
| e. From Fourth-Year Stock = (4e) × 1.250 ........... | — | — | — | 0 | 0 |
| f. From Fifth-Year Stock = (4f) × 1.200 ........... | — | — | — | — | 24,000 |
| (6) End-of-Year LIFO Inventory at Original Costs = Sum of Lines (5a) through (5f) ...... | $110,000 | $ 75,000 | $ 98,750 | $ 80,750 | $104,750 |

C$ denotes dollars of purchasing power for the base year.

See also Exhibit 10.5 for illustration of LIFO layers for this example.

ventory. This is the amount obtained by summing the most recent invoice costs for the physical amounts in ending inventory.* It is equal to the amount that would be reported for ending inventory under FIFO.

**2.** Obtain a price index series for goods of the sort in the LIFO pool being analyzed. The U.S. Labor Department makes such series available. One price index number is needed for each year since the firm has been on LIFO (or, more precisely, since the date of the earliest LIFO layer).† The method does not require the index number for the base year to be ''1.000,'' but examples are easier to work with if the base-year price index number is 1.000. We assume here that the price series has been rescaled, if necessary, to set the base-year index number to 1.000.**

**3.** Convert the current cost of ending inven-

tory for each year into common units by dividing the numbers on line (1) for each year by the index number on line (2) for that year.

**4.** Starting with the base year, sort the common unit amounts on line (3) into LIFO layers. Label each layer with its year of acquisition. (Note in Exhibits 10.4 and 10.5 that once a firm dips through old layers, those layers never reemerge.)

**5.** Convert the common unit amount for each layer into its historical cost: Multiply the amount for the layer from line (4) by the price index number on line (2).‡

**6.** Sum the historical costs of the layers to derive the dollar-value LIFO ending inventory.

## Cost-Flow Assumption for LIFO Layers

The steps described in the preceding section for dollar-value LIFO are those commonly used, but they are not fully consistent with a LIFO assumption. LIFO means last-in, first-out. During any year when inventory decreases, LIFO means that the most recently preceding year's layers are assumed to be used. During any year when inventory increases, amounts will be added to inventory. Exhibit 10.6 illustrates a year of inventory increase. Under assumption (I) the first few purchases for the current year go into the LIFO layer for the current year. Under assumption (II) the last purchases go into the LIFO layer. The method for dollar-value LIFO typically used makes assumption (II): that the last few purchases of the year make up the LIFO layer for the current year. That assumption is made when the price index is selected to convert the new LIFO layer for a particular year, line (4), to current prices, line (5). Because most firms use the price index for the end of the year from line (2), the layer for that year consists of end-of-year costs. If the year's layer is to be from the first purchases of the year, then the price index for the start of the year must be used on

10.16

---

*It may also be obtained by using only the most recent invoice cost per unit and extending that per unit cost to the entire ending inventory. During periods of rising prices this method will generally yield a slightly larger number for current cost of ending inventory than does FIFO.

†Most descriptions of dollar-value LIFO assume a price index number representing prices near the end of each year, but, as we discuss later, a price index number for the beginning of the period is more appropriate.

**To convert an index series so that a given number is replaced by 1.000, divide all numbers in the series by the given number. To give two examples, suppose that the price index series for home appliances and for clothes show:

|         | Appliances | Clothes |
|---------|-----------|---------|
| Year 13 | 132.46 | 150.0 |
| Year 14 | 137.54 | 156.0 |
| Year 15 | 143.73 | 166.0 |
| Year 16 | 150.08 | 179.0 |
| Year 17 | 154.92 | 195.0 |
| ⋮ | | |
| Year 20 | 184.35 | 240.0 |

Assume that year *14* is to be the base year. Then all numbers in the Appliance series are divided by 137.54 and all numbers in the Clothes series are divided by 156.0. The resulting rescaled series are as follows:

|         | Appliances | Clothes |
|---------|-----------|---------|
| Year 13 | 0.963 | 0.962 |
| Year 14 | 1.000 | 1.000 |
| Year 15 | 1.045 | 1.064 |
| Year 16 | 1.091 | 1.147 |
| Year 17 | 1.126 | 1.250 |
| ⋮ | | |
| Year 20 | 1.340 | 1.538 |

---

‡If the price index number for the base year is not 1.000, then the description of this step becomes more cumbersome but is arithmetically equivalent.

*Exhibit 10.5*
**LIFO Layers for Exhibit 10.4**

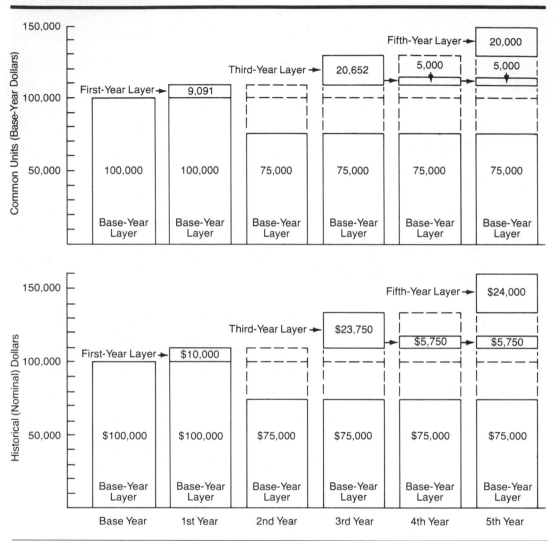

line (5). Firms seeking the maximum possible advantage from LIFO will compute the amounts for layers of a given year by using the price index for the early purchases. They will use start-of-year price index numbers on line (5) even though end-of-year prices are used in line (2) to compute ending inventory at base-year prices.

10.17     Some accountants and financial analysts use the terms "LIFO/FIFO," "LIFO/ LIFO," and "LIFO/weighted-average" in describing cost-flow assumptions. By this double label they distinguish those LIFO companies who compute the cost of a given year's LIFO layer assuming FIFO–(II) in Exhibit 10.6, assuming LIFO–(I) in Exhibit 10.6, or assuming weighted-average cost flow for the year.

A LIFO/weighted-average firm, using dollar-value LIFO, will use on line (5) price in-     10.18

*Exhibit 10.6*
**Source of LIFO Layer within a Year**
**(I) From First Purchases**
**(II) From Last Purchases**

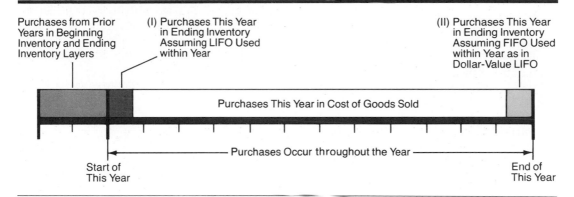

Purchases from Prior Years in Beginning Inventory and Ending Inventory Layers

(I) Purchases This Year in Ending Inventory Assuming LIFO Used within Year

(II) Purchases This Year in Ending Inventory Assuming FIFO Used within Year as in Dollar-Value LIFO

Purchases This Year in Cost of Goods Sold

————— Purchases Occur throughout the Year —————

Start of This Year

End of This Year

dex numbers representing the average costs for the year rather than the year-end costs used by LIFO/FIFO firms or the beginning-of-year costs used by LIFO/LIFO firms.

## Estimating Cost of Ending Inventory and Cost of Goods Sold

10.10   This section presents techniques that are based on a single concept but are used for two different purposes. We discuss the gross margin method, the retail inventory method, and the dollar-value LIFO retail method.

### Purposes of the Techniques

10.20   To count every item in inventory is generally expensive, whether one counts physical units or dollar values of items in inventory. Firms try to count as seldom as possible while satisfying generally accepted accounting principles and the need for effective inventory control.

10.21   **Estimating Cost of Goods Sold with No Data on Ending Inventory** In many businesses using periodic inventory systems, adequate inventory control can be achieved by taking a physical inventory once each year

at the end of the year. Many firms must, however, issue quarterly financial statements. Quarterly income cannot be measured without an estimate of cost of goods sold. Financial position cannot be measured without an estimate of ending inventory. The *gross margin method,* discussed below, can be used to obtain estimates of cost of goods sold and inventory during an accounting period.

**Estimating Amounts in a Retail Enterprise** Recall your experience as a customer   10.22 in a department store or grocery store. Think about the data you, as a customer, encounter. For each item in the store, you may see nothing more than a retail, or selling, price. You might find code numbers describing the merchandise. When you purchase the item, the store typically records only the amount of the sale and, perhaps, the department from which the item comes. Only occasionally does it record anything else specific about the item sold. The store generally knows only these items:

1. The cost of all the items it has purchased.

2. The total of the selling prices (retail, not cost) of the goods it has put out for sale.

3. The total of the selling prices of the goods it has sold (that is, sales).

The store keeps track of retail selling prices of beginning inventory, purchases, sales, and ending inventory. It does not keep track of the *costs* of the items sold, and therefore cannot compute directly the *cost* of ending inventory. Accounting requires data on costs.

10.23    The *retail inventory method* enables us to derive satisfactory estimates of the *cost* of goods sold and the *cost* of ending inventory from data on the retail selling price of goods sold and the relation between cost and retail price of goods available for sale.

10.24    **Foundation of the Gross Margin and Retail Inventory Methods** The common foundation of the gross margin method and the retail inventory methods is the fact that most businesses mark up the cost of similar kinds of merchandise by a relatively constant percentage to obtain selling prices. For example, nearly every college bookstore sets the selling price of a textbook 25 percent more than its cost to the bookstore. Put another way, the manager of the bookstore would say that the gross margin (= retail selling price less cost) is 20 percent of selling price.* To take another example, men's clothing in a department store is likely to carry a selling price twice the cost to the store. The selling price of most types of retail items stands in a relatively constant percentage to their costs. This fact is used in estimating Ending Inventory and Cost of Goods Sold under the gross margin and retail inventory methods.

---

*This is one of the most confusing areas in business terminology. If you buy a share of stock for $8 and sell it for $10, both you and your stockbroker would call that a 25 percent (= $2/$8) *gain*. You would compute the gain percentage with the denominator being original cost. A retailer, however, speaks of the *markup* on an item selling for $10 that cost $8 as being 20 percent (= $2/$10). The retailer uses selling price, not cost, as the denominator. It seems illogical to do so, but it is common practice and the effective participant in the business world will have to understand these differences in terms.

## The Gross Margin Method

Estimating cost of goods sold when there are  10.25  no data on ending inventory can be done with the *gross margin* method. It is sometimes also called the "gross profit" method. The method is used also to reconstruct inventory accounts when inventory and inventory records have been lost or destroyed and when, for whatever reason, counting ending inventory is not expedient.

The *gross margin percentage* is  10.26

$$\text{Gross Margin Percentage} = \frac{\text{Selling Price} - \text{Acquisition Cost}}{\text{Selling Price}}.$$

Refer to the data at the top of Exhibit 10.7, where the gross margin method is illustrated (in parallel with the retail method discussed later). Data available include the cost of beginning inventory, the cost of purchases (net), net sales measured at selling prices of goods sold, and the gross margin percentage. (Throughout this section we refer to net purchases and net sales. Computation of net purchases and net sales is relatively straightforward once discounts, allowances, returns, freight charges, taxes, and the like are considered. For the most part, we do not complicate the illustrations with these items, which are discussed in Chapters 7 and 9.)

The steps in the gross margin method are  10.27  as follows:

**1.** Compute the acquisition cost of goods available for sale using amounts from the beginning inventory and net purchases during the period.

**2.** Ascertain the gross margin percentage using historical data, current pricing policies, and similar sources of information.

**3.** Compute net sales for the current period.

**4.** Multiply net sales for the current period by the gross margin percentage. Subtract the resulting total gross margin from net sales to obtain the cost of goods sold.

**5.** Use the inventory equation to compute the cost of ending inventory.

In the example in Exhibit 10.7, the cost of ending inventory is

$$\frac{\text{Ending}}{\text{Inventory}} = \frac{\text{Beginning}}{\text{Inventory}} + \frac{\text{Purchases}}{\text{at Cost}} - \frac{\text{Estimated } Cost}{\text{of Goods Sold.}}$$

$$\$165,000 = \$150,000 + \$195,000 - (1.00 - .25) \times \$240,000.$$

## Retail Inventory Methods

10.28  In the gross margin method, we use the gross margin percentage, derived from a firm's usual markup on cost in setting selling prices, to estimate cost of goods sold. The gross margin percentage is defined as follows:

$$\frac{\text{Gross Margin}}{\text{Percentage}} = \frac{\text{Selling Price} - \text{Acquisition Cost}}{\text{Selling Price}}.$$

In the retail inventory method an equivalent percentage, the *cost percentage,* is used to estimate the cost of ending inventory. The cost percentage is defined as follows:

$$\frac{\text{Cost}}{\text{Percentage}} = 1 - \frac{\text{Gross}}{\begin{array}{c}\text{Margin}\\\text{Percentage}\end{array}} = \frac{\text{Acquisition Cost}}{\text{Selling Price}}.$$

The cost percentage and the gross margin percentage always sum to one. Knowing or using one, therefore, is equivalent to knowing or using the other.

10.29  Exhibit 10.7 illustrates the retail method in its simplest form. The illustration parallels that for the gross margin method to show how closely the two methods resemble each other.

10.30  The steps in the retail method are as follows:

**1.** Compute the acquisition cost and selling price of goods available for sale using amounts from the beginning inventory plus net purchases during the period.

**2.** Compute the cost percentage for goods available for sale from **(1)**.

**3.** Compute the total selling prices of ending inventory.

**4.** Multiply the selling price of goods in ending inventory by the cost percentage to estimate the *cost* of ending inventory.

**5.** Use the inventory equation to compute cost of goods sold.

The remainder of this section discusses complications caused by the realities of retail business operations.

## Retail Operations and Terminology

10.31  The preceding discussion of the retail method assumes that once an item is purchased and given a selling price, the selling price does not change. In reality, merchants change the selling prices of goods from time to time, increasing prices for popular items in short supply (snowblowers in Chicago in February) and decreasing them for out-of-style, out-of-season items or merchandise otherwise less in demand than had been originally anticipated.

10.32  When a retailer acquires items for inventory, the items are given a selling price. The difference between original selling price and cost is technically called a *markon,* but many retailers, accountants, and other business people use the term *markup* or *original markup.* When, for whatever reason, the originally established retail price is increased, the difference between the new and the old selling prices is technically called *markup,* but because that term is also used for markon, the term *additional markup* is used. (We use the terms "original markup" for the original difference and "additional markup" for the subsequent increases.) If a selling price is lowered, the reduction in selling price is called either a "markup cancellation" or a "markdown," depending on what has happened. If there had previously been an additional markup, the reduction is called a *markup cancellation,* and if there had been only the original markup (markon), then the reduction is called a *markdown.* If, after a markdown, prices are later increased, the increase is called a *markdown cancellation.* The amounts labeled markup cancellation and markdown cancellation do not exceed the amounts for the additional markups or markdowns that are being cancelled. (The reason is given later.)

10.33  Exhibit 10.8 illustrates these terms. Refer

*Exhibit 10.7*
**Gross Margin and Retail Inventory Methods Compared**

### DATA FOR ILLUSTRATIONS

| | At Cost | At Selling Price |
|---|---|---|
| Beginning Inventory, January 1 | $150,000 | $200,000 |
| Purchases (Net), January 1–March 31 | 195,000 | 260,000 |
| Sales, Net, January 1–March 31 | — | 240,000 |
| Cost of Goods Sold, January 1–March 31 | Computed from Gross Margin Percentage in Gross Margin Method / Computed from Inventory Equation in Retail Method | — |
| Ending Inventory, March 31 | Computed from Inventory Equation in Gross Margin Method / Computed from Cost Percentage in Retail Inventory Method | Not Needed in Gross Margin Method / Physically Counted and Prices Summed in Retail Method |
| Name of Critical Percentage | Gross Margin Percentage / Cost Percentage Calculated | |
| Source of Critical Percentage | Given, 25% | |

### GROSS MARGIN METHOD

| | At Cost | At Selling Price |
|---|---|---|
| Beginning Inventory | $150,000 | |
| Purchases | 195,000 | |
| Goods Available for Sale | $345,000 | |
| Gross Margin in Dollars on Sales Estimated from Gross Margin Percentage (Given) × Selling Price of Goods Sold: | | |
| Selling Price of Goods Sold | | $240,000 |
| Less Gross Margin at 25% | | (60,000) |
| Less Estimated Cost of Goods Sold: Net Sales Revenue in Dollars Less Gross Margin in Dollars [$240,000 − (.25 × $240,000)] | 180,000 | |
| Cost of Ending Inventory | $165,000 | |

### RETAIL INVENTORY METHOD

| | At Cost | At Selling Price |
|---|---|---|
| Beginning Inventory | $150,000 | $200,000 |
| Purchases | 195,000 | 260,000 |
| Goods Available for Sale | $345,000 | $460,000 |
| Cost Percentage Estimated from: | | |
| $\dfrac{\text{Cost of Goods Available}}{\text{Selling Price of Goods Available}} = \dfrac{\$345,000}{\$460,000} = 75.0\%$ | | |
| Ending Inventory (Counted and Selling Prices Summed) | | 220,000 |
| Less: Cost of Ending Inventory (Estimated as Cost Percentage × Selling Price of Ending Inventory) = .75 × $220,000 | 165,000 | |
| Cost of Goods Sold | $180,000 | |

to item F in Exhibit 10.8. The acquisition cost is $12, the original markup is $8 (original selling price of $20), additional markup is $4 (selling price now $24), markup cancellation was first $3 (selling price now $21), followed by another price reduction of $5 (consisting of markup cancellation of $1 and markdown of $4, yielding a selling price of $16), followed by a markdown cancellation of $2 (selling price now $18). This example is merely illustrative; seldom would so much price change occur on any one item.

## Illustrations of Retail Inventory Method

10.34   Exhibit 10.8 shows data used in this section to illustrate the various choices and complications of the retail method. That exhibit shows the history of six kinds of items, A–F, bought for a retail store. All items cost $12, and the original markup for all items is

$8. After the original markup, each of the six items has a different history of additional markups, markdowns, markup cancellations, and markdown cancellations. Goods available for sale include a total of 6,000 items of the six types: 1,000 in beginning inventory and 5,000 purchased. Unrealistically, we assume that all purchases for the 6-month period occurred in January. This assumption makes presentation simpler without oversimplifying. The dollar totals of beginning inventory, purchases, original markups, later selling price adjustments, and ending inventory appear at the bottom of Exhibit 10.8.

Exhibit 10.9 summarizes the transactions   10.35 and events for these six items from January through June. The first column shows the acquisition cost of beginning inventory plus purchases during the 6-month period. The second column shows the beginning inventory and purchases at selling prices together with the amounts of additional markups,

---

*Exhibit 10.8*
### Data for Retail Inventory Method
### Illustrating All Selling Price Adjustments

| Month | Event | A | B | C | D | E | F |
|---|---|---|---|---|---|---|---|
| | | | | Dollars per Item | | | |
| January | Cost | $12 | $12 | $12 | $12 | $12 | $12 |
| | Original Markup (Markon) | 8 | 8 | 8 | 8 | 8 | 8 |
| February | Additional Markup | | 4 | | 4 | 4 | 4 |
| March | Markdown | | | (2) | | | |
| April | Markup Cancellation | | | | (3) | (3) | (3) |
| May | Markup Cancellation | | | | | (1) | (1) |
| | Markdown | | | | | (4) | (4) |
| June | Markdown Cancellation | | | | | | 2 |
| | Final Selling Price | $20 | $24 | $18 | $21 | $16 | $18 |

| | At Cost | At Selling Price |
|---|---|---|
| | | Dollar Totals |
| January 1, Beginning Inventory | $11,000 | $ 20,000 |
| January 1–June 30, Purchases (Net) | 61,000 | 100,000 |
| Additional Markups | | 16,000 |
| Markup Cancellations | | (11,000) |
| Markdowns | | (10,000) |
| Markdown Cancellations | | 2,000 |
| Sales (Net) | | (91,800) |
| June 30, Ending Inventory | | $25,200 |

*Exhibit 10.9*
**Steps in Carrying Out Retail Inventory
Method Illustrating Choice of Cost
Percentages and All Selling Price
Adjustments**

| | At Cost (1) | At Selling Price (2) | Cost Percentage (3) = (1)/(2) |
|---|---|---|---|
| I. and II. Calculation of Cost Percentage and Final Selling Price of Goods Available for Sale: | | | |
| Beginning Inventory ................. | $11,000 | $ 20,000 | |
| Net Purchases ...................... | 61,000 | 100,000 | |
| Goods Available for Sale before Any Selling Price Adjustments .......... | $72,000 | $120,000 | (i) 60.0% |
| Additional Markups ................ | | 16,000 | |
| Goods Available for Sale after All Markups ........................ | $72,000 | $136,000 | (ii) 52.9% |
| Markup Cancellations .............. | | (11,000) | |
| Goods Available for Sale after All Markups and Markup Cancellations . | $72,000 | $125,000 | (iii) 57.6%[c] |
| Markdowns ....................... | | (10,000) | |
| Markdown Cancellations ............ | | 2,000 | |
| Goods Available for Sale after All Sales Adjustments .................... | $72,000 | $117,000 | (iv) 61.5% |
| III. Calculation of Selling Price of Ending Inventory: | | | |
| Goods Available for Sale after All Sales Adjustments .................... | | $117,000 [a] | |
| Less: Net Sales .................... | | (91,800) | |
| Ending Inventory ................... | | $ 25,200 [b] | |

| | Most Conservative (ii) | Conventional Lower of Cost or Market (iii)[c] | Average Cost Approximation (iv) |
|---|---|---|---|
| IV. Calculation of Cost of Ending Inventory: | | | |
| Selling Price of Ending Inventory ..... | $25,200 | $ 25,200 | $25,200 |
| × Cost Percentage ................. | ×.529 | ×.576 | ×.615 |
| Cost of Ending Inventory ........... | $13,331 | $ 14,515 | $15,498 |
| V. Calculation of Cost of Goods Sold from Inventory Equation: | | | |
| Cost of Goods Available for Sale ...... | $72,000 | $ 72,000 | $72,000 |
| Less: Cost of Ending Inventory ....... | (13,331) | (14,515) | (15,498) |
| Cost of Goods Sold ................ | $58,669 | $ 57,485 | $56,502 |

Note: Remarks on the cost percentages appear on the facing page.

Remarks on Cost Percentages:

**(i)** Complement of the gross margin percentage; rests on unreasonable assumption that all selling price adjustments relate to units sold.

**(ii)** Most conservative in its effects on ending inventory, cost of goods sold, and net income; rests on assumptions that most markup cancellations and net markdowns apply to units in ending inventory; probable choice for tax reporting, where allowed.

**(iii)** Conventional method; usually called "lower of cost or market" because it is more conservative than **(iv)**, but for no other reason; rests on assumption that net markups apply primarily to units sold and net markdowns apply to units in ending inventory.

**(iv)** Least conservative in its effects on ending inventory, cost of goods sold, and net income; rests on the assumption that selling price adjustments are equally likely to apply to units sold and units in ending inventory; if assumption is valid, provides valuations of ending inventory approximating acquisition cost.

[a]Note that, whereas selling price adjustments are either included in or excluded from the various cost percentages, all selling price adjustments are included in the computation of the selling price of goods available for sale.

[b]The ending inventory at selling prices can either be **(1)** estimated using the selling price of goods available for sale and net sales for the period, or **(2)** computed based on an actual physical inventory. In retail establishments a physical inventory is taken at least once each year to verify the inventory amounts shown on the books.

[c]Commonly used method is **(iii)**. The cost percentage results from taking all markups and markup cancellations into account but not markdowns or markdown cancellations.

markup cancellations, markdowns, and markdown cancellations. Goods available for sale have an acquisition cost of $72,000 and final selling price after all adjustments of $117,000. With sales of $91,800 during the period, the ending inventory at selling prices is $25,200. This ending inventory amount on the books should be verified periodically by a physical inventory.

10.36    To convert the ending inventory at selling prices to ending inventory at acquisition cost requires multiplying the $25,200 ending inventory at selling prices by a cost percentage. There are several cost percentages that might be calculated depending on which selling price adjustments are included in the computations. Column (3) of Exhibit 10.9 shows four possible cost percentages.[*] Herein lies the only real difficulty and the source of virtually all confusion about the retail inventory method: Which cost percentage should be used?[†] In practice, the third

---

[*]A fifth, taken after markdowns, but before markdown cancellations, could be shown. Because that cost percentage is never used (so far as we know), it has been omitted.

[†]That the different percentages are so close numerically should not lead you to assume that the difference is immaterial. Be aware that in the typical retail operation, cost of goods sold is a number 15 to 20 times as large as net income. A 1-percent change in cost of goods sold implies a 15- to 20-percent change in gross margin. The relation between the cost percentage and cost of goods sold is complicated by the rate of inventory turnover, but a one or two percentage point difference between cost percentages can easily have a material impact on net income. See Problem **P10.13**.

cost percentage—the one marked **(iii)**—is used. This cost percentage takes all markups and markup cancellations into account but not markdowns nor markdown cancellations.

Note that in all four cost percentages, the numerator is the acquisition cost of goods available for sale of $72,000. The denominator amounts differ with respect to their inclusion or exclusion of selling price adjustments. The first cost percentage excludes all selling price adjustments, the second includes markups only, the third includes markups and markup cancellations, and the fourth includes all selling price adjustments.    10.37

Now observe the effect of using different cost percentages on the calculation of ending inventory and cost of goods sold at acquisition cost.[‡] The lower portion of Exhibit 10.9 shows that the most conservative measure of ending inventory and cost of goods sold is obtained by using the *lowest* cost percentage (52.9 percent in this example). The lower the cost percentage, the smaller will be the ending inventory at acquisition cost. All else being equal, the smaller the amount of ending inventory, the larger will be cost of goods sold and the smaller will be net income. The smallest cost percentage is obtained by including markups in the denomi-    10.38

---

[‡]Whether the various types of selling price adjustments are included in or excluded from the cost percentages, all selling price adjustments are included in the computation of the selling price of goods available for sale.

nator but excluding markup cancellations, markdowns, and markdown cancellations.*

10.39 The least conservative measure of ending inventory and cost of goods sold is obtained by using the *highest* cost percentage (61.5 percent in this example). More of the acquisition cost of goods available for sale is allocated to the units in ending inventory and less to goods sold relative to other cost percentages.

10.40 The other two cost percentages (57.6 percent and 60.0 percent) provide amounts for ending inventory and cost of goods sold that lie between the most and least conservative.

10.41 **Choosing a Cost Percentage** There is no generally accepted accounting principle for choosing among the four cost percentages. In practice, most accountants use the third cost percentage shown in Exhibit 10.9, 57.6 percent. The following discussion indicates some of the factors to be considered in selecting a cost percentage.

10.42 The first cost percentage shows the normal markup on purchases before any selling price adjustments. It is equal to one minus the gross profit percentage used in the gross profit method. This first cost percentage presumes that all markups and markdowns relate to the units sold. Thus the ending inventory includes units whose prices were initially set using the firm's normal markup and not subsequently changed. This latter assumption is probably unreasonable in most cases. To understand why this is unreasonable requires an understanding of the dynamics of price setting and the movement of goods.

10.43 Businesses are not charities; they attempt to maximize income over long periods of time. Businesses price goods to maximize income. They change prices as selling conditions suggest, raising prices for goods when demand exceeds forecasts and lowering prices when demand seems to fall short of expectations. It then seems reasonable to

*A still smaller cost percentage could be obtained by including markdown cancellations as well. It seems illogical, however, to include markdown cancellations without first including markdowns.

deduce that underpriced goods will sell faster and overpriced goods slower than "correctly" priced goods. Markup cancellations and markdowns are signs of overpriced goods. Ending inventory is likely to contain a larger-than-random percentage of formerly overpriced goods than of underpriced goods—the underpriced goods are more likely to have been sold. Thus, the ending inventory is likely to consist of a larger-than-random percentage of goods overpriced at some stage of their history for which markdowns have been taken. Thus, the assumption underlying this first percentage, that all markups and markdowns relate to units sold, is not usually justifiable.

10.44 The second cost percentage includes markups but excludes all other selling price adjustments. Using this cost percentage provides the most conservative measure of ending inventory and cost of goods sold. If the valuation objective is to state ending inventory at an amount approximating lower of cost or market, we feel that this second cost percentage should be used. The ending inventory is likely to include a larger-than-random percentage of goods that have been overpriced at some stage in their history. Such goods are most likely to have market price less than cost and to require a writedown. Without comparing acquisition costs and replacement costs for every item in inventory, it is impossible to determine *how much* of a writedown is needed. The second cost percentage at least provides the largest writedown of the four percentages illustrated.

10.45 The third cost percentage includes markups and markup cancellations but excludes markdowns and markdown cancellations. When most writers speak of the "conventional retail method" or the "retail method approximating lower of cost or market," they are referring to the use of this third cost percentage. We can find no convincing theoretical reasons for the use of this third percentage that do not apply even more strongly to the second cost percentage. Some writers, for example, argue that net markups (markups less markup cancellations) most likely apply to units sold,

*Exhibit 10.10*
**Illustration of Dollar-Value Retail
LIFO Inventory Valuation**

Price index for December 31 of base year = 1.000.
Selling price of inventory on December 31 of base year was $100,000.
Cost percentage for base year was 60.0%; other
cost percentages in line (6) are assumed.

| | First Year | Second Year | Third Year | Fourth Year | Fifth Year |
|---|---|---|---|---|---|
| (1) End-of-Year Inventory at Retail Selling Prices of Goods ...................... | $120,000 | $90,000 | $110,000 | $100,000 | $120,000 |
| (2) Price Index for Retail Prices of Goods .... | 1.100 | 1.200 | 1.150 | 1.250 | 1.200 |
| (3) End-of-Year Inventory in Base-Year Selling Price ............................... | $109,091 | $75,000 | $ 95,652 | $ 80,000 | $100,000 |
| (4) LIFO Inventory Layers at Base-Year Selling Prices: | | | | | |
| a. From Base-Year Stock .............. | C$100,000[a] | C$75,000 | C$75,000 | C$75,000 | C$75,000 |
| b. From First Year .................... | 9,091 | 0 | 0 | 0 | 0 |
| c. From Second Year ................. | — | 0 | 0 | 0 | 0 |
| d. From Third Year ................... | — | — | 20,652 | 5,000 | 5,000 |
| e. From Fourth Year .................. | — | — | — | — | 0 |
| f. From Fifth Year ................... | — | — | — | — | 20,000 |
| [Sum of Lines (4a) through (4f) = Line (3)] | | | | | |
| (5) LIFO Inventory Layers at Selling Price in Year of Acquisition: | | | | | |
| a. From Base-Year Stock = (4a) × 1.000 .......................... | $100,000 | $75,000 | $ 75,000 | $ 75,000 | $ 75,000 |
| b. From First-Year Stock = (4b) × 1.100 .......................... | 10,000 | 0 | 0 | 0 | 0 |
| c. From Second-Year Stock = (4c) × 1.200 .......................... | — | 0 | 0 | 0 | 0 |
| d. From Third Year Stock = (4d) × 1.150 .......................... | — | — | 23,750 | 5,750 | 5,750 |
| e. From Fourth-Year Stock = (4e) × 1.250 .......................... | — | — | — | 0 | 0 |
| f. From Fifth-Year Stock = (4f) × 1.200 . | — | — | — | — | 24,000 |
| (6) Cost Percentage by Year ................ | 61.5% | 59.0% | 62.0% | 58.0% | 61.9% |
| (7) LIFO Inventory Layers at Cost in Year of Acquisition: | | | | | |
| a. (5a) × .600 ...................... | $ 60,000 | $ 45,000 | $ 45,000 | $ 45,000 | $ 45,000 |
| b. (5b) × .615 ...................... | 6,150 | 0 | 0 | 0 | 0 |
| c. (5c) × .590 ...................... | — | 0 | 0 | 0 | 0 |
| d. (5d) × .620 ...................... | — | — | 14,725 | 3,565 | 3,565 |
| e. (5e) × .580 ...................... | — | — | — | 0 | 0 |
| f. (5f ) × .619 ...................... | — | — | — | — | 14,856 |
| (8) End-of-Year LIFO Inventory at Acquisition Cost = Sum of Lines (7a) through (7f) .. | $ 66,150 | $ 45,000 | $ 59,725 | $ 48,565 | $ 63,421 |

[a]C$ denotes dollars of purchasing power for the base year.

whereas net markdowns (markdowns less markdown cancellations) apply more often to units in ending inventory. By excluding net markdowns from the cost percentage, the markdowns are implicitly treated as losses of the period rather than part of the valuation of ending inventory. This argument applies equally well to the second cost percentage. The second cost percentage, moreover, treats markup cancellations implicitly as losses of the period. As with markdowns, markup cancellations indicate overpriced goods, goods that have a more-than-random probability of being in ending inventory. We cannot justify accounting's choice of **(iii)** rather than **(ii)**. If conservatism is the goal, then the cost percentage after additional markups, but before markup cancellations, should be used.

10.46    The fourth cost percentage includes all selling price adjustments in the denominator. Using this cost percentage presumes that selling price adjustments apply equally to units sold and to units in ending inventory. If this assumption is realistic, then using the fourth cost percentage provides a valuation of ending inventory approximating acquisition cost.

## Summary Illustrations of Retail Methods

10.47    Exhibit 10.11 illustrates the calculation of ending inventory and cost of goods sold for four variations of the retail method: conventional (lower of cost or market) retail method, FIFO retail method, LIFO retail method, and dollar value LIFO method. The illustrations are based on the data in Exhibit 10.8 and the additional assumption that the retail prices of these goods increased by 10 percent during the six-month period ending June 30.

## Dollar-Value Retail Method LIFO

10.48    This chapter has shown the rationale for using dollar-value, rather than physical-unit, LIFO and the rationale for tracking retail selling prices of goods sold, rather than cost of goods sold. Most retailers who use LIFO actually use a combination of the dollar-value method and the retail method. This section illustrates the combination.

10.49    If one understands the fundamental principles of dollar-value LIFO and of the retail method, then the combination adds only a little complexity. The fundamentals are the common-dollar layering of dollar-value LIFO and the use of a cost percentage to convert selling prices to costs in the retail method.

10.50    The accountant calculates end-of-current-year retail selling prices of ending inventory. From that number the cost of ending inventory must be computed. Under a LIFO cost-flow assumption, two steps are involved:

**1.** Building up layers of selling prices, first in common units, then in terms of actual dollars (using a price index).

**2.** Converting selling prices to costs (using a cost percentage).*

10.51    The layering of selling prices occurs before the cost percentage is applied to derive costs. Because selling prices, not costs, are layered, a price index of selling prices, not of costs, is required. Exhibit 10.10 illustrates the process using the same numbers as in Exhibit 10.4 with appropriate changes in the captions. Note that the cost percentages for each year are presented at step (6) and are used then, only after layers of selling prices have been found. [In practice, because the data on line (6) are known at the start, not computed as one of the steps, this line would be shown at the top of most presentations, along with the data on lines (1) and (2), which are also known at the start.]

10.52    A final complication in using dollar-value retail method LIFO involves computing the cost percentage. Exhibit 10.9 computes the cost percentage from goods available for

---

*It seems simpler to convert selling prices to costs before doing the layering. This leads to incorrect results, as Problem **10.27** explores.

*Exhibit 10.11*
**Illustrations of Variations of Retail Inventory Methods**

| Basic Data | At Cost | At Selling Price |
|---|---|---|
| Beginning Inventory (January 1) | $11,000 | $ 20,000 |
| Gross Purchases (during period) | 65,000 | 106,000 |
| Purchase Returns (during period) | (4,000) | (6,000) |
| Additional Markups (during period) | | 16,000 |
| Markup Cancellations (during period) | | (11,000) |
| Markdown Cancellations (during period) | | (10,000) |
| Markdown Cancellations (during period) | | 2,000 |
| Goods Available for Sale (during period) | | $127,000 |
| Less: Sales ($93,500 gross sales less $1,700 sales returns) | | 91,800 |
| Ending Inventory (June 30) | | $ 25,200 |

Acquisition cost of items increase by 10 percent during six-month period.

| Conventional Retail Method | At Cost | At Retail |
|---|---|---|
| Beginning Inventory | $11,000 | $ 20,000 |
| Gross Purchases | 65,000 | 106,000 |
| Less: Purchase Returns | (4,000) | (6,000) |
| Additional Markups | | 16,000 |
| Less: Markup Cancellations | | (11,000) |
| Total | $72,000 | $125,000 |

Cost to Retail Ratio: $72,000/$125,000 = .576
Deduct:

| | At Cost | At Retail |
|---|---|---|
| Sales | | $ 93,500 |
| Less: Sales Returns | | (1,700) |
| Markdowns | | 10,000 |
| Less: Markdown Cancellations | | (2,000) |
| Total Deductions | | $ 99,800 |
| Ending Inventory at Retail | | $ 25,200 |
| Ending Inventory at Cost, Conventional Lower-of-Cost-or-Market Retail ($25,200 × .576) | 14,515 | |
| Cost of Goods Sold | $57,485 | |

| FIFO Historical Retail Method | At Cost | At Retail |
|---|---|---|
| Beginning Inventory | $11,000 | $ 20,000 |
| Gross Purchases | 65,000 | $106,000 |
| Less: Purchase Returns | (4,000) | (6,000) |
| Add: Additional Markups | | 16,000 |
| Markdown Cancellations | | 2,000 |
| Less: Markdowns | | (10,000) |
| Markup Cancellations | | (11,000) |
| Net Purchases | $61,000 | $ 97,000 |
| Total Goods Available for Sale | $72,000 | $117,000 |

*Exhibit 10.11 (continued)*

|  | At Cost | At Retail |
|---|---|---|
| Cost of Purchases to Retail Price of Purchases Ratio:<br>$61,000/$97,000 = .629 | | |
| Less: | | |
|   Sales | | $ 93,500 |
|   Less: Sales Returns | | (1,700) |
|     Total Deductions from Goods Available for Sale | | $ 91,800 |
| Ending Inventory at Retail | | $ 25,200 |
| Ending Inventory at FIFO Cost ($25,200 × .629) | 15,851 | |
| Cost of Goods Sold | $56,149 | |

| **LIFO Retail Method** | At Cost | At Retail |
|---|---|---|
| Beginning Inventory | $11,000 | $ 20,000 |
| Gross Purchases | 65,000 | $106,000 |
| Less: Purchase Returns | (4,000) | (6,000) |
| Add: Additional Markups | | 16,000 |
|     Markdown Cancellations | | 2,000 |
| Less: Markdowns | | (10,000) |
|     Markup Cancellations | | (11,000) |
| Net Purchases | $61,000 | $ 97,000 |
|   Total Goods Available for Sale | $72,000 | $117,000 |
| Cost of Purchases to Retail Ratio, Computed from Purchases Only:<br>$61,000/$97,000 = .629. | | |
| Less: | | |
|   Sales | | $ 93,500 |
|   Less: Sales Returns | | (1,700) |
|   Net Sales | | $ 91,800 |
| Ending Inventory at Retail | | $ 25,200 |
| Ending Inventory at LIFO Cost: | | |
|   Beginning Inventory | $11,000 | 20,000 |
|   Layer Added ($5,200 × .629 = $3,271) | 3,271 | $ 5,200 |
| Total Inventory at LIFO Cost | $14,271 | |
| Cost of Goods Sold ($72,000 − $14,271) | $57,729 | |

| **Dollar Value LIFO Method** | Dollar Value LIFO Cost | Retail |
|---|---|---|
| Beginning Inventory at January 1 Prices | $11,000 | $ 20,000 |
| Add: Increase in Retail Prices Due to Price Changes: $20,000 × .10 | | 2,000 |
| Beginning Inventory at June 30 Prices | | $ 22,000 |
| Add Incremental Layer: | | |
|   At Retail ($25,200 − $22,000) | | 3,200 |
|   At Dollar Value LIFO Cost: $3,200 × .629[a] | 2,013 | |
| Ending Inventory at Retail | | $ 25,200 |

*Exhibit 10.11 (continued)*

| | Dollar Value LIFO Cost | Retail |
|---|---|---|
| Ending Inventory at Dollar Value LIFO Cost ..................................... | $13,013 | |
| Cost of Goods Available for Sale[b] ......................................... | $72,000 | |
| Less: Cost of Ending Inventory ............................................ | 13,013 | |
| Cost of Goods Sold ........................................................ | $58,987 | |

[a]$61,000/$97,000 = .629; see panel above on LIFO Retail Method for computation.

[b]See panel above on LIFO Retail Method for computation.

*Exhibit 10.12*

**Calculating Cost Percentage and
Final Selling Price of Goods
Available for Sale (Step III) for Retail
Method Using LIFO Cost Flow
(Data from Exhibit 10.9)**

| | At Cost | At Selling Price | Cost Percentage |
|---|---|---|---|
| Net Purchases ............................................. | $61,000 | $100,000 | |
| Additional Markups ....................................... | | 16,000 | |
| Markup Cancellations ..................................... | | (11,000) | |
| Markdowns ............................................... | | (10,000) | |
| Markdown Cancellations .................................. | | 2,000 | |
| Purchases after All Adjustments to Selling Prices ............... | $61,000 | $ 97,000 | 62.9% |
| Beginning Inventory ...................................... | [a] | 20,000 | |
| Goods Available for Sale .................................. | | $117,000 | |

[a]Cost of beginning inventory not shown here because it is not used in the calculation.

sale. Because the cost percentage is used to derive the costs for a particular year, it should not be contaminated with data from other years. Because LIFO beginning inventory contains costs going back to the base year, the gross margin or markup on beginning inventory is irrelevant in computing the current year's cost percentage. Consequently, the cost percentage for LIFO is derived from data on net purchases only, excluding costs of beginning inventory. Moreover, all price adjustments are assumed to have been made to items purchased during the current year—that is, the cost percentage is computed after adjusting selling prices of purchases with markdowns and markdown cancellations, as well as net markups.* Exhibit 10.12 illustrates the computation of the LIFO cost percentage using the data of Exhibit 10.9.

*The justification for excluding markdowns in the conventional retail method is that doing so "approximates lower of cost or market." Because the tax code does not permit LIFO to be used with lower of cost or market, it requires the use of the less conservative (cost-based) cost percentage when the retail method is used with LIFO. The tax requirement by itself would not dictate using the more conservative cost percentage for financial reporting (see the discussion in Chapter 9 of LIFO conformity and cost basis), but it is certainly easier not to have to worry about using different cost percentages for tax and financial reporting. Hence, we and others use the cost-based version of the cost percentage (after net markdowns) in illustrating dollar-value retail LIFO.

## Summary

10.53 This chapter has presented various accounting techniques for inventory and cost of goods sold. The techniques include methods actually used for computing ending inventories, the gross margin method, the retail method, and dollar-value LIFO. We have attempted to justify the need for each of these methods and to motivate each of the steps.

## Questions and Short Cases

**10.1** Review the meaning of the following concepts or terms discussed in this chapter.
- **a.** LIFO layer.
- **b.** Dollar-value LIFO.
- **c.** Gross margin method.
- **d.** Retail inventory method.
- **e.** Dollar-value retail LIFO.

**10.2** Inventory valuations appear only on the balance sheet. How is it, then, that inventory valuations affect net income for the period?

**10.3** Summarize the treatment of markups, markup cancellations, markdowns, and markdown cancellations in calculating the cost percentage under the conventional retail inventory method.

**10.4** The conventional method of applying dollar-value LIFO results in a combination of LIFO and FIFO valuations. Explain.

**10.5** In applying the dollar-value LIFO retail method, amounts from the beginning inventory are excluded from the calculation of the cost percentage. Explain.

**10.6** (Adapted from CPA examinations) A department store using the conventional retail inventory method estimates the cost of its ending inventory as $290,000. An accurate physical count reveals only $220,000 of inventory at lower of cost or market. What factors may have caused the difference between the computed inventory and the physical count?

**10.7** At the end of each accounting period, the accountant must check to see that all items purchased near the end of the period are properly counted both in purchases and in ending inventory while items not to be included in inventory are excluded both from the amount recorded as purchases and from the count of physical inventory. Throughout this question we assume that a periodic inventory method is used.*

Exhibit 10.13 shows for Error Company schedules computing cost of goods sold, an income statement, and an ending balance sheet for two periods. Exhibit 10.14 shows the effect

---

*If a perpetual inventory method is used, then the accounts will at all times indicate a cost of goods sold. From that amount, a "book" ending inventory figure can be computed and compared with the amount of ending inventory obtained from a physical count. Errors in recording purchases will show up as discrepancies between the book and physical amounts of ending inventory. When such differences arise, the accountant must check for inventory errors of the sort described in this section. Because a discrepancy between book and physical inventory counts can occur for other reasons—shrinkages of various sorts in inventory—an excess of book inventory over physical inventory does not necessarily signal an error. An excess of physical inventory over book inventory usually does signal a recording error.

*Exhibit 10.13*
**Error Company**
**Data for Illustration of Effects of**
**Inventory Errors (Question 10.7)**

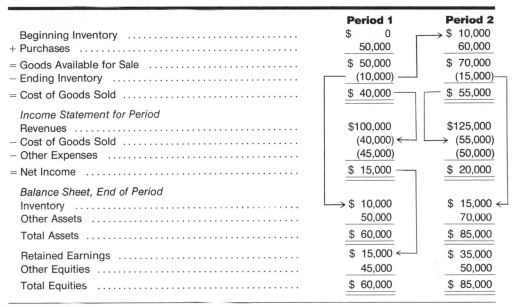

| | Period 1 | Period 2 |
|---|---|---|
| Beginning Inventory | $      0 | $ 10,000 |
| + Purchases | 50,000 | 60,000 |
| = Goods Available for Sale | $ 50,000 | $ 70,000 |
| − Ending Inventory | (10,000) | (15,000) |
| = Cost of Goods Sold | $ 40,000 | $ 55,000 |
| *Income Statement for Period* | | |
| Revenues | $100,000 | $125,000 |
| − Cost of Goods Sold | (40,000) | (55,000) |
| − Other Expenses | (45,000) | (50,000) |
| = Net Income | $ 15,000 | $ 20,000 |
| *Balance Sheet, End of Period* | | |
| Inventory | $ 10,000 | $ 15,000 |
| Other Assets | 50,000 | 70,000 |
| Total Assets | $ 60,000 | $ 85,000 |
| Retained Earnings | $ 15,000 | $ 35,000 |
| Other Equities | 45,000 | 50,000 |
| Total Equities | $ 60,000 | $ 85,000 |

on items in the financial statements of various kinds of errors. The reader should trace through the financial statements the effects of the errors described to verify the impact reported in Exhibit 10.14. It is easy to skip over Exhibit 10.14, mistakenly thinking one understands the effects of inventory errors.

**a.** What is the effect on total assets of a firm if it excludes items bought on account from the recorded Purchases for a period but the items are counted in ending inventory?

**b.** What is the effect on net income for the period of that error?

**10.8**   The Wilson Company sells chemical compounds made from expensium. The company has used a LIFO inventory-flow assumption for many years. The inventory of expensium on January 1, 1975, consisted of 2,000 lb from the inventory bought in 1971 for $30/lb. The following schedule shows purchases and physical ending inventories of expensium for the years 1975 through 1980.

| Year | Purchase Price per Pound during Year | Cost of Units Purchased | End-of-Year Inventory |
|---|---|---|---|
| 1975 | $48 | $240,000 | 2,000 lb |
| 1976 | 46 | 296,000 | 2,200 lb |
| 1977 | 48 | 368,000 | 3,000 lb |
| 1978 | 50 | 384,000 | 3,600 lb |
| 1979 | 50 | 352,000 | 2,600 lb |
| 1980 | 52 | 448,000 | 4,000 lb |

Because of temporary scarcities, expensium is expected to cost $62/lb during 1981 but to fall back to $52/lb in 1982. Sales for 1981 are expected to require 7,000 lb of expensium. The

*Exhibit 10.14*
**Effects of Various Inventory Errors on Items in Financial Statements**
**Error Company (See Exhibit 10.12)**
**(Question 10.7)**

**Dollar Amount by Which Item Reported Is Too Large (+) or Too Small (−); Income Taxes Ignored**

| Error[a] | Ending Inventory | | Cost of Goods Sold | | Net Income for | | | Retained Earnings at End of | |
|---|---|---|---|---|---|---|---|---|---|
| | Period 1[b] | Period 2 | Period 1 | Period 2 | Period 1 | Period 2 | Two-Period Total | Period 1 | Period 2 |
| (1) No Error Made | $ 0 | $ 0 | $ 0 | $ 0 | $ 0 | $ 0 | $ 0 | $ 0 | $ 0 |
| (2) Period-1 Beginning Inventory Overstated by $1,000 | 0 | 0 | +1,000 | 0 | −1,000 | 0 | −1,000 | −1,000 | −1,000 |
| (3) Purchases for Period 1 Understated by $1,000, but These Items Properly Included in Period-1 Ending Inventory | 0 | 0 | −1,000 | 0 | +1,000 | 0 | +1,000 | +1,000 | +1,000 |
| (4) Purchases for Period 1 Understated by $1,000 and Items Excluded from Period-1 Ending Inventory. Items Counted as Period-2 Purchases | −1,000[c] | 0 | 0 | 0 | 0 | 0 | 0 | 0 | 0 |
| (5) Period-1 Ending Inventory (and Period-2 Beginning Inventory) Overstated by $1,000, but Period-2 Ending Inventory Correct | +1,000 | 0 | −1,000 | +1,000 | +1,000 | −1,000 | 0 | +1,000 | 0 |
| (6) Ending Inventory for Period 1 (and Beginning Inventory for Period 2) Understated by $1,000; Ending Inventory for Period 2 Understated by $600. Errors Remain Uncorrected throughout Both Periods | −1,000 | −600 | +1,000 | −400 | −1,000 | +400 | −600 | −1,000 | −600 |

[a]Errors can occur in Beginning Inventory, Purchases, Ending Inventory as Recorded in Accounts, Ending Inventory as Physically Counted. All items not mentioned for a given example are assumed correct.

[b]Equal to Period-2 Beginning Inventory.

[c]The balance sheet remains in balance, however, because Accounts Payable (for Purchases) are also understated by $1,000.

purchasing agent suggests that the inventory of expensium be allowed to decrease from 4,000 to 600 lb by the end of 1981 and to be replenished to the desired level of 4,000 lb early in 1982.

The controller argues that such a policy would be foolish. If inventories are allowed to decrease to 600 lb, then the cost of goods sold will be extraordinarily low (because the older LIFO purchases will be consumed) and income taxes will be extraordinarily high. Furthermore, he points out that the diseconomies of smaller orders during 1981, as required by the purchasing agent's plan, would lead to about $1,000 of extra costs for record keeping. These costs would be treated as an expense for 1981. He suggests that 1981 purchases should be planned to maintain an end-of-year inventory.

Assume that sales for 1981 do require 7,000 lb of expensium, that the prices for 1981 and 1982 are as forecast, and that the income tax rate for Wilson Company is 40 percent.

Calculate the cost of goods sold and end-of-year LIFO inventory:

a. For each of the years 1975 through 1980.
b. For 1981, assuming that the controller's advice is followed so that inventory at the end of 1981 is 4,000 lb.
c. For 1981, assuming that the purchasing agent's advice is followed and inventory at the end of 1981 is 600 lb.

Assuming that the controller's, rather than the purchasing agent's, advice is followed, calculate:

d. The tax savings for 1981.
e. The extra cash costs for inventory.
f. Using the results derived so far, what should Wilson Company do?
g. Would your advice be different if Wilson Company used a FIFO cost-flow assumption?

**10.9** This question is designed to explore the degree to which various computations of the cost percentage in the retail method lead to ending inventory valuations that approximate cost in lower-of-cost-or-market valuations.

The Nordhauser Company begins a year with no inventory. During month 1 it purchases four units, prices them, later adds additional markup, and then sells one. In month 2 it cancels some of the additional markup on the remaining three units and then sells another unit. In month 3 it cancels the rest of the additional markup on the remaining two units, reduces price still further by markdowns, and sells one unit. It ends the 3-month period with one unit. Replacement cost of units and selling price set by Nordhauser Company vary exactly proportionally: Selling prices are increased (or decreased) as replacement costs increase (or decrease), and vice versa, by the same percentages. Exhibit 10.15 summarizes the events of the 3 months.

a. For the end of month 1, calculate the following: actual cost of ending inventory, lower-of-actual-cost-or-market value of ending inventory, and two estimates of ending inventory using the retail method with cost percentages computed (1) before additional markups and (2) after additional markups. Which cost percentage estimates ending inventory more closely approximating the cost of ending inventory? The lower-of-cost-or-market value of ending inventory?

b. For the end of month 2, calculate the following: actual cost of ending inventory, lower-of-actual-cost-or-market value of ending inventory, and three estimates of ending inventory using the retail method with cost percentages computed (1) before additional markups, (2) after additional markups but before markup cancellations, and (3) after markup cancellations. In applying the retail method, use data for the 2-month period as a whole. That is, ignore the calculations in part **a** and assume that the books are being closed for the first time at the end of month 2. Which cost percentage estimates ending inventory more

*Exhibit 10.15*
**Nordhauser Company**
**Events of 3 Months to Illustrate**
**Computation of Cost Percentage**

| Month | Start of Month per Unit | | Events of Month | End of Month per Unit | |
| | Replacement Cost | Selling Price | | Replacement Cost | Selling Price |
|---|---|---|---|---|---|
| 1 | $200 | $240 | Buy 4 units, put them on sale for $240 each. | | |
| | | | Additional markups on all 4 units of $60 each. | | |
| | | | Then, sell 1 unit for $300. | $250 | $300 |
| 2 | 250 | 300 | Markup cancellations of $30 each on 3 units remaining. | | |
| | | | Sell 1 unit for $270. | 225 | 270 |
| 3 | 225 | 270 | Markup cancellations of $30 each on 2 units remaining. | | |
| | | | Markdowns of $60 each on 2 units remaining. | | |
| | | | Sell one unit for $180. | 150 | 180 |

closely approximating the actual cost of ending inventory? Lower-of-cost-or-market value of ending inventory?

c. For the end of month 3, calculate the following: actual cost of ending inventory, lower-of-cost-or-market value of ending inventory, and four estimates of ending inventory using the retail method with cost percentages computed (1) before additional markups, (2) after additional markups but before markup cancellations, (3) after markup cancellations but before markdowns, and (4) after markdowns. In applying the retail method, use data for the 3-month period as a whole. That is, ignore the calculations in parts a and b, and assume that the books are being closed for the first time at the end of month 3. Which cost percentage estimates ending inventory more closely approximating the actual cost of ending inventory? Lower-of-cost-or-market value of ending inventory?

d. Repeat part c, assuming the following. Month 1 event, additional markup and sale, is as in part c. In month 2, one unit is sold for $300, but there are no changes in selling prices. One unit is sold in month 3 for $300. There are no markup cancellations or markdowns until the end of month 3, when the single remaining unit is reduced to $180. The replacement cost of units is $180 at the end of month 3.

e. What can you conclude from this exercise about choosing a calculation for the cost percentage in applying the retail method?

**10.10** Refer to the data in Exhibit 10.8. In this question consider only the sales price adjustments through the end of March, those for items A, B, and C. Sales through March are $48,400. Ending inventory is $73,600. Exhibit 10.16 summarizes the data through March 31.

Compute cost percentages, cost of ending inventory, and cost of goods sold for each of the following assumptions.

a. Include original markup, additional markup, but ignore markdowns in the cost percentage. Compute cost of goods sold and cost of ending inventory on March 31.

*Exhibit 10.16*
**Data for Retail Inventory
Method Markups and Markdowns
Only (Question Q10.10)**

| | | Dollars per Items | | |
|---|---|---|---|---|
| **Month** | **Event** | **A** | **B** | **C** |
| January | Cost .................................................... | $12 | $12 | $12 |
| | Original Markup (Markon) ............................. | 8 | 8 | 8 |
| February | Additional Markup ..................................... | | 4 | |
| March | Markdown ............................................. | | | (2) |
| | Final Selling Price .................................... | $20 | $24 | $18 |

| | At Cost | At Selling Price |
|---|---|---|
| | **Dollar Totals** | |
| January 1, Beginning Inventory ...................................... | $12,000 | $ 20,000 |
| January 1–March 31, Purchases ...................................... | 60,000 | 100,000 |
| Additional Markups ............................. | | 4,000 |
| Markdowns ..................................... | | (2,000) |
| Sales ......................................... | | (48,400) |
| March 31, Ending Inventory ........................................ | | $73,600 |

**b.** Include all sales price adjustments in the cost percentage. Compute cost of goods sold through March and cost of ending inventory on March 31.

**c.** Which of the above two sets of computations is more conservative?

**d.** Which set should be used?

## Problems and Exercises

**10.11**   The Haskell Company uses the dollar-value LIFO method of inventory valuation. Given the following data on inventory valued at end-of-year prices and an index of prices, compute the ending inventory at LIFO cost for each of the 4 years 1978 through 1981.

| Year | Inventory at End-of-Year Prices | Price Index at End of Year |
|---|---|---|
| 1977 | 500 | 100 |
| 1978 | 750 | 115 |
| 1979 | 900 | 130 |
| 1980 | 825 | 122 |
| 1981 | 650 | 120 |

**10.12**   The inventory of the Marby Company on December 31 of year 1 amounts to $240. The company decides to use the dollar-value method of costing inventories during year 2. On December 31 of year 2, the inventory is $273 at current prices. The price levels of December 31 for years 1 and 2 are 100 and 105, respectively.

Compute the inventory value at December 31, year 2, under the dollar-value LIFO method.

**10.13**   A flood destroys all of the merchandise of the Fishley Company on March 4. The following information is available:

| | |
|---|---:|
| Inventory, January 1 ................................. | $2,000 |
| Sales to March 4 .................................... | 8,000 |
| Purchases to March 4 ............................... | 8,400 |
| Freight-in to March 4 ............................... | 350 |
| Purchase Returns to March 4 ........................ | 30 |
| Gross Margin Percentage, Based on Selling Price ....... | 30% |

Compute the approximate cost of inventory on hand at March 4.

**10.14**   Refer to the data of the preceding problem.
  **a.** Assume that the gross margin percentage based on cost is 30 percent. Will the ending inventory increase or decrease?
  **b.** Assume that the gross margin percentage based on selling price is 25 percent. Will the ending inventory increase or decrease?
  **c.** Assume that the gross margin percentage based on cost is 50 percent. Will the ending inventory increase or decrease?

**10.15**   The merchandise inventory of Parks Store was destroyed by fire on July 4. The accounting records were saved. They provided the following information:

| | |
|---|---:|
| Cost of Merchandise Inventory on Hand, January 1 ................................. | $ 46,000 |
| Purchases of Merchandise, January 1 to July 4 ..................................... | 98,000 |
| Sales, January 1 to July 4 ...................................................... | 120,000 |

The average retail markup over cost of the goods sold during the year before the fire was 50 percent of the acquisition cost.
  **a.** Use the gross margin method to estimate the cost of the goods on hand at the time of the fire.
  **b.** Give the journal entry to record the loss assuming that it was uninsured.
  **c.** Give the journal entry to record the loss assuming that all goods were fully insured for their acquisition cost.

**10.16**   Refer to the data in the preceding problem. Assume that the store owner does not know the average retail markup over cost for the destroyed goods. The accounting records show that the total sales revenue during the 4 years preceding the fire amounted to $1,000,000 and the total cost of goods sold over the same period was $650,000.
  **a.** Assuming that the ratio of sales prices to cost of goods sold for the last 4 years holds for this year, estimate the cost of the goods destroyed in the fire.
  **b.** Assume the same facts as above, except that the $1,000,000 represents the original selling price of the goods sold during the last 4 years. Certain goods were marked down before sale so that the actual sales revenue was only $975,000. Assuming that the same percentage of goods were marked down by the same price during the first 6 months of this year as in the previous 4 years, estimate the cost of the goods destroyed by the fire.

**10.17**   (Adapted from CPA Examination.) On November 21 a fire at Hodge Company's warehouse caused severe damage to its entire inventory of Product Tex. Hodge estimates that all usable damaged goods can be sold for $10,000. The following information was available from Hodge's accounting records for Product Tex:

| | |
|---|---|
| Inventory at November 1 ........................................................ | $100,000 |
| Purchases from November 1 to date of fire ........................................ | 140,000 |
| Net sales from November 1 to date of fire ........................................ | 220,000 |

Based on recent history, Hodge had a gross margin on Product Tex of 30 percent of net sales. Calculate the estimated loss on the inventory in the fire, using the gross margin method.

**10.18**   (Adapted from CPA Examination.) The Grand Department Store, Inc., uses the retail inventory method to estimate ending inventory for its monthly financial statements. The following data pertain to a single department for the month of October:

| | |
|---|---|
| Inventory, October 1: | |
| At Cost ........................................................................ | $ 20,000 |
| At Retail ...................................................................... | 30,000 |
| Purchases (exclusive of freight and returns): | |
| At Cost ........................................................................ | 100,151 |
| At Retail ...................................................................... | 146,495 |
| Freight-in ...................................................................... | 5,100 |
| Purchase Returns: | |
| At Cost ........................................................................ | 2,100 |
| At Retail ...................................................................... | 2,800 |
| Additional Markups .......................................................... | 2,500 |
| Markup Cancellations ........................................................ | 265 |
| Markdowns (net) .............................................................. | 5,300 |
| Sales .......................................................................... | 135,730 |

Using the conventional retail method, prepare a schedule computing estimated lower-of-cost-or-market inventory for October 31.

**10.19**   (Adapted from CPA Examination.) The Red Department Store uses the retail inventory method. Information relating to the computation of the inventory at December 31 is as follows:

| | Cost | Retail |
|---|---|---|
| Inventory at January 1 ........................................... | $ 32,000 | $ 80,000 |
| Sales .............................................................. | | 600,000 |
| Purchases ........................................................ | 270,000 | 590,000 |
| Freight in ......................................................... | 7,600 | |
| Markups .......................................................... | | 60,000 |
| Markup cancellations ............................................ | | 10,000 |
| Markdowns ....................................................... | | 25,000 |
| Markdown cancellations ......................................... | | 5,000 |
| Estimated normal shrinkage is 2% of sales. | | |

Calculate the estimated ending inventory at the lower of average cost or market at December using the retail inventory method.

**10.20**   McKeen's Store first began using LIFO in year 1 and uses the dollar-value LIFO method. Refer to the accompanying data on its inventories of sporting goods and desk calculators.

|  | Sporting Goods | | Desk Calculators | |
|---|---|---|---|---|
|  | Current Cost of Ending Inventory | Price Index | Current Cost of Ending Inventory | Price Index |
| Year 1 | $100,000 | 0.750 | $100,000 | 1.250 |
| Year 2 | 132,000 | 0.900 | 135,000 | 1.125 |
| Year 3 | 104,000 | 0.975 | 160,000 | 1.000 |
| Year 4 | 108,000 | 1.125 | 210,000 | 0.875 |

a. Compute the historical cost of ending inventory of sporting goods for years 1–4.

b. Compute the historical cost of ending inventory of desk calculators for years 1–4.

10.21 Winship Company has been using dollar-value LIFO since year 1. Its inventory quantities have increased steadily since then. The accompanying schedule presents data on ending inventory at its current replacement cost at the end of each of 3 years, acquisition cost using dollar-value LIFO, and the price index used in the calculations. Compute the missing amounts, represented by "?" in the schedule.

**Winship Company**
**Ending Inventory**

|  | At Current Replacement Cost | At LIFO Acquisition Cost | Price Index |
|---|---|---|---|
| Year 1 | $ ? | $ 75,000 | 1.00 |
| Year 2 | 81,000 | ? | .90 |
| Year 3 | 126,500 | 111,500 | ? |

10.22 The Algrim Corporation lost most of its inventory in a fire in December just before the year-end physical inventory was taken. Its gross margin percentage is 20 percent of sales. The corporation's books disclosed the following:

| | |
|---|---|
| Beginning Inventory | $ 150 |
| Purchases for the Year | 4,900 |
| Freight-in | 100 |
| Purchase Returns | 300 |
| Sales | 5,280 |
| Sales Returns | 480 |

After the fire, merchandise with a selling price of $250 was on hand, undamaged. Damaged merchandise on hand had an original selling price of $180 and a salvage value of $70. Compute the amount of the loss as a result of the fire, assuming that the corporation had no insurance coverage.

10.23 (Adapted from CPA Examination.) The Barometer Company manufactures one product. On December 31, 1978, Barometer adopted the dollar-value LIFO inventory method. The inventory on that date using the dollar-value LIFO inventory method was $200,000.

Inventory data are as follows:

| Year | Inventory at Respective Year-End Prices | Price Index (Base Year 1978) |
|---|---|---|
| 1979 | $231,000 | 1.05 |
| 1980 | 299,000 | 1.15 |
| 1981 | 300,000 | 1.20 |

Compute the inventory at December 31, 1979, 1980, and 1981, using dollar-value LIFO.

**10.24**  Cunningham Company uses the conventional retail method of calculating cost of ending inventory and cost of goods sold. Its cost percentage was computed after taking into account both additional markups and markup cancellations. Beginning inventory had cost $100 and had selling prices of $160. Purchases for the period of $1,000 had been originally marked up to $1,500. Sales for the period at retail prices amounted to $1,740. There were additional markups and some markup cancellations. Ending inventory was counted at retail selling prices. Consider parts **a** and **b** independently.

    **a.** The cost percentage was 55 percent, and markup cancellations amounted to $60. Calculate the amount of additional markups, the selling prices of ending inventory, the cost of ending inventory, and the cost of goods sold.

    **b.** Additional markups were $240, and the selling prices of ending inventory totaled $20. Calculate the cost percentage, markup cancellations, cost of ending inventory, and cost of goods sold.

**10.25**  Wolfson Company uses the retail method of computing cost of goods sold and a FIFO cost-flow assumption. Its unaudited income statement for a recent quarter showed:

| | |
|---|---|
| Revenues | $100,000 |
| Cost of Goods Sold | (60,000) |
| Other Expenses except Taxes | (35,000) |
| Income Taxes at 40% | (2,000) |
| Net Income | $  3,000 |

Cost of goods sold was computed from the following schedule:

| | At Cost | At Selling Price | Cost Percentage |
|---|---|---|---|
| Goods Available for Sale | $84,000 | $140,000 | 60.0% |
| Less: Ending Inventory | 24,000[a] | 40,000 | |
| Goods Sold | $60,000 | $100,000 | |

[a]$24,000 = .60 × $40,000.

Markdowns of $10,000 were mistakenly included in computing the cost percentage. If markdowns had been excluded, then the denominator of the cost percentage calculation would have been $150,000 and the cost percentage would have been 56.0 percent. Management wonders if such a trivial error, cost percentage of 60.0 percent used instead of 56.0 percent, really makes enough difference to warrant preparing a new income statement.

    **a.** Compute net income for the quarter assuming that the cost percentage is 56.0 percent rather than 60.0 percent.

    **b.** Is the difference in income trivial? Would you judge that the company's accountant ought to prepare a revised quarterly report given this size change?

c. The size of the change depends critically on the rate of inventory turnover. Rework part **a** assuming that the cost of goods sold resulted from the calculation shown below.

| | At Cost | At Selling Price | Cost Percentage |
|---|---|---|---|
| Goods Available for Sale ................. | $66,000 | $110,000 | 60.0% |
| Less: Ending Inventory .................... | 6,000 | 10,000 | |
| Goods Sold ........................... | $60,000 | $100,000 | |

This calculation was also in error because markdowns were improperly included in the cost percentage; the cost percentage should have been 56.0 percent and the cost of goods available for sale before markdowns should have been $117,857 (= $66,000/.56).

d. What dollar amount of markdowns were improperly included in the denominator of the cost percentage calculation of 60.0 percent in part **c**?

e. Make a general statement about the effect on net income as the cost percentage varies.

**10.26** The Jericho Variety Store uses the LIFO retail inventory method. Information relating to the computation of the inventory at December 31 follows:

| | Cost | Retail |
|---|---|---|
| Inventory, January 1 .............................................. | $ 29,000 | $ 45,000 |
| Purchases ......................................................... | 120,000 | 172,000 |
| Freight-in ......................................................... | 20,000 | |
| Sales ............................................................. | | 190,000 |
| Net Markups ....................................................... | | 40,000 |
| Net Markdowns ..................................................... | | 12,000 |

Assume that there was no change in the price index during the year. Compute the inventory at December 31 using the LIFO retail inventory method.

**10.27** The controller of Levy Company wrote the following note to the company's outside auditor, who had not yet completed the year's audit. How should the auditor reply?

"Last year, the first year when we used LIFO, the cost percentage derived from purchase data was 60.0 percent. This year, our retail prices came under great pressure and the cost percentage rose to 90.0 percent. We computed dollar-value, retail method LIFO ending inventory as follows:

| | Last Year | This Year |
|---|---|---|
| Retail Prices of Ending Inventory .......................... | $100,000 | $115,500 |
| Multiplied by Cost Percentage ............................. | ×.600 | ×.900 |
| Cost of Ending Inventory ................................... | $ 60,000 | $103,950 |
| Divided by Price Index for Cost of Retail Goods ............. | ÷1.000 | ÷1.100 |
| Common Unit Costs of Inventory ........................... | C$ 60,000 | C$ 94,500 |
| Which Is Split into Layers of Common Units: | | |
|     Last Year ......................................... | C$ 60,000 | C$ 60,000 |
|     This Year ......................................... | — | C$ 34,500 |
| Which Are Converted into Dollars of Cost in Year of Acquisition, | | |
|   Multiplying by Price Index: | | |
|     Last Year (C$ × 1.000) .......................... | $ 60,000 | $ 60,000 |
|     This Year (C$ × 1.100) .......................... | — | 37,950 |
| To Give LIFO Cost of Ending Inventory .................... | $ 60,000 | $ 97,950 |

We don't understand why retail prices can go up by 10 percent for the year (1.000 to 1.100), quantity of goods as measured in retail prices can go up by 15.5 percent for the year (from $100,000 to $115,500) so that real quantities of retail goods have gone up by 5 percent ($100,000 to $115,500/1.100) and yet the cost of ending inventory has gone up by 63 percent (from $60,000 to $97,500). How can that happen?''

10.28   Stober Company uses the dollar-value retail LIFO method of computing cost of ending inventory and cost of goods sold. It began using the method in year 1. Its ending inventories increased in physical quantity and price every year thereafter. Refer to the accompanying data and compute the missing numbers represented by "?" in the schedule.

### Stober Company

| | Cost of Ending Inventory | Cost Percentage | Retail Prices of Ending Inventory | Price Index Used |
|---|---|---|---|---|
| Year 1 | $48,000 | ?% | $ 80,000 | 1.00 |
| Year 2 | 70,260 | 70.0% | ? | 1.06 |
| Year 3 | 82,910 | 55.0% | 149,500 | ? |

10.29   The following data are available for Hanouille's Store for a year:

| | Cost | Selling Price |
|---|---|---|
| Inventory, January 1 | $26,900 | $ 40,000 |
| Markdowns | | 10,500 |
| Additional Markups | | 19,500 |
| Markdown Cancellations | | 6,500 |
| Markup Cancellations | | 4,500 |
| Purchases | 86,200 | 111,800 |
| Sales | | 122,000 |
| Purchase Returns and Allowances | 1,500 | 1,800 |
| Sales Returns and Allowances | | 6,000 |

Assume that additional markups and markdowns apply to purchases and that the price index for these retail goods has increased by 10 percent during the year. Compute Hanouille's cost of year-end inventory and cost of goods sold for the year using each of the following methods in turn.
a. Conventional retail method.
b. FIFO historical cost retail method.
c. LIFO retail method, ignoring changes in the price index for these retail goods.
d. Dollar-value LIFO retail method, which takes into account changes in the price index for retail goods.

# Chapter 11
## *Plant Assets:*
## *Acquisition and Disposition*

11.1 All assets represent future service potentials. They may be divided into two categories: **(1)** those whose potential will be used in the near future, current assets, and **(2)** those whose potential will be used over many periods, noncurrent assets. The latter category is usually divided into three parts: plant assets, considered in this chapter and the next; intangible assets, discussed in Chapter 13; and investments, discussed in Chapter 14.

11.2 The term "fixed assets" is sometimes used to refer to the broad concept of noncurrent assets and is sometimes used more narrowly to refer to plant assets. The term "fixed assets" is gradually falling into disuse, a development we applaud. Plant assets are not confined to factories but include land, buildings, and equipment of wholesale, retail, and service enterprises as well.

11.3 A survey of the titles used in a recent year for plant assets by the 30 companies in the Dow-Jones Industrial Index showed the following:

| Title of Section | Number of Companies |
| --- | --- |
| Property, Plant, and Equipment | 19 |
| Property or Properties | 3 |
| Fixed Assets | 1 |
| Plant and Properties | 2 |
| Plant, Rental Machines, and Other Property | 1 |
| Plant and Equipment | 1 |
| Land, Buildings, and Equipment | 1 |
| Telephone Plant | 1 |
| Owned Properties | 1 |

11.4 Companies in extractive industries usually include their natural resources and timber property in plant assets. Chapter 13 discusses such assets, frequently described as "wasting assets."

11.5 The service potential of plant assets is used over many periods. The process of accounting for the use of the service benefits of buildings, equipment, furniture, and fixtures is described as "depreciation." The service potential of land is assumed not to be reduced by use, so land is not depreciated.

11.6 This chapter discusses the accounting for the acquisition and disposition of plant assets. Chapter 12 discusses the depreciation of plant assets.

## Acquisition of Plant Assets

### Valuation at Cost of Purchased Assets

11.7 At acquisition, plant assets are recorded at the amount of the cash or cash-equivalent purchase price. Both new and used assets are recorded at acquisition cost. Normally, each acquisition results from an arm's-length market transaction by two independent parties, both presumed to be acting rationally in their own self-interest. This estab-

**11-1**

lishes a strong likelihood that cost is the best measure of value at the time of acquisition.

11.8 For plant assets, as for all others, acquisition cost means cash cost but includes the full cost required to prepare the asset for its intended use. Thus, cash discounts and trade discounts as well as any imputed interest are deducted from invoice price, whereas freight-in, installation costs, and similar items are added to invoice price to determine the full cash cost of the plant asset.

### Prudent Cost and Lucky Buys

11.9 In some rare cases, one knows at the time of completion or delivery of an asset that the acquisition cost differs significantly from the market value. This may be due to changes in demand or supply conditions or other unanticipated events that occur during the construction of the plant assets. Accounting practice seems to be governed by the asymmetric lower-of-cost-or-market rule in such cases. An asset is written down if its acquisition cost exceeds fair market value at the delivery date. If fair market value ("prudent cost") is higher at delivery date, however, no recognition of this fact is customarily made in the accounts. Assets are not generally valued at more than acquisition cost, and "lucky buys" are not recognized as income until they are realized by arms'-length transactions with independent third parties.

### "Original Cost"

11.10 The acquisition of used plant assets is recorded at the agreed purchase price. The book value of the assets on the seller's records is not relevant. One exception relates to plant assets of companies subject to public utility regulation. In that industry, each plant asset is recorded at "the cost of such property to the person first devoting it to the public service." This amount is described as the "original cost" of the property. (Opponents of this valuation approach say that a more appropriate title would be "aboriginal cost.") Any excess amount paid over the book value—original cost less accumulated depreciation—for used property acquired by a subsequent utility purchaser is excluded from the basic plant account used for

rate making. The merit of such a procedure for public utility regulation is debatable, but it is clearly inappropriate for nonregulated businesses. There is no reason to expect the seller's book value to indicate the fair market value some periods after acquisition when technology and prices change.

### Rehabilitation

11.11 The cost of restoring or improving used property, acquired in a run-down condition, to an acceptable condition is described as *rehabilitation*. Because the property's condition is known at acquisition and is reflected in the purchase price, planned rehabilitation expenditures should be added to the plant cost at the time the rehabilitation expenditures are made. If, for example, a used bulldozer is acquired for $8,000 and $2,000 is spent for rehabilitation before it can be used, then the $2,000 should be added to the asset's cost; total cost is $10,000. Expenditures for rehabilitation should be added to the asset account even when they are called repairs, which are usually expensed.

11.12 When several used properties are acquired and rehabilitation takes several years, computing which expenditures are for ordinary repairs (expenses) and which are for rehabilitation (capitalized as assets) is more difficult.

### "Inventory" of Replacement Parts

11.13 At the time equipment is acquired, the prudent owner will often acquire, in addition, a stock of replacement parts, sometimes at substantial cost. Firms frequently acquire replacement parts in large quantities at the time the original asset is acquired because the terms offered by the manufacturer make such lump-sum acquisitions more cost effective than item-by-item purchases over the life of the main asset.

11.14 Although such parts are often called "inventory," they are not inventory in the sense that the word should be used. *Inventory* means a stock of items held for sale or for future processing leading to a sale. Replacement parts are not held for sale but to maintain the productive capacity of the main asset. The future benefits of replacement parts come only from their being able to help to keep the main asset in service. The parts will lose their service potential when the main asset is retired from service; the future benefits of such parts may expire as they sit idle on the shelf ready for use. Because replacement parts lose their service potential as the life of the main asset expires, the cost of replacement parts is part of the cost of the main asset. The cost of replacement parts should be written off the books—depreciated—just as the main asset is depreciated. Calling such items "inventory," as is sometimes done, does not change the essential nature of these items. Accounting for such replacement parts as though they are inventory—leaving their cost on the balance sheet until the parts are used or retired—is, we think, wrong. Generally accepted accounting principles do not address this subject; our view results from application of accounting theory.

11.15 **Example** A major airline acquires a fleet of eight new wide-bodied jets, each costing around $30 million. At the same time, it acquires the equivalent of two spare airplanes—airplanes on the shelf—in the form of replacement parts. It expects never to use most of these parts, but acquiring them at the same time as the original fleet produces substantial economies of purchasing (savings in expected total cost). The manufacturer is able to increase production runs slightly and tool the replacement parts at small incremental cost. The cost of the two "airplanes on the shelf" should be treated just like the airplanes themselves, depreciated over the useful life of the airplanes. (Group and composite methods, introduced in the next chapter, may be used for these airplanes and parts.)

## Valuation of Self-Constructed Assets

11.16 When a firm constructs its own assets, the basic principle concerning valuation is clear. The firm should include in the valuation of the asset all reasonable costs necessary to bring the asset to a functioning condition. The cost of all materials used and the wages of employees who work on the project are included in the cost of the project. In certain situations, costs of self-construction require more attention. The following sections describe them.

### Land with Existing Structures

11.17 Sometimes a building is to be constructed on a newly acquired site with an existing building on it. If the existing building is immediately torn down to prepare the site for the new building, the cost of demolition of the existing building, less any salvage proceeds, is a cost of getting the land ready for its intended use and should be included in the cost of the land.

11.18 A more troublesome problem arises if the site is acquired several years before construction of the new building is to occur. How should the cost of the property be divided between the land and the existing building? Normally, the purchase price would be allocated, as the later section on "basket purchases" explains, on the basis of the relative fair market values of the properties acquired. Because the building is to be demolished, it should be valued at the present value of the anticipated rentals to be received over the period until the building is demolished, discounted at an appropriate rate. If the purchaser plans to use the building until demolition, an estimate of the fair market rental rate is required. The purchase price less the building valuation is allocated to the land.

### Assignment of Overhead

11.19 When buildings or machinery and equipment are self-constructed, how much overhead or general and administrative costs should be allocated to those assets? When the overhead or general and administrative costs increase as a result of construction, the plant asset clearly should be charged for the incremental costs. Problems arise only for fixed overhead or general and administrative costs, costs that do not increase as a result of construction. The great majority of overhead and general and administrative costs are fixed.

11.20 Three approaches have been suggested:

**1.** Use a direct costing approach; assign no fixed costs to the plant asset.

**2.** Follow an absorption costing approach; allocate fixed costs to construction on the basis used for the allocation of such costs to jobs or processes.

**3.** Follow an opportunity-cost approach; assign to the constructed plant assets a charge for the profits foregone because the fixed resources were used for construction, rather than regular production and sales activity.

11.21 Of the three approaches, the last is the most appealing conceptually, but measurement problems are so great that it is almost never used in practice. Chapter 9 indicates our preference for a direct costing approach to inventory valuation. Following reasoning similar to that in Chapter 9, we prefer method **1** for the valuation of self-constructed plant assets, but it is doubtful if that approach conforms to generally accepted accounting principles. The absorption costing approach for self-constructed assets is more widely used in practice.

11.22 **Income Tax Reporting Issues** For tax reporting, the advantage of the direct costing method is clear in most cases. Certain costs are deducted immediately in direct costing but are capitalized and amortized under absorption costing. In 1974, the U.S. Supreme Court held that depreciation charges on equipment used for revenue-producing purposes and for self-constructed plant assets could not be assigned entirely to revenue-producing activities, but must be allocated between the two activities.* The Court, in explaining its decision, said:

An additional pertinent fact is that capitalization of construction-related depreciation by the taxpayer who does its own construction work maintains

---

*Commissioner v. Idaho Power Co. (418 US 1), 1974.

parity with the taxpayer who has its construction work done by an independent contractor. The depreciation on the contractor's equipment incurred during the performance of the job will be an element of cost charged by the contractor for his construction services, and the entire cost, of course, must be capitalized by the taxpayer having the construction work performed.

Two years later the Tax Court extended that 11.23 ruling, saying:†

We are persuaded that only the full cost absorption method as here applied, will correctly reflect income [for income tax purposes].**

## Interest during Construction

When the construction period is long, should 11.24 interest on expenditures during the construction period be included in the cost of the plant and equipment being built? The question may also arise with purchased plant assets when substantial advances to suppliers are made long before delivery of the plant asset. Three ways of dealing with the problem have been used; all were at one time in conformity with generally accepted accounting principles. They are

**1.** Capitalize no interest during construction.

**2.** Capitalize interest paid on funds specifically borrowed for the construction project. (Generally accepted accounting principles require a variant of this rule. Interest on borrowed funds, only, is capitalized, but the funds need not have been borrowed for the specific project. The current rules are discussed more fully below.)

**3.** Capitalize interest on all funds used for

---

†Louisville & Nashville Railroad Co. v. Commissioner (66 TC 962), 1976.

**In 1967, in the Fort Howard Paper case (49 TC 275), the Tax Court had permitted the use of a direct costing approach in a situation where the company had followed that approach for many years and the Internal Revenue Service had not previously objected. The later cases went to some lengths to point out that the specialized facts in the Fort Howard Paper case could not be applied generally.

construction, whether or not separately identifiable with the project.

11.25   The first method considers interest as a cost of financing and not a cost of construction. This view is accepted throughout the rest of accounting; for example, no interest charge is added to the cost of inventories held during the period.

11.26   The second method views interest on funds borrowed for construction as a cost akin to costs of materials purchased and labor hired for construction. It limits interest included in plant to interest costs actually incurred and avoids recognizing imputed interest on funds provided by the owner. An argument against this approach is that no funds are costless; to charge interest for borrowed funds, but not for ownership funds, is inconsistent. The results produced by this method are the least satisfactory of the three, since the cost of an asset differs merely because of the way its construction is financed.

11.27   The third method—capitalizing interest on all funds used—is based on the view that the cost of financing is an economic cost of construction and should be included in the cost of the self-constructed asset in the same way as labor or material. Even though interest on ownership funds is an imputed or "opportunity" cost, proponents of this view say that it is an essential cost and thus should be included in the cost of the asset. They point out that if the asset were purchased rather than self-constructed, interest on investment would likely be included as a factor in the purchase price. Opponents of this view note that if interest on ownership funds is capitalized in the asset account with a debit, then a credit to income may be required:

Building under Construction  ....... 10,000
    Interest Revenue  .............        10,000
Capitalize $10,000 of implicit interest
costs.

They object to recognizing income for this implicit interest, noting that income results from using assets, not acquiring them, and that no arm's-length transaction has oc-

curred. If the asset carries implicit interest now, depreciation charges will be higher later. They prefer not to show either interest revenue now or the related higher depreciation over the life of the asset.

**Rate to be Used**   If the third method is   11.28
used, estimating the overall cost of funds becomes necessary. This estimation process has troubled writers in the field of finance for generations. Some companies that capitalize interest have, however, used the borrowing rate, rather than the overall cost of funds, and applied that rate to all funds used for construction. As explained below, the FASB now requires that the actual borrowing rate be used.

**History of Accounting Practice** Public util-   11.29
ity firms have capitalized interest during construction for many years; the accounting is discussed below. Most land development companies have also done so, but until recently few other nonregulated firms capitalized interest during construction. For a variety of reasons, some companies began to do so in the early 1970s. For example, the Sears Roebuck and Company annual report for the year ending January 31, 1974, contains the following footnote:

Effective February 1, 1973, the Company adopted the accounting policy of capitalizing the carrying costs, real estate taxes and interest, of construction-in-progress and land held for future use. Under this new policy, all amounts capitalized will be amortized to earnings over the depreciable life of the structure when the property is placed in economic use. The effect of this prospective change was to increase net income for the year ended January 31, 1974, by $14,100,000 ($.09 per share).

Reports for later years explain:   11.30

Carrying costs (real estate taxes and interest) of construction-in-progress and land held for future use [are deferred], to the extent market value is not exceeded, [and depreciated] over the depreciable life of the structure when placed in economic use. Interest capitalized is based on the cost of land and construction and the average cost of borrowed funds.

11.31 The Securities and Exchange Commission became concerned by the move to capitalizing interest, and it issued *Accounting Series Release No. 163* in 1974 to deal with this matter. It says:

Accordingly, the Commission concludes that companies . . . which had not, as of June 21, 1974, publicly disclosed an accounting policy of capitalizing interest costs shall not follow such a policy in financial statements . . . after June 21, 1974.

Thus, no additional companies began capitalizing interest after 1974, but those that were before then were permitted to continue.

11.32 **Current Rules** The FASB issued *Statement No. 34* in 1979. It requires capitalization of interest as part of an asset's cost if "an asset requires a period of time in which to carry out the activities necessary to bring it to that condition and location." The FASB explains that the "historical cost of acquiring an asset includes the costs necessarily incurred to bring it to the condition and location necessary for its intended use."*

11.33 *Assets Qualifying for Interest Capitalization* The FASB recognizes that the capitalization of interest and its subsequent amortization may result in financial statements that do not differ materially from those where interest is expensed. Interest capitalization is not required in those circumstances. Subject to this customary materiality constraint, interest is capitalized on assets constructed for a firm's own use or constructed as discrete projects for sale or lease to others (such as ships or real estate developments). Interest is not to be capitalized for three kinds of assets:†

**1.** Inventories that are routinely manufactured or otherwise produced in large quantities on a repetitive basis (such as aging whiskey or tobacco).

**2.** Assets ready for use, whether used or not.

**3.** Assets not ready for use, where no work (broadly defined) is being done to get them ready for use. For example, consider a partially complete nuclear electric generating plant which has been under construction for several years but is now not being finished pending settlement of litigation between regulators and conservationists. When construction resumes, capitalization of interest must resume.

*Amount of Interest to Be Capitalized* The 11.34 amount of interest to be capitalized is based on the entity's actual borrowings and interest payments. It is intended to be that portion of interest cost incurred during the assets' acquisition periods that theoretically could have been avoided if the assets had not been acquired. If there is a specific new borrowing in connection with the qualifying asset, the interest rate on that borrowing is used. If the expenditures on plant exceed such specific new borrowings, the interest rate to be applied to such excess is the weighted average of rates applicable to other borrowings of the enterprise. Of course, in some cases, there may not be specific new borrowings; then the average interest rate on old borrowings is used to compute the total amount to be capitalized. Interest capitalized is compounded; that is, interest capitalized for a given period is based on all costs previously incurred, including interest capitalized in preceding periods. The amount of interest capitalized is recorded as a reduction of interest expense for the period. The total amount of interest capitalized cannot exceed total interest costs for the period, so no credit to interest income is reported. Of course, the reduction in interest expense serves to increase final net income during the construction period.

Both the total amount of interest cost for 11.35 a period and the portion capitalized, if any, must be disclosed.

**Example** To illustrate the provisions of 11.36 *Statement No. 34,* assume that a firm has the following long-term debt structure in 1981:

---

*Financial Accounting Standards Board, *Statement No. 34* (1979), par. 6.

†These requirements are summarized from pars. 8, 9, and 10 of FASB *Statement No. 34.*

Mortgage at 10% Interest on Building
    under Construction ............... $1,200,000
Other Recent Borrowings at 11%
    Interest ......................... 2,000,000
Older Debt at a Weighted-Average
    Interest Rate of 9% .............. 8,000,000

The average interest rate for other borrowings is calculated as follows:

| | | |
|---|---|---|
| $ 2,000,000 at 11% | ................. | $ 220,000 |
| 8,000,000 at 9% | ................. | 720,000 |
| $10,000,000 | | $ 940,000 |

$940,000/$10,000,000 = 9.4%

The account for Land and Building under Construction has an average balance during 1981 of $2,000,000. The entries would be:

Interest Expense ............. 1,060,000
    Interest Payable .......... 1,060,000
To record all interest; ($1,200,000
× .10) + ($2,000,000 × .11) +
($8,000,000 × .09).

Plant ....................... 195,200
    Interest Expense .......... 195,200
To capitalize interest into Plant;
($1,200,000 × .10) + ($800,000 ×
.094).

Interest cost for the year, $1,060,000, and the portion capitalized, $195,200, are to be disclosed in the financial statements for 1981.

**11.37** **Funds Statement Effects** No special adjustments are required in the statement of changes in financial position for interest capitalized during construction. Funds that were originally expended for interest payments have been reallocated to plant. In the Other Uses section of the statement, the amount shown for funds used for plant acquisition will be made up of the total of the debits to the plant account, including the amount for interest during construction.

## Interest during Construction for Public Utilities

**11.38** Public utilities have capitalized interest during construction for many years. The rationale is that public utility customers should pay the full cost of producing the services they receive—nothing more and nothing less. Current customers should not have to pay the interest cost on plants being built to serve the next generation of customers. The next generation should be charged with the full cost of the plant now being built, including explicit and implicit interest on the funds expended for the plant.

**11.39** This argument for capitalization of interest is similar to that in FASB *Statement No. 34,* but most public utilities have followed a different recording procedure. The debit for interest during construction is made to the plant account as before, but the credit is to a revenue account, Interest during Construction, rather than to the account for Interest Expense. This difference does not affect the amount of net income; as compared with the FASB procedure, it merely increases the amount of both revenue and of expense by the amount of capitalized interest.

## Property Taxes on Land Held for Later Sale or Use

**11.40** A problem somewhat similar to interest during construction arises in connection with property taxes on land held for resale or use. For example, if a firm acquires land today for use or resale in 3 years, how should property taxes in the period between purchase and sale be treated? Assume management estimates that it is cheaper to buy the land today and pay property taxes for 3 years than to buy the land in 3 years. Then the property taxes should properly be capitalized, because they were necessary to make the land available for its intended use at its lowest cost. Assume, on the other hand, that the land is acquired today to be used or sold this year, but there are unanticipated delays and the land is not used or sold for 3 years. Then the case for capitalization is much weaker.

**11.41** The tax laws permit the current deduction for all property taxes. Charging all property taxes to expense currently is often done in financial reporting as well. *Accounting Research Bulletin No. 43* states: "While it is sometimes proper to capitalize in property accounts the amount of real estate taxes applicable for property which is being developed for use or sale, these taxes are generally regarded as the expense of doing business."*

## Acquisition by Gift

11.42 Accounting generally assumes a rational economic world. One of the frequently used phrases of rational economics is, "There is no such thing as a free lunch." Ordinarily, we would not expect a business entity to receive gifts. Occasionally, however, a local government unit may offer to donate a plant site, and sometimes even a building, if the firm will promise to locate its plant there. The arrangements usually involve a commitment by the firm to employ a certain number of people for a given period of time—200 people for 5 years, for example.

11.43    Strict adherence to the historical (acquisition) cost principle might seem to call for a zero valuation for property acquired by such gifts. However, the logical foundation for the acquisition-cost principle is that acquisition cost is usually the best measure of value at acquisition. If it is clear that value differs materially from cost at the moment of acquisition, fair market value of the asset acquired is the valuation basis used. Accounting Principles Board *Opinion No. 29* states that "a nonmonetary asset received in a nonreciprocal transfer should be recorded at the fair value of the asset received." (A nonreciprocal transfer is defined in the *Opinion* as "a transfer of assets or services in one direction . . . from another entity to the enterprise." Donations are an example of a nonreciprocal transfer.) The account credited for a gift is Donated Capital, a shareholders' equity account, to be distinguished from Contributed Capital, discussed in Chapter 21. An illustrative entry, assuming

that the fair market value of the acquired assets is found to be $400,000, is

| | | |
|---|---|---|
| Land | 100,000 | |
| Building | 300,000 | |
| Donated Capital | | 400,000 |

Title to the property may not be transferred 11.44 until the conditions concerning employment are met. If, however, the company plans to comply with the conditions, the assets should be recognized in the balance sheet with footnote disclosure of the conditions that remain to be met.

## Lump-Sum Acquisitions

A business may acquire several different as- 11.45 sets for a single, lump-sum price. For example, a business may acquire the land, buildings, and equipment of a used factory at a single price for the whole facility. Such an acquisition, frequently called a "basket purchase," requires allocation of the lump-sum cost among the assets acquired. Accounting Principles Board *Opinion No. 16* describes the allocation by saying: "A portion of the total cost is . . . assigned to each individual asset acquired on the basis of its fair value."†

Calculating the fair value of individual 11.46 assets is not easy. Fair market values are usually based on such factors as tax assessments, insurance coverages, independent appraisals, or management estimates. Valuations on the seller's books are not normally a significant factor in determining the fair value of assets acquired.

In many cases, the sum of the fair values 11.47 of the individual assets acquired exceeds the lump-sum purchase price. If the sum of the individual fair values is $1,000,000 and the lump-sum purchase price is $900,000, each asset acquired will be allocated a valuation equal to 90 percent (= $900,000/$1,000,000) of its estimated fair value.

---

*Committee on Accounting Procedure, *Accounting Research Bulletin No. 43, Restatement and Revision of Accounting Research Bulletin* (1953), chap. 10A, par. 17.

†Accounting Principles Board *Opinion No. 16, Business Combinations* (1970), par. 68.

## Method of Payment for Acquisition

11.48   Payment for the acquisition of any asset may be made before the asset is received, at the time of receipt, or subsequent to receipt. Payment may be made by transferring cash or by transferring some other asset, or by a combination. Cash payment at the time of receipt of the plant asset is straightforward. All discounts are deducted from the valuation, and costs of delivery and installation are added.

### Payment in Advance

11.49   Sometimes when plant assets are ordered, the supplier may require a substantial advance payment. Many major plant assets, such as nuclear generating plants or large oil tankers, are built to special order after the purchaser signs a contract with the supplier. Such contracts usually provide for progress payments to be made as the asset reaches certain stages of completion.* Funds received sooner are more valuable than funds received later. Analysis suggests that the contract price for such assets should be lower if the purchaser makes payments in advance of delivery of the asset.

11.50   FASB *Statement No. 34* requires that the purchaser capitalize the interest cost implicit in the advance payment.† The valuation for the asset is increased above the contract price by the amount of capitalized interest. The amount is capitalized in the same way as that illustrated earlier in paragraph 11.36. The entries might be

Jan. 1
| | | |
|---|---|---|
| Advances to Suppliers | 100,000 | |
|    Cash | | 100,000 |

To record contractual payment to supplier of plant assets. Contract price is $500,000.

The equipment is delivered on the last day of the year, and payment is made:

---

*Chapter 8 discusses such contracts from the supplier's viewpoint.
†FASB *Statement No. 34* (1979), par. 9.

Dec. 31
| | | |
|---|---|---|
| Equipment | 500,000 | |
|    Cash | | 400,000 |
|    Advances to Suppliers | | 100,000 |

Payment of contract amount.

| | | |
|---|---|---|
| Equipment | 10,000 | |
|    Interest Expense | | 10,000 |

Borrowings carry a 10% rate. Implicit interest for 1 year at that rate on the advance payment of $100,000 is included in the equipment cost.

### Deferred-Payment Contracts

11.51   Plant assets are frequently acquired on contracts that permit deferred payments for the asset. The obligation to pay may take the form of a note, mortgage, bond, equipment obligation contract, or other instrument. If the deferred payment contract provides for explicit interest payments at a rate that reflects current market conditions at the time the contract was signed, then the plant asset is recorded at the contract price and interest expense is recorded each period in the amount of explicit interest paid or payable.

11.52   Sometimes, however, the deferred-payment contract does not provide for explicit interest charges. In that case, the valuation assigned to the plant asset should be its cash-equivalent price, which is equal to the present value of the payments to be made, discounted at a realistic rate. If the seller offers the equipment for a realistic cash price, then that price is the valuation assigned to the plant asset even when the asset is acquired on a deferred-payment plan. The interest rate implicit in the contract can be determined with methods explained in Appendix B. If the deferred-payment contract calls for equal periodic payments, then the computation is straightforward. Assume that a dealer is willing to sell an extruding machine for $100,000 cash or $16,275 per year for 10 years. The plant asset is assigned a valuation of $100,000. The discount rate implicit in the contract is 10 percent: $100,000/$16,275 = 6.144; Appendix Table 4, 10-percent column, shows a factor of approximately 6.144 for a 10-percent rate.

11.53    If no cash equivalent price is available, an appropriate discount rate must be estimated to calculate the present value of the periodic payments. That present value is the current acquisition cost. The objective is to approximate the interest rate that the buyer and seller would have agreed upon in an arms'-length loan from seller to buyer. To restate the example, assume that the dealer is willing to sell an extruding machine for payments of $16,275 a year for 10 years and that 10 percent is an appropriate borrowing rate for this purchaser. Then the valuation to be assigned to the plant asset is approximately $100,000 (= $16,275 × 6.14457; see Appendix Table 4, 10-period row, 10-percent column).

11.54    Whether the implicit interest rate is found from the cash price or the implicit cash price is found from the interest rate, the entries during the first 2 years, assuming that a note was given, would be

January 1, 1981

| | | |
|---|---:|---:|
| Machinery | 100,000 | |
|     Notes Payable (Net) | | 100,000 |

To record acquisition and note. The note might be recorded for $162,750 with a contra account for the discount of $62,750. See Chapter 17.

December 31, 1981

| | | |
|---|---:|---:|
| Interest Expense | 10,000 | |
| Notes Payable (Net) | 6,275 | |
|     Cash | | 16,275 |

Interest at 10% on $100,000 net opening balance of notes. Part of payment discharges interest; remainder repays part of principal. The balance of the loan is now $93,725 (= $100,000 − $6,275). Plug for the amount reducing the loan balance.

December 31, 1982

| | | |
|---|---:|---:|
| Interest Expense | 9,373 | |
| Notes Payable (Net) | 6,902 | |
|     Cash | | 16,275 |

Interest expense is 10% of the outstanding loan balance, $93,725. Interest Expense rather than the Machinery account is debited because this interest charge occurs while the asset is in use rather than during its construction period.

## Plant Assets Acquired by Issuing Securities

11.55    Plant assets are sometimes acquired in nonmonetary transactions. In describing such acquisitions, APB *Opinion No. 29* says:

The Board concludes that in general accounting for nonmonetary transactions should be based on the fair values of the assets (or services) involved which is the same basis as that used in monetary transactions. Thus, the cost of a nonmonetary asset acquired in exchange for another nonmonetary asset is the fair value of the asset surrendered to obtain it. . . . The fair value of the asset received should be used to measure the cost if it is more clearly evident than the fair value of the asset surrendered.*

11.56    One type of nonmonetary transaction is the issue of securities for plant assets. If the acquiring company's securities are traded on an established stock exchange, then the market value of the securities issued is a satisfactory measure of the valuation of the plant asset acquired. If the securities are not actively traded, then an appraisal may be necessary to determine the fair value of the plant assets acquired. In the first case, the fair value of the securities determines the valuation assigned to the plant assets. In the latter case the appraisal of the plant assets determines the valuation assigned to the securities issued. The par or stated value of the securities issued is not a proper valuation of the plant assets acquired.

## Plant Assets Acquired in Trade-in Transactions

11.57    Sometimes new plant assets are acquired by trading in old assets. This is a particularly common practice for automobiles. The accounting for trade-in transactions depends on the data available about the fair value of the old asset traded in, the fair value of the new asset acquired, and whether or not the two assets are similar. Three general approaches to recording trade-ins have been

---

*Accounting Principles Board, APB *Opinion No. 29, Accounting for Nonmonetary Transactions* (May 1973), par. 18; footnote references omitted.

used. They can be described as (1) the new-asset method, (2) the used-asset market method, and (3) the book value method. To use the new-asset method, one must know the fair market price for the new asset. This may be the list price or some price less than list. (Readers will be familiar with the phenomenon that some automobiles, hi-fi equipment, and cameras can be purchased for cash at a price less than list.) To use the used-asset market method, one must know the fair market value of the old asset being traded in. This number can sometimes be estimated by consulting price quotations in secondhand markets, such as the "blue" and "red" books for automobiles. Whether one uses the new-asset method or the used-asset market method basically depends on which information is more reliable—the estimate of the fair market price of the new asset or the estimate of the used asset's fair market value.

11.58    To illustrate the methods, assume that an old asset cost $25,000 and has $15,000 of accumulated depreciation (after recording depreciation to the date of the trade-in). The old asset thus has a book value of $10,000. Also assume that the list price of the new asset is $43,000, but it can be purchased for $40,000 cash. Hereafter, the list price is irrelevant and the cash price of $40,000 is the fair market price for the new asset. The old asset has a fair market value of $8,000. The method of recording the trade-in depends on which of the pieces of information (new asset price of $40,000 or old asset value of $8,000) is judged more reliable. The old asset and $28,000 in cash are given for the new asset. Cash given in a trade-in is called *boot*. The generic entry for the trade-in transaction is

| | | |
|---|---|---|
| New Asset ...................... | *x* | |
| Accumulated Depreciation ......... | 15,000 | |
| Loss or Gain on Retirement ........ | *y* or | *y* |
|     Cash ...................... | | 28,000 |
|     Old Asset ................... | | 25,000 |

11.59   **1.** The new-asset method assumes that the fair market value of the new asset is the best measure of fair value at the date of acquisition. Thus, $x = \$40,000$; $y$ is a plug ($= \$2,000$ credit). If $y$ requires a credit plug, then there

is a gain on retirement; if $y$ requires a debit plug, then there is a loss on retirement of the old asset.

**2.** The used-asset market method assumes that the price quotation in the used-asset market is the best measure of fair value at the date of acquisition. Thus $y$ is calculated by subtracting the used-asset value from the book value. If the difference is positive, then there is a loss and $y$ is a debit. If the difference is negative, then there is a gain and $y$ is a credit. In the example, $y = \$10,000 - \$8,000$, so there is a loss of $2,000. The new asset is recorded by plugging for $x$ once $y$ is known: $x = \$28,000 + \$25,000 - \$15,000 - \$2,000 = \$36,000$.

**3.** The book value method assumes that the fair value of the old asset is equal to its book value. Consequently, there is neither gain nor loss on retirement ($y = 0$). The new asset is recorded by plugging for $x$ ($= \$28,000 + \$25,000 - \$15,000 = \$38,000$).

The recording of trade-in transactions under   11.60 generally accepted accounting principles is guided by the provisions of APB *Opinion No. 29.* The method used for recording trade-in transactions depends on whether the new asset's or the used asset's market price is a better indicator of fair value, whether there is a gain or loss indicated on retirement, and whether the new and old assets are "similar productive assets."* The basic approach is to use the new-asset method (1) or the used-asset market method (2), depending on which valuation is considered a more reliable estimate of fair value.

**Loss on Trade-in** If, when applying the   11.61 basic approach, a loss is calculated on the retirement of the old asset, the full amount of the loss is recognized currently. Thus, in the previous example, if the used-asset market were considered more reliable, then the required entry would be

---

*Ibid., par. 3(e), defines productive assets as "assets held for or used in the production of goods or services by the enterprise." Similar productive assets are defined as "productive assets that are of the same general type, that perform the same function or that are employed in the same line of business."

```
New Asset  ......................   36,000
Accumulated Depreciation  .........   15,000
Loss on Retirement  ..............    2,000
     Cash  .......................          28,000
     Old Asset  ..................          25,000
```
Used asset market price more reliable; plug for a loss; record loss; plug for new asset cost.

11.62 **Gain on Trade-in** If, however, a gain is calculated on the retirement, then the form of the entry depends on whether or not the old asset and the new asset are "similar productive assets." If they are not similar, then the gain is recognized currently. Thus, in the earlier example, if the new asset value were considered more reliable and the assets were not similar, the entry would be

```
New Asset  ......................   40,000
Accumulated Depreciation  .........   15,000
     Gain on Retirement  ..........          2,000
     Cash  .......................          28,000
     Old Asset  ..................          25,000
```
List price of new asset more reliable; plug for gain on retirement; report gain because assets are dissimilar.

11.63 If the assets are similar and no cash is received on the trade, then no gain is recognized and the recording follows the book value method (3). The justification for not recording gain is that trading one asset for a similar asset does not constitute the "culmination of an earning process,"* but merely a preparatory step to providing goods or services to customers. In the example, if the assets were considered similar, the entry would be

```
New Asset  ......................   38,000
Accumulated Depreciation  .........   15,000
     Cash  .......................          28,000
     Old Asset  ..................          25,000
```
Market value of new asset more reliable; plug for gain; do not report gain because assets are similar; reduce new asset cost by amount of gain suppressed.

11.64 **Cash Received by Purchaser** In rare cases, the firm making the trade-in receives cash,

---

*Ibid., par. 21. The phrase generally means that the goods have not been sold to a final consumer.

also called *boot*. This would occur if the asset traded in had a fair value greater than the fair value of the asset acquired.

**1.** If the fair value of the asset traded in is less than its book value, a loss is recognized.

**2.** If the fair value of the asset traded in is greater than its book value (and also greater than the fair value of the asset acquired, resulting in a receipt of cash), the full gain is recognized if the assets are not similar.

**3.** If the assets are similar, only a portion of the gain is recognized. The portion recognized is equal to the fraction, cash received divided by total value of consideration received. Total value of consideration received is the sum of the cash received and the fair value of the new asset. In some cases the fair value of the new asset can be determined only by subtracting the amount of cash received from the fair value of the asset traded in.† The justification for recognizing a portion of the gain is based upon the view that a portion of the asset traded in has been sold for cash and a portion exchanged for a similar, new asset. When an asset is dis-

---

†An algebraic expression for these rules may help. Use the following notation:

$G$ = Gain to Be Recognized
$C$ = Cash Received in Trade-in
$F$ = Fair Market Value of Asset Received
$B$ = Book Value of Asset Given Up
$A$ = Cost to Be Recorded for New Asset Acquired.

Then

$$G = [(C + F) - B]\, \frac{C}{C + F}$$

and

$$A = B - \left(B \times \frac{C}{C + F}\right).$$

In the example in the next paragraph of the text,

$$\$1{,}500 = [(\$12{,}000 + \$4{,}000) - \$10{,}000]\, \frac{\$4{,}000}{\$16{,}000}$$

and

$$\$7{,}500 = \$10{,}000 - \left(\$10{,}000 \times \frac{\$4{,}000}{\$4{,}000 + \$12{,}000}\right).$$

posed of for cash, gain or loss must be recognized.

11.65    As an example of the last situation, assume that an asset that cost $25,000 and has accumulated depreciation of $15,000 is traded for a new asset with a current cash price of $12,000, and $4,000 of cash is received. The gain is $6,000 [= ($12,000 + $4,000) − ($25,000 − $15,000)]. The portion of the gain recognized is 25 percent [= $4,000/($4,000 + $12,000)]. The gain to be recognized is $1,500 (= $6,000 × .25), and the valuation assigned to the new asset can be determined only by plugging. It is $7,500 (= $25,000 − $15,000 − $4,000 + $1,500). The entry is

| | | |
|---|---|---|
| New Asset ...................... | 7,500 | |
| Accumulated Depreciation ......... | 15,000 | |
| Cash .......................... | 4,000 | |
|     Old Asset .................... | | 25,000 |
|     Gain on Retirement .......... | | 1,500 |

11.66    **Summary of Accounting for Trade-in Transactions** These complex rules of accounting for trade-in transactions can be summarized as follows:

1. A determination is made as to whether the list price of the new asset or the trade-in allowance on the old asset most clearly reflects market value.

2. Using the valuation most clearly reflecting market value from 1, a gain or loss on the trade-in is computed. This gain or loss is recognized, with two exceptions:

   a. If the assets exchanged serve similar productive uses and no cash is received, any gain indicated from the trade-in is not recognized. The gain not recognized reduces the cost of the new asset received. A loss is recognized.

   b. If the assets exchanged serve similar productive uses and cash is received, a portion of the gain indicated from the trade-in is recognized. The proportion of the gain recognized is equal to the percentage that the cash received bears to the total value of the consideration received.

The decision rules for determining the recognition of gain or loss on the trade-in are illustrated in Figure 11.1.

11.67 **Income Tax Treatment** For income tax reporting, no gain or loss may be recognized on a trade-in. The book value method must be used. In many cases, the valuation assigned to the acquired asset on the financial records differs from that shown on tax records because gain or loss upon retirement is recognized on the financial records but not on the tax return. A timing difference results, requiring the recognition of deferred income taxes. Chapter 20 describes the accounting for deferred taxes.

---

*Figure 11.1*
**Decision Rules for Determining the Recognition of Gain or Loss on a Trade-in**

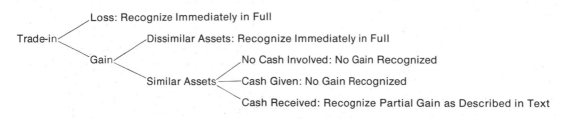

Source: From a suggestion by Professor Leon Hanouille, Syracuse University, Syracuse, New York.

## Anticipated Removal Costs

11.68   Removal costs are incurred when an asset is retired from service. For example, a contract may require the destruction of a building at the end of its intended life; or a coal mining company may agree to restore a strip mining site at the completion of mining operations to a condition similar to its original, natural state. Conceptually, removal costs are the same as negative salvage value. The next chapter explains that removal costs are added to the cost of the asset in computing depreciation charges.

## The Investment Tax Credit

11.69   Since 1962, with occasional suspensions, both businesses and individuals have been able to reduce their income taxes payable by a credit arising from the acquisition of plant assets. The credit is known as the "investment (tax) credit" and can equal some percentage (usually 10 percent) of the cost of equipment acquired during the period. Chapter 20 discusses and illustrates accounting for the investment tax credit.

## Costs Subsequent to Acquisition

11.70   After a plant asset is acquired, many costs related to its continued use are incurred. Should these costs be charged to current operations, or should they be treated as an addition to the cost of the plant asset? The question is sometimes worded, "Should such costs be expensed or capitalized?" (Describing all charges to operations as expenses is not fully satisfactory because the debit is frequently made to a Work-in-Process Inventory account rather than to an expense account.)

11.71   The conceptual basis for making the expense–capitalize decision is clear. Costs incurred to increase the future benefits to be derived from a plant asset should be capitalized; costs that merely help to maintain the given level of services should be expensed. The criteria for determining whether future benefits have been increased are as follows:

**1.** The quantity of services to be received from the asset has been increased by extending its service life or increasing the volume of services rendered during the original estimated service life, or

**2.** The quality of services furnished by the asset has been improved, or both.

Although the concept is clear, the determination that there has been an increase in future benefits is frequently difficult to make in practice.

11.72   Frequently, considerable analysis and judgment are required before the expense –capitalize decision can be made. Many firms limit practical problems by arbitrarily specifying that all expenditures below a specified minimum, say, $500 or $1,000, are automatically charged to expense.

11.73   Costs incurred subsequent to acquisition fall into four major categories:

**1.** Repairs and maintenance.

**2.** Rearrangement and moving.

**3.** Replacements and improvements.

**4.** Additions.

A fifth category, anticipated removal costs, was discussed in the contexts of acquisition and retirement.

## Repairs and Maintenance

11.74   Regular repair and maintenance expenditures are usually required on a more-or-less continuous basis to keep the plant assets in good operating condition. Included are the costs of lubrication, cleaning, repair parts and supplies, repair labor, and related items. Repair and maintenance expenditures do not increase the productive power of an asset or prolong its economic service life, but merely maintain the originally anticipated useful life. Distinguishing them from expenditures for improvements and replacements, however, can be difficult.

**11.75   Unit of Property Determines Accounting**
Whether an item is treated as a repair or a replacement frequently depends on the detail of the recording of plant assets. If plant assets are defined in terms of complete units, such as a truck or a building, the cost of a new set of tires or of a new roof is treated as a repair. On the other hand, if plant assets are recorded in greater detail in terms of structural elements subject to separate depreciation, then the cost of replacing such items is not treated as a repair but is capitalized in the plant asset accounts.

**11.76**   *Example* A truck is expected to last for 10 years if the engine is completely replaced every 4 years and the tires are replaced every 2 years. If the cost of the truck as a complete unit is depreciated over 10 years, then the cost of new engines and tires is an expense in the year incurred. The truck, however, can be divided into three asset accounts: engine, tires, and chassis. The engine is depreciated over 4 years, the tires over 2 years, and the chassis over 10 years. Then, the costs incurred for new tires and engines are capitalized as replacements. The unit of property—truck versus tires, engines, and chassis—to be used is a matter of accounting convenience in most cases. Whatever unit is chosen will determine the subsequent accounting. For tax purposes, the separate accounting for components of a building is not allowed after the 1981 change in the tax law.

## Rearrangement and Moving

**11.77**   The cost of rearranging and moving machinery and equipment to secure greater efficiency in production or reduce operating costs in future periods should be capitalized. Estimating the number of periods of future benefit from the rearrangement, and thus the amortization period, is difficult. If the measurable benefit from the rearrangement does not clearly extend into future periods, then the costs should be expensed as incurred. If, when the asset was first acquired, it was expected to remain in one place, then moving costs are expenses. If, on the other hand, relocation was anticipated, then capitalizing moving costs seems theoretically preferred.

## Replacements and Improvements

Replacements and improvements (some-   **11.78**
times referred to as "betterments") are nonrecurring expenditures that increase the service potential of plant assets beyond the service potential originally anticipated. The increased service potential results from factors such as increasing the rate of output, lowering the operating cost, or increasing the remaining service life of a plant asset.

Replacement involves the removal of a   **11.80**
major component of a plant asset and the substitution of a new component of the same type or the same operating capability. An improvement also involves the removal of a major component of a plant asset, but the component substituted has materially superior operating characteristics.

Replacements and improvements both result in an increase in the book value of the plant assets. Repairs, on the other hand, are charged to expense as incurred. Frequently, distinguishing a replacement or improvement from a repair is difficult. The basic distinction is whether the expenditure increases the future service potential of the plant asset (capitalize) or merely maintains the existing level of service (expense).

If future service potential has been in-   **11.81**
creased, the expenditure should be capitalized. Under generally accepted accounting principles, the capitalization may be accounted for in one of three ways depending on the circumstances:

**1.** *Substitution.* This approach recognizes that an old element of plant has been retired and replaced by a new one. Two separate events are recorded. First, the old element is retired with a credit to Plant, a debit to Accumulated Depreciation and a debit or credit to Loss or Gain on Retirement. Then, the cost of the new element is recognized by a debit to the plant account and a credit to Cash or some other account depending on the means of payment. This method of recording is soundest conceptually, but it can be applied only when the cost and accumulated depreciation of the element of plant retired are known. The method is especially appropriate when individual elements of an asset, such as tires on a truck or a roof on a building, are recorded and depreciated separately.

**2.** *Capitalize the new cost.* In this approach, the cost of the new element is debited to Plant (with a credit to Cash or other means of payment) and no other entry is made. This approach is justified when sufficient depreciation has been taken on the element retired to reduce its book value almost to zero, an unlikely case. This approach may be practicable if neither the cost nor accumulated depreciation of the element retired is known. Improvements are frequently recorded in this way.

**3.** *Debit accumulated depreciation.* In this approach, the cost of the new element is debited to Accumulated Depreciation (with a credit to Cash or other means of payment), and no other entry is made. This approach is likely to be followed when there is a replacement that extends the estimated service life of the asset. It is viewed as a recovery of past depreciation charges. This approach has little conceptual justification, because even if the replaced element were fully depreciated, the changing cost of elements of plant makes it most unlikely that the new cost would equal past depreciation. This approach may be a practical way of accounting for the replacements if the accumulated depreciation on the item replaced is not known.

### Additions

11.82    *Additions* are extensions or expansions of an existing plant asset. Adding an extra wing to a hospital is an addition to a building; adding an additional feature to an existing paper-making machine is an addition to equipment. An addition is clearly a capital expenditure that is debited to the plant account at full acquisition cost.

11.83    The addition extends or expands an existing asset. Has any part of the future service potential of the existing plant asset been diminished because of the addition? Assume that an existing wall has to be torn down to add the wing. Should the cost of that wall be removed from the plant account? If so, should the cost of removing it be treated as an expense of the period of construction or as part of the cost of the addition? Practice varies in dealing with these items. Conceptually, the proper treatment depends on the firm's original intent. First, assume it had anticipated that an addition would be needed later, but that building the original structure first and then adding the wing was cheaper than building the whole larger structure at the outset. Then, the cost of the removed wall should be retained and the cost of removal should be viewed as part of the cost of the addition. If the firm had not anticipated the need for the addition, the cost of removing the old wall is an expense. Conceptually, the cost of the removed wall and its accumulated depreciation should also be removed from the plant account, and a loss recognized, but this entry is seldom made.

## Valuation Subsequent to Acquisition

11.84    At acquisition, the cost of an asset acquired in an arm's-length transaction represents its value. After acquisition, plant assets are depreciated as described in the next chapter. Because of general inflation and changing market conditions for specific assets, the cost less accumulated depreciation of plant assets may, as time passes, differ widely from their current value. Chapter 26 discusses accounting for changing prices. The next sections briefly consider valuation subsequent to acquisition for plant assets by methods different from those traditionally used. The methods considered are the following:

**1.** Constant-dollar accounting, involving adjustments for changes in the general price level.

**2.** Current-cost accounting, involving adjustments for changes in specific prices.

## Constant-Dollar Measuring Unit

11.85    Inflation is a continuing phenomenon in our economic world. Put simply, inflation means that the dollar buys a smaller general market basket of goods than it did previously; looked at another way, the same general market basket of goods costs more. Changes in the purchasing power of the dollar are usually described as changes in the general price level. Constant-dollar accounting changes the measuring unit for assets as the general price level changes. The historical cost basis remains in use, but the measuring unit is changed from nominal dollars to dollars of constant purchasing power.

11.86    Proponents of constant-dollar accounting draw an analogy from foreign exchange adjustments. Assume that a firm has a plant in England that cost 200,000 pounds, one in the Netherlands that cost 400,000 guilders, and a third in the United States that cost 300,000 dollars. No one would add those three numbers together to say that the firm had 900,000 (= 200,000 + 400,000 + 300,000) units of plant. They say, quite properly, that the valuations must be expressed in a common measuring unit before they can be summed. However, accountants regularly add $200,000 of plant purchased in 1967, $400,000 of plant purchased in 1974, and $300,000 of plant purchased in 1981 and say that there is $900,000 of plant. Yet the difference in purchasing power between the 1967 dollar and the 1981 dollar may be greater than the difference between the dollar and the pound or the guilder. Supporters of constant-dollar accounting say that the valuations of assets should be expressed in units of the same purchasing power.

11.87    The FASB requires constant-dollar accounting disclosures. *Statement No. 33* requires larger firms ($125 million or more of inventories and plant or $1 billion or more of total assets) to show as supplemental information, among other items, the valuation of plant assets, adjusted for changes in the general price level. The index required by the FASB for measuring changes in the general price level is a consumer price index published by the Department of Labor. If the index was 100 in 1967 and 270 in 1981, then the original cost of the plant acquired in 1967 would be translated to 540,000 (= 200,000 × 270/100) 1981 dollars for presentation in the 1981 financial statements.

## Current-Cost Basis

11.88    The current-cost basis values plant assets at the current cost of replacing the *services* of the plant assets. Current cost may differ from reproduction cost whenever new technology becomes available. Replacing the service potential of an asset (for example, by substituting computerized controlling devices to save expensive fuel and labor) may be less expensive than reproducing a physically identical asset. Current-cost accounting deals with changes in specific prices; constant-dollar accounting deals with changes in the general price level. Chapter 26 discusses both.

## Retirement of Plant Assets

11.89    Plant assets may be retired by sale, exchange, or abandonment. They may also be lost involuntarily as a result of a casualty such as a fire or flood. Whatever the cause of disposition, depreciation of the asset should be recorded up to the date of disposition. At that date, the cost of the retired asset and the accumulated depreciation related to it should be removed from the accounts. There will usually be a gain or loss upon disposition to be recognized at that time. Such gains or losses had been frequently reported as extraordinary items, but APB *Opinion No. 30* provides that they should be shown as part of the income from continuing operations. If, however, the disposition of plant assets is part of "the disposal of a segment of a business," *Opinion No. 30* requires that the gain or loss on disposition of those plant assets be included with the other gains and losses from the disposal of the segment. A segment, for this purpose, must represent a separate line of business or class of customers. The sum of the gains or losses on disposal of a segment is shown below income from continuing operations and before extraordinary items, as Chapter 2 explains.

11.90    The gain or loss upon retirement of a plant asset effectively recognizes that depreciation charges in earlier years were in error. Depreciation is based on estimates of economic service life and of salvage value that are affected by many subsequent events. New inventions, development of new materials, and changing prices, to name a few, may occur in an unexpected fashion and make the actual events differ from the estimates. Such deviations from estimates are normal in a dynamic world; including the gain or loss that results from deviations from estimates in the normal operating section of the income statement seems justified.

## Abandonment of Plant Assets

11.91    In rare cases, a plant asset may be disposed of without the owner's receiving any salvage proceeds or paying any disposal costs. If, even rarer, the asset is fully depreciated, the abandonment entry is merely a debit to Accumulated Depreciation and a credit to the asset. If the asset is not fully depreciated, a loss on abandonment is recognized. More commonly, there will be some salvage value or disposal cost. These proceeds should be taken into account in calculating gain or loss upon retirement of the asset.

## Sale of Plant Assets

11.92    Plant assets are frequently sold while they have substantial economic value. The distinction between abandonment, considered in the previous section, and sale of plant assets is one of degree only. A sale could be considered an abandonment with large retirement proceeds. Assume that a machine costing $100,000 has $70,000 of accumulated

depreciation and is sold for $25,000. The entry to record the sale is

| | | |
|---|---|---|
| Cash | 25,000 | |
| Accumulated Depreciation | 70,000 | |
| Loss upon Disposal | 5,000 | |
| Machinery | | 100,000 |

If the proceeds of sale had been $36,000, there would have been a gain upon disposal of $6,000.

## Exchanges of Plant Assets

The accounting for exchanges of plant assets   11.93 was discussed earlier in this chapter in the section on trade-ins. The frequency of trade-ins is affected by the income tax regulations. As mentioned in the earlier section, no gain or loss is recognized on a trade-in for income tax reporting. The recording follows the book-value method described earlier. In practice, firms considering a trade-in implying a loss will sell the old asset directly rather than trading it in. In this way, the firm will be able to recognize the loss currently for tax purposes. Then, they will acquire the new asset entirely for cash. If the firm expects to gain upon disposing of an old asset, it is more likely to trade in the asset rather than selling it directly. The gain is not recognized or taxed; it reduces the basis of the new asset.

## Involuntary Conversions

The services of a plant asset are sometimes   11.94 lost through a casualty such as a fire or flood or by condemnation by the government for a public purpose. Frequently, the insurance proceeds or the amount granted in condemnation are spent to acquire replacement property. Such an event, loss of an asset followed by its replacement, is an *involuntary conversion*. The recording of involuntary conversions had not been uniform until the FASB issued *Interpretation No. 30* in 1979. The FASB requires that gain or loss, as appropriate, be recognized.

   For example, assume that certain land and   11.95 buildings owned by a firm are condemned by the state as the site for a new civic auditorium. The land and buildings cost $400,000 and have accumulated depreciation of $240,000. Because of increased property values in that area, the firm is awarded $300,000 in the condemnation proceedings. Assume further that new land and buildings costing $500,000 are acquired to replace those condemned. The $300,000 proceeds, $50,000 of additional cash, and proceeds of a mortgage for $150,000 are given as consideration. The accounting is carried out in two steps, first recording the disposition of the old asset and then recording the acquisition of the new:

| | | |
|---|---:|---:|
| Cash ........................ | 300,000 | |
| Accumulated Depreciation ....... | 240,000 | |
| Land and Buildings ......... | | 400,000 |
| Gain on Disposal of Land and Buildings ............... | | 140,000 |

To record proceeds of condemnation of building.

| | | |
|---|---:|---:|
| Land and Buildings ............. | 500,000 | |
| Cash ..................... | | 350,000 |
| Mortgage Payable .......... | | 150,000 |

To record acquisition of land and buildings.

The gain upon disposition of land and buildings is treated in the same way as other gains on disposition, as an item of income from continuing operations.

11.96 If the assets are not replaced, then only the first entry to record the asset disposition and the gain or loss is required.

11.97 **Other Methods** Previously, two other possible approaches were in use and considered acceptable. One approach offset the gain against the cost of the new acquisition, so no gain was recognized. The valuation assigned to the new land and buildings was $360,000 (= $500,000 − $140,000). The other approach recognized the gain, but treated it as an extraordinary item. Neither of these approaches is now permitted by FASB *Interpretation 30.*

11.98 **Tax Reporting** For tax purposes, the taxpayer has the choice of treating the event as an involuntary conversion or an ordinary sale of a plant asset and purchase of a new

one. If there is a gain and all of the proceeds are reinvested in a similar new asset, the taxpayer should treat the transaction as an involuntary conversion. No gain need be recognized for tax purposes. Because the gain must be recognized for financial reporting, a timing difference is created and deferred taxes must be recognized; see Chapter 20. On the other hand, if there is a loss on disposition, the taxpayer should not normally treat the transaction as an involuntary conversion but as a normal sale and purchase. In this case the loss is deductible currently.

**Partial Loss, Without Replacement** If 11.99 plant assets are damaged by fire or other casualties, and are repaired rather than replaced, the accounting follows the same general pattern. If the property is insured, and the insurance covers the exact repair costs, no loss is recognized. If repair costs to restore the property to its original service potential exceed the insurance proceeds, a loss in the amount of the difference is recognized. If the expenditures improve the asset beyond its approximate service potential before the casualty, the cost should be apportioned between the loss and the asset improvement accounts.

## Retirement of Plant Assets in the Statement of Changes in Financial Position

Retirement of a plant asset frequently re- 11.100 quires special treatment in the statement of changes in financial position. A loss upon disposition is an expense that does not require the use of working capital and thus requires an addback to net income in calculating funds provided by operations. Working capital was used when the asset was acquired.

**Gain on Disposition** Reporting a gain upon 11.101 disposition of noncurrent assets in the funds statements presents irreconcilable goals. First, because the funds are generated by disposition of noncurrent assets, we would like to show all of the funds as an "Other Source" of funds, Proceeds of Sale of Noncurrent Assets. Second, because the gain is included in income from continuing operations, we would like to show the funds from the gain as part of funds from continuing operations. The source of funds cannot be shown in both places. Two treatments are possible, and both are seen in practice:

**1.** All the proceeds of disposition are shown as an "Other Source" of funds; a subtraction from net income is required for the amount of the gain. Reported funds from operations exclude the amount of the gain.

**2.** No adjustment to net income is made in showing funds from operations. The "Other Source" of funds from disposition of a noncurrent asset must show an amount equal to the book value of the asset retired. An appropriate title is Proceeds from Sale of Noncurrent Assets at Book Value.

11.102  Exhibit 11.1 illustrates both treatments for the sale described earlier in this chapter, in which an asset with a book value of $30,000 is sold at a gain for $36,000. Exhibit 11.1 assumes that this is the only transaction for the period, so the effects of this transaction can be isolated. We prefer the first method because all funds generated by the disposal are reported on a single line in the statement of changes in financial position. We use that method throughout this book in describing the funds statement effects of disposal of noncurrent assets at a gain.* Those who use the second method should not omit the words "Book Value" from the label on the line in the "Other Sources" section, or confusion is almost certain to result.

---

*The AICPA prepares a looseleaf reporting service (with bound annual volumes), *Technical Practice Aids* (available from Commerce Clearing House). The AICPA compiles replies by its Technical Information Service to inquiries from practicing accountants. The views expressed in *Technical Practice Aids "are not official"* opinions of the AICPA. In Section 1300.09, the following answer is given to an inquiry about which of the two methods is correct for reporting gains on disposal of noncurrent assets. The reply states:

Reporting the book value of property sold as a source of funds [treatment **(2)**, above] continues to be used in practice. But, adjusting income or loss from operations by the gain or loss on the sale of the property and reporting the entire proceeds as a source

---

## Exhibit 11.1
### Illustration of Alternative Funds Statement Presentations of Gain on Disposal of Noncurrent Asset

**Asset with Book Value of $30,000 Is Sold for $36,000**

**1. All Proceeds Shown as "Other Source" of Funds**[a]

| | |
|---|---|
| Net Income | $ 6,000 |
| Subtract Gain Not Producing Funds from Operations | (6,000) |
| Funds Provided by Continuing Operations | $   0 |
| Other Sources: Proceeds of Sale of Noncurrent Assets | 36,000 |
| Total Sources of Funds | $36,000 |

**2. Gain Produces Funds from Operations**

| | |
|---|---|
| Net Income | $ 6,000 |
| Funds Provided by Continuing Operations | $ 6,000 |
| Other Sources: Proceeds of Sale of Noncurrent Asset at Book Value | 30,000 |
| Total Sources of Funds | $36,000 |

[a]This is the preferred alternative. See discussion in text.

## The Plant Ledger

11.103  The preceding discussion has indicated the need for adequate records for the various plant assets. Adequate records provide a description of each asset, the vendor from whom acquired, the date acquired, its location in the plant, and its cost. They also include a depreciation schedule, described in the next chapter. For small equipment items, the use of a separate record for each item is often not considered practicable; in-

---

of nonoperating funds specifically conforms to the requirements in paragraph 14 of Accounting Principles Board *Opinion No. 19.* . . . [Excerpts from the paragraph are then shown.]

Although we use the inquiries and replies of AICPA *Technical Practice Aids* frequently in constructing questions and cases, we do not cite it as authority for generally accepted accounting principles because of the express disclaimer in the volume itself. Still, we are heartened by the agreement of the Technical Information Service with our view.

ventory sheets—with a line for each item or group—are used. The development of computer-based records has made the maintenance of detailed plant records more practicable.

11.104    There may be one or more aggregate or controlling plant asset accounts. Each of the controlling accounts summarizes details in the detailed plant accounts. The detailed plant accounts are commonly known as a "plant ledger."

## Summary

11.105    Plant assets, like most other assets, are recorded at cash-equivalent cost at the time of acquisition. Where the acquisition is made other than by immediate cash payment, the cash equivalent of the means of payment must be found. For deferred payment promises, the present value of the promised payments must be calculated. If securities are transferred, the fair market value of the securities given up is generally the measure of the cost of the plant assets. If there is a trade-in, the fair market values of the asset received and of the asset traded in are critical factors in the calculation of the valuation of the new asset.

11.106    When additions and improvements are made that increase the service potential of the asset by extending its life or making it more efficient, they are capitalized and charged as a cost to future periods.

11.107    When the plant asset is disposed of, gain or loss is recognized by comparing the disposition proceeds or trade-in value with book value at the disposition date.

## Questions and Short Cases

**11.1**    Review the meaning of the following concepts or terms discussed in this chapter.

a. Plant assets versus fixed assets.
b. Wasting assets versus renewable resources.
c. Prudent cost.
d. Lucky buy.
e. Aboriginal cost.
f. Rehabilitation versus repair.
g. Direct costing versus absorption costing.
h. Interest during construction.

i. Opportunity cost.
j. Donated capital versus contributed capital.
k. Basket purchase.
l. Implicit interest.
m. Trade-in.
n. Similar productive assets.
o. Boot.
p. Removal costs.
q. Maintenance versus repair.
r. Replacement versus improvement.

s. Rearrangement.
t. Betterment.
u. Historical cost stated in constant dollars versus current cost.
v. Retirement versus abandonment.
w. Involuntary conversion.
x. Plant ledger.
y. AICPA *Technical Practice Aids*.

**11.2**    a. What is the general rule for valuing plant assets acquired by purchase?
b. What is the rule for valuing plant assets acquired by gift?
c. What principle reconciles these apparently different answers?

**11.3**    a. Is accounting symmetric when it subtracts "imprudently incurred costs" from the cost of the asset but does not add the "amount of luck" in a "lucky buy" to the cost of an asset?
b. If not, what justifies the asymmetry?

**11.4**    "Showing both acquisition cost and accumulated depreciation amounts separately provides a rough indication of the relative age of the firm's long-lived assets."
a. Assume that the Lavin Company acquired an asset with a depreciable cost of $100,000

several years ago. Accumulated depreciation as of December 31, recorded on a straight-line basis, is $60,000. The depreciation charge for the year is $10,000. What is the asset's depreciable life? How old is the asset?

b. Assume straight-line depreciation. Devise a formula that, given the depreciation charge for the year and the asset's accumulated depreciation, can be used to determine the age of the asset.

11.5 Why is it convenient for accounting to distinguish between land on the one hand and buildings and equipment on the other?

11.6 What principles (none are discussed in this book) might justify the use of "aboriginal cost" in public utility rate regulation?

11.7 The discussion in this chapter of the unit of property—e.g., truck versus tires, engines, and chassis—does not say which of the approaches is preferable. That vagueness results both from lack of guidance from generally accepted accounting principles and from the authors' lack of a strong opinion on the subject. Which method do you think better and why?

11.8 a. Describe three methods of accounting for replacements.
b. Which of these methods can be used for improvements? Why can't the others be used?

11.9 a. Why does accounting for trade-ins require different treatment in some cases for similar and dissimilar assets? Evaluate the reasoning.
b. Why does accounting for trade-ins require different treatment in some cases for gains and losses? Evaluate the reasoning.

11.10 Consider the acquisition of an asset with a single-payment, noninterest-bearing note for $100,000 payable in 3 years. Note that accounting requires that the asset be recorded at the present value of the note, say, $75,000, and the difference—$25,000 in this case—be accrued as expense over 3 years.

A skeptic wonders, "Why bother?" The asset's depreciation will be $75,000 and the $25,000 will be interest expense. If the asset were merely recorded at $100,000, then its depreciation would be $100,000.

Reply to the skeptic.

11.11 Consider a firm with no borrowings and, hence, no interest costs. The FASB forbids capitalization of interest during construction under these circumstances. Opponents of the FASB position say that when payments are made far in advance of receipt of a plant asset, the cost of the asset must be increased by the implicit interest on the funds paid sooner, rather than later, even though there is no borrowing. The credit would be to a revenue account.

a. Why is this treatment suggested?
b. Throughout, this book emphasizes that income over long-enough time periods is cash in less cash out. Note that here income would be recorded even though no cash is coming in. Resolve the apparent contradiction.

11.12 What principles (a) support the capitalization of interest on discrete projects, such as ships or shopping centers, prepared for sale to others, but (b) forbid capitalization of interest on manufactured products routinely produced in large quantities, such as tobacco, that take as long or longer to produce from start to finish than a shopping center? (Hint: Refer to paragraphs 10 and 45 of FASB *Statement No. 34.*)

11.13   Consider the production of each of the following items which are produced for sale to others. In each of these cases, costs for items produced are accumulated item by item. (Using the terminology of cost accounting, the "job-order method," not the "process-costing method," is used.) Assume that the manufacturer incurs sufficient interest cost that capitalization of interest during the construction period would make the financial statements with capitalization of interest materially different from those without capitalization. In which of the following cases would interest be capitalized during construction?
   a. Construction company building a single office building, at a cost of $10 million.
   b. Construction company building five office buildings, each costing $10 million.
   c. Construction company building 100 office buildings, each costing $10 million.
   d. Construction company building one single-family house, costing $100,000.
   e. Construction company building five single-family houses, each costing $100,000.
   f. Construction company building 100 single-family houses, each costing $100,000.
   g. Vineyard producing a single vintage of fine wine, which it ages for 6 years before sale.
   h. Vineyard producing three vintages of fine wine, aging each for 6 years before bringing it to market, with a new batch of wine being put into production every 2 years.
   i. Vineyard producing six vintages of fine wine, each aging 6 years before being brought to market, with a new batch being put into production each year.

11.14   Describe the allocation of the cost of a basket purchase to its individual items. Distinguish among three cases, as follows. The estimates of the fair market value of the individual, separately identifiable items sum to an amount:
   a. Exactly equal to acquisition cost of the group.
   b. More than the acquisition cost of the group.
   c. Less than the acquisition cost of the group. (How can this happen?)

11.15   The word "repair" is used in two different ways in describing work done on factory machines to bring them up to full working order. Sometimes the word "repair" means costs debited to Work-in-Process Inventory and sometimes it means costs debited to an expense or loss account.
     Distinguish between repairs that are debited to an asset account and those that are debited to an expense or loss account.

11.16   Sometimes property taxes on land held for later use are debited to an asset account and sometimes they are debited to an expense account.
   a. Distinguish between the cases.
   b. What analogy can be drawn between the problem for property taxes, treated here, and for "repairs," treated in the preceding question?

11.17   For each of the following costs, indicate the kind of account debited:
   (1) Work-in-Process Inventory.
   (2) Some other asset account.
   (3) Expense.
   a. Cost of office machine.
   b. Cost of oil and new type bars used to repair office typewriter that broke down in normal use.
   c. Cost to repair damage caused by vandals who poured glue into office machine.
   d. Cost of factory production machine.
   e. Cost of oil and new parts used to repair factory machine that broke down in normal use.
   f. Cost to repair damage caused by vandals who poured paint into factory machine.

**11.18** Describe the treatment of overhead costs incurred in constructing an asset. In answering, distinguish between costs that would have been incurred anyway and incremental costs.

**11.19** **a.** Describe the treatment of interest costs incurred in constructing an asset. In answering, distinguish among interest costs that would have been incurred anyway, incremental borrowing costs, and opportunity costs on funds already on hand that remove the need to borrow additional funds.

**b.** Why should the opportunity cost of interest not earned on the company's own funds because they were used to finance the construction of a building be treated differently from the explicit interest cost on funds borrowed to finance the construction of the building?

**11.20** Consider an airline's inventory of replacement parts acquired for use for its current fleet of airbuses. Assume that these parts cannot be used for planes other than airbuses.

**a.** Why does the airline care if the cost of these parts is accounted for as "inventory" or as a depreciating asset?

**b.** Which method is it likely to prefer for tax purposes and why?

**11.21** The Jensen Company bought two used tractors from Black Company for $10,000 each. The tractors are not identical. Jensen Company knew that one of the tractors required an extensive engine "repair," expected to cost about $3,000. The repair was made and actually cost $3,200. Jensen Company thought that the second tractor was in fine working order when it was purchased but found, upon putting it to work, that certain bearings needed replacing. The cost of this repair was $3,200.

**a.** What costs should be recorded in the asset accounts for the two tractors?

**b.** If the amounts recorded above are different, then distinguish between the two "repairs."

**11.22** Generally accepted accounting principles require that gain or loss be recognized on involuntary conversions, whereas tax rules allow deferral of the gain or loss. Why should there be a difference?

**11.23** (Adapted from CPA Examination.) Webben & Sons, Inc., purchased land, together with a building standing on it, as the site for an additional plant that it planned to construct. The corporation obtained bids from several contractors for demolition of the old building and construction of the new building, but finally rejected all bids and undertook the construction using company labor, facilities, and equipment. Construction was almost completed by the close of the year.

All transactions relating to these properties were charged or credited to an account titled Real Estate. The various items in that account are summarized below. Separate Land and Buildings accounts should be set up. All of the items in the Real Estate account should be reclassified.

Indicate the disposition of each lettered item below. Although there may be other appropriate dispositions not listed, you need not use them. Consider only the following five possibilities:

**(1)** Transfer to Land account.

**(2)** Transfer to Buildings account.

**(3)** Transfer to a revenue (or gain) account.

**(4)** Transfer to an expense (or loss) account.

**(5)** Make some other disposition of the item.

You may recommend a reclassification involving two or more of the above accounts. For each item for which you recommend (5), "some other disposition," provide an explanation of the nature of that disposition and the reasons for your recommendation.

**a.** Contract price of "package" purchase (land and old building).

**b.** Legal fees relating to conveyance of title.

**c.** Invoice cost of materials and supplies used in construction.

**d.** Direct costs arising from demolition of old building.

**e.** Discounts earned for early payment of item **c.**

**f.** Total issuing costs on bonds issued during the year. Proceeds were used to finance construction.

**g.** Interest accrued to end of year on bonds mentioned above.

**h.** "Interest" charge based on company funds used to acquire the plant site and assigned by the client to "create a cost of acquisition comparable to that which would have resulted had funds been borrowed for this purpose."

**i.** Total depreciation on equipment used during construction period partially for construction of building and the remainder of the time for regular operations.

**j.** Total cost of excavation.

**k.** Proceeds of sale of materials salvaged from razing of old building.

**l.** Net cost of temporary structures (tool sheds, construction offices, etc.) erected for use in construction activity.

**m.** Cost of building permits and licenses.

**n.** Architects' fees.

**o.** Allocated portion of certain corporation engineering executives' salaries (based on time devoted to planning and supervision of construction).

**p.** Other allocated overhead for the period covering the razing of the old building, excavation, and construction of the new building.

**q.** Allocated portions of employees' wages for the period of excavation and of construction of the new building.

**r.** Payment of property taxes on land and old building, owed by the former owner and assumed by Webben & Sons, Inc.

**s.** Special municipal assessments for sidewalk and street pavings necessitated by the altered use of the site.

**t.** Premiums for insurance against natural hazards during construction.

**u.** Premium rebates for certain of the above policies surrendered before completion of construction.

**v.** Total of employer's share of full year's social security taxes for all employees who worked on the construction.

**w.** Uninsured claims paid for injuries sustained during construction (aggregate amount $3,000).

**x.** Installation costs for newly acquired machinery installed in completed wings of the building.

**y.** Estimated profit on construction of new building to date (computed as follows: Lowest contractor's bid multiplied by percentage of building completion on December 31, less new building construction costs through December 31).

**11.24** (Adapted from CPA Examination.) Lexton Corporation acquired a new machine by trading in an old asset and paying $24,000 in cash. The old machine originally cost $40,000 and had accumulated depreciation at the date of exchange of $30,000. The new machine could have been purchased outright for $50,000 cash.

This transaction could be recorded by either of the two following methods:

**Method 1**

| | | |
|---|---|---|
| Machinery | 50,000 | |
| Accumulated Depreciation | 30,000 | |
|     Gain on Disposal of Fixed Assets | | 16,000 |
|     Cash | | 24,000 |
|     Machinery | | 40,000 |

**Method 2**

| | | |
|---|---|---|
| Machinery | 34,000 | |
| Accumulated Depreciation | 30,000 | |
|     Cash | | 24,000 |
|     Machinery | | 40,000 |

a. Identify the reason for recording the above transaction using method 1.

b. Identify the reason for recording the above transaction using method 2.

c. Using the required method, give the entry to record the above transaction if the new machine had a nominal list price of $52,000 and was commonly selling for $50,000 cash, assuming Lexton Corporation was allowed $28,000 for its old asset, which is a machine used for the same purpose as the new machine.

**11.25** A utility acquiring a nuclear generating plant knows that substantial costs, currently estimated to be $40 million, will be incurred in approximately 50 years to "decommission" the plant—to retire the plant and dispose of the spent nuclear fuel in the approved fashion. How should these expected decommissioning costs be accounted for at the time the plant is acquired?

**11.26** a. Which attribute of a person, height or girth, is useful to know?

b. Distinguish between the measurement of height in inches and in centimeters.

c. Use the distinctions drawn above to distinguish between the constant-dollar amounts for an asset and their current cost.

**11.27** a. A firm's garage was constructed several decades ago, in part, of a special red cedar wood that today is available only from the Philippine Islands at very high prices. In calculating the current cost of the garage, why is the high current price of red cedar wood largely irrelevant?

b. Distinguish between the reproduction cost of an asset and the current cost of replacing productive capacity of the asset.

**11.28** (Adapted from AICPA *Technical Practice Aids*.) Beaver Corporation owns a log pond that it dredged during the current year at a cost of $350,000. The useful life of the pond was thereby extended by several years. Should the dredging cost be expensed or capitalized?

**11.29** (Adapted from AICPA *Technical Practice Aids*.) A company acquired land and developed it into a ski resort. It incurred costs for cutting trees, clearing and grading the land, and constructing ski lifts. It sold some of the cut timber to a local lumber mill. How should these costs and receipts be treated? Differentiate costs that are expensed immediately, capitalized into a nondepreciable land account, and capitalized into a depreciable plant account.

**11.30** (Adapted from AICPA *Technical Practice Aids*.) A manufacturer entered into a long-term supply contract with a customer. The customer agreed to purchase all of the manufacturer's product for several years. At the end of the contract term the customer has the option to purchase the manufacturer's plant for $10 million. The plant is recorded in the manufacturer's records in the following accounts: Land, Buildings, and Equipment; and Accumulated Depreciation on Buildings and Equipment. At the end of the contract term, the manufacturer gives $3 million to the customer and retains ownership of the plant. How should the expenditure of $3 million be recorded?

**11.31** The balance sheet of Woolf's Department Store shows a building with an original cost of $800,000 and accumulated depreciation of $660,000. The building is being depreciated on a straight-line basis over 40 years. The remaining depreciable life of the building is 7 years. On January 2 of the current year, an expenditure of $28,000 was made on the street-level displays of the store. Indicate the accounting for the current year if the expenditure of $28,000 was made under each of the following circumstances. Each of these cases is to be considered independently of the others, except where noted. Ignore income tax effects.

   **a.** Management decided that improved displays would make the store's merchandise seem sufficiently more attractive that the displays are a worthwhile investment.

   **b.** A violent hailstorm on New Year's Day had destroyed the display windows previously installed. There was no insurance coverage for this sort of destruction. New windows are installed that are physically identical to the old windows. The old windows had a book value of $28,000 at the time of the storm.

   **c.** Vandals had destroyed the display windows on New Year's Day. There was no insurance coverage for this sort of destruction. New windows are installed that are physically identical to the old windows. The old windows had a book value of $28,000 at the time of the destruction.

   **d.** The old displays contained windows that were constructed of nonshatterproof glass. Management had previously considered replacing its old nonshatterproof windows with new ones but had decided that there was *zero* benefit to the firm in doing so. New shatterproof windows are installed because a new law was passed requiring that all stores must have shatterproof windows on the street level. The alternative to installing the new windows was to shut down the store. In responding to this part, assume *zero* benefits result from the new windows. Part e below considers the more realistic case of some benefits.

   **e.** Management had previously considered replacing its old, nonshatterproof windows with new ones, but decided that the new windows would produce future benefits of only $7,000 and so were not a worthwhile investment. However, a new law (see part **d**) now requires it to do so, and the new windows are installed.

**11.32** The Dixie Company acquired all the properties of the Montgomery Company. The consideration given was $2.5 million cash and Dixie Company First Mortgage Bonds with a par value of $40 million. An appraisal of the property by Dixie engineers showed that it had a replacement cost in new condition of $52 million and a current value, as is, of $40 million. Dixie's bonds sell in the market place for 96 percent of par. The bonds exchanged for Montgomery property could have been issued for cash of $38.4 million.

   Shortly after taking over the Montgomery property, Dixie sold one plant, realizing $600,000 after paying sales commissions. It removed and scrapped several machines, realizing $50,000 cash and spare parts worth $200,000. These retirements were planned at the time the purchase of the Montgomery property was considered. The replacement cost new of the assets scrapped was estimated to be $3 million.

   The engineer in charge of appraisals stated that the retained elements of purchased property were of modern construction in first-class shape and that if Dixie were to acquire such property new at the time of purchase, the cost would be approximately $49 million.

   Give journal entries to record this acquisition.

**11.33** (Adapted from CPA Examination.) Among the principal topics related to the accounting for the property, plant, and equipment of a company are acquisition and retirement.

a. What expenditures should be capitalized when equipment is acquired for cash?

b. Assume that the market value of equipment acquired is not measurable by reference to a similar purchase for cash. Describe how the acquiring company should calculate the capitalizable cost of equipment purchased by exchanging it for each of the following:

(1) Bonds having an established market price.

(2) Common stock not having an established market price.

(3) Similar equipment having a determinable market value.

c. Describe the factors that determine whether expenditures relating to property, plant, and equipment already in use should be capitalized.

d. Describe how to account for the gain or loss on the sale of property, plant, and equipment for cash.

## Problems and Exercises

**11.34**   On March 1, one of the buildings owned by the Metropolitan Storage Company was destroyed by fire. The cost of the building was $100,000; the balance in the Accumulated Depreciation account at January 1, the start of the accounting period, was $38,125. A service life of 40 years with a zero salvage value had been estimated for the building. The company uses the straight-line method. The building was not insured.

a. Give the journal entries made at March 1.

b. If there have been no alterations in the service life estimate, when was the building acquired?

**11.35**   Icerman Company wanted to acquire new land for a plant site. It found two reasonable properties for which the asking price was $100,000 each. Rather than purchase either property immediately, it retained the services of a lawyer and a real estate appraiser to give advice. It paid fees totaling $10,000—$6,000 to the appraiser and $4,000 to the lawyer—for their advice. It purchased one of the parcels for $100,000. What is the cost of the land?

**11.36**   McIntyre Company wanted to acquire new land for a plant site. It found a reasonable property for which the asking price was $100,000. Rather than purchase the land immediately, the company acquired a 60-day option to acquire the land for $100,000. The option cost $5,000, which was paid in cash on April 1. On May 15, McIntyre Company exercised its option and paid an additional $100,000 for the land.

a. What is the cost of the land?

b. Same general facts as above, except that McIntyre Company found two reasonable properties. The company paid $5,000 to each of the current owners for 60-day options to acquire their parcels. The company is allowed to buy none, one, or both of the properties. On May 15, the company made its decision and bought one of the parcels for $100,000. It let the other option lapse. What is the cost of the land?

c. Same as part **b**, except that the second option was sold to another buyer on May 15 for $2,000.

d. Same as part **b**, except that the second option was sold to another buyer on May 15 for $7,000.

**11.37**   (Adapted from CPA Examination.) On January 1, the Lock Company sold property to the Key Company that had originally cost Lock $600,000. Key gave Lock a $900,000 noninterest-bearing note payable in six equal annual installments of $150,000. The first payment was due (and was made) on the date of sale. There was no established market value of the property sold, but the prevailing interest rate for notes of this type was 15 percent with Lock as the borrower and 12 percent with Key as the borrower.

a. Compute the gain or loss Lock should record on sale of property.

b. Prepare a schedule showing the amount for Lock's note receivable from Key at the end of the year of sale and 1 year after that.

11.38    In negotiating the purchase price of property, says Kenneth Harney, it is "far better to get a 10-percent-down, 30-year seller-financed loan at one or two percentage points below the going market . . . than to haggle over . . . sale price." Consider a property with an appraised fair market value of $100,000 when mortgage rates are 12 percent. Assume that mortgage payments are made annually, at the end of each year.

     Consider two alternative offers the buyer, Harney Company, can make to the seller:

(1) Offer $95,000 by giving a $20,000 cash payment and a 30-year mortgage for $75,000 at 12 percent, annual payments of $9,311.

(2) Offer "$100,000" by giving a $10,000 ("10-percent-down") cash payment and a 30-year mortgage for $90,000 at 10 percent, annual payments of $9,547, even though the fair market rate is 12 percent.

     The student who has completed all parts of this problem will rightly question whether a rational seller of property will be indifferent between these two offers. The point of the problem is that economic substance differs substantially between the two offers.

a. What cost is recorded for the property if it is acquired under the financing plan outlined in (1)?

b. What cost is recorded for the property if it is acquired under the financing plan outlined in (2)?

c. Describe the accounting subsequent to acquisition for plan (1) and show the journal entries for the first year after purchase.

d. Describe the accounting subsequent to acquisition for plan (2) and show the journal entries for the first year after purchase.

e. Does the accounting difference between financing plans (1) and (2) adequately reflect the real "economic" differences between the two plans? Why? Which plan would you prefer as buyer? Why?

11.39    (This problem cannot easily be worked with pencil, paper, and the compound interest tables at the end of this book. Do not attempt it unless you have a calculator with the ability to do annuity and present-value computations.) Refer to the preceding problem. Consider a property with an appraised value of $100,000 when mortgage rates are 12 percent for 30-year loans. Assume a mortgage covering 100 percent of the price.

     At what interest rate used in computing 30 annual payments to be made at the end of each year should the buyer be indifferent between giving a mortgage for $100,000 computed at that rate and a purchase price of $95,000 financed at a rate of 12 percent?

11.40    (Adapted from CPA Examination.) Ellford Corporation received a $400,000 low bid from a reputable manufacturer for the construction of special production equipment needed by Ellford in an expansion program. Because the Company's own plant was not operating at capacity, Ellford decided to construct the equipment there and recorded the following production costs related to the construction:

| | |
|---|---:|
| Services of Consulting Engineer | $ 10,000 |
| Work Subcontracted | 20,000 |
| Materials | 200,000 |
| Plant Labor Normally Assigned to Production | 65,000 |
| Plant Labor Normally Assigned to Maintenance | 100,000 |
|     Total | $395,000 |

Management prefers to record the cost of the equipment under the incremental cost method. Approximately 40 percent of the Corporation's production is devoted to government supply contracts, which are all based in some way on cost. The contracts require that any self-constructed equipment be allocated its full share of all costs related to the construction.

The following information is also available:

(1) The above production labor was for partial fabrication of the equipment in the plant. Skilled personnel were required and were assigned from other projects. The maintenance labor would have been idle time of nonproduction plant employees who would have been retained on the payroll whether or not their services were used.

(2) Payroll taxes and employee fringe benefits are approximately 30 percent of labor cost and are included in manufacturing overhead cost. Total manufacturing overhead for the year was $5,630,000.

(3) Manufacturing overhead is approximately 50 percent variable and is applied on the basis of production labor cost. Production labor cost for the year for the Corporation's normal products totaled $6,810,000.

(4) General and administrative expenses include $22,500 of executive salary cost and $10,500 of postage, telephone, supplies, and miscellaneous expenses identifiable with this equipment construction.

a. Prepare a schedule computing the amount that should be reported as the full cost of the constructed equipment to meet the requirements of the government contracts. Any supporting computations should be in good form.

b. Prepare a schedule computing the incremental cost of the constructed equipment.

c. What is the greatest amount that should be capitalized as the cost of the equipment? Why?

11.41   The Parrish Company buys a large machine from the Thompson Tool Company on January 1. The payment terms are $10,000 to be paid on delivery and $10,000 plus interest at 6 percent on the unpaid balance at December 31 of this and each of the next 4 years. The six payments are $10,000 (now), $13,000 (= $10,000 + .06 × $50,000), $12,400 (= $10,000 + .06 × $40,000), $11,800, $11,200, $10,600. A realistic interest rate for obligations of this sort is 10 percent per year. The machine is estimated to have a 10-year service life with no salvage value.

a. What amount should be recorded as the cost of the machine to the Parrish Company?

b. Record all entries for the first 2 years on the books of the Parrish Company.

c. Record the entries for this year on the books of the Thompson Tool Company. Assume that the company regularly manufactures and sells machines of this sort. The machine cost $40,000 to manufacture.

11.42   Happy Pappy's Manufacturing Company borrows $1 million by giving a 12-percent, interest-bearing note to the Sola Bank. It is a demand note, due whenever the bank wishes. The bank treats the note, in effect, as a floating-rate loan. The proceeds of the loan are used for several business purposes. The note is the only borrowing of the company. During the term of the loan, Happy Pappy's drills for natural gas to be used as fuel in heating its plant. At the beginning of the current year, Happy Pappy's incurs $600,000 to drill the gas well and to install pumping equipment. The process of laying the pipeline to the well takes 3 years. Although the company will accumulate costs for the pipeline asset in a separate account, the work on the entire project continues throughout the 3-year period so that capitalization of interest on the natural gas well is required. At the end of each year, the company capitalizes interest into the account for the cost of the natural gas.

a. Assume that the interest rate on the demand, floating-rate note is 12 percent for each of the 3 years. What is the book value of the natural gas well at the end of the current year and each of the next 2 years?

   b. Assume that the interest rate is 12 percent for the current year, 15 percent for the next year, and 10 percent for the third year. What is the book value of the natural gas at the end of each of the 3 years?

   c. Assume that the principal amount of the note is only $650,000 and that the interest rate is 12 percent per year for each of the 3 years. What is the book value of the natural gas at the end of each of the 3 years?

**11.43**   Copeland Company was organized in year 1 to carry out long-term construction projects. It undertook a few separate projects during each of several years and borrowed various amounts on long-term notes during each of the several years. Interest is to be capitalized into the Construction-in-Process account. Exhibit 11.2 shows the borrowing history over the first 4 years. Assume that all new borrowing and retirement of old debt occurs on the first day of each year. None of the borrowings are specific to any individual project. Treat each of the following problems as independent of the others.

   a. Assume that the average balance in the Construction-in-Process account for year 1 is $800,000. What amount of interest is capitalized into that account for the year?

   b. What is the weighted-average interest rate on borrowings outstanding at the end of year 3?

   c. Assume that the Construction-in-Process account began year 4 with a balance of $5 million, that $7 million of new costs other than capitalized interest were added to that account, and that $4 million of construction was completed and removed from the account. Assume that additions and deletions for the account occurred evenly throughout the year. What is the balance in the Construction-in-Process account at the end of year 4 after capitalizing interest?

   d. Assume that the Construction-in-Process account had an average balance during year 4 of $5.1 million. What amount of interest is capitalized into the Construction-in-Process account for year 4?

**11.44**   The Chisholm Manufacturing Company purchased a plot of land for $50,000 as a plant site. There was a small office building on the plot, conservatively appraised at $8,000, which the company will continue to use with some modification and renovation. The company had plans drawn for a factory and received bids for its construction. It rejected all bids and

*Exhibit 11.2*
**Copeland Construction Company**
**Borrowing History**

| Year | Total Borrowings Outstanding Beginning of Year (1) | New Borrowings for Year[a] (2) | Interest Rate on New Borrowings (3) | Debt Retired at Start of Year[a] (4) | Interest Rate on Debt Retired (5) | Total Borrowings Outstanding End of Year (6) |
|---|---|---|---|---|---|---|
| 1 ..... | $          0 | $1,000,000 | 10% | $          0 | — | $1,000,000 |
| 2 ..... | 1,000,000 | 2,000,000 | 12 | 400,000[b] | 10% | 2,600,000 |
| 3 ..... | 2,600,000 | 3,000,000 | 15 | 1,200,000[c] | 12 | 4,400,000 |
| 4 ..... | 4,400,000 | 2,000,000 | 10 | 0 | — | 6,400,000 |

[a]All new borrowings and retirement of old borrowings assumed to occur on the first day of each year.
[b]Year 1 borrowing.      [c]Year 2 borrowing.

decided to construct the plant itself. Below are listed additional items that management feels should be included in plant asset accounts.

| | |
|---|---:|
| (1) Materials and Supplies | $250,000 |
| (2) Excavation | 12,000 |
| (3) Labor on Construction | 138,000 |
| (4) Cost of Remodeling Old Building into Office Building | 9,000 |
| (5) Interest on Money Borrowed by Chisholm[a] | 5,000 |
| (6) Interest on Chisholm's Own Money Used | 13,000 |
| (7) Cash Discounts on Materials Purchased | 6,000 |
| (8) Supervision by Management | 10,000 |
| (9) Workman's Compensation Insurance Premiums | 8,000 |
| (10) Payment of Claim for Injuries Not Covered by Insurance | 3,000 |
| (11) Clerical and Other Expenses of Construction | 8,000 |
| (12) Paving of Streets and Sidewalks | 4,000 |
| (13) Architect's Plans and Specifications | 3,000 |
| (14) Legal Costs of Conveying Land | 2,000 |
| (15) Legal Costs of Injury Claim | 1,000 |
| (16) Income Credited to Retained Earnings Account, Being the Difference between the Foregoing Cost and the Lowest Contractor's Bid | 15,000 |

[a]This borrowing was Chisholm's only borrowing during the construction period.

Show in detail the items to be included in the following accounts: Land, Factory Building, Office Building, and Site Improvements. Explain why you excluded any items from the four accounts.

**11.45** (Adapted from CPA Examination.) Selected accounts included in the property, plant and equipment section of the Kingston Corporation's balance sheet at January 1, had the following balances:

| | |
|---|---:|
| Land | $175,000 |
| Land improvements | 90,000 |
| Buildings | 900,000 |
| Machinery and Equipment | 850,000 |

During the year the following transactions occurred:

(1) A tract of land was acquired for $125,000 as a potential future site.

(2) A plant facility consisting of land and building was acquired from the Nostrand Company in exchange for 10,000 shares of Kingston's common stock. On the acquisition date, Kingston's stock had a closing market price of $45 per share on a national stock exchange. The plant facility was carried on Nostrand's books at $89,000 for land and $130,000 for the building at the exchange date. Current appraised values for the land and building, respectively, are $120,000 and $240,000.

(3) Items of machinery and equipment were purchased at a total cost of $300,000. Additional costs were incurred as follows:

| | |
|---|---:|
| Freight and Unloading | $ 5,000 |
| Sales and Use Taxes | 12,000 |
| Installation | 25,000 |

(4) Expenditures totaling $75,000 were made for new parking lots, streets and sidewalks at the corporation's various plant locations. These expenditures had an estimated useful life of fifteen years. Disregard the related accumulated depreciation accounts and prepare a

detailed analysis of the changes in each of the following balance sheet accounts for the year:

a. Land
b. Land improvements
c. Buildings
d. Machinery and equipment

11.46   In each of the following situations, compute the amounts of revenue, gain, expense, and loss to be shown on the income statement for the year and the amount of assets to be shown on the balance sheet as of the end of the year. Show the journal entry or entries required, and provide reasons for your decisions. Straight-line amortization is used. The reporting period is the calendar year. The situations are independent of each other, except where noted.

a. Because of a new fire code, a department store must install additional fire escapes on its building. The fire escapes are acquired for $28,000 cash on January 1. The building is expected to be demolished 7 years from the date the fire escapes were installed.

b. Many years ago, a firm acquired shares of stock in the General Electric Company for $100,000. On December 31, the firm acquired a building with an appraised value of $1 million. The company paid for the building by giving up its shares in the General Electric Company at a time when equivalent shares traded on the New York Stock Exchange for $1,050,000.

c. Same data as part **b**, except that the shares of stock represent ownership in Small Timers, Inc., whose shares are traded on a regional stock exchange. The last transaction in shares in Small Timers, Inc., occurred on December 27. Using the prices of the most recent trades, the shares of stock of Small Timers, Inc., given in exchange for the building have a market value of $1,050,000.

d. A company drills for oil. It sinks 10 holes during the year at a cost of $1 million each. Nine of the holes are dry, but the tenth is a gusher. By the end of the year, the oil known to be recoverable from the gusher has a net realizable value of $40 million. No oil was extracted during the year. Chapter 13 gives the answer to this question required by generally accepted accounting principles. What do you think the answer should be?

e. A film producer incurred costs of $12 million during the year to produce a movie for television. The contract with the television network specifies that the film will be shown twice—once during the current year and once during the next year. The network is to pay $10 million during the current year and $5 million within one month of showing the film during the next year.

f. Same data as in part **e**, but the network has the additional option to show the film still a third time 2 years from now for an additional fee of $5 million, payable only if the option is exercised.

g. The same film producer mentioned above incurred costs of $3 million to produce an *avant-garde* film. No network has yet purchased rights to show the film. In the past, the producer has generally recovered only one-third of the costs of such speculative films.

11.47   Oxnard Company wishes to acquire a 5-acre site for a new warehouse. The land it wants is part of a 10-acre site that the owner insists be purchased as a whole for $18,000. The company purchases the land, spends $2,000 in legal fees for rights to divide the site into two 5-acre plots, and immediately offers half of the land for resale.

a. The two best offers are
   (1) $12,000 for the east half, and
   (2) $13,000 for the west half.
   The company sells the east half. What is the cost of the west half kept and the gain or loss on sale of the east half?

    **b.** The two best offers are

    **(1)** $5,000 for the east half, and

    **(2)** $12,000 for the west half.

    The company sells the west half. What is the cost of the east half kept and the gain or loss on sale of the west half?

**11.48** The City of Meridin has developed certain industrial property as part of a program to attract industry. On January 1, the city made a donation of land and a plant building to the Fallsboro Corporation. There were some conditions attaching to the gift. The Fallsboro Corporation agreed to employ 500 people or more on average for a period of 5 years. If the corporation fulfilled this agreement, the title to the land and building would pass to the corporation at the end of 5 years. If the average employment was fewer than 500 people, then the corporation agreed to purchase the property for $340,000 at the end of 5 years, $50,000 in cash and a 10-year mortgage for $290,000 at the then-current mortgage rate. On January 1, the property was appraised at $40,000 for the land and $400,000 for the building, and the building had an estimated service life of 20 years.

    **a.** Assume that the corporation fulfilled the conditions. Describe the accounting for this conditional gift during the 5-year period, presenting appropriate journal entries.

    **b.** Assume that the corporation is unable to fulfill the conditions. Prepare the journal entry or entries necessary to record the purchase of the property 5 years hence.

**11.49** Southside Development Corporation acquired a parcel of land on July 1, 1980, for $50,000. The tract was sold on July 1, 1981, for $38,000.

    An index of the general price level on various dates is as follows:

| | |
|---|---|
| July 1, 1980 | 100 |
| December 31, 1980 | 115 |
| July 1, 1981 | 125 |
| December 31, 1981 | 140 |

    **a.** Compute the amount of gain or loss recognized during 1981 relating to this property under the acquisition cost valuation method, assuming that changes in the general purchasing power of the dollar are ignored.

    **b.** Restate the gain or loss recognized during 1981 on the sale of the tract from its nominal dollar amount to amounts based on the general purchasing power of the dollar. Use dollars of purchasing power on December 31, 1981.

**P11.50** Refer to the data in Problem **4.27** at the end of Chapter 4 for the Calhoun Company. Assume in the Supplementary Information that the proceeds of sale of the equipment amount to $400, rather than $1,000. As a result, net income is reduced from $45,000 to $44,400, and dividends are reduced from $20,000 to $19,400. All other items remain unchanged. Prepare a statement of changes in financial position for the year, defining funds as working capital.

**11.51** Refer to the data in Problem **4.27** at the end of Chapter 4 for the Calhoun Company. Assume in the Supplementary Information that the proceeds of sale of the equipment amount to $3,000, rather than $1,000. As a result, net income is increased from $45,000 to $47,000, and dividends are increased from $20,000 to $22,000. All other items remain unchanged. Prepare a statement of changes in financial position for the year, defining funds as working capital.

**11.52** In *Statement No. 33,* the FASB defines the "current cost" of a used asset. When prices of similar assets in second-hand markets are available, the current cost of the owned asset is the cost of a similar asset in the second-hand market. (Consider, for example, a 3-year-old, four-door sedan of standard design with the usual optional equipment, for which prices can be ascertained from dozens of different used-car dealers.) When prices for similar used assets are not available, the FASB says (paragraph 180 of *Statement No. 33*) that the current cost of a used asset may be estimated by "the buying price of a new improved asset less an allowance for the operating disadvantages of the asset owned (higher operating costs or lower output potential) and an allowance for depreciation calculated according to an acceptable accounting method. This approach yields what may be described as a measurement of the current cost of the service potential of the asset owned."

Assume that the Functional Pricing Company owns an asset that cost $100,000, is 4 years old, and is being depreciated on the straight-line method over a 10-year life. This asset requires labor and materials costing $80,000 per year to produce 10,000 units of product that sell for $50 each. No second-hand market prices for this asset are available. A new machine costs $175,000, has a 6-year life and can produce 10,000 units of product identical to those produced by the old machine. The operating costs for labor and materials to operate the new machine are only $60,000 per year. The discount rate appropriate under the circumstances is 10 percent per year.

a. What is the present value of the operating cost savings of $20,000 (= $80,000 − $60,000) per year for 6 years? (Assume that all cash flows occur at the end of the year.)

b. What is the "current cost," as defined by the FASB, of the used asset?

c. Same general facts as above except the new machine will last 10 years, not 6 years. What is the "current cost" of the used asset already owned by the Functional Company?

11.53 Repairs and maintenance are normally treated as operating expenses of the period in which they are incurred. If interim statements are issued during the year, an accrual approach is sometimes used. The method is similar in concept to the allowance method for uncollectibles. This procedure requires an estimate of the repair and maintenance costs for the year. The estimated repair and maintenance charges are then allocated to each interim period on a time (equal amount each month or quarter) or units-of-production basis.

Some accountants suggest that this accrual procedure be used to smooth the annual charges for repairs over the life of the asset if they are substantial in amount and are expected to vary substantially from year to year. The suggestion has received little support because of the substantial problems involved in estimating total repair costs over the life of the asset and because such a procedure would tend to obscure the fact that repair costs do increase as the asset gets older. FASB *Statement No. 5* forbids such accruals. See the discussion in Chapter 15.

Assume that repair and maintenance costs for the year are estimated to be $100,000. Actual expenditures during the year total $96,000; by quarter, they are $10,000, $48,000, $15,000, and $23,000. Repair and maintenance costs are allocated equally to each quarter.

The entries in the first quarter would be

---

| | | |
|---|---|---|
| Repair Expense ................................................ | 25,000 | |
|     Estimated Repair Liability .............................................. | | 25,000 |
| Accrue "allowance" for repairs. | | |

| | | |
|---|---|---|
| Estimated Repair Liability ................................................. | 10,000 | |
|     Cash, Wages Payable, etc. ............................................ | | 10,000 |
| Charge actual repairs for quarter. | | |

---

The $15,000 credit balance in the Estimated Repair Liability account appears among the current liabilities on the interim balance sheet. The income statement reports Repair Expense of $25,000.

a. Prepare entries for the next three quarters, so that the estimated liability is reduced to zero by the end of the fourth quarter.

b. Assume, now, that the actual repair expenditures for the year were $103,000, not $96,000. What amount is debited to Repair Expense for the fourth quarter?

11.54  (Adapted from CPA Examination.) Many companies insure their plant assets against loss. Many insurance policies have a "co-insurance" clause, for example, an 80-percent co-insurance requirement. The firm purchasing the insurance must co-insure with the insurance company up to 80 percent of the asset's value. That is, the insurance company requires that the insured property be covered by insurance in dollar amount at least equal to the value of the property multiplied by the co-insurance percentage. Thus, a company with property worth $1 million would be required, under an 80-percent co-insurance requirement, to carry at least $800,000 of insurance. Otherwise, actual losses might not be fully reimbursed. If a co-insurance clause exists, the insurance company will pay the lowest of the following three amounts:

(1) The face amount of the insurance policy.

(2) The actual loss (at fair market value).

(3) An amount equal to

$$\text{Actual Loss} \times \frac{\text{Face Amount of Insurance Policy}}{\text{Co-insurance Percentage} \times \text{Value of Property}}.$$

Rule (2) applies only when insurance coverage actually purchased is greater than or equal to the value of the property multiplied by the co-insurance percentage. A property with a $1 million fair market value insured for $600,000 (face amount of policy) damaged in a fire entitles the insured company to receive the following amounts:

| Dollar Amount of Damage | Rule Applicable Above | Amount Paid by Insurance Company |
|---|---|---|
| $ 10,000 | (3) | $ 7,500 |
| 600,000 | (3) | 450,000 |
| 900,000 | (1) | 600,000 |

If the insured company carries more than one policy on the same property, each with co-insurance clauses, then the amounts to be recovered from the insurance companies in case of loss are computed for each policy as though it is the only policy.

Homer, Inc., has two fire insurance policies. Policy A covers the office building at a face value of $360,000, and the furniture and fixtures at a face value of $108,000. Policy B covers only the office building at an additional face value of $140,000. Each policy is with a different insurance company. A fire caused losses to the office building and the furniture and fixtures. Exhibit 11.3 summarizes the relevant data.

Compute the amount due from each insurance company for the loss on each asset category. Show computations in good form.

11.55  Refer to the Simplified Funds Statement for a Period in Exhibit 4.13. Nine of the lines in the statement are numbered. Line (2) should be expanded to say "Additions for Expenses and Other Charges Against Income Not Using Funds," and line (3) should be expanded to say "Subtractions for Revenues and other Credits to Income Not Producing Funds from Operations." Ignore the unnumbered lines in responding to the questions below.

Assume that the accounting cycle is complete for the period and that all of the financial statements have been prepared. Then, it is discovered that a transaction has been overlooked. That transaction is recorded in the accounts and all of the financial statements are

*Exhibit 11.3*
**Homer, Inc.**
**Data for Co-insurance Calculations**

| | Furniture and Fixtures | Office Building | |
|---|---|---|---|
| Insurance Policy | A | A | B |
| Fair Market Value of the Property before Fire | $150,000 | $700,000 | $700,000 |
| Fair Market Value of the Property after Fire | 20,000 | 420,000 | 420,000 |
| Face of Insurance Policy | 108,000 | 360,000 | 140,000 |
| Co-insurance Requirement | 80% | 80% | 80% |

corrected. Define *funds* as *working capital*. For each of the following transactions, indicate which of the numbered lines of the funds statement is affected and by how much. Ignore income tax effects.

a. A machine that cost $10,000 and that has $7,000 of accumulated depreciation is sold for $4,000 cash.

b. A machine that cost $10,000 and that has $7,000 of accumulated depreciation is sold for $2,000 cash.

c. A machine that cost $10,000 and that has $7,000 of accumulated depreciation is traded in on a similar new machine. The new machine has a cash price of $12,000. A trade-in allowance for the old machine of $4,000 is given, so that $8,000 cash is paid.

d. A fire destroys a warehouse. The loss is uninsured. The warehouse cost $80,000 and at the time of the fire had accumulated depreciation of $30,000.

e. Refer to the facts of part d. Inventory costing $70,000 was also destroyed. The loss was uninsured.

11.56 O'Keefe Company manufactures small machine tools. Its inventory turnover (= cost of goods sold/average inventory during year) is about 3. The company uses a FIFO cost-flow assumption. During the current year, inventory increased. It depreciates its plant assets over 7 years, using the straight-line method. Below are described several transactions and the incorrect way these events were recorded. Indicate the effect of the mistake (overstatement, understatement, no effect) on each of the following items:

(1) Plant Assets (Net of Depreciation), end of current year.

(2) Selling, General, and Administrative Expenses for the current year.

(3) Cost of Goods Sold for the current year.

(4) Total Assets, end of next year.

(5) Net Income for next year.

(6) Owners' Equity, end of next year.

For example, if the effect of recording is that net income is too low and correcting the error will increase net income, then the right response is *understatement*.

a. During the current year, expenditures for testing a new factory machine were debited to Work-in-Process Inventory.

b. During the current year, the company completed (self-) construction of a warehouse for finished goods, but failed to charge any general supervisory overhead costs of construction to the plant account. All were expensed.

c. The local electric utility installed new time-of-day metering devices to enable peak-load pricing of electricity. The O'Keefe Company paid the utility a $5,000 deposit, which will be returned in 3 years if the meters have not been negligently damaged by the company. O'Keefe Company debited this payment to Work-in-Process Inventory.

d. Maintenance cost of office machines was debited to Accumulated Depreciation on Plant Assets.

e. Maintenance of factory machines was debited to Accumulated Depreciation on Plant Assets.

f. In the current year, O'Keefe acquired new land to be used for a warehouse. It incorrectly debited the cost of independent appraisals of the property to general expenses, rather than to a plant account.

g. O'Keefe Company carried out a significant rearrangement of its factory plant layout during the current year and properly accounted for all costs that were recorded. A bill from Stephens Moving Company will not arrive until the next year. When it is paid, the amount will be debited to a general expense account.

# Chapter 12
# *Depreciation*

12.1 Chapter 11 characterized plant assets as bundles of service potential to be used up over several periods. This chapter treats the measurement and reporting of the using up of the service potential of plant assets; that using up is called "depreciation."

12.2 Through a process of evolution in accounting terminology, the use of the term *depreciation* is restricted to the expiration of the cost of plant assets. Although in popular speech *depreciation* is often associated with a decline in market value of any kind of property, its accounting usage is more restricted in two ways: (1) In accounting, depreciation refers to the expiration of the acquisition cost (or other basis) of an asset, which is unlikely to coincide with its decline in market value; and (2) depreciation has been restricted to expiration of plant assets. Special terms are used for the decline in recorded costs of assets other than plant assets. *Depletion* refers to the allocation of costs of wasting assets, or natural resources, over time. The general term *amortization* is used for the process of allocating the costs of intangibles over time. The next chapter treats depletion and amortization. Merchandise and materials may become shopworn or obsolete, but the accounting recognition of this fact is described as an "inventory adjustment" rather than as depreciation.

12.3 The investment in a depreciating asset is the price paid for a series of future services. The asset account may well be considered as a prepayment, similar in many respects to prepaid rent or insurance—a payment in advance for services to be received. As the asset is used in each accounting period, an appropriate portion of the investment in the asset is treated as the cost of the service received and is recognized as an expense of the period or as part of the cost of goods produced during the period.

## The Causes of Depreciation

12.4 The causes of depreciation are the causes of decline in an asset's service-rendering potential and of its ultimate retirement. The services or benefits provided by land do not ordinarily diminish over time, so land is not depreciated. Many factors lead to the retirement of assets from service, but the causes of decline in service potential can be classified as either *physical* or *functional*. The physical factors include such things as ordinary wear and tear from use, chemical action such as rust or electrolysis, and the effects of wind and rain. The most important functional or nonphysical cause is *obsolescence*. Inventions, for example, may result in new equipment, the use of which reduces the unit cost of production to the point where continued operation of the old asset is not economical, even though it may be relatively unimpaired physically. Retail stores often replace display cases and storefronts long before they are worn out in order to keep the appearance of the store as attractive as their competitors'. Changed economic conditions may also become functional causes of depreciation, such as when an old airport becomes inadequate and must be abandoned, and a new, larger one is built to meet the requirements of heavier traffic. Or consider that an increase in the cost of gasoline causes a reduction in demand for recreational vehicles, which results in reduced operations in automobile manufacturing and a reduced economic life for the manufacturing plant.

12.5 Identifying the specific causes of depreciation is not essential for considering the fundamental problem of its measurement. It is enough to know that almost any physical asset will eventually have to be retired from service and that in some cases the retirement will become necessary at a time when physical deterioration is negligible. The specific causes do become important, however, when the attempt is made to estimate the useful life of an asset.

## Depreciation as a Decline in Value

12.6 Depreciation is frequently used in ordinary conversation to mean a decline in value. Such an interpretation may be fundamentally sound when applied to the entire service life of a plant asset—there certainly is a decline in the value of an asset from the time it is acquired until it is retired from service. A decline in asset values is not, however, a satisfactory description of the charge made to the operations of each accounting period. One incorrect inference from such a description is that if, in a given period of time, there has been an increase in the value of an asset, such as an increase arising from increasing prices for the asset, then there has been no depreciation during that period.

Rather, there have been two partially offsetting processes: (1) an unrealized holding gain on the asset, which usually is not recognized in historical cost accounting, and (2) depreciation of the asset's historical cost. As Chapter 5 indicated, a holding gain is an increase in the market price of an asset since the time the asset was acquired or last revalued.

12.7 Further, the word *value* has so many uses and connotations that it is not a serviceable term for a definition. (The noun *value* should seldom be used in accounting without a qualifying adjective.) If depreciation is defined as a decline in value and the undepreciated balance of an asset account as a "present" value, it is usually necessary to explain that, under generally accepted accounting principles, it is value to the going concern based on historical cost, not on current selling prices or current replacement costs. The word *value* is not entirely inappropriate in describing an element of depreciation, but is not helpful in isolating its essence.

## Summary of Depreciation Concepts

12.8 Depreciation is a process of cost allocation, not one of valuation. This chapter discusses the problems of *allocating* assets' costs to the periods of benefit. A depreciation problem will exist whenever (1) capital is invested in services to be rendered by a plant asset, and (2) at some reasonably predictable date in the future the asset will have to be retired from service with a residual value less than its acquisition cost. The problem is to interpret and account satisfactorily for the diminution from acquisition cost to residual value.

12.9 Note especially that replacing the asset is *not* essential to the existence of depreciation. Depreciation is the expiration or disappearance of service potential from the time the plant asset is put into use until the time it is retired from service. Whether or not the asset is replaced does not affect the amount or treatment of its depreciation.

## Depreciation Accounting Problems

12.10   There are three principal accounting problems in allocating the cost of an asset over time:

**1.** Ascertaining the depreciation basis of the asset.

**2.** Estimating its useful service life.

**3.** Deciding on the pattern of expiration of services over the useful service life.

### Calculating the Periodic Charge

12.11   Ascertaining the amount of the periodic charge for depreciation is not an exact process. The cost of the plant asset is a *joint cost* of the several benefited periods. That is, each of the periods of the asset's use benefits from its services. There is usually no logically correct way to allocate a joint cost. The depreciation process seeks to assign reasonable periodic charges that reflect a careful and systematic method of calculation.

12.12   Whenever it is feasible to do so, depreciation should be computed for individual items such as a single building, machine, or truck. Where many similar items are in use and each one has a relatively small cost, individual calculations may be impracticable and the depreciation charge is usually calculated for the group as a whole. Furniture and fixtures, tools, and telephone poles are examples of assets that are usually depreciated in groups. Depreciation of individual assets, sometimes described as "unit depreciation," is described first. Depreciation of groups of assets, referred to as "group or composite depreciation," is then described.

### Depreciation Basis of Plant Assets

12.13   Depreciation charges are usually based on the acquisition cost of the asset less (except for declining-balance methods described later) the estimated residual value—the amount to be received when the asset is retired from service. As inflation has become recognized as a major economic problem, there has been increasing recognition that basing depreciation charges on acquisition costs will not in most cases charge to expense amounts sufficient to maintain the productive capacity of the business. Basing depreciation on acquisition costs will enable a business to provide for maintenance of its financial position measured in dollars but not of its physical productive capacity in periods of rising prices.

12.14   As Chapters 11 and 26 indicate, the Financial Accounting Standards Board has required both depreciation measured in constant dollars and depreciation based on current costs to be disclosed as supplementary information for large firms. The formal financial statements continue to use the acquisition cost basis for depreciation.

### Estimating Salvage Value

12.15   The total depreciation of an asset over its life is the difference between its acquisition cost and the amount that can be received for the asset when it is retired from service, either in a cash sale or as a trade-in allowance. The amount received is described as the asset's "salvage value," or "residual value." Estimates of salvage value are necessary for making the depreciation calculations. (The terms *salvage value* and *residual value* refer to the estimated proceeds on disposition of an asset less all removal and selling costs. Salvage value must be an estimate at any time before the asset is retired. Hence, before retirement, the terms *salvage value* and *estimated salvage value* are synonymous.)

12.16   For buildings, common practice assumes a zero salvage value. This treatment rests on the assumption that the cost to be incurred in tearing down the building will approximate the sales value of the scrap materials recovered. For other assets, however, the salvage value may be substantial, and should be estimated and taken into account in making the periodic depreciation charge. This is particularly true where it is planned to retire an asset while it still has substantial value. For example, a car rental firm will replace

*Figure 12.1*
**Patterns of Depreciation:**
**Book Value over Life of Asset**

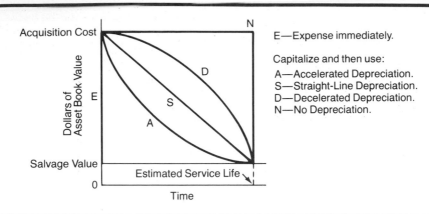

E—Expense immediately.

Capitalize and then use:
A—Accelerated Depreciation.
S—Straight-Line Depreciation.
D—Decelerated Depreciation.
N—No Depreciation.

its automobiles at a time when other owners can use the cars for several more years. The rental firm will be able to realize a substantial part of acquisition cost from the sale of used cars. Past experience usually forms the best basis for estimating salvage value.

12.17    Salvage values can be negative. (Consider, for example, the expected "decommissioning" costs of a nuclear power-generating plant. At the time the plant is constructed the expected costs for safe dismantling at retirement are larger than the expected salvage proceeds.) *Negative salvage values* are generally treated arithmetically just the opposite of positive salvage values. The amount of salvage value is subtracted from cost (in the case of negative salvage value, the expected net cost of removal is added to cost) to derive the amount to be depreciated.

12.18    Estimates of salvage value are necessarily subjective. Disputes over estimated salvage value in the past have led to many disagreements between Internal Revenue Service agents and taxpayers. Partly to reduce such controversy, the Internal Revenue Code was amended in 1962 and again in 1971 to reduce the significance of salvage value in calculating depreciation for tax purposes. The Economic Recovery Tax Act of 1981 provides

that salvage value may be completely ignored in tax calculations. The illustrations and problems in this text assume, however, that salvage value is to be taken into account in calculating depreciation unless explicit contrary statements are made.

## Estimating Service Life

The second factor in the depreciation calculation is the estimated economic service life of the asset. In making the estimate, both the physical and the functional causes of depreciation must be taken into account. Experience with similar assets, corrected for differences in the planned intensity of use or alterations in maintenance policy, is usually the best guide for this estimate.    12.19

The Economic Recovery Tax Act of 1981 abandons the use of the term "depreciation" entirely in calculating taxable income and provides instead for an "Accelerated Cost Recovery System" (ACRS). The "cost recovery" charge is exactly comparable to depreciation, but it provides for an accelerated write-off of the depreciable asset. Service lives of three years for automobiles and other light vehicles and five years for almost all other equipment are prescribed for ACRS; service lives of 10 or 15 years are    12.20

prescribed for various types of buildings. A taxpayer may elect to use longer service lives, but such elections are rare.

12.21    The lives prescribed in ACRS are in most cases shorter, and in many cases much shorter, than the likely economic service life of the assets. The Congress was aware of this difference but it established the shorter service lives for tax purposes in an effort to stimulate investment in depreciable assets and thus to speed up technological advances.* The difference between depreciable lives for tax purposes and estimated economic service lives is so great that most firms make separate calculations of depreciation for tax and financial reporting purposes using different service lives for each. This difference adds to the deferred tax problem discussed in Chapter 20.

12.22    Despite the abundance of data from experience, estimating economic service lives is the most difficult task in the entire depreciation calculation. Making proper allowances for obsolescence is particularly difficult because obsolescence results for the most part from forces external to the firm. Unless the estimator possesses prophetic powers, it is likely that the estimates will prove to be incorrect. For this reason, the estimates of useful service life of important assets or groups of assets should be reconsidered every few years. Estimating the "true" economic life of an asset with a long life, as required for financial reporting, is a difficult and troublesome process.

## Pattern of Expiration of Services

12.23    Once the acquisition cost has been calculated and both salvage value and service life have been estimated, the total of depreciation charges for the whole life of the asset

---

*Reductions in income tax rates for businesses tend to be politically unpopular. Congress can effectively reduce taxes for businesses using depreciable assets by allowing their costs to be depreciated over shorter lives for tax reporting purposes. Some who study the political process argue that the primary purpose of shortening depreciable lives for tax reporting purposes is to reduce taxes for businesses in a politically acceptable way.

*Figure 12.2*
**Patterns of Annual Depreciation Charge over Life of Asset**

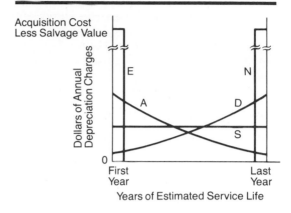

has been determined. There then remains the problem of selecting the pattern for allocating those charges to the specific years of the life. There are five basic patterns for such allocations. They are labeled E, A, S, D, and N in Figure 12.1.

12.24    If salvage value is assumed to be zero, then, of course, the salvage value line coincides with the horizontal axis and the entire acquisition cost is depreciated.

12.25    The patterns are discussed in more detail in the next section. A represents *accelerated* depreciation; S, *uniform* or *straight-line* depreciation; D, *decelerated* depreciation. (Understanding the terms "accelerated" and "decelerated" is easier if you compare the depreciation charges in the early years to straight-line depreciation, as in Figure 12.2.) Patterns A and S are much more commonly used than D. Pattern E, of course, represents immediate expensing of the item; all costs are charged to the period when the cost is incurred. This pattern is discussed further in Chapter 13 on intangibles. Pattern N represents the situation, such as for land, where there are no periodic amortization charges. The asset is shown on the books at acquisition cost until it is sold or otherwise retired.

12.26 Figure 12.1 illustrates the book value of the asset during various periods of its life. The pattern of depreciation charges can also be depicted by showing the annual depreciation charges over the life of the asset. The same five patterns illustrated in Figure 12.1 are shown in Figure 12.2. The important point to recognize is that the areas under each of the five curves in Figure 12.2 are equal. All are equal to acquisition cost less estimated salvage value.

## Depreciation Methods

12.27 All depreciation methods seek to allocate, reasonably and systematically, the acquisition cost of an asset minus its estimated salvage value to the periods of its use. The allocation can be made either on the basis of use or on the basis of time. The use basis, also known as the "production basis," is conceptually superior if obsolescence is not a primary factor in causing retirement. However, because estimating the likely number of units of use of a plant asset is usually even more difficult than estimating its likely service life, the great majority of plant assets are depreciated on a time basis.

12.28 The use basis is almost always applied by a straight-line method; that is, each unit of use is assigned an equal charge. When a time basis is used, any of several methods may be employed. The time bases discussed here are the following:

**1.** Straight-line method (Pattern S of Figures 12.1 and 12.2).

**2.** Declining-balance method (Pattern A of Figures 12.1 and 12.2).

**3.** Sum-of-the-years'-digits method (Pattern A of Figures 12.1 and 12.2).

**4.** Compound interest method (Pattern D of Figures 12.1 and 12.2; paragraph 12.54 explains that it is not generally accepted).

12.29 Three methods are used for calculating depreciation in the years of acquisition and retirement:

**1.** Depreciation may be charged only for that portion of the period during which the asset is used.

**2.** Depreciation may be charged for one-half of a year in the year of acquisition and one-half of a year in the year in which the asset is retired. This approach is called the "half-year convention."

**3.** A full year's depreciation may be taken in the first year for assets acquired in the first half of the year, and no depreciation may be taken in the first year on assets acquired in the second half of the year; for assets retired in the first half of the year, no depreciation is taken in the retirement year, but if retirement occurs in the second half of the year, a full year's depreciation is taken.

ACRS for tax purposes requires a modified form of the second method. Depreciation for one-half of a year is charged in the year of acquisition, but the remainder of the cost is written off in the remaining full years of asset life. (This effectively reduces service life for equipment for tax purposes from five years to four and one-half years.) For financial reporting, any of the three methods is acceptable but should be followed consistently. In addressing problems in this text, the first method should be used in making the depreciation calculation unless explicit contrary instructions are given.

## Production, or Use, Method

12.30 Many assets are not used uniformly over time. Manufacturing plants often have seasonal variations in operation so that certain machines may be used 24 hours a day at one time and 8 hours or less a day at another time of year. Trucks are not likely to receive the same amount of use in each month or year of their lives. The time methods of depreciation may, then, result in depreciation charges for such assets not reflecting usage patterns.

12.31 When the rate of usage varies from period to period and when the total usage of an asset over its life can be estimated reliably, a depreciation charge based on actual usage during the period may be justified. For example, depreciation of a truck for a period could be based on the ratio of miles driven during the period to total miles expected to be driven over the truck's life. The depreciation cost per unit (mile) of use is

$$\text{Depreciation Cost per Unit} = \frac{\text{Acquisition Cost} - \text{Estimated Salvage Value}}{\text{Estimated Number of Units}}$$

The arithmetic of the calculation is simple, but it is necessary to keep a special record of the units of operation of each asset or of the number of units produced. If a truck that costs $38,000 and has an estimated salvage value of $1,200 is expected to be driven 100,000 miles before it is retired from service, then the depreciation per mile is $.368 [= ($38,000 − $1,200)/100,000]. Then, if the truck is operated 1,000 miles in a given month, the depreciation charge for the month is 1,000 × $.368 = $368.

12.32    If the production method is used, depreciation becomes a variable cost of output. Total depreciation cost for the period will vary with output, but depreciation cost per unit will be fixed. If the straight-line (time) method is used, the total depreciation cost for the period is fixed, but the cost per unit varies.

### The Straight-Line (Time) Method

12.33   The allocation method that is used most commonly for financial reporting is known as the straight-line method. It was used almost exclusively until 1954, when the income tax laws were revised to recognize other depreciation methods for general use. Under the straight-line method, the cost of the asset, less any estimated salvage value, is divided by the number of years of its expected life in order to arrive at the annual depreciation:

$$\text{Annual Depreciation} = \frac{\text{Acquisition Cost} - \text{Estimated Salvage Value}}{\text{Estimated Life in Years}}.$$

For example, if a machine costs $12,000, has an estimated salvage value of $1,000, and has an expected useful life of 5 years, the annual depreciation will be $2,200 [= ($12,000 − $1,000)/5]. Occasionally, instead of a positive salvage value, the cost of removal exceeds the gross proceeds on disposition. This excess of removal costs over gross proceeds should be added to the cost of the asset in making the calculation. Thus, if a building is constructed for $370,000, and it is estimated that it will cost $50,000 to remove it at the end of 25 years, the annual depreciation would be $16,800 [= ($370,000 + $50,000)/25].

12.34    A common practice, especially when the salvage value is assumed to be zero, is to apply an appropriate percentage, known as the depreciation rate, to the *acquisition cost* in order to calculate the annual charge. The rate is chosen so that it will charge the entire acquisition cost off over the estimated life. A rate of 10 percent will write off the cost of an asset in 10 years, a rate of 25 percent in 4 years, and so on.

### Accelerated Depreciation

12.35    The efficiency and earning power of many plant assets decline as the assets grow older. Cutting tools lose some of their precision; printing presses are shut down more frequently for repairs; rentals in an old office building are lower than those in its gleaming new neighbor. These examples show the tendency of some assets to provide more and better services in the early years of their lives while requiring increasing amounts of maintenance as they grow older. Where this is the case, methods that recognize progressively smaller depreciation charges in successive periods may be justified. Such methods are referred to as *accelerated depreciation* methods because the depreciation charges in the early years of the asset's life are larger than in later years. Accelerated depreciation leads to a pattern such as A in Figures 12.1 and 12.2. For convenience, the depreciation charges for a year, however they are determined, are allocated on a straight-line basis to periods *within* the year.

### Declining-Balance Methods

12.36    The *declining-balance method* is one accelerated depreciation method. In this method, the depreciation charge is calculated by multiplying the *net book value* of the asset (acquisition cost less accumulated depreciation) at the start of each period by a fixed rate. The estimated salvage value is not subtracted from the cost in making the depreciation calculation, as is the case with other depreciation methods. Because the net book value declines from period to period, the result is a declining periodic charge for depreciation throughout the life of the asset.* The rate most commonly used is the maximum one that was permitted until 1981 for income tax purposes, which ordinarily is twice the straight-line rate. When this rate is used, the method is called the *double-declining-balance* method. Thus, for example, an asset with an estimated 10-year life would be depreciated at a rate of 20 percent (= $^1/_{10} \times 2$) per year of the book value at the start of the year. To take another example, if a machine costing $5,000 is purchased on January 1, 1981, and it is estimated to have a 5-year life, a 40-percent (= $^1/_5 \times 2$) rate would be used. The depreciation charges would be calculated as shown in Exhibit 12.1.

12.37    The undepreciated cost as of December 31, 1985, as shown in Exhibit 12.1, is $389 (= $648 − $259). This amount is unlikely to equal the salvage value at that time. The problem is usually anticipated and solved by adjusting depreciation in the later years of the asset's life. The asset should not be depreciated below salvage value. If the salvage value is large, the asset is likely to be depreciated to that value before the end of the estimated service life and the last period(s) will

have no depreciation charges. If the salvage value is small, the firm can switch in the last years of asset life to writing off the undepreciated cost minus salvage value in straight-line fashion.

Refer again to Exhibit 12.1. If the asset    12.38 had an estimated salvage value of $200, the depreciation charges in 1984 and 1985 would be $440 a year (net book value at January 1, 1984, of $1,080 less the estimated salvage value of $200 divided by the 2 years of remaining life). In general, the switch to the straight-line method for the remaining life is made when the switch will produce a greater depreciation charge than the one resulting from continued application of the double-declining-balance method. For assets with zero salvage value, this ordinarily occurs with the double-declining-balance method in the period following the midpoint of the service life.

If the asset were acquired at mid-year, de-    12.39 preciation in 1981 would be $1,000 (= $^1/_2 \times$ .40 × $5,000). Depreciation in 1982 would be based on the book value at January 1, 1982, of $4,000 and would be $1,600 (= .40 × $4,000). Similar calculations would be made for each following year.†

Although double-declining-balance rates    12.40 have been most common, the declining-balance method can be used with any rate that is deemed appropriate. The Internal Revenue Code prior to 1981 prescribed 150 percent (i.e. $1^1/_2$ times the straight-line rate) and 125 percent (i.e. $1^1/_4$ times the straight-line rate) as the maximum rates to be used for depreciation of certain types of real property. In the preceding example of an asset costing $5,000 with a 5-year life and zero salvage value, 150-percent declining balance would have depreciation in the first year of

---

*Under the declining-balance method, as strictly applied, the fixed depreciation rate used is one that will charge the cost less salvage value of the asset over its service life. The formula for computing the rate is

$$\text{Depreciation Rate} = 1 - \sqrt[n]{\frac{s}{c}} = 1 - \left(\frac{s}{c}\right)^{1/n}.$$

In this formula $n$ = estimated periods of service life, $s$ = estimated salvage value, and $c$ = cost.

Estimates of salvage value have a profound effect on the rate. Unless a positive salvage value is assumed, the rate is 100 percent—that is, all depreciation is charged in the first period. For an asset costing $10,000, with an estimated life of 5 years, the depreciation rate is 40 percent per period if salvage value is $778, but it is 60 percent if salvage value is $102.

The effect of small changes in salvage value on the rate and the seeming mathematical complexity of the formula have resulted in widespread use of approximations or rules of thumb instead of the formula.

---

†When assets are acquired at any time other than year-end, special problems may arise in computing periodic depreciation. Under declining-balance methods, there is a problem only for the first, partial period where the charge is computed as the full period's charge multiplied by the fraction of the full period that the first, partial period represents. After that, the general rule—multiply book value at the start of the period by the depreciation rate—holds in each period. For the sum-of-the-years'-digits method, described next, mid-period acquisition complicates the calculation in every period.

*Exhibit 12.1*
**Double-Declining-Balance**
**Depreciation Asset with 5-Year Life,**
**$5,000 Cost**

| Year | Acquisition Cost (1) | Accumulated Depreciation as of Jan. 1 (2) | Net Book Value as of Jan. 1 (1) − (2) (3) | Depreciation Rate (4) | Depreciation Charge for the Year = (3) × (4) (5) |
|---|---|---|---|---|---|
| 1981 | $5,000 | $     0 | $5,000 | .40 | $2,000 |
| 1982 | 5,000 | 2,000 | 3,000 | .40 | 1,200 |
| 1983 | 5,000 | 3,200 | 1,800 | .40 | 720 |
| 1984 | 5,000 | 3,920 | 1,080[a] | .40 | 432 |
| 1985 | 5,000 | 4,352 | 648 | .40 | 259 |
| 1986 | 5,000 | 4,611 | 389 | — | — |

[a]If the asset had a zero salvage value, the firm would switch to straight-line write-off over the remaining life, or $540 (= $1,080/2) a year for the last 2 years.

$1,500 [= $5,000 × (1.50 × $^1/_5$)]. Depreciation in the second year would be $1,050 (= $3,500 × .30). The undepreciated balance at the end of the second year would be $2,450 (= $5,000 − $1,500 − $1,050). Because straight-line write-off of the remaining balance over the remaining life of $817 (= $2,450/3) is greater than the declining balance write-off for year 3 of $735 (= $2,450 × .30), a switch to straight-line would be made in the third year and depreciation in the last three years would be $817, $817, and $816.

## Sum-of-the-Years'-Digits Method

12.41   Another accelerated depreciation method is the *sum-of-the-years'-digits method*. Under this method, the depreciation charge is determined by applying a fraction, which diminishes from year to year, to the acquisition cost less estimated salvage value of the asset. The numerator of the fraction is the number of periods of remaining life at the beginning of the year for which the depreciation calculation is being made. The denominator is the sum of all such numbers, one for each year of estimated service life; if the service life is *n* years, the denominator for the sum-of-the-years'-digits method is 1 + 2 + . . . + *n*.*

The method is illustrated by again considering an asset costing $5,000 purchased January 1, 1981, which has an estimated service life of 5 years and an estimated salvage value of $200. The sum of the years' digits is 15 (= 1 + 2 + 3 + 4 + 5).† The depreciation charges are calculated in Exhibit 12.2.   12.42

If the asset were acquired at mid-year, depreciation in 1981 would be $800 (= $^1/_2 × ^5/_{15}$ × $4,800). Depreciation in 1982 would be made up of two parts, the remaining half of the first year's charge and the first half of the second year's charge. The amount would be $1,440 [ ($^1/_2 × ^5/_{15}$ × $4,800) + ($^1/_2 × ^4/_{15}$ × $4,800)]. Similar computations would be made for each of the following years.   12.43

## Compound Interest Methods

Compound interest methods of depreciation are not widely used in financial accounting, but they are theoretically sound for many management decisions. For plant assets producing equal annual net inflows of cash, compound interest depreciation leads to a pattern like D in Figures 12.1 and 12.2. The straight-line and accelerated methods described earlier in this chapter are both simpler than the compound interest methods, but they do have one flaw, discussed next,   12.44

*A useful formula for summing the numbers 1 through *n* is 1 + 2 + . . . + *n* = *n* (*n* + 1)/2.

†That is, according to the formula given in the previous footnote: 1 + 2 + 3 + 4 + 5 = 5 × 6/2 = 15.

*Exhibit 12.2*
**Sum-of-the-Years'-Digits Depreciation
Asset with 5-Year Life, $5,000 Cost,
and $200 Estimated Salvage Value**

| Year | Acquisition Cost Less Salvage Value (1) | Remaining Life in Years (2) | Fraction = (2)/15 (3) | Depreciation Charge for the Year = (3) × (1) (4) |
|---|---|---|---|---|
| 1981 | $4,800 | 5 | $5/15$ | $1,600 |
| 1982 | 4,800 | 4 | $4/15$ | 1,280 |
| 1983 | 4,800 | 3 | $3/15$ | 960 |
| 1984 | 4,800 | 2 | $2/15$ | 640 |
| 1985 | 4,800 | 1 | $1/15$ | 320 |
| | | | | $4,800 |

that the compound interest method is designed to correct.

12.45 **Rate of Return on Investment** To illustrate both the compound interest method and the flaws in the other methods, consider an asset that costs $11,400 and has an estimated service life of 5 years with no salvage value. Assume further that it was estimated when this asset was acquired that it would increase cash flows (increase revenues or decrease operating expenses other than depreciation) by $3,000 per year. A plant asset costing $11,400 and yielding an annuity of $3,000 per year for 5 years has an internal rate of return of approximately 10 percent per year.* (See the discussion in Appendix B.) In this context, the internal rate of return is called the "earning rate."

12.46 The depreciation charge each year under the compound interest method is found from the following formula:

$$\begin{array}{l}\text{Compound} \\ \text{Interest} \\ \text{Depreciation} \\ \text{for Year} \end{array} = \begin{array}{l}\text{Cash} \\ \text{Flow} \\ \text{for the} \\ \text{Year} \end{array} - \left(\begin{array}{l}\text{Earning} \\ \text{Rate}\end{array} \times \begin{array}{l}\text{Undepreciated} \\ \text{Balance at} \\ \text{Beginning} \\ \text{of Year}\end{array}\right)$$

12.47 Management is often evaluated on the rate of return on investment (ROI) it produces. The rate of return on investment is defined

*$11,400/$3,000 = 3.80. See Appendix Table 4, 5-period row for the amount closest to 3.80. At 10 percent, the factor is 3.79079, so the implicit rate is slightly less than 10 percent.

to be net income for the period divided by the book value of assets for the period. Ordinarily, some average of the entire year's assets is used in the denominator. To keep this example simple, the book value of assets at the beginning of the year is used for the denominator. Exhibit 12.3 shows the rate-of-return calculation for the asset when depreciation is calculated with the straight-line, the sum-of-the-years'-digits and the compound interest methods.

12.48 Note that when the straight-line method is used in the example, the rates of return range from 6.3 percent in 1981 to 31.6 percent in 1985. The fluctuations in the rate of return implied by the sum-of-the-years'-digits method are even more severe in this assumed case of equal annual cash inflows. A flaw in the straight-line and accelerated methods is that they show increasing rates of return on the investment in the plant asset as time passes if the asset produces roughly equal annual net cash inflows. If cash flows from the asset decline over time (more down time, lower rents, higher repair costs, etc.), this flaw in those methods becomes less significant but rarely disappears. The compound interest method is designed to give *equal rates* of return each year of the asset's life; see column (6).

12.49 **Pattern of Charges** As the example illustrates, when equal annual cash flows are assumed, the compound interest method re-

*Exhibit 12.3*
**Illustration of Rate-of-Return
Calculation for 5-Year Asset Costing
$11,400 with 3,000 Annual Cash Flow**

| Year (1) | Book Value at Start of Year = Cost − Accumulated Depreciation (2) | Net Cash Flow (Given) (3) | Depreciation Charge (Calculated) (4)[a] | Income = (3) − (4) (5) | Percentage Rate of Return = [(5)/(2)] × 100 (6) |
|---|---|---|---|---|---|
| | | **Straight-Line Method** | | | |
| 1981 .......... | $11,400 | $3,000 | $2,280 | $ 720 | 6.3% |
| 1982 .......... | 9,120 | 3,000 | 2,280 | 720 | 7.9 |
| 1983 .......... | 6,840 | 3,000 | 2,280 | 720 | 10.5 |
| 1984 .......... | 4,560 | 3,000 | 2,280 | 720 | 15.8 |
| 1985 .......... | 2,280 | 3,000 | 2,280 | 720 | 31.6 |
| | | **Sum-of-the-Years'-Digits Method** | | | |
| 1981 .......... | $11,400 | $3,000 | $3,800 | $ [800] | −7.0% |
| 1982 .......... | 7,600 | 3,000 | 3,040 | [ 40] | −0.5 |
| 1983 .......... | 4,560 | 3,000 | 2,280 | 720 | 15.8 |
| 1984 .......... | 2,280 | 3,000 | 1,520 | 1,480 | 64.9 |
| 1985 .......... | 760 | 3,000 | 760 | 2,240 | 294.7 |
| | | **Compound Interest Method (Rate of Return = 10%)** | | | |
| 1981 .......... | $11,400 | $3,000 | $1,860 | $1,140 | 10.0% |
| 1982 .......... | 9,540 | 3,000 | 2,046 | 954 | 10.0 |
| 1983 .......... | 7,494 | 3,000 | 2,251 | 749 | 10.0 |
| 1984 .......... | 5,243 | 3,000 | 2,476 | 524 | 10.0 |
| 1985 .......... | 2,767 | 3,000 | 2,723[b] | 277 | 10.0 |

[a]See text for descriptions of calculations for column (4).

[b]Rounding error. If an earning rate of 9.905% were used, then the rounding error would be eliminated.

sults in increasing depreciation charges over time. The depreciation charge of $1,860 in 1981 is calculated by deducting from the cash flow of $3,000 the earning rate times the book value of the asset at the start of the year; $1,860 = $3,000 − (.10 × $11,400). The depreciation charge for 1982 is calculated as $3,000 − [.10 × ($11,400 − $1,860)] = $2,046.

12.50   If cash flows from the asset decline over time, then the increases in depreciation charges year by year under this method diminish and there may even be decreasing depreciation charges if the cash flows decline rapidly enough. If, in the example, total cash flows remain at $15,000, but are $5,000, $4,000, $3,000, $2,000, and $1,000 from the first to fifth years, respectively, depreciation charges would decline each year as shown in Exhibit 12.4.

The compound interest method illustrated here is sometimes called the "sinking fund method." Another compound interest method, described as the "annuity method," shows the *same net expense* each year but recognizes larger depreciation charges offset by interest income.   12.51

As the examples illustrate, the compound interest method produces equal rates of return on investment each year. That method can be justified on theoretical grounds as follows.   12.52

An asset is acquired because of its future benefits. Amortization traces the reduction in the asset's book value as the future benefits are used up. The compound interest method of depreciation writes off the asset's cost for a period in direct proportion to the present-value dollars of benefit from the asset that have been received during the pe-   12.53

*Exhibit 12.4*
**Illustration of Compound Interest
Method with Declining Cash Flows**

| Year (1) | Book Value at Start of Year (2) | Net Cash Flow (Given) (3) | Income (Calculated) (4)[a] | Depreciation Charges (3) − (4) (5) | Percentage Rate of Return[b] [(4)/(2)] × 100 (6) |
|---|---|---|---|---|---|
| 1981 ........... | $11,400 | $5,000 | $1,482 | $3,518 | 13.0% |
| 1982 .......... | 7,882 | 4,000 | 1,025 | 2,975 | 13.0 |
| 1983 .......... | 4,907 | 3,000 | 638 | 2,362 | 13.0 |
| 1984 .......... | 2,545 | 2,000 | 331 | 1,669 | 13.0 |
| 1985 ...... .... | 876 | 1,000 | 114 | 886[c] | 13.0 |

[a]Column (4) = column (2) × .13.

[b]Calculations of the 13% internal rate of return appear in Example 23 of Appendix B.

[c]Rounding error of $10 (= $886 − $876). Exact earnings rate is slightly less than 13.03%.

riod. A little experimentation with the examples should convince you that compound interest depreciation writes off an asset's cost in exact "straight-line" proportion to the number of present value dollars of benefit that have been generated by the asset during the period.*

12.54 To use the compound interest method requires estimates of cash flows for each year of the asset's life. Accurate estimates are hard to make, but management can use the same estimates for calculating depreciation that were used to make the decision to acquire the asset in the first place. Despite its logical advantages, the compound interest method is found in practice only in rare public utility situations. It is the least conservative method of recording depreciation. Most accountants would say that it is not in accord with generally accepted accounting principles.

## Factors to Consider in Choosing the Depreciation Method

12.55 To the individual firm, depreciation is a factor in the calculation of income reported on the financial statements as well as a de-

*The decelerated pattern of depreciation charges occurs in many cases because even though a large chunk of future cash flows may have been received, all of the remaining cash flows are 1 year closer to being received. The loss of future benefits can be largely offset (even more than offset) by "interest" earnings on the future cash flows now 1 year closer to being received.

duction from otherwise taxable income on tax returns. The firm need not choose the same depreciation method for both financial and tax reporting purposes (and probably should not).

**Financial Reporting** The goal in financial 12.56 reporting for long-lived assets is to seek a statement of income that realistically measures the expiration of the economic benefits of those assets. The only difficulty is that no one knows, in any satisfactory sense, just what portion of the service potential of a long-lived asset expires in any one period. The cost of the plant asset is a joint cost of the several periods of use, and there is no logical way of allocating joint costs. All that can be said is that financial statements should report depreciation charges based on reasonable estimates of asset expirations so that the goal of fair presentation can more nearly be achieved.

A recent issue of *Accounting Trends and* 12.57 *Techniques*, the AICPA's annual survey of the accounting practices of 600 large corporations, shows that the straight-line method was used for financial reporting purposes by more than 90 percent of the firms.

**Tax Reporting** It seems clear that the goal 12.58 of the firm in selecting a depreciation method for tax purposes should be to maximize the present value of the reductions in tax payments from claiming depreciation. When tax rates remain constant over time and there is a flat tax rate (for example, all income taxed at a 46 percent rate), this goal can usually be achieved by maximizing the present value of the depreciation deductions from otherwise taxable income. That is, for tax purposes the asset should be written off as quickly as possible. Of course, a firm can deduct only the acquisition cost, less salvage value, from otherwise taxable income over the life of the asset. Earlier deductions are, however, worth more than later ones because a dollar saved today is worth more than a dollar saved tomorrow.

In the Economic Recovery Tax Act of 1981, Congress not only specified the service lives to be used in measuring "cost recovery" in the calulation of taxable income, but also specified the percentage of cost to be charged off each year of that life. Property put in service in the years from 1981 through 1984 is subject to one set of rates; the rates are increased for property acquired in 1985 and increased again for property acquired in 1986 and thereafter. The prescribed rates for the major classes of personal property are shown in Exhibits 12.5 and 12.6.

12.59

---

## Exhibit 12.5
### Accelerated Cost Recovery System Depreciation Rates for Property Placed in Service 1981 – 1984

| Recovery Year | Percentage of Cost of Property Class | | |
|---|---|---|---|
| | 3 Year | 5 Year | 10 Year |
| 1 | 25% | 15% | 8% |
| 2 | 38 | 22 | 14 |
| 3 | 37 | 21 | 12 |
| 4 | | 21 | 10 |
| 5 | | 21 | 10 |
| 6 | | | 10 |
| 7 | | | 9 |
| 8 | | | 9 |
| 9 | | | 9 |
| 10 | | | 9 |
| Total | 100% | 100% | 100% |

---

## Exhibit 12.6
### Accelerated Cost Recovery System Depreciation Rates for Property Placed in Service in 1985 and in Years after 1985

| Recovery Year | 1985 Acquisitions Property Class | | 1986 and Later Acquisitions Property Class | |
|---|---|---|---|---|
| | 3 Year | 5 Year | 3 Year | 5 Year |
| 1 | 28% | 18% | 33% | 20% |
| 2 | 47 | 33 | 45 | 32 |
| 3 | 24 | 25 | 22 | 24 |
| 4 | | 16 | | 16 |
| 5 | | 8 | | 8 |
| | 100% | 100% | 100% | 100% |

12.60    The prescribed rates generally reflect the following combinations of depreciation methods: 1981 to 1984, 150-percent declining balance switching to straight line; 1985, 175-percent declining balance switching to sum-of-the-years'-digits; 1986 and thereafter, 200-percent declining balance with switch to sum-of-the-years'-digits; all switches being made at the optimum point. The major exception to these general rules occurs for 5-year property in 1981 to 1984. The second-year charge should 26 percent [= 85 percent $\times (1.50 \times {}^1/_5)$] but the amount allowed is only 22 percent. This was apparently done to reduce the tax revenue loss in the early years from the introduction of ACRS.

12.61    Companies are not allowed to offset losses in one year against taxable income indefinitely into the future; Chapter 20 discusses tax loss carryforwards. Companies with large tax losses and few prospects of offsetting income in the foreseeable future may prefer not to use the shorter ACRS lives. A company may elect to use longer lives for all property in a particular class acquired in a given year. The optional lives are:

| ACRS life | Optional life |
|---|---|
| 3 years ....................... | 5 or 12 years |
| 5 years ....................... | 12 or 25 years |
| 10 years ....................... | 25 or 35 years |
| 15 years ....................... | 35 or 45 years. |

If an optional recovery life is elected, straight-line depreciation must be used. The half-year convention applies, and salvage value is ignored. Throughout this book, we tend to ignore the cases where a rational taxpayer delays tax losses and accelerates taxable income in order to preserve chances of using tax losses to offset taxable income in the future. Those cases are rare, however, and the least and latest rule has widespread applicability.

12.62    Management has an obligation in a competitive economy to carry on operations so as to minimize all costs—that is, to minimize the present value of those costs over the long run. Failure to minimize costs hinders the attempt of the competitive market economy to allocate resources efficiently.

Management's obligation to reduce costs applies to taxes as well as to other costs, and, in most circumstances, the present value of taxes is minimized by taking depreciation as rapidly as is legally possible.

## Accounting for Periodic Depreciation

12.63    The debit made in the entry to record periodic depreciation is usually either to an expense account or to a production cost account such as Work-in-Process Inventory. In a manufacturing concern, the depreciation of factory buildings and equipment is a production cost, a part of the work-in-process and finished product cost. Depreciation on sales equipment is a selling expense. Depreciation on office equipment is a general or administrative expense. The matching credit for periodic depreciation could logically be made directly to the asset account affected, such as buildings or equipment. Although such an entry is sometimes made, it is customary to credit a special contra-asset account so that the acquisition cost of the asset will be left undisturbed and the total amount written off through depreciation can be readily observed.* The effect on net assets, however, is precisely the same as a direct credit to the asset account. We have used Accumulated Depreciation as the title of the account to be credited.

12.64    The entry to record periodic depreciation of office facilities, a period expense, is

| | | |
|---|---|---|
| Depreciation Expense ................ | 1,500 | |
| Accumulated Depreciation ........ | | 1,500 |

The entry to record periodic depreciation of manufacturing facilities, a product cost, is

| | | |
|---|---|---|
| Work-in-Process Inventory ............ | 1,500 | |
| Accumulated Depreciation ........ | | 1,500 |

The Depreciation Expense account is closed at the end of the accounting period as a part of the regular closing-entry procedure. The

---

*Assume you know that an asset cost $10,000, is depreciated on a straight-line basis at $1,000 per year, and has accumulated depreciation of $4,000. Then you can deduce that the asset is expected to last 10 years and is now 4 years old. Such useful deductions are not possible unless both cost and accumulated depreciation are revealed in separate accounts.

Work-in-Process Inventory account is an asset. Product costs, such as depreciation on manufacturing facilities, are accumulated in the Work-in-Process account until the goods being produced are completed and transferred to Finished Goods Inventory. The Accumulated Depreciation account remains open at the end of the period and is shown on the balance sheet as a deduction from the asset to which it refers. The balance in the Accumulated Depreciation account usually represents the total charges to accounting periods prior to the balance sheet date for the depreciation on assets currently in use. The difference between the balance of the asset account and the balance of its accumulated depreciation account (with possibly an adjustment for salvage value) represents the amount that will presumably be charged to future accounting periods. This difference is called the *book value* of the asset.

12.65  In preparing a statement of changes in financial position, the periodic depreciation charge is an addback in the "operations" section, because it represents an expense (or production cost) that does not use funds but instead uses a noncurrent asset.

### Depreciation Disclosures

12.66  Information about depreciation practices and amounts has always been of prime interest to financial statement readers. The Accounting Principles Board recognized this in *Opinion No. 12* by saying:*

Because of the significant effects on financial position and results of operations of the depreciation method or methods used, the following disclosures should be made in the financial statements or in notes thereto:

**a.** Depreciation expense for the period,

**b.** Balances of major classes of depreciable assets, by nature or function, at the balance-sheet date,

**c.** Accumulated depreciation, either by major classes of depreciable assets or in total, at the balance-sheet date, and

**d.** A general description of the method or meth-

---

*Accounting Principles Board, *Opinion No. 12, Omnibus Opinion—1967* (1967), par. 5.

ods used in computing depreciation with respect to major classes of depreciable assets.

Accounting Principles Board *Opinion No.*  12.67
*22* on *Disclosure of Accounting Policies* (1972) cites depreciation methods as an example of disclosure commonly required. The financial statements of International Corporation in the Appendix illustrate the required disclosure in Note 1.

Financial Accounting Standards Board  12.68
*Statement No. 33* (1979) requires supplementary disclosure by large firms of depreciation on both a constant-dollar basis and a current-cost basis. In addition, the current cost of the plant "assets' remaining service potential" must be included in the supplementary disclosure.

## Changes in Periodic Depreciation

When a plant asset is acquired, estimates of  12.69
service life and salvage value must be made in order to calculate periodic depreciation. The estimates are based on past experience with similar assets, production plans for the future, and all other pertinent information available. As time passes, new information and events may indicate that the original estimates are now incorrect and should be revised. Unexpected physical deterioration or unforeseen technological developments may indicate that estimated service life should be shortened; improved maintenance policies or a slowing of technological change may result in expectation of a longer life than originally estimated. Changing the depreciation schedule to reflect the new estimates is a relatively common and desirable accounting practice.

Misestimates of the useful life of an asset  12.70
may become apparent at any time during its life. It is usually possible to improve the degree of accuracy of the estimates as the time of retirement approaches. If it appears that the misestimate will be relatively minor, an adjustment usually is not made. If the misestimate appears to be material, corrective action must be taken if the effect of the previous estimation error is to be kept at a min-

imum. The generally accepted procedure for treating revisions of estimates is prescribed in Accounting Principles Board *Opinion No. 20* and reaffirmed in Financial Accounting Standards Board *Statement No. 16*. The procedure makes no adjustment for the past misestimate, but spreads the remaining undepreciated balance less the revised estimate of salvage value over the new estimate of remaining service life of the asset. We feel that a more logical procedure would be to make an adjustment of past periods' earnings for the misestimate of the past periods, and use the revised rate of depreciation for the remaining portion of the life of the asset. Such an adjustment is not permitted under generally accepted accounting principles, however.

To illustrate the accounting for changes in 12.71 periodic depreciation, assume the following facts illustrated in Figure 12.3. An office machine was purchased on January 1, 1976, for $9,200. It was estimated that the machine would be operated for 10 years with a salvage value of $200. On December 31, 1981, before the books are closed for the year, it is decided that, in light of the evidence presently available, a total useful life of 15 years with the same salvage estimate of $200 would be a more reasonable estimate. The depreciation charge recorded for each of the years from 1976 through 1980 under the straight-line method would have been $900 [= ($9,200 − $200)/10].

If the revised estimate of service life were 12.72 ignored, the original annual depreciation

**Figure 12.3**

**Illustration of Revised Depreciation Schedule. Asset's Service Life Estimate Is Increased from 10 to 15 Years during the Sixth Year. The Straight-Line Method Is Used. Asset Cost $9,200 and Has Estimated Salvage Value of $200.**

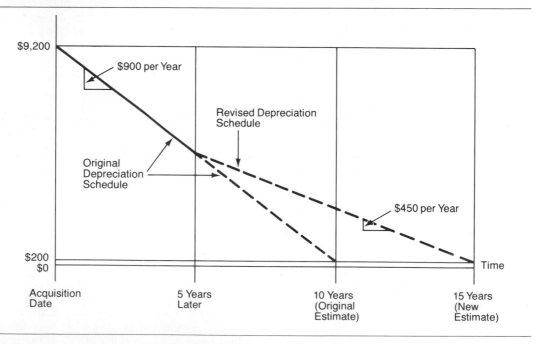

charge of $900 would be continued through 1985. The years 1986 to 1990 would receive no charge to operations for the use of the machine. The Accumulated Depreciation account would remain undisturbed for those years until the machine was retired from service. Thus, during the last 5 years that the machine was in service, no charge for depreciation would be made.

12.73    The accepted procedure for recognizing this substantial increase in service life is to revise the future depreciation so that the correct total will presumably be accumulated in the Accumulated Depreciation account at the end of the revised service life. In our example, the total amount of acquisition cost yet to be depreciated before the 1981 adjustments is $4,500 [= ($9,200 − $200) − $4,500]. The new estimate of the *remaining* life is 10 years, so the new annual depreciation charge is $450 (= $4,500/10). The only change in the accounting procedure is to substitute the new amount of $450 for the former annual depreciation of $900. The depreciation entry on December 31, 1981, and each year thereafter would be

Depreciation Expense . . . . . . . . . . . . . . . . . . . 450
    Accumulated Depreciation . . . . . . . . . . .        450
To record depreciation on revised basis.

## Group and Composite Depreciation

12.74    The previous sections discuss depreciation calculated on individual assets, the "unit basis." Many companies, however, find it advantageous to account for certain kinds of assets on a group or composite basis. *Group basis* and *group method* refer to depreciation of a collection of assets that are similar in nature, such as sewing machines in a shoe factory; *composite method* refers to depreciation of a collection of assets that are dissimilar, such as all equipment used in manufacturing shoes. From an accounting standpoint there is no distinction between the group and composite methods. The same procedures are followed and the same entries are made for both.

## Calculation of Group and Composite Depreciation

The procedures for both group and composite depreciation are generally the same. First, find a group depreciation rate. Second, in each year multiply that rate by the acquisition cost of the assets remaining in the group to find the depreciation charge for the year. When an asset is retired from the group, remove its cost from the asset account and remove sufficient amounts from the Accumulated Depreciation account so that there is no gain or loss on retirement of the asset. Four methods of finding the group depreciation rate are described next; then they are illustrated.    12.75

1. Compute the group depreciation rate as the reciprocal of the longest-lived asset in the group. This method results in lower depreciation charges than the other methods; it is generally thought of as too "unconservative" for financial reporting.

2. Compute the group depreciation rate as the reciprocal of the unweighted average life of assets in the group. This method can be used for groups of assets with similar lives.

3. Compute a depreciation rate as the ratio of the sum of each asset's annual depreciation charge divided by the acquisition cost of the entire group. This method is most often used in practice. It is somewhat simpler than the fourth method, below, and more accurate than either of the first two methods.

4. Compute a weighted-average depreciation rate for the group taking into account, for each asset, both its cost and its life.

All of these methods work similarly when the assets have the same life. To the degree the lives of the assets in the group differ, the methods give different results. Problem **12.54** at the end of this chapter explores some of the differences. Exhibit 12.7 illustrates the four methods of finding the group depreciation rate. We assume a group of assets costing $75,000 acquired on January 1. Estimated salvage value of the individual assets sum to $4,800, so the amount to be depreciated is $70,200.

*Exhibit 12.7*
**Four Methods of Computing
the Group Depreciation Rate**

**ASSUMPTIONS**

| Machine Number | Acquisition Cost | Estimated Salvage Value | Amount to Be Depreciated | Estimated Service Life in Years | Annual Straight-Line Depreciation |
|---|---|---|---|---|---|
| 101 ................. | $15,000 | $1,800 | $13,200 | 8 | $1,650 |
| 102 ................. | 22,500 | 1,500 | 21,000 | 10 | 2,100 |
| 103 ................. | 28,500 | 1,500 | 27,000 | 12 | 2,250 |
| 104 ................. | 9,000 | 0 | 9,000 | 5 | 1,800 |
| Totals ............... | $75,000 | $4,800 | $70,200 | | $7,800 |

**1. From Longest-Lived Item**

Group Depreciation Rate = $1/12$ years = 8.3 percent per year.

**2. From Average Life of Items**

Group Depreciation Rate = $\dfrac{1}{(8 + 10 + 12 + 5)/4}$ = 11.4 percent per year.

**3. From Ratio of Sum of Individual Depreciation Charges to Cost of Assets in Group**

Group Depreciation Rate = $\dfrac{\$1,650 + \$2,100 + \$2,250 + \$1,800}{\$15,000 + \$22,500 + \$28,500 + \$9,000}$

$= \dfrac{\$7,800}{\$75,000}$ = 10.4 percent per year.

**4. From Weighted-Average Cost and Life for Each Asset**

| Year of Group's Life | Cost of Machines in Use during Year |
|---|---|
| 1 ............................................................... | $ 75,000[a] |
| 2 ............................................................... | 75,000 |
| 3 ............................................................... | 75,000 |
| 4 ............................................................... | 75,000 |
| 5 ............................................................... | 75,000 |
| 6 ............................................................... | 66,000[b] |
| 7 ............................................................... | 66,000 |
| 8 ............................................................... | 66,000 |
| 9 ............................................................... | 51,000[c] |
| 10 ............................................................... | 51,000 |
| 11 ............................................................... | 28,500[d] |
| 12 ............................................................... | 28,500 |
| | $732,000 |

Group Depreciation Rate = $\dfrac{\text{Costs to be Depreciated}}{\substack{\text{Cost of Assets in Use, Summed} \\ \text{over All Years of Group's Life}}}$

$= \dfrac{\$70,200}{\$732,000}$ = 9.6 percent per year.

[a]Cost of machines 101, 102, 103, and 104.

[b]Cost of machines 101, 102, and 103.

[c]Cost of machines 102 and 103.

[d]Cost of machine 103.

12.76    In general, the group need not survive intact from the day it is acquired until the day it is retired. Assets can be added to the group or retired from the group at any time. The dollar amount of the depreciation charge will change as the assets in the group change, but the depreciation rate, once found, is generally used throughout the life of the group. It should be recomputed if the composition of the group changes substantially.*

12.77    The straight-line or declining-balance methods can be used to compute the yearly charge for the group depreciation account. The sum-of-the-years'-digits method does not lend itself to group depreciation because the assets in the group need not all be the

---

*Note that the procedure for calculating depreciation on a straight-line basis under the composite method differs in one important way from that used in the unit method. In the unit method, the service life of the asset being depreciated is estimated. The depreciation rate is the reciprocal of the service life. The depreciation charge for the year is found as this rate multiplied by the *depreciable basis* (= acquisition cost less salvage value). In the composite method, the depreciation rate is calculated and applied to *acquisition cost,* not the depreciable basis. The composite service life is not the reciprocal of the depreciation rate, because the composite service life relates to the depreciable basis whereas the depreciation rate relates to acquisition cost. (When estimated salvage value is zero, so that acquisition cost equals depreciable basis, the composite service life is the reciprocal of the depreciation rate.)

It is customary to base the depreciation rate on acquisition cost because additions to and retirements from the composite group are likely to be made on a regular basis. Each time a change is made, the composite depreciation rate applied to the depreciable basis would have to be changed unless the estimated service life and salvage value of the addition or retirement were equal to the average estimated service life and salvage value of the earlier group. This would rarely be the case.

If the depreciation rate related to acquisition cost were calculated each time an addition to the group was made, that rate would also change. It is customary, however, under the composite method not to recalculate the depreciation rate as additions to the group are made unless the group's composition is substantially altered. In this way, it is not necessary to estimate service life or salvage value for additions to the original group.

If the group is a vintage group, no additions to the original group are made in subsequent years. Thus, either a depreciation rate based on acquisition cost or depreciable basis can be used.

same age and the numerator of the fraction for calculating the depreciation charge can be indeterminate.

The year's depreciation charge is calcu-  12.78 lated as either (1) some fraction of the acquisition cost of the assets in the group (if the straight-line method is used), or (2) some fraction of the book value of the assets in the group (if the declining-balance method is used). The depreciation charge can never be larger than the current book value of the assets in the group.

The major difference between group depreciation and unit methods is the treatment of asset retirements. The group method assumes, in effect, that although items have the same expected service life, some individual items will be retired earlier than average and others will remain in use longer than average. Items retired from a group are assumed to be sold, or otherwise disposed of, *at book value.* Consequently, a gain or loss is not recognized on retiring assets from a group until either (1) the last item in the group has been retired, (2) the group has a book value of zero, or (3) accumulated depreciation after acquisition date becomes zero, whichever of these three comes first. There is not uniform agreement on criterion (3) for recognizing a loss. Some would debit the Accumulated Depreciation account with the cost less proceeds of disposition, thereby creating a debit balance in the Accumulated Depreciation account. Following this procedure, recognition of loss would be deferred until one of the first two criteria was met.

## Composite Depreciation
## Journal Entries

Journal entries for the first 3 years of life of  12.80 the group of assets assumed in Exhibit 12.7 are illustrated below. The group is assumed to have been acquired January 1, 1979. We use the third method of finding the depreciation charge, $7,800 per year in this example. Machine 104 is sold at December 31, 1980, yielding cash proceeds of $4,000. A new machine costing $12,000 is acquired and added to the composite group at that date. New acquisitions for a given group do not alter the depreciation rate under the composite method for that group, so no information on the estimated service life of the new machine is needed. The example assumes that all depreciation charges are product costs.

Dec. 31, 1979
| | | |
|---|---|---|
| Work-in-Process Inventory | 7,800 | |
| Accumulated Depreciation | | 7,800 |

Dec. 31, 1980
| | | |
|---|---|---|
| Work-in-Process Inventory | 7,800 | |
| Accumulated Depreciation | | 7,800 |

| | | |
|---|---|---|
| Cash | 4,000 | |
| Accumulated Depreciation | 5,000 | |
| Machinery and Equipment | | 9,000 |

Machine 104 is retired. The debit to Accumulated Depreciation is the amount that will result in no gain or loss on retirement being recognized.

| | | |
|---|---|---|
| Machinery and Equipment | 12,000 | |
| Cash and Payables | | 12,000 |

Machine 105 is acquired.

Dec. 31, 1981
| | | |
|---|---|---|
| Work-in-Process Inventory | 8,112 | |
| Accumulated Depreciation | | 8,112 |

Depreciation at 10.4 percent on new cost of $78,000 (= $75,000 − $9,000 + $12,000).

12.81 **Flow Assumption for Retirements** In the preceding example, the specific asset retired was identified and removed from the composite account. Group depreciation generally assumes that the items in the group are sufficiently alike that the time-saving method of group depreciation is warranted. Therefore, the burdensome task of determining which particular assets have been retired and their original cost is not necessary. Rather, a flow assumption can be made, much the same as the flow assumption made in valuing inventories.

The easiest flow assumption to implement in group depreciation, and the one most consistent with the theory of group depreciation, is the weighted-average flow assumption. Thus, for example, assume that a group consists of 1,000 telephone poles, which were purchased at many different times and together originally cost $160,000. If 150 poles are retired during a period, the weighted-average flow assumption would imply that $24,000 (= $160,000 × 150/1,000) of acquisition costs are retired.

12.83 When the group consists of relatively unlike items, such as a group of all office furniture and equipment, then a FIFO flow assumption is easier to implement. For example, as typewriters are retired, we assume that the first typewriter purchased is the first retired, and so on.

## Depreciation Based on Other Than Nominal Dollar Measurements of Acquisition Cost

12.84 All of the previous discussion of depreciation has assumed an acquisition cost basis for depreciation calculations. In a period of inflation, however, depreciation based on acquisition cost usually is not a realistic measure of the decline of economic usefulness of the asset. It is merely an allocation of acquisition cost to periods of benefit. To make depreciation charges reflect the current conditions of the business, supplemental disclosure of depreciation on a constant-dollar basis and on a current-cost basis is required.

12.85 **Current Cost** Chapter 11 explained that *FASB Statement No. 33* requires large firms to show the current cost of the productive capacity of plant assets in the footnotes. *Statement No. 33* also requires that depreciation charges based on amortization of the current cost of the plant assets be shown in the notes.

12.86 **Constant Dollar** The FASB in *Statement No. 33* also requires the supplementary disclosure of depreciation calculated in constant-dollar terms. The calculation of the valuation of a plant asset in constant-dollar terms is explained in Chapters 11 and 26. If the acquisition cost of an asset measured in nominal dollars is $100, but in constant dollars of 1982, general purchasing power is C$150, then the depreciation charges on a constant-dollar basis of the asset would be 150/100 times depreciation based on acquisition cost.*

12.87    Assume a plant asset was acquired 4 years ago for $10,000 when the general price index was 100. It was estimated that the asset would have a service life of 10 years with no salvage value. The straight-line depreciation method is used. Four years later the current cost of the asset is $16,000 and the general price index is 150. Depreciation on an acquisition cost basis would be $1,000 (= .10 × $10,000). Depreciation on a current cost basis would be $1,600 (= .10 × $16,000), assuming depreciation is based on year-end replacement cost. Depreciation of acquisition cost measured in constant dollars is C$1,500 (= 150/100 × .10 × $10,000).

## Retirement and Replacement Systems

12.88    The depreciation methods considered thus far assign the depreciable basis to the periods benefited by the asset in a systematic and rational manner. Two alternative methods recognize expense, not by period of use, but only when the asset is retired. These two methods are the retirement method and the replacement method. These alternatives should not be designated as "depreciation methods," but frequently are.

12.89    The retirement method charges the cost of the asset retired, less any salvage proceeds, to expense in the period of retirement. The replacement method charges the acquisition cost of the asset that replaces the retired asset, less the salvage proceeds of the retired asset, to expense in the period the replacement asset is acquired. In neither case is any depreciation recognized during the periods of use of the plant asset. Under the replace-

ment method, the book value of the asset account at all times is equal to the full acquisition cost of the first units of property of each type acquired. Under the retirement method, the book value of the asset account for all periods after the replacement occurs is equal to the full cost of the replacement assets less the salvage proceeds of the assets retired. The retirement method corresponds to line N on Figures 12.1 and 12.2. Under the replacement method, whenever an asset is replaced, the cost of the replacement asset is charged to expense, which corresponds to line E in those figures.

12.90    The retirement and replacement methods are sometimes used in public utility and railroad accounting where large numbers of interrelated, relatively low-cost items must be accounted for, such as telephone poles or railroad tracks and ties. These methods are also frequently used for low-cost items such as hand tools. As an example, if 10 telephone poles are acquired in 1971 for $60 each and are replaced in 1982 for $100 each when the salvage value of the old poles is $5 each, the accounting would be as follows:

**Retirement Method**

| | | |
|---|---|---|
| Plant Assets ........................ | 600 | |
| Cash ......................... | | 600 |

To acquire assets in 1971.

| | | |
|---|---|---|
| Retirement Expense ................. | 550 | |
| Salvage Receivable ........ ........ | 50 | |
| Plant Assets .. ............... | | 600 |

To record retirement and expense in 1982.

| | | |
|---|---|---|
| Plant Assets ........................ | 1,000 | |
| Cash ......................... | | 1,000 |

To record acquisition of new assets in 1982.

**Replacement Method**

| | | |
|---|---|---|
| Plant Assets ........................ | 600 | |
| Cash ......................... | | 600 |

To acquire assets in 1971.

| | | |
|---|---|---|
| Replacement Expense .............. | 950 | |
| Salvage Receivable ................. | 50 | |
| Cash ......................... | | 1,000 |

To record replacement expense on old assets in amount quantified by net cost of replacement in year 1982.

*Amounts expressed in constant-dollar measuring units are designated C$. See Chapter 26 for a fuller discussion.

12.91 The retirement method is like FIFO in that the cost of the first assets is recorded as expense, and the cost of the second assets is put on the balance sheet. The replacement method is like LIFO in that the cost of the second assets determines the expense and the cost of the first assets remains on the balance sheet.

12.92 The replacement method has some justification in current cost accounting in what is described as a "sustained-yield situation." The purpose of current cost data is to provide financial statement users with relevant information about the current economics of a business. If an asset, such as a tract of timber, is managed so that given the regular replacement and maintenance policy it never wears out, then the current operating costs for replacement and maintenance reported in the historical cost income statement already represent the current economics of the business.

12.93 As an example, suppose that a company owns 20 acres of timberland, that timber takes 20 years to grow to the stage where it can be harvested, that the company has 1 acre of newly planted timber, 1 acre of 1-year old timber, 1 acre of 2-year old timber . . . , 1 acre of 19-year-old timber, that it harvests the 1 acre of matured timber each year, that it replants that acre, and that it maintains the entire forest with proper weeding, fertilizing, and so on. Such a company can go on forever harvesting 1 acre of timber each year without ever having to replace the timberland asset as a whole. Replacement cost data are not required to make the income statement reflect the current economics of the business. Current-value data on the balance sheet would, of course, provide additional useful information.

nancial press often defines funds from operations as net income plus depreciation. This leads some financial writers to describe depreciation as a "source of funds." Such a description is clearly and unquestionably wrong. Funds from operations come from revenues from customers, not by making accounting entries. In fact, depreciation expense results from an outflow of funds in an earlier period that is only now being recognized as an operating expense. The following example illustrates the fact that depreciation does not produce funds. Assume first that the Jonathan Manufacturing Company has net income of $20,000 resulting from revenues of $125,000, expenses other than depreciation of $95,000, and $10,000 of depreciation. Now assume that depreciation increases to $25,000 while other expenses and revenues are unchanged; net income is $5,000. (Ignore income taxes in both examples.) Exhibit 12.8 shows that changes in depreciation do not affect funds from operations; funds from operations would be the same, $30,000, in both examples.

12.95 Depreciation does help determine cash flow, however, by its effect on the measurement of taxable income and thus tax expense. The more rapid the rate of depreciation charges for tax purposes, the slower the rate of tax payments. For this reason, short service lives for tax purposes stimulate acquisition of depreciable assets and are viewed as significant in increasing the rate of capital formation. In the United States, in the last third of a century, as well as in most other Western countries, there has been much tinkering with the depreciation provisions (sometimes called "capital consumption allowances") of the tax laws to stimulate new investment and to speed up the rate of economic growth.

## Depreciation and Cash Flows

12.94 Chapter 4 noted that in the statement of changes in financial position, depreciation is added back to net income in calculating funds provided by operations. It is an expense that does not use funds currently. Because it is added back to net income, the fi-

## Summary

12.96 The goal of depreciation accounting is to allocate, in a systematic, rational manner, the depreciable basis of a plant asset to the periods that benefit from the asset's being used. The depreciable basis in historical cost accounting is acquisition cost less salvage

*Exhibit 12.8*
**Impact of Depreciation
on Funds from Operations
Jonathan Manufacturing Company
Year 1982**

**Depreciation $10,000**

| Income Statement | | Funds from Operations | |
|---|---|---|---|
| Revenues | $125,000 | Net Income | $20,000 |
| Expenses except Depreciation | (95,000) | Add Back Expenses Not Using | |
| | $ 30,000 | Working Capital: | |
| Depreciation Expense | (10,000) | Depreciation | 10,000 |
| Net Income | $ 20,000 | Total Funds from Operations | $30,000 |

**Depreciation $25,000**

| Income Statement | | Funds from Operations | |
|---|---|---|---|
| Revenues | $125,000 | Net Income | $ 5,000 |
| Expenses except Depreciation | (95,000) | Add Back Expenses Not Using | |
| | $ 30,000 | Working Capital: | |
| Depreciation Expense | (25,000) | Depreciation | 25,000 |
| Net Income | $ 5,000 | Total Funds from Operations | $30,000 |

value. The period (or number of units) of benefit—the depreciable life—is calculated by judgment or by experience. The pattern of depreciation charges over the asset's life is usually based on some conventional method. The most common methods in practice are straight-line, double-declining-balance, and sum-of-the-years'-digits.

12.97   Different methods are commonly used for financial reporting and tax reporting.

Straight-line depreciation is used most frequently for financial reporting, and tax reporting is based on prescribed ACRS lives and methods.

12.98   As part of the effort to reflect the effects of inflation on financial statements, larger firms are required to present supplemental information on depreciation charges based both on general price level–adjusted historical cost and on current cost.

## Questions and Short Cases

**12.1**   Review the meaning of the following concepts or terms discussed in this chapter.

a. Depreciation.
b. Depletion.
c. Amortization.
d. Obsolescence.
e. Unit depreciation versus composite or group depreciation.
f. Salvage value, residual value, estimated salvage value.
g. Service life, depreciable life, economic life.
h. ACRS lives.
i. Half-year convention.

j. Straight-line versus accelerated depreciation.
k. Straight-line use versus straight-line time depreciation.
l. Declining-balance methods.
m. Sum-of-the-years'-digits method.
n. Compound interest method.
o. Rate of return on investment.

p. Rule of least and latest.
q. Changes in estimates.
r. Current cost depreciation.
s. Retirement accounting.
t. Replacement accounting.
u. Sustained-yield forestry.
v. Depreciation as a source of funds.

**12.2**   Distinguish among amortization, depreciation, and depletion.

**12.3**   "Accounting for depreciating assets would be greatly simplified if accounting periods were only long enough or the life of the assets short enough." What is the point of the quotation?

**12.4**   "The major purpose of depreciation accounting is to provide funds for the replacement of assets as they wear out." Do you agree? Explain.

**12.5**   Distinguish between physical and functional causes of depreciation.

**12.6**   "Unless an asset declines in value, it will not be depreciated." Why does the careful accountant not use the word *depreciation* to mean a decline in value?

**12.7**   Why is the term *estimated salvage value* generally a redundancy?

**12.8**   One writer stated that: "Depreciation expense was the chief source of funds for growth in most major industries." A reader criticized this statement by replying:

The fact remains that if the companies listed had elected, in any year, to charge off $10 million more depreciation than they did charge off, they would not thereby have added one dime to the total of their funds available for plant expansion or for increasing inventories or receivables. Therefore, to speak of depreciation expense as a source of funds has no significance in a discussion of fundamentals.

Comment on these statements, including income tax effects.

**12.9**   Why is it generally unnecessary to state a special rule for the treatment of negative salvage value?

**12.10**  In 1971 the Internal Revenue Code was amended to provide for depreciable lives for tax purposes from 20 percent less of the guideline lives previously established to 20 percent more of the guideline lives. The Secretary of the Treasury announced that depreciable lives could be chosen within a 40-percent range. A noted accountant remarked that the government could have allowed a range of choices of 100 percent (from 20 percent less to 80 percent more) with virtually the same effects on tax collections as the 40-percent range. What did the accountant mean?

**12.11**  Payments made later are less burdensome than payments made sooner. Assume a profitable investment in plant assets—one whose cash inflows have present value sufficiently higher than the present value of expected cash outflows. Assume that the cash outflows are so large (in absolute, undiscounted amounts) that the total undiscounted net cash inflows are negative. Still, the project is profitable because the present value of the future outflows is small. For example, the owner of a coal mine might receive a substantial payment from an electric utility today for strip mining rights. The owner expects to incur costs in 15 years to restore the site that will exceed the amount of cash received today. The present value of the site restoration costs is, however, less than the amount received today. How should this case of negative depreciable basis (cost less salvage value is negative) be treated?

**12.12**  Describe the two purposes of compound interest depreciation.

**12.13**  Under certain conditions compound interest depreciation can lead to negative depreciation charges. Consider, for example, an asset costing $1,000 with only one cash flow, $1,210, two years hence. The earnings rate on this asset is 10 percent per year. The depreciation charge for the first year is −$100. Explain the phenomenon of negative depreciation.

**12.14**   Distinguish between the goals of choosing a depreciation method or a depreciable life for financial reporting and for tax reporting.

**12.15**   Recollect the accounting for a manufacturing firm. A manufacturing firm records depreciation on factory machinery (or equipment or buildings) with an entry such as the following:

| | | |
|---|---|---|
| Work-in-Process Inventory | 10,000 | |
|     Accumulated Depreciation (Factory Machinery) | | 10,000 |

Assume that none of the work in process was completed during the current accounting period. All sales were made from Finished Goods Inventory, and there were no transfers from Work-in-Process Inventory to Finished Goods Inventory.

**a.** Under these unrealistic assumptions, trace the effects of the above entry on the balance sheet accounts. Think about the totals of current assets, all assets, liabilities, and all equities.

**b.** What is the effect of the above entry on working capital?

**c.** Aside from income tax effects, can depreciation be a source of funds? Explain.

**d.** What can you generalize from the above answers to a more realistic situation where part of the goods produced during the current period were sold?

**12.16**   It is the policy of the Victoria Company to recondition its buildings and equipment each year so that they are maintained in perfect repair. In view of the substantial costs involved in such a practice, one of the vice presidents says that there is no need to recognize depreciation. Do you agree?

**12.17**   When new information about an asset's depreciable life becomes available, that information is used only prospectively, affecting only future depreciation charges. Accounting does not allow revision of prior periods' depreciation charges so that financial statements appear as though the new information had been known all along. Refer to Figure 12.3. Explain why promulgators of accounting principles might prefer that management not be able to restate prior periods' depreciation charges for changes in estimates.

**12.18**   Explain why some theorists think that the nature of group depreciation suggests that only a weighted-average flow assumption be used for computing the cost of assets retired from the group before the end of the group's life.

**12.19**   **a.** Distinguish both the retirement method and the replacement method from conventional depreciation methods.

**b.** Distinguish between the retirement method (FIFO flow) and the replacement method (LIFO flow).

**12.20**   (Adapted from AICPA *Technical Practice Aids*.) Dukes Company has been depreciating its typewriters on a straight-line, individual-unit basis. Starting in the current year it has begun using accelerated depreciation for newly acquired typewriters, which are essentially identical to the old ones. It retains straight-line depreciation for the old ones. Comment on this procedure.

**12.21**   (Adapted from AICPA *Technical Practice Aids*.) APB *Opinion No. 12* requires that the financial statements disclose depreciation "expense" for the year. In a manufacturing firm some depreciation is debited to Work-in-Process Inventory and becomes expense only when the goods are sold. How should depreciation charged to Work-in-Process Inventory be treated in the required disclosure?

The AICPA response is that the amount of depreciation "expense" may be disclosed as the sum of amounts that have been charged to manufacturing costs and to expense accounts.

Comment on the distortions caused by this answer, if any, and the reasons for the answer.

**12.22**   (Adapted from AICPA *Technical Practice Aids*.) Swieringa Company acquires used apartment buildings with kitchen appliances installed. The appliances have substantially shorter service lives than the buildings. What depreciation policy is appropriate for the buildings and the appliances?

**12.23**   (Adapted from AICPA *Technical Practice Aids*.) Morse Company has a contract with the city that reimburses Morse for all costs of running a hospital, including depreciation on the building. The company constructed a new hospital and demolished the old one when its estimated remaining depreciable life was 5 years. At the time of demolition the old hospital had a book value of $200,000. Morse Company proposes to continue depreciation of the $200,000 book value over the remaining 5 years of life so that it can collect reimbursement for depreciation. Comment.

**12.24**   (Adapted from AICPA *Technical Practice Aids*.) Banchet's Restaurant owns a substantial amount of silverware and dishes. These items are of classic design and have been used in the restaurant for many decades. Banchet's Restaurant plans to continue using these patterns indefinitely. Banchet knows the cost of the original purchase of silverware and dishes, the physical losses each year through breakage and theft, and the cost of dishes and silverware purchased as replacements. How should Banchet's Restaurant account for its silverware and dishes?

**12.25**   (Adapted from AICPA *Technical Practice Aids*.) A hospital anticipates increasing replacement costs for its medical equipment, which has a relatively short economic life because of rapid technical obsolescence. Each year it sets aside an amount of cash equal to 60 percent of the depreciation charges for the year in a fund with which to replace assets. It proposes to make the following journal entries (assuming a year in which depreciation on existing equipment is $100,000):

| | | |
|---|---:|---:|
| Depreciation Expense | 100,000 | |
|     Accumulated Depreciation | | 100,000 |
| | | |
| Replacement Fund for Replacement of Equipment | 60,000 | |
|     Cash | | 60,000 |
| | | |
| Replacement Expense | 60,000 | |
|     Estimated Costs of Replacement | | 60,000 |
| The account credited will appear among the estimated liabilities. | | |

Comment on this treatment.

**Q12.26**   (Adapted from AICPA *Technical Practice Aids*). Dyckman Company maintains an inventory of tuxedos, shoes, and related items that are rented to individuals. Each item has an estimated life of only 2 years. Additional items are purchased as required. At the end of each year a complete physical inventory of items is taken. Which of the following methods, if any, is appropriate accounting for these items?

   a. Use the retirement method, which is equivalent to treating the items as inventory, expensing costs only as the assets are retired from service.

   b. Use the replacement method, expensing costs of new items acquired to replace old ones and capitalizing costs of new items not replacing old ones.

   c. Expense all items as acquired.

   d. Depreciate all items over 2 years as individual units.

   e. Depreciate all items in a single group, using a depreciation rate of 50 percent per year.

12.27   The Southern Union Railroad uses the replacement method of accounting for all its track, ties, ballast, and tie plates. It expenses replacements and capitalizes betterments. How would it treat each of the following costs?

   a. Fifty miles of main line track are installed where there was none before. The line contains "100-pound" rail.

   b. Costs are incurred to replace 2,000 rail ties.

   c. Several sections of rail are replaced with "100-pound" rail.

   d. A new siding is constructed where there was none before.

   e. Ten miles of "100-pound rail" are removed and reinstalled on a branch line to a warehouse that previously had no rail service. The 10 miles of main line are replaced with heavy-duty "140-pound" rail.

   f. The ballast (the rocks and gravel under the ties) is removed and replaced with new ballast comparable in quality to that originally installed.

   g. Tie plates, damaged in a derailment, are replaced.

   h. A new switch is installed so that one line can be more conveniently connected to another.

12.28   Because the accountant wishes to show both original cost and accumulated depreciation in separate accounts for plant assets, the accounting for them on a current-cost basis presents some problems not seen in current-cost accounting for inventories and other assets. These problems are sometimes called the problems of "catch-up" depreciation or "backlog" depreciation.

   Vancil Company owns a machine with a 10-year life that had an original cost 3 years ago of $16,000 and has a current replacement cost in new condition at the start of the current year of $20,000. At the start of the fourth year, the asset has 70 percent of its useful life remaining, current cost of the asset in its as-is, used condition is $14,000, and accumulated depreciation is $6,000. At the end of the year, consistent with a 10-year life, the asset has 60 percent of its useful life remaining, but the replacement cost of a new asset with comparable productive capacity has increased to $25,000. Assuming straight-line depreciation at a 10-percent rate, the asset must be shown on the balance sheet at the end of the third year with a gross current cost of $25,000, accumulated depreciation of $10,000, and net current cost of $15,000. Exhibit 12.9 summarizes these assumptions.

   Exhibit 12.10 illustrates the possible accounting treatments. Line (ii), for example, shows depreciation based on average replacement cost during the year. [This is the treatment required by the FASB in *Statement No. 33* (1979).]

   Using a 10-percent rate, the depreciation charge is $2,250, rather than the $1,600 based on historical cost. The required journal entries would be

(1) Depreciation Charge Based on Historical Cost  . . . . . . . . . . . . . . . . . . . . . . . . . . . . . . . 1,600
    Additional Depreciation Charge Based on Replacement Cost  . . . . . . . . . . . . . . . . . .   650
        Accumulated Depreciation  . . . . . . . . . . . . . . . . . . . . . . . . . . . . . . . . . . . . . . . . . . .   2,250
    The above entries recognize depreciation based on average replacement cost during the year.

---

*Exhibit 12.9*
**Vancil Company**
**Assumed Data for Illustration of**
**Catch-up Depreciation**

---

Machine Costs $16,000, Has 10-Year Life, Was 3 Years Old at Start of Year, and Is Depreciated on Straight-Line Basis at the Rate of 10% per Year

| | Start of Year | End of Year |
| --- | --- | --- |
| Percentage of Economic Life Remaining ..................................... | 70% | 60% |
| Replacement Cost of Similar Machine in New Condition ...................... | $20,000 | $25,000 |
| Replacement Cost of Similar Used Machine with Similar Productive Capacity ................................................................ | (14,000) | (15,000) |
| Required Accumulated Depreciation ........................................ | $ 6,000 | $10,000 |

---

(2) Asset (at Cost New) ...................................................... 5,000
                 Accumulated Depreciation for Catch-up ................................. 1,750
                 Unrealized Holding Gain .............................................. 3,250

These entries recognize increased cost of a new asset (debit of $5,000) and increased accumulated depreciation for the amount of asset's service already expired by the time of the calculation. The amount is whatever is necessary to give total accumulated depreciation of $10,000 at year-end [credit of $1,750 = $10,000 − ($6,000 + $2,250)]. The remaining credit is the total holding gain for the year. Part of the holding gain is realized in the next entry.

(3) Unrealized Holding Gain ................................................. 650
                 Realized Holding Gain ................................................ 650

These entries acknowledge the amount of holding gain realized during the year—the excess of replacement cost depreciation charges over historical cost depreciation charges.

The first journal entry recognizes depreciation charges for the year. The second entry adjusts the asset's cost to replacement cost new and adjusts accumulated depreciation to show that our asset was *not* new at the start of the year. The amount of catch-up depreciation is determined by working backwards from knowing the required amount of accumulated depreciation at year-end ($10,000) and subtracting from that amount the sum of accumulated depreciation at the beginning of the year ($6,000), plus all depreciation charges for the year ($2,250). Thus catch-up depreciation is $1,750 = $10,000 − ($6,000 + $2,250). In addition, the second entry shows the holding gain recognized because of the increase in current value of the used asset. Part of the holding gain is realized during the year via depreciation expense. The unrealized holding gain on inventories or marketable securities is realized when items are sold and their costs become charges against income. Similarly, unrealized holding gain on plant is realized in the period when the increased depreciation charges become expenses on the income statement.

The realized holding gain is equal to the excess of replacement cost depreciation over historical cost depreciation—$650 in the example—as shown in the third entry.

Current-cost depreciation need not, in principle, be based on average current cost during the year. It could be based on current cost at the start of the year, as shown on line **(i)**, or at the end of the year, as shown on line **(iii)**. Line **(iv)** shows the treatment allowed by the French tax authorities in the 1950s. In this treatment, depreciation for tax purposes was allowed to be large enough to encompass the catch-up depreciation as well as the charge for the current year.

*Exhibit 12.10*
**Vancil Company**
**Possible Accounting Treatments**
**for Catch-up Depreciation**
**and Holding Gains**

| | Debits | | | Credits | |
| --- | --- | --- | --- | --- | --- |
| **Depreciation Charge for Year Based on Current Cost** | **To Asset Account at Year-End (1)a** | **+ Current-Cost Depreciation Charge for Year (2)b** | **= To Accumulated Depreciation for Year's Charge (3)b** | **+ To Accumulated Depreciation at Year-End for Catch-up Depreciation (4)c** | **+ Holding Gain for Year (5)d** |
| (i) At Start of Year | $5,000 | $2,000 | $2,000 | ? | ? |
| (ii) Average for Year | 5,000 | 2,250 | 2,250 | 1,750 | $3,250 |
| (iii) At End of Year | 5,000 | 2,500 | 2,500 | ? | ? |
| (iv) French Tax Method | 5,000 | 4,000 | 4,000 | ? | ? |

| | **Calculation of Realized Holding Gain for Year Assuming Historical Cost of Asset of $16,000** | | | **Net Increase Credit in Unrealized Holding Gain Account for Year (9)g** |
| --- | --- | --- | --- | --- |
| | **Current Cost Depreciation Charge (6)b** | **− Historical Cost Depreciation Charge (7)e** | **= Realized Holding Gain for Year (8)f** | |
| (i) At Start of Year | $2,000 | $1,600 | ? | ? |
| (ii) Average for Year | 2,250 | 1,600 | $650 | $2,600 |
| (iii) At End of Year | 2,500 | 1,600 | ? | ? |
| (iv) French Tax Method | 4,000 | 1,600 | ? | ? |

aTo increase cost of new asset to $25,000 from $20,000.

bTen percent of depreciable basis for first three rows: row 1—$20,000, row 2—$22,500; row 3—$25,000. In row 4, the $4,000 depreciation is computed so that accumulated depreciation at year-end is $10,000: $4,000 = $10,000 − $6,000.

cAmount to force accumulated depreciation at year-end to $10,000: $10,000 − $6,000 − amount in column (3).

dPlug for equal debits and credits for entire entry: (5) = (1) + (2) − (3) − (4) = (1) − (4).

e$16,000 × 0.10.

f(6) − (7).

g(5) − (8).

Fill in numbers for the 12 question marks, "?," shown in columns (4), (5), (8), and (9). The differences among the treatments result in different depreciation charges and different amounts of realized holding gains. Note, however, in column (9) how the increase in unrealized holding gains is independent of the particular current value used for computing periodic depreciation charges.

## Problems and Exercises

12.29 Prepare journal entries for the following transactions:
(1) A piece of office equipment is purchased for $850 cash.
(2) Depreciation for 1 year of $85 is recorded.
(3) The equipment is sold for $400. At the time of the sale, the Accumulated Depreciation shows a balance of $425. Depreciation of $85 for the year of the sale has not yet been recorded.

12.30 Give the journal entries for the following selected transactions of the Eagle Manufacturing Company. The company uses the straight-line method of calculating depreciation and closes its books annually on December 31.
(1) A machine is purchased on November 1, 1970, for $30,000. It is estimated that it will be used for 10 years and that it will have a salvage value of $600 at the end of that time. Give the journal entry for the depreciation at December 31, 1970.
(2) Record the depreciation for the year ending December 31, 1971.
(3) In August 1976 it is decided that the machine will probably be used for a total of 12 years and that its scrap value will be $400. Record the depreciation for the year ending December 31, 1976.
(4) The machine is sold for $1,000 on March 31, 1981. Record the entries of that date, assuming that depreciation is recorded as indicated in (3).

12.31 In each case below, the firm uses the straight-line method of depreciation and closes its books annually on December 31. Recognize all gains and losses currently.

a. A cash register was purchased for $300 on January 1, five and one-half years ago. It was depreciated at a rate of 10 percent. On June 30 of this year, it was sold for $200, and a new cash register was acquired for $500. The bookkeeper made the following entry to record the transaction:

| | | |
|---|---|---|
| Store Equipment | 300 | |
| Cash | | 300 |

b. A used truck was acquired in May for $4,000. Its cost when new was $6,000, and the bookkeeper made the following entry to record the purchase:

| | | |
|---|---|---|
| Truck | 6,000 | |
| Accumulated Depreciation | | 2,000 |
| Cash | | 4,000 |

c. A testing mechanism was purchased on April 1, two and one-quarter years ago, for $600. It was depreciated at a 10-percent annual rate. On June 30, it was stolen. The loss was not insured, and the bookkeeper made the following entry:

| | | |
|---|---|---|
| Theft Loss | 600 | |
| Testing Mechanism | | 600 |

Give correcting or adjusting entries for the above cases.

**12.32**  Assume that an asset is expected to last for 4$\frac{1}{2}$ years and is acquired at mid-year. Use sum-of-the-years'-digits depreciation. Assume $\frac{1}{2}$ year of depreciation is taken in the year of acquisition. What fractions of the asset's life are depreciated in each of the 5 years the asset is in service?

**12.33**  Roche Trucking Company has found after several years experience that its trucks last 4 years before being retired. The current cost of a truck is $65,800.
  **a.**  What is the annual depreciation rate under the declining-balance method (*not* the double-declining-balance method) if the expected salvage value 4 years hence is $13,000?
  **b.**  What is the annual depreciation rate under the declining-balance method (*not* the double-declining-balance method) if the expected salvage value 4 years hence is $8,530?

**12.34**  Calculate the depreciation charge for the first and second year of the asset's life in the following cases.

| Asset | Cost | Estimated Salvage Value | Life (Years) | Depreciation Method |
|---|---|---|---|---|
| **a.** Blast Furnace | $800,000 | $25,000 | 20 | Double-Declining-Balance |
| **b.** Warehouse | 500,000 | 50,000 | 45 | Straight-Line |
| **c.** Typewriter | 400 | 40 | 8 | Sum-of-the-Years'-Digits |
| **d.** 'Lathe | 6,000 | 500 | 10 | Double-Declining-Balance |
| **e.** Ferris Wheel | 7,600 | 400 | 12 | Straight-Line |
| **f.** Electric Cart | 5,500 | 1,300 | 6 | Sum-of-the-Years'-Digits |

**12.35**  On January 1, the Central Production Company acquired a new turret lathe for $36,000. It was estimated to have a useful life of 4 years and no salvage value. The company closes its books annually on December 31. Indicate the amount of the depreciation charge for each of the 4 years under:
  **a.**  The straight-line method.
  **b.**  The declining-balance method at twice the straight-line rate.
  **c.**  The sum-of-the-years'-digits method.
  **d.**  Assume now that the lathe was acquired on April 1. Indicate the amount of the depreciation charge for this year and each of the next four calendar years using the sum-of-the-years'-digits method.

**12.36**  A machine is acquired for $8,900. It is expected to last 8 years and to be operated for 25,000 hours during that time. It is estimated that its salvage value will be $1,700 at the end of that time. Calculate the depreciation charge for each of the first 3 years using:
  **a.**  The straight-line (time) method.
  **b.**  The sum-of-the-years'-digits method.
  **c.**  The declining-balance method using a 25-percent rate (the maximum rate allowed).
  **d.**  The units-of-production method. Operating times are as follows: first year, 3,500 hours; second year, 2,000 hours; third year, 5,000 hours.

**12.37**  The Wolf Company bought factory equipment costing $25,000 on March 31 of Year 1. The equipment is estimated to have an economic service life of six years, after which it will have a salvage value of $4,000. The Company calculates depreciation in the year of acquisition by the number of months an asset is in use.

    **a.** Calculate the depreciation charge on this machine for Year 1 assuming the use of:
      **(1)** The straight-line method
      **(2)** The sum-of-the-year's-digits method
      **(3)** The double-declining-balance method
      **(4)** The 150-percent-declining-balance method.
    **b.** Repeat the instructions of **a** for Year 2.

**12.38**    The Slowpoke Shipping Company buys a new truck for $10,000 on January 1, 1979. It is estimated to last 6 years and to have a salvage value of $1,000. Early in 1981, a mechanic reports that the truck will last only an additional 2 years, or 4 years in total. The company closes its books on December 31. Present a table showing the depreciation charges for each year from 1979 to 1982 and give the adjusting entry made in 1981. Follow the instructions for each of the following methods.
    **a.** The straight-line method.
    **b.** The sum-of-the-years'-digits method.
    **c.** The declining-balance method with depreciation at twice the straight-line rate. The remaining undepreciated cost less salvage value is to be written off in the last year.

**12.39**    The Linder Manufacturing Company acquires a new machine for $7,200 on July 1, 1976. It is estimated to have a service life of 6 years and then to have a salvage value of $900. The company closes its books annually on June 30.
    **a.** Compute the depreciation charges for each year of the asset's life assuming the use of:
      **(1)** The straight-line method.
      **(2)** The sum-of-the-years'-digits method.
      **(3)** The declining-balance method, with a rate twice the straight-line rate.
    **b.** Assume that the machine is sold for $700 on October 30, 1981. Give the journal entries that would be made on that date under each of the methods in part **a.**

**12.40**    The Twombly Company purchased a new automobile in May 1978. The automobile cost $8,800. It was estimated that the automobile would be driven for 100,000 miles before being traded in and that its salvage value at that time would be $800.
    Odometer readings are as follows:

| | |
|---|---:|
| Dec. 31, 1978 | 12,000 |
| Dec. 31, 1979 | 50,000 |
| Dec. 31, 1980 | 82,000 |
| June 16, 1981 | 98,000 |

On June 16, 1981, the automobile was traded in for a new one with a list price of $10,000. The old automobile had a fair market value of $800, but the dealer allowed $1,500 on it toward the list price of the new one. The balance of the purchase price was paid by check.
    **a.** Compute the depreciation charges for each year through 1980 using a "production" or "use" method.
    **b.** Record the entries for June 16, 1981, assuming that the list price of the new automobile is unreliable whereas the fair market value of the old is reliable.
    **c.** Record the entries for June 16, 1981, assuming that there were no reliable estimates for the fair market value of the old automobile.

**12.41**    Dr. Kadlac buys a new car every year at a list price of $18,000. He trades in a 1-year-old car and pays $7,500 cash. Operating the car is a legitimate business expense. Dr. Kadlac depre-

ciates the car using a 3-year life. After 15 years of following this practice, Dr. Kadlac discovered that the book value of the new car for tax purposes was identical every year.
a. What is that book value if Dr. Kadlac uses straight-line depreciation?
b. What is the book value if Dr. Kadlac uses double-declining-balance depreciation?
c. What is the book value if Dr. Kadlac uses sum-of-the-years'-digits depreciation?

12.42   Assume that the Internal Revenue Service would allow certain assets used for business purposes to be depreciated by assuming no salvage value either on a straight-line basis with a depreciable life of $2^1/_2$ years or on an accelerated basis (double-declining-balance or sum-of-the-years'-digits) with a depreciable life of 3 years. Which of the three depreciation methods leads to the largest present value of depreciation expenses for an asset costing $6,000?
a. Assume a discount rate of 10 percent.
b. Assume a discount rate of 20 percent.
c. What is the result for discount rates between 10 and 20 percent per year? (Round present-value factors to three digits and calculations to the nearest dollar.)

12.43   The Alexander Company acquired three used machine tools for a total price of $49,000. Costs to transport the machine tools from the seller to Alexander Company's factory were $1,000. The machine tools were renovated, installed, and put to use in manufacturing the firm's products. The costs of renovation and installation were as follows:

|  | **Machine Tool A** | **Machine Tool B** | **Machine Tool C** |
|---|---|---|---|
| Renovation Costs | $1,700 | $800 | $950 |
| Installation Costs | 300 | 550 | 250 |

The machine tools have the following estimated remaining lives: tool A—4 years; tool B—10 years; tool C—6 years.
a. Assume that each machine tool is capitalized in a separate asset account and that the remaining life of each machine tool is used as the basis for allocating the joint costs of acquisition. Compute the depreciable cost of each of the three machine tools.
b. Present journal entries to record depreciation charges for years 1, 5, and 8, given the assumption in part a. Use the straight-line method.
c. Assume that the three machine tools are treated as one composite asset in the accounts. If management decides to depreciate the entire cost of the composite asset on a straight-line basis over 10 years, what is the depreciation charge for each year?
d. Which treatment, a or c, should management of the Alexander Company probably prefer for tax purposes and why?

12.44   Prepare journal entries for the transactions below.
7/1/1978   The Acme Tool Rental Shop purchases 10 electric typewriters for cash at a cost of $400 each. It is estimated that they will have a life of 10 years.
12/31/1978   Record the depreciation from July 1 to December 31, 1978. The straight-line method is used with a 10-percent rate applied to original cost. The books are closed for the year.
4/1/1979   A sticking key causes one machine to short circuit, which causes damage and reduces the machine to scrap. A claim is filed with the insurance company for its book value, $370.
5/1/1979   A manual typewriter is purchased for cash to replace the destroyed machine. The cost of the unit is $200, and the life is 10 years. Salvage value is estimated to be zero. Do not change the depreciation rate.

|  |  |
|---|---|
| 5/15/1979 | The insurance company sends a check for $300 to settle the claim, which Acme accepts. |
| 12/31/1979 | Record the depreciation on the machines for the year. The books are closed. |
| 12/31/1980 | Before closing the books for the year, the remaining life of the electric type-writers is found to be only 4 more years. The life estimate for the manual unit is to remain unchanged. In the light of these new facts, compute depreciation for the year. |
| 7/1/1981 | It is decided to turn in the manual typewriter for an electrical unit. The dealer allows $100 for the manual typewriter on the cost of the new electric unit. The cash price of the new machine is $500. The balance is paid in cash. The new machine has an estimated life of 10 years and $50 salvage value. |
| 12/31/1981 | Depreciation for the year is recorded. The books are closed. |

**12.45** A machine with a life of 5 years is purchased for $10,652. The cash flows that will occur because of ownership of the asset are estimated as follows:

| | |
|---|---:|
| Jan. 1, 1981 | −$10,652 |
| Dec. 31, 1981 | +1,000 |
| Dec. 31, 1982 | +2,000 |
| Dec. 31, 1983 | +3,000 |
| Dec. 31, 1984 | +4,000 |
| Dec. 31, 1985 | +5,000 |

a. Compute the internal rate of return on these cash flows.

b. Compute the annual depreciation charges for this asset using the compound interest method.

**12.46** An asset is purchased for $5,000 on January 1, 1981, and is expected to have no salvage value at the end of its 5-year life.

Taking into account all costs and revenues produced by the ownership of this asset, the net cash flows are estimated as follows:

| | |
|---|---:|
| Jan. 1, 1981 | −$5,000 |
| Dec. 31, 1981 | +1,000 |
| Dec. 31, 1982 | +1,100 |
| Dec. 31, 1983 | +1,200 |
| Dec. 31, 1984 | +1,300 |
| Dec. 31, 1985 | +1,392 |

a. Compute the internal rate of return on these cash flows.

b. Compute the annual depreciation charges under the compound interest method.

**12.47** On July 1, 1979, the Hankton Company installed a processing unit in one of its plants at a cost, including freight and installation, of $546,000. The company anticipated significant technological developments within the next several years. Although the equipment had an expected physical life of 12 to 15 years, Hankton estimated it would be obsolete by the end of 5 years.

Late in 1980, new equipment featuring automatic controls came on the market. The new equipment was expected to make the old equipment obsolete 4 years hence.

Early in 1981, Hankton discovered that its equipment could be modernized by adding an automatic control system, which was done April 1, 1981, at a cost of $83,300. The modernized equipment is expected to have a life of 10 years from the time it was put into service.

Prepare a schedule showing depreciation charges for each of the years 1979, 1980, 1981, and 1982. Use the straight-line method.

**12.48** The Peters Processing Company acquired 100 similar factory machines on January 1, Year 1 for $200,000. It is estimated the machines will have an average life of 5 years and no salvage value. The company uses the group depreciation method. Retirements of machines, all occuring at the end of the year, were:

| | |
|---|---|
| Year 3 —  8 machines | Year 5 — 44 machines |
| Year 4 — 24 machines | Year 6 — 10 machines |

a. Give the entries Peter Processing Company made with regard to these machines for Years 1 through Year 6.

b. What is the balance in the Machinery account at December 31, Year 6?

c. What is the balance in the Accumulated Depreciation account at December 31, Year 6?

**12.49** Assume that an asset cost $5,000 and has expected salvage value of $200 at the end of its expected 5-year life. The asset is expected to return net cash flows as follows at the end of each year, starting with the end of the current year: $2,450; $1,980; $1,460; $980; and $460 at the end of the fifth year.

a. Prepare a schedule of depreciation charges based on the straight-line method. Compute the rate of return on the asset using the cash flow less depreciation for the year as the numerator and the book value at the start of the year as the denominator.

b. Repeat part **a** using sum-of-the-years'-digits depreciation.

c. Compute the internal rate of return on the cash flows from the asset: −$5,000, +$2,450, . . ., +$660 (= $460 plus salvage of $200).

d. Repeat part **a** using compound interest depreciation and the earnings rate found in part **c**.

**12.50** Nelson Corporation uses the group method of depreciation on its fleet of delivery trucks. All trucks are placed in a single group where such treatment is allowed by the tax regulations and are assumed to have zero salvage value.

The group was first established in 1979. For simplicity, it is assumed that truck purchases and retirements take place on December 31 of each year. Exhibit 12.11 shows data on acquisitions and retirements.

### Exhibit 12.11
### Nelson Company

| | Purchases | | Retirements | | |
|---|---|---|---|---|---|
| Year | Number of Trucks | Cost per Truck | Number of Trucks | Cost per Truck | Proceeds per Truck |
| 1979 ................. | 10 | $30,000 | — | — | — |
| 1980 ................. | 8 | 31,000 | 1 | $30,000 | $10,000 |
| 1981 ................. | 4 | 32,000 | 2 | 30,000 | 8,000 |
| 1982 ................. | 0 | — | — | — | — |

Compute the depreciation charges for 1980, 1981, and 1982 on the group method.

a. Use the straight-line method and a 20-percent annual rate.

b. Use the double-declining-balance method and a rate of 40 percent.

**12.51** The Acme Rental Company rents heavy-duty rug shampooing machines on a week-to-week basis. The expected life of a machine is 10 years. Exhibit 12.12 shows a summary of purchases and disposals of machines for the first 5 years of the firm's existence.

*Exhibit 12.12*
**Acme Rental Company**

| End of Year | Acquisitions | Total Cost | Retirements | Retirement Proceeds |
|---|---|---|---|---|
| 0 ............................ | 10 | $100,000 | 0 | 0 |
| 1 ............................ | 2 | 21,000 | 1 | $3,000 |
| 2 ............................ | 0 | 0 | 1 | 2,500 |
| 3 ............................ | 0 | 0 | 1 | 2,000 |
| 4 ............................ | 3 | 35,000 | 1 | 1,000 |
| 5 ............................ | 0 | 0 | 0 | 0 |

The company adopted the group method of depreciation for its rug shampooing machines. All machines are placed in a single group when tax regulations permit such treatment. Compute depreciation for the first 5 years assuming a FIFO flow for retirements and zero salvage value. Round computed amounts to the nearest $10.

a. Use the straight-line method.

b. Use the declining-balance method at twice the straight-line rate.

12.52 Mueller Steel Products Company uses a number of electric cranes consisting of a chassis, motor, and truck. The crane chassis has a normal service life of 12 years, the truck lasts 6 years and must be overhauled at the end of every 3 years, and the motor requires a major overhaul at the end of each 2 years and must be replaced every 4 years.

The operating history of crane 25A is as follows:

Jan., year 1      Purchased crane for $50,000. Estimated cost of components: chassis, $24,000; truck, $18,000; motor, $8,000.

Dec., year 2      Overhauled motor at cost of $600.

Dec., year 3      Overhauled truck at cost of $2,400.

Dec., year 4      Replaced motor at cost of $9,600.

Dec., year 6      Overhauled motor at cost of $680; replaced truck at cost of $21,000.

Dec., year 8      Replaced motor at cost of $10,000.

Dec., year 9      Overhauled truck at cost of $2,900.

Dec., year 10      Overhauled motor at cost of $800.

Dec., year 12      Scrapped crane; scrap value covered cost of dismantling and removal.

The company depreciates its cranes at the straight-line rate of 14 percent per year. The cost of motor and truck overhauls is charged to expense, and the cost of replacing motors and trucks is debited to the Accumulated Depreciation account.

The assistant controller has suggested that the company revise its accounting procedure as follows. Separate property records would be maintained for motors, trucks, and chassis. Annual depreciation on each component would be computed by totaling the cost of the component and the estimated cost of the overhaul (in the case of motors and trucks) and dividing by the estimated service life. The cost of major overhauls would be debited to Accumulated Depreciation. Components would be retired from the property account and any gain or loss recorded at the time of replacement. The controller feels that this procedure would not make any significant difference in the pattern of operating charges, and asks the assistant to prepare a comparative history using crane 25A as an example, showing the results under the company's present policy and the results under the assistant's suggested procedure.

a. Prepare a schedule summarizing the operating history of crane 25A, showing the balance in the asset account, the accumulated depreciation, and the total charge to expense for depreciation and repairs for each of the 12 years under the company's present procedures.

b. Prepare a similar schedule summarizing the operating history of crane 25A assuming that the company had followed the assistant's suggested procedure. Assume that the cost of the first overhauls is estimated as follows: motor, $600; truck, $2,400. Subsequent overhauls are estimated at the cost actually incurred in making the last overhaul. Include supporting schedules showing the computation of revised depreciation charges after the replacement of a component, and the gain or loss at the time of retirement.

c. Evaluate the two procedures and explain why you would or would not recommend that the assistant's suggestion be adopted.

**P12.53**  The data in Exhibit 12.13 show assumed acquisitions and retirements from a group of small vehicles. Using those data and the depreciation methods described in each part of the problem, prepare a schedule showing each of the following items for each of the 6 years of the group's life:

(1) Number of vehicles in use, start of year.
(2) Cost of vehicles in use, start of year.
(3) Book value of vehicles in use, start of year.
(4) Depreciation charge for year for group.
(5) Amount credited to asset account for retirements.
(6) Amount debited to cash for proceeds of retirement.
(7) Amount debited to Accumulated Depreciation on retirement.
(8) Gain (Cr.) or loss (Dr.) on retirement.
(9) Accumulated depreciation on books at the end of the year.

a. Use straight-line group depreciation, a rate of 25 percent of cost per year, and assume FIFO flow of retirements.

b. Use straight-line group depreciation, a rate of 25 percent of cost per year, and assume weighted-average flow of retirements.

c. Use straight-line group depreciation, a rate of 25 percent of cost per year, and assume specific identification of retirements.

d. Use double-declining-balance group depreciation charged at the rate of 50 percent of book value per year.

e. Use straight-line unit (*not* group) depreciation with a rate of 25 percent of original cost per year until retirement or until cost is fully depreciated.

---

*Exhibit 12.13*
**Asset Acquisitions and Retirements
for Group Depreciation**

| End of Year | Retirements[a] Number from First Purchase | Retirements[a] Number from Second Purchase | Proceeds from Disposition | Purchases[a] Number | Purchases[a] Cost |
|---|---|---|---|---|---|
| 0 | — | — | — | 10 | $120,000 |
| 1 | — | — | — | — | — |
| 2 | 4 | — | $6,000 | 3 | 45,000 |
| 3 | 3 | — | 5,000 | — | — |
| 4 | 2 | 1 | 3,000 | — | — |
| 5 | 1 | 1 | 2,000 | — | — |
| 6 | — | 1 | 1,000 | — | — |

[a]All retirements take place on the last day of the year, just before purchases are made.

12.54   The Skillern Oil Company purchased a fleet of 100 fully equipped trucks on January 1 of year 1 for $3,000,000. The controller of the firm decided to use group depreciation procedures on these trucks and estimated the appropriate group rate from data shown in Exhibit 12.14.

The company had followed standard group depreciation procedures and recorded no gain or loss when the trucks were retired.

At the end of year 7, when the last truck had been retired, the controller prepared the following summary showing the company's actual experience with this fleet:

| Year | Number of Trucks Retired | Salvage Received |
|------|--------------------------|------------------|
| Year 1 | 4 | $ 86,000 |
| Year 2 | 11 | 164,000 |
| Year 3 | 28 | 401,800 |
| Year 4 | 42 | 248,000 |
| Year 5 | 8 | 25,000 |
| Year 6 | 5 | 9,000 |
| Year 7 | 2 | 2,800 |
| | 100 | $936,600 |

a. Reconstruct the asset and related accumulated depreciation account as it would have appeared had the controller's estimates been exactly realized and the computed rate of 21 percent used as a basis for recording depreciation. Would the controller's rate have produced accurate results if the assumptions had turned out to be correct? Why or why not?

b. Compute the group depreciation rate on the basis of the controller's original estimates using the weighted average cost and life of each asset. (See Exhibit 12.7.)

c. On the basis of hindsight, that is, the actual record of experience with this fleet, compute the group rate that should have been used in depreciating this fleet of trucks.

d. Using the rate computed in part **c**, reconstruct the asset and accumulated depreciation accounts to show that the rate would produce a zero balance in the allowance for depreciation account at the end of year 7.

---

*Exhibit 12.14*
**Skillern Oil Company**

| End of Year (1) | Number of Trucks to Be Retired (2) | Original Cost (3) | Estimated Total Salvage (4) | Depreciation Base (5) | Average Yearly Depreciation (6) |
|------|------|------|------|------|------|
| Year 1 | 5 | $ 150,000 | $105,000 | $ 45,000 | $ 45,000 |
| Year 2 | 20 | 600,000 | 360,000 | 240,000 | 120,000 |
| Year 3 | 30 | 900,000 | 297,000 | 603,000 | 201,000 |
| Year 4 | 30 | 900,000 | 180,000 | 720,000 | 180,000 |
| Year 5 | 15 | 450,000 | 30,000 | 420,000 | 84,000 |
| | | $3,000,000 | | $2,028,000 | $630,000 |

The group depreciation rate was estimated as:

$$\frac{\$630,000}{\$3,000,000} = .21.$$

Column (5) = column (3) − column (4).
Column (6) = column (5)/life (1).

12.55   (Adapted from CPA Examination.) Thompson Corporation, a manufacturer of steel products, began operations on October 1, 1980. The accounting department of Thompson has started

*Exhibit 12.15*
**Thompson Corporation**
**Fixed Asset and Depreciation**
**Schedule for Fiscal Years Ended**
**September 30, 1981, and**
**September 30, 1982**

| Assets | Acquisition | Cost | Salvage | Depreciation Method | Estimated Life in Years | Depreciation Expense Year Ended September 30, 1981 | Depreciation Expense Year Ended September 30, 1982 |
|---|---|---|---|---|---|---|---|
| Land A ......... | Oct. 1, 1980 | $   a | N/A | N/A | N/A | N/A | N/A |
| Building A ...... | Oct. 1, 1980 | b | $47,500 | Straight-Line | c | $14,000 | d |
| Land B ......... | Oct. 2, 1980 | e | N/A | N/A | N/A | N/A | N/A |
| Building B ...... | Under Construction | 210,000 to Date | — | Straight-Line | 30 | — | f |
| Donated Equipment .... | Oct. 2, 1980 | g | 2,000 | 15% Declining-Balance | 10 | | h | i |
| Machinery A .... | Oct. 2, 1980 | j | 5,500 | Sum-of-the-Years'-Digits | 10 | | k | l |
| Machinery B .... | Oct. 1, 1981 | m | — | Straight-Line | 15 | — | n |

N/A—Not applicable.

the fixed-asset and depreciation schedule presented as Exhibit 12.14. The data already on the schedule are correct. The following information comes from the company's records and personnel.

(1) Depreciation is computed from the first of the month of acquisition to the first of the month of disposition.

(2) Land A and Building A were acquired from a predecessor corporation. Thompson paid $812,500 for the land and building together. At the time of acquisition, the land had an appraised value of $72,000 and the building had an appraised value of $828,000.

(3) Land B was acquired on October 2, 1980, in exchange for 3,000 newly issued shares of Thompson's common stock. At the date of acquisition, the stock had a par value of $5 per share and a fair value of $25 per share. During October 1980, Thompson paid $10,400 to demolish an existing building on this land so it could construct a new building.

(4) Construction of Building B on the newly acquired land began on October 1, 1981. By September 30, 1982, Thompson had paid $210,000 of the estimated total construction costs of $300,000. Estimated completion and occupancy are July 1983.

(5) Certain equipment was donated to the corporation by a local university. An independent appraisal of the equipment when donated placed the fair value at $16,000 and the salvage value at $2,000.

(6) Machinery A's total cost of $110,000 includes installation expense of $550 and normal repairs and maintenance of $11,000. Salvage value is estimated as $5,500. Machinery A was sold on February 1, 1982.

(7) On October 1, 1981, Machinery B was acquired with a down payment of $4,000 and the remaining payments to be made in 10 annual installments of $4,000 each beginning October 1, 1982. The prevailing interest rate was 8 percent.

Compute the missing quantities labeled **a–n**. Show supporting computations in good form.

12.56  Jones Manufacturing Corporation depreciates its machinery using the straight-line method over a 10-year life with zero estimated salvage value. A full year's depreciation is taken in the year of acquisition and none in the year of disposal. Acquisitions, which took place evenly over the appropriate years, were as follows: 1979, $500,000; 1980, $100,000; 1981,

$200,000. An index of the average general price level during 1979 was 120, during 1980 was 160, and during 1981 was 180. The general price index on December 31, 1981, is 200.

a. Compute the amount of depreciation expense for 1981 and the book value of the machinery on December 31, 1981, using the acquisition cost valuation method as conventionally reported.

b. Repeat part **a**, using the acquisition cost valuation method restated for general price level changes. Round conversion factors used to two decimal places (for example, 200/120 = 1.67).

12.57 The FASB requires that the total increase in current cost of assets be disaggregated into a "real" portion and an "inflation component." The real portion is equal to the portion of the increase in the asset's value in excess of the increase caused by the change in general prices. If a specific asset costing $100 increases in value 15 percent during a period of general inflation of 10 percent, then the nominal holding gain is $15 (= $100 × 1.15 − $100), the inflation component of the holding gain is $10 (= $100 × .10), and the real holding gain is $5 (= $15 − $10).

Refer to the data in the preceding problem. Assume that at the end of 1981 the machinery has a current cost new of $1.5 million and a current cost used, as is, of $1 million. Compute the total holding gain on these assets as of December 31, 1981, and disaggregate the holding gain into an inflation component and a real component. (Note that you are *not* asked for the holding gain and its components for 1981, but for the entire life of the asset.)

# Chapter 13
## *Amortization of Natural Resources and Intangibles*

13.1 Under a historical, or acquisition, cost accounting system, costs incurred to obtain goods and services are treated either as expenses of the period in which the costs are incurred (if the goods or services are consumed in the current period) or capitalized as assets (if the goods or services will be consumed in future periods). When the goods or services are consumed in those future periods, all, or a portion, of the assets' costs is recognized as an expense.

13.2 Previous chapters have discussed the application of these cost, asset, and expense concepts to inventories, prepayments, and depreciable assets. This chapter discusses their application to (1) costs incurred in acquiring, exploring, developing, and extracting natural resources, and (2) costs incurred in acquiring and developing intangible assets, such as patents, copyrights, and goodwill. Although natural resources are not intangible assets, the issues involved in accounting for natural resources and intangible assets are so similar that we discuss them together. In exploring for new deposits of natural resources or developing marketable patents or product innovations, substantial expenditures are made with the hope that a small percentage (as low as one-half of one percent in the drug industry) will turn out to be so successful that the entire exploration venture is worthwhile.

## Accounting for Nonrenewable Natural Resources

13.3 Natural resources include such items as oil, gas, iron ore, sulfur, and uranium. Natural resources are *wasting assets,* or *nonrenewable resources,* because their extraction or removal results in the physical consumption of a portion of the natural resource. In most cases, replacement occurs only by an act of nature. For *renewable resources* such as forests or orchards, replacement occurs naturally in the growth process.

13.4 The process of exploring for, developing, and extracting natural resources that are wasting assets generally involves the following steps:

1. Acquisition of property or property rights—Property with potential natural resources is either purchased outright or leased from others with the understanding that any natural resources discovered will be shared by the lessor and lessee.

2. Exploration—The property is explored to determine the existence of recoverable natural resources.

3. Development—If recoverable natural resources are discovered, the property is developed to gain access to the natural resources and to permit their extraction or removal.

**13-1**

**4.** Production—The natural resources are extracted, treated, and stored until the time of sale.

13.5 During the acquisition and exploration stages, it is not known if natural resources will be discovered on a particular parcel of land. If natural resources are discovered, the development stage begins. If natural resources are not discovered, the search activity on that parcel of land is abandoned.

13.6 The issues in accounting for natural resources are similar to those for depreciable assets:

**1.** Which costs should be recognized as expenses in the period incurred and which costs should be capitalized as assets to be amortized ("depleted" is the term used for natural resources) over future periods?

**2.** For those costs capitalized as assets, what pattern of amortization, or depletion, should be used?

## Determining the Cost Basis for Depletion

13.7 As discussed in previous chapters, all costs incurred in preparing an asset for its intended use should be capitalized as part of the cost of the asset. The cost of manufactured inventories includes the raw materials, direct labor, and overhead costs incurred in their production. The cost of machinery and equipment includes, in addition to the invoice price, any transportation, installation, and breaking-in costs. Likewise, a natural resource property should theoretically include all acquisition, exploration, and development costs incurred to prepare the property for the extraction of natural resources. Once extracted, the inventory of natural resources should include depletion on the property itself plus the cost of extraction, treatment, and storage.

13.8 The application of these general principles to natural resource activities is more complex than for manufactured inventories, machinery, and equipment, because a substantial proportion of the acquisition and exploration costs incurred does not result in the discovery of recoverable natural resources. An important question is when these nonproductive costs should be recognized as an expense or a loss.

13.9 Two historical cost methods of accounting for natural resources are commonly used: **(1)** successful-efforts costing, and **(2)** full costing.

**Successful-Efforts Costing** Under success- 13.10 ful-efforts costing, each parcel of property is treated as a separate accounting unit. All acquisition and exploration costs incurred on the property are initially capitalized as assets. In the period when it is determined that a particular property does not contain recoverable natural resources, the acquisition and exploration costs initially capitalized are treated as an expense or a loss. The acquisition and exploration costs on properties for which exploration efforts are successful are carried forward as assets (hence the term "successful-efforts costing"). To the acquisition and exploration costs are added the development costs incurred to prepare the property for extraction of the natural resources. Thus, the cost basis for depletion under successful-efforts costing includes acquisition, exploration, and development costs on each property with recoverable natural resources.

*Example 1* Texas Oil Company incurred ac- 13.11 quisition and exploration costs during 1980 as follows:

| Site | Acquisition Costs | Exploration Costs |
|---|---|---|
| Parcel A | $ 5,000,000 | $12,000,000 |
| Parcel B | 2,000,000 | 6,000,000 |
| Parcel C | 3,000,000 | 12,000,000 |
| Total | $10,000,000 | $30,000,000 |

Recoverable oil is discovered early in January 1981 on parcel B. Exploration efforts on parcel A and parcel C are discontinued immediately. Development costs of $20,000,000 are incurred on parcel B to prepare the site for the extraction of oil. It is estimated that parcel B has 8,000,000 barrels of recoverable oil. The current market value of oil is $20 per barrel.

The $32,000,000 of acquisition and explo- 13.12 ration costs on parcel A and parcel C is treated as an expense of 1981 under successful-efforts costing. The cost basis for depletion on parcel B is $28,000,000 (= $2,000,000 + $6,000,000 + $20,000,000). Depletion will be charged at the rate of $3.50 (= $28,000,000/8,000,000 bbl) per barrel used or sold.

13.13 **Full Costing** Under full costing, all parcels of property in some broad area, such as a geographic region or a country, are treated as the accounting unit. Acquisition and exploration costs incurred within this accounting unit are capitalized as assets. As long as recoverable natural resources are discovered somewhere within this accounting unit (region or country), *all* acquisition and exploration costs incurred (both those resulting in successful and those resulting in unsuccessful efforts) are treated as part of the cost of the recoverable natural resources so long as the market value of the resources discovered is at least equal to the total acquisition and exploration costs. Development costs are also capitalized to obtain the total, or full, cost basis for depletion.

13.14 *Example 2* Refer to the data for Texas Oil Company in Example 1. The cost basis for depletion on parcel B under full costing is the total acquisition and exploration cost on all three parcels of $40,000,000 (= $10,000,000 + $30,000,000) plus the development costs on parcel B of $20,000,000 for a total of $60,000,000. Because the market value of the recoverable reserves is $160,000,000 (= 8,000,000 bbl × $20), the entire $60,000,000 of acquisition, exploration, and development cost is capitalized as the cost of parcel B. Depletion will be charged at the rate of $7.50 (= $60,000,000/8,000,000 bbl) per barrel used or sold.

13.15 **Evaluation of Successful-Efforts and Full Costing** Advocates of successful-efforts costing argue that it better reflects the risks and returns from current operations. The costs of acquiring and exploring properties that turn out to be nonproductive are treated as expenses or losses in the period when the property is determined to be nonproductive. These losses are not submerged in the cost of productive properties and recognized piecemeal over several future periods, as is effectively done under full costing. Advocates also contend that successful-efforts costing is more consistent with other generally accepted accounting principles. For example, each long-term construction contract is treated as a separate accounting unit. If it is determined that losses will be incurred on a particular contract, the loss is recognized immediately.

13.16 Advocates of full costing contend that it better reflects the decision process that underlies exploration activity. In order to discover a single productive site, many nonproductive sites, or "dry holes," must be explored. Decision makers think in terms of the total investment required to discover that single productive site. They view the costs, voluntarily incurred, of the nonproductive sites as part of the inevitable cost of locating productive sites (much the same as normal spoilage costs are considered part of the cost of good units produced by a manufacturing firm).

13.17 **Official Position** Financial Accounting Standards Board *Statement No. 19,* issued in 1977, stipulated that successful-efforts costing would be the only method permitted *for oil- and gas-producing activities.* In 1978, however, the Securities and Exchange Commission ruled* that either successful-efforts costing or full costing would be acceptable for oil and gas properties. The SEC's position was in response to pressures from users of full costing, primarily small exploration and drilling companies, who would have had to report net losses under successful efforts costing, whereas they reported net income under full costing. In this case, the SEC effectively overruled the Financial Accounting Standards Board in establishing acceptable accounting principles.† In *State-*

---

*Accounting Series Release No. 253,* SEC (1978).
†Some accountants believe that the SEC actually was over-ruling the wishes of Congress rather than of the FASB. In 1975, Congress passed a law which required uniform standards of accounting in the petroleum industry by the end of 1977. FASB *Statement No.19* was a response to that law. The FASB had earlier indicated that it preferred to delay its ruling on oil and gas accounting until after its conceptual framework had been put into place.

*ment No. 25,* the FASB suspended those portions of *Statement No. 19* that pertained to the required use of successful-efforts accounting.* The accounting for oil and gas activities is currently being studied intensively by the FASB. The SEC has expressed its support for these efforts, implicitly shifting responsibility for setting standards for oil and gas activities back to the private sector.**

13.18 Although an official pronouncement has not been issued on the acceptability of successful-efforts costing and full costing for natural resource activities other than oil and gas, both methods are widely used in practice.

13.19 **Application of Successful-Efforts Costing** Financial Accounting Standards Board *Statement No. 19* establishes the guidelines for applying the successful-efforts costing method. These guidelines are summarized as follows:

1. Costs incurred to purchase, lease, or otherwise acquire a property are capitalized when incurred.

2. The costs of drilling exploratory wells, including depreciation on drilling equipment, are capitalized when incurred.

3. Acquisition and exploration costs incurred on properties with "proved reserves" continue to be capitalized as assets. Such costs on properties on which "proved reserves" are not found are charged to expense. Proved reserves are defined as "those quantities of crude oil, natural gas, and natural gas liquids which, upon analysis of geological and engineering data, appear with reasonable certainty to be recoverable in the future from known oil and gas reserves under existing economic and operating conditions."†

4. Development costs incurred to **(a)** gain access to and prepare well locations for drilling, **(b)** drill and equip development wells, **(c)** acquire, construct, and install production facilities, and **(d)** provide improved recovery systems are capitalized.

5. The capitalized amounts of acquisition, exploration, and development costs form the cost basis for depletion.

6. In addition to depletion, the following production, or lifting, costs are included in the cost of oil and gas inventories: **(a)** cost of labor to operate wells and related equipment, **(b)** repairs and maintenance, **(c)** materials, supplies, and fuel consumed in operating wells and related equipment, **(d)** property taxes and insurance relating to wells and equipment, and **(e)** severance taxes.

**Application of Full Costing** The SEC has 13.20 issued guidelines for the application of the full-costing method.†† These guidelines are summarized as follows:

1. Cost centers must be established on a country-by-country basis.

2. All costs associated with property acquisition, exploration, and development activities should be capitalized within the appropriate cost center.

3. Within each cost center, capitalized costs, less accumulated amortization and related deferred income taxes, should not exceed an amount equal to the sum of: **(a)** the present value of the future net revenues (cash flows) from proved oil and gas reserves, and **(b)** the lower-of-cost-or-market value of unproved properties included in costs being amortized. If the unamortized costs capitalized within a cost center exceed this cost center ceiling, the excess must be charged to expense. The imposition of a ceiling on the total costs capitalized results in a type of lower-of-cost-or-market valuation for depletable property.

4. Costs relating to the production, or removal, of oil and gas reserves are charged to expense when incurred.

The treatment of production costs as period expenses, instead of product costs as under successful-efforts costing, lacks theoretical justification. Lifting costs, like acquisition, exploration, and development costs, are necessary costs to prepare natural resources for sale and should be treated as product costs. The treatment of such costs as period

*Financial Accounting Standards Board, *Statement of Financial Accounting Standards No. 25* (1979).

**Accounting Series Release No. 289*, SEC, (1981).

†*Accounting Series Release No. 253,* SEC (1978), app. C.

††*Securities and Exchange Commission Release No. 33–5968* (1978); and *Accounting Series Release No. 258, SEC* (1978).

expenses under full costing can be justified only if natural resources are sold soon after extraction takes place (that is, inventories of natural resources are minimal). Even then, such treatment is merely expedient, not theoretically justified.

## Computation of Depletion

13.21 For financial reporting purposes, depletion is generally calculated using the unit-of-production method. The "unit" used is some physical measure of output (for example, tons or barrels). For income tax purposes, a firm may calculate depletion using either the unit-of-production method based on the cost basis of the property or the percentage-depletion method based on the sales revenue from depletable properties.

13.22 **Unit-of-Production Method** The unit-of-production method for depletable assets is similar to the unit-of-production method for depreciable assets. The periodic charge for depletion is calculated as follows:

$$\text{Periodic Charge for Depletion} = \frac{\text{Cost Basis of Depletable Property}}{\text{Estimated Quantity of Proved Reserves}} \times \frac{\text{Quantity of Proved Reserves Extracted During the Period}}{}$$

13.23 *Example 3* Refer to the data for Texas Oil Company in Example 1. The cost basis for depletion under successful-efforts costing was determined to be $28,000,000, and the estimated proved reserves were 8,000,000 barrels. Depletion of $3.50 per barrel (= $28,000,000/8,000,000) is recognized as oil is extracted. During 1981, 1,200,000 barrels were extracted at a production cost of $3,600,000. Depletion for 1981 is $4,200,000 (= 1,200,000 × $3.50). The total cost of the 1,200,000 barrels is $7,800,000 (= $4,200,000 + $3,600,000).

13.24 *Example 4* Refer to the data for Texas Oil Company in Example 2. The cost basis for depletion under full costing was determined to be $60,000,000. With estimated proved reserves of 8,000,000 barrels, the depletion rate is $7.50 per barrel (= $60,000,000/8,000,000). Depletion on the

1,200,000 barrels extracted during 1981 is $9,000,000 (= 1,200,000 × $7.50).

13.25 *Example 5* Assume that the full costing method was used by Texas Oil Company in 1981. The book value of the depletable property at the end of 1981 is $51,000,000 (= $60,000,000 − $9,000,000). During 1982, 1,500,000 barrels are extracted. Depletion for 1982 is $11,250,000 (= 1,500,000 × $7.50). The book value of the property at the end of 1982 is $39,750,000 (= $60,000,000 − $9,000,000 − $11,250,000).

13.26 *Example 6* Assume that during 1983 it is ascertained that the remaining proved reserves total only 4,500,000 barrels instead of the originally estimated 5,300,000 (= 8,000,000 − 1,200,000 − 1,500,000). This revision in proved reserves is considered a change in an accounting estimate which must be corrected during the current and future periods. A correction of prior years' depletion amounts is not permitted.* The revised depletion rate for 1983 is $8.83 per barrel (= $39,750,000/4,500,000). If 2,000,000 barrels are extracted during 1983, total depletion is $17,660,000 (= 2,000,000 × $8.83).

13.27 **Percentage Depletion** The Internal Revenue Code permits firms in some cases to calculate depletion using either the unit-of-production method or the percentage-depletion method. The percentage-depletion method is not permitted for financial reporting purposes. Percentage depletion is equal to a specified percentage times the sales revenue (defined in the Code as "gross income") from a depletable property. Percentage depletion may continue to be claimed even after the book value of depletable property has been reduced to zero. Percentage depletion is no longer permitted for most oil and gas producers, but for those small producers for whom it is permitted the percentage is currently 22 percent. The specified percentages for other natural resources range between 5 and 22 percent.

13.28 *Example 7* If Texas Oil Company sold 1,100,000 of the 1,200,000 barrels extracted

---

*Accounting Principles Board, *Opinion No. 20* (1971).

*Exhibit 13.1*
**Effects of Successful-Efforts Costing
and Full Costing on Financial Statements
of Texas Oil Company for the Year 1981**

| Balance Sheet | Successful-Efforts Costing | Full Costing |
|---|---|---|
| Crude Oil Inventory: | | |
| ($7,800,000/1,200,000) × 100,000 .......................... | $ 650,000 | — |
| ($9,000,000/1,200,000) × 100,000 .......................... | — | $ 750,000 |
| Depletable Natural Resources: | | |
| $28,000,000 − $4,200,000 .................................. | $ 23,800,000 | — |
| $60,000,000 − $9,000,000 .................................. | — | $51,000,000 |
| **Income Statement** | | |
| Sales (1,100,000 × $20) ................................... | $ 22,000,000 | $22,000,000 |
| Less Cost of Goods Sold: | | |
| ($7,800,000/1,200,000) × 1,100,000 ......................... | (7,150,000) | |
| ($9,000,000/1,200,000) × 1,100,000 ......................... | — | (8,250,000) |
| Gross Margin ............................................. | $ 14,850,000 | $13,750,000 |
| Less Acquisition and Exploration Costs from Unsuccessful Efforts | (32,000,000) | — |
| Less Production Costs on Crude Oil Extracted .................. | — | (3,600,000) |
| Income (Loss) before Other Expenses and Income Taxes ......... | $(17,150,000) | $10,150,000 |

during 1981 at a price of $20 per barrel, sales revenue would be $22,000,000. If it qualified for use of percentage depletion, a deduction of $4,840,000 (= .22 × $22,000,000) could be used in calculating taxable income for 1981.

## Effects of Successful-Efforts Costing and Full Costing on Financial Statements

13.29 Exhibit 13.1 summarizes the effects of successful-efforts costing and full costing on the financial statements of Texas Oil Company for 1981. It is assumed that 1,100,000 of the 1,200,000 barrels extracted are sold at a price of $20 per barrel.

13.30 The valuation of ending inventory of natural resources on the balance sheet will almost always be larger under full costing than under successful-efforts costing, because acquisition and exploration costs from unsuccessful exploration activities are treated as product costs under full costing. Partially offsetting this effect, however, is the treatment of production, or removal, costs as a period expense instead of as a product cost under full costing. The valuation of depletable property at the end of each period will usually be larger under full costing because of the capitalization of costs relating to unsuccessful efforts.

The two costing methods can have a sig- 13.31 nificant impact on the income statement and on the amount of net income for a period. Cost of goods sold differs between the two methods because different cost elements are included in product costs. Note that the acquisition and exploration costs of unsuccessful exploration activities are treated as a period expense under successful-efforts costing, whereas production (removal) costs are treated as a period expense under full costing. As is the case for Texas Oil Company, income under full costing usually exceeds income under successful-efforts costing, primarily because of the treatment of acquisition and exploration costs related to unsuccessful exploration efforts. In the example of Texas Oil Company, the ratio of unsuccessful to successful efforts was 2 to 1. In reality, the ratio ranges from 8 to 1 up to 15 to 1. Thus, income under full costing can be significantly higher than under successful-efforts costing.

## Journal Entries for Successful-Efforts Costing and Full Costing

13.32   Exhibit 13.2 presents the journal entries for 1980 and 1981 for Texas Oil Company under successful-efforts costing and full costing. Note the following:

1. Acquisition and exploration costs are debited to the Deferred Acquisition and Exploration Cost account when incurred. This account is classified either under "Property, Plant, and Equipment" or "Intangible Assets" on the balance sheet. Under successful-efforts costing, a separate account is maintained for each parcel of property. Under full costing, only one account need be maintained, because all three parcels of property are within one country.

2. When crude oil is discovered, the appropriate amount in the Deferred Acquisition and Exploration Cost account is transferred to the Depletable Natural Resources account. Under successful-efforts costing, the amount is the costs incurred on parcel B. Under full costing, the amount is the costs incurred on all three parcels. The acquisition and exploration costs incurred on parcel A and parcel C are treated as expenses under successful-efforts costing when the exploration process is abandoned.

3. Development costs are capitalized as part of the cost of the depletable natural resource under both methods.

4. Depletion for the year is debited to the Crude Oil Inventory account under both methods. This entry is similar to the treatment of depreciation on production equipment as part of the cost of manufactured inventories (that is, debit to Work-in-Process Inventory). Because the cost bases for depletion under successful-efforts costing and full costing are different, the amounts of depletion for the year are different.

5. Production costs are treated as a product cost under successful-efforts costing and as a period expense under full costing.

6. When revenue is recognized at the time of sale, the usual entries are made to record sales revenue and cost of goods sold.

## Reserve-Recognition Accounting

13.33   As discussed in Chapter 7, revenue is typically recognized at the time goods and services are sold. At this time, a buyer has been identified and an exchange price established. An assessment of the credit standing of the customer permits a reasonable estimate of the amount of cash that will be received. The costs of generating the revenue have either been incurred or future costs can be accurately estimated. Thus, the time of sale is the critical event in the earnings process. Costs incurred prior to the time of sale are treated as assets.

13.34   Some accountants argue that the time of sale is not the appropriate time to recognize revenue for oil, gas, and other natural resources. Instead, revenue should be recognized at the time that proved reserves are discovered. The theoretical rationale is summarized as follows:

1. The discovery of natural resources is the most significant event affecting the economic value of a firm involved in natural resource activities.

2. The earnings process of firms engaged in natural resource activities follows reasonably discrete steps (acquisition of property, exploration to determine the existence of proved reserves, development of site to permit extraction of proved reserves, extraction of proved reserves, sale of natural resources extracted). The time within this earnings process when natural resources are discovered can be easily identified. Costs associated with each of these discrete steps have either been incurred at the time of discovery or future costs can be estimated.

3. Given the demand for most natural resources, particularly oil and gas, the marketability of natural resources at prices at or above current levels is reasonably assured.

*Exhibit 13.2*

## Journal Entries for 1980 and 1981 for Texas Oil Company under Successful-Efforts Costing and Full Costing

| Transaction | Successful-Efforts Costing | | Full Costing | |
|---|---|---|---|---|
| **1.** Acquisition and Exploration Costs Incurred (1980) | Deferred Acquisition and Exploration Costs—Parcel A ...... 17,000,000<br>Deferred Acquisition and Exploration Costs—Parcel B ...... 8,000,000<br>Deferred Acquisition and Exploration Costs—Parcel C ...... 15,000,000<br>Cash ...... | 40,000,000 | Deferred Acquisition and Exploration Costs—Parcels A, B, and C ...... 40,000,000<br>Cash ...... | 40,000,000 |
| **2.** Discovery of Crude Oil on Parcel B (1981) | Depletable Natural Resource ...... 8,000,000<br>Deferred Acquisition and Development Costs—Parcel B ......<br>Acquisition and Exploration Expenses ...... 32,000,000<br>Deferred Acquisition and Exploration Costs—Parcel A ......<br>Deferred Acquisition and Exploration Costs—Parcel C ...... | 8,000,000<br><br><br>17,000,000<br>15,000,000 | Depletable Natural Resource ...... 40,000,000<br>Deferred Acquisition and Exploration Costs ...... | 40,000,000 |
| **3.** Development Costs Incurred (1981) | Depletable Natural Resource ...... 20,000,000<br>Cash ...... | 20,000,000 | Depletable Natural Resource ...... 20,000,000<br>Cash ...... | 20,000,000 |
| **4.** Depletion on Crude Oil Extracted (1981) | Inventory of Crude Oil ...... 4,200,000<br>Accumulated Depletion ...... | 4,200,000 | Inventory of Crude Oil ...... 9,000,000<br>Accumulated Depletion ...... | 9,000,000 |
| **5.** Production Costs Incurred (1981) | Inventory of Crude Oil ...... 3,600,000<br>Cash ...... | 3,600,000 | Production Expenses ...... 3,600,000<br>Cash ...... | 3,600,000 |
| **6.** Sale of Crude Oil (1981) | Cash ...... 22,000,000<br>Sales Revenue ......<br>Cost of Goods Sold ...... 7,150,000<br>Inventory of Crude Oil ......<br>[($4,200,000 + $3,600,000)/1,200,000)<br>× 1,100,000 = $7,150,000] | 22,000,000<br><br>7,150,000 | Cash ...... 22,000,000<br>Sales Revenue ......<br>Cost of Goods Sold ...... 8,250,000<br>Inventory of Crude Oil ......<br>($9,000,000/1,200,000)<br>× 1,100,000 = $8,250,000 | 22,000,000<br><br>8,250,000 |

*Exhibit 13.3*
**Valuation of Proved Reserves
of Texas Oil Company
at the Beginning of 1981**

| Year (1) | Barrels Expected to Be Sold (2) | Expected Net Cash Flows (3) | Present Value Factor at 10% [f] (4) | Present Value of Expected Cash Flows (5) |
|---|---|---|---|---|
| 1981 | — | $(20,000,000) | 1.00000 | $(20,000,000) |
| 1981 | 1,100,000 | 18,400,000[a] | .90909 | 16,727,256 |
| 1982 | 1,500,000 | 25,500,000[b] | .82645 | 21,074,475 |
| 1983 | 2,000,000 | 34,000,000[c] | .75131 | 25,544,540 |
| 1984 | 1,800,000 | 30,600,000[d] | .68301 | 20,900,106 |
| 1985 | 1,600,000 | 27,500,000[e] | .62092 | 17,075,300 |
| | 8,000,000 | | | $ 81,321,677 |

[a](1,100,000 × $20) − (1,200,000 × $3) = $18,400,000.
[b](1,500,000 × $20) − (1,500,000 × $3) = $25,500,000.
[c](2,000,000 × $20) − (2,000,000 × $3) = $34,000,000.
[d](1,800,000 × $20) − (1,800,000 × $3) = $30,600,000.
[e](1,600,000 × $20) − (1,500,000 × $3) = $27,500,000.
[f]See Table 2 at the end of the book.

13.35 Thus, it is argued, the criteria for revenue recognition are satisfied at the time of discovery.

13.36 *Reserve recognition accounting* is a method of accounting by which proved oil and gas reserves are recognized as assets and as income at the time of discovery. The SEC currently requires only the supplementary disclosure of information about proved oil and gas reserves using reserve recognition accounting.* The proved reserves are not formally recognized on the books as assets or as income under the SEC rules. The next section illustrates reserve recognition accounting according the the SEC's rules and shows the journal entries that would be made if proved reserves were formally recorded in the accounts.

13.37 **Reserve-Recognition Accounting Procedures** The procedures for applying the reserve-recognition method are summarized as follows:

**1.** Proved oil and gas reserves are recognized as assets and as income at the time of

*Accounting Series Release No. 253, SEC (1978).

discovery. The reserves are stated at the present value of the future cash inflows expected from the sale of such reserves net of future cash outflows for development and production costs *based on current economic conditions* (that is, current prices, costs, competitive conditions) and a discount rate of 10 percent.

**2.** Changes in the valuation of proved reserves after the time of discovery as a result of changed economic or technological conditions are added to (or subtracted from) the valuation of the asset and recognized as income (or loss).

**3.** All acquisition and exploration costs are recognized as expenses in the period incurred, regardless of whether they result in successful or unsuccessful exploration efforts.

13.38 *Example 8* Refer to the data for Texas Oil Company in Example 1. During 1981, 8,000,000 barrels of proved reserves are discovered on parcel B. Assume that these reserves are expected to be extracted and sold during the years 1981 through 1985 as shown in column (2) of Exhibit 13.3. Column (3) lists the expected future net cash flows from parcel B. Development costs of $20,000,000 will be incurred during 1981. To simplify the calculations of the present value of the cash flows, it is assumed that the development costs are incurred immediately at the time of discovery. The expected cash flows from selling the barrels are based on a current selling price of $20 per barrel. The cash outflow for production costs is based on the current cost of $3 a barrel (= $3,600,000/1,200,000 bbl). It is assumed that 100,000 more barrels will be extracted than will be sold each year except for 1985. To simplify the illustration, it is assumed that cash flows relating to sales and production costs occur at the end of each year. The net present value of the proved reserves at the time of discovery in 1981 is $81,321,677. The following journal entries would be made during 1980 and 1981 under the reserve-recognition accounting method:

```
1980
Acquisition and Exploration
    Expenses  ..............  40,000,000
    Cash  ................           40,000,000
To recognize acquisition and
exploration costs as ex-
penses of the period when
incurred.
```

```
1981
Proved Oil Reserves (asset) . 81,321,677
    Unrealized Income from
        Proved Oil Reserves
        (income)  ............        81,321,677
To recognize proved oil re-
serves as an asset and as
income at the time of discov-
ery.
```

```
1981
Proved Oil Reserves  ........ 20,000,000
    Cash  ................          20,000,000
To recognize development
costs incurred.
```

Exhibit 13.3 indicates that development costs are a *negative* element in the valuation of proved reserves. Once these costs have been incurred (and, therefore, removed from future cash flows), the valuation of proved reserves increases:

```
1981
Proved Reserves  ........... 10,132,168
    Interest Revenue  .......         10,132,168
To recognize interest revenue
for the increase in valuation
of proved reserves because
future cash flows are nearer,
$10,132,168 [= .10 ×
($81,321,677 + $20,000,000)].
```

```
1981
Proved Oil Reserves  ......... 3,600,000
    Cash  ..................         3,600,000
To recognize production cost
incurred in extracting
1,200,000 bbl of oil during
1981.
```

```
1981
Cash  ..................... 22,000,000
    Proved Oil Reserves  ....        22,000,000
To recognize sale of 1,100,000
bbl extracted during 1981 at
$20 per bbl.
```

13.39 Exhibit 13.4 presents an analysis of changes in the valuation of proved oil reserves during 1981 to 1985. Income for 1981 includes the unrealized income from proved reserves of $81,321,677 and interest revenue of $10,132,168. Income during the years 1982 to 1985 only includes interest revenue.

## Disclosure of Information Regarding Natural Resources

13.40 While the FASB is studying the accounting for oil and gas activities, the SEC has ruled that companies should continue to use either successful efforts or full costing in preparing their financial statements. The SEC has expressed concern, however, that these accounting methods, which are based on historical cost data, do not accurately reflect the assets and income of oil and gas activities. The SEC feels that information about the economic value of proved reserves is useful and should be disclosed in notes to the financial statements. Until the FASB completes its study of oil and gas accounting and requires some form of supplementary

*Exhibit 13.4*
**Valuation of Proved Reserves
for Texas Oil Company**

| Year (1) | Valuation at Beginning of Year (2) | Interest Revenue (3) | Development Costs (4) | Production Costs (5) | Sales Revenue (6) | Valuation at End of Year (7) |
|---|---|---|---|---|---|---|
| 1981 ........ | $81,321,677 | $10,132,168 | $20,000,000 | $3,600,000 | $22,000,000 | $93,053,845 |
| 1982 ........ | 93,053,845 | 9,305,385 | — | 4,500,000 | 30,000,000 | 76,859,230 |
| 1983 ........ | 76,859,230 | 7,685,923 | — | 6,000,000 | 40,000,000 | 50,545,153 |
| 1984 ........ | 50,545,153 | 5,054,515 | — | 5,400,000 | 36,000,000 | 24,999,668 |
| 1985 ........ | 24,999,668 | 2,500,332[a] | — | 4,500,000 | 32,000,000 | — |

[a]Does not equal .10 × $24,999,668 due to rounding of present value factors.
(2) = (7) of previous period.
(3) = .10 × (2), except for 1981.
(4), (5), (6) given.
(7) = (2) + (3) + (4) + (5) − (6).

disclosure of proved reserves, companies are required to report certain supplementary information about proved reserves following reserve recognition accounting. The following information must be disclosed.*

1. Quantities and annual changes in quantities of proved oil and gas reserves.

2. Costs incurred in exploration, development, and production activities.

3. Capitalized costs relating to oil- and gas-producing activities.

4. Historical information on cash flow and value of transfers from producing oil and gas.

5. Cash flow and value of transfers from estimated future production of proved oil and gas reserves, calculated on the basis of current economic conditions.

6. Present value of cash flows from estimated future production of proved oil and gas reserves using a 10-percent discount rate.

# Accounting for Intangible Assets

## Definition of Intangible Assets

13.41    Accountants have had difficulty developing a precise definition of an intangible asset.

_____
*Accounting Series Release No. 253, SEC (1978).*

Accounting Principles Board *Opinion No. 17* is devoted entirely to intangibles, but never defines the term. Some accountants define intangible assets as resources that lack physical existence. Accounts receivable and prepayments, however, lack physical existence but are not considered intangible assets. Other accountants include as intangible assets those resources for which the existence and timing of future benefits are difficult to observe and verify. Copyrights and trademarks fit into this definition and are usually considered intangible assets.

13.42    Most accountants simply resort to a listing of resources that are considered intangible assets, recognizing that the items included do not have common characteristics. Included among intangible assets might be copyrights, patents, trademarks, goodwill, organization costs, franchises, leaseholds, and similar items. The characteristics underlying these intangibles vary in the following ways:

**Identifiability** Some intangible assets, such as copyrights and franchises, are separately identifiable, whereas others, such as goodwill, represent a combination of factors or attributes that cannot be separately identified.

**Separability** Some intangible assets, such as patents, can be sold by the firm, whereas others, such as organization costs and goodwill, cannot be severed, or sold. They have significance only when considered in relation with other assets.

**Manner of Acquisition** Some intangible assets are developed internally, whereas others are acquired in an external market transaction.

**Expected Period of Benefit** Some intangible assets, such as copyrights and patents, have a legally defined limited life, whereas others, such as trademarks and organization costs, have an indefinite life.

## Accounting Valuation and Measurement Issues

13.43    The general principles relating to the capitalization of costs discussed in Chapter 5 are particularly difficult to apply in the case of intangibles. The inability to observe the physical existence of most intangibles makes it difficult to ascertain whether a particular expenditure is made for benefits received during the current period (an expense) or for benefits to be received in future periods (an asset). Also, the inability to observe the consumption of benefits over time makes the allocation of costs to the periods of benefit an arbitrary process. An even more difficult decision is whether benefits are actually being consumed over time (requiring amortization of the intangible asset) or whether the asset sustains itself (as, perhaps, with organization costs or goodwill). The application of the general principles of cost capitalization and asset amortization to intangible assets, therefore, can be subjective.

13.44    Generally accepted accounting principles* distinguish between intangible assets that are specifically identifiable and those that are not and between intangible assets developed internally by a firm and those purchased externally.

13.45    **1.** *Specifically Identifiable and Internally Developed* Costs incurred internally in developing specifically identifiable intangible assets (for example, trademarks, trade names, copyrights) can either be capitalized and subsequently amortized (over a period not exceeding 40 years) or expensed when incurred. A major exception involves expenditures on research and development (discussed later in this chapter), which must be expensed when incurred in almost all cases.

13.46    **2.** *Specifically Identifiable and Externally Acquired* The cost of specifically identifiable intangible assets acquired from another firm or individual must be capitalized as an asset. The cost should be amortized over the expected period of benefit (but not more than 40 years).

13.47    **3.** *Not Specifically Identifiable and Internally Developed* The cost of developing good customer relations, a reputation for quality products and services, and other elements of goodwill must be expensed when incurred.

13.48    **4.** *Not Specifically Identifiable and Externally Acquired* The excess of the purchase price for a group of assets (as when one company acquires another company) over the market values of identifiable tangible and intangible assets is considered goodwill. The excess cost must be capitalized as goodwill and amortized over the expected period of benefit (but not more than 40 years).

13.49    The requirements that costs incurred in acquiring intangible assets externally be capitalized and that costs incurred internally for research and development and goodwill development be expensed when incurred eliminate the need to decide whether a particular expenditure is for benefits already received or for benefits to be received in future periods. The requirement that all costs capitalized be amortized over the expected period of benefit, but not more than 40 years, eliminates the need to decide whether a particular intangible has a definite or indefinite life. The requirement that the straight-line (time) method of amortization be used (unless another systematic method is more appropriate given the pattern of benefits) largely eliminates the need to select an amortization

---

*Accounting Principles Board, *Opinion No. 17* (August 1970); and Financial Accounting Standards Board, *Statement of Financial Accounting Standards No. 2* (1974).

method. Thus, much of the subjectivity in the valuation of intangible assets and the amortization of capitalized costs has been removed by the enactment of rules lacking theoretical justification.

13.50    Generally accepted accounting principles for intangible assets have been criticized as follows:

**1.** The costs incurred in developing some intangible assets internally (for example, a patent resulting from research and development expenditures) must be expensed when incurred, whereas the cost incurred in acquiring intangibles in external market transactions must be capitalized and amortized. Thus, a firm that purchases a patent from another firm or individual will report the patent as an asset on its balance sheet. Another firm owning an equally valuable patent developed internally will not show the patent on its balance sheet and will have reported higher expenses.

**2.** The requirement that research and development costs incurred internally in developing intangible assets be expensed when incurred fails to recognize the economic nature of these costs. Expenditures are made on research and development primarily for the future benefits a firm expects to realize. Assigning a zero valuation to these potential benefits results in an understatement of assets on the balance sheet. Also, it fails to distinguish firms that are successful from those that are not successful in research activity. The arguments for capitalizing costs incurred for wide-ranging research and development efforts with occasional success are identical with those for capitalizing the cost of unsuccessful efforts under the full costing method for natural resource activities.

**3.** The requirement that all intangibles capitalized as assets be amortized (that is, all purchased intangibles plus internally developed, specifically identifiable intangibles for which a firm chooses to capitalize the costs) replaces professional judgment with an arbitrary rule. Whether or not amortization is appropriate depends on the particular circumstances in each case. In some cases, the facts might indicate that the value of the intangible is being maintained or increased. In such cases, amortization is not appropriate. In other cases, the useful life may be determinable and amortization over the estimated period of benefit is appropriate. In all cases, professional judgment instead of arbitrary rules should guide the amortization of intangibles.

**4.** The selection of 40 years as the maximum amortization period is arbitrary and lacks theoretical justification.

13.51    The pronouncements on intangible assets reflect the judgment of standard-setting bodies that objectivity, verifiability, and uniformity are more important in generating useful financial statements than granting firms discretion in setting capitalization and amortization policies.

## Accounting for Specific Intangible Assets

13.52    The accounting for specific intangibles is discussed in the sections that follow.

13.53    **Research and Development Costs** Financial Accounting Standards Board *Statement No. 2* establishes the required accounting for research and development costs incurred by a firm. "Research" and "development" are defined as follows:

*Research* is planned search or critical investigation aimed at discovery of new knowledge with the hope that such knowledge will be useful in developing a new product or service . . . or a new process or technique . . . or in bringing about a significant improvement to an existing product or process.

*Development* is the translation of research findings or other knowledge into a plan or design for a new product or process or for a significant improvement to an existing product or process whether intended for sale or use. It includes the conceptual formulation, design, and testing of product alternatives, construction of prototypes, and operation of pilot plants. It does not include routine or periodic alterations to existing products, production lines, manufacturing processes, and other ongoing operations even though those alterations may represent improvements and it does not include market research or market testing activities.*

13.54    Excluded from research and development activity according to *Statement No. 2* are research and development activities conducted for others under a contractual arrangement (which are accounted for like other long-term contracts) and exploration and development activities by firms involved in extractive industries (discussed earlier in this chapter).

13.55    Research and development costs that must be charged to expense when incurred include the following elements:

1. Materials, equipment, and facilities— The cost of materials, equipment, and facilities acquired or constructed for research and development activities that have no alternative future use beyond their use in a particular research and development project are considered research and development costs at the time the costs are incurred. The cost of materials, equipment, and facilities that are acquired or constructed for research and development activities and that have alternative future uses in research and development products or otherwise should be capitalized when acquired. The cost of materials consumed and depreciation on equipment and facilities used are included in research and development costs.

2. Personnel—Salaries, wages, and related costs of personnel engaged in research and development activities are included in research and development costs.

3. Intangibles purchased from others—The cost of patents and other intangibles purchased from others that have alternative future uses in research and development products or otherwise should be capitalized and amortized. The amortization of those intangibles is included in research and development costs. If the purchased intangibles have no alternative future use beyond their

use in a particular research and development project, their cost is included in research and development cost at the time the cost is incurred.

4. Contract services—The cost of services performed by others in connection with research and development activities of an enterprise is included in research and development cost when incurred.

5. Indirect costs—Research and development costs include a reasonable allocation of indirect costs. However, general and administrative costs that are not clearly related to research and development activities should not be included in research and development costs.

All costs that are defined as "research and 13.56 development costs" are treated as an expense in the period in which the costs are incurred. The amount charged to expense each period should be disclosed in the financial statements or notes.

**Patents** A *patent* is a right granted by the 13.57 federal government to exclude others from manufacturing, using, or selling a claimed design, product, or plan or from using a claimed process or method of manufacture for a period of 17 years. Just because a firm has received a patent, however, is no guarantee that the patent has any economic value or that the useful life of the patent will last 17 years. If a process is not useful, it will have no economic value. If a product does not meet with consumer acceptance, it will have no economic value. A patent may be superseded by the development of another product or process that is more economical, efficient, or otherwise advantageous. Finally, a patent granted by the U.S. Patent Office may be withdrawn if the firm receiving the patent is unable to defend itself successfully against patent infringement suits.

Financial Accounting Standards Board 13.58 *Statement No. 2* requires that research and development costs incurred internally to develop products or processes that ultimately become patented be expensed when incurred. Thus, the only patents that appear among intangible assets on the balance sheet

---

*Financial Accounting Standards Board, *Statement of Financial Accounting Standards No. 2* (1974).

are those purchased externally. They are reported at amortized acquisition cost.

13.59   The cost of a purchased patent includes, in addition to the price paid for the patent, any government fees, attorneys' fees, and other costs incurred in its acquisition. The cost of a lawsuit resulting in the successful defense of the patent should also be capitalized, because such suits establish the legal rights of the owner. The cost of an unsuccessful lawsuit, along with any amounts previously capitalized for the patent, should be expensed in the period in which the court decision is rendered.

13.60   All amounts capitalized for a patent should be amortized over the expected useful life of the patent. In rapidly growing technological industries, this useful life may be as short as 4 or 5 years. In other cases, the useful life may be the full 17 years. The straight-line (time) method of amortization is normally used. If a patent has a cost of $20,000 and a 4-year expected useful life, the entry at the end of each year is

```
Patent Amortization Expense or Work-
  in-Process Inventory .............. 5,000
    Accumulated Amortization ........     5,000
To record patent amortization as either a
period expense (patent on selling or ad-
ministrative facilities) or a product cost
(patent on manufacturing facilities, pro-
cesses, or products)
```

The SEC requires the separate disclosure of the cost and accumulated amortization of intangible assets. The disclosures may be made either in the financial statements or in the notes.*

13.61   If it is decided that a patent has a shorter or longer useful life than initially anticipated, a change in the amortization period is required. This change in useful life is considered a change in an *accounting estimate*. The book value of the patent at the time of the change must be amortized over the remaining expected useful life. An adjustment of amortization expense of prior years is not permitted.†

**Copyrights**   A *copyright* gives the holder   13.62 certain rights to published material. The copyright period is equal to the life of its creator plus 50 years. If the copyright is held by a firm, then the life is 75 years from first publication. Copyrights, like patents, can be sold or assigned to others.

The costs of copyrights developed inter-   13.63 nally by a firm can either be capitalized and then amortized or treated as an expense when incurred. The costs of copyrights purchased from another firm or individual must be capitalized and then amortized.

The amortization period for a copyright is   13.64 its expected useful life. For most literary works, the expected useful life is significantly shorter than the legal life of the copyright. Even for certain classic books, songs, and other compositions, where the useful life may extend for the full legal life of the copyright, the maximum amortization period for accounting purposes is 40 years.** Amortization using the straight-line (time) method is normally used.

**Franchises**   As discussed in Chapter 8,   13.65 many consumer products are now marketed through franchises. The franchisee normally pays an initial franchise fee for the right to use the franchisor's name, sell its products, and benefit from advertising carried out by the franchisor.‡ In addition, periodic fees are paid by the franchisee for goods or services purchased from the franchisor.

At the time a franchise is acquired by a   13.66 franchisee, the initial franchise fee should be capitalized as an asset stated at the present value of the payments to be made. For example, assume that a franchise is acquired for an initial franchise fee of $30,000. The franchisee pays $5,000 immediately and signs a note agreeing to pay the remainder over 5 years plus interest at 10 percent. The 10-percent rate is considered a reasonable borrowing rate for the franchisee. (See the

---

*Accounting Series Release No. 280, SEC (1980).
†Accounting Principles Board, *Opinion No. 20* (July 1971).

---

**Accounting Principles Board, *Opinion No. 17* (August 1970).
‡McDonald's is the franchisor. The local owner is the franchisee.

discussion of interest imputation in Chapter 8 for the accounting when the stated interest rate is considered an unreasonable borrowing rate.) The following entry is made:

| | | |
|---|---|---|
| Franchise ...................... 30,000 | | |
| Cash ...................... | 5,000 | |
| Note Payable ................ | 25,000 | |

13.67 The franchise should be amortized over the expected period of benefit. As with patents and copyrights, this period may be shorter than the legal life of the franchise. Some franchises, called *perpetual franchises,* have an unlimited life. In these cases, the maximum amortization period allowed is 40 years.

13.68 **Operating Rights** An operating right is a permit issued by a governmental agency allowing a firm to conduct business in a certain specified geographical area. Because only a limited number of operating rights are usually granted in each such geographical area, the operating right has future benefits and is considered an asset. Operating rights may be acquired directly by a firm from a governmental agency or acquired indirectly when another firm holding such operating rights is purchased.

13.69 In the past, the Interstate Commerce Commission issued operating rights to interstate motor carriers to transport specified commodities over specified routes with limited competition. The cost of these operating rights was usually treated as an asset and amortized as appropriate.*

13.70 The Motor Carrier Act of 1980, however, eliminated most of the benefits of operating rights. The Act provides for easier entry into the motor carrier industry by new carriers and for easier route expansion by existing carriers. Most restrictions on routes and commodities that could be carried were removed. Thus, it is questionable whether operating rights have future benefits justifying their continued recognition as assets.

13.71 FASB *Statement No. 44*† stipulates that the unamortized cost of interstate operating rights of motor carriers be immediately charged to income. If the criteria of APB *Opinion No. 30* are met, these costs may be treated as an extraordinary item in the income statement. The immediate write-off of such unamortized costs reflects the Board's view that any future benefits of operating rights are now too uncertain to justify their recognition as an asset.

**Leaseholds and Leasehold Improvements** 13.72 A *lease* is a contractual agreement between a lessor and a lessee in which the lessor agrees to let the lessee use a particular piece of property for a specified period of time.** The lessee must make periodic lease payments. As discussed more fully in Chapter 18, leases may be of three general types: **(1)** short-term operating leases, **(2)** long-term operating leases, and **(3)** long-term capital leases.

13.73 Short-term operating leases, such as for rental of an automobile or temporary office facilities, present few accounting problems. Lease payments are treated as expenses in the period when the rental services are received. Amounts paid in advance are treated as prepayments and included among current assets on the balance sheet.

13.74 Long-term *capital* leases involve lease arrangements in which the lessee is essentially making an installment purchase of the property. If certain conditions are met and a particular lease is classified as a "capital lease," then both the leased asset and a lease liability must be recognized by the lessee. The leased asset is depreciated over the life of the lease.

13.75 There are some long-term leases that do not meet the criteria for being classified as long-term capital leases. For example, a firm might sign a lease to occupy several floors in a large office building for a period of 20 years or more. Such leases, treated as long-term operating leases, often require the lessee to

---

*Operating rights acquired after October 31, 1970, the effective date of APB *Opinion No. 17,* were amortized over a maximum period of 40 years. Operating rights acquired before this date were typically not amortized.

†Financial Accounting Standards Board, *Statement of Financial Accounting Standards No. 44* (1980).

**The lessor is the landlord; the lessee is the tenant.

make substantial payments at the inception of the lease in addition to any other periodic payments. This initial payment is for an asset known as a *leasehold*. For example, if a public accounting or law firm rented several floors of an office building for a 20-year period and paid $1 million upon signing of the lease, the following entry would be made:

```
Leasehold ................... 1,000,000
    Cash  ..................         1,000,000
```

Assuming that this expenditure is not merely a rental deposit, the $1 million payment must be amortized over the period of the lease much the same as the initial franchise fee is amortized over the life of the franchise. If the rental period exceeds 40 years, the maximum amortization period is 40 years.

13.76   Firms renting facilities under long-term operating leases often make changes to the leased premises. For example, new walls or partitions, carpets, lights, or other items may be installed. Buildings or other structures may be constructed on leased land. Most lease agreements state that any improvements made to the leased property become the property of the lessor at the completion of the lease. Leasehold improvements should be capitalized and amortized over the shorter of the life of the improvement or the life of the lease. If the lease has a renewal option and the likelihood of renewal is high, then the renewal period should be considered in determining the amortization period. If the probability of renewal is uncertain, then only the initial lease period should be considered in determining the amortization period. In no case may the amortization period exceed 40 years.

13.77   Leaseholds and leasehold improvements are sometimes classified under "Property, Plant, and Equipment," instead of under "Intangible Assets," on the balance sheet.

13.78   **Trademarks and Trade Names** A *trademark* or *trade name* is a word or symbol affixed to a product, its package, or its dispenser, which uniquely identifies the firm's products and services. A *trademark right* or a *trade name right* is a right to exclude competitors from using words or symbols that may be confusingly similar to the firm's trademarks or trade names. Trademarks and trade names can be registered with the federal government. Registrations last 20 years and are renewable as long as the trademark or trade name is being used. Trademark and trade name rights, on the other hand, derive their legal status from common law, which holds that the rights continue to accrue to the firm as long as it continues to use the trademark or trade name.* Thus, trademark and trade name rights have an infinite life.

13.79   The economic value of most trademark and trade name rights is created over time as a result of providing quality products and services, conducting effective advertising, and similar activities. The cost of such activities can be either capitalized and amortized or expensed when incurred. Because of the difficulties in deciding which portion of advertising and similar expenditures is for current benefits and which portion is for future benefits, almost all firms expense these costs in the period incurred. Trademark rights or trade name rights purchased from others must be capitalized. Even though trademark and trade name rights have an indefinite life as long as they continue to be used, their cost must be amortized over their expected useful life up to a maximum period of 40 years.

13.80   **Organization Costs** A newly formed corporation will usually incur legal, accounting, administrative, and other costs in obtaining its corporate charter and organizing its activities. These costs can either be expensed when incurred or capitalized and amortized

---

*The name "thermos bottle" used to be a trade name. Its owner did not vigorously pursue its rights, and gradual use of this name by others has made the term generic, available to all. Kimberly-Clark takes pains to protect its trademark, "Kleenex," from use by others, as does The Coca Cola Company with the name "Coke." In recent years, the Federal Trade Commission has attempted, without success, to argue that "Formica" and "ReaLemon" should now, for various reasons, be treated as generic names, available to anyone.

over subsequent periods. Even though organization costs have an indefinite life as long as the corporation remains in existence, the maximum amortization period is 40 years. Organization costs can be amortized in income tax returns over a 5-year period, so that period is also frequently used for amortization in the financial records.

13.81    Some newly organized firms have an extended development stage before any revenues are generated. For example, a firm may engage in research and development activity for several years before a commercially feasible product is developed. A firm may search for natural resources for several years before recoverable reserves are located, extracted, and sold. Such firms are considered "development-stage enterprises."

13.82    An important accounting question is whether costs incurred by development-stage companies should be capitalized when incurred and subsequently matched against revenues generated or whether the costs should be treated as an expense in the period incurred. Financial Accounting Standards Board *Statement No. 7* requires that the financial statements of development-stage companies be prepared in conformance with generally accepted accounting principles applicable to established operating firms. Thus, research and development costs incurred by a development-stage company must be treated as an expense in the period when the costs are incurred even though there may be no revenues against which the costs can be matched. Costs incurred by a development-stage company engaged in natural resource exploration can be accounted for using either the successful-efforts costing method or the full costing method.

13.83    The financial statements of a development-stage company must clearly disclose that the firm's activities are developmental and that the financial statements are for a development-stage company.

**Goodwill**    *Goodwill* is considered by APB 13.84 *Opinion No. 17* to be an intangible asset that is not specifically identifiable, has an indeterminate life, is inherent in a continuing business, and relates to a firm as a whole. All costs incurred by a firm in developing, 13.85 maintaining, or restoring goodwill must be treated as an expense in the period incurred.

Goodwill is recognized for accounting purposes only when one firm acquires the common stock or assets of another firm in a business combination accounted for using the purchase method (discussed in advanced financial accounting principles texts). The price paid for the acquired company will in many cases exceed the market value of the specifically identifiable tangible and intangible assets acquired. This excess is considered goodwill. The excess amount paid might be attributable to the acquired firm's reputation for quality products or services, its superior managerial talent, its well-trained labor force, or other factors.*

Goodwill is initially recorded at the excess 13.86 price paid. Even though goodwill has an indeterminate useful life, it must be amortized under generally accepted accounting principles over a period not exceeding 40 years. Goodwill amortization is not, however, deductible in computing taxable income each year.

--------

*Calculating the price to be paid for another company is a topic discussed in finance textbooks.

## Questions and Short Cases

13.1    Review the meaning of the following concepts or terms discussed in this chapter.
   a. Natural resources, or wasting assets.
   b. Acquisition, exploration, development, and product costs for natural resources.
   c. Successful-efforts costing.
   d. Full costing.
   e. Unit-of-production depletion method.
   f. Percentage depletion method.
   g. Reserve-recognition (discovery-value) accounting.
   h. Proved reserves.

i.  Intangible assets.
j.  Specifically identifiable, internally developed intangible assets.
k.  Specifically identifiable, externally purchased intangible assets.
l.  Not specifically identifiable, internally developed intangible assets.
m. Not specifically identifiable, externally purchased intangible assets.
n.  Research and development costs.

o.  Patent.
p.  Copyright.
q.  Franchise.
r.  Leasehold.
s.  Leasehold improvement.
t.  Trademark and trade name.
u.  Trademark right and trade name right.
v.  Organization costs.
w.  Development-stage enterprise.
x.  Goodwill.

**13.2**   "The distinction between successful efforts and full costing relates to the definition of the accounting unit." Explain.

**13.3**   Discuss the theoretical rationale for the following:
   a.  Successful-efforts costing.
   b.  Full costing.

**13.4**   Indicate whether each of the following statements more accurately describes successful-efforts costing or full costing for extractive industries.
   a.  This method results in the smallest cumulative net income.
   b.  This method usually results in the largest valuation of ending inventory of natural resources.
   c.  This method results in the largest amount of depletion per unit (barrel, ton) of natural resources extracted.
   d.  This method results in the earliest recognition of production (removal) costs as an expense.
   e.  This method results in the smallest book value for depletable property on the balance sheet.

**13.5**   *Accounting Series Release No. 258* of the SEC places an upper limit on the amount of costs that can be capitalized under full costing. Standard-setting bodies have not placed a similar upper limit in the case of successful-efforts costing. Suggest reasons for this differential treatment.

**13.6**   *Accounting Series Release No. 258* of the SEC requires that production (removal) costs be expensed when incurred under full costing, whereas FASB *Statement No. 19* requires that such costs be treated as product costs under successful-efforts costing. Suggest reasons for this differential treatment.

**13.7**   "Depreciation for a period may appropriately be debited to Depreciation Expense in some cases, but depletion for a period should never be debited to Depletion Expense." Explain.

**13.8**   Distinguish between cost depletion and percentage depletion, both as to the basis for depletion and the calculations made.

**13.9**   "Percentage depletion is inconsistent with historical-cost accounting." Explain.

**13.10**   Revenue is normally recognized at the time goods are sold or services are rendered. What justification can you suggest for recognizing revenue earlier than the time of sale in natural resource industries?

**13.11** Define reserve-recognition accounting. To which of the asset-valuation methods in Chapter 5 does revenue-recognition accounting most closely relate? Explain.

**13.12** Under reserve-recognition accounting, proved reserves are recorded at the present value of the future cash inflows from selling natural resources net of the future cash outflows for development and production costs. What is the theoretical rationale for netting cash outflows for development and production against cash inflows from sales?

**13.13** "The controversy regarding successful-efforts costing versus full costing is of no consequence when reserve-recognition accounting is used." Explain.

**13.14** Distinguish among amortization, depreciation, and depletion.

**13.15** Summarize generally accepted accounting principles for each of the following types of intangibles:
a. Specifically identifiable and internally developed.
b. Specifically identifiable and externally acquired.
c. Not specifically identifiable and internally developed.
d. Not specifically identifiable and externally acquired.

**13.16** What is the justification under generally accepted accounting principles for treating intangibles developed internally differently from intangibles purchased in external market transactions?

**13.17** What is the justification under generally accepted accounting principles for treating specifically identifiable, internally developed intangibles differently from internally developed intangibles that are not specifically identifiable?

**13.18** Research and development costs must be expensed when incurred. Describe the theoretical strengths and weaknesses of this accounting treatment.

**13.19** "Requiring all firms to treat research and development costs as an expense in the period incurred may result in less, instead of more, comparability between the financial statements of various firms." Explain.

**13.20** Indicate whether or not each of the following costs should be included in research and development costs according to the definitions in FASB *Statement No. 2:*
a. Cost of laboratory research aimed at discovering new knowledge.
b. Design and engineering costs related to the relocation of equipment within a plant.
c. Construction of a pilot plant that is not of sufficient scale to make production commercially feasible.
d. Cost of a market survey to determine consumer acceptability of a new product.
e. Legal costs in connection with a patent application.
f. Cost of testing preproduction prototypes of a new product.

**13.21** Intangible assets differ in the following dimensions:
(1) Some are specifically identifiable, whereas others are not.
(2) Some can be sold by a firm, whereas others cannot be severed from the firm as a whole.
(3) Some have definite lives, whereas some have indefinite lives.
With respect to each of the three dimensions above, classify each of the following intangibles:
a. Patents.                          c. Franchises.
b. Copyrights.                       d. Leaseholds.

e. Leasehold improvements.
f. Trademark and trade name rights.

g. Organization costs.
h. Goodwill.

**13.22** What is the maximum period over which the following costs can be recognized as an expense?

a. A 4-year old patent purchased from its creator and owner.

b. A leasehold improvement with an estimated useful life of 10 years. The lease has 8 years remaining and no renewal option.

c. Same as part **b**, except that the lease has 14 years remaining and no renewal option.

d. Research and development costs.

e. Organization costs.

f. A copyright purchased from the estate of its creator. The creator died 2 years ago.

g. Same as part **f**, except that the creator died 15 years ago.

h. Goodwill.

i. A trade name of a product acquired from another firm in a business combination.

j. Initial franchise fee paid for perpetual franchise rights.

**13.23** "Specifically identifiable, internally developed intangible assets are more similar to tangible assets than they are to intangible assets that are not specifically identifiable and internally developed, such as goodwill." Do you agree? Why or why not?

**13.24** In 1981, Epstein Company acquired the assets of Falk Company. The assets of Falk Company included various intangibles. Discuss the accounting for the acquisition in 1981 and in later years for each of the items described below.

a. Epstein Company has a registered trademark on "Thyrom" for thyristors. Epstein Company thought that the trademark had a fair market value of $60,000. It expects to continue making and selling Thyrom thyristors indefinitely.

b. The design patent covering the ornamentation of the containers for displaying Thyrom thyristors expires in 5 years. The Epstein Company thought that the design patent had a fair market value of $20,000 and expects to continue making the containers indefinitely.

c. An unpatented trade secret on a special material used in manufacturing thyristors was viewed as having a fair market value of $250,000.

d. Refer to the trade secret in part c. Suppose that in 1982 a competitor discovers the trade secret but does not disclose the secret to other competitors. How should the plans for accounting be changed?

e. During 1981, the Epstein Company produced a sales promotion film, *Using Thyristors for Fun and Profit*, at a cost of $25,000. The film is licensed to purchasers of thyristors for use in training their employees and customers. The film is copyrighted.

**13.25** Respond to Question 2.19 in Chapter 2.

## Problems and Exercises

**13.26** Utah Copper Company was organized during January 1981. The company is engaged in exploring, mining, and selling copper. The successful-efforts method of costing is used. Record the following transactions of Utah Copper Company for 1981 and 1982.

(1) During 1981, acquisition and exploration costs of $600,000 were incurred on site A and paid in cash. In addition, depreciation on equipment used in exploration totaled $100,000.

(2) During 1981, acquisition and exploration costs of $800,000 were incurred on site B and paid in cash. In addition, depreciation on equipment used in exploration totaled $200,000.

*Exhibit 13.5*
**Louisiana Petroleum Company Operating
Data for 1981 through 1986**

| | 1981 | 1982 | 1983 | 1984 | 1985 | 1986 |
|---|---|---|---|---|---|---|
| Acquisition and Exploration Costs: | | | | | | |
| Parcel A ........... | $17,250,000 | $ 750,000 | — | — | — | — |
| Parcel B ........... | 25,000,000 | 10,000,000 | — | — | — | — |
| Development Costs: | | | | | | |
| Parcel A ............. | — | 7,000,000 | — | — | — | — |
| Production Costs ........ | — | 500,000 | $1,250,000 | $2,250,000 | $3,000,000 | $1,500,000 |
| Barrels Discovered ....... | — | 5,000,000 | — | — | — | — |
| Barrels Extracted ........ | — | 500,000 | 1,000,000 | 1,500,000 | 1,500,000 | 500,000 |
| Barrels Sold ............. | — | 450,000 | 1,000,000 | 1,500,000 | 1,500,000 | 550,000 |
| Selling Price per Barrel ... | $22 | $23 | $24 | $25 | $26 | $27 |

(3) On January 2, 1982, copper was discovered on site A. It is estimated that the site contains 25,000,000 pounds of copper. Exploration efforts on site B were immediately discontinued.

(4) During 1982, development costs of $300,000 were incurred on site A and paid in cash. In addition, depreciation on equipment used in the development work totaled $100,000.

(5) During 1982, production costs of $600,000 were incurred in extracting 2,000,000 pounds of copper.

(6) During 1982, 1,600,000 pounds of copper were sold for $1.10 per pound.

**13.27** Louisiana Petroleum Company was organized during March 1981 to search, extract, and sell crude oil. Exploration rights were acquired on two parcels of land (parcel A and parcel B) in Louisiana in April 1981. Exploration work began soon thereafter and continued into early 1982. Oil was discovered on parcel A during January 1982, and the search process was abandoned on parcel B. Operating data for 1981 through 1986 are summarized in Exhibit 13.5. All costs are paid in cash. A FIFO cost-flow assumption is used.

a. Calculate the amount of income before other expenses and income taxes for each of the years 1981 through 1986 using successful-efforts costing.

b. Repeat part **a** using full costing.

c. Calculate the amount shown on the balance sheet at the end of each year for Crude Oil Inventory, Deferred Acquisition and Exploration Costs, and Depletable Natural Resources (net) under successful-efforts costing.

d. Repeat part **c** using full costing.

**13.28** Refer to the data in the preceding problem for Louisiana Petroleum Company. Calculate the amount of income before other expenses and income taxes for 1981 and 1982, using reserve-recognition accounting as prescribed by *Accounting Series Release No. 253*. Assume that all cash flows occur at the end of each year. Keep in mind that the valuation of proved reserves must be based on current selling prices and current production costs.

**13.29** Oklahoma Oil and Gas Company began a search for oil off of the coast of Texas early in 1981. Acquisition and exploration costs incurred totaled $6,000,000 during 1981 and $3,000,000 during 1982. Oil was discovered on July 1, 1982. Recoverable reserves were estimated to be 3,000,000 barrels. Assume that development costs of $6,000,000 were incurred immediately on July 1, 1982. The current selling price per barrel of oil is $20. The firm anticipates that production costs to remove the oil from the ground will be $6 a barrel and paid in cash as incurred. The proved reserves are expected to be extracted and sold evenly over the years 1983 through 1988 as follows:

| | |
|---|---|
| 1983 ............................. | 300,000 bbl |
| 1984 ............................. | 500,000 bbl |
| 1985 ............................. | 600,000 bbl |
| 1986 ............................. | 600,000 bbl |
| 1987 ............................. | 600,000 bbl |
| 1988 ............................. | 400,000 bbl |

a. Calculate the valuation of proved reserves on July 1, 1982, under reserve-recognition accounting according to *Accounting Series Release No. 253*.
b. Give the journal entries under the reserve-recognition accounting method for 1981, 1982, and 1983.
c. Early in January 1984, the selling price of oil increases to $22 a barrel, the production costs increase to $7 a barrel, and the estimate of proved reserves is decreased by 100,000 barrels. Thus, during 1988, 300,000 barrels instead of 400,000 will be sold. Describe how this information would be reflected in the financial statements under reserve-recognition accounting.

13.30   (Adapted from CPA Examination.) On July 1, 1981, Miller Mining, a calendar-year corporation, purchased the rights to a copper mine. Of the total purchase price, $2,800,000 was appropriately allocable to the copper. Estimated reserves were 800,000 tons of copper. Miller Mining expects to extract and sell 10,000 tons of copper per month. Production began immediately. The selling price is $25 per ton. Miller Mining uses percentage depletion (15 percent) for income tax purposes.

To aid production, Miller Mining also purchased some new equipment on July 1, 1981. The equipment cost $76,000 and had an estimated useful life of 8 years. However, after all of the copper is removed from the mine, the equipment will be of no use to Miller Mining and will be sold for an estimated $4,000.

a. If sales and production conform to expectations, what is the amount of depletion for financial reporting purposes for 1981?
b. If sales and production conform to expectations, what is the amount of depletion recognized for income tax purposes for 1981?
c. If sales and production conform to expectations, what is the amount of depreciation on the new equipment for 1981 if the straight-line method is used?

13.31   Arizona Mining Company is engaged in the search, extraction, and sale of iron ore. The costs incurred during 1981, 1982, and 1983 on two sites, site A and site B, are as follows:

| | **1981** | **1982** | **1983** |
|---|---|---|---|
| Acquisition Costs: | | | |
| Site A ............................................ | $100,000 | — | — |
| Site B ............................................ | 100,000 | — | — |
| Exploration Costs: | | | |
| Site A ............................................ | 500,000 | $600,000 | $300,000 |
| Site B ............................................ | 700,000 | 800,000 | 200,000 |
| Development Costs: | | | |
| Site B ............................................ | — | — | 700,000 |

Recoverable iron ore was discovered on site B early in 1983. It is estimated that the site contains 10,000 tons of iron ore. Exploration efforts were discontinued on site A in 1983 after it was decided that the site would be nonproductive.

During 1984, 2,000 tons of iron ore were extracted at a production cost of $400,000 and then sold. During 1985, 3,000 tons were extracted at a production cost of $660,000 and then sold. At the end of 1985, it is estimated that site B has 2,000 tons of iron ore remaining to be extracted. During 1986, the remaining 2,000 tons are extracted at a production cost of $500,000 and then sold.

a. Calculate the amount of depletion for each of the years 1981 through 1987 assuming that the successful-efforts costing method is used.

b. Calculate the amount of depletion for each of the years 1981 through 1987 assuming that the full costing method is used.

**13.32** Diversified Petroleum Company incurred costs of $20,000,000 to acquire, explore, and develop a parcel of property expected to yield 40,000,000 barrels of crude oil. The crude oil is expected to be extracted and sold as follows:

| Year | Number of Barrels Extracted and Sold | Expected Selling Price per Barrel |
|------|--------------------------------------|-----------------------------------|
| 1981 ......... | 5,000,000 bbl | $20 |
| 1982 ......... | 8,000,000 | 22 |
| 1983 ......... | 8,000,000 | 23 |
| 1984 ....... | 10,000,000 | 25 |
| 1985 ......... | 9,000,000 | 26 |
|  | 40,000,000 bbl | |

a. Calculate the amount of depletion for each year, using the unit-of-production method.

b. Calculate the amount of depletion for each year, using the percentage depletion method as permitted for income tax purposes.

**13.33** Offshore Oil Exploration Corporation was organized in 1979 to search for oil off of the coast of Louisiana. Acquisition and exploration costs incurred between 1979 and 1981 totaled $15,000,000. Of this amount, 96 percent relates to sites that turned out to be nonproductive and were abandoned early in 1981. The remaining 4 percent of the acquisition and exploration costs relate to sites that are expected to be productive. Development costs totaling $1,000,000 were incurred during 1980 and 1981 on these productive sites.

The company uses the full costing method. Selling prices remained stable at $20 per barrel between 1981 and 1985. Production expenses are based on the number of barrels extracted instead of the number of units sold and remained stable during the 5-year period.

Partial income statements and certain balance sheet data for Offshore Oil Exploration Corporation for the years 1981 through 1985 are shown in Exhibit 13.6.

Calculate the amounts for each of the income statement and balance sheet accounts in Exhibit 13.6, assuming the successful-efforts costing method had been used.

**13.34** Oil Exploration Corporation was organized during January 1981 to search, extract, and sell crude oil. Exploration rights on three parcels of land (parcel A, parcel B, and parcel C), all located in Texas, were acquired during February 1981. Exploration efforts began in March 1981 and continued into 1982. Recoverable reserves were discovered on parcel B early in 1982. Exploration efforts on parcel C were discontinued late in 1982 and on parcel A late in 1983 after it was found that these sites did not contain recoverable reserves. Operating data

*Exhibit 13.6*
**Offshore Oil Exploration Company
Partial Income Statements and
Balance Sheet Amounts**

| Year Ended December 31: | 1981 | 1982 | 1983 | 1984 | 1985 |
|---|---|---|---|---|---|
| Sales .............. | $ 1,000,000 | $ 2,000,000 | $ 3,000,000 | $4,000,000 | $5,000,000 |
| Cost of Goods Sold .. | (800,000) | (1,600,000) | (2,400,000) | (3,200,000) | (4,000,000) |
| Gross Margin ....... | $ 200,000 | $ 400,000 | $ 600,000 | $ 800,000 | $1,000,000 |
| Production Expenses . | (150,000) | (225,000) | (325,000) | (425,000) | (525,000) |
| Selling and Administrative Expenses ........ | (5,000) | (10,000) | (15,000) | (20,000) | (25,000) |
| Income before Income Taxes ........... | $ 45,000 | $ 165,000 | $ 260,000 | $ 355,000 | $ 450,000 |

| December 31: | 1981 | 1982 | 1983 | 1984 | 1985 |
|---|---|---|---|---|---|
| Inventory of Crude Oil .............. | $ 400,000 | $ 600,000 | $ 800,000 | $1,000,000 | $1,200,000 |
| Number of Barrels ... | 25,000 | 37,500 | 50,000 | 62,500 | 75,000 |
| Depletable Natural Resources (net) ... | $14,800,000 | $13,000,000 | $10,400,000 | $7,000,000 | $2,800,000 |
| Remaining Recoverable Reserves (barrels) . | 925,000 | 812,500 | 650,000 | 437,500 | 175,000 |

for 1981, 1982, and 1983 are summarized in Exhibit 13.7. All costs incurred are paid in cash. All sales are made for cash.

a. Give the journal entries for each of the years 1981, 1982, and 1983 to reflect the transactions above using the successful-efforts costing method. A first-in, first-out cost-flow assumption is used.

b. Repeat part a using the full costing method.

c. Prepare a partial income statement for each of the 3 years under successful-efforts costing and under full costing.

d. At what amounts would the accounts Crude Oil Inventory, Deferred Acquisition and Exploration Costs, and Depletable Natural Resources (net) be shown on the balance sheet at the end of each year under the successful-efforts and full costing methods?

13.35   High Flyer Company was organized on January 1981. Selected transactions during 1981 are as follows:

(1) Legal, accounting, and other costs incurred during January 1981 in organizing the corporation totaled $20,000.

(2) A patent was acquired for $12,000 from its creator. At the time of acquisition on February 1, 1981, it was expected to have a useful life of 10 years. On July 1, 1981, however, the federal government banned products made from the patent from the market because of safety hazards.

(3) A franchise was received from National Auto Parts Corporation on January 2, 1981. High Flyer Company paid $6,000 down and agreed to pay the remainder of the $24,000 initial franchise fee over the next 3 years plus interest at 10 percent. The franchise period is 10 years.

*Exhibit 13.7*
**Oil Exploration Corporation**
**Operating Data for 1981, 1982, and 1983**

| Acquisition and Exploration Costs: | 1981 | 1982 | 1983 |
|---|---|---|---|
| Parcel A | $3,000,000 | $2,500,000 | $1,750,000 |
| Parcel B | $5,000,000 | $3,000,000 | — |
| Parcel C | $7,000,000 | $2,000,000 | — |
| Development Costs: | | | |
| Parcel B | — | $2,000,000 | — |
| Production Costs: | | | |
| Parcel B | — | $ 400,000 | $ 600,000 |
| Barrels Discovered | — | 2,000,000 bbl | — |
| Barrels Extracted | — | 250,000 bbl | 300,000 bbl |
| Barrels Sold | — | 200,000 bbl | 325,000 bbl |
| Selling Price per Barrel | — | $20 per bbl | $22 per bbl |

(4) High Flyer Company incurred the following costs in connection with its research and development activity during 1981:

| Personnel | $10,000 |
|---|---|
| Materials | 5,000 |
| Indirect Costs | 3,000 |

A new product was created from the research work and a patent received on the product late in 1981. Production of the product will begin early in 1982. Because of the unique nature of the product, it is expected to provide future benefits to High Flyer Company for 5 years.

(5) Advertising costs of $15,000 were incurred during 1981 to expose the Company's name to customers.

High Flyer Company wishes to report the most favorable earnings performance permitted under generally accepted accounting principles for 1981. For each of the five items above, indicate the minimum amount that can be reported as an expense for 1981 under generally accepted accounting principles.

**13.36** The general ledger of Markham Corporation lists the following as of December 31, 1981:

| | |
|---|---|
| Organization Costs | $20,000 |
| Deposit with Advertising Agency (will be used to promote goodwill) | 10,000 |
| Excess of Cost over Market Values of Identifiable Tangible and Intangible Assets of Acquired Subsidiary | 25,000 |
| Trademark | 12,000 |
| Research and Development Costs | 35,000 |
| Prepaid Rent (rental paid in advance on lease expiring next year) | 5,000 |

Indicate the amount shown as "intangible assets" on the balance sheet of Markham Corporation on December 31, 1981.

**13.37** The general ledger accounts of Scientific Technologies Corporation lists the following for 1981:

| | |
|---|---:|
| **(1)** Salaries of personnel involved in basic research. Commercially feasible products from this group of personnel are not expected for at least 5 years | $50,000 |
| **(2)** Materials used in constructing a prototype of a new product expected to be produced after additional testing is completed | 3,500 |
| **(3)** Design and engineering costs to adapt a plant for the manufacture of a new product | 10,000 |
| **(4)** Automobile acquired for use by the research staff. The automobile has a 3-year life and a $1,500 estimated salvage value | 6,000 |
| **(5)** Salary of the vice-president in charge of research and development | 60,000 |
| **(6)** Used automobiles acquired for use in testing the crash-sustaining power of a new bumper. The automobiles will be sold for a total of $500 when testing is completed in 2 years | 4,500 |
| **(7)** Cost of a patent on a process acquired from its creator. The patented process is to be used in research and development work. It has a remaining legal life of 5 years but an economic life to scientific technologies of 3 years | 45,000 |
| **(8)** Cost of research and development work done by an outside agency | 10,000 |

Compute the amount of research and development costs for 1981. The straight-line method of depreciation and amortization is used by the company.

13.38 Wilcox Corporation rented office space in a choice downtown location for 5 years beginning January 1, 1981. The annual rent is $28,000. In order to obtain the lease, Wilcox Corporation paid a bonus of $50,000. No option to renew the lease is provided for in the rental agreement. Wilcox Corporation made substantial alterations to the interior of the building (moved certain walls, added windows). The alterations, which cost $30,000, are expected to have a useful life for another 30 years, the remaining estimated life of the building. In addition, carpets, light fixtures, and partitions costing $11,000 were added. The latter alterations have an economic life of 10 years and $1,000 salvage value. At the end of 5 years, their estimated salvage value is $3,000.

a. How should each of the above costs be treated for financial reporting purposes?

b. How would your answer to part **a** have differed if the lease had a renewal option for 10 additional years and the likelihood of renewal was high?

# Chapter 14
# *Investments in Securities*

14.1   A firm usually invests in securities to achieve one of two different goals: to help ensure liquidity or to seek special economic benefits by its security ownership. When a firm holds cash for reasons of liquidity, it forgoes interest earnings on that cash. Such a firm will usually invest much of its cash needed for liquidity in securities such as U.S. Treasury notes or commercial paper that can be converted quickly into cash. Securities held for liquidity are classified as current assets; Chapter 6 discusses the accounting for marketable securities held as current assets.

14.2   This chapter primarily treats investments in securities held for reasons not related to a firm's operating liquidity. The chapter discusses the investment characteristics of such securities as well as the accounting for their acquisition, holding, and disposition.

## Types of Investments

14.3   Two basic types of securities exist: *contractual*, or *debt*, securities and *equity* securities. *Hybrid securities* combine features of both basic types.

## Contractual Securities (Monetary Assets)

Contractual securities specify that certain   14.4
amounts of cash will be paid on certain future dates. Examples include notes, bonds, mortgages, installment receivables, and lease receivables. Such instruments are often called "monetary items" because they are claims to specific amounts of cash.

## Equity Securities

Equity securities represent a residual claim   14.5
to ownership in another firm. Examples include common shares, options, rights, and warrants. Holders of such securities rank behind holders of specific monetary claims in event of liquidation and bear the predominant risk of the firm's failure, but in return are entitled to the rewards of a successful firm. Equity securities do not provide for specific cash payments. Holders of such securities can frequently sell them in public markets, such as the New York Stock Exchange. In the sense that the securities can quickly be turned into cash, they are liquid; because the amount of cash proceeds depends on market conditions at the time of sale, they are not necessarily reliable ways to provide for liquidity. When liquidity is the

primary goal, the securities are classified as Marketable Securities, a current asset.

14.6    Long-term investments in equity securities of other firms are usually made either because these appear to be an attractive investment or so that the investor firm can gain some influence over the operations of the investee firm. Accounting for passive investments differs from those where the goal is influence or control. Passive investments in equity securities are accounted for with the lower-of-cost-or-market method, whereas controlling investments are accounted for with the equity method or in consolidated statements. Appendix 14.1 discusses consolidated statements.

## Hybrid Securities

14.7    Hybrid securities contain both specific promises to pay like debt and claims like owners' equity. Examples include preferred shares and convertible bonds. A preferred share promises a preferred claim to a specific dividend but seldom has a maturity date. A convertible bond contains promises typical of a bond, but can be swapped for (converted into) equity securities, usually common shares.

## Acquisition of Investments

14.8    Securities are initially recorded at acquisition cost. Cost is the cash or cash-equivalent market value of other assets given in exchange for the securities acquired. Cost includes all outlays, such as brokerage fees and transfer taxes, required to make the acquisition. Accounting Principles Board *Opinion No. 29* states that when securities are acquired in exchange for other assets, then "fair value of a nonmonetary asset transferred to or from an enterprise in a nonmonetary transaction should be determined by reference to estimated fair values of assets or services received in exchange or other available evidence."*

_____

*Accounting Principles Board, APB *Opinion No. 29* (May 1973), par. 25.

## Basket Purchase

When more than one security is acquired in 14.9 a single transaction, the acquisition cost must be allocated among the securities. Ideally, the acquisition cost should be allocated based on the relative market values of individual securities. If market value data are not available, the accountant can either wait for market value data to emerge or rely on expert appraisal.

**Example** Joyce Company purchases 1,000 14.10 units of a new offering of securities in Consolidated Food Products Company (CFP) for $252,000, including broker's commissions of $2,000. Each unit consists of one share of $100-par-value, 8-percent preferred stock and two shares of $2-par-value common stock. The preferred shares are a new issue, but the common shares trade on the Midwest Stock Exchange. On the day the units are purchased, the market price of the common shares is $50 per share. The journal entry to record this purchase is

| | | |
|---|---|---|
| Investment in CFP Common Shares | 100,800 | |
| Investment in CFP Preferred Shares | 151,200 | |
| Cash | | 252,000 |

Common shares are allocated $100,000 (= $50 per share × 2 shares per unit × 1,000 units) of cost before commissions. Preferred shares are allocated the balance of $250,000 cost before commissions. Commissions are allocated $100,000/$250,000 = 40 percent or $800 to common shares and 60 percent or $1,200 to preferred shares.

## Exchange or Conversion

One security, voluntarily acquired, can 14.11 sometimes be *exchanged* for another security (possibly with some cash included in the transaction), as when stock warrants are exercised. Generally accepted accounting principles require that fair market values be used in recording the asset received in exchange. Whether the fair market value of the asset given up or the fair market value of the asset received is used depends on which is more objectively measurable.* Using the fair market value of the items given up typically involves recognizing gain or loss on the disposition on those items. This process is illustrated later in the chapter in the discussion of stock warrants.

14.12 Calculating the acquisition cost of shares obtained by *conversion* of other securities is controversial. Some theorists adhere strictly to the historical cost principle of awaiting an arm's-length transaction before substituting current market values for originally recorded acquisition costs. They would transfer the acquisition cost of the old securities to the new securities received on conversion. An allocation of old, recorded costs may be necessary if more than one kind of security is received. The allocation would be carried out using historical cost principles. Other theorists argue that a conversion of securities, even an involuntary one, is an arm's-length transaction with outsiders, so that the market values on the date of conversion should be used to record the exchange. We prefer the latter treatment, although the former seems to be more widely used. Both treatments are acceptable accounting procedures.

14.13 **Example** A firm holds a convertible bond of Consolidated Foods Products Company (CFP) with a recorded acquisition cost of $980. The firm converts the bond into 20 common shares of the same company. On

the conversion date, the market price of the common is $60 per share. Those advocating the carryover of the acquisition cost would record:

| | | |
|---|---|---|
| Investment in CFP Common Shares | ...... | 980 |
| Investment in CFP Convertible Bonds . | | 980 |

Valuation of the common shares received is the same as that of the bond given up.

Those advocating that the event be treated as an arm's-length transaction would record:

| | | |
|---|---|---|
| Investment in CFP Common Shares | .... | 1,200 |
| Investment in CFP Convertible | | |
|   Bonds | ...................... | 980 |
| Gain on Conversion of Bonds | ...... | 220 |

Valuation of the common shares is calculated from the market price of shares on date of conversion. A gain appears on the income statement for the period.

Some theorists would use the first entry, carrying over the cost basis, when the conversion is involuntary or forced, but the second when the conversion is voluntary.

## Disposition of Investments: Cost-Flow Procedures

14.14 When the investor owns several shares or certificates of the same security issue purchased at different prices and sells some of the securities, but not the entire holding, the cost of the securities sold must be computed. The problem is analogous to that of finding costs for items sold from inventory. Because transactions tend to be infrequent and because which particular securities are sold can make a large difference in reported income, the certificates actually sold are specifically identified in most sales of securities. Each time a particular security is sold, its acquisition cost is found from the records. When specific identification is not used, FIFO (first-in, first-out) is usually assumed because the tax rules require FIFO in those cases. Investments in mutual funds may be accounted for with a weighted-average cost-flow assumption.

---

*Paragraph 18, APB *Opinion No. 29* (1973), says in part, "Thus, the cost of a nonmonetary asset acquired in exchange for another nonmonetary asset is the fair value of the asset surrendered to obtain it, and a gain or loss should be recognized on the exchange. The fair value of the asset received should be used to measure the cost if it is more clearly evident than the fair value of the asset surrendered." Without going into great detail here, we report that some theorists argue, at least implicitly by their treatment of such transactions, that paragraph 21 of APB *Opinion 29* overrides paragraph 18. The reader is invited to study paragraphs 18, 21, and 22 of APB *Opinion No. 29* to see the "interpretation" (some call it "legal accounting") that is necessary to deduce GAAP from its source documents.

## Valuation in General

14.15 Securities remaining in a firm's possession must be valued on each balance sheet. The valuation methods used for investments in securities include the cost basis, the lower-of-cost-or-market basis, and the equity basis (resulting from using the "equity method"). Both the cost and lower-of-cost-or-market bases have been discussed earlier in this book, although lower of cost or market for investments involves some details presented only in this chapter. This chapter also describes the equity method. (Try not to confuse the term "equity method" with the term "equity securities," which may or may not be accounted for with the equity method.)

14.16 The valuation method used depends on

1. The marketability of the securities,

2. Whether they are contractual or equity, and

3. The relationship between the investor and the investee firm.

The cost method is used for investments in nonmarketable equity securities and for some investments in contractual securities, although the lower-of-cost-or-market method can be used if market prices are available. The cost method is used for individual investments in marketable equity securities when the investor firm does not possess significant control of the investee firm, but the lower-of-cost-or-market method is used for the portfolio of such investments. The investor firm uses the equity method when owning the equity securities gives it significant control over the investee firm.

14.17 APB *Opinion No. 18* says that ownership of 20 percent or more of the voting shares is sufficient to exercise control. When the investor owns more than 50 percent of the voting shares of the investee firm (and thus can surely control it), the investor firm will either use the equity method or, more often, will consolidate the investee's financial statements with its own. The next several sections discuss valuation methods and reporting procedures for investments.

## Investments in Contractual Securities: The Cost Method

14.18 Under the cost method, investments are recorded at acquisition cost, including all brokerage fees and other costs of transfer. Later, when dividends or interest is received in cash, the Cash account is debited and an appropriately titled revenue account—Dividend Revenue or Interest Revenue—is credited. For investments in contractual securities, market fluctuations in interest rates complicate the general procedure. Chapter 5 introduced this procedure, which is reviewed and illustrated again here.

### Valuation of Contractual Securities

14.19 A contractual security is a promise to pay specified amounts of cash at specified future dates. The market value of a promised series of payments depends on the interest rate used by the marketplace to discount the payments.

14.20 **Structure of Interest Rates** Interest is the price paid or collected for the use of money. Just as there is no one price of bread (which depends on the size of the loaf and the quality of the ingredients used in the dough), there is no one price of money. Interest rates depend in part on the length of time the loan is to be outstanding and the quality (creditworthiness) of the borrower. Generally, the shorter the time of the loan and the higher quality the borrower, the lower the interest rate.* Interest rates also fluctuate over time as the demand and supply for money change. The interest rate applicable to a loan on the day it is made will only by coincidence be the applicable market interest rate at some other time. As market interest rates

---

*Occasionally, however, interest rates for short-term loans are higher than for loans to the same borrower for long-term loans. Although this relation was observed during at least two significant periods in the last decade, it is generally thought to be unusual. The relation between interest rates and length of loan or time until maturity of the loan is often called the *yield curve.*

*Exhibit 14.1*
**Illustration of Use of "Historical"
Interest Rate in Accounting for
Bonds by Issuer and Investor**

| Date | Market Interest Rate (%) | Event | Interest Rate (%) Used in Historical Cost Accounting by | | | |
|---|---|---|---|---|---|---|
| | | | Issuing Corporation | Investor A | Investor B | Investor C |
| Year 1 .... | 10 | Issuing corporation issues bonds with yield of 10%; investor A buys $2 million of face value and investor B buys $1 million of face value of these bonds .......... | 10 | 10 | 10 | — |
| Year 2 .... | 12 | Investor A sells $1 million face value of bonds (at a loss) to investor C ........... | 10 | 10 | 10 | 12 |
| Year 3 .... | 8 | Investor A sells $1 million face value of bonds (at a gain) to investor B ........... | 10 | — | 10, 8[a] | 12 |
| Year 4 .... | 9 | Investor C sells $500,000 face value of bonds (at a gain) to investor B ........... | 10 | — | 10, 8, 9[b] | 12 |

[a]For purchase of $1 million face value in year 1, 10% is used; for purchase of $1 million face value in year 3, 8% is used.
[b]For purchase of $500,000 face value in year 4, 9% is used.

change, the market value of a promise to pay a fixed sum of cash will change. The higher the interest rate, the lower is the market value of a fixed sum of cash to be collected in future. The lower the interest rate, the higher is the market value of a fixed sum.

14.21    Although the interest rate applicable to a contractual security changes over time (and the value of the security changes inversely), historical cost accounting uses the historical interest rate—the one in effect the day the loan was made—in accounting for that security throughout the time the security is held. Exhibit 14.1 illustrates the use of historical interest rates by the issuer and several investors.

## The Cost Method for Contractual Securities

14.22    The following example explains and illustrates steps in accounting for an investment in a contractual security under the cost method.

**Example** Five years ago, on January 1, the 14.23 Macaulay Corporation issued 8-percent, semiannual coupon bonds at par with face amount of $10 million. Coupons are due each July 1 and January 1 for 15 years. The company promised to pay $400,000 (= $10,000,000 × .08/2) each 6 months for 15 years and the $10 million principal 15 years from the issue date. At the time the bonds were issued, the market required Macaulay Corporation to pay 8 percent interest per year, compounded semiannually.*

On January 2 of the current year, Investor 14.24 Company purchases $100,000 of face value of these bonds in the market place as an investment. The bonds mature 10 years from the date of purchase by Investor Company. On the date of purchase by Investor, the in-

---

*This is *not* the same as 8 percent per year; see the discussion in Appendix B under the heading, "Changing the Compounding Period."

terest rate Macaulay Corporation would have to pay to borrow for 10 years is 10 percent, compounded semiannually, or 5 percent per 6-month period. The bonds cost Investor Company $87,538. (This amount is derived below.) The steps in accounting for these bonds by Investor parallel the four steps for monetary items introduced in Chapter 5.

**1.** Compute the initial cash payment made by the investor and the implied effective interest on the security. Sometimes both of these amounts are known. More often, either the price of the investment is stated or the interest rate is stated; the other must be computed.

**a.** To compute the cash payment when the interest rate is known (10 percent compounded semiannually in the example), multiply each of the contractual payments by the present-value factor (as from the tables at the back of this book) appropriate for that payment. In the example of the Macaulay Corporation bonds, we use Table 2 for the present value of the single-payment principal amount due in 10 years and Table 4 for the present value of the coupon payments:

| | |
|---|---:|
| Present value of $100,000 to be received 10 years hence. Table 2 shows that the present value of $1 to be received in 20 (six-month) periods discounted at the rate of 5 percent per period is $.37689; $100,000 × .37689 = $37,689 ...... | $37,689 |
| Present value of $4,000 to be received at the end of each of the next 20 six-month periods. Table 4 shows that the present value of $1 to be received at the ends of each of the next 20 periods discounted at the rate of 5 percent per period is $12.46221; $4,000 × 12.46221 = $49,849 ........................ | 49,849 |
| Total present value ................ | $87,538 |

**b.** To compute the market interest rate (5 percent compounded semiannually in the example), from a given bond price and given contractual interest payments is

called "finding the internal rate of return." Appendix B illustrates the process. If the investment is a bond and bond tables, such as Table 6 at the back of this book, are at hand, then the interest rate can be read from the table. Turn to Table 6; locate the cell in the 10-year column and 10-percent row. Note that the price quoted as a percentage of par value is 87.5378.

**2.** Record a journal entry debiting the Investment account with the amount paid and crediting Cash. The journal entry is

```
Jan. 2
Investment in Bonds  ..............  87,538
    Cash  .......................           87,538
To record purchase of bond invest-
ment.
```

**3.** At any contractual payment date or at the end of an accounting period, compute interest revenue as the book value of the investment at the beginning of the period multiplied by the interest rate at the date of acquisition, 10 percent compounded semiannually in the example (5 percent per 6-month period). Debit the amount of interest to the Investment account, increasing it, and credit the amount to Interest Revenue. If cash is received, debit Cash and credit the Investment account, reducing it. The following entries assume that the books are closed annually.* The entries made on July 1 and December 31 of the current year and on January 1 of the next year would be as follows:

```
July 1
Investment in Bonds  ................  4,377
    Interest Revenue  ...............           4,377
Interest revenue is interest rate times
book value on January 2: .05 × $87,538 =
$4,377.
```

---

*The accountant may wish to show amounts to be received in cash within the next year as Interest Receivable, instead of having the amount "buried" in the Investment account. If so, and if cash is to be received within a year of any closing date, the amounts may be debited to Interest Receivable and credited to Interest Revenue. We do not illustrate this set of entries in the example.

```
Cash ............................. 4,000
    Investment in Bonds ............      4,000
```
Coupons for $4,000 are redeemed for cash. The Investment account now has a balance of $87,915 = $87,538 + $4,377 − $4,000.

14.25  The two entries at July 1 could instead be combined in a single entry:

```
Cash ............................. 4,000
Investment in Bonds .................  377
    Interest Revenue ...............      4,377
```

The two entries shown below for December 31 could similarly be combined in a single entry.

Dec. 31
```
Investment in Bonds .................. 4,395
    Interest Revenue ...............      4,395
```
Interest revenue is .05 × $87,915.

```
Interest Receivable .................. 4,000
    Investment in Bonds .............      4,000
```
Coupons for $4,000 of interest recognized this year will be redeemed for cash. The Investment account now has a balance of $88,310 = $87,915 + $4,395 − $4,000.

Jan. 1
```
Cash ............................. 4,000
    Interest Receivable .............      4,000
```
Coupons for $4,000 are redeemed.

The Investment account would increase over time because the interest revenue each period exceeds the cash received from coupons. Exhibit 14.2 shows an amortization schedule detailing the amounts of the periodic journal entries.

14.26  **Effects on Statement of Changes in Financial Position**  The statement of changes in financial position shows funds from operations as the first and most important source of funds. Whenever operations do not produce funds in dollar amounts equal to revenues, an adjustment of net income must be made in deriving funds from operations. The investment in Macaulay Corporation's bonds illustrates an event that produces funds in an amount less than revenues.

Some of the interest revenue is reflected in an increase in the Investment account, instead of in cash or interest receivable.

The amounts in column (5) of Exhibit 14.2   14.27 are added to the Investment account, instead of being received in cash. When the bond matures, these amounts are collected as the excess of the face value over the original purchase price. Funds provided by the bond investment for any period are less than revenue recognized by the amount in column (5) of Exhibit 14.2. These amounts must be subtracted from income in deriving funds from operations for the period. In preparing the statement of changes in financial position, the changes in the long-term asset account for Investments must be explained. That account increases by the amounts in column (5) of Exhibit 14.2. In preparing the work sheet for the funds statement, the debit to the Investment account to explain the change is matched with a credit to the Working Capital account in the "Net Loss and Subtractions" section.

**Example Extended: Purchase Date Differ-   14.28 ent from Interest Collection Date**  Assume that Investor Company purchased the bonds of Macaulay Corporation on March 1 of the current year, instead of on January 2. The market interest rate remains 10 percent, compounded semiannually. The market price of the $100,000 bonds would be $87,661.* Two months have gone by since the last payment date, so the prior owner is entitled to receive $1,333 (= $^2/_6$ × $4,000) of the $4,000 interest coupon due on the next interest payment date, July 1. The confir-

---

*$87,661 is the present value of the bond 9 years and 10 months from the date of maturity. The formula at the top of Table 6 at the back of the book can be used to find the market value of a bond, even for fractional numbers of periods such as in this case:
Market Value in Percent of Par for 8% Semiannual Coupon Bond Maturing in 9 Years and 10 Months

$$= \frac{8}{.10} + \left(100 - \frac{8}{.10}\right)(1 + .05)^{-(2 \times 9^{10}/_{12})}$$
$$= 80 + 20 \times (1.05)^{-19.667}$$
$$= 80 + 20 \times 0.38307$$
$$= 80 + 7.66138$$
$$= 87.66138$$

---

*Exhibit 14.2*
**Amortization Schedule for $100,000 of 8%, 10-Year Bonds Purchased for $87,538 to Yield 10%, Compounded Semiannually**

---

**Semiannual Journal Entries**

Dr. Investment in Bonds ............................. Amount in Column (3)

    Cr. Interest Revenue ............................. Amount in Column (3)

To record interest revenue. The Investment account begins the period with the balance in column (2) and is increased by the amount of interest revenue.

Dr. Cash ........................................... 4,000

    Cr. Investment in Bonds ......................... 4,000

To record cash receipt. The Investment account increases, net, during a period by the amount in column (5) and starts the next period with the amount in column (6).

---

| Period (6-Month Intervals) (1) | Book Value at Start of Period (2) | Interest Revenue (3) | Interest Coupon (4) | Interest Not Received in Cash Added to Investment Account (5) | Book Value at End of Period (6) |
|---|---|---|---|---|---|
| 0 | — | — | — | — | $87,538 |
| 1 | $87,538 | $4,377 | $4,000 | $377 | 87,915 |
| 2 | 87,915 | 4,395 | 4,000 | 395 | 88,310 |
| 3 | 88,310 | 4,416 | 4,000 | 416 | 88,726 |
| 4 | 88,726 | 4,436 | 4,000 | 436 | 89,162 |
| 5 | 89,162 | 4,458 | 4,000 | 458 | 89,620 |
| 6 | 89,620 | 4,481 | 4,000 | 481 | 90,101 |
| 7 | 90,101 | 4,505 | 4,000 | 505 | 90,606 |
| 8 | 90,606 | 4,531 | 4,000 | 531 | 91,137 |
| 9 | 91,137 | 4,557 | 4,000 | 557 | 91,694 |
| 10 | 91,694 | 4,585 | 4,000 | 585 | 92,278 |
| 11 | 92,278 | 4,614 | 4,000 | 614 | 92,892 |
| 12 | 92,892 | 4,645 | 4,000 | 645 | 93,537 |
| 13 | 93,537 | 4,677 | 4,000 | 677 | 94,214 |
| 14 | 94,214 | 4,711 | 4,000 | 711 | 94,924 |
| 15 | 94,924 | 4,746 | 4,000 | 746 | 95,671 |
| 16 | 95,671 | 4,784 | 4,000 | 784 | 96,454 |
| 17 | 96,454 | 4,823 | 4,000 | 823 | 97,277 |
| 18 | 97,277 | 4,864 | 4,000 | 864 | 98,141 |
| 19 | 98,141 | 4,907 | 4,000 | 907 | 99,048 |
| 20 | 99,048 | 4,952 | 4,000 | 952 | 100,000 |

Note: Calculations were made carrying results to nearest tenth of one cent, but are rounded to nearest dollar for presentation here.

Column (3) = .05 × column (2).
Column (5) = column (3) − $4,000.
Column (6) = column (2) + column (5).

mation slip giving details of the purchase price would indicate (in part):

| | |
|---|---|
| Bonds of Macaulay Corporation ........ | $87,661 |
| Accrued Interest to Date of Purchase ... | 1,333 |
| Purchase Price (Excluding Commissions and Taxes) ........................ | $88,994 |

The purchase of the investment could be recorded as

March 1
| | | |
|---|---|---|
| Investment in Bonds .............. | 87,661 | |
| Interest Receivable ............... | 1,333 | |
| Cash ...................... | | 88,994 |

Then, on July 1, the entry would be

July 1
| | | |
|---|---|---|
| Investment in Bonds ................. | 255 | |
| Interest Receivable ................. | 2,667 | |
| Interest Revenue ............... | | 2,922 |

Interest is principal × rate × time. In this case the time is two-thirds of a 6-month interest-earning period.* Thus, interest revenue is $87,661 principal × .05 interest rate × $2/3$ = $2,922. The interest is split between that to be received in cash when the coupons are redeemed ($2,667 = $4,000 − $1,333) and that to be added to the Investment account ($255 = $2,922 − $2,667, increasing it).

| | | |
|---|---|---|
| Cash ..... ,,................... | 4,000 | |
| Interest Receivable ........... | | 4,000 |

Redemption of interest coupons, cash is received.

The book value of the investment is now $87,916 (= $87,661 + $255), the amount shown for the end of the first period in Exhibit 14.2. The accounting from the second period on is the same as in the preceding example.

14.29 **Sale of Investment before Maturity** Refer to the data in Exhibit 14.2. Assume that

---

*The text illustrates the simple interest computation for this first, partial period because simple interest is virtually always used in practice for partial interest-earning periods. The compound interest calculation is $88,994 × [(1.05^{2/3} − 1] = $2,942.

Investor Company sells the bonds 3 years and 8 months after having acquired them—during period 8. The book value of the Investment account, as shown on the line for the start of period 8, is $90,606. The interest revenue accrued from the last coupon payment until the date of sale must be recorded. That amount is (calculated at simple interest) $90,606 × .10 × $2/12$ = $90,606 × .05 × $2/6$ = $1,510. The entry to record accrued interest is

March 1
| | | |
|---|---|---|
| Investment in Bonds ................. | 1,510 | |
| Interest Revenue ............... | | 1,510 |

To record interest revenue accrued from last preceding coupon payment until date of sale. The book value of the investment after this entry is $92,116 (= $90,606 + $1,510).

If the bonds are sold for more than $92,116, say $95,000 (market interest rate is less than the historical interest rate so that the market value of the bonds exceeds their book value), a gain results:

| | | |
|---|---|---|
| Cash .......................... | 95,000 | |
| Investment in Bonds .......... | | 92,116 |
| Gain on Sale of Bond Investment ................. | | 2,884 |

If the bonds are sold for less than $92,116, say, $90,000 (market interest rate is greater than the historical rate so that the market value of the bonds is less than their book value), then a loss results:

| | | |
|---|---|---|
| Cash .......................... | 90,000 | |
| Loss on Sale of Bond Investment ... | 2,116 | |
| Investment in Bonds .......... | | 92,116 |

The net income for the period of sale is affected by both the interest revenue and the gain or loss on sale. If the interest were not recognized, perhaps because of an oversight, the net income for the period would not be affected; the gain would be larger or the loss smaller by the amount of the nonrecorded interest.

**Summary of Cost Method** Under the cost    14.30
method, the investment is initially recorded

at cost. At the end of any period, or at any interest payment date, interest revenue is calculated as the book value of the investment multiplied by the historical interest rate—the interest rate applicable to the investment on the day it was first made. The amount of interest is added to (debited to) the Investment account. Any cash receipts are deducted from (credited to) the Investment account. The cost method is used for notes, bonds, and mortgages held as investments.

## Investments in Equity Securities: Minority Ownership

14.31 Businesses acquire equity securities of other firms for various reasons. The accounting for such investments depends on the reasons and the percentages of ownership acquired. Figure 14.1 summarizes the conditions for using the various methods.

14.32 Businesses may acquire equity securities of another firm as a long-term investment.

Long-term investments in equity securities are generally intended to be either passive or controlling. A passive investment is one where the owning firm hopes to accumulate wealth by sharing in the good fortunes and good management of another firm. (In this sense, individual purchases of shares of stock are usually passive.)

14.33 Often, a firm will acquire shares of another company with the notion of directing its activities, controlling the investee firm for purposes thought advantageous for the investor firm. One company can control, or at least strongly influence, another even when it owns 50 percent or less of the voting shares. Ownership of 50 percent or less is called *minority ownership*. Appendix 14.1 discusses majority ownership, where control is assured.

14.34 The accounting for passive investments differs from the accounting for controlling investments. Passive investments, where no control is sought or exercised, are accounted for with the lower-of-cost-or-market method. The method is similar to that explained in Chapter 6 for marketable equity securities,

## Figure 14.1
### Accounting for Ownership of Equity Securities

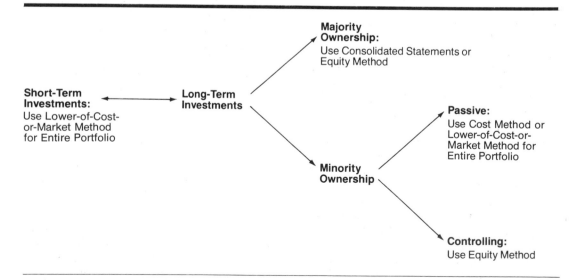

but is different enough to warrant separate explanation here. When the investor firm owns sufficient shares to exercise control, the investor uses the equity method or consolidated statements.

## Valuation of Passive Investments in Equity Securities

14.35   Equity securities are initially recorded at acquisition cost, including the purchase price plus any commissions, taxes, and other costs incurred to acquire the securities. Dividends on marketable securities are recognized as income when declared. The valuation of investments in equity securities after acquisition may, however, depart from strict historical cost accounting.

## Cost Method

14.36   The investor company may acquire *non*marketable equity securities as an investment in another company. In that case, the investor company will carry the investment at *cost* because market values are unavailable. The investor's Investment account shows original cost. The investor treats dividends declared by the owned company as revenue, credited to a Dividend Revenue account. In rare situations, firms declare dividends larger than income. The investor's share of the excess of cumulative dividends over cumulative income since acquisition will be credited to its Investment account as a return *of* investment, rather than credited to Investment Revenue as a return *on* investment. If market values become known, then the lower-of-cost-or-market method is used.

## Lower-of-Cost-or-Market Method

14.37   Financial Accounting Standards Board *Statement No. 12* (1975) requires that the *portfolio* of investments in marketable equity securities (that is, common stock, preferred stock, stock options, and warrants) be stated at the lower of acquisition cost or market at the end of each period. Under the *lower-of-cost-or-market method*, the decrease in the market value of a portfolio of equity securities classified as investments is not recognized as a loss during the period when the decrease occurs as is done for marketable securities classified as current assets. Instead, the debit is to an account such as Net Unrealized Loss on Investments in Marketable Equity Securities, which is an owners' equity contra account. The account appears in the owners' equity section, usually between Additional Paid-in Capital and Retained Earnings. The account always has a debit balance and is, thus, subtracted from the other amounts (credit balances) of owners' equity.

14.38   The credit to reduce the carrying amount of the noncurrent asset, Investment in Marketable Equity Securities, is made to an account contra to the Investment account. The contra is usually called Allowance for Excess of Cost of Investments in Marketable Equity Securities over Market Value. Using a separate contra account enables the simultaneous identification of both the acquisition cost and the amount of decline in the market value of the portfolio. Separate identification of the cost and current market value, when below cost, is required because subsequent increases in the market value of the portfolio up to the original acquisition costs are restored to the net asset balance with debits to the asset contra account, Allowance for Excess. . . . The credits are to the owners' equity contra, Net Unrealized Loss . . . , reducing its debit balance and, therefore, increasing owners' equity.

14.39   The investment portfolio may never be stated at an amount greater than the original acquisition cost; that is, the asset contra, or allowance, account can never have a debit balance. The Net Unrealized Loss account may never have a credit balance. The footnote to paragraph 6.75 in Chapter 6 discusses the FASB's choice of applying the lower-of-cost-or-market valuation rule to the entire portfolio, instead of security by security. The procedures for applying the lower-of-cost-or-market method to Investments are illustrated below.

## Exhibit 14.3
### Data for Illustration of Accounting for Investments in Marketable Equity Securities

| Security | Date Acquired | Acquisition Cost | Market Value 12/31/1977 | 12/31/1978 | 12/31/1979 | 12/31/1980 | 12/31/1981 |
|---|---|---|---|---|---|---|---|
| A Company ...................... | 11/1/77 | $10,000 | $11,000 | $13,000 | $ 14,000 | $12,000 | $10,000 |
| B Company ...................... | 12/1/77 | 20,000 | 18,000 | 17,000 | 18,000 | —[a] | — |
| C Company ...................... | 2/1/78 | 30,000 | — | 26,000 | 33,000 | 34,000 | —[b] |
| D Company ...................... | 4/1/78 | 40,000 | — | 41,000 | 37,000 | 30,000 | 35,000 |
| Total ............................ | | | $29,000 | $97,000 | $102,000 | $76,000 | $45,000 |

[a]Holding of B Company sold during 1980 for $18,500.

[b]Holding of C Company sold during 1981 for $32,000.

14.40 **Example** Nurnberg Company acquired marketable equity securities as passive investments during 1977 and 1978 as shown in Exhibit 14.3. The entry to record the investments in A Company and B Company during 1977 is

```
Investments  ....................  30,000
    Cash  .......................          30,000
```

The data in Exhibit 14.3 parallel those in Exhibit 6.4, and the discussion here parallels that in Chapter 6 for current assets.

14.41 *Unrealized Loss* At the end of 1977, the portfolio of investments (that is, the securities of A Company and B Company) had an aggregate acquisition cost of $30,000 (= $10,000 + $20,000) and an aggregate market value of $29,000 (= $11,000 + $18,000). A write-down of $1,000 is required to recognize the unrealized decline in value:

```
Net Unrealized Loss on Investments in
   Marketable Equity Securities ........ 1,000
      Allowance for Excess of Cost of
         Investments in Marketable Equity
         Securities over Market Value  ...        1,000
Entry to adjust credit balance in allow-
ance account to $1,000.
```

The Unrealized Loss account appears on the balance sheet at the end of 1977 as an own-ers' equity contra. The Allowance account is shown as an account contra to Investments on the balance sheet at the end of 1977. Exhibit 14.4 illustrates the required disclosures.

The entry to record the acquisitions during 1978 is   14.42

```
Investments  ......................  70,000
    Cash  .......................          70,000
```

At the end of 1978, the portfolio of investments in marketable equity securities has an aggregate acquisition cost of $100,000 (= $10,000 + $20,000 + $30,000 + $40,000) and an aggregate market value of $97,000 (= $13,000 + $17,000 + $26,000 + $41,000). The unrealized loss is now $3,000 (= $100,000 − $97,000). The allowance account before adjustment has a balance carried over from 1977 of $1,000. Thus, an additional write-down of $2,000 is required at the end of 1978:

```
Net Unrealized Loss on Investments in
   Marketable Equity Securities ........ 2,000
      Allowance for Excess of Cost of
         Investments in Marketable Equity
         Securities over Market Value  ...        2,000
```
Aggregate decline below cost is $3,000. Adjustment of $2,000 is needed to increase credit balance in allowance account and the debit balance in the unrealized loss account from $1,000 to $3,000.

*Exhibit 14.4*
**Items in Income Statement and Balance Sheet of Nurnberg Company Illustrating Transactions in Investments in Marketable Equity Securities**

| | 1977 | 1978 | 1979 | 1980 | 1981 |
|---|---|---|---|---|---|
| **Excerpts from Income Statement for Year** | | | | | |
| Other Items (Assumed) before Taxes ..... | $200,000 | $200,000 | $200,000 | $200,000 | $200,000 |
| Realized Gain (Loss) on Sale of Investments in Marketable Equity Securities ........................ | — | — | — | (1,500) | 2,000 |
| Income before Taxes ................... | $200,000 | $200,000 | $200,000 | $198,500 | $202,000 |
| **Excerpts from Balance Sheet Items at Year-End** | | | | | |
| **Asset Section** | | | | | |
| Investments in Marketable Equity Securities at Cost ................... | $ 30,000 | $100,000 | $100,000 | $ 80,000 | $ 50,000 |
| Less Allowance for Excess of Cost of Investments in Marketable Equity Securities over Market Value ........ | (1,000) | (3,000) | — | (4,000) | (5,000) |
| Marketable Securities at Lower of Cost or Market .......................... | $ 29,000 | $ 97,000 | $100,000[a] | $ 76,000 | $ 45,000 |
| **Owners' Equity Section** | | | | | |
| Net Unrealized Loss on Investments in Marketable Equity Securities (Debit Balance) .................... | ($ 1,000) | ($ 3,000) | — | ($ 4,000) | ($ 5,000) |

[a] The captions on the balance sheet or the notes must disclose that the market value on December 31, 1979, is $102,000.

The portfolio of investments appears on the December 31, 1978, balance sheet at its market value of $97,000 (= $100,000 acquisition cost less $3,000 allowance). Owners' equity is reduced by $3,000 of unrealized losses on investments.

14.43 *Recovery of Unrealized Loss* Taking the example one step further, assume that there were no acquisitions or dispositions of investments during 1979 but that the market value of the portfolio at the end of 1980 was $102,000. The portfolio of securities has increased to an amount greater than original acquisition cost, but only the increase to the original acquisition cost is recorded in the accounts. The entry is

Allowance for Excess of Cost of
    Investments in Marketable Equity
    Securities over Market Value ....... 3,000
        Net Unrealized Loss on
            Investments in Marketable Equity
            Securities ....................        3,000
To increase valuation of marketable securities to original cost.

This entry brings the balance in both the Allowance account and the Unrealized Loss account to zero. The Investment account now shows an amount equal to original cost, not current market value.

*Realized Gain or Loss through Sale* When 14.44 an individual equity security investment is sold, the realized gain or loss is the difference between the selling price and the acquisition cost of the individual security, regardless of the related balance in the Allowance account. For example, assume that the securities of B Company were sold during 1980 for $18,500. The entry to record the sale during 1980 is

| | | |
|---|---|---|
| Cash .......................... | 18,500 | |
| Realized Loss on Sale of Investments in Marketable Equity Securities ... | 1,500 | |
| Investments ................. | | 20,000 |

To recognize realized loss of $1,500 (= $20,000 original cost − $18,500).

The realized loss is included in net income for 1980.

14.45 Because the lower-of-cost-or-market method is applied to the entire investment portfolio, instead of security by security, the amount of the decline in market value below cost is not recorded separately for each security. (In many cases, gains on some securities offset losses on others.) Therefore the correct balance for the allowance account must be recomputed at the end of each period. The aggregate acquisition cost of the investment portfolio at the end of 1980 is now $80,000 (= $10,000 + $30,000 + $40,000). The aggregate market value of the portfolio at the end of 1980 is $76,000 (= $12,000 + $34,000 + $30,000). Thus, the allowance account should have a $4,000 balance. Because the allowance account has a zero balance carried over from 1979, the following entry is necessary at the end of 1980 to bring the allowance account to $4,000:

| | | |
|---|---|---|
| Net Unrealized Loss on Investments in Marketable Equity Securities ........ | 4,000 | |
| Allowance for Excess of Cost of Investments in Marketable Equity Securities over Market Value ... | | 4,000 |

To bring both credit balance in allowance account and debit balance in owners' equity contra account to $4,000.

The securities are shown at $76,000 on the December 31, 1980, balance sheet in Exhibit 14.4.

14.46 *Realized Gain and Unrealized Loss* The data for 1981 illustrate the simultaneous realization of a gain on sale of one security, and further unrealized losses on securities still held. Holdings of C Company that had cost $30,000 are sold for $32,000. The journal entries are

| | | |
|---|---|---|
| Cash .......................... | 32,000 | |
| Investments ................. | | 30,000 |
| Realized Gain on Sale of Investments in Marketable Equity Securities ............ | | 2,000 |

Sale of holding of C Company for $2,000 more than original cost.

| | | |
|---|---|---|
| Net Unrealized Loss on Investment in Marketable Equity Securities ..... | 1,000 | |
| Allowance for Excess of Cost of Investments in Marketable Equity Securities over Market Value ..................... | | 1,000 |

Securities held have aggregate market value $5,000 (= $10,000 + $40,000 − $10,000 − $35,000) less than cost. Balance carried over from 1980 in Allowance account was $4,000; this entry increases it to $5,000.

**Transfer of Securities between Current** 14.47 **and Noncurrent Portfolios** The same holding of equity securities may be classified either as a current asset, Marketable Securities, or as a noncurrent asset, Investment, depending on the intentions of the owning company. A security can be transferred from the current asset portfolio to the noncurrent asset portfolio or vice versa. If the market price of the security is less than cost on the date of transfer, generally accepted accounting principles require a "dual transaction assumption." FASB *Statement No. 12* (paragraph 10) requires that a transfer of a security between portfolios be treated as though the security were sold for cash at the time of transfer and immediately repurchased at the same price. Thus, the transfer between portfolios establishes a realized loss and a new cost basis. Assume, for example, that equity securities had been purchased for $10,000 and held as a current asset while the market price declined to $8,000. The investment has been accounted for using the lower-of-cost-or-market basis explained in Chapter 6. If the firm decides to reclassify the investment as a long-term investment, the following entry is made:

Realized Loss on Reclassification of
  Marketable Security as a
  Noncurrent Asset .............. 2,000
Investments (Noncurrent Asset) ...... 8,000
    Marketable Securities (Current
      Asset) ..................... 10,000

The loss appears on the income statement for the year; the cost basis of the noncurrent asset is $8,000; subsequent increases in market value, even to $10,000, are not recognized in the accounts.

At the end of the period, a new required balance, if any, will be computed for the Allowance account. The appropriate adjusting entry will adjust the balance from its current zero or credit balance to the correct zero or credit balance. No entry need be made at this time. See the description in step 3 in paragraph 14.51.

14.48    If, on the date of transfer, the market value is greater than cost, then a journal entry is made debiting the portfolio to which the security is being added and crediting the portfolio from which it is being transferred. The amount is the original cost of the shares.

14.49  **Nontemporary Declines in Market Value**
The accountant may decide that a decline in market value of an investment in a given marketable equity security is not temporary.* When the accountant determines that the decline is not temporary, then an entry is made in effect assuming that the security is sold and then repurchased at the current market price on the date of that determination. That is, the accountant **(1)** records a realized loss equal to the difference between

historical cost and the current market value and **(2)** establishes a new cost basis equal to the current market value. The realized loss and revaluation of the booked amount of "cost" is recorded security by security in the Investment portfolio, not for the entire portfolio considered as a whole.

14.50    Refer to the data in Exhibit 14.3. If, for example, it were decided in 1979 that security D's decline in current market value to $37,000 was not temporary, the following entry would be made:

Realized Loss Caused by Permanent
  Decline in Value of Investment in
  Security D ........................ 3,000
    Investments ..................... 3,000

To record loss on permanent decline and to write down the $40,000 cost of investment to current market value, $37,000.

Note that the credit is not to the Allowance account, but to the primary Investment account. Even if subsequent increases in value should occur, these will not be recognized in the accounts. A new cost basis has been established. At the end of the period, the accountant may need to adjust balances in the Allowance account and the Unrealized Loss account so that the amounts in those accounts are equal to the difference between the sum of the costs of the equity securities and the sum of their market values at the end of the period.

14.51  **Order of Procedures for Lower-of-Cost-or-Market Method** Students often find the

---

*We do not know how the accountant arrives at the judgment that some declines in market price are temporary whereas others are not, nor do GAAP give guidance on how such a decision is to be made. GAAP merely state (FASB *Statement No. 12,* par. 21) that "a determination must be made as to whether a decline in market value below cost of an individual security is other than temporary." People who can make such determinations correctly more often than would be predicted by chance outcome alone should not be working as accountants, but should be getting rich purchasing the securities whose declines are "temporary." FASB *Statement No. 12* refers to an article in the April 1975 *Journal of Accountancy* on this matter, but that article says merely that (p. 70) "The value of

investments in marketable securities classified as noncurrent assets may decline because of general market conditions that reflect prospects of the economy as a whole or prospects of a particular industry. Such declines may or may not be indicative of the ability to ultimately recover the carrying amount of investments. The auditor should consider all available evidence to evaluate the carrying amount of the securities." The article gives no further guidance on determining whether or not the decline is temporary. Subsequently, FASB *Interpretation No. 11* (1976) added, in par. 3, the following: "In judging whether or not decline in market value below cost at the balance sheet date is other than temporary, a gain or loss realized on subsequent disposition or changes in market price occurring after the date of the financial statements but prior to their issuance shall be taken into consideration along with other factors."

treatment of the various events relating to investments in marketable securities confusing: the recording of realized gains or losses (through sale, reclassification from current to noncurrent or vice versa, or determination that declines are not temporary), the recording of unrealized losses, the recovery of unrealized losses, and the valuation of the allowance account. Confusion will be minimized and the final answer more likely to be correct if the transactions are analyzed and recorded in the following order:

**1.** Record any realized gains or losses, from whatever source (sale, reclassification from current to noncurrent portfolio or vice versa, determination that a decline is not temporary).

**2.** Compare the market value of the portfolio at the end of the period with its cost to ascertain the required credit balance in the allowance account (= cost less market value if cost exceeds market value and zero otherwise).

**3.** Prepare a journal entry to adjust the allowance account from its current zero or credit balance to its required credit or zero balance.

   **a.** If the adjustment requires a credit to the Allowance account, then the debit is to the Unrealized Loss account, which appears only on the balance sheet.

   **b.** If the adjustment requires a debit to the allowance account, the credit is to the Unrealized Loss account, which appears only on the balance sheet.

14.52   One principle may help you in dealing with application of the lower-of-cost-or-market method to portfolios of marketable equity securities. The principle is this: Individual securities are carried at cost, not at the lower of cost or market with separate valuation allowances; only the portfolio is valued at lower of cost or market. The only exception to this rule is the "dual transaction assumption" of a presumed sale and repurchase made when a decline in market value is judged permanent or when a security is transferred between portfolios. Even then, however, the credit to reduce the investment to cost is made to the Investment account,

not to the Allowance account. The Investment account is a "controlling account" showing the sum of all of the recorded original costs of all the individual securities in the portfolio. When a security is removed from the portfolio, its original cost must be taken out of the Investment account.

**Effect of Lower of Cost or Market on Statement of Changes in Financial Position**   14.53   Use of lower of cost or market for investments in marketable equity securities can affect income in four ways:

**1.** Revenue from dividends declared.

**2.** Realization of gain or loss through sale of securities.

**3.** Assumed realization of loss when a security is transferred either way between current and noncurrent portfolios.

**4.** Assumed realization of loss when decline in market value is judged permanent.

Dividend declarations provide funds. No adjustment to net income in calculating funds from operations is required for dividend revenue. None of the other effects on income, loss in cases **2**, **3**, and **4** or gain in case **2**, affects working capital *provided by continuing operations*. The amounts of the loss should be added back to net income in deriving funds provided by operations. The gain on sale is accompanied by an increase in funds—cash is received when the investment is sold—but those funds are not produced by operations. The funds result from an "Other Source," Disposition of Noncurrent Asset Investment. Consequently, even when there is realized gain on sale of a long-term investment, the amount of the gain is subtracted from net income in deriving funds provided by operations. All of the working capital is shown as provided by the sale of the noncurrent asset, below the operations section. This treatment parallels that for gain on disposition of long-term plant assets, discussed in Chapter 11. (See paragraph 11.101.)

14.54   Using lower of cost or market for investments sometimes involves crediting the asset contra account, Allowance for Decline in Market Value of Investments in Marketable

Equity Securities, and debiting the owners' equity contra account, Net Unrealized Losses on Investments in Marketable Equity Securities. Such entries occur at the end of the period when the Allowance account is adjusted to write down the portfolio's net balance to its current market value. The opposite entry—debit Allowance and credit Unrealized Loss—occurs when the Allowance account is adjusted to write up the portfolio's net balance from its current amount below original cost to a larger amount, still not greater than original cost. Such entries should be reflected in the statement of changes in financial position in the "Other Sources" and "Other Uses" sections, but in practice are seldom seen.* When market values have declined and the net asset is written down, there is an "Other Use" of funds for Decrease in Owners' Equity through Increase in Unrealized Loss and an "Other Source" of funds for the Decrease in Carrying Value of Investments. When market values later increase and the net investment asset is written up, there is an "Other Use" of funds for Increase in Carrying Amount of Investments and an "Other Source" of funds for Increase in Owners' Equity through Decrease in Unrealized Loss.

14.55 **Disclosure Requirements** The acquisition cost and market value of the equity securities in the Investment portfolio at the end of the period must be reported. To make the required adjusting entry, these two amounts must be compared with the acquisition cost and market value of the equity securities in the portfolio at the start of the period, even though the individual equity securities in the portfolio may have changed drastically during the period. The financial statements must include the following disclosures relating to investments in marketable equity securities:

1. Aggregate cost and aggregate market value of the portfolio at each balance sheet date.

2. The gross unrealized gain on all marketable equity securities on which there are gains at the most recent balance sheet date.

3. The gross unrealized loss on all marketable equity securities on which there are losses at the most recent balance sheet date.†

4. The change in the Unrealized Loss account reported in the equity section of the balance sheet.

5. Any significant changes in the net unrealized gain or loss or the net realized gain or loss after the most recent balance sheet date but prior to the issuance of the financial statements. These disclosures parallel those listed in Chapter 6 for equity securities held as current assets.

**Exempt Industries** FASB *Statement No. 12* does not apply to nonprofit organizations, mutual life insurance companies, and employee benefit plans, but it does apply to mutual savings banks and other profit-seeking    14.56

---

*The requirement for this disclosure is paragraph 13 of APB *Opinion No. 19* (March 1971), which preceded FASB *Statement No. 12* on lower of cost or market by 4 years. We infer the requirement described in the body of the text; it cannot be found explicitly in APB *Opinion No. 19*. The analogy of these changes in noncurrent assets and noncurrent equities with those actually described in par. 13 of APB *Opinion No. 19* is so strong, in our opinion, that they should be treated the same as transactions explicitly mentioned there.

†The FASB reports in par. 31 of *Statement No. 12* that it chose to apply the lower-of-cost-or-market valuation basis to the entire portfolio, rather than to each security individually, which would be more conservative, because most firms look on their portfolio as a "collective asset." To decide whether or not such a view is theoretically defensible requires an understanding of modern portfolio theory, which is beyond the scope of this book. (We think it is defensible.) The FASB defended its choice of the whole-portfolio application as follows. *Statement No. 12* requires that disclosure of the gross gains on all securities with gains be separate from the disclosure of the gross losses on all securities with losses. From these two disclosures, the reader can ascertain the extent to which the balance sheet valuation results from offsetting gains on some securities against losses on others. (If the lower-of-cost-or-market valuation basis were applied security by security, rather than to the entire portfolio, the net balance sheet amount would usually be lower than the amount currently reported. The general rule is that in applying the lower-of-cost-or-market basis security by security, the net balance sheet amount would be the original cost of all securities less the amount of gross losses on securities where there are losses.)

mutual enterprises. In addition, companies in industries with specialized industry accounting practices for marketable securities, such as investment companies, broker-dealers, stock life insurance companies, and casualty insurance companies, may continue to follow the specialized accounting practices.

14.57 **Evaluation of Lower of Cost or Market** The lower-of-cost-or-market valuation method provides only a partial solution to accounting for investments in marketable securities. Since at least 1939, accounting theorists have argued that marketable securities should be shown at market value, whether greater or less than cost. Their marketability makes valuing them on a current basis reasonably objective. The market value of the securities is the most relevant value for assessing a firm's current financial position. The FASB has taken the position, however, that permitting the write-up of marketable securities to an amount greater than acquisition cost would be too drastic a departure from historical cost accounting. The case for market values for marketable securities is so strong that upward revaluations from acquisition cost may soon become part of generally accepted accounting principles. Keep in mind that the total gain (or loss) on the holding of a security is the difference between the cash received upon disposal less the original cash cost; over long enough time periods, income equals cash-in less cash-out. The write-downs and write-ups, if any, merely allocate that income to the various accounting periods between the date of purchase and of sale as market conditions change.

## Share Purchase Agreements: Rights, Warrants, and Options

14.58 Certain financial instruments permit their holder to acquire shares of stock in another firm at a stated price for a given time period. Some of these instruments—stock rights, stock warrants, and call options—may be treated as passive equity investments. Others—stock options—are not.

14.59 **Stock Options** A stock option is generally granted in lieu of cash salary to selected employees. It generally specifies that the employee can purchase a specific number of shares at a specific price for a given time span, called the *exercise period*. The exercise period need not begin immediately and can depend on such future events as the profitability of the company or the continued employment of the person receiving the option. Such options are generally not transferable. Because the employee is not allowed to sell it to an investor, there are no accounting problems from the investor's point of view for stock options. Chapter 22 discusses the issuing company's accounting for employee stock options.

**Call and Put Options** One person can 14.60 promise to sell to another a given number of a company's shares, usually 100 shares, at a fixed price for a given time span, such as 3 months or 6 months. The holder of the promise has the option to acquire the securities during the fixed time span for the fixed price. The option, referred to as a *call option,* therefore has value. The value of the option depends on several factors:

**1.** The current relationship between the option's exercise price and the current market price of the underlying shares. The greater the current market price, the more valuable is the option. (When the market price is greater than the exercise price, the option is said to be "in the money.")

**2.** The length of time during which the option is exercisable. The longer the exercise period, the more valuable is the option.

**3.** The volatility of the price of shares under option. The more stable the underlying shares, the less valuable is an option to acquire the shares.

In recent years public exchanges have been 14.61 organized to trade call options in many major public corporations. Investors can acquire these options in the marketplace. The accounting for call options presents no new problems—they are recorded at cost and they are part of the portfolio of *current* marketable equity securities, and, as such, are accounted for with the lower-of-cost-or-market method as discussed in Chapter 6. If the option is exercised, the valuation of the securities acquired is equal to the cost of the option plus the cash given up. If the option lapses, it is written off and a loss is recognized.

14.62    Put options are similar to call options except that the option gives the holder the right to sell at a fixed price, rather than to buy, the shares under option. Put options are also treated as part of the portfolio of current marketable equity securities.

14.63    **Stock Rights and Warrants** Stock rights are normally received by existing shareholders without additional cash investment. Stock warrants are usually purchased by the investor from the issuing corporation. Both instruments specify the price at which a new share may be acquired and how many rights or warrants must be turned in along with the cash in exchange for the new share. The period during which a right can be exercised is usually short—less than 2 months, whereas a warrant's exercise period may be for many years. Both rights and warrants are usually transferable between holders and, as such, are traded in public markets as marketable equity securities. Whether warrants and rights are classified as current or as noncurrent marketable equity securities depends on management intention in holding them.

14.64    **Accounting for Stock Rights** Stock rights are received by existing shareholders in proportion to their current holdings—one right per share, for example. The issuing company specifies the number of rights and the amount of cash required for a new share as well as the expiration date of the offer. During the period between issue of the rights and their expiration, the rights may be traded in the marketplace. Three dates are important for understanding stock rights: the date the rights offer is announced, the date when the rights are issued, and the expiration date of the rights. From the time the rights offering is announced until the time the rights themselves are issued, the existing shares are said to be *rights-on*. After the rights are issued, they may be traded separately from the shares and the shares are said to be *ex-rights*.

Rights received from the issuing company    14.65 are a portion of the investor's interest in the owned corporation. The carrying amount for the investment has not changed, but recorded cost must be allocated between the previously owned shares and the new rights. Assume, for illustration, that Owning Company owns 10,000 shares of C Company which are carried on its books in the account Investment in C Company Stock for $80,000. Owning Company receives 10,000 rights. Five rights and $20 cash are required for one new share in C Company. The market value of C Company shares was $32 rights-on just before the rights were issued and $30 ex-rights just after. The market price of the rights alone is $2.* The cost, as contrasted to the market value, of the rights is determined by allocating the book value of the shares as follows:

$$\frac{\$2 \text{ Market Value per Right}}{\$32 \text{ Market Value per Share Rights-on}} \times \$80,000 \text{ Cost of Investment}$$

$$= \$5,000 \text{ Cost Allocated to Rights}$$

The journal entry to separate the already-booked cost between shares and rights is

*In some situations, the investor needs to approximate the theoretical market value of the stock after a rights offering. An estimate can be made by summing the present market price of the shares that must be held to permit the acquisition of one new share and the cash payment required to acquire one new share; then this total is divided by the number of shares existing after exercise of the right. The difference between the existing price of a share of stock and the theoretical price ex-rights is, of course, the theoretical value of the right received by present shareholders. This relationship can be expressed as follows:

$$\frac{P(m/n) + C}{(m/n) + 1} = P - nR \quad \text{or} \quad P - nR = C + mR$$

$$\text{or} \quad R = \frac{P - C}{m + n}$$

where

$P$ = Market Price of a Share, Rights-on (that is, before the issue of the rights)

$m$ = Number of Rights Required to Acquire One New Share

$n$ = Number of Rights Received for Each Share Held, Usually Equal to One

$C$ = Cash Payment Required to Acquire One New Share upon Exercise of $m$ Rights

$R$ = Estimated Market Price of One Right.

Investment in C Company Rights ...... 5,000
    Investment in C Company Stock ..         5,000
To allocate cost to rights from stock;
rights carry cost of $0.50 (= $5,000/
10,000 shares) each.

When the rights are exercised, they are accounted for at cost.* The cost of the rights and the cash exchanged become the cost of the new shares. Assume that half the rights are exercised when rights have a fair market value of $2.05 each. Owning Company swaps 5,000 rights and $20,000 for 1,000 new shares. The entry is

Investment in C Company Stock .... 22,500
    Cash ......................     20,000
    Investment in C Company
        Rights ....................     2,500
To record cost of 1,000 shares acquired with rights and cash.

Of the remaining rights, assume that 4,000 are sold for $2.10 each and the remaining 1,000 rights are allowed to lapse. (Lapse of rights worth $2.10 each would be foolish, but we let them lapse so that the accounting can be illustrated. Occasionally rights become worthless before they are exercised because of a drop in the market price of the stock.) The entries are

Cash .............................. 8,400
    Investment in C Company Rights ..    2,000
    Gain on Sale of Stock Rights .....    6,400

Loss on Expiration of Stock Rights .... 500
    Investment in C Company Rights ..    500

The gain or loss affects reported net income for the period.

_____

*In spite of our interpretations of APB *Opinion No. 29*, par. 18, discussed in the footnote to paragraph 14.11 above, we think gain or loss is not recognized on exercise of rights. The rights were not explicitly purchased by the firm as are warrants, discussed next. Rights are received because shares have been purchased in the past and are part of the prior investment. The ownership conveyed with the rights issue is analogous to a stock dividend. The owning firm must exercise its rights (or not sell off the shares received as a stock dividend) to keep its percentage interest in the investee firm intact. Whereas the purchase of warrants is a transaction completed when the warrants are sold or exercised, the receipt of rights is not the start of a transaction; the original share purchase was the start. In this sense, the exercise of stock rights is much like subsequent payments on stock subscription agreements, discussed in Chapter 21.

**Accounting for Stock Warrants** Stock war-    14.66
rants are acquired by purchase, either from the issuing company or from another owner. Investments in stock warrants are treated like investments in any other equity security. They are recorded at cost and added to the portfolio of investments accounted for at the lower of cost or market. If, later, the warrants are exercised, then their market value on the date of exercise is transferred to the cost of the shares they were used to acquire and gain or loss upon exercise is recognized.† For example, assume that Owning Company acquires warrants to purchase 100 shares of D Company. The warrants are exercisable for 5 years at a price of $40 per share. The warrants cost $10 each, $1,000 in total. Sometime after acquisition, when their market price is $14, they are exercised. The journal entries are

Investment in D Company Warrants ... 1,000
    Cash .........................     1,000
To record cost of warrants purchased.

Investment in D Company Stock ...... 5,400
    Cash .........................     4,000
    Investment in D Company
        Warrants ....................     1,000
    Gain on Exchange of Warrants ...      400
Exercise of warrants, using $4,000 cash, to acquire 100 shares. Warrants have increased in value by $4 (= $14 − $10) since acquisition. The gain is recognized on the exchange.

The price of the rights or warrants may fluctuate in the market place. Using lower of cost or market, the portfolio of equity securities containing rights or warrants may carry a book value different from original cost. Whatever the balance in the Allowance account, the exchange of rights or warrants is treated as a sale. Gain (or loss) recognized is equal to the market price on the exchange date less the cost of the rights or warrants. The cost is removed from the Investment account. At the end of the accounting period, the net book value of the remaining portfolio may be different from its market value. If so, the Allowance account

_____

†See APB *Opinion No. 29* (1973), par. 18, and our discussion in the footnote to paragraph 14.11 above.

balance is recomputed to adjust the portfolio's net amount to market value.

## Stock Dividends and Stock Splits

14.67   For reasons discussed more fully in Chapter 23, firms sometimes distribute additional shares of stock in the form of stock dividends and stock splits. Both stock dividends and stock splits involve the distribution of additional shares of stock to the current owners of outstanding shares. The firm receiving additional shares treats them similarly whether they are received through stock dividends or stock splits. Chapter 23 explains how the issuing firm accounts differently for the two.

14.68   When the investor company receives additional shares of stock from a stock dividend or a stock split, it changes the cost basis *per share* of the shares it then owns. The receipt of the shares does not itself involve income recognition.* The owning firm's rights of ownership have been spread over more pieces of paper. The total cost of the investment remains unchanged; the number of shares evidencing ownership increases; the cost per share declines.

14.69   For example, assume that the Owning Company has 10,000 shares of A Company, which are currently carried on the books at $110,000, or $11 per share, and 500 shares of B Company, which are currently carried on the books for $50,000, or $100 per share. A Company declares a 10-percent stock dividend, distributing one new share to holders for each 10 shares currently held. Owning Company receives 1,000 new shares. (If an investor does not hold a number of shares evenly divisible by 10, then the issuing company will not usually issue a fractional share but will pay cash equal to the market value of a fractional share. The investor receiving the cash will debit Cash and credit the Investment account, because all the cash received is viewed as reducing the cost of the remaining investment.) Owning Company need make no journal entry upon receiving its additional 1,000 shares of A Company

stock. It merely notes that the number of shares has increased from 10,000 to 11,000, and the cost basis per share decreases from $11 (= $110,000/10,000 shares) to $10 (= $110,000/11,000 shares). If it sells 2,000 shares for $25 per share, the entry is

| | | |
|---|---|---|
| Cash ........................... | 50,000 | |
|    Investment in A Company ...... | | 20,000 |
|    Gain on Sale of Investment .... | | 30,000 |

Sale for $25 per share of 2,000 costing $10 per share.

14.70   Assume that B Company declares a four-for-one stock split and distributes 1,500 additional shares to Owning Company. (B Company might issue 2,000 shares and recall the outstanding 500 shares, but this would be unusual.) Owning Company makes no journal entry, but notes that the cost per share has been decreased to $25 per share.

14.71   Occasionally, a firm will declare a *reverse* stock split, issuing one new share for each, say, four shares outstanding. It will issue new shares and recall the outstanding shares. Then the owning company's cost basis per share will be increased, in this case by a factor of four, but the *total* cost of the new shares will be the same as the old shares.

## Controlling Investments: The Equity Method

14.72   Under the lower-of-cost or-market method, the owner of an investment typically recognizes income or loss on the income statement when it becomes entitled to receive dividends or when it sells shares at a gain or loss.† When the owner of the shares can control the operations of the owned, investee company, then the owner can manipulate its own reported income by controlling the dividend policy of the owned company. The lower-of-cost-or-market method may not adequately reflect income of the owning company when it controls the investee company. The *equity method* is designed to provide a better measure of the owning com-

---

*Accounting Research Bulletin No. 43,* AICPA (1953), chap. 7B, par. 6. In almost all cases, such receipts are not taxable income.

†In addition, reclassifying securities from the noncurrent portfolio to the current portfolio or determining declines in market value to be permanent also causes losses to be recognized in income.

pany's income and financial position under these circumstances. In the rest of this section the owning company is called Company P (for purchaser or parent) and the owned, investee company is called Company S (for seller or subsidiary).

14.73 **Required Use of the Equity Method** When Company P can exercise "significant influence" over the operating and financial policies of Company S, generally accepted accounting principles require that P's investment in S be reported using the equity method, as described in APB *Opinion No. 18*. To ascertain when significant influence can be exercised involves judgment. For the sake of objectivity, generally accepted accounting principles presume that P can influence S and should use the equity method when P owns 20 percent or more of the common stock of S. The equity method is required even when less than 20 percent is owned when management and accountants agree that Company P exercises significant influence over Company S.* In some cases, the owner could exercise complete control if it owned 5 to 10 percent of the outstanding voting shares. In rare cases, ownership of 20 percent or more of the voting shares does not signify control, and the requirement for use of the equity method is waived. This would occur, for example, if Company P had agreed in settlement of legal proceedings not to vote the shares it owned in Company S.

## Equity Method: Procedures

14.74 Under the equity method, the initial purchase of an investment is recorded at cost. Company P treats as income (or revenue) each period its proportionate share of the earnings, not the dividends, of Company S. Dividends declared by S are then treated by P as a reduction in its Investment in S. Suppose that P acquires 30 percent of the outstanding shares of S for $600,000. The entry to record the acquisition is

*Financial Accounting Standards Board, *Interpretation No. 35,* "Criteria for Applying the Equity Method of Accounting for Investments in Common Stock" (May 1981).

**(1)**

| | | |
|---|---|---|
| Investment in S | 600,000 | |
| Cash | | 600,000 |

Investment made in 30% of Company S.

Between the time of the acquisition and the end of P's next accounting period, S reports income of $80,000. P, using the equity method, records

**(2)**

| | | |
|---|---|---|
| Investment in S | 24,000 | |
| Revenue from Investments | | 24,000 |

To record 30% of income earned by investee accounted for using the equity method. Revenue account title often used in practice is Equity in Income of Unconsolidated Affiliates.

If S declares a dividend of $30,000 to holders of common stock, P is entitled to receive $9,000 and records

**(3)**

| | | |
|---|---|---|
| Dividends Receivable | 9,000 | |
| Investment in S | | 9,000 |

To record dividends receivable from investee accounted for using the equity method and the resulting reduction in the investment account.

Notice that the credit is to the Investment in S account. P records income earned by S as an *increase* in investment. The dividend becomes a return of capital or a *decrease* in investment.†

---

†Students often have difficulty understanding journal entry **(3)**, particularly the credit by the investor when a dividend is declared by the investee company. The transactions and entries are analogous to an individual's ordinary savings account at a local bank. Assume that you put $600,000 in a savings account, that later interest of 4 percent (or $24,000) is added by the bank to the account, and that still later you ask the bank to withdraw $9,000 from the savings account, depositing the $9,000 in your checking account. Journal entries **(1)** – **(3)** in the text could be recorded for these three events with slight changes in the account titles: Investment in S changes to Savings Account, Revenue from Investments changes to Interest Revenue, and Dividends Receivable changes to Cash in Bank. The cash withdrawal reduces the amount invested in the savings account. Similarly, the declaration of a cash dividend by an investee company accounted for with the equity method reduces the investor's investment in the company.

14.75    Suppose that S subsequently reports earnings of $100,000 and also declares dividends of $40,000. P's entries are

**(4)**

| | | |
|---|---|---|
| Investment in S ................ | 30,000 | |
|     Revenue from Investments ... | | 30,000 |

**(5)**

| | | |
|---|---|---|
| Dividends Receivable ............ | 12,000 | |
|     Investment in S ............. | | 12,000 |

To record revenue and dividends from investee, accounted for using equity method.

P's Investment in S account now has a balance of $633,000 as follows:

**Investment in S**

| | | | |
|---|---|---|---|
| (1) | 600,000 | 9,000 | (3) |
| (2) | 24,000 | 12,000 | (5) |
| (4) | 30,000 | | |
| Bal. | 633,000 | | |

If P now sells one-fourth of its shares for $152,000, P's entry to record the sale is

**(6)**

| | | |
|---|---|---|
| Cash ........................ | 152,000 | |
| Loss on Sale of Investment in S .. | 6,250 | |
|     Investment in S ............. | | 158,250 |

($1/4 \times \$633,000 = \$158,250$.)

14.76    An investment accounted for using the equity method is shown in the Investments section of the balance sheet. The amount shown is generally equal to the acquisition cost of the shares plus P's share of S's undistributed earnings since the date the shares were acquired. On the income statement, P shows its share of S's income as a revenue each period. (The financial statements of the investee, S, are not affected by the accounting method used by the investor, P.)

## Equity Method Effects on the Statement of Changes in Financial Position

14.77    Accounting for investments using the equity method generally requires an adjustment to net income to calculate Funds Provided by Operations. Suppose that Company P prepares its financial statements at the end of a year during which transactions **(1)**–**(3)**, above, occurred. P's revenue from its investment in S is $24,000. This amount is the revenue recognized in transaction **(2)**.

14.78    P's income (ignoring income tax effects) increased $24,000 because of its investment. However, P's working capital increased by only $9,000 [transaction **(3)**] as a result of S's dividend declaration. Consequently, there must be a *subtraction* from net income of $15,000 (= $24,000 − $9,000) in calculating Funds Provided by Operations, to show that working capital did not increase by as much as the amount of revenue recognized under the equity method.

14.79    In preparing P's statement of changes in financial position for the first year using the T-account method, the following change in a noncurrent asset account must be explained:

**Investment in S**

| | | |
|---|---|---|
| Bal. | 0 | |
| Bal. | 615,000 | |

The work sheet entries to explain this debit change of $615,000 would be

| | | |
|---|---|---|
| Investment in S ................ | 600,000 | |
|     Working Capital (Use— | | |
|       Acquisition of Investment) . | | 600,000 |

To recognize use of funds for an investment in a noncurrent asset.

| | | |
|---|---|---|
| Investment in S ................ | 15,000 | |
|     Working Capital (Subtraction | | |
|       —Undistributed Income | | |
|       under Equity Method) ..... | | 15,000 |

To recognize that working capital was not increased by the full amount of revenue under the equity method.

Keep in mind that these two entries are not formally made in the accounting records, but are made only in the work sheet used for preparing the statement of changes in financial position.

## Equity Method Illustrated in Annual Report

14.80    Exhibits A.1, A.2, and A.3 (in Appendix A) show the income statement, balance sheet, and statement of changes in financial position of the International Corporation. The balance sheet, Exhibit A.2, shows investments of approximately $289 million as of year-end 1981.

14.81 The income statement for 1981 shows income of $14.5 million from the investments accounted for on the equity method as "Equity in Income (Loss) from Nonconsolidated Subsidiaries and Affiliated Companies." This income did not produce working capital because the subsidiaries and affiliated companies did not declare dividends. Thus, the funds statement, Exhibit A.3, shows a subtraction of $14.5 million in deriving "Working Capital Provided by Continuing Operations." For the year 1980, the nonconsolidated subsidiaries and affiliates had losses of $32.3 million. The parent's equity in these losses is shown on the income statement as an amount reducing net income. On the funds statement in Exhibit A.3, the amount is added back in deriving funds provided by operations because it did not use working capital. Instead, this loss reduced a noncurrent asset account, Investments.

## Complications in Using the Equity Method

14.82 The equity method as described above is simple enough to use. To make financial reports using the equity method more realistic, generally accepted accounting principles require some modification of the entries under certain circumstances.*

14.83 **Deferred Taxes** Even though S does not declare all of its earnings in dividends, P reports its proportionate share of S's earnings as income. But this income to P is not currently taxable. Consequently, there may be an entry for deferred taxes. See the discussion in Chapter 20.

14.84 **Excess of Cost over Book Value** The acquisition cost of P's shares can exceed P's proportionate share of the book value of the net assets (= assets minus liabilities), or shareholders' equity of S, at the date of acquisition. For example, assume that P acquires 25 percent of the stock of S for $400,000 when the total shareholders' equity of S is $1 million. The excess of P's cost over book value acquired is $150,000 (= $400,000 − .25 × $1,000,000). This excess can arise for one or both of two reasons:

**1.** The value of S's recorded assets exceeds their booked amounts.

**2.** Company S has unrecorded *goodwill,* which is discussed in Chapter 13 on intangibles.

The excess of purchase price over the market value of identifiable assets acquired must be amortized over a period not exceeding 40 years.† The amortization reduces both the investment account and income of the period of amortization. Assume, for example, that the $150,000 excess of cost of P's investment over S's book value results from $130,000 excess of current value over book value of plant assets and $20,000 of goodwill. S's plant assets are being depreciated over, say, 20 years, and P decides to amortize the goodwill over 40 years (the longest period allowed). Each year Company P will make the following entry in addition to whatever entries were necessary to record its share of earnings and dividends:

Amortization Expense . . . . . . . . . . . . . . . . 7,000
    Investments in S . . . . . . . . . . . . . . . . 7,000
Income and the Investment account are both reduced by amortization of extra cost of plant, $6,500 = $130,000/20, and of goodwill, $500 = $20,000/40. This expense does not use funds; an addition to net income is required in deriving funds from operations.

The debit might be to Revenue from Investments instead of to Amortization Expense.

**Excess of Book Value over Cost** If P's cost 14.85

---

*Accounting Principles Board, APB *Opinion No. 18* (March 1971).

†Accounting Principles Board, APB *Opinion No. 17*(August 1970).

of shares is less than the book value of those shares as recorded on S's books, then S's net assets presumably are worth less than their book value. Depreciation and other expenses on S's income statement are based on S's book values; these are too large relative to the amounts P paid for them. Hence from P's viewpoint, S's income (particularly P's share of it) is understated. To compensate for the understatement, the excess of book value over cost of the shares owned by P is amortized to P's investment revenue over the life of the assets, increasing it. The debit is to the investment account. Assume, for example, that P's investment in S cost $80,000 less than the book value of the shares on S's books. P decides that the excess applies to assets being depreciated on average over 10 years. (This will be a difficult determination to make in practice.) For the first 10 years P owns the investment in S, it will make the following entry each year (in addition to whatever others may be required):

```
Investment in S  .................... 8,000
    Revenue from Investments  ......       8,000
To amortize to income one-tenth of the
excess of S's book value over cost of P's
shares in S. This revenue does not
provide funds; a subtraction from net
income is required in deriving funds
from operations.
```

**After Investment, Losses Exceed Cost** Assume that after P purchases S's shares, S has net losses. Using the equity method, P will record its share of those losses with a debit to the account Revenue from Investments (or perhaps Losses from Investments) and credits to the Investment account. If S's losses persist, P's investment account will reduce to zero. P will generally cease recording further losses in the books, but will make note of its share of these further losses. If S subsequently has positive net income, then P will record as revenues its share of that income only after the unrecorded losses have been recouped. Exhibit 14.5 illustrates this treatment. If P has guar-     14.86

---

## Exhibit 14.5
### Illustration of Equity Method When Investee Sustains Losses

| Year | Events of Year |
|---|---|
| 0 | P purchases 25% of S's shares for $100,000 at end of year. |
| 1 | S earns $ 60,000; P's share is $15,000. |
| 2 | S loses $140,000; P's share is $35,000 |
| 3 | S loses $180,000; P's share is $45,000. |
| 4 | S loses $200,000; P's share is $50,000. |
| 5 | S loses $40,000; P's share is $10,000. |
| 6 | S earns $80,000; P's share is $20,000. |
| 7 | S earns $100,000; P's share is $25,000. |

| Year | P's Account Investment in S Start of Year | P's Recorded Revenue (Loss) from Investment In S for Year | P's Unrecorded Revenue (Loss) for Year[a] | P's Account Investment in S End of Year | P's Cumulative Unrecorded Loss[a] |
|---|---|---|---|---|---|
| 1 | $100,000 | $15,000 | — | $115,000 | — |
| 2 | 115,000 | (35,000) | — | 80,000 | — |
| 3 | 80,000 | (45,000) | — | 35,000 | — |
| 4 | 35,000 | (35,000) | ($15,000) | 0 | $15,000 |
| 5 | 0 | 0 | (10,000) | 0 | 25,000 |
| 6 | 0 | 0 | 20,000 | 0 | 5,000 |
| 7 | 0 | 20,000 | 5,000 | 20,000 | 0 |

[a]These accounts do not appear in the financial statements.

anteed S's obligations or has made some other commitment for financial support of S, then P will recognize losses so long as S has losses. The resulting credit balance in the Investment account will be shown as a liability, with the account title changed to something like Obligation to Creditors of Investee Company.

14.87 **Changing to the Equity Method** P may gradually acquire a controlling interest in S. When P first acquires shares in S, the number of shares may be less than the, say, 20 percent required for control. Over time, P acquires more shares until, at a given time, it owns sufficient shares to control S. Until the last purchase that provides control, P does not use the equity method. It will use instead the lower-of-cost-or-market method. When the controlling shares are acquired, P

adjusts its books so that the books appear as they would have if P had been using the equity method all along. This general procedure is described in more detail in Chapter 23 under the heading, "Change in an Accounting Principle." The accounting is like that for a prior-period adjustment. The following journal entries, based on data in Exhibit 14.6, illustrate the treatment.

Jan., Year 1
Investment in S ................. 100,000
    Cash ..................... 100,000
Record investment.

During Year 1
Dividends Receivable or Cash .... 5,000
    Dividend Revenue ........... 5,000
Record revenue from dividends under lower-of-cost-or-market method.

---

*Exhibit 14.6*
**Illustration of Change to Equity Method Resulting from Gradual Acquisition of Controlling Interest**

| Date | Events |
|---|---|
| Jan., Year 1 ................. | P Company acquires 10% of the shares of S for $100,000. At this time S's net assets have a book value of $700,000. The $30,000 excess of P's $100,000 cost over book value acquired of $70,000 (= .10 × $700,000) is attributed to undervalued assets being amortized over 8 years. P uses the lower-of-cost-or-market method of accounting for its investment in S. |
| Dec., Year 1 ................. | S earned income of $90,000 during Year 1 and declared dividends of $50,000. P's investment portfolio has increased in market value. |
| Dec., Year 2 ................. | S earned income of $100,000 during Year 2 and declared dividends of $60,000. P's investment portfolio has increased in market value. |
| Jan., Year 3 ................. | P acquires an additional 15% of the shares of S for $210,000. At this time S's net assets have a book value of $1,000,000. The $60,000 excess of P's cost of $210,000 over book value acquired of $150,000 (= .15 × $1,000,000) is attributed to undervalued assets being depreciated over 6 years. |
| Dec., Year 3 ................. | S earned income of $140,000 and declared dividends of $80,000. |

**ACCOUNTING IF EQUITY METHOD WERE USED IN ALL 3 YEARS**

| Year | Investment Start of + Year | Share of – Earnings | Share of – Dividends | Amortization of Excess of Cost over = Book Value | Investment End of Year |
|---|---|---|---|---|---|
| 1 ..................... | $100,000 + | $ 9,000 – | $ 5,000 – | $ 3,750[b] = | $100,250 |
| 2 ..................... | 100,250 + | 10,000 – | 6,000 – | 3,750[b] = | 100,500 |
| 3 ..................... | 310,500[a] + | 35,000 – | 20,000 – | 13,750[c] = | 311,750 |

[a]$100,500 + $210,000 = $310,500.

[b]$1/8 × [$100,000 − (.10 × $700,000)] = $3,750.

[c]$1/8 × [$100,000 − (.10 × $700,000)] + 1/6 × [$210,000 − (.15 × $1,000,000)] = $13,750.

During Year 2
Dividends Receivable or Cash .... 6,000
    Dividend Revenue .......... 6,000

Jan., Year 3
Investment in S ................. 210,000
    Cash ..................... 210,000
To record cost of additional investment.

Jan., Year 3
Investment in S ................. 500
    Retained Earnings .......... 500
To adjust Investment to $310,500, the amount that would be shown if equity method had been used all along. The credit adjusts Retained Earnings directly, bypassing this year's income statement.

During Year 3
Dividends Receivable or Cash .... 20,000
Investment in S ................. 15,000
    Investment Revenue ......... 35,000
To record P's 25% share of earnings for year.

Dec., Year 3
Amortization Expense ........... 13,750
    Investment in S ............. 13,750
To record amortization of excess of cost over book value for the year.

The last pair of entries, for Year 3, might well be combined:

Dividends Receivable or Cash ...... 20,000
Investment in S .................. 1,250
Amortization Expense ............ 13,750
    Investment Revenue .......... 35,000

14.88    **Changing from the Equity Method** The investor company P may sell some of its shares in S, reducing its holdings sufficiently so that it cannot exercise control, or the investee company S may increase the number of shares outstanding so that the shares owned by P are insufficient for it to exercise control. In either case, P will stop using the equity method and use the lower-of-cost-or-market method. The amount shown for the investment is the amount remaining in the Investment account after the shares are sold. That is, the effects of P's having used the equity method are left in the Investment

account. The balance in the Investment account is *not* changed to reflect the balance that would be there if lower of cost or market had been used all along.

## Summary of Accounting for Minority and Majority Investments in Equity Securities

14.89 Businesses acquire stock in other businesses for a variety of reasons in a variety of ways. The acquisition of stock of another company is generally recorded as follows:

Investment in S ........................... X
    Cash or Other Consideration Given ...... X

The investment account is recorded at the amount of cash given or the market value of other consideration exchanged.

14.90 The accounting for the investment subsequent to acquisition depends on the ownership percentage and the marketability of the shares. The cost method is used for nonmarketable, passive investments. The lower-of-cost-or-market method is used for the portfolio of marketable, passive investments, generally investments of less than 20 percent of the voting shares. The equity method is used when the investor can exert significant influence, generally by owning 20 percent but not more than 50 percent of the voting stock of another company. Consolidated statements are usually prepared when the parent owns more than 50 percent of the voting shares of another company, but the equity method may be used. Exhibit 14.7 summarizes the accounting for investments subsequent to the acquisition.

## Other Investment Accounts

14.91 Two other investment accounts—special-purpose funds and life insurance—merit special treatment.

### Investments in Special-Purpose Funds

14.92 Firms sometimes deposit cash in earmarked funds to provide for specific purposes at spe-

---

*Exhibit 14.7*

**Effects of Various Methods
of Accounting for Investments
in Equity Securities**

---

| Method of Accounting | Balance Sheet | Income Statement | Statement of Changes in Financial Position |
|---|---|---|---|
| Cost method for nonmarketable equity securities. | Investment account shown at acquisition cost. | Dividends declared by investee shown as revenue of investor. Gains and losses (from original cost) are reported in income only as realized. | Revenues from dividends produce working capital. Sales of investments generate working capital shown in their entirety as an "Other Source." The gain (or loss) reported on sale does not produce (or use) funds from operations; a subtraction for gain from (or addition for loss to) net income is required to derive funds from operations. |
| Lower-of-cost-or-market method for marketable equity securities (generally when ownership percentage is less than 20%). | Investment account shown at lower of acquisition cost or current market value as a noncurrent asset. Unrealized losses resulting from decline in market value below cost are credited to an asset contra and debited to an unrealized loss account that is shown as a negative component of owners' equity. | Dividends declared by investee shown as revenue of investor. Gains and losses (from original cost) are reported in income only as realized by sale. Losses are also recognized upon reclassification from noncurrent to current or vice versa and by determination that declines in market value are not temporary. | Sale of investments generates working capital shown in its entirety as an "Other Source." The related gain (or loss) increases (or decreases) income but does not produce (or use) funds from operations. The amount of gain (loss) is subtracted from (added to) income in deriving funds from operations. When a loss is realized through reclassification or permanent decline of a security not yet sold, there is an addback to net income for the loss not using funds in deriving funds from operations. |
| Equity method (generally when ownership percentage is at least 20% but not more than 50%). | Investment account shown at cost plus share of investee's net income less share of investee's dividends since acquisition. | Equity in investee's net income shown as revenue in period during which investee earns income.[b] | Equity in investee's undistributed earnings is subtracted from net income to derive working capital provided by operations of investor. Working capital from operations is thus increased only by the amount of dividend declarations. |

*Exhibit 14.7 (continued)*

| **Method of Accounting** | **Balance Sheet** | **Income Statement** | **Statement of Changes in Financial Position** |
| --- | --- | --- | --- |
| Consolidation method (generally when ownership percentage is greater than 50%).[a] | Investment account is eliminated and replaced with individual assets and liabilities of subsidiary. Minority interest in subsidiary's net assets shown among equities. | Individual revenues and expenses of subsidiary are combined with those of parent. Minority interest in subsidiary's net income shown as a subtraction. | Individual sources and uses of working capital of subsidiary are combined with those of parent. Minority interest in net income is added to net income to obtain working capital provided by operations. |

[a]Appendix 14.1 discusses these details.

[b]If the cost of the investment exceeds the investor's share of the book value of the underlying net assets, then the excess must be amortized over a period not exceeding 40 years. The periodic amortization reduces the investment account and increases amortization expense. This expense does not use working capital and must, therefore, be added to net income in deriving working capital from operations.

cific later times. This section discusses such funds, which are slightly different from those discussed in Chapter 6. The funds considered there involved essentially two purposes:

1. Revolving funds established to provide coins and currency where those items are needed, such as for change funds and petty cash funds.

2. Special bank accounts, such as for payroll or dividend or interest disbursements. The goal of such funds is to allow the primary cash account to be credited with a given sum that is to be disbursed in smaller amounts to many recipients. The accounting for the many disbursements can be separated from the primary task of keeping the firm's records, allowing better control than would be convenient if all disbursements were handled from the primary cash account.

14.93   The special-purpose funds treated here either are required by specific provisions of contracts between the firm and others or are voluntarily set up by the firm to accumulate funds for the future. Examples of the former include sinking funds (to pay off long-term debt), stock redemption funds (to retire stock, usually preferred shares), and pension funds (to provide for employee pension payments). Examples of the latter include plant expansion funds (to provide cash for acquiring new plant) and, in principle, contingency funds (to provide funds for some as-yet-undefined problem). Cash is so scarce in business these days that the latter sort of fund is seldom seen.

Funds required because of specific contract provision are usually administered by trustees who are independent of the firm. Voluntary funds are usually managed within the firm. The cash deposited in either of these types of funds is invested. When funds are created to provide specific amounts at specific future times, the investment is usually in bonds (or mortgages) with maturity dates near the time that payment is required.*

14.94

---

*A better strategy even than investing in bonds with maturity date near the time funds are needed is to invest in bonds whose *duration* is equal to the amount of time to elapse before the funds are needed. A discussion of duration, a measure of a financial investment's time horizon used in modern financial management, is beyond the scope of accounting. The duration measure was devised to deal with the problem caused by bonds providing cash distributions in the form of coupon payments arriving on one date and requiring reinvestment because they cannot be used to discharge the obligation until some later date. At the time bonds are originally acquired, one cannot be sure what the reinvestment rate will be for coupons to be received later.

14.95 **Accounting for Funds** Funds created to satisfy contractual provisions are, themselves, of two types.

**1.** Some funds are created to satisfy an obligation of the firm. The firm is responsible for the eventual payment of a contractual amount whether or not the fund has accumulated the specific amount at maturity; conversely, if the fund has more than necessary, then the firm gets back the excess.*

**2.** In other cases, the firm satisfies its obligations merely by paying contractually specified amounts to a fund administered outside the firm. Once the firm makes the required payments, it has no further liability. The beneficiaries of the fund bear the risks that the amount in the fund will be inadequate at some future time and are entitled to the extra rewards if the amounts are more than necessary. The firm making deposits to the second type of fund has no problem in accounting for the fund. It merely debits expense and credits cash as the contractual payments are made.†

---

*Under circumstances where a firm is liable for an obligation whether or not the fund has sufficient amounts at maturity to pay off the obligation, one may wonder about the reason for having a fund at all. What purpose does the fund serve? The assets of a fund can legally be earmarked for a certain purpose, such as paying off bondholders. If a bankruptcy were to occur and there were no special funds for paying off bondholders, those creditors would not be entitled to any special treatment when the firm's assets were divided among all the creditors. It is generally thought that bondholders can assure themselves some additional protection against a firm's insolvency or bankruptcy by requiring a legally separate sinking fund for the retirement of the bonded indebtedness. (Modern financial theory makes one skeptical of the benefit to bondholders. Bonds with sinking funds required by the indenture are generally safer investments than those without; the market generally requires smaller interest payments on safer bonds than on less safe bonds. Thus bondholders who require a sinking fund are not getting something for nothing. The sinking fund comes at the cost of lower interest than the bondholder could have had for general corporate debentures with no sinking fund protection.)

†Under some circumstances, for example, if the firm had settled a lawsuit and had become liable to pay amounts to damaged customers over a long period of time, it would have debited a loss account and credited liability at the time the lawsuit was settled. Then the contractual payments to the fund would be debited, not to expense, but to the liability account.

Accounting techniques for funds are necessary when the fund is to satisfy the firm's, as opposed to the fund's, contractual obligations or when the fund is set up voluntarily by the firm. The accounting records must be capable of recording each of the following sorts of transactions: **(1)** the transfer of assets to the fund, **(2)** investment transactions in the fund, **(3)** revenues from investment earnings, **(4)** expenses of managing the fund, and **(5)** payouts from the fund. 14.96

**Illustration of Bond Sinking Fund** Owning 14.97 Company issues $1 million of bonds that mature in 10 years. The bond indenture requires that cash be set aside in a bond sinking fund to be administered by a bank acting as trustee. Ten cash payments are to be paid altogether. There will be nine equal annual installments, starting 1 year from today; the tenth payment will be made to the fund at the end of the tenth year to bring the amount in the fund up to $1 million; if there should be more than $1 million in the fund at the end of the tenth year, Owning Company will get back the excess. Owning Company decides that investments in the fund can earn 8 percent and that expenses of managing the fund will be about $1,000 per year. Using the methods described in Appendix B of this book, Owning Company calculates that 10 periodic annual payments of about $70,000 will accumulate at 8 percent interest to $1 million while paying for $1,000 per year in expenses.** Assume that Owning Company makes a cash deposit of $70,000 to the fund at the end of the first year and that during the second year, earnings of the fund are $5,500 while expenses are $1,100. The journal entries for the fund through the end of the second year might be as follows:

**End of First Year:**

Investment in Bond Sinking
    Fund ................... 70,000
       Cash ................ 70,000
To establish fund.

---

**Table 3 at the back of the book, 8-percent column, 10-payment row, shows the future value of annuity in arrears for 10 payments to be $14.48656 per dollar of payment. Because $1 million is required, the annual payment for maturity is $1,000,000/14.48656 = $69,029.50. That payment plus expected expenses of $1,000 amounts to approximately $70,000 per year.

**End of Second Year:**

| | | |
|---|---|---|
| Investment in Bond Sinking Fund .................. | 5,500 | |
|     Sinking Fund Revenue . | | 5,500 |

To record earnings of investments in fund.

| | | |
|---|---|---|
| Sinking Fund Expense ..... | 1,100 | |
|     Investment in Bond Sinking Fund ........ | | 1,100 |

To record expenses paid from sinking fund assets.

| | | |
|---|---|---|
| Investment in Bond Sinking Fund .................. | 70,000 | |
|     Cash ................. | | 70,000 |

Second payment to fund.

14.98   Owning Company reports the revenue and expense amounts in its income statement each year. The Investment in Bond Sinking Fund is Owning Company's asset.

14.99     Assume, further, that after the required deposit at the end of the ninth year, the fund has a balance of $875,000, the earnings of the fund for the tenth year are $75,000, and the expenses for the tenth year are $1,300. At the end of the tenth year, the last payment is made to the fund and the manager of the fund retires the bonds. The entries at the end of the tenth year would be as follows:

| | | |
|---|---|---|
| Sinking Fund Expense ..... | 1,300 | |
| Investment in Bond Sinking Fund .................... | 125,000 | |
|     Sinking Fund Revenue ... | | 75,000 |
|     Cash ................... | | 51,300 |

To record revenue and expense of fund for year 10 as well as the cash payment to bring amount in fund up to $1 million.

| | | |
|---|---|---|
| Bonds Payable ............. | 1,000,000 | |
|     Investment in Bond Sinking Fund ......... | | 1,000,000 |

To record effect of fund trustee's paying off bonds with fund's assets.

In addition, there would be entries each period for the recording of interest expense and the payment of cash for interest coupons. Chapter 17 illustrates these entries.

14.100  **Fund Investments in Firm's Securities**
Many funds are set up to provide for the redemption or retirement of the firm's own securities, such as the retirement of bonds in the example above. In practice, such funds often invest their cash in the bonds that are to be retired with the fund. When the fund invests in the bonds to be retired, many of the bonds will have been effectively retired before redemption because the fund will have repurchased them. Such bonds are not effectively outstanding. At the maturity date of the bonds, the firm will be responsible only for sufficient funds to redeem the outstanding bonds. The accounting problem when the fund acquires the firm's own bonds arises for the treatment of interest expense and revenue on the firm's bonds acquired by the fund. Should the firm recognize interest expense on the bonds held by the sinking fund which is offset by interest revenue from the investments in the fund? Generally accepted principles provide no clear answer to this question. We believe that the answer depends on who holds the fund and the terms of the bond indenture.

**1.** If the firm itself manages the fund, instead of an outside trustee, then the purchase of the firm's bond should be treated as a redemption and retirement of the bond as explained in Chapter 17, with gain or loss (an extraordinary item) recognized if the price paid for the bond differs from its current book value.

**2.** If an outside trustee manages the fund, but the trustee *must* invest its cash in the bonds to be retired, then purchases of the bond should be treated as above, with gain or loss (not an extraordinary item) recognized as the bonds are purchased.

**3.** If an outside trustee manages the fund and the trustee is free to invest in any instrument it thinks best, then investments in the firm's own bonds should be treated no differently from investments in other instruments. All bonds are treated as outstanding, with interest expense recognized by the firm and interest revenue recognized by the fund (and the firm).

14.101  We have discussed funds for redemption of *bonds*. If the fund is to retire *preferred stock*, then the treatment in case **3** would lead to the firm being able to record income from its own dividends declarations: The firm declares a dividend on preferred stock; the fund receives the dividend and records fund investment revenue, to be reported by the firm owning the fund.* Because this possibility is conceptually displeasing, we recommend that the accounting for funds established for redemption of preferred shares always record the purchase of the firm's own shares as a retirement of shares. There will be no further dividend declarations on these shares. As Chapter 21 discusses, there is never gain nor loss recognized on repurchase of a firm's own shares. Rather, if the purchase price of the shares exceeds their book value, the difference is debited to Additional Paid-in Capital, not to a Loss account or Retained Earnings. If the price is less than book value, the difference is credited to Additional Paid-in Capital account, not to a Gain or Retained Earnings account.

## Cash Value of Life Insurance Policies

14.102 Two basic kinds of life insurance are term insurance and whole-life insurance. *Term insurance* provides only insurance protection. The policy promises a payment to the beneficiary if the insured person dies while the policy is in force but is worthless at the end of its term if the insured lives. *Whole-life* insurance (sometimes called *permanent insurance*) combines term insurance with a savings account.† At any time during the policy's life, including its expiration date,

the savings account portion has a cash value. The owner of the policy may redeem the policy for its cash value or may borrow against it the cash value, while keeping the policy in force. The term *cash surrender value* is sometimes used. At any time, the cash value of a whole-life policy is an asset of the policy's owner. Because most policy owners intend to keep policies in effect for an indefinite period, the asset is a long-term investment.

When a company buys life insurance on 14.103 an employee's life, either the company will own the policy and be its beneficiary, or the employee will own the policy and have the right to name the beneficiary. If the employee owns the policy, then the premium for the policy is an expense of the company and compensation to the employee.** If the insured dies while the policy is in force, the cash value disappears and the face amount of the policy, less any amounts owed to the insurance company (such as for overdue premiums, policy loans, or interest on policy loans), becomes payable to the beneficiary of the policy.

**Insurance Premiums** Insurance premiums 14.104 on company-owned policies are separated into two parts. The portion of the premium paid for current insurance protection is an expense. The portion of the premium paid for savings is an asset called Cash Value of Life Insurance. Any collections in excess of the cash value because of the insured's death are revenues reported as part of income for the year of death. For tax report-

---

*In the case of bond interest, the interest revenue of the fund and interest expense of the firm offset each other.

†One might wonder why people choose to have a savings account through an insurance policy. The primary economic justification results from there being no taxes on the earnings of insurance investments. If cash is invested directly in a savings account, the interest revenue will be taxed currently to its owner. If cash is invested in a whole-life insurance policy, the earnings on the savings account's cash value are not taxed to the owner of the policy, either as earned or later, when paid to the policyholder. Because interest expense is usually deductible for tax purposes, some individuals

arrange to borrow to hold whole-life insurance which earns tax-free interest, generating large aftertax returns on investment. The Internal Revenue Service rules on these matters are complicated enough so that one should investigate before embarking on a tax-shelter plan based on borrowing to carry whole-life insurance.

**Certain amounts of term insurance can be purchased as compensation for the employee; although the amount of the premium is a deduction to the employer for tax purposes, it is not taxable income to the employee. Thus, company-provided term insurance can be a fringe benefit for which the tax collector pays part of the costs.

ing, the insurance premium is not deductible and the eventual collection of any death benefit is not taxable income.

14.105   **"Dividends" on Insurance** In addition, most whole-life insurance policies provide for the payment to the policy owner of an annual cash "dividend".* In financial accounting, this dividend should be treated as a reduction in insurance expense, although treatment as revenue is not wrong. (The effect on income is the same, either way.) For tax reporting, the dividend is never taxable to the recipient (because the related insurance expense is not deductible for taxes). These differences between revenue or expense for financial reporting and taxable income or deductions for company-owned life insurance on employees are permanent differences between financial and taxable income. Chapter 20 discusses such permanent differences in income tax reporting.

14.106   **Example** Exhibit 14.8 illustrates the accounting for a whole-life insurance policy owned by the company. The data at the top of the exhibit show premiums, cash values, expected dividends, and actual dividends for the first 5 years of the policy's life. The journal entries below account for the first 2 years of the policy's life. A problem at the end of the chapter continues the accounting through the next several years.

---

*The term "dividend" is a misnomer. The dividend is usually guaranteed and is thus similar to interest. Accrual of the dividend as time passes is therefore appropriate. Most insurance companies paying dividends on whole-life policies are *mutual* companies, owned by the policyholders, rather than *stock* companies, owned by investors who are not generally policyholders. Because policyholders in mutual companies bear the ultimate risks and rewards of insurance underwriting experience, the premiums on life insurance policies are set conservatively high, with the expectation that amounts left over after the payment of death benefits will be returned to continuing policyholders. Thus, cash dividends are merely returns of insurance premiums that had purposefully been set higher than necessary in the first place. Stock companies charge lower initial premiums than do mutual companies but do not return any "profit" to policyholders. Instead, the shareholders of stock companies bear the risks and are entitled to the rewards of residual ownership.

14.107   When dividends received differ from those expected, the difference is considered a change in accounting estimates and is treated as an adjustment to the amount of Insurance Expense of the period when the dividend is received. If the Insurance Expense account ends the year with a credit balance, then the amount in that account is shown on the income statement as Income from Savings on Insurance Policy Net of Premium Expense. In later policy years, the increase in the cash value of a whole-life policy plus the dividends can exceed the premium for the year. The net excess is part of the income from the insurance policy.

14.108   Although the dividends and cash value do not contractually accrue throughout the year, the accounting treats them as though they do. Because life insurance premiums are paid in advance, there is no question that the dividend and increase in cash value will become receivable at year-end. The only uncertainty is the amount of the dividend.

## Summary

14.109   Firms invest in both contractual securities and equity securities of others. The investor company uses the cost method for contractual securities. The interest rate on the date of acquisition of the investment is used throughout the life of the investment.

14.110   The investor firm uses the lower-of-cost-or-market method for passive investments in equity securities. For controlling investments when majority ownership is not present, the investor uses the equity method. For majority-owned investments, the investor uses the equity method or prepares consolidated statements.

## Appendix 14.1: Investments in Equity Securities, Majority Ownership

14.111   When a firm owns more than 50 percent of the voting stock of another company, the firm is a *majority* investor and can control

---

*Exhibit 14.8*
**Illustration of Accounting for
Company-Owned Whole-Life
Insurance Policy
Policy Dated July 1; Company's
Business Year Ends December 31**

| Policy Year | Premium Due at Start of Year | Cash Value at Start of Year | Cash Value at End of Year | Dividends Expected at End of Year | Cash Dividends Actually Paid |
|---|---|---|---|---|---|
| | **Data for Policy at Time of Purchase** | | | | |
| 1 | $6,000 | $ 0 | $ 2,150 | $1,420 | $1,400 |
| 2 | 6,000 | 2,150 | 5,000 | 1,430 | 1,460 |
| 3 | 6,000 | 5,000 | 9,600 | 1,530 | 1,550 |
| 4 | 6,000 | 9,600 | 14,200 | 1,740 | 1,700 |
| 5 | 6,000 | 14,200 | 19,000 | 1,970 | 2,000 |

**Journal Entries for First Two Policy Years**

Year 1

July 1     Prepaid Insurance ...................................................... 6,000
          Cash ............................................................... 6,000
        To record payment of first annual premium.

Dec. 31    Cash Value of Life Insurance ............................................. 1,075
        Dividend Receivable on Life Insurance ...................................... 710
        Insurance Expense ..................................................... 1,215
          Prepaid Insurance ................................................. 3,000
        Although neither cash dividend expected nor the cash value contractually exists until the
        end of the first full policy year, accrual accounting recognizes both as the year passes.
        One-half the amount of the expected dividend, $710, and one-half the contractual cash
        value, $1,075, become assets as one-half of the first year's premium expires. The remain-
        der of the prepaid insurance expired is allocated to expense by plugging.

Year 2

June 30    Dividends Receivable on Life Insurance ........................................ 710
        Cash Value of Life Insurance ............................................. 1,075
        Insurance Expense ..................................................... 1,215
          Prepaid Insurance ................................................. 3,000
        Expiration of rest of first year's premium allocated to dividend, to cash value and, with
        plug, to expense.

July 1     Prepaid Insurance ...................................................... 6,000
          Cash ............................................................... 6,000
        To record payment of premium for second year.
        Cash ................................................................. 1,400
          Dividends Receivable on Life Insurance ..................................... 1,400
        When the dividend check arrives, it is for only $1,400, instead of the expected $1,420; the
        receivable account has a $20 debit balance at this point.

*Exhibit 14.8 (continued)*

**Journal Entries for First Two Policy Years (continued)**

| | | | |
|---|---|---:|---:|
| Dec. 31 | Dividends Receivable on Life Insurance | 695 | |
| | Cash Value of Life Insurance | 1,425 | |
| | Insurance Expense | 880 | |
| | Prepaid Insurance | | 3,000 |

To record expiration of one-half year's premium and accrual of one-half year of dividends and cash value. The Dividends Receivable account had a $20 debit balance; the amount debited to that account is the amount required to bring the balance to $715, one-half the year's expected dividend.

| | | | |
|---|---|---:|---:|
| June 30 | Dividends Receivable on Life Insurance | 715 | |
| | Cash Value of Life Insurance | 1,425 | |
| | Insurance Expense | 860 | |
| | Prepaid Insurance | | 3,000 |

Expiration of second year's insurance coverage is allocated to dividend expected, to cash value, and to expense.

the other company. In most cases, the financial statements of the majority-owned *subsidiary* are combined, or *consolidated,* with those of the parent. In some instances, however, consolidated financial statements are not prepared. Instead, the investment is reported using the equity method. Whether consolidated statements are prepared or the equity method is used depends on the consolidation policy of the firm, which is discussed later in this section. The detailed procedures for preparing consolidated financial statements are discussed in advanced accounting principles texts.

## Reasons for Legally Separate Corporations

14.112   There are many reasons why a business firm prefers to operate as a group of legally separate companies, rather than as a single legal company. From the standpoint of the parent company, the more important reasons for maintaining legally separate subsidiary companies include the following:

**1.** To allocate the financial risk. Separate corporations may be used for mining raw materials, transporting them to a manufacturing plant, producing the product, and selling the finished product to the public. If any one part of the total process proves to be unprofitable or inefficient, the corporation performing the particular step can be dissolved or sold and the required goods or services purchased from other sources without seriously interfering with the operations of other corporations in the group. Losses from insolvency will fall only on the owners and creditors of the one subsidiary corporation.

**2.** To meet more effectively the requirements of state corporation laws and tax legislation. If an organization does business in a number of states, it is often faced with overlapping and inconsistent taxation, regulations, and requirements. It may be more economical to organize separate corporations to conduct the operations in the various states.

**3.** To expand with a minimum of capital investment. A firm may absorb another company by acquiring a controlling interest in its voting stock. The result may be accomplished with a substantially smaller capital investment, as well as with less difficulty and inconvenience, than if a new plant had been constructed or a complete merger were arranged.

## Purpose of Consolidated Statements

14.113 For a variety of reasons, then, a single economic entity may exist in the form of several legally separate companies. (The General Electric Company, for example, consists of about 150 legally separate companies.) Consolidated financial statements present the results of operations, financial position, and changes in financial position of an affiliated group of corporations under the control of a parent essentially as if the group of corporations were a single economic entity. The parent and each subsidiary corporation are legally separate entities, but they operate as one. Consolidated financial statements generally provide more useful information to the shareholders of the parent corporation than would separate financial statements of the parent and each subsidiary.

14.114 Consolidated financial statements also generally provide more useful information than does using the equity method. The parent, because of its voting interest, can effectively control the use of the subsidiary's assets. Consolidation of the individual assets and equities of both the parent and the subsidiary provides a more realistic picture of the operations and financial position of the single economic entity. In a legal sense, consolidated statements merely supplement, and do not replace, the separate statements of the individual corporations, although it is common practice to present only the consolidated statements in published annual reports.

## Consolidation Policy

14.115 Consolidated financial statements are generally prepared when all of the following three criteria are met:

**1.** The parent owns more than 50 percent of the voting stock of the subsidiary.

**2.** There are no important restrictions on the ability of the parent to exercise control of the subsidiary.

**3.** The asset and equity structure of the subsidiary is not significantly different from that of the parent.

Ownership of more than 50 percent of the subsidiary's voting stock implies an ability to exert control over the activities of the subsidiary. For example, the parent can control the subsidiary's corporate policies and dividend declarations. There may be situations, however, where control of the subsidiary's activities cannot be carried out effectively, despite the ownership of a majority of the voting stock. For example, the subsidiary may be located in a foreign country that has severely restricted the withdrawal of funds from that country. Or the subsidiary may be in bankruptcy and under the control of a court-appointed group of trustees. In these cases, the financial statements of the subsidiary probably will not be consolidated with those of the parent. When the parent owns more than 50 percent of the shares and can exercise control, but consolidated statements are not prepared, then the equity method must be used.

14.116 If the asset and equity structure of the subsidiary is significantly different from that of the parent, the subsidiary's financial statements are frequently not consolidated with those of the parent and the equity method is used. For example, consolidated statements might not be prepared if the parent is a manufacturing concern with heavy investments in property, plant, and equipment, whereas the subsidiary is a finance or insurance company with large holdings of cash, receivables, and marketable securities. The presentation of consolidated financial statements of corporations with significantly different asset and equity structures is sometimes thought to submerge potentially important information about the individual corporations. This is particularly true when the assets of the subsidiary are not, by law, fully available for use by the parent, such as when the subsidiary is a bank or an insurance company.

14.117  **Example 1** American Telephone and Telegraph Company (AT&T) conducts its activities through many subsidiaries organized under the laws of various states (for example, New England Telephone Company, Southern Bell, Pacific Telephone and Telegraph). AT&T owns all, or a significant percentage, of the common shares of each of these subsidiaries. It can therefore exert control over the activities of the subsidiaries much the same as if the subsidiaries were branches or divisions. AT&T often raises capital in the debt and equity markets and distributes it to the subsidiaries. In evaluating the operations and financial position of AT&T, it is more useful to consider all of the assets under its control, not just those of the parent, many of whose assets are investments. Consolidated statements are also easier to comprehend than separate statements for each of its many operating subsidiaries. AT&T also owns Western Electric, the manufacturer of most of AT&T's telephone equipment. Because Western Electric is a manufacturing company whereas most of the other subsidiaries operate telephone systems, AT&T chooses not to consolidate Western Electric, but to use the equity method for it.

14.118  **Example 2** General Motors, General Electric, and Westinghouse, among others, have wholly owned finance subsidiaries. These subsidiaries make many of their loans to customers who wish to purchase the products of the parent company. The financial statements of these subsidiaries are not consolidated with those of the parent company. The assets of these subsidiaries are largely receivables. It is argued that statement readers might be misled as to the relative liquidity of these firms if consolidated statements were prepared and the assets of the parent, largely noncurrent manufacturing plant and equipment, were combined with the more liquid assets of the finance subsidiary.

14.119  **Example 3** Sears, Roebuck & Co. and J. C. Penney Company are large retailers. Each has organized a separate subsidiary to finance customers' purchases and another separate subsidiary to sell insurance. Sears consolidates the finance subsidiary, but not the insurance subsidiary (Allstate). Penney's consolidates neither, but uses the equity method for both.

14.120  **Example 4** A major mining corporation owns a mining subsidiary in South America. The government of the country enforces stringent control over cash payments outside the country. The company is not able to control the use of all the assets, despite the ownership of a majority of the voting shares. Therefore, it does not prepare consolidated statements with the subsidiary.

14.121  **Disclosure of Consolidation Policy** The summary of significant accounting principles in financial statements includes a statement about the consolidation policy of the parent. If a significant majority-owned subsidiary is not consolidated, then its financial statements are often included in the notes to the financial statements. For example, Note 1 for the International Corporation in Exhibit A.4, Appendix A indicates that all significant majority-owned subsidiaries are consolidated with the exception of its finance company and its real estate development company. For these, the equity method is required and used. The financial statements of the finance company are themselves presented in Note 11 of Exhibit A.4.

## Understanding Consolidated Statements

14.122  This section discusses items necessary to understand consolidated statements: intercompany eliminations, the meaning of consolidated income and retained earnings, the nature of the minority interest, and the consolidated statement of changes in financial position.

14.123  **Intercompany Eliminations** The items on consolidated statements are little more than the sum of the items on the financial statements of the corporations being consolidated. Consolidated statements are intended to reflect the results that would be achieved if the affiliated group of companies were a single company. The amounts resulting from a summation of the accounts of the companies being consolidated must therefore be adjusted to eliminate double counting and intercompany transactions.

14.124    For example, a parent may lend funds to its subsidiary. If the separate balance sheets were merely added together, those funds would be counted twice: once as the notes receivable on the parent's books and again as the cash or other assets on the subsidiary's books. Consolidated balance sheets eliminate intercompany transactions that would not be reported for a single, integrated enterprise. Thus, the note receivable of the parent and the note payable of the subsidiary are eliminated in preparing the consolidated balance sheet.

14.125    To take a more complex example, the parent's balance sheet shows an asset, Investment in Subsidiary. The subsidiary's balance sheet shows its individual assets. If the two balance sheets were merely added together, the sum would show both the parent's investment in the subsidiary's assets and the assets themselves. The parent's balance sheet item, Investment in Subsidiary, must therefore be eliminated from the sum of the balance sheets. Because the consolidated balance sheet must maintain the accounting equation, corresponding eliminations must be made on the right-hand side as well.

14.126    To understand the eliminations from the right-hand side of the balance sheet, recall that the right-hand side shows the sources of the firm's financing. The subsidiary is financed by creditors (liabilities) and by owners (shareholders' equity). Assume that the parent owns 100 percent of the subsidiary's voting shares. Then the assets on the consolidated balance sheet of the single economic entity are financed by the creditors of both companies and by the parent's shareholders. That is, the equities of the consolidated entity are the liabilities of both companies but the shareholders' equity of the parent alone. If the shareholders' equity accounts of the subsidiary were added to those of the parent, then the financing from the parent's shareholders would be counted twice (once on the parent's books and once

on the subsidiary's books). Hence, when the parent's investment account is eliminated from the sum of the two companies' assets, the accounting equation is maintained by eliminating the shareholders' equity accounts of the subsidiary. Exhibit 14.9 illustrates the hypothetical consolidation of a 100-percent-owned company accounted for on the equity method.

Similarly, certain intercompany transac-    14.127 tions must be eliminated from the sum of income statement accounts so that the operating performance of the consolidated entity can be meaningfully presented. For example, if a manufacturing parent sells goods to a subsidiary which, in turn, sells the goods to the public, then the sum of individual income statements would double-count sales and costs of goods sold. Suppose that the parent sells to the subsidiary but that the subsidiary has not yet sold the goods to the public. The parent will have recorded profits on the sale, but from the standpoint of the overall economic entity, no profits for shareholders have actually been realized because the items are still in the inventory of the overall economic entity. Consequently, profits from the parent's sales to subsidiaries that have not been realized by subsequent sales to outsiders are eliminated from consolidated net income and balance sheet amounts. The consolidated income statement attempts to show sales, expenses, and net income figures that report the results of operations of the group of companies as though it were a single company.

**Consolidated Income and Retained Earn-**    14.128 **ings** The amount of consolidated net income for a period is the same as the amount that would be reported if the parent company used the equity method of accounting for the intercorporate investment. That is, consolidated net income is equal to

| Parent Company's Net Income | + | Parent's Share of Subsidiary's Net Income | − | Profit (or Plus Loss) on Intercompany Transactions |
|---|---|---|---|---|

The principal differences between the consolidated income statement and the income statement where the subsidiary is accounted for under the equity method are the components of income presented. When a consolidated income statement is prepared, the individual revenues and expenses of the subsidiary (less intercompany adjustments) are combined with those of the parent. When the equity method is used for an unconsolidated subsidiary, the parent's share of the subsidiary's net income minus gain (or plus loss) on intercompany transactions is shown on a single line of the income statement with a title such as "Equity in Earnings (Loss) of Unconsolidated Subsidiary." (See, for example, the income statement of International Corporation in Exhibit A.1, in Appendix A. That income statement is a consolidated income statement. The company has, however, "subsidiaries and affiliates" that are not consolidated but are accounted for with the equity method.)

14.129    The amount shown on the consolidated balance sheet for retained earnings is likewise the amount that would be reported if the parent company used the equity method of accounting for the intercorporate investment. That is, consolidated retained earnings is equal to

| Parent's Retained + Earnings | Parent's Share of the Change in Subsidiary's Retained Earnings Since Acquisition | Profit (or Plus Loss) − on Intercompany Transactions |
|---|---|---|

14.130    **Minority Interest in Consolidated Subsidiary** In many cases, the parent will not own 100 percent of the voting stock of a consolidated subsidiary. The owners of the remaining shares of voting stock are called *minority shareholders*, or the *minority interest*.* These shareholders continue to have a proportionate interest in the net assets (= total assets minus total liabilities) of the subsidiary as shown on the subsidiary's separate corporate records. They also have a proportionate interest in the earnings of the subsidiary.

--------

*Do not confuse this minority interest in a consolidated subsidiary with a firm's own minority investments, discussed earlier. The minority *interest* belongs to others outside the parent and its economic entity. The parent's minority *investments* are merely those for which the parent owns less than 50 percent of the shares.

When there is a minority interest, should   14.131 the consolidated statements show only the parent's share of the assets and equities of the subsidiary, or should they show all of the subsidiary's assets and equities together with the minority interests in them? The generally accepted accounting principle is to show all of the assets and equities of the subsidiary, because the parent, with its controlling voting interest, can effectively direct the use of all the assets and liabilities, not merely an amount equal to the parent's percentage of ownership. The consolidated balance sheet and income statement in these instances must, however, disclose the interest of the minority shareholders in the subsidiary that has been consolidated.

The amount of the minority interest   14.132 shown on the balance sheet generally results from multiplying the common shareholders' equity of the subsidiary by the minority's percentage of ownership. For example, if the common shareholders' equity (or assets minus liabilities) of a consolidated subsidiary totals $500,000 and the minority owns 20 percent of the common stock, then the minority interest shown on the consolidated balance sheet is $100,000 (= .20 × $500,000).

The minority interest is typically pre-   14.133 sented among the equities on the consolidated balance sheet between the liabilities and shareholders' equity. See, for example, the International Corporation consolidated balance sheet in Exhibit A.2 in Appendix A. Note that "Minority Interest" is shown among the liabilities but is not clearly labeled as one. This presentation is typical of many published financial statements. We think that the right-hand side of the balance sheet should contain only liabilities and owners' equity items, so that the minority interest should be classified as one or the other. The minority interest does not meet the criteria to be a liability discussed in Chapter 15, because there is no maturity date. The minority interest might be classified as an indeterminate-term liability, much the same as deferred taxes.

The amount of the minority interest in the   14.134 subsidiary's income shown on the consolidated income statement is generally the re-

*Exhibit 14.9*

**Conversion of Accounting of International Credit Company, a 100%-Owned Subsidiary, from Equity Basis to Consolidation with the Parent, International Corporation**
*(Dollar Amounts in Millions)*

| International Credit Company | | Equity Method (as Reported) | International Corporation — Adjustments to Consolidate Credit Company | | Consolidated (Hypothetical) |
|---|---|---|---|---|---|
| | **Income Statement** | | Debit | Credit | |
| $ 141.7 | Revenues (other than from Credit Company) ...... | $5,917.2 | | $ 141.7 (1) | $6,058.9 |
| | Equity Method Revenues from Credit Company ...... | 11.4 | (1) $ 11.4 | | — |
| | Total Revenues ...... | $5,928.6 | | | $6,058.9 |
| 130.3 | Total Expenses (Including Discontinued Operations) ...... | 5,763.4 | (1) 130.3 | | 5,893.7 |
| $ 11.4 | Net Income ...... | $ 165.2 | | | $ 165.2 |
| | **Balance Sheet** | | | | |
| $1,143.9 | All Assets Except Investment in Credit Company ...... | $4,714.5 | (2) 1,143.9 | | $5,858.4 |
| | Investment in Credit Company ...... | 151.8 | | 151.8 (2) | — |
| | Total Assets ...... | $4,866.3 | | | $5,858.4 |
| $ 992.1 | Liabilities (including Minority Interest) ...... | $2,864.6 | | 992.1 (2) | $3,856.7 |
| 151.8 | Owners' Equity ...... | 2,001.7 | | | 2,001.7 |
| $1,143.9 | Total Equities ...... | $4,866.3 | $1,285.6 | $1,285.6 | $5,858.4 |

Sources: International Corporation statements condensed from those in Appendix A, where the Credit Company is accounted for on the equity method. The adjustments shown convert the accounting to consolidated statements.

International Credit Company statements condensed from those in Note 11 to financial statements for International Corporation.

Adjustments: Adjustment (1) adds all of the Credit Company revenues ($141.7) and expenses ($130.3) to those of the parent and removes the parent's equity method revenue ($11.4).

Adjustment (2) adds all of the Credit Company's assets ($1,143.9) to those of the parent, removes the parent's investment account ($151.8), and adds all of the Credit Company's liabilities ($992.1) to those of the parent.

sult of multiplying the *subsidiary's* net income by the minority's percentage of ownership. The consolidated income is allocated to show the portions applicable to the parent company and the portion of the subsidiary's income applicable to the minority interest. Refer again to International Corporation's consolidated income statement shown in Exhibit A.1. Notice the deduction of $2.5 million for the "Minority Interest in Net Income of Consolidated Subsidiaries" before the consolidated net income figure. The consolidated net income includes only that portion of net income of subsidiary companies allocable to the shareholders of International Corporation. Typically, the minority interest in the subsidiary's income is shown as a deduction in calculating consolidated net income.

14.135 **Statement of Changes in Financial Position** Two items may appear in the consolidated statement of changes in financial position that do not usually appear on single-company statements.

14.136    The first item in consolidated funds statements that does not appear in single-company statements is the addback to net income for the minority interest in earnings. As we pointed out in the discussion of minority interest above, International Corporation shows a deduction of $2.5 million for the minority's share of earnings before the final net income figure in Exhibit A.1. This deduction did not require the use of any working capital. Consequently, there must be an addback to derive "Working Capital Provided by Continuing Operations" in the consolidated statement of changes in financial position. International Corporation shows the addback of $2.5 million in its statement of changes in financial position, Exhibit A.3, as "Minority Interest in Net Income of Consolidated Subsidiaries."

14.137    Second, the amortization of goodwill may appear in consolidated income statements. Goodwill is discussed in Chapter 13. Just like other amortization charges, amortization of goodwill causes a reduction in reported net income without using funds. Therefore, there must be an addback to net income in the amount of that amortization in order to derive the amount of funds provided by operations. Often, however, as in the case of the consolidated statement of changes in financial position of International Corporation shown in Exhibit A.3, the amount of this amortization is so small that it does not warrant separate disclosure and is included with "Other" items.

## Limitations of Consolidated Statements

The consolidated statements do not replace those of individual corporations; rather, they supplement those statements and aid in their interpretation. Creditors must rely on the resources of one corporation and may be misled if forced to rely entirely on a consolidated statement that combines the data of a company in good financial condition with those of one verging on insolvency. Dividends can legally be declared only from the retained earnings of one corporation. Where the parent company does not own all of the shares of the subsidiary, the outside or minority shareholders can judge the dividend constraints, both legal and financial, only by an inspection of the subsidiary's statements.   14.138

In the best of all possible worlds, parent corporations would report on their own and their subsidiaries' operations in both single-company and consolidated statements. Many companies show both statements in their Form 10-K reports to the SEC. Generally accepted accounting principles do not require the publication of both single-company and consolidated reports. Only the consolidated report need be published. Few U.S. corporations publish separate financial statements for both the parent and the subsidiaries as single companies, other than in their Form 10-K.   14.139

## Consolidated Statements and the Equity Method Compared

Exhibit 14.9 shows the income statement and balance sheet condensed from Appendix A for International Corporation and its   14.140

100-percent-owned but nonconsolidated subsidiary, International Credit Company. The Credit Company is accounted for with the equity method. Exhibit 14.9 shows how the income statement and the balance sheet would look if the Credit Company were consolidated instead of being accounted for on the equity method. Certain financial statement ratios (discussed in Chapter 25), such as the debt-equity ratio and the rate of return on assets, computed from the consolidated statements differ significantly from the same ratios computed from the equity-method statements.

## Questions and Short Cases

**14.1** Review the meaning of the following concepts or terms discussed in this chapter.

a. Contractual securities.
b. Conversion versus exchange.
c. Equity securities.
d. Hybrid securities.
e. Basket purchase.
f. Investments (noncurrent).
g. Convertible bond.
h. Cost method.
i. Lower of cost or market.
j. Equity method.
k. Consolidated statements.
l. Market value of debt securities.
m. Stock dividend.
n. Stock right.
o. Stock split.
p. Stock option.
q. Call option.
r. Put option.
s. Stock warrant.
t. Sinking fund.
u. Cash value of life insurance.

**14.2** What amount is recorded for an investment acquired in exchange for nonmonetary assets?

**14.3** Distinguish between the nature of temporary investments and long-term investments. Give examples of each type. How can securities of the same kind be carried by one company as a short-term investment and by another company as a long-term investment?

**14.4** How is the acquisition cost of a basket purchase of two securities allocated if the market price of only one security is known? If no market prices are known? If both prices are known?

**14.5** Distinguish between face value of bonds, market value of bonds, maturity value of bonds, par value of bonds, and principle value of bonds.

**14.6** Why is interest revenue accrued between interest payment dates on investments in bonds but dividend revenue is not accrued between dividend payment dates on investments in stock?

**14.7** How is "significant influence" determined when a corporation acquires less than a 50-percent interest in another corporation?

**14.8** The distinction between voting and nonvoting shares is not important for investments that might be accounted for at lower of cost or market but is for investments that might be accounted for with the equity method. Why?

**14.9** Distinguish between the cost and equity methods of accounting for long-term equity investments subsequent to the acquisition date.

**14.10** Distinguish between lower of cost or market applied to the acquisition of securities classified as noncurrent assets and to the acquisition of securities classified as current assets.

**14.11**   Describe the accounting used for a controlling investment when cost is less than the book value of the company acquired.

**14.12**   Describe the accounting treatment of an investment in equity securities that grows gradually from passive to controlling.

**14.13**   How does the investor account for a stock dividend received? For a stock split on an investment?

**14.14**   Distinguish between a stock right and a stock warrant. What are their similarities?

**14.15**   Company P owns convertible bonds in Company S with a book value of $100,000. Company P converts its bonds into common shares with a market value of $120,000. How should Company P account for this conversion?

**14.16**   Company P acquired 40 percent of the shares of Company S for $100,000 at a time when Company S reported assets of $500,000 and liabilities of $300,000. How should Company P account for this investment?

**14.17**   The following item appears on a consolidated balance sheet: Minority Interest in Subsidiary Companies. What does it represent?

**14.18**   Consider stock acquired on the market after a subsidiary had been in existence for several years. The consolidated balance sheet does not include an item of "goodwill." What are the possible explanations?

**14.19**   **a.** Why is it impossible to determine from a consolidated balance sheet the amount of retained earnings legally available for dividends, either for the parent company or for the subsidiary company?
**b.** Indicate some of the types of eliminations that may be necessary in the preparation of a consolidated income statement.

**14.20**   Why is the equity method sometimes called a *one-line consolidation?*

**14.21**   Company P acquires 100 percent of the stock of Company S at a time when Company S has negative retained earnings, that is, a deficit. P pays more for S than the book value of S's owners' equity. How can this happen?

**14.22**   The Annoppers Copper Corporation has, for many years, consolidated the financial position and results of operations of its South American copper mining facility. During the last year, the government of the country in which the mine is located has expropriated the plants of two other U.S. corporations. These two other companies were engaged in manufacturing operations. Should the Annoppers Copper Corporation continue to consolidate the financial statements of its South American facility in its statements issued to shareholders?

**14.23**   (Adapted from AICPA *Technical Practice Aids.*) Company P owns 30 percent of the shares of Company S. It uses the equity method for this investment because it can exercise significant influence over the operations of Company S. Company P uses the percentage-of-completion method for its own long-term construction contracts. Company S constructs office and apartment buildings under long-term construction contracts. It recognizes revenue using the completed-contract method.

May Company P recognize its share of Company S's income on long-term construction contracts as measured under the percentage-of-completion method?

14.24    (Adapted from AICPA *Technical Practice Aids*.) Patell Company owns a 40-percent interest in an investment in a "hedge fund." This is a partnership of investors who speculate in the common stock of small companies whose shares are traded in public markets. The "hedge fund" accounts for its investments at market value, reporting income when shares increase in value, whether or not these gains are realized. The hedge fund reports to the partners both realized and unrealized gains, as well as both cost and market value of the portfolio.

How should Patell Company account for its investment in the hedge fund?

14.25    (Adapted from AICPA *Technical Practice Aids*.) Company P acquired 50 percent of the shares of Company S by giving to Company S the right to use certain computer programs that Company P had developed and expensed at the time of development. The other 50 percent of the shares in Company S were purchased for cash for $150,000 by another company. Company P debited investment for $150,000 and credited income for $150,000. Thereafter Company P used the equity method for its investment.

Comment on this accounting procedure.

14.26    (Adapted from AICPA *Technical Practice Aids*.) Horngren Company thinks its president and founder is a virtually irreplaceable asset of the company. It has purchased a $5 million life insurance policy on the president's life with the company as beneficiary. The company does not show the cash value of the life insurance policy as an asset. The company argues that the death of the president would be such a terrible loss for the company that even the collection of $5 million would not be adequate compensation.

Is the accounting for the life insurance policy acceptable?

14.27    (Adapted from AICPA *Technical Practice Aids*.) Company P purchased 15 percent of the voting shares of Company S. Company P also made a loan to Company S that is convertible into shares of Company T, a subsidiary of Company S. For as long as the loan is outstanding, Company P is contractually entitled to several seats on the board of directors of Company S, but the guaranteed number of seats is less than a majority. Company P also owns rights to purchase shares in Company S.

What accounting method, lower of cost or market or equity, should Company P use for its investment in Company S?

14.28    Company A owns 51 percent of the voting stock of Company B. Company B owns 51 percent of the voting stock of Company C. Company C owns 51 percent of the voting stock of Company D. Company D owns 51 percent of the voting stock of Company E. Notice that Company A effectively controls Companies B, C, D, and E. Company A decides that it wishes to control Company Z. Company Z has $30 million of assets and $22 million of liabilities. Company Z's outstanding voting stock sells in the market place for $10 million. Suppose that Company A acquires control of Company Z by having Company E purchase 51 percent of the voting stock of Company Z for $5.1 million. Company E "raises" the cash needed to acquire voting control of Company Z by not declaring dividends that would otherwise be declared. Companies D, C, and B ordinarily add to their dividend declarations the amounts received in dividends from their own investments.

What cash receipt does the management of Company A forgo by having Company E purchase the stock of Company Z in this fashion? Ignore income tax effects.

14.29    (Adapted from AICPA *Technical Practice Aids*.) Company B is 100-percent owned by Company A. Company B exchanged its 100-percent investment in Company C for a 43-percent investment in Company D. The market value of the shares of Company D received by Company B differed from the book value of its investment in Company C. Should the gain or loss on exchange of shares be reported as a realized gain or loss in the year of exchange?

**14.30**   In 1979, a committee of the AICPA considered ruling that *all* majority-owned subsidiaries should be consolidated, so that the equity method should not be an option, even when the operations of the subsidiary are unlike those of the parent. Condensed financial statements for General Motors Corporation and its 100-percent-owned subsidiary, General Motors Acceptance Corporation (GMAC), are shown in Exhibit 14.10. GM's primary mission is producing transportation equipment. GMAC's primary mission is financing those purchases by lending funds to customers.

Using whatever reasoning and financial statement ratios you think appropriate, suggest how either the proponents or the opponents of the change on the AICPA committee might use these statements to bolster their arguments.

---

*Exhibit 14.10*
**Condensed Balance Sheet of General Motors Corporation Accounting for GMAC with Equity Method (Dollar Amounts in Billions)**

| | |
|---|---:|
| All Assets Except Investment in GMAC | $25.0 |
| Investment in GMAC[a] | 1.7 |
| Total Assets | $26.7 |
| Liabilities | $10.9 |
| Owners' Equity | 15.8 |
| Total Equities | $26.7 |

[a]GMAC is General Motors Acceptance Corporation: GMAC's assets are $23.6 billion; its liabilities are $21.9 billion.

**14.31**   This case illustrates the impact that consolidation policy can have on financial statements and financial statement analysis. Sears, Roebuck & Co. and J. C. Penney Company are large retailers who have similar operations. Both companies have organized financing subsidiaries. Each subsidiary borrows funds in credit markets and lends the funds to customers who purchase goods or services for the retailers. Each subsidiary is 100-percent owned by its parent company. Sears consolidates its financing subsidiary (Sears, Roebuck Acceptance Corp.) in published financial statements. Penney's uses the equity method for its financing subsidiary (J. C. Penney Financial Corporation) and shows the separate financial statements of the financing subsidiary in notes to the published financial statements.

In this problem we focus on the debt ratio, because the effects are easy to illustrate. Other ratios could be used as well. Throughout this text, we define the debt-equity ratio as

$$\text{Debt-Equity Ratio} = \frac{\text{Total Liabilities}}{\text{Total Equities}}.$$

Many financial analysts prefer to use a form of the debt ratio such as

$$\frac{\text{Debt}}{\text{Ratio}} = \frac{\text{Total } Long\text{-}Term \text{ Debt}}{\text{Total Shareholders' Equity}}.$$

*Exhibit 14.11*
**J. C. Penney and Sears**
**(All Dollar Amounts in Millions)**

| | J. C. Penney Company | | | Sears, Roebuck & Co. |
|---|---|---|---|---|
| | Financial Statements as Issued (1) | Financing Subsidiary Statements as Shown in Notes (2) | Hypothetical Financial Statements If Subsidiary Were Consolidated (3) | Financial Statements as Issued (4) |
| Total Assets .............. | $3,483.8 | $1,458.1 | ? | $12,711.5 |
| Total Liabilities ........... | 1,567.2 | 1,078.9 | ? | 6,774.6 |
| Long-Term Debt ........... | 355.5 | 517.0 | ? | 1,563.5 |
| Shareholders' Equity ....... | 1,916.6 | 379.2 | ? | 5,936.9 |
| Debt-Equity Ratio (Total Liabilities/Total Equities) .. | 45.0% | 72.3% | 58.0% | 53.3% |
| Long-Term Debt/ Shareholders' Equity ..... | 18.5% | 136.3% | 45.5% | 26.3% |

Such analysts feel that this version of the debt ratio focuses more attention on the risk of companies being analyzed. (The notion is that the percentage of current liabilities to total equities is to a large degree determined by the nature of the business and that so long as current assets are as large as current liabilities, the percentage of current liabilities in total equities is not important.)

Exhibit 14.11 shows pertinent data for both Sears and Penney's from recent financial statements. Both versions of the debt ratio mentioned above are presented. The data for Sears are taken directly from the financial statements. For Penney's, the exhibit shows data from the published balance sheet in column (1) and data from the statements of the financing subsidiary in column (2) and presents a column for Penney's hypothetical financial statements assuming consolidation of the financing subsidiary. Column (3) represents the accounting for Penney's that is analogous to Sears' accounting.

a. Complete column (3) for Penney's. (The ratios shown are correct; you can check your work from them.)

b. As measured by the debt ratios (and ignoring other factors—see Problem P25.31), which company appears to be the more risky? Which company do you think is more risky and why?

c. Assume that the managements of Penney's and Sears are both considering additional long-term financing to raise funds. Managements of both companies are concerned about how the marketplace will react to new debt financing on the one hand or new common share issues on the other. How are financial analysts who are concerned with risk (as measured in part by debt ratios) likely to react to these two companies? How are managements of the two companies likely to react in making their financing decisions if they anticipate the reaction of financial analysts?

## Problems and Exercises

14.32   On January 1, Buyer Company acquired common stock of X Company. At the time of acquisition, the book value and fair market value of X Company's net assets were $100,000.

During the year, X Company earned $25,000 and declared dividends of $20,000. How much income would Buyer Company report for the year from its investment under the assumption that Buyer Company:

a. Paid $15,000 for 15 percent of the common stock and uses the cost method for its investment in X Company?

b. Paid $20,000 for 15 percent of the common stock and uses the cost method for its investment in X Company?

c. Paid $30,000 for 30 percent of the common stock and uses the equity method to account for its investment in X Company?

d. Paid $40,000 for 30 percent of the common stock and uses the equity method to account for its investment in X Company? Give the maximum income that Buyer Company can report from the investment.

14.33 The CAR Corporation manufactures computers in the United States. It owns 75 percent of the voting stock of Charles of Canada, 80 percent of the voting stock of Alexandre de France (in France), and 90 percent of the voting stock of R Credit Corporation (a finance company). The CAR Corporation prepares consolidated financial statements consolidating Charles of Canada, using the equity method for R Credit Corporation, and using the lower-of-cost-or-market method for its investment in Alexandre de France. Data from the annual reports of these companies are given below.

| | Percentage Owned | Net Income | Dividends | Accounting Method |
|---|---|---|---|---|
| CAR Corporation Consolidated . | — | $1,000,000 | $ 70,000 | — |
| Charles of Canada ............ | 75% | 100,000 | 40,000 | Consolidated |
| Alexandre de France .......... | 80 | 80,000 | 50,000 | LCM[a] |
| R Credit Corporation ......... | 90 | 120,000 | 100,000 | Equity |

[a]LCM = lower of cost or market.

a. Which, if any, of the companies is incorrectly accounted for by CAR according to generally accepted accounting principles?

Assuming the accounting for the three subsidiaries shown above to be correct, answer the following questions

b. How much of the net income reported by CAR Corporation Consolidated is attributable to the operations of the three subsidiaries?

c. What is the amount of the minority interest shown on the income statement and how does it affect net income of CAR Corporation Consolidated?

d. If all three subsidiaries had been consolidated, what would have been the net income of CAR Corporation Consolidated?

e. If all three subsidiaries had been consolidated, what would be the minority interest shown on the income statement?

14.34 A parent company owns shares in one other company. It has owned them since the other company was formed. The parent company alone has retained earnings of $100,000. The consolidated balance sheet shows no goodwill and retained earnings of $160,000. Consider each of the following questions independently of the others.

a. If the parent owns 80 percent of its consolidated subsidiary, what are the retained earnings of the subsidiary?

b. If the subsidiary has retained earnings of $96,000, what fraction of the subsidiary does the parent own?

c. If the subsidiary had not been consolidated but instead had been accounted for by the equity method, how much revenue in excess of dividends received would the parent have recognized from the investment since acquisition?

14.35 During the current year, Buyer Corporation purchased machinery for $20,000, its fair market value, from its wholly owned subsidiary. The machinery had been carried on the books of the subsidiary at a cost of $30,000 and had accumulated depreciation of $16,000. What net book values for this machinery would be shown on:
a. Buyer Corporation's single-company books?
b. Consolidated balance sheet for Buyer and its subsidiary?

14.36 Lesala Corporation purchased most of the common stock of its subsidiary 2 years ago. The subsidiary earned $1 million this year, but declared no dividends. An excerpt from Lesala Corporation's financial statements for this year is shown in Exhibit 14.12.
a. What percentage of the consolidated subsidiary does Lesala Corporation own?
b. Goodwill arising from the acquisition of the consolidated subsidiary is being amortized using the straight-line method to show the minimum charges allowed by generally accepted accounting principles. What was the excess of the subsidiary's market value as a going concern over the market value of the actual assets shown on its books as of the date of acquisition? Assume that the acquisition occurred on January 1, two years ago.

---

*Exhibit 14.12*
**Lesala Corporation**
**Consolidated Statement of**
**Changes in Financial Position**
**for This Year**

---

**Sources of Working Capital:**

| | | |
|---|---:|---:|
| Consolidated Net Income | | $3,000,000 |
| Addback Charges Not Requiring Working Capital: | | |
| Depreciation of Plant | $150,000 | |
| Amortization of Goodwill Arising from Acquisition of Consolidated Subsidiary | 10,000 | |
| Minority Interest in Earnings of Consolidated Subsidiary | 200,000 | 360,000 |
| Total Working Capital from Operations | | $3,360,000 |

---

14.37 Sealco Enterprises published the consolidated income statement for the year that is shown in Exhibit 14.13.

The unconsolidated affiliate retained 20 percent of its earnings of $100,000 during the year, having paid out the rest as dividends. The consolidated subsidiary earned $200,000 during the year and declared no dividends.
a. What percentage of the unconsolidated affiliate does Sealco Enterprises own?
b. What dividends did Sealco Enterprises receive from the unconsolidated affiliate during the year?
c. What percentage of the consolidated subsidiary does Sealco Enterprises own?

*Exhibit 14.13*
**Sealco Enterprises**
**Consolidated Income Statement**
**for the Year**

**Revenues:**

| | | |
|---|---:|---:|
| Sales | | $1,000,000 |
| Equity in Earnings of Unconsolidated Affiliate | | 40,000 |
| Total Revenues | | $1,040,000 |
| **Expenses:** | | |
| Cost of Goods Sold (Excluding Depreciation) | | $ 650,000 |
| Administrative Expenses | | 100,000 |
| Depreciation Expense | | 115,000 |
| Amortization of Goodwill | | 5,000 |
| Income Tax Expenses: | | |
|    Currently Payable | $42,000 | |
|    Deferred | 10,000 | 52,000 |
| Total Expenses | | $ 922,000 |
| Income of the Consolidated Group | | $ 118,000 |
| Less Minority Interest in Earnings of Consolidated Subsidiary | | 30,000 |
| Net Income to Shareholders | | $  88,000 |

**d.** Prepare the "working capital provided by operations" section of the Sealco Enterprises Consolidated Statement of Changes in Financial Position for the year assuming that

   **(i)** The statement starts with net income to shareholders:

   **(ii)** The statement shows only revenues and expenses that involve working capital.

**14.38**  Refer to the Simplified Funds Statement for a Period in Exhibit 4.13 at the end of Chapter 4. Nine of the lines in the statement are numbered. Line (2) should be expanded to say "Additions for Expenses, Losses, and Other Charges against Income Not Using Funds," and line (3) should be expanded to say "Subtractions for Revenue, Gains, and Other Credits to Income Not Producing Funds from Operations." Ignore the unnumbered lines in responding to the questions below.

   Assume that the accounting cycle is complete for the period and that all of the financial statements have been prepared. Then it is discovered that a transaction has been overlooked. That transaction is recorded in the accounts, and all of the financial statements are corrected. Define *funds* as *working capital*. For each of the following transactions or events, indicate which of the numbered lines of the funds statement is affected and by how much. Ignore income tax effects.

   **a.** An affiliate accounted for on the equity method earns $10,000 and declares dividends of $4,000.

   **b.** An affiliate accounted for on the equity method reports a loss for the year of $5,000.

   **c.** Minority interest in income of a consolidated subsidiary is recognized in the amount of $20,000.

   **d.** Minority interest in the losses of a consolidated subsidiary is recognized in the amount of $8,000.

   **e.** Securities that cost $10,000 and had a market value of $10,000 at the end of last year are transferred from the Investment account (noncurrent asset) to the Marketable Securities (current asset) account at a time when the market value is $8,000.

f. Securities that cost $10,000 and had a market value of $10,000 at the end of last year are transferred from the Investment account to the Marketable Securities (current asset) account at a time when the market value is $12,000.

g. The *investment* in the portfolio of equity securities accounted for with the lower-of-cost-or-market method is written down from $10,000 to $8,000.

h. The market value of the portfolio of equity securities accounted for as *current assets* (Marketable Securities) is $5,000 less than the net amount shown for the same portfolio on the balance sheet at the end of the previous accounting period. The amount in the allowance contra to the Marketable Securities account is changed.

i. The market value of the portfolio of marketable equity securities in the preceding part **h** increases $3,000 by the end of the next accounting period. The amount in the allowance contra to the Marketable Securities account is changed.

**14.39** Tillich Corporation had taken out a $100,000 life insurance policy insuring the president's life. The president died on January 1 of the current year at a time when the cash value of the insurance policy was correctly recorded in the records at $23,500. The policy year runs from January 1 through December 31. The postclosing trial balance on December 31 of the year just ended showed Life Insurance Dividends Receivable on this policy of $2,700. No life insurance premium is due for the current year when the president died.

a. How much cash does the insurance company owe Tillich Corporation?

b. Record the journal entry for the receipt of $100,000 cash by the company for the death benefit.

**14.40** On January 2, year 1, Holt Company purchased for $700,000 shares representing 10 percent of the voting stock of House Company. On that date the assets of House Company exceeded its liabilities by $3 million. During year 1, House Company earned $500,000 and declared $200,000 of dividends. During year 2, House Company earned $1 million and declared $300,000 of dividends. On January 2, year 3, Holt Company purchased another 20 percent of the voting shares of House Company at their book value. The book value of House Company's net assets was $4 million. During year 3, House Company earned $1.2 million and declared dividends of $400,000.

Prepare journal entries for these transactions on the books of Holt Company, which uses a 40-year period to amortize the excess of cost over book value of investments acquired. Show supporting calculations.

**14.41** The Verr Company issued rights to existing shareholders of its stock. Four rights and cash could be exchanged for one additional share. After the announcement of the offering, the shares traded rights-on for $100 each. The rights had a fair market value of $10 each. How much was required in the exchange to accompany the four rights in order for the holder to acquire one new share?

**14.42** Chia Company issued rights to existing shareholders. Each share outstanding was issued one right. Five rights and $42 could be exchanged for one new share. Just after the rights offering, the existing shares traded rights-on for $60. What is the value of one right just after the rights offering?

**14.43** During January, Allen Company acquired shares in two other companies as passive, long-term investments. Neither investee declared dividends during the year. The cost of these investments and their December 31 market values are shown here. Allen Company owners' equity accounts on December 31, after all closing entries, included:

a. Prepare an adjusting entry for December 31.

| Common Shares | $5,000,000 |
|---|---|
| Additional Paid-in Capital | 6,500,000 |
| Retained Earnings | 7,400,000 |

### Allen Company Investments

| Long-Term Investments | January 15 Cost | December 31 Market Value |
|---|---|---|
| Investment One | $1,446,000 | $1,478,000 |
| Investment Two | 2,340,000 | 1,900,000 |
| Total | $3,786,000 | $3,378,000 |

b. Prepare financial statement disclosures including footnotes as required for the year-end balance sheet.

**14.44**  Prepare the journal entries required for the following transactions, using the effective-interest method.

Year 1
4/1    Bonds of the Ritchie Company with a par value of $15,000 are purchased as a long-term investment at 95 plus accrued interest. The bonds pay interest of 8 percent annually on December 1. They mature in 6 years and 8 months from the purchase date. The effective yield is 9 percent per year.

12/1    Interest of $1,200 is received on the Ritchie Company bonds.

12/31    Adjusting entries are made.

Year 2
6/1    One-third of the bonds are sold for 97 plus accrued interest.

**14.45**  Astley Company has a credit balance of $500,000 in its Bonds Payable account on January 1 representing the proceeds of 7-percent semiannual coupon bonds issued at par several years ago. Interest is payable on April 1 and October 1 of each year. On June 21 of the current year Astley Company sends $10,000 to the sinking fund trustee for the bonds. The trustee purchases $12,000 face value of Astley Company bonds for $10,000, which includes interest accured since April 1. Thus, the total payment to the bondholder selling back their bonds is $10,000. The sinking fund is shown as an investment by Astley Company. The trustee is *not* obligated to invest its cash receipts in Astley Company bonds. All sinking fund items of cash and securities are included in a single Sinking Fund investment account. The accounting period is the calendar year.
a. Prepare journal entries for April 1, June 21, and October 1, assuming that the bonds in the hands of the trustee are treated as outstanding bonds and receive interest.
b. Prepare journal entries for April 1, June 21, and October 1, assuming that Astley Company bonds in the hands of the trustee are treated as retired and canceled.
c. Which of the treatments above do you think provides a more realistic presentation of economic reality?

**14.46**  Refer to the data given in the text for the 5-year whole-life insurance policy. Exhibit 14.8 shows journal entries for the first two policy years.
    Show journal entries for the last three policy years. Note that in years when the increase

in the cash value plus dividends exceeds the policy premium, there will be an account Income from Life Insurance Policy Savings in Excess of Insurance Expense.

**14.47** The Reserve Coal Company paid $100,000 to a sinking fund trustee under the provisions of a bond indenture. It recorded the following journal entries:

| | | |
|---|---|---|
| Sinking Fund Investment | 100,000 | |
|     Cash | | 100,000 |
| Retained Earnings | 100,000 | |
|     Retained Earnings Appropriated for Sinking Fund | | 100,000 |

Make any entries required to correct the recording of this event.

**14.48** The Newton Corporation bought 40 percent of the shares of the Centre Company common stock for $6 per share on January 1, year 1. At that time Centre's balance sheet showed net assets of $40,000, common stock ($1 par value) of $5,000, and retained earnings of $35,000. The excess of book value acquired over purchase price is attributed to assets with a remaining life of 5 years.

Centre Company reported net income for year 1 of $12,500 and paid cash dividends of $3,750 on December 31, year 1. The market value of Centre Company was $7 per share on December 31, year 1.

On January 2, year 2, Newton Corporation sold 500 shares of Centre Company stock for $7 per share.

**a.** Prepare journal entries to record these events assuming that the Newton Company does *not* exercise significant influence over the Centre Company during year 1 and, therefore, uses the lower-of-cost-or-market method.

**b.** Prepare journal entries to record the events using the equity method.

**14.49** On December 31, 1979, the Raelis Company acquired as an investment 1,000 shares of the Zales Corporation common stock for $16,000. These shares represent 25 percent of the Zales Corporation's outstanding stock. This is the only noncurrent marketable equity security held by Raelis Company. At date of acquisition, the book value of Zales Corporation's net assets was $64,000.

Zales Corporation declared and paid a cash dividend of $2 per common share on June 1, 1980; it reported net income of $4,000 for the year. The market value of the investment was $12,000 at December 31, 1980.

On June 1, 1981, the Zales Corporation declared and paid a dividend of $1 per share. Zales Corporation reported a net income for 1981 of $6,000. Its market value per share was $13.50 on December 31, 1981.

**a.** Prepare journal entries to record the above transactions on the Raelis Company's books assuming that it cannot exercise significant influence over the Zales Corporation and therefore uses the lower-of-cost-or-market basis. Assume that the Raelis Company closes its books on December 31.

**b.** Prepare journal entries to record the above transactions on the Raelis Company's books assuming that the investment in the Zales Corporation is carried on the equity basis.

**c.** Compute the carrying value of the investment in the Zales Corporation stock on December 31, 1981, under both the lower-of-cost-or-market method and the equity method.

**14.50** (Adapted from CPA Examination.) On January 1, Avow, Inc., purchased 30 percent of the outstanding common stock of Depot Corporation for $129,000 cash. Avow is accounting for this investment on the equity method. On the date of acquisition, the fair value of Depot's net assets was $310,000. Avow has ascertained that the excess of the cost of the investment over its share of Depot's net assets has an indeterminate life. Depot's net income for the year ended December 31 was $90,000. During the year Depot declared and paid cash dividends of $10,000. There were no other transactions between the two companies.

a. At what amount should the investment have been recorded on January 1?

b. Ignoring income taxes, Avow's statement of income for the year ended December 31 should include what amount for equity in net income of Depot Corporation?

14.51    (Adapted from CPA Examination.) On January 1, Year 1 Jeffries, Inc., paid $700,000 for 10,000 shares of Wolf Company's voting common stock which was a 10 percent interest in Wolf. At that date the net assets of Wolf totaled $6,000,000. The fair values of all of Wolf's identifiable assets and liabilities were equal to their book values. Jeffries does not have the ability to exercise signficant influence over the operating and financial policies of Wolf. Jeffries received dividends of $0.90 per share from Wolf on October 1, Year 1. Wolf reported net income of $400,000 for the year ended December 31, Year 1.

On July 1, Year 2, Jeffries paid $2,300,000 for 30,000 additional shares of Wolf Company's voting common stock which represents a 30 percent investment in Wolf. The fair values of all of Wolf's identifiable assets net of liabilties were equal to their book values of $6,500,000. As a result of this transaction, Jeffries has the ability to exercise significant influence over the operating and financial policies of Wolf. Jeffries received dividends of $1.10 per share from Wolf on April 1, Year 2, and $1.35 per share on October 1, Year 2. Wolf reported net income of $500,000 for the year ended December 31, Year 2, and $200,000 for the six months ended December 31, Year 2. Jeffries amortizes goodwill over a forty-year period.

a. Prepare a schedule showing the income or loss before income taxes for the year ended December 31, Year 1, that Jeffries should report from its investment in Wolf in its income statement issued in March, Year 2.

b. During March, Year 3 Jeffries issues comparative financial statements for Year 1 and Year 2. Prepare schedules showing the income or loss before income taxes for the years ended December 31, Year 1 and Year 2, that Jeffries should report from its investment in Wolf. Show supporting computations in good form.

14.52    Prepare journal entries to record the following transactions of a sinking fund established to retire bonds of Sheltin Company.

a. Cash of $10,000 is transferred from the cash account to the sinking fund account.

b. Darans Corporation 6 percent annual coupon bonds with par value of $4,000, maturing in 4 years, are purchased for $3,600. The effective yield to maturity is 9 percent.

c. Interest payment of $240 is received on Darans Corporation bonds. Interest revenue is recognized for one year on these bonds.

d. Sinking fund expenses of $85 are paid from sinking fund cash.

e. Dividends of $300 are received on an investment in Maximum Company's preferred stock.

f. Investments carried in the fund at $17,000 are sold for $14,800.

g. The fund contained $21,655 after disposing of all investments and paying all expenses. $18,000 of this amount is used to retire the bonds at the maturity date. The remaining cash balance is returned to the general account.

14.53    Shown here are data for a whole-life insurance policy Keller Company purchased on the president's life. The policy year runs from October 1 through September 30.

### Keller Company's Life Insurance Policy

| Policy Year | Annual Gross Premium | Estimated Dividend at End of Year | Guaranteed Cash Value Increase at End of Year |
|---|---|---|---|
| 1 | $3,000 | $420 | $ 100 |
| 2 | 3,000 | 460 | 700 |
| 3 | 3,000 | 480[a] | 2,500 |
| 4 | 3,000 | 520 | 2,560 |

[a]Dividend received on October 10 was $505.

The books are closed annually on December 31. Dividends from the insurance policy were as projected in the exhibit except that at the end of the third policy year, the dividend received was actually $505. Annual dividends checks arrive on October 10. Insurance premiums are paid annually on October 1. In any year when the Insurance Expense account has a credit balance, the account is retitled Revenue from Insurance Savings and shown on the income statement for the year.

a. Prepare journal entries for this insurance policy for the first 4 years of its life. Make journal entries for October 1, October 10, December 31, and September 30 of each policy year.

b. What is insurance expense (revenue) for the calendar year, January 1 of the first policy year through December 31 of the second policy year?

c. What is insurance expense (revenue) for the calendar year, January 1 of the third policy year through December 31 of the fourth policy year?

**14.54** The Bergen Company executed the following transactions in the shares of common stock of the Holland Company.

| Date | Shares Purchased and Prices | | Cash Disbursed |
|---|---|---|---|
| Jan. 2, Year 1 ..................... | 200 Shares | $100 | $20,000 |
| Aug. 1, Year 1 ..................... | 40 Shares | 124 | 4,960 |
| Sept. 1, Year 3 .................... | 45 Shares | 50 [a] | 2,250 |
| Jan. 2, Year 4 ..................... | 100 Shares | 90 | 9,000 |
| | | | $36,210 |

[a] Rights exercised; market value of rights same as on August 15 of Year 3.

| Date | Shares Sold and Price | | Cash Received |
|---|---|---|---|
| Sept. 1, Year 1 ........................... | 80 Shares | $125 | $10,000 |
| Feb. 20, Year 4 ........................... | 420 Shares | 100 | 42,000 |

The stock initially had a par value of $10 per share. On January 1, year 2, the par value was reduced to $5 when a 2-for-1 stock split became effective.

On July 1, year 2, a 25-percent stock dividend was issued. On August 15, year 3, rights were issued to shareholders to buy one share for $50 and four rights. Bergen Company received one right for each share owned. At this date, the stock had a market price of $80 rights-on. Bergen Company computed the cost to be assigned to the rights. It debited an Investment in Rights account and credited the Investment in Stock account. The amounts credited to the Investment in Stock account were allocated equally to each of the 400 shares then owned. The rights that were not exercised were sold on September 5, year 3, for $.50 per right more than their market value as computed on August 15, year 3.

The Bergen Company uses a first-in, first-out cost flow assumption for security transactions.

a. Record all transactions for years 1–4 in journal entry form. Show supporting calculations.

b. How many shares remain after February 20, year 4, and what is their cost?

**14.55** The Calvert Company executed the following transactions for securities in its investment account.

Feb. 1    Purchased 1,000 shares of Food Products Company for $8 per share and 1,000 shares of Stainless Steel Company for $31 per share. Brokerage costs were $96 for the first purchase and $1,000 for the second.

Apr. 30   The company buys $10,000 par value, 9-percent, semiannual coupon bonds of Union Electric Company. Interest is payable on April 1 and October 1 of each year. The price of the bonds is 103 percent of par plus accrued interest. In addition, transaction costs were $50. The bonds have an effective yield on cost, including brokerage fees of 8.2 percent, compounded semiannually.

May 1     Food Products Company declares a dividend of $.40 per share, one-quarter of which is designated as a capital distribution, not income. Such capital distributions are credited to the cost of the investment, reducing it, not to a revenue account. (Reported income will be larger in the period when the investment is sold because its cost has been reduced by this entry.) The dividend check arrived on May 31.

June 10   1,000 rights are received on shares of Stainless Steel Company. The rights enable Calvert to purchase 100 additional shares of Stainless Steel Company for a cash payment of $2,800. The market value of Stainless shares, rights-on, is $50 per share.

June 30   The Stainless rights are exercised. The fair market value today of the rights owned by Calvert is $2,400.

July 1    Calvert Company opens a new trading account for temporary investments with the brokerage firm of Isgur & Roberts, Inc., and deposits $15,000 in the account.

July 5    200 shares of Midvale Steel are bought through Isgur & Roberts for $50 per share. Transaction costs are $95.

Oct. 1    Interest on Union Electric Bonds is recorded. The coupons are redeemed at the bank for cash on October 5.

Nov. 1    200 shares of Midvale Steel are sold from the account with Isgur & Roberts. Proceeds of the sale are $53 per share less $120 transaction costs.

Dec. 10   The 100 shares of Stainless Steel acquired through rights exercised are sold for $55 per share. Transactions costs are $60.

Dec. 31   Market values are as follows:

| | |
|---|---|
| Food Products Company Shares | $ 8 per Share |
| Midvale Steel Company Shares | $46 per Share |
| Stainless Steel Company Shares | $30 per Share |
| Union Electric Company Bonds | 101% of Par |

a. Record journal entries for these events. Show supporting calculations.

b. What is the pretax effect on income for the year from these transactions?

14.56   General Products (G. P.) Company manufactures heavy-duty industrial equipment and consumer durable goods. In order to enable its customers to make convenient credit arrangements, G. P. Company organized General Products Credit Corporation several years ago. G. P. Credit Corporation is 100 percent owned by G. P. Company. G. P. Company accounts for its investment in G. P. Credit Corporation using the *equity method*. G. P. owns shares of many other companies and consolidates several of them in its financial statements. Refer to the comparative balance sheets and income statements for the two companies in Exhibits 14.14 and 14.15.

a. Given that G. P. Company accounted for its investment in G. P. Credit Corporation on the equity method, identify for the year the components of G. P. Company's income that are attributable to the Credit Corporation's dividends and earnings.

b. Assume that G. P. Company had accounted for its investment in the Credit Corporation using the lower of cost or market method and that market value has exceeded book value continually since acquisition.

(i) Show the components of G. P. Company's income from the Credit Corporation and compute how much larger or smaller G. P. Company's income would have been for the year than was reported.

*Exhibit 14.14*
**General Products Company
and Consolidated Affiliates**

| | (In Millions of $) December 31 |
|---|---:|
| **Balance Sheet** | |
| Investment in G. P. Credit Corporation | $ 260.0 |
| Other Assets | 7,141.8 |
| Total Assets | $ 7,401.8 |
| Total Liabilities | $ 4,317.2 |
| Shareholders' Equity | 3,084.6 |
| Total Equities | $ 7,401.8 |
| **Income Statement** | **For the Year** |
| Sales | $10,387.6 |
| Equity in Net Earnings of Credit Corporation | 41.1 |
| Total Revenues | $10,428.7 |
| Expenses | (9,898.7) |
| Net Income | $ 530.0 |

(ii) Identify any G. P. Company balance sheet accounts that would have different balances, and calculate the differences from what is shown in the actual statements and what would be shown had the alternative treatment been used.

c. Assume that G. P. Company had accounted for its investment in the G. P. Credit Corporation by *consolidating* it. Perform the same computations as required in (i) and (ii) of part **b** above for the year. Notice that when a 100-percent-owned affiliate accounted for with the equity method is consolidated, the effect on balance sheet totals and subtotals can be summarized as follows:

(i) Total owners' equity on the parent's books remains unchanged.

(ii) Total liabilities on the parent's books increases by the amount of the affiliate's total liabilities (assuming no intercompany receivables and payables).

(iii) Total assets on the parent's books increases net by an amount equal to the affiliate's liabilities. (All of the affiliate's assets are recorded onto the parent's books, but the parent's investment in the affiliate, an amount equal to the affiliate's owners' equity, is removed. The net effect is to increase assets by the amount of the affiliate's total assets − affiliate's owners' equity = affiliate's liabilities.)

d. Compute the following ratios for G. P. Company from the annual report as published for the year. (Refer to Exhibit 25.11 for definitions of these ratios.)

(i) Rate of return on assets. (Insufficient information is given to allow an addback to the numerator for interest payments net of tax effects; ignore that adjustment to net income which is ordinarily required. Use the year-end balance of total assets for the year's average.)

(ii) Debt-equity ratio.

e. For the year compute the two ratios required in part **d,** assuming that G. P. had consolidated the Credit Corporation rather than accounting for it with the equity method. Use the information derived in part **c.**

f. Compare the results in parts **d** and **e.** What conclusions can you draw from this exercise about comparing financial ratios for companies consolidating their subsidiaries with those of companies that do not?

*Exhibit 14.15*
**General Products Credit Corporation**

| Balance Sheet | (In Millions of $) December 31 |
|---|---|
| Total Assets | $2,789.5 |
| Total Liabilities | $2,529.5 |
| Capital Stock | $ 110.0 |
| Retained Earnings | 150.0 |
| Shareholders' Equity | $ 260.0 |
| Total Equities | $2,789.5 |

| Statement of Income and Retained Earnings | For the Year |
|---|---|
| Revenues | $ 319.8 |
| Less: Expenses | 278.7 |
| Net Income | $ 41.1 |
| Less: Dividends | 33.0 |
| Earnings Retained for Year | $ 8.1 |
| Retained Earnings at Jan. 1 | 141.9 |
| Retained Earnings at Dec. 31 | $ 150.0 |

**14.57** (Adapted from CPA Examination.) Craig Corporation enters all investment-related transactions in a single Investment account, to be adjusted at year-end. All of the entries in that account for a recent year are listed in Exhibit 14.16, together with dates and explanations for the entry.

Additional information required to make proper adjusting and correcting entries for the Investment account and several other accounts is given next.

1. The fair market values for each security on various dates are reported in the schedule on the next page.

| Security | March 15 | April 30 | June 28 | September 30 | October 31 |
|---|---|---|---|---|---|
| Ace Tool Company Common Stock | $25 | | | | $42 |
| Bymore Sales Company Common Stock | | | $8 | $14 | |
| Mascot, Inc., Preferred Stock | 20 | | | | |
| Mascot, Inc., Common Stock | 10 | $13 | 15[a] | 16 | |
| Mascot, Inc., Common Stock Rights | | | 3 | 4 | |
| Standard Service, Inc., Common Stock | 17 | | | | |
| Azuma Mines, Inc., Bonds | | 100 | | 100 | 102 |
| Azuma Mines, Inc., Common Stock | | | | 65 | |
| Kevin Instruments, Inc., Common Stock | 28 | 30 | | | |

[a]Ex-rights.

*Exhibit 14.16*
**Craig Corporation**
**Analysis of Investments**
**for the Year Ended December 31**

| Date | | Debit | Credit |
|---|---|---|---|
| | **(a)** | | |
| | **Ace Tool Company Common Stock** | | |
| Mar. 15 .......... | Purchased 1,000 shares @ $25 per share. ......... | $ 25,000 | |
| June 28 .......... | Received 50 shares of Bymore Sales Company common stock as a dividend on Ace Tool Company common stock (memorandum entry in general ledger). | | |
| Sep. 30 .......... | Sold 50 shares of Bymore Sales Company common stock @ $14 per share. ................................... | | $ 700 |
| Oct. 31 .......... | Awarded 500 shares of Ace Tool Company common stock to selected members of Craig's management as an incentive award and accounted for as employee compensation. .................................. | | 12,500 |
| | **(b)** | | |
| | **Mascot, Inc., Common and Preferred Stock** | | |
| Mar. 15 .......... | Purchased 600 units of common and preferred stock @ $36 per unit. Each unit consists of one share of preferred and two shares of common stock. ....... | 21,600 | |
| Apr. 30 .......... | Sold 300 shares of common stock @ $13 per share. .......... | | 3,900 |
| June 28 .......... | Received 900 common stock rights. Each right entitles the holder to purchase one share of common stock for $12 (memorandum entry in general ledger). | | |
| Sep. 30 .......... | Exercised 450 common stock rights to acquire 450 shares of common stock @ $12 per share. ........ | 5,400 | |
| Sep. 30 .......... | Sold remaining 450 common stock rights @ $4 per right. .................................................... | | 1,800 |
| | **(c)** | | |
| | **Standard Service, Inc., Common Stock** | | |
| Mar. 15 .......... | Purchased 10,000 shares @ $17 per share. ........ | 170,000 | |
| Oct. 31 .......... | Received dividend of $.75 per share. ....................... | | 7,500 |
| | **(d)** | | |
| | **Azuma Mines, Inc., Convertible Bonds** **(Due Sep. 30, 1983, with interest at** **7% payable Mar. 31 and Sep. 30)** | | |
| Apr. 30 .......... | Purchased 40 $1,000 bonds @ $100 plus accrued interest. ..................................... | 40,233 | |
| Sep. 30 .......... | Received interest due. .................................... | | 1,400 |
| Sep. 30 .......... | Converted 10 bonds into 200 shares of Azuma Mines common stock. ........................................... | | 10,000 |
| Sep. 30 .......... | Received 200 shares of common stock on conversion of bonds. ............................... | 10,000 | |
| Oct. 31 .......... | Sold the remaining 30 bonds @ $102 plus interest for one month. The interest was credited to interest revenue. ............................................... | | 30,600 |

---

*Exhibit 14.16 (continued)*

| Date | | Debit | Credit |
|---|---|---|---|
| | **(e)** | | |
| | **Kevin Instruments, Inc., Common Stock** | | |
| Mar. 15 ......... | Purchased 4,000 shares @ $28 per share. ......... | $112,000 | |
| Apr. 30 ......... | Purchased 2,000 shares @ $30 per share. ......... | 60,000 | |
| June 28 ......... | Received dividend of $.40 per share. ....................... | | $2,400 |
| | **(f)** | | |
| | **Other Investment** | | |
| Oct. 31 ......... | Reacquired 1,600 shares of its own (Craig) outstanding common stock @ $14 per share with the intention of retiring them. ................... | 22,400 | |

2. Assume that in accordance with Craig's practice, no gain was recognized on conversion of the Azuma convertible bonds into Azuma common stock.

3. Standard Service, Inc., has only one class of stock authorized, and there were 30,000 shares of its common stock outstanding throughout the year. Craig's cost of its investment in Standard was not materially different from its equity in the recorded values of Standard's net assets; recorded values were not materially different from fair values (individually or collectively). Standard's net income from the date of acquisition of Craig's investment to December 31 was $336,000. There were no intercompany transactions requiring elimination.

4. Kevin Instruments, Inc., has only one class of stock authorized, and there were 40,000 shares of its common stock outstanding throughout the year. Craig's cost of its investment in Kevin was not materially different from its equity in the recorded values of Kevin's net assets; recorded values were not materially different from fair values (individually or collectively). Kevin's net income from the date of acquisition of Craig's investment to December 31 was $120,000. There were no intercompany transactions requiring elimination.

5. All other investments of Craig are widely held, and Craig's percentage of ownership in each is nominal (5 percent or less).

Prepare adjusting entries classified by security analyzed; use letters **a** through **f** corresponding to the data in the accompanying exhibits. Ignore brokerage charges, transfer taxes, and income taxes. Show supporting calculations in good form.

14.58 (Adapted from CPA Examination.) Exhibit 5.2 in Chapter 5 illustrates a procedure for accounting for all monetary assets. The illustrations are simplified because the interest-collection dates correspond to period-end dates. In practice, interest dates generally are not at accounting period-ends. Even so, the method in Exhibit 5.2 can still be applied, but knowing which "historical interest rate" to use requires an understanding of the effects of changing the compounding period. For example, an interest rate of 18 percent compounded semiannually—9 percent per six months—is not the same as $1^1/_2$ percent per month. See the discussion in Appendix B, where it is pointed out that 9 percent for six months is equivalent to $(1.09)^{1/6} - 1 = 1.4467$ percent per month. The following problem appeared in a recent CPA Examination.

On June 1 of Year 1, Warner, Inc. purchased as a long-term investment 800 of the $1,000 face value, 8-percent bonds of Universal Corporation for $738,300. The bonds were purchased to yield 10 percent interest compounded semiannually. Interest is payable semiannually on December 1 and June 1. The bonds mature on June 1, Year 5. Warner uses the effective interest method of amortization. On November 1, Year 2, Warner sold the bonds for $785,000. This amount includes the appropriate accrued interest.

*Exhibit 14.17*

**Amortization Schedules to Illustrate Accounting for Monetary Assets when Interest-Collection Dates Differ from End-of-Period Dates**

**Amortization Schedule Based on Semiannual Compounding for Use in Straight-Line Allocation to Sub-periods**

| Date (1) | Book Value Before Computations (2) | + | Interest (3)[a] | − | Cash Received (4) | = | Book Value After Computations (5) |
|---|---|---|---|---|---|---|---|
| **Year 1** | | | | | | | |
| June 1 | | | | | | | $738,300 |
| Dec. 1 | $738,300 | | $36,915 | | $32,000 | | 743,215 |
| | | | | | | | |
| **Year 2** | | | | | | | |
| June 1 | 743,215 | | 37,161 | | 32,000 | | 748,376 |
| Dec. 1 | 748,376 | | 37,419 | | 32,000 | | 753,795 |

Column (3) = .05 × Number in Column (2).

**Amortization Schedule Based on Compounding Every Payment Date and Every Adjusting Entry Date**

5 percent compounded semiannually is equivalent to:

$(1.05)^{1/6} - 1 =$ .8165 percent per month

or

$(1.05)^{5/6} - 1 =$ 4.1496 percent per 5 months

| Date (1) | Book Value Before Computation (2) | + | Interest (3) | − | Cash Received (4) | = | Book Value After Computations (5) |
|---|---|---|---|---|---|---|---|
| **Year 1** | | | | | | | |
| June 1 | | | | | | | $738,300 |
| Dec. 1 | $738,300 | | $36,915[a] | | $32,000 | | 743,215 |
| Dec. 31 | 743,215 | | 6,068[b] | | — | | 749,283 |
| Total | | | $42,983 | | | | |
| | | | | | | | |
| **Year 2** | | | | | | | |
| June 1 | 749,283 | | 31,092[c] | | 32,000 | | 748,376 |
| Nov. 1 | 748,376 | | 31,055[c] | | — | | 779,430 |
| Total | | | $62,147 | | | | |

[a]6-month period; Column (2) × .05

[b]1-month period; Column (2) × .008165

[c]5-month period; Column (2) × .04196

The CPA Examination question required a schedule showing the income or loss before income taxes from the bond investment that Warner should record for the years ended December 31, Year 0 and Year 1, with supporting computations in good form.

Exhibit 14.17 gives amortization schedules for this bond investment. The top panel assumes compounding every six months at the rate of 5 percent per six month period. Interest from sub-periods such as one month or five months is merely the corresponding fraction, such as $1/6$ or $5/6$, of the interest for the entire six-month period. This is the method used in the "unofficial" answer to the examination question. The second panel deals with each period separately, whatever its length, using an interest rate appropriate for the length of period. That is, if the interest rate is 5 percent for six months, the second panel uses a rate of .8165 percent for one-month intervals (because $1.05^{1/6} - 1 = .008165$) and 4.1496 percent for five-month periods (because $1.05^{5/6} - 1 = 4.1496$ percent). Using these exact interest rates enables one to use the procedures of Exhibit 5.2 without any modification.

The following journal entries could be made in the first year under the two methods. The straight-line allocation data come from the top panel of Exhibit 14.17 and the exact computation data come from the bottom panel.

|  | Straight-Line Allocation to Sub-periods | | Exact Computation for Sub-periods | |
|---|---|---|---|---|
| **June 1, Year 1** | | | | |
| Bond Investment | 738,300 | | 738,300 | |
|   Cash | | 738,300 | | 738,300 |
| **December 1, Year 1** | | | | |
| Cash | 32,000 | | 32,000 | |
| Bond Investment | 4,915 | | 4,915 | |
|   Interest Revenue | | 36,915 | | 36,915 |
| **December 31, Year 1** | | | | |
| Receivable | 6,194 | | 6,068 | |
|   Interest Revenue | | 6,194 | | 6,068 |
|     $1/6 \times \$37,161 = \$6,194$. | | | | |

a. Compute interest revenue and gain on sale of the investment for Year 2, using the straight-line method for allocation of interest to sub-periods. (This is the method illustrated in the CPA Examination answer.)

b. Compute interest revenue and gain on sale of the investment for Year 2, using the exact method of allocation of interest to sub-periods.

c. Comment on the advantages and disadvantages of each of these methods.

d. Demonstrate that income over the life of the investment is equal to cash-in less cash-out, independent of the method of allocating that income to interest for Year 1, interest for Year 2, and gain on sale in Year 2.

# Part Three
# Liability Recognition and Related Expenses

# Chapter 15
# *Liability Recognition and Valuation: Underlying Concepts*

15.1 Chapters 16 through 20 discuss generally accepted accounting principles for each major type of liability—accounts payable, bonds payable, warranties payable, and so on. This chapter considers the concept of an accounting liability and various valuation bases. This material provides the conceptual base for understanding the specific accounting principles and procedures discussed in the next five chapters.

## Liability Recognition

15.2 The concept of an accounting liability has developed historically in parallel with issues of revenue, expense, and asset recognition. Acquisition of the asset inventory on account creates a liability. Using labor services results in either a product cost or a period expense and creates a liability. Receipts of cash as advances from customers create a liability. Accounting's emphasis on revenues, expenses, and asset recognition, with liabilities being created only as necessary to provide equal debits and credits, has resulted in an incohesive theory of accounting liabilities. Questions of liability recognition have been more difficult than those of liability valuation in historical cost accounting: once the accountant makes the sometimes difficult decision to recognize a liability, the

amount, as explained below, is generally the net present value of the future cash payments.

## Criteria for Liability Recognition

15.3 An obligation is generally recognized as a liability of an entity if it satisfies four criteria:*

**1.** The obligation involves a probable future sacrifice of resources—a future transfer of cash, goods, or services or the foregoing of a future cash receipt.

**2.** The obligation is discharged by the specific enterprise.

**3.** The transaction or event giving rise to the entity's obligation has already occurred.

**4.** The amount of the obligation and the time of its settlement are measurable with reasonable accuracy.

15.4 Note two aspects of an accounting liability. First, the obligation need not be a legally enforceable claim against the enterprise. Any probable future transfer of resources is recognized as a liability. The transfer can be made "probable" by custom or moral re-

---

*Financial Accounting Standards Board, *Statement of Financial Accounting Concepts No. 3* (December 1980), pars. 17 and 29.

sponsibility as well as by law. Second, knowing the identity of the specific recipients of the future cash, goods, or services is not necessary. An example of a liability that is neither legally binding nor to a specific person is an informal warranty on products sold. Some retail stores, for example, advertise that refunds will be given to customers dissatisfied for any reason. The estimated amount to be paid to customers for sales that have already occurred is a liability. Note both the lack of a legal obligation and knowledge of the eventual specific recipient. As long as an obligation to transfer resources is probable, it is recognized as a liability.

## Application of Criteria for Liability Recognition

15.5   The criteria for liability recognition may appear to be straightforward and subject to unambiguous interpretation. Unfortunately, this is not so. Various obligations of an enterprise fall along a continuum with respect to how well they satisfy these criteria. Exhibit 15.1 classifies obligations into six groups. Each of these groups is discussed next.

15.6   **Obligations with Fixed Payment Dates and Amounts**  The obligations that most

clearly satisfy the liability recognition criteria are those for which the payment amounts and due dates are fixed, usually by contract, and for which the enterprise has already received benefits. Most obligations arising from borrowing arrangements fall into this category. A firm receives the benefit of having funds available for its use. The borrowing agreement specifies the timing and amount of interest and principal payments.

**Obligations with Fixed Payment Amounts**   15.7
**but Estimated Payment Dates**  Most current liabilities fall into this category. Amounts payable to suppliers, employees, and governmental agencies are relatively fixed, either by oral agreement, written agreement, or legal statute. These obligations will normally be settled within a few months after they have been incurred. The settlement date, although not known precisely, can be estimated with sufficient accuracy to warrant recognizing a liability.

**Obligations for Which Both Timing and**   15.8
**Amount of Payment Must Be Estimated**
Obligations in this group require estimation because the specific future recipients of cash, goods, or services cannot be identified at the time the obligation becomes a liability. In addition, the amount of resources to be transferred in the future cannot be precisely

*Exhibit 15.1*
### Classification of Accounting Liabilities

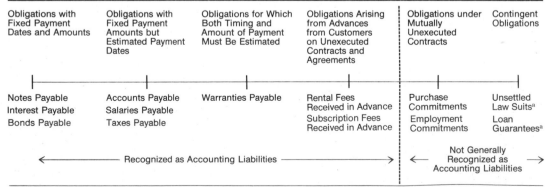

| Obligations with Fixed Payment Dates and Amounts | Obligations with Fixed Payment Amounts but Estimated Payment Dates | Obligations for Which Both Timing and Amount of Payment Must Be Estimated | Obligations Arising from Advances from Customers on Unexecuted Contracts and Agreements | Obligations under Mutually Unexecuted Contracts | Contingent Obligations |
|---|---|---|---|---|---|
| Notes Payable | Accounts Payable | Warranties Payable | Rental Fees Received in Advance | Purchase Commitments | Unsettled Law Suits[a] |
| Interest Payable | Salaries Payable | | Subscription Fees Received in Advance | Employment Commitments | Loan Guarantees[a] |
| Bonds Payable | Taxes Payable | | | | |
| ← Recognized as Accounting Liabilities → | | | | ← Not Generally Recognized as Accounting Liabilities → | |

[a]If certain criteria for a loss contingency are met, these obligations are recognized as liabilities. See the discussion later in this chapter.

computed. For example, when products are sold under a warranty agreement, a firm promises to replace defective parts or perform certain repair services for a specified period of time. At the time of sale, the firm can neither identify the specific customers who will receive warranty benefits nor ascertain the amounts of their claims. Past experience, however, often provides the information for estimating the likely proportion of customers who will make claims and the probable average amount of their claims. As long as the probable amount of the obligation can be estimated, the fourth criterion is satisfied. The selling price of goods sold under warranty includes an explicit or implicit charge for the warranty services. Thus, the receipt of cash or the right to receive cash in the sales transaction benefits the firm and creates the warranty liability. (As Chapter 16 discusses, the accounting here is similar in concept and method to the allowance method for receivables introduced in Chapter 7.)

15.9   **Obligations Arising from Advances from Customers on Unexecuted Contracts and Agreements** A firm sometimes receives cash from customers in advance for goods or services to be provided in a future period. For example, cash may be received in advance on rental property owned by a firm. A magazine publisher may receive subscription fees in advance of the subscription period. Organizations and associations may receive membership dues prior to the membership period. The receipt of this cash could be recognized as revenue, as with the sale of products under warranty plans. In the cases described above, however, the required transfer of resources (goods or services) will occur in the future. Revenue recognition generally requires that goods be delivered or that services be performed. Receipt of cash in advance creates a liability equal to the cash received. The liability might conceivably be recorded at the expected cost of delivering the promised goods or services, but doing so would require recognizing the profit on the transaction before the transaction was complete.

**Obligations under Mutually Unexecuted Contracts** Mutually unexecuted contracts arise when two entities agree to make a transfer of resources but *neither* entity has yet made a transfer. For example, a firm may agree to supply its customers with specified amounts of merchandise over the next 2 years. Or a firm may agree to pay its president a certain sum as compensation over the next 5 years. A bank may agree to provide lines of credit to its business customers in the event that funds are needed in the future. Because neither party has transferred resources, no accounting liability has been created. This category of obligation, called executory contracts, differs from the preceding two, where the contracts or agreements were partially completed. With warranty agreements, a firm receives cash but has not fulfilled its warranty obligation. With rental, subscription, and membership fees, a firm receives cash but has not provided the required goods or services.   15.10

Obligations under mutually unexecuted contracts are generally not recognized as accounting liabilities. If the amounts involved are material, the nature of the obligation and its amount must be disclosed in notes to the financial statements.   15.11

**Contingent Obligations** An event whose outcome today is unknown may create an obligation for the future transfer of resources. For example, a firm may be a defendant in a lawsuit, the outcome of which depends on the results of legal proceedings. The obligation is *contingent* on future events.   15.12

Contingent obligations may or may not be recognized as accounting liabilities. Financial Accounting Standards Board *Statement No. 5* requires an estimated loss from a contingency (called a *loss contingency*) to be recognized if and only if both of the following conditions are met:   15.13

**1.** Information available prior to the issuance of the financial statements indicates that it is probable that an asset has been impaired or that a liability has been incurred, and

**2.** The amount of the loss can be reasonably estimated.

15.14 The first criterion for a recognition of a loss contingency rests on the probability, or likelihood, that an asset has been impaired or a liability has been incurred. Generally accepted accounting principles do not provide guidance as to what probability cutoff defines *likely* or *probable*. One definition might interpret the words to mean that any event with probability greater than 50 percent is "probable" or "likely." We suspect that the interpretation in practice is to use a cutoff closer to 90 percent.*

15.15 The second criterion is that the amount of the loss can be reasonably estimated. Again, generally accepted accounting principles do not define "reasonably estimated" in any precise terms. Instead, if the amount of the loss can be narrowed to a range, however large, it is considered to be measured with sufficient precision to be recognized. The amount of the loss is the most likely estimate within the range. If no amount within the range is thought to be more likely than any

---

*Consider the following three events:

**Event A:** A lawsuit is filed against a firm. The probability is .90 that the firm will lose. If it loses, the amount of the loss will most likely be $100,000. In a statistical sense, the expected loss is $90,000 (= .90 × $100,000). Assume that the standard deviation of the expected loss is $30,000.

**Event B:** A firm does not carry fire insurance on its 1,000 different stores. The probability of loss at any one store is .009 and the expected loss if there is a fire is $10,000. The total loss has an expected value of $90,000 (= 1,000 × .009 × $10,000) and a standard deviation of $30,000.

**Event C:** A firm issues "cents-off" coupons in its cereal boxes. Ten million coupons for 10 cents each are issued. The probability of redemption for any one coupon is .09. The expected cost of the promotion is $90,000 and the standard deviation is $30,000.

These three events, somewhat stylized for presentation here, are assumed to be the same statistically and economically. Yet accounting treats them differently. Event A is recorded as an expense or loss and a liability of $100,000. Event B will not be recorded at all until an actual loss occurs. Event C is recorded as an expense and an estimated liability of $90,000. Events A and C are "probable," whereas event B would be viewed as "possible," not "probable."

other, then the amount at the lower end of the range should be chosen.†

15.16 Obligations meeting both of the above tests are referred to as "loss contingencies." Only a few situations are likely to meet both of these tests, however. One example suggested by the FASB is a toy manufacturer that has sold products that were later discovered to have a safety hazard. The toy manufacturer thinks it likely that it will have to pay damages to customers. Test **2** is met if experience or other information enables the manufacturer to make a reasonable estimate of the loss.

15.17 Potential obligations that do not meet the two tests are not recognized as accounting liabilities. If the amounts potentially involved are significant, however, disclosure in the notes is required. See, for example, the disclosure of contingencies by International Corporation in Note 20 to its financial statements in Appendix A at the back of the book.

15.18 *Example 1* A common potential obligation of small, closely held firms arises in connection with loan guaranties. Corporate owner-officers or other major shareholders might obtain personal loans from a local bank. To add security to the lending arrangement, the firm may agree to repay the bank if the shareholder fails to do so. If on the balance sheet date, loan repayment by the shareholder as required appears probable, then only a potential obligation—not an accounting liability—exists. If, on the other hand, the shareholder has failed to make the required payments or evidence indicates that the individual will not be able to make the required payments when due, then the criteria for a loss contingency are likely to be satisfied. Hence, a liability should be recognized.

15.19 *Example 2* A second potential cost is sometimes seen in the context of self-insurance. The scope of some firm's operations is sufficiently broad and the risk of losses is sufficiently diversified that the firm may choose

---

†Financial Accounting Standards Board, *Interpretation No. 14* (1976).

to "self-insure." That is, rather than obtain a formal insurance policy and pay the required premiums, the firm merely absorbs any losses itself. (Self-insurance means no insurance.) Prior to the issuance of FASB *Statement No. 5,* firms self-insuring would spread out the effect of actual losses on earnings by using the allowance method. An entry would be made each period debiting Self-Insurance Expense and crediting Estimated Losses from Self-Insurance. The Estimated Losses from Self-Insurance would appear among the liabilities on the balance sheet much the same as Estimated Warranty Liability. When actual losses occurred, such as from a fire, the Estimated Losses account would be debited and the account for the particular asset destroyed would be credited. FASB *Statement No. 5* forbids recognizing liabilities for self-insurance. The allowance method is, therefore, *not* acceptable for self-insurance. If an actual loss occurs under self-insurance arrangements, it must be recognized at the time of the loss, not earlier through spreading. If a loss has not occurred as of the date of the balance sheet, then no liability is recognized.*

## Controversial Issues of Liability Recognition

15.20    Most obligations discussed in the preceding sections clearly either were liabilities or were not liabilities. Controversy has continued, however, regarding whether or not obligations arising from leases, pensions, deferred taxes, and convertible debt should be recognized as accounting liabilities. The issues involved are discussed here briefly and explored in greater depth in later chapters.

15.21    **Leases** Firms often acquire the rights to use buildings, equipment, and other assets under leasing arrangements. Some leases cover only a short period, such as an automobile leased by the day. Other leases cover a longer term. They may or may not run for the entire economic life of the leased assets. Some leases are cancelable by merely returning the leased property and paying the rental for the period the asset was used. Other leases are noncancelable. Regardless of the extent of asset usage, lease payments must be made for the life of the lease.

15.22    The lease controversy concerns whether long-term noncancelable leases create assets (leaseholds) and liabilities at the time they are signed. Those favoring the recognition of a lease asset and liability argue that the leasing arrangement is in substance nothing more than a method of financing the acquisition of rights to use property. In economic substance, they say, rights to use property are the same as owning property. A firm could borrow funds from its bank and then purchase the property for cash. Alternatively, when a firm acquires use of property under a long-term noncancelable lease and makes periodic payments to the lessor, it has carried out the same economic transactions. Because an asset (property) and a liability to the bank are recognized in the first case, consistency suggests that an asset (leasehold) and a liability should be recognized in the second case as well.

15.23    Those who oppose recognizing lease assets and liabilities argue that leases are mutually unexecuted contracts at the time they are signed. Neither party has transferred resources and, therefore, no liability has been created. The event that creates a liability, according to this view, is the use over time of the leased asset. The accounting suggested, therefore, is the recognition of a liability as payments become due.

15.24    Chapter 18 discusses the specific criteria established by the FASB for answering the lease recognition question. In general, short-term or cancelable leases are not recognized as liabilities, whereas long-term noncancelable leases equivalent to financing the purchase of an asset are recognized as assets and liabilities.

---

*In the past, firms had used the allowance method for self-insurance losses as a means of smoothing income. The FASB concluded that income smoothing had become the principal purpose of accruing estimated losses. Because catastrophic losses occur irregularly, the FASB decided that the income pattern of a company with occasional catastrophic losses should be irregular, not smoothed.

15.25 **Pensions** When a firm adopts a pension plan, it typically gives existing employees "credit" for service prior to the plan's adoption. The credit takes the form of reducing the number of years in the future that the employee must work to qualify for the pension or increasing the eventual retirement benefits, or both. When the plan is adopted, the firm incurs a future obligation because of past events (prior employee service). Should this *prior service obligation* (now referred to as *actuarial accrued liability;* see Chapter 19) be recognized as an accounting liability?

15.26 Those favoring liability recognition argue that the labor services giving rise to the prior service obligation have already been received. The pension is an as-yet-unpaid part of the compensation for those labor services and should be recognized as a liability.

15.27 Opponents of liability recognition argue that the granting of retroactive benefits is not part of compensation for past services. Instead, it is intended to enhance employee morale and productivity and, therefore, is part of future compensation. Because all benefits are expected to be received in the future, there has been no transfer of resources (labor services) as of the date the plan is adopted and, therefore, no pension liability.

15.28 Under current generally accepted accounting principles, most prior service obligations from pension plans are not recognized as liabilities. Chapter 19 discusses this complex and controversial topic.

15.29 **Deferred Income Taxes** Firms commonly use different methods of accounting for income tax and financial reporting purposes. For example, a firm will probably use ACRS depreciation for income for tax purposes and the straight-line method for financial reporting. During the early years of an asset's life, depreciation claimed on the tax return will exceed depreciation expense reported in the financial statements. During later years, book depreciation will exceed tax depreciation. These differences in depreciation expense create timing differences between tax and book income. An item, revenue or ex-

pense, that appears in the financial statements in one period but on the tax return in another period is called a *timing difference*. Over a period of years, these timing differences will reverse and net out to zero.

15.30 Should income tax expense in each year be **(1)** the income taxes actually payable for the year based on taxable income or **(2)** the income taxes that will ultimately be payable in the current and future years based on the current year's income reported in the financial statements? Under current generally accepted accounting principles, income tax expense must be based on the financial statement (or book) income amounts. Because book income usually exceeds taxable income, the debit to Income Tax Expense will exceed the credit to Current Income Taxes Payable. The remaining credit must be made to a Deferred Income Taxes account and classified among the equities on the balance sheet. Is this Deferred Income Taxes account a liability?

15.31 Proponents of recognition argue that benefits have been received by a firm in the form of lower current tax payments.* Resources will be transferred in the future when the timing differences reverse. The criteria for liability recognition are therefore satisfied.

15.32 Opponents argue that neither the first nor the fourth criterion for liability recognition is met. Deferred taxes become payable only if a reversal of the timing difference actually occurs. For a particular asset, timing differences do reverse. However, if all timing differences of a firm are considered in the aggregate, timing differences are not likely to reverse. That is, total depreciation claimed on the tax return may never be less for any year than total depreciation expense in the financial statements. A growing firm, for example, will find that the cost of new assets in the early years of their lives when tax depreciation exceeds book depreciation will always exceed the cost of old assets in their

---

*If you have not previously been exposed to deferred tax accounting, you should not expect to understand fully the arguments presented here.

later years when book depreciation exceeds tax depreciation. The credit balance in the Deferred Income Taxes account will, therefore, continually grow. Not only is there no obligation to make a future transfer of resources, but the timing of any eventual settlement cannot be estimated with reasonable accuracy. In addition, the amount of any future payment is uncertain because future tax rates are uncertain.

15.33   Most firms classify Deferred Income Taxes between liabilities and shareholders' equity on the equities side of the balance sheet but include its amount in neither total liabilities nor total shareholders' equity. Chapter 20 discusses deferred income taxes in greater depth.

15.34   **Convertible Bonds** Firms sometimes borrow funds with issues that give the holder of the bonds two options: **(1)** The bonds can be held as bonds—the holder receives periodic interest payments and the principal repayment at maturity; or **(2)** the bonds can be converted into a contractually specified number of preferred or common shares. Are these convertible bonds a liability of the issuing firm?

15.35   The first three criteria for liability recognition are clearly met. Cash is currently received by a specific enterprise, obligating it to transfer cash in the future if the bonds are repaid at maturity. If the bonds are converted into preferred or common stock, the firm foregoes the cash that would have been received if the shares were sold on the open market at the time of conversion. The problem occurs because the amount and timing of settlement of the obligation may not be measurable with reasonable accuracy. If conversion is likely to take place, one can argue that the fourth criterion is not met.

15.36   Generally accepted accounting principles treat all convertible bonds as liabilities until conversion occurs. This uniform treatment of convertible bonds results from the inability of standard-setting bodies to develop a reasonably objective procedure for distinguishing convertible bonds, unlikely to be converted and are thus debt, from convertible bonds that are likely to be converted and are thus components of owners' equity.

15.37   **Summary** The purpose of this discussion of leases, pensions, deferred taxes, and convertible bonds has been to indicate the difficulties often encountered in applying the criteria for liability recognition. A set of unambiguous liability criteria that would clearly signal whether or not a particular obligation is an accounting liability would be difficult to develop.

## Liability Valuation

15.38   Most liabilities require a future cash payment of a specific amount (for example, accounts payable, salaries payable, taxes payable, bonds payable). Liabilities that require the future transfer of goods or services (for example, warranties and subscriptions) may also be thought of as requiring future cash payments, because the goods or services must first be either acquired or produced by the firm. Liabilities could conceivably be measured using one of two valuation methods: **(1)** amount of cash ultimately payable, or **(2)** present value of cash amount ultimately payable.

### Amount Ultimately Payable

15.39   One of the criteria for recognizing a liability is that there exists an obligation to make a future sacrifice of resources. This sacrifice is a future transfer of cash (or cash equivalent value of goods or services). The amount of this expected cash transfer could be used as the valuation basis for measuring accounting liabilities.

15.40   The principal weakness of using the amount ultimately payable is that it ignores the fact that the payment will not be made immediately. Accounts, salaries, and taxes payable will not be paid for several weeks or months. Bonds and other long-term debt may not be paid for many years. Because interest can be earned on cash that is not paid out immediately, the amount ultimately payable and the present value of that amount differ.

## Present Value of Amount Payable

15.41  A second valuation basis for liabilities is the present value of the future cash flows. To calculate a present value, a discount rate must be selected. Two discount rates merit consideration. One possibility is to use the market rate of interest appropriate to the risk level of the particular liability at the time the liability was initially incurred. This rate is referred to as the *historical market rate*. The other possibility is to use the *current market rate* appropriate to the particular liability. These two interest rates are the same at the time a liability first arises, but generally differ thereafter.

15.42  **Historical Market Rate** Assume, for example, that a firm wished to acquire a machine costing $39,927 on January 1, 1981. To finance the acquisition, it borrowed the necessary funds from a local bank. The firm agreed to repay the loan, including interest, at the rate of $10,000 a year at the end of each of the next 5 years. This loan implicitly carries an interest rate of 8 percent. To see this, compute the present value of an annuity of $10,000 payable at the end of each of the next 5 years discounted at 8 percent per year: $39,927 = $10,000 × 3.9927; see Table 4 at the back of the book. The journal entry to record the loan is

Jan. 1, 1981
Cash .......................... 39,927
    Note Payable ................ 39,927
To record a bank loan, repayable at
the rate of $10,000 per year for 5 years
at an implicit interest rate of 8 percent.

As Chapters 8 and 17 discuss, it is common practice to credit Note Payable for the amount payable ($50,000) and debit Discount on Note Payable, a contra account to Note Payable, for the discount ($10,073 = $50,000 − $39,927).

15.43  At the end of 1981, after the first $10,000 payment has been made, there will be four remaining payments. The present value of these

four remaining payments discounted at the historical interest rate for this loan of 8 percent is $33,121 (= $10,000 × 3.3121); see Table 4, 4-period row, 8-percent column. This is the amount at which the liability would be stated at the end of 1981. The journal entries made during 1981 to obtain this end-of-year valuation are as follows:

Dec. 31, 1981
Interest Expense .................. 3,194
    Note Payable ................ 3,194
To recognize interest expense at 8
percent on the amount of the loan
outstanding at the beginning of 1981
($39,927 × .08).

Dec. 31, 1981
Note Payable .................... 10,000
    Cash ........................ 10,000
To recognize the payment of principal
and interest on the bank loan.

The Note Payable account will show the following during 1981:

| | |
|---|---|
| Balance, January 1, 1981 .............. | $39,927 |
| Plus: Interest for 1981 ................. | 3,194 |
| Less: Payment of Principal and Interest | (10,000) |
| Balance, December 31, 1981 ........... | $33,121 |

As shown above, $33,121 is the present value of the remaining four payments discounted at the historical market, or interest, rate of 8 percent.

**Current Market Rate** The historical market  15.44 rate and the current market rate are the same amount at the time a liability is initially recognized. Over time, however, market rates change in response to changes in the borrower's creditworthiness and changes in the demand for and supply of money. An increase in the demand for housing by consumers will increase the demand for money and tend to drive up interest rates. A repurchase of outstanding government securities by the federal government will increase the money supply and tend to reduce short-term interest rates. Instead of using the historical market rate, liabilities might be valued at each balance sheet date using the *current market* *rate* appropriate to the risk level of the particular liability. For example, assume that the market rate appropriate to the bank loan discussed above increased from 8 percent to 10 percent on December 31, 1981. The present value of the four remaining payments discounted at 10 percent is $31,699 (= $10,000 × 3.1699). The journal entries made for this loan during 1981 to achieve this end-of-the-year valuation are as follows:

Jan. 1, 1981
Cash .......................... 39,927
 Note Payable ................   39,927
To record a bank loan, repayable at
the rate of $10,000 per year for 5 years
at an implicit interest rate of 8 percent.

Dec. 31, 1981
Interest Expense .................. 3,194
 Note Payable ..................   3,194
To record interest expense at 8 percent,
the current market rate throughout
1981.

Dec. 31, 1981
Note Payable ..................... 10,000
 Cash ......................   10,000
To record the payment of principal
and interest.

Dec. 31, 1981
Note Payable ..................... 1,422
 Unrealized Holding Gain .......   1,422
To state the note at $31,699, the present value of the remaining cash flows
at the current market rate of 10 percent, and to record a holding gain:
$39,927 + $3,194 − $10,000 −
$31,699 = $1,422.

Under the assumption that the market rate remained at 8 percent throughout 1981, the first three entries are identical to those made earlier. (If the market rate had changed *during* 1981, then the amount in the second entry would be different.) The fourth entry is new. This entry recognizes the effect of the change in the current market rate on the valuation of the liability on December 31, 1981. The firm has an unrealized holding gain as a result of owing ("holding") debt that accumulates interest at 8 percent when current loans of comparable risk require interest at

10 percent. The bank, on the other hand, has an unrealized holding loss, because it has loaned funds at 8 percent that could be loaned currently at 10 percent.

15.45  Exhibit 15.2 provides amortization schedules* for the 5 years of this loan using the present-value valuation basis and both the historical and current market rates. The top panel shows the amounts using the historical market rate of 8 percent throughout the life of the loan. Interest expense each period is equal to 8 percent times the liability at the beginning of the year. The liability is increased for the interest accrual and then decreased for the $10,000 payment. The liability at the end of the period is equal to the present value of the remaining cash flows discounted at 8 percent. Of the total $50,000 paid during the 5-year period, $10,073 represents interest and $39,927 represents a repayment of the principal amount borrowed.

15.46  The lower panel shows the amortization schedule using the current market rate. For 1981, the current rate was 8 percent, the same as the historical market rate. Interest expense is equal to 8 percent times the beginning of the period liability. On December 31, 1981, the current market rate increases from 8 percent to 10 percent. The present value of the remaining four cash payments discounted at 10 percent is $31,699. The difference between this amount and the book value of the liability of $33,121 (= $43,121 − $10,000) is an unrealized holding gain. For 1982, interest expense is equal to 10 percent of the beginning of the period liability. The end-of-the-period valuation of $24,869 equals the present value of the three remaining payments discounted at 10 percent. Interest expense for 1983 again equals 10 percent of the beginning-of-the-period liability. On December 31, 1983, the current market rate decreases from 10 percent to 7 percent. The present value of the two remaining pay-

---

*The term *amortization* in the context of a liability refers to the periodic write-up or write-down of the liability so that at maturity the book value and maturity value of the liability are the same. For the loan illustrated here, the value at maturity on December 31, 1985, should be $10,000 (the amount of the last payment).

*Exhibit 15.2*
**Amortization Schedule for $39,927
Loan Repaid with Interest in Five
Annual Installments of $10,000 Each
(Effective-Interest Method)**

| Year (1) | Liability at Beginning of Year (2) | Interest Expense (3) | Liability at End of Year before Payment[e] (4) | Cash Payment (5) | Liability at End of Year after Payment (6) | Holding Gain or (Loss)[f] for Year (7) |
|---|---|---|---|---|---|---|
| **Based on Historical Market Rate of 8%** | | | | | | |
| 1981 ..... | $39,927[a] | $ 3,194[b] | $43,121 | $10,000 | $33,121 | — |
| 1982 ..... | 33,121 | 2,650[b] | 35,771 | 10,000 | 25,771 | — |
| 1983 ..... | 25,771 | 2,062[b] | 27,833 | 10,000 | 17,833 | — |
| 1984 ..... | 17,833 | 1,427[b] | 19,260 | 10,000 | 9,260 | — |
| 1985 ..... | 9,260 | 740[b] | 10,000 | 10,000 | — | — |
| Total ... | | $10,073 | | $50,000 | | |
| **Based on Current Market Rate of 8% (1981), 10% (1982, 1983), 7% (1984, 1985)** | | | | | | |
| 1981 ..... | $39,927[a] | $ 3,194[b] | $43,121 | $10,000 | $31,699 | $1,422[g] |
| 1982 ..... | 31,699 | 3,170[c] | 34,869 | 10,000 | 24,869 | — |
| 1983 ..... | 24,869 | 2,487[c] | 27,356 | 10,000 | 18,080 | (724)[h] |
| 1984 ..... | 18,080 | 1,266[d] | 19,346 | 10,000 | 9,346 | — |
| 1985 ..... | 9,346 | 654[d] | 10,000 | 10,000 | — | — |
| Total ... | | $10,771 | | $50,000 | | $ 698 |

[a]Present value of an annuity for $10,000 for 5 years discounted at 8%.

[b]8% × amount in column (2) for the year.

[c]10% × amount in column (2) for the year.

[d]7% × amount in column (2) for the year.

[e]Column (4) = column (2) + column (3) for the year.

[f]Column (7) = column (2) + column (3) − column (5) − column (6).

[g]Present value at 8% ($33,121) minus present value at 10% ($31,699).

[h]Present value at 10% ($17,356) minus present value at 7% ($18,080).

ments discounted at 7 percent is $18,080. The difference between this amount and the book value of the liability on December 31, 1983, of $17,356 (= $27,356 − $10,000) is an unrealized holding loss. Interest expense for 1984 and 1985 is based on the 7-percent current rate times the beginning-of-the-period liability. Note that total interest expense of $10,771 less the net holding gain of $698 equals $10,073. This is the same amount recognized as total interest expense over the 5-year period using the historical rate. Recall from discussions in previous chapters that over long-enough time periods, income is equal to cash in less cash out. Here, cash in is $39,927 and cash out is $50,000. The choice of valuation basis—using the historical market rate versus current market rates—affects the amount of interest expense and holding gain or loss each period, but the total effect on net income over the life of the loan is the same.

The accounting procedures illustrated in Exhibit 15.2 state the liability both initially and at the end of each period at the present value of the remaining cash flow (using either the historical or the current market rate). Interest expense each period results from multiplying the beginning-of-the-period liability by the appropriate interest rate. This procedure is referred to as the *effective-interest method of amortization*. We use the

15.47

*Exhibit 15.3*
**Amortization Schedule for $39,927**
**Loan Repaid with Interest in Five**
**Annual Installments of $10,000 Each**
**(Straight-Line Method)**

| Year (1) | Liability at Beginning of Year (2) | Interest Expense[a] (3) | Liability at End of Year before Payment (4) | Cash Payment (5) | Liability at End of Year after Payment (6) |
|---|---|---|---|---|---|
| 1981 | $39,927 | $ 2,015 | $41,942 | $10,000 | $31,942 |
| 1982 | 31,942 | 2,015 | 33,957 | 10,000 | 22,957 |
| 1983 | 22,957 | 2,015 | 25,972 | 10,000 | 15,972 |
| 1984 | 15,972 | 2,015 | 17,987 | 10,000 | 7,987 |
| 1985 | 7,987 | 2,013 | 10,000 | 10,000 | — |
| Total | | $10,073 | | $50,000 | |

[a]$10,073/5, except in the last year, where the amount is a plug to force the total to $10,073.

effective-interest method throughout the discussion of long-term liabilities. Another method, called the "straight-line method," discussed next, has been widely used in the past.

## Present Value of Amount Payable and Straight-Line Amortization

15.48 The difference between the amount ultimately payable ($50,000) and the amount borrowed ($39,927 in the illustration) represents the total cost of borrowing. The present-value approach using the historical market rate recognizes this amount as interest expense over the life of the loan. The present-value approach using the current market rate recognizes this amount as both interest expense and holding gain or loss. An alternative procedure simply recognizes an equal amount of the $10,073 difference between the amount borrowed and the amounts payable as interest expense each period. This procedure is referred to as the *straight-line method* of amortization.

15.49 The straight-line method states the liability initially at the amount received. As discussed previously, this amount is equal to the present value of the future cash flows discounted at the market rate of interest at the time of the loan. The journal entry on January 1, 1981, in the example, is the same as before:

Jan. 1, 1981
Cash ........................... 39,927
    Note Payable ................. 39,927
To record bank loan.

Interest expense for 1981 is equal to one-fifth of $10,073, or $2,015 (actually, $2,014.60 = $10,073/5). The journal entry to recognize interest expense is

Dec. 31, 1981
Interest Expense ............. ..... 2,015
    Note Payable ................. 2,015
To record interest expense at one-fifth of $10,073 (= $50,000 − $39,927).

The following journal entry records the $10,000 payment:

Dec. 31, 1981
Note Payable .................... 10,000
    Cash ....................... 10,000
To record the payment of principal and interest.

The liability at the end of 1981 using the straight-line method is recorded in the accounts at $31,942 (= $39,927 + $2,015 − $10,000). This amount is best described as the initial present value of remaining cash payments less straight-line amortization (recognition) of interest. After initial recognition, the liability is no longer stated on the balance sheet at a present value amount (except by coincidence). Exhibit 15.3 presents an amortization schedule for the straight-line method.

## Evaluation of Valuation Methods

15.50 **Amount Ultimately Payable** The valuation of liabilities at the amount ultimately payable provides a measure of the future sacrifice of resources that will be required to pay the obligation. The major weakness of this valuation method is that it ignores the interest element implicit in the delayed payment. Because the balance sheet is prepared as of a current date, it is more appropriate to state liabilities at the current, or present equivalent, value of the future sacrifice of resources (that is, the present value of the future cash flows).

15.51 **Present Value of Amount Payable: Historical Market Rate** This valuation method explicitly recognizes the interest element in delayed payments relating to liabilities. The historical market rate is generally relatively easy to ascertain. In the case of some bank loans, the interest rate is stated in the loan agreement. In cases where the rate is not stated explicitly (as in the illustration in the preceding sections), the rate can be computed by finding the interest rate that will discount the future cash payments to the present so that their present value is equal to the amount of the loan. (Appendix B at the back of the book describes this process, called "finding the internal rate of return.") A similar procedure can be followed for bonds issued on the open market.

15.52 The main weakness of this valuation method is that it ignores changes in current market rates and the resulting changes in the market value of the debt itself while liabilities are outstanding. Liabilities are, therefore, not stated at the current amounts at which they could be discharged.

15.53 **Present Value of Amount Payable: Current Market Rate** This valuation method recognizes both the interest element in delayed payments relating to liabilities and the holding gains and losses arising from changes in current interest rates. As in

Chapter 5's discussion of historical versus current cost valuations for assets, however, finding the appropriate current market rate may be difficult. For bonds and similar securities traded on organized security exchanges, the current market price unambiguously implies a single current market rate for that security. The current market price is equal to the present value of the future cash flows discounted at the current market rate appropriate to the bond or other security. To discover the current market rate for bank loans and other obligations not traded in organized security markets is more difficult. It requires consultation with bankers regarding the interest rate they would currently charge on loans of comparable amounts and risk levels as existing liabilities. Estimating the current market rate is less objective than knowing the historical market rate.

15.54 **Present Value of Amount Payable: Straight-Line Amortization** The main strength of this valuation method is its computational simplicity. If the amounts reported as liabilities on the balance sheet and interest expense on the income statement under the straight-line method are not materially different from the corresponding amounts reported using the effective-interest method, then a case can be made for the straight-line method on the grounds of computational ease.

15.55 This valuation method is subject to three criticisms, however. First, the liability is not stated each period at the present value of the remaining cash flows. Second, the valuation method has no conceptual meaning; it might be described as an amortized initial present-value amount. Third, interest expense is the same amount each period despite the fact that the amount of the outstanding liability changes. The straight-line method essentially averages out interest over the life of the liability.

## Generally Accepted Accounting Principles Relating to Liability Valuation

15.56 The generally accepted methods for valuing liabilities depend on the particular liability.

15.57 **Obligations with Fixed Payment Dates and Amounts** Accounting Principles Board *Opinion No. 21* requires that liabilities requiring future cash payments beyond 1 year and not related to the normal operating activities of a firm be stated at the present value of the future cash flows using the historical market rate. If the resulting amounts are not materially different, however, the present-value valuation method coupled with straight-line amortization may be used. Thus, bonds, notes, mortgages, leases, and similar liabilities are stated at their present-value amount using the historical market rate. Using a current market rate in the present-value calculation departs from historical cost accounting and is not permitted.

15.58 *Illustration* Exhibit 15.4 shows the accounting for five types of long-term monetary liabilities stated at the present value of future cash flows. These examples are the mirror images of those shown in Exhibit 5.2, where the valuation of long-term monetary assets is discussed. As with monetary assets, the accounting for each of these monetary liabilities follows a common procedure:

1. Compute the initial amount of cash received by the borrower and the historical interest rate. Sometimes, both of these will be known; sometimes the cash received will be known and the interest rate must be inferred by calculation. Sometimes, as Exhibit 15.4 illustrates in all five cases, the interest rate is known and the initial cash received must be computed.

(a) To compute the initial amount of cash received given the contractual payments and the market interest rate, multiply each of the contractual payments by the present-value factor (as from Table 2 at the back of the book) for a single payment of $1 to be received in the future. Exhibit 15.4 shows the present-value factors at 10-percent interest for payments to be received in 1 year (0.90909) and in 2 years (0.82645).

(b) To compute the market interest rate given the initial cash proceeds and the series of contractual payments requires finding the *internal rate of return* of the series of cash flows. Appendix B illustrates this process.

Exhibit 15.4 shows that only the 10-percent coupon bond and the level payment note have initial cash proceeds equal to $1,000. The difference in amounts arises because each of the items has a different present value, in spite of the fact that each, loosely speaking, would be called a "$1,000 liability."

2. Record a journal entry debiting cash and crediting the monetary liability with the amount of cash received. In this presentation showing the common theme, we use the generic account title "Monetary Liability," although in practice more descriptive titles would be used, as would some contra accounts (for the 8-percent bond and single-payment note) or adjunct account (for the 12-percent bond).

3. At a contractual payment date or at the end of an accounting period, whichever comes first, compute interest expense as the book value of the liability at the beginning of the period multiplied by the historical interest rate. Debit the computed amount to interest expense and credit the liability account, increasing its book value.

If a cash payment is made, credit cash and debit the liability, reducing the book value of the liability. The book value of the liability is equal to beginning balance plus interest expense recorded less cash payments made, if any.

Exhibit 15.4 does not illustrate this fact directly, but if you were to return to step 1 at this point and compute the present value of the remaining contractual payments, using the historical interest rate (10 percent in the examples), then that present value would equal the book value computed after step 3.

4. At each payment date, or at each period-end closing date, repeat step 3. Eventually, when the final payment is made (as illustrated at the bottom of Exhibit 15.4), the entire amount of the liability plus interest will have been discharged. The remaining liability is zero.

# Exhibit 15.4
## Accounting for Long-Term Monetary Liabilities Based on the Present Value of Future Cash Flows

| | Single-Payment Note of $1,000.00 Maturing in 2 Years | | | Two-Year Annual Coupon Bond—10% ($100) Coupons | | |
|---|---|---|---|---|---|---|
| | Amount | Dr. | Cr. | Amount | Dr. | Cr. |
| **1.** Compute Present Value of Future Contractual Payments Using Historical Interest Rate on Day Monetary Liability Is First Recorded. Rate is 10.0% | | | | | | |
| (a) 1 Year Hence | $ 0 | | | $ 100.00 | | |
| (b) 2 Years Hence | 1,000.00 | | | 1,100.00 | | |
| Multiply Payment by Present-Value Factors (Table 2) | | | | | | |
| .90909 × (a) | 0 | | | 90.91 | | |
| .82645 × (b) | 826.45 | | | 909.09 | | |
| (c) Total Present Value | $ 826.45 | | | $1,000.00 | | |
| **2.** Record Initial Liability and Cash or Other Assets Received from Step 1. | | | | | | |
| Dr. Cash or Other Assets | | 826.45 | | | 1,000.00 | |
| Cr. Monetary Liability | | | 826.45 | | | 1,000.00 |
| **3.** First Recording (Payment Date or End of Period): End of First Year | | | | | | |
| (a) Compute Interest Expense as Monetary Liability × Historical Interest Rate | | | | | | |
| Amount on Line 1(c) × 0.10. | $ 82.64 | | | $ 100.00 | | |
| (b) Record Interest Expense | | | | | | |
| Dr. Interest Expense | | 82.64 | | | 100.00 | |
| Cr. Monetary Liability | | | 82.64 | | | 100.00 |
| (c) Record Cash Payment (If Any) | | | | | | |
| Dr. Monetary Liability | | — | | | 100.00 | |
| Cr. Cash | | | — | | | 100.00 |
| (d) Compute Book Value of Monetary Liability | | | | | | |
| Beginning Balance | $ 826.45 | | | $1,000.00 | | |
| Add Interest Expense | 82.64 | | | 100.00 | | |
| Subtotal | $ 909.09 | | | $1,100.00 | | |
| Subtract Cash Payment (If Any) | — | | | (100.00) | | |
| = Ending Balance | $ 909.09 | | | $1,000.00 | | |
| **4.** Second Recording (End of Second Year) | | | | | | |
| (a) Compute Interest Expense as Monetary Liability × Historical Interest Rate Amount on Line 3(d) × .10 | $ 90.91 | | | $ 100.00 | | |
| (b) Record Interest Expense | | | | | | |
| Dr. Interest Expense | | 90.91 | | | 100.00 | |
| Cr. Monetary Liability | | | 90.91 | | | 100.00 |
| (c) Record Cash Payment (If Any) | | | | | | |
| Dr. Monetary Liability | | 1,000.00 | | | 1,100.00 | |
| Cr. Cash | | | 1,000.00 | | | 1,100.00 |
| (d) Compute Book Value of Monetary Liability | | | | | | |
| Beginning Balance | $ 909.09 | | | $1,000.00 | | |
| Add Interest Expense | 90.91 | | | 100.00 | | |
| Subtotal | $1,000.00 | | | $1,100.00 | | |
| Subtract Cash Payment (If Any) | (1,000.00) | | | (1,100.00) | | |
| = Ending Balance | $ 0 | | | $ 0 | | |

*Exhibit 15.4*
**Continued**

| Two-Year Annual Coupon Bond—8% ($80) Coupons | | | Two-Year Annual Coupon Bond—12% ($120) Coupons | | | Level-Payment Note Annual Payments of $576.19 | | |
|---|---|---|---|---|---|---|---|---|
| Amount | Dr. | Cr. | Amount | Dr. | Cr. | Amount | Dr. | Cr. |
| $ 80.00 | | | $ 120.00 | | | $ 576.19 | | |
| 1,080.00 | | | 1,120.00 | | | 576.19 | | |
| 72.73 | | | 109.09 | | | 523.81 | | |
| 892.57 | | | 925.62 | | | 476.19 | | |
| $ 965.30 | | | $1,034.71 | | | $1,000.00 | | |
| | 965.30 | | | 1,034.71 | | | 1,000.00 | |
| | | 965.30 | | | 1,034.71 | | | 1,000.00 |
| $ 96.53 | | | $ 103.47 | | | $ 100.00 | | |
| | 96.53 | | | 103.47 | | | 100.00 | |
| | | 96.53 | | | 103.47 | | | 100.00 |
| | 80.00 | | | 120.00 | | | 576.19 | |
| | | 80.00 | | | 120.00 | | | 576.19 |
| $ 965.30 | | | $1,034.71 | | | $1,000.00 | | |
| 96.53 | | | 103.47 | | | 100.00 | | |
| $1,061.83 | | | $1,138.18 | | | $1,100.00 | | |
| (80.00) | | | (120.00) | | | (576.19) | | |
| $ 981.83 | | | $1,018.18 | | | $ 523.81 | | |
| $ 98.18 | | | $ 101.82 | | | $ 52.38 | | |
| | 98.18 | | | 101.82 | | | 52.38 | |
| | | 98.18 | | | 101.82 | | | 52.38 |
| | 1,080.00 | | | 1,120.00 | | | 576.19 | |
| | | 1,080.00 | | | 1,120.00 | | | 576.19 |
| $ 981.83 | | | $1,018.18 | | | $ 523.81 | | |
| 98.18 | | | 101.82 | | | 52.38 | | |
| $1,080.01 | | | $1,120.00 | | | $ 576.19 | | |
| (1,080.00) | | | (1,120.00) | | | (576.19) | | |
| $ 0[a] | | | $ 0 | | | $ 0 | | |

[a]Rounding error of $.01.

**15.59** **Obligations with Fixed Payment Amounts but Estimated Payment Dates** Most of a firm's short-term obligations arising from its normal operating activities (for example, accounts payable, salaries payable, taxes payable) require fixed payments but do not have fixed payment dates. When the time that will elapse before payment is made is relatively short, there will be only minor differences between the amount ultimately payable and the present value of that amount. The discounting process is, therefore, ignored on the grounds of computational ease and immateriality. Under these conditions, these obligations are stated at the amount ultimately payable.

**15.60** **Obligations for Which Both Timing and Amount Must Be Estimated** Obligations requiring long-term future cash payments, such as for pensions, are stated at the present value of the estimated future cash flows. (As we study in Chapter 19, however, prior service obligations arising from pension plans are seldom recognized as liabilities; the amounts are disclosed in the notes.) Obligations, other than advances from customers, that will be settled with goods or services rather than cash (warranties, coupons) are stated at the estimated cost of providing the goods or services. Even though the timing of "payment" in this case may be delayed for several years, the discounting process is generally ignored in the valuation process (see Problem **15.18**).

**Obligations Arising from Advances from** **15.61** **Customers on Unexecuted Contracts and Agreements** As discussed earlier in the chapter, advances from customers for future rent, subscription, and similar items are not recognized as revenue when cash is received. Instead the cash receipt creates a liability equal to the amount of cash received.

**Summary of Liability Valuation** Liabilities **15.62** may be classified into two groups for purposes of valuation. *Monetary liabilities* are those payable in a fixed future amount of cash. If these obligations will be paid within the next year, they are normally stated at the amount payable. If the payment period exceeds 1 year, they are stated at the present value of the future cash flows. *Nonmonetary liabilities* are those payable in goods or services. Obligations arising from transactions where revenue has already been recognized (for example, warranties on products sold) are stated at the estimated future cost of the warranty services. Obligations arising from advances from customers for future goods or services are stated at the amount of cash received.

## Questions and Short Cases

**15.1** Review the meaning of the following concepts or terms discussed in this chapter.

a. Criteria for recognition of an accounting liability.

b. Obligations with fixed payment dates and amounts.

c. Obligations with fixed payment amounts but estimated payment dates.

d. Obligations for which both timing and amount of payment must be estimated.

e. Obligations arising from advances from customers on unexecuted contracts and agreements.

f. Obligations under mutually unexecuted contracts.

g. Contingent obligations.

h. Loss contingency.

i. Amount of cash ultimately payable as the basis for liability valuation.

j. Present value of amount payable based on the historical market interest rate as the basis for liability valuation.

k. Present value of amount payable based on the current market interest rate as the basis for liability valuation.

l. Unrealized holding gain or loss on long-term liability.

m. Effective-interest method of amortization.

n. Straight-line method of amortization.

**15.2**   Indicate whether or not each of the following items is recognized as an accounting liability. If a liability is recognized, indicate how the amount of the liability would be determined.

   a. A tenant's obligation to maintain a rented office building in good repair.
   b. The amount payable by a firm for a newspaper advertisement that has appeared but for which payment is not due for 30 days.
   c. An obligation to deliver merchandise to a customer next year for which cash has been received.
   d. A reputation for not paying bills promptly.
   e. Wages earned by employees during the current year but not payable until the next accounting period.
   f. An obligation by a pet food company to distribute pet toys to customers who return coupons attached to the labels of cans of pet food.
   g. An obligation to the firm's president for salary and bonus earned during the past year.
   h. Same as part **g**, but for amounts payable to the president in future years under a 5-year employment contract.
   i. An obligation of a firm that acted as guarantor on a loan by a major shareholder. The shareholder has been judged bankrupt and will therefore be unable to pay.
   j. A contractual obligation of a company for payment for landscaping services to be performed next month.
   k. A damage claim by a customer who was injured on the firm's premises. The case has not yet come to trial.

**15.3**   How does the accounting for partially unexecuted and mutually unexecuted contracts differ?

**15.4**   Does the recognition of a loss contingency always give rise to a liability? Explain.

**15.5**   While shopping in a supermarket on July 5, 1979, a customer slipped on the floor and sustained back injuries. On January 15, 1980, the customer sued the supermarket for $500,000. The case came to trial on April 30, 1980. The jury's verdict was rendered on June 15, 1980, with the supermarket found guilty of gross negligence. A damage award of $350,000 was granted to the customer. The supermarket, on June 25, 1980, appealed the decision to a higher court on the grounds that certain evidence had not been admitted by the lower court. The higher court ruled on November 1, 1980, that the evidence should have been admitted. The lower court reheard the case beginning on March 21, 1981. The jury, on April 20, 1981, again found the supermarket guilty of gross negligence. On May 15, 1981, the supermarket paid the $350,000 judgment.

   When should a loss from these events be recognized by the supermarket? Explain your reasoning.

**15.6**   Indicate whether each of the following statements is true or false and why.

   a. The valuation of long-term monetary liabilities at the present value of the future cash flows using the market interest rate at the time the liability was initially recorded results in reporting unrealized holding gains and losses as market interest rates change.
   b. The use of the effective-interest method of amortization for long-term monetary liabilities based on the historical market interest rate results in an amount for interest expense each period that is a constant percentage of the book value of the liability at the beginning of the period.
   c. The issuance of 8-percent, $1,000 face-value coupon bonds when the market interest rate is 10 percent results in an issue price greater than $1,000.
   d. At the beginning of the current period, a firm issued 10-percent coupon bonds at par value. During the period, the market interest rate for these bonds decreased to 8 percent. If the

bonds were stated at the present value of the future cash flows using the current market interest rate, this firm would show an unrealized holding loss.

e. If market interest rates increase between the time a bond is issued and the end of the current accounting period, valuation of long-term monetary liabilities at the present value of the future cash flows using the historical market interest rate will result in reporting these liabilities at a lower amount than if the current market interest rate were used in discounting.

f. The straight-line method of amortization for long-term monetary liabilities results in an equal amount of interest expense each period while the bonds are outstanding.

g. The issuance of 10-percent, $1,000 face-value coupon bonds when the market interest rate is 10 percent, results in an issuance price less than $1,000.

h. The valuation of a single-payment, long-term, noninterest-bearing note will increase each period prior to maturity by the amount of interest expense for the period.

i. The valuation of an annual coupon bond issued for less than its face value will increase each period prior to maturity by the amount of interest expense for the period.

j. When bonds are initially issued for an amount greater than their face value, interest expense each period while the bonds are outstanding will be greater than the coupon payments made.

15.7 (Adapted from CPA Examination.)

a. The two basic requirements for the accrual of a loss contingency are supported by several basic concepts of accounting. Three of these concepts are periodicity (time periods), measurement, and objectivity.

Discuss how the two basic requirements for the accrual of a loss contingency relate to the three concepts listed above.

b. The following three *independent* sets of facts relate to (1) the possible accrual or (2) the possible disclosure by other means of a loss contingency.

*Situation I.* A company offers a 1-year warranty for the product that it manufactures. A history of warranty claims has been compiled, and the probable amount of claims related to sales for a given period can be determined.

*Situation II.* Subsequent to the date of a set of financial statements, but prior to the issuance of the financial statements, a company enters into a contract that will probably result in a significant loss to the company. The amount of the loss can be reasonably estimated.

*Situation III.* A company has adopted a policy of recording self-insurance for any possible losses resulting from injury to others by the company's vehicles. The premium for an insurance policy for the same risk from an independent insurance company would have an annual cost of $2,000. During the period covered by the financial statements, there were no accidents involving the company's vehicles that resulted in injury to others.

Discuss the accrual and/or type of disclosure necessary (if any) and the reason(s) why such disclosure is appropriate for each of the three independent sets of facts above.

15.8 The accounts listed below appear on the financial statements of a company. Describe the valuation basis probably used for each account.

a. Current Income Taxes Payable.

b. Mortgage Payable.

c. Estimated Liability under Trading Stamp Redemption Plan.

d. Rental Fees Received in Advance.

e. Noninterest-Bearing Note Payable to Bank (due in 6 years).

f. Noninterest-Bearing Note Payable to Bank (due in 6 months).

g. Current Maturities of Long-Term Debt.

h. Withheld Income Taxes (from employees' paychecks).

i. Estimated Obligation from Lawsuit.

## Problems and Exercises

**15.9**   Give all of the required journal entries during 1981 in accordance with generally accepted accounting principles to account for each of the following independent transactions.

a. A firm issued a $20,000, single-payment, noninterest-bearing note on January 2, 1981, in the acquisition of a tract of land. The interest rate appropriate to the note was 10 percent on January 2, 1981, and 12 percent on December 31, 1981. The note is due on December 31, 1984.

b. Sales of a company during 1981, all on account, totaled $300,000. The merchandise sold had an acquisition cost of $160,000. The merchandise is sold under a 3-year warranty plan. The estimated costs of providing warranty services on these sales are 1981: $2,000; 1982: $12,000; 1983: $9,000. Actual costs incurred for 1981 coincided with expectations. The market interest rate appropriate to the warranty obligation is 8 percent.

c. A firm has been sued by a competitor for $10 million on the grounds of patent infringement. The firm feels that there is a .30 probability that it will lose the case. If the case is lost, the loss is expected to be $6 million.

d. A firm issued a $20,000, 8-percent note on January 2, 1981, in the acquisition of land. The note requires interest payments on December 31 of each year and matures on December 31, 1983. The market interest rate appropriate to the note was 10 percent on January 2, 1981, and 12 percent on December 31, 1981.

e. On December 30, 1981, a magazine publisher received $40,000 as subscription fees for 1982 magazine issues and $20,000 as subscription fees for 1983 magazine issues. The estimated cost of producing the magazines for these subscriptions is $32,000 in 1982 and $16,000 in 1983. Assume that all costs are incurred at the end of each year and that the market rate of interest appropriate for these subscription fees on December 30, 1981, was 8 percent.

f. A firm signed a contract on December 28, 1981, agreeing to provide $50,000 of merchandise to various customers during the next two years ($30,000 in 1982 and $20,000 in 1983). The estimated cost of the merchandise is 70 percent of the selling price. Assume that all cash flows occur at the end of each year and that the appropriate market rate of interest on December 28, 1981, was 10 percent.

**15.10**   Give all the journal entries during 1981 in accordance with generally accepted accounting principles to account for each of the following independent transactions. The accounting period is the calendar year in all cases.

a. On January 2, 1981, a firm acquired a tract of land. It gave an 8-percent, interest-bearing note in the face amount of $30,000 as consideration. The note provides for the payment of interest on December 31 of each year and the repayment of principal on December 31, 1985. The market interest rate appropriate for this note was 12 percent on January 2, 1981.

b. Sales of a company during 1981, all for cash, totaled $200,000. The merchandise sold had an acquisition cost of $125,000. Attached to the label of each product was a 10-cents-off coupon. The company expects coupons totaling $1,500 to be presented for payment during 1981, $1,300 to be presented for payment during 1982, and $700 to be presented for payment during 1983. Assume that all payments will be made on December 31 of each year. Payments during 1981 totaled $1,500.

c. Bonds with a face value of $1,000,000 and a 10-percent coupon interest rate were issued on January 2, 1981. The bonds require interest payments on December 31 of each year and mature in 15 years from the date of issue. The effective-interest method of amortization is used. The market interest rate appropriate for these bonds was 12 percent on January 2, 1981.

d. A company acted as guarantor on a note of a major shareholder. The note is a noninterest-bearing note totaling $20,000 and is due on June 31, 1983. The shareholder was declared bankrupt on July 1, 1981, and there is no expectation that the note will be paid by the shareholder at maturity. The market interest rate appropriate for this note was 12 percent on July 1, 1981.

15.11  Lebanon Graphics Corporation issued a $10,000 noninterest-bearing note on January 2, 1981, in the acquisition of a piece of equipment. The note matures on December 31, 1984. The equipment has a 10-year life, zero estimated salvage value, and is depreciated using the straight-line method. The market rate of interest appropriate to this note was 8 percent on January 2, 1981, but increased to 10 percent on December 31, 1981.

a. Give the journal entries relating to the acquisition and use of this equipment during 1981, assuming that the historical market interest rate is used in discounting.

b. Repeat part **a** but use the current market interest rate in discounting.

15.12  Campbell Corporation issued $500,000 face-value, 10-percent coupon bonds on January 2, 1981. The bonds require annual interest payments on December 31 of each year and mature in 10 years. The market rate of interest appropriate to the bonds on the date of issue was 8 percent. On December 31, 1981, the interest rate appropriate to these bonds increased to 10 percent. On December 31, 1982, the interest rate increased to 12 percent. On December 31, 1983, the interest rate decreased to 10 percent. The market interest rate remained at 10 percent through the end of 1984.

Prepare an amortization schedule for these bonds similar to Exhibit 15.2 using:

a. The historical market interest rate.

b. The current market interest rate.

15.13  Generally accepted accounting principles require that long-term monetary liabilities be stated at the present value of the future cash flows discounted at the market rate of interest appropriate to the particular monetary liability at the time it was recorded. Give the journal entries during 1981 and 1982 for each of the following monetary liabilities recorded on January 2, 1981. The accounting period is the calendar year.

a. Single-payment, noninterest-bearing note of $5,000 maturing on December 31, 1982. The appropriate market rate of interest is 8 percent. The note was issued in the acquisition of land.

b. Level-payment note with payments of $3,000 on December 31 of each of the years 1981 through 1983. The interest rate appropriate to the note is 7 percent. The note was issued in the acquisition of land.

c. Annual-coupon bond with 10-percent coupons and $10,000 face amount. The bonds require interest payments on December 31 of each year and mature on December 31, 1985. The market rate of interest appropriate to the bonds is 8 percent.

15.14  Give the journal entries during 1981 and 1982 for each of the following monetary liabilities recorded on January 2, 1981. The accounting period is the calendar year.

a. Single-payment, noninterest-bearing note of $10,000 maturing on December 31, 1983. The appropriate market rate of interest is 12 percent. The note was issued in exchange for a tract of land.

**b.** Annual coupon bonds with 10-percent coupon payments and $10,000 face value. The bonds require interest payments on December 31 of each year and mature on December 31, 1982. The market rate of interest at the time the bonds were issued was 12 percent.

**c.** Level-payment note with payments of $2,000 on December 31 of each of the years 1981 through 1984. The interest rate appropriate to the note is 10 percent. The note was issued in exchange for a tract of land.

**15.15** Melisitom Company issued $1,000,000 face-value, 10-percent coupon bonds on January 2, 1981. The bonds require annual interest payments on December 31 of each year and mature in 20 years. The market rate of interest appropriate to the bonds on the date of issue was 12 percent.

**a.** Compute the issue price of these bonds.

**b.** Prepare an amortization schedule for these bonds for 1981 through 1985 similar to the top portion of Exhibit 15.2, using the effective-interest method of amortization.

**c.** Prepare an amortization schedule for these bonds for 1981 through 1985 similar to Exhibit 15.3, using the straight-line method of amortization.

**15.16** Williams Corporation issued $1,000,000 face-value, 8-percent coupon bonds on January 2, 1981. Interest payments are required on December 31 of each year, and the bonds mature in 20 years. The market interest rate appropriate to these bonds was 10 percent at the time of issue.

**a.** Compute the issue price of these bonds.

**b.** Give the journal entries to account for these bonds during 1981 assuming that a separate Discount on Bonds Payable account is not used.

**c.** Give the journal entries to account for these bonds during 1981 assuming that a separate Discount on Bonds Payable account is used.

**d.** Calculate the book value of the bonds on December 31, 1981, assuming that a separate discount account is not used.

**e.** Repeat part **d** assuming that a separate discount account is used.

**15.17** Generally accepted accounting principles require that long-term monetary liabilities be stated at the present value of the future cash flows discounted at the market rate of interest appropriate to the monetary items at the time they were initially recorded. APB *Opinion No. 21* specifically excludes from present value valuation obligations under warranties. Warranties, being nonmonetary liabilities, are stated at the estimated cost of providing warranty goods and services in the future.

Assume that the estimated future costs of a 3-year warranty plan on products sold during 1981 are as follows:

| Year | Expected Cost |
|---|---|
| 1982 | $ 400,000 |
| 1983 | 600,000 |
| 1984 | 300,000 |
| Total | $1,300,000 |

Actual costs coincided with expectations both as to timing and amount.

**a.** Prepare the journal entries for each of the years 1981 through 1984 for this warranty plan following current generally accepted accounting principles.

**b.** Prepare the journal entries for each of the years 1981 through 1984 for this warranty plan assuming that the warranty liability is stated at the present value of the future costs discounted at 10 percent. To simplify the calculations, assume that all warranty costs are incurred on December 31 of each year.

c. What theoretical arguments can be offered for the valuation basis in part **b**?

15.18 Alexander Company signs an agreement with an electric utility to provide that utility with coal. Under the agreement, the utility will reimburse all operating costs of mining coal, dollar for dollar. In addition, the electric utility will pay $10 million in cash today for this privilege. At the time the deal is made, the coal mine is recorded on the Alexander Company's books for $1 million. The company estimates that 10 years from today, the coal mine will be exhausted of coal and abandoned. When the mine is abandoned, the company will spend $15 million to repair the landscape and return the site to its natural state.

a. What is the amount of net income or net loss expected from this contract for the 10 years taken as a whole?

b. What portion of the total income or loss from part **a** should be recognized during each of the 10 years? State any assumptions that you feel are necessary in order to respond to this question.

# Chapter 16
## Current Liabilities

16.1 The preceding chapter introduced the basic concepts of liabilities. This chapter discusses the accounting for current liabilities, those with due dates 1 year or less. If the firm uses some other basis for classifying its assets as current or noncurrent, such as one operating cycle, then the same basis is used for classifying liabilities.

### Definition of Current Liabilities

16.2 Generally accepted accounting principles define *current liabilities* as

obligations whose liquidation is reasonably expected to require the use of existing resources properly classifiable as current assets, or the creation of [new] current liabilities.*

A current liability need not require the use of cash immediately. It can be replaced by another current liability. When that liability comes due, it can in turn be replaced by another current liability, and so on indefinitely. Still, each of the individual items appears as a current liability between the time it becomes a liability and the later time when it is discharged.

___

*Accounting Research Bulletin No. 43*, AICPA (1953), chap. 3A.

### Measurement of Current Liabilities

Monetary liabilities are discharged by the payment of cash and are generally shown at the present value of the amounts to be paid. Future payments are discounted at the interest rate applicable when the liability was recorded—the historical interest rate. Applying present-value measurement to current liabilities is usually judged more trouble than it is worth. The difference between the amount eventually paid and its present value is usually immaterially small; current monetary liabilities therefore appear at the amounts of cash (or cash-equivalent value of other consideration) expected to be disbursed to satisfy the obligation. 16.3

Nonmonetary liabilities are discharged by the delivery of a good or service. An automobile manufacturer provides warranty services to those who purchase its products; a publisher delivers magazines to subscribers and satisfies its obligation to those who paid for subscriptions in advance; a landlord lets tenants use a building and satisfies its obligation to those who paid rent in advance. Usually the promise to provide an ancillary good (toys from cereal coupon redemptions) or ancillary service (product warranties) in the future accompanies the sale of the firm's principal product (cereal or automobiles) 16.4

**16-1**

during the current period. In that case, revenue from the sales of both the principal product and the ancillary product is normally recognized during the current period. An estimate of the future cost of the ancillary product or service must be made currently. The amount of the estimate is debited to expense and credited to a liability account. The liability is then stated at the estimated future cost of providing the ancillary good or service. Recall from Chapter 15 that cash flows associated with such future costs are not discounted to their present value in measuring the amount of the nonmonetary liability.

16.5   Often, the promise to provide a future good or service arises solely from the receipt of cash in the current period; no good or service has yet been provided. Revenue is then recognized in the later period when the good or service is provided. A liability is recognized currently in the amount of the cash received. Ordinarily the seller will be able to supply the goods or services at a smaller cost than this amount; otherwise the seller would not be expecting a profit. Accounting recognizes the liability at the amount of cash received. To record only the expected cost of discharging the obligation would imply recognizing profit at the time of cash collection, not as the services are rendered. Only when the seller expects that the cost of fulfilling the obligation will exceed the amount of cash to be received will the obligation be shown at its expected cost. In that case, the loss is recognized with a debit to a Loss account as soon as it becomes apparent that there will be one; the credit increases the amount of the liability account.

# Presentation of Current Liabilities

16.6   Generally accepted accounting principles do not require any particular ordering of items within the current liability section of the balance sheet. Most firms attempt to order items from most current to least current, but this is not necessarily easy to do in practice. For example, suppose that Accounts Payable include items due in 1 week and others due in 3 months, whereas Notes Payable include only items due in 60 days. Which of these two items is more current? (A weighted average might be taken, but this calculation is generally not worth the trouble.)

## Offset against Assets

A firm might acquire short-term government 16.7 notes that mature on the date an income tax payment is due. The accountant might consider offsetting the asset, Notes, against the liability, Taxes Payable, on the balance sheet. Such offsetting of specific assets and specific liabilities is generally not permitted.* The underlying concept is that *all* of the equities finance *all* of the assets. The offsetting of one asset against one liability misrepresents reality except where the specific right of offset exists. For example, firm A may hold an account receivable from firm B, while firm A owes firm B via a note payable. The note specifically states that firm B may withhold payment of its accounts payable to firm A until the note is discharged by firm A. In this case, the receivables and payables relating to these transactions can be netted. If the net amount is a debit, it is included among the assets. If the net amount is a credit, it is shown among the liabilities. Neither firm is required to offset; either may. Another exception arises when governmental bodies (state or local; the federal government has not done so in many years) issue notes, usually discount notes offering no explicit interest payments and priced below maturity value, which are acceptable for the payment of taxes. The notes mature in the "relatively near future." If a firm acquires such a note, intending to pay taxes with the proceeds at maturity, it may offset the asset and liability.†

## Debt to Be Refinanced

Occasionally, firms owing amounts legally 16.8 due within 1 year will plan to borrow cash to repay the now-existing loan. The new bor-

---

*Accounting Principles Board, *Opinion No. 10* (1966).
†Ibid.

rowing will mature more than 1 year hence. Because the new debt will be noncurrent, the old debt will not use up current assets or be replaced with current liabilities. Under these conditions firms have often shown the present debt, current though it may be, as a noncurrent liability. In order to improve its apparent liquidity position (as measured by the current ratio or the quick ratio), a firm often prefers to show current debts as noncurrent. Prior to 1973, many firms were reclassifying current debt as noncurrent in the hope, or with only moderate expectation, that the debt might be refinanced as noncurrent debt.

16.9 In 1973, the SEC issued *Accounting Series Release No. 148,* which allowed firms to reclassify current debt as noncurrent only if: (1) the borrower had an option, noncancelable by the lender, to refinance the debt; (2) the new debt would mature more than 1 year after the balance sheet date; and (3) the borrower intended to refinance the debt.

16.10 In 1975, the FASB issued *Statement No. 6* affirming the SEC's rule. The FASB relaxed it in two ways:

1. The financing agreement need not be noncancelable by the lender on the balance sheet date if by the time the balance sheet is issued, the firm has a financing agreement in hand;

2. The firm may show the debt as noncurrent if it both has the ability and intends to replace the current debt with owners' equity, rather than with noncurrent debt.

16.11 FASB *Statement No. 6* contains several subparagraphs of guidance for the accountant attempting to decide whether or not the conditions are met. Those confronted with a problem of whether or not certain short-term debts can be shown as noncurrent should consult FASB *Statement No. 6.*

## Specific Current Monetary Liabilities

16.12 This section discusses the accounting problems of the various current monetary liabilities.

## Accounts Payable

16.13 Accounts payable, or trade accounts payable, normally arise from the purchase of goods or services. The debts exist in the form of open accounts (when the purchaser signs a general agreement to pay for goods or services received according to specified terms), rather than in the form of individual promissory notes. End-of-period procedures for accounts payable require careful attention to amounts that are owed and those not yet owed. Goods are generally sold with an F.O.B. (free-on-board) point where the goods become the property of the buyer, not the seller. The F.O.B. point may be the seller's warehouse or the carrier (truck or railroad). In those cases, goods that have not yet arrived at the buyer's premises are still part of the buyer's inventory, and the related payables should be recorded. Items shipped F.O.B. purchaser become the inventory of the purchaser and a payable only after they are received by the purchaser.

16.14 Chapter 9 discussed the net and gross price methods of recording discounts on items purchased. Whatever convention is used for recording the asset should also be used for the related payable. If the net price method is used, then losses should be accrued at the end of the accounting period for discounts lapsed on accounts not yet paid. To illustrate, assume that $1,000 of raw materials are purchased subject to a 2-percent discount that, through oversight, was not taken. The account remains unpaid at the end of the period. The entries are

Raw Materials Inventory . . . . . . . . . . . . . . . . 980
    Accounts Payable . . . . . . . . . . . . . . . . . 980
To record purchase of $1,000 gross; net amount due, $980.

Loss on Lapsed Discounts . . . . . . . . . . . . . 20
    Accounts Payable . . . . . . . . . . . . . . . . . 20
End-of-period adjusting entry required to record lapsed discounts on bills not yet paid.

Entries accruing the loss are rare in well-run firms. Such firms seldom slip up and lose the discount; if they do, the amounts are generally immaterially small.

## Notes Payable

16.15 The accounting for the short-term Notes Payable discussed here is the mirror image of the accounting for the current asset, short-term Notes Receivable, discussed in Chapter 7. Whenever a note appears as a receivable on the books of the holder, it appears as a payable among the liabilities of the maker. Notes payable arise from the same situations as do notes receivable, and they have the same arrangements as to interest, length of life, number of payees, and so on.

16.16 **Interest-Bearing Notes** Compound interest calculations (see Appendix B) are not generally used for periods shorter than 1 year.* The general formula for the calculation of interest for periods shorter than one year is

$$\begin{array}{c} \text{Base} \\ \text{(Principal or Face)} \end{array} \times \begin{array}{c} \text{Interest} \\ \text{Rate} \end{array} \times \text{Time} = \text{Interest}.$$

To illustrate the accounting for interest-bearing notes, refer to the illustration in paragraph 7.55 in Chapter 7, in which Mullen Company sold goods to Suren Company for $30,000 on July 1 and received a 60-day, 12-percent note due on August 30. The discussion in Chapter 7 considered this transaction from the view of Mullen Company, who sold the goods and received the note. The accounting for this transaction from the view of Suren Company, who purchased the goods and issued the note, is discussed next.

16.17 The issue of a 60-day, 12-percent, $30,000 note on July 1 by the Suren Company to the Mullen Company would be recorded by the Suren Company at its face value as follows:

---

*The schedule of cash payments for principal and interest on an interest-bearing debt is specified in the debt contract. The portion of the cash payments representing principal and the portion representing interest are usually based on compound interest computations. The accounting for these short-term notes is computationally easier if simple rather than compound interest is used at dates prior to maturity. The use of simple interest computations tends to understate interest relative to the amounts using compound interest computations. Because the difference is usually immaterially small, the accounting is based on simple interest computations.

July 1
| | | |
|---|---:|---:|
| Inventory | 30,000 | |
|   Notes Payable | | 30,000 |

Assuming the accounting period of the Suren Company to be the calendar year, the entry upon payment at maturity would be

August 30
| | | |
|---|---:|---:|
| Notes Payable | 30,000 | |
| Interest Expense | 600 | |
|   Cash | | 30,600 |

Assuming that the accounting period of the Suren Company is 1 month, the entries for adjustment of interest at the interim date and the payment at maturity would be

July 31
| | | |
|---|---:|---:|
| Interest Expense | 300 | |
|   Interest Payable | | 300 |

August 30
| | | |
|---|---:|---:|
| Notes Payable | 30,000 | |
| Interest Payable | 300 | |
| Interest Expense | 300 | |
|   Cash | | 30,600 |

Chapter 7 illustrates several alternatives to collection at maturity. The entries by the maker mirror those of the holder.

16.18 **Noninterest-Bearing Notes: Theoretically Preferred Treatment** Noninterest-bearing notes indicate a face amount that is also the maturity value. The basic elements of such a note might read: "Sixty days after date (July 1), the Butler Company promises to pay to the order of the Dryer Company the amount of $30,000." Although no explicit rate of interest is given, the value of the note prior to maturity is less than the maturity value of $30,000. The difference is the implicit interest, which theoretically should be recognized. For example, if the credit standing of the Butler Company would permit it to borrow at 12 percent, then the present value of the note on July 1 is approximately $29,400 (= maturity value of $30,000 less discount of 12 percent for 60 days, or $600).† The note could be recorded at $29,400 and

---

†The rounded calculation is $29,412 = $30,000/(1.02), where 60/360 × 12 percent = 2 percent, implying a discount factor of 1.02.

the $600 difference between the present value and the maturity value recognized as interest expense over the 60-day period. If the note were given for inventory with an invoice price of $29,400, the entries would be

```
July 1
Inventory ........................ 29,400
Discount on Notes Payable ........    600
      Notes Payable ...............         30,000
```

Payment at maturity, assuming an annual closing, would be

```
August 30
Interest Expense .................    600
      Discount on Notes Payable .....         600
To record interest expense.

Notes Payable ...................  30,000
      Cash ......................         30,000
To pay off note.
```

16.19   If the Butler Company closed its books monthly, on July 31 it would credit the discount account for $300 and debit the Interest Expense account. Upon payment at maturity, an additional $300 of Interest Expense would be recognized.

16.20   *"Prepaid Interest" Does Not Exist* The payment of interest can take place only after the borrower has had the use of the borrowed funds. Because interest is the price for the use of borrowed funds, any effort to pay the interest in advance simply reduces the amount of the actual proceeds of the loan. Thus, there is no such thing as "prepaid interest." The difference, $600 in the example above, between the face value of the note and the amount of the proceeds of the loan should be labeled as Discount on Notes Payable and treated as a contra account to Notes Payable. The discount is shown on the balance sheet as a deduction from the face amount of the note in order to indicate the effective liability with regard to the note. It should not be shown as the asset "prepaid interest."

16.21   **Noninterest-Bearing Notes: Usual Treatment in Practice** Short-term, noninterest-bearing notes are usually recorded at the amount of cash to be paid, not the present

value of that amount, because the difference between the two amounts is usually immaterially small. The note—assuming that it was given for the purchase of inventory costing $30,000—would be recorded at $30,000.

```
July 1
Inventory ........................ 30,000
      Notes Payable ...............         30,000
```

The entry at maturity would be

```
August 30
Notes Payable .................... 30,000
      Cash ......................         30,000
```

This accounting procedure for short-term, noninterest-bearing notes results in recognizing all of the cost as inventory and none as interest expense. If cash is received in exchange for a short-term, noninterest-bearing note payable, then the note is recorded at the amount of cash received, which is typically less than the maturity value of the note. The difference between the maturity value and the cash received is interest that is debited to Interest Expense and credited to Note Payable over the life of the note. This accounting parallels that for long-term noninterest-bearing notes payable.

## Current Portions of Long-Term Debt

16.22   Portions of long-term debt payable within the next year from a firm's general cash account are classified as current liabilities. The maturing portion of a serial bond issue, for example, is a current liability even though the remainder of the bond issue will mature more than 1 year hence.

16.23   Chapter 14 describes "sinking" funds of cash accumulated for retirement of debt; such funds are usually shown as noncurrent assets. When a maturing bond issue is to be paid off with cash from a sinking fund, the balance sheet should show both the fund and the maturing debt as current or both as noncurrent. Otherwise, financial statement analysis of current assets and liabilities will give the wrong data for assessing liquidity. We prefer that current portions of maturing debt and related funds both be shown as current items. Some accountants think that the sinking fund investment should be shown entirely as a noncurrent asset and, therefore, that the current portion of long-term debt to be discharged with those funds should also appear as a noncurrent liability.

## Interest Payable

16.24 Interest payable usually results from an adjusting entry at the end of an accounting period. Interest on trade notes, notes payable to banks, installment contracts, bonds, and mortgages can be lumped together in one Interest Payable account. The payments due on installment contracts and mortgages typically contain, however, elements of both interest and principal repayment. If current portions of these long-term debts are shown in the current liability section of the balance sheet, the amounts for interest need not be separated from the amounts for principal. Only in rare cases, when material amounts of interest payable have a legally different status from other interest payable, such as interest payable on bonds in default, should such amounts be separated from other interest payable.

## Dividends Payable

16.25 Courts have held generally that, once declared by the board of directors, a dividend may not be revoked and has the same legal status as any other unsecured debt, such as accounts payable. The account Dividends Payable appears among current liabilities if the amounts are material. Dividend arrearages on preferred stock issues (see Chapter 21) are not legal liabilities because the dividends have not been declared. Footnote disclosure is required for dividends in arrears. Stock dividends do not create current liabilities; see the discussion in Chapter 23.

## Wages and Salaries Payable

16.26 Compensation of employees results in current liabilities payable both to the employees and to governments for various withholdings and payroll taxes. The liability to employees arises because pay periods and accounting periods do not coincide. At the end of the accounting period, an adjusting entry must be made accruing wages and salaries earned since the last payday. Calculating the amount payable for a portion of a pay period can be time consuming, particularly when employees are paid on an hourly basis. Estimating the expense since the last payday and the related liability is an acceptable procedure.

**Bonus Plans** Often key employees, or in 16.27 some cases all employees, are promised a bonus based on operating performance. The calculation of the amount of the bonus can involve some algebra that the accountant should understand. The bonus is an expense reducing income and is an allowable deduction in computing taxable income, so that the amount of the bonus affects income tax expense. Because the bonus often depends on net income, and net income depends on the amount of the bonus, simultaneous equations must be set up and solved. The statement of the bonus plan specifies the treatment of both income taxes and the bonus itself in the computation of income eligible for the bonus.

Assume that a company has $100,000 of 16.28 income before taxes and bonus payments and that income taxes are computed at 40 percent of taxable income. Assume also that the bonus plan provides for a bonus of 10 percent of income. The bonus plan can be stated in several ways, each implying a different calculation.

**1.** In the simplest plan, the bonus is a fixed percentage of prebonus, pretax income, $10,000 (= .10 × $100,000) in the example.

**2.** Assume next that the employees are entitled to a bonus of 10 percent of *pretax* income and that the bonus itself is an expense. Thus, we cannot merely compute the bonus as 10 percent of $100,000. Rather, the bonus is computed as

$$\text{Bonus} = \text{Bonus Rate} \times (\text{Pretax Income before Bonus} - \text{Bonus})$$

$$= \frac{\text{Bonus Rate} \times \begin{array}{l}\text{Pretax}\\\text{Income}\\\text{before}\\\text{Bonus}\end{array}}{1 + \text{Bonus Rate}}.$$

In the example,

$$\text{Bonus} = .10 \times (\$100,000 - \text{Bonus})$$
$$= \frac{10,000}{1.10} = \$9,091.$$

The calculation can be checked by noting that $9,091 = .10 \times ($100,000 − $9,091)$.

**3.** Finally, assume that the bonus is derived *after taxes* and the bonus is counted as an expense. That is,

$$\text{Taxes} = \text{Tax Rate} \times (\text{Pretax Income before Bonus} - \text{Bonus})$$
$$= .40 \times (\$100,000 - \text{Bonus}).$$

and

$$\text{Bonus} = \text{Bonus Rate} \times (\text{Pretax Income before Bonus} - \text{Bonus} - \text{Taxes})$$
$$= .10 \times (\$100,000 - \text{Bonus} - \text{Taxes}).$$

Substituting the tax equation into the bonus equation gives

$$\text{Bonus} = .10 \times \begin{bmatrix} \$100,000 - \text{Bonus} \\ - .40 \times (\$100,000 \\ - \text{Bonus}) \end{bmatrix}$$
$$= \$10,000 - .10\,\text{Bonus} - .04 \times (\$100,000 - \text{Bonus})$$
$$\text{Bonus} (1 + .10 - .04) = \$10,000 - \$4,000$$
$$\text{Bonus} = \frac{\$6,000}{1.06} = \$5,660.$$

The calculation can be checked by noting that $5,660 = .10 \times [$100,000 − $5,660 − .40 ($100,000 − $5,660)]$.

**16.29**    Elementary algebra, using variables for taxes and the bonus as well as known pretax, prebonus income and tax rates, will find the amounts in all cases. The only problem is setting up the proper algebraic representation of the bonus plan from its verbal description. The accountant can help the firm in its working of the bonus plan so that the implied calculation is unambiguously derivable from the description. It is usually helpful if verbal descriptions of bonus plans are accompanied by worked-out examples so that the intended meaning is clearer than it might be otherwise.

## Payroll Taxes and Employee Withholdings Payable

**16.30**    An employee earns a wage. Some of that wage is owed by the employee to governments for income taxes and for social security taxes. The employee may owe other amounts for union dues and insurance plans. These amounts are subtracted from the nominal, or gross, wages otherwise paid the employees.

**16.31**    In addition, the employer must pay various taxes and may have agreed to pay for fringe benefits because wages were earned.* Employers owe federal social security (FICA, for Federal Insurance Contributions Act) taxes for each employee as well as both federal and state unemployment compensation (FUTA, for Federal Unemployment Tax Act) taxes. The amounts for FICA and FUTA tax rates vary over time. The numbers used in the examples here are approximately correct.†

**16.32**    Assume that employees earn $100,000 and that the employees' withholding rate for federal income taxes averages 20 percent and for state income taxes averages 4 percent. Assume also that employees owe 7 percent for social security, payments aggregating $500 for union dues to be withheld by the employer, and $3,000 for employee pay-

---

*Labor economists have generally agreed that in spite of the law's formality—that the employer "pays" part of the social security tax and the employee pays part— the reality is that the employee in effect pays all of the taxes. When employers consider hiring, they understand the total costs—wages plus taxes—that the hiring will entail. If the employee is worth, say, $15,000, then the employer will be willing to pay up to that amount and is only secondarily concerned with how much of the total cost goes to the government and how much goes to the employee. The employee is concerned with after-tax compensation. Insofar as after-tax compensation is less than the cost to the employer, a barrier to hiring may exist. Consider, for example, a case in which the employer is willing to pay $15,000 or less and the employee will work only if the after-tax compensation is $12,000 or more. If various governments take more than $3,000 in taxes from the total compensation of $15,000, then this employee will not work for this employer.

†Readers interested in exact tax rates should consult a current tax manual, such as those published by Commerce Clearing House, Prentice-Hall, and others.

ments to various health insurance plans. The employer owes, in addition, 7 percent for social security and 3.5 percent for FUTA, but these taxes are due on only $40,000 of gross payroll. (Federal unemployment insurance taxes are generally levied on only the first few thousand dollars of wages per employee.) A part (2.7 percent) of the FUTA tax is paid to the state government and the rest (0.8 percent) is paid to the federal government. In addition, the employer owes $4,500 for payments to insurance plans and estimates that the current period's share of the year's bonus pool payable to employees is $1,200. These data would be recorded as shown below. We show two entries to separate the explicit withholdings from employees' nominal wages and the employers' compensation payments not included in nominal wages.

| | | |
|---|---|---|
| Wage and Salaries Expense | 100,000 | |
| U.S. Withholding Taxes Payable | | 20,000 |
| State Withholding Taxes Payable | | 4,000 |
| FICA Taxes Payable | | 7,000 |
| Union Dues Payable | | 500 |
| Insurance Premiums Payable | | 3,000 |
| Wages and Salaries Payable | | 65,500 |

To record gross wages and salaries nominally due employees, withholdings, and plug for amount payable to employees.

| | | |
|---|---|---|
| Wage and Salaries Expense | 14,100 | |
| FICA Taxes Payable | | 7,000 |
| FUTA Taxes Payable to U.S. | | 320 |
| FUTA Taxes Payable to State | | 1,080 |
| Insurance Premiums Payable | | 4,500 |
| Estimated Bonus Payable | | 1,200 |

Employer's wage expense for amounts not paid directly to employees.

The bonus estimate would not be recorded if the eventual amount due could not be reasonably estimated.

16.33    On payday, the employer pays $65,500 to employees, discharging the employer's liability for wages and salaries. Checks are written at various times to the federal government, the state government, the union,

and the insurance company. Such checks might be written as often as twice per week or as seldom as once per calendar quarter. The insurance premiums might be paid only once per year, in advance, resulting in an asset, Prepaid Insurance. In that case, the credit when wages are recognized is to the asset account.

## Income Taxes Payable

16.34   Chapter 20 discusses the computation of income tax *expense,* which generally differs from income taxes *payable* for periods as short as 1 year. (Income tax expense and income taxes payable in total might be equal only over a period as long as the life of the firm.) This section discusses the accounting for income taxes that are currently *payable.* Income tax rates vary over time and with amounts of taxable income. This section assumes that all taxable income is taxed at the rate of 40 percent.*

16.35   Corporations must generally pay quarterly installments during a year of the amount of estimated tax for that year. They must pay according to a schedule that depends on the fiscal year used for tax reporting. The following description assumes a company with a tax year corresponding to the calendar year. By April 15 of the current year, 25 percent of the *estimated* taxes payable for the current year must be paid. By June 15, 50 percent must be paid. By September 15, 75 percent must be paid, and by December 15, all of the *estimated* taxes for the year must be paid. Then, soon after the end of the year the company computes its *actual* tax bill. One-half of the excess of the actual amount over the estimated amount (now already paid) must be paid by March 15, and the rest of the excess must be paid by June 15.

16.36   Exhibit 16.1 illustrates the procedures over several quarterly payments. The related journal entries are of two kinds:

---

*Information about current tax rates can be found in the tax manuals published by Commerce Clearing House, Prentice-Hall, and others.

*Exhibit 16.1*
**Estimating Quarterly Income Tax Payments and Final Payments of Actual Taxes**

| | Estimates of Taxable Income for | | Amounts Payable for Income Taxes of | |
|---|---|---|---|---|
| Date | Year 1 | Year 2 | Year 1 | Year 2 |
| **Year 1** | | | | |
| April 15 | $1,000,000 | — | $100,000 [a] | — |
| June 15 | 1,000,000 | — | 100,000 [b] | — |
| September 15 | 1,000,000 | — | 100,000 [c] | — |
| December 15 | 1,000,000 | — | 100,000 [d] | — |
| | | | | |
| **Year 2** | | | | |
| March 15 | 1,100,000* | — | 20,000 [e] | — |
| April 15 | — | $1,100,000 | | $110,000 [f] |
| June 15 | 1,100,000* | 1,100,000 | 20,000 [e] | 110,000 [g] |
| September 15 | — | 1,200,000 | — | 140,000 [h] |
| December 15 | — | 1,300,000 | — | 160,000 [i] |
| | | | | |
| **Year 3** | | | | |
| March 15 | — | 1,350,000* | — | 10,000 [j] |
| June 15 | — | 1,350,000* | — | 10,000 [j] |

*Actual, not estimated, amounts.

Year 1 Estimates of Taxes

[a] $.25 \times [.40 \times (\$1,000,000)]$
[b] $.50 \times [.40 \times (\$1,000,000)] - \$100,000$
[c] $.75 \times [.40 \times (\$1,000,000)] - \$200,000$
[d] $1.00 \times [.40 \times (\$1,000,000)] - \$300,000$
[e] $.50 \times [.40 \times (\$1,100,000)] - \$400,000$

Year 2 Estimates of Taxes

[f] $.25 \times [.40 \times (\$1,100,000)]$
[g] $.50 \times [.40 \times (\$1,100,000)] - \$110,000$
[h] $.75 \times [.40 \times (\$1,200,000)] - \$220,000$
[i] $1.00 \times [.40 \times (\$1,300,000)] - \$360,000$
[j] $.50 \times [.40 \times (\$1,350,000)] - \$520,000$

| | | |
|---|---|---|
| Income Tax Expense | 100,000 | |
| Income Taxes Payable | | 100,000 |

To accrue quarterly payment.

| | | |
|---|---|---|
| Income Taxes Payable | 100,000 | |
| Cash | | 100,000 |

To make payment.

The illustration shows changing estimates of taxable income in the second year. Although in principle such changes as these will occur and should be accounted for as shown, the income tax regulations allow a company to use a single estimate throughout the year in many cases. That estimate can be the taxes payable for the preceding year. Thus, in practice, the computation of the quarterly payment is as illustrated for year 1, not complicated with changing estimates as in year 2.

If, at the end of a year, it happens that actual taxes are *less* than the estimate, so that payments have exceeded the amounts due, then the excess of payments over the amounts due will be reclassified as an asset, Prepaid Income Taxes. The adjusting entry, assuming an excess of $8,000, is

16.37

Dec. 31

| | | |
|---|---|---|
| Prepaid Income Taxes | 8,000 | |
| Income Tax Expense | | 8,000 |

Payments for estimated taxes exceeded tax liability for the year by $8,000. An asset for this amount is shown on the balance sheet.

When the payments for the next year come due, say, on April 15, the entry, assuming that the payment for the estimate of taxes due is $110,000, is

```
Income Tax Expense  . . . . . . . . . . .  110,000
     Prepaid Income Taxes  . . . . . . .            8,000
     Income Taxes Payable  . . . . . . .          102,000
```
A check for only $102,000 need be sent, because the firm overpaid during the preceding year.

## Sales and Excise Taxes Payable

16.38 Various governments impose sales or excise taxes based on the level or rate of sales. The federal government, for example, taxes gasoline sales; many state and local governments impose a sales tax as a percentage of sales. Amounts for sales taxes are charged to customers as a percentage of each sale with total tax rounded up. Generally, amounts are due the taxing authority as a percentage of total sales for the period. There may be a small difference between amounts collected from customers and amounts paid to governments. These differences present no special accounting problems. Revenues typically include all amounts collected from customers. A revenue contra for taxes is used; amounts due the governments are shown as a liability at the balance sheet date. The journal entries might be as follows:

```
Cash and Accounts Receivable .  1,048,000
     Sales Revenue  . . . . . . . . . .          1,048,000
To record 100,000 sales to cus-
tomers of items costing $9.98
each with sales tax of 5% added:
$9.98 × 1.05 = $10.48.
```

```
Sales Tax Collected (a revenue
     contra)  . . . . . . . . . . . . . . . . . .     49,900
     Sales Tax Payable  . . . . . . .              49,900
Sales taxes due the government
are 5% of total sales subject to
tax; $998,000 is taxed.
```

Note in this example that the firm has collected from customers $100 [= ($1,048,000 − $998,000) − $49,900] more than it must remit in taxes. This amount is effectively ex-

tra revenue to the collecting firm. In some jurisdictions, the firm is allowed to keep a portion of the sales taxes otherwise due as a collection fee. Although it is usually not worth the trouble, theory suggests that the portion allowed as a collection fee be separately reported, along with some estimate of the expenses of collection. Many firms treat sales taxes as an expense, rather than as a revenue contra.

## Property Taxes

16.39 The accounting problems for property taxes arise only because the amounts for them often become known after the period to which they relate. The taxing body (city or county, for example) will have an assessed valuation of each property in its records. The assessments themselves are changed periodically. At a specified time, the city will divide the amount of required or budgeted property tax receipts for the year by the sum of the assessed valuations for all the property in its jurisdiction to calculate the property tax rate. Sometime after the tax year is over, the city will send a tax bill to each property owner equal to the overall rate multiplied by the specific property's assessed valuation. The bill itself may be payable in installments. Sometimes the actual amount of the bill is not known until the final payment; earlier installments are based on the preceding year's bill. Generally accepted accounting principles in most cases require that property tax expense be estimated and accrued throughout the tax year as time passes.*

## Estimated Current Liabilities

16.40 This section discusses current liabilities whose amounts are not contractually specified and therefore can only be estimated.

---

*ARB No. 43, chap. 10A, par. 14. Paragraph 10 of chap. 10A of ARB No. 43 lists eight alternative methods of accounting for property taxes and suggests that in some cases methods other than the preferred one will make most sense. The interested reader should consult ARB No. 43 for details not presented here.

## Compensated Absences

16.41   Employers often promise to provide paid vacations to employees or to pay employees for days they are away from work because of sickness or jury duty. The FASB refers to such absences as *compensated absences* and requires that employers debit expense (or product cost) and credit liability for compensation for future absences if all of the following conditions are met:*

**1.** The employer's obligation to compensate employees results from employees' past service;

**2.** The obligation relates to employees' rights that

**a.** vest (employees have a legal right to be paid even if employment terminates before the compensated absence is actually taken), or

**b.** accumulate if the rights are not sick-pay benefits (that is, once earned, any unused rights can be carried over, at least in part, to periods subsequent to the ones in which they were earned);

**3.** Payment of the compensation is probable; and

**4.** The amount can be reasonably estimated.

If the first three conditions are met, but the amounts cannot be reasonably estimated, then the facts must be disclosed. Note that the second rule has an exception for sick-pay benefits: if an employer regularly pays employees who are sick but has no obligation to do so, then the employer is not required to accrue a liability, even though the rights accumulate. The FASB views such compensated absences as contingent liabilities merely to be disclosed rather than accrued. The contingency is the employee's sickness. By the same reasoning, compensation for jury duty is not accrued but is charged to expense (or product cost) as paid.

Assume, for example, that employees'   16.42
wages and fringe benefits other than for compensated absences average $200 per day. Assume that in the current period employees earned a vested right to 250 days of paid vacation and accumulated nonvested rights to 100 paid sick days. The journal entries would be:

Wage Expense and Work-in-Process
   Inventory ...................... 50,000
      Estimated Liability for Compen-
         sated Absences ............         50,000
Accrue benefits for vacation pay only:
250 days × $200 per day = $50,000.
Split debits between wage expense
and product cost, depending on nature of employment and work done.

If, during the period, employees took 100 days of paid vacation and were paid for 60 sick days, then the journal entries would be:

Estimated Liability for Compensated
   Absences ...................... 20,000
      Wages Payable or Cash .......         20,000
Debit wages paid or payable for vacations to estimated liability account:
100 days × $200 per day = $20,000.

Wage Expense and Work-in-Process
   Inventory ...................... 12,000
      Wages Payable or Cash .......         12,000
Nonvested sick-pay benefits are not
accrued but are debited to expense or
product cost as paid: 60 days × $200
per day = $12,000.

The notes to the financial statements at the end of the period would disclose, if material, a contingent liability for up to $8,000 (= 40 days × $200 per day) for sick-pay benefits accumulated but not vested.

## Premiums and Coupons Offered to Customers

The reader may have seen "cents-off" cou-   16.43
pons offered as inducement to buy a firm's goods. These "cents-off" coupons are one form of premium offered to customers in one accounting period that may not be used by the customer until a later accounting period. Other examples are offers on packages ("send in the boxtop") and certificates sent

---

*Financial Accounting Standards Board, *Statement of Financial Accounting Standards No. 43*, "Accounting for Compensated Absences," 1980, pars. 6 and 7.

to shareholders entitling the shareholder to a discount at any retail outlet. The offering firm must estimate the cost of its liability for redemption in future periods. If the estimate can be made with reasonable precision, the firm will debit Promotion Expense or Selling Expense and credit a liability account in the period the offer is made. Because the amounts can usually be estimated within some range, FASB *Statement No. 5* and *Interpretation No. 14* on loss contingencies require such accruals. The accountant studies similar promotional plans and uses the results of those studies to develop a range of estimates of promotion expenses for this period. The minimum amount from the range of estimates is chosen unless some other estimate appears to be better.

16.44    Entries might be the following:

| | | |
|---|---|---|
| Promotion Expense | 10,000 | |
| Liability for Coupon Redemptions | | 10,000 |

Accrual of estimated liability for redemptions of coupons distributed to customers this period.

| | | |
|---|---|---|
| Liability for Coupon Redemptions | 8,500 | |
| Cash | | 8,500 |

Payments to customers this period for redemptions of coupons this period.

If all coupon redemptions are debited to Promotion Expense as cash is paid, the adjusting entry need only adjust the existing balance in the liability account to an appropriate amount at the end of the period.

16.45    **Trading Stamps** Some retailing firms purchase trading stamps from firms that promise customers specific goods for certain numbers of stamps. The retailing firm that purchases trading stamps has no liability for outstanding, unredeemed trading stamps. That liability accrues to the trading stamp firm. The trading stamp firm must estimate as expenses each period the cost of redeeming the stamps and set up corresponding liabilities, current or noncurrent, depending on the expected time until redemption.

## Deposits

16.46    Firms often collect cash from customers as a deposit, such as for soft drink bottles.

When the customer fulfills a certain obligation, the cash is returned. Accounting problems arise only when all funds left on deposit are not expected to be claimed by customers. Then, the firm must estimate an amount of revenue from the "sale" of items to customers, such as soft drink bottles, and the expense of providing the services, such as the cost of the soft drink bottles lost, broken, and otherwise not returned. The problems of estimation can involve tricky statistical procedures, but the accounting for the estimates, once derived, involves no new principles. Entries might be as follows:

| | | |
|---|---|---|
| Soft Drink Bottle Inventory | 80,000 | |
| Cash or Accounts Payable | | 80,000 |

New bottles purchased this accounting period for use in selling soft drinks to customers. Inventory of bottles may be treated as a plant asset.

| | | |
|---|---|---|
| Cash | 120,000 | |
| Sales | | 100,000 |
| Customer Deposits Payable for Bottles | | 20,000 |

To record cash received from customers for sales of and deposits on soft drink bottles. Customer Deposits is a liability account.

| | | |
|---|---|---|
| Customer Deposits Payable for Bottles | 8,000 | |
| Revenue from Unclaimed Bottle Deposits | | 8,000 |

Estimate of amounts never to be returned to customers because of unreturned bottles.

| | | |
|---|---|---|
| Cost of Bottles Not Returned | 7,000 | |
| Soft Drink Bottle Inventory | | 7,000 |

A cost-flow assumption is used to remove from the asset account the cost of the bottles estimated not to be returned and report that amount as an expense.

Some state or local governments require that the firm pay the state for unclaimed deposits, under various "lost or unclaimed property" laws. The amounts involved may be disputed by the government and the firm, but, once they are calculated, the accounting is straightforward.

## Product Warranties and Guarantees

16.47   Firms often make promises to customers to repair or replace faulty or unsatisfactory goods. In practice the terms *warranty* and *guarantee* are used. In precise terminology, *guarantee* means a promise to fulfill another person's obligation if the person fails to do so. A retailer who co-signs a supplier's note at the bank, promising to repay the debt if the supplier fails to do so, "guarantees" it. Until information becomes available that the actual borrower is likely to default, the guarantee is a contingent obligation, disclosed only in notes to financial statements. When firms make promises about their own products, the precise term is *warranty* or *product warranty*.

16.48   When firms make promises about their own goods and services, they do so because they find that profits are thereby increased. These firms have found that customers who expect the firm to back its products are more likely to buy goods and services or are more likely to pay higher prices. Firms making such promises can either sell zero defective goods or repair defective goods. Only under unusual circumstances (such as a photographic firm providing a camera for a voyage to the moon or a manufacturer of cardiac pacemakers) would it pay a manufacturer to be sure that all products are not defective. In most cases, it is cheaper to repair or replace goods than to have such stringent quality control that there are no defective products or unsatisfied customers. In the usual case, then, the firm expects on the day it sells products that some portion of the sales will later require servicing under the warranty agreement. Because the future expenditure of assets is expected on the date of sale, accounting requires that the warranty expense be recognized in the period of sale—as a use of assets bolstering revenue—not in the later period when the promise is fulfilled. The treatment parallels the allowance method for uncollectible accounts where the firm debits a revenue contra in the period of sale for sales it does not expect to collect. The allowance method does not wait until specific accounts are uncollectible to recognize the resulting reduction in net income. FASB *Statement No. 5*

and *Interpretation No. 14* require accrual of estimated warranty costs when these costs can be estimated within some range, as most firms selling consumer products can do.

16.49   The issue in accounting for goods sold under warranty is whether the firm should recognize *all* expected profits during the period of sale or whether some of the profits should await the period when warranty work is done. When firms have substantial warranty work to do, some theorists argue that the warranty work should itself be treated as a profit center with its own revenues and expenses. The profit center should be able to report profits. This treatment is required when the warranty or a service contract is sold separately from the product itself. Some argue that the treatment should be used even when the warranty or service contract is sold as an integral part of the product. Such accounting requires an allocation of part of the overall sales revenue to the sales of the warranty.

16.50   Others, such as we, view warranty work, even in substantial amounts, as a means of boosting sales. With this interpretation, warranty work should generally be treated as a cost center, without its own profits. The only exception occurs when service contracts are sold separately. The accounting should mirror the firm's intent: If the firm uses warranties to boost sales, then separate profit-center accounting is not as suitable as accounting for warranties at expected costs. When the firm plans to profit from warranty service in addition to the regular margins on sales, the warranty activities should be accounted for as a profit center. Whether the repair work is treated as a cost center or a profit center for internal reporting need not influence the firm's choice of accounting methods for external reporting.* For example, a firm might decide that the nature of its warranties and repair activities suggest cost-center reporting for financial accounting even though the repair services are treated as a profit center for internal reporting and evaluation. The following entries illustrate the two methods.

---

*Geraldine Dominiak first suggested this distinction to us.

## Cost-Center Approach (Warranty Expense)

Accounts Receivable ............ 900,000
    Sales ..................... 900,000
Sale of goods with warranty attached.

Warranty Expense ............. 27,000
    Estimated Warranty Liability .. 27,000
Three percent of sales revenue expected to be spent for warranty replacements and repairs.

Estimated Warranty Liability ...... 9,000
    Cash, Repair Parts Inventory,
      Accounts Payable ......... 9,000
Repairs made on faulty products.

16.51 The goal is to estimate the cost of providing warranty services for specific sales and to accrue that amount as expense and estimated liability in the period of sale. By the time the warranty period expires for those sales, the amount in the Estimated Warranty Liability account for the sales will ideally be zero. (Of course, there will be other sales in subsequent periods involving their own warranties and credits to the Estimated Liability account, so its balance will probably grow over time.)

## Profit-Center Approach (Warranty Sales)

Accounts Receivable ............ 900,000
    Sales ..................... 855,000
    Advances from Customers ... 45,000
Five percent of sales revenues is allocated to warranty revenue. Because cash is collected before the service is provided, the credit is to the nonmonetary liability account.

Advances from Customers ....... 15,000
    Warranty Revenue .......... 15,000
One-third of the expected faulty goods are returned for repair.

Warranty Expense ............. 9,000
    Cash, Repair Parts Inventory,
      Accounts Payable ......... 9,000
Assets used in making warranty repairs are debited to an expense account.

16.52 Note that the revenue in the period of sale in this treatment is less than the revenue net of warranty expense in the cost-center treatment. The revenue from warranty repairs exceeds the expense of repairs in the period when the repairs are made. Thus the income from the transactions is the same under either method after all warranty work is complete. The profit-center approach delays revenue recognition until warranty work is done. This method is more conservative but justifiable, in our opinion, only when warranty work is planned as a profit center.

## Estimated Losses on Purchase and Sales Commitments

16.53 When a firm contracts to buy goods at some future date but at a price agreed upon today, it will suffer an economic loss if the price of the goods to be delivered declines in the future. Paragraph 9.69 discussed the accounting for the losses that result. When an account such as Loss on Purchase Commitments is debited, the current liability, Estimated Liability for Purchase Cost in Excess of Market Value, is credited. When the goods arrive and are paid for, the expenditure is not all debited to the inventory account. Rather, an amount equal to the market value on the delivery date is debited to inventory and the excess of the expenditure over that market value is debited to the Estimated Liability account. This process results in reflecting the loss on purchase commitments in income when the loss becomes apparent rather than having the inventory carried at higher-than-normal costs with the income reduction occurring in the period of sale.*

16.54 Similarly, firms can make supply commitments at fixed prices that turn out to be too low. The firm will debit a loss account as soon as it learns of the loss, rather than wait for the loss to be realized through sale at a price less than cost. For example, assume that a manufacturer of nuclear generating

---

*If, after the goods are received and recorded, the Estimated Liability account still has a credit balance, then that account is closed and a recovery of loss is recognized in income (debit Estimated Loss account and credit Recovery of Loss account).

plants has obligated itself to deliver 1,000 lb of uranium to its customers for $10/lb. It discovers that the cost of uranium has risen to $40/lb. It will make the following entry:*

Loss on Supply Commitments ...... 30,000
   Allowance for Losses on Supply
     Commitments ..............           30,000

The allowance account appears on the balance sheet among the liabilities.

## Advances on Unexecuted Contracts

16.55   Firms sometimes receive cash in advance of providing goods or services. Examples include newspaper and magazine subscriptions, tickets for future performances, rent collected in advance, insurance premiums collected in advance, and payments on supply contracts, such as the uranium in the preceding example. All these collections have in common the incurring of an obligation to provide a good or service, rather than to pay cash. The firm hopes that the cost of providing the service will be less than the amount of cash collected; otherwise the firm will not profit from the transaction. When the cash is collected, the firm must debit cash for the amount received and credit some account. Generally accepted accounting principles require that a liability be credited for the amount of cash collected, rather than the expected cost of providing the service, so long as the firm expects to profit from the transaction. The account credited can have various specific names, depending on the context, but we find that the concept is mastered faster if all such accounts are given the same title—Advances from Customers.

16.56   The account Advances from Customers is a nonmonetary liability because the obligation requires the rendering of goods or services rather than the payment of a specific amount of cash. It is a liability because it is a legal obligation due at a definite or reasonably definite time and the firm has received a past benefit (it collected cash). Some writers call this account "deferred revenue." Although it is true that later this account will be debited when a revenue account is credited, we find that the title "deferred revenue" clouds understanding.

16.57   Illustrative entries for collections in advance and the eventual providing of the service are as follows:

Cash ........................ 100,000
   Advances from Customers ...         100,000
Collections from subscribers for 10 issues of a local magazine.

Magazine Inventory ............. 8,000
   Cash and Accounts Payable ..        8,000
Production of one issue of the magazine.

Advances from Customers ....... 10,000
   Revenue from Subscriptions .       10,000
Delivery of magazines to subscribers.

Cash and Accounts Receivable ... 4,000
   Revenue from Newsstand
     Sales ...................       4,000
Cash sales to newsstands.

Cost of Magazines Sold ........ 7,200
   Magazine Inventory ........       7,200
Part of the inventory is held for later sale of back issues. This entry records the cost of magazines sent to subscribers and sold to newsstands.

## Summary

16.58   The principles discussed in Chapter 15 requiring that liabilities be recorded when the payments are reasonably certain and can be estimated with reasonable precision apply to current liabilities as well as to noncurrent liabilities. Current liabilities present few conceptual problems. A monetary liability account is credited with the cash or cash-equivalent amount expected to be paid to discharge the obligation. The debit is typi-

---

*The reader may wonder about recognizing all of the loss on a transaction that itself has not yet been recorded. The FASB, too, is perplexed about this phenomenon and has it under study. See the discussion in *Statement of Financial Accounting Concepts No. 3*, December 1980, pars. 174–176.

cally either to an expense or to an asset, although another liability may be debited (as when notes payable replace accounts payable), or owners' equity can be debited (when dividends are declared). A nonmonetary liability account is credited when cash or a cash-equivalent amount is received in return for a future good or service. If revenue is recognized when the cash is received, such as when goods are sold under warranty, then the nonmonetary liability is stated at the estimated future cost of the services—warranty repairs in this case. If revenue recognition is postponed until the good or service is provided, such as when cash for magazine subscriptions is collected in advance, the nonmonetary liability is stated at the amount of cash received.

## Questions and Short Cases

**16.1** Review the meaning of the following concepts or terms discussed in this chapter.
   a. Current liability.
   b. Monetary liability versus nonmonetary liability.
   c. Offset of liability and asset.
   d. Debt to be refinanced.
   e. F.O.B. point.
   f. Net price method
   versus gross price method.
   g. Interest-bearing versus noninterest-bearing notes.
   h. Prepaid interest.
   i. Dividend arrearages.
   j. Bonus plan.
   k. FICA.
   l. FUTA.
   m. Warranty versus guarantee.
   n. Profit-center method versus cost-center method for warranties.
   o. Executory contract.
   p. Advances from customers.

**16.2** Why is stating a general rule for ordering liabilities within the category of current liabilities hard, whereas stating a general rule for classifying liabilities as either current or noncurrent is relatively easy?

**16.3** a. Under what conditions may a firm show current liabilities as noncurrent because of expected refinancing?
   b. Why might it wish to do so?

**16.4** Why does the balance sheet not show assets offset against liabilities when the firm intends to use a specific asset to discharge a specific liability?

**16.5** A firm knows that it has a $1 million payment due 3 months hence. It is the final, "balloon" payment of a series of installment payments that began several years ago. It has purchased a $1 million U.S. Treasury note maturing on the date its own payment is due. The firm intends to deliver the maturity proceeds of $1 million of the Treasury note to discharge its own liability.

   How should the $1 million liability and the $1 million asset be presented in the financial statements?

**16.6** How does a noninterest-bearing note provide a return to the lender of the funds?

**16.7** a. Distinguish between the theoretically preferred method and the method used in practice for short-term noninterest-bearing notes.
   b. Explain how the *timing* of expense recognition can be drastically different between these two methods, although the amounts may be small.

**16.8**  Why does this book state that prepaid interest does not exist? Bankers and other participants in the business world, however, often use the term. Explain the difference between these two positions.

**16.9**  Why does income tax expense for a period differ from income taxes paid during that period?

**16.10**  Why do corporations' installment payments for estimated taxes for a year change much less often than estimates of taxable income for that year change?

**16.11**  Why should dividends, once declared, become legal obligations of the corporation, with legal standing equal to that of wages payable or accounts payable?

**16.12**  What is the difference between a sales tax and an excise tax?

**16.13**  Why does a company that gives trading stamps to its customers usually not have a problem of estimating a liability for the cost of goods to be given to customers who redeem their stamps?

**16.14**  Brealey Company negotiated a 5-year loan for $1 million with its bank. The terms of the loan require that the interest rate can be changed as the bank chooses, but that the company can repay the loan at any time. Interest is to be paid quarterly. How should Brealey Company classify this note on its balance sheet?

**16.15**  A noted accountant once remarked that the optimal number of faulty TV sets for the General Electric Company to sell is "not zero" even if GE promises to repair all faulty GE sets that break down, for whatever reason, within 2 years of purchase. Why is the optimal number "not zero"?

**16.16**  Refer to the discussion in paragraph 7.36, where the reductions in income for expected uncollectibles are shown as a revenue contra for the period of sale, not an expense for the later period when uncollectibility becomes known. Estimated warranty costs are subtracted from income for the period of sale, not in the later period when the repair is made. Why is this item called "warranty expenses" rather than being treated as a revenue contra?

**16.17**  **a.** In times of rising prices and increasing sales volume, which method, the cost-center method or the profit-center method of accounting for warranties and their associated costs, will report higher income?
   **b.** Under what conditions will the two methods have the same effect on reported income for a period?

**16.18**  Edwards Company maintains a series of revolving loans at its bank for $100,000. The loans are evidenced by a note payable. Each note matures 2 months after the date of issue. For the past several years, Edwards Company has signed a new note upon maturity of the old note; the company has never discharged the series of notes with a cash payment, although it does pay interest on each maturity date. Edwards Company and its bank plan to continue the arrangement indefinitely. Edwards Company suggests that the $100,000 liability for note payable should be classified as a long-term liability because it is not expected to require cash payment for several years, at least. Respond to the suggestion.

**16.19**  Why is the Customer Deposits account a liability when, clearly, cash is an asset?

16.20    Bonus plans state that a bonus will be paid as some percentage of "eligible income." Eligible income is sometimes computed after taxes and sometimes before taxes. Eligible income is sometimes computed after the bonus itself is subtracted and sometimes before. Which treatments are likely to be most effective in achieving the goals of the bonus?

16.21    How should each of the following appear in the financial statements?
   a.  Cash dividends payable.
   b.  Stock dividends issuable.
   c.  Estimated costs for repairs to be made next accounting period.
   d.  Accrued wages.
   e.  Rent received from tenants in advance.
   f.  Losses estimated from lawsuits currently in court.
   g.  Customer deposits on shipping pallets returnable at any time up to 2 years hence.
   h.  Current installments of serial bonds.
   i.  Estimated income taxes payable but not yet paid.
   j.  Amounts for loans taken out by officers of the company that the company has guaranteed.
   k.  Loans made to officers by the company.

16.22    (Adapted from AICPA *Technical Practice Aids*.) The state in which Bell Company has its work force allows the employer to choose the method of payment of unemployment insurance premiums. The employer may either
   (1) Pay a percentage of wages, or
   (2) Reimburse the state directly for unemployment claims.
   The Bell Company chose the second option. May it account for unemployment compensation by debiting expense for a period with the expected dollar amount of claims while crediting a liability account for the estimated liability?

16.23    (Adapted from AICPA *Technical Practice Aids*.) Rice Company received a series of billings from the federal government for interest and penalties related to Rice Company's inadvertent late payment during the past year of federal withholding taxes for employees. By the balance sheet date, billings for $25,000 had been received. By the time the financial statements were prepared, another $5,000 of billings had arrived and another $10,000 were expected. How should these actual and expected billings be treated by Rice Company?

16.24    (Adapted from AICPA *Technical Practice Aids*.) Sterling Company franchises distributorships for oxygen inhalator units. The licensee (franchisee) leases the units from Sterling Company but pays an initial leasing fee for each unit before it is shipped. Subsequent lease payments are made by the licensee as the unit is used. The franchise agreement specifies that the licensee can terminate the franchise agreement, return the units, and have a portion of the initial fee returned. The portion returnable to the licensee is inversely proportional to the time the unit has been used; the longer the unit is used, the smaller the refund. When the units are returned, they are in sufficiently good condition that they can be redistributed by Sterling Company at little or no rehabilitation and repair cost.
   How should Sterling Company account for the initial leasing fee?

16.25    (Adapted from CPA Examination.) The Supple Food Company distributes to consumers coupons which may be presented to grocers for discounts on certain products of Supple. The coupons cannot be redeemed by the consumer more than six months from the date of original issue by Supple. The grocers are reimbursed when they send the coupons to Supple. In Supple's experience, 40 percent of such coupons are redeemed, and generally one month elapses between the date a grocer receives a coupon from a consumer and the date Supple receives it. During the current year Supple issued two separate series of coupons as follows:

| Issued On | Total Value | Consumer Expiration Date | Amount Disbursed as of 12/31 |
|---|---|---|---|
| 1/1 | $100,000 | 6/30 | $34,000 |
| 7/1 | 120,000 | 12/31 | 40,000 |

What liability for unredeemed coupons should appear on the December 31 balance sheet?

**16.26**   (Adapted from CPA Examination.) Royal Corporation's liabilities at December 31, 1981 were as follows:

| | |
|---|---|
| Trade accounts payable .......................................................... | $100,000 |
| 16 percent notes payable issues November 1, 1981, maturing July 1, 1982 ............. | 30,000 |
| 14 percent debentures payable issued February 1, 1981, final installment due February 1, 1986, balance at December 31, 1981, including annual installment of $50,000 due February 1, 1982 ........................................ | 300,000 |
| | $430,000 |

Royal's December 31, 1981, financial statements were issued on March 31, 1982. On January 5, 1982, the entire $300,000 balance of the 14 percent debentures was refinanced by issuance of a long-term obligation. In addition, on March 1, 1982, Royal consummated a non-cancelable agreement with the lender to refinance the 17 percent note payable on a long-term basis, on readily determinable terms that have not yet been implemented. Both parties are financially capable of honoring the agreement, and there have been no violations of any of the agreement's provisions.

a.  What is the total amount of Royal's short-term obligations that may properly be excluded from current liabilities at December 31, 1981?

b.  Assume the same facts for Royal Corporation's liabilities, except that the agreement with the lender to refinance the 16 percent note payable on a long-term basis is cancellable at any time upon ten days' notice by the lender. What is the total amount of Royal's short-term obligations that may properly be excluded from current liabilities at December 31, 1981?

**16.27**   In its balance sheet as of December 31, the Norwood Corporation reported current assets of $1,500,000 and current liabilities of $600,000, including a cash dividend of $110,000 declared by the board of directors near the end of the year. The bond indenture for an issue of Norwood Corporation bonds provides that "the company shall maintain current assets in an amount at least twice as large as its current liabilities. If at any time the amount of current assets falls below this amount, no dividends shall be paid on common stock until the company's working capital position meets the above-stated standard (after taking into account the dividend)."

Early in January of the following year, the company received a letter from the trustee for the bondholders asking for detailed information about several items on its year-end financial statement. Subsequently the trustee wrote to the president of Norwood Corporation stating that the dividend declared in December violated the bond contract. Excerpts from the trustee's letter are cited below:

Included among your current assets is prepaid insurance of $20,500. According to information furnished by your accountant, $8,500 of these premiums apply to insurance coverage for the year following your balance sheet; the remainder of the premiums are for insurance coverage 2 years or more after the balance sheet date. Thus $12,000 of the prepaid insurance should not be classified as a current asset, because these costs will be charged against revenues earned in subsequent years.

Included in your inventories is $60,000 of spare parts and supplies used in maintaining your manufacturing equipment. These spare parts will ultimately be converted into long-term assets, and therefore classifying them as a part of current assets is improper.

Among the long-term liabilities on the balance sheet are notes payable of $120,000. These notes were given to finance acquisition of a building currently owned and being rented to others. The notes are secured by an assignment of the rental proceeds and will be paid from the proceeds of these rents. The notes mature at the rate of $20,000 each month, beginning 6 months after the balance sheet date, and are therefore properly classified as a current liability.

According to our analysis, your current assets are overstated in the amount of $72,000 (= $12,000 + $60,000), and your current liabilities are understated by $120,000. If these corrections were made, current assets would be less than twice as large as current liabilities. The dividend declaration on common stock is therefore in violation of the bond indenture. You should rescind this dividend declaration immediately.

The president of Norwood Corporation has referred this letter to you. Write a memorandum to the president commenting on the points in the trustee's letter. State your recommendation on the question of rescinding the dividend declaration.

16.28  Some accountants argue that the condition related to rights that vest or accumulate is unnecessary for deciding when a liability for a compensated absence has been incurred. These accountants argue that the crux of the matter is whether the employer's obligation results from past service or whether its existence depends on future absences. Comment. (Hint: See the dissent to FASB *Statement No. 43*.)

## Problems and Exercises

16.29  Acker Company estimated its income tax liability for the year to be $1 million. It must make quarterly payments on its income taxes based on the estimated amount payable for the year in excess of $100,000. What is the amount of each quarterly payment?

16.30  Lantz Company has 1 million shares of common stock outstanding with a par value of $10 per share. It declared a $1 cash dividend per share. Prepare journal entries for this event.

16.31  What is the interest rate implicit in a noninterest-bearing note with face value of $10,000 maturing in 6 months given in exchange for goods with a fair market value of $9,260?

16.32  Edmonds Company borrowed funds from its bank on October 1 of year 1. It signed two notes, each for $48,000, each due 1 year later, and each providing for interest at the appropriate market rate of 20 percent per year. One note was interest bearing (interest due on maturity), and the other was noninterest bearing. Edmonds Company closes its books for the year on December 31.

In parallel columns, one for each note, show the following items:

a. Cash received on signing the note.

b. Interest expense for the year ending December 31.

c. Interest payable on balance sheet for December 31.

d. Amount in the Notes Payable (net) account on December 31.

e. Interest expense for year 2.

f. The total expense over the life of the loan.

g. The amount of cash paid to the bank on maturity in year 2.

16.33  On December 15, the Martin Company secured a loan from the First National Bank on its 2-month, noninterest-bearing note for $3,000. The bank discounts the note at an 8-percent rate, giving cash to Martin Company of $2,960. The note is paid at maturity. The Martin Company closes it books monthly. Present entries on the books of the Martin Company for the life of the note.

16.34  The Kamax Company issued a $2,400 note to the Berin Company to be applied on account. The note is dated November 15, bears interest at 10 percent, and matures on the following March 15. The note is paid at maturity. Present entries on the books of the Kamax Company for the life of the note, assuming that the books are closed annually on December 31.

16.35  On May 20, the Muriel Company received a note from R. M. Maxwell to be applied on account. The note is dated April 20 and is due October 20. The face value is $900; it bears interest at 8 percent per annum; the maker is B. F. McGrath. Maxwell is given credit for the face value plus one month's accrued interest. The note is paid by the maker at maturity. Present entries on the books of the Muriel Company for the note. The Muriel Company closes its books annually at June 30.

16.36  Refer to the data of the preceding problem. Present entries on the books of B. F. McGrath for the note. McGrath issued the note to Maxwell on account. McGrath's books are closed quarterly on March 31, June 30, etc.

16.37  Refer to the data of the second preceding problem. Present entries on the books of R. M. Maxwell for the note. Maxwell's books are closed annually at December 31.

16.38  On December 1, the Mellon Company obtained a 90-day loan at the Lindell State Bank on its noninterest-bearing note for $4,500. The bank discounted the note at the rate of 8 percent per annum, paying cash of $4,410. On the maturity date, March 1, the note was renewed for another 30 days, with a check being issued to the bank for the interest applicable to the 30-day period in March. The Mellon Company closes its books annually at December 31. Present entries on the books of the Mellon Company to record the issue of the note, the year-end adjustment, the renewal of the note on March 1, and the payment at maturity of the renewed note.

16.39  Refer to the data in the preceding problem. Present entries for the following variations in the settlement of the note of the Mellon Company on March 1, its original maturity date:

a. The original note is paid at maturity on March 1.

b. The note is renewed under the same terms on March 1, except that the new note bears interest at a rate of 12 percent per year.

c. The note is renewed on March 1 for 90 more days as a noninterest-bearing note under the original terms, except that the bank has raised its discount rate from 8 percent to 12 percent. On March 1, the company pays the bank interest for 90 days in advance.

**16.40** Consider the following transactions:

| | |
|---|---|
| Nov. 6, 1980 ......... | The Castles Wholesale Company receives a $2,700, noninterest-bearing, 3-month note from a customer, the Swan Sales Company. The note is discounted at 8% per annum (simple interest), and the resulting value is applied to the Swan account. |
| Dec. 16, 1980 ........ | The note is endorsed and transferred to the Cook Manufacturing Company to apply on account. The note is discounted at an 8% rate from its face value. In addition, the Castles Wholesale Company is allowed a 1% cash discount on the invoice amount of the account being discharged by the transfer of the note. That is, every $99 of (discounted) value of the note given up by Castles Wholesale Company discharges $100 of accounts payable to Cook Manufacturing Company. |
| Jan. 6, 1981 ......... | The Cook Manufacturing Company discounts the note at the Wydown National Bank at a rate of 8% per annum. |
| Feb. 6, 1981 ......... | The Swan Sales Company requests permission to pay only $300 on the notes at this date. In accordance with an agreement among the parties concerned, the Swan Sales Company issues a new $2,400, 3-month, 9% note, payable to the Wydown National Bank, which was endorsed and guaranteed by the Castles Wholesale Company and the Cook Manufacturing Company. |
| May 6, 1981 ......... | The Swan Sales Company pays the note and interest in full. |

All discounting is done with recourse. Present entries for the notes and interest, including adjusting entries at the close of the accounting periods, on the books of:
**a.** The Swan Sales Company, which closes its books quarterly (March 31, June 30, etc.).
**b.** The Castles Wholesale Company, which closes its books annually on December 31.
**c.** The Cook Manufacturing Company, which closes its books annually on December 31.

**16.41** On December 1, the Percival Company obtained a 90-day loan for $12,600 from the Twin City State Bank at an annual interest rate of 10 percent. On the maturity date the note was renewed for another 30 days, with a check being issued to the bank for the accrued interest. The Percival Company closes its books annually at December 31.
**a.** Present entries on the books of the Percival Company to record the issue of the note, the year-end adjustment, the renewal of the note, and the payment of cash at maturity of the renewed note.
**b.** Present entries at maturity date of the original note for the following variations in the settlement of the note of the Percival Company.
   **(1)** The original note is paid at maturity.
   **(2)** The note is renewed for 30 days; the new note bears interest at 12 percent per annum. Interest on the old note was not paid at maturity.

**16.42** (Adapted from AICPA *Technical Practice Aids*.) A private school has a reporting year ending June 30. It hires teachers for the 10-month period September of one year through June of the following year. It contracts to pay teachers in 12 monthly installments over the period September of one year through August of the next year. For the current academic year, the total contractual salaries to be paid to teachers is $360,000. How should this amount be accounted for in the financial statements issued June 30, at the end of the academic year?

**16.43** Chan Company's payroll records for April indicate that $100,000 wages were earned by factory employees. Of that amount, $30,000 was withheld for income taxes, $7,000 for FICA taxes, and $900 for union dues. In addition, the employer owed $7,000 for FICA taxes and $3,200 for FUTA taxes. Prepare journal entries to record this information.

**16.44**   Snodell Company recorded wages and salaries for the month amounting to $120,000. It also recorded its share of various payroll taxes. Of the $120,000, $15,000 was received by employees who had already earned the maximum amount taxed for social security taxes and is not subject to social security (FICA) taxes. Both the employer and employee are liable for 8-percent FICA taxes on the taxable amounts of $105,000. FUTA taxes are levied only on the employer. FUTA tax rates are 2.8 percent for state and .7 percent for federal taxes of taxable payroll. For purposes of FUTA, taxable payroll for the month is $80,000. Amounts withheld from employees' paychecks for income taxes were $25,000 for federal taxes, $5,000 for state taxes, and $1,000 for city taxes. In addition, $3,000 was withheld from employee paychecks for their voluntary contributions to an investment fund managed by the Gibraltar Insurance Company. Snodell Company is engaged solely in retailing operations.
  **a.** Prepare journal entries to record these events.
  **b.** What is the net increase in amounts payable caused by these transactions?

**16.45**   Cleveland Department Store had 1 million sales transactions during the year. Each transaction was for some dollar amount and 95 cents; the average sales transaction was $20.95. Total sales for the year were $20,950,000. The store charges sales tax at the rate of 6 percent of the amount on the sales invoice but remits to the taxing authorities 5.5 percent of the total, store-wide sales amount for the year. The store is allowed to keep the difference as a collection fee.
  By how much do collections of sales taxes differ from amounts remitted to the taxing authorities?

**16.46**   The Myrtle Lunch sells coupon books that patrons may use later to purchase meals. Each coupon book sells for $17 and has a face value of $20. That is, each book can be used to purchase meals with menu prices of $20. On July 1, redeemable unused coupons with face value of $1,500 were outstanding. During July, 250 coupon books were sold; during August, 100; during September, 100. Cash receipts exclusive of coupons were $1,200 in July, $1,300 in August, and $1,250 in September. Coupons with a face value of $2,700 were redeemed by patrons during the 3 months.
  **a.** If the Myrtle Lunch had a net income of $500 for the quarter ending September 30, how large were expenses?
  **b.** What effect, if any, do the July, August, and September coupon sales and redemptions have on the liabilities and owners' equities reported on the September 30 balance sheet?

**16.47**   The Jones Company sells service contracts to repair copiers at $300 per year. When the contract is signed, the $300 fee is collected and the Service Contract Fees Received in Advance account is credited. Revenues on contracts are recognized on a quarterly basis during the year in which the coverage is in effect. On January 1, 1,000 service contracts were outstanding. Of these, 500 expired at the end of the first quarter, 300 at the end of the second quarter, 150 at the end of the third quarter, and 50 at the end of the fourth quarter. Sales and service during the year came to these amounts (assume that all sales occurred at the beginning of the quarter):

|  | Sales of Contracts | Service Expenses |
|---|---|---|
| First Quarter | $120,000 (400 contracts) | $50,000 |
| Second Quarter | 240,000 (800 contracts) | 60,000 |
| Third Quarter | 90,000 (300 contracts) | 45,000 |
| Fourth Quarter | 60,000 (200 contracts) | 55,000 |

**a.** Prepare journal entries for the first three quarters of the year for the Jones Company. Assume that quarterly reports are prepared on March 31, June 30, and September 30.

**b.** What is the balance in the Service Contract Fees Received in Advance account on December 31?

**16.48**   Hagerman Company puts coupons in the packages of goods it sells. The coupons, which have no expiration date, can be redeemed for merchandise. Experience shows that 30 percent of coupons issued are redeemed. At the start of the current year, the liability for coupon redemptions was $100,000. During the year, coupons redeemable for merchandise costing $1,000,000 were issued, and coupons were redeemed for merchandise costing $250,000. What amount of liability for future coupon redemptions appears on the balance sheet for the end of the year?

**16.49**   A chemical company's operations in a certain plant are extremely dangerous. Commercial insurance premiums are so high that the company self-insures for injuries at the plant. During the current year, just ended, there was no loss caused by injury. The current year was judged unusually fortunate because in each year for the last decade injuries had cost an average of $100,000 per year. Management is sure that next year the company will not be so fortunate. What entry should be made at the end of the current year to reflect management's best estimate that next year the expected losses will cost $125,000?

**16.50**   Foster Company has a profit-sharing plan for employees. It provides that the company will contribute to a fund an amount equal to one-fourth of its net income after taxes (and profit-sharing expense) each year. Income before profit-sharing computations and income taxes for the year is $9.2 million. Income taxes are 40 percent of taxable income. Compute the amount of profit-sharing expense, income tax expense, and net income for the year.

**16.51**   Sheldahl Company has a bonus plan for employees that promises a bonus equal to 75 percent of "eligible income." The "eligible income" is defined as net income (after taxes and bonus) less an amount equal to 10 percent of the average balance of owners' equity for the year. Average owners' equity is computed as one-half the sum of beginning and ending balance sheet amounts for owners' equity. Ending owners' equity amount *after* net income for the year is recorded. Owners' equity was $2,260,000 at the start of the year and was also $2,260,000 at the end of the year before closing entries. Income before taxes and bonus was $2,400,000. Income taxes are 40 percent of taxable income.

Compute the amounts of bonus expense, income tax expense, net income, and ending owners' equity.

**16.52**   Cox Company received $100,000 cash and made commitments to sell 10,000 items for $10 each at a time when it estimated that its cost would be $8 per item. Later, it received $60,000 cash and made commitments to sell an additional 4,000 units for $15 when it estimated that its cost would be $12 per item. At the end of the year, the commitments are still outstanding, but all items have been ordered, with orders and prices confirmed by the supplier, at a cost of $11 per unit. Delivery costs are expected to average $.50 per unit. Record these transactions in the records of Cox Company.

**16.53**   Anderson Company sells appliances, all for cash. All acquisitions of appliances during a year are debited to the Merchandise Inventory account. The company provides warranties on all its products, guaranteeing to make repairs within 1 year of the date of sale as required for any of its appliances that break down. The company has many years of experience with its products and warranties.

*Exhibit 16.2*
**Anderson Company**
**Trial Balances**

| | Adjusted Preclosing | | Postclosing | |
|---|---|---|---|---|
| **Trial Balance—End of Year 1** | **Dr.** | **Cr.** | **Dr.** | **Cr.** |
| Estimated Liability for Warranty Repairs ...... | | $   3,000 | | $   3,000 |
| Merchandise Inventory .................... | $  100,000 | | $100,000 | |
| Sales ...................................... | | 800,000 | | |
| Warranty Expense ........................ | 18,000 | | | |
| All Other Accounts ........................ | 882,000 | 197,000 | 110,000 | 207,000 |
| Totals .................................. | $1,000,000 | $1,000,000 | $210,000 | $210,000 |

| | Unadjusted Trial Balance | |
|---|---|---|
| **Trial Balance—End of Year 2** | **Dr.** | **Cr.** |
| Estimated Liability for Warranty Repairs .......................... | $   14,000 | |
| Merchandise Inventory ...................................... | 820,000 | |
| Sales ...................................................... | | $1,000,000 |
| Warranty Expense ......................................... | — | — |
| All Other Accounts ......................................... | 266,000 | 100,000 |
| Totals ..................................................... | $1,100,000 | $1,100,000 |

Exhibit 16.2 shows trial balances for the Anderson Company at the ends of year 1 and year 2. The trial balances for the end of year 1 are the Adjusted Preclosing Trial Balance (after all adjusting entries have been properly made) and the final Postclosing Trial Balance. The trial balance shown for the end of year 2 is taken before any adjusting entries of any kind, although entries have been made to the Estimated Liability for Warranty Repairs account during year 2 as repairs have been made. Anderson Company closes its books once each year.

At the end of year 2, the management of Anderson Company analyzes the appliances sold within the preceding 12 months. All appliances in the hands of customers that are still covered by warranty are classified as follows: those sold on or before June 30 (more than 6 months old), those sold after June 30 but on or before November 30 (more than 1 month, but less than 6 months old), and those sold on or after December 1. One-half of one percent of the appliances sold more than 6 months ago are estimated to require repair, 5 percent of the appliances sold 1 to 6 months before the end of the year are estimated to require repair, and 8 percent of the appliances sold within the last month are assumed to require repair. From this analysis, management estimated that $5,000 of repairs still would have to be made in year 3 on the appliances sold in year 2. Ending inventory on December 31, year 2, is $120,000.

a. What were the total acquisitions of merchandise inventory during year 2?
b. What is the cost of goods sold for year 2?
c. What was the dollar amount of repairs made during year 2?
d. What is the Warranty Expense for year 2?
e. Give journal entries for repairs made during year 2, for the warranty expense for year 2, and for cost of goods sold for year 2.

16.54  Purdy Company's payroll for October is summarized in Exhibit 16.3. By October, some of the employees have already received wages in excess of those to which payroll taxes apply. Assume that the state unemployment compensation premium (charged to the employer) is

*Exhibit 16.3*
**Purdy Company**
**November Payroll Data**

| | | Employee Income Taxes Withheld | Amount Subject to Tax | | |
|---|---|---|---|---|---|
| | | | | FUTA | |
| Payroll | Wages Earned | | FICA | State | Federal |
| Factory ........................ | $100,000 | $25,000 | $ 90,000 | $35,000 | $35,000 |
| Sales .......................... | 60,000 | 12,000 | 55,000 | 4,000 | 4,000 |
| Office .......................... | 40,000 | 15,000 | 10,000 | — | — |
| Total ....................... | $200,000 | $52,000 | $155,000 | $39,000 | $39,000 |

2.7 percent of covered wages and the rate for the federal portion is .8 percent. The FICA rate is 8 percent of covered wages for the employer and 8 percent for the employee.

**a.** Prepare journal entries for these payroll-related events.

**b.** By how much have Purdy Company's liabilities increased?

16.55   The Pennsylvania Steel Company files its income tax returns on a calendar-year basis and issues financial statements quarterly as of March 31, June 30, and so on. All income taxes are estimated or paid at the rate of 40 percent of taxable income. The following data are applicable to the company's income tax for year 1.

**Year 1**

| | |
|---|---|
| March 31 ......... | It is estimated that total taxable income for year 1 will be about $1.5 million. The first quarter's financial statements are prepared. |
| April 15 ......... | The first payment on estimated taxes is made. |
| June 15 ......... | It is now estimated that total taxable income for the year will be about $1.7 million. The second payment on estimated taxes is made. |
| June 30 ......... | The second quarter's financial statements are prepared. |
| Sept. 15 ......... | It is now estimated that total taxable income for the year will be about $1.6 million. The third payment on estimated taxes is made. |
| Sept. 30 ......... | The third quarter's financial statements are prepared. |
| Dec. 15 .......... | It is now estimated that total taxable income for the year will be about $1.75 million. The fourth payment on estimated taxes is made. |
| Dec. 31 .......... | Income for the year is $1,775,000. Financial statements for the year are prepared. |

**Year 2**

| | |
|---|---|
| March 15 ......... | The first payment of the balance of taxes for year 1 is made. |
| June 15 ......... | The second payment of tax balance for year 1 is made. |

**a.** Prepare schedules showing
   (1) For tax returns: estimated taxes for year, cumulative payments due, and payment made for each payment date.
   (2) For financial statements: tax expenses for the quarterly reports and annual report.
**b.** Record the transactions related to year 1 income taxes in journal entry form.
**c.** Present the T-accounts for Cash, Prepaid Income Taxes (if necessary), Income Taxes Payable, and Income Tax Expense.

16.56   Merilyn Hackett is the principal owner and manager of Word Algebra, a seller of word-processing supplies. Hackett's company sells magnetic diskettes, print wheels, CRT tables, and other equipment for use with modern word-processing computers. Among its products are devices that hold the data being processed. The device looks something like a 45-rpm phonograph record and, because it is extremely flexible plastic rather than inflexible metal, it is called a "floppy disk." One of the recent innovations in this business is the dual disk track machine, a machine that can read two disks simultaneously. In year 1, Hackett devised a promotion for the company's dual track disks. She decided to include in each box of 10 disks a card telling of the promotion. Ten such cards are redeemable during the period Labor Day–Thanksgiving of year 2 for a T-shirt that Hackett has had specially designed. The shirt contains their company's slogan. Hackett offers $10 to any man and $15 to any woman who will wear these T-shirts in the 10-km Lake Front Race early in year 3, one of the highlights of the outdoor season.

Such a promotion as this has never been put on before. Hackett estimates that 80,000 boxes of diskettes (or floppy disks), each containing one promotion card, will be sold— 20,000 in year 1 and 60,000 in year 2. She estimates that 30 percent of those will be redeemed for T-shirts. She is sure that the percentage redeemed will be in the range of 20 to 40 percent. The T-shirts will be made to order after the cards are turned in and are expected to cost $5 each in these quantities, but might cost as much as $5.50 each. Hackett is even less sure of this, but she estimates that of the T-shirts distributed, 20 percent will be worn in the race and three-fourths of those will be worn by women. She uses a 10-percent discount rate in computing present values.

a. How should Word Algebra account for this promotion on its financial statements issued at the end of year 1? Give journal entries and supporting computations in good form.

b. Assume that 20,000 boxes are sold in year 1, that 64,000 are sold in year 2, that 35 percent of the cards are redeemed, and that the T-shirts cost $5.20 each. Other estimates remain unchanged. How should Word Algebra account for this promotion on its financial statement at the end of year 2? Give journal entries and computations in good form.

16.57   Krasny Company sells washing machines. During the year it sold 1,000 machines per month, 12,000 in total, for $360 each. Each machine is guaranteed for 1 year from the first of the month following the sale against defects in materials and in workmanship. Management estimates that it will incur a total of $48,000 to service the 12,000 machines during their warranty periods. The cost to produce and sell each machine, not including warranty costs, is $200. The company uses a perpetual inventory method and records the following journal entry at the time of sale:

| | | |
|---|---|---|
| Accounts Receivable | 360 | |
| Cost of Goods Sold | 200 | |
| Warranty Expense | 4 | |
|     Estimated Warranty Liability | | 4 |
|     Inventory | | 200 |
|     Sales Revenue | | 360 |

As warranty repairs are performed for customers, the cost of the repairs is debited to the Estimated Warranty Liability account. On December 31, the credit balance in that account is $36,000; the balance on January 1 was zero.

Before preparing financial statements for the year, management decides that it will use profit-center accounting for its warranty work and that the sale of a washing machine for $360 includes a "warranty policy" with fair market value of $12.

a. Assume that the profit-center approach had been used throughout the year. Prepare journal entries that would have been made for the year.

b. Prepare adjusting entries to convert the financial records to profit-center accounting from the method actually used.

c. Prepare an analysis showing the difference in pretax income for the year under the profit-center method of accounting for warranties and the warranty-expense method of accounting for warranties of Krasny Company.

16.58 (Adapted from CPA Examination.) The Trumb Radio Corporation manufactures television tubes and sells them with a 6-month warranty under which defective tubes will be replaced without a charge. On December 31, year 1, the Estimated Warranty Liability account had a credit balance of $510,000.

The company started out in year 2 expecting 8 percent of the dollar volume of sales to be returned. However, because of the introduction of new models during the year, this estimated percentage of returns was increased to 10 percent on May 1. It is assumed that no tubes sold during a given month are returned in that month. Each tube is stamped with a date at time of sale so that the warranty may be properly administered. The following table of percentages indicates the likely pattern of sales returns during the 6-month period of the warranty, starting with the month following the sale of tubes.

| Month Following Sale | Percentage of Total Returns Expected |
|---|---|
| First | 20% |
| Second | 30 |
| Third | 20 |
| Fourth through Sixth—10% Each Month | 30 |
| Total | 100% |

Gross sales of tubes were as follows for the first 6 months of year 2:

| Month | Amount |
|---|---|
| January | $3,600,000 |
| February | 3,300,000 |
| March | 4,100,000 |
| April | 2,850,000 |
| May | 2,000,000 |
| June | 1,800,000 |

The company's warranty also covers the payment of freight cost on defective tubes returned and on new tubes sent out as replacements. This freight cost runs approximately 10 percent of the sales price of the tubes returned. The manufacturing cost of the tubes is roughly 80 percent of sales price, and the salvage value of returned tubes averages 15 percent of their sales price. Returned tubes on hand are thus valued in inventory at 15 percent of their original sales price. The Estimated Warranty Liability account had a balance of $80,250 on June 30 of year 2.

a. Compute the required balance for the Estimated Warranty Liability account for June 30 of year 2.

b. Prepare the appropriate adjusting entries for warranty items as of June 30 of year 2.

16.59 The following events relate to compensated absences of the Matulich Company; give journal entries and explanations for each. The events are related to one another. Assume throughout the problem that the total cost of employees' compensation other than for compensated absences is $200 per day. Ignore income taxes and payroll taxes.

a. Office employees earn vested rights to 10 vacation days.

b. Factory employees earn nonvested, but accumulating, rights to 20 vacation days.

c. Office employees earn nonvested, accumulating rights to 10 sick days.

d. Factory employees earn vested rights to 15 sick days.

e. An office employee is paid for 4 vacation days.

f. An office employee is paid for 2 sick days.

g. A factory employee is paid for 3 days of jury duty.

h. An office employee has not been absent from work for sickness for several years. This employee has accumulated 75 sick days as of the end of this year. Only 60 of those days carry over to next year. The records are adjusted on December 31 to reflect this employee's loss of 15 accumulated sick days.

i. Same facts as in the preceding part, but the employee is paid a $2,000 bonus at the time the accumulation is reduced. The bonus is not part of the formal labor contract nor has it ordinarily been paid in the past when accumulated sick days have been carried over in reduced amounts.

# Chapter 17
# Noncurrent Liabilities: Mortgages, Notes, and Bonds

17.1 This chapter and the following two discuss obligations that require payments more than 1 year hence. A thorough knowledge of noncurrent liabilities requires understanding of compound interest and present-value computations. In these computations, payments made at different times are made comparable by taking into account the interest that cash can earn over time. Appendix B at the back of this book explains and illustrates the computations necessary for understanding the discussion of noncurrent liabilities.

17.2 The principal noncurrent liabilities are mortgages, notes, bonds, and leases. The significant differences between noncurrent and current liabilities, aside from the differences in length of time to maturity, are that: (1) interest on noncurrent liabilities is ordinarily paid at regular intervals during the life of an obligation, whereas interest on short-term debt is usually paid in a lump sum at maturity; (2a) the principal of noncurrent obligations is often paid back in installments, or (2b) special funds are accumulated by the borrower for retiring noncurrent liabilities.

## Liabilities as a Form of Long-Term Financing

17.3 A firm seeking new long-term capital has essentially two choices. It can issue new shares of capital stock (preferred or common), thereby changing the proportional interest of current owners. Or it can raise capital by issuing long-term debt. Raising funds by borrowing does not affect the proportional interest of current owners. More important, interest on indebtedness is deductible for income tax purposes, whereas dividends on common and preferred stock are not. Thus, a 10-percent bond issue will have a lower aftertax cost than a 7-percent preferred stock issue, as long as the marginal tax rate is more than 30 percent. At a 46-percent tax rate, the aftertax cost of the 10-percent bonds is 5.4 percent.

17.4 Writers in corporate finance disagree on whether or not the overall cost of capital of a firm can be reduced by using long-term debt as a means of obtaining capital. The traditional view holds that there is an optimum mix of equity (capital stock) and debt (bonds or notes) that will minimize the firm's cost of capital. This view holds that by issuing securities with differing degrees of risk, the firm can appeal to the preferences of different groups of investors, and, by the right combination, minimize its cost of capital. Another view holds that the cost of capital is independent of the financing instruments used but instead depends only on the risk and potential return of the assets used in the business. Although debt may be issued at a lower rate than the presently prevailing cost for common stock, the effect of the issuance of debt is to increase the risk of the residual equity (common stock) and thus to increase its cost. The overall cost of capital made up of the lower-rate debt and the now higher-cost common stock will be unaffected.

17.5 Many firms issue long-term debt instruments because their cost is lower than the rate currently being earned on the investments. This is known as providing "leverage" by borrowing. The potential rewards to financial leverage are great. If the firm can borrow funds for, say, a fixed 11-percent rate and invest them in projects that earn 20 percent, the difference accrues to the benefit of the owners of common shares. The potential rewards of leverage are, however, offset by the increased riskiness of the firm to the owners. Leverage is discussed more fully in Chapter 25.

17.6 Large amounts of long-term debt imply large amounts of fixed interest charges that must be met each period if the firm is to remain solvent. If the firm cannot meet its required debt-service payments (whether for bonds, mortgages, leases, or pensions), owners will find their investments much less valuable than before. Whether a given firm should use debt financing or ownership equity and whether it even makes a difference in the long run when all factors are considered are questions beyond the scope of financial accounting. These issues are discussed in corporate finance books.

## Procedures for Recording Noncurrent Monetary Liabilities

17.7 Accounting for all noncurrent monetary liabilities generally follows the same procedures. Those procedures are outlined next. We illustrate their application to various long-term liabilities throughout the rest of this chapter. The initial liability is recorded at the present value of all payments to be made. These payments are discounted at the market rate of interest appropriate to the liability when it is incurred. Historical cost accounting uses the market interest rate at the time the liability is recorded in three ways. First, at the time of initial recording,

it is used to compute the present value of the payments to be made. Second, it is used to compute the amount of interest expense throughout the life of the liability. Third, it can be used at any time to compute the present value of the remaining payments to be shown on the balance sheet.* A portion of each cash payment represents interest expense. Any excess of cash payment over interest expense is used to reduce the liability itself (often called the *principal*). If a given payment is not sufficient to discharge the entire interest expense that has accrued since the last payment date, then the liability principal is increased by the amount of the deficiency. Refer to Exhibit 15.4 for a comprehensive illustration of these principles.

17.8 Retirement of long-term liabilities can occur in several ways, but the recording is the same. The net amount shown on the books for the obligation is debited, the asset given up in return (usually cash) is credited, and any difference is recognized as a gain or loss upon retirement of the debt.

## Mortgages

17.9 A mortgage is a contract in which the lender is awarded legal title to certain property of the borrower, with the provision that the title reverts to the borrower when the loan is repaid in full. (In a few states, the lender merely acquires a lien on the borrower's property rather than legal title to it.) The mortgaged property is security for the loan. The customary terminology designates the lender as the "mortgagee" and the borrower as the "mortgagor."†

17.10 As long as the mortgagor meets the obligations under the mortgage agreement, the mortgagee does not have the ordinary rights of an owner to possess and use the property. If the mortgagor defaults on either the principal or interest payments, the mortgagee

---

*This last use does *not* result from a required calculation. Normally, the remaining balance in a noncurrent liability account (including its adjunct or contra account) is correct if the initial amount recorded is correct and if interest expense has been recorded in the fashion described in the text.

†When you borrow money to finance your loan purchase, you give the bank a mortgage, not vice versa.

can usually arrange to have the property sold for his or her benefit through a process called *foreclosure*. The mortgagee has first rights to the proceeds from the foreclosure sale for satisfying any unpaid claim. If there is an excess, it is paid to the mortgagor. If the proceeds are insufficient to pay the remaining loan, the lender becomes an unsecured creditor of the borrower for the unpaid balance. A mortgage, therefore, is a "recourse" loan.

## Accounting for Mortgages

17.11  Some of the more common problems in accounting for mortgages are presented in the following illustration.

17.12    On October 1, 1980, the Midwestern Products Company borrows $30,000 for 5 years from the Home Savings and Finance Company to obtain funds for additional working capital. As security, Midwestern Products Company gives Home Savings and Finance Company title to several parcels of land that it owns and that are on its books at a cost of $50,000. The interest rate is 8 percent per year compounded semiannually, with payments due on April 1 and October 1. Midwestern agrees to make 10 equal payments of $3,700 each over the 5 years of the mortgage so that when the last payment is made on October 1, 1985, the loan and all interest will have been paid. The Midwestern Products Company closes its books annually on December 31. (The derivation of the semiannual payment of $3,700 is shown in Example 11 in Appendix B at the end of the book.)

17.13    The entries from the time the mortgage is issued through December 31, 1981, are as follows:

October 1,1980
| | | |
|---|---|---|
| Cash | 30,000 | |
| Mortgage Payable | | 30,000 |

Loan obtained from Home Savings and Finance Company for 5 years at 8% compounded semiannually.

December 31, 1980
| | | |
|---|---|---|
| Interest Expense | 600 | |
| Interest Payable | | 600 |

Adjusting entry: Interest expense on mortgage from 10/1/1980 to 12/31/1980 (.04 × $30,000 × 3/6).

April 1, 1981
| | | |
|---|---|---|
| Interest Expense | 600 | |
| Interest Payable | 600 | |
| Mortgage Payable | 2,500 | |
| Cash | | 3,700 |

Cash payment made requires an entry. Interest expense on mortgage from 1/1/1981 to 4/1/1981, payment of 6 months' interest, and reduction of loan by the difference, $3,700 − $1,200 = $2,500.

October 1, 1981
| | | |
|---|---|---|
| Interest Expense | 1,100 | |
| Mortgage Payable | 2,600 | |
| Cash | | 3,700 |

Cash payment made requires an entry. Payment of interest for the period 4/1/1981 to 10/1/1981. Interest expense for the period is $1,100 [= .04 × ($30,000 − $2,500)]. The loan is reduced by the difference, $3,700 − $1,100 = $2,600.

December 31, 1981
| | | |
|---|---|---|
| Interest Expense | 498 | |
| Interest Payable | | 498 |

Adjusting entry: Interest expense from 10/1/1981 to 12/31/1981 [.04 × ($30,000 − $2,500 − $2,600) × 3/6].

Exhibit 17.1 presents an "amortization schedule" for this mortgage. It shows the allocation of each $3,700 payment between interest and repayment of principal. (The last payment, $3,685 in this case, often differs slightly from the others because of the cumulative effect of rounding errors.) Amortization schedules indicate both the amounts that are recorded each period and the amount of the outstanding loan at the end of each period.

**Foreclosure** Assume that the Midwestern  17.14 Products Company experiences a major, uninsured loss in February 1982 (during the third 6-month period in Exhibit 17.1) and is unable to make the required $3,700 payment on April 1, 1982. The Home Savings and Finance Company forecloses, the mortgaged property is sold at auction by the sheriff, and $40,000 is realized from the sale after deducting legal fees and other costs. The mortgagee receives a payment equal to the sum of the remaining principal, $24,900, and the

*Exhibit 17.1*

**Amortization Schedule for $30,000 Mortgage, Repaid in 10 Semiannual Installments of $3,700, Interest Rate of 8%, Compounded Semiannually**

**Semiannual Journal Entry**

Dr. Interest Expense ................................. Amount in Column (3)

Dr. Mortgage Payable ................................ Amount in Column (5)

    Cr. Cash .......................................... Amount in Column (4)

| 6-Month Period (1) | Mortgage Principal Start of Period (2) | Interest Expense for Period (3) | Payment (4) | Portion of Payment Reducing Principal (5) | Mortgage Principal End of Period (6) |
|---|---|---|---|---|---|
| 0 | | | | | $30,000 |
| 1 .............. | $30,000 | $1,200 | $3,700 | $2,500 | 27,500 |
| 2 .............. | 27,500 | 1,100 | 3,700 | 2,600 | 24,900 |
| 3 .............. | 24,900 | 996 | 3,700 | 2,704 | 22,196 |
| 4 .............. | 22,196 | 888 | 3,700 | 2,812 | 19,384 |
| 5 .............. | 19,384 | 775 | 3,700 | 2,925 | 16,459 |
| 6 .............. | 16,459 | 658 | 3,700 | 3,042 | 13,417 |
| 7 .............. | 13,417 | 537 | 3,700 | 3,163 | 10,254 |
| 8 .............. | 10,254 | 410 | 3,700 | 3,290 | 6,964 |
| 9 .............. | 6,964 | 279 | 3,700 | 3,421 | 3,543 |
| 10 .............. | 3,543 | 142 | 3,685 | 3,543 | 0 |

Column (2) = column (6) from previous period.

Column (3) = .04 × column (2).

Column (4) is given, except row 10, where it is the amount such that column (4) = column (2) + column (3).

Column (5) = column (4) − column (3).

Column (6) = column (2) − column (5).

interest due on April 1, 1982, $996. The remaining $14,104 is turned over to Midwestern. Because the mortgaged land was carried on the books at $50,000, a $10,000 loss must be recognized in reporting net income for 1982. The entry to record the foreclosure is

April 1, 1982

| | | |
|---|---|---|
| Cash ........................... | 14,104 | |
| Mortgage Payable ................. | 24,900 | |
| Interest Expense .................. | 498 | |
| Interest Payable ................... | 498 | |
| Loss on Disposition of Land through Foreclosure of Mortgage ........ | 10,000 | |
|     Land ...................... | | 50,000 |

If the proceeds of the foreclosure sale are less than $25,896 (= $24,900 + $498 + $498), then the total debt due Home Savings and Finance Company is not discharged. The lender in a mortgage loan usually has full *recourse* to the assets of the borrower. That is, the lender who is not paid in full with the proceeds of the foreclosure sale becomes an unsecured creditor of the borrower. The lender will look to the borrower's other assets for payment of the remaining debt. If the borrower goes into bankruptcy, then the lender, together with other creditors, will have a claim on the remaining assets.

## Long-Term Notes and Contracts

Real estate is often purchased on a *land contract*. Equipment is frequently acquired on

17.15

the installment plan, and the liability is called an *equipment contract*. Payments on such contracts are usually made monthly. Sometimes an explicit interest rate is provided in the contract, whereas in other cases so-called *carrying charges* are added to the purchase price, and the total is divided over a certain number of months without any specific charge being indicated for interest. A common arrangement, particularly in the case of real estate, is to have a regular monthly payment which is applied first to interest accrued since the last payment, with the balance of the payment reducing the principal.

17.16    Generally accepted accounting principles require that the liability be stated at the present value of the future cash payments using the appropriate interest rate for the borrower on the date of the loan.* The difference between the present value and the face value of the liability represents interest to be recognized over the period of the loan. If the note is recorded at its maturity value, then the interest, or discount, must be recorded in a contra account. A preferable but seldom used method is to record the liability at its net present value without the use of a contra account. The next two sections discuss two acceptable ways to compute the present value of the liability.

## Base Interest Rate on Market Value of Asset

17.17    The first approach uses the market value of the assets acquired as a basis for computing the present value of the liability. For example, assume that a piece of equipment has a list price of $12,000 but can be bought for $10,500 cash. The equipment is purchased in return for a single-payment note with face amount of $13,500 payable in 3 years. The implied interest rate is about 8.74 percent per year or about 4.28 percent compounded semiannually. (That is, $1.0874^3 \times \$10,500$ and $1.0428^6 \times \$10,500$ are both approximately equal to $13,500.) Using the approx-

---

*Accounting Principles Board, *APB Opinion No. 21*, "Interest on Receivables and Payables" (1971).

imate semiannual rate of 4.28 percent for six-month periods and the approximate annual interest rate of 8.74 percent for annual periods, the entries would be:

| | | |
|---|---|---|
| Equipment ...................... | 10,500 | |
| Discount on Long-Term Note | | |
| Payable ...................... | 3,000 | |
| Long-Term Note Payable ...... | | 13,500 |

To record purchase of equipment using the known cash price. The discount implicit in the note is inferred from the known cash price of the equipment.

At the end of each accounting period that intervenes between the acquisition of the equipment and repayment of the note, journal entries would be made to recognize interest expense. Assume that the first accounting period ends 6 months after the note is issued and that the second accounting period ends 1 year later, 18 months after the original issue. The entries would be:

(1)

| | | |
|---|---|---|
| Interest Expense .................. | 449 | |
| Discount on Long-Term Note | | |
| Payable .................. | | 449 |

Entry made 6 months after issue of note. Interest is .0428 × $10,500. The amount is not paid in cash but is added to the principal amount of the liability by a reduction in the amount of the discount. The entry to the discount account is a credit. Liabilities increase with credits, whether the amount is credited directly to the liability or to its contra.

(2)

| | | |
|---|---|---|
| Interest Expense .................. | 957 | |
| Discount on Long-Term Note | | |
| Payable .................. | | 957 |

Entry made 1 year after entry above, 1½ years after issue of note. Interest assuming annual compounding is .0874 × ($10,500 + $449).

(3)

| | | |
|---|---|---|
| Interest Expense .................. | 1,041 | |
| Discount on Long-Term Notes | | |
| Payable .................. | | 1,041 |

Entry made 1 year after entry (2). Interest is $1,041 = .0874 × ($10,500 + $449 + $957) = .0874 × $11,906.

(4)

| | | |
|---|---|---|
| Interest Expense ................. | 553 | |
| Discount on Long-Term Note | | |
| Payable .................... | | 553 |

Entry made $1/2$ year after entry (3) at maturity of note to reduce discount to zero. Interest is $13,500 − ($11,906 + $1,041) = $553, which is approximately equal to .0428 × ($11,906 + $1,041) = $554. The difference is the accumulated rounding error caused by using an approximation to the implicit interest rate.

(5)

| | | |
|---|---|---|
| Long-Term Note Payable ......... | 13,500 | |
| Cash ...................... | | 13,500 |

To repay note at maturity.

The discount is completely amortized by the time the single payment of $13,500 is made. Of that amount, $3,000 represents interest accumulated on the note since its issue.

## Use Market Interest Rate to Establish Market Value of Asset and Present Value of Note

17.18    If undeveloped land had been purchased with the same 3-year note, the firm might not be able to establish the current market value of the asset acquired. The firm would then use the interest rate it would have to pay for a similar loan in the open market to find the present value of the note. This is the second acceptable method for quantifying the amount of the liability. Suppose that the market rate for notes such as the one above is 8 percent compounded annually, rather than $8^3/4$ percent. The present value at 8 percent per year of the $13,500 note due in 3 years is $10,717 (= $13,500 × .79383; see Appendix Table 2 at the back of the book, 3-period row, 8-percent column). The entry to record the purchase of land and payment with the note would be

| | | |
|---|---|---|
| Land .......................... | 10,717 | |
| Discount on Long-Term Note | | |
| Payable ..................... | 2,783 | |
| Long-Term Note Payable ...... | | 13,500 |

To record purchase of land. Cost of land is inferred from known interest rate.

The discount on the note would then be amortized following the same procedure shown previously.

## Explicit Interest Not Equal to Market Rate

17.19    Some notes state interest rates that do not reasonably approximate the interest rate appropriate for the borrower under the circumstances. That explicit interest payments are paid does not necessarily imply that the interest rate appropriately reflects market conditions and, hence, that the face value of the note is its present value. Consider the equipment referred to above that has a list price of $12,000 but can be bought for $10,500 cash. Assume that Alexis Company acquires this equipment using a 3-year note with face value of $12,000 and requiring annual interest payments of 7 percent of the face value, or $840 per year. The accountant might be tempted to record the equipment at $12,000 cost and report interest expense of $840 per year over the 3-year life of the note. This treatment is not acceptable. Because the cash price of the equipment is $10,500, the borrower is paying a higher rate of interest than 7 percent. The rate implicit in this contract is about 12.2 percent. (Example 21 in Appendix B for Alexis Company illustrates the derivation of the 12.2-percent rate.)

17.20    APB *Opinion 21* requires that the accounting for the equipment and the note be based on the 12.2-percent rate appropriate for the borrower and the $10,500 cash price of the asset. The top panel of Exhibit 17.2 gives the details of the journal entries made each year. The entry upon acquisition would be

| | | |
|---|---|---|
| Equipment ...................... | 10,500 | |
| Discount on Note Payable ......... | 1,500 | |
| Note Payable ................. | | 12,000 |

Record asset at fair market value.

17.21    In cases like this, the accountant might feel more confident in an estimate of the interest rate appropriate for the borrower/purchaser than the estimate of the cash price of the asset. Assume, for example, that the accountant thought a 12-percent annual interest rate appropriate for this purchaser. The present

*Exhibit 17.2*
**Amortization Schedules
for a 3-Year Note with Face Value
of $12,000 Calling for 7%
Annual Interest Payments**

**Annual Journal Entry for Interest**
Dr. Interest Expense  . . . . . . . . . . . . . . . . . . . . . . . . . . . . . . . . . . .   Amount in Column (3)
    Cr. Cash  . . . . . . . . . . . . . . . . . . . . . . . . . . . . . . . . . . . . . . . .   Amount in Column (4)
    Cr. Note Payable (or Discount on Note Payable)  . . . . . .   Amount in Column (5)

| Year (1) | Note Principal Start of Year (2) | Interest Expense for Period (3) | Payment (4) | Interest Added to Principal (5) | Note Principal End of Year (6) |
|---|---|---|---|---|---|
| **I. Known Present Value of Note of $10,500, Implying 12.2% Effective Interest Rate (See Alexis Company Example in Appendix B)** | | | | | |
| 0 | | | | | $10,500 |
| 1 . . . . . . . . . . . . . | $10,500 | $1,281 | $840 | $441 | 10,941 |
| 2 . . . . . . . . . . . . . | 10,941 | 1,335 | 840 | 495 | 11,436 |
| 3 . . . . . . . . . . . . . | 11,436 | 1,404 | 840 | 564 | 12,000 |
| **II. Known Effective Interest Rate of 12.0%, Implying a Present Value of $10,560** | | | | | |
| 0 | | | | | $10,560 |
| 1 . . . . . . . . . . . . . | $10,560 | $1,267 | $840 | $427 | 10,987 |
| 2 . . . . . . . . . . . . . | 10,987 | 1,318 | 840 | 478 | 11,465 |
| 3 . . . . . . . . . . . . . | 11,465 | 1,375 | 840 | 535 | 12,000 |

Column (2) = column (6) from previous year.

Column (3) = interest rate of .122 in panel I and .12 in panel II × oolumn (2) except in last year, where the amount is a plug so that $12,000 − $11,436 ⊢ $840 − $1,404 In panel I and $12,000 − $11,465 + $840 = $1,375 in panel II.

Column (4) is given by the terms of the note.

Column (5) = column (3) − column (4).

Column (6) = column (5) + column (2) = column (2) ⊢ oolumn (3) − column (4).

value of a $12,000 note with $12,000 face value and 7-percent annual interest payments maturing in 3 years discounted at 12 percent is $10,560, computed as shown below.

Present value of $840 per year paid at the end of each of the next 3 years, discounted at 12 percent, using factor from Appendix Table 4, 3-period row, 12-percent column):
$840 × 2.40183  . . . . . . . . . . . . . . . . . . . . . . . .   $ 2,018

Present value of $12,000 single payment paid 3 years hence, discounted at 12 percent, using factor from Appendix Table 2, 3-period row, 12-percent column: $12,000 × .71178  . . . . . . . . . . . . . . . . . . . . . . . . . . .   8,542

Total present value  . . . . . . . . . . . . . . . . . . . . . .   $10,560

Then, the asset is recorded at a cost of $10,560, and interest expense on the note is based on the amortization schedule in the bottom panel of Exhibit 17.2.

17.22   APB *Opinion No. 21* implies that the accountant will often be able to estimate the appropriate interest rate and not the effective cash price of the asset. It provides guidance about estimating the interest rate to be used in finding the effective cash price of the asset.* The process is called "interest imputation"; the estimated rate is called the "imputed rate."

17.23   A note that is the long-term liability of the borrower is a long-term asset of the lender.

*APB *Opinion No. 21,* pars. 13 and 14.

Generally accepted accounting principles require the lender to state the asset in the Long-Term Note Receivable account at its present value net of its discount. The rate at which the lender discounts the note should in theory be the same as that used by the borrower, but in practice the two rates often differ. Chapters 7 and 14 illustrate the lender's accounting.

### Funds Statement Effects of Interest Imputation

17.24 The amortization of discount over the life of a long-term note when the explicit interest rate is less than the effective interest rate is an item of expense not using funds in the amount of the expense. The funds statement must show an addback to net income for the amounts of interest expense not using funds. In Exhibit 17.2, these are the amounts in column (5).

# Bonds

17.25 Mortgages or notes are used whenever the funds being borrowed can be obtained from a small number of sources. When large amounts are needed, the firm may have to borrow from the general investing public through the use of a bond issue. Bonds are used primarily by corporations and governmental units. The distinctive features of a bond issue are as follows:

**1.** A *bond indenture,* or agreement, is drawn up, which shows in detail the terms of the loan and the rights and duties of the borrower and other parties to the contract.

**2.** *Bond certificates* are used. Engraved certificates are prepared, each one representing a portion of the total loan. The usual minimum denomination in business practice is $1,000, although smaller denominations are used occasionally. Government bonds are issued in denominations as small as $100.

**3.** If property is pledged as security for the loan (as in a mortgage bond), then a *trustee* is named to hold title to the property serving as security. The trustee acts as the represen-

tative of the bondholders and is usually a bank or trust company.

**4.** An agent is appointed, usually a bank or trust company, to act as *registrar* and *disbursing agent*. The borrower deposits interest and principal payments with the disbursing agent, who distributes the funds to the bondholders.

**5.** Many bonds are *coupon bonds*. Coupons are attached to the bond certificate covering the interest payments throughout the life of the bond. When a coupon comes due, the bondholder cuts it off and deposits it with a bank. The bank sends the coupon through the bank clearing system to the disbursing agent for payment, which is deposited in the bondholder's account at the bank.

**6.** Bonds are frequently *registered as to principal,* which means that the bondholder's name appears on the bond certificate and on the records of the registrar. Sometimes both the principal and interest of bonds are registered, in which case the interest payments are mailed directly to the bondholder and coupons are not used. Registered bonds are easily replaced if lost, but the transfer from one holder to another is cumbersome. Unregistered bonds may be transferred merely by delivery, whereas registered bonds have to be assigned formally from one holder to another.

**7.** The entire bond issue is usually issued by the borrower to an investment banking firm, or to a group of investment bankers known as a *syndicate,* which takes over the responsibility of reselling the bonds to the investing public. Members of the syndicate usually bear the risks and rewards of interest-rate fluctuations during the period while the bonds are being sold to the public.

### Types of Bonds

17.26 *Mortgage bonds* carry a mortgage on real estate as security for the repayment of the loan. *Collateral trust bonds* are usually secured by stocks and bonds of other corporations. The most common type of corporate bond, except in the railroad and public utility industries, is the *debenture bond*. This type carries no special security or collateral;

instead, it is issued on the general credit of the business. To give added protection to the bondholders, provisions are usually included in the bond indenture that limit the amount of subsequent long-term debt that can be incurred. *Convertible bonds* are debentures that the holder can exchange, possibly after some specific period of time has elapsed, for a specific number of shares of capital stock.

17.27    Almost all bonds provide for the payment of interest at regular intervals, usually semiannually. The amount of interest is typically expressed as a percentage of the principal. For example, an 8-percent, 10-year semiannual coupon bond with face or principal amount of $1,000 promises to pay $40 every 6 months. The first payment generally occurs 6 months after the bond issue date, until a total of 20 payments is made. At the time of the final $40 coupon payment, the $1,000 principal is also due. The coupon rate is 8 percent in this case. The principal amount of a bond is its face, or par, value. The terms *face value* and *par value* are used synonymously in this context. In general, the par amount multiplied by the coupon rate equals the amount of cash paid per *year,* whether in quarterly, semiannual, or annual installments. By far the majority of corporate bonds provide for semiannual coupon payments. A bond can be issued and subsequently traded in the marketplace below par, at par, or above par.

## Proceeds of a Bond Issue

17.28    The amount received by the borrower may be more or less than the par value of the bonds issued. The difference arises primarily because there is a difference between the coupon rate printed on the bond certificates and the interest rate the market requires the firm to pay to borrow under the circumstances. If the coupon rate is less than the market rate for this firm, then the bonds will sell for less than par. The difference between par and selling price is called the *discount* on the bond. If the coupon rate is larger than the rate the market requires, the bonds will sell above par. The difference between selling price and par is called the *premium* on the bond.

The presence of a discount or premium in and of itself indicates nothing about the credit standing of the borrower. A firm with a credit standing that would enable it to borrow funds at $9^1/_4$ percent might issue 9-percent bonds that would sell at a discount, whereas another firm with a lower credit standing that would require it to pay $9^3/_4$ percent on loans might issue bonds at 10 percent, which would sell at a premium.

17.29

**Marketing Arrangements and Issuing Costs**  Bonds may be issued directly by the borrowing company. Small, new companies dealing in a local market may find direct issuance the most cost-effective way to reach the market. Most bond issues (and nearly all dollar amounts raised with bond issues) are, however, marketed through investment bankers. The banker "underwrites" the issue. *Underwriting* a bond issue means promising the borrower a fixed amount of funds, taking the risk of price fluctuations between the date of making the promise and issuing the bonds to the lenders, handling many of the legal aspects of the bond issue, as well as arranging for printing and distribution of the certificates. Thus the issuing company is selling "wholesale" to the investment banker, who resells, like a retailer. The net proceeds received by the issuer will not be equal to the total amounts paid for the bonds by their purchasers, the lenders, because of brokerage commissions required by the investment banker. The issuing company, in our opinion, should account only for the net proceeds received. The implied interest rate used in computing interest expense over the life of the bond issue will then be somewhat higher than the lenders are receiving. APB *Opinion No. 21* requires, however, that the net credit to Bonds Payable should be for the amounts of cash paid by the lenders;* the difference between the

17.30

---

*The net amount can be credited directly to Bonds Payable, or the par value can be credited to Bonds Payable with the appropriate debit (plug) made to Discount on Bonds Payable (or the appropriate credit plug made to Premium on Bonds Payable).

amount credited to Bonds Payable and the amount received, debited to Cash, is shown as an asset, Bond Issue Costs, to be amortized over the life of the bond issue.* In our opinion, this refinement does not add anything of conceptual importance.

17.31    The following illustrations cover the calculations of the proceeds of a bond issue when the market interest rate is equal to, more than, and less than the coupon rate.

17.32    **Bonds Issued at Par** The Macaulay Corporation issues $100,000 face value of 8-percent semiannual coupon debenture bonds. The bonds are dated July 1, 1981, and are due July 1, 1991. Coupons are dated July 1 and January 1. The coupon payments promised at each interest payment date total $4,000. Assuming that the issue was taken by L. Fisher and Company, investment bankers, on July 1, 1981, at a rate to yield 8 percent compounded semiannually and that there is no brokerage commission, the calculation of the proceeds to Macaulay would be as follows.

(a)
Present value of $100,000 to be paid at the
   end of 10 years ..................... $ 45,639
(Appendix Table 2 at the back of the book shows the present value of $1 to be paid in 20 periods at 4% per period to be $.45639; $100,000 × .45639 = $45,639.)

(b)
Present value of $4,000 to be paid each 6
   months for 10 years ................. 54,361
(Appendix Table 4 shows the present value of an ordinary annuity of $1 per period for 20 periods discounted at 4% to be $13.59033; $4,000 × 13.59033 = $54,361.)
Total proceeds ........................ $100,000

The issue price would be stated as 100 (that is, 100 percent of par), which implies that the market rate was 8 percent compounded semiannually, the same as the coupon rate.

---

*APB *Opinion No. 21*, par. 16. This treatment, which we question on theoretical grounds, has also been questioned by the Financial Accounting Standards Board in paragraph 161 of *Statement of Finanacial Accounting Concepts No. 3* (1980).

**Bonds Issued at Discount** Assuming that the bonds were issued at a price to yield 9 percent compounded semiannually, the calculation of the proceeds would be shown below. The reason that "8-percent" bonds can be issued to yield 9 percent is discussed in paragraph 17.42. (The tables at the back of the book do *not* include columns for $4\frac{1}{2}$ percent.)†    17.33

(a)
Present value of $100,000 to be paid at the
   end of 10 years ..................... $41,464
(Present value of $1 to be paid in 20 periods at $4\frac{1}{2}$% per period is $0.41464; $100,000 × 0.41464 = $41,464.)

(b)
Present value of $4,000 to be paid each 6
   months for 10 years ................. 52,032
(Present value of an ordinary annuity of $1 per period for 20 periods, discounted at $4\frac{1}{2}$% per period = $13.00794; $4,000 × 13.00794 = $52,032.)
Total proceeds ........................ $ 93,496

If the issue price were stated on a conventional pricing basis in the market at 93.50 (93.50 percent of par), the issuing price would be $93,500. This amount implies a market yield of slightly less than 9 percent compounded semiannually.

**Bonds Issued at Premium** Assuming that the bonds were issued at a price to yield 7 percent compounded semiannually, the calculation of the proceeds would be as follows. (The tables at the back of the book do not include columns for $3\frac{1}{2}$ percent.)**    17.34

(a)
Present value of $100,000 to be paid at the
   end of 10 years ..................... $ 50,257
(Present value of $1 to be received in 20 periods at $3\frac{1}{2}$% per period is $0.50257; $100,000 × 0.50257 = $50,257.)

---

†A calculator with an exponent feature can be used to show that $(1.045)^{-20} = 0.41464$. The formula at the top of Appendix B Table 4 can be used to compute the present value of an annuity for 20 periods discounted at 4.5 percent per period: $13.008 = (1 - .41464)/.045$.

**$(1.035)^{-20} = 0.50257$; $(1 - 50257)/.035 = 14.21240$.

(b)

| | |
|---|---|
| Present value of $4,000 to be paid each 6 months for 10 years .................. | 56,850 |

(Present value of an ordinary annuity at $1 per period for 20 periods, discounted at 3½% per period = $14.21240; $4,000 × 14.21240 = $56,850.)

| | |
|---|---|
| Total proceeds ...................... | $107,107 |

If the issue price were stated on a conventional pricing basis in the market at 107.11 (107.11 percent of par), the issuing price would be $107,110.* This price would imply a market yield of slightly less than 7 percent compounded semiannually.

## Bond Tables

17.35 Fortunately, these tedious calculations need not be made every time a bond issue is analyzed. Special bond tables have been prepared to show the results of calculations like those just described. Examples of such tables are included in the tables at the back of the book. Table 5 in the Appendix shows for 6-percent, semiannual coupon bonds the price as a percent of par for various market interest rates (yields) and years to maturity. Table 6 shows market rates and implied prices for 8-percent, semiannual coupon bonds. (Some modern electronic calculators are capable of making the calculations represented by these tables in a few seconds.)

17.36 The percentages of par shown in these tables represent the present value of the bond indicated. Because the factors are expressed as a percent of par, they have to be multiplied by 10 to find the price of a $1,000 bond.

---

*In many contexts, bond prices are quoted in dollars plus thirty-seconds of a dollar. A bond selling for about 107.107 percent of par would be quoted at 107³/₃₂, which would be written as 107.3. In order to read published bond prices, you must know whether the information after the "decimal" point refers to fractions expressed in one-hundredths or in thirty-seconds. (If you are reading published bond prices and see any number larger than 31 after the decimal point, you can be sure that one-hundredths are being used. If you see many prices, but none of the numbers shown after the point is larger than 31, then you can be reasonably sure that thirty-seconds are being used.) In this book, we use decimal fractions, that is, one-hundredths.

If you have never used bond tables before, turn to Table 6 following Appendix B and find in the 10-year column the three different prices for the three different market yields used in the preceding example. Notice further that a bond will sell at par if and only if it has a market yield equal to its coupon rate.

17.37 These tables are useful whether a bond is being issued by a corporation or resold later by an investor. The approach to determining the market price will be the same in either case, although the years to maturity will be less than the original term of the bond when it is resold. The following generalizations can be made regarding bond prices:

**1.** When the market rate equals the coupon rate, the market price will equal par.

**2.** When the market rate is greater than the coupon rate, the market price will be less than par.

**3.** When the market rate is less than the coupon rate, the market price will be greater than par.

## Accounting for Bonds Issued at Par

17.38 The following illustration covers the more common problems associated with bonds issued at par.

17.39 We use the data presented in the previous sections for the Macaulay Corporation, in which the bonds were issued at par, and we assume that the books are closed semiannually on June 30 and December 31. The entry at the time of issue would be

| July 1, 1981 | | |
|---|---|---|
| Cash ........................ | 100,000 | |
| Debenture Bonds Payable ... | | 100,000 |

$100,000 of 8%, 10-year bonds issued at par.

The entries for interest would be made at the end of the accounting period and on the interest payment dates. Entries through January 2, 1982, would be

| December 31, 1981 | | |
|---|---|---|
| Interest Expense ............... | 4,000 | |
| Interest Payable ............ | | 4,000 |

To record accrual of 6 months' interest.

January 2, 1982

| | | |
|---|---|---|
| Interest Payable ................ | 4,000 | |
| Cash ...................... | | 4,000 |

To record payment of 6 months' interest.

17.40 **Bonds Issued between Interest Payment Dates** The actual date when a bond is issued seldom coincides with one of the payment dates. Assuming that these same bonds were actually brought to market on August 1, rather than July 1, and were issued at par, the purchaser of the bond would be expected to pay Macaulay Corporation for 1 month's interest in advance. After all, on the first coupon Macaulay Corporation promises a full $4,000 for 6 months' interest, but would have had the use of the borrowed funds for only 5 months. The purchasers of the bonds would pay $100,000 plus 1 month's interest of $667 (= .04 × $100,000 × $1/6$) and would get the $667 back when the first coupons were redeemed. The journal entries made by Macaulay Corporation, the issuer, would be

August 1, 1981

| | | |
|---|---|---|
| Cash ........................ | 100,667 | |
| Bonds Payable ............. | | 100,000 |
| Interest Payable ............ | | 667 |

To record issue of bonds at par between interest payment dates. The purchasers pay an amount equal to interest for the first month but will get it back when the first coupons are redeemed.

December 31, 1981

| | | |
|---|---|---|
| Interest Expense ............... | 3,333 | |
| Interest Payable ............ | | 3,333 |

Accrual of interest for 5 months = .04 × $100,000 × $5/6$. The Interest Payable account now has a credit balance of $4,000 (= $667 + $3,333).

January 2, 1982

| | | |
|---|---|---|
| Interest Payable ................ | 4,000 | |
| Cash ...................... | | 4,000 |

To record payment of 6 months' interest.

Note that interest expense in 1981 amounts to only $3,333, even though the first coupons total $4,000. After the first coupon payment date, the accounting will be identical for bonds originally issued on an interest payment date or between interest payment dates.

## Accounting for Bonds Issued at a Discount

17.41 The following illustration covers the more common problems associated with bonds issued at a discount.

17.42 Assume the data presented for the Macaulay Corporation, in which the bonds were issued for $93,500 to yield approximately 9 percent compounded semiannually and the books are closed on June 30 and December 31. The entry at the time of issue would be

July 1, 1981

| | | |
|---|---|---|
| Cash ......................... | 93,500 | |
| Discount on Debenture Bonds Payable ..................... | 6,500 | |
| Debenture Bonds Payable .... | | 100,000 |

$100,000 of 8%, 10-year bonds issued at a discount.

The discount is primarily an indication that 8 percent is not a sufficiently high rate of interest for the bonds to bring their face value in the open market. Because the market requires approximately 9 percent compounded semiannually, Macaulay actually acquires the use of only $93,500. Macaulay agrees to pay to bondholders the face value of $100,000 when the bond matures as well as the 20 semiannual payments of $4,000 each. The difference between the par value and the amount of proceeds, $6,500, represents additional interest that will be paid as a part of the face value at maturity. Thus the total interest that must be charged to the periods during which the loan is outstanding is $86,500 (periodic payments totaling $80,000 plus the $6,500 included in the principal payment at maturity). Two acceptable methods of allocating the total interest of $86,500 to the periods of the loan are the effective-interest method and the straight-line method.

## Interest Expense under the Effective-Interest Method

17.43 Interest *payable* each period is equal to the coupon interest rate multiplied by the principal or face amount of the liability. Interest

*Exhibit 17.3*
**Effective-Interest Discount
Amortization Schedule for
$100,000 of 8%, 10-Year Bonds
Issued for 93.5% of Par to Yield 9%,
Interest Payable Semiannually**

**Semiannual Journal Entry**

Dr. Interest Expense ............................... Amount in Column (3)
    Cr. Cash ......................................... Amount in Column (4)
    Cr. Discount on Debenture Bonds Payable .......... Amount in Column (5)

| Period (6-Month Intervals) (1) | Liability at Start of Period (2) | Effective Interest: 4½% per Period (3) | Coupon Rate: 4% of Par (4) | Discount Amortization (5) | End of Period Unamortized Discount (6) | End of Period Net Liability (7) |
|---|---|---|---|---|---|---|
| 0 | | | | | $6,500.00 | $93,500.00 |
| 1 ........ | $93,500.00 | $ 4,207.50 | $ 4,000.00 | $ 207.50 | 6,292.50 | 93,707.50 |
| 2 ........ | 93,707.50 | 4,216.84 | 4,000.00 | 216.84 | 6,075.66 | 93,924.34 |
| 3 ........ | 93,924.34 | 4,226.60 | 4,000.00 | 226.60 | 5,849.06 | 94,150.94 |
| 4 ........ | 94,150.94 | 4,236.79 | 4,000.00 | 236.79 | 5,612.27 | 94,387.73 |
| (calculations continued for 20 periods) | | | | | | |
| 20 ........ | 99,521.53 | 4,478.47 | 4,000.00 | 478.47 | 0 | 100,000.00 |
| Total ................... | | $86,500.00 | $80,000.00 | $6,500.00 | | |

Column (2) = column (7) from previous period.
Column (3) = .045 × column (2).
Column (4) is given.
Column (5) = column (3) − column (4).
Column (6) = column (6) from previous period − column (5) of this period.
Column (7) = column (2) + column (5) = $100,000.00 − column (6).

*expense* each period under the effective-interest method is equal to the market rate at the time the bonds were originally issued multiplied by the amount of the bond liability shown on the books at the beginning of the interest period. When bonds are initially issued at a discount, the amount of interest expense will exceed the coupon payment at each payment date. In the example, on the first interest payment date the interest expense is $93,500 × .045 = $4,207.50. Only $4,000 will be paid in cash at that time. The remaining $207.50 will reduce the Discount on Debenture Bonds Payable account (from $6,500 to $6,292.50) and increase the net amount of the liability shown on the balance sheet. The amount of effective liability for the next 6-month period is $93,707.50 (= $93,500.000 + $207.50). In the second 6-month period, interest expense will be computed on a new, larger dollar amount. Interest will exceed that of the first 6-month period: $93,707.50 × .045 = $4,216.84. Interest expense increases each period as the amount effectively borrowed increases.

The periodic interest expense recorded in the accounting records must include both the coupon payment and an expense representing an allocation of an appropriate part of the discount. This process of allocating the discount as extra interest expense over the life of the bond is called *amortization*. An amortization schedule like the one shown in Exhibit 17.3, which assumes an annual market yield of 9 percent with interest compounded and payable semiannually, would be prepared.

The interest expense for a period, shown

17.44

17.45

in column (3), is calculated by multiplying the net liability at the start of the period [column (2)] by the market rate on the bond issue *at the time of issue*. Because the market yield at issue is 9 percent compounded semi-annually, the market rate for the 6-month period is 4¹/₂ percent. The net liability [column (7)] is increased at the end of each 6-month period by the amount of discount amortization for the period.

17.46    The interest-related entries through June 30, 1982, would be as follows:

December 31, 1981
Interest Expense  . . . . . . . . . . . . . .  4,207.50
  Discount on Debenture
    Bonds Payable  . . . . . . . . .           207.50
  Interest Payable  . . . . . . . . . . .     4,000.00
To record accrual of interest and amortization of discount for 6 months.

January 2, 1982
Interest Payable  . . . . . . . . . . . . . . .  4,000.00
  Cash  . . . . . . . . . . . . . . . . . . .          4,000.00
To record payment of interest for 6 months.

June 30, 1982
Interest Expense  . . . . . . . . . . . . . .  4,216.84
  Discount on Debenture Bonds
    Payable  . . . . . . . . . . . . . . .              216.84
  Interest Payable  . . . . . . . . . . . .           4,000.00
To record accrual of interest and amortization of discount for the second 6 months.

The series of entries will continue with an increasing amount of amortization each 6-month period until the entire discount is amortized by the maturity date, July 1, 1991. Exhibit 17.3 shows interest expense in column (3) and the credit to the Discount account in column (5) for each of the entries. This method is often called the ''effective-interest method'' of accounting for bond discount.

17.47    The Discount on Debenture Bonds Payable account is a contra-liability account, because the discount represents additional interest that will be paid as part of the face value at maturity. The Discount on Debenture Bonds Payable should be shown on the balance sheet as a deduction from the liability account, Debenture Bonds Payable. The balance sheet for December 31, 1981, would show

Debenture Bonds Payable  . $100,000.00
Less: Discount on
  Debenture Bonds
    Payable  . . . . . . . . . . . . . .    6,292.50 $93,707.50

## Interest Expense under the Straight-Line Method

17.48    The amortization of bond discount by the effective-interest method results from using a constant interest rate over the life of the bond issue, 4.5 percent per 6 months in the example. Because the amount of the principal liability increases each period, the amount of interest expense increases each period. Some accountants find the calculations of the effective-interest method too tedious and too hard to understand. They often use the *straight-line method* of amortizing bond discount. In the straight-line method, the *amount* of interest expense is constant each period; because the amount of the principal liability increases, the implied interest rate decreases.

17.49    Under the straight-line method, the amount of discount to be amortized every 6 months is the total discount to be amortized over the life of the bond divided by the number of half-years of the bond's life. In this illustration, the semiannual straight-line amortization of bond discount is $325 (= $6,500/20) per 6 months until the discount is fully amortized at the maturity date.

The entries to record the interest expense through January 2, 1982, would be

December 31, 1981
Interest Expense  . . . . . . . . . . . . . . . . . . . .  4,325
  Interest Payable  . . . . . . . . . . . . . . . .          4,000
  Discount on Debenture Bonds
    Payable  . . . . . . . . . . . . . . . . . . . . .           325
To record the accrual of interest and amortization of discount for 6 months.

January 2, 1982
Interest Payable  . . . . . . . . . . . . . . . . . . . .  4,000
  Cash in Bank  . . . . . . . . . . . . . . . . . . .          4,000
To record payment of 6 months' interest.

Similar entries with identical dollar amounts would be made every 6 months throughout the life of the bond issue.

## Preferred Method of Amortizing Bond Discount

17.50   In practice, many companies use the straight-line method of amortizing bond discount. Most of the accountants working in these companies were trained in the era preceding inexpensive calculating devices. They act as though the calculations required by the effective-interest method are too tedious to be done regularly. The effective-interest method may appear more difficult, but it is based on the same concepts and procedures used for all long-term liabilities illustrated in Chapter 15 and in this chapter.

## Amortization of Bond Discount in the Statement of Changes in Financial Position

17.51   The amortization of discount requires special treatment in the statement of changes in financial position. Assuming that the straight-line method of amortizing bond discount is used, interest expense reported for the first 6 months is $4,325: $4,000 in coupon payments and $325 in discount amortization. Notice that only $4,000 of working capital was used for the expense. There was an increase in Interest Payable of $4,000 followed by discharge of that current liability with a cash payment. The remainder of the interest expense, $325, is an increase in the net noncurrent liability Debenture Bonds Payable less Discount on Debenture Bonds Payable. Consequently, there must be an *addback* to net income in determining "funds provided by operations" in the statement of changes in financial position. The amount of the addback is the amount of the expense that did not use working capital, $325. Under the effective-interest method, the addback is the amount in column (5) of the amortization schedule, $207.50 in the first period and $478.47 in the last.

## Accounting for Bonds Issued at a Premium

17.52   The following illustration covers the more common problems associated with bonds issued at a premium.

17.53   Assume now that, for whatever reason (such as the company's fine credit standing), the marketplace requires a return of only 7 percent from investments in Macaulay Corporation bonds. If Macaulay Corporation promises to pay $80 interest each year for every bond issued (in the form of 8-percent coupons), then the marketplace is willing to pay more than $1,000 for the bond. (The marketplace, is, under these assumptions, willing to pay $1,000 for a bond of Macaulay Corporation promising only $70 per year.) It will pay enough more so that the total cash payments by Macaulay Corporation, $40 per 6-month period plus $1,000 paid in 10 years, will exactly equal a 7-percent rate on the original price paid for the bond. The earlier calculation showed that amount to be approximately $1,071 (paragraph 17.34).

17.54   We assume that Macaulay Corporation issues $100,000 of par-value, 8-percent, semi-annual coupon bonds to mature in 10 years. It receives $107,100. The books are closed on June 30 and December 31 of each year. The entry at the time of issue would be

July 1, 1981
| | | |
|---|---|---|
| Cash ..................... | 107,100 | |
|    Debenture Bonds Payable ... | | 100,000 |
|    Premium on Debenture Bonds | | |
|      Payable ................. | | 7,100 |

$100,000 of 8%, 10-year bonds issued at a premium. The premium is recorded in a separate liability-adjunct account.

The extra $7,100 received by Macaulay Corporation at the time of issue represents an extra amount that the market is willing to lend in return for being paid $80 per year, rather than $70 per year, per bond. Because the market required only $70 per year but is being paid $80 per year, a portion of each coupon payment represents a return of the principal amount lent to Macaulay Corporation. Macaulay Corporation borrowed

$107,100. Observe that interest for the first 6-month period under the effective-interest method is only $3,748.50 (= .035 × $107,100). Macaulay Corporation pays $4,000 in cash at the end of the first 6-month period. The difference, $251.50 (= $4,000.00 − $3,748.50), is a partial return of principal to the lenders.

17.55    When the bonds are issued at a premium, an amortization schedule such as the one shown in Exhibit 17.4 is prepared. The total premium amortization (sum of the partial principal repayments) over the life of the bond issue will be exactly $7,100. The journal entries made on December 31, 1981, to recognize interest expense and on January 2, 1982, to record the interest payment would be

December 31, 1981
Interest Expense ............... 3,748.50
Premium on Debenture Bonds
    Payable .................... 251.50
        Interest Payable ............ 4,000.00
To record the accrual of inter-
est and amortization of premium
for 6 months.

January 2, 1982
Interest Payable ................ 4,000.00
    Cash .................... 4,000.00
To record payment of 6 months'
interest.

---

## Exhibit 17.4
### Effective-Interest Premium Amortization Schedule for $100,000 of 8%, 10-Year Bonds Issued for 107.1% of Par to Yield 7%, Interest Payable Semiannually

**Semiannual Journal Entry**
Dr. Interest Expense ................................... Amount in Column (3)
Dr. Premium on Debenture Bonds Payable ............... Amount in Column (5)
   Cr. Cash ......................................... Amount in Column (4)

| Period (6-Month Intervals) (1) | Liability at Start of Period (2) | Effective Interest 3½% per Period (3) | Coupon Rate 4% of Par (4) | Premium Amortization (5) | End of Period Unamortized Premium (6) | End of Period Net Liability (7) |
|---|---|---|---|---|---|---|
| 0 | | | | | $7,100.00 | $107,100.00 |
| 1 ........ | $107,100.00 | $ 3,748.50 | $ 4,000.00 | $ 251.50 | 6,848.50 | 106,848.50 |
| 2 ........ | 106,848.50 | 3,739.70 | 4,000.00 | 260.30 | 6,588.20 | 106,588.20 |
| 3 ........ | 106,588.20 | 3,730.59 | 4,000.00 | 269.41 | 6,318.79 | 106,318.79 |
| 4 ........ | 106,318.79 | 3,721.16 | 4,000.00 | 278.84 | 6,039.95 | 106,039.95 |
| (calculations continued for 20 periods) | | | | | | |
| 20 ........ | 100,483.09 | 3,516.91 | 4,000.00 | 483.09 | 0 | 100,000.00 |
| Total .................... | | $72,900.00 | $80,000.00 | $7,100.00 | | |

Column (2) = column (7) from previous period.

Column (3) = .035 × column (2).

Column (4) is given.

Column (5) = column (4) − column (3).

Column (6) = column (6) from previous period − column (5) of this period.

Column (7) = column (2) − column (5) = $100,000.00 + column (6).

Entries similar to these but with different amounts will continue until July 1, 1991, when the bond premium will be completely amortized and the face value of the bonds will be paid.

17.56 The Premium on Debenture Bonds Payable account, like the parallel discount account when the market rate exceeds the coupon rate, represents an adjustment in the amount of borrowing. When premium is amortized, either at an interest-payment date or at the end of an accounting period, the journal entry shows that interest expense is *less* than the amount of cash paid out for redemption of coupons.

17.57 The interest expense on the loan each period is the effective interest rate at time of issue, 3.5 percent per 6-month period in the example, multiplied by the amount of the principal borrowed each period. The amount of interest expense declines from period to period. Because $4,000 cash is paid each period, the amount of principal repaid must therefore *increase* from period to period.

17.58 The Premium on Bonds Payable account is an adjunct to, or an addition to, the liability account Debenture Bonds Payable.

17.59 **Straight-Line Amortization of Bond Premium** As in the case of discount amortization, a straight line method could be used. In the straight line method, the amount of premium amortization recorded each period will be constant. In the example, the total premium to be amortized over 20 six-month periods is $7,100. The amount to be amortized each 6-month period is $355 (= $7,100/20). The entry every 6 months is

| | | |
|---|---|---|
| Interest Expense | 3,645 | |
| Premium on Debenture Bonds Payable | 355 | |
| Cash | | 4,000 |

Because the principal amount borrowed each period declines, this results in showing an ever-increasing interest rate. In the effective-interest method, the interest rate is constant and the dollar amount of premium amortization increases.

## Amortization of Bond Premium in the Statement of Changes in Financial Position

17.60 When the amount of interest expense is less than the amount of cash that is paid for interest expense, there must be an adjustment on the funds statement. More funds are used for the semiannual payment than are reported as interest expense. Thus, in deriving funds provided from operations, the amount of premium amortization [column (5) of Exhibit 17.4] might be *subtracted* from net income. Alternatively, because the extra funds were used as a reduction of the effective liability, the amount of premium amortization might be shown as an "other" use of funds (debt retirement) below funds provided by operations.

## Bond Retirement

17.61 Many bonds remain outstanding until the stated maturity date. The company pays the final coupon, $4,000 in the Macaulay example, and the face amount, $100,000 in the example, on the stated maturity date. The retirement of bonds originally issued at par is illustrated here. (The entry recognizing expense and payment is shown as one for convenience.)

July 1, 1991

| | | |
|---|---|---|
| Interest Expense | 4,000 | |
| Debenture Bonds Payable | 100,000 | |
| Cash | | 104,000 |

Retirement of bonds at maturity along with payment of final coupons and recognition of interest expense.

**Refunding at Maturity** A growing, profitable firm will seldom want to reduce the amount of its outstanding bonded indebtedness. When one bond issue matures, the firm will usually float another to take its place. We have heard that American Telephone and Telegraph has not reduced outstanding debt since Alexander Graham Bell borrowed a dollar to build the first telephone. Bond issues in large, profitable com-

17.62

panies are protected by the high credit standing of the issuer. The market does not worry about the source of funds to be used to repay bonds at maturity. It is not concerned that the borrowing firm will often issue new bonds to repay the old. Such new issues are often called "refunding bond issues." The refunding of outstanding debt at maturity is accounted for as two separate transactions: the retirement of the old bonds and the issue of the new bonds.

17.63    Often, the market requires—through the bond indenture or in other ways—that the borrower make specific plans for repayment of the bond issue at maturity. A later section discusses such contractual provisions for bond retirement.

17.64    **Retirement before Maturity** It is not unusual for a firm to enter the marketplace and to purchase its own bonds before maturity. Interest rates constantly change. Assume that Macaulay Corporation originally issued its bonds at par to yield 8 percent compounded semiannually. Assume that 5 years later, on July 1, 1986, interest rates in the marketplace have increased so that the market then requires a 10-percent interest rate to be paid by Macaulay Corporation. Refer to Appendix Table 6 at the back of the book, 5-year column, 10-percent row, where you will see that 8-percent bonds with 5 years until maturity will sell in the marketplace for 92.2783 percent of par if the current interest rate is 10 percent compounded semiannually.

17.65    The marketplace is not constrained by the principles of historical cost accounting. Even though Macaulay Corporation continues to show the Debenture Bonds Payable on the balance sheet at $100,000, the marketplace puts a price of only $92,278 on the entire bond issue. From the point of view of the marketplace, these bonds are the same as bonds issued on July 1, 1986, at an effective yield of 10 percent and so carry a discount of $7,722 (= $100,000 − $92,278).

17.66    If Macaulay Corporation goes out into the marketplace on July 1, 1986, to purchase, say, $10,000 of par value of its own bonds, it would have to pay only $9,228 (= .92278 ×

$10,000) for those bonds. The journal entries it would make at the time of purchase are*

July 1, 1986
| | | |
|---|---|---|
| Interest Payable .................... | 4,000 | |
|      Cash ......................... | | 4,000 |

To record payment for coupons, as usual.

| | | |
|---|---|---|
| Debenture Bonds Payable .......... | 10,000 | |
|      Cash ......................... | | 9,228 |
|      Gain on Retirement on Bonds ... | | 772 |

To record purchase of bonds for less than the current amount shown in the accounting records. The gain is an extraordinary item.

The adjustment to give equal debits and credits in the second journal entry is recorded as a gain. The gain arises because the firm is able to retire a liability recorded at one amount, $10,000, for a cash payment, $9,228, which is less than that amount. This gain actually occurred as interest rates increased between 1981 and 1986. In historical cost accounting, the gain is reported only when realized—in the period of bond retirement. This phenomenon is analogous to a firm's purchasing marketable securities, holding those securities as prices increase, selling the securities in a subsequent year, and reporting all the gain in the year of sale. It is caused by the historical cost accounting convention of recording amounts at historical cost and not recording increases in wealth until those increases are realized in arm's-length transactions with outsiders.

17.67    During the 1970s, interest rates jumped upward from their levels in the 1960s. Many companies had issued bonds at prices near par with coupon rates of only 3 or 4 percent per year in the 1960s. When interest rates in the 1970s jumped to 10 or 12 percent per year, these bonds sold in the marketplace for substantial discounts. Many companies went into the marketplace and repurchased their

---

*If the bonds were originally issued either at a discount or at a premium, then the appropriate part of the discount or premium account is retired along with the Bonds Payable account. The treatment parallels that for the simultaneous retirement of the accounts for a plant asset and its accumulated depreciation.

own bonds, recording substantial gains in the process. (In one year Pan American World Airlines was able to report profits after 7 consecutive years of losses. Pan Am had gains on bond retirement that year in excess of the entire amount of net income.)

17.68　Because there is no alternative in historical cost accounting to showing a gain (or loss) on bond retirement (the debits must equal the credits) and because the FASB is reluctant to let companies manage their own reported income by repurchasing bonds, it has required that gains and losses on voluntary bond retirements prior to maturity be reported in the income statement as *extraordinary* items.* Such items are included in net income but shown in a separate section of the income statement; see the discussion in Chapter 2.

17.69　*Funds Statement Effects* Neither the gain nor loss on bond retirement affects funds provided by extraordinary items. If a gain on bond retirement is recorded, then there must be a subtraction in computing funds provided by extraordinary items. If a loss is recorded, then there must be an addition in computing funds from extraordinary items.

## Contractual Provisions for Bond Retirement

17.70　To increase the likelihood that they will receive the face value of bonds at maturity, lenders often require that the borrower make advance provisions for payments at maturity. These requirements take the form of sinking funds and serial bond issues. The lenders do not get something for nothing. If they require special funds or early repayment, they will get a smaller interest return than otherwise.

17.71　To protect against drastic declines in interest rates after a bond is issued, the borrower may include a ''call provision,'' which permits the borrower to retire the bond early. The bond issuer does not get something for nothing. If it requires the lender to

accept repayment of funds at the borrower's discretion, the bond issuer will have to pay a higher interest rate than otherwise.

17.72　This section discusses various contractual provisions for bond retirement. Sinking funds and serial bond issues are generally thought to benefit the lenders, whereas call provisions are generally thought to benefit the borrower.

17.73　**Sinking Fund Bonds** Sinking funds of cash are designed to accumulate amounts required to retire bond issues. A more descriptive title is ''bond-retirement fund.'' Such funds are usually removed from the control of the borrower and given to a trustee. The trustee receives sums of cash, invests the funds in appropriate ways, and uses the accumulated funds to pay off the bonds. (Chapter 14 explains the accounting for the fund as an investment.) The trustee acts for the benefit of the lenders and acts in accord with the provisions of the bond indenture. Often, the trustee will find it useful to invest the cash it receives in the same bonds the fund will be used to retire. Not only will the fund be serving its intended purpose of paying off the bond issue, but also the yield on the fund investments could well be higher than the trustee could earn on investments otherwise thought prudent. That is, the trustee might be willing to invest funds in a low grade, high-yield bond only when the low-grade bond is the very issue to be retired from the fund.

17.74　When the sinking fund trustee invests in the bonds to be retired, the purchase is treated as a retirement of the bond and a gain or loss is recognized for the difference between the book value and the open-market cost of the bonds reacquired. If the purchase by the trustee is to satisfy a sinking fund requirement, then the resulting gain or loss is *not* an extraordinary item.† Recall the earlier discussion where we pointed out GAAP's reluctance to let firms manage their own incomes by voluntary debt retirement. In this case, the retirement is not voluntary;

---

*Financial Accounting Standards Board, *Statement of Financial Accounting Standards No. 4* (1975).

†Ibid., par. 8.

the retirement was planned when the bonds were first issued. Whether the retirement would be a gain or loss could not then be anticipated; the actual gain or loss does not result from attempted income manipulation.

17.75 **Serial Bond Issues** Bond retirement funds systematically accumulate cash for retirement but present an important problem. The rate of return generated by the bond retirement fund is uncertain, so no one can be sure that the amounts required to be invested in the fund will be the correct amounts. To solve the problem of uncertain investment returns on retirement funds, some bond indentures call for the bonds to mature serially, over time. For example, one-tenth of an outstanding bond issue might mature each year for 10 years. Such bonds are called a *serial bond issue*. A serial bond issue of this sort is the same as 10 separate issues, each with a different maturity date. Because the bonds were all originally marketed at one time, these bonds are thought of as a single issue. Calculating the interest rate for a serial bond issue involves finding an internal rate of return. The example for Lexie's Fashionables in Appendix B illustrates the computation of initial issue proceeds, of the effective interest rate, and of the amortization schedule for a serial bond issue. Once the rate is known, the effective-interest method for amortizing bond discount or premium can be used for serial bond issues. In earlier days, before calculating devices were as inexpensive as they are now, accountants devised various averaging methods for accounting for discount or premiums on a serial bond issue so that the straight-line method could be used. Now that calculators are so inexpensive, serial bonds ought to be accounted for with the effective-interest method, avoiding problems of computing an approximation to discount or premium amortization.

17.76 **Callable Bonds** A common provision gives the issuing company the right to retire portions of the bond issue before maturity if it so desires, but does not require it do so. In order to facilitate such reacquisition and retirement of a part of the bond issue, the bond indenture usually provides that the bonds shall be *callable*. That is, the issuing company will have the right to reacquire its bonds at prices specified in the bond indenture. The *call price* is usually set a few percentage points above the par value and declines as the maturity date approaches. Because the call provision may be exercised by the issuing company at a time when the market rate of interest is less than the coupon rate, callable bonds usually are sold in the marketplace for something less than otherwise similar, but noncallable, bonds.

17.77 Assume, for example, that a firm had issued 12-percent semiannual coupon bonds at par, but market interest rates and the firm's credit standing at a later date would currently allow it to borrow at 8 percent. The firm would be paying more to borrow the face value than it would have to pay if the bonds were issued currently. If $100,000 par value bonds issued at par are called at 105, the entry, in addition to the one to record the accrued interest expense, would be

| | | |
|---|---|---|
| Debenture Bonds Payable | 100,000 | |
| Loss on Retirement of Bonds | 5,000 | |
| Cash | | 105,000 |

Bonds called and retired.

This loss, like the analogous gain, recognized on bond retirement must be classified as an extraordinary item in the income statement.

17.78 If the bonds were originally issued at a discount (or premium), then the appropriate portion of the unamortized discount (or premium) must also be retired when the bonds are called or otherwise retired. Suppose that $100,000 par value bonds were issued at a premium several years ago and that the unamortized premium is now $3,500. If $10,000 par value bonds are called at 105, the entry to record the retirement would be

| | | |
|---|---|---|
| Bonds Payable | 10,000 | |
| Premium on Bonds Payable | 350 | |
| Loss on Retirement of Bonds | 150 | |
| Cash | | 10,500 |

Partial retirement of bonds originally issued at a premium. The loss is an extraordinary item.

The market rate of interest a firm must pay depends on two factors: the general level of interest rates and its own creditworthiness. If the market rate of interest has risen since bonds were issued (or the firm's credit rating has declined), the bonds will sell in the market at less than issue price. A firm that wanted to retire such bonds would not *call* them, because the call price is typically greater than the issue price. Instead the firm would purchase its bonds in the open market and realize a gain on the retirement of bonds.

## Convertible Bonds

17.79    Convertible bonds are typically semiannual coupon bonds like those discussed above, but with one added feature. The holder of the bond can *convert,* or "trade in," the bond for shares of capital stock. The number of shares to be received when the bond is converted into stock, the dates when conversion can occur, and other details are specified in the bond indenture. Convertible bonds are usually callable.

17.80    Investors often find convertible bonds attractive. The owner is promised a regular interest payment. In addition, should the company business be so successful that its share prices rise on the stock market, the holder of the bond can convert the investment from debt into equity. The creditor has become an owner and can share in the good fortune of the company.* Of course, an investor does not get something for nothing. Because of the potential participation in the earnings of the company once the bonds are converted into common shares, an investor in the bonds must accept a lower interest rate than would be received if the bonds were not convertible into stock. From the company's point of view, convertible bonds allow borrowing at lower rates of interest than is required on ordinary debt, but the company

---

*In recent years the brokerage commission fees on convertible bonds have often been less than those for comparable dollar amounts of investments in the underlying common shares.

must promise to give up an equity interest if the bonds are converted. The purchaser of the convertible bond is paying something for the option to acquire common stock later. Thus, a portion of the proceeds from the issue of convertible bonds actually represents a form of capital contribution even though it is not so recorded.

## Issue of Convertible Bonds

17.81    Assume, for example, that the Lorraine Company's credit rating would allow it to issue $100,000 of ordinary 10-year, 11-percent semiannual coupon bonds at par. The firm prefers to issue convertible bonds with a lower coupon rate. Assume that Lorraine Company issues at par $100,000 of 10-year, 8-percent semiannual coupon bonds, but each $1,000 bond is convertible into 50 shares of Lorraine Company $5-par-value common stock. The entire issue is convertible into 5,000 shares. Appendix Table 6 (for 8-percent coupon bonds) indicates that 8-percent, 10-year semiannual (nonconvertible) coupon bonds sell for about 82 percent of par when the market rate of interest is 11 percent. Thus, if the 8-percent convertible bonds can be issued at par, the conversion feature must be worth 18 percent of par. Then 18 percent of the proceeds from the bond issue is actually a capital contribution by the bond buyers for the right to acquire common stock later. It is *not* a loan. The logical entry to record the issue of these 8-percent convertible bonds at par would be

| | | |
|---|---|---|
| Cash ....................... | 100,000 | |
| Discount on Convertible Bonds .. | 18,000 | |
|    Convertible Bonds Payable .. | | 100,000 |
|    Additional Paid-in Capital .... | | 18,000 |

Issue of 8% semiannual coupon convertible bonds at a time when ordinary 8% bonds could be issued for 82% of par.

Notice that calculating the amounts for this entry requires that we know what the proceeds would be of an issue of nonconvertible bonds that are otherwise similar to the convertible bonds. Because auditors are often unable to ascertain this information in a reasonably objective manner, generally acceptable accounting principles do not allow the logical journal entry above. Instead, the following, simpler entry is required:*

Cash ......................... 100,000
      Convertible Bonds Payable ...        100,000
Issue of convertible bonds at par.

This entry effectively treats convertible bonds just like ordinary, nonconvertible bonds and records the value of the conversion feature at zero. (Generally accepted accounting principles do recognize the potential issue of common stock implied by the conversion feature in the calculations of earnings-per-share figures. See the discussion in Chapter 22.)

## Conversion of Bonds

17.82   To carry the illustration further, assume that the common stock of the Lorraine Company increases in the market to $30 a share so that one $1,000 bond, which is convertible into 50 shares of stock, can be converted into stock with a market value of $1,500. If the entire convertible bond issue were converted into common stock at this time, then 5,000 shares of $5-par-value stock would be issued upon conversion.

17.83   **Using Book Value of Bonds** The usual entry to record the conversion of bonds into stock ignores current market prices in the interest of simplicity and merely shows the swap of stocks for bonds at their book value.

Convertible Bonds Payable ...... 100,000
      Common Stock—$5 Par .....        25,000
      Additional Paid-in Capital ....        75,000
To record conversion of 100 convertible bonds with book value of $100,000 into 5,000 shares of $5-par-value stock.

17.84   **Using Market Value of Shares** An allowable alternative treatment recognizes that

market prices provide information useful in quantifying the market value of the shares issued. Under the alternative treatment, when the market price of a share is $30 and the fair market value of the 5,000 shares issued on conversion is $150,000, the journal entry made would be

Convertible Bonds Payable ....... 100,000
Loss on Conversion of Bonds ....  50,000
      Common Stock—$5 Par .....        25,000
      Additional Paid-in Capital ....        125,000
To record conversion of 100 convertible bonds into 5,000 shares of $5-par-value stock at a time when the market price of a share is $30.

The entry above is the equivalent of the following two entries:

Cash ......................... 150,000
      Common Stock—$5 Par .....        25,000
      Additional Paid-in Capital ....        125,000
To record issue of 5,000 shares of $5-par-value stock at $30 per share.

Convertible Bonds Payable ...... 100,000
Loss on Retirement of Bonds ....  50,000
      Cash ....................        150,000
Retirement by purchase for $150,000 of 100 convertible bonds carried on the books at $100,000.

**Using Market Value of Bonds** Still another   17.85
acceptable alternative for recording the conversion uses the market price of the bonds on the date of conversion. Assume that the market value of the convertible bonds of Lorraine Company was $1,600 on the conversion date. Even though the stock into which the bonds can be converted is worth only $1,500, the bonds sell for $1,600.† The entry to record conversion using the market price of the bonds is

Convertible Bonds Payable ...... 100,000
Loss on Conversion of Bonds ....  60,000
      Common Stock—$5 Par .....        25,000
      Additional Paid-in Capital ....        135,000

---

*Accounting Principles Board, *Opinion No. 14* (1969). The APB stated that, in reaching its conclusions, less weight was given to the practical difficulties than to some other considerations, spelled out in the *Opinion*. We concur with the dissent to this *Opinion* expressed by several members of the Board.

---

†There are several causes of this "premium," for example, interest coupons' exceeding dividends on shares and differences in transaction costs. Some texts on corporate finance and investments explain these causes of premiums on convertible bonds.

The effects on total shareholders' equity of all three methods are identical. Only the classification of amounts as Retained Earnings and Additional Paid-in Capital differs.

## Troubled Debt Restructurings

17.86 A firm with long-term liabilities outstanding may experience difficulty and find itself unable to discharge its liabilities as they come due. Rather than declare bankruptcy or be placed into bankruptcy by its creditors, the borrower may negotiate a less burdensome set of payments with the lender. To take a simple example, assume that Happy Pappy's Wine Company borrows $10,000, agreeing to repay $11,000 one year hence (implying a 10-percent interest rate). Just after the loan is made, Happy Pappy's experiences a major uninsured fire loss. Rather than declare bankruptcy and let the lender await the outcome of a long court proceeding after which it might get nothing, Happy Pappy's agrees with the lender to repay $11,000, not 1 year hence, but 5 years hence. Such a negotiated agreement by a borrower in financial difficulty with a lender is called a "troubled debt restructuring" by the FASB in *Statement No. 15*. The critical aspect of a troubled debt restructuring is that the lender makes concessions to a borrower in financial difficulty that the lender would not otherwise consider. The lender judges that the new, negotiated terms are the best it can get; the lender makes the best deal it can for itself in a difficult situation when it perceives that the alternative to renegotiating the loan is getting much less than it was promised or, perhaps, nothing at all.

17.87 The FASB's *Statement** on troubled debt restructurings deals with three types of situations:

**1.** The borrower gives the lender assets or equities to settle the debt.

**2.** The borrower agrees to pay the lender cash less than originally promised or later

---

*Financial Accounting Standards Board, *Statement of Financial Accounting Standards No. 15* (1977) is the source of the principles described in this section.

than originally promised (or both), but still more in total, before discounting, than the book value of the loan.

**3.** The borrower agrees to pay the lender cash whose undiscounted amount totals less than the book value of the loan.

Each of these is discussed below.

### Final Settlement with Assets or Equities

17.88 The borrower may give the lender assets or equities to discharge the debt. The borrower has no further obligations to the lender. (For example, Happy Pappy's might give the lender wine with a fair market value of $8,000 in full settlement of the debt.) The transaction is recorded using the fair market value of the assets or equities given up, assuming that the borrower is acting as a willing seller selling to a willing buyer. Gain or loss to be included in ordinary income results from the difference between the fair market value and the book value of the asset transferred. (Note that if the asset transferred has previously been written down to market, then the loss has similarly been reported as part of ordinary income.) Then, the borrower records a gain on the transaction equal to the difference between the book value of the debt retired and the fair market value of the assets or equities transferred. Like the gain on other voluntary debt retirements, the gain is an extraordinary item. The lender records the assets received at their fair market value and reports the loss as an *ordinary* item, not an extraordinary item.

17.89 Assume the borrower transfers wine to the lender to settle the debt of $10,000. The wine had cost $8,500 and has a fair market value of $8,000. The borrower records:

| | | |
|---|---|---|
| Note Payable | 10,000 | |
| Loss in Transfer of Wine | 500 | |
| Wine Inventory | | 8,500 |
| Gain on Settlement of Note | | 2,000 |

Note is paid off in full by delivering wine that cost $8,500 and has a fair market value of $8,000. The loss is ordinary. The gain is extraordinary.

The lender records:

| | | |
|---|---:|---:|
| Wine | 8,000 | |
| Loss on Settlement of Note | 2,000 | |
|     Note Receivable | | 10,000 |

Acceptance of assets in payment of loan; an ordinary loss results.

17.90  Similar treatment is used if Happy Pappy's gave shares of its common stock having a fair market value of $8,000 to the lender in complete settlement of the loan. The borrower has only the $2,000 extraordinary gain in this case.

## Prospective Cash Payments Greater Than Book Value

17.91  The lender may allow the borrower to stretch out payments on the loan or reduce the total undiscounted payments to be made (or both), but the total of the cash payments to be made over the life of the new loan exceeds (or equals) the book value (including accrued interest) of the loan. (This is the case for Happy Pappy's described earlier.) In this case, neither the borrower nor the lender reports gain or loss. Rather, the book value of the loan is left undisturbed and the new implicit interest rate is computed for the negotiated loan as though it were a new loan. This new rate is used in accounting for the loan over the remainder of its life. In the example in which Happy Pappy's agreed to pay $11,000 five years hence, the implicit interest rate has become 1.924 percent.* Thus the entries will be:

---

*Appendix B illustrates finding the implicit interest rate by a trial-and-error procedure. It points out that when there is only one payment involved, the implicit rate can be found analytically. In this case $10,000 \times (1 + r)^5 = \$11,000$; $(1 + r)^5 = \$11,000/\$10,000$; $r = (1.10)^{1/5} - 1$; $r = .01924$. That the right answer is between 1.5 and 2.0 percent can be seen by scanning the 5-period row of Appendix Table 1 and noting that $1.00 grows to $1.10 in five periods at some interest rate between 1.5 and 2.0 percent per period.

| By Borrower | 1st Year | 2nd Year | 3rd Year | 4th Year | 5th Year |
|---|---|---|---|---|---|
| Interest Expense | 192 | 196 | 200 | 204 | 208 |
|   Note Payable | 192 | 196 | 200 | 204 | 208 |

To record interest expense as 1.924% of book value. Book value increases each year by the amount of interest added to principal for single-payment note.

The lender will make entries of similar amounts each year, debiting Note Receivable and crediting Interest Revenue.

## Prospective Cash Payments Less Than Book Value

17.92  The lender may allow the borrower to repay cash amounts whose undiscounted sum is less than (or equal to) the current book value of the loan (including accrued interest). (For example, the lender allows Happy Pappy's to agree to repay $9,000 cash 2 years hence.) The book value of the loan is reduced by both the borrower and the lender to this undiscounted sum of future promised payments. Then the difference between the original book value and the undiscounted sum is an extraordinary gain to the borrower and an ordinary loss to the lender. As the borrower pays cash, it debits Note Payable and credits Cash. As the lender receives cash, it debits Cash and credits Note Receivable. There is neither interest expense to the borrower nor interest revenue to the lender.

## Summary of Troubled Debt Restructurings

17.93  The treatment of gain and interest expense by the borrower is symmetric with the treatment of loss and interest revenue by the lender with two exceptions. First, whereas the borrower's gain is extraordinary (because of the voluntary nature of the debt retirement), the lender's loss is ordinary. At the time of the restructuring, the borrower may have been carrying the Note Payable in its records at an amount slightly different from the amount of the Note Receivable's book value in the lender's records. After the restructuring, the amounts will be the same; thus the amount of gain to the borrower may differ slightly from the loss of the lender in cases **1** and **3** described in paragraph 17.87.

17.94    FASB *Statement No. 15* contains details of the implementation for these principles, such as how to treat combinations of transactions when settlement of part of the loan is made and the rest is stretched out. It also discusses why, in case **2** described above, the FASB chose not to allow the lender to record loss and the borrower to record gain. The reasoning rests on the statement that a negotiated restructuring "does not involve transfers of resources or obligations," and therefore no transaction has occurred.* Book values must be left undisturbed as much as possible, consistent with historical cost accounting.

## Weakness of Accounting for Troubled Debt Restructurings

17.95    The reader who has understood the fundamentals of present-value analysis can see that when the terms of repayment of a loan are stretched out or the amounts to be paid are reduced, then the lender has effectively forgiven part of the debt. Consider the restructuring where the lender allows Happy Pappy's to discharge the $11,000 debt 5 years hence rather than 1 year hence. Assume that Happy Pappy's borrowing rate remains 10 percent per year after the fire.† Whereas the present value of $11,000 due in 1 year discounted at 10 percent is $10,000, the present value of $11,000 due in 5 years discounted at 10 percent is only $6,830 (= $11,000 × 0.62092; see Appendix Table 2, 5-period row, 10-percent column). The present value of the debt has decreased by $3,170 (=

*FASB, *Statement No. 15* (1977), par. 145.

†Realistically, the interest rate Happy Pappy's would have to pay is likely to increase because of its major loss. We do not complicate the example with that feature, which adds nothing to the concepts.

$10,000 − $6,830). The renegotiation has resulted in a gain of $3,170 to the borrower and a loss of $3,170 to the lender because the present value of the loan has declined by $3,170. (From the lender's point of view, the fire may be thought of as causing a loss of almost the entire $10,000, and the renegotiation as enabling the lender to get back $6,830 of the loan. Either way, the net effect is that the lender has chosen a course of action that combined with the fire makes it worse off by $3,170 as measured by present values.) The logical way to record this renegotiation is

**Borrower's Records**

Note Payable (or Discount on Note
    Payable) .......................... 3,170
        Gain on Renegotiation of Loan  ...          3,170
To record effect of renegotiating loan. The loan will be amortized using a 10% rate over the next 5 years so that by maturity, the loan will have a book value of $11,000. Interest expense for the first year after renegotiation is $683 (= .10 × $6,830), for the second is $751 [= .10 ($6,830 + $683)], and so on.

**Lender's Records**

Loss on Renegotiation of Loan  ....... 3,170
        Note Receivable .................          3,170
To record loss equal to the difference between book value of loan and its value after the renegotiation. Interest revenue over the next 5 years will be recorded in the same amounts as the borrower records interest expense.

Generally accepted accounting principles do  17.96 *not* treat troubled debt restructurings this way. The FASB does not view the renegotiation of a loan in a troubled debt restructuring as an arm's-length transaction implying the need to recognize gain to the borrower and loss to the lender in all cases.

We disagree with generally accepted ac-  17.97 counting principles. We think that a renegotiation is an arm's-length transaction. The lender may not be as free to bargain as it would with someone who had not yet borrowed, but those borrowings occurred in the past. The forward-looking lender has negotiated the best deal it could under the circumstances. It was not coerced. In general, we think that when a business does something voluntarily, historical cost accounting ought to record that event as a transaction.

17.98    At the time the FASB was considering this subject, many bank loans involving substantial amounts were in default. Bankers told the FASB that if they were required to report losses on debt restructurings, then they would not engage in restructuring. The regulations to which banks are subject look to historical cost accounting books, not necessarily to the substance of transactions. The banks felt that even though the reality of economic loss is not changed by the accounting for the restructuring, whether or not the historical cost records show loss would make a big difference to them because of regulators' behavior. Although we deplore the FASB statement on this subject, we understand how the regulation of banks and their importance to our economy may have led to the actual result. The fault, if any, ultimately lies in the bank regulators' reliance on accounting that ignores changes in the current value of monetary instruments as interest rates or paying ability of borrowers, or both, change.

## Summary

Historical cost accounting treats all noncurrent monetary liabilities similarly. The initial present value of the monetary item is recorded using the contractual payments and the current market interest rate. That rate is called the *historical rate* for later calculations. At any interim payment or closing date, interest expense is computed by multiplying the historical interest rate by the book value of the liability. That amount is debited to Interest Expense and credited to the liability, increasing it. Any cash payment is used to reduce the principal amount of the liability, resulting in a new book value for the start of the next period.    17.99

At the end of any period, after all entries and cash payments, if any, the book value of the monetary item is equal to the remaining contractual payments discounted to present value using the historical interest rate.    17.100

When the liability is discharged and the amount of cash or cash equivalent value of other consideration given up is less than (or greater than) the book value of the liability, then gain (or loss) results (exceptions apply in the gain of troubled debt restructurings). The gain or loss is classified as extraordinary when long-term liabilities are voluntarily retired.    17.101

## Questions and Short Cases

17.1    Review the meaning of the following concepts or terms discussed in this chapter.

a. Long-term versus short-term financing.
b. Debt versus equity financing.
c. Financial leverage.
d. Mortgage, mortgagor, mortgagee.
e. Foreclosure.
f. Amortization schedule.
g. Recourse loan versus nonrecourse loan.
h. Interest-bearing versus noninterest-bearing notes.
i. Implicit interest rate.
j. Imputed interest rate.
k. Bond indenture versus bond certificate.
l. Mortgage bonds, collateral trust bonds, debenture bonds.
m. Face value or par value versus market value of bonds.
n. Bond discount versus bond premium.
o. Underwriting.
p. Effective-interest versus straight-line amortization.
q. Refunding bond issue.
r. Extraordinary gain or loss on bond retirement.
s. Sinking fund bonds versus serial bonds.
t. Callable bonds.
u. Troubled debt restructuring.
v. Convertible bonds.
w. Historical interest rate versus market interest rate.

17.2   Under what conditions is a short-term liability classified as long-term? Under what conditions is a long-term liability classified as short-term?

17.3   What factors determine the amount of money a firm actually receives when it offers a bond issue to the market?

17.4   Why do noninterest-bearing notes have a smaller value at the time of issue than at time of maturity?

17.5   What are the relative advantages and disadvantages of the straight-line method versus the effective-interest method of bond discount (or premium) amortization?

17.6   Why might a lender voluntarily agree to accept less than the contractually promised amount from a borrower in a troubled debt restructuring?

17.7   Aside from length of time to maturity, what feature(s) distinguish short-term from long-term financing?

17.8   Theorists argue about the optimal financial structure of a corporation. What is the nature of the controversy?

17.9   What is meant by the statement "leverage is a two-edged sword"?

17.10  In what sense is the historical cost accounting for noncurrent liabilities subsequent to the date of issuance based on historical costs?

17.11  Why is the recording of gain or loss upon retirement of noncurrent debt by the issuer treated as an extraordinary item?

17.12  All else being equal, why are interest rates on recourse loans generally lower than on nonrecourse loans?

17.13  Assume that a borrower gives a lender a mortgage on property and later fails to make payments; the property is sold at foreclosure, but the proceeds of sale are insufficient to repay the lender all that is owed. What then typically happens?

17.14  What is the purpose of an amortization schedule for a long-term loan?

17.15  State a method for calculating the interest rate for a debt given in exchange for cash.

17.16  State two ways of computing the interest rate for a debt given in exchange for consideration other than cash. Which of these two is preferable?

17.17  What function does a bond underwriter serve?

17.18  Why do bonds of "AAA"-rated companies (good credit risks) sometimes sell at a discount, whereas bonds of "B"-rated companies (poor credit risks) sometimes sell at a premium?

17.19  What feature of some modern pocket calculators makes computations of present values of noncurrent debts much easier than before?

17.20 The following questions compare the effective-interest method and the straight-line method of amortizing bond discount and bond premium.

a. Which method gives higher interest expense in the first year for a bond issued at a discount?

b. Which method gives higher interest expense in the first year for a bond issued at a premium?

c. Which method gives higher interest expense in the last year for a bond issued at a discount?

d. Which method gives higher interest expense in the last year for a bond issued at a premium?

e. Which method involves the larger adjustment to net income in deriving funds provided by operations in the first year for a bond issued at a discount?

f. Which method involves the larger adjustment to net income in deriving funds provided by operations in the first year for a bond issued at a premium?

17.21 For whose protection are bonds made callable, and what is being protected? Why might we be skeptical that call features provide the intended protection?

17.22 For whose protection are bonds issued as serial bonds, and what is being protected? Why might we be skeptical that serial bonds' features provide the intended protection?

17.23 Under what conditions is gain or loss on bond retirements before maturity not reported as an extraordinary item by the issuer? Why is there an exception to the general rule?

17.24 Sinking fund trustees are liable for the results of imprudent investments that turn sour. In what sense does the acquisition of the issuing company's bonds for the sinking fund allow the trustee to make "imprudent" investments with a guarantee of not being liable for bad performance?

17.25 A noted accountant once said that the time of a troubled debt structuring is the *last* date at which a write-down of debt ought to be made, not the first date on which it should be considered. What did this accountant have in mind?

17.26 Why does the required treatment of a troubled debt restructuring, which generally does not allow the recognition of lender's loss and borrower's gain on restructuring, require such recognition when the debt is settled and canceled at the time of the restructuring?

17.27 Why are convertible bonds thought attractive instruments? Why might we be skeptical of such thoughts?

17.28 State two methods of treating the conversion of a convertible bond into common shares. What is the effect of each on income for the period? What is the effect of each on total owners' equity at the end of the period?

17.29 If a company borrows $1,000,000 by issuing, at par, 20-year, 8-percent bonds with semiannual coupons, the total interest expense over the life of the issue is $1,600,000 (= 20 × .08 × $1,000,000). If a company undertakes a 20-year financing lease or mortgage with an implicit borrowing rate of 8 percent, the annual lease payments are $1,000,000/9.81815 = $101,852. (See Appendix Table 4 at the end of the book, 20-period row, 8-percent column.) The total lease payments are $2,037,040 (= 20 × $101,852), and the total interest expense over the life of the lease or mortgage is $1,037,040 (= $2,037,040 − $1,000,000). Why are the amounts of interest expense different for these two means of borrowing for the same length of time at identical interest rates?

**17.30** (Adapted from AICPA *Technical Practice Aids*.) Landau Company acquired merchandise on account for $10,000 from Gianni Company. The payment agreement provides that so long as Landau Company acquires, and promptly pays for, goods in sufficient quantity that it has at least $10,000 of goods from Gianni Company in inventory at all times, then the payment for the original purchase can be postponed indefinitely. Title to all of the goods passes from Gianni Company to Landau Company when the goods are received by Landau Company. Landau intends to keep sufficient inventory on hand at all times so that payment of the $10,000 will be postponed indefinitely.

How should the amount payable for the $10,000 be presented by Landau Company?

**17.31** (Adapted from CPA Examination.) One way for a corporation to accomplish long-term financing is through the issuance of long-term debt instruments in the form of bonds.
   **a.** Describe how to account for the proceeds from bonds issued with detachable stock purchase warrants.
   **b.** Contrast a serial bond with a term (straight) bond.
   **c.** For a five-year term bond issued at a premium, why would the amortization in the first year of the life of the bond differ using the interest method of amortization instead of the straight-line method? Include in your discussion whether the amount of amortization in the first year of the life of the bond would be higher or lower using the interest method instead of the straight-line method.
   **d.** When a bond issue is sold between interest dates at a discount, what journal entry is made and how is the subsequent amortization of bond discount affected? Include in your discussion an explanation of how the amounts of each debit and credit are determined.
   **e.** Describe how to account for and classify the gain or loss from the reacquisition of a long-term bond prior to its maturity.

## Problems and Exercises

**17.32** Indicate the presentation of each of the following items in the balance sheet.
   **a.** Noninterest-bearing Notes Payable for $10,000 due 15 months hence.
   **b.** Credit balance in accounts receivable for individual customers who have paid in full for goods, but who have returned some of them and not yet received a refund.
   **c.** Amounts withheld from employees' wages for income taxes.
   **d.** Amounts received from customers for goods to be delivered in the next accounting period.
   **e.** Amounts received from customers as payments on long-term contracts when the goods are to be delivered 3 years hence. The completed-contract method of revenue recognition is used.
   **f.** Same as part **e** except that the percentage-of-completion method of revenue recognition is used.
   **g.** Serial bonds payable, $100,000 due in each of the next 5 years.
   **h.** Stock dividends payable.

**17.33** (Adapted from CPA Examination.) On January 1 the Hopewell Company issued 8-percent annual coupon bonds that had a face value of $1,000,000. Interest is payable at December 31, each year. The bonds mature ten years after the issue date. The bonds were issued to yield a rate of 10 percent.

Compute the total amount received from the sale of the bonds.

**17.34** The Bartley Company issues 8-percent semiannual coupon bonds maturing in 20 years. The face amount of the bonds is $1 million. The bonds were issued for a price of 94.3183 percent of par. In addition, Bartley Company incurred issue costs of $8,992 in bringing the bonds to market. What interest rate will be used in applying the effective-interest method of amortizing bond discount over the life of the bonds?

**17.35** The Holmes Sales Company sells a building lot to Ruth Watson on September 1 for $27,000. The down payment is $3,000, and minimum payments of $265 a month are to be made on the contract. Interest at the rate of 1 percent per month on the unpaid balance is deducted from each payment, and the balance is applied on the principal. Payments are made as follows: October 1, $265; November 1, $265; December 1, $600; January 2, $265. Prepare a schedule showing payments, interest and principal, and remaining liability at each of these dates. Round amounts to the nearest dollar.

**17.36** Lynne Michals secures a mortgage loan of $56,000 from the Oakley National Bank. The terms of the mortgage require monthly payments of $830. The interest rate to be applied to the unpaid balance is 9 percent per year.

Calculate the distribution of payments for the first 4 months between principal and interest and present the new balance figures. Round amounts to the nearest dollar.

**17.37** On June 1, the Southern Oil Company purchases a warehouse from F. S. Brandon for $60,000, of which $10,000 is assigned to the land and $50,000 to the building. There is a mortgage on the property payable to the Dixie National Bank, which, together with the accrued interest, will be assumed by the purchaser. The balance due on the mortgage is $24,000. The mortgage provides that interest at the rate of 10 percent per annum on the unpaid balance and $2,000 of the principal will be paid on April 1 and October 1 of each year. A 10-year second mortgage for $15,000 originally issued to F. S. Brandon is assumed by the purchaser. The second mortgage bears interest at the rate of 12 percent per annum, payable on June 1 and December 1. A check is drawn to complete the purchase. Prepare journal entries for the Southern Oil Company for June 1, October 1, and December 1. The company closes its books once a year on December 31.

**17.38** On September 1, 1981, Howell Stores, Inc., issues 20-year, first mortgage bonds with a face value of $1,000,000. The proceeds of the issue are $1,060,000. The bonds bear interest at the rate of 8 percent per annum, payable semiannually at March 1 and September 1. Howell Stores, Inc., closes its books annually at December 31. (Round amounts to the nearest dollar.)

**a.** Present dated journal entries related to the bonds from September 1, 1981, through September 1, 1982, inclusive. Assume that Howell Stores, Inc., uses the straight-line method to amortize the bond premium.

**b.** Repeat instructions for part **a,** but assume that the company uses an effective-interest method. The effective-interest rate to be used is 7.4 percent, compounded semiannually.

**17.39** The Bellcat Company borrowed $100,000 by giving a mortgage to the First Federal Savings and Loan Association. It agreed to make monthly payments of $1,053 for 25 years, implying an interest rate of 12 percent, compounded monthly. On January 1 of this year the mortgage had been outstanding for 5 years and had an unpaid balance of $95,650. Bellcat Company made no payments this year. On March 1, the lender foreclosed the loan, sold the property for $92,000, and kept the proceeds. The book value of the property on the date of sale was $85,000. Because the proceeds of sale did not fully recompense the lender, it sent a bill to Bellcat Company for the balance due. Bellcat Company recorded that amount as a payable.

a. How much did Bellcat Company owe the lender on March 1?

b. Record journal entries made by Bellcat Company on March 1, assuming that no entries for this mortgage had been made during the current year.

17.40   McBurney Company acquires a minicomputer from Windham's Computer Store. The cash price of the computer is $25,284. McBurney Company gives a 3-year interest-bearing note with maturity value of $30,000. The note requires annual interest payments of 9 percent of face value, $2,700 per year. The interest rate implicit in the note is 16 percent per year.

a. Prepare an amortization schedule for the note.

b. Prepare journal entries for McBurney Company over the life of the note.

17.41   The Ruland Company purchased an automobile from Stark's Auto Agency. The automobile had a list price of $12,000, but discounts of 10 to 15 percent from list price are common in purchases of this sort. Ruland Company paid for the automobile by giving a noninterest-bearing note due 2 years from the date of purchase. The note had a face value of $13,500. The rate of interest that Ruland Company paid to borrow on secured 2-year loans ranged from 11.5 to 12.5 percent during the period when the purchase occurred.

a. Record the acquisition of the automobile on Ruland Company's books assuming that the fair market value of the automobile was computed assuming a 10-percent discount from list price. What interest rate will be used throughout the loan for computing interest expense?

b. Record the acquisition of the automobile on Ruland Company's books assuming that the estimated interest rate Ruland Company must pay to borrow is deemed reliable and is 12 percent per year.

c. Record the acquisition of the automobile on Ruland Company's books assuming that the interest rate Ruland Company must pay to borrow is 1 percent per month.

d. What is the lowest amount at which the automobile might be recorded in Ruland Company's records?

e. Prepare journal entries to record the loan and to record interest over two years, assuming that the automobile is recorded at $11,157 and the interest rate implicit in the loan is 10 percent per year.

f. Throughout, this book has stressed that over long-enough time periods, total expense is equal to cash outflow. In what sense is the total expense for this transaction the same, independent of the interest rate (and, therefore, the interest expense)?

17.42   In 1981, the Central Power Company issued $2 million bonds in two series, A and B. Each series had face amount of $1 million and was issued at prices to yield 7 percent. Issue A contained semiannual 6-percent coupons. Issue B contained 8-percent semiannual coupons. In 1982, Central Power issued series C, with face amount of $1 million. This issue contained 8-percent semiannual coupons; the effective yield at time of issue was 8.6 percent. Issues A, B, and C all mature 30 years from issue date. Answer the following questions for issue A. Round amounts to the nearest dollar.

a. What is the issuing price of the bonds?

b. Make the journal entry for the date of bond issue.

c. Using the effective-interest method, show the journal entries made on the first semiannual interest payment date.

d. Repeat part c for the second and third payment dates.

e. Show the semiannual entry if straight-line amortization of discount (or premium) is used.

17.43 Refer to the data in Problem **P17.42.** Work the problem for issue B.

17.44 Refer to the data in Problem **P17.42.** Work the problem for issue C.

17.45 Refer to the Simplified Funds Statement for a Period in Exhibit 4.13. Nine of the lines in the statement are numbered. Line (2) should be expanded to say "Additions for Expenses, Losses, and Other Charges against Income Not Using Funds," and line (3) should be expanded to say "Subtractions for Revenues, Gains, and Other Credits to Income Not Producing Funds from Operations." Ignore the unnumbered lines in responding to the questions below.

Assume that the accounting cycle is complete for the period and that all of the financial statements have been prepared. Then it is discovered that a transaction has been overlooked. That transaction is recorded in the accounts and all of the financial statements are corrected. Define *funds* as *working capital*. For each of the following transactions, indicate which of the numbered lines of the funds statement is affected and by how much. Ignore income tax effects except when taxes are explicitly mentioned.

a. Bonds are issued for $100,000 cash.

b. Bonds with a fair market value of $100,000 are issued for a building.

c. Bonds with a book value of $100,000 are retired for $90,000 cash.

d. Bonds with a book value of $100,000 are called for $105,000 cash and retired.

e. Interest expense on bonds is recorded using the effective-interest method. The bonds have a face value of $100,000 and a book value at the beginning of the current period of $90,000. The coupon rate is 8 percent, paid semiannually, and the bonds were originally issued to yield 10 percent, compounded semiannually.

f. Interest expense on bonds is recorded using the effective-interest method. The bonds have a face value of $100,000 and a book value at the beginning of the current period of $105,000. The coupon rate is 8 percent, paid semiannually, and the bonds were originally issued to yield 6 percent, compounded semiannually.

17.46 Posey Company issued 20-year, 6-percent, semiannual coupon bonds 15 years ago at 104.776 percent of par. Posey Company uses the effective-interest method and records bond premium in a separate, adjunct account. Today the bonds sell in the marketplace to yield 9 percent to maturity. The Posey Company retires $100,000 of face value of these bonds by a cash purchase. Prepare the journal entry to record the reacquisition of its own bonds by the Posey Company.

17.47 Gray Company issues 10-year, 10-percent semiannual coupon bonds. Compute the initial issue proceeds per $1,000 bond, assuming that the market rate of interest, compounded semiannually, is as follows:

a. 8 percent.

b. 10 percent.

c. 12 percent.

17.48 Wheeler Company issued $800,000 of 10-percent *annual* coupon bonds maturing serially over a 5-year period. The bonds were issued to yield 12 percent when interest is computed with the effective-interest method. The interest payment date of the bonds corresponds to the date at the end of the reporting year for accounting purposes. The proceeds of issue were $756,253. The bonds mature $100,000 each at the end of the first, second, and third years of the issue, $200,000 at the end of the fourth year, and $300,000 at the end of the fifth year.

a. Verify that the amount of the initial issue proceeds is $756,253.

b. Construct an amortization schedule for these bonds and present journal entries for each of the 5 years the bonds are outstanding. (Hint: Refer to Appendix B, where an example like this is illustrated.)

17.49  (Adapted from CPA Examination.) On December 1, Year 1, the Cone Company issued its 7-percent, $2,000,000 face value bonds for $2,200,00, plus accrued interest. Interest is payable on November 1 and May 1. On December 31, Year 2, the book value of the bonds, including unamortized premium was $2,100,000. On July 1, Year 3, Cone reacquired the bonds at 98 percent of par value, plus accrued interest. Cone uses the straight-line method for the amortization of bond premium.

Compute the gain or loss on this extinguishment of debt.

17.50  Arnett Company has outstanding $10,000,000 par value, 12-percent coupon bonds. The effective rate (market rate at time of issue) on these bonds was 11 percent. The book value of the bonds today, an interest payment date, is $10,200,000 before interest accrual. The bonds are called for 103 percent of par. Arnett Company makes the semiannual interest accrual and the required cash payments to pay interest and to retire the bonds.

Record the journal entries for these transactions. Use a Premium on Bonds Payable account.

17.51  (Adapted from CPA Examination.) The board of directors of Nelson Company authorized a $1 million issue of 10-percent coupon, convertible 20-year bonds dated March 1 of the current year, year 1. Interest at the rate of 5 percent of par value is payable March 1 and September 1 of each year. The conversion agreement provides that up to 5 years from the date of issue, each $1,000 bond can be converted into six shares of $100-par-value common stock, and that interest accrued to the date of conversion will be paid in cash. After 5 years, each $1,000 bond can be converted into only five shares of common, and interest accrued to the date of conversion will be paid in cash.

The Company sold the entire issue on June 30 of the current year. The purchasers of the bond paid 97.12 percent of par plus accrued interest for the period March 1 through June 30. The company makes adjusting entries each month and closes its books once per year, on December 31. All interest is paid when due. On February 1 of year 3, a holder of $20,000 of face value of bonds converts them into common shares. Use the straight-line method of amortizing bond discount to:

a.  Prepare journal entries for the following dates: year 1—June 30, September 1; year 2 — December 31, including closing entries; year 3—February 1, December 31, including closing entries.

b.  Prepare a schedule presenting the balance in the Discount on (Convertible) Bonds account as of December 31, year 3.

17.52  The Hartley Company issues $1 million of face value 8-percent, semiannual coupon bonds. Buyers paid 98.05 percent of par value for these bonds, which mature in 20 years. Each $1,000 bond is convertible into 20 shares of $5-par-value common, which has a market price of $30 per share on the date the bonds are issued. Similar nonconvertible debt could have been issued at par only if the coupon rate on the bonds were 11 percent. The underwriting costs would have been the same as for the convertible bonds.

a.  What journal entry is made at time of issue?

b.  Assume use of the effective-interest method. What interest rate will be used in accounting for these bonds while they remain outstanding?

c.  What is the market value of the conversion feature on the date of issue? Show a journal entry for the issue date that, although not generally acceptable, would distinguish the value of the debt from the value of the equity in this issue.

17.53 (Adapted from CPA Examination.) To answer this problem requires certain material in Chapter 22. Before attempting to answer this problem, refer to the discussion in Chapter 22 of the difference between convertible bonds and debt issued with detachable warrants.

Incurring long-term debt with an arrangement whereby lenders receive an option to buy common stock during all or a portion of the time the debt is outstanding is a frequently used corporate financing practice. In some situations the result is achieved through the issuance of convertible bonds; in others the debt instruments and the warrants to buy stock are separate.

a. (1) Describe the differences that exist in current accounting for original proceeds of the issuance of convertible bonds and of debt instruments with separate warrants to purchase common stock.

(2) Discuss the underlying rationale for the differences described in (1) above.

(3) Summarize the arguments that have been presented for the alternative accounting treatment.

b. At the start of the year AB Company issued $6,000,000 of 7-percent notes along with warrants to buy 400,000 shares of its $10-par-value common stock at $18 per share. The notes mature over the next 10 years starting 1 year from date of issuance, with annual maturities of $600,000. At the time, AB had 3,200,000 shares of common stock outstanding and the market price was $23 per share. The company received $6,680,000 for the notes and the warrants. For AB Company, 7 percent was a relatively low borrowing rate. If offered alone, at this time, the notes would have been issued at a 20- to 24-percent discount. Prepare journal entries for the issuance of the notes and warrants for the cash consideration received.

17.54 (Problem developed from material prepared by Shyam Sunder.) Subsequent to the initial issue, the semiannual entries for semiannual coupon bonds may be regarded as consisting of three elements. For illustration, consider two bonds: the first issue of a premium with interest expense of $3,150 and coupon payment of $4,000; the second issue at a discount with interest expense of $3,150 and coupon payment of $2,500.

First consider the journal entries for these bonds in three stages:

| | **Premium Bond** | **Discount Bond** |
|---|---|---|
| (1) Interest Expense ................................. | 3,150 | 3,150 |
| Interest Payable .............................. | 3,150 | 3,150 |
| Recognize interest expense and the associated current liability. | | |
| (2) Interest Payable .................................. | 3,150 | 3,150 |
| Cash ........................................ | 3,150 | 3,150 |
| Make payment on the current liability. | | |
| (3) Bond Premium .................................. | 850 | |
| Cash ........................................ | 850 | |
| Record repayment of principal for premium bond. | | |
| Cash ......................................... | | 650 |
| Bond Discount ............................. | | 650 |
| Increase in debt for discount bond. | | |

Now examine the effect of each of the three elements of this transaction on net income and working capital:

| Entry | Premium Bond | | Discount Bond | |
|---|---|---|---|---|
| | Net Income | Working Capital | Net Income | Working Capital |
| (1) ................. | $-3,150 | $-3,150 | $-3,150 | $-3,150 |
| (2) ................. | 0 | 0 | 0 | 0 |
| (3) ................. | 0 | -850 | 0 | +650 |
| Total .............. | $-3,150 | $-4,000 | $-3,150 | $-2,500 |

The total effect of the transaction on working capital is equal to the amount of cash paid, $4,000 for the premium bond and $2,500 for the discount bond. However, there is some disagreement on which of the three elements of the transaction should be counted as the part of "operations" of the firm. If all three elements are counted as "operations," we must subtract $850 (add $650 for the discount bond) from net income to arrive at funds from operations. Those who regard the third element as not a part of "operations" will not add or subtract anything to net income and list $850 as other uses of funds (partial payment of bond principal) for the premium bond and $650 as additional long-term borrowing (other sources of funds) for the discount bond.

a. Assume that inventory costing $7,000 is sold for a long-term, noninterest-bearing receivable with a face value of $10,000. Record journal entries for this transaction.

b. Prepare a schedule, similar to the one above for the bonds issued at a discount and at a premium, showing the effect of the transaction of the entries on net income and on working capital. Describe the effect on funds from operations of two alternative treatments of this event.

17.55  The City Bank made a $100,000, interest-bearing loan to Wriston Company several years ago. The note requires interest payments of $4,000 every 6 months and a payment of $100,000 plus $4,000 five years from today. The implied interest rate was reasonable at the time the loan was made.

Today, Wriston Company is nearly insolvent and asks City Bank to renegotiate the loan. Wriston Company offers to pay $100,000 five years from today if all interest charges are forgiven for the next 5 years. The bank accepts this offer.

a. Assume that City Bank's book value of the loan to Wriston Company is $100,000. Define the bank's "economic loss" to be the difference between the book value and the present value of the newly promised cash flows discounted at the current interest rate of 20 percent per year. Assume that Wriston Company's book value for the liability is $100,000. Define its "economic gain" to be the difference between book value and the present value of the newly promised cash flows discounted at the current interest rate of 20 percent. What is the amount of economic loss to City Bank and economic gain to Wriston Company? Comment on the definitions of "economic gain" and "economic loss" used in this problem.

b. Following generally accepted accounting principles, what amount of gain or loss does Wriston Company record upon renegotiation?

c. Following generally accepted accounting principles, what amount of gain or loss does City Bank record upon renegotiation?

17.56  One year ago, Wriston Company gave a 15-percent, interest-bearing note for $20,000 to Mercantile Supply Company for office equipment. Interest is to be paid annually at the end of each year. The fair market value of the equipment was $20,000, and the appropriate interest rate for Wriston Company's borrowings was 15 percent per year. The note matures 3 years from today. Wriston Company fails to make the payment due today. Because Wriston Company is nearly insolvent, it approaches management of Mercantile Supply Company and asks that the loan be renegotiated.

Show the accounting on both Wriston Company's records and on Mercantile Supply Company's records for each of the negotiation outcomes described below. Record all payments or events described through final settlement of the note. Interest for the first year has been accrued on the books of both Wriston Company and Mercantile Supply Company.

a. Mercantile Supply Company repossesses the equipment. The equipment has a net book value on Wriston Company's books of $15,000. After repossession, Mercantile spends $2,000 to restore the equipment to salable condition and then sells it for $9,000.

b. Mercantile forgives the interest due today, but both parties agree that future contractual payments will be made on schedule. All future payments are made on schedule. The interest rate implicit in the renegotiated stream of payments is approximately 9 percent per year. Verify that rate and use it in your calculations.

c. Mercantile forgives all interest payments in return for a promise that Wriston will pay the $20,000 face amount of the note 2 years hence. Wriston fulfills its promise.

d. Mercantile accepts a $1,000 payment today and agrees to accept $1,000 per year until the maturity date of the note, 3 years hence, when it will receive the face value of $20,000 plus another $1,000. Wriston makes all three payments on schedule. The interest rate implicit in the renegotiated stream of payments is approximately 1.5 percent per year. Verify that rate and use it in your calculations.

e. Mercantile refuses to renegotiate the loan; it forces Wriston into bankruptcy. Six months later, Mercantile gets back its equipment, which has a net realizable value of $8,000, and receives a cash settlement of $3,000. The transaction is completed. In this case, record only the entries for Mercantile Supply Company. (The entries for a bankrupt company are beyond the scope of this text.)

17.57 (Adapted from CPA Examination.) Your client, Realm Manufacturing, Inc., is planning to issue new bonds at a lower interest rate in order to extinguish currently outstanding bonds. You have been asked to assist with some calculations regarding these transactions. The following data relate to the original (outstanding) bonds and the new bonds to be issued by Realm:

| | Original Bond Issue | New Bond Issue |
|---|---|---|
| Face Value | $20,000,000 | $20,000,000 |
| Coupon Rate | 6% | 5% |
| Call Premium | 4% | $4^1/_2$% |
| Expired Life | 5 years | — |
| Remaining Life to Maturity | 15 years | 15 years |
| Issued at (Percent of Par) | $98^1/_2$ | 100 |
| Total Issue Costs | $120,000 | $135,000 |

The new issue is to be sold and then 1 month later the original issue is to be redeemed. This overlapping month's interest on the original issue is *not* to be considered a miscellaneous cost of acquisition in computing the gain or loss. Note that under this plan, the new issue will mature one month sooner than the old issue would mature if it were to remain outstanding.

All discounts and issue costs are amortized on a straight-line basis because that method is not materially different from the "effective interest" method of amortization. Interest is paid annually.

All cash flows are assumed to occur at year end.

The federal income tax rate is 40 percent. Do not ignore income tax effects in carrying out the following steps.

a. Compute Realm's accounting gain or loss on the early extinguishment of the original (outstanding) bonds.

b. Compute the net cash investment based on the difference between the net cash outflow to redeem the original issue and the amount raised by the new issue.

c. Compute the net cash benefit per year based on the difference between the annual net cash outlay required on the original issue and the annual net cash outlay required on the new issue.

17.58   Serial bonds are not always accounted for with the effective-interest method. Exhibit 17.5 shows the calculation of the discount to be amortized under the "bonds-outstanding method" for a $1 million bond issued for $910,000 cash. This method is a "straight-line" method and was used extensively before APB *Opinion No. 21* and the advent of inexpensive computing devices. The serial bond issue contains 10-percent annual coupons and matures in 8 years, with $200,000 maturing at the end of the fourth, fifth, sixth, seventh, and eighth years of the issue.

17.59   On January 1 of year 1, Keller Company's $10 par value common shares were selling in the marketplace for $18 per share. At that time, Keller Company issued $1,000,000 par value of 6-percent, convertible bonds due in ten years. The bonds have semiannual coupons. The bonds can be called at any time for 101 percent of par. The conversion option allowed bond-holders to exchange each $1,000 par value bond for forty shares of common stock. The bonds were issued at $977,990 to yield 6.3 percent compounded semiannually. At the time of issue, an issue of nonconvertible bonds at par by the Keller Company would have required interest of 9 percent per year, compounded semiannually. Record journal entries for each of the following events.

a. Original issue of the bonds.

b. Six months after the date of issue, holders of $50,000 of par value of the bonds exchange their bonds for common shares at a time when the shares are selling for $26 each. Use the

**Exhibit 17.5**
**Serial Bond Issue Discount**
**of $90,000 Amortized with**
**the Bonds-Outstanding Method**

| Year (1) | Bonds Outstanding during Year (2) | Column (2) Divided by Total of Column (2) (3) | Discount to Be Amortized for Year (4) |
|---|---|---|---|
| 1 | $1,000,000 | 10/60 | $15,000 |
| 2 | 1,000,000 | 10/60 | a |
| 3 | 1,000,000 | b | 15,000 |
| 4 | 1,000,000 | 10/60 | c |
| 5 | 800,000 | 8/60 | 12,000 |
| 6 | 600,000 | d | 9,000 |
| 7 | e | 4/60 | f |
| 8 | 200,000 | 2/60 | g |
| Total | $6,000,000 | 60/60 | $90,000 |

a.–g.  Fill in the lettered blanks in Exhibit 17.5.

h. Prepare journal entries for issue of the bonds and at the end of each of the 8 years they are outstanding.

book value of the bonds to derive amounts. These bondholders are entitled to, and collect, interest for the six-month period just ended.
c. Six months later interest expense is recorded.
d. What is the book value of the bonds after the events of part **c**?

17.60 Refer to the data in the preceding problems.
a. Use Table 5 to help verify that the book value of the bonds outstanding four years later (five years after initial issue) is $936,924 (= $986,236 × 950/1,000) before adjusting entries.
b. Five years after date of original issue, holders of $350,000 par value of bonds exchange their bonds for common shares. At that time, the shares are selling for $30 each. Use the market value of the shares to derive amounts. The bondholders are entitled to, and collect, interest for the six-month period then ended.

17.61 Refer to the data in the preceding two problems. Nine and one-half years after date of issue, the common shares are selling in the marketplace for $35 per share, and the bonds for $1,410 each. Keller Company calls the bonds for redemption. $590,000 par value of the bonds are converted. Use the market value of the bonds to derive amounts. The remaining $10,000 of bonds are not converted, probably because of oversight by their owners, and are redeemed at call price plus accrued interest to date of call. The redemption occurs on the original maturity date of the bonds.
a. Use Table 5 to help verify that the book value of the 600 bonds still outstanding nine and one-half years after issue, before adjusting entries, is $997.136 per bond, $598,282 in total.
b. Record the entries made for interest and for conversion of 590 bonds. Assume interest coupons are presented for only 590 bonds.
c. Record entries made on redemption of the last 10 bonds. These bonds are *not* entitled to interest payments after call date.

# Chapter 18
# *Leases*

18.1 In a lease, the owner of property (the landlord or lessor) allows the user of the property (the tenant or lessee) to rent it for a specified period, but not to buy it outright. The lessor retains various rights in the property, primarily the right to have it returned at the end of the lease term. The lease term might be as short as a few minutes (for a metered parking space) or as long as several decades (for a shopping center site).

18.2 The reader may correctly wonder why leases are discussed in the context of liabilities. For every lessee with a liability and lease-related expenses, there is a lessor with an asset and lease-related revenues. As the accounting for leases has developed over the years, the major issues have involved lessee accounting. For this reason, we discuss leases in the chapters on long-term liabilities. This chapter discusses lease accounting by both the lessee (tenant) and the lessor (landlord).

## Issues in Lease Accounting

18.3 Generally accepted accounting principles have been concerned with lease accounting since at least the late 1940s. The FASB had no greater problem in the decade of the 1970s than leases—eight of the first thirty

FASB *Statements* and six of the first thirty FASB *Interpretations* concern leases. The issues in lease accounting involve the difference between renting an asset and effectively owning it. The critical question is who, the lessor or the lessee, bears the risks and is entitled, in turn, to the potential rewards from the asset.

## Operating Leases: Rent

18.4 Apartment dwellers rent an apartment by the year; a telephone user rents telephone equipment by the month; a reader rents a book from the library for a week; a traveling executive rents a car for a day. All of these acts are commonly thought of as renting. The tenant or lessee (renter is an ambiguous word) promises to pay for the use of the property, perhaps with payment depending on the amount of use (such as miles driven) during the lease term. The lessee makes entries such as the following at the time of each payment:

```
Rent Expense (or Prepaid Rent) ....   500
    Cash  .......................          500
```
To record payment for rent. Typical building leases call for payments in advance; automobile rentals are typically paid at the end of the rental period.

The landlord receives the payment and makes the following entry:

Cash ......................... 500
    Rent Revenue (or Rental Fees
       Received in Advance) ....... 500
The landlord credits revenue if the service has been rendered; the landlord credits a nonmonetary liability if the service will be rendered in the future.

In addition, the landlord makes adjusting entries for depreciation on the asset at the end of each accounting period:

Depreciation Expense ............ 10,000
    Accumulated Depreciation ..... 10,000
Depreciation on fleet of automobiles for the past 3 months.

18.5    Under generally accepted accounting principles, a lease is defined as an *operating lease* if it fails the test to be classified as the kind of lease that is not an operating lease, called a *capital lease*. Roughly, in an operating lease, the tenant acquires some of the future benefits of the asset being rented and expects to, or has the right to, return the asset to its owner while the asset still has considerable service potential. In this chapter, the verb *rent* means to lease an asset under an operating lease.

18.6    In accounting for operating leases, the tenant records rent expense. The lessor records rent revenue, retains the asset on its balance sheet, and records depreciation as appropriate.

18.7    **Long-Term Operating Leases** Operating leases are not necessarily characterized by lease periods of a year or less. Chapter 13 pointed out that a lessee might acquire the right to use office space in a building by signing a long-term lease, say, for 5 years. The lessee has the right to use the office space for a period of time significantly shorter than the life of the building and must return the rented premises to the lessor at the end of the lease period. Such long-term leases are operating leases, not capital leases. A lessee signing such a long-term operating lease debits Prepaid Rent (if rents are paid in advance)

or Leasehold Improvements (if the lessee makes improvements to the rented premises to benefit itself, such as for elegant paneling or carpets or special lighting fixtures). Assume that $230,000 cash is spent on signing a 5-year lease: $100,000 for permanent alterations of the office space, $60,000 for the first year's rent in advance, and $70,000 for the second year's. The lessee's entries might be:

Prepaid Rent (Current Asset) ..... 60,000
Prepaid Rent (Noncurrent Asset) . 70,000
Leasehold Improvements ........ 100,000
    Cash ..................... 230,000
To record payments upon signing lease.

At the end of the first year, entries record the expiration of the current asset, prepaid rent, the reclassification of the noncurrent asset as a current asset, and the amortization of the improvements:

Rent Expense ................... 60,000
    Prepaid Rent (Current Asset) .. 60,000
To record expiration of the current year's prepaid rent.

Prepaid Rent (Current Asset) ..... 70,000
    Prepaid    Rent    (Noncurrent
      Asset) ................... 70,000
To reclassify the prepayment for the second year as a current asset.

Amortization Expense ........... 20,000
    Leasehold Improvements .... 20,000
In spite of the fact that the improvements may last longer, they are amortized over the life of the lease, 5 years; $100,000/5 = $20,000.

The landlord-lessor makes the following entry upon signing the lease:

Cash ........................ 130,000
    Rental Fees Received in
      Advance (Current) ......... 60,000
    Rental Fees Received in
      Advance (Noncurrent) ..... 70,000
Receipt of cash from tenants for 2 years' rent in advance. The accounts credited are like Advances from Customers.

At the end of the first year, the following entry parallels the tenant's:

18.8

Rental Fees Received in Advance
   (Noncurrent) . . . . . . . . . . . . . . . . . . 70,000
    Rental Fees Received in
      Advance (Current) . . . . . . . . . 10,000
    Rent Revenue . . . . . . . . . . . . . . 60,000
Reclassification of second year's
rent as a current nonmonetary liability and recognition of revenue
for first year's use of rented premises.

The lessor also recognizes depreciation and other expenses on the rented property. One might wonder why the lessor does not debit an asset account for the leasehold improvement: the lessor cannot count on the improvement being of value, or even being on hand, after the lease term; moreover, the lessor has not acquired anything through an arm's-length transaction.

## Capital Leases: Installment Sale and Purchase

18.9 An airline acquires an airplane. Rather than pay for it with cash or borrow in the form of a mortgage or secured note, it signs a non-cancelable contract called a lease. The lease requires payments whose present value is approximately the same as the purchase price. At the end of the lease term, the property is returned to the lessor. At the time the lease is signed, however, the expected salvage of the property at the end of the lease term is near zero. Such leasing contracts are in every economic respect like an installment sale by the lessor and an installment purchase by the lessee.

18.10 Why might an airline prefer to sign a long-term noncancelable lease for an airplane, rather than purchase the airplane outright using the more straightforward long-term, noncancelable installment note? To see why the airline might prefer the lease, consider the accounting if it signs the installment note.

18.11 **Accounting for Installment Purchases** Assume that an airline agrees to buy an airplane for $30 million and to pay for it with 15 end-of-year installments of $5 million each (implying an interest rate of about 14.5 per-

cent per year). The airline debits equipment for $30 million and credits Installment Note Payable, a long-term liability, for $30 million. It will record both depreciation expense of $2 million (= $30 million/15 years) on the airplane each year and interest expense of over $4.3 million (= .145 × $30 million) during the first year of the lease. Taxes, insurance, and other costs will also be recognized as an expense each year. Total expense in the first year exceeds $6.3 million.

18.12 Now, assume that the airline rents the airplane for $5 million per year (the cash payment as required by the installment purchase) and accounts for the transaction as an operating lease. Rent expense of $5 million will be recognized each year. In contrast to the installment purchase, the airline has less debt on the balance sheet (no $30 million long-term Note Payable) and smaller expenses in the early years of the lease.* All else being equal, most managements would prefer to show lower amounts of debt and lower amounts of expense.

18.13 Lease accounting problems arose because lessees were able to structure lease agreements that were in economic substance installment purchases of property but were accounted for as operating leases. These leases came to be known as off-balance-sheet financing because they enabled the lessee to acquire most of the service potential of the asset without showing either the asset or, more important, the liability on its balance sheet. Since FASB *Statement No. 13* was issued in 1976, the accounting for leases has come closer to reflecting economic substance, but it still has some way to go.†

## The Problem of Executory Contracts

18.14 Historical cost accounting does not recognize an asset or the related liability to pay for it until there has been mutual perfor-

---

*Later, we show that over the life of the asset, the two methods of accounting will have the same total expense. Only the timing differs.
†Financial Accounting Standards Board, "Accounting for Leases" *Statement of Financial Accounting Standards No. 13* (1976).

mance. Recall that the existence of a liability implies some past or current benefit. Assume, for example, that a firm signs a 5-year employment contract with its president. The firm is obligated to pay and the president is obligated to work for 5 years. Accounting does not, however, recognize an asset for the future benefits it expects to receive from the president, nor does it recognize a liability for the present value of the promised payments. Chapter 15 discussed the fact that the signing of executory contracts, such as long-term employment contracts, is not an accounting event. No mutual performance has taken place.

18.15    Long-term leases covering only part of an asset's life are likewise considered executory contracts.* For example, an 8-year lease on an airplane expected to have a 15-year useful life is an executory contract. At the time of signing, all of the performance under the contract is viewed as taking place in the future. The lessee will use the airplane during the 8 years and will pay the lessor amounts due under the lease agreement. Accounting does not require the lessee to record an asset for the right to use the airplane for 8 years in the amount of the present value of the contractual 8 payments; neither must the lessee record a liability for the present value of those 8 payments. If it did, then managements would not be able to keep long-term lease financing off the balance sheet. Accounting has been reluctant to change its long-standing rules about recording the assets and liabilities implied in executory contracts.

18.16    We think that the criterion of mutual performance has been satisfied at the time the 8-year lease described above is signed. The lessee has acquired the legal right to possess and use the property for the term of the lease. As long as lease payments are made when due, the lessor cannot interfere with the lessee's use of the leased asset. In many long-term leasing arrangements, the lease is

---

*FASB *Statement No. 13* allows leases covering up to 75 percent of the asset's life to be treated as operating leases.

noncancelable. Thus, a transaction has occurred that affects the financial position of a firm in a way that can be measured with virtual certainty. In our opinion, this transaction satisfies the criteria for an accounting event and ought to be recognized.

FASB *Statement No. 13* requires that    18.17 long-term leases meeting certain conditions be classified as capital leases. The leased asset and the related liability are recorded in the accounts. Thus, although these leases are executory contracts, their signing is recognized as an accounting event. Many other long-term, noncancelable leases, however, do not satisfy the criteria for classification as capital leases. Such leases, as with most other executory contracts, are not recorded in the accounts but are treated as operating leases. The FASB will likely continue to struggle with accounting for leases until it changes the rules regarding the recognition of assets and liabilities for long-term, noncancelable executory contracts.

## Symmetry of Accounting: Lessors and Lessees

Before FASB *Statement No. 13* was issued    18.18 in 1976, a lessor could account for a long-term noncancelable lease as though it had *sold* the asset on a long-term installment note. The lessee, meanwhile, could account for the lease as an operating lease, *not* an installment purchase. Millions of dollars of assets were on no one's books: The accounting presumed that the lessor had sold the asset but the lessee had merely rented it. Since FASB *Statement No. 13,* the same criteria generally apply to both lessors and lessees. It is easier to understand when a lease is considered an operating lease and when a capital lease than it was before 1976.

The next section contrasts operating lease    18.19 accounting and capital lease accounting for a simple case. Then we discuss the criteria currently used in accounting for classifying leases as operating leases or capital leases. The authoritative pronouncements on lease accounting, more than 15 FASB *Statements* and *Interpretations,* contain many details not explored here. The reader who understands this chapter should be prepared to tackle any particular problem by seeking answers in the pronouncements.

## Lessee Accounting

### Example Data

18.20  Assume that User Company wants to acquire a minicomputer produced by Manufacturing Company. The minicomputer has a 3-year life and costs $30,000. User Company is responsible for property taxes, maintenance, and repairs of the computer whether leased or purchased.

18.21   Assume that the lease is signed January 1, year 1, and that payments on the lease are due on December 31, year 1, year 2, and year 3. In practice, lease payments are usually made in advance, but the computations in the example are simpler if we assume payments at the end of the year. The interest rate implicit in the lease is 12 percent. Compound interest computations show that each lease payment is about $12,500. (The present value of $1 paid at the end of this year and each of the next 2 years is about $2.40 when the interest rate is 12 percent per year. See Table 4 at the end of the book. Because the lease payments must have a present value of $30,000, each payment must be about $30,000/2.40 = $12,500.)

### Operating Lease Accounting by Lessee

18.22  In operating lease accounting, the lessee makes no entry on January 1 of year 1, when the lease is signed, and the following entry on December 31 of years 1, 2, and 3:

Rent Expense .................... 12,500
    Cash ....................... 12,500
To recognize annual expense of leasing computer.

The lessor's accounting is described later.

### Funds Statement Effects of Operating Leases

In an operating lease, Rent Expense equals   18.23
cash paid or payable for the lease. No special adjustment is required to net income in deriving funds from operations. Lease payments in advance are debited to Prepaid Rent, an element of funds, and credited to Cash, an element of funds. There is no net effect on funds. If the lessee signs a long-term operating lease, such as a 5-year lease on office space, and makes payments covering more than the next year, there is an "Other Use" of funds for acquisition of a long-term asset, which might be called Prepaid Rent or Leasehold.

### Capital Lease Accounting by Lessee

In capital lease accounting, the lessee rec-   18.24
ognizes the signing of the lease as the simultaneous acquisition of a long-term asset, called a *leasehold,* and the incurring of a liability for lease payments. At the time the lease is signed, both the leasehold and the liability are recorded on the books at the present value of the liability—$30,000 in the example.*

The entry made at the time User Com-   18.25
pany signs its 3-year lease is:

Asset   Computer Leasehold . ..,, 30,000
    Liability—Present Value of
      Lease Obligations ...........       30,000
To recognize acquisition of asset and the related liability.

At the end of the year, two separate entries are made. The leasehold must be amortized over its useful life. The first entry made at the end of each year recognizes the amortization of the leasehold asset. Assuming that User Company uses straight-line amortization of its leasehold, the entry made at the end of each of the 3 years is:

---

*FASB *Statement No. 13* requires that the lease liability be segregated into its current and noncurrent portions. We do not illustrate this refinement here.

Amortization Expense (on Computer
  Leasehold) .................... 10,000
    Accumulated Amortization of
      Computer Leasehold ........ 10,000

The second entry made at the end of each year recognizes the lease payment, which is part payment of interest on the liability and part reduction in the liability itself. The entries made at the end of each of the 3 years are based on an amortization schedule such as that shown in Exhibit 18.1.

**Dec. 31, Year 1:**

Interest Expense ................. 3,600
Liability—Present Value of Lease
  Obligations .................... 8,900
    Cash ...................... 12,500

To recognize lease payment, interest on liability for year (.12 × $30,000 = $3,600), and plug for reduction in the liability. The present value of the liability after this entry is $21,100 (= $30,000 − $8,900).

**Dec. 31, Year 2:**

Interest Expense ................. 2,532
Liability—Present Value of Lease
  Obligations .................... 9,968
    Cash ...................... 12,500

To recognize lease payment, interest on liability for year (.12 × $21,100 = $2,532), and plug for reduction in the liability. The present value of the liability after this entry is $11, 132 (= $21,000 − $9,968).

**Dec. 31, Year 3:**

Interest Expense ................. 1,368
Liability—Present Value of Lease
  Obligations .................... 11,132
    Cash ...................... 12,500

To recognize lease payment, interest on liability for year, and reduction in the liability. Interest expense is a plug. The present value of the liability after this entry is zero (= $11,132 − $11,132).

In the capital lease method, the total expense over the 3 years is $37,500, consisting    18.26

---

## Exhibit 18.1

### Amortization Schedule for $30,000 Lease Liability, Repaid in Three Annual Installments of $12,500 Each, Interest Rate of 12 Percent, Compounded Annually

**ANNUAL JOURNAL ENTRY**

Dr. Interest Expense ..................................... Amount in Column (3)
Dr. Liability—Present Value of Lease Obligations ......... Amount in Column (5)
  Cr. Cash .......................................... Amount in Column (4)

| Year (1) | Lease Liability Start of Year (2) | Interest Expense for Year (3) | Payment (4) | Portion of Payment Reducing Lease Liability (5) | Lease Liability End of Year (6) |
|---|---|---|---|---|---|
| 0 | | | | | $30,000 |
| 1 ........... | $30,000 | $3,600 | $12,500 | $ 8,900 | 21,100 |
| 2 ........... | 21,100 | 2,532 | 12,500 | 9,968 | 11,132 |
| 3 ........... | 11,132 | 1,368 | 12,500 | 11,132 | 0 |

Column (2) = column (6), previous period.

Column (3) = .12 × column (2), except in year 3, where it is a plug = column (4) − column (2).

Column (4): given.

Column (5) = column (4) − column (3).

Column (6) = column (2) − column (5).

of $30,000 (= $10,000 + $10,000 + $10,000) for amortization expense and $7,500 (= $3,600 + $2,532 + $1,368) for interest expense. This is exactly the same as the total expense recognized under the operating lease method described above. Total expense over the life of the lease equals cash outflow. The difference between the operating lease method and the capital lease method is the *timing* of the expense recognition and the entries in income statement and balance sheet accounts. The capital lease method recognizes both the asset and the liability. It recognizes expense sooner than does the operating lease method. Exhibit 18.2 compares the two methods.

## Funds Statements Effects of Capital Leases on the Lessee

18.27 The lessee's statement of changes in financial position for the period when it signs a capital lease shows a nonoperating source of funds from the issue of long-term debt in the form of a lease and a nonoperating use of funds for the acquisition of noncurrent assets. In later periods, cash payments are made; part of the cash is for interest expense, reducing net income, and part reduces the liability for future lease payments. The amounts of the payments used for interest and for reduction in the liability are shown in an amortization schedule such as

that shown in Exhibit 18.1. All of the interest expense uses funds. The expenses also include amortization of the noncurrent asset, Leasehold. Thus, an addback is required in calculating funds from operations for amortization not using funds.

To summarize, consider the data in Exhibit 18.1 and the funds statement for User Company for the second year of its capital lease. Income declines by $12,532 (= $10,000 of amortization expense and $2,532 of interest expense). Ten thousand dollars is added back to net income in deriving funds provided by operations for amortization not using funds; operations show a $2,532 net use of funds for interest. In addition, funds of $9,968 are used to reduce the noncurrent liability for lease payables.* The total uses of funds of $12,500 (= $2,532 + $9,968) match the cash payment of $12,500.

18.28

## Effects of Lease Accounting on Lessee

In this simple example, expense under the capital lease method is only slightly larger than expense under the operating lease method in the first year. In more realistic cases where the lease extends over 20 years,

18.29

*Technically, funds of $9,968 are used to reduce the current portion of the liability, and then $9,968 of the noncurrent portion of the liability is reclassified as current. The net effect is to reduce the noncurrent liability by $9,968.

*Exhibit 18.2*
**Comparison of Lessee's Expense Recognized Under Operating Lease and Capital Lease Methods**

| | Expense Recognized Each Year under | | |
|---|---|---|---|
| | Operating Lease | Capital Lease | |
| Year 1 ............................................ | $12,500 | $13,600 | (= $10,000 + $3,600) |
| Year 2 ............................................ | 12,500 | 12,532 | (= 10,000 + 2,532) |
| Year 3 ............................................ | 12,500 | 11,368 | (= 10,000 + 1,368) |
| Total ............................................ | $37,500[a] | $37,500 | (= $30,000[b] + $7,500[c]) |

[a]Rent expense.   [b]Amortization expense.   [c]Interest expense.

the expense in the first year under the capital lease method may be 25 percent larger than under the operating lease method. In the last year, expenses under operating lease accounting can exceed those under capital lease accounting by large amounts.*

18.30 Most lessees prefer to use the operating lease method whenever they can for two reasons:

**1.** The income reported in financial statements is higher in the early years than it would be under the capital lease method.

**2.** There is no need to show a Present Value of Lease Obligations account as a liability on the balance sheet. Thus, the debt-equity ratio is not significantly affected under the operating lease method.

## Some Details from FASB Rules Involving a Lessee's Capital Lease

18.31 The preceding discussion omits details the reader may encounter in practice. Three are discussed here: the residual value, the im-

---

*Approximating the last row of an amortization schedule is just as easy as the first. Consider that the final cash payment must discharge the remaining principal and interest on that principal for the last period. That is

$$\frac{\text{Final Cash}}{\text{Payment}} = \frac{\text{Principal}}{\text{Repayment}} + \text{(Interest on Principal Repayment)}.$$

$$\frac{\text{Final Cash}}{\text{Payment}} = \frac{\text{Principal}}{\text{Repayment}} \times (1 + \text{Interest Rate}).$$

$$\frac{\text{Principal}}{\text{Repayment}} = \frac{\text{Final Cash Payment}}{1 + \text{Interest Rate}}.$$

In the example in Exhibit 18.1, the final cash payment is $12,500, and the interest rate is 12 percent. Thus, the final principal repayment is approximately $11,161 (= $12,500/1.12), and the interest expense for the last period can be approximated in either of two ways as $1,339 (= .12 × $11,161 = $12,500 − $11,161).

The approximation will be exact if the exact implicit interest rate is used; in this example, the implicit interest rate to equate three payments of $12,500 to a present value of $30,000 is not exactly 12 percent but is closer to 12.0444 percent. To compute the total expense (= depreciation + interest) for the last year of the life of a capital lease, one must know how much of the cash payment is interest and how much is principal repayment. One need not compute the entire amortization schedule (a tedious job by hand, but trivial with a computer) to approximate the amount of interest expense.

---

plicit interest rate versus incremental borrowing rate comparison, and executory costs.

**Residual Value** At the end of the lease term, the asset is returned to the lessor. At that time, it may have a value. At the start of the lease term, the estimate of that value is called the estimated *residual value*. In some circumstances, the lessee agrees in the lease contract to guarantee a residual value. That is, if the lessor finds the asset is worth less than the guaranteed amount, then the lessee must pay the difference to the lessor. Guaranteed residual values are part of contractual minimum lease payments. 18.32

*Example* User Company agrees to make three annual lease payments in arrears of $12,500 and guarantees that the value of the asset at the end of the lease term will be at least $3,000. Assume that the interest rate is 12 percent, compounded annually. We have already seen that the present value of the three lease payments is $30,000. The present value of the guaranteed residual value of $3,000 is $2,135 (= $3,000 × .71178; Table 2, 3-period row, 12-percent column). The lessee would record both the leasehold asset and lease obligation at $32,135 (= $30,000 + $2,135). 18.33

Even when the residual value is not guaranteed, it can affect the lessee's analysis, calculations, and accounting, as described next. 18.34

**Implicit Interest Rate and Incremental Borrowing Rate** The interest rate that equates the present value of the minimum lease payments plus the estimated residual value (whether guaranteed or not) of an asset to the fair market value of the asset at the inception of the lease is the *implicit interest rate* in the lease.† In the example in Exhibit 18.1, a 12-percent interest rate was implicit 18.35

---

†See Examples 21 and 22 in Appendix B for illustrative calculations. Note that a residual value must be guaranteed to be part of the "contractual minimum lease payments," but need not be guaranteed to be part of the computation of the implicit rate of return. For this latter purpose, an estimate will do.

in the series of three lease payments of $12,500 that had a present value of $30,000. In general, the lessee's incremental *borrowing rate,* the interest rate for secured loans of duration similar to those in the lease, may differ from the implicit interest rate. The lessee will generally use the lower of the implicit interest rate or its incremental borrowing rate for its calculations.* The amount recorded for the leasehold asset cannot exceed the fair market value of the asset, if it is known.

18.36 *Example* The interest rate implicit in the lease illustrated in Exhibit 18.1 is 12 percent. If User Company has an incremental borrowing rate of 12 percent or larger, then it will record the lease asset and lease obligations at $30,000 and use a 12-percent rate throughout the life of the lease. If User Company's incremental borrowing rate is less than 12 percent, say 10 percent, then the calculations will be as follows. Assume there is no residual value. Then the contractual lease payments have a present value of $31,086 (= $12,500 × 2.48685; Table 4, 3-period row, 10-percent column). So long as the fair market value of the asset is not less than $31,086, the lease asset and the lease obligation will be recorded at $31,086.† The 10-percent rate will be used throughout the life of the lease in accounting for the liability. Interest expense for the first year of the lease would be $3,109 (= .10 × $31,086) and amortization expense for the first year would be $10,362 (= $31,086/3).

18.37 **Executory Costs** Generally, costs for insurance, maintenance, property taxes, and the like will be incurred over the life of the leased asset, just as they are incurred for

owned assets. These costs, called *executory costs,* are often paid directly by the lessee, who debits an appropriate expense account as the costs are incurred. Sometimes, however, the lessor will pay such costs of ownership. In that case, each lease payment includes amounts for executory costs as well as for interest and principal on the lease obligations. The lessee excludes the amount of executory costs from the contractual lease payments in computing implicit interest rates and present values.

*Example* In the lease of Exhibit 18.1, assume that Manufacturing Company is responsible for property taxes on the minicomputer of $1,000 per year. The lease contract specifies that each of the three annual payments is to be $13,500. So long as User Company can estimate the amount of each $13,500 that is for property taxes ($1,000 in this case), it will exclude that amount from the contractual lease payments and base its calculations, as in Exhibit 18.1, on the difference—$12,500 (= $13,500 − $1,000). 18.38

## Lessor Accounting

**Operating Lease Accounting by Lessor** 18.39
Assume that the minicomputer cost Manufacturing Company $18,000. The company uses straight-line depreciation. The operating lease treatment involves the following entries each year:

| | | |
|---|---|---|
| Cash | 12,500 | |
|     Rent Revenue | | 12,500 |
| Receipt of cash for rent at the end of the year. | | |

| | | |
|---|---|---|
| Depreciation Expense | 6,000 | |
|     Accumulated Depreciation on | | |
|       Leased Machines | | 6,000 |
| To record expense (= $18,000/3) at the end of the year. | | |

## Funds Statement Effects

The operating lease method reports revenues to the lessor equal to the amounts of cash received or receivable for leases. No special adjustment to net income is required 18.40

---

*The lower the interest rate used to discount future payments, the larger is their present value. Prior to FASB *Statement No. 13,* there had been concern that lease transactions had given rise to off-balance-sheet financing. In requiring that the financing appear on the balance sheet, the FASB has chosen the rate that will make the amount of the debt larger rather than smaller.

†If the fair market value is less than $31,086, then the lease asset and obligation will be recorded at that lower amount.

*Exhibit 18.3*

**Comparison of Lessor's Revenue and Expense under Operating Lease and Capital Lease Methods**

| | Operating Lease Method | | | Capital Lease Method | | |
|---|---|---|---|---|---|---|
| | Revenues − | Expenses = | Income | Revenues − | Expenses = | Income |
| Start of Year 1 ............... | — | — | — | $30,000[b] | $18,000[c] | $12,000 |
| End of | | | | | | |
| Year 1 ............... | $12,500 | $ 6,000[a] | $ 6,500 | 3,600[d] | — | 3,600 |
| Year 2 ............... | 12,500 | 6,000[a] | 6,500 | 2,532[d] | — | 2,532 |
| Year 3 ............... | 12,500 | 6,000[a] | 6,500 | 1,368[d] | — | 1,368 |
| Totals ............. | $37,500 − | $18,000 = | $19,500 | $37,500 − | $18,000 = | $19,500 |

[a]Depreciation: $18,000/3.   [b]Sales price.   [c]Cost of goods sold.   [d]Interest revenue; see Exhibit 18.1.

in deriving funds from operations. The lessor subtracts depreciation expense that does not use funds in calculating net income; the addback to net income for depreciation in calculating funds from operations is the same as for any other depreciation expense.

## Capital Lease Accounting by Lessor

18.41   The capital lease treatment reports as though Manufacturing Company sold the computer and received an installment note for three payments of $12,500 each. The implicit interest rate is 12 percent per year. The entries upon signing the lease, assuming a perpetual inventory method, are:

Installment Note Receivable ........ 30,000
    Sales Revenue ................     30,000
To record present value of notes and sales revenue.*

---

*As with lease liabilities, FASB *Statement No. 13* requires that receivables arising from lessors' capital leases be disaggregated into current and noncurrent portions. We have not illustrated that refinement here. When the amounts receivable are split between current and noncurrent receivables, the subsequent calculation of interest revenue and the resulting journal entries will be easier if the current portions of the receivables are recorded at their present value, not their undiscounted amounts. Showing current receivables at present value, although not generally done, is allowed. We recommend that practice where, as here, the computation of compound interest, using the effective interest method, involves both current and noncurrent principal amounts.

Cost of Goods Sold ............... 18,000
    Finished Goods Inventory ......     18,000
To record cost of minicomputer sold.

The effect is to recognize a $12,000 (= $30,000 − $18,000) gross margin on the "sale."

18.42   At the end of each year, Manufacturing Company receives a cash payment and makes an entry with amounts similar to those made by User Company, also based on the amortization schedule in Exhibit 18.1. For example, the entry at the end of the second year would be:

Cash .......................... 12,500
    Interest Revenue .............     2,532
    Installment Note Receivable ....     9,968

Interest revenue is the implicit interest rate, 12 percent, multiplied by the book value of the receivable at the start of the year; plug for the reduction in the installment receivable.

18.43   Exhibit 18.3 compares the revenue and expense for the lessor, Manufacturing Company, over the 3 years. Note that its net income totals $19,500 (= $37,500 − $18,000) under both accounting treatments. Over long enough time spans, income is cash in less cash out. Only the timing of income differs. The capital lease method shows all of the manufacturing profit or gross margin in the year of sale and only interest revenue over the life of the lease. Under the operating lease method, the operating profit and the implicit interest are both spread over 3 years. Lessors have, other things being equal, preferred the capital lease method for financial reporting because it reports income earlier.

18.44 **Funds Statement Effect of Capital Leases on Lessor** The lessor's statement of changes in financial position for the period when it signs a capital lease includes an operating source of funds in the amount of the selling price and operating use of funds in an amount equal to the cost of the asset leased. Because these amounts are already included in the calculation of net income, no addback or subtraction is required in deriving funds from operations. Current assets, however, do not increase by the full amount of the selling price. A portion of the lease receivable is noncurrent. Thus, a nonoperating use of funds in the amount of the increase in noncurrent assets (receivables) must be shown. As Chapter 7 points out, the "sale" of an asset involving a note or lease receivable might be thought of as sale for cash and then the immediate investment of a portion of the cash in a noncurrent receivable.*

18.45     In each subsequent period, interest revenue produces an inflow of funds. Part of the cash payments received from the lessee are repayments of the receivable. Each receipt of cash results in an increase in funds of $12,500: part from operations (interest revenue) and part from redemption of a noncurrent receivable.† The amounts are split between operations and redemption of noncurrent receivable shown in the amortization schedule in Exhibit 18.1.

---

*At the end of the first year, funds will increase because the receivable for the second lease payment will be reclassified from noncurrent to current. Whether that amount is shown at face value or at present value affects the amount of funds reported as used during the year for the investment in the long-term receivable. We omit the complications required to carry this example far enough to illustrate with numbers.

†As noted with lease liabilities, the redemption is of a *current* receivable. However, a noncurrent receivable of equal amount must be reclassified as current. The net effect therefore is a redemption of a noncurrent receivable.

## Some Details from FASB Rules Involving a Lessor's Capital Lease

18.46 The details of accounting for lessor's capital leases involve terminology somewhat more complicated than we have illustrated. This section illustrates the following terms used in *Statement No. 13* in describing the accounting for lessor's capital leases.

**Gross Investment in Lease** Undiscounted sum of minimum lease payments plus the undiscounted estimated residual value.

**Net Investment in Leases** Present value of minimum lease payments plus present value of estimated residual value discounted at the implicit interest rate.

**Unearned Income** The difference between the gross investment in the lease and the net investment in the lease.

**Sales Revenue** The present value of the minimum lease payments plus any *guaranteed* residual value.

**Cost of Sales** The cost of the leased asset "sold" reduced by the present value of the estimated residual value. (Because the lessor recovers part of the cost of the leased asset when the residual value is realized, the present value of that recovery reduces the economic burden of putting the asset in the hands of the lessee.)

**Initial Direct Costs** The lessor's direct incremental costs, such as for sales commissions and legal fees, to negotiate and consummate the lease transaction.

18.47 *Example* Manufacturing Company manufactures a machine with an estimated economic life of five years. It leases the machine to Using Company on a noncancelable basis. Using Company agrees to pay $25,000 per year at the end of each year for five years. Collectibility of the installments is reasonably assured, and Using Company will pay all executory costs. The estimated residual value at the end of the lease term is $20,000. Total manufacturing cost of the machine is $25,000, and initial direct costs are $1,000. The interest rate implicit in the lease is 20 percent per year. The machine is to be returned by Using Company at the end of the lease term. Exhibit 18.4 illustrates the var-

*Exhibit 18.4*
**Illustration of Terms Used in
FASB Statement No. 13 for
Lessor's Capital Leases**

Lease term is 5 years.
Annual lease payments in arrears are $25,000 each.
Manufacturing cost of asset is $25,000.
Initial direct cost is $1,000.
Unguaranteed residual value is $20,000.
Interest rate implicit in lease is 20 percent per year.

| | |
|---|---:|
| Gross Lease Receivables (Undiscounted Sum of Minimum Lease Payments = 5 × $25,000) ...... | $125,000 |
| Gross Amount of Estimated Residual Value ............................................... | 20,000 |
| Gross Investment in Lease (Undiscounted Sum of Lease Receivables and Estimated Residual Value) ................................................................................. | $145,000 |
| Unearned Income (Plug Required to Reduce Gross Investment in Lease to Net Investment, Below) ................................................................................... | (62,197) |
| Net Investment in Lease [Present Value of Minimum Lease Payments Plus Present Value of Estimated Residual Value = ($25,000 × 2.99061)[a] + ($20,000 × .40188)[b] = $74,765 + $8,038] ................................................................................. | $ 82,803 |
| Sales Price of Asset (Present Value of Contractual Lease Payments = $25,000 × 2.99061[a]) ...... | $ 74,765 |
| Less: Cost of Sales [Cost of Goods Sold Reduced by Present Value of Estimated Residual Value = $25,000 − ($20,000 × .40188)[b] = $25,000 − $8,039] ............................... | (16,962) |
| Initial Indirect Costs ................................................................ | ( 1,000) |
| Gross Margin on Signing Lease ....................................................... | $ 56,803 |

[a]Table 4, 5-period row, 20-percent column.
[b]Table 2, 5-period row, 20-percent column.

ious intermediate computations made by the lessor.

18.48    FASB *Statement No. 13* suggests balance sheet presentation for lessor capital leases that implies the following journal entries:

| | | |
|---|---:|---:|
| Gross Investment in Lease ........ | 145,000 | |
| Cost of Sales ................... | 16,962 | |
| Unearned Income ........... | | 62,197 |
| Finished Goods Inventory ..... | | 25,000 |
| Sales Revenue .............. | | 74,765 |

Summary entry for investment in lease and associated revenues.

| | | |
|---|---:|---:|
| Expense for Initial Direct Costs .... | 1,000 | |
| Various Assets and Liabilities .. | | 1,000 |

Record expense for sales commissions, legal fees, and the like.

The first of these entries is difficult to follow because it condenses so many steps. It is equivalent to the following series of entries:

| | | |
|---|---:|---:|
| Gross Lease Receivables ......... | 125,000 | |
| Sales Revenue ............. | | 74,765 |
| Discount on Gross Lease Receivables ............. | | 50,235 |

Record sales revenue at present value of receivables; show receivables at undiscounted amount with discount in contra account to reduce to present value.

| | | |
|---|---:|---:|
| Cost of Sales ................... | 16,962 | |
| Investment in Residual Value of Leased Asset ................. | 8,038 | |
| Finished Goods Inventory .... | | 25,000 |

Record cost of sales and lessor's asset, which is the present value of the estimated residual value to be realized in five years.

| | | |
|---|---:|---:|
| Gross Investment in Lease ....... | 125,000 | |
| Gross Lease Receivables ..... | | 125,000 |

Reclassification of receivables account into a single investment account that will record all aspects of the lease: receivables and residual value.

| Discount on Gross Lease | | |
|---|---|---|
| Receivables .................. | 50,235 | |
| Unearned Income ........... | | 50,235 |

Reclassification of discount on receivables.

| Gross Investment in Lease ....... | 20,000 | |
|---|---|---|
| Investment in Residual Value of | | |
| Leased Asset ............. | | 8,038 |
| Unearned Income ........... | | 11,962 |

Aggregation of residual value into gross, undiscounted amount with discount included in Unearned Income along with the discount on the lease receivables. Thus, the difference between the estimated residual value and the present value of that amount will be recognized as interest revenue over the term of the lease as the balance in the Unearned Income account is amortized.

The above five entries have the combined effect of the entry shown at the beginning of this paragraph. Only the net investment in the lease, $82,663 (see Exhibit 18.4), need be included in the balance sheet, but then, the details of the gross investment and unearned income are disclosed in notes.

## Criteria for Classifying Leases

18.49    The accounting goal for leases is to place the asset on the books of the party enjoying the risks and rewards of the asset and to record liabilities for its debt financing. The lease asset is to appear on one set of books—either the lessor's or the lessee's—but not on both. The current rules for leases virtually ensure that the accounting for a lease transaction is symmetric between the lessor and the lessee. If the lessee treats it as an operating lease, the lessor will also do so. Exceptions to perfect symmetry are discussed below.

18.50    The criteria are stated for a capital lease. All leases not meeting these criteria are operating leases.

## Capital Lease for Lessee

The lessee treats a lease as a capital lease— conveying the risks and rewards of an asset from the lessor to the lessee— if *any* of the following four conditions is satisfied:    18.51

**1.** The lease transfers ownership of the property to the lessee by the end of the lease term; or

**2.** The lease contains a bargain purchase option;* or

**3.** The lease term is equal to 75 percent or more of the estimated economic life of the property; or

**4.** The present value at the inception of the lease† of the contractual lease payments is greater than or equal to 90 percent of the market value of the lessor's property at that time, reduced by the dollar amounts of investment credit to which the lessor is entitled.

There are some exceptions to the rules and many details. To become an expert on the details of lease accounting requires study of the many pronouncements issued. Our objective is to develop a sufficient understanding of the issues involved and the general guidelines included in authoritative pronouncements so that the pronouncements can be searched when dealing with specific questions.    18.52

If the goal of lease accounting is to capture the economic substance of who owns the asset, then the most important of the criteria    18.53

---

*A *bargain purchase option* exists when the lessee has the contractual right to purchase the leased asset sometime during the lease term for a price that appears, at the start of the lease, to be sufficiently less than the estimated fair market value of the asset on the date the option can be exercised so that the option seems likely to be exercised. When there is a bargain purchase option, the present value of the lease liability is equal to the present value of the bargain purchase option plus the present value of all lease payments until the bargain purchase option can be exercised. Payments after the bargain purchase option date are ignored in the calculation of the lease's present value.
†"Inception of the lease" is a technical term defined in FASB *Statement No. 13* (1976), par. 5.

listed above is the fourth. A lease is a capital lease if the lessor gets a fair return from investing in the leased asset. Those who construct lease contracts have been able to structure agreements that do not satisfy any of the first three criteria but still transfer the risks and rewards of ownership from the lessor to the lessee.

18.54 **Example** Assume that Manufacturing Company owns a computer with a fair market value of $100,000 and an economic life of five years. It estimates the residual value of the computer to be $20,000 in three years, but it realizes that the used computer business is subject to great uncertainty about future values. User Company offers to lease the computer for a three-year term, paying $35,038 per year at the end of this and each of the next two years. User Company's incremental borrowing rate is 15 percent per year. The present value of the three lease payments is $80,000 (= $35,038 × 2.28323; Table 4, 3-period row, 15-percent column). If a lease were constructed with no *guaranteed* residual value, then that lease would be an operating lease for both lessee and lessor because the present value of the contractual minimum lease payments is only $80,000, which is less than 90 percent of the fair market value of the lessor's asset.

18.55 Such an arrangement is, however, unsatisfactory to the lessor, Manufacturing Company. Although it estimates the residual value three years hence to be $20,000, that value is uncertain. If the value turns out to be less than $20,000, then Manufacturing Company will end up losing. Manufacturing Company in turn suggests that a three-year lease for payments of $35,038 is satisfactory only if User Company guarantees the residual value of $20,000. That is, at the end of the lease term, if the fair market value of the computer is less than $20,000, then User Company will pay Manufacturing Company the difference. Under these circumstances, the lease will be a capital lease for both lessor and lessee. Typically, however, lessees have not wanted to show the obligations for lease payments on their balance sheets.

18.56 One method used in lease transactions can satisfy both the lessor and the lessee. The lessee agrees to pay for an insurance policy that will guarantee the residual value. Assume that Insurance Company will sell a policy that guarantees the residual value of the computer to be at least $20,000 in three years. Manufacturing Company is indifferent as to who guarantees the residual value, so long as it is guaranteed. If the insurance premium payments have present value at the inception of the lease not greater than $10,000, then both lessor and lessee can achieve their goals. Assume the insurance policy can be bought for a single payment of $7,000 at the inception of the lease. Then the payments made by the lessee, User Company, have present value of only $87,000 (= $80,000 + $7,000), which is less than 90 percent of the fair market value of the lessor's asset. Thus, the lessee treats the lease as an operating lease and the obligations for the lease payments will not appear on its balance sheet. Meanwhile the lessor, Manufacturing Company, is relieved of the risk of a residual value different from its estimate.

18.57 Until accounting principles require the capitalization of obligations for executory contracts, whatever their term, it seems likely that lessees will be able to avoid treating many long-term leases as assets financed by balance sheet liabilities.

## Lessor's Additional Criteria for a Capital Lease

18.58 For a seller to record sales revenue, there must be little or no unpredictability about cash collection. Refer to the discussion in Chapters 7 and 8. For a lessor to treat a lease as a sale, the lessor must be reasonably able to predict the amount to be collected and must be reasonably certain that there are no substantial amounts of unreimbursable future expenditures that the lessor might have to make.* Such future expenditures might

---

*FASB *Statement No. 13* (1976), par. 8. Chapter 8 discusses how the seller treats unpredictability of cash collection from its customers on installment sales. Note that the required treatment by the lessor of unpredictable cash collections from the lessee differs from the usual treatment of unpredictable cash flows as discussed in Chapter 8. When a seller accepts a long-term receivable and is uncertain about the

be required under unusual warranty agreements or to reimburse the lessee for obsolescence. A lessor will treat a lease as a capital lease if any one of the four criteria listed earlier for lessees is met *and* both of the following criteria are also met:

**1.** Collectibility of the minimum lease payments is reasonably predictable.

**2.** No important uncertainties surround the amount of unreimbursable future costs to be incurred by the lessor. (If the lessor can make reasonable estimates of future costs it must incur for maintenance, insurance, taxes, and the like, the mere fact that such estimates are required is not itself an important uncertainty.)

18.59 Thus, we see that on rare occasions a lease can be treated as a capital lease by the lessee (because at least one of the four criteria is satisfied) but as an operating lease by the lessor (because the lessor is uncertain about future cash flows). No lease can, in principle, be classified as a capital lease (sale) by the lessor, but as an operating lease (rent) by the lessee.

## Further Classification of Leases by Lessors

18.60 In the capital lease examples used so far in this chapter, the lessor was a manufacturer. Often, a manufacturer will sell its product outright to a bank or other financial institution, which will then, in effect, lend money to the user by leasing the asset to the user.

18.61 Dozens of companies have been formed

---

amounts of cash to be collected, then the seller will use either the installment method or the cost-recovery-first method. Installment method accounting defers the gross margin on the sale and recognizes portions of each cash collection as cost recovery and profit. Analogous accounting for lessor's leases leads to income recognition patterns not substantially different from the lessor's operating lease method. Cost-recovery-first accounting defers all income recognition until sufficient cash is collected to recover all costs. It would delay income until the later periods of the lease's life and report income later than under the operating lease method. For the reasons in Chapter 8, paragraph 8.34, we think the analog of the cost-recovery-first method should be used when lessor's cash collections are unpredictable. See Problem **18.51.**

since the 1960s whose major business is to "lend" money to users of equipment. These financial institutions often "sell" assets to users via long-term, noncancelable leases. Leases, rather than long-term installment sales contracts, are used because the users had been able, prior to FASB *Statement No. 13,* to treat the acquisition of the leasehold as an operating lease. Some managers have, in addition, believed that leasing is superior to borrowing as a method of financing a long-term asset. A later section of this chapter discusses the benefits of lease financing.

18.62 When one who normally sells goods (for example, a manufacturer) becomes a lessor under a capital lease, the lease is called a *sales-type lease.* When one who normally lends funds acquires an asset and then becomes a lessor under a capital lease, the lease is called a *direct-financing lease.* There is little conceptual difference between the two. There is no manufacturing profit to the lessor in a direct-financing lease. In sales-type leases, the manufacturer reports a profit or gain in the period the lease is signed equal to the difference between the present value of the lease receivables and the cost of the goods "sold." In later periods, interest revenue is recognized on the lease receivables. The capital leases illustrated in this chapter are sales-type leases. In a direct-financing lease, no profit or gain accrues to the lessor on signing the lease. The present value of the lease payments receivable is set equal to the lessor's cost of the asset. The only income to a direct-financing lessor is interest revenue over the life of the lease.

18.63 **Example** Manufacturing Company produces a specialized machine tool at a cost of $60,000. The machine tool has a fair market value of $100,000 and an economic life of ten years. Lessee Company, whose incremental borrowing rate is 15 percent, signs a lease agreeing to pay $19,925 (= $100,000/5.01877; Table 4, 10-period row, 15-percent column) in arrears for ten years. If Manufacturing Company leases the asset to Lessee Company, then Manufacturing Company will treat the lease as a sales-type lease. If, on the other hand, Manufacturing Company sells the machine tool to the First National Bank Leasing Company, which leases it to Lessee Company, then the Manufacturing Company will record the transaction as a sale of the property. In either case, Manufacturing Company will recognize revenues of $100,000 and cost of goods sold of $60,000, with a gross margin of $40,000 on the transaction. The First National Bank Leasing Company will treat the lease with Lessee Company as a direct-financing lease. The accounting by Lessee Company will be the same regardless of whether it leases the machine from Manufacturing Company under a sales-type lease or from First National Bank Leasing Company under a direct-financing lease.

18.64 In a sales-type lease, the lessor recognizes manufacturing profit at the inception of the lease as well as interest revenue during the lease term. In a direct-financing lease, the lessor's only revenue is interest during the lease term. Although there are no other important conceptual differences between the two types of lessor capital leases, one detail is treated differently in sales-type leases and direct-financing leases. *Initial direct costs* are costs such as sales commissions, legal fees, and costs of investigating the credit-worthiness of the lessee incurred by the lessor to consummate the transaction. These costs are expenses of the period incurred in sales-type leases (as in operating leases). For direct-financing leases, however, such costs are added to the cost basis of the asset on the books of the lessor and are amortized (depreciated) along with the cost of the asset being leased. In the example above, assume that the machine tool has a fair market value of $96,000, and the First National Bank Leasing Company incurs initial direct costs of $4,000 in closing the transaction. If the First National Bank Leasing Company were the lessor, and it paid $96,000 for the asset, the $4,000 costs incurred to close the deal would be debited to the asset account. The implicit interest rate for the lease would be computed on the basis of an investment of $100,000 and would be found to be 15 percent.

## Leveraged Leases

18.65 Another form of leasing agreement has so perplexed those who set accounting principles that special rules have been written for these leases, called *leveraged leases*.

18.66 A leveraged lease involves as lessor, here called "Lessor," an investor who has substantial other taxable income. Lessor borrows funds from some lender, here called "Bank." Lessor uses some of its own ("equity") funds and the borrowings from Bank to acquire an asset from the manufacturer. The asset is leased to the lessee, here called "User." The lease is a long-term noncancelable lease that meets the criteria to be a lessor's direct-financing capital lease. User makes periodic lease payments; Bank collects the payments as debt service on its loan to Lessor and remits any extra funds to Lessor. Lessor owns the asset and can claim an investment credit on its acquisition cost in the year of acquisition and accelerated cost recovery (depreciation) on its tax return. The investment credit, the depreciation deductions, and interest expense on Lessor's loan from Bank reduce Lessor's income taxes otherwise payable, saving cash.

18.67 The reductions in income taxes from investment credits, accelerated cost recovery, and interest result in reductions of income taxes otherwise payable by Lessor and thus effectively lead to positive net cash flows to Lessor in the early years of the asset's life. In later years, there is no investment credit, the use of accelerated cost recovery has reduced the depreciation deductions for taxes, and the portion of payments made to Bank representing deductible interest expense has declined. As time passes, Lessor has smaller tax losses and thus has reduced cash inflows. Eventually, there is taxable income that results in cash outflows. The fact that the cash inflows in the early years have larger present value then than the later cash outflows makes the deal profitable from Lessor's point of view.

18.68 Normally, lessors have cash outflows (for acquisition of the asset to be leased) followed by cash inflows (from the lessee). The general principles for recognizing income on monetary assets (explained in Chapter 5) are followed: find an interest rate that when multiplied by book value of the investment gives interest revenue for the period. The book value of the investment at the beginning of the period is increased by the addition of such interest and reduced by any cash receipts.

18.69    In a leveraged lease, the lessor's pattern of cash flows has three phases: (1) cash outflow (for acquisition of the asset), (2) cash inflow (from tax benefits and lease receipts), and (3) net cash outflow (for income taxes net of lease receipts*). During the middle phase, cumulative cash inflows have been positive, but future cash expenditures for income taxes will exceed lease receipts, so there will be future net cash outflows. During the middle phase, the lessor temporarily holds cash that will have to be paid out later for income taxes. Part of the lessor's benefit from the transaction is the earnings on this cash.

18.70    The methods introduced in Chapter 5 (for monetary assets) and in Chapter 15 (for monetary liabilities) could be applied to the entire transaction as follows. Find a single implicit rate of return for the entire series of cash flows: outflow, inflow, outflow. Use that rate to compute interest revenue in years when there is a net asset or to compute interest expense in the years when there is a net liability. This method is called the *integral investment method* in paragraph 109 of FASB *Statement No. 13*, which explains why this method is not allowed.

18.71    The major reason why the simple integral investment method is not allowed is this. During the middle phase of the project, the lessor temporarily holds cash to be paid later for income taxes. That cash will earn a return for the lessor, but the amount of earnings on the cash is uncertain at the time the lease is signed. Accounting wishes to be conservative and not include any effects of those earnings in income until the cash from the earnings is actually received. Thus, a method called the *separate phases method*

has been devised for the three phases. The method treats the first and last phases, when the present value of the future cash inflows exceeds the present value of the cash outflows, separately from the middle phase, when the net present value of the future outflows exceeds that of the inflows.

18.72    One unfortunate aspect of the required accounting for leveraged leases becomes evident when the undiscounted cash outflows exceed the undiscounted cash inflows. If outflows exceed inflows, independent of the timing, then the entire excess of outflows over inflows must be recognized as a loss when the lease is signed.†

18.73    A lease is a leveraged lease if

**1.** It is a direct-financing, capital lease, *and*

**2.** There are three parties to the lease—the lessee, the lessor, and a lender who provides financing to the lessor, *and*

**3.** The lender has no right to the lessor's assets other than the leased asset and the lessee's payments,** *and*

---

†FASB *Statement No. 13* (November 1976), par. 45. Recognizing such loss ignores economic reality but is consistent with other situations where a loss is recognized on a profitable transaction. Consider the following problem, first presented in Chapter 15. Assume that Alexander Company signs an agreement with an electric utility to provide that utility with coal. The agreement states that the utility will reimburse all operating costs of mining coal, dollar for dollar. In addition, the electric utility will pay $10 million in cash today for this privilege. At the time the deal is made, the coal mine is recorded on Alexander Company's books for $1 million. The company estimates that 10 years from today the coal mine will be exhausted of coal and abandoned. When the mine is abandoned, the company will spend $15 million to restore the landscape to its natural state. Is Alexander Company's venture profitable? Accounting thinks not: Costs are $16 million (= $1 million + $15 million) and revenues are only $10 million; a loss of $6 million must be recorded today. Accounting fails to recognize that the present value of the $15 million to be spent in 10 years is much less than $15 million. The present value is about $5.8 million if the discount rate is 10 percent per year and is smaller for higher discount rates. Thus it is a sensible business decision for Alexander Company to make an agreement such as the one described here, *even though the accountant would report it as a losing venture.*

**Such a loan is called a *nonrecourse loan* (see Chapter 7). A nonrecourse loan reduces the borrower's risk by confining its exposure to the collateral. Because the risk to the lender increases, it charges a higher interest rate than otherwise.

---

*In the last period, there may be net cash inflows from the residual value of the asset. These cash inflows do not add another phase because the accounting problem ends at the time the residual value is recovered and the lease term is complete.

**4.** The lessor's investment during some periods of the life of the lease increases because of net cash outflows.*

Such leases are called leveraged leases because the lessor has borrowed funds to finance the purchase of the asset; the financing is leveraged. See the discussion of long-term financing at the beginning of Chapter 17.

## Sale and Leaseback

18.74 A firm may sell property and immediately lease it back from its new owner. The terms of the combined sale and leaseback make the deal equivalent to outright borrowing with the asset as collateral. The user/lessee pays maintenance, insurance, and taxes. Periodic payments amortize the lender/lessor's purchase price of the leased asset and provide revenue in the form of interest. At the end of the lease term, property rights in the asset usually return to the user/lessee in one of several ways.

18.75 Because of generally rising prices, the fair market value of the property on the date of a sale and leaseback will likely exceed the user's book value before the sale. If so, the usual accounting for the sale implies that the user recognizes a gain equal to the difference between the selling price and the user's book value.

18.76 Generally accepted accounting principles have long required that the gain from sale in a sale and leaseback not be reported as income but be amortized over the life of the lease.† Instead of the user's recording a gain on sale and larger amortization expenses over the lease term, it bases amortization expenses over the life of the leaseback on the book value of the property at the time of the sale. The user excludes deferred gain from income in the period of sale because the sale is not an arm's-length transaction. The lender/lessor might be willing to pay any price for the asset suggested by the user/lessee so long as the leaseback arrangement compensated the lender/lessor for that price with a reasonable return for the amount invested. If the fair market value of the asset sold is *less* than its book value on the date of sale and leaseback, then the loss on sale will be reported in the user/lessee's income for the period of sale. This asymmetry results from accounting's conservatism.

18.77 Most leases resulting from sale and leaseback are capital leases. The asset Leasehold initially appears on the user/lessee's records at the net present value of the future payments reduced by the amount of deferred gain, which is a net amount equal to the book value of the asset before the transaction.

## Sale and Leaseback Illustrated

18.78 User Company owns a building that cost $3,000,000, that has $1,100,000 of accumulated depreciation, and that has a fair market value of $2,600,000. The building is sold for $2,500,000 to Lessor Company and leased back over a 20-year term, with lease payments of $400,000 to be made at the end of each year. The implicit interest rate is 15.03 percent per year, which we round to 15 percent for calculations.** The leaseback is a capital lease because the user has a bargain purchase option to acquire the property for $1,000 at the end of the lease term. The journal entries at the time of the sale and initial leaseback might be as shown in Exhibit 18.5. The Deferred Gain account that appears on the User/Lessee's balance sheet is an asset contra much like the Deferred Gross Margin account on installment sales discussed in Chapter 8. The user/lessee need not use

---

*Ordinarily, the book value of many assets declines over time because of amortization. The book value of this leasehold declines in some periods, then increases in others, and then declines to zero in the last year or two.

†FASB *Statement No. 13* (1976), pars. 32–34 covers sale and leaseback transactions, but the rules go back as far as *Accounting Series Release No. 95* (1962) and APB *Opinion No. 5* (September 1964).

---

**Using the methods described in Appendix B, we find the implicit interest rate $r$ from trial-and-error estimates by solving:

$$\frac{1 - (1 + r)^{-20}}{r} \times \$400,000 = \$2,500,000.$$

See also Table 4, 20-period row, 15-percent column.

## Exhibit 18.5
### Journal Entries for Sale and Leaseback

Asset with book value of $1.9 million sold for $2.5 million and leased back over 20-year term with annual payments of $400,000, implying interest at the rate of 15 percent per year.

*The entries on signing the lease would be:*

**User/Lessee**

| | | |
|---|---|---|
| Cash | 2,500,000 | |
| Accumulated Depreciation | 1,100,000 | |
|     Building | | 3,000,000 |
|     Deferred Gain | | 600,000 |

To record sale. Gain does not appear in income; Deferred Gain is a balance sheet account contra to the asset Leasehold set up in the next entry.

| | | |
|---|---|---|
| Leasehold | 2,500,000 | |
|     Present Value of Lease | | |
|         Obligation | | 2,500,000 |

To record leaseback by setting up asset and the related liability.

The balance sheet of the user/lessee shows:

| | |
|---|---|
| Leasehold | $2,500,000 |
| Less: Deferred Gain | 600,000 |
|     Leased Asset Net | $1,900,000 |

**Lessor**

| | | |
|---|---|---|
| Building | 2,500,000 | |
|     Cash | | 2,500,000 |

| | | |
|---|---|---|
| Lease Receivable | 2,500,000 | |
|     Building | | 2,500,000 |

Sale of property for book value and recognition of long-term receivable. This is a direct-financing lease with no profit at the date of sale.

*One year later, the entries would be:*

**User/Lessee**

| | | |
|---|---|---|
| Interest Expense | 375,000 | |
| Present Value of Lease | | |
|     Obligation | 25,000 | |
|     Cash | | 400,000 |

Interest is 15% of liability; plug for $25,000 reduction in liability.

| | | |
|---|---|---|
| Amortization Expense | 125,000 | |
|     Accumulated Amortization | | |
|         on Leasehold | | 125,000 |

Amortization expense of leasehold is like depreciation on building. Amount is book value of lease divided by 20-year life: $2,500,000/20.

| | | |
|---|---|---|
| Deferred Gain | 30,000 | |
|     Amortization Expense | | 30,000 |

Amortization of gain reduces amortization expense from $125,000 to $95,000, the amount that would appear if the asset were depreciated at book value before sale and leaseback: $1,900,000/20 = $95,000.

**Lessor**

| | | |
|---|---|---|
| Cash | 400,000 | |
|     Interest Revenue | | 375,000 |
|     Lease Receivable | | 25,000 |

Interest is 15% of the receivable; plug for $25,000 reduction in asset.

straight-line amortization for the leasehold (unless the leased asset is land*). Whatever amortization method and time span are used for amortization of the asset are used for amortization of the deferred gain. Thus the net amortization expense after amortization of deferred gain, $95,000 (= $125,000 − $30,000) in the example, is the same as it would have been had amortization been based on the book value of the property before its sale and leaseback.

18.79 The lessee's interest expense declines each year, while the amounts of each lease payment reducing lease liabilities increase. The lessor's interest revenue declines each year; the portion of each payment received representing repayment of principal increases.

## Financial Statement Disclosure of Leases

18.80 FASB *Statement No. 13* lists the disclosures required for leases both by lessees (paragraph 16) and by lessors (paragraph 23). It illustrates the required disclosures in Appendix D. We summarize highlights below.

### Lessee Disclosure

18.81 Generally, the lessee shows the gross amount of assets recorded under capital leases, less accumulated amortization in a separate contra account, and the present value of lease liabilities separated between current and noncurrent liabilities. Disclosure in notes describes the leasing arrangements (including information about contingent rental payments) and provides data about lease payments by year over the next 5 years. The gross amounts of minimum lease payments are listed separately by year for each of the following 5 years, and its total for subsequent years. From those minimum lease payments the interest component is subtracted to arrive at the net present value of the minimum payments. The details of gross contractual payments totaling $250

million with net present value of $140 million might appear in the 1981 notes as follows:

**Schedule of Minimum Lease Payments (in Millions)**

| | |
|---|---:|
| 1982 | $47 |
| 1983 | 37 |
| 1984 | 33 |
| 1985 | 29 |
| 1986 | 16 |
| Subsequent Years | 88 |
| Total Minimum Lease Payments | $250 |
| Less: Amounts for Interest (Average 10% Rate) | 110 |
| Present Value of Minimum Lease Payments | $140 |

Note 19 to the financial statements of International Corporation in Appendix A shows this required disclosure in an alternative format.

18.82 For relatively new long-term leases with realistic interest rates (10 percent or more per year), the bulk of the gross lease payment is for future interest. For example, in the 20-year sale and leaseback transaction illustrated in Exhibit 8.5, the contractual payments at the inception of the lease are $8 million (= 20 × $400,000) and $5.5 million of that amount is for interest.

### Lessor Disclosure

18.83 Generally, the lessor shows the present value of expected lease receivables as an asset, with separate amounts for gross contractual receivable, for executory costs (insurance, maintenance, taxes, and the like), for amounts not expected to be collectible (allowance for uncollectibles), for estimated amounts of residual values at end of lease terms, and for amounts of interest included in the net amounts of expected collectibles. The resulting figure is the lessor's net investment in the leased asset. The disclosure could be as follows:

**Schedule of Lease Investments (in Thousands)**

| | |
|---|---:|
| Total Contractual Lease Receivables | $1,120 |
| Less: Amounts for Insurance, Maintenance, and Taxes | ( 100) |
| Less: Allowance for Uncollectibles | ( 20) |
| Net Lease Receivables | $1,000 |
| Less: Interest Component of Receivables | ( 400) |
| Plus: Estimated Residual Values at Ends of Lease Terms (Not Guaranteed) | 50 |
| Net Investment in Capital Leases | $ 650 |

---

*Although the owner of land does not amortize it because of land's perpetual life, the lessee of land has an asset, the leasehold, with a finite life, the lease term.

## Leases as a Form of Financing

18.84 Chapter 17 discussed the costs and benefits of financing through long-term borrowing. This chapter explained that capital leases are a form of long-term borrowing and that accounting attempts to report the economic substance of these lease transactions. If accounting requires lessees to report the present value of all contractual lease payments as debt, then the phenomenon of off-balance-sheet financing disappears. Lease financing will, however, probably continue for other, nonaccounting reasons. The benefits of lease financing often result from government regulations.

## Real (Contrasted to Accounting) Benefits of Leasing

18.85 The use of leases may allow the investment credit to be passed from a user (lessee) who cannot fully benefit from it because of low taxable income to another taxpayer (lessor), who can. (This benefit explains some leveraged lease transactions.)

18.86    Some government contracts permit the suppliers to be reimbursed for direct costs ("cost-plus" contracts), but not general financing costs of the supplier. In some cases, the contractor might find leasing an asset (where total lease payments including financing costs are all direct, reimbursable costs) preferable to outright ownership (where the financing costs are indirect and not reimbursable).

18.87    Lease contracts can provide ways to alter the risks and rewards of ownership of long-term assets that are not easily achieved with other contracts. For example, the use of leases for parts of an asset's life, perhaps with sublease provisions, permits different owners to arrange for asset ownership at different times.

    Tax advisors often suggest that leases may permit tax deductions that would not otherwise be allowed. For example, one can amortize the leasehold for land but cannot deduct depreciation for the land itself.

18.89 **Example** User Company wants to acquire land costing $1 million as a plant site. It can buy the land, financing it through a mortgage at 10 percent interest, making mortgage payments over 30 years of $106,000 per year. If it does so, then only a portion of each payment is deductible interest expense, whereas the remainder is repayment of principal. (See, for example, the mortgage amortization schedule in Chapter 17, Exhibit 17.1.) The amount of deductible interest is a large portion of early payments—$100,000 in the first year—but a small portion of later payments—only about $9,600 of the last payment.* If User Company leases the land, making payments of $106,000 per year at the end of each of the next 30 years, each payment is totally deductible for taxes. At the end of the lease term, the land must remain with the lessor. Otherwise, the tax authorities consider the transaction an installment purchase of nondepreciable land, rather than a lease. The user gives up the right to own the land 30 years hence, but that may be a small price to pay in order to make all expenditures for the asset tax deductible over the next 30 years.

    Some managers and accountants believe, 18.90 incorrectly we think, that leasing usually provides financing *more* preferable than borrowing in order to make a purchase. The Garden Winery case at the end of this chapter explores the effect of outright cash purchase, leasing, and borrowing to purchase as alternatives.

## Summary

Leases are either operating leases or a form 18.91 of long-term financing. Accounting attempts, not always successfully, to reflect the economic substance of lease transactions, reporting the asset on the books of the party bearing the risks and rewards of its ownership.

    So long as lessees cannot use leases as a 18.92 form of off-balance-sheet financing, there are no *accounting* benefits to leasing. Since

---

*See footnote to paragraph 18.29. $106,000/1.10 = $96,364. Thus, the last payment includes $96,364 of principal repayment and only $9,636 (= $106,000 − $96,364) of interest.

1976, generally accepted accounting principles have reduced the amount of long-term leasing disguised as off-balance-sheet financing. Whether or not lease financing is superior to other forms of financing probably depends more on governmental regulations than it does on the patterns of the debt service payments, which are likely to have similar economic impact whatever form of financing is chosen.

## Questions and Short Cases

18.1 Review the meaning of the following concepts or terms discussed in this chapter.
   a. Lease.
   b. Lessee versus lessor.
   c. Operating lease versus capital lease.
   d. Leasehold.
   e. Installment sales and purchases.
   f. Executory contract.
   g. Off-balance-sheet financing.
   h. Symmetry of accounting by lessor and lessee.
   i. Bargain purchase option.
   j. Inception of the lease.
   k. Sales-type lease versus direct-financing lease.
   l. Leveraged lease.
   m. Recourse loan versus nonrecourse loan.
   n. Sale and leaseback transaction.

18.2 Why is the question, "Who bears the risks and enjoys the potential rewards of an asset?" important for lease accounting?

18.3 What are the important differences, if any, between short-term and long-term operating leases?

18.4 a. Distinguish between the economic reality of a capital lease and that of an installment sale/purchase.
   b. Distinguish between the lessor's accounting for a capital lease and for an installment sale.
   c. Distinguish between the lessee's accounting for a capital lease and for an installment purchase.

18.5 a. Why are executory contracts, such as an employment contract with the firm's president, not capitalized as assets and liabilities by the firm?
   b. What, if anything, distinguishes the executory contract of a 5-year operating lease from a 5-year employment contract?

18.6 What advantages would result if accounting principles were changed so that all executory contracts were capitalized as assets and liabilities for the net present value of the contractual payments? What disadvantages would result?

18.7 Under what conditions does a lessee record a lease as a capital lease? As an operating lease?

18.8 Under what conditions does a lessor record a lease as a capital lease? As an operating lease?

18.9 a. What asymmetry in accounting for leases did FASB *Statement No. 13* cure?
   b. What asymmetry in accounting for leases remains in spite of FASB *Statement No. 13*?

18.10 Consider a lessor's capital leases. What are the important economic distinctions and the important accounting distinctions between sales-type leases and direct-financing leases?

**18.11**   Why do separate accounting rules exist for recording the transactions of the equity participant in leveraged leases?

**18.12**   **a.** What is the economic substance of a sale and leaseback transaction?
**b.** What is the essence of the accounting for such transactions?

**18.13**   Lessor Company, as manufacturer/lessor, entered into a lease agreement with Lessee Company, as lessee. Both companies accounted for the lease as an operating lease, whereas both
companies should have accounted for it as a capital (sales-type) lease. What effect (understated, overstated, none) does this error have on each of the following items in the financial
statements of Lessor Company for the first year of the lease?
**a.** Assets.                                       **d.** Expense.
**b.** Liabilities.                                  **e.** Net income.
**c.** Revenue.                                      **f.** Retained earnings.

**18.14**   Respond to items **a–f** in the preceding question for Lessee Company for the first year of the
lease.

**18.15**   Refer to the preceding two questions. Assume that Lessor Company is not a manufacturer
and the capital lease is a direct-financing lease.
What is the effect on Lessor Company's total assets at both the beginning and end of the
first year resulting from the error of classifying the capital lease as an operating lease? Explain
your reasoning.

**18.16**   Why is the capital lease a common form of financial instrument?

**18.17**   Describe the difference, if any, in the lessor's treatment of guaranteed and unguaranteed
residual values.

**18.18**   Describe the difference, if any, in the lessee's treatment of guaranteed and unguaranteed
residual values.

**18.19**   Consider the lessor's treatment of initial direct costs in sales-type leases and direct-financing
leases.
**a.** Describe the difference in treatment.
**b.** What justifies this difference?

**18.20**   (Adapted from AICPA *Technical Practice Aids*.) Ohlson Company is a retailer with stores at
many different locations. When it finds a new store site suitable for its operations, it purchases the land and building. Within a few months of purchase, the retailer arranges a sale
and leaseback with some financing institution.
**a.** Assume that the retailer has had many years of experience in these sorts of transactions
and that it has always been able to arrange a sale and leaseback within 6 months of purchase. How should Ohlson Company account in its December 31 financial statements for
a site acquired for $2.5 million on November 1?
**b.** Assume the same facts as above except that one site costing $1.75 million has been owned
for 15 months. A suitable sale and leaseback has not yet been arranged for this site. There
is no way of ascertaining when a suitable sale and leaseback will be arranged. How should
Ohlson Company account for this site?

**18.21**   (Adapted from AICPA *Technical Practice Aids*.) Krogstad Company owns a commercial building. It leases the street-level locations to retailers and the upper floors as offices. In order to secure a lease from a certain retail tenant on the street level, Krogstad Company incurred substantial costs in altering the physical layout of the walls and electrical wiring. Subsequent tenants are unlikely to find these alterations usable. How should the cost of these alterations be accounted for?

18.22 (Adapted from AICPA *Technical Practice Aids*.) Lorange Company is a lessor who assigns, without recourse, its capital lease agreements to a financing institution to which it is completely unrelated. The financing institution collects monthly lease payments from the lessees. On the date of assignment, the financing institution pays a fee to Lorange Company. How should Lorange Company account for the fee it receives? Consider two alternatives:
**(i)** Credit revenue at the time of assignment.
**(ii)**Revenue to be spread over the life of the lease as additional income each month.

18.23 (Adapted from CPA Examination.)
**a.** Capital leases and operating leases are the two classifications of leases described in FASB pronouncements, from the standpoint of the **lessee.**
   **(1)** Describe how a capital lease would be accounted for by the lessee both at the inception of the lease and during the first year of the lease, assuming the lease transfers ownership of the property to the lessee by the end of the lease.
   **(2)** Describe how an operating lease would be accounted for by the lessee both at the inception of the lease and during the first year of the lease, assuming equal monthly payments are made by the lessee at the beginning of each month of the lease. Describe the change in accounting, if any, when rental payments are not made on a straight-line basis.
**b.** Sales-type leases and direct financing leases are two of the classifications of leases described in FASB pronouncements, from the standpoint of the **lessor.**
   Compare and contrast a sales-type lease with a direct financing lease as follows:
**(1)**Gross investment in the lease.
**(2)**Amortization of unearned interest income.
**(3)**Manufacturer's or dealer's profit.

18.24 This question explores the required accounting by lessors for changes in estimates of residual value. The rules for such changes are not discussed in this chapter; they appear in FASB *Statement No. 13,* paragraph 17d. These rules require at least an annual review of estimated residual values. If the review suggests that the value has increased or *temporarily* decreased, then there is no adjustment. If the value has decreased and the decrease is not temporary, then a loss must be recognized for that period, with a corresponding reduction in the net investment in the lease.
   Assume a lessor's sales-type lease with four years remaining. The minimum lease payments are $20,000 per year, in arrears, and the estimated residual value has been $30,000. The interest rate implicit in the lease is 10 percent. The gross investment in the lease is $110,000 (= $20,000 × 4 + $30,000) and the net investment in the lease at the end of the current year, *after* all adjusting entries except for review of residual value estimate, is $83,887 (= $20,000 × 3.16987 + $30,000 × .68301).
   A review of current market conditions suggests that the residual value will be $10,000, not $30,000, and that this decline in value is not temporary. At the time of the estimate the interest rate implicit in new leases of this sort has, because of general inflation, increased to 20 percent per year.
**a.** In computing the loss from decline in residual value, which interest rate should be used? (No specific guidance on this question appears in this chapter or in FASB *Statement No. 13,* but the answer emerges from consideration of general principles.)

    **b.** What is the loss to be recognized in adjusting the estimate of residual value to $10,000 from $30,000?

    **c.** What journal entries will accomplish the recognition of the loss?

**18.25**   Review the accounting procedures described in Chapter 12 for treating changes in estimates with respect to salvage value of depreciable assets. Does the treatment described in the preceding question for changes in estimates of residual value seem to be consistent or inconsistent with that treatment? Explain.

**18.26**   A well-known company with a financing subsidiary promotes its leasing activities (as lessor) with material containing the following statements. Evaluate these statements.

**Retain Favorable Tax Advantages**

Many companies in capital-intensive industries are not in a position to use investment tax credits to full advantage. Neither can they benefit from accelerated depreciation. Yet these companies often need new equipment. Leasing offers a solution to the problem: The lessee can assign tax-benefits—benefits it cannot use—to the lessor in exchange for reduced lease payments. No other form of equipment financing provides this important advantage.

**Conserve Cash**

Normally, leasing affords 100-percent financing. There are no down payments or compensating balances. If a company ties up its cash to purchase equipment, the earning power of the cash itself is lost. But if the same company were to lease equipment, it could still put the cash into other, profitable investments. It is for this reason that, in the long run, leasing can help maximize the use of a company's resources. Leasing gives a company the opportunity to use more equipment or to spend less for equipment. Leasing, in fact, can often do both.

**Match Income and Expense, and Stay within Capital Budgets**

If a company purchases equipment, it immediately pays for the last day of production as well as the first. But leasing allows the payment for equipment to be made from the income generated by its use. Furthermore, lease payments can be tailored to fit even the tightest capital equipment budgets. Combined, these attributes make leasing an effective way for companies to sustain rapid growth.

**Reduce the Impact of Inflation**

If inflation continues, a company that purchases capital equipment will find in the future that the true value of its depreciation allowance has been reduced. But companies that lease equipment will benefit from a reduction in the true value of future lease payments. It is for this reason that leasing can provide an effective hedge against inflation; and to maximize the advantage, many companies choose to lease depreciating assets such as equipment, while purchasing appreciating assets such as property.

**Preserve Other Sources of Financing**

Growing companies need many sources of financial assistance. When they lease equipment, companies preserve the flexibility to use alternative credit sources in other ways. If a company leases its income-producing equipment, it can still use its bank lines of credit for short-term needs, or it can hold them open in anticipation of future capital requirements.

**Control the Use of Equipment**

It is the use—not the ownership—of equipment that generates income. A unit of equipment has the same productive capacity regardless of whether it is leased or owned. When equipment is leased, however, its disposition is much easier. At the end of the lease period, the equipment can be leased again, can be purchased, or can be returned to the lessor. The decision is made on the basis of whether the equipment is still profitable, not whether it is owned.

*Exhibit 18.6*

**Annual Net Cash Flows and Net Present Values of Alternatives Available to Garden Winery Company for Acquiring Use of Asset Costing $10,000 (Discount Rate Is 15 Percent per Year; Income Taxes are 40 Percent of Pretax Income)**

| End of Year (1) | Pretax Cash Inflows Less Cash Outflow Expense[a] (2) | Depreciation[b] (3) | Lease Payments (4) | Total = (5) | Interest Expense[c] + (6) | Principal Repayment[d] (7) | Pretax Income[e] (8) | Income Tax Expense[f] (9) | Net Cash Inflows (Outflows)[g] (10) | Present Value of Net Cash Flows at 15%[h] (11) |
|---|---|---|---|---|---|---|---|---|---|---|
| **Purchase Asset Outright; No Borrowing** | | | | | | | | | | |
| 0 | — | — | — | — | — | — | — | — | ($10,000) | ($10,000) |
| 1 | $ 5,000 | $ 2,500 | — | — | — | — | $2,500 | $1,000 | 4,000 | 3,478 |
| 2 | 4,500 | 2,500 | — | — | — | — | 2,000 | 800 | 3,700 | 2,798 |
| 3 | 4,000 | 2,500 | — | — | — | — | 1,500 | 600 | 3,400 | 2,236 |
| 4 | 3,000 | 2,500 | — | — | — | — | 500 | 200 | 2,800 | 1,601 |
| | $16,500 | $10,000 | | | | | $6,500 | $2,600 | $ 3,900 | $ 113 |
| **Lease Asset; Lease Payment Made at the End of Each Period** | | | | | | | | | | |
| 0 | — | — | — | — | — | — | — | — | — | — |
| 1 | $ 5,000 | — | $ 3,292 | — | — | — | $1,708 | $ 683 | $ 1,025 | $ 891 |
| 2 | 4,500 | — | 3,292 | — | — | — | 1,208 | 483 | 725 | 548 |
| 3 | 4,000 | — | 3,292 | — | — | — | 708 | 283 | 425 | 279 |
| 4 | 3,000 | — | 3,292 | — | — | — | (292)[i] | (117)[i] | (175) | (100) |
| | $16,500 | | $13,168 | | | | $3,332 | $1,332 | $ 2,000 | $ 1,618 |
| **Purchase Asset; Borrow $10,000 at 12 Percent to Be Repaid in Four Annual Installments** | | | | | | | | | | |
| 0 | — | — | — | — | — | — | — | — | $ 0[j] | $ 0 |
| 1 | $ 5,000 | $ 2,500 | — | $ 3,292 = | $1,200 + | $2,092 | $1,300 | $ 520 | 1,188 | 1,033 |
| 2 | 4,500 | 2,500 | — | 3,292 = | 949 + | 2,343 | 1,051 | 420 | 788 | 596 |
| 3 | 4,000 | 2,500 | — | 3,292 = | 668 + | 2,624 | 832 | 333 | 375 | 247 |
| 4 | 3,000 | 2,500 | — | 3,292 = | 351 + | 2,941 | 149 | 59 | (351) | (201) |
| | $16,500 | $10,000 | | $13,168 | $3,168 + | $10,000 | $3,332 | $1,332 | $ 2,000 | $ 1,675 |

[a]Amounts given.

[b]Straight-line method; $10,000 cost/4-year life.

[c]Twelve percent of outstanding loan. Outstanding loan is $10,000 less cumulative principal repayments shown in column (7).

[d]Lease payment $3,292 less portion allocated to interest expense from column (6).

[e]Amount in column (2) less amounts in columns (3), (4), and (6).

[f]Forty percent of amount in column (8).

[g]Amount in column (2) less amounts in columns (4), (5), and (9).

[h]Amount in column (10) multiplied by present-value factor for 15 percent discount rate: 1.00000 for cash flow at end of year 0; .86957 for cash flows at end of year 1; .75614 for cash flows at end of year 2; .65752 for cash flows at end of year 3; and .57175 for cash flows at end of year 4.

[i]Assume sufficient other taxable income that this loss reduces taxes otherwise payable.

[j]At the end of year 0, $10,000 is borrowed and used immediately to acquire asset; this number is + $10,000 − $10,000 = $0.

**Obtain Favorable Balance Sheet Treatment**

When correctly structured, some leases can qualify as operating leases for the purpose of the lessee's accounting treatment. Operating lease payment obligations are not capitalized on the lessee's balance sheet as a liability.

18.27   This case considers leasing as a form of financing. All of the firm's equities finance all of its assets. The only exceptions are nonrecourse loans, such as those described in this chapter in the context of leveraged leases.

In a nonrecourse loan, the lender's collateral is a single asset (or asset group), rather than the full faith and credit of the borrower. Generally, loans, even those secured with specific collateral, provide that the lender can seek repayment of the loan from all revenues or any asset of the business, not just the collateral, if the borrower defaults. Because all of the assets generally support all of the borrowing, it rarely makes sense to think of any one equity as financing any one asset. A specific asset may have been acquired with the proceeds of a specific issue of debt or owners' equity. Once acquired, however, the asset does not differ from all other assets, and the debt or equity does not differ from all other debt or equity. These principles are often overlooked by those promoting lease financing and by some managers considering lease financing.

**Data** Exhibit 18.6 presents data for the evaluation of a proposed asset acquisition by Garden Winery Company. The asset costs $10,000. If purchased, the asset is to be depreciated on a straight-line basis for tax purposes over four years. The asset provides cash inflows before taxes of $5,000 in the first year, $4,500 in the second year, $4,000 in the third year, and $3,000 in the fourth year. The firm uses a discount rate of 15 percent in evaluating investment decisions but can borrow at a lower rate, 12 percent per year.

Managerial accounting and finance texts discuss the difference between a firm's cost of capital (used for investment decisions) and its borrowing rate. Here, it is sufficient for you to know that in evaluating investment decisions, firms consider the cost of all capital, not just the lower cost of debt financing. As the discussion of borrowing in Chapter 17 pointed out, additional borrowing makes the firm more risky; this raises the return required by those who are asked to provide owners' equity capital. Thus the net cost of borrowing is not only the explicit interest but also the increased cost of owners' equities.

**Cash Purchase** The top panel of Exhibit 18.6 evaluates an investment in the asset costing $10,000 when the income tax rate is 40 percent and a discount rate of 15 percent is used. The present value of the net cash flow ($10,000 outflow at the start of the first year, and aftertax inflows from $4,000 to $2,800 at the end of the four years) is greater than zero when discounted at a 15-percent cost of capital. The investment, therefore, is a worthwhile undertaking.

**Lease** The middle panel shows a similar calculation to evaluate a lease suggested to the Garden Winery Company by an outside leasing firm. The leasing company is willing to lend at 12 percent. Payments of $3,292 for four years will amortize a loan of $10,000. The lease payments are deductible expenses for tax purposes. The lessee does not own the asset and thus has no depreciation deductions. The net, aftertax cash flows are discounted at 15 percent. The net present value is $1,618, much larger than the $113 net present value from outright purchase analyzed in the top panel. Some managers note this larger present value and conclude that leasing is superior to outright ownership.

**Borrow-Purchase** Next, consider ownership financed through borrowing on a mortgage or note. The bottom panel of Exhibit 18.6 analyzes the borrowing from a bank on an installment note or mortgage requiring annual payments in arrears at 12 percent. If one lender—a leasing company—will lend at 12 percent, then presumably another lender—such as a bank—will similarly be willing to lend at 12 percent. In the borrow-buy case, the user has tax deductions for depreciation and interest. An amortization schedule shows how much of each payment is deductible interest and how much is nondeductible repayment of principal. The net present value of the aftertax cash flows is $1,675, slightly larger than those from leasing but much larger than those from cash purchase. When accelerated depreciation is used for tax purposes in this example, borrow-purchase appears even more attractive than leasing.

Whether leasing appears preferable to borrow-purchase or vice versa also depends on the level of interest rates. One of the questions below requires that you work through this example with a cost of capital discount rate of 10 percent and a borrowing rate of 8 percent.

a. Why do leasing and borrowing appear more attractive than cash purchase?

b. Should management of Garden Winery acquire the asset? How should it be financed?

c. Assume that the cash outflow in the first year were reduced by $250. Then the results in the first panel of Exhibit 18.6 would show a negative net present value, while those in the bottom two panels would remain positive. How would this one change in the cash flows affect your answers in parts **a** and **b**?

d. Compute figures like those in Exhibit 18.6, using a cost of capital of 10 percent per year and a debt rate of 8 percent per year. How do these conditions affect your answers above?

# Problems and Exercises

18.28    Spiceland Leasing Company acquired equipment for $50,000 of cash and leased it to a lessee for 3 years. The lease payments of $11,260 each are made at the end of each of the 3 years. At the end of 3 years, the equipment is returned to the lessor, Spiceland Leasing Company. On the date the lease agreement was signed, Spiceland Leasing Company estimated that the residual value of the equipment 3 years hence would be $32,250. What is the lessor's interest rate implicit in the lease?

18.29    (Adapted from CPA Examination.) The Jackson Company manufactured a piece of equipment at a cost of $7 million, which it held for resale from January 1 to June 30 at a price of $8 million. On July 1, Jackson leased the equipment to the Crystal Company for a 3-year period. The lease is appropriately recorded as an operating lease for accounting purposes. Equal monthly payments under the lease are $115,000 and are due on the first of the month. The first payment was made on July 1. The equipment is being depreciated on a straight-line basis over an 8-year period with no residual value expected.

a. What expense should Crystal record as a result of the above facts for the current year ended December 31? Show supporting computations in good form.

b. What income or loss before income taxes should Jackson record as a result of the above facts for the year ended December 31? Show supporting computations in good form.

18.30    (Adapted from CPA Examination.) The Truman Company leased equipment from the Roosevelt Company on October 1. The lease is appropriately recorded as a purchase for accounting purposes for Truman and as a sale for accounting purposes for Roosevelt. The lease is for an eight-year period. Equal annual payments under the lease are $600,000 and are due on October 1 of each year. The first payment was made on October 1. The cost of the equipment on Roosevelt's accounting records was $3 million. The equipment has an estimated useful life of eight years with no residual value expected. Truman uses straight-line depreciation and takes a full year's depreciation in the year of purchase. The rate of interest contemplated by Truman and Roosevelt is 10 percent. The present value of an annuity of $1 in advance for eight periods at 10 percent is $5.868.

a. What expense should Truman record as a result of the above facts for the year ended December 31? Show supporting computations in good form.

b. What income or loss before income taxes should Roosevelt record as a result of the above facts for the year ended December 31? Show supporting computations in good form.

**18.31**   (Adapted from CPA Examination.) On February 20, Riley, Inc., purchased a machine for $1,200,000 for the purpose of leasing it. The machine is expected to have a ten-year life, no residual value, and will be depreciated on the straight-line basis. The machine was leased to Sutter Company on March 1, for a four-year period at a monthly rental of $18,000. There is no provision for the renewal of the lease or purchase of the machine by the lessee at the expiration of the lease term. Riley paid $60,000 in commissions associated with negotiating the lease in February.

a. What expense should Sutter record as a result of the above facts for the year ended December 31?

b. What income or loss before income taxes should Riley record as a result of the above facts for the year ended December 31?

**18.32**   Colantoni Company has calculated that the annual payment in arrears to amortize a $3,000,000 loan at 8-percent interest is $266,482.

a. What is rent expense for the first year of an operating lease when the rent payment is $266,482?

b. What is lease expense for the first year of a capital lease for use of an asset costing $3,000,000, requiring annual payments in arrears of $266,482? Use straight-line amortization of leasehold.

c. How much larger in percentage terms is the expense in the first year under the capital lease than under the operating lease?

d. What is interest expense in the last year of the lease, assuming the capital lease method?

e. Repeat parts **a–d**, assuming an interest rate of 10 percent per year and an annual payment of $318,238.

**18.33**   Assume that Federal Department Stores, Incorporated, is about to sign four separate leases for stores in four separate shopping centers. Each of the stores would cost $10 million if purchased outright and has an economic life of twenty years. Assume that the company currently must pay interest at the rate of 10 percent per year on long term borrowing when sound collateral backs the loan. The lease payments are to be made at the end of each year in all four cases.

Based on the information given here, decide whether each of the four leases should be accounted for as an operating lease or as a capital lease. Give your reasoning.

|  | Lease Term | Annual Lease Payment |
| --- | --- | --- |
| a. Seaview Mall | 16 Years | $1,100,000 |
| b. Normandale Center | 16 Years | 1,215,000 |
| c. Eastbrook Haven | 12 Years | 1,250,000 |
| d. Palos Parkview | 12 Years | 1,395,000 |

**18.34**   Assume that the Trans Western Airlines Company is about to sign a lease for 15 years to acquire the use of a new airplane. The interest rate used to compute the lease payments, which are to be made annually at the end of each year, is 12 percent per year. At the start of the lease, the present value of the lease payments is to be $30 million.

  **a.** Verify that the annual lease payment is $4,404,730.

  **b.** Assuming that the lease is accounted for as an operating lease, compute:

   **(i)** Total rent expense over 15 years.

   **(ii)** Rent expense for the first year.

  **(iii)** Rent expense for the fifteenth year.

  **c.** Assuming that the lease is accounted for as a capital lease, and that asset amortization is straight-line, compute:

   **(i)** Total expense related to using the asset over 15 years.

   **(ii)** Expense relating to using the asset in the first year.

  **(iii)** Expense relating to using the asset in the fifteenth year. (Hint: Refer to the footnote to paragraph 18.29 in this chapter, where the method of deriving the last row of an amortization table is given.)

  **d.** Which method of accounting for the lease, operating or capital, is Trans Western Airlines Company likely to prefer for its financial statements and why?

  **e.** Assume that the airplane's fair value in the hands of the lessor is $30 million. What is the largest annual lease payment that Trans Western Airlines Company could make to the lessor for 15 years without disqualifying the lease from operating lease treatment in financial statements?

  **f.** Which method of accounting for the lease is Trans Western Airline Company likely to prefer for tax purposes and why?

**18.35** The Carom Company plans to acquire, as of January 1, 1981, a computerized cash register system that costs $100,000 and that has a five-year life and no salvage value. The company is considering two plans for acquiring the system.

  **(1)** Outright purchase. To finance the purchase, $100,000 of par-value, 10-percent semiannual coupon bonds will be issued January 1, 1981, at par.

  **(2)** Lease. The lease requires five annual payments to be made on December 31, 1981, 1982, 1983, 1984, and 1985. The lease payments are such that they have a present value of $100,000 on January 1, 1981, when discounted at 10 percent per year.

Straight-line amortization methods will be used for all depreciation and amortization computations.

  **a.** Verify that the amount of the required lease payment is $26,380 by constructing an amortization schedule for the five payments. Note that there will be a $2 rounding error in the fifth year. Nevertheless, you may treat each payment as being $26,380 in the rest of the problem.

  **b.** What balance sheet amounts will be affected if plan **(1)** is selected? If plan **(2)** is selected, the lease is cancelable, and the operating lease treatment is used? If plan **(2)** is selected, the lease is noncancelable, and the capital lease treatment is used?

  **c.** What will be the total depreciation and interest expenses for the five years under plan **(1)**?

  **d.** What will be the total expenses for the five years under plan **(2)** if the lease is accounted for as an operating lease? As a capital lease?

  **e.** Why are the answers in part **d** the same? Why are the answers in part **c** different from those in part **d**?

  **f.** What will be the total expenses for the first year, 1981, under plan **(1)**? Under plan **(2)** accounted for as an operating lease? Under plan **(2)** accounted for as a capital lease?

  **g.** Repeat part **f** for the fifth year, 1985.

**18.36** Refer to the Simplified Funds Statement for a Period in Exhibit 4.13. Nine of the lines in the statement are numbered. Line (2) should be expanded to say "Additions for Expenses, Losses, and Other Charges against Income Not Using Funds," and line (3) should be expanded to say "Subtractions for Revenues, Gains, and Other Credits to Income Not Producing Funds from Operations." Ignore the unnumbered lines in responding to the questions below.

Assume that the accounting cycle is complete for the period and that all of the financial statements have been prepared. Then it is discovered that a transaction has been overlooked. That transaction is recorded in the accounts and all of the financial statements are corrected. Define *funds* as *working capital*. For each of the following transactions, indicate which of the numbered lines of the funds statement is affected and by how much. Ignore income tax effects except where taxes are explicitly mentioned.

For the following questions, assume that an asset with an economic life of 10 years costing $100,000 is leased for $19,925 per year, paid at the end of each year. Assume that all lease receivables and payables are classified as noncurrent on the balance sheet.

**a.** The lessor, using the operating lease method, records depreciation for the year.

**b.** The lessor, using the operating lease method, records receipt of a cash payment for the year.

**c.** The lessee, using the operating lease method, records payment of cash at the end of the year.

**d.** The lessor, using the capital lease method, records receipt of cash for the first year and uses an interest rate of 15 percent per year.

**e.** The lessee, using the capital lease method, records payment of cash for the first year and uses an interest rate of 15 percent per year.

18.37  Rentee Company has an incremental borrowing rate of 18 percent. As lessee, it signs a four-year noncancelable lease for an asset with fair market value of $100,000, agreeing to make annual payments at the end of this year and each of the next three—four payments in total—of $38,629. The present value of an annuity of $1 in arrears for four years discounted at 18 percent is 2.69006.

**a.** At what amount will Rentee Company capitalize its leasehold asset and related lease liability at the start of the lease term?

**b.** What interest rate will Rentee Company use throughout the life of this lease?

**c.** What is the interest expense for the first year of the lease?

**d.** What is the amortization expense for the first year of the lease?

**e.** Why might Rentee Company voluntarily agree to such a lease?

18.38  The manufacturing cost of an asset in inventory is $80,000. The cost of sale of this asset is $62,707 in a sales-type capital lease covering a six-year term with an implicit interest rate of 15 percent.

What is the estimated residual value of this asset?

18.39  The financial statements of Strawcab Company, a lessor, show a gross investment in a sales-type lease of $90,000 and a net investment in the lease of $67,102. Investigation of the lease's details reveals that this particular lease has four years to run, requires annual payments in arrears of $20,000 each, and the estimated residual value of the leased asset is $10,000.

**a.** What is the interest rate implicit in the lease?

**b.** What is the unearned income at the date of the balance sheet containing these data?

**c.** What will be the unearned income at the end of the next year?

18.40  Tenant Company signs an eleven-year noncancelable lease, agreeing to make payments at the end of this year and each of the next ten of $19,925 each. Its incremental borrowing rate is 15 percent per year. The lease contract specifies that at the end of the eighth year, after the payment of $19,925 is made, Tenant Company has the option to purchase the asset from the lessor for $32,395. At the time the lease is signed, the estimated fair market value of the asset at the end of the eighth year is $48,000. The option is a bargain purchase option.

    a. What is the present value of eleven contractual lease payments?

    b. What is the present value of the first eight contractual lease payments plus the present value of the option purchase price?

    c. At what amount will Tenant Company record the lease asset and liability?

    d. What is interest expense for the first year of the lease?

    e. What is the amortization expense for the first year of the lease? (Hint: Use the estimate of fair market value analogously to estimated salvage value and amortize over eight years.)

**18.41** Lessor Company and Lessee Company enter into a five-year capital lease agreement that meets one of the criteria to be a capital lease. The lease payments are to be $2,983, made annually at the end of this year and each of the next four—five payments in total. Lessee Company's incremental borrowing rate is 18 percent. Lessor Company estimates that the residual value of the asset will be $2,000 at the end of the five-year lease term. Lessee Company is aware of this fact and that the fair market value of the asset is $11,000 when the lease term begins. Compute each of the following amounts.

    a. The implicit interest rate in the lease.

    b. The interest rate Lessee Company will use in computing interest expense each period.

    c. The amount Lessee Company will show as net lease obligations on its balance sheet at the start of the lease.

    d. Interest expense for the first year of the lease.

    e. Amortization expense for the first year of the lease.

**18.42** Refer to the data in the preceding problem. Assume that Lessor Company estimates the residual value of the asset as $5,175 (rather than $2,000) at the end of the five-year lease term. Compute each of the amounts asked for in parts **a–e** of Problem **P18.13**.

**18.43** Manufacturing Company has produced a boxcar at a cost of $44,000. It leases the boxcar to Renting Railroad on a noncancelable basis for three years, agreeing to accept equal annual payments of $20,000 at the end of this year and each of the next two. Manufacturing Company estimates that the boxcar will have a residual value of $16,000 in three years, when it is returned by the railroad. The interest rate implicit in the lease is 10 percent per year. The initial indirect costs of executing the lease represent sales commissions and are $1,000. Renting Railroad will pay all executory costs. The lease satisfies the criteria to be a sales-type capital lease for Manufacturing Company, the lessor. The following questions refer to Manufacturing Company.

    a. What is the gross investment in the lease?

    b. What is the net investment in the lease?

    c. What is the unearned income at the inception of the lease?

    d. What are the revenues on signing the lease?

    e. What is the cost of sales for the boxcar leased?

    f. Construct an amortization schedule for the net investment in the lease covering its three-year life.

    g. Prepare journal entries for all transactions of the lease term, including the return of the boxcar at the end of the lease term.

**18.44** Refer to the data in the preceding problem. Assume that immediately after having the boxcar returned at the end of the lease term Manufacturing Company sells the boxcar to Buying Railroad. Prepare journal entries for Manufacturing Company using each of the following sale prices:

    a. $16,000.

    b. $18,000.

    c. $15,000.

**18.45**   Refer to the data in the preceding two problems. Assume that at the outset Manufacturing Company sells the boxcar to the First National Leasing Company for $61,758. The First National Leasing Company incurs initial direct costs of $2,485 to lease the boxcar to Renting Railroad for three years, on the same terms described above—payments of $20,000 per year for three years with estimated (unguaranteed) residual value of $16,000. First National Leasing Company, as lessor, treats this lease as a direct-financing lease. The following questions refer to First National Leasing Company.

a. Verify that the interest rate implicit in the lease is 8 percent per year and that unearned income is $11,757.

b. Prepare an amortization schedule to be used over the life of the lease.

c. Prepare journal entries for the life of the lease, starting with the acquisition of the boxcar for cash and continuing through the return of the boxcar at the end of the third year.

**18.46**   (Adapted from CPA Examination.) Cannon, Inc., was incorporated in 1980 to operate as a computer software service firm with an accounting fiscal year ending August 31. Cannon's primary product is a sophisticated on-line inventory control system; its customers pay a fixed fee plus a usage charge for using the system.

Cannon has leased a large, BIG-1 computer system from the manufacturer. The lease calls for a monthly rental of $30,000 for the 144 months (12 years) of the lease term. The estimated useful life of the computer is 15 years.

Each scheduled monthly rental payment includes $5,000 for full-service maintenance on the computer to be performed by the manufacturer. All rentals are payable on the first day of the month. The computer was installed and the lease agreement was signed on August 1, 1981.

The lease is noncancelable for its 12-year term, and it is secured only by the manufacturer's chattel lien on the BIG-1 system. The lease is to be accounted for as a capital lease by Cannon; it will be amortized by the straight-line method with no expected salvage value. Borrowed funds for this type of transaction would cost Cannon 12 percent per year (1 percent per month). Following is a schedule of the present value of an annuity of $1 for selected periods discounted at 1 percent per period when payments are made at the beginning of each period.

| Periods (Months) | Present Value of an Annuity of $1 Discounted at 1% per Period |
|---|---|
| 1 | 1.000 |
| 2 | 1.990 |
| 3 | 2.970 |
| 143 | 76.658 |
| 144 | 76.899 |

Prepare all journal entries Cannon should have made in its accounting records during August 1981 relating to this lease. Give full explanations and show supporting computations for each entry. Remember August 31, 1981, is the end of Cannon's fiscal accounting period, and it will be preparing financial statements on that date. Do not prepare closing entries.

**18.47**   The chapter illustrations of accounting for capital leases by the lessee always used straight-line amortization of the leasehold asset. If compound interest depreciation is used instead, an interesting result occurs.

Refer to the data for the lessee in Exhibit 18.1. Assume that the net cash flows to the lessee from using the leased computer are exactly $12,500 per year. Thus, the internal rate of return on the asset (with a $30,000 cost) is 12 percent per year.

a. Construct a depreciation schedule for the leasehold asset using the compound interest method and a 12-percent earnings rate.

b. Compute total lease expense for each year.

c. The result of part **b** is not coincidence, but always occurs. State the generalization that appears to be correct from the exercise just completed.

18.48 User Company owns a building that cost $5,000,000, that has $3,500,000 of accumulated depreciation, and that has a fair market value of $2,800,000. The building is sold for $2,000,000 to Lessor Company and leased back over a 10-year term, with lease payments of $400,000 to be made at the end of each year. The leaseback is a capital lease because the user has a bargain purchase option.

a. Verify that the interest rate implicit in the lease is approximately 15 percent per year. (The rate is closer to 15.098 percent per year. Using the 15-percent rate in the rest of the problem simplifies arithmetic computations.)

b. Prepare journal entries made on the date of sale and leaseback by both User Company and Lessor Company. Use a 15-percent rate.

c. Prepare the presentation for the balance sheet of User Company for the date of the sale and leaseback.

d. Prepare journal entries for both User Company and Lessor Company made 1 year after the date of sale and leaseback, assuming that the accounting year and the lease year end at the same time. Use a 15-percent rate. User Company uses straight-line amortization.

18.49 Pan American World Air Lines (Pan Am) leased three Boeing 707 aircraft in 1963 from Sally Leasing Company (Sally). The aircraft had a purchase price of $6.64 million each. The leases covered 13-year terms, were noncancelable, contained no purchase options, and required monthly payments of $71,115. The rental cost per month of $71,115 was several hundred dollars less than Pan Am would have had to pay for conventional financing at the then-prevalent interest rate.

a. What, if anything, did Pan Am give up in return for its savings of several hundred dollars per month for 13 years? What, if anything, did Sally Leasing Company get for giving up several hundred dollars per month for 13 years?

b. Who bore the risks and rewards of ownership in these leases?

c. Verify that the interest rate implicit in the lease contract is about three-fourths of 1 percent per month.

d. Assume that FASB *Statement No. 13* had been in effect when these leases were signed. How would the leases be accounted for?

18.50 (Adapted from CPA Examination.) Computer Systems, Inc. (CSI), a small computer-service company, was established on July 1, 1979. Although it had no revenue during its first year of existence, it did develop 12 general computer programs for a total cost of $48,500. At June 30, 1980, the $48,500 cost of the programs was deferred, whereas all general, administrative, and selling expenses for the year were expensed.

CSI leases its programs to customers for 3 years but retains custody of and title to the programs. CSI runs the leased programs on its own equipment and bills its customers (the lessees) a monthly charge for operating time.

In addition to the general programs, CSI develops programs tailored especially to a customer's needs. These tailored programs are also leased to customers for 3 years and, like the general programs, are controlled by CSI, which bills for operating time. At June 30, 1980, no tailored programs had been developed.

Minor modifications of a general program sometimes are made to meet a lessee's specific

*Exhibit 18.7*
**Data for CSI Leases for Keller**

| | Type A-1 | Type A-2 | Type B-1 | Type B-2 |
|---|---|---|---|---|
| Total Lease Revenue | $6,600 | $6,300 | $15,600 | $18,300 |
| Total Initial Program Modification Costs | 330 | 300 | — | — |
| Total Program Development Costs | — | — | 3,000 | 3,300 |
| Charges for Operating Time for Year Ended June 30, | | | | |
| 1981 | 900 | 849 | 1,200 | 1,275 |
| 1982 | 990 | 975 | 1,278 | 1,299 |
| 1983 | 1,098 | 1,002 | 1,350 | 1,374 |
| Customer Requested Modification Costs for Year Ended June 30, | | | | |
| 1981 | 111 | — | — | — |
| 1982 | — | 108 | 210 | — |
| 1983 | — | — | — | 123 |

needs. Modification of a general program or development of a tailored program is undertaken immediately after a lease is executed.

The general programs are leased under a type A lease agreement, whereas the tailored programs are leased under a type B agreement.

Following are the provisions of the type A agreement: The lease can be renewed after 3 years; the program cannot be purchased; the total charge for the lease must be made in installments of 40 percent the first year, 35 percent the second year, and 25 percent the third year; any initial program modification costs are absorbed by CSI and amortized over 3 years; any later customer program modification requests are billed to the customer at cost.

The provisions of the type B agreement follow: The lease can neither be renewed nor canceled; the program can be purchased for $1 at the end of the lease; the total charge for the lease must be made in installments of 50 percent the first year, 30 percent the second year, and 20 percent the third year. CSI receives the first, 50-percent payment before it commences work on the program. After initial acceptance by the customer of the program results, any customer program modification requests are billed to the customer at cost.

The executives of CSI have considerable expertise in the computer service–bureau industry. They have estimated that the 12 general programs will have an economic life of 6 to 9 years and will earn an estimated total lease revenue of $1,212,500. They have selected to amortize the deferred development costs of the 12 general programs over the estimated lease revenue ($.04 per dollar of lease revenue).

On July 1, 1980, CSI signed two type A and two type B lease agreements with Keller, Inc. All four leases expire June 30, 1983. Other pertinent data are given in Exhibit 18.7.

Using a 7-percent interest rate, the present values at July 1, 1980, of future lease payments due from Keller follow: type A-1, $6,240; type A-2, $5,957; type B-1, $14,898; and type B-2, $17,478. The annual lease payments are made on the first day of the year. CSI accounts for the type A leases under the operating lease method and the type B leases under the capital lease method.

**a.** For the data presented in the problem, prepare a schedule of revenues and expenses by type of lease with Keller for the years ended June 30, 1981, 1982, and 1983. Round all calculations to the nearest dollar. Prepare in good form any supporting schedules you feel necessary. Ignore income taxes. Organize your answer sheet as follows:

| | Type A Leases | Type B Leases |
|---|---|---|
| Lease Rental Revenue: | | |
| 1981 .................................................... | | |
| 1982 .................................................... | | |
| 1983 .................................................... | | |
| Sale of Programs: | | |
| 1981 .................................................... | | |
| 1982 .................................................... | | |
| 1983 .................................................... | | |
| Interest Revenue: | | |
| 1981 .................................................... | | |
| 1982 .................................................... | | |
| 1983 .................................................... | | |
| All Other Revenues: | | |
| 1981 .................................................... | | |
| 1982 .................................................... | | |
| 1983 .................................................... | | |
| Amortization of Program and Initial Program Modification Costs: | | |
| 1981 .................................................... | | |
| 1982 .................................................... | | |
| 1983 .................................................... | | |
| All Other Expenses: | | |
| 1981 .................................................... | | |
| 1982 .................................................... | | |
| 1983 .................................................... | | |

**b.** On July 1, 1981, CSI sold various auxiliary equipment with a net book value of $15,000 to Hope, Inc., for $20,000. Because the collection of the sales price was questionable, CSI retained title to the equipment until Hope made the last payment. Hope made a down payment of $2,000 and signed an 8-percent note due in eight equal quarterly payments of $2,457 each, including interest, beginning September 30, 1982. During 1981, CSI incurred $750 selling expenses in the sale of this equipment. Based on the installment sales method of accounting, prepare a schedule of all revenues and expenses for the above transaction for the year ended June 30, 1982. Assume that all payments are made in accordance with the agreement. Ignore income taxes. Round all computations to the nearest dollar.

**18.51** Refer to the data and example in Exhibit 18.3. Assume that the lessor "sold" the equipment to the lessee on an installment basis. The lessee is to make three annual payments, one at the end of each year, of $12,500 each.
**a.** Prepare columns analogous to those in Exhibit 18.3 showing income each period, assuming the lessor used the installment method of revenue recognition.
**b.** Repeat part **a**, using the cost-recovery-first method of revenue recognition.

**18.52** Beckett Computers manufactured a computer at a cost of $80,000. The computer ordinarily sells for $100,000 cash. A customer, Mori Company, wishes to acquire the computer but prefers to finance the acquisition with a long-term noncancelable lease. Mori Company wishes to arrange the terms of the lease so that it will be an operating lease for itself, the lessee, while Beckett Computers wants the lease drawn so that it will be a capital lease (sale) for itself, the lessor.

The computer is expected to have a useful life of eight years, but rapid technological change is expected. Today, the fair market value of the computer is expected to be only $15,000 in five years. Mori Company's debt rate is 15 percent per year. Beckett Computers proposes that Mori Company sign a five-year noncancelable lease requiring five payments (each to be made at the end of the year) of $25,357. Meanwhile, Beckett Company will take out an insurance policy with Lloyd's of London to guarantee the residual value of the computer. Five years from the beginning of the lease, Lloyd's will take possession of the computer and will pay Beckett Computers $15,000. Lloyd's will charge Beckett Computers an insurance premium to cover its risks.* Beckett Computers will make a single payment to Lloyd's on the date the lease begins but will pass along the charge for the insurance policy to Mori Company. Thus, Mori Company's total contractual payments for the five-year lease are payments for the insurance policy on signing the lease and five payments of $25,357, one at the end of each of the five years of the lease.

How large can the insurance premium be while still allowing Beckett Company to use the capital lease method, and Mori Company to use the operating lease method?

**18.53** (Adapted from CPA Examination.) Dumont Corporation, a lessor of office machines, purchased a new machine for $500,000 on December 31, Year 1, which was delivered the same day (by prior arrangement) to Finley Company, the lessee. The following information relating to the lease transaction is available:

● The leased asset has an estimated useful life of seven years which coincides with the lease term.

● At the end of the lease term, the machine will revert to Dumont, at which time it is expected to have a residual value of $60,000 (none of which is guaranteed by Finley).

● The 10-percent investment tax credit on the asset cost is retained by Dumont and is expected to be realized in its Year 1 income tax return.

● Dumont's implicit interest rate (on its net investment) is 12 percent, which is known by Finley.

● Finley's incremental borrowing rate is 14 percent at December 31, Year 1.

● Lease rentals consist of seven equal annual payments, the first of which was paid on December 31, Year 1.

● The lease is appropriately accounted for as a direct financing lease by Dumont and as a capital lease by Finley. Both lessor and lessee are calendar-year corporations and depreciate all fixed assets on the straight-line basis.

Information on present value factors is as follows:

Present value of $1 for seven periods at 12 percent ............................ 0.452
Present value of $1 for seven periods at 14 percent ............................. 0.400
Present value of an annuity of $1 in advance for seven periods at 12 percent ......... 5.111
Present value of an annuity of $1 in advance for seven periods at 14 percent ......... 4.889

**a.** Compute the annual rental under the lease.
**b.** Compute the amounts of the gross lease rentals receivable and the unearned interest revenue that Dumont should disclose at the inception of the lease on December 3, Year 1.
**c.** What expense should Finley record for the year ended December 31, Year 2.

**18.54** (Adapted from CPA Examination.) Nelson, Inc., manufactures and markets nationally two types of high-tolerance milling and machining equipment. The first type (Nelson's product

---

*In the late 1970s, Lloyd's suffered the largest underwriting losses in its history from deals such as these. The bottom dropped out of the used computer market because of unexpectedly rapid technological change and price decreases by IBM. Leasing companies, such as Beckett in this example, thought they were protected. Lloyd's and other insurors have claimed in litigation, however, that for several reasons they do not owe the full amounts the leasing companies thought they were entitled to receive.

line since its business started 50 years ago) is manually operated; the second (introduced 5 years ago after significant research and development) is automated. Both types have estimated useful lives of 15 years or more.

For 20 years, approximately 10 percent of the old-line equipment has been leased; approximately 80 percent of the automated equipment has been leased since being introduced. Nelson refers to the lease agreement for the old-line equipment as type I, and that for the automated equipment as type II. The major provisions follow.

(1) *Terms*. Both lease types have a primary noncancelable term with an option to purchase or renew for a second noncancelable term with a second purchase option. For type I leases, the primary and second terms are 8 years and 5 years; for type II, the terms are 6 years and 3 years.

(2) *Payments*. The type I lease requires equal monthly payments in the primary term to provide a 10-percent return with the present value of the lease equal to the cash selling price of the equipment. Monthly payments in the second term are 25 percent of the payments in the primary term.

The type II lease requires equal monthly payments in the primary term to produce a 10-percent return, with the present value of the lease equal to the cost of the equipment (based on full absorption costing). Monthly payments in the second term are set to provide a 10-percent return, with the present value of the payments equal to the purchase option price at the end of the primary term. Monthly payments in both terms are increased for the estimated cost of a maintenance program.

(3) *Purchase option prices*. Type I lessees may purchase the equipment at the end of the primary term for 10 percent of the present value of the lease at issue date. The equipment may be purchased for $100 at the end of the second term.

Type II lessees may purchase the equipment at the end of the primary and second terms for 50 percent and 25 percent, respectively, of the present value of the lease at issue date.

(4) *Maintenance*. Type I lessees are responsible for maintenance. Nelson provides type II lessees with a complete maintenance program, including equipment replacement if necessary.

(5) *Return of equipment*. Nelson agrees to accept equipment F.O.B. lessee's dock at the end of either the primary or second term of both type I and type II leases.

(6) *Other responsibilities of lessees*. For both types of leases, the lessee is responsible for (a) insurance coverage, (b) payment of property taxes, and (c) damage to the equipment through negligent use.

Nelson's type I lease experience is that 10 percent of the lessees return the equipment at the end of the primary term, 30 percent exercise their renewal options and then purchase at the end of the second term, and 60 percent exercise the purchase option at the end of the primary term. There is a ready market for used equipment returned.

Nelson has had limited experience with the type II lease and equipment, but management expects or recognizes the following three points.

(7) A higher percentage of equipment will probably be returned at the end of the primary term. Management plans to re-lease equipment returned at rates essentially comparable to the second term payments or sell the equipment at approximately the purchase option price at the end of the primary term.

(8) Maintenance costs may differ from estimates, as there has been insufficient experience to evaluate; however, management's opinion is that the payment made by the lessee will be adequate considering all present information.

(9) The marketability of returned equipment is uncertain; the market has not been tested yet.

a. Identify Nelson's type I leases as either capital or operating leases; give reasons for your conclusion.

**b.** Identify Nelson's type II leases as either capital or operating leases; give reasons for your conclusion.

**c.** Early this year, Nelson arranged for its bank to purchase all of its type II leases (including title to the equipment) for a present value computed by discounting future payments at 12 percent. In the event of lessee default, sales are subject to recourse, requiring Nelson to repurchase the lease or substitute a new lease in its place. Nelson agreed to meet its maintenance commitments. It also agreed to use its best efforts to sell any returned equipment for a 10-percent sales commission.

Explain how Nelson should account for and report in its financial statements the sale of type II leases to the bank. Support your conclusions with underlying theoretical justification.

**18.55**   The leveraged lease is a direct-financing lease involving at least three parties: a lessee, a long-term lender, and a lessor who is the equity participant. The financing provided by the long-term lender is nonrecourse debt to the lessor. The lessor's cash flows typically involve an initial outflow, subsequent inflows, then outflows, then inflows.

Column (1) of Exhibit 18.8 illustrates a series of leveraged-lease cash flows. The data come from an example used in Appendix E of FASB *Statement No. 13*. The cash flows are the lessor's. The lessor acquires an asset costing $1 million and borrows $600,000 from the long-term lender at 9 percent, to be repaid in 15 equal annual installments on the last day of each year. Thus the lessor's initial net cash outflow is $400,000. The asset is leased for 15 years with lease payments from lessee to lessor of $90,000 per year, payable on the last day of each year. The lessor is assumed to have other pretax income sufficiently large so that accounting losses from accelerated cost recovery and interest expense in the early years of the lease can be used to reduce cash payments for income taxes. The asset is assumed to have a residual value of $20,000, which will be realized on the last day of the sixteenth year. Column (1) of Exhibit 18.8 shows the net cash inflows (outflows) for each year. These cash flows are the starting point of the problem addressed here.

The FASB requires that the lessor compute the implicit rate of return from the projected cash flows on the net investment in the periods when the net investment is positive. That rate of return multiplied by the net investment for a period is the income for the period, and the remaining cash flows of that period are allocated to reduce the amount of investments. The net investment in the example is $400,000 at the start of the first year and is reduced by that portion of cash flows not allocated to income of the year. There is, by definition, no income during periods in which the lessor's investment is negative.

The computation of the implicit interest rate depends on knowing the periods for which the net investment is positive, but knowing when net investment is positive requires knowing the implicit interest rate.* The implicit interest rate for the lessor's leveraged lease cash flows in Exhibit 18.8 is 8.647 percent per year.

Based on the description of the accounting for leveraged leases in this discussion, fill in the blanks in Exhibit 18.8 represented by the letters **a** through **i**.

**18.56**   Refer to the data for the leveraged lease in the preceding problem. The cash flow data shown in the first column have an implicit interest rate of 9.2575 percent per year.

**a.** Construct an amortization schedule showing the income that results from using the integral investment method for leveraged leases. Show the following columns:

(1) Year Number (starting with year 0),

---

*An algorithm for finding the implicit rate appears in D. F. Shanno and R. L. Weil, "The Separate Phases Method of Accounting for Leveraged Leases: Properties of the Allocating Rate and an Algorithm for Finding It," *Journal of Accounting Research* 14 (Autumn 1976), pp. 348–356.

---

*Exhibit 18.8*
**Illustration of Leveraged Lease
Income Based on Appendix E of
FASB Statement No. 13**

| Year | Cash Inflow (Outflow) during Year[a] (1) | Income for Year (2) | Net Investment at Year-End[b] (3) |
|---|---|---|---|
| 0 | $(400,000) | — | $400,000 |
| 1 | 169,421 | $ 34,588 | 265,167 |
| 2 | 119,923 | 22,929 | a. |
| 3 | 89,769 | 14,542 | 92,946 |
| 4 | b. | 8,037 | 29,458 |
| 5 | 53,182 | c. | (21,177) |
| 6 | 18,616 | 0 | d. |
| 7 | (9,553) | 0 | (30,240) |
| 8 | (11,108) | e. | (19,132) |
| 9 | (12,803) | 0 | (6,329) |
| 10 | f. | 0 | 8,320 |
| 11 | (16,663) | 719 | 25,702 |
| 12 | (18,857) | g. | 46,781 |
| 13 | h. | 4,045 | 72,074 |
| 14 | (23,856) | 6,232 | 102,162 |
| 15 | (26,698) | 8,834 | 137,694 |
| 16 | 149,600 | i. | 0 |
| Totals | $116,601 | $116,601 | |

[a]Initial investment is $400,000.

[b]Item in this column for year $t$ is equal to preceding amount in this column for year $t - 1$, minus cash inflow or plus cash outflow for year $t$ from column (1) plus income for the year $t$, column (2).

Sources:

Column (1) = column (8) of Schedule 2 of Appendix E of FASB *Statement No. 13.*

Column (2): computed; see text.

Column (3): computed; see text.

---

(2) Investment, Start of Year = Column (5) from Preceding Year,

(3) Income (Expense) for Year = Column (2) × .092575,

(4) Cash Receipts (Outflows) for Year = Column (1) of Exhibit 18.8, and

(5) Investment, End of Year = Column (2) + Column (3) − Column (4).

b. Compare the income in the third column of the answer to part **a** for the integral investment method with that in the second column of Exhibit 18.8 for the separate phases method. Which method of recognizing income on a leveraged lease is more conservative?

# Chapter 19
# *Pensions*

Under a pension plan, an employer promises to make payments to employees after retirement. Private pension plan systems have grown in number and size over the last several decades so rapidly that the major asset of many individuals is the present value of their pension benefits. The basic operations of a pension plan are simple, but the concepts can be lost in a variety of details. In a pension plan:

**1.** The employer sets up a pension plan, specifying the eligibility of employees, the types of promises made to employees, the method of funding, and the pension plan administrator. Typically, the plan's funding agent is a bank or insurance company.*

**2.** Each period, the employer computes a pension expense according to some formula. The employer debits Pension Expense for that amount and credits Pension Liability. This process is called "expensing pension obligations."

**3.** The employer transfers cash to the plan each period according to some formula. The employer generally debits Pension Liability

---

*Pension law differentiates between the *plan administrator* (one with fiduciary responsibility for the plan) and the *funding agent* (who holds and invests funds). In this chapter, we do not distinguish between these two functions.

and credits Cash. This process is called "funding pension liabilities." The amounts expensed each period in step **2** are *not* necessarily the same as the amounts funded in this step.

The preceding steps comprise the employer's accounting for pensions. The employer is sometimes called the "plan sponsor."

The following steps are carried out for the pension plan by the plan administrator, who maintains the accounting records of the pension plan.

**1.** The plan receives cash each period from the plan sponsor. In the accounting records of the pension plan, Cash is debited and Pension Liability to Employees is credited.

**2.** As time passes, payment dates approach. The pension plan debits Interest Expense and credits Pension Liability to Employees for the increase in present value of the pension liability. Meanwhile, the funds received are invested to generate income. The pension plan debits Cash Received from Earnings and credits Investment Revenue. The interest expense and investment income are not part of the employer's (sponsor's) income for the period but are reported in separate financial statements of the pension plan.

**3.** The plan makes payments to those entitled to receive them. The plan debits Pension Liability to Employees and credits Cash.

As you study pension accounting, keep in mind the distinction between accounting by the plan sponsor and by the plan administrator.

19.3    Accounting Principles Board *Opinion No. 8* and Financial Accounting Standards Board *Statement No. 36** govern the *employer's* accounting and reporting for pension plans. FASB *Statement No. 35* governs the accounting and reporting for pension plans.† The FASB is expected to issue a new pronouncement within the next year or two that will revise APB *Opinion No. 8*.

## Introduction to Pension Plans

19.4    There are almost as many different kinds of pension plans as there are employers who have them. The basic variables of a pension plan are the following:

**1.** Its requirement for contributions by employers and employees.

**2.** Vesting provisions.

**3.** Funding provisions.

**4.** The kinds of promises made by the employer.

Each of these variables is now explained and discussed.

## Contributions

19.5    Under a *noncontributory* plan, the employee makes no explicit contribution of funds to the pension plan; only the employer contributes. Under a *contributory* plan, both the

---

*Accounting Principles Board, APB *Opinion No. 8,* "Accounting for the Cost of Pension Plans," 1966; Financial Accounting Standards Board, *Statement of Financial Accounting Standards No. 36,* "Disclosure of Pension Information," 1980.

†Financial Accounting Standards Board, *Statement of Financial Accounting Standards No. 35,* "Accounting and Reporting for Defined Benefit Pension Plans," 1980.

employee and the employer contribute, but they do not necessarily contribute equal amounts. Employees retain a claim to their explicit contributions under virtually all plans. The employee's rights to the employer's contributions are determined by the *vesting* provisions. The rest of this chapter considers noncontributory plans or, if the plan is contributory, only the employer's contributions.

## Vesting Provisions

An employee's rights to a benefit under a   19.6
pension plan may be fully vested, partially vested, or not vested. When the rights are *fully vested,* the pension benefits cannot be taken away from the employee. (These benefits are partially insured by an agency of the federal government.) If the rights are not vested, the employee will lose all rights to the employer's contributions if he or she leaves the company before retirement. Under *partially vested* (or "graded vesting") plans, rights vest gradually. For example, an employee in the fifth year of work might have no vested rights, but after 10 years' employment, the pension rights would be 50 percent vested, and by 15 years, all rights would be vested. The nature of vesting provisions influences the present value of the expected pension liabilities generated during an accounting period. If employees leave their jobs, their benefit rights—and therefore the employer's liabilities—are smaller when the benefits are only partially vested than when the benefits are fully vested.

Federal pension law (the Pension Reform   19.7
Act of 1974, called the *Employee Retirement Income and Security Act* or *ERISA*) requires that an employee's benefits from contributions by the employer must become vested according to one of several formulas. These generally provide for full vesting by the time the employee has worked for the employer for 15 years.

## Funding Provisions

A pension plan may be *fully funded* or *par-*   19.8
*tially funded.* Under a fully funded plan, the employer pays cash to an outside trustee

such as a trust company, equal to the present value of all expected pension liabilities. Partially funded plans have cash available in an amount less than the present value of all pension obligations. ERISA mandates certain minimum funding requirements for corporate pension plans.

## Employer Promises

19.9  Employers make essentially two different kinds of pension promises to employees:

**1.** A few employers make promises about the amounts to be contributed to the pension plan without specifying the benefits to be received by retired employees. Such plans are referred to as *defined-contribution plans*. Employer inputs or contributions to the plan are defined. The amounts eventually received by employees depend on the investment performance of the pension fund.

**2.** Most employers make promises about the amount each employee will receive during retirement without specifying the amounts the employer will contribute to the plan. These plans are referred to as *defined-benefit plans*. Payments to employees are defined. The employer must make contributions to the plan so that those amounts plus the investment earnings of the plan are large enough to make the payments promised to the retired employees.

19.10  **Defined-Contribution Plans** In a defined-contribution plan, the employer promises to contribute an amount determined by formula to each employee's pension account. Zenith Radio Corporation, for example, promises to contribute between 6 and 12 percent of an employee's income before the contribution (the exact amount depending on some other factors) to the pension plan each year. An employee's share in the company's pension fund depends on his or her annual compensation. Another employer might agree to contribute an amount equal to 5 percent of an employee's salary to a pension fund. Subject to reasonable investment risks, the funds are managed to produce as large a series of payments as is possible during the employee's retirement. No specific promises are made to employees about the amount of the eventual pension. Inputs are defined; total payments depend on investment performance.

The accounting for defined-contribution     19.11 plans is particularly simple. If the employer contributes $55,000 to a trustee to be managed for employees' retirement benefits, the journal entry under generally accepted accounting principles is

| | | |
|---|---|---|
| Pension Expense | ................. 55,000 | |
| Cash | ........................ | 55,000 |

Other than periodically overseeing the activ-  19.12 ities of the plan to insure that investment policies are being prudently carried out, the employer's obligation under the pension plan is largely completed once the cash is paid to the plan. Neither the assets of the pension plan nor the amounts expected to be paid to retired employees appear in the employer's financial statements. The income from pension fund investments each period is not included in the net income of the employer, but in separate financial statements of the plan.

**Defined-Benefit Plans** Under a defined-  19.13 benefit plan, the employer promises the employee a series of payments at retirement based on a formula. The typical formula takes into account the employee's length of service and some measure of average or maximum earnings. For example, the employer might promise to pay during retirement an annual pension equal to 25 percent of the maximum annual salary earned during working years for an employee who has been employed for 5 years. The percentage might increase to 26 percent for 6 years of service, and so on, so that an employee with 40 years of service would get a pension equal to 60 percent of his or her maximum salary during the working years. The defined-benefit formula is

$$\begin{array}{l}\text{Pension Benefit} \\ \text{per Year during} = (.20 + .01n) \times \\ \text{Retirement}\end{array} \begin{array}{l}\text{Maximum} \\ \text{Salary} \\ \text{during} \\ \text{Employment}\end{array}$$

where $n$ is the number of years of the employee's employment.* Payments are defined by formula; the exact amount to be paid later to employees is not known currently and therefore must be estimated. This amount depends on factors such as mortality, inflation, employee turnover, and retirement age.

19.14     The employer must set aside funds currently and in the future to fulfill its pension obligations to employees. The amount set aside depends, among other factors, on the rate of return to be earned on pension fund investments. Because defined-benefit pension plans are based on numerous estimates, such plans must be able to cope with misestimates as they become apparent.

19.15   **Comparison of Types of Promises** Most corporate pension plans are defined-benefit plans. ERISA makes defined-contribution plans relatively more attractive than they had been previously. The number of defined-contribution plans is increasing, but such plans remain a small minority. Some employees prefer a defined-benefit plan because it reduces the employee's risk in planning for retirement. Some employers tend to prefer defined-contribution plans because of the reduced uncertainty of pension expenses and contributions. The plan used in any given firm is likely to be the result of labor-management negotiations. Later sections discuss defined-benefit plans in more detail.

# Generally Accepted Accounting Principles by Employers for Defined-Benefit Plans

## Concepts and Terminology

19.16     The examples below illustrate the essential concepts and terminology for defined-bene-

fit pension plans. They are based on Exhibit 19.5, which appears later in this chapter.

**Example 1** On December 31, 1981, a firm   19.17 adopts a pension plan that promises to pay retired employees an annual pension equal to a stated percentage of their maximum salary during their working years. The percentage is equal to 20 percent plus 1 percent for each year worked according to the following formula:

$$\text{Annual Pension} = \begin{pmatrix} .20 + .01 \times \\ \text{Number of} \\ \text{Years Worked} \end{pmatrix} \times \begin{array}{c} \text{Maximum} \\ \text{Salary} \\ \text{Earned} \end{array}.$$

The pension is to be paid for 20 years, one payment at the end of each year during retirement.† Pension funds are expected to earn 6 percent per year.

    John Wilson, one of the firm's employees,   19.18 began work on January 1, 1981, at a salary of $10,000 per year. By the date of the pension plan's adoption, December 31, 1981, Wilson had earned an annual pension of $2,100 [= (.20 + .01) × $10,000]. Assume that Wilson will work for 40 years before retiring, 39 years more after the plan is adopted. The pension will be paid for 20 years. The payments of $2,100 each will be made at the ends of the 41st, 42nd, . . . , 60th years. (See Figure 19.1.) On the date of Wilson's retirement, the end of the 40th year, the payments of $2,100 each have present value of $24,086 (= $2,100 × 11.46992; Table 4, 20-period row, 6-percent column). The present value of these payments on December 31, 1981, the date of the adoption of the plan, is $2,482 [= $24,086 × .10306; Table 2, 39-period row, 6-percent

---

*The formula used here, and throughout the rest of this chapter, is simplified for ease of exposition. Typically, the pension is based on an average of several years' salary, rather than on the highest salary, because the income tax laws require such an average if pension contribuions are to be deductible for tax purposes.

†In reality, employees would expect a pension for as long as they (or their spouses) live, and the calculation of the expected total pension to be paid is complex, involving "commutation tables"—a combination of mortality tables and present-value tables. One cannot merely take the *expected* number of years of life, say 20, for an individual as input to a simple annuity calculation to compute the present value of expected pension costs for that individual. This book does not illustrate the detailed actuarial calculations. Appendix B discusses life contingent annuities to illustrate the problem and why the computation is more complex than one might think.

*Figure 19.1*
**Illustration of Events for Example 1**

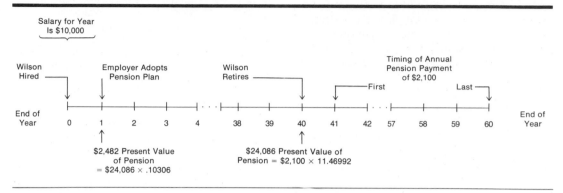

column would show $(1.06)^{-39} = .10306$]. The present value of the benefits earned as of any given date is called the *accumulated benefits* of the pension plan. In the example, the accumulated benefits on December 31, 1981, are $2,482.

19.19 Assume that, upon adoption of the pension plan, the employer immediately recognizes as an expense and fully funds the accumulated benefits of the pension plan. The journal entries on the books of the employer and on the books of the pension plan are as follows:

**Employer**
December 31, 1981
Pension Expense .................... 2,482
    Pension Liability ................ 2,482
To recognize an expense and a liability for benefits earned to date upon adoption of a pension plan.

Pension Liability .................... 2,482
    Cash ......................... 2,482
To fund the pension liability.

**Pension Plan**
December 31, 1981
Cash .............................. 2,482
    Pension Liability to Employees .... 2,482
To record receipt of cash from plan sponsor.

January 1, 1982
Investments ........................ 2,482
    Cash ......................... 2,482
To record acquisition of investments by the pension plan.

The pension plan investments earn at an as- 19.20 sumed rate of 6 percent per year. During the 39 years between receipt of the $2,482 contribution from the employer and the employee's retirement, the plan will earn revenue from its investments. The plan will also recognize interest expense on the Pension Liability to Employees as the payment of the pension approaches. The plan's liability to pay pension benefits increases with the passage of time. The pension plan's journal entries over the 39 years for the earnings on the contribution of $2,482 would be:

Investments ....................... 21,604
    Investment Revenue (Interest,
    Dividends, etc.) ............. 21,604
Recording cumulative earnings over 39 years on investment. $21,604 = $2,482 \times (1.06)^{39} - $2,482 = $24,086 - $2,482.

Interest Expense .................. 21,604
    Pension Liability to Employees . 21,604
To record increase in liability for payments as they come closer to being due.

The Pension Liability to Employees is 19.21 $24,086 (= $2,482 + $21,604) by the end of the 40th year. Over the 40-year period, the employer would have recognized an expense of only $2,482 for the first-year pension, the initial contribution. The remaining amount necessary to cover John Wilson's pension from his first year of work of $21,604 (= $24,086 − $2,482) would be generated from pension fund investments. This example ignores the employer's expenses for pension benefits earned during the years between the first and retirement. Example 2 considers these benefits and the related expenses.

19.22 **Example 2** Refer to the data in Example 1. During 1982, John Wilson earned a salary of $11,000. By the end of 1982, Wilson had earned rights to an annual pension of $2,420 [= (.20 + .02) × $11,000]. The annual pension has increased both because he worked one more year and because the salary base on which pension benefits are calculated has increased. The present value at the end of year 40 of 20 annual payments in arrears of $2,420 each discounted at 6 percent is $27,757 (= $2,420 × 11.46992). The present value of these payments at the end of the current year is $3,032 (= $27,757 × .10924; Table 2, 38-period row, 6-percent column). Thus, accumulated benefits at the end of 1982 are $3,032. The $550 increase in accumulated benefits from $2,482 at the end of 1981 to $3,032 at the end of 1982 results from two factors: (1) interest during 1982 on accumulated benefits as of December 31, 1981, because the pension is one year closer to being paid, and (2) an increased pension caused by an additional year of employment at a higher salary. These two components can be seen as follows:

1. Interest during 1982 on accumulated benefits as of December 31, 1981. (Because the employer paid $2,482 to the pension plan at the end of the first year, this interest will appear in the plan's accounts.) Interest on benefits of $2,482 is $149 (= $2,482 × .06) . . . . . . . . . . . . . . . . . . . . . . . . . . . . . . $149

2. Increased pension due to an additional year of employment at a higher salary. Because an extra year has been worked, the defined-benefit formula grants a pension larger by $100 {= [(.20 + .02) − (.20 + .01)] × $10,000]}. The raise causes the eventual pension to be higher by .22 (= .20 + .01$n$) of the amount of the raise; .22 × $1,000 = $220. Thus, the eventual pension will be

$320 (= $100 + $220) larger as a result of the extra year of work at a larger salary. The present value at the end of year 40 of the entire pension stream increases by $3,670 (= $320 × 11.46992). The present value of $3,670 at the end of year 2 is $401 (= .10924 × $3,670) . . . . . . . . . . . . . . . . . . . . . .   401

Total increase in present value of accumulated benefits = $3,032 − $2,482 . . . . . . . . .   $550

The portion of the increase in accumulated benefits due to an employee's services for one more year of work is referred to as the *normal cost* of the pension plan, $401 in this example.* Assume that the employer recognizes the normal cost as an expense of 1982 and funds this amount on December 31, 1982. The entries on the books of the employer and on the books of the pension fund are as follows:

19.23

**Employer**
December 31, 1982
Pension Expense . . . . . . . . . . . . . . . . . . . . . . . 401
    Pension Liability . . . . . . . . . . . . . . . . . . . .   401
To record pension expense and pension liability for the normal cost of the pension plan for 1982.

December 31, 1982
Pension Liability . . . . . . . . . . . . . . . . . . . . . . . 401
    Cash . . . . . . . . . . . . . . . . . . . . . . . . . . . . .   401
To fund the pension liability.

---

*Confusion often arises as to whether normal cost for the current year includes interest on normal cost accrued in prior years ($149 in this example). The confusion arises because of a failure to distinguish between normal cost *expense* and normal cost *liability*.

Normal cost expense for a period is the increase in accumulated benefits from the beginning of the period to the end of the period, assuming that all years' normal costs since the inception of the pension plan have been funded as they have been accrued. Because these amounts have been funded, the increase in accumulated benefits due to the benefits' being one year closer (that is, the interest on prior years' normal cost) is an expense of the pension fund, not of the employer. Thus, normal cost expense of the employer does not include interest on normal cost accrued in prior years.

The normal cost liability, on the other hand, is equal to that portion of accumulated benefits at any date attributable to employees' service since inception of the plan. The normal cost liability is thus the sum of prior periods' normal cost expense (recognized by the employers) and the interest thereon. The normal cost liability is not separately labeled and disclosed as such but is included in the pension plan's total liabilities.

**Pension Plan**
December 31, 1982
Interest Expense ....................... 149
  Pension Liability to Employees .......  149
To record interest on pension liability of $2,482 previously recorded: .06 × $2,482 = $149.

December 31, 1982
Cash ................................. 149
  Pension Fund Revenue .............  149
To record revenue earned from pension fund investment during 1982 at 6 percent: $2,482 × .06 = $149. Note that the revenue recognized here is the same dollar amount as the interest expense in the preceding entry.

December 31, 1982
Cash ................................. 401
  Pension Liability to Employees .......  401
To record receipt of cash from plan sponsor.

19.24 The assets of the pension fund are now as follows:

| | |
|---|---|
| Investments (from 12/31/81 contribution) . | $2,482 |
| Cash (from revenues earned on investments during 1982) ............. | 149 |
| Cash (from 12/31/82 contribution by the employer) ......................... | 401 |
|   Total Pension Fund Assets .......... | $3,032 |

The assets in the pension fund precisely equal the accumulated benefits earned under the pension plan as of December 31, 1982. The employer has recognized as an expense a total of $2,883 (= $2,482 + $401). The plan has recognized interest expense of $149. The sum of the amounts recognized by the employer as expenses, $2,883, and the amount of interest expense on pension fund liabilities of $149 equals the total accumulated benefit of $3,032. The total cost is split between the employer's pension expenses and the plan's interest expense. For a given set of assumptions and outcomes, the *total* pension cost will not change. The timing of the employer's payments to the plan will, however, determine how much of the total cost is reported by the employer and how much by the plan.

19.25 **Example 3** Assume the same facts as in examples 1 and 2, but that the employer makes all funding payments to the pension plan at the end of the *second* year, 1982. (Under current federal regulations, it would have to make some funding payments at the end of 1981, but the pension concepts will be clearer if you consider the employer's accounting if it does not immediately fund all obligations.) The employer makes the following entries for Wilson's pension:

**Employer**
December 31, 1981
Pension Expense .................... 2,482
  Pension Liability .................  2,482
To recognize expense for pension earned during 1981.

December 31, 1982
Interest Expense .................... 149
  Pension Liability .................  149
Interest on Pension Liability accrued for one year at 6 percent: .06 × $2,482 = $149.

Pension Expense .................... 401
  Pension Liability .................  401
To recognize expense of pension earned during 1982. The Pension Liability is now $3,032 = $2,482 + $149 + $401.

Pension Liability .................... 3,032
  Cash .........................  3,032
To fund liability with payment to pension plan.

The pension plan receives the cash of $3,032, invests it, and records the following entries:

**Pension Plan**
December 31, 1982
Cash ............................... 3,032
  Pension Liability to Employees ....  3,032
Receive cash and set up liability.

Investments ........................ 3,032
  Cash .........................  3,032
To invest cash.

19.26 Note that the pension plan now has assets of $3,032 and liabilities of $3,032, the same as at the end of Example 2. The employer has more expense in Example 3 ($3,032 = $2,482 + $149 + $401) than in Example 2 ($2,883 = $2,482 + $401). The difference occurs because the employer in Example 3 did not contribute cash to the pension fund at the end of 1981. The pension fund was therefore unable to earn the $149 (= .06 × $2,482) generated in Example 2. The required contribution by the employer at the end of 1982, and therefore the employer's cost, must be larger by $149. Revenue generated by the pension fund during 1982 is smaller by $149 than if the employer had made the contribution at the end of 1981.

19.27    These examples illustrate a general principle: the employer's total pension-related expenses depend on its funding policy; the combined pension-related expenses of the employer and the pension plan together, however, are independent of the employer's timing of funding payments. The student who recalls that the combined employer–plan pension expense is unaffected by the employer's funding policy is less likely to be confused by the possible variation in the individual components of the total. If the employer funds early, its expenses will be smaller but those of the fund will be larger. If the employer funds later, its expenses will be larger but the fund's will be smaller.*

19.28    **Example 4** Refer to the data for John Wilson in Examples 1 and 2. Instead of adopting the pension plan at the end of 1981, assume that the employer adopts the plan on December 31, 1990. The annual pension is again equal to 20 percent plus 1 percent for each year worked times the maximum annual salary earned. At the time the pension plan is adopted, Wilson has worked for 10 years. He earns a salary of $23,600 during 1990. The employer agrees to give all employees credit for the years worked prior to adoption of the plan, so Wilson receives credit for the 10 years he has worked. His annual pension during retirement will be $7,080 [= (.20 + .10) × $23,600].

The present value of a periodic payment    19.29 of $7,080 paid for 20 periods discounted at 6 percent is $81,207 (= 7,080 × 11.46992). The present value of these payments on December 31, 1990, the date the pension plan is adopted, is $14,139 (= $81,207 × .17411; Table 2, 30-period row, 6-percent column). See Figure 19.2.

APB *Opinion No. 8* refers to the present    19.30 value of benefits earned prior to the adoption of a pension plan as the "past service cost" of the plan, $14,139 in this example. FASB *Statement No. 35* uses the actuarial term *supplemental actuarial value* for the present value of benefits earned prior to the adoption of the plan. In 1981, the Joint Committee on Pension Terminology adopted the term *actuarial accrued liability* and we shall use that term throughout.†

On the date a pension plan is adopted, the    19.31 accumulated benefits and the actuarial accrued liability of the plan will be the same. On subsequent dates, accumulated benefits will increase both because the pension payments are nearer and because employees work additional years at higher salaries. These factors are part of the normal cost liability of the plan.** Thus, at any date:

   Accumulated Benefits
−  Normal Cost Liability for All Years Worked
=  Actuarial Accrued Liability.

Part of the actuarial accrued liability will be expensed each year and part (perhaps a different amount) will be funded. The part not

---

*Jack L. Treynor, editor of the *Financial Analysts Journal*, writing under his pseudonym Walter Bagehot, was the first we know of to suggest that understanding the financial effects of pension plans would be easier if one considers the "consolidated" financial statements of the employer and the plan. See Walter Bagehot, "Risk and Reward in Corporate Pension Funds," *Financial Analysts Journal* 28 (January–February 1972), pp. 80–84; and J. L. Treynor, W. Priest, and P. Regan, *The Financial Reality of Pension Funding under ERISA* (Homewood, Ill.: Dow-Jones-Irwin, 1976), Chapter 3.

---

†More technically, and more correctly, whether or not actuarial accrued liability even exists and its amount when it does exist depend on the actuarial cost method used. That is, a pension plan can be adopted and credit given to employees for past years of service, but no actuarial or accounting obligation for the cost of that credit comes into being. Rather, the actuarial cost method in use takes the credit into account *prospectively*, by adjusting the amount of funding (or expense) in each future period for the cost of the credit. The discussion here assumes use of an actuarial cost method, such as entry age normal, where an amount for actuarial accrued liability is created on adoption of the plan. These issues are discussed later in the chapter and in problem **19.42**.

**See the note to paragraph 19.23, which explains the difference between normal cost (expense) and the normal cost liability.

*Figure 19.2*
**Illustration of Events for Example 4**

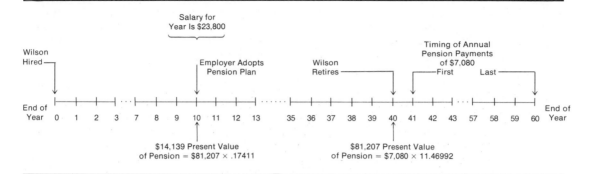

yet expensed is called the *unrecognized* or *unamortized actuarial accrued liability*. The part that has not yet been funded is called the *unfunded actuarial accrued liability*.

## Current Service Benefits: Normal Cost

19.32 Generally accepted accounting principles* require the employer with a defined-benefit plan to recognize the normal cost† of the pension plan as an expense of the period. ERISA generally requires that the liabilities generated during the period for normal costs be funded in the current period. Because federal law requires the current funding of normal costs, most companies show no Pension Liability account for *current service* on their balance sheets.

## Supplemental Actuarial Value

19.33 The present value of benefits earned prior to adoption or sweetening** of a plan are referred to as the plan's actuarial accrued lia-

---

*Accounting Principles Board, APB *Opinion No. 8* (November 1966).

†See the note to paragraph 19.23. Normal cost is the increase in accumulated benefits during a period that would have occurred if the plan had been in effect from the earliest date of any employee's covered service and all normal costs had been funded as accrued, year by year.

**Sweetening* refers to an increase in pension benefits resulting from a change in the pension formula. For

bility.‡ Generally accepted accounting principles do not permit the immediate recognition of the plan's actuarial accrued liability as an expense at the time it is adopted or sweetened. ERISA does not require (but

example, the annual percentage for calculating the pension payments might be increased from .01 to .015 in these examples. Most employers make the benefits of sweetening retroactive and generate further *actuarial accrued liability*.

‡The term *supplemental actuarial value* first entered the accounting vocabulary in 1980 (FASB *Statement No. 35*) after having been adopted by the actuarial profession several years earlier. The new term displaced two older terms, *past service cost* and *prior service cost*, used in APB *Opinion No. 8* because of actuarial terminology current in 1966. In 1981 the Joint Committee on Pension Terminology (of several professional actuarial societies) issued an exposure draft recommending that the term "supplemental actuarial value" no longer be used, and that a new term, *actuarial accrued liability* be used instead. The exposure draft defines the actuarial accrued liability for a given actuarial cost method (described in this chapter below) as the portion of the "actuarial present value of pension plan benefits . . . . not provided for by future normal costs." The FASB issued a *Discussion Memorandum*, "Employers' Accounting for Pension and Other Post Employment Benefits," in February 1981. This DM uses the terms "past service cost" and "prior service cost", as well as "actuarial accrued liability." It avoids the term "supplemental actuarial value." The accounting profession is likely to be confused about terminology for several years. Many accountants still use the terms "past service cost" and "prior service cost" (because of APB Opinion *No. 8*), while some are attempting to modernize their terms by using "supplemental actuarial value" (because of FASB *Statement No. 35*). Now, that term seems likely to be discarded within a year or two.

allows) that the actuarial accrued liability be immediately funded. The actuarial accrued liability is gradually recognized as an expense and gradually funded over a period of years after plan adoption or sweetening.

19.34    A justification for not immediately recognizing the expense and liability associated with a plan's actuarial accrued liability is that any benefits to the firm from making pension benefits retroactive will be realized in the future from better employee morale and increased productivity. Under this interpretation, the cost of these retroactive benefits must be matched against future rather than past revenues. The question as to whether an accounting liability exists for unfunded actuarial accrued liability has been the subject of much discussion and debate.

19.35    **Assessment of Required Accounting for Actuarial Accrued Liability** Accounting treats an obligation as a liability if the obligation will likely require an amount to be transferred at a future time in return for a past or current benefit.* We think the obligation to employees for actuarial accrued liability meets these criteria and ought to be shown as a liability. Generally accepted accounting principles, in effect, say that the benefits are to be received in the future, as employees continue their working careers, so that it is appropriate to amortize the amounts over the future working careers of those who will receive the pension just adopted or just made more generous.†

19.36    Other accounting theorists are equally

---

*FASB *Statement of Financial Accounting Concepts No. 3,* (May 1980), par. 17 and 29.

†We suspect that the reason actuarial accrued liabilities are not shown as liabilities is in part political, not theoretical. When a plan is adopted or made more generous, the actuarial accrued liability is generally a large number, relative to liabilities on the balance sheet. The potential increase in liabilities is so unpalatable to management that it might be reluctant to grant and sweeten pensions if the amounts had to be currently reported as liabilities. Labor prefers that pension accounting not impede management's granting generous pensions. Thus, the promulgators of accounting principles are pressured both by labor and by management not to require immediate recognition of liabilities for actuarial accrued liability.

concerned about the asset side of the question: APB *Opinion No. 8* justifies amortizing actuarial accrued liability over the future by appealing to its future service potential to the firm (that is, improved employee productivity). If we accept the logic of APB *Opinion No. 8,* then a pension fund asset for the future service potential (and the related pension liability) should be recognized. These theorists compare the generally accepted accounting for actuarial accrued liability with the following accounting for a machine costing $100,000 with a depreciable life of 20 years acquired under an installment purchase plan with payments over 10 years. Do not debit Machine asset for $100,000 or credit Notes Payable for $100,000 when the asset is acquired. Instead, each year debit Depreciation Expense, debit Interest Expense (for the interest accumulated since the last interest accrual), and credit Cash. Such accounting for a machine uses the cash basis, not the accrual basis, and is unacceptable. The analogous accounting for actuarial accrued liability should be, these accountants argue, equally unacceptable.**

**Recognition of Actuarial Accrued Liability: Largest Amounts** The obligation for actuarial accrued liability arises on adoption or sweetening of a pension plan. The employer gradually recognizes the obligation with debits to Pension Expense and credits to Pension Liability. This process is called "amortizing actuarial accrued liability." The unrecognized amount accumulates interest. APB *Opinion No. 8* governs the amounts (and timing) of expense for actuarial accrued liability. A variety of factors make it difficult to provide a simple statement about the minimum and maximum *periods* over which actuarial accrued liability can be amortized.    19.37

In the not-unusual case where pension    19.38 funding by the employer is equal each year to the amount of pension expense, the rule for the largest dollar amount of pension expense related to actuarial accrued liability is reasonably simple. In these cases, the larg-

---

**Professor Blaine A. Ritts first called this argument to our attention.

est *dollar amount* a firm can recognize is 10 percent of the initial amount of actuarial accrued liability created by that adoption or sweetening. Assume, for example, that a defined-benefit plan adopted five years ago created actuarial accrued liability of $1,000,000 at that time. It was sweetened two years ago, creating an additional $400,000 of actuarial accrued liability. For the first three years, the maximum amounts expensed would be $100,000 (= $1,000,000 × .10) per year. After that, the maximum amounts expensed could be $140,000 (= $1,000,000 × .10 + $400,000 × .10) until the actuarial accrued liability arising upon adoption of the plan and its accumulating interest are fully amortized. The maximum expense then drops to $40,000 until the $400,000 amount and its interest are fully recognized. (The case of unequal expense and funding is discussed later in the chapter.)

19.39    No general statement can be made about how long it takes to recognize the entire amount as an expense. The actuarial accrued liability amount accumulates interest each year as the time for making pension payments to employees gets nearer. It decreases as portions of the actuarial accrued liability are recognized as an expense. The length of time until full amortization depends on the interest rate.*

---

*One interesting sidelight to the history of pension accounting is the APB's requirement in *Opinion No. 8* that amounts charged for actuarial accrued liability cannot be larger in any year than 10 percent of its initial amount. Note that if interest rates exceed 10 percent per year, then those maximum amounts do not even cover interest charges on the unamortized amount, and it will grow, not shrink, over time. If the interest rate is 5 percent, then 14.2 years are required for a $1 payment per period to amortize a present value of $10. At 6 percent, 16 years are required; at 9 percent, 27 years are required; at 9.9 percent, about 50 years are required. The Internal Revenue Service allows deductions for actuarial accrued liability to be no larger than the amount that will amortize the past service cost over 10 years. The APB apparently translated the IRS *10-year* rule into a *10-percent-per-year* rule, forgetting about the interest accumulation on unamortized amounts. We suspect that firms which fund actuarial accrued liability at maximum rates allowed for tax reporting would be allowed to report those amounts as expense, even though they are larger than

**Example 5**  Refer to Example 4 discussed       19.40
earlier. The actuarial accrued liability of the pension plan on December 31, 1990, the date of adoption, was $14,139. The maximum amount of the supplemental actuarial value that could be recognized as an expense during 1991 is $1,413.90 (= .10 × $14,139). If we assume that $1,413.90 is funded as of December 31, 1991, then the actuarial accrued liability on December 31, 1991, is as follows:

| | |
|---|---|
| Actuarial Accrued Liability, December 31, 1990 .............. | $14,139.00 |
| Plus Interest at 6 Percent during 1991; $14,139 × .06 .............. | 848.34 |
| Less Amount Expensed and Funded | (1,413.90) |
| Unamortized Actuarial Accrued Liability, December 31, 1992 ...... | $13,573.44 |

The rates of recognition of actuarial accrued liability can exceed the amounts implied by the rules above when interest rates are high and vesting provisions are generous. We do not discuss those details here.

**Recognition of Actuarial Accrued Lia-**       19.41
**bility: Smallest Amounts**  The smallest of actuarial accrued liability that can be recognized as an expense (in addition to expense for normal costs) under APB *Opinion No. 8* is interest on the amount of unfunded actuarial accrued liability ($848.34 = .06 × $14,139, in Example 4 above). The principal amount is never amortized. Vested amounts must be amortized over no more than 30 years, however. ERISA requires vesting of all accumulated benefits by one of three rules discussed later in the chapter. Thus, in practice, the slowest rate at which the actuarial accrued liability can be amortized is often determined by the vesting provision. Because amounts can vest gradually and, once vested, can be amortized to expense gradually, there is no simple way to state the minimum amount of expense. Firms tend to re-

---

the amounts allowed in APB *Opinion No. 8*. If the expense is not reported for the full amount deducted on the tax return, deferred taxes (discussed in Chapter 20) arise for this timing difference. Firms tend to want to fund slowly under most circumstances, so this problem is unlikely to arise.

port as expense the amounts they fund. Because the amount of required funding is relatively straightforward, the amounts expensed usually are not quite as complicated as we make them seem here. We discuss funding periods next.

## Funding of Actuarial Accrued Liability

19.43 A firm can fund actuarial accrued liability as fast as it wishes. If the funding exceeds the amounts expensed, a Prepaid Pension Benefits account with a debit balance appears on the balance sheet. Prior to the passing of ERISA in 1974, there were no minimum funding requirements. The bankruptcy of a few companies, notably Studebaker, with many employees who were promised pensions but never collected them, prompted Congress to require funding of pensions. ERISA requires actuarial accrued liabilities, including interest on the unfunded amounts, existing in 1973 or before to be funded over 40 years or less and amounts arising since 1973 to be funded over 30 years or less.

19.44 **Illustration of Different Expensing and Funding Rates and Periods** When the expense and funding for actuarial accrued liability differ, a balance sheet account for Pension Liability or Prepaid Pension Benefit arises. To provide the data for illustrating such situations, Exhibit 19.1 shows amortization schedules for two possible expense and funding combinations. In all cases, the present value of actuarial accrued liability is $100,000. The interest rate is 10 percent per year. The future value at the end of year 5 of $100,000 compounded at 10 percent per year is $161,051. The top two panels of Exhibit 19.1 show how amounts recognized as expense over 3 or 5 years amortize the $100,000 present value at 10-percent interest. The bottom two panels show how amounts funded over 3 or 5 years accumulate sums whose present value is $100,000, which grows to $161,051 in 5 years. The amortization periods illustrated are shorter (and the amounts, greater) than those allowed by APB *Opinion No. 8* but are used for ease of illustration.

**Expensing Faster Than Funding** The top 19.45 panel of Exhibit 19.2 illustrates expensing over 3 years and funding over 5 years. To recognize the actuarial accrued liability, $40,211 per year ($40,213 in the third year) in column (4), debit Expense and credit Liability. As cash of $26,380 is paid to the plan trustee each year ($26,378 in the 5th year), the Liability account is debited and Cash is credited. Because funding is slower than expensing, a credit balance builds up in the Liability account. This credit balance, like any other noncurrent liability, accumulates interest. Column (2) shows the amounts of interest charged to Expense and credited to the Liability account. The amounts for interest expense are usually reported as part of pension expense and are sometimes called "interest equivalents" or "amounts equivalent to interest." These amounts are interest; they are called by these terms which include the word "equivalent" because no cash payment for interest is required. The cash flows out of the firm when the Pension Liability is funded. The interest is added to the liability just as interest is added to a long-term "noninterest-bearing" note. The journal entries for year 3 would be as follows:

```
Year 3
Pension Expense (Recognition of
   Actuarial Accrued Liability) ....... 40,213
Pension Expense (Interest
   Equivalent) .................... 2,904
Pension Liability ................       43,117
To expense a portion of the actuarial
accrued liability and interest on credit
balance in Pension Liability account.
Amounts are in columns (2) and (4) of
Exhibit 19.2.


Pension Liability .................. 26,380
   Cash ......................       26,380
To fund part of liability according to a
5-year funding schedule. The credit
balance in Pension Liability is re-
duced, but not by as much as it in-
creased in the preceding entry. The in-
terest for the next year will be higher
than for this year.
```

Note that the balance in the pension fund at 19.46 the end of year 5 is $161,051. Of this amount, $131,898 came from contributions by the

*Exhibit 19.1*
**Amortization Tables to Illustrate Expensing and Funding of $100,000 of Actuarial Accrued Liability ($161,051 Future Value) over Different Time Spans (Interest Rate is 10% per Year with Payments at End of Year)**

| Year (1) | Principal Amount at Start of Year (2) | Interest (Expense in Top Panels; Revenue in Bottom Panels) on Amount in Column (2) (3) | Amount Expensed (Top Panels) or Funded (Bottom Panels) (4) | Amount Reducing Principal (5) | Principal Amount at End of Year (6) |
|---|---|---|---|---|---|
| **Amounts of Expense Required to Amortize $100,000 Debt over 5 Years** | | | | | |
| 0 | | | | | $100,000 |
| 1 | $100,000 | $10,000 | $26,380 | $16,380 | 83,620 |
| 2 | 83,620 | 8,362 | 26,380 | 18,018 | 65,602 |
| 3 | 65,602 | 6,560 | 26,380 | 19,820 | 45,782 |
| 4 | 45,782 | 4,578 | 26,380 | 21,802 | 23,980 |
| 5 | 23,980 | 2,398 | 26,378 | 23,980 | 0 |
| **Amounts of Expense Required to Amortize $100,000 Debt over 3 Years** | | | | | |
| 0 | | | | | $100,000 |
| 1 | $100,000 | $10,000 | $40,211 | $30,211 | 69,789 |
| 2 | 69,789 | 6,979 | 40,211 | 33,232 | 36,557 |
| 3 | 36,557 | 3,656 | 40,213 | 36,557 | 0 |
| **Amounts Required to Fund a $161,051 Future Value over 5 Years** | | | | | |
| 1 | $   0 | $   0 | $26,380 | | $  26,380 |
| 2 | 26,380 | 2,638 | 26,380 | | 55,398 |
| 3 | 55,398 | 5,540 | 26,380 | | 87,318 |
| 4 | 87,318 | 8,732 | 26,380 | | 122,430 |
| 5 | 122,430 | 12,243 | 26,378 | | 161,051 |
| **Amounts Required to Fund a $161,051 Future Value over 3 Years** | | | | | |
| 1 | $   0 | $   0 | $40,211 | | $  40,211 |
| 2 | 40,211 | 4,021 | 40,211 | | 84,443 |
| 3 | 84,443 | 8,444 | 40,213 | | 133,100 |
| 4 | 133,100 | 13,310 | 0 | | 146,410 |
| 5 | 146,410 | 14,641 | 0 | | 161,051 |

employer, and $29,153 was generated by pension fund investments. The total amount contributed was recognized as an expense, $131,898 (= $120,635 + $11,263) over the five years.

19.47   The decision to fund pension liabilities at a rate slower than the rate of expense recognition is not necessarily a poor decision. Funds retained by the firm can be invested to generate a return. If the aftertax return generated from investments by the firm exceeds the pretax return that can be generated by pension fund investments, then the firm may wish to fund the minimum amounts permitted by ERISA.* Given that income of a pension fund is not subject to income taxes, the firm must earn almost twice the pretax return on internal investments than

---

*Recent research in finance suggests that the firm may maximize the wealth of its owners by funding pension obligations as fast as possible and then investing the pension fund solely in bonds. The reasoning is beyond the scope of an accounting text. See Fischer Black, "The Tax Consequences of Long-Run Pension Policy," *Financial Analysts Journal* 36 (July–August 1980), pp. 21–28.

*Exhibit 19.2*

**Illustration of Expensing and Funding
Supplementary Actuarial Value
at Different Rates
(Beginning Actuarial Accrued
Liability = $100,000. Interest Rate Is
10 Percent per Year)**

| | | | | | | | | | |
|---|---|---|---|---|---|---|---|---|---|
| | **Company's Records** | | | | | | | **Pension Fund Records** | |
| | **During Year** | | | | **End of Year** | | | | |
| **Year** | **Interest Expense on Pension Liability Dr.** | **Interest Revenue on Prepaid Pension Benefits Cr.** | **Pension Expense for Actuarial Accrued Liability Dr.** | **Credit to Cash = Debit to Pension Liability** | **Prepaid Pension Benefit Dr.** | **Pension Liability Cr.** | **Principal Amount of Actuarial Accrued Liability Disclosed in Notes** | **Earnings for Year** | **Balance in Fund at End of Year** |
| **(1)** | **(2)** | **(3)** | **(4)** | **(5)** | **(6)** | **(7)** | **(8)** | **(9)** | **(10)** |
| Expense over 3 Years; Fund over 5 Years | | | | | | | | | |
| 0 ....... | $ | $ — | $ | $ — | $ — | $ | $100,000 | $ 0 | $ 0 |
| 1 ....... | 0 | — | 40,211 | 26,380 | — | 13,831 | 69,789 | 0 | 26,380 |
| 2 ....... | 1,383 | — | 40,211 | 26,380 | — | 29,045 | 36,557 | 2,638 | 55,398 |
| 3 ....... | 2,904 | — | 40,213 | 26,380 | — | 45,782 | 0 | 5,540 | 87,318 |
| 4 ....... | 4,578 | — | 0 | 26,380 | — | 23,980 | 0 | 8,732 | 122,430 |
| 5 ....... | 2,398 | — | 0 | 26,378 | — | 0 | 0 | 12,243 | 161,051 |
| Totals .. | $11,263 | | $120,635 | $131,898 | | | | $29,153 | |
| Expense over 5 Years; Fund over 3 Years | | | | | | | | | |
| 0 ....... | | | | | 0 | — | 100,000 | 0 | 0 |
| 1 ....... | — | 0 | 26,380 | 40,211 | 13,831 | — | 83,620 | 0 | 40,211 |
| 2 ....... | — | 1,383 | 26,380 | 40,211 | 29,045 | — | 65,602 | 4,021 | 84,443 |
| 3 ....... | — | 2,905 | 26,380 | 40,213 | 45,781 | — | 45,782 | 8,444 | 133,100 |
| 4 ....... | — | 4,578 | 26,380 | 0 | 23,979 | — | 23,980 | 13,310 | 146,410 |
| 5 ....... | — | 2,398 | 26,378 | 0 | 0 | — | 0 | 14,641 | 161,051 |
| Totals .. | | $11,263 | $131,898 | $120,635 | | | | $40,416 | |

Column (2) = amount in column (7) from previous year × .10.

Column (3) = amount in column (6) from previous year × .10.

Column (4)   from Exhibit 19.1, column (4).

Column (5)   from Exhibit 19.1, column (4).

Column (6) = column (6) from previous year + column (3) − column (4) + column (5).

Column (7) = column (7) from previous year + column (2) + column (4) − column (5).

Column (8)   from Exhibit 19.1, column (6), top panels.

Column (9) = amount in column (10) from previous year × .10.

Column (10)  from Exhibit 19.1, column (6), lower panels.

the return generated by pension fund investments for minimum funding to be worthwhile.

19.48 **Funds Statement Effects** Virtually all pension-related events are part of continuing operations. Thus, all effects of pensions on funds appear in the section reporting funds from operations.* The cash amounts paid are sometimes less than the amounts expensed in the early years and greater in the later years. Thus, in the early years (the first addbacks and subtractions from net income to show no net effect on funds from operations. We think that such treatment is inconsistent with the theory that justifies the gradual amortization of actuarial accrued liability. If that amount were set up as a liability all at once when the pension plan was adopted, then treating the debt repayments as a nonoperating use would be justified. Because the actuarial accrued liability amortization is viewed as providing a current benefit, the amounts disbursed to fund should be viewed as part of current operations.

*A possible alternative treatment shows the creation of Pension Liability as an other source of funds and its discharge as an other use of funds with appropriate

three years in the example of three-year expensing and five-year funding) there will be an addback to net income for expense using less funds than amounts of the expense. In the third year, the addback is for $16,737 (= $43,117 − $26,380). In the later years (years 4 and 5 in the example), the amount of funds used exceeds the expense reported. There will be a subtraction in adjusting net income for funds used in excess of expense recognized. This subtraction is analogous to the treatment of amortization of bond premium, where more cash is disbursed than the amount of interest expense. For example, in the fifth year of the example, expense is only $2,398 (for interest equivalent), but $26,378 of cash is disbursed to the pension fund. The $23,980 (= $26,378 − $2,398) excess is subtracted from net income to show that operations used more funds than were reported as expense.

19.49   **Funding Faster Than Expensing** The bottom panel of Exhibit 19.2 illustrates funding of actuarial accrued liability faster than expensing. Actuarial accrued liability is recognized, $26,380 per year (26,378 in the 5th year) from column (4), with debits to expense and credits to liability. As cash is paid to the plan trustee, $40,211 per year ($40,213 in the third year), the liability is debited and cash is credited. Because funding is faster than expensing, a *debit* balance builds up in the Pension Liability account. This account is then renamed Prepaid Pension Benefits and is shown among the assets. Like all noncurrent monetary assets, it accumulates interest. The amounts of interest are added to the asset account and credited, as in column (3), to an income statement account. The amounts for interest revenue are called "interest equivalents" or "amounts equivalent to interest" because no cash is ever received. The amounts are typically reported as a reduction in Pension Expense rather than as a separate interest revenue account.*

---

*The reporting issue here is exactly the same as that for implicit interest on funds used during construction, discussed in Chapter 11. There, we noted that the FASB treatment of implicit interest was to credit an expense account, whereas public utilities have for many years credited a revenue account.

The journal entries for year 3 of the example would be as follows:   19.50

| Year 3 | | |
|---|---|---|
| Pension Expense (Recognition of Actuarial Accrued Liability) ...... 26,380 | | |
| Pension Expense (Interest Equivalent) ................ | | 2,905 |
| Pension Liability (or Prepaid Pension Benefits) .......... | | 23,475 |

To expense a portion of actuarial accrued liability and to reduce expense for interest equivalent earned on prepaid pensions. Amounts are in columns (4) and (3) of Exhibit 19.2.

| | | |
|---|---|---|
| Pension Liability (or Prepaid Pension Benefits) ..................... 40,213 | | |
| Cash ...................... | | 40,213 |

Funding accords with a 3-year schedule. The debit balance in Prepaid Pension Benefits increases so that interest equivalent earned next year will be larger than for this year.

Note that the balance in the pension fund at the end of year 5 is also $161,051, as in the previous example. Of this amount, $120,635 came from contributions by the employer, and $40,416 was generated by pension fund investments. The total amount contributed was recognized as expense ($131,898 − $11,263) over the five years. The firm's "cost" of the pension plan is less in this case ($120,635) than in the preceding example ($131,898). Because of the more rapid funding here, a larger portion of the required fund of $161,051 came from revenues generated by pension fund investments.

**Funds Statement Effects** The funds statements effects here are similar to those discussed above, except that the timing is reversed. In early years, more funds are used than the amount of expense, and in later years, less. Thus, in early years, a subtraction is required to compute funds from operations, and in later years, an addition.   19.51

**Constancy of Combined Employer—Plan Expense** The combined expense of the combined economic entity—employer and pension plan—is constant, $161,051 in either case. The employer has pension expense for   19.52

*Exhibit 19.3*
**Illustrating Constancy of Combined Employer and Pension Plan Expense for Pension Plan (Based on Exhibit 19.2)**

| | Expense over 3 Years; Fund over 5 Years | Expense over 5 Years; Fund over 3 Years |
|---|---|---|
| Employer: | | |
| Interest Expense (Revenue) on Pension Liability (Prepaid Pension Asset) .......... | $ 11,263 | $ (11,263) |
| Amortization of Actuarial Accrued Liability and Accrued Interest .................. | 120,635 | 131,898 |
| Employer's Total Expense ................................................ | $131,898 | $120,635 |
| Pension Fund's Interest Expense on Liability to Employees ....................... | 29,153 | 40,416 |
| Combined Pension-Related Expense .......................................... | $161,051 | $161,051 |

unrecognized supplemental actuarial value and interest expense on its balance sheet amounts for Pension Liabilities (or interest revenue on pension funding in excess of pension expense). The pension fund has interest expense on its Liability for Pensions to Employees. The sum of these amounts is constant, independent of the expensing and funding patterns, so long as the interest on the pension plan's investments is the same as assumed in the pension calculations. See Exhibit 19.3. The current disclosure rules for the employer, listed below, do *not* require, however, that the plan's operations—revenues and expenses—be reported in the employer's financial statements. The financial statements of the *plan* will report these operations, but the plan's full statements need not be reported by the employer.

## Summary of Employer's Accounting for Defined-Benefit Pension Plans

19.53   APB *Opinion No. 8* preceded ERISA. It established certain limitations on the amounts of pension expense that an employer can recognize each year. Although some of these limitations have been superseded in practice by ERISA's requirements, the accounting student may want to be familiar with the terminology so long as APB *Opinion No. 8* is still part of generally accepted accounting principles.

**Defined Minimum Amount of Annual Pension Expense**  The smallest amount of   19.54 pension expense an employer can report for a year is the sum of:

1. Normal cost;

2. Amounts equivalent to interest on unfunded actuarial accrued liability; and

3. An amount for vested benefits.

The means of computing an amount for vested benefits, explained in paragraph 17 of APB *Opinion No. 8,* are sufficiently complex that we omit the details from this book.

**Defined Maximum Amount of Annual Pension Expense**  The largest amount of   19.55 pension expense an employer can report for the year is the sum of:

1. Normal cost;

2. Ten percent of actuarial accrued liability arising from adoption of the pension plan (called "past service cost" in APB *Opinion No. 8);*

3. Ten percent of the increases in actuarial accrued liability arising on amendment (usually a sweetening) of the plan (called increases in "prior service costs" in APB *Opinion No. 8);* and

4. Amounts equivalent to interest on the difference between pension obligations that have been debited to expense and the funding of the resulting liabilities. If cumulative

*Exhibit 19.4*
**Illustration of Calculations Required to Compute Defined Minimum and Maximum Pension Expenses**

| Pension Expense | Year 1 | | | Year 2 | | |
|---|---|---|---|---|---|---|
| | Defined Minimum Expenses | Defined Maximum Expense | Pension Funding | Defined Minimum Expense | Defined Maximum Expense | Pension Funding |
| Normal Costs ........................... | $200,000[a] | $200,000[a] | | $225,000[a] | $225,999[a] | |
| Amount Equivalent to Interest on Unfunded Actuarial Accrued Liability ................. | 60,000[b] | | | 67,369[e] | | |
| Amount for Vested Benefits ................. | 0[a] | | | 0[a] | | |
| Ten Percent of Actuarial Accrued Liability (Adoption of Plan) ........................ | | 100,000[c] | | | 100,000[c] | |
| Ten Percent of Increase in Actuarial Accrued Liability (Sweetening of Plan) ............... | | — | | | 15,000[g] | |
| Interest Expense (Credit) on Difference Between Amounts Expensed and Amounts Funded in Preceding years .......................... | — | 0 | | | .06 × (X − $287,185)[f] | |
| Total ...................................... | $260,000 | $300,000 | | $292,369 | Total Depends on Preceding Expenses Recognized | |
| **Pension Funding** | | | | | | |
| Normal Costs ........................... | | | $200,000[a] | | | $225,000[a] |
| Actuarial Accrued Liability | | | | | | |
| Adoption ............................ | | | 87,185[d] | | | 87,185[d] |
| Sweetening ........................... | | | — | | | 13,078[h] |
| Total Funding Payments ..................... | | | $287,185 | | | $325,263 |

[a]Given.

[b]$1,000,000 × .06 = $60,000.

[c]$1,000,000 × .10 = $100,000.

[d]See Table 4, 20-percent row, 6-percent column for factor of 11.46992: $100,000/11.46992 = $87,185.

[e]($1,000,000 × 1.06 − $87,185) × .06 = $972,815 × .06 = $58,369 on initial adoption; $150,000 × .06 = $9,000 on sweetening: $67,369 = $58,369 + $9,000.

[f]X represents the amount of pension expense recognized in the first year.

[g]$150,000 × .10 = $15,000.

[h]$150,000/11.46992 = $13,078.

expenses exceed cumulative funding, then this interest is potential expense and increases the maximum. If cumulative funding exceeds cumulative expenses, then this interest is equivalent to revenue and reduces the defined maximum.

19.56 **Illustration of Defined Minimum and Maximum Pension Expense Calculations** Schipper Company adopts a pension plan at the start of year 1, creating $1 million of actuarial accrued liability. Normal costs for year 1 are $200,000. At the start of year 2, the plan is sweetened, creating an additional $150,000 supplemental actuarial value. Normal costs for year 2 are $225,000. The interest rate used in pension calculations is 6 percent per year. Supplemental actuarial value

is funded over 20 years with payments made at year end. None of the pension benefits are vested by the end of year 2. Exhibit 19.4 shows the computation of the maximum and minimum pension expense for each of the two years. Because the computation of the defined maximum depends on the amount of previously recognized pension expense, the amount shown for the defined maximum is stated as a formula for the second year.

## Required Disclosures for Defined-Benefit Plans by Employers

19.57 FASB *Statement No. 36* requires that the employer make the following disclosures with respect to its defined-benefit plans:

**1.** A statement that a pension plan exists,

identifying or describing the employee groups covered.

**2.** A statement of the firm's accounting and funding policies.

**3.** The pension expense for the period.

**4.** The nature and effect of significant matters affecting comparability for all periods presented, such as changes in actuarial cost methods, amortization of actuarial accrued liability, or treatment of actuarial gains and losses.

**5.** The actuarial present value of vested accumulated plan benefits based on the accrued benefit actuarial cost method (discussed in Appendix 19.1).

**6.** The actuarial present value of nonvested accumulated plan benefits based on the accrued benefit actuarial cost method.

**7.** The plan's net assets available for benefits.*

**8.** The assumed rates of return used in computing actuarial present values of vested and nonvested accumulated benefits.

**9.** The date as of which the benefit information was computed.

Note 4 to the financial statements of International Corporation illustrates the required disclosures (see Appendix A).

## Generally Accepted Accounting Principles by the Plan for Defined-Benefit Pensions

19.58 The pension plan receives the cash paid by the employer/sponsor and invests it until it must be paid to pensioners. The plan keeps its own accounting records and makes disclosures according to rules in FASB *Statement No. 35*. The major provisions of *Statement No. 35* are as follows:

**1.** The pension fund reports its assets, usually investments of various sorts, at fair market value, a laudable departure from the accounting for most investments described in Chapter 14.

**2.** The liabilities of the pension fund must be computed using the accrued benefit actuarial cost method.

**3.** Actuarial gains and losses, including unrealized holding gains and losses on pension fund investments, are included in the net income of the plan each year as they arise.

**4.** The following information about the pension fund must be disclosed each year in the notes to the financial statements of the plan:

**a.** A statement that includes information regarding the net assets available for benefits as of the end of the plan year.

**b.** A statement showing the principal reasons for changes in net assets available for benefits during the year, including net appreciation or depreciation in fair value of significant classes of investments, investment income, contributions received from the employer and employees, benefits paid to participants, and administrative expenses.

**c.** Information regarding the actuarial present value of plan benefits as of either the beginning or end of the plan year. The beginning-of-the-year valuation date is acceptable because of the time often required to calculate the present value of accumulated benefits.

**d.** Information regarding the effects of significant factors affecting the year-to-year changes in actuarial present value of accumulated plan benefits, such as changes in actuarial cost methods, treatment of actuarial gains and losses, and the interest rate used in discounting.

Note 4 to the financial statements of International Corporation illustrates the required disclosures by the pension fund (see Appendix A).

## Summary

19.59 Pension plans generally are either defined-contribution plans or defined-benefit plans.

---

*The excess of accumulated plan benefits [the sum of items (5) and (6)] over the net assets in the plan [item (7)] can be a staggeringly large amount.

In defined-contribution plans, the employer debits Pension Expense and credits Cash for amounts paid to a pension plan administrator. The administrator manages the funds for the benefit of the individual employee, who is paid whatever amounts have accumulated by the time of retirement.

19.60    In defined-benefit plans, the employer recognizes pension expense for normal costs and funds that amount with a payment to the pension plan. An obligation for actuarial accrued liability arises when pension plans are adopted or sweetened and the employees are given credit for years of service prior to the date of adoption or sweetening. These obligations are not immediately recognized as liabilities. Instead they are gradually debited to expense and credited to liability. The resulting liability may be funded at rates slower than, equal to, or faster than the obligations have been recognized.

19.61    When obligations are recognized faster than they are funded, a credit balance appears on the employer's balance sheet for Pension Liability. When obligations are funded faster than they are recognized, a debit balance appears on the employer's balance sheet for Prepaid Pension Benefits.

19.62    The pension plan will have assets (cash received from employer and earned on investments acquired) and liabilities to employees for pension payments. The pension plan reports its liabilities using the accrued benefit actuarial cost method and values its assets at current market value.

## Appendix 19.1: Some Complexities of Defined-Benefit Pension Plans

19.63    The actuarial computations underlying pension plan accounting are complex. In practice, the accountant will receive from an actuary information necessary for making the accounting entries described in the chapter. This appendix describes and illustrates certain details of defined-benefit pension plans. The accountant who understands these details will be in a better position to advise management and to understand the economic facts about pensions. The appendix discusses (1) actuarial cost methods, (2) the interest rate used, (3) the treatment of actuarial gains and losses, and (4) the effect of vesting.

19.64    Exhibit 19.5 shows data for a simplified defined-benefit pension plan. The data are derived from the pension plan discussed in Examples 1 and 2 earlier in this chapter. An employee starts work in year 1, earning $10,000 per year. Salary increases are approximately 10 percent per year through year 10 and approximately 5 percent per year thereafter, assuming the employee continues to work. The computations assume that the benefits will be paid with certainty. Vesting provisions are illustrated later. The formula for the annual pension starting at the end of year 40 is

$$\text{Annual Pension} = \begin{pmatrix}.20 + .01 \times \\ \text{Number of} \\ \text{Years Worked}\end{pmatrix} \times \begin{matrix}\text{Maximum} \\ \text{Salary} \\ \text{Earned}\end{matrix}$$

In words, the employee will receive 60 percent of the maximum salary earned if employment continues for 40 years. For every year less than 40, the percentage is reduced by 1 point. Thus, if the employee stops work after 10 years (and benefits are vested), then the pension is $7,080. This pension does not commence until retirement, with the first payment being made at the end of year 41.

19.65    Column (2) shows the annual salary. Column (3) for each row shows the annual pension starting in year 41 if the employee stops work after the year shown for that row. The employee is assumed to receive pension payments for exactly 20 years.* Column (4) shows the value at the end of year 40 of the 20-year pension promised to the employee. Column (5) shows the present value of these benefits at the end of the current year, referred to as "accumulated benefits." Column (6) shows interest for the current year on accumulated benefits as of the beginning of the year (that is, the increase during the current year in the present value of accumulated benefits earned as of the beginning of the year). Column (7) shows normal cost

---

*See note to paragraph 19.17.

*Exhibit 19.5*
**Illustration for Calculation of Pension
Costs in Defined-Benefit Plan**

Annual Pension is Amount in Column (3) for Last Year of Employment[a]
Pension Paid in Arrears for Exactly 20 Years, First Payment Occurs at the End of Year 41
Salary Starts at $10,000 per Year and Increases during Years of Employment by 10% per Year for 9 Years
and by 5% per Year Thereafter

| | | | Interest Accumulated or Discounted at 6% per Year | | | |
|---|---|---|---|---|---|---|
| Current Year (1) | Salary for Current Year (2) | Annual Pension Starting at End of Year 40[a] (3) | Present Value at End of Year 40 of 20 Annual Pension Payments of Amounts in Column (3) (4) | Accumulated Benefits = Present Value of Pension at End of Current Year (5) | Interest for Current Year on Accumulated Benefits at Start of Year[b] (6) | Normal Cost for Current Year (7) |
| 1 ..... | $ 10,000 | $ 2,100 | $ 24,086 | $ 2,482 | $ — | $ 2,482 |
| 2 ..... | 11,000 | 2,420 | 27,757 | 3,032 | 149 | 401 |
| 3 ..... | 12,100 | 2,783 | 31,921 | 3,696 | 182 | 482 |
| 4 ..... | 13,300 | 3,192 | 36,612 | 4,494 | 222 | 576 |
| 5 ..... | 14,600 | 3,650 | 41,865 | 5,447 | 270 | 683 |
| 6 ..... | 16,100 | 4,186 | 48,013 | 6,622 | 327 | 848 |
| 7 ..... | 17,700 | 4,779 | 54,815 | 8,013 | 397 | 994 |
| 8 ..... | 19,500 | 5,460 | 62,626 | 9,704 | 481 | 1,210 |
| 9 ..... | 21,400 | 6,206 | 71,182 | 11,692 | 582 | 1,406 |
| 10 ..... | 23,600 | 7,080 | 81,207 | 14,139 | 702 | 1,745 |
| 11 ..... | 24,800[c] | 7,688 | 88,181 | 16,274 | 848 | 1,287 |
| 12 ..... | 26,000 | 8,320 | 95,430 | 18,669 | 976 | 1,419 |
| 19 ..... | 36,600 | 14,274 | 163,722 | 48,160 | 2,533 | 3,536 |
| 20 ..... | 38,400 | 15,360 | 176,178 | 54,933 | 2,890 | 3,883 |
| 36 ..... | 83,800 | 46,928 | 538,260 | 426,353 | | |
| 37 ..... | 88,000 | 50,160 | 575,331 | 483,059 | 25,581 | 31,125 |
| 38 ..... | 92,400 | 53,592 | 614,696 | 547,077 | 28,984 | 35,034 |
| 39 ..... | 97,000 | 57,230 | 656,424 | 619,268 | 32,825 | 39,366 |
| 40 ..... | 101,900 | 61,140 | 701,271 | 701,271 | 37,156 | 44,847 |

**Notes and Sources**

[a]Formula is

Annual Pension = [.20 + (.01 × Years of Employment)] × Maximum Salary.

If the employee stops working at the end of a given year, then the pension shown in column (3) for that year is paid starting at the end of year 41.

[b]Because normal costs are generally funded as they are expensed, the amounts in this column are the interest expense of the pension plan.

[c]Salary increases of approximately 5% per year start here.

Column (2) given.

Column (3) = [.20 + .01 × column (1)] × column (2).

Column (4) = column (3) × 11.46992; see Table 4, 20-period row, 6% column.

| Continued (6% per Year) | Interest Accumulated or Discounted at 8% per Year | | | | |
|---|---|---|---|---|---|
| Normal Cost for Current Year Plus Interest on Accumulated Benefits from Preceding Year (8) | Present Value at End of Year 40 of 20 Annual Pension Payments of Amounts in Column (3) (9) | Accumulated Benefits = Present Value of Pension at End of Current Year (10) | Interest for Current Year on Accumulated Benefits at Start of Year[b] (11) | Normal Cost for Current Year (12) | Normal Cost for Current Year Plus Interest on Accumulated Benefits from Preceding Year (13) |
| $   2,482 | $ 20,618 | $   1,025 | $   — | $ 1,025 | $   1,025 |
| 550 | 23,760 | 1,276 | 82 | 169 | 251 |
| 664 | 27,324 | 1,584 | 102 | 206 | 308 |
| 798 | 31,339 | 1,963 | 127 | 252 | 379 |
| 953 | 35,836 | 2,424 | 157 | 304 | 461 |
| 1,175 | 41,099 | 3,002 | 194 | 384 | 578 |
| 1,391 | 46,921 | 3,702 | 240 | 460 | 700 |
| 1,691 | 53,607 | 4,567 | 296 | 569 | 865 |
| 1,988 | 60,931 | 5,607 | 365 | 675 | 1,040 |
| 2,447 | 69,512 | 6,908 | 449 | 852 | 1,301 |
| 2,135 | 75,482 | 8,101 | 553 | 640 | 1,193 |
| 2,395 | 81,687 | 9,469 | 648 | 720 | 1,368 |
| 6,060 | 140,144 | 27,840 | 1,916 | 2,042 | 3,958 |
| 6,773 | 150,807 | 32,355 | 2,227 | 2,288 | 4,515 |
| | 460,746 | 338,662 | | | |
| 56,706 | 492,478 | 390,945 | 27,093 | 25,190 | 52,283 |
| 64,018 | 526,174 | 451,110 | 31,276 | 28,889 | 60,165 |
| 72,191 | 561,893 | 520,271 | 36,089 | 33,072 | 69,161 |
| 82,003 | 600,282 | 500,282 | 41,622 | 38,389 | 80,011 |
| $701,271 | | | | | $600,282 |

Column (5) = column (4)/(1.06)$^{[40 - \text{column (1)}]}$; see Table 2, row for [40 − column (1)] periods, 6% column.

Column (6) = .06 × column (5) last year.

Column (7) = column (5) this year − column (5) last year − column (6) this year.

Column (8) = column (6) + column (7).

Column (9) = column (3) × 9.81815; see Table 4, 20-period row, 8% column.

Column (10) = column (9)/(1.08)$^{[40 - \text{column (1)}]}$; see Table 2, row for [40 − column (1)] periods, 8% column.

Column (11) = .08 × column (10) last year.

Column (12) = column (10) this year − column (10) last year − column (11) this year.

Column (13) = column (11) + column (12).

for the current year.* Recall that normal cost is equal to the increase in accumulated benefits in column (5) that does not represent interest on the beginning-of-the-year accumulated benefits [see column (6)]. Columns (4), (5), (6), (7), and (8) show present value amounts assuming that all sums accumulate interest or are discounted at 6 percent per year. Columns (9), (10), (11), (12), and (13) show similar data for interest rates of 8 percent per year.

## Actuarial Cost Methods

19.66 The computations of accumulated benefits in column (5) and the amounts in columns (6) and (7) are based on the following assumptions:

**1.** When the formula is used to compute the pension, the total years of employment are equal only to the number of years worked by the end of the current year.

**2.** Similarly, the maximum salary input to the formula used to compute the pension is equal to the maximum salary earned by the end of the current year.

19.67 No estimate is made of the actual number of years this employee will work, although actuaries can estimate total years of employment with reasonable precision for large numbers of workers. Also, no estimate is made of the actual maximum salary this employee is likely to earn, although the amount is almost surely going to be larger than the current year's salary. Actuaries can attempt to estimate such amounts, but the estimate is likely to have a greater margin of error

than the estimate of total years of employment. As a result of not estimating the parameters for length of service and future wages, the normal cost is small in early years and increases dramatically in later years as the impact of increasing salary and years of service affect the computations.

19.68 The assumptions made about earnings history and other factors taken into account in computing the accumulated benefits constitute the *actuarial cost method* of the pension plan. Exhibit 19.5 uses the *accrued benefit* actuarial cost method. FASB *Statements No. 35* and *No. 36* require that accumulated benefits be measured by the employer and by the pension fund using the accrued benefit actuarial cost method. (They do *not* say that the employer must use the accrued benefit actuarial cost method in computing annual pension expense; see discussion below.) Several other actuarial cost methods, often used for expensing and funding pension plans, are known as "projected benefit" methods. These allow estimates of the future to be incorporated. The projected benefit methods include:†

**1.** Entry age normal method.

**2.** Attained age normal method.

**3.** Aggregate cost method.

**4.** Individual level premium method.

19.69 None of these projected benefit methods imply an upward tilt in the schedule of pension costs, analogous to columns (6), (7), and (8) or columns (11), (12), and (13) of Exhibit 19.5. These other methods imply level costs or declining costs. The projected benefit methods recognize much larger percentages of the total pension cost in earlier years than does the accrued benefit method. The projected benefit methods listed here are ranked from the method that recognizes expenses

---

*Note the pattern of normal costs—large in the first year, then dropping in amount substantially, and increasing gradually thereafter. This pattern—large in the "first" year, then small, and increasing thereafter—will occur in general. The "first" year is, however, the first year that benefits become vested, not necessarily the first year that an employee works. Exhibit 19.5 assumes immediate, full vesting so the large normal costs are shown for the first year of employment.

---

†These four projected benefit methods and the accrued benefit method are explained and contrasted for accountants in William A. Dreher, "Alternatives Available under APB *Opinion No. 8:* An Actuary's View," *Journal of Accountancy* 124, no. 3 (September 1967), pp. 37–51.

most uniformly over time, with relatively constant amounts each year (entry age normal), to the method that recognizes more of the cost in early years and less later (individual level premium).

19.70    To make an analogy with depreciation, entry age normal is like straight-line, whereas the individual level premium method is like the most accelerated method allowed. In contrast, the accrued benefit method is like decelerated depreciation, the compound interest method discussed in Chapter 12, where charges *increase* with the passage of time.* Figure 19.3 depicts graphically the pattern of pension expense under each of these actuarial cost methods.

19.71    Firms are still free to choose the actuarial cost method used in calculating *pension expense*.† Because various actuarial cost methods can lead to significantly different amounts for pension expense, accumulated benefits, and supplemental actuarial value, the amounts reported by firms have not been comparable. FASB *Statements No. 35* and *No. 36* require that all firms and pension funds now use the accrued benefit cost method for disclosing *accumulated plan benefits*. This requirement increases the comparability of reported pension information.

19.72    The required uniformity may be a mixed blessing, however. Some have argued that the method selected by the FASB, the accrued benefit method, is the least desirable

---

*Here, as elsewhere in accounting, the issue is the *timing* of expense recognition. To use the data in column (8) of Exhibit 19.5, by the end of year 40 all actuarial cost methods will have reported $701,271 of expense. The projected benefit methods recognize much larger percentages of this amount in the early years than does the accrued benefit method. Which actuarial cost method should be used? This is a question of allocating costs over time, much like the question of choosing a depreciation method for an asset.

†Two alternatives to actuarial cost assumptions were sometimes used before APB *Opinion No. 8*. These methods recognized all expenses after the employee's working career was ended, not during the years of employment. These methods are the "terminal funding method" and the "pay-as-you-go method." They are not currently allowed.

---

## Figure 19.3
### *Illustration of Actuarial Cost Methods*

**Accrued Benefit Method**

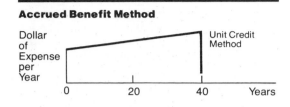

**Projected Benefit Methods**

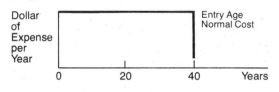

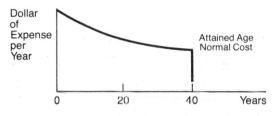

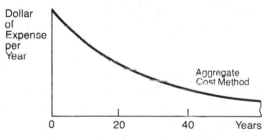

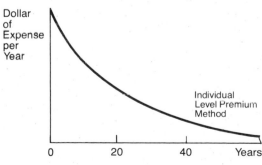

Source: Dreher, see footnote to paragraph 19.68.

of the actuarial cost methods that could have been chosen. It has been argued that accumulated plan benefits at the end of each year are significantly understated because the accrued benefit method does not take into account projected future years of employment or projected future salary increases. The accrued benefit method is theoretically justifiable, it is argued, if employees are effectively hired anew each year. The accrued benefit method will then correctly reflect the incremental pension cost of an additional year of work.

## Effect of Interest Rate Assumed

19.73　In computing accumulated benefits (and normal costs), the FASB allows the use of the current market rate of interest for discounting future payments and for assumed earnings on pension funds. In recent years, inflation has increased so that 8 percent, rather than 6 percent, is not an unusual current interest rate. Columns (10) and (12) of Exhibit 19.5 show accumulated benefits and normal costs for an 8-percent rate. The reader can see the effects of changing the rate. Using a higher interest rate in the discounting reduces the total pension costs [compare columns (8) and (13)] recognized during the employee's working years.

19.74　Amounts to be paid to employees are determined by formula. The interest rate assumed does *not* affect the amount of cash paid to employees. It affects in various ways the amounts of pension expense charged against income of the company and the amounts of interest assumed to be earned by the fund.* The earnings in the pension fund are assumed larger because of an assumed larger interest rate; as a result, pension ex-

pense is smaller. In pension calculations, the conservative assumption is the lower interest rate.

## Actuarial Gains and Losses of the Plan

Even the best estimates are only estimates.　19.75
Inevitably, employees will quit or die at rates different from projections. Inevitably, earnings on funds invested for future payments will differ from amounts projected. Deviations between pension projections and outcomes are called *actuarial gains and losses* of the pension plan. Before 1980, actuarial gains and losses were amortized in some regular fashion over future periods. Since FASB Statement No. 35, these amounts are now reflected in the plan's income (or loss) as they occur. All unrealized holding gains and losses on pension or fund investments appear in the pension plan's income statement in the year they occur. There are no longer any special accounting problems for actuarial gains and losses.

## Vested Benefits

Column (5) of Exhibit 19.5 shows the accu-　19.76
mulated benefits by year. It assumes immediate, 100 percent vesting. To illustrate the vesting requirements, Exhibit 19.6 shows results from two different minimum vesting formulas allowed by ERISA:

**1.** Five- to fifteen-year rule. The employee must have vested rights equal to 25 percent of the accumulated benefits by the end of the fifth year of employment and 100 percent by the end of the fifteenth year. The percentage must increase by at least 5 percentage points each year for the years six through ten, and 10 percentage points each year thereafter, so that it is 100 by the fifteenth year.

**2.** Ten-year rule. The employee must have vested rights in 100 percent of the accumulated benefits by the end of the tenth year of employment.

A third allowable vesting rule, called the　19.77
"Rule of 45," is not illustrated in Exhibit

---

*As usual, total expense over long enough time periods equals cash outflow. In the case of pensions, however, the employer pays cash to the pension fund and the fund later pays the employee. The total expenses of these two entities equal the cash paid to pensioners. The cash paid to the plan by the employer, however, depends on the interest rate assumed. The higher the assumed rate, the smaller the required cash payments (and expenses) of the employer, because of the larger assumed earnings on the investments of the fund.

*Exhibit 19.6*
**Illustration of Two Minimum Vesting Formulas**
**Based on Accumulated Benefits**
**in Exhibit 19.5**

| End of Year (1) | Accumulated Pension Benefit (2) | 5- to 15-Year Rule | | 10-Year Rule | |
|---|---|---|---|---|---|
| | | Percentage Vested (3) | Amount Vested (4) | Percentage Vested (5) | Amount Vested (6) |
| 1 | $ 2,482 | 0% | $ 0 | 0% | $ 0 |
| 2 | 3,032 | 0 | 0 | 0 | 0 |
| 3 | 3,696 | 0 | 0 | 0 | 0 |
| 4 | 4,494 | 0 | 0 | 0 | 0 |
| 5 | 5,447 | 25 | 1,362 | 0 | 0 |
| 6 | 6,622 | 30 | 1,987 | 0 | 0 |
| 7 | 8,013 | 35 | 2,085 | 0 | 0 |
| 8 | 9,704 | 40 | 3,882 | 0 | 0 |
| 9 | 11,692 | 45 | 5,261 | 0 | 0 |
| 10 | 14,139 | 50 | 7,070 | 100 | 14,139 |
| 11 | 16,274 | 60 | 9,764 | 100 | 16,274 |
| 12 | 18,669 | 70 | 13,068 | 100 | 18,669 |
| 13 | 21,428 | 80 | 17,142 | 100 | 21,428 |
| 14 | 24,602 | 90 | 22,142 | 100 | 24,602 |
| 15 | 28,155 | 100 | 28,155 | 100 | 28,155 |
| 16 | 32,226 | 100 | 32,226 | 100 | 32,226 |

Column (2) taken from Exhibit 19.5, 6% interest assumption, column (5).

Columns (3) and (5) constructed from the Pension Reform Act of 1974 (ERISA), Section 411.

Column (4) = column (2) × column (3).

Column (6) = column (2) × column (5).

19.6. Under this rule, an employee with five or more years of employment must have at least 50 percent of accumulated benefits vested by the time the employee's age plus years of employment total forty-five. By the time the employee has worked ten years and age plus years of service equals or exceeds fifty-five the accumulated benefits must be 100-percent vested. This rule contains various other details not mentioned here.*

19.78    At the time of any pension computation, an estimate is made of the annual pension to be paid to the retired employees during their retirement years. The amount of estimated pension payments is in part a function of the vesting provision. The more generous the vesting provision, all else being equal, the larger the expected payments to a given class of employees. In terms of our simple example, the less generous the pension's vesting provisions, the smaller would be the numbers in early years in column (3) of Exhibit 19.5.

Vested benefits are legal obligations by    19.79 the employer to the employee. People who

*See Section 411 of the Pension Reform Act of 1974 (ERISA).

are owed money often require that collateral be pledged as security to protect their loans. Employees with pension promises find it hard to require that the employer provide collateral for unfunded vested benefits. Some employees have not received promised pension benefits after the employer went bankrupt. Congress, to protect the claims of employees' promised pensions, established (in ERISA) the Pension Benefit Guarantee Corporation (PBGC). PBGC charges an insurance premium per employee to all employers with defined-benefit pension plans. Then, PBGC guarantees the employee with vested rights some pension benefit in case the employer becomes bankrupt and is unable to pay.\* From the employer's point of view, the insurance premium, an additional component of pension expense not

illustrated in our simple examples, creates no accounting problems.

19.80      PBGC has the right under some circumstances, not yet clearly spelled out in the law (ERISA) or its resulting regulations, to take over the employer's assets if the PBGC judges that its risks (of having to pay pensions to employees) "begin to increase unreasonably." The contingency that PBGC may take over a corporation's assets to satisfy potential pension claims creates interesting theoretical problems but no difficult accounting ones. Accounting treats contingencies with footnote disclosure. The auditor may judge that seizure of the corporation's assets is likely. In that case, the auditor will require a detailed footnote explanation and may even provide only a qualified opinion. No accounting entries will be made for a going concern. The special accounting problems for bankrupt companies are treated in some advanced accounting texts.

---

\*PBGC limits the total payments to any employee to an amount specified by law.

## Questions and Short Cases

**19.1**    Review the meaning of the following concepts or terms discussed in this chapter.

**a.** Pension plan.
**b.** Contributory versus noncontributory plans.
**c.** Fully vested versus partially vested plans.
**d.** Fully funded versus partially funded plans.
**e.** Defined-contribution versus defined-benefit plans.
**f.** Deferred-compensation contract.
**g.** ERISA.
**h.** Pension Benefit Guarantee Corporation.

**i.** Normal cost expense.
**j.** Normal cost liability.
**k.** Commutation table.
**l.** Accrued benefit versus projected benefit actuarial cost methods.
**m.** Terminal funding.
**n.** Pay-as-you-go.
**o.** Five- to fifteen-year rule, ten-year rule, and "rule of 45."
**p.** Actuarial accrued liability.
**q.** Pension obligation versus pension liability.

**r.** Expensing versus funding of supplemental actuarial value.
**s.** Interest equivalent.
**t.** Pension plan versus pension fund.
**u.** Actuarial gains and losses.
**v.** Accumulated plan benefits.
**w.** Deferred-compensation plan.

**19.2**    What journal entries are made by the employer for employees' contributions to contributory pension plans?

**19.3**    What are the economic and accounting differences between a defined-benefit pension plan and a defined-contribution plan?

**19.4**    "The law does our employees a disservice. It forces us to fund pension costs with an independent trustee who must follow rules of prudent investment behavior. The trustee is limited to investments that today promise a rate of return of only 10 percent per year. If we could keep the funds in the company, we could invest them in our own new projects that we expect to return 25 percent per year." Comment.

19.5   a. What is an actuarial cost method?
     b. What actuarial cost methods are acceptable for accounting by a plan sponsor (employer)?
     c. What actuarial methods are acceptable for accounting by a pension plan?

19.6   a. Distinguish the accrued benefit actuarial cost method from the projected benefit actuarial cost methods.
     b. For a given defined-benefit formula, describe the effects on expense over the life of a work force using an accrued benefit actuarial cost method relative to one of the projected benefit methods.

19.7   Name and describe three vesting rules that will satisfy ERISA's minimum vesting requirements.

19.8   Describe the Pension Benefit Guarantee Corporation and its potential claim on a firm's net assets.

19.9   Why does the amendment ("sweetening") of a defined-benefit plan increase actuarial accrued liability, whereas a change with the same cost in a defined-contribution plan does not increase actuarial accrued liability?

19.10   How can a pension plan protect the employer?

19.11   Compare a nonvested (no longer legal) with a vested pension plan. Who supposedly benefits from vesting provisions? Why are we skeptical that the benefits accrue to the intended beneficiary?

19.12   a. Distinguish between the pension plan sponsor and the pension plan administrator.
     b. Distinguish between the accounting by the pension plan and the accounting by the pension sponsor.

19.13   Sometimes normal cost includes interest and sometimes it does not. Explain.

19.14   a. Describe the conditions under which a firm with a defined-benefit plan will have pension "expense equivalent to interest" on its income statement.
     b. Describe the condition under which a firm with a defined-benefit plan will have pension "revenue equivalent to interest" on its income statement.

19.15   The chapter states that an excess of net assets over accumulated plan benefits of a pension plan may be artificial, caused by differences in accounting principles. Explain.

19.16   An accountant had the following discussion with a young student who had never before heard of pensions and asked what they were.

*Accountant:* You know that your grandfather no longer works, but still must have money to live. During his working life, he saved for retirement. If he had worked for a large company, the company would have. . . .

*Student:* But they take it out of the paycheck, don't they?

*Accountant:* No. . . . Well, yes, it's cash you would otherwise get.

*Student:* Why? Don't they trust you?

*Accountant:* That's right. They are afraid that if you were paid in cash, you might not save it. . . .

*Student:* And then later, you would come screaming for help.

*Accountant:* Yes. There's another reason for pensions. If the company were to pay you $100, then. . . .

*Student:* They don't tax pensions, do they?

At this point the accountant stopped to consider that this student, who had not previously studied pensions, has had several major insights. What are they?

19.17 When a company adopts a defined-benefit pension plan giving credit to current employees for past service, actuarial accrued liability, perhaps in large amounts, arises. This amount is merely disclosed in notes and is gradually recognized. This chapter criticizes the failure to recognize actuarial accrued liability as a liability.

   a. How do generally accepted accounting principles justify not recording a liability?

   b. Assume, contrary to generally accepted accounting principles, that the amount was immediately credited to liability when it came into existence. What accounts might be debited? Give justifications that might be used to justify debiting an asset account, an expense account, or a direct debit to Retained Earnings.

19.18 A defined-benefit pension plan promises a certain amount to the pensioner. Assume that this certain amount is paid. This book has emphasized that over long enough time periods, expense is equal to cash paid out. But this chapter has shown that the interest rate assumed in making expense calculations for a company's pension expenses affects the total amount of expense recognized. Refer to the totals in columns (8) and (13) of Exhibit 19.5 to compare total pension expense using 6-percent and 8-percent interest assumptions, respectively. Resolve the apparent contradiction.

19.19 The Hicks Company is adopting a pension plan. Two plans are being considered. Both of the proposed pension plans are defined-benefit plans. The benefits actually paid to a given retired ex-employee who actually qualifies for benefits are to be the same for whichever of the two proposed plans is adopted.

   a. Who, the employee or The Hicks Company, is more likely to bear the risks and rewards of fluctuating market returns on funds invested to pay the pensions?

   In each of the parts below, explain which of the two plans is likely to be less costly from the standpoint of The Hicks Company and why. If the costs are likely to be the same in both of the plans, then explain why.

   b. Contributory plan or noncontributory plan.

   c. Plan with benefits fully vested in 5 years or plan with benefits fully vested in 10 years.

   d. Fully funded plan or partially funded plan.

19.20 (Adapted from CPA Examination.) Many companies have pension plans for their employees. Accounting for the cost of pension plans is a complex subject in which many technical terms are encountered.

   a. Describe normal cost.

   b. Describe vested benefits. Include in your discussion what the actuarially computed value of vested benefits represents.

   c. How should actuarial gains and losses directly related to the operation of a pension plan be accounted for?

*Figure 19.4*
**Time Line for Deferred
Compensation Case**

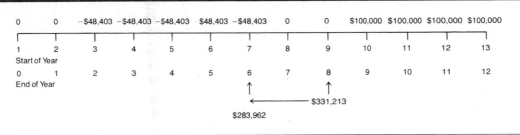

d. What disclosures concerning pension plans should be made in the company's financial statements or notes?

**19.21**  (Adapted from AICPA *Technical Practice Aids.*) Bargainier Company and its president entered into an employment contract. The contract stipulated that if the president of the company died while employed by Bargainier, the company would pay $500 a month to the president's spouse for life. Shortly after the contract was signed, the president died. The present value of $500 per month for the remainder of the spouse's life is $40,000. Prior to the president's death, the company had accrued $2,500 of Deferred Compensation Expense and had credited Deferred Compensation Payable. In addition, $750 of deferred compensation had been earned between the date of the last accrual and the president's death. Record these events.

**19.22**  This case explores some of the accounting problems of deferred-compensation contracts. The answers to the questions must be deduced from general knowledge of compound interest, amortization schedules for liabilities, and the accounting for pensions.

Assume that a firm agreed in year 1 to employ an executive for 5 years starting on January 1 of year 2 and to pay a salary for those 5 years. In addition, the firm promises $100,000 per year for 4 years starting on January 1 of year 10. Deferred compensation is accrued over the 5 years of employment, years 2, 3, 4, 5, and 6. Expense recognition does not start until employment starts in year 2. The accrual should be completed by the end of year 6, when employment ceases. A simple accrual of $80,000 per year for the 5 working years will accumulate a sum of $400,000, which will eventually be necessary. Such a simple accrual ignores compound interest and is not acceptable.

Assume that an interest rate of 8 percent per year is appropriate. The generally accepted accounting for this deferred compensation accrues $48,403 compensation expense each year for the years 2 through 6 and interest expense each year.

The methods illustrated in Appendix B for deferred annuities are used as follows to find the amount, $48,403. On January 1 of year 9, the present value, discounted at 8 percent, of the $100,000 payment to be made at the start of the 4 years, year 10 through year 13, is $331,213 (= $100,000 × 3.31213; see Table 4, 4-period row, 8-percent column). The present value of that $331,213 on January 1 of year 7, just after the employment has stopped, is $283,962 (= $331,213 × .85734; see Table 2, 2-period row, 8-percent column). To accumulate a sum of $283,962 at the end of year 6 (= start of year 7) with equal annual payments at the end of years 2, 3, 4, 5, and 6 requires annual payments of $48,403 (= $283,962/5.86660; see

Table 3, 5-period row, 8-percent column). The time line for this series of payments is shown in Figure 19.4.

**a.** Construct an amortization schedule for this deferred compensation plan for year 1 through year 13. Use six columns: the year, liability at the start of each year, compensation payment at the start of the year (payments made only at the start of years 10–13), interest expense for year on liability (computed at 8 percent), deferred compensation expense accrued at end of year ($48,403 at the end of each of years 2–6), and total liability at end of year.

**b.** Prepare journal entries for the deferred compensation plan for each year, year 2 through year 13.

## Problems and Exercises

**19.23**   A defined-benefit pension plan uses the following formula, stated in terms of three parameters, $x$, $y$, and $z$,

Annual Pension = $(x + yn) \times$ Average Salary Paid over $z$ Highest-Paid Years of Employment

where $n$ is the number of years of employment.

**a.** Are pension costs likely to go up or down as $x$ is increased?
**b.** As $y$ is increased?
**c.** As $z$ is increased?

**19.24**   Refer to Exhibit 19.5. Assume that the pension plan is adopted at the end of year 20.

**a.** How much does actuarial accrued liability computed at 6 percent interest differ from its amount computed at 8 percent?
**b.** All else being equal, will actuarial accrued liability be larger or smaller for a larger assumed interest rate?

**19.25**   Refer to Exhibit 19.5. Compute the amounts for the row corresponding to current year 21, assuming that the salary for this year, column (2), is $40,300.

**19.26**   Refer to the data in Exhibit 19.5.

**a.** What would actuarial accrued liability be if the plan is adopted at the end of year 10 and the interest-rate assumption is changed to 4 percent per year?
**b.** To 10 percent per year?

**19.27**   The firm must choose a single vesting rule for all of its employees. The Chadwick Company must pick a vesting rule for its two employees, whose employment history is summarized below.

|  | Accrued Benefit | Years of Employment |
|---|---|---|
| Employee A | $10,000 | 8 |
| Employee B | 15,000 | 12 |

Compute the minimum amount of vested benefits under both the 5- to 15-year rule and the 10-year rule.

**19.28**   (Adapted from CPA Examination.) Liberty Company, a calendar-year corporation, adopted a pension plan at the beginning of year 1. The plan is noncontributory. Liberty used an appropriate actuarial cost method to compute its annual normal pension cost for year 1 and year 2 as $15,000 and $16,000, respectively. These amounts were properly expensed and funded at the end of each year.

The actuarially computed amount of actuarial accrued liability on January 1 of year 1 is $100,000. This amount was paid to the pension plan trustee on January 1 of year 1. The amount of actuarial accrued liability is to be expensed at the maximum rates allowed by generally accepted accounting principles. The interest rate to be used is 8 percent per year.

a. Prepare journal entries for the funding of actuarial accrued liability at the beginning of year 1.

b. Prepare journal entries for pension expenses for both year 1 and year 2. Provide explanations with each entry.

19.29   Refer to the Simplified Funds Statement for a Period in Exhibit 4.13. Nine of the lines in the statement are numbered. Line (2) should be expanded to say "Additions for Expenses, Losses, and Other Charges against Income Not Using Funds," and line (3) should be expanded to say "Subtractions for Revenues, Gains, and Other Credits to Income Not Producing Funds from Operations." Ignore the unnumbered lines in responding to the questions below.

Assume that the accounting cycle is complete for the period and that all of the financial statements have been prepared. Then it is discovered that a transaction has been overlooked. That transaction is recorded in the accounts and all of the financial statements are corrected. Define *funds* as *working capital*. For each of the following transactions, indicate which of the numbered lines of the funds statement is affected and by how much. Ignore income tax effects except where taxes are explicitly mentioned.

Make clear any assumptions you think are necessary to answer the questions unambiguously.

a. A pension plan is adopted; actuarial accrued liability of $100,000 arises.

b. Actuarial accrued liability is funded in the amount of $80,000.

c. Actuarial accrued liability is expensed in the amount of $50,000.

d. Normal costs of $40,000 are expensed and funded.

e. Interest expense equivalents are recognized on Pension Liabilities in the amount of $10,000.

f. Interest revenue equivalents are recognized on Prepaid Pension Benefits in the amount of $5,000.

g. Actuarial accrued liability of $60,000 is recognized as expense and $40,000 of that amount is funded.

19.30   On January 1, Year 1, Dodd Company adopted a pension plan with defined benefits. At the time of adoption, credit was given to current employees for past years of service. The amount of actuarial accrued liability at that time was $900,000. The amount is being expensed and funded over 10 years assuming 10-percent interest. Normal costs have been $100,000 per year.

At the end of Year 3, the plan is sweetened. Employees are given credit for all prior service. Actuarial accrued liability as of the beginning of Year 4 increased by $200,000 because of the sweetening. Normal cost for Year 4 will increase to $150,000.

The increase in actuarial accrued liability will be expensed over 15 years and funded over 20 years. The original amount of actuarial accrued liability arising upon adoption of the plan is to be expensed and funded as originally planned.

a. What is the amount of actuarial accrued liability on January 1, Year 4, just after the adoption of the amended plan?

b. What pension-related amounts, if any, appear on the balance sheet at the end of Year 3?

**19.31**  Refer to the scenario in the preceding problem.
  **a.** Prepare journal entries for Year 3.
  **b.** Prepare journal entries for Years 4 and 5, assuming no change in stated assumptions.

**19.32**  On January 1, 1981, Kayco Company instituted a pension plan. The actuarial accrued liability—the present value of the past service benefits awarded to current employees—is $1,200,000. The present value of the benefits earned by employees during both 1981 and 1982 is $700,000 at the end of each of those years. Kayco Company designates the Retirement Insurance Company as the trustee of the pension plan and deposits all funding payments with the insurance company at the end of each year. Interest on unfunded liabilities is accrued at a rate of 8 percent per year. Kayco Company plans to fund an amount each year equal to the pension expense recognized for the year.
  Ignore the defined minimum and maximum limits on pension expenses in working this problem. Show the journal entries that Kayco Company would make on December 31, 1981 and 1982, for its pension plan and related expenses under the following two assumptions:
  **a.** Actuarial accrued liability is amortized over 10 years.
  **b.** Actuarial accrued liability is amortized over 30 years.

**19.33**  (This problem should not be attempted until the previous one has been worked.) Refer to the actuarial accrued liability data for Kayco Company presented in the preceding problem. Assume that the amount is amortized over 10 years, that all expenses are funded as recognized, and that interest on the unfunded amount of prior service cost accrues at the rate of 8 percent per year.
  **a.** What amount of unfunded obligation for actuarial accrued liability would be disclosed in the footnotes to Kayco Company's financial statements issued for December 31, 1981?
  **b.** What amount of unfunded obligation for actuarial accrued liability would be disclosed in the footnotes to Kayco Company's financial statements issued for December 31, 1982?

**19.34**  Exhibit 19.7 shows amortization schedules for expensing and funding a present value of $100,000 over a 4-year period. These data are analogous to those shown in Exhibit 19.1 for 3- and 5-year periods. Ignore the defined minimum and maximum limits on pension expenses in working this problem.
  **a.** Assume that actuarial accrued liability of $100,000 is expensed over 4 years and funded over 5 years. Prepare an exhibit similar to Exhibit 19.2.
  **b.** Show journal entries made by the pension sponsor for the first, third, and fifth years.

**19.35**  Refer to Exhibit 19.7. Ignore the defined minimum and maximum limits on pension expenses in working this problem.
  **a.** Actuarial accrued liability of $100,000 is expensed over 4 years and funded over 3 years. Prepare an exhibit similar to Exhibit 19.2. Continue the calculations through 5 years.
  **b.** Show journal entries made by the pension sponsor for the first, third, and fifth years.

**19.36**  On January 1 of year 1, Pomeranz Company discontinues its informal pension arrangements for employees and adopts a formal pension plan. The actuarially computed costs are to be funded through a pension trust, administered by a local bank.
  Until year 1, Pomeranz Company had debited to expense each year the cash paid to retired ex-employees (pensioners) under the informal pension plan. Four hundred pensioners had received $6 million in the preceding year and will receive the same amounts in year 1 and year 2. Pension benefits are paid on December 31 of each year. The present value on January 1 of year 1 of the promises made to the 400 pensioners is actuarially estimated to be $48 million on January 1. The entire $48 million is to be funded on January 1 of year 1.

*Exhibit 19.7*
**Amortization Tables to Illustrate Expensing
and Funding of $100,000 of Actuarial
Accrued Liability over Different Time
Spans (Interest Rate is 10% per Year)**

| Year (1) | Principal Amount at Start of Year (2) | Interest on Amount in Column (2) (3) | Amount Expensed (Top Panel) or Funded (Bottom Panel) (4) | Amount Reducing Principal (5) | Principal Amount at End of Year |
|---|---|---|---|---|---|
| **Amounts of Expense Required to Amortize $100,000 Debt over 4 Years** | | | | | |
| 0 ............ | | | | | $100,000 |
| 1 ............ | $100,000 | $10,000 | $31,547 | $21,547 | 78,453 |
| 2 ............ | 78,453 | 7,845 | 31,547 | 23,702 | 54,751 |
| 3 ............ | 54,751 | 5,475 | 31,547 | 26,072 | 28,679 |
| 4 ............ | 28,679 | 2,868 | 31,547 | 28,679 | 0 |
| | | | | | |
| **Amounts Required to Fund a $161,051 Future Value over 4 Years** | | | | | |
| 1 ............ | $    0 | $    0 | $31,547 | | $  31,547 |
| 2 ............ | 31,547 | 3,155 | 31,547 | | 66,249 |
| 3 ............ | 66,249 | 6,625 | 31,547 | | 104,421 |
| 4 ............ | 104,421 | 10,442 | 31,547 | | 146,410[a] |
| 5 ............ | 146,410 | 14,641 | 0 | | 161,051 |

[a]Note that this amount has a present value of $100,000 at the start of year 1: $146,410 $\times$ (1.10)$^{-4}$ = $100,000.

The pension plan gives credit to 3,500 current employees for all years of employment, even those worked before adoption of the plan. As a consequence, the actuarial accrued liability for those 3,500 employees is computed. It amounts to $35 million. It is to be funded in 15 equal annual installments of $4,601,582 at the end of each year, starting with the end of year 1. Normal service costs for current service of the 3,500 employees is actuarially estimated as $5 million per year and is funded on December 31 of each year, when the expense for normal service costs is recognized. A 10 percent interest rate is assumed throughout.

Management proposes to report the effects of the pension plan and its adoption as follows:

(1) Debit Retained Earnings with the present value of the supplemental actuarial value of $6 million for the 400 pensioners, net of taxes, because it relates to wages long ago debited to expense and closed to Retained Earnings.

(2) Amortize actuarial accrued liability for the current work force of $35 million over 25 years.

(3) Debit normal costs for current service of $5 million to expense each year.

(4) For tax reporting, all normal costs plus 10 percent of actuarial accrued liability is to be deducted from otherwise taxable income until the amount is fully amortized.

A 40-percent income tax rate is assumed throughout.

a. Is the plan to fund all of the actuarial accrued liability for pensioners in accord with generally accepted accounting principles? With ERISA? Regardless of your answer, assume throughout the rest of this problem that the answers are *yes*.

b. Derive the $4,601,582 amount of funding for actuarial accrued liability for current employees.

c. Is the proposed accounting in accord with generally accepted accounting principles? If not, why not?

    d. Compute the minimum amount of expense that can be recognized for both year 1 and year 2 under generally accepted accounting principles. That is, assume that actuarial accrued liability is not amortized for financial reporting. What differences between reported expense, reported in the financial statement, and deductions on the tax return arise if this treatment is used for financial reporting, whereas the tax deduction for pensions is computed as explained in (4), above? What amount of *unamortized* actuarial accrued liability will be disclosed in notes at the end of each of these years? What pension-related accounts and what amounts will appear on the balance sheet at the end of year 1 and year 2?

**19.37** Refer to the scenario for Pomeranz Company in the preceding problem. Assume that 10 years have elapsed. A new study of pension costs and related assumptions is made. The study indicates that because of higher-than-anticipated interest rates and favorable investment experience, the pension fund balance now is larger than it was projected to have been 2 years from now. Because the company has had a bad year, it decides not to make any payments to the pension fund and not to recognize any pension expense for the year.

    What counsel can you give management about its plan to eliminate pension expense and funding for this year?

**19.38** The following information is available about Ronen Company's pension plan:

| | |
|---|---:|
| Actuarial Accrued Liability Arising on Adoption of Plan ............................. | $900,000 |
| Unfunded Portion of Original Amount of Actuarial Accrued Liability at Start of Year ................................................................. | 600,000 |
| Pension Liability on Balance Sheet at Start of Year ............................. | 200,000 |
| Pension Expense for Current Year .............................................. | 150,000 |
| Cash Paid to Pension Plan Administrator by Employer during Current Year (on December 31) ........................................................ | 120,000 |
| Normal Cost for Current Year ................................................. | 63,259 |

Ronen Company uses a 6-percent interest rate in all pension calculations.

    a. What is the interest equivalent for the current year that is part of the defined minimum pension expense?

    b. What is the interest equivalent for the current year that is part of the defined maximum pension expense?

**19.39** Refer to the data in the preceding problem. Over how many years is Ronen Company amortizing to expense the actuarial accrued liability arising on adoption of the plan?

**19.40** Ingberman Company adopted a defined-benefit pension plan on January 1 of year 1. Normal costs of the plan are $10,000 for year 1 and $12,000 for year 2. Normal costs are funded each year at year-end. Actuarial accrued liability (past service cost) arising at inception of the plan is $80,000. An employee's pension benefits vest after that employee has worked for 3 years beyond the adoption date of the plan. Actuarial accrued liability is funded over 15 years, with equal annual payments of $15,761 on December 31 of each year. Actuarial accrued liability is amortized to expense over 6 years at a rate of $7,707 per year.

    a. Verify that the interest rate being used in this pension plan is 5 percent per year.

    b. What is the defined minimum pension expense for year 1?

    c. What is the defined maximum pension expense for year 1?

    d. What is the defined minimum pension expense for year 2?

    e. What is the defined maximum pension expense for year 2, assuming the pension expense for year 1 was its defined maximum?

    **f.** What is pension expense for year 1?

    **g.** What is pension expense for year 2?

    **h.** Give the journal entry for year 1 for pension expense and funding.

    **i.** Give the journal entry for year 2 for pension expense and funding.

**19.41**   Refer to the data in the preceding problem. Work parts **b–g**, assuming funding of actuarial accrued liability over 6 years ($15,761 per year) and expensing over 15 years ($7,707 per year).

**19.42**   (Developed from materials prepared by Katherine Schipper and Roman L. Weil.) This problem explores the relation between actuarial "cost" methods for pension funding and accounting expense attribution methods for pension costs. Actuarial cost methods were developed by actuaries to suggest *funding* patterns to assist business in accumulating over long time spans amounts of cash adequate to pay pensions. An emphasis on funding without placing undue burdens on any one year led actuaries to attend to *smoothness* of cash flows in devising the methods. Accounting has not, however, generally allowed smoothness of expenditures to determine expense recognition patterns: to the accountant, a cash expenditure leads to an asset if there is a future benefit; an expense is recognized for the period when the future benefit expires.

    The phrase *expense attribution*, rather than the more usual phrases, *expense allocation* and *cost allocation*, is used to distinguish between accounting problems and funding problems. Actuaries have for many years used the term "cost allocation," where an accountant might use the term "funding pattern." In the following discussion, the phrase *cost allocation* is used in its historical, actuarial sense, and the phrase *expense attribution* is used for the accounting problem.

*Simplified Pension Example*

    This problem develops the issues of expense attribution and funding patterns by using a simple pension example.

    Suppose a firm promises an employee for each year of employment, a bonus equal to 20 percent of the annual salary at the end of a three-year period. This bonus is payable only if the person is still employed at the end of three years.

    To take a concrete example, assume an executive earning $100,000 for the first year whose wage is estimated to be $120,000 by the end of the second year and $150,000 by the end of the third year. Throughout, assume an interest rate of ten percent per year. At the end of the first year the executive earns $100,000 per year and is believed to be likely to stay employed for two more years. The end-of-first-year estimate of the nominal amount of bonus at the end of the third year is $90,000 (= $150,000 × .20 × 3).

*Benefit Allocation Methods vs. Cost Allocation Methods*

    The taxonomy of actuarial cost methods distinguishes *benefit allocation methods* from *cost allocation methods*. The FASB has preserved this distinction between benefit allocation and cost allocation methods in its writings about pensions. In a benefit allocation method, the actuarial present value of a discrete dollar amount of pension benefit is separately computed for each year of credited service. In a cost allocation method, an estimate is first made of the total amount to be paid to the employee at retirement. That amount is then apportioned in some systematic way among the years the employee works. Various allocating methods can be used; methods discussed in the literature include straight-line (equal amounts to each year) and percentage of salary (amounts allocated to a year in proportion to that year's salary as a fraction of the total career earnings). If amounts are computed for an individual, then allocated to that individual's work years before the amounts for a given year are summed over all employees, the method is known as an *individual* method. Amounts may also be aggregated across individuals before being allocated to years, in which case the method is known as an *aggregate* method.

*Benefit Allocation Methods*

Benefit allocation methods divide into two classes: (1) those based on accumulated or accrued benefits, making no projections about the future earnings or employment pattern of the employee, and (2) those based on projected or estimated benefits to be earned over the work life of the employee. Exhibit 19.8 illustrates these methods.

*Accumulated Benefit Method.* At the end of the first year, the employee is earning $100,000 per year and has worked for one year. Under the accumulated benefit method, the expected bonus based on the first year of work is $20,000 (= $100,000 × 1 year × .20) and the obligation at the end of the first year is computed to be $16,529 (= $20,000 × $1.10^{-2}$). If accounting is to recognize a liability for this bonus, the amount to be recognized is $16,529, because there is an obligation for $16,529 where there was none at the start of the year. At the end of the second year, the total accumulated benefits amount to $48,000 (= $120,000 × 2 years × .20), so the benefit accumulated during the second year is $28,000 (= $48,000 − $20,000). The present value of this obligation at the end of the second year is $43,636 (= $48,000 × $1.10^{-1}$). If accounting is to record these obligations as expenses, the second year's expense totals $27,107 (= $43,636 − $16,529). Part of this expense ($1,653 = .10 × $16,529) is an amount equivalent to interest on the $16,529 obligation from the first year; part reflects the application of the higher salary to the first year's work; and part is attributable to the second year's work. (If the $16,529 were funded at the end of the first year, the earnings on the fund during the second year might offset the interest on the liability during the second year; this point is discussed later.) By the end of the third year the accumulated benefit is $90,000 (= $150,000 × 3 years × .20), and the obligation is also $90,000 because the payment is now due. The accounting obligation to be recognized for the third year is $46,364 (= $90,000 − $43,636).

Exhibit 19.8 summarizes this approach in the first column labeled Accumulated Benefit Method Based on Accrued Benefits. This method is sometimes known as a "benefit allocation method based on salary earned."

*Projected Benefit Methods.* Under the projected benefit method, the benefit for any year is based on expectations about salary. In the example, the benefit for the first year is based on the expected final salary of $150,000. It is computed as $30,000 (= $150,000 × 1 year × .20), so the obligation at the end of the first year is $24,793 (= $30,000 × $1.10^{-2}$). Note that the "projection" involves wages only, not total years of employment. The accounting obligation that might be recognized for the first year is also $24,793. At the end of the second year, the total accumulated benefits amount to $60,000 (= $150,000 × 2 years × .20), which have a present value of $54,545 (= $60,000 × $1.10^{-1}$). If these obligations are recognized as expenses, then the expense for the second year is $29,752 (= $54,545 − $24,793). This expense includes interest of $2,479 (= $24,793 × .10) on the obligation from the first year and expense for compensation of $27,273 (= $29,752 − $2,479). The second column of Exhibit 19.8 shows the components of expense for each of the three years. This method is known as the "projected benefit method based on years of service."

In the method described above, each year is given equal weight in computing the benefit for a year. Another method is the "projected benefit method based on compensation." Under this method, the annual deferred compensation benefit is assumed to be equal to a fraction of each year's salary that is constant over time. Because the sum of all (estimated) salaries is $370,000 (= $100,000 + $120,000 + $150,000) and the (estimated) deferred payment is $90,000, the benefits attributable to each year is 24.32 percent (= $90,000/$370,000) of each year's salary. The third column of Exhibit 19.8 shows the components of expense for each of the three years under the projected benefit method based on compensation.

*Cost Allocation Methods*

Cost allocation methods allocate to the years of work the total benefit to be paid (estimated at the end of the first year of the example to be $90,000). Cost allocation methods, unlike

## Exhibit 19.8
### Methods of Attributing Compensation Expense to Periods

$$\text{Lump-Sum Payment} = \begin{matrix}\text{Annual} \\ \text{Salary Rate} \\ \text{End of} \\ \text{Third Year}\end{matrix} \times \begin{matrix}\text{Number of} \\ \text{Years of} \\ \text{Work}\end{matrix} \times .20$$

| | |
|---|---|
| Salary at End of First Year | = $100,000 |
| Salary Estimate for End of Second Year | = 120,000 |
| Salary Estimate for End of Third Year | = 150,000 |

| | Benefit Allocation Method Based on | | | Cost Allocation Method Based on | |
|---|---|---|---|---|---|
| | | Projected Benefit Calculated as a Function of | | | |
| | Accumulated (or Accrued) Benefits | Years of Service | Compen- sation | Years of Service | Compen- sation |
| | (1) | (2) | (3) | (4) | (5) |
| **Year 1** | | | | | |
| Deferred Compensation Expense ..... | $16,529[a] | $24,793[d] | $20,103[g] | $27,190[j] | $22,333[m] |
| | | | | | |
| **Year 2** | | | | | |
| Amount Equivalent to Interest ........ | $ 1,653[b] | $ 2,479[e] | $ 2,010[h] | $ 2,719[k] | $ 2,233[n] |
| Deferred Compensation Expense ..... | 25,454* | 27,273* | 26,536[i] | 27,190[l] | 26,799[o] |
| Total Year-2 Expenses ............... | $27,107[c] | $29,752[f] | $28,546 | $29,909 | $29,032 |
| | | | | | |
| **Year 3** | | | | | |
| Amount Equivalent to Interest ........ | $ (1) | $ (6) | $ (11) | $ (16) | $ (21) |
| Deferred Compensation Expense ..... | (2) | (7) | (12) | (17) | (22) |
| Total Year-3 Expenses ............... | $ (3) | $ (8) | $ (13) | $ (18) | $ (23) |
| Three-year Total Expenses ....... | $90,000 | $90,000 | $90,000 | $90,000 | $90,000 |
| | | | | | |
| **Summary and Reconciliation** | | | | | |
| Deferred Compensation Expense ..... | $ (4) | $ (9) | $ (14) | $ (19) | $ (24) |
| Amounts Equivalent to Interest ....... | (5) | (10) | (15) | (20) | (25) |
| Three-year Total Expenses ....... | $90,000 | $90,000 | $90,000 | $90,000 | $90,000 |

*Indicates a plugged or forced calculation. Other numbers are calculated as indicated in the following notes.

a. ($100,000 × 1 × .20) × $1.10^{-2}$

b. .10 × $16,529

c. [($120,000 × 2 × .20) × $1.10^{-1}$] − $16,529

d. ($150,000 × 1 × .20) × $1.10^{-2}$

e. .10 × $24,793

f. [($150,000 × 2 × .20) × $1.10^{-1}$] − $24,793

Note that $\dfrac{(\$150,000 \times 3 \times .20)}{\$100,000 + \$120,000 + \$150,000} = .243243$

g. .243243 × $100,000 × $1.10^{-2}$

h. .10 × $20,103

i. (.243243 × $120,000) × $1.10^{-1}$

j. Amount of an ordinary annuity accumulated for three years at ten percent is $3.31; $90,000/3.31 except in Year 3, where it is $1 more to correct for rounding error.

k. .10 × $27,190

Note that if

[($100,000P) × $1.10^2$] + [($120,000P) × 1.10] + $150,000P = $90,000

then $P = \dfrac{\$ 90,000}{\$403,000} = .223325$

m. $100,000 × .223325

n. .10 × $22,333

o. $120,000 × .223325

benefit allocation methods, take into account at each calculation the estimated number of total years to be worked, rather than focusing only on the work done by the end of the period when the calculation is being made. Like the projected benefit methods, cost allocation methods also take into account estimates of future wages.

*Years of Service.* When allocated amounts are based on expected years of service, equal amounts are assigned to each year. An ordinary annuity of $1 in arrears for three periods accumulated at 10 percent per period has a future value of $3.31. Thus an annuity of $36,190 (= $90,000/3.31) will accumulate at 10 percent interest to $90,000. See column (4) of Exhibit 19.8.

*Cost Proportional to Salary.* Another method of allocation assigns amounts to each period in proportion to the salary earned. A factor of proportionality of expected payment to total discounted salaries is solved for. This factor is then multiplied by the salary in each period so that the resulting amounts, accumulated at interest, will sum to the total costs to be allocated. The fifth column of Exhibit 19.8 illustrates this method. The proportionality factor is solved for at note *m* to that exhibit.

*Generalizations about the Expense Attribution Methods*

If we assume that the accounting system recognizes the obligations incurred by the employer as expenses, then various generalizations can be made about the expense attribution methods and their actuarial cost method analogs.

*Total Expense is Constant over All Methods.* Exhibit 19.8 demonstrates that *total* expense over the life of the compensation plan (or of the employer and the plan together) is equal to the cash expenditure of $90,000. Part of the expense each period may be shown as compensation expense and part as an "amount equivalent to interest."

*Accumulated Benefits Approach.* The compensation component of annual expense increases more rapidly throughout the employee's career with an accumulated benefits approach than under the other methods—projected benefit or cost allocation—because each year the full effect of another year of service and higher wages is recognized. None of this impact has been anticipated.

*Benefits Approach vs. Cost Allocation Approach.* Everything else being equal, a cost allocation approach implies larger funding payments in the early years than does a benefits approach, because it takes into account the estimated total years of work. For any calculation, the cost allocation approach attempts to estimate the total costs to be incurred over the life of the plan and to allocate them to the various periods. The benefit approach uses only the elapsed work history to a given point in making calculations for a period. While the projected benefit approach uses estimates of future salary in periodic computations, it does not use estimates of eventual number of years worked.

*Years-of-Service vs. Compensation Approaches.* The years-of-service approach, other things being equal, treats every year equally in assigning costs to years, while the compensation approaches assign costs to each year in proportion to that year's salary as a fraction of all salaries expected to be earned. Because salaries generally increase over time, the compensation approaches generally show smaller compensation cost in the early years than do the years-of-service approaches.

No universally applicable generalization can be made comparing allocations of projected benefits based on years of service against cost allocations based on compensation. In Exhibit 19.8, the former—column (2)—shows a larger first-year expense than the latter—column (5)—but that result is happenstance.

*Individual vs. Group Effects.* In the simple example, the "work force" of one person ages at the rate of one year for every year of elapsed calendar time. Generally, the average age and salary of a group of employees will not increase as rapidly as the average age and salary of a single employee. Thus differences in the methods across a group of employees will not be as dramatic as in this example for a single exployee.

*Giving Employees Credit for Years of Service Prior to a Plan Change*

The term *plan change* encompasses both a change in an existing plan and the adoption of a new plan. Refer to the example of Exhibit 19.8, but assume that the plan is not adopted until the executive has been employed for one year. At the *end* of the first year, the business makes the same promise as before, again requiring that the executive remain employed for two more years—three in total—to receive the deferred compensation. Exhibit 19.9 shows the extension of the example to illustrate a plan change.

Generally, when a defined benefit plan is changed and the benefit is partly a function of the number of years of service, the benefit is based on all of a given employee's work years, not merely the years elapsing between the plan change and retirement. Assume that the employee's right to receive the benefit is fully *vested;* relaxing this assumption changes the amounts in the calculations, but not the concepts. By adopting a plan change that gives credit for prior years of service, the employer incurs an obligation for *actuarial accrued liability* to be discharged later.

*Funding After a Plan Change.* After a plan change, the actuary selects an actuarial cost method for computing an amount to be funded in *each* time period after the change. The actuary calls the periodic amount the *normal cost* or the *normal actuarial cost.* Under some actuarial cost methods, the sum of all normal cost plus interest accumulating on those amounts will be sufficient to build a fund to pay *all* of the benefits promised by a given plan change, including both benefits associated with work done before the plan change and benefits to be earned after the plan change. Put another way, the present value of normal costs in these cases equals the present value of the benefits promised by the plan change. In such cases the actuary says there is no actuarial accrued liability resulting from the plan change. Column (4) of Exhibit 19.9 illustrates such an actuarial cost method.

If the present value of the future normal costs resulting from application of a particular actuarial cost method is less than the present value of the benefits generated by the plan change, then the shortage is called actuarial accrued liability and is given special treatment in the funding plan. That is, an additional funding series will be generated to cover this shortage in funding from normal costs. The accrued actuarial liability, if any, is a residual resulting from the characteristics of the actuarial cost method used in computing the "normal," periodic costs after the plan change. Columns (1), (2), and (3) of Exhibit 19.9 illustrate actuarial cost methods that generate actuarial accrued liability.

*Which Actuarial Cost Methods Generate Actuarial Accrued Liability?* Actuarial cost methods are applied to individuals before being summed for the group, or they are applied in aggregate to the entire group. If an individual actuarial cost method is based on the age of the employee at the time of the plan change (the "attained age") rather than the age of the employee when work commenced (the "entry age"), then the actuarial method will spread all the cost of all obligations, including those arising on plan adoption, over the remaining work life of the employee. If the individual method for computing normal costs is based on the entry age of the employee, then the sum of the normal costs for all years subsequent to the plan change will be insufficient to build the fund to a level to cover the years of work before the plan change. Column (3) of Exhibit 19.9 illustrates an entry-age calculation. Columns (1) and (2), which are analogous to the first two columns of Exhibit 19.8 in that they are based on benefit methods, rather than cost allocation methods, lead to an actuarial accrued liability at the time of a plan change.

If the actuarial cost method is an aggregate method, then there is no actuarial accrued liability. The periodic "normal" cost for each period subsequent to the plan change is defined and derived so that the present value of future normal costs at the time of the plan change equals the present value of the future benefits to be paid.

*Summary of Exhibit 19.9.* Exhibit 19.9 is designed to highlight the essential characteristics of actuarial cost methods in the context of a plan change.

## Exhibit 19.9
### Actuarial Cost Methods for Determining Existence and Amount of Actuarial Accrued Liability

| | Benefit Allocation Method Based on | | Cost Allocation Method Based on Individual Years of Service | |
|---|---|---|---|---|
| | Accumulated Benefits | Projected Benefits As A Function of Years of Service | Entry Age Normal | Attained Age Normal[a] |
| | (1) | (2) | (3) | (4) |
| **End of Year 1** | | | | |
| Actuarial Accrued Liability Created ............. | $16,529[b] | $24,793[e] | $27,190[g] | — |
| **Year 2** | | | | |
| Interest on Unrecognized Actuarial Accrued Liability ................................. | $ 1,653[c] | $ 2,479[f] | $ 2,719[h] | $ — |
| Amount Equivalent to Interest on Recognized Expenses .................................. | — | — | — | — |
| Deferred Compensation Expense ............. | 25,454[b] | 27,273[e] | 27,190[g] | 42,857[i] |
| Amortization of Actuarial Accrued Liability ..... | 8,265[d] | 12,397[d] | 13,595[d] | — |
| Total Year-2 Expenses ....................... | $35,372 | $42,149 | $43,504 | $42,857 |
| **Year 3** | | | | |
| Interest on Unrecognized Actuarial Accrued Liability ................................. | $ (26) | $ (34) | $ (42) | $ (50) |
| Amount Equivalent to Interest on Recognized Costs .................................... | (27) | (35) | (43) | (51) |
| Deferred Compensation Expense ............. | (28) | (36) | (44) | (52) |
| Amortization of Actuarial Accrued Liability ..... | (29) | (37) | (45) | (53) |
| Total Year-3 Expenses ...................... | $54,628 | $47,851 | $46,496 | $47,143 |
| Three-year Total Expenses ............... | $90,000 | $90,000 | $90,000 | $90,000 |
| **Summary and Reconciliation** | | | | |
| Deferred Compensation Expense ............. | $ (30) | $ (38) | $ (46) | $ (54) |
| Amounts Equivalent to Interest on Expenses Recognized ............................... | (31) | (39) | (47) | (55) |
| Amortization of Actuarial Accrued Liability ..... | (32) | (40) | (48) | (56) |
| Interest on Unrecognized Actuarial Accrued Liability ................................. | (33) | (41) | (49) | (57) |
| Three-year Total Expenses ............... | $90,000 | $90,000 | $90,000 | $90,000 |

a. Because there is only one employee covered, a column based on the Aggregate Level Dollar Cost actuarial method would give the same numbers as in this column. See the discussion in the problem description.

b. See Exhibit 19.8, column (1).

c. .10 × $16,529.

d. Amortize actuarial accrued liability over 2 years:
$16,529/2 = $ 8,264.50.
$24,793/2 = $12,396.50.
$27,190/2 = $13,595.

e. See Exhibit 19.8, column (2).

f. . 10 × $24,793.

g. See Exhibit 19.8, column (4).

h. .10 × $27,190.

i. The future value of a two-period annuity of $1 in arrears accumulated at 10 percent per period is $2.10; $90,000/2.10 = $42,857.

1. Total expenses over the life of the plan are independent of the actuarial cost methods, although the allocation of the components of expense among
   - deferred compensation expense,
   - amounts equivalent to interest on deferred compensation expense already recognized,
   - amortization of accrued actuarial liability, and
   - interest on unrecognized actuarial accrued liability is a function of the actuarial cost method chosen.
2. At the time of the plan change, whether an actuarial accrued liability arises or not depends on the computation of the amounts to be funded in each of the subsequent periods.
3. If there is an actuarial accrued liability—an amount uncovered by future normal costs— then the amount is a residual, a function of the method of computing the future normal costs.

*A Major Difference between Actuarial Science and Accounting.* The difference between the actuary's emphasis on funding and the accountant's emphasis on expense and liability recognition is easy to see in Exhibit 19.9. The actuary devises a rule for computing a periodic funding amount subsequent to a plan change and calls that amount *normal cost*. If the sum of normal costs and interest equivalents thereon (that is, the present value of normal costs) is sufficient to accumulate the fund required by the plan change, then there is no actuarial accrued liability. If, on the other hand, the actuary's rule for computing the annual funding amount and interest thereon is insufficient to accumulate the fund required by the plan change, then and only then does actuarial accrued liability arise. Furthermore, the amount of the actuarial accrued liability is a residual and a function of the actuarial cost method chosen.

This notion may seem alien to accountants. To an accountant, past events and future cash flows, not future voluntary funding patterns, determine whether or not a liability exists and its amount. A plan change creates an obligation that has a fixed (though perhaps uncertain) series of future cash flows. One need not know how the future cash flows are to be funded to decide
   - whether or not the adoption of a plan change creates an obligation,
   - whether or not that obligation deserves to be called an accounting liability, and
   - the procedure for computing its amount.

a. Fill in the missing numbers, (1) − (25), in Exhibit 19.8
b. Fill in the missing numbers, (26) − (57), in Exhibit 19.9.

## Chapter 20
## *Income Taxes*

**20.1** Income tax expense for many firms may be as much as 40 percent or more of income before taxes. Proper measurement of income tax expense can have a significant impact on net income for a period. This chapter discusses the measurement of income tax expense and related liabilities and the disclosure of information about income taxes in the financial statements. Our attention is directed to **(1)** the effect of differences between financial statement (book) income* and taxable income on the measurement of income tax expense, **(2)** the accounting recognition of investment tax credits, and **(3)** the treatment of net operating losses.

## Accounting for Differences between Book and Taxable Income

**20.2** Income taxes payable and income tax expense are calculated by multiplying a *tax rate* times a *tax base*. Income taxes payable

---

*The term "financial statement income," although descriptive, is somewhat cumbersome. Throughout this chapter, we use the term *book income* to refer to net income before taxes reported in the financial statements and *taxable income* to refer to the amount reported on the income tax return. Similarly, the terms *book purposes* and *tax purposes* differentiate the financial statements from the income tax return.

for a period are determined by multiplying taxable income as prescribed by law by the income tax rate applicable to that period's taxable income. Perhaps the most controversial issue in accounting for income taxes is the question of the tax base to be used in calculating income tax expense for financial reporting purposes. The controversy arises because income before taxes reported in the financial statements differs in most cases from taxable income. There are two principal causes of these differences: **(1)** permanent differences, and **(2)** timing differences.

**20.3** Interest on municipal bonds is an example of a *permanent difference* between book and taxable income. Such interest is a revenue of the firm for financial reporting purposes but is never subject to income taxation. The Congress, in an effort to achieve particular governmental policy objectives, has permitted certain revenues to be excluded from taxation and barred the deduction of certain expenses. The top part of Exhibit 20.1 lists some of the more common permanent differences.

**20.4** The use of different depreciation methods for book and tax purposes creates a *timing difference* between book and taxable income. A firm using Accelerated Cost Recovery System depreciation for tax and the straight-line method for book will report larger depreciation for tax than for book purposes during the earlier years of an

*Exhibit 20.1*

**Examples of Permanent and Timing Differences**

**Permanent Differences**

1. Interest on state or local government obligations.
2. Interest expense on debt incurred to purchase tax-exempt securities (such as state or local government obligations).
3. Life insurance proceeds received by a firm on the life of one of its officers or employees.
4. Premiums paid for life insurance on an officer or employee when the firm is the beneficiary.
5. Eighty-five percent of dividends received by one U.S. corporation from another U.S. corporation.
6. Fines and expenses resulting from activities that are a violation of the law.
7. Amortization of goodwill.
8. Percentage depletion recognized for tax purposes in excess of the cost of depletable property.

**Timing Differences**

Type 1: Revenues included in pretax book income earlier than recognized for tax purposes.

1. Income from installment sales recognized at the time of sale for book purposes and at the time of cash collection using the installment method for tax purposes.
2. Income from long-term contracts recognized using the percentage-of-completion method for book purposes and the completed-contract method for tax purposes.

Type 2: Revenues included in taxable income earlier than recognized for book purposes.

1. Rental, subscription, and similar advances received prior to the period in which goods or services are rendered.

Type 3: Expenses subtracted earlier in determining pretax book income than deducted in determining taxable income.

1. Loss from the write-down of marketable equity securities under the lower-of-cost-or-market method recognized for book purposes at the time of the write-down and for tax purposes at the time the securities are sold.
2. Warranty, pension, and similar estimated costs recognized for book purposes in the period when goods are sold or services are rendered and for tax purposes when cash payments are made.

Type 4: Expenses deducted earlier in determining taxable income than subtracted in determining pretax book income.

1. Depreciation calculated using ACRS for tax purposes and the straight-line method for book purposes.
2. Intangible drilling and development costs deducted when incurred for tax purposes but capitalized and amortized for book purposes.

asset's life. During later years, book depreciation on that asset will exceed tax depreciation. Over the life of the asset, *total* depreciation for tax and book purposes will be the same. Only the timing of the charges differ.

20.5 Firms often use different accounting methods for tax and book purposes. For tax purposes, a firm selects those accounting methods that will minimize the present value of income tax payments (maximize the present value of income tax savings). This strategy is often referred to as the "least-and-latest rule." That is, pay the least amount of taxes as late as possible within the law. For financial reporting purposes, the objective is usually to select those accounting methods that most realistically reflect periodic earnings performance and financial position. Given these different reporting objectives, it is not surprising to find firms using different methods of accounting for tax and book. The accounting system must be designed to accommodate both sets of accounting methods. The lower part of Exhibit 20.1 lists some of the more common timing differences.

The issues involved in selecting a tax base 20.6

for computing income tax expense for financial reporting purposes can be better understood by referring to Exhibit 20.2. Column (1) shows that a firm generated revenues from sales and from interest on municipal bonds. Expenses were incurred for cost of goods sold, depreciation, and selling and administration. Column (6) shows the amounts reported on the firm's income tax return. The amounts in Column (1) and column (6) differ for two reasons: **(a)** interest on municipal bonds is not subject to income taxation and is therefore excluded from column (6) (a permanent difference), and **(b)** depreciation claimed for tax purposes of $15 exceeds the amount recognized for book purposes of $10 because of the use of different depreciation methods (a timing difference).

20.7    Income tax payable is based on the amount of taxable income in column (6). If

the income tax rate is 40 percent, then $2 (= .40 × $5) of income taxes will be payable currently. But what is the tax base for computing income tax expense for financial reporting purposes?

Four possible treatments are shown in Exhibit 20.2:    20.8

A. Tax base includes permanent differences and uses amounts from the tax return for timing differences.

B. Tax base includes permanent differences and uses amounts from the books for timing differences.

C. Tax base excludes permanent differences and uses amounts from the tax return for timing differences.

D. Tax base excludes permanent differences and uses amounts from books for timing differences.

---

**Exhibit 20.2**
**Calculation of Income Tax Expense**
**Using Various Tax Bases**
**(Income Tax Rate Is 40%)**

| | (1) On the Books | (2) A | (3) B | (4) C | (5) D | (6) On the Income Tax Return |
|---|---|---|---|---|---|---|
| | | Tax Base for Calculating Income Tax Expense | | | | |
| Sales ..................................... | $100 | $100 | $100 | $100 | $100 | $100 |
| Interest on Municipal Bonds ............... | 20 | 20 | 20 | — | — | — |
| Total ........................... | $120 | $120 | $120 | $100 | $100 | $100 |
| Cost of Goods Sold ..................... | $ 50 | $ 50 | $ 50 | $ 50 | $ 50 | $ 50 |
| Depreciation Expense ................... | 10 | 15 | 10 | 15 | 10 | 15 |
| Selling and Administrative Expenses ........ | 30 | 30 | 30 | 30 | 30 | 30 |
| Total ............................ | $ 90 | $ 95 | $ 90 | $ 95 | $ 90 | $ 95 |
| Tax Base ............................. | $ 30 | $ 25 | $ 30 | $ 5 | $ 10 | $ 5 |
| Income Tax Payable at 40% ............... | | | | | | $ 2 |
| Income Tax Expense at 40% of Tax Base Above ............................ | | $ 10 | $ 12 | $ 2 | $ 4 | |
| Pretax Book Income ..................... | | $ 30 | $ 30 | $ 30 | $ 30 | |
| Income Tax Expense .................... | | 10 | 12 | 2 | 4 | |
| Net Income ............................ | | $ 20 | $ 18 | $ 28 | $ 26 | |

**Definition of Possible Tax Bases:**
A. Tax base includes permanent differences and uses amounts from tax return for timing differences.
B. Tax base includes permanent differences and uses amounts from books for timing differences.
C. Tax base excludes permanent differences and uses amounts from tax return for timing differences.
D. Tax base excludes permanent differences and uses amounts from books for timing differences.

20.9  The first two treatments (A and B) can be eliminated. Because permanent differences are never subject to tax, it would be inappropriate to make a tax provision for them. Permanent differences should be excluded from the tax base in determining both income taxes payable and income tax expense.

20.10  Under treatment C, income tax expense is calculated using taxable income as the tax base. Income tax expense is therefore equal to the taxes actually payable for the period. No recognition is given to the tax effects of timing differences between book and taxable income.

20.11  Under treatment D, income tax expense is calculated using pretax book income less permanent differences as the tax base. Income tax expense is composed of two elements: **(1)** income taxes actually payable for the period, and **(2)** a charge (or credit) for the tax effects of timing differences between book and taxable income.

20.12  Generally accepted accounting principles require that treatment D be followed (that is, income tax expense be based on pretax book income excluding permanent differences).* The principal justification rests on the matching convention of accrual accounting. Under the matching convention, all costs either already incurred or expected to be incurred in the future in generating revenues during the current period are matched against those revenues in measuring earnings. The view of generally accepted accounting principles is that income taxes saved currently because book income exceeds taxable income will be paid later when the timing differences reverse and taxable income exceeds book income. These additional taxes paid when timing differences reverse are treated as an expense of the period when timing differences originate, much the same as estimated warranty costs are an expense of the period when products are sold and revenue is recognized. The process of providing deferred taxes for timing differences is referred to as *interperiod tax allocation*.

---

*Accounting Principles Board, *Accounting Principles Board Opinion No. 11* (1967), par. 34.

## Illustration of Interperiod Tax Allocation

20.13  Exhibit 20.3 illustrates the mechanics of interperiod tax allocation. For the firm illustrated, the only difference between book and taxable income is depreciation on a truck costing $10,000. The truck is depreciated using ACRS over three years for tax and the straight-line method over five years for book. Book and taxable income before depreciation and income taxes is $10,000 in each year. Income tax *expense* in each year is based on pretax book income of $8,000, reflecting straight-line depreciation. In year 1, only $3,000 of income tax is currently payable. The difference between income tax expense of $3,200 (= .40 × $8,000) and income taxes payable of $3,000 is credited to the Deferred Income Taxes account. The amount credited is equal to the difference between pretax book and taxable income caused by timing differences multiplied by the tax rate [$200 = .40($8,000 − $7,500)]. In year 2, pretax book income exceeds taxable income by $1,800 and the Deferred Income Taxes account is increased by $720 [= .40($8,000 − $6,200)]. The Deferred Income Taxes account has a balance of $920 at the end of year 2. The $920 amount represents the *cumulative* difference between book and taxable income times the income tax rate [$920 = .40($8,000 + $8,000 − $7,500 − $6,200)]. During year 4, the timing difference reverses. Depreciation recognized for book of $2,000 exceeds depreciation for tax of zero. Taxes currently payable of $4,000 exceed income tax expense of $3,200. The $800 difference [$800 = .40($8,000 − $10,000)] is debited to Deferred Income Taxes. This amount represents a portion of the income taxes provided in years 1, 2, and 3. A similar entry is made in year 5 for the reversal of the remaining $800 of deferred taxes. At the end of year 5, cumulative depreciation on the truck is the same for book and tax. Because there are no timing differences remaining to reverse, the balance in the Deferred Income Taxes account relating to this truck is zero.

20.14  The lower portions of Exhibit 20.3 present alternative sets of journal entries to record

*Exhibit 20.3*
**Illustration of Interperiod Tax Allocation**

| | Book | Tax | | | | |
|---|---|---|---|---|---|---|
| | Years 1-5 | Year 1 | Year 2 | Year 3 | Year 4 | Year 5 |
| Income before Depreciation and Income Taxes .................. | $10,000 | $10,000 | $10,000 | $10,000 | $10,000 | $10,000 |
| Depreciation Expense ................. | 2,000 | 2,500 | 3,800 | 3,700 | — | — |
| Income before Income Taxes .......... | $ 8,000 | | | | | |
| Taxable Income ...................... | | $ 7,500 | $ 6,200 | $ 6,300 | $10,000 | $10,000 |
| Income Tax Expense at 40% ......... | $ 3,200 | | | | | |
| Income Tax Payable—Current at 40% .. | | $ 3,000 | $ 2,480 | $ 2,520 | $ 4,000 | $ 4,000 |

**Combined Journal Entry for Current and Deferred Income Taxes**

| | Year 1 | Year 2 | Year 3 | Year 4 | Year 5 |
|---|---|---|---|---|---|
| Income Tax Expense ......... | 3,200 | 3,200 | 3,200 | 3,200 | 3,200 |
| Deferred Income Taxes ....... | — | — | — | 800 | 800 |
| Deferred Income Taxes ..... | 200 | 720 | 680 | — | — |
| Income Tax Payable— Current ................. | 3,000 | 2,480 | 2,520 | 4,000 | 4,000 |

**Separate Journal Entries for Current and Deferred Income Taxes**

| | Year 1 | Year 2 | Year 3 | Year 4 | Year 5 |
|---|---|---|---|---|---|
| Income Tax Expense ......... | 3,000 | 2,480 | 2,520 | 4,000 | 4,000 |
| Income Tax Payable— Current ................. | 3,000 | 2,480 | 2,520 | 4,000 | 4,000 |
| Income Tax Expense ......... | 200 | 720 | 680 | — | — |
| Deferred Income Taxes ..... | 200 | 720 | 680 | — | — |
| Deferred Income Taxes ....... | — | — | — | 800 | 800 |
| Income Tax Expense ....... | — | — | — | 800 | 800 |

income taxes. Both produce the same results. In the first of the two parts, current and deferred taxes for each year are recognized in a single entry. In the second of the two parts, current and deferred taxes are recognized in separate entries. The latter journal entries demonstrate more clearly the manner in which income taxes relating to timing differences are allocated between periods. During years 1, 2, and 3, when timing differences originate, Income Tax Expense is increased and the Deferred Income Taxes account is credited. During years 4 and 5, when timing differences reverse, Income Tax Expense is decreased and the Deferred Income Taxes account is debited. The process of interperiod tax allocation is one of shifting expenses to the period when timing differences originate from the period when they reverse.

## Partial versus Comprehensive Allocation

Although many accountants agree with the general concept of interperiod tax allocation, there are two views as to its application. Some favor partial allocation, whereas others favor comprehensive allocation. Only comprehensive allocation is permitted under generally accepted accounting principles.  20.15

20.16 **Partial Allocation** The general presumption under partial allocation is that income tax expense for the current period is the amount payable. Advocates of partial allocation argue that deferred taxes should not be provided for book/tax differences that are recurring and tend to roll over. That is, some timing differences reverse but are replaced with similar types of timing differences originating in the period. Under partial allocation, deferred taxes are provided only for nonrecurring timing differences, when the future reversal is not expected to be replaced with a similar timing difference originating in the period. For example, an isolated installment sale of a plant in which the gross profit is recognized at the time of sale for book and as cash collections are received using the installment method for tax purposes would require a deferred tax provision under the partial allocation approach. On the other hand, no deferred taxes would be provided for book/tax differences related to depreciable assets because, for a stable or growing firm, reversals of timing differences on some assets are continually replaced with originating timing differences on other assets. The balance in the Deferred Income Taxes account will either remain stable or increase. Because a net reversal will not occur in the future, it is inappropriate to provide currently for deferred taxes.

20.17 Advocates of partial allocation concede that timing differences on individual assets, such as a single machine, will reverse in the future. However, income taxes are not assessed on the income generated from each asset and liability of a firm. Income taxes are assessed on aggregate income (all revenues less all expenses). If a firm replaces its assets as they wear out or increases its operating capacity, book income will continually exceed taxable income and no net reversals of depreciation timing differences will take place. Even if a firm does not always replace its assets as they wear out, net reversals may not occur. In order for there to be no net reversals, all that is required is that the dollar amount expended each year for depreciable assets not decline. With inflation, the cost of new assets increases. Thus, even if

assets are not always replaced as they wear out, the dollar investment each year may remain stable or even increase because of higher purchase prices. Inflation makes the reversal of deferred taxes even less likely. Moreover, firms are not likely to stay profitable and remain in business for very long if their operating capacity continually deteriorates. If a firm begins incurring losses under such circumstances, it will not pay income taxes anyway.*

**Comprehensive Allocation** Under comprehensive allocation, deferred taxes are provided for any item that enters into taxable income in a period different from when it enters into the computation of pretax book income, regardless of whether the difference is recurring or nonrecurring. Advocates of comprehensive allocation offer the following arguments: 20.18

**1.** Comprehensive allocation emphasizes matching expenses with related revenues under accrual accounting. The focus is on when the benefits from tax savings should be recognized in measuring income tax expense. Partial allocation emphasizes cash outlays and the likelihood that taxes will or will not become payable in the future.

**2.** Comprehensive allocation is more consistent with the accounting for liabilities that roll over, such as accounts payable. New accounts payable continually replace accounts being paid, much the same as originating timing differences replace timing differences that reverse. Each creditor's account is accounted for separately, even though aggregate accounts payable continue to roll over. Consistency requires that timing differences

---

*The issue of whether there are any, many, or few firms that find taxes payable exceeding tax expense because of reversals of timing differences has been addressed empirically by several writers in an interchange in the *Journal of Accountancy,* April 1977, pp. 53–59. The data show that in an examination of 3,100 companies over 19 years (nearly 60,000 company-years), there are about 700 cases (slightly more than 1 percent) of a firm remaining profitable while its depreciable assets shrink in size for the year so that tax depreciation exceeds book depreciation.

related to a particular asset or liability likewise be accounted for separately.*

**3.** Comprehensive allocation is more objective. Under partial allocation, it is difficult to develop a sufficiently precise set of guidelines to follow in selecting the timing differences for which deferred taxes would and would not be provided. Firms therefore would have considerable flexibility in determining the amount of income tax expense.

20.19 **Official Position** Accounting Principles Board *Opinion No. 11*† requires that comprehensive allocation be followed. Although not stated explicitly by the Board, one suspects that the greater objectivity of comprehensive allocation was an important factor in the Board's decision.

20.20 Although comprehensive allocation is required by APB *Opinion No. 11* in almost all cases, APB *Opinion No. 23*** introduced the possibility of using partial allocation in certain specific instances. *Opinion No. 23* deals with the question of whether deferred taxes should be provided for undistributed earnings of majority-owned subsidiaries. For financial reporting purposes, the parent recognizes its share of the subsidiary's net income in the period earned through consolidation or through use of the equity method. This income, however, is not subject to income taxation to the parent until a dividend or other cash distribution is received. Because of its voting interest, the parent can control if, and when, a dividend will be paid. *Opinion No. 23* states:

The presumption that all undistributed earnings will be transferred to the parent company may be overcome, and no income taxes should be ac-

crued by the parent company, if sufficient evidence shows that the subsidiary has invested or will invest undistributed earnings indefinitely or that the earnings will be distributed in a tax-free liquidation.‡

20.21 This provision has become known as the "indefinite reversal criterion." If the criterion is met, undistributed earnings of subsidiaries are considered permanent, instead of timing, differences. On the other hand, if the parent or investor owns less than 50 percent of the voting stock of another company and uses the equity method to account for the investment (that is, 20-percent to 50-percent ownership), then it must provide deferred taxes for the difference between the income recognized for book (its share of earnings of affiliates) and the dividends received each year. In this case, the parent is presumed not to have a sufficient voting interest to control the payment of dividends.***

20.22 The indefinite reversal criteria have subsequently been applied to foreign currency translation gains and losses (covered in advanced accounting principles texts).†††

## Methods of Interperiod Tax Allocation

20.23 Three methods of interperiod tax allocation have been suggested: **(1)** deferral method, **(2)** liability method, and **(3)** net-of-tax method. Only the deferral method is allowed under generally accepted accounting principles.

20.24 **Deferral Method** Under the deferral method, the income taxes saved currently because book income exceeds taxable income are set up as a *deferred credit* on the balance sheet. This deferred credit is then allocated to in-

---

*Advocates of partial allocation counter with the argument that income taxes payable and accounts payable are different. Income taxes are assessed on the aggregate income of the firm, not on the income related to individual assets. In addition, deferred income taxes are not a legal liability, as are accounts payable. If a firm ceases operations, accounts payable must be paid, but not deferred taxes.
†Accounting Principles Board, *Accounting Principles Board Opinion No. 11* (1967), par. 34.
**Accounting Principles Board, *Accounting Principles Board Opinion No. 23* (1972).

‡Accounting Principles Board, *Accounting Principles Board Opinion No. 23* (1972), par. 12. The *Opinion* provides for similar treatment for investments in corporate joint ventures, "bad debt reserves" of savings and loan associations, and "policyholders" surpluses" of stock life insurance companies.
***Accounting Principles Board, *Accounting Principles Board Opinion No. 24* (1972).
†††Financial Accounting Standards Board, *Statement of Financial Accounting Standards No. 52* (1981), par. 23.

come of future periods when the timing differences reverse as a reduction in income tax expense.

20.25 The measurement of deferred taxes under the deferral method emphasizes the income taxes actually saved during the current period. The income tax rate in effect when timing differences originate is used to make the deferred tax provision. Deferred taxes are not altered subsequently if tax rates change or new taxes are imposed. For example, Exhibit 20.3 shows that $200, $720 and $680 were saved in years 1, 2 and 3, respectively, based on an income tax rate of 40 percent, and these amounts were credited to the Deferred Income Taxes account. Even if the income tax rate increased to 45 percent for year 4 and year 5, the debits to Deferred Income Taxes in those years would still be based on the 40 percent rate that prevailed when the timing differences originated. Thus, $800 would be debited to Deferred Income Taxes in year 4 and year 5. Once the original measurements of the deferred tax credit (or charge) have been made, they are not altered under the deferral method. All that remains is to allocate the deferred taxes to the period in which the timing differences reverse.

20.26 **Liability Method** Under the liability method, income taxes expected to be paid when timing differences reverse are set up as a liability on the balance sheet. The liability is then reduced in future periods when income taxes payable exceed income tax expense.

20.27 The measurement of deferred taxes under the liability method emphasizes the income taxes that will be payable in future periods. The income tax rate expected to be in effect when timing differences reverse is used to make the deferred tax provision. For example, the deferred tax provision in year 1, year 2, and year 3 in Exhibit 20.3 would be based on an income tax rate of 45 percent if that were the rate expected to be in effect in year 4 and year 5 when the timing differences reverse.

20.28 To be consistent with other long-term liabilities, deferred taxes under the liability method should be stated at the present value of the expected cash outflows for deferred income taxes.

**Net-of-Tax-Method** Under the net-of-tax 20.29 method, the tax effects of timing differences (determined by either the deferral or liability method) are treated as adjustments to the valuation of individual assets or liabilities and related revenues or expenses. For example, a truck costing $10,000 might be viewed as providing two types of future benefits: the benefit from using the truck to transport a product and the benefit from saving income taxes by deducting depreciation in determining taxable income. If the income tax rate is 40 percent, the $10,000 truck might be thought of as encompassing two elements: a $6,000 benefit attributable to future productive services and a $4,000 benefit attributable to future tax savings. The $6,000 benefit can be allocated to the periods of benefit as depreciation expense using the straight-line or some other depreciation method. Likewise, the $4,000 tax savings benefit would be recognized as part of depreciation expense as these tax savings are realized. For example, assume that the $6,000 benefit is allocated equally to each of the 5 years of useful life. The $4,000 tax savings benefit is allocated to each of the 3 years as depreciation is claimed for tax purposes using ACRS. The journal entry to record depreciation for year 1 is

| | | |
|---|---|---|
| Depreciation Expense (productive services) | 1,200 | |
| Depreciation Expense (tax savings) | 1,000 | |
| Accumulated Depreciation (productive services) | | 1,200 |
| Accumulated Depreciation (tax savings) | | 1,000 |

An alternative approach to accomplishing this dual allocation of cost is to recognize depreciation on the total cost of the asset ($2,000 = $10,000/5) each year and then to add to Depreciation Expense an amount equal to the tax effect of the excess of tax over book depreciation. The journal entry would be

Depreciation Expense
  ($2,000 + $200) .................. 2,200
    Accumulated Depreciation
    ($10,000/4) ................... 2,000
    Deferred Taxes [.4($2,500 −
    $2,000)] ..................... 200

The depreciable asset would be shown on the balance sheet at the end of year 1 as

| Depreciable Assets | | Year 1 |
| --- | --- | --- |
| Cost .............................. | | $10,000 |
| Less: Accumulated Depreciation ... | 2,000 | |
| Deferred Taxes ............. | 200 | (2,200) |
| Net Depreciable Assets ................ | | $ 7,800 |

Because both depreciation expense and the book value of the machine are adjusted for the tax effects of timing differences, this method is referred to as the net-of-tax method.

20.30    **Official Position** Accounting Principles Board *Opinion No. 11* requires that the deferral method be used, "since it provides the most useful and practical approach to interperiod tax allocation and the presentation of income taxes in the financial statements."* The deferral method was selected for many of the same reasons that comprehensive allocation was selected instead of partial allocation.

**1.** The deferral method emphasizes the measurement of current tax savings from timing differences and the allocation of those benefits to future periods. The liability method, on the other hand, emphasizes cash outlays expected to be made in the future for income taxes.†

**2.** The deferral method is more objective than the liability method, because no estimates or assumptions must be made about

---

*Accounting Principles Board, *Accounting Principles Board Opinion No. 11* (1967), par. 34.

†Because deferred taxes are viewed as deferred charges and credits instead of receivable and payables, it is considered inappropriate to account for deferred taxes on a discounted (present value) basis.

---

the timing of reversals, existence of sufficient taxable income in the period of reversal, or future tax rates.

**3.** The deferral method (as well as the liability method) results in separate disclosure of deferred tax provisions in the income statement and balance sheet instead of being submerged in the valuation of individual assets or liabilities and revenues or expenses as under the net-of-tax method.

The most serious weakness of the deferral    20.31
method is the lack of conceptual foundation or theoretical rationale for the deferred tax credit. The credit does not have the usual attributes of an accounting liability (see discussion in Chapter 15), nor is it like an owner's claim on the assets of a firm.** The Board apparently placed greater emphasis on the income statement and the objectivity of measuring income tax expense under the deferral method than on the balance sheet and the theoretical consistency of deferred tax credits with other equities of a firm.

## Basis for Applying the Deferral Method

The deferred tax provision for a period can    20.32
be calculated using **(1)** an individual-item basis, or **(2)** a group-of-similar-items basis.

**Individual-Item Basis** The basis, or unit, of    20.33
accountability for deferred taxes may be each asset or liability giving rise to a timing difference. For example, separate records might be kept of the originating and reversing timing differences on each machine, automobile, warranty liability, and so on. The individual-item basis of providing for deferred taxes was illustrated in Exhibit 20.3.

The individual-item approach requires a    20.34
considerable amount of record keeping. It is usually used only for large, nonrecurring timing differences, such as gains or losses on sales of buildings or other major assets.

---

**For additional discussion of deferred credits, see Robert T. Sprouse, "Accounting for What-You-May-Call-Its," *Journal of Accountancy* 122 (October 1966), pp. 43–53.

20.35   **Group-of-Similar-Items Basis** A more common approach is to group similar assets together in measuring deferred taxes. For example, all assets depreciated using ACRS for tax purposes and the straight-line method for book purposes might be grouped together. Or all long-term contracts accounted for using the completed-contract method for tax and the percentage-of-completion method for book might be grouped together.

20.36   There are two alternative methods of calculating the deferred tax provision for a period, once these similar assets or liabilities have been grouped: **(1)** gross-change method, and **(2)** net-change method.*

20.37   *Gross-Change Method* Under the gross-change method, the deferred tax provision for a particular period is the net of two calculations:

**1.** Income tax effects of similar timing differences originating in the current period based on the current income tax rate.

**2.** Income tax effects of similar timing differences reversing in the current period based on the income tax rate in effect in prior periods when deferred taxes were originally provided. Some assumption (FIFO, LIFO, weighted-average) may be required to determine the year of origination of a timing difference that reverses in the current period.

The upper part of Exhibit 20.4 illustrates the gross-change method under the assumption that the tax rate decreased from 45 percent to 40 percent.†

20.38   *Net-Change Method* Under the net-change method, the deferred tax provision for a par-

---

*Accounting Principles Board, *Accounting Principles Board Opinion No. 11* (1967), par. 37.

†Professor Gere Dominiak points out that the individual-item basis and the group-of-similar-items basis using the gross-change method are essentially the same. Both approaches require information on the year timing differences originate, the year they reverse, and the tax rate in each year. The only difference we can see is that the individual-items basis would use specific identification in determining the tax rate for originating differences, whereas the group-of-similar-items basis would probably use a flow assumption.

---

*Exhibit 20.4*

**Illustration of the Gross-Change and Net-Change Methods of Providing for Deferred Taxes**

| | |
|---|---:|
| Current Income Tax Rate .............. | 40% |
| Income Tax Rate When Timing Differences Originated ............... | 45% |
| Pretax Income per Books .............. | $500,000 |
| Timing Differences Originating in 1981 .. | (100,000) |
| Timing Differences Reversing in 1981 ... | 70,000 |
| Taxable Income ...................... | $470,000 |
| Income Tax Payable: $470,000 × .40 .... | $188,000 |

Income Tax Expense—Gross-Change Method:

| | | |
|---|---:|---:|
| Current Income Taxes ............... | | $188,000 |
| Deferred Income Taxes: | | |
| Originating: $100,000 × .40 . | $40,000 | |
| Reversing: $70,000 × .45 ... | (31,500) | 8,500 |
| Total .......................... | | $196,500 |

Income Tax Expense—Net-Change Method:

| | | |
|---|---:|---:|
| Current Income Taxes ............... | | $188,000 |
| Deferred Income Taxes: | | |
| Net Originating and Reversing Timing Differences ............ | $30,000 | |
| Times Current Tax Rate .. | × .40 | 12,000 |
| Total ......................... | | $200,000 |

---

ticular period is the result of a single calculation. The *net* timing difference for similar items (that is, originating differences netted against reversing differences) is multiplied by the current tax rate. The lower part of Exhibit 20.4 illustrates the net-change method. Note that income tax expense under the net-change method is simply the current income tax rate times the pretax book income (excluding any permanent differences).

20.39   If income tax rates do not change over time, the gross- and net-change methods result in identical deferred tax provisions. If tax rates do change, the balance in the Deferred Income Taxes account under the net-change method may have no relationship to the tax effects of cumulative timing differences, because amounts are added to the account at the income tax rate in effect when timing differences originate but are subtracted from the account at the income tax

*Exhibit 20.5*
**Illustration of the Calculation**
**of Income Taxes with and without**
**a Timing Difference**

|  | With Timing Difference | Without Timing Difference |
|---|---|---|
| Income before Depreciation and Income Taxes .................... | $30,000 | $30,000 |
| Depreciation: Assuming Timing Difference ........................ | (4,000) | — |
| Depreciation: Assuming No Timing Difference .................... | — | (10,000) |
| Income before Income Taxes ............................. | $26,000 | $20,000 |
| Income Tax: | | |
| .15 × $25,000 ............................................ | $3,750 | $ — |
| .18 × $1,000 ............................................ | 180 | — |
| .15 × $20,000 ............................................ | — | 3,000 |
| Total Income Tax ............................................ | $3,930 | $3,000 |

rate in effect when timing differences reverse. Although the net-change method is easier to apply and is acceptable, the gross-change method is considered theoretically preferable because, in principle at least, the balance in the Deferred Income Taxes account will become zero when no timing differences remain to reverse.

20.40 **Other Complexities of the Deferral Method** Although the calculation of deferred taxes in practice follows the general principles discussed thus far in this chapter, significant complexities often arise. For example, we have assumed that a single income tax rate applies to all types of timing differences. In practice, corporations are subject to graduated tax rates. Inclusion of a particular item in income may push a firm into a higher or lower tax rate category. In addition, the tax rate applicable to a particular timing difference (for example, depreciation) may differ from the tax rate applicable to other timing differences (for example, gains on sale of land). The general approach for measuring the tax effect of a particular timing difference is to measure the differential between income taxes computed with and without inclusion of the timing difference that creates the difference between book and taxable income.

20.41 To illustrate, assume that income taxes are imposed at a rate of 15 percent on the first $25,000 of taxable income and 18 percent on amounts between $25,000 and $50,000. A particular firm has income of $30,000 before depreciation and taxes; its taxable income before depreciation is, in this case, also $30,000. Depreciation expense is $4,000 for book purposes and $10,000 for tax purposes; a timing difference results from the use of different depreciation methods. Exhibit 20.5 demonstrates the calculation of income tax expense with and without inclusion of the timing difference for depreciation. The first column assumes that a timing difference does exist. Income before income taxes is calculated using the $4,000 of depreciation reported for financial reporting. The second column assumes that a timing difference does not exist. Income before income taxes is calculated using the $10,000 of depreciation reported on the income tax return. The incremental income taxes caused by the timing difference are $930 (= $3,930 − $3,000). The journal entry to recognize income taxes for the year is

| Income Tax Expense .............. $3,930 | | |
|---|---|---|
| Income Taxes Payable ........ | | $3,000 |
| Deferred Income Taxes ........ | | $930 |

Note that deferred income taxes have been provided on the $6,000 timing difference at an effective rate of 15.5 percent (= $930/$6,000). This rate differs from either of the statutory tax rates because the timing difference laps over the two graduated tax rate income levels.

20.42 In the problems at the end of the chapter, it is assumed that a single income tax rate applies to all timing differences to limit the complexity of the problems.

20.43 **Classification of Deferred Income Taxes** The balance sheet classification of deferred or prepaid income taxes arising from timing differences is determined in two steps:

**1.** Deferred or prepaid taxes relating to a specific asset or liability are classified as current or noncurrent, depending on the classification of the related asset or liability. Deferred or prepaid taxes are related to an asset or liability "if reduction of the asset or liability causes the timing difference to reverse."* Deferred or prepaid taxes not related to a specific asset or liability are classified as current or noncurrent based on the expected reversal date of the timing difference, given the particular firm's criteria for classifying assets and liabilities as current and noncurrent.

Deferred taxes relating to depreciation timing differences would be classified as noncurrent because depreciable assets are classified as noncurrent. Deferred taxes relating to undistributed earnings of subsidiaries cannot be related to a particular asset or liability on the balance sheet. The deferred taxes will reverse when the subsidiary pays a dividend to the parent. The classification of deferred taxes in this case depends on when dividends are expected to be received.

**2.** All deferred and prepaid taxes classified as current are grouped together. If the net amount is a debit (net Prepaid Income Taxes), it is classified as a current asset. If the net amount is a credit (net Deferred Income Taxes), it is classified as a current liability. Similarly, all deferred and prepaid taxes classified as noncurrent are grouped together. If the net amount is a debit, it is classified as a noncurrent asset. If the net

*Financial Accounting Standards Board, *Statement of Financial Accounting Standards No. 37* (July 1980), par. 4.

amount is a credit, it is classified as a noncurrent liability. Thus, amounts relating to the tax effects of timing differences will appear at most in two places in the balance sheet: (1) either as a current asset or as a current liability, and (2) either as a noncurrent asset or as a noncurrent liability.

# Accounting for Investment Tax Credits

20.44 In order to stimulate investment in machinery and equipment, Congress has passed tax laws that permit the purchaser of machinery and equipment to claim a tax credit based on the new investment. The credit is applied to reduce the purchaser's income tax *liability* to the federal government. The rate of the credit and the property eligible for the credit have varied through the years as Congress has amended the tax laws. In this chapter, we shall assume that a 10-percent credit applies on all machinery and equipment purchases.†

20.45 To illustrate the accounting for the investment credit, assume that during 1981 a firm had pretax book income of $1,200,000 and taxable income of $1,000,000. The $200,000 difference is a timing difference related to depreciation. The income tax rate is 40 percent. During 1981, the firm purchased $900,000 of equipment with an estimated service life of 10 years.

20.46 The journal entry to record income tax expense excluding the effects of the investment credit is

| | | |
|---|---|---|
| Income Tax Expense | 480,000 | |
| Income Tax Payable— | | |
| Current | | 400,000 |
| Deferred Income Taxes | | 80,000 |

†The investment credit provisions are much more complex. The investment credit rate depends on the property class to which the machinery and equipment are assigned under the ACRS system. Propery in the 3-year class receives a 6 percent credit. Property in the 5-year, 10-year, or 15-year class receives a 10 percent credit. The credit may not exceed a stated percentage of the tax liability (recently, the first $25,000 of tax liability plus 80 percent of the tax liability in excess of $25,000) with appropriate carrybacks and carryforwards.

A partial journal entry to record the investment tax credit of $90,000 (= .10 × $900,000) is

```
Income Tax Payable—Current ....... 90,000
      Account or Accounts to Be
         Credited ................      90,000
```

Income taxes payable to the government are reduced by the amount of the tax credit in the year in which the assets are placed in service. Thus, Income Taxes Payable—Current is always debited for the amount of the credit allowed. But what is the account credited? That is, what recognition is given to the credit for financial reporting purposes? There are two acceptable methods of accounting for the investment credit: **(1)** the flow-through method, and **(2)** the deferral method.*

## Flow-through Method

20.47   Under the flow-through method, the benefit of the investment credit is recognized as a reduction in income tax expense *in the year in which it reduces current income taxes payable*. The journal entry to record the investment credit under the flow-through method in the previous example is

```
Income Tax Payable—Current ..... 90,000
      Income Tax Expense ..........     90,000
```

20.48   This method derives its name from the fact that the benefits of the tax credit "flow through" to income in the year the credit is allowed for tax purposes. The flow-through method affects the balance sheet only through its effect on Retained Earnings, which is increased because of the smaller income tax expense.

## Deferral Method

20.49   Under the deferral method of accounting for the investment credit (not to be confused with the deferral method of interperiod tax

---

*Accounting Principles Board, *Accounting Principles Board Opinion No. 4* (1964).

allocation), the benefit of the investment credit is recognized as a reduction of income tax expense *over the life of the property giving rise to the credit*. In the example, the entry in 1981, the year of acquisition, is

```
Income Tax Payable—Current ...... 90,000
      Income Tax Expense ..........         9,000
      Deferred Investment Credit .....        81,000
```

Income Taxes Payable is reduced by the full amount of the credit. For financial reporting purposes, the benefits of the $90,000 tax reduction are recognized as a reduction in Income Tax Expense at the rate of $9,000 per year for each of the 10 years of the asset's life. Thus, $81,000 of the $90,000 is a *deferred credit* to be allocated to future periods as a reduction of Income Tax Expense.

20.50   The journal entry during each of the years 1982 through 1990 is

```
Deferred Investment Credit ........... 9,000
      Income Tax Expense ............        9,000
```

20.51   Income Tax Expense is reduced by the full amount of the credit under both methods, but over different time periods. Under the deferral method, income tax expense for any year includes not only a part of the current year's credit but also portions of investment credits relating to earlier years that are still being amortized. The Deferred Investment Credit account is shown on the right-hand side of the balance sheet, usually between liabilities and shareholders' equity. It, like Deferred Income Taxes, is a deferred credit. Deferred Income Taxes relates to the tax effects of timing differences between pretax book income and taxable income. Deferred Investment Credits represents tax credits realized in prior years that are being amortized into income over the lives of the related assets. The account is similar to the Deferred Gross Margin account arising from installment sales. It has a credit balance that will eventually increase income for a period and Retained Earnings thereafter. Until a critical event occurs—collection of cash in the installment setting or the passage of time in the investment credit setting—owners' equity is not increased.

## Selection of Method

20.52 Theoretical arguments can be offered for both the flow-through and the deferral methods. Advocates of the flow-through method liken the investment credit to a reduction of the effective tax rate in the year the firm complies with governmental goals (that is, investing in machinery and equipment). They also argue that the cash savings are realized during the period of acquisition, and should therefore be recognized in measuring that period's performance. Deferral-method advocates argue that the credit effectively reduces the initial cost of acquiring the property. Because firms generate earnings from using facilities, not from acquiring them, the benefits of the credit, or cost reduction, should be recognized over the useful lives of the facilities. Advocates of the flow-through method counter that property acquisitions and the tax credit result from two entirely separate events, which differ in that: **(1)** the cash retained can be used for purposes other than capital investment, and **(2)** the credit depends on more than investment in property; it can be used only if the purchaser has sufficient taxable income to claim the credit.

20.53 In addition to theoretical considerations, the choice between these two methods may depend on their financial statement impact. The flow-through method results in an earlier recognition of the investment credit in income. If the volume of acquisitions varies significantly from year to year, however, the flow-through method may result in widely varying amounts of income tax expense relative to pretax income. The deferral method, on the other hand, tends to smooth out the effects of the investment credit on earnings by recognizing credits piecemeal over the lives of the related assets. The deferral method results in reporting a deferred credit on the right-hand side of the balance sheet. Not only may such a credit be difficult for a financial statement user to understand, but the user might include the deferred credit among liabilities in calculating the debt/equity ratio and other ratios of capital structure risk.

The flow-through method is far more com- 20.54 monly used in practice. Both methods are acceptable.

## Unused Investment Credits

A firm may not be able to take advantage of 20.55 investment credits allowable on acquisitions during a period because **(1)** it has a net loss for tax purposes and pays no income taxes, or **(2)** the allowable credit based on acquisitions made exceeds the maximum credit permitted by law. In these cases, the income tax law permits unused investment credits first to be carried back to offset taxes paid in prior years and then to be carried forward to offset taxes otherwise payable in future years.*

To illustrate the accounting for unused in- 20.56 vestment credits, refer to the earlier example in this section. A credit of $90,000 was allowable on acquisitions made during 1981. The earlier journal entries assumed that all of this credit could be used to offset taxes payable for 1981. Assume now that, because of limitations in the tax law, only $60,000 can be used to offset 1981 taxes. The $30,000 unused credit is carried back to offset taxes paid in the preceding 3 years. Assume that income taxes previously paid had been as follows: 1978, $5,000; 1979, $20,000; 1980, $25,000. The $30,000 unused credit would be carried back to offset the $5,000 taxes paid in 1978, the $20,000 taxes paid in 1979, and $5,000 of the $25,000 taxes paid in 1980.†
The journal entry to record the investment

---

*As a result of changes in the income tax law brought about by the Economic Recovery Tax Act of 1981, a firm with unused investment tax credits can also sell these tax credits (and ACRS depreciation deductions) to another firm that has sufficient taxable income to take advantage of them. The accounting for the purchase and sale of tax benefits is discussed later in the chapter.

†For simplicity, the example assumes that the investment credit carry-back results in a refund of 100 percent of the taxes paid in the earlier years. As the footnote to paragraph 20.44 explains, the credit will result in a refund of only a stated percentage of taxes paid in earlier years.

credit *in 1981* under the flow-through and deferral methods would be as follows:

**Flow-through Method**

| | | |
|---|---:|---:|
| Income Tax Refund Receivable ..... | 30,000 | |
| Income Tax Payable—Current ...... | 60,000 | |
|     Income Tax Expense ......... | | 90,000 |

**Deferral Method**

| | | |
|---|---:|---:|
| Income Tax Refund Receivable ..... | 30,000 | |
| Income Tax Payable—Current ...... | 60,000 | |
|     Income Tax Expense ......... | | 9,000 |
|     Deferred Investment Credit ..... | | 81,000 |

20.57    Assume that instead of the amounts shown above, income taxes paid in prior years had been as follows: 1978, $5,000; 1979, $10,000; 1980, $12,000. The $30,000 unused credit would be carried back 3 years and offset the $27,000 taxes paid during these years. The journal entries under the flow-through and deferral methods would be as follows:

**Flow-through Method**

| | | |
|---|---:|---:|
| Income Tax Refund Receivable ..... | 27,000 | |
| Income Tax Payable—Current ..... | 60,000 | |
|     Income Tax Expense ......... | | 87,000 |

**Deferral Method**

| | | |
|---|---:|---:|
| Income Tax Refund Receivable ..... | 27,000 | |
| Income Tax Payable—Current ..... | 60,000 | |
|     Income Tax Expense ......... | | 8,700 |
|     Deferred Investment Credit ..... | | 78,300 |

20.58    The remaining credit of $3,000 allowed on acquisitions during 1981 must be carried forward to offset taxes otherwise payable during the next 15 years. An important theoretical question is whether or not an unused investment credit carryforward should be recognized as an asset (a receivable from the government) and as a reduction in income tax expense prior to the year in which the unused credit actually reduces income taxes payable. That is, should accounting recognition be given *in 1981* to the $3,000 unused investment credit carryforward?

20.59    If there is a high probability that the firm will be able to use the $3,000 unused credit to offset its tax liability during the next 15 years, a case can be made on theoretical grounds for recognizing the credit as an asset during 1981. The Accounting Principles Board took a more conservative view, how-

ever, in stating that "a carryforward of unused investment credits should ordinarily be reflected only in the year in which the amount becomes 'allowable,' in which case the unused amount would not appear as an asset."* Material amounts of unused credits should be disclosed in the notes to the financial statements.

20.60    To take this illustration one step further, assume that the firm is able to take full advantage of the $3,000 unused credit in 1982. The journal entries under the flow-through and deferral method in 1982 are as follows:

**Flow-through Method**

| | | |
|---|---:|---:|
| Income Tax Payable—Current ........ | 3,000 | |
|     Income Tax Expense ............ | | 3,000 |

**Deferral Method**

| | | |
|---|---:|---:|
| Income Tax Payable—Current ........ | 3,000 | |
|     Income Tax Expense ............ | | 333 |
|     Deferred Investment Credit ....... | | 2,667 |

To recognize the investment credit carried forward and the amortization of the benefit over the remaining 9 years of the asset's useful life.

# Accounting for Net Operating Losses

20.61    Firms that operate at a net loss *for tax purposes* for a year can carry the loss back and offset taxable income of the preceding 3 years. A refund of taxes previously paid will be made by the government. If the net loss exceeds the taxable income of the 3 preceding years (after certain statutory adjustments), the remaining net loss can be carried forward to offset taxable income generated during the next 15 years.

## Tax Loss Carrybacks

20.62    The carryback of a net operating loss results in a refund of tax previously paid. For ex-

---

*Accounting Principles Board, *Accounting Principles Board Opinion No. 4* (1964), par. 16. The FASB is currently reconsidering the accounting for investment credit carry forward in light of the increase in the carry forward period from 7 to 15 years brought about by the Economic Recovery Tax Act of 1981.

ample, assume that a net operating loss of $100,000 in 1981 is carried back to offset $100,000 of taxable income during the preceding 3 years. Taxes previously paid on this $100,000 of taxable income are $40,000. The journal entry to record the tax loss carryback in the loss year is

Income Tax Refund Receivable ..... 40,000
    Account or Accounts to be
       Credited .................. 40,000

20.63  The accounting issue is whether the benefits of the loss carryback should be recognized in the determination of net income **(1)** for the period(s) to which the loss is carried back (as a prior-period adjustment), or **(2)** in the period of the loss. APB *Opinion No. 11* requires that the benefits of the loss be recognized in the loss year, ''since realization is assured.''* The account credited in the entry above is Income Tax Expense. The notes to the financial statements should indicate that income tax expense for the year has been reduced by a net operating loss carryback.

## Tax Loss Carryforwards

20.64  Net operating losses, to the extent that they exceed taxable income of the preceding 3 years, are carried forward. Assume that in the first year of operations, a firm incurs a net operating loss of $100,000. Because the firm has no prior years' taxable income to which the loss can be carried back, it must be carried forward. The tax benefits of this net operating loss carryforward could conceivably be recognized:

**1.** In the loss year.

**2.** In the carryforward year as an element in determining net income.

**3.** In the carryforward year as a prior-period adjustment.

20.65  To illustrate the effect on income and retained earnings of these three possibilities, assume that pretax accounting income and taxable income during 1982 are $500,000 and that the income tax rate is 40 percent. Ex-

hibit 20.6 indicates the effects on net income and retained earnings of each possibility.

20.66  Recognition of the tax benefits of the loss carryforward in the loss year provides the best matching of income taxes and income or loss, both in the year of the loss and in the year of the carryforward. This approach is most consistent with interperiod tax allocation, where the income tax follows the income. Recognition of the tax benefits in the loss year, however, requires that a receivable be set up for the anticipated tax benefit. Establishment of an asset may be questionable because realization of the benefits of the tax loss requires that the firm generate taxable income in the future. Income prospects are always uncertain. They are usually even more uncertain if the firm has operated at a loss and has been unable to offset that loss against prior years' taxable income. They may be most uncertain for a new company without an established earnings record.

20.67  Recognition of the tax benefits in the carryforward year as an element in determining net income results in its inclusion in income in the year legal rights to receive a refund have been established. Under this approach, an asset is not recognized until these rights have been assured. A poorer matching of income tax expense and income (loss) results, however. In the year of the loss, no income taxes are recognized. In the carryforward year, income taxes on the income (loss) of two periods are recognized.

20.68  Recognition of the tax benefits in the carryforward year as a prior-period adjustment might be viewed as a compromise between the preceding two approaches. An asset is not recognized in the loss year. In addition, income tax expense in the carryforward year is not distorted by including income taxes related to two years' incomes and losses.

20.69  The Accounting Principles Board established acceptable methods of accounting for net operating loss carryforwards as follows:

The Board has concluded that the tax benefits of loss carry*forwards* should not be recognized until they are actually realized, except in unusual circumstances when realization is *assured beyond any reasonable doubt* at the time the loss carry*forwards* arise. When the tax benefits of loss

*Accounting Principles Board, *Accounting Principles Board Opinion No. 11* (1967), par. 44.

*Exhibit 20.6*
**Possible Methods of Recognizing Tax
Loss Carryforward Benefits**

| | | Tax Loss Benefit Recognized in | |
| | | Carryforward Year as: | |
| **1981** | **Loss Year** | **Income** | **Prior-Period Adjustment** |
|---|---|---|---|
| Operating Loss | $(100,000) | $(100,000) | $(100,000) |
| Tax Benefit of Net Operating Loss | 40,000 | — | — |
| Net Loss, 1981 | $ (60,000) | $(100,000) | $(100,000) |
| **1982** | | | |
| Operating Income before Tax | $ 500,000 | $ 500,000 | $ 500,000 |
| Income Tax Expense | (200,000) | (200,000) | (200,000) |
| Tax Benefit of Net Operating Loss Carryforward | — | 40,000 | — |
| Net Income, 1982 | $ 300,000 | $ 340,000 | $ 300,000 |
| Beginning Retained Earnings, 1982 | $ (60,000) | $(100,000) | $(100,000) |
| Tax Benefit of Net Operating Loss Carryforward | — | — | 40,000 |
| Beginning Retained Earnings—Adjusted | $ (60,000) | $(100,000) | $ (60,000) |
| Net Income, 1982 | 300,000 | 340,000 | 300,000 |
| Ending Retained Earnings, 1982 | $ 240,000 | $ 240,000 | $ 240,000 |

carry*forwards* are not recognized until realized in full or in part in subsequent periods, the tax benefits should be reported in the results of operations of those periods as extraordinary items.*

20.70   Thus, the second approach illustrated in Exhibit 20.6 is generally followed, except that the tax benefit of the loss carryforward is segregated as an extraordinary item instead of being included in the determination of income tax expense for the period. The following journal entry would be made in the carryforward year:

Income Tax Payable—Current  . . . . . .  40,000
  Tax Benefit of Net Operating Loss
  Carryforward (an Extraordinary
  Credit)  . . . . . . . . . . . . . . . . . . . .  40,000

20.71   If certain criteria are met, however, it may be possible to recognize the benefits of the

*Accounting Principles Board, *Accounting Principles Board Opinion No. 11* (1967), par. 45 (emphasis in original). As the footnote to paragraph 20.59 indicates, the FASB is likewise reconsidering the accounting for net operating loss carryforwards.

loss in the loss year (the first approach illustrated in Exhibit 20.6). APB *Opinion No. 11* states:

Realization of the tax benefit of a loss carry*forward* would appear to be assured beyond any reasonable doubt when both of the following conditions exist: **(a)** the loss results from an identifiable, isolated and nonrecurring cause and the company either has been continuously profitable over a long period or has suffered occasional losses which were more than offset by taxable income in subsequent years, and **(b)** future taxable income is virtually certain to be large enough to offset the loss carry*forward* and will occur soon enough to provide realization during the carry*forward* period.†

20.72   If the tax benefits of an operating loss are recognized in the loss year, the asset and income effect should be computed using the tax rates expected to be in effect when the benefit of the tax loss carryforward is realized in the carryforward year. Any subse-

†Ibid., par. 47 (emphasis in original).

quent changes in tax rates should be accounted for in the period of change as an adjustment of the asset and of income tax expense. If the tax rate of 40 percent in effect in 1981 is expected to be in effect in 1982, then the following entry would be made *in 1981:*

```
Income Tax Receivable—Tax Loss
   Carryforward .................. 40,000
      Income Tax Expense ......... 40,000
```

When the loss actually offsets taxable income of 1982, the following entry would be made:

```
Income Tax Payable—Current ...... 40,000
   Income Tax Receivable—Tax
      Loss Carryforward .......... 40,000
```

Note that when the benefits of operating loss carryforwards are recognized in the year of the loss, there is no income effect in the subsequent year when the operating loss carryforward offsets taxable income and taxes payable.

## Tax Loss Carrybacks and Timing Differences

20.73  The accounting for net operating loss carrybacks is more complicated if a firm uses different methods of accounting for tax and book purposes. For example, assume that a firm has pretax book and taxable income as shown in Exhibit 20.7. The refund receivable from the government will be based on the amounts reported for tax purposes and the amount of taxes actually paid in prior periods. The tax loss of $150,000 is carried back to 1978, 1979, and 1980 to offset $150,000 (= $30,000 + $50,000 + $70,000) of taxable income. If the income tax rate is 40 percent, then a refund of $60,000 (= .40 × $150,000) is receivable from the government. Hence, Income Tax Refund Receivable is debited for $60,000.

20.74  The tax benefit recognized for financial reporting purposes is based on the amounts of income and income tax expense reported for book purposes. The $160,000 book loss in 1981 is carried back to 1978, then to 1979, and finally to 1980 to offset $160,000 of previously reported book income. With an income tax rate of 40 percent, the tax benefit

of this book loss carryback is $64,000 (= .40 × $160,000). This amount is credited to Income Tax Expense in 1981.

The journal entry thus far is          20.75

```
Income Tax Receivable ............ 60,000
Account Debited .................. 4,000
   Income Tax Expense .......... 64,000
```

To complete the entry, some account must be debited for $4,000. The account debited is Deferred Income Taxes. Recall that the Deferred Income Taxes account includes the tax effects of *cumulative* timing differences between book and taxable income. As a result of carrying back the operating loss in 1981, cumulative book income is $90,000 (= $50,000 + $80,000 + $120,000 − $160,000). Cumulative taxable income is $10,000 (= $30,000 + $50,000 + $80,000 − $150,000). Cumulative timing differences are therefore $80,000 (= $90,000 − $10,000). The Deferred Income Taxes account should have a balance of $32,000 (= .40 × $80,000). Because the Deferred Income Taxes account had a balance of $36,000 at the beginning of 1981, it must be debited for $4,000 to bring the balance down to $32,000.

The full entry to record the tax loss carryback is therefore          20.76

```
Income Tax Receivable ............ 60,000
Deferred Income Taxes ............ 4,000
   Income Tax Expense .......... 64,000
```
The account credited is a "negative expense" account; it reduces expenses and increases income for the year.

The accounting procedures for net operating          20.77 loss carrybacks when timing differences exist are summarized as follows:

**1.** Determine the amount of the refund from the government by carrying back the current period's tax loss and offsetting it against taxable income of the preceding 3 years. The refund is equal to the taxes paid on this offsetting income (that is, tax rate times offsetting taxable income).

**2.** Determine the amount of the carryback benefit for financial reporting purposes by carrying back the current period's book loss and offsetting it against pretax book income of the preceding 3 years. The benefit recog-

*Exhibit 20.7*
**Tax Loss Carrybacks and Timing Differences**

|  | 1978 | 1979 | 1980 | 1981 |
|---|---|---|---|---|
| Pretax Book Income | $50,000 | $80,000 | $120,000 | $(160,000) |
| Taxable Income | 30,000 | 50,000 | 80,000 | (150,000) |
| Timing Differences | 20,000 | 30,000 | 40,000 | (10,000) |
| Deferred Tax Expense: 40% | 8,000 | 12,000 | 16,000 | ? |
| Balance in Deferred Income Taxes Account | 8,000 | 20,000 | 36,000 | ? |

nized is equal to the income tax expense on this offsetting book income.

**3.** Determine the *cumulative* timing difference between book and taxable income after carrying back the operating loss. Then, multiply the cumulative timing difference by the income tax rate to determine the appropriate balance in the Deferred Income Taxes account. Adjust the Deferred Income Taxes account to the desired ending balance.

20.78   Although not discussed here, similar complexities are encountered in accounting for operating loss carryforwards when timing differences exist.

## Purchase and Sale of Tax Benefits

20.79   A firm that acquires depreciable assets can usually claim an investment tax credit in the year of acquisition and reduce taxes otherwise payable. In addition, the assets can be depreciated over their ACRS life. These depreciation deductions reduce taxable income and thereby save income taxes.

20.80   Prior to the Economic Recovery Tax Act of 1981, these tax benefits could be obtained only by the purchaser of the depreciable assets. Changes in the tax law, however, now permit the purchasing firm to sell these tax benefits to another firm. The sale of the tax benefits is beneficial to the selling firm when it has little or not taxable income and therefore cannot take full advantage of the tax benefits. The purchase of the tax benefits is beneficial to the purchasing firm if it can acquire them for an amount that is less than the present value of the tax benefits to be realized.

20.81   In order for the purchaser of the tax benefits to be able to take advantage of them, the purchaser must be viewed as the "owner" of the assets *for tax purposes* (but not necessarily for legal purposes). There are various arrangements to transfer "ownership" to the purchaser, the most common of which is through a leasing arrangement.

20.82   *Example* Trans National Airlines (TNA) acquires equipment costing $100,000 on January 1, Year 1. The equipment has a 5-year ACRS life and qualifies for a 10-percent investment tax credit. Because TNA has operated at a net loss for the past several years and expects to do so for the next several years, it anticipates that it will be unable to take advantage of the investment credit and ACRS depreciation deductions. TNA has agreed to sell these tax benefits to MBI, Inc., a profitable company that can take advantage of them. The "sale" is arranged as follows:

**1.** TNA will sell the equipment to MBI as of January 1, Year 1. MBI will pay $35,242 immediately and sign a note promising to pay $13,805 on December 31 of each of the next 10 years. For tax purposes, MBI will be viewed as the owner of the equipment and entitled to the investment credit and depreciation deductions.

**2.** MBI will lease the equipment back to TNA for a period of 10 years. The annual lease payment of $13,805 will be due on December 31 of each year. TNA will have the option to purchase the equipment at the end of the lease period for $1.

20.83 The only cash that changes hands in this case is the $35,242 payment on January 1, Year 1. The subsequent payments on the note by MBI exactly offset the lease payments by TNA. The substance of this transaction is that MBI has paid $35,242 for a 10-percent investment credit and tax savings from future depreciation deductions.

20.84 As this book goes to press, the Financial Accounting Standards Board has not issued a final standard on the accounting for the purchase and sale of tax benefits. Its most recent exposure draft* proposes the following accounting:

1. Where there is a legal right of offset, the seller should record neither the Note Receivable from the buyer nor the Lease Liability payable to the buyer. Instead, the seller should recognize immediately as revenue the initial amount of cash received ($35,242 in this example).

2. The buyer should record neither the Note Payable to the seller nor the Lease Receivable from the seller where there is a legal right of offset. Instead, the initial amount paid ($35,242 in this example) should be debited to an investment account. The difference between the tax benefits to be realized by the buyer and the cost of the investment in the tax benefits should be recognized as income over the time periods that the benefits are realized. The proposed procedure follows essentially an effective interest approach in which an imputed rate of return is multiplied times a beginning-of-the–period balance sheet amount to find the income for the period.

20.85 Problem 20.52 at the end of the chapter explores the accounting for the purchase and sale of tax benefits in greater depth using the above example.

## Income Taxes and the Statement of Changes in Financial Position

20.86 Cash, working capital, or funds defined in other ways may not be reduced by the full

*Financial Accounting Standards Board, "Accounting for the Sale or Purchase of Tax Benefits through Tax Leases," (March, 1982).

amount of income tax expense for a period. When funds are defined as working capital, the following additions or subtractions must be made to net income to derive working capital provided by operations:

1. Net *noncurrent* deferred income tax expense (arising from timing differences relating to noncurrent assets and liabilities or to timing differences not expected to reverse within one year) does not use working capital and should be added to net income in calculating working capital provided by operations. Net *current* deferred income tax expense (arising from timing differences relating to current assets and liabilities or to timing differences expected to reverse within one year) is viewed as using working capital and therefore an addback to net income is not required.

2. The investment credit realized during an accounting period effectively provides working capital by reducing the cash outflow for income taxes. Because the investment credit realized is treated as an immediate reduction in income tax expense under the flow-through method, no adjustment to net income is required to calculate working capital provided by operations. Under the deferral method, however, the investment credit realized during an accounting period is treated as a deferred credit. Only the amortization of current and prior years' investment credits reduces income tax expense. To calculate working capital provided by operations, the credit amortized must be subtracted from, and the credit realized must be added to, net income. This result can be accomplished by simply adding the *net credit change* in the Deferred Investment Credit account (that is, the amount realized minus the amount amortized) to net income. Alternatively, if there is a *net debit change* in the Deferred Investment Credit account (that is, the amount amortized minus the amount realized), it should be subtracted from net income to derive working capital from operations.

20.87 The procedures outlined above are also followed when funds are defined as "cash." There is one exception, however. When cash flow provided by operations is calculated, both the net current and the net non-current deferred income tax expense are added to net income. The net current deferred income tax expense uses working capital but does not use cash.

## Disclosure of Income Tax Information

20.88   The amount of information required to be disclosed about a firm's income tax expense has increased significantly in recent years as a result of a series of pronouncements by the Accounting Principles Board, the Financial Accounting Standards Board, and the Securities and Exchange Commission. Some of the more important disclosures are listed below. Many of these disclosures are illustrated in the financial statements of International Corporation in Appendix A at the back of the book.

1. Income before income taxes separated as to amounts from the United States and from foreign sources.*
2. The components of income tax expense, segregated along three different dimensions:
   a. Taxes currently payable plus the net amounts, if any, applicable to (i) timing differences, (ii) operating losses, and (iii) net deferred investment credits.†
   b. Amounts applicable to United States federal income taxes, to foreign income taxes, and to other (state and local) income taxes.**
   c. Amounts applicable to income from continuing operations, discontinued operations, extraordinary items, and changes in accounting principles (referred to as *intraperiod tax allocation*).‡

20.89   The income statement of International Corporation in Exhibit A.1 and the income tax note (Note 5, Exhibit A.4) illustrate these required disclosures. Observe the separation of income taxes on continuing and discontin-

ued operations in the income statement. The allocation of income taxes *within a period* to each type, or category, of income permits the user of the financial statements to understand better the relationship between income tax expense and each type of income. For example, the overall effective tax rate (income tax expense divided by income before taxes) of International Corporation for 1981 is 33.6 percent [=$83.7/($165.2 + $83.7)]. The effective rate on discontinued operations, however, is 43.0 percent [= $10.1/($13.4 + $10.1)], whereas the effective rate on continuing operations is 34.4 percent [= $93.8/($178.6 + $93.8)].

3. A reconciliation between the amount of income tax expense and an amount computed by multiplying pretax book income by the applicable statutory federal tax rate. The reconciliation should include the amounts for all significant reconciling items.***

20.90   The reconciliation shown in Note 5 for International Corporation includes the tax effects of lower foreign tax rates, the investment tax credit, and state and local taxes. Other items commonly included in the reconciliation are the tax effects of lower capital gain rates, percentage depletion, disallowance of goodwill amortization for tax purposes, and nonrecognition of taxes on undistributed earnings of subsidiaries.

4. With respect to deferred taxes:
   a. The amounts of material individual timing differences (for example, depreciation, warranty costs, and so on) that comprise the deferred tax provision for the year.†††
   b. Segregation on the balance sheet of the net current amount and the net noncurrent amount of deferred taxes. The classification of deferred taxes as current and noncurrent depends on the classification of the assets or liabilities for which deferred taxes were provided or to the expected reversal date of the timing difference (see discussion in paragraph 20.43). Deferred taxes on installment sales would be current; deferred taxes on depreciable assets

---

*Accounting Series Release No. 280,* SEC (1980).
†*Accounting Series Release No. 149,* SEC (1973).
**Ibid.
‡Accounting Principles Board, *Accounting Principles Board Opinion No. 11* (1967), par. 52.

---

***Accounting Series Release No. 149,* SEC (1973).
†††Ibid.

would be noncurrent.* (Note that deferred charges and deferred credits are netted in determining the net current and the net noncurrent deferred tax amounts.)

**c.** The amount of deferred taxes that have *not* been provided on the cumulative undistributed earnings of subsidiaries because of the "indefinite reversal criteria."†

20.91 Note 5 to the financial statements of International Corporation indicates that timing differences relate to depreciation, long-term contracts, and warranties. The balance sheet in Exhibit A.2 lists "Deferred Current Income Taxes" among current liabilities and "Deferred Noncurrent Income Taxes" among noncurrent liabilities. Note 5 indicates that deferred taxes have not been provided on $275 million of undistributed earnings of subsidiaries as of December 31, 1981.

**5.** With respect to investment credits:

**a.** The method of accounting for the investment credit (either flow-through or deferral) and the amounts involved, if material.**

**b.** Disclosure either in the income statement or notes of the amounts of any investment credits carried back from the current year or carried forward to the current year.‡

**c.** Material amounts of unused investment credits.***

20.92 Note 1 to the financial statements of International Corporation indicates that the flow-through method is used for the investment credit, except that the deferral method is used on assets leased to others. The first paragraph of note 5 indicates that an investment credit of $12.9 million is recognized for 1981. This total is comprised of both flow-through method amounts and amortization of deferral method amounts. Also disclosed is the deferred investment credit still remaining to be amortized.

**6.** With respect to net operating losses:

**a.** Refunds of past taxes or offsets to future taxes arising from the recognition of operating loss carrybacks or carryforwards should be disclosed separately and classified either as current or noncurrent, depending on when realization is expected to occur.†††

**b.** When the tax benefit of an operating loss carryforward is realized in full or in part in a subsequent period, and has not been previously recognized in the loss period, then the tax benefit should be reported as an extraordinary item in the income statement of the carryforward period.****

**c.** Amounts of any operating loss carryforwards not recognized in the loss period should be disclosed.††††

20.93 International Corporation did not report any information about net operating losses during 1980 or 1981.

## Summary

20.94 The major issues involved in accounting for income taxes revolve around questions of timing:

**1.** Should the benefits of tax savings from using different methods of accounting for book and tax be recognized in the period when the timing differences originate or the period when they reverse? (Generally accepted accounting principles state when they reverse.)

**2.** Should the benefits of investment tax credits be recognized in the period when the credit reduces taxes payable or over the lives of the related assets? (Generally accepted accounting principles state that either is acceptable.)

**3.** Should the benefits realized from investment credit and net operating loss carrybacks be recognized in the current year or as a prior-period adjustment of the year to which the credits or losses are carried back? (Generally accepted accounting principles state current year.)

---

*Financial Accounting Standards Board, *Statement No. 37* (1980), par. 4.

†Accounting Principles Board, *Accounting Principles Board Opinion No. 23* (1972), par. 14.

**Accounting Principles Board, *Accounting Principles Board Opinion No. 4* (1964), par. 11.

‡Ibid. par. 16.

***Ibid.

---

†††Accounting Principles Board, *Accounting Principles Board Opinion No. 11* (1967), par. 58.

****Ibid., par. 61.

††††Ibid., par. 63.

**4.** Should the potential benefits of unused investment credit and operating loss carry-forwards be recognized in the current year or in the future year when the credits or losses reduce taxes payable? (Generally accepted accounting principles state, in general, the future year.)

20.95 This diversity of treatments suggests the lack of a well-established, internally consistent theory of accounting for income taxes. The only guiding theme appears to be conservatism in reporting income. Fortunately, the expanded disclosure of income tax information in the past decade permits the financial statement user to make any adjustments to reported data that are considered appropriate. For example, if either no or partial interperiod allocation of income taxes, instead of comprehensive allocation, is deemed appropriate, all or part of the deferred tax provision can be eliminated. If the flow-through method of accounting for the investment credit is preferable, deferral amounts can usually be transformed to flow-through amounts.

## Questions and Short Cases

20.1    Review the meaning of the following concepts or terms discussed in this chapter:

   **a.** Permanent difference.
   **b.** Timing difference.
   **c.** Interperiod tax allocation.
   **d.** Partial interperiod tax allocation.
   **e.** Comprehensive interperiod tax allocation.
   **f.** Indefinite reversal criteria.
   **g.** Deferral method.
   **h.** Liability method.
   **i.** Net-of-tax method.
   **j.** Originating timing differences.
   **k.** Reversing timing differences.
   **l.** Individual-items basis of providing deferred taxes.
   **m.** Similar-items basis (gross-change method) of providing deferred taxes.
   **n.** Similar-items basis (net-change method) of providing deferred taxes.
   **o.** Flow-through method of accounting for investment credits.
   **p.** Deferral method of accounting for investment credits.
   **q.** Investment tax credit carryback.
   **r.** Investment tax credit carryforward.
   **s.** Net operating loss carryback.
   **t.** Net operating loss carryforward.
   **u.** Intraperiod tax allocation.
   **v.** Current versus noncurrent classification of deferred income taxes.

20.2    Describe the theoretical rationale for interperiod tax allocation.

20.3    "Interperiod tax allocation is primarily a measurement issue, whereas intraperiod tax allocation is primarily a disclosure issue." Explain.

20.4    "Both interperiod and intraperiod tax allocation involve matching." Explain.

20.5    You have been called to testify before a Congressional committee on income taxation. One committee member states: "My staff has added up the amounts shown for Deferred Income Taxes on the balance sheets of the largest 500 U.S. corporations. If we collected these amounts immediately, we could reduce the national deficit by billions of dollars. After all, I have to pay my taxes as they become due each year. Why shouldn't corporations have to do the same?" How would you respond?

20.6    "Deferred income taxes might be viewed as an interest-free loan from the government." Do you agree? Why or why not?

20.7     Under what circumstances will the Deferred Income Taxes account be reduced to a zero balance?

20.8     Give one example of an originating timing difference that leads to each of the following:
    **a.** Current deferred tax credit.
    **b.** Noncurrent deferred tax credit.
    **c.** Current deferred tax debit (prepaid income taxes).
    **d.** Noncurrent deferred tax debit (prepaid income taxes).

20.9     The financial reporting objectives discussed in Chapter 1 place heavier emphasis on measuring and predicting cash flows than was the case when interperiod tax allocation was first required in the late 1960s. Discuss the possible implications of this greater concern for cash flows on interperiod tax allocation.

20.10     Summarize the theoretical arguments for each of the following:
    **a.** Partial allocation of interperiod income taxes.
    **b.** Comprehensive allocation of interperiod income taxes.

20.11     Because of its voting interest, a parent corporation can control if and when a dividend is to be paid by a subsidiary. Deferred taxes need not be provided by a parent for its equity in a subsidiary's earnings if management of the parent firm intends that such earnings will be permanently reinvested (that is, the timing of any reversal is indefinite). Can a similar case be made for not providing deferred taxes for depreciation timing differences? Why or why not?

20.12     "The measurement of deferred taxes under the deferral method emphasizes the period when timing differences originate, whereas the measurement of deferred taxes under the liability method emphasizes the period when timing differences reverse." Explain.

20.13     Summarize the theoretical arguments for each of the following:
    **a.** The deferral method of interperiod tax allocation.
    **b.** The liability method of interperiod tax allocation.

20.14     "The deferral method and the liability method of interperiod tax allocation are concerned primarily with measurement, whereas the net-of-tax method is concerned primarily with disclosure." Explain.

20.15     Summarize the arguments for each of the following:
    **a.** The individual-items basis for providing deferred taxes.
    **b.** The group-of-similar-items basis (gross-change method) for providing deferred taxes.
    **c.** The group-of-similar-items basis (net-change method) for providing deferred taxes.

20.16     A particular firm had no cumulative differences between book and taxable income. Its Deferred Income Taxes account, however, had a credit balance before adjusting entries are made for the year. What is the likely explanation?

20.17     Summarize the theoretical arguments for each of the following:
    **a.** The flow-through method of accounting for the investment credit.
    **b.** The deferral method of accounting for the investment credit.

20.18   A professor states: "Investment credits *for tax purposes* are almost always accounted for on a flow-through basis. Unless there are carrybacks or carryforwards, there is no such thing as the deferral method of accounting for the investment credit for tax purposes." Explain.

20.19   Compare and contrast the Deferred Income Taxes and the Deferred Investment Credit accounts.

20.20   How do deferred investment credits under the deferral method differ from investment credit carryforwards?

20.21   Distinguish between an investment credit carryback and a net operating loss carryback. How is each accounted for under generally accepted accounting principles?

20.22   Distinguish between an investment tax credit carryforward and a net operating loss carryforward. How is each accounted for under generally accepted accounting principles?

20.23   "Deferred income taxes relating to depreciation timing differences have no affect on working capital or cash flows either at the time they originate or at the time they reverse." Do you agree? Why or why not?

20.24   "Deferred investment credits (under the deferral method) have no effect on working capital or cash flows either at the time the credit originates (is realized) or at the time it is amortized." Do you agree? Why or why not?

20.25   What is the purpose of intraperiod tax allocation?

20.26   (Adapted from CPA Examination.) Burns Company, an installment seller of furniture, records sales on the accrual basis for financial reporting purposes but on the installment method for tax purposes. As a result, $50,000 of deferred income taxes have been accrued as of December 31, 1981. In accordance with trade practice, installment accounts receivable from customers are shown as current assets, although the average collection period is approximately 3 years.

    At December 31, 1981, Burns Company has recorded a $20,000 deferred income tax debit arising from a book accrual of noncurrent deferred compensation expense that is *not* presently tax deductible for tax purposes until the compensation is paid.

    Also, at December 31, 1981, Burns has accrued $15,000 of deferred income taxes resulting from the use of accelerated depreciation for tax purposes and straight-line depreciation for financial reporting purposes.

    How should the deferred income taxes be shown on Burns' December 31, 1981, balance sheet?

20.27   The Securities and Exchange Commission requires that a reconciliation be provided between income tax expense and an amount computed by multiplying pretax book income by the applicable statutory federal tax rate. What is the purpose of such disclosures?

20.28   Indicate whether each of the following items gives rise to a permanent difference or to a timing difference for which deferred taxes must be provided.
    a. Estimated warranty costs of $6,000 applicable to the current year's sales have not been paid.
    b. Percentage depletion deducted on the tax return exceeds the cost of depletable property by $45,000.

c. Rental fees received in advance of $25,000 are deferred on the books but appropriately included in taxable income.

d. Life insurance premiums on officers' lives of $2,000 are paid and recorded as an expense for book purposes. The company is the beneficiary.

e. Gross profit of $80,000 is excluded from taxable income because a firm has appropriately used the installment method for tax purposes while recognizing all of the gross profit from the installment sale at the time of the sale for financial reporting.

f. The investment credit realized as a reduction of income taxes payable exceeds the amount recognized for book purposes under the deferral method by $8,000.

g. There is a difference of $10,000 in depreciation expense because property has one basis for depreciation for book purposes and a different basis for tax purposes. Thus total depreciation over the life of the property for tax and book purposes will differ.

h. Dividends of $15,000 are received on marketable equity securities. Of this amount, only $2,250 is included in taxable income.

i. A company properly uses the equity method to account for its 30-percent investment in another company. The investee pays dividends that are about 10 percent of its annual earnings.

j. Same as part **i**, except that the ownership percentage is 60 percent.

20.29 Three companies have each recently made investments in equipment designed to save fuel. The equipment purchased by each company costs $100,000 and has a 10-year service life. In each of the three cases, the company was entitled to a $10,000 investment tax credit when it purchased the asset during the current year. The income taxes otherwise payable of all three companies were reduced by $10,000 during the current year. In all three companies management had made careful studies of the costs and benefits of acquiring the new equipment.

Management of Company A decided that the equipment purchased would provide operating cost savings with a present value of $150,000. The company is delighted to acquire the asset.

Management of Company B decided that the equipment it purchased would provide operating cost savings with a present value of $90,000. The equipment was worth acquiring only because of the investment credit.

Management of Company C decided that the equipment it purchased provided operating cost savings with a present value of $94,000. The equipment was acquired only because the investment credit made the investment worthwhile.

a. Discuss the considerations management of each of these companies might give to accounting for the investment credit.

b. What can you conclude from this question about the appropriate method of accounting for the investment credit to reflect management decision making?

## Problems and Exercises

20.30 Pierced Earring Company reported the following amounts for book and tax purposes for its first 3 years of operations:

|  | 1981 | 1982 | 1983 |
|---|---|---|---|
| Pretax Book Income | $150,000 | $140,000 | $220,000 |
| Taxable Income | 120,000 | 160,000 | 170,000 |

The differences between book and taxable income are attributable to the use of different depreciation methods. The income tax rate was 45 percent during all years.

**a.** Give the journal entry to record income tax expense for each year.

**b.** Assume, for this part, that $5,000 of interest on state and municipal bonds was included in the pretax book income amounts shown above for each year but properly excluded from taxable income. Give the journal entry to record income tax expense for each year.

**20.31**  The accounting records of Kelley Corporation indicate the following for 1981 through 1984:

|  | **1981** | **1982** | **1983** | **1984** |
| --- | --- | --- | --- | --- |
| Pretax Book Income ........................ | $80,000 | $150,000 | $120,000 | $200,000 |
| Timing Differences ......................... | (20,000) | (35,000) | 25,000 | (50,000) |
| Permanent Differences ..................... | (5,000) | 6,000 | (4,000) | 8,000 |
| Taxable Income ............................ | $55,000 | $121,000 | $141,000 | $158,000 |

The income tax rate is 40 percent during each year. Give the journal entry to record income tax expense for each of the 4 years.

**20.32**  Equilibrium Company adopted a program of purchasing a new machine each year. It uses ACRS depreciation on its income tax return and straight-line depreciation on its financial statements. Each machine costs $1,000 installed and has a depreciable life of 8 years for financial reporting. The assets are written off over 5 years for tax purposes using the following percentages: .15, .22, .21, .21, .21.

**a.** Calculate depreciation for each of the first 10 years in accordance with ACRS depreciation.

**b.** Calculate depreciation for each year in accordance with the straight-line method of depreciation.

**c.** Calculate the annual difference in depreciation from parts **a** and **b**.

**d.** Calculate the annual increase or decrease in the Deferred Income Tax Liability account. Assume a 40-percent tax rate and straight-line depreciation in financial reports.

**e.** Calculate year-end balances for the Deferred Income Tax Liability account.

**f.** If Equilibrium Company continues to follow its policy of buying a new machine every year, what will happen to the balance in the Deferred Income Taxes account?

**20.33**  The following events are recorded on the books of the K. Schipper Company during a recent year.

**1.** Machinery costing $100,000 is acquired. Estimated service life is 8 years, with no salvage value.

**2.** Installment sales of $800,000 are made; cost of goods sold is $600,000. During the year, $500,000 of this amount is collected.

**3.** The estimated future warranty liability on sales is charged to warranty expense for the year and amounts to $100,000. Actual expenditures for warranty repairs under the agreements during the year total $25,000. Tax regulations require that deductions from revenues for warranty expense cannot exceed actual expenditures for that purpose.

**4.** Outlays for research and development are $50,000. Management estimates that benefits of this R&D outlay will accrue to the company over a 5-year period.

Recall the "least-and-latest rule," and make the unrealistic assumption that only these four events occurred during the year. Compute the income before taxes, tax liabilities, and income after taxes for the K. Schipper Company. If there is a difference between tax expense and tax currently payable, indicate how this difference is recorded. Assume a tax rate of 40 percent. Use straight-line depreciation and completed-sales revenue recognition for financial reports. Use ACRS depreciation and installment method of income recognition for tax purposes. The machinery will be depreciated over 5 years for tax purposes using the following percentages: .15, .22, .21, .21, .21.

20.34   With the exception of the accounting for rental fees and warranties, Largay Mower Company uses the same methods of accounting for tax and book purposes. Rental fees are collected for at most 1 year in advance. The warranty period runs for 1 year after sale. The following analysis has been prepared:

| **Pretax Book Income** | 1981 | 1982 | 1983 |
|---|---|---|---|
| Income Excluding Rent and Warranties | $40,000 | $70,000 | $60,000 |
| Rent Earned | 5,000 | 25,000 | 30,000 |
| Estimated Warranty Cost | (10,000) | (15,000) | (20,000) |
| Income before Taxes | $35,000 | $80,000 | $70,000 |
| **Taxable Income** | | | |
| Income Excluding Rent and Warranties | $40,000 | $70,000 | $60,000 |
| Rent Collected | 20,000 | 30,000 | 40,000 |
| Warranty Expenditures Made | (4,000) | (12,000) | (17,000) |
| Taxable Income | $56,000 | $88,000 | $83,000 |

The income tax rate was 40 percent during all years.

a. Prepare the journal entry to record income tax expense for each year.
b. Describe briefly how the journal entries in part **a** would have changed if the tax rate had changed during the 3-year period.
c. Describe briefly how the journal entries in part **a** would have changed if the warranty period was 5 years.

20.35   The income statement of Robinson's Electronics Company for 1981 is shown in Exhibit 20.8. Determine the amount of income tax expense (both current and deferred) for 1981. The income tax rate is 45 percent. Deferred taxes are provided using the net-change method.

20.36   (Adapted from CPA Examination.) On January 1, 1981, Lodge Company sold machinery on the following terms: The buyer signed a noninterest-bearing note requiring annual payments of $1,000 per year for 10 years, with the first payment to be made on December 31, 1981. Had the buyer tried to arrange financing for the acquisition through an independent financing institution, a 10-percent rate of interest would have been charged. In this situation Accounting Principles Board *Opinion No. 21* requires that interest be imputed for financial reporting purposes.

Assume that, for income tax purposes, interest must also be imputed, but at a rate of 5 percent. Lodge's income tax rate is 40 percent.

a. What amount should Lodge Company record as the discount on this note for financial reporting purposes as of January 1, 1981?
b. What amount of interest revenue should Lodge Company recognize from this note during 1981?
c. What amount of deferred taxes should Lodge Company report relating to the sale of the machinery on January 1, 1981?
d. What amount of deferred taxes should Lodge Company report relating to interest revenue for 1981?

*Exhibit 20.8*
**Robinson's Electronics Company**
**Income Statement**

**Revenues:**

| | |
|---|---:|
| Sales | $500,000 |
| Rentals (Note 1) | 25,000 |
| Income from Long-Term Contracts (Note 2) | 80,000 |
| Equity in Earnings of Unconsolidated Subsidiaries (Note 3) | 120,000 |
| Interest on Corporate Bonds | 32,000 |
| Interest on State Government Bonds | 46,000 |
| Total Revenues | $803,000 |

**Expenses:**

| | |
|---|---:|
| Cost of Goods Sold | $310,000 |
| Depreciation (Note 4) | 105,000 |
| Warranties (Note 5) | 25,000 |
| Selling and Administration | 136,000 |
| Goodwill Amortization | 15,000 |
| Unrealized Loss from Price Decline of Marketable Securities (Note 6) | 10,000 |
| Total Expenses (Except Income Taxes) | $601,000 |
| Income before Income Taxes | $202,000 |
| Income Tax Expense—Current | ? |
| —Deferred | ? |
| Net Income | ? |

**Note 1.** All rental amounts are received in advance of the rental period. During 1981, a total of $20,000 of rental amounts was received in cash.

**Note 2.** Income from long-term contracts is recognized using the percentage-of-completion method for book and the completed-contract method for tax. Income from long-term contracts under the completed-contract method was $95,000 during 1981.

**Note 3.** Of the equity in earnings of unconsolidated subsidiaries, it is anticipated that $80,000 will be retained for growth and diversification. Dividends of $25,000 were received from these subsidiaries during 1981.

**Note 4.** Depreciation is based on ACRS for tax and the straight-line method for book. Depreciation under ACRS for 1981 is $163,000.

**Note 5.** Actual expenditures for warranty services during 1981 totaled $18,000.

**Note 6.** The lower-of-cost-or-market method is used for marketable securities.

20.37   Whitmyer Popcorn Company purchased five popping machines on January 2, 1981, for $6,000 each. The machines have an expected service life of 8 years and zero estimated salvage value. The machines will be depreciated using ACRS depreciation for tax and the straight-line method for book. ACRS depreciation for these machines is as follows: .15, .22, .21, .21, .21. The income tax rate in 1981 is 42 percent. The rate is expected to increase to 46 percent beginning January 1, 1986.

   a. Determine the amount of deferred tax provision relating to these machines for each of the years 1981 to 1985, using the deferral method.

   b. Repeat step a, but assume that the liability method is used. Ignore present-value complexities for this part.

   c. What would be the amount of the deferred tax provision for 1981 if the liability method were used and present-value calculations were incorporated? Assume that deferred taxes roll over on a FIFO basis, all tax provisions and tax payments are made at the end of each period, and the discount rate is 10 percent.

    **d.** Which of the three methods above is permitted under generally accepted accounting principles?

**20.38** Trailhound Delivery Services, Inc., which began business in 1981, uses an accelerated depreciation method for tax purposes and the straight-line method for book purposes. A schedule of originating and reversing timing differences relating to its depreciation accounts is shown in Exhibit 20.9.

---

*Exhibit 20.9*
**Trailhound Delivery Services, Inc.**

| Year | Originating Timing Difference | Year and Amount of Reversal | | | | |
|------|------|------|------|------|------|------|
| | | **1982** | **1983** | **1984** | **1985** | **1986** |
| 1981 | $50,000 | $5,000 | $10,000 | $30,000 | $ 5,000 | $ — |
| 1982 | 60,000 | — | 8,000 | 32,000 | 18,000 | 2,000 |
| 1983 | 40,000 | — | — | 10,000 | 22,000 | 6,000 |
| 1984 | 55,000 | — | — | — | 15,000 | 23,000 |

---

Pretax income and the income tax rate for each of the years 1981 to 1984 are as follows:

| Year | Pretax Income | Income Tax Rate |
|------|------|------|
| 1981 | $200,000 | 40% |
| 1982 | 230,000 | 42% |
| 1983 | 210,000 | 44% |
| 1984 | 240,000 | 46% |

Assume that the only timing differences relate to depreciation and that there are no permanent differences.

    **a.** Give the journal entry to record income tax expense for each of the years 1981 to 1984, assuming that the deferred tax provision is based on the gross-change method for similar items.

    **b.** Repeat step **a,** but assume that the deferred tax provision is based on the net-change method for similar items.

**20.39** Dees Oil Company uses different methods of accounting for book and tax purposes as follows:

    **1.** Depreciation is calculated using ACRS tax and the straight-line method for book.

    **2.** Income from the rental of facilities is recognized when cash is received for tax and when rental services are provided for book. Rental fees received in advance are treated as current liabilities.

These are the only timing differences between book and taxable income. There are no permanent differences.

    Timing differences relating to depreciation are shown in Exhibit 20.10, and timing differences relating to rent revenue are shown in Exhibit 20.11.

*Exhibit 20.10*
**Dees Oil Company—Depreciation**

| Year | Originating Differences | Reversing Differences That Originated in Year: | | | | |
|------|------------------------|------|------|------|------|------|
|      |                        | 1978 | 1979 | 1980 | 1981 | 1982 |
| 1981 | $200,000 | $25,000 | $30,000 | $50,000 | $ — | $ — |
| 1982 | 220,000 | 10,000 | 20,000 | 25,000 | 60,000 | — |
| 1983 | 160,000 | 5,000 | 10,000 | 15,000 | 40,000 | 80,000 |

*Exhibit 20.11*
**Dees Oil Company—Rent Revenue**

| Year | Originating Differences | Reversing Differences That Originated in Year: | | | |
|------|------------------------|------|------|------|------|
|      |                        | 1979 | 1980 | 1981 | 1982 |
| 1981 | $110,000 | $20,000 | $50,000 | $ — | $ — |
| 1982 | 140,000 | — | 40,000 | 80,000 | — |
| 1983 | 170,000 | — | — | 30,000 | 100,000 |

Pretax book income and the income tax rate for each of the years 1978 through 1983 are as follows:

| Year | Pretax Book Income | Income Tax Rate |
|------|--------------------|-----------------|
| 1978 | $  800,000 | 48% |
| 1979 | 900,000 | 48% |
| 1980 | 700,000 | 46% |
| 1981 | 1,000,000 | 40% |
| 1982 | 600,000 | 42% |
| 1983 | 1,200,000 | 42% |

a. Give the journal entry to record income tax expense for each of the years 1981 to 1983, assuming that the deferred tax provision is based on the gross-change method for similar items.

b. Repeat step **a,** but use the net-change method for similar items.

20.40   The data in Exhibit 20.12 relate to the activities of Whitley Organ Company for the years 1981 to 1985.

*Exhibit 20.12*
**Whitley Organ Company**

|  | 1981 | 1982 | 1983 | 1984 | 1985 |
|--|------|------|------|------|------|
| Pretax Book Income and Taxable Income .......... | $1,000,000 | $2,000,000 | $3,000,000 | $4,000,000 | $5,000,000 |
| Cost of Machinery and Equipment Acquired ...... | 400,000 | 600,000 | 800,000 | 1,000,000 | 1,200,000 |
| Income Tax Rate .......... | 40% | 40% | 43% | 44% | 46% |
| Investment Tax Credit Rate .. | 10% | 10% | 12% | 12% | 14% |

The machinery and equipment acquired, which fully qualify for the investment tax credit, are depreciated over a 10-year life for financial reporting.

a. Give the journal entries to record income tax expense and to recognize investment credits for each year using the flow-through method (two entries required for each year).

b. Repeat step **a,** but use the deferral method.

20.41 The Libby Company has income tax expense before any investment credits of $100,000 each year. At the start of the first year, it acquires an asset with a depreciable life of 4 years. Assume that the asset qualifies for an investment credit of $4,000.

a. Record income taxes and the entries related to the investment credit for the 4 years of the asset's life using the flow-through method.

b. Record entries related to income taxes and the investment credit for the 4 years of the asset's life using the deferral method.

20.42 Refer to the data in the preceding problem for the Libby Company. Assume that each year the Libby Equilibrium Company acquires an asset with a depreciable life of 4 years. Each year the asset acquired qualifies for an investment credit of $4,000 and income tax expense before any investment credits is $100,000.

a. Record entries related to income taxes and the investment credit for each of the first 5 years using the flow-through method.

b. Record entries related to income taxes and the investment credit for each of the first 5 years using the deferral method.

c. Assuming that Libby Equilibrium Company's income taxes, asset acquisitions, and investment credits continue in the following years as in the first 5 years, describe the effects on the financial statements of the two methods of accounting for the investment credit.

d. Assume the same data as in part **c,** but that the new asset's cost increases by 10 percent each year and that the amount of the investment credit earned increases by 10 percent each year. Describe the effects on the financial statements of the two methods of accounting for the investment credit.

20.43 The following data relate to the activities of Langston's Supermarkets, Inc., for the years 1978 to 1981.

| | 1978 | 1979 | 1980 | 1981 |
|---|---|---|---|---|
| Pretax Book Income | $12,000 | $16,000 | $21,000 | $24,000 |
| Timing Differences | (3,000) | (4,000) | (6,000) | (8,000) |
| Taxable Income | $ 9,000 | $12,000 | $15,000 | $16,000 |
| Investment Credit on Acquisitions during the Year | $ 3,000 | $ 4,000 | $ 5,200 | $10,000 |
| Income Tax Rate | 40% | 40% | 42% | 44% |

Langston uses the flow-through method of accounting for the investment credit.

Give the journal entries to record income tax expense and to recognize the investment credit for 1981 (two entries required). Assume that available investment credits can be used to offset 100 percent of the tax liability in any year.

20.44 Hargrave Airlines discloses its pretax book income and taxable income as well as income taxes paid for the years 1978 to 1980 as follows:

| | 1978 | 1979 | 1980 |
|---|---|---|---|
| Pretax Book Income and Taxable Income | $460,000 | $780,000 | $1,200,000 |
| Income Taxes Paid | 200,000 | 350,000 | 540,000 |

As a result of a strike that closed down all operations for 5 months, Hargrave Airlines operated at a pretax book loss and taxable loss of $3,000,000 during 1981. The strike was resolved during 1981, with the employees' union signing a new 5-year contract. The income tax rate for 1981 and future years is 40 percent.

a. Give the journal entries to record income taxes for 1981.

b. Prepare a partial income statement for 1981 beginning with pretax book income. Describe any disclosures that you feel should be made.

c. Assume that pretax book income and taxable income for 1982 is $1,600,000. Give the journal entries to record income tax expense for 1982.

d. Prepare a partial income statement for 1982 beginning with pretax book income. Describe any disclosures that you feel should be made.

e. Assume that the strike was resolved in 1981 but that, because significant differences still exist between labor and management, only a 1-year contract was signed. A strike is therefore a distinct possibility in future years. Repeat steps a through d.

20.45  The accounting records of Pratt Pampered Baby Products reveal the following information:

| | 1978 | 1979 | 1980 | 1981 |
|---|---|---|---|---|
| Pretax Book Income | $50,000 | $20,000 | $10,000 | $(95,000) |
| Timing Differences | (20,000) | 10,000 | 15,000 | 10,000 |
| Permanent Differences | (5,000) | (6,000) | (6,000) | (5,000) |
| Taxable Income | $25,000 | $24,000 | $19,000 | $(90,000) |
| Deferred Tax Provision at .40 | $8,000 Cr. | $4,000 Dr. | $6,000 Dr. | ? |
| Balance in Deferred Income Taxes Account at Year-End | $45,000 | $41,000 | $35,000 | ? |

a. Prepare the journal entry to record income taxes for 1981, giving consideration to any benefits of net operating loss carrybacks. The income tax rate is 40 percent in all years.

b. Calculate the amount of net operating loss carryforward for tax and book purposes at the end of 1981. Any benefits of the net operating loss carryforward are not assured beyond reasonable doubt at the end of 1981.

20.46  Jones Shoe World, Inc., which was organized in 1978, operates retail shoe stores in shopping centers throughout the United States. The following data relate to the operations of Jones Shoe World for 1978 to 1981. The income tax rate is 40 percent for all years. Benefits of net operating loss carryforwards are not recognized as assets. There are no permanent differences between book and taxable income.

| | 1978 | 1979 | 1980 | 1981 |
|---|---|---|---|---|
| Pretax Book Income | $20,000 | $60,000 | $100,000 | $(80,000) |
| Timing Differences | (20,000) | (40,000) | (30,000) | 10,000 |
| Taxable Income | $ 0 | $20,000 | $ 70,000 | $(70,000) |
| Deferred Tax Provision at .40 | $ 8,000 | $16,000 | $ 12,000 | ? |
| Balance in Deferred Income Taxes Account | 8,000 | 24,000 | 36,000 | ? |

a. Prepare the journal entry to record income taxes for 1981, giving consideration to any benefits of net operating loss carrybacks.

b. Assume instead of the above that the pretax book loss for 1981 was $110,000 and that the taxable loss was $100,000. Give the journal entry to record income taxes for 1981.

c. Assume instead of the above that the pretax book loss for 1981 was $70,000 and that the taxable loss was $80,000. Give the journal entry to record income taxes for 1981.

d. Assume instead of the above that the pretax book loss for 1981 was $200,000 and that the taxable loss was $160,000. Give the journal entry to record income taxes for 1981.

**20.47** The income statement of Elliott Figurine Company for 1981 reveals the following:

**Income Statement:**

| | | |
|---|---:|---:|
| Continuing Operations: | | |
| Income before Income Taxes | | $1,000,000 |
| Income Tax Expense: | | |
| Current | $316,000 | |
| Deferred | 48,000 | 364,000 |
| Total—Continuing Operations | | $ 636,000 |
| Extraordinary Items: | | |
| Tax Benefit of Net Operating Loss Carryforward | | 50,000 |
| Net Income | | $ 686,000 |

The comparative balance sheet reveals the following:

| | December 31, 1980 | December 31, 1981 |
|---|---:|---:|
| Income Tax Payable—Current | $ 50,000 | $ 66,000 |
| Deferred Income Taxes | 540,000 | 588,000 |
| Deferred Investment Credits | 120,000 | 160,000 |

A note to the financial statements indicated that an investment credit of $60,000 was realized during 1981 as a reduction in income taxes payable.

Prepare the journal entries for income taxes during 1981 that fully account for the changes in the three balance sheet accounts as listed above.

**20.48** Refer to the Simplified Funds Statement for a Period in Exhibit 4.13 (Question **4.15**). Nine of the lines in the statement are numbered. Line (2) should be expanded to say "Additions for Expenses and Other Charges against Income Not Using Funds," and line (3) should be expanded to say "Subtractions for Revenues and Other Credits to Income Not Producing Funds from Operations." Ignore the unnumbered lines in responding to the questions below.

Assume that the accounting cycle is complete for the period and that all of the financial statements have been prepared. Then it is discovered that a transaction has been overlooked. That transaction is recorded in the accounts and all of the financial statements are corrected. Define funds as working capital. For each of the following transactions, indicate which of the numbered lines of the funds statement is affected and by how much. Assume an income tax rate of 40 percent of taxable income.

a. Pretax financial statement income is $200,000. Depreciation claimed on the tax return exceeds depreciation expense on the financial statements by $50,000. An entry is made to record income tax expense.

b. Pretax financial statement income is $300,000 and the income tax rate is 40 percent of taxable income. Warranty deductions allowed on the tax return are less than warranty expense on the financial statements by $40,000. An entry is made to record income tax expense.

c. Municipal bond interest of $10,000 is received. No previous entry had been made for this interest. All effects of this transaction, including income tax effects, if any, are recorded.

d. During the year, assets qualifying for the investment credit are acquired. The assets have a 10-year life, and tax credits of $10,000 are realized. The flow-through method is used. Record the effects of the investment credit for the year the assets are acquired.

e.  Refer to the data in part **d** and record the effects of the investment credit for the year after the assets are acquired.

f.  Refer to the data in part **d,** but assume now that the deferral method is used. Record the effects of the investment credit for the year the assets are acquired.

g.  Refer to the data in part **d,** but assume now that the deferral method is used. Record the effects for the year after the assets are acquired.

**20.49**  (Adapted from CPA Examination.) The Mikis Company has supplied you with information regarding its 1981 income tax expense for financial statement reporting as follows:

The provision for current income taxes (exclusive of investment tax credits) was $600,000 for the year ended December 31, 1981. Mikis made estimated tax payments of $550,000 during 1981.

Investment tax credits of $100,000 arising from fixed assets put into service in 1981 were taken for income tax reporting in 1981. Mikis defers investment tax credits and amortizes them to income over the productive life of the related assets for financial statement reporting. Unamortized deferred investment tax credits amounted to $400,000 at December 31, 1981, and $375,000 at December 31, 1980.

Mikis generally depreciates fixed assets using the straight-line method for financial statement reporting and various accelerated methods for income tax reporting. During 1981 depreciation on fixed assets amounted to $900,000 for financial statement reporting and $950,000 for income tax reporting. Commitments for the purchase of fixed assets amounted to $450,000 at December 31, 1981. Such fixed assets will be subject to an investment tax credit of 10 percent.

For financial statement reporting, Mikis has accrued estimated losses from product warranty contracts prior to their occurrence. For income tax reporting, no deduction is taken until payments are made. At December 31, 1980, accrued estimated losses of $200,000 were included in the liability section of Mikis' balance sheet. Based on the latest available information, Mikis estimates that this figure should be 30 percent higher at December 31, 1981. Payments of $250,000 were made in 1981.

In 1977, Mikis acquired another company for cash. Goodwill resulting from this transaction was $800,000 and is being amortized over a 40-year period for financial statement reporting. The amortization is not deductible for income tax reporting.

Mikis has a wholly owned subsidiary. In 1981, this subsidiary had net income of $100,000. No earnings were remitted to Mikis in 1981. Mikis anticipates that $70,000 of these earnings will be retained from growth and diversification. Dividends paid are subject to the 85 percent dividend exclusion (see Exhibit 20.1).

Premiums paid on officers' life insurance amounted to $80,000 in 1981. These premiums are not deductible for income tax reporting.

Assume that the U.S. income tax rate was 48 percent.

a.  What amounts should be shown for **(1)** provision for current income taxes; **(2)** provision for deferred income taxes; and **(3)** investment tax credits recognized in Mikis' income statement for the year ended December 31, 1981? Show supporting computations in good form.

b.  Identify any information in the fact situation that was not used to determine the answer to **(1),** and explain why this information was not used.

**20.50**  (Adapted from CPA Examination.) Your firm has been appointed to examine the financial statements of Clark Engineering, Inc. (CEI) for the 2 years ended December 31, 1981, in conjunction with an application for a bank loan. CEI was formed on January 2, 1973, by the nontaxable incorporation of the Clark family partnership.

Early in the engagement you learned that the controller was unfamiliar with income tax accounting and that no tax allocations have been recorded.

During the examination considerable information was gathered from the accounting records and client employees regarding interperiod tax allocation. This information has been audited and is as follows (with dollar amounts rounded to the nearest $100):

1. CEI uses the direct write-off method for tax purposes and the allowance method for book purposes. The balance of the Allowance for Doubtful Receivables account at December 31, 1979, was $62,000. Following is a schedule of accounts written off and the corresponding year(s) in which the related sales were made.

| Year(s) in Which Sales Were Made | Year in Which Accounts Written Off | |
|---|---|---|
| | 1981 | 1980 |
| 1979 and Prior | $19,800 | $29,000 |
| 1980 | 7,200 | — |
| 1981 | — | — |
| | $27,000 | $29,000 |

The following is a schedule of changes in the Allowance for Doubtful Receivables account for the 2 years ended December 31, 1981:

| | Year Ended December 31 | |
|---|---|---|
| | 1981 | 1980 |
| Balance at Beginning of Year | $66,000 | $62,000 |
| Accounts Written Off during the Year | (27,000) | (29,000) |
| Provision for Estimated Uncollectibles | 38,000 | 33,000 |
| Balance at End of Year | $77,000 | 66,000 |

2. Following is a reconciliation between net income per books and taxable income:

| | Year Ended December 31 | |
|---|---|---|
| | 1981 | 1980 |
| 1. Net Income per Books | $333,100 | $262,800 |
| 2. Federal Income Tax Payable during Year | 182,300 | 236,800 |
| 3. Taxable Income Not Recorded on the Books This Year: | | |
| Deferred Sales Commissions | 10,000 | |
| 4. Expenses Recorded on the Books This Year Not Deducted on the Tax Return: | | |
| (a) Allowance for Doubtful Receivables | 11,000 | 4,000 |
| (b) Amortization of Goodwill | 8,000 | 8,000 |
| 5. Total of Lines 1 through 4 | 544,400 | 511,600 |
| 6. Income Recorded on the Books This Year Not Included on the Tax Return: | | |
| Tax-Exempt Interest—Watertown 5% Municipal Bonds | 5,000 | |
| 7. Deductions on the Tax Return Not Charged against Book Income this Year: | | |
| Depreciation | 83,700 | 38,000 |
| 8. Total of Lines 6 and 7 | 88,700 | 38,000 |
| 9. Taxable Income (Line 5 Less Line 8) | $455,700 | $473,600 |

3. Assume that income tax rates are as follows:

   1979 and prior years: 60 percent

   1980: 50 percent

   1981: 40 percent

4. In December 1981, CEI entered into a contract to serve as distributor for Brown Manufacturer, Inc.'s engineering products. The contract became effective December 31, 1981, and $10,000 of advance commissions on the contract were received and deposited on December 31, 1981. Because the commissions had not been earned, they were accounted for as a deferred credit to income on the balance sheet at December 31, 1981.

5. Goodwill represents the excess of cost over fair value of the net tangible assets of a retiring competitor that were acquired for cash on January 2, 1976. The original balance was $80,000.

6. Depreciation on plant assets transferred at incorporation and acquisitions through December 31, 1979, have been accounted for on a straight-line basis for both financial and tax reporting. Beginning in 1980, all additions of machinery and equipment have been depreciated using ACRS for tax reporting but the straight-line method for financial reporting. Company policy is to take a full year's depreciation in the year of acquisition and none in the year of retirement. There have been no sales, trade-ins, or retirements since incorporation. Exhibit 20.13 is a schedule disclosing significant information about depreciable property and related depreciation:

---

*Exhibit 20.13*
**Clark Engineering, Inc.**

| Asset | Cost | Life | Annual Straight-Line Amount* | ACRS Depreciation 1981 | ACRS Depreciation 1980 | Depreciation Taken through December 31, 1979 |
|---|---|---|---|---|---|---|
| Buildings | $1,190,000 | 20 & 50 years | $31,000 | | | $380,000 |
| Machinery and Equipment: | | | | | | |
| Transferred at Incorporation or Acquired through December 31, 1979 | 834,000 | Various | 45,900 | | | 495,800 |
| Acquisitions since December 31, 1979: | | | | | | |
| 1980 | 267,000 | 6 years | 38,000 | $ 63,700 | $ 76,000 | |
| 1981 | 395,000 | 6 years | 58,000 | 116,000 | | |
| Total Asset Cost | $2,686,000 | | | | | |

**Total Depreciation Expense**

| | 1981 | 1980 | Through December 31, 1979 |
|---|---|---|---|
| For Book Purposes | $172,900 | $114,900 | $875,800 |
| For Tax Purposes | $256,600 | $152,900 | $875,800 |

*After giving appropriate consideration to salvage value.

---

a. Prepare a schedule calculating (1) the balance of deferred income taxes at December 31, 1980 and 1981, and (2) the amount of the timing differences between actual income tax payable and financial income tax expense for 1980 and 1981. Round all calculations to the nearest $100. Assume that the gross-change method of providing for deferred taxes is used.

b. Independent of your solution to part **a** and assuming data shown below, prepare the section of the income statement beginning with pretax accounting income to disclose properly income tax expense for the years ended December 31, 1981 and 1980.

|  | **1981** | **1980** |
|---|---|---|
| Pretax Accounting Income | $480,400 | $465,600 |
| Taxes Payable Currently | 182,300 | 236,800 |
| Year's Net Timing Difference—Dr. (Cr.) | 28,100 | (24,500) |
| Balance of Deferred Tax at End of Year—Dr. (Cr.) | (44,200) | (16,100) |

**20.51** (Adapted from CPA Examination.) You have been retained to assist the office manager of Dom Corp. in developing certain year-end financial information for the corporation. Dom is a domestic corporation, files its tax return on the accrual basis, and is engaged in the manufacture of office supplies and furniture. Dom's accounts had been adjusted properly as of December 31, 1980.

Dom's trial balance before adjustment at December 31, 1981, the close of its fiscal year, follows:

|  | **Debit** | **Credit** |
|---|---|---|
| Cash | $ 45,120 | |
| Inventory | 70,000 | |
| Installment Accounts Receivable | 85,000 | |
| Note Receivable | 20,000 | |
| Deferred Income Tax | 37,880 | |
| Fixed Assets (net of depreciation) | 178,000 | |
| Investment in Serv Corp. Stock | 260,000 | |
| Accounts Payable | | $ 31,000 |
| Note Payable | | 100,000 |
| Rental Fees Received in Advance | | 6,000 |
| Capital Stock | | 250,000 |
| Retained Earnings | | 135,000 |
| Sales | | 600,000 |
| Cost of Goods Sold | 360,000 | |
| Operating Expenses | 105,000 | |
| Dividend Revenue—Serv Corp. | | 15,000 |
| Rental Revenue | | 24,000 |
| Total | $1,161,000 | $1,161,000 |

The following information has been gathered from the accounting records and verified to be correct.

1. **Installment accounts receivable** Income on installment sales is included in the income tax return in the period of collection rather than in the period of sale.

| | | **Installment Receivables** | |
|---|---|---|---|
| **Sales** | **Gross-Profit Percentage** | **December 31, 1980** | **December 31, 1981** |
| 1979 | 25% | $10,000 | — |
| 1980 | 30 | 41,000 | $25,000 |
| 1981 | 40 | — | 60,000 |

2. **Note receivable** The note was received on July 1, 1981, in exchange for the sale of office desks and was recorded in the sales account at the face amount. The note is noninterest bearing and matures July 1, 1983. The face amount of the note does not reasonably represent the present value of the consideration given. The present value of $1.00, due at the

end of two periods in the future, discounted at the prevailing rate of 6 percent, is $.89 (rounded to two decimal places).

3. **Deferred income tax** The only entry charged to this account during 1981 is a debit of $43,000 representing payments on the 1981 estimated tax liability.

4. **Investment in Serv Corp. stock** On January 2, 1981, Dom Corp. purchased 80 percent of the outstanding common stock of Serv Corp. for $260,000 cash. Serv Corp. is a domestic corporation and an accrual basis taxpayer. It sells insurance. Because the investor and investee corporations are not economically related, preparation of consolidated statements is not deemed appropriate.

   On the date of acquisition, the recorded net assets of Serv Corp. had a fair market value and a book value of $230,000. Any goodwill arising from the acquisition is to be amortized over 20 years using the straight-line method.

   The 1981 calendar-year earnings per the Serv Corp. income statement were $55,000. Dividend income per the Dom Corp. trial balance represents actual cash distributions received in 1981. There is no intention to reinvest undistributed earnings of Serv Corp. indefinitely in the future.

5. **Note payable** The note is noninterest bearing and was issued in exchange for cash borrowed from a supplier. It matures 5 years from October 1, 1981. The loan was negotiated in connection with a $100,000 purchase contract for the supplier's product, at prices above the prevailing market rate. The present value of $1.00 due at the end of five periods in the future, discounted at the prevailing rate of 6 percent, is $.75 (rounded to two decimal places).

   Seventy-five percent of the merchandise purchased under this contract is included in cost of goods sold, and 25 percent is included in the ending inventory.

6. **Rental fees received in advance** This represents rent received in advance from a tenant who occupies a portion of the building owned by Dom Corp. There is unrestricted use of the funds. The rent is $2,000 per month, and 1 month's rent was received in advance at the end of 1980 for January 1981.

   a. Prepare a comparative schedule of pretax accounting income and taxable income, including supporting schedules of sales, cost of goods sold, present-value computations, and investment income. For financial accounting purposes, recognize all present-value concepts where indicated but assume that this method is not acceptable for income tax purposes. Discounts and/or premiums should be amortized on the straight-line basis. Do not impute any interest in computing taxable income.

   b. Independent of your answer to part **a**, prepare a schedule analyzing deferred income taxes for the year ended December 31, 1981, showing the amount of deferred tax attributable to each variation between pretax accounting income and taxable income, including the reversal of any timing differences that originated in a prior period. Differences arising from the application of present-value concepts should be treated as timing differences. Assume that the effective tax rate is 40 percent for all computations.

20.52 This problem explores the accounting for the purchase and sale of tax benefits using data presented in paragraph 20.82 in the chapter. Recall that Trans National Airlines (TNA) purchases equipment costing $100,000 on January 1, Year 1. The equipment has a 5-year ACRS life and qualifies for a 10-percent investment tax credit. TNA "sells" the tax benefits of the investment credit and ACRS deductions to MBI, Inc., for $35,242. The "sale" takes place using a sale and leaseback arrangement.

a. Give the journal entry made by the seller for the receipt of $35,242 on January 1, Year 1, in accordance with the procedure outlined in paragraph 20.84

b. Give the journal entry made by the buyer for the payment of the $35,242 on January 1, Year 1, in accordance with the procedure outlined in paragraph 20.84.

c. Assume that the tax savings from the investment credit and ACRS deductions at the end of each of the next five years are as follows:

| End of Year | Tax Savings |
|---|---|
| 1 | 16,900 |
| 2 | 10,120 |
| 3 | 9,660 |
| 4 | 9,660 |
| 5 | 9,660 |

The interest rate that will discount these tax savings to $35,242 is approximately 20 percent. Complete the following table showing the computation of income and return of investment for each of the 5 years.

| Investment- Beginning of Year (1) | Tax Savings Realized (2) | Income- 20% of Column (1) (3) | Return of Invest- ment (4) | Investment- End of Year (5) |
|---|---|---|---|---|
| $35,242 | $16,900 | | | $25,390 |
| 25,390 | 10,120 | | | 20,348 |
| 20,348 | 9,660 | | | 14,758 |
| 14,758 | 9,660 | | | 8,050 |
| 8,050 | 9,660 | | | |

*Part Four*
**Shareholders' Equity**

# Chapter 21
# *Shareholders' Equity: Capital Transactions*

21.1   The economic resources of a firm come essentially from two major sources. Nonowners, or creditors, provide funds; these sources of funds are shown on the balance sheet as *liabilities*. Owners also provide funds; the sources of these funds are shown on the balance sheet as *owners' equity*. Because ownership in a corporation is evidenced by shares of stock, the owners' equity is referred to as shareholders' equity or stockholders' equity.

21.2   A distinction is made in accounting for shareholders' equity between (1) capital contributions by owners and (2) earnings generated from such capital. This distinction has more legal than economic significance. The claims of owners on the assets of a firm are measured by the total of shareholders' equity, regardless of the specific accounts (common stock, retained earnings) to which this total is allocated. The accounting for shareholders' equity, however, has evolved from various legal considerations. The distinction between capital and earnings generated from capital therefore presents a useful scheme for organizing the study of shareholders' equity. This chapter considers the accounting for the issue and reacquisition of shares. Chapter 22 discusses accounting for dilutive securities and the calculation of earnings per share. Chapter 23 focuses on accounting for retained earnings.

## Corporate Form and Ownership

This chapter is concerned exclusively with 21.3 corporations. The accounting for other types of business entities (sole proprietorships, partnerships) is discussed in advanced accounting principles texts. The corporation is a widely used form of business organization in the United States for at least two major reasons:

1. It facilitates the raising of capital through several features. The corporation raises funds by issuing shares of stock, and the public can acquire shares in varying amounts. Individual investments can range from a few dollars to hundreds of millions of dollars. The corporate form provides the shareholder with limited liability. That is, should the corporation become insolvent, creditors' claims are limited to the assets of the corporate entity. The assets of the individual owners are not subject to the claims of the corporation's creditors. On the other hand, creditors of partnerships and sole proprietorships have a claim on both the owners' personal and business assets in settlement of such firms' debts.

2. It permits the continuity of management and operations despite ongoing changes in ownership. Shares of stock can be sold or

otherwise transferred by current owners to others without affecting the continuity of operations. In other types of business entities, withdrawal of an owner or partner usually brings the entity to an end.

21.4 The corporation is a legal entity separate from its owners. Capital contributions are made by individuals or other entities under a contract between themselves and the corporation. The rights and obligations of a shareholder are determined by:

**1.** The corporation laws of the state in which incorporation takes place.

**2.** The articles of incorporation, or *charter*. This is the agreement between the firm and the state in which the business is incorporated. The enterprise is granted the privilege of operating as a corporation for certain stated purposes and of obtaining its capital through the issue of shares of stock.

**3.** The bylaws of the corporation. Bylaws are adopted by the board of directors and act as the rules and regulations under which the internal affairs of the corporation are conducted.

**4.** The stock contract. Each type of capital stock has its own provisions as to such matters as voting, sharing in earnings, distribution of earnings, and sharing in assets in case of dissolution.

## Classes of Shares

21.5 Corporations are often authorized to issue more than one class of shares, each representing ownership in the business. Most shares issued are either *common* or *preferred*. Occasionally, there may be several classes of common or preferred shares. Each share of stock has the same rights and privileges as every other share of the same class. All corporations must have at least one class of shares. They are usually called "common shares," but they may be designated by another name, such as Class A shares. Preferred shares may, but need not, be issued by a corporation.

21.6 *Common* shares have a residual claim to earnings of the corporation after commitments to preferred shareholders have been satisfied. Frequently, common shares are the only voting shares of the company. In the event of corporate dissolution, all of the proceeds of asset disposition, after settling the claims of creditors and required distributions to preferred shareholders, are distributable to the common shareholders.

21.7 *Preferred stock* is granted special privileges. Although these features vary considerably from issue to issue, a preferred share usually entitles its holder to dividends at a certain rate, which must be paid before dividends can be paid to common shareholders. Sometimes, though, these dividends may be postponed or omitted, according to the provisions of the issue. If the preferred dividends are *cumulative*, then all current and previously postponed dividends must be paid before any dividends can be paid on common shares. Most preferred shares are cumulative.

21.8 Preferred stock may also be *participating*. Participating preferred stock and common stock share in any dividends paid after a dividend equal to the preferred dividend rate has been paid to both preferred and common shareholders. The participation in any excess dividends is frequently based on the total par value of the capital contributed by each class of stock. For example, assume that 6-percent, participating preferred stock with a total par value of $100,000, and common stock with a total par value of $200,000 are outstanding. Dividends of $30,000 are declared. The dividends are paid as follows:

| | |
|---|---:|
| To Participating Preferred: .06 × $100,000. | $ 6,000 |
| To Common: .06 × $200,000 ........... | 12,000 |
| Total ......................... | $18,000 |
| Excess: $30,000 − $18,000 ............. | $12,000 |
| Allocated to: | |
| Preferred: $100,000/$300,000 × | |
| $12,000 ...................... | $ 4,000 |
| Common: $200,000/$300,000 × | |
| $12,000 ...................... | $ 8,000 |

The participating feature gives the preferred stock attributes of both preferred and common stock, because preferred shareholders receive a certain minimum dividend and can share in all dividends paid in excess of some specified amount.

21.9 Most preferred shares issued by corporations in recent years have been *callable*. Callable preferred shares may be reacquired by the corporation at a specified price, which will vary according to a predetermined time schedule. Callability is commonly thought to be for the benefit of the corporation. If sufficient financing is otherwise available, especially if that alternative financing is available at a lower cost than the rate previously fixed for the preferred shares, a corporation may wish to reduce the relatively fixed commitment of preferred dividends (as compared to common). It can do so by calling the preferred shares. The corporation has the option to call the shares. This callable feature is valuable to the corporation but makes the shares less attractive to potential owners. Other things being equal, noncallable shares will be issued for a higher price than will callable shares. Thus, the degree to which the corporation benefits by making shares callable is not clearcut.

21.10 Some preferred shares issued in recent years have been subject to mandatory redemption requirements. These preferred shares must be redeemed at specified times and in specified amounts. In contrast, callable preferred shares are redeemable at the option of the issuer. The mandatory redemption feature gives these preferred shares attributes of long-term debt. Both types of securities have fixed maturity dates. *Accounting Series Release No. 268*\* requires that preferred shares with a mandatory redemption requirement be disclosed separately from other preferred and common shares and that the amount of capital contributed by preferred shareholders with mandatory requirements be excluded from total shareholders' equity. *ASR No. 268,* however, does not require that these preferred shares be included among long-term debt on the balance sheet. If they are not,

the amount appears between liabilities and owners' equity. The notes to the financial statements must disclose the redemption terms and the amount and timing of required redemptions during the succeeding 5 years.

Preferred shares with a conversion feature 21.11 have become increasingly popular. *Convertible preferred shares* may be converted into a specified amount of common shares at specified times by their owner. The conversion privilege may appear advantageous to both the individual shareholder and the corporation. The preferred shareholder enjoys the security of a relatively assured dividend as long as the shares are held. The shareholder also has the opportunity to realize capital appreciation by converting the shares into common stock if the market price of the common shares rises sufficiently. Because of this feature, the change in the market price of convertible preferred shares will often parallel changes in the market price of the common shares.

The firm may also benefit from the conversion option. By including it in the issue, the company is usually able to specify a lower dividend rate on the preferred than otherwise would have been required to issue the shares for a given price.

A major consideration in the issue of preferred shares is that dividends are not deductible in calculating taxable income. However, bond interest is deductible. Thus, the aftertax cost of borrowing may be less than the aftertax cost of issuing preferred shares, even though the interest rate on the bonds is higher than the preferred stock dividend rate.

Separate accounts are used for each class 21.14 of shares. On the balance sheet, each class of shares is shown separately, often with a short description of the major features of the shares. Customarily, preferred shares are listed before common shares on the balance sheet.

## Par Value and No-Par Shares

Shares of capital stock often have a *par,* or 21.15 nominal, value per share specified in the ar-

---

\**Accounting Series Release No. 268,* SEC (1979).

ticles of incorporation and printed on the face of the stock certificates. The par value of common stock has some legal significance but little economic significance. For legal reasons, accountants separate par value from other contributed capital amounts. Shares assigned a certain par value will almost always sell on the stock market at a price different from par. Also, *the book value of a share of common stock*—the total common shareholders' equity divided by the number of shares outstanding—is almost always greater than the par value of the shares, in part because retained earnings are usually positive. The par value rarely denotes the worth of the shares, except perhaps at the date of original issue. Readers of financial statements can usually assume merely that the par value of all common shares is the minimum investment that has been made by the shareholders in the corporation. Par value of preferred stock is more meaningful. The dividend rate specified in the preferred stock contract (for example, 8 percent) is almost always based on par value. Any preference as to assets in liquidation that preferred shareholders may have is usually related to the par value of the preferred shares.

21.16 Although preferred shares usually have a par value, common shares without a par value are widely used. When no-par-value shares are issued, customary practice assigns a *stated* value to the no-par shares, which has much the same effect as assigning the shares a par value. Some state corporation laws require the directors to assign a stated value to each no-par share. The stated value can usually be changed from time to time at the discretion of the board of directors.

## Accounting for the Issue of Capital Stock

21.17 Capital stock, either preferred or common, may be issued for cash or for a noncash consideration. In some cases, capital stock is issued by a subscription agreement or as part of a package issue of securities. The sections that follow discuss the accounting for each of these types of stock issues.

## Issue for Cash Consideration

Capital stock is most commonly issued for cash. In offering shares for sale to the public, corporations usually incur legal, accounting, administrative, and other costs. All such costs should theoretically be netted against the cash received in recording the issuance of the stock on the books. This accounting treatment is consistent with the accounting for the acquisition of inventory or fixed assets, where all costs incurred in preparing these assets for their intended uses are capitalized as part of the cost of the assets. This treatment of issuance costs also permits the distinction between capital and earnings generated from capital to be maintained. Most firms, however, treat issue costs as expenses of the period in which such costs are incurred. This accounting treatment probably follows from the immediate deductibility of such costs in reporting taxable income.  21.18

**Contributions in Excess of Par or Stated Value**  Capital stock, particularly common stock, is usually issued for an amount greater than its par or stated value. As discussed earlier, the par or stated value of a share of stock is set to satisfy certain legal requirements of the state of incorporation and usually bears no relationship to the economic value of the shares. For example, individuals who purchase newly issued shares from a corporation some years after the corporation began operations normally pay a higher price per share to compensate current shareholders for the additional capital that has been accumulated by the retention of earnings and the increase in value of the firm's assets. Even the original shareholders of a firm may have contributed more per share than the par or stated value.  21.19

One approach to recording the issue of capital stock for more than its par or stated value is to debit Cash and credit Preferred  21.20

Stock or Common Stock for the cash received. In this way, the capital contributed by each class of owner may be recorded in a single account.

21.21    One awkward convention in accounting requires that the amount received from issuing stock be allocated between the par or stated value of the shares and amounts received in excess of par or stated value. This convention evolved out of a desire to disclose the *legal capital* of a firm. In an effort to protect creditors, state corporation laws stipulate that a corporation cannot distribute dividends to shareholders from legal capital. In many states, legal capital was initially defined as the aggregate par or stated value of the outstanding shares of stock. Accountants attempted to report this legal capital amount by crediting Preferred Stock or Common Stock for the par or stated value of shares issued. Additional Paid-in Capital or Capital Contributed in Excess of Par or Stated Value was credited for amounts received in excess of par or stated value of shares issued. The definition of legal capital now, however, varies widely among the states. In some states it includes only the par or stated values of the shares. In others, it also includes part or all of the amounts received in excess of par or stated value. The result is that the amount disclosed in the balance sheet as the aggregate par or stated value of outstanding shares is not likely to represent the legal capital of the firm. If information about the amount of legal capital is considered useful, then disclosure of the amount in a note to the financial statements seems a more effective mechanism than segregating amounts in the body of the balance sheet.

21.22    The journal entry to record the issue of common (or preferred) stock for cash in an amount greater than par or stated value is

| | | |
|---|---|---|
| Cash | | X |
| Common (or Preferred) Stock—Par (or Stated) Value | | Y |
| Additional Paid-in Capital | | X-Y |

21.23    The account credited for amounts received in excess of par or stated value was formerly labeled "Capital Surplus." This terminology is no longer considered acceptable,* because it suggests an excess available for distribution to owners. The account titles Additional Paid-in Capital or Capital Contributed in Excess of Par or Stated Value are more commonly used.

Because shares ordinarily have no maturity date, the Additional Paid-in Capital account remains on the books indefinitely as a partial measure of contributions by shareholders. This account differs from Premium on Bonds, considered in Chapter 17, in two respects. Additional Paid-in Capital appears in the shareholders' equity section of the balance sheet, whereas Premium on Bonds is shown in the liability section; Additional Paid-in Capital is not amortized, whereas Premium on Bonds is amortized over the life of the bonds to which the premium relates.    21.24

## Issue for Noncash Consideration

Capital stock may be issued for property, property rights, intangible assets, or for services. A question arises as to the valuation to be placed on such transactions. *Accounting Research Bulletin No. 43*† establishes the guideline that the transaction should be recorded based either on the value of the shares issued or on the value of the goods or services received, whichever is more clearly determinable. For a large, publicly held corporation, the market value of the shares issued will probably be more readily determinable. For a small, closely held corporation, the value of the consideration received may be the better indicator.    21.25

Particularly troublesome valuation problems arise when shares are issued to promoters of a newly formed corporation. A market value for neither the shares nor for the services may be readily apparent. Under these circumstances, the Securities and Exchange Commission may require that no    21.26

---

*Accounting Research Bulletin No. 43,* AICPA (1953), chap. 1A.

†Ibid., chap. 5.

value be assigned to the shares issued for the services received.

## Subscriptions for Capital Stock

21.27 Corporations, particularly those in the formative stage, may issue subscriptions to purchase shares of their stock to potential investors. Investors typically make a down payment in cash and sign a note agreeing to pay the remainder of the purchase price at some later date or on an installment basis. The shares of stock are not issued until the full purchase price has been received.

21.28 An important question involving shares sold on a subscription basis is whether recognition should be given only to the cash received or to the full amount of the contract price. The response to this question depends on whether the issuance of subscriptions to prospective shareholders is considered an accounting event.

21.29 Some accountants argue that, except for the down payment, an accounting event has not occurred. The subscription arrangement involves merely an unperformed (executory) contract by both parties. Shares of stock will be issued in the future if all payments are made as prescribed. Until the amounts are received and shares are issued, no recognition should be given to the subscription arrangement. Amounts received are credited either to a liability or a shareholders' equity account, depending on whether amounts received are refundable (liability) or forfeited (shareholders' equity) if the full subscription price is not received.

21.30 Other accountants argue that the subscription arrangement should be recognized as an accounting event. An agreement has been reached that affects the financial position of the firm. An assessment of the potential investors' financial conditions permits the firm to estimate the amount of cash that will be received and the probability that shares will be issued.

21.31 To illustrate the accounting entries made if the full stock subscription price is recognized, assume that subscriptions are received for the purchases of 10,000 shares of $1-par-value common stock for $6 per share.

Subscribers make a down payment of $2 per share and agree to pay the remainder of the purchase price 6 months later. The entry to record this transaction is

| | | |
|---|---|---|
| Cash | 20,000 | |
| Stock Subscriptions Receivable | 40,000 | |
|     Common Stock—Subscribed | | 10,000 |
|     Additional Paid-in Capital— | | |
|         Subscribed Common Stock | | 50,000 |

When the remainder of the purchase price is received, two entries are made:

| | | |
|---|---|---|
| Cash | 40,000 | |
|     Stock Subscriptions | | |
|         Receivable | | 40,000 |

| | | |
|---|---|---|
| Common Stock—Subscribed | 10,000 | |
| Additional Paid-in Capital— | | |
|     Subscribed Common Stock | 50,000 | |
|         Common Stock | | 10,000 |
|         Additional Paid-in Capital | | 50,000 |

21.32 It is not clear whether or not stock subscriptions give rise to an accounting event under generally accepted accounting principles. Recall from Chapter 3 that events are recognized as accounting events if they **(1)** have already occurred, **(2)** affect the financial position of individual business entities, and **(3)** can be measured with a reasonable degree of precision.* Stock subscriptions exhibit many of the same characteristics as unfilled purchase orders and sales agreements, which are not recognized as accounting events. The impact of these events on the financial position of the firm will occur in the future when goods and cash are exchanged. Similar arguments can be made in the case of stock subscriptions. The Securities and Exchange Commission has consistently maintained that receivables for capital stock subscriptions should not be shown as assets at a given balance sheet date unless the receivable has been collected prior to the date the financial statements are issued. The receivable must be shown as a contra account to shareholders' equity. This method

---

*Financial Accounting Standards Board, *Statement of Financial Accounting Concepts No. 1* (1978), pars. 17–21.

of disclosure results in a zero net effect on assets, liabilities, and shareholders' equity. The same results could be achieved by not recording the subscription in the accounts but, instead, disclosing the existence of the subscription arrangement in a note to the financial statements.

### Issue in a Package

21.33   Two or more securities may be issued as a unit. For example, a unit might consist of one share of common stock, one share of convertible preferred stock, and one nonconvertible $100 bond sold for a unit price of $200. The unit price should be allocated to each security based on the relative market values of the securities at the time of issue. For example, if the common stock and preferred stock were selling for $80 and $40, respectively, and bonds with interest rates, terms, and other characteristics similar to the bond in the package were selling at par, then the $200 issue price of the unit would be allocated among the securities based on the market value of each security as a percentage of the combined market value of the three securities ($220 = $80 + $40 + $100). The allocation is as follows:

| | |
|---|---:|
| Common Stock: $80/$220 × $200 ...... | $ 72.73 |
| Preferred Stock: $40/$220 × $200 ...... | 36.36 |
| Bond: $100/$220 × $200 .......... | 90.91 |
| Total ........................ | $200.00 |

### Donated Capital

21.34   Municipalities and governmental agencies may grant a corporation certain rights or property as an inducement to locate manufacturing or other operations in a particular area. The grant is usually in the form of an outright donation or a donation contingent upon the employment of a specified number of individuals or occupancy for a specified period of time.

21.35   Although the corporation does not issue shares of capital stock for such donated property or rights, the donation is a source of capital to the firm. If no legal obligation exists to return the property, then the dona-

tion must accrue to the benefit of the shareholders of the firm.

21.36   There are two viewpoints as to the accounting for donated capital. One view holds that there is no acquisition cost to the firm of donated capital and, therefore, no asset should be recognized. Any benefits from capital donations will be realized through lower costs in the current and future periods.

21.37   Opponents of this view argue that an exchange has taken place—an economic resource has been received in exchange for a promise to locate in a particular area and satisfy certain employment or other conditions—and that this exchange gives rise to an accounting event. The exchange should be measured based on the market value of the property or rights received.

21.38   Generally accepted accounting principles require that the second approach be followed.* For example, assume that land is donated to a corporation as an inducement to locate a plant in a particular city. The market value of the land, based on prices for comparable industrial plant sites, is found to be $2 million. The journal entry to record the land received as a donation is

| | | |
|---|---:|---:|
| Land ..................... | 2,000,000 | |
| Additional Paid-in | | |
| Capital—Donated | | |
| Capital ............... | | 2,000,000 |

Note the use of the term "donated" instead of "contributed" in the account title. Contributed capital in accounting refers to investments by shareholders.

## Accounting for the Reacquisition of Capital Stock

21.39   Corporations may temporarily or permanently reacquire previously issued stock. The general principle underlying the accounting for reacquired stock is that a firm should not recognize net income from deal-

---

*Accounting Principles Board, *Accounting Principles Board Opinion No. 29* (May 1973), par. 18.

ing in its own stock. "Gains" from reacquiring shares for less than their initial issue price or reselling reacquired shares for more than their reacquisition price represent additional contributions of capital, and not sources of earnings. On the other hand, "losses" of a corporation from dealing in its own stock may be debited directly to Retained Earnings (but not to Net Income) in some cases but are usually charged to Additional Paid-in Capital.*

## Redemption of Preferred Stock

21.40    As discussed earlier, some preferred stock issues are callable by the corporation. By calling, or redeeming, such shares, the corporation eliminates a group of owners who are senior to the common shareholders. It also saves funds that would be required in the future to pay preferred stock dividends.

21.41    The call price for preferred stock is usually greater than the initial issue price. This excess is referred to as a *call premium*. When preferred stock is redeemed, the Preferred Stock and Additional Paid-in Capital—Preferred Stock accounts are debited for an amount equal to the initial issue price. The call premium is usually debited to Retained Earnings, thereby being viewed as an additional dividend on the preferred stock. If the issue is called at an amount less than the issue price, the difference between the issue price and the call price is credited to Additional Paid-in Capital. For example, if preferred stock with a $100,000 par value and a $102,000 initial issue price is called at $105,000, the journal entry is

| | | |
|---|---:|---:|
| Preferred Stock | 100,000 | |
| Additional Paid-in Capital— | | |
| Preferred Stock | 2,000 | |
| Retained Earnings | 3,000 | |
| Cash | | 105,000 |

If the call price is $101,000, the journal entry is

| | | |
|---|---:|---:|
| Preferred Stock | 100,000 | |
| Additional Paid-in Capital— | | |
| Preferred Stock | 2,000 | |
| Additional Paid-in Capital— | | |
| Common Stock | | 1,000 |
| Cash | | 101,000 |

Because all of the preferred stock is being redeemed, it is appropriate that the Additional Paid-in Capital—Preferred Stock account be reduced to zero. The credit of $1,000 to Additional Paid-in Capital accrues to the benefit of the common shareholders.

## Redemption of Common Stock

A firm may likewise reacquire its own shares    21.42 of common stock. In some cases, the reacquired shares are permanently canceled. For example, the shares of a company may be owned 60 percent by the members of a particular family and 40 percent by the general public. The firm may reacquire the 40 percent owned by the general public in an effort to eliminate public ownership (a process referred to as *going private*).

The accounting for redemptions of common stock is somewhat more complicated    21.43 than that for redemptions of preferred stock. The issues involved can perhaps be best understood using an example. Consider the following amounts for a particular firm:

| | |
|---|---:|
| Common Stock, $10 par value, | |
|    1,000,000 shares outstanding | $10,000,000 |
| Additional Paid-in Capital | 1,000,000 |
| Retained Earnings | 15,000,000 |
|    Total Shareholders' Equity | $26,000,000 |

Now assume that 100,000 shares of common stock are redeemed for $18 per share and then canceled. This transaction might be recorded in at least three ways.

---

*The exclusion from net income of "gains" and "losses" from dealings in a firm's own stock can be traced historically to a concern that management, with its access to inside information, might purchase or sell shares at a time which is beneficial to the corporation and detrimental to shareholders and investors. Excluding such "gains" and "losses" from net income supposedly makes management less likely to deal in its own stock as a means of increasing earnings. It is now unlawful for a firm or its management to use inside information to gain advantage in the purchase and sale of its own stock.

**1.** Charge the difference between the redemption price and the par value of the shares redeemed to Additional Paid-in Capital.

| | | |
|---|---|---|
| Common Stock | 1,000,000 | |
| Additional Paid-in Capital | 800,000 | |
| Cash | | 1,800,000 |

**2.** Charge the difference between the redemption price and the par value of the shares redeemed to Retained Earnings.

| | | |
|---|---|---|
| Common Stock | 1,000,000 | |
| Retained Earnings | 800,000 | |
| Cash | | 1,800,000 |

**3.** Charge the difference between the redemption price and the par value of the shares redeemed proportionately to Additional Paid-in Capital and Retained Earnings.

| | | |
|---|---|---|
| Common Stock | 1,000,000 | |
| Additional Paid-in Capital ($1/16$ × $800,000) | 50,000 | |
| Retained Earnings ($15/16$ × $800,000) | 750,000 | |
| Cash | | 1,800,000 |

21.44    The first entry presumes that redemptions of common stock are capital transactions. Any "losses" from such redemptions should be charged to Additional Paid-in Capital until the balance in that account is zero. Only then should Retained Earnings be reduced.

21.45    The second entry assumes that all of the difference between the redemption price and the par value of the shares redeemed is due to the retention of earnings.

21.46    The third entry combines the reasoning of the first two. The increase in market price to $18 a share is due to the accumulated effects of both capital transactions and to the retention of earnings.

21.47    Any of these three methods of accounting for "losses" on redemptions of common stock are permitted under generally accepted accounting principles.* Note that *total* shareholders' equity is the same under all three methods. Only the distribution of

*Accounting Principles Board, *Accounting Principles Board Opinion No. 6* (October 1965), par. 12a.

amounts among shareholders' equity accounts will differ. "Gains" on such redemptions are always credited to Additional Paid-in Capital. This treatment of "gains" is consistent with the convention of not crediting, or increasing, Retained Earnings for dealings in a firm's own shares.

## Reacquisition as Treasury Stock

21.48    Instead of redeeming and then retiring shares of capital stock, a corporation may reacquire its own shares with the intention of reissuing the shares in the future. Such shares are referred to as *treasury stock* or *treasury shares*. Among the more common reasons suggested for the acquisition of capital stock as treasury shares are the following:

**1.** The shares will be issued to employees under stock option plans. By using previously issued, instead of newly issued, shares for this purpose, the proportionate interest of the remaining shareholders is not reduced, or diluted.

**2.** The shares will be used to acquire another firm in a business combination. Comments similar to those above regarding dilution apply here also.

**3.** The shares are acquired as a worthwhile use for idle funds. Treasury shares are not entitled to dividends nor to vote, because they are not considered "outstanding" shares for these purposes.

21.49    Two acceptable methods of accounting for treasury shares are **(1)** the par-value method and **(2)** the cost method.

21.50    **Par-Value Method** Under the par-value method, shares reacquired as treasury stock are accounted for as if the shares had been redeemed and retired. When the shares are reissued, the transaction is recorded as if the shares were newly issued shares. To illustrate the journal entries under the par-value method, assume that the shareholders' equity accounts are the same as in the previous section (Common Stock, $10,000,000; Additional Paid-in Capital, $1,000,000; Retained

Earnings, $15,000,000). Now, 50,000 of the 1,000,000 outstanding shares are acquired as a temporary investment for $18 per share and held as treasury stock. The journal entry to record the acquisition of the shares is as follows:

```
Common Stock ................. 500,000
Additional Paid-in Capital ........ 400,000
    Cash ..................... 900,000
```

Although the shares are not legally retired, this journal entry records the acquisition of treasury shares as if retirement has occurred. There is one important exception, however. "Losses" from the acquisition of treasury stock are debited to Additional Paid-in Capital relating to that class of stock to the extent there is a credit balance in this account. Any excess "losses" are charged to Retained Earnings.*

21.51    Now, assume that the shares are reissued for $22 per share. The journal entry is the same as if the shares were newly issued shares.

```
Cash ........................ 1,100,000
    Common Stock ........... 500,000
    Additional Paid-in Capital .. 600,000
```

Assume, instead, that the shares are reissued for $15 per share. The journal entry is

```
Cash ........................ 750,000
    Common Stock ........... 500,000
    Additional Paid-in Capital ... 250,000
```

21.52    **Cost Method** Under the cost method, either the Treasury Stock—Preferred or the Treasury Stock—Common account is debited with the total amount paid for the shares.

```
Treasury Stock—Common ..... 900,000
    Cash .................... 900,000
```

---

*Ibid., par. 12b. The Board did not state its rationale for permitting "losses" on redemptions of common stock to be charged to retained earnings but requiring that "losses" on *treasury stock transactions* be charged to Additional Paid-in Capital as long as there is a sufficient balance in this account. The Board's reasoning is perhaps an extension of the concern that management will purchase and resell its own stock in the short run in an effort to affect reported earnings and Retained Earnings. Given the legal restrictions against such actions, we find this logic unconvincing.

When the treasury shares are later reissued, Cash is debited with the amount received and the Treasury Stock—Common account is credited. It is unlikely, of course, that the reissue price will precisely equal the amount paid to acquire the treasury shares. If the reissue price is greater than the acquisition price, the excess is credited to Additional Paid-in Capital. For example, the reissue of the treasury shares in this example for $22 per share is recorded as follows:

```
Cash ........................ 1,100,000
    Treasury Stock—Common .     900,000
    Additional Paid-in Capital  ..     200,000
```

If the reissue price is less than the acquisition price, the difference should be debited to Additional Paid-in Capital, as long as there is a sufficient credit balance in that account. If there is not, the additional balancing debit is made directly to Retained Earnings. If the treasury shares are reissued for $15 per share, the journal entry is

```
Cash ........................ 750,000
Additional Paid-in Capital ....... 150,000
    Treasury Stock—Common .     900,000
```

**Balance Sheet Disclosure of Treasury Stock** Under the par-value method, individual shareholders' equity accounts are reduced when treasury shares are acquired. When the cost method is used, the balance in the Treasury Stock—Common account is subtracted from total shareholders' equity (that is, Treasury Stock—Common is a contra account to shareholders' equity). The top panel of Exhibit 21.1 shows the shareholders' equity section of the balance sheet immediately after treasury stock is acquired under the par-value and cost methods. Note that total shareholders' equity is the same under the two methods. The amounts in the individual accounts are, of course, different.     21.53

The middle and lower panels of Exhibit 21.1 show the shareholders' equity after the shares are reissued for $22 per share and $15 per share, respectively. Note that, once the treasury stock is resold, total shareholders' equity and the balance in each shareholders' equity account are the same under the two     21.54

Exhibit 21.1

**Disclosure of Treasury Stock under Par-Value and Cost Methods**

|  | Par-Value Method | Cost Method |
|---|---|---|
| **After Acquisition of Treasury Stock** | | |
| Common Stock | $ 9,500,000 | $10,000,000 |
| Additional Paid-in Capital | 600,000 | 1,000,000 |
| Retained Earnings | 15,000,000 | 15,000,000 |
| Total | $25,100,000 | $26,000,000 |
| Less Cost of Treasury Stock | — | (900,000) |
| Total Shareholders' Equity | $25,100,000 | $25,100,000 |
| **After Reissue for $22 per Share** | | |
| Common Stock | $10,000,000 | $10,000,000 |
| Additional Paid-in Capital | 1,200,000 | 1,200,000 |
| Retained Earnings | 15,000,000 | 15,000,000 |
| Total Shareholders' Equity | $26,200,000 | $26,200,000 |
| **After Reissue for $15 per Share** | | |
| Common Stock | $10,000,000 | $10,000,000 |
| Additional Paid-in Capital | 850,000 | 850,000 |
| Retained Earnings | 15,000,000 | 15,000,000 |
| Total Shareholders' Equity | $25,850,000 | $25,850,000 |

methods of accounting for the treasury stock.

21.55 Some firms classify the Treasury Stock—Common account as an asset. The rationale for this method of presentation is that the treasury shares will provide the firm with future benefits (that is, cash will be received when the shares are reissued). Although inclusion of treasury stock as an asset is permitted under some circumstances,* the rationale for this method of presentation has been questioned. It creates the paradoxical situation of a corporation owning part of itself.

## Donated Stock

21.56 Shareholders may occasionally donate to a corporation a portion of their shares owned. If the shares are then retired, an entry must be made debiting Preferred Stock or Common Stock for the par or stated value of the shares and crediting Additional Paid-in Capital for a like amount. If the shares are held by the corporation with the intention of reissuing them, they are accounted for as treasury shares. Under the par-value method, an entry is made debiting Preferred Stock or Common Stock for the par or stated value of the shares, with the credit to Additional Paid-in Capital—Donated Stock rather than to Cash. When the shares are reissued, the transaction is recorded as if the shares sold were newly issued stock. Under the cost method, the Treasury Stock—Preferred or Treasury Stock—Common account is debited and the Additional Paid-in Capital—Donated Stock account is credited for the market value of the donated shares.† When the shares are reissued, they are accounted for as other treasury stock for which the cost method is used.

---

*Accounting Research Bulletin No. 43, AICPA (1953), chap. 1A, par. 4.

†Accounting Principles Board, Accounting Principles Board Opinion No. 29 (May 1973), par. 18.

## Financial Statement Disclosures of Contributed Capital

21.57 The following types of information regarding contributed capital are usually disclosed, either in the balance sheet or in a note to the financial statements:

**1.** The par value, number of shares authorized, and the number of shares issued for each class of capital stock.

**2.** The nature of the rights of each class of preferred stock (dividend rate, cumulative versus noncumulative status of dividends, convertibility and conversion rates, callability and call price, mandatory redemption requirements, and any voting rights).

**3.** The number of shares held as treasury stock.

21.58 Many of these disclosures are illustrated for International Corporation in Note 18 (in Ex-

hibit A.4) to the financial statements in Appendix A at the back of the book.

Generally accepted accounting principles also require that disclosures be made of the principal reasons for changes in all contributed capital accounts.* The disclosures should indicate the number of shares and dollar amounts involved. Note 18 to the financial statements of International Corporation illustrates the type of disclosures typically made. During 1979 and 1980, the transactions disclosed involve the acquisition of treasury stock and the reissue of the treasury stock to employees and to other individuals in a business combination. During 1981, preferred stock was redeemed, treasury stock was acquired, and treasury stock was reissued to employees. 21.59

---

*Accounting Principles Board, *Accounting Principles Board Opinion No. 12* (December 1967), par. 10.

## Questions and Short Cases

**21.1** Review the meaning of the following concepts or terms discussed in this chapter.

a. Distinction between capital and earnings generated from capital.

b. Corporate charter or articles of incorporation.

c. Corporate bylaws.

d. Capital stock contract.

e. Cumulative versus noncumulative preferred stock.

f. Participating versus nonparticipating preferred stock.

g. Callable versus noncallable preferred stock.

h. Convertible versus nonconvertible preferred stock.

i. Preferred stock with mandatory redemption requirements.

j. Par-value versus no-par-value common stock.

k. Legal capital.

l. Donated capital versus donated stock.

m. Capital Surplus versus Additional Paid-in Capital accounts.

n. Treasury stock.

o. Cost method versus par-value method of accounting for treasury stock.

**21.2** One of the objectives in accounting for shareholders' equity is to distinguish **(1)** capital transactions from **(2)** the generation of earnings from capital. Give three examples from this chapter in which either capital transactions affect retained earnings or earnings transactions affect contributed capital.

**21.3** Compare and contrast the accounts Premium on Bonds Payable and Additional Paid-in Capital—Preferred Stock, both as to the reasons they arise and the accounting methods used.

**21.4**   Compare and contrast the accounting for donated capital and donated stock.

**21.5**   "Our firm acquired 10,000 shares of our own common stock for $12 a share as a short-term investment. When the price increased to $16, the shares were sold for a total gain of $40,000 (= 10,000 × $4). You accountants won't let us recognize this gain in measuring net income for the current year. Yet if shares of another corporation had been purchased, the gain would have been recognized as an element of net income." Comment, including possible reasons for this difference in the accounting treatment of gains on sales of stock.

**21.6**   How is the accounting for the redemptions of common stock similar to and different from the accounting for the acquisition of treasury stock under the par-value method?

**21.7**   Indicate whether or not each of the following is acceptable under generally acceptable accounting principles:
   **a.** Showing treasury stock as an asset.
   **b.** Recognizing "losses" from sale of treasury stock as an element of net income.
   **c.** Crediting "gains" from the resale of treasury stock to Additional Paid-in Capital.
   **d.** Including the market value of donated stock in Retained Earnings.
   **e.** Charging the call premium on preferred stock redeemed to Retained Earnings.
   **f.** Treating Stock Subscriptions Receivable as a negative amount in the shareholders' equity section of the balance sheet.

**21.8**   How will the shareholders' equity section of the balance sheet differ if the par-value method rather than the cost method of accounting for treasury stock is used?

**21.9**   "When common shares are issued in the acquisition of a basket purchase of assets, the assets are recorded at their market values." Do you agree?

**21.10**   Give three examples of owners' equity accounts that might have debit balances (other than expense accounts).

**21.11**   Distinguish between each of the following pairs of items:
   **a.** Callable preferred shares and convertible preferred shares.
   **b.** Callable preferred shares and preferred shares with mandatory redemption requirements.
   **c.** Participating and nonparticipating preferred shares.
   **d.** Cumulative versus noncumulative preferred shares.

## Problems and Exercises

**21.12**   (Adapted from CPA Examination.) Tomasco, Incorporated, began operations in January 1977 and had the following reported net income or loss for each of its first 5 years of operations:

| | | |
|---|---:|---|
| 1977 | $ 150,000 | Loss |
| 1978 | 130,000 | Loss |
| 1979 | 120,000 | Loss |
| 1980 | 250,000 | Income |
| 1981 | 1,000,000 | Income |

At December 31, 1981, the Tomasco capital accounts were as follows:

| | |
|---|---:|
| Common stock, par value $10 per share; authorized 100,000 shares; issued and outstanding 50,000 shares ................................................. | $ 500,000 |
| 4% nonparticipating noncumulative preferred stock, par value $100 per share; authorized, issued, and outstanding 1,000 shares ........................... | 100,000 |
| 8% fully participating cumulative preferred stock, par value $100 per share; authorized, issued, and outstanding 10,000 shares ........................... | 1,000,000 |

Tomasco has never paid a cash or stock dividend. There has been no change in the capital accounts since Tomasco began operations. The appropriate state law permits dividends only from retained earnings.

Prepare a work sheet showing the maximum amount available for cash dividends on December 31, 1981, and how it would be distributable to the holders of the common shares and each of the preferred shares. Show supporting computations in good form.

21.13 The following events relate to shareholders' equity transactions of the Richardson Copper Company during the first year of its existence. Present journal entries for each of the transactions.

a. January 2. Articles of incorporation are filed with the State Corporation Commission. The authorized capital stock consists of 5,000 shares of $100 par-value preferred stock which offers a 5-percent annual dividend, and 50,000 shares of no-par common stock. The original incorporators are issued 1,000 shares of common stock for $20 per share; cash is collected for the shares. A stated value of $5 per share is assigned to the common stock.

b. January 6. 100 shares of common stock are issued to the corporate attorney for services rendered in organizing the corporation. Organization costs are treated as an expense in the first year of operations.

c. January 7. 15,000 shares of common stock are issued for cash at $20 per share.

d. January 8. 2,800 shares of preferred stock are issued for cash at $102.

e. January 10. The tangible assets of Wilson Copper Works are acquired in exchange for 600 shares of preferred stock and 10,000 shares of common stock. The tangible assets acquired have appraised values as follows: inventories, $40,000; land, $45,000; buildings, $80,000; and equipment, $95,000. The market value of the stock is considered more reliable than the appraised values of the assets.

f. July 1. 500 shares of common stock are acquired for $24 a share and held as treasury stock. The cost method is used.

g. August 1. 500 shares of preferred stock are acquired for $101 per share and held as treasury stock. The cost method is used.

h. October 1. 200 shares of common stock held as treasury stock are reissued for $22 per share.

i. December 1. The preferred stock reacquired on August 1 is permanently retired.

21.14 The following events relate to shareholders' equity transactions of West Corporation during its first year of existence. Present journal entries for each of these transactions.

a. January 5. Articles of incorporation are filed with the state. The authorized capital stock consists of 10,000 shares of $100-par-value preferred stock, which offers a 6-percent cumulative dividend, and 50,000 shares of $10-par-value common stock.

b. January 20. 20,000 shares of common stock are issued for $15 per share. Accounting, legal, and other issuing costs of $4,000 are paid in cash. West Corporation treats issue costs as an expense of the period.

c. January 25. Subscriptions are received for 5,000 shares of common stock. Purchasers paid $20,000 down and signed notes agreeing to pay the balance due of $65,000 on October 1, 1981.

d. February 18. Land and building are acquired by issuing 5,000 shares of common stock. The market value of the stock, which is traded in the over-the-counter market, is determined to be $20 per share on February 18. The land has an appraised value of $21,000 and the building has an appraised value of $84,000 on the date of acquisition. The market value of the stock is considered more reliable than the appraised values of the assets.

e. February 20. The city of Plainview has granted West Corporation the right to operate without paying property taxes for its first year, as an inducement to locate in the city. The property taxes that would have been paid are $2,500.

f. March 5. 4,000 shares of preferred stock are issued for $105 per share. Legal, accounting, and other issuing costs of $15,000 are incurred. In settlement of these costs, 750 shares of common stock are issued. The market value of the stock on March 5 is $20 per share.

g. July 15. 1,000 shares of common stock are acquired on the open market for $24 per share and held as treasury stock. The cost method is used.

h. September 1. 500 shares of preferred stock are purchased on the open market for $103 and retired.

i. October 1. Subscribers to 4,900 shares of common stock pay the remaining amounts due of $63,700 and the common shares are issued. Subscribers to the remaining 100 shares forfeit their down payment.

j. November 24. 600 shares of common stock held as treasury stock are sold on the open market for $27 per share. A brokerage commission of $1 per share is deducted, with the net proceeds of $26 per share paid to West Corporation.

k. December 1. A shareholder owning 500 common shares donates them to West Corporation. The shares are retired.

**21.15**   The shareholders' equity of Logue Corporation on December 31, 1980, the end of its first year of operations, is shown in Exhibit 21.2.

---

*Exhibit 21.2*
**Logue Corporation**
**Shareholders' Equity**
**December 31, 1980**

| | |
|---|---|
| Preferred Stock, $100 par value, 5% cumulative dividend, issued for par, callable at $105, 10,000 shares outstanding ......................................... | $1,000,000 |
| Preferred Stock, $100 par value, 3% noncumulative dividend, each share convertible into 5 shares of common stock, 5,000 shares outstanding ..................... | 500,000 |
| Common Stock, $10 par value, 200,000 issued and outstanding .................. | 2,000,000 |
| Additional Paid-in Capital—Convertible Preferred Stock ......................... | 10,000 |
| Additional Paid-in Capital—Common Stock ..................................... | 600,000 |
| Retained Earnings ........................................................... | 80,000 |
| Total Shareholders' Equity ............................................. | $4,190,000 |

---

Record in journal entry form the following transactions during 1981.

Jan. 5.   200 shares of callable preferred stock are called for $105 per share and retired.

Jan. 18.   5,000 shares of common stock are acquired for $16 a share and held as treasury stock. The cost method is used.

Feb. 6.   500 shares of convertible preferred stock are acquired on the open market for $103 per share and retired.

Feb. 22.   2,000 shares of common stock held as treasury stock are reissued for $14 per share.

**21.16**   (Adapted from CPA Examination.) The Amlin Corporation was incorporated on January 1, 1981, with the following authorized capitalization:

20,000 shares of common stock, no par value, stated value of $40 per share.

5,000 shares of 5-percent cumulative preferred stock, par value $10 per share.

During 1981, Amlin issued 12,000 shares of common stock for a total of $600,000, and 3,000 shares of preferred stock at $16 per share. In addition, on December 20, 1981, subscriptions for 1,000 shares of preferred stock were taken at a purchase price of $17 per share. These subscribed shares were paid on January 2, 1982.

**a.** Give the journal entries to record these transactions and events during 1981 and 1982.

**b.** How would your entries in part **a** have differed if the subscribed shares were paid for on July 15, 1982, after the 1981 annual report had been issued?

**21.17**   (Adapted from CPA Examination.) The shareholders' equity of Sola Corporation as of December 31, 1980, was as follows:

| | |
|---|---:|
| Common Stock, $20 par value, authorized 150,000 shares, issued and outstanding 100,000 shares | $2,000,000 |
| Additional Paid-in Capital | 400,000 |
| Retained Earnings | 200,000 |
| Total | $2,600,000 |

On March 1, 1981, Sola reacquired 10,000 shares for $240,000. The following transactions occurred during 1981 with respect to treasury stock acquired:

June 1.          Sold 3,000 of the 10,000 shares for $84,000.
August 1.        Sold 2,000 of the 10,000 shares for $42,000.
September 1.     Retired remaining 5,000 shares.

**a.** Give the journal entries to record the events relating to the treasury stock during 1981, assuming that the cost method is used and that "losses" on retirements are charged to Additional Paid-in Capital.

**b.** How would your answer to part **a** have differed if "losses" on retirements were charged to Retained Earnings?

**c.** How would your answer to part **a** have differed if "losses" on retirements were apportioned between Additional Paid-in Capital and Retained Earnings? The balance in Retained Earnings on September 1, 1981 was $294,000.

**21.18**   The shareholders' equity accounts of Magee Corporation on December 31, 1980, revealed the following:

**Shareholders' Equity**

| | |
|---|---:|
| Common Stock, $10 par value, 50,000 shares issued and outstanding | $500,000 |
| Additional Paid-in Capital | 8,000 |
| Retained Earnings | 200,000 |
| Total Shareholders' Equity | $708,000 |

On January 3, 1981, 2,000 shares of common stock are acquired for $15 a share and held as treasury stock. On February 15, 1981, 500 shares of treasury stock are reissued for $17 a share. On March 28, 1981, 1,000 shares of treasury stock are reissued for $13 a share.

a. Give the journal entries to record these treasury stock transactions using the cost method.

b. Give the journal entries to record these treasury stock transactions using the par-value method.

c. Assuming that net income for 1981 was $15,000 and the $5,000 of dividends were declared and paid, prepare the shareholders' section of the balance sheet of Magee Corporation on December 31, 1981.

21.19　The Worman Company began business on January 1. Its balance sheet on December 31 contains the shareholders' equity section shown below.

---

### Exhibit 21.3
### Worman Company
### Shareholders' Equity
### as of December 31

| | |
|---|---:|
| Capital Stock ($5 par value) | $ 50,000 |
| Additional Paid-in Capital | 252,800 |
| Retained Earnings | 25,000 |
| Less: 600 Shares Held in Treasury | (16,800) |
| Total Shareholders' Equity | $311,000 |

---

During the year, Worman Company engaged in the following capital stock transactions:

1. Issued shares for $30 each.
2. Acquired a block of 1,000 shares for the treasury in a single transaction.
3. Reissued some of the treasury shares.

Assuming that these were the only capital stock transactions during the year, answer the following questions:

a. How many shares were issued for $30 each?

b. What was the price at which the treasury shares were acquired?

c. How many shares were reissued from the block of treasury shares?

d. What was the price at which the treasury shares were reissued?

e. What journal entries must have been made during the year?

21.20　Refer to Exhibit 4.13 in Chapter 4 (Question 4.15), where a simplified funds statement is presented. For each of the transactions below, indicate the number(s) of the line(s) in Exhibit 4.13 that would be affected assuming that funds are defined as working capital. If net income is affected, be sure to indicate if it increases or decreases net income. Ignore income tax effects.

a. Preferred shares are issued for cash.

b. Common shares are exchanged for land, building, and equipment.

c. Treasury shares are acquired on the open market (cost method is used).

d. Treasury shares are acquired on the open market (par-value method is used).

e. Land and building are donated to a firm by its local government.

f. Treasury shares are reissued for a higher price than was paid for them (cost method is used).

g. Preferred shares are redeemed for a larger amount than their initial issue price.

h. A shareholder donates 10,000 shares of common stock to a firm.

i. Subscriptions to 20,000 shares of common stock are received. No cash is exchanged at this time.

j. Refer to part i. Subscribers pay the subscription price and the shares are issued.

k. Shares of convertible preferred stock are exchanged for shares of common stock.

21.21 The information in Exhibit 21.4 relates to the shareholders' equity accounts of Lipscomb Corporation on December 31, 1981. From this information, prepare in good form the shareholders' equity section of the balance sheet for Lipscomb Corporation on December 31, 1981.

21.22 (Adapted from CPA Examination.) During May, Year 1, Gilroy, Inc., was organized with 3,000,000 authorized shares of $10 par value common stock, and 300,000 shares of its common stock were issued for $3,300,000. Net income through December 31, Year 1, was $125,000.

On July 3, Year 2, Gilroy issued 500,000 shares of its common stock for $6,250,000. A 5 percent stock dividend was declared on October 2, Year 2, and issued on November 6, Year 2, to shareholders of record on October 23, Year 2. The market value of the common stock was $11 per share on the declaration date. Gilroy's net income for the year ended December 31, Year 2, was $350,000

During Year 3 Gilroy had the following transactions:

1. In February Gilroy reacquired 30,000 shares of its common stock for $9 per share. Gilroy uses the cost method to account for treasury stock.

2. In June Gilroy sold 15,000 shares of its treasury stock for $12 per share.

3. In September each shareholder was issued (for each share held) one stock right to purchase two additional shares of common stock for $13 per share. The rights expire on December 31, Year 3. (See discussion of stock rights in paragraphs 22.9 and 22.10.)

4. In October 250,000 stock rights were exercised when the market value of the common stock was $14 per share.

5. In November 400,000 stock rights were exercised when the market value of the common stock was $15 per share.

---

*Exhibit 21.4*
**Lipscomb Corporation**
**Shareholders' Equity**
**December 31, 1981**
**(Problem 21.21)**

| | |
|---|---:|
| Preferred Stock Authorized ($100 par value) | $400,000 |
| Common Stock Authorized ($10 par value) | 600,000 |
| Unissued Preferred Stock | 100,000 |
| Unissued Common Stock | 200,000 |
| Subscriptions Receivable, Preferred | 15,000 |
| Subscriptions Receivable, Common | 30,000 |
| Preferred Stock Subscribed | 20,000 |
| Common Stock Subscribed | 40,000 |
| Treasury Stock—Common (4,000 shares at cost) | 38,000 |
| Additional Paid-in Capital—Preferred | 9,000 |
| Additional Paid-in Capital—Common | 180,000 |
| Retained Earnings | 260,000 |

6. On December 15, Year 3, Gilroy declared its first cash dividend to shareholders of $0.20 per share, payable on January 10, Year 4, to shareholders of record on December 31, Year 3.
7. On December 21, Year 3, in accordance with the applicable state law, Gilroy formally retired 10,000 shares of its treasury stock and had them revert to an unissued basis. The market value of the common stock was $16 per share on this date.
8. Net income for Year 3 was $750,000.

Prepare a schedule of all transactions affecting the common stock (shares and dollar amounts), additional paid-in capital, retained earnings, and the treasury stock (shares and dollar amounts) accounts and the amounts that would be included in Gilroy's balance sheet at December 31, Year 1, Year 2, and Year 3, based on the above facts.

# Chapter 22
## *Shareholders' Equity: Dilutive Securities and Earnings per Share*

**22.1**  In addition to issuing preferred or common stock, corporations may issue various types of securities that can be converted into shares of common stock. One example is convertible bonds, discussed in Chapter 17. Another example is convertible preferred stock, described briefly in Chapter 21. A corporation may also issue or sell rights to acquire shares of its common stock. For example, stock options may be issued to employees, permitting them to purchase shares of common stock at a lower price than the market price of the shares on the date the options are exercised. Stock warrants may be attached to a bond or preferred stock issue, permitting the holders to acquire shares of common stock at a specified price.

**22.2**  When securities are converted into, or exchanged for, shares of common stock, it is possible that the relative equity interest of the previous shareholder group will be reduced, or diluted. This section discusses the accounting for various types of potentially dilutive equity securities. Later parts of the chapter consider the treatment of dilutive securities in the calculation of earnings per share.

## Convertible Preferred Stock

**22.3**  Convertible preferred stock is initially recorded the same as any other issue of capital stock. For example, assume that 1,000 shares of $100-par-value convertible preferred stock are issued for $120 per share. The journal entry is

| | | |
|---|---:|---:|
| Cash ........................ | 120,000 | |
|     Convertible Preferred Stock— | | |
|       Par .................... | | 100,000 |
|     Additional Paid-in Capital— | | |
|       Preferred Stock .......... | | 20,000 |

**22.4**  At the time of conversion, shares of outstanding preferred stock are exchanged for shares of common stock. Typically, no cash or other resources are exchanged. Thus, no additional contributions are made by shareholders. Because no additional contributions are made, the total amount of contributed capital should remain unchanged. All that has occurred is that one type of equity claim has been substituted for another. In order to reflect the change in equity claims without changing total contributed capital, the conversion of preferred into common stock should be recorded at the *book value* of the preferred shares. For example, if each share of preferred stock can be exchanged for five shares of $10-par-value common stock, the journal entry is

| | | |
|---|---:|---:|
| Convertible Preferred Stock—Par . | 100,000 | |
| Additional Paid-in Capital— | | |
|     Preferred Stock .............. | 20,000 | |
|     Common Stock (5,000 shares | | |
|       × $10) .................. | | 50,000 |
|     Additional Paid-in Capital— | | |
|       Common Stock .......... | | 70,000 |

**22-1**

22.5  If the par value of the common shares issued exceeds the book value of the preferred stock, the difference is debited to Retained Earnings. For example, if the par value of the common stock in the example above were $25 per share, the following entry would be made:

| | | |
|---|---|---|
| Convertible Preferred Stock—Par . | 100,000 | |
| Additional Paid-in Capital— | | |
|     Preferred Stock ............... | 20,000 | |
| Retained Earnings ............. | 5,000 | |
|     Common Stock (5,000 shares | | |
|       × $25) ................... | | 125,000 |

The preferred shareholders are viewed as having received a dividend of $5,000 at the time of conversion.

22.6  Some accountants argue that the conversion of preferred stock into common stock is a change in economic substance, not merely one of form, so that the conversion should be recorded at the market value of the shares exchanged. After conversion, the fixed commitment for preferred stock dividends no longer exists. Other things being equal, this should increase the cash available to the firm and reduce the risk of the common stockholders. Using market values to record the exchange is also consistent with the recording of reciprocal exchanges of assets and liabilities, where market values are used.*

22.7  Assume that the par value of the common stock is $10 per share, the market price of the common stock is $30 per share, and a decision is made to convert the 1,000 preferred shares into 5,000 shares of common stock. The entry to record the conversion using market, instead of book, values is

| | | |
|---|---|---|
| Convertible Preferred Stock ...... | 100,000 | |
| Additional Paid-in Capital— | | |
|     Preferred Stock ............... | 20,000 | |
| Retained Earnings .............. | 30,000 | |
|     Common Stock (5,000 shares | | |
|       × $10) ................... | | 50,000 |
|     Additional Paid-in Capital | | |
|       (5,000 shares × $20) ....... | | 100,000 |

The preferred shareholders are viewed as having received a dividend of $30,000 and

---

*Accounting Principles Board, *Accounting Principles Board Opinion No. 29* (May 1973).

immediately contributed this amount back to the corporation.

22.8  Note that total shareholders' equity is the same under both the book-value and market-value methods. The amounts shown as contributed capital and as retained earnings will be different. Either of these two methods of accounting for convertible preferred stock is acceptable, although the book-value method is most commonly followed in practice.

## Stock Rights

22.9  Rights to purchase additional shares of stock are sometimes given to existing shareholders. Stock rights are typically of short duration (several months), are transferable, and are often traded in public markets. Stock rights are ordinarily associated with attempts by a firm to raise new capital from its shareholders. The purchase price for the shares specified in the stock right is usually less than the market value of the shares.

22.10  A journal entry is not required when stock rights are issued to shareholders. When the rights are exercised, an entry is made debiting Cash for the proceeds and crediting Preferred or Common Stock and Additional Paid-in Capital accounts. If financial statements are issued while stock rights are outstanding, a note to the financial statements should indicate the number of authorized but unissued shares that may be issued under the stock rights arrangement.

## Stock Options

22.11  Officers, managers, and other employees (hereafter collectively referred to as employees) are often given the right to purchase shares of stock of a corporation through stock options. Stock options may be used as a means of (1) promoting employee ownership in a corporation and, thereby, increasing employee interest and loyalty to the firm, and (2) providing additional compensation to employees.

22.12  In contrast to stock rights granted to shareholders, stock options granted to employees are usually of longer duration (the option period may run for several years) and are nontransferable. The number of shares that can be purchased by each employee and the option (exercise) price may be set at the time the stock option is granted or may be contingent on certain future events, such as growth rates in earnings or changes in stock prices.

22.13 The principal accounting issues related to stock options are as follows:

**1.** Does the benefit to employees from a stock option represent additional compensation?

**2.** If additional compensation is present, how is the benefit element in the stock option measured?

**3.** During which accounting period(s) is the benefit element in a stock option recognized as an expense in measuring net income?

22.14 Some accountants argue that *some* stock options are noncompensatory in nature. Some option plans, for example, are designed primarily to assist a corporation in raising capital or in promoting employee ownership and interest in the firm. Plans that are not designed primarily as a means of providing additional compensation do not give rise to compensation expense according to this view.

22.15 Other accountants argue that *all* stock options are essentially a means of providing additional compensation to employees. The benefit realized by employees from purchasing shares of stock for a smaller amount than would be required to purchase the shares on the open market is an element of compensation. The compensation expense related to the stock option, if it can be measured satisfactorily, should be recognized in measuring net income either during the period when the option is granted (compensation for current services) or during future periods (compensation for services to be received in the future). Because the benefit element in most stock option plans cannot be measured satisfactorily at the time the option is granted, a zero valuation is arbitrarily assigned under generally accepted accounting principles.

Thus, most option plans, although compensatory in nature, are accounted for as if they were noncompensatory. The treatment under generally accepted accounting principles of compensatory stock option plans differs from that for noncompensatory plans.*

## Noncompensatory Plans

22.16 A stock option plan that has all of the following four characteristics is considered a noncompensatory plan by Accounting Principles Board *Opinion No. 25:*

1. Substantially all full-time employees meeting limited employment qualifications may participate.
2. Stock is offered to eligible employees equally or based on a uniform percentage of salary or wages.
3. The time permitted for exercise of an option is limited to a reasonable period.
4. The discount from the market price of the stock is no greater than would be reasonable in an offer of stock to shareholders or others.

22.17 Under most noncompensatory stock option plans, the option price is set equal to the market price of the stock *at the time the option is granted.* At this time, the employee is not viewed as having received any benefits, because the employee must pay the same amount for a share of stock as would a non-employee on the open market.† Any benefits realized later by the employee because the option price is less than the market price *at the time the option is exercised* is viewed as a gain from speculation by the employee and not as compensation for services rendered.

22.18 When a noncompensatory stock option is granted, no formal entry is made on the cor-

---

*Accounting Research Bulletin No. 43,* AICPA (1953), chap. 13B; and Accounting Principles Board, *Accounting Principles Board Opinion No. 25* (1972).

†This view flies in the face of economic reality. The option to buy anything for a fixed period of time at a fixed price is generally worth something. The longer the fixed period of time, the more valuable the option. *The Wall Street Journal* daily shows quotations for stock options where the exercise price is greater than or equal to the current market value of shares. These options virtually always have positive market values.

poration's books. For example, assume that options to purchase 1,000 shares of a corporation's $10-par-value common stock are granted to employees on December 31, 1981. The option price of $25 is equal to the market price of the stock on this date. The firm would maintain internal records of the number of shares subject to option, the option price, and the names of specific employees holding the options. No journal entry would be made at this time, however.

22.19    When stock options under a noncompensatory plan are exercised, the journal entry made treats the transaction simply as an issue of shares at the option price. For example, if options to acquire 400 shares are exercised on July 1, 1982, when the shares are selling in the open market for $30 per share, the entry is

July 1, 1982
Cash (400 shares × $25)  ........... 10,000
    Common Stock (400 shares ×
        $10)  ...................... 4,000
    Additional Paid-in Capital  ....... 6,000

The employees realized a savings of $2,000 by purchasing shares for $10,000 that have a market value of $12,000 (= 400 × $30) on July 1, 1982. This savings is not recognized as compensation if the plan satisfies the requirements for being noncompensatory.

## Compensatory Plans

22.20    All plans that do not meet the requirements for a noncompensatory plan are considered compensatory plans. For example, a stock option plan exclusively for corporate executives would be classified as "compensatory," because all full-time employees do not participate in the plan. Compensation expense is recognized in a compensatory plan in an amount equal to the difference between the market price and the option price on the *measurement date*. The measurement date is the first date on which are known (1) the number of shares that an individual employee is entitled to receive and (2) the option or purchase price, if any.* It is

_____
*Accounting Principles Board, *Accounting Principles Board Opinion No. 25* (October 1972), par. 10.

not necessary that the option be exercisable on the measurement date.

As with noncompensatory plans, the option price in most compensatory plans is set equal to the market price of the shares on the date the option is granted. The measurement date is, therefore, the date the option is granted. Because the option price is set equal to the market price on that date, no compensation expense is recognized. In the previous illustration, options to acquire 1,000 shares of common stock at $25 per share were granted to employees on December 31, 1981. If this plan were considered compensatory instead of noncompensatory, the measurement date would be December 31, 1981. Because the market price was equal to the option price on this date, there would be no compensation expense recognized, even though this is a compensatory plan. The journal entries to record the transactions under this plan are identical to those illustrated earlier for the noncompensatory case. Thus, even though the plan is considered a compensatory one, it is accounted for as if it were noncompensatory.

22.21

Assume, instead of the above arrangement, that options to acquire 1,000 shares of common stock were granted to employees on December 31, 1981. The option price is to be $5 less than the market price of the shares on the date the options are exercised. In this case, the measurement date is the date of exercise, because this is the earliest date when the option price is known. If options to purchase 400 shares of common stock are exercised on July 1, 1982, when the market price is $30 per share, then the option price is $25 per share (= $30 − $5). Compensation expense of $2,000 (= 400 shares × $5) must be recognized. A question arises as to the accounting periods in which the compensation should be recognized as an expense. *Accounting Research Bulletin No. 43* states that "if the period for which payment for services is being made by the issuance of the stock option is not specifically indicated in the offer or agreement, the value of the option should be apportioned over the periods of service for which the payment of compensation seems appropriate

22.22

in the existing circumstances."* This provision would appear to provide firms with considerable freedom in the timing of the expense recognition. Most firms tend to recognize the compensation expense in the period when the measurement is made. In the example illustrated here, the following entries would be made on July 1, 1982:

```
July 1, 1982
Compensation Expense  . . . . . . . . . . . .  2,000
    Additional Paid-in Capital  . . . . . . .        2,000
To recognize compensation equal to the
difference between the market price and
the option price on July 1, 1982 ($2,000 =
400 × $5).
```

```
July 1, 1982
Cash (400 × $25)  . . . . . . . . . . . . . . . . . .  10,000
    Common Stock (400 × $10)  . . . . .          4,000
    Additional Paid-in Capital  . . . . . . .        6,000
To record the receipt of the option price
and the issuance of common stock.
```

### Disclosure of Stock Options

22.23  The following information regarding stock option plans must be disclosed:†

**1.** The status of the option plan at the end of each period, including the number of shares under option, the option price, and the number of shares to which options are currently exercisable.

**2.** The number of shares issued during the period upon the exercise of options and the option price.

22.24  Note 17 to the financial statements of International Corporation in Appendix A presents an example of the required disclosures. (See Exhibit A.4).

### Stock Appreciation Rights

22.25  Because of changes in the income tax laws and because of lackluster performance of the stock market in recent years, many executives have found stock option plans less attractive as a form of compensation than before. Corporations have in many cases substituted stock appreciation rights for stock options. A *stock appreciation right* is a promise made to an employee to pay cash to that employee at a future date. The amount is the difference between the market price of a certain number of shares on a given future date and some base price designated on the date the rights are granted. The granting of stock appreciation rights is a form of compensation. Generally accepted accounting principles (FASB *Interpretation No. 28,* 1978)** measure the amount of compensation as the excess of the market value of the shares over the base price set when the rights were granted. Subsequent changes, either increases or decreases, in the market value of the shares after the date of the grant result in a change in the measure of compensation. The amount of compensation is charged to expense over the period (during which the employee performs the services) that must elapse before the stock appreciation right can be exercised.

### Stock Warrants

22.26  Corporations may sell *stock warrants* to individuals who are not shareholders. The holder of the warrant can acquire shares of capital stock by returning the warrant plus a specified amount of cash. Warrants differ from stock rights and stock options in three important respects: **(1)** Warrants are issued to individuals who are not shareholders or employees, **(2)** warrants are sold for cash, and **(3)** the total purchase price (warrant price plus required cash remittance) usually exceeds the market price of the stock on the date the warrants are sold.

22.27  To illustrate the accounting for stock warrants, assume that a corporation sells warrants permitting the holder to purchase 10,000 shares of $5-par-value common stock for $20 per share. The warrants are sold for $15,000 cash. The journal entry to record the sale of the warrants is

```
Cash  . . . . . . . . . . . . . . . . . . . . . . . . .  15,000
    Common Stock Warrants  . . . .          15,000
```

---

*Accounting Research Bulletin No. 43, AICPA (1953), Chap. 13B, par. 14.

†Ibid., Chap. 13B, par. 15.

---

**FASB *Interpretation No. 28,* "Accounting for Stock Appreciation Rights and Other Variable Stock Option or Award Plans," 1978.

The Common Stock Warrants account is normally included with Additional Paid-in Capital on the balance sheet.

22.28    When the warrants are returned with the required cash, the following entry is made:

```
Cash (10,000 × $20) ............  200,000
    Common Stock Warrants ........   15,000
        Common Stock (10,000 × $5) .           50,000
        Additional Paid-in Capital ....        165,000
```

If the warrants expire without being exercised, the entry is

```
Common Stock Warrants ........   15,000
    Additional Paid-in Capital  ....            15,000
```

22.29    Warrants may also be issued as a "bonus" or "sweetener" with other securities. For example, warrants to purchase shares of common stock may be attached to a bond or preferred stock issue. An important theoretical question is whether **(1)** all of the proceeds from the sale of the combined security should be allocated to the bond or preferred stock, or **(2)** whether a portion of the proceeds should also be allocated to the warrant.

22.30    Advocates of a dual allocation argue that the bond or preferred stock and the warrant derive their value from different sources and should, therefore, be accounted for separately. The market value of the bond and preferred stock will be related primarily to the level of interest rates. The value of the warrant will be related primarily to the market price performance of the underlying common stock, which in turn will be related to the profitability of the firm.

22.31    Those arguing against a dual allocation point out the measurement difficulties in allocating the total proceeds between the two securities. To make a meaningful allocation, it is necessary that the market prices of the individual securities be found. When the securities are issued as a unit, finding such market values may be difficult.

22.32    Generally accepted accounting principles make a distinction between bonds or preferred stock issued with *detachable* and *nondetachable stock warrants.*

## Detachable Stock Warrants

22.33    When bonds or preferred stocks are issued with detachable stock warrants, the holder essentially has two securities. Actions taken with respect to one security are independent of actions taken with respect to the other. For example, the warrants could be sold on the open market immediately after acquisition, whereas the bonds could be held until maturity.

22.34    When bonds or preferred stocks are issued with detachable stock warrants, each of the securities will have a separate market value. Generally accepted accounting principles require that the issue price of the combined security be allocated to the bonds or preferred stock and the warrants based on their relative market values at the time of issuance.* For example, assume that 10,000 shares of $10-par-value preferred stock are issued, with each share having a detachable stock warrant. By returning five warrants and $20 in cash, the holder can purchase one share of $5-par-value common stock. The preferred stock with detachable warrants is issued for $15 per share. The market value of the preferred stock is determined to be $12 per share and the market value of each warrant is determined to be $4 at the time of issue. The journal entry to record the issue is

```
Cash (10,000 × $15) ............  150,000
    Preferred Stock (10,000 ×
        $10) ...................             100,000
    Additional Paid-in Capital—
        Preferred Stock (.75 ×
        $150,000 = $112,500;
        $112,500 − $100,000 =
        $12,500) ................             12,500
    Additional Paid-in Capital—
        Stock Warrants (.25 ×
        $150,000) ..............             37,500
```

| | | |
|---|---|---|
| Preferred Stock: 10,000 × $12 ... $120,000 | 75% |
| Stock Warrants: 10,000 × $4 .... 40,000 | 25% |
| Total ................. $160,000 | 100% |

---

*Accounting Principles Board, *Accounting Principles Board Opinion No. 14* (March 1969), par. 16.

The accounting for the warrants subsequent to initial issuance is identical to the procedures illustrated in the preceding sections when warrants are sold outright to the general public. For example, if holders of 4,000 warrants return the warrants with $16,000 in cash, 800 shares of $5-par-value common stock will be issued. The journal entry to record the transaction is

```
Cash  ........................   16,000
Additional Paid-in Capital—Stock
  Warrants (4,000/10,000 ×
  $37,500) ...................   15,000
    Common Stock (800 × $5)  ..            4,000
    Additional Paid-in Capital—
      Common Stock  ..........             27,000
```

## Nondetachable Stock Warrants

22.35  When bonds or preferred stock are issued with nondetachable stock warrants, the holder essentially has one security. Either the security can be held as an investment in a bond or preferred stock or the security (plus the required cash) can be exchanged for common stock. When the stock warrants are nondetachable, the security is equivalent to a convertible bond or convertible preferred stock. Under such circumstances, the market value of the bond or preferred stock and the warrant are inseparable. Generally accepted accounting principles require that all of the proceeds from issuing these securities be allocated to the bonds or preferred stock.* The journal entry to record the issuance of 10,000 shares of $10-par-value preferred stock with nondetachable stock warrants for $15 per share is

```
Cash (10,000 × $15) ...........  150,000
    Preferred Stock (10,000 ×
      $10)  ....................            100,000
    Additional Paid-in Capital—
      Preferred Stock  ..........            50,000
```

22.36  If holders of 4,000 shares of preferred stock return the preferred shares with nondetachable warrants plus $16,000 in cash, then 800

shares of $5-par-value common stock will be issued. The journal entry is

```
Cash  .........................   16,000
Preferred Stock (4,000 × $10) ......   40,000
Additional Paid-in Capital—Preferred
  Stock  .........................   20,000
    Common Stock (800 × $5) .....            4,000
    Additional Paid-in Capital—
      Common Stock ............             72,000
```

Note the similarity between this journal entry and the entry to record the conversion of convertible preferred stock into common stock. The principal difference in the case of preferred stock with nondetachable stock warrants is that cash is usually involved in the transaction.  22.37

## Calculation of Earnings per Share

Earnings per share of common stock is considered by many investors to be an important measure for assessing the profitability of a firm. Earnings-per-share† amounts for corporations are prominently reported in the financial press. Financial analysts commit considerable time to forecasting future earnings per share for various companies.  22.38

Generally accepted accounting principles require that earnings-per-share amounts be disclosed in the income statement.** If a firm has income, gains, or losses from discontinued operations or extraordinary gains or losses, separate earnings-per-share amounts must be disclosed for each of these types of income. The calculation of earnings per share depends on a corporation's capital structure. Firms that do not have outstanding convertible bonds or convertible preferred stock that can be turned into common stock or options or warrants that can be exchanged for common stock are considered to have *simple capital structures*. Firms that have outstanding securities that can be converted into, or exchanged for, common  22.39

---

*Ibid.

†All future references to ''earnings per share'' refer to earnings per share of common stock.
**Accounting Principles Board, *Accounting Principles Board Opinion No. 15* (1969), par. 12.

stock are considered to have *complex capital structures*.

## Simple Capital Structures

22.40 Firms with simple capital structures report a single earnings-per-share amount. The calculation is as follows:

$$
\begin{aligned}
\text{Earnings per Share (simple capital structure)} &= \frac{\text{Net Income Applicable to Common Stock}}{\text{Weighted Average Number of Common Shares Outstanding}} \\
&= \frac{\text{Net Income} - \text{Preferred Stock Dividends}}{\text{Weighted Average Number of Common Shares Outstanding}}.
\end{aligned}
$$

22.41 The number of shares outstanding during each day of the year is weighted by the number of days such shares are outstanding. For example, if 200,000 shares are outstanding on January 1, 1981, 10,000 shares are acquired as treasury stock on April 1, 1981, 100,000 new shares are issued on July 1, 1981, and 4,000 of the treasury shares are resold on October 1, 1981, the calculation of the weighted average number of shares outstanding for 1981 is as follows:

| | |
|---|---:|
| $200{,}000 \times {}^{90}/_{365}$ ................. | 49,315 |
| $190{,}000 \times {}^{91}/_{365}$ ................. | 47,370 |
| $290{,}000 \times {}^{92}/_{365}$ ................. | 73,096 |
| $294{,}000 \times {}^{92}/_{365}$ ................. | 74,104 |
| Weighted Average ........... | 243,885 shares |

## Complex Capital Structures

22.42 Since the mid-1960s, increasing use has been made by corporations of securities that can be converted into, or exchanged for, shares of common stock. Because these securities do not represent outstanding common stock, they have no effect on the denominator of earnings per share as calculated for a simple capital structure. If the securities are converted into, or exchanged for, shares of common stock, however, they will increase the weighted average of shares outstanding and could reduce, or dilute, earnings per share. Given the importance of earnings-per-share amounts to investors and other users of financial statements, it is desirable that this *potential dilution* be reflected in some

manner in the reported earnings-per-share amounts. Accounting Principles Board *Opinion No. 15* requires that firms with complex capital structures (that is, firms with convertible securities or stock options and warrants) report two earnings-per-share amounts: **(1)** primary earnings per share and **(2)** fully diluted earnings per share.

**Primary Earnings per Share** Primary earnings per share is the amount of earnings applicable to each share of outstanding common stock and common stock equivalent. *Common stock equivalents* are securities whose principal value arises from their capability of being converted into, or exchanged for, common stock, instead of for their own periodic cash yields over time. Stock options and warrants are always common stock equivalents. Their only value arises from their capability of being used to acquire shares of common stock. Convertible bonds and convertible preferred stock may or may not be common stock equivalents. A test is used to determine if the return from these convertible securities at the date of their issue is substantially below the return available from other bond and preferred stock investments. If so, the presumption is that the securities derive their value primarily from their conversion privilege and are, therefore, common stock equivalents. If not, then the convertible security is not considered a common stock equivalent and does not enter into the calculation of primary earnings per share. As discussed next, they would enter into the calculation of fully diluted earnings per share. Primary earnings per share is calculated as follows:

22.43

$$
\text{Primary Earnings per Share (complex capital structure)} = \frac{\text{Net Income Applicable to Common Stock} + \text{Adjustments for Common Stock Equivalents}}{\text{Weighted Average Number of Common Shares Outstanding} + \text{Weighted Average Number of Common Shares Issuable from Common Stock Equivalents}}.
$$

**Fully Diluted Earnings per Share** As the title implies, fully diluted earnings per share indicates the maximum potential dilution

22.44

that would occur if all options, warrants, and convertible securities were exchanged for common stock. This amount, therefore, represents the maximum limit of possible dilution that could take place on the date of the balance sheet. All securities convertible into or exchangeable for common stock, whether or not classified as common stock equivalents for purposes of calculating primary earnings per share, enter into the determination of fully diluted earnings per share. Convertible securities that do not meet the test for classification as a common stock equivalent are labeled "other potentially dilutive securities." Fully diluted earnings per share is calculated as follows:

$$
\begin{array}{l}
\text{Fully Diluted} \\
\text{Earnings per} \\
\text{Share} \\
\text{(complex} \\
\text{capital} \\
\text{structure)}
\end{array}
=
\frac{
\begin{array}{c}
\text{Net Income} \\
\text{Applicable} \\
\text{to Common} \\
\text{Stock}
\end{array}
+
\begin{array}{c}
\text{Adjustments} \\
\text{for Common} \\
\text{Stock} \\
\text{Equivalents}
\end{array}
+
\begin{array}{c}
\text{Adjustments} \\
\text{for Other} \\
\text{Potentially} \\
\text{Dilutive} \\
\text{Securities}
\end{array}
}{
\begin{array}{c}
\text{Weighted} \\
\text{Average} \\
\text{Number of} \\
\text{Common} \\
\text{Shares} \\
\text{Outstanding}
\end{array}
+
\begin{array}{c}
\text{Weighted} \\
\text{Average} \\
\text{Number of} \\
\text{Common} \\
\text{Shares} \\
\text{Issuable} \\
\text{from} \\
\text{Common} \\
\text{Stock} \\
\text{Equivalents}
\end{array}
+
\begin{array}{c}
\text{Weighted} \\
\text{Average} \\
\text{Number of} \\
\text{Common} \\
\text{Shares} \\
\text{Issuable} \\
\text{from} \\
\text{Other} \\
\text{Potentially} \\
\text{Dilutive} \\
\text{Securities}
\end{array}
}
$$

22.45   **Summary** The general principles underlying the calculation of earnings per share for firms with complex capital structures may be summarized as follows:

**General Rule:** Firms with capital structures that include securities that can be converted into, or exchanged for, shares of common stock must report the effects of potential dilution in two earnings-per-share amounts: **(1)** primary earnings per share, and **(2)** fully diluted earnings per share.

**Antidilutive Exception:** If the effect of adjusting earnings per common share outstanding (that is, earnings per share calculated as for a firm with a simple capital structure) for a common stock equivalent or other potentially dilutive security is to increase earnings per share or to reduce the net loss per share for a particular year (that is, the effect is antidilutive), that particular security is excluded from the computations for that year.

**Immateriality Exception:** If primary or fully diluted earnings per share is not different by at least 3 percent from earnings per common share outstanding (that is, earnings per share calculated as for a firm with a simple capital structure), then

the earnings-per-share amount (primary, fully diluted, or both) that is not materially different from earnings per common share outstanding need not be disclosed.

## Adjustments for Convertible Securities

The adjustments to calculate primary and   22.46 fully diluted earnings per common share for convertible bonds or convertible preferred stock can be summarized as follows:

**Two-Thirds Rule:** If the cash yield of a convertible security (that is, cash payments per year/initial issue price) at the date of issue is less than two-thirds of the bank prime interest rate* at that time, then the convertible is a "common stock equivalent." If the cash yield is greater than or equal to two-thirds of the bank prime interest rate, then the convertible security is not a "common stock equivalent" but is an "other potentially dilutive security."

**Permanent Classification Rule:** The classification of a convertible security as either a "common stock equivalent" or an "other potentially dilutive security" is made at the time the security is issued and is not changed during subsequent periods while the security is outstanding.

**If-Converted Method:** The effect of convertible securities on earnings-per-share calculations (primary and/or fully diluted) is based on the assumption that the securities were converted into shares of common stock at the beginning of the earliest period reported on (unless the securities were issued subsequent to the beginning of this earliest period, in which case the calculations assume conversion as of the date of their issue).

**Two-Thirds Rule** The two-thirds rule is the   22.47 test used to ascertain whether a convertible security derives most of its value from its conversion privilege or whether its value derives primarily from its own cash yield. If the cash yield is significantly lower than market interest rates at the time of issue,

---

*The FASB has proposed that the average Aa corporate bond yield be used instead of the bank prime interest rate. See "Determining Whether a Convertible Security is a Common Stock Equivalent," *Proposed Statement of Financial Accounting Standard* (November 1981).

then accounting presumes that the security is viewed by the market more as common stock than as a bond or preferred stock. If the cash yield is similar to current market rates, then accounting presumes that the market views the security more as a bond or preferred stock than as a common stock.

22.48    To provide a degree of objectivity to the process of ascertaining whether particular convertible security issues behave more like bonds or preferred stock or more like common stock, APB *Opinion No. 15* specifies the two-thirds rule. There is no particular logic to the use of the bank prime interest rate (which applies to short-term bank loans to low-risk customers) or to the two-thirds cut off point. The bank prime interest rate is readily available, however, and the two-thirds rule can be applied unambiguously in most cases. To illustrate the application of the two-thirds rule, consider the following illustrations.

22.49    *Example 1* Monroe Corporation issued 8-percent convertible bonds on July 1, 1979. The bonds have a face value of $1,000,000, mature in 20 years from the date of issue, and are issued at par. Each $1,000 bond is convertible into 10 shares of $10-par-value common stock. The bank prime interest rate on July 1, 1979, is 11 percent.* The cash yield on these bonds (cash payments per year divided by the initial market price) is 8 percent. Two-thirds of the bank prime interest rate is 7.33 percent (= $^2/_3$ × .11). Because the cash yield exceeds two-thirds of the bank prime interest rate, these convertible securities are not "common stock equivalents." They are "other potentially dilutive securities."

22.50    *Example 2* Washington Corporation issued 8-percent convertible bonds on July 1, 1981. The bonds have a face value of $1,000,000, mature in 20 years, and are issued at 123.115 percent of par (that is, the issue price is

*The bank prime interest rate used in the examples and problems in this chapter do not necessarily coincide with the actual bank prime interest rates on the dates shown.

$1,231,150). Each $1,000 bond is convertible into 20 shares of $10-par-value common stock. The bank prime interest rate on July 1, 1981, is 10 percent. The cash yield on the bonds at the time of issue is 6.50 percent (= $80,000/$1,231,150). Because the cash yield (not the nominal yield) is less than 6.67 percent (= $^2/_3$ × .10), these convertible bonds are "common stock equivalents."

22.51    *Example 3* Jefferson Corporation issued 50,000 shares of $100-par-value convertible preferred stock on July 1, 1976, for $102. The shares carry a dividend rate of 5 percent and are convertible into common stock at the rate of five common shares for each share of preferred stock. The bank prime interest rate on July 1, 1976, was 8 percent. The cash yield at the time of issue was 4.90 percent (= $5/$102). Because this yield is less than two-thirds of the bank prime interest rate, the convertible preferred stock is a "common stock equivalent."

22.52    The cash yield on a convertible security may change after issue because of a change in the contractual dividend or interest rate. Then, the lowest return during the first 5 years after issue is used in applying the two-thirds rule.

**Permanent Classification Rule** Once a convertible security has been classified as a "common stock equivalent" or an "other potentially dilutive security" at the time of issue, it retains this classification for all future periods as long as the convertible security is outstanding (that is, until it is either actually converted into common stock or redeemed by the corporation). Changes in conditions may make the probability of actual conversion low. Nonetheless, if a particular security meets the test for classification as a "common stock equivalent" at issue, it must continue to be treated as such in earnings-per-share calculations.

**If-Converted Method** The if-converted method is used for including the effects of convertible securities in the calculation of primary and fully diluted earnings per share. *For purposes of calculating primary and fully diluted earnings per share only,* the assumption is made that convertible securities are converted into common stock. Adjustments are required in the numerator and denominator of earnings per share under the if-converted method.

22.55    In the numerator, the aftertax effects of interest on convertible bonds and dividends on preferred stock that were subtracted in determining net income available to common stock must be added back. If convertible bonds had been converted as of the beginning of the period, no interest expense on such bonds would have been subtracted in determining net income. Because interest expense has actually been subtracted, it must be added back. The effect of interest expense on net income is not the amount of interest expense recognized, however. Interest expense is deductible in calculating taxable income. By deducting interest expense, there is a savings in income taxes equal to interest expense times the marginal tax rate. The net effect of interest on net income is therefore $(1.0 -$ Marginal Tax Rate$) \times$ (Interest Expense).

22.56    If convertible preferred stock had been converted as of the beginning of the period, dividends on preferred stock would not have been subtracted from net income in determining net income available to common stock. The preferred stock dividends must, therefore, be added back. The amount added back is the full amount of the dividend, because preferred dividends, unlike interest, are not deductible in calculating taxable income.

22.57    In the denominator, the number of shares of common stock that would have been issued if the convertible securities had been converted must be added to the weighted average of common shares actually outstanding.

22.58    The examples below build on the three examples discussed earlier in this section and illustrate the mechanics of the if-converted method. In all cases, the current year is 1981 and the marginal income tax rate is 40 percent.

22.59    *Example 4* Refer to Example 1 for Monroe Corporation. The convertible bonds were

found to be "other potentially dilutive securities." If these convertible securities had been converted as of the beginning of 1981, interest expense on these bonds of $80,000 $(= .08 \times \$1,000,000)$ would not have been subtracted in determining net income. An addback in the numerator of fully diluted earnings per share in the amount of $48,000 $[= (1.0 - .40)(\$80,000)]$ is, therefore, necessary. The conversion rate is 10 shares of common stock for each $1,000 bond. Thus, upon conversion of the $1,000,000 of bonds, 10,000 shares $(= 1,000$ bonds $\times 10)$ of common stock would have been issued. Because these bonds were initially issued prior to the beginning of the period reported on (that is, 1981), the 10,000 additional shares of common stock are assumed to be outstanding for all of 1981.

22.60    *Example 5* Refer to Example 2 for Washington Corporation. The convertible bonds were determined to be "common stock equivalents." The numerator of both primary and fully diluted earnings per share must be adjusted for interest expense recognized during 1981. At an issue price of $1,231,150, the bonds were priced on the market to yield 6 percent (that is, the present value of the future interest payments plus present value of the maturity amount, both discounted at 6 percent per year, will yield a present value of $1,231,150). Interest expense under the effective interest method on these bonds from July 1, 1981, the date of issue, to December 31, 1981, is $36,935 $[= (.06 \times \$1,231,150 \times {}^{6}/_{12})]$. The addback to net income in the numerator is, therefore, $22,161 $[= (1.00 - .40)(\$36,935)]$. Note that the *market yield* on these bonds of 6 percent is not the same as the *cash yield* of 6.50 percent used to ascertain if the convertible security is a common stock equivalent.

22.61    The denominator of primary and fully diluted earnings per share must likewise be adjusted. The conversion rate is 20 shares of common stock for each $1,000 bond. Thus, upon conversion of the $1,000,000 of bonds, 20,000 shares $(= 1,000$ bonds $\times 20)$ of common stock would be issued. Because these convertible bonds were issued on July 1,

1981, the effect on the weighted average of common shares in the denominator is only 10,000 (= .5 × 20,000) additional shares.

22.62 Assuming that these convertible bonds continue to be outstanding in subsequent years, the addback of interest expense in the numerator will reflect a full year's interest. Similarly, the 20,000 additional shares of common stock issuable upon conversion will receive a full year's weight in the denominator.

22.63 *Example 6* Refer to Example 3 for Jefferson Corporation. The convertible preferred stock was determined to be a common stock equivalent at the time of its issuance in 1976. To extend this example, assume that all of the preferred stock was actually converted into common stock on July 1, 1981. During the first 6 months of 1981, the convertible preferred stock is considered a common stock equivalent. During the second 6 months of 1981, the convertible preferred stock did not exist. In its place were 250,000 shares of outstanding common stock.

22.64 In calculating net income available to common stock, preferred stock dividends during the first 6 months of the year of $125,000 (= .025 × $5,000,000) would have been subtracted. In calculating primary and fully diluted earnings per share for 1981, this amount must be added back to net income available to common stock, because conversion is assumed as of the beginning of the year. Because the preferred stock was not outstanding during the second 6 months of 1981, no dividends for this period have been subtracted in determining net income available to common stock. No addback is therefore necessary in computing primary and fully diluted earnings per share.

22.65 The denominator must likewise be increased for the additional common shares that would have been outstanding during the first 6 months of 1981 if conversion had taken place on January 1, 1981. The additional 250,000 shares weighted for one-half of the year is 125,000 shares. Because conversion actually took place on July 1, 1981, the weighted average of common shares outstanding already includes the effect of the 250,000 shares issued at the time of conversion, weighted for the last half of the year.

## Adjustments for Stock Options and Warrants

22.66 The adjustments to calculate primary and fully diluted earnings per share for stock options and warrants can be summarized as follows:

**Common Stock Equivalent Rule:** Stock options and warrants are always considered common stock equivalents, because their only value derives from their capability of being exchanged for common stock.

**Treasury Stock Method:** The effect of stock options and warrants on earnings-per-share calculations (primary and fully diluted) is based on the assumption that shares of common stock would be purchased on the open market with any cash proceeds received at the time stock options or warrants are exercised. Only the incremental shares (shares issued under options or warrants minus shares reacquired on the open market) enter into the calculation of primary and fully diluted earnings per share.

**Separation Rule:** The treasury-stock method is applied to each class or type of stock option and warrant separately each period. If the effect is dilutive, the particular option or warrant is included in the calculation of primary and fully diluted earnings per share for that period. If the effect is antidilutive, the particular option or warrant is excluded from the calculation of primary and fully diluted earnings per share for that period.

22.67 **Common Stock Equivalent Rule** Stock options and warrants have no cash yield on their own. Their value comes from their being exchangeable for common stock. Stock options and warrants are, therefore, always considered "common stock equivalents." They may not always enter into the calculation of primary and fully diluted earnings per share, however. Options and warrants, as discussed more fully in the next section, are included only if their effect is dilutive.

**22.68** **Treasury Stock Method** *For purposes of computing primary and fully diluted earnings per share only,* any cash hypothetically received upon the exercise of options or warrants is assumed to be used to purchase shares of common stock on the open market. The incremental shares (shares issued under options and warrants minus shares reacquired) enter into the calculation of primary and fully diluted earnings per share. The effect would be dilutive only when the market price of the shares exceeds the option price. Otherwise, more shares will be purchased than issued and the effect will be antidilutive. The treasury-stock method need not be applied until the market price exceeds the option price for substantially all of 3 consecutive months. For purposes of calculating primary earnings per share, the average market price is used in applying the treasury-stock method. If market prices do not change significantly during the year, a simple average of the four quarters' average prices can be used. If market prices do change significantly, then the treasury-stock method should be applied using the average price for each quarter separately. The resulting incremental shares for each quarter are then weighted by one-fourth to calculate the average incremental shares for the year. For purposes of calculating fully diluted earnings per share, the higher of the average market price or the market price at the end of each period is used in the calculations. A higher market price means that fewer shares would be purchased with the cash received, and the incremental shares issued (shares issued minus shares repurchased) would be larger. With a larger number of incremental shares, the denominator would be larger and fully diluted earnings per share would be smaller (that is, reflecting the *maximum* potential dilution).

**22.69** *Example 7* Lincoln Corporation issued stock options to employees on December 31, 1980, permitting them to purchase 20,000 shares of common stock for $30 per share. The average market price during 1981 was $32 per share. The market price on December 31, 1981, was $34 per share. Because the market price did not change significantly during the year, the treasury-stock method is applied using the average market price for the year. The cash proceeds upon exercise of the options are $600,000 (= 20,000 × $30). In calculating primary earnings per share, 18,750 shares (= $600,000/$32) are assumed to be purchased. The incremental shares issued would, therefore, be 1,250 shares (= 20,000 − 18,750). If these options were outstanding for all of 1981, 1,250 shares would be added to the denominator in calculating primary earnings per share. In calculating fully diluted earnings per share, the higher ending market price of $34 would be used. A total of 17,647 shares (= $600,000/$34) is assumed to be purchased. The incremental shares issued, to be included in the denominator of fully diluted earnings per share, are 2,353 shares (= 20,000 − 17,647).

**22.70** *Example 8* Refer to the data for Lincoln Corporation in Example 7. Assume that the average price and ending market price for each quarter of 1981 were as follows:

|  | **Average** | **End of Quarter** |
|---|---|---|
| First Quarter .......... | $25 | 28 |
| Second Quarter ........ | 31 | 31 |
| Third Quarter .......... | 40 | 43 |
| Fourth Quarter ........ | 32 | 34 |

Because the market price of the shares changed significantly during the year, the treasury-stock method must be applied using the average and ending market prices for each quarter separately.

**22.71** Consider first the calculation of primary earnings per share. During the first quarter, the option price exceeds the average market price. Because the effect of applying the treasury-stock method would be antidilutive, the stock options are excluded from the calculation of earnings per share. During the second quarter, the average market price exceeds the option price for the first time. If we assume that the market price exceeded the option price for substantially all of the second quarter, then the treasury-stock method will be applied beginning in the second quarter. The application of the treasury-stock method for primary earnings per share will result in 1,824 incremental shares as follows:

Second Quarter: $600,000/$31 = 19,355;
  (20,000 − 19,355) × (.25) .............. 161
Third Quarter: $600,000/$40 = 15,000;
  (20,000 − 15,000) × (.25) .............. 1,250
Fourth Quarter: $600,000/$32 = 18,750;
  (20,000 − 18,750) × (.25) .............. 313
    Incremental Shares, ................. 1,824

22.72 Similar calculations apply in the case of fully diluted earnings per share, except that the market price at the end of each quarter is used if that price exceeds the average of the quarter. The application of the treasury-stock method for fully diluted earnings per share is

Second Quarter: $600,000/$31 = 19,355;
  (20,000 − 19,355) × (.25) .............. 161
Third Quarter: $600,000/$43 = 13,953;
  (20,000 − 13,953) × (.25) .............. 1,512
Fourth Quarter: $600,000/$34 = 17,647;
  (20,000 − 17,647) × (.25) .............. 588
    Incremental Shares ................. 2,361

22.73 **Separation Rule** Each class or type of stock option or warrant is considered separately (see exception below) in applying the treasury-stock method. Thus, the effects of some options or warrants may be dilutive, while the effects of others will be antidilutive. In general, when the market price used in applying the treasury-stock method exceeds the cash received per share at the time the option or warrant is exercised, the effect will be dilutive. When the market price is less than the cash received per share, the effect will be antidilutive. A particular class of option or warrant may be dilutive in some years and antidilutive in other years. Likewise, a particular class of option may be antidilutive for purposes of calculating primary earnings per share but dilutive for purposes of calculating fully diluted earnings per share.

*Example 9* Refer to the three stock option 22.74 plans of Adams Corporation in Exhibit 22.1. Plan A is identical to the plan in Example 7 except for the ending market price. Because the average and ending market prices are higher than the option price, the effect of the options under plan A will be dilutive for both primary and fully diluted earnings per share (incremental shares issued of 1,250 and 5,000, respectively). For plan B, the option price exceeds both the average and the ending market price. Because the effect of in-

---

*Exhibit 22.1*
### Stock Option Plans of Adams Corporation

|  | Plan A | Plan B | Plan C |
|---|---|---|---|
| Common Shares Issuable under Option Plan ............................ | 20,000 | 20,000 | 20,000 |
| Option Price per Share ................................................. | $30 | $45 | $36 |
| Average Market Price—1981 ........................................... | $32 | $32 | $32 |
| Ending Market Price, December 31, 1981 ............................... | $40 | $40 | $40 |
| Common Shares Assumed Purchased for Primary Earnings per Share: |  |  |  |
| $600,000/$32 ......................................................... | 18,750 |  |  |
| $900,000/$32 ......................................................... |  | 28,125 |  |
| $720,000/$32 ......................................................... |  |  | 22,500 |
| Common Shares Assumed Purchased for Fully Diluted Earnings per Share: |  |  |  |
| $600,000/$40 ......................................................... | 15,000 |  |  |
| $900,000/$40 ......................................................... |  | 22,500 |  |
| $720,000/$40 ......................................................... |  |  | 18,000 |

cluding the options under plan B would be antidilutive, these options are excluded from all earnings-per-share calculations for 1981. If the price increases above the option price of $45 in the future, the options under plan B would enter into the earnings-per-share calculations. For plan C, the option price lies between the average market price and the higher ending market price. The effect of plan C is antidilutive on primary earnings per share and is, therefore, excluded from the calculations for 1981. The effect is dilutive, however, on fully diluted earnings per share and would enter into the calculations for 1981.

22.75    There is one exception to the separation test. If the number of common shares that would be issued if all outstanding options and warrants were exercised exceeds 20 percent of the number of common shares actually outstanding at the end of the period, all option and warrant plans are aggregated together, regardless of whether individually they are dilutive or antidilutive. In applying the treasury-stock method under these circumstances, the cash proceeds received from all option and warrant plans are presumed to be used in the following order:

**1.** Common shares up to a maximum of 20 percent of the outstanding shares at the end of the period are purchased.

**2.** Any remaining cash is used to reduce any short- or long-term debt of the issuer.

**3.** Any remaining cash is then invested in U.S. government securities or commercial paper.

Steps **2** and **3** require adjustment to the numerator as well as the denominator of earnings-per-share amounts. The effects of these three steps are then aggregated. If the net aggregate effect is dilutive, all of these computations enter into earnings-per-share calculations. If the net aggregate effect is antidilutive, all computations are omitted from the calculations. In the few cases where the 20-percent exception applies in practice, it is seldom necessary to go beyond step **2**.

## Summary Illustration of Earnings-per-Share Calculations

If the above rules seem complicated, it is because they are. The Accounting Principles Board's original opinion specifying the calculations is more than 60 pages long, and a year after the opinion was issued, an unofficial interpretation of more than 100 pages was issued to explain and interpret the opinion itself. The following illustration is adapted from that unofficial interpretation.*    22.76

Assume the data in Exhibit 22.2 about the capital structure and earnings for the Layton Ball Corporation for the year 1981.    22.77

A useful starting point is to determine whether or not each convertible security is a common stock equivalent.    22.78

**Is the Convertible Preferred Stock a Common Stock Equivalent?** The cash yield to buyers at the time of issue in 1967 was 5 percent (= $1/$20). Because the cash yield exceeds two-thirds of the bank prime interest rate (4 percent = $2/3 \times 6$ percent), the convertible preferred stock is not a "common stock equivalent." It is, therefore, an "other potentially dilutive security." In calculating fully diluted earnings per share, the preferred stock dividend for 1981 of $1,500 must be added back to "net income available for common" in the numerator. An additional 1,500 shares is added to the weighted average of outstanding shares in the denominator.    22.79

**Are the Convertible Bonds a Common Stock Equivalent?** The cash yield to buyers at the time of issue in 1969 was $4^{1}/_{6}$ percent, because the bonds were issued at par. Because the cash yield is less than two-thirds of the bank prime interest rate (4.5 percent = $2/3 \times 6.75$ percent), the convertible bonds are a "common stock equivalent." Annual interest expense is $4,167 (= .041667 $\times$ $100,000). If these bonds were converted,    22.80

---

*"Computing Earnings per Share: Unofficial Accounting Interpretation of APB *Opinion No. 15*," AICPA (July 1970).

*Exhibit 22.2*
**Layton Ball Corporation**
**Capital Structure and Earnings**
**For the Year 1981**

| | |
|---|---|
| Number of Common Shares Outstanding on December 31, 1981 | 27,000 |
| Number of Common Shares Outstanding during 1981 (weighted average) | 25,000 |
| Market Price per Common Share on December 31, 1981 | $25 |
| Weighted-Average Market Price per Common Share during 1981 | $20 |
| Options Outstanding during 1981: | |
|     Number of Shares Issuable on Exercise of Options | 1,000 |
|     Exercise Price | $15 |
| Warrants Outstanding during 1981: | |
|     Number of Shares Issuable on Exercise of Warrants | 2,000 |
|     Exercise Price | $30 |
| Convertible Preferred Stock Outstanding (March 1967 issue): | |
|     Number of Shares | 1,500 |
|     Shares of Common Issuable on Conversion (per share) | 1 |
|     Dividends per Share | $1 |
|     Market Price at Time of Issue | $20 |
|     Prime Rate at Time of Issue | 6% |
| Convertible Bonds Outstanding (December 1969 issue): | |
|     Number | 100 |
|     Shares of Common Issuable on Conversion (per bond) | 10 |
|     Coupon Rate | $4\frac{1}{6}\%$ |
|     Proceeds per Bond at Issue (= par value) | $1,000 |
|     Prime Rate at Time of Issue | $6\frac{3}{4}\%$ |
| Net Income for 1981 | $95,000 |
| Tax Rate for 1981 | 40% |

interest expense would be reduced and net income increased. The aftertax increase in net income from eliminating interest expense is $2,500 [= (1.00 − .40) × ($4,166.70)]. Thus, $2,500 would be added back to net income in the numerator of both primary and fully diluted earnings per share. Upon conversion, 1,000 (= 100 × 10) shares of common stock would be issued. These additional shares are added to the weighted average of shares outstanding in the denominator of primary and fully diluted earnings per share.

22.81    A second step is to find out whether each option and warrant is dilutive or antidilutive.

22.82   **Are the Options Dilutive?** Because both the average and end-of-the-period market price of the common stock exceeds the option price, the options are dilutive. For primary earnings per share, the cash proceeds

of $15,000 (= 1,000 × $15) would be used to purchase 750 shares (= $15,000/$20) on the open market. The net incremental shares issued of 250 (= 1,000 − 750) would be added to the denominator of primary earnings per share. For fully diluted earnings per share the cash proceeds of $15,000 would be used to purchase 600 shares (= $15,000/$25). The net incremental shares issued of 400 (= 1,000 − 600) would be added to the denominator of fully diluted earnings per share.

**Are the Warrants Dilutive?** Because the 22.83 average and end-of-the-period market prices of the common stock are less than the exercise price on the warrants, their effect on earnings per share would be antidilutive. The warrants are therefore excluded from earnings-per-share calculations for 1981.

It is important to check the total number 22.84

*Exhibit 22.3*
**Preliminary Earnings-per-Share Calculations for Layton Ball Corporation**

|  | Options | Warrants | Convertible Preferred Stock | Convertible Bonds |
|---|---|---|---|---|
| Common Stock Equivalent . . . . . . . . . . . . . . . . . . | Yes | Yes | No | Yes |
| Dilutive: Primary . . . . . . . . . . . . . . . . . . . . . . . . . | Yes | No[a] | [b] | [b] |
|        Fully Diluted . . . . . . . . . . . . . . . . . . . . . . | Yes | No[a] | [b] | [b] |
| Addback to Net Income: |  |  |  |  |
|    Primary . . . . . . . . . . . . . . . . . . . . . . . . . . . | — | — | — | $2,500 |
|    Fully Diluted . . . . . . . . . . . . . . . . . . . . . . . | — | — | $1,500 | $2,500 |
| Addition to Common Shares Outstanding: |  |  |  |  |
|    Primary . . . . . . . . . . . . . . . . . . . . . . . . . . . | 250 | — | — | 1,000 |
|    Fully Diluted . . . . . . . . . . . . . . . . . . . . . . . | 400 | — | 1,500 | 1,000 |

[a]Exercise price exceeds average and ending market price.

[b]Whether or not each convertible security is dilutive depends on the earnings-per-share base used. See discussion in text.

of shares issuable under options and warrants to determine if the 20-percent aggregation rule applies. If the number of shares issuable under options and warrants exceeds 20 percent of the number of common shares outstanding at the end of the year, all options and warrants must be aggregated to determine their net dilutive or antidilutive effect. The 3,000 (= 1,000 + 2,000) shares issuable under options and warrants are equal to only 11.1 percent (= 3,000/27,000) of the shares outstanding on December 31, 1981, so the aggregation rule does not apply. The results of the analysis so far are summarized in Exhibit 22.3.

22.85 **Are the Convertibles Dilutive?** Note that we cannot yet determine whether the convertible preferred stock and convertible bonds will have a dilutive or an antidilutive effect on earnings per share. Because both the numerator and denominator of earnings per share (primary and fully dilutive) are increased when a convertible security is included in the calculations, including a particular convertible security can increase, instead of decrease, earnings per share. Earnings per share will be increased if the amount added to the numerator (that is, the aftertax interest expense or the preferred stock dividend) for each share added to the denominator exceeds earnings per share before the adjustment. For the convertible bonds, for example, $2.50 (= $2,500/1,000) is added to the numerator for each share added to the denominator. If earnings per share before any adjustment for the convertible bonds is less than $2.50, then inclusion of the convertible bonds would be antidilutive. These bonds would be excluded from the calculations for 1981. If, on the other hand, earnings per share before any adjustment is greater than $2.50, the inclusion of the convertible bonds would be dilutive and they would be included in the calculations.

22.86 Deciding whether each convertible security has a dilutive or antidilutive effect, in principle, requires calculating earnings per share (primary and/or fully diluted) for each possible combination of convertible securities. The amount to be reported as earnings per share is the lowest of the amounts computed. If there are $n$ classes of convertible securities, there will be $2^n$ such combinations. For example, there is only one convertible security that is a common stock equivalent. Thus, there will be two combinations ($2^1 = 2$) to check for primary earnings per share:

1. Convertible bonds are excluded from the calculations.

2. Convertible bonds are included in the calculations.

22.87   For fully diluted earnings per share, there are two convertible securities and, therefore, four combinations ($2^2 = 4$) to check:

1. Convertible bonds and preferred stock are both excluded from the calculations.

2. Convertible bonds are included and preferred stock is excluded in the calculations.

3. Convertible bonds are excluded and preferred stock is included in the calculations.

4. Convertible bonds and preferred stock are both included in the calculations.

It is not necessary to add the stock options and warrants to these possible combinations, because no amount is normally added to the numerator in earnings-per-share calculations.*

---

*A short-cut procedure for finding the combination of convertible securities that will provide the lowest earnings-per-share amount is provided by S. Davidson and R. Weil (*Journal of Accountancy,* December 1975, pp. 45–47). The short-cut procedure is summarized as follows. The key to the short cut is the calculation of the "charge against earnings per common share embodied in a convertible security," or CANY. A convertible preferred stock paying a $5-per-share annual dividend and convertible into five shares of common stock has a CANY of $1 ($5 per share preferred dividend added to numerator of earnings per common share/5 common shares added to denominator of earnings per common share) for each convertible preferred share outstanding. A convertible bond paying $80 in interest and convertible into 20 shares of common stock has a CANY of $2.40 [= $(1 - .40) \times$ $80/20 shares] assuming a 40-percent tax rate. The short-cut procedure is as follows:

1. Compute earnings per share including stock options and warrants but excluding all convertible securities. Call the result tentative earnings per share (TEPS).
2. Compute CANY for each convertible security and list them from smallest to largest.
3. Compare the CANY at the top of the list with TEPS.
   a. If CANY is greater than or equal to TEPS, then this and all other convertible securities are an-

**Earnings per Common Share Outstanding**   The starting point is to calculate earnings per share based on the weighted average number of common shares outstanding. The calculation is

$$\frac{\text{Net Income} - \text{Preferred Stock Dividends}}{\text{Weighted Average Number of Common Shares Outstanding}} = \frac{\$95,000 - \$1,500}{25,000 \text{ Shares}} = \frac{\$3.74}{\text{per Share}}$$

This basic earnings-per-share amount is adjusted in calculating primary and fully diluted earnings per share. It is also used for ascertaining whether the calculated amounts of primary and fully diluted earnings per share are different enough (3-percent materiality test) to warrant separate disclosure.

**Primary Earnings per Share**   The stock options and convertible bonds must be considered in the calculations. Primary earnings per share is the lower of the following two amounts:

1. Earnings per share, assuming exercise of the options but excluding the convertible bonds,

$$\frac{\$95,000 - \$1,500}{25,000 + 250} = \$3.70 \text{ per Share.}$$

2. Earnings per share, assuming exercise of the options and conversion of the convertible bonds,

$$\frac{\$95,000 - \$1,500 + \$2,500}{25,000 + 250 + 1,000} = \$3.66 \text{ per Share.}$$

Because the result of the second calculation is smaller than the first, the convertible bonds are dilutive and primary earnings per share is $3.66.

---

tidilutive. TEPS is therefore earnings per share (either primary or fully diluted as appropriate).
   b. If CANY is less than TEPS, then this convertible security is dilutive. Compute a new TEPS taking into account the convertible security.
4. Return to step 3 for the next CANY.
5. Repeat the process until either the last CANY is exhausted or the last CANY equals or exceeds TEPS.

22.88

22.89

22.90 **Fully Diluted Earnings per Share** The stock options, convertible preferred stock, and convertible bonds must be considered in the calculations. Fully diluted earnings per share is the lowest of the following four amounts:

**1.** Earnings per share assuming exercise of the options but excluding the convertible bonds and preferred stock,

$$\frac{\$95,000 - \$1,500}{25,000 + 400} = \$3.68 \text{ per Share.}$$

**2.** Earnings per share assuming exercise of the options, inclusion of the bonds, and exclusion of the preferred stock,

$$\frac{\$95,000 - \$1,500 + \$2,500}{25,000 + 400 + 1,000} = \$3.64 \text{ per Share.}$$

**3.** Earnings per share assuming exercise of the options, exclusion of the bonds, and inclusion of the preferred stock,

$$\frac{\$95,000 - \$1,500 + \$1,500}{25,000 + 400 + 1,500} = \$3.53 \text{ per Share.}$$

**4.** Earnings per share, assuming exercise of the options and including the bonds and preferred stock,

$$\frac{\$95,000 - \$1,500 + \$1,500 + \$2,500}{25,000 + 400 + 1,500 + 1,000} = \$3.49 \text{ per Share.}$$

Fully diluted earnings per share would be reported as $3.49.

22.91   Note that in applying the 3-percent materiality test, primary earnings per share is within the 3-percent immateriality range (.97 × $3.74 = $3.63), whereas fully diluted earnings per share is outside this range. Layton

Ball Corporation would, therefore, report its earnings per share for 1981 as follows:

| | |
|---|---|
| Earnings per Common Share Outstanding . | $3.74 |
| Fully Diluted Earnings per Share . . . . . . . . . . | $3.49 |

Disclosure of primary earnings per share is not required in this case.

## Summary

22.92 The dilution of an owner's equity investment in a corporation is of concern to the owner because of its possible effect on both the market price per share and the owner's proportionate voting interest. During the past two decades, corporations have increasingly used various dilutive securities as a means of obtaining capital. Holders of dilutive securities have the right to acquire shares of common stock at terms that are usually more attractive than purchasing the shares on the open market.

22.93   The principal accounting issues for dilutive securities have centered on (1) their recognition and valuation, particularly regarding their status as debt versus owners' equity securities, and (2) their effect on the calculation of earnings per share. Two earnings-per-share amounts must be calculated if a firm has a significant amount of dilutive securities in its capital structure. Primary earnings per share measures the earnings attributable to outstanding common shares plus shares issuable relating to dilutive securities that are substantially equivalent to common stock. Fully diluted earnings per share measures the maximum potential dilution that could occur if all dilutive securities were turned into shares of common stock.

## Questions and Short Cases

**22.1** Review the meaning of the following concepts or terms discussed in this chapter:
   **a.** Book value versus market value basis of recording conversions of preferred stock.
   **b.** Stock subscriptions versus stock rights.
   **c.** Stock rights versus stock options versus stock warrants.
   **d.** Compensatory versus noncompensatory stock option plans.
   **e.** Bonds or preferred stock with detachable versus nondetachable stock warrants.
   **f.** Dilution.

g. Earnings per outstanding common share.

h. Simple versus complex capital structure.

i. Primary earnings per share.

j. Fully diluted earnings per share.

k. Common stock equivalent.

l. Other potentially dilutive security.

m. Antidilution exception.

n. Three-percent immateriality exception.

o. Two-thirds rule for convertible securities.

p. Cash yield.

q. Nominal yield.

r. Market yield.

s. Permanent classification rule for convertible securities.

t. If-converted method for convertible securities.

u. Common stock equivalency rule for stock options and warrants.

v. Treasury-stock method for stock options and warrants.

w. Separation rule for stock options and warrants.

x. Twenty-percent exception to treasury-stock method for stock options and warrants.

**22.2** One of the objectives in accounting for shareholders' equity is to distinguish (1) capital transactions from (2) the generation of earnings from capital. Give three examples from this chapter where either capital transactions affect retained earnings or earnings transactions affect contributed capital.

**22.3** If a firm exchanges a fleet of trucks for a tract of land, APB *Opinion No. 29* requires that the land be recorded at its fair market value if readily determinable. If not, then the fair market value of the fleet of trucks given should be used in recording the valuation of the land received. If holders of a firm's convertible preferred stock exercise their options and convert the preferred stock into shares of common stock, the exchange can be recorded using either the book value of the preferred stock or the market value of the preferred or common stock exchanged. Suggest reasons why market values must generally be used in the case of exchanges of assets but that either book or market values can be used in exchanges of ownership interests.

**22.4.** Distinguish between stock subscriptions and stock rights, both as to their purpose and to the methods of accounting used.

**22.5** Distinguish between compensatory and noncompensatory stock option plans, both as to their nature and the methods of accounting used.

**22.6** Distinguish between bonds (or preferred stock) with detachable versus nondetachable stock warrants, both as to their nature and the methods of accounting used.

**22.7** Distinguish among the roles of the cash yield, nominal yield, and market yield in applying the two-thirds rule for convertible securities.

**22.8** "A convertible security that is classified as a common stock equivalent will enter into the calculation of primary earnings per share each year until it is either redeemed by the corporation or converted into common stock." Do you agree? Why or why not?

**22.9** A corporation has the following convertible securities outstanding:

$10,000,000 of 6-percent convertible bonds issued at par; each $1,000 bond is convertible into 100 shares of common stock.

$10,000,000 of $100-par-value convertible preferred stock issued at par; each share carries a cumulative annual dividend of $6 and is convertible into 10 shares of common stock.

The corporation president stated: "Our earnings-per-share calculations are simplified, because the convertible bonds and preferred stock have an identical impact on primary and fully diluted earnings per share each year." Do you agree? Why or why not?

22.10    "Stock options and warrants are always considered common stock equivalents and enter into the calculation of primary and fully diluted earnings per share each year." Do you agree? Why or why not?

22.11    For each convertible security, primary and/or fully diluted earnings per share must be calculated by both excluding and then including the convertible security to determine if the effect is dilutive or antidilutive. Why are similar calculations not required for stock options and warrants?

22.12    In applying the treasury-stock method, the average market price during the period is used in calculating primary earnings per share, but the higher of the average or ending market price is used in calculating fully diluted earnings per share. What is the rationale for this difference in the market prices used?

22.13    A particular stock option plan may be antidilutive for primary earnings per share and dilutive for fully diluted earnings per share. Such a plan, however, could not be dilutive for primary earnings per share and antidilutive for fully diluted earnings per share. Why is this the case?

22.14    Stock options for 10,000 shares of common stock were issued to employees 2 years ago and have not yet been exercised. These options were dilutive and entered into the calculations of primary and fully diluted earnings per share during each of the preceding 2 years. During the current year, these stock options, although still outstanding, were not included in the calculation of primary and fully diluted earnings per share. What possible reasons might there be for such exclusions?

22.15    Refer to the schedule reproduced in Exhibit 22.4, which shows employee stock option data for the General Products Company (GP). At December 31, 1981, there were 2.7 million options outstanding to purchase shares at an average of $54 per share. Total shareholders' equity at December 31, 1981, was about $2.5 billion.
   a. If GP were to issue 2.7 million shares in a public offering at the market price per share on December 31, 1981, what would be the proceeds of the issue?
   b. If GP were to issue 2.7 million shares to employees who exercised all outstanding stock options, what would be the proceeds of the issue?
   c. Are GP's shareholders better off under **a** or under **b**?
   d. The text accompanying the stock option data in the GP annual report reads, in part, as follows:

Option price under these plans is the full market value of General Products common stock on date of grant. Therefore, participants in the plans do not benefit unless the stock's market price rises, thus benefiting all share owners. . . .

GP seems to be saying that shareholders are not harmed by these options, whereas your answers to parts **a** and **b** show shareholders are worse off when options are exercised than when shares are issued to the public. Attempt to reconcile GP's statement with your own analysis in parts **a** and **b**.

*Exhibit 22.4*
**General Products Company**
**Disclosure of Employee**
**Stock Options**

| Stock Options | Shares Subject to Option | Average per Share | |
|---|---|---|---|
| | | Option Price | Market Price |
| Balance at December 31, 1979 ......... | 2,388,931 | $45 | $72 |
| Options Granted ..................... | 475,286 | 77 | 77 |
| Options Exercised .................... | (297,244) | 42 | 76 |
| Options Terminated .................. | (90,062) | 45 | — |
| Balance at December 31, 1980 ......... | 2,476,911 | 50 | 83 |
| Options Granted ..................... | 554,965 | 75 | 75 |
| Options Exercised ................... | (273,569) | 42 | 74 |
| Options Terminated .................. | (58,307) | 52 | — |
| Balance at December 31, 1981 ......... | 2,700,000 | 54 | 77 |

22.16 (Adapted from CPA Examination.) On January 1, 1981, as an incentive to greater performance in their duties, Recycling Corporation adopted a qualified stock option plan to grant corporate executives nontransferable stock options to 500,000 shares of its unissued $1.00-par-value common stock. The options were granted on May 1, 1981, at $25 per share, the market price on that date. All of the options were exercisable 1 year later and for 4 years thereafter, providing that the grantee was employed by the Corporation at the date of exercise.

The market price of this stock was $40 per share on May 1, 1982. All options were exercised before December 31, 1982, at times when the market price varied between $40 and $50 per share.

a. What information on this option plan should be presented in the financial statements of Recycling Corporation at (1) December 31, 1981, and (2) December 31, 1982? Explain why this is acceptable.

b. It has been said that the exercise of such a stock option would dilute the equity of existing shareholders in the Corporation. (1) How could this happen? Discuss. (2) What condition could prevent a dilution of existing equities from taking place in this transaction? Discuss.

22.17 (Adapted from CPA Examination.) Raun Company had the following account titles on its December 31, 1981, trial balance:
Six-percent cumulative convertible preferred stock, $100 par value
Premium on preferred stock
Common stock, $1 stated value
Premium on common stock
Retained earnings

The following additional information about the Raun Company was available for the year ended December 31, 1981:

1. There were 2,000,000 shares of preferred stock authorized, of which 1,000,000 were outstanding. All 1,000,000 shares outstanding were issued on January 2, 1978, for $120 a share. The bank prime interest rate was 8.5 percent on January 2, 1978, and was 10 per-

cent on December 31, 1981. The preferred stock is convertible into common stock on a one-for-one basis until December 31, 1987; thereafter the preferred stock ceases to be convertible and is callable at par value by the company. No preferred stock has been converted into common stock, and there were no dividends in arrears at December 31, 1981.

2. The common stock has been issued at amounts above stated value per share since incorporation in 1966. Of the 5,000,000 shares authorized, there were 3,500,000 shares outstanding at January 1, 1981. The market price of the outstanding common stock has increased slowly, but consistently, for the last 5 years.

3. The company has an employee stock option plan by which certain key employees and officers may purchase shares of common stock at 100 percent of the market price at the date of the option grant. All options are exercisable in installments of one-third each year, commencing 1 year after the date of the grant, and expire if not exercised within 4 years of the grant date. On January 1, 1981, options for 70,000 shares were outstanding at prices ranging from $47.00 to $83.00 a share. Options for 20,000 shares were exercised at $47.00 to $79.00 a share during 1981. No options expired during 1981, and additional options for 15,000 shares were granted at $86.00 a share during the year. The 65,000 options outstanding at December 31, 1981, were exercisable at $54.00 to $86.00 a share; of these, 30,000 were exercisable at that date at prices ranging from $54.00 to $79.00 a share.

4. The company also has an employee stock purchase plan by which the company pays one-half and the employee pays one-half of the market price of the stock at the date of the subscription. During 1981, employees subscribed to 60,000 shares at an average price of $87.00 a share. All 60,000 shares were paid for and issued late in September 1981.

5. On December 31, 1981, there was a total of 355,000 shares of common stock set aside for the granting of future stock options and for future purchases under the employee stock purchase plan. The only changes in the shareholders' equity for 1981 were those described above, 1981 net income, and cash dividends paid.

a. Prepare the shareholders' equity section of the balance sheet of Raun Company at December 31, 1981; substitute, where appropriate, Xs for unknown dollar amounts. Use good form and provide full disclosure. Write appropriate footnotes as they should appear in the published financial statements.

b. Explain how the amount of the denominator should be determined to compute primary earnings per share for presentation in the financial statements. Be specific as to the handling of each item. If additional information is needed to determine whether an item should be included or excluded or the extent to which an item should be included, identify the information needed and how the item would be handled if the information were known. Assume Raun Company had substantial net income for the year ended December 31, 1981.

## Problems and Exercises

22.18  (Adapted from CPA Examination.) In January 1981, Orlando, Incorporated, issued for $105 per share, 8,000 shares of $100-par-value convertible preferred stock. One share of preferred stock can be converted into three shares of Orlando's $25-par-value common stock at the option of the preferred shareholder. In August 1981, all of the preferred stock was converted into common stock. The market value of the common stock at the date of the conversion was $30 per share.

   Give the journal entries to record the issue of the preferred stock and its subsequent conversion into common stock.

22.19   On December 31, 1980, Bradley Corporation issued stock options to various employees permitting them to purchase 10,000 shares of $5-par-value common stock for $15 a share. Employees holding options for 6,000 shares exercised the options on November 30, 1981. Give the journal entries relating to this stock option plan during 1980 and 1981 under each of the four independent cases below.

| Type of Plan | a<br>Noncom-<br>pensatory | b<br>Noncom-<br>pensatory | c<br>Compen-<br>satory | d<br>Compen-<br>satory |
|---|---|---|---|---|
| Market Price: | | | | |
| December 31, 1980 .................. | $15 | $16 | $15 | $16 |
| November 30, 1981 .................. | $18 | $18 | $18 | $18 |

22.20   (Adapted from CPA Examination.) On July 18, 1981, the Amos Corporation granted nontransferable options to certain of its key employees as additional compensation. The options permit the purchase of 20,000 shares of Amos' common stock at a price of $30 per share. On the date of the grant, the market value of the stock was $42 per share. The options are exercisable beginning January 2, 1982, and expire on December 31, 1983. On February 3, 1982, when the stock was selling for $45 per share, half of the options were exercised. On April 6, 1983, when the stock was selling for $53 per share, the other half of the options were exercised.

Determine the amount of compensation expense to be recognized by Amos Corporation during 1981, 1982, and 1983.

22.21   **a.** On September 15, 1981, Hill Company issued 20,000 shares of $100-par-value, 6-percent, noncumulative preferred stock for $105 per share. Each share carried with it a detachable warrant to purchase one share of $5-par-value common stock for $20 per share. On December 20, 1981, holders of warrants to purchase 15,000 shares of common stock exercised their warrants. The market value of the preferred stock was $102.90 per share and of the warrants was $4.20 per warrant on September 15, 1981. Give the journal entries to record the issuance of the preferred stock and warrants on September 15, 1981, and the exercise of the warrants on December 20, 1981.

**b.** Assume the same information as in part **a**, except that the warrants are nondetachable and each warrant can be exchanged for five shares of common stock. No cash payment is required at time of conversion to common stock. Give the journal entries to record the issuance of the preferred stock and warrants on September 15, 1981, and the exercise of warrants to purchase 75,000 shares (= 15,000 × 5) on December 20, 1981.

22.22   (Adapted from CPA Examination.) On July 1, 1981, Round Company issued for $530,000 a total of 5,000 shares of $100-par-value, 7-percent, noncumulative preferred stock along with one detachable warrant for each share issued. Each warrant contains a right to purchase one share of Round's $10-par-value common stock for $15 per share. The market price of the preferred stock on July 1, 1981, was $102.90 per share and of the rights was $2.10 per right. On October 31, 1981, when the market price of the common stock was $19 per share and the market value of the rights was $3.00 per right, 4,000 rights were exercised.

Give the journal entries to record the transactions on July 1 and October 31.

22.23   Taylor Corporation has a simple capital structure. Net income for 1981 was $500,000. On December 31, 1980, 200,000 common shares were outstanding. The following information relates to its common stock:

| | |
|---|---|
| Jan. 1, 1981 ...... | 100,000 shares of common stock are redeemed and retired. |
| March 1, 1981 .... | 5,000 shares of common stock are acquired and held as treasury stock. |
| April 1, 1981 ..... | 10,000 shares of common stock are issued on the open market. Of this total, 5,000 shares come from the treasury shares acquired on March 1, 1981. |
| June 1, 1981 ..... | 1,000 shares of common stock are redeemed and retired. |
| Aug. 1, 1981 ..... | 2,000 shares of common stock are acquired and held as treasury stock. |
| Nov. 1, 1981 ...... | 1,500 of the shares of common stock acquired on August 1, 1981, are resold on the open market. |

Compute the earnings per share for 1981. Prepare a separate schedule to show the calculation of the weighted-average number of shares outstanding. Assume a 365-day year.

22.24   (Adapted from CPA Examination.) Information concerning the capital structure of the Petrock Corporation is as follows:

| | December 31 | |
|---|---|---|
| | **1980** | **1981** |
| Common Stock ......................................... | 90,000 Shares | 90,000 Shares |
| Convertible Preferred Stock ............................. | 10,000 Shares | 10,000 Shares |
| 8% Convertible Bonds .................................. | $1,000,000 | $1,000,000 |

During 1981, Petrock Corporation paid dividends of $1.00 per share on its common stock and $2.40 per share on its preferred stock. The preferred stock is convertible into 20,000 shares of common stock but is not considered a "common stock equivalent." The 8-percent convertible bonds, originally issued at par, are convertible into 30,000 shares of common stock and are considered common stock equivalents. The net income for the year ended December 31, 1981, was $285,000. Assume that the income tax rate was 40 percent.
a. Calculate primary earnings per share.
b. Calculate fully diluted earnings per share.

22.25   On December 31, 1980, Williamson Corporation granted stock options to various employees permitting them to acquire 20,000 shares of common stock at $20 per share. The market price on December 31, 1980, was $18 per share.
   During 1981, earnings per share of outstanding common stock was $2.00 (= $400,000/200,000 shares). Compute the amount of primary and fully diluted earnings per share for 1981, assuming that the average and ending market prices of the common stock for each quarter were as follows:

| | **Average** | **End of Quarter** |
|---|---|---|
| First Quarter ............................................ | $19 | $20 |
| Second Quarter ......................................... | 22 | 21 |
| Third Quarter ........................................... | 18 | 20 |
| Fourth Quarter .......................................... | 24 | 28 |

You may assume that the market price exceeded $20 per share for substantially all of the second quarter of 1981.

22.26   Refer to Exhibit 4.13 in Chapter 4 (Question **4.15**), where a simplified funds statement is presented. For each of the transactions below, indicate the number(s) of the line(s) in Exhibit 4.13 that would be affected assuming that funds are defined as working capital. If net income is affected, be sure to indicate if it increases or decreases net income. Ignore income tax effects.

a. Shares of convertible preferred stock are issued on the open market.

b. Noncompensatory stock options are granted to various employees.

c. Refer to part **b**. The options are exercised by employees, who pay cash for the shares issued.

d. Compensatory stock options are granted to various employees. The amount of compensation is measurable at the date of the grant.

e. Refer to part **c**. The options are exercised by employees, who pay cash for the shares issued.

f. Shares of outstanding convertible preferred stock are exchanged for shares of common stock.

g. Bonds with detachable stock warrants are issued for cash.

h. Refer to part **g**. The warrants are exercised. Holders of the warrants pay the agreed-upon price and the common shares are issued.

**22.27**   Set up a work sheet with the following columns:

| Item | Primary Earnings per Share | Fully Diluted Earnings per Share |
|---|---|---|

Earnings per common share outstanding has been computed for the period. For each of the independent items below, indicate the incremental adjustment made to the numerator and to the denominator of earnings per common share outstanding to calculate primary and fully diluted earnings per share for 1981. The income tax rate is 46 percent.

a. $5,000,000, 5-year bank loan, due 1986. The interest rate for the first 4 years is 10 percent annually; the fifth-year interest rate is 6 percent. The loan was obtained when the bank prime interest rate was 8 percent.

b. The 1980 employee stock purchase plan granted the right to various individuals to purchase 10,000 shares of common stock at $50 per share (the market price on the date of the grant) at any time during the next 3 years. The average market price during 1981 was $55 per share, whereas the price on December 31, 1981, was $48 per share.

c. On June 1, 1981, 1,000 shares of the firm's common stock were acquired on the open market for $52 per share. These shares were sold for $55 per share on November 1, 1981.

d. $5,000,000 convertible debentures, 7 percent, due January 1, 1991. Each $1,000 bond is convertible into 20 shares of common stock. The bonds were issued at $800 each. At the time of issuance on January 1, 1981, the bank prime interest rate was 8 percent. The straight-line method of amortizing bond discount is used.

e. Same as part **d**, except that the debentures were issued on April 1, 1981. The bank prime interest rate was still 8 percent.

f. The 1981 stock option plan granted to each of the top five officers offers the right to acquire 1,000 common shares per year during each of the next 3 years. At the time of the grant, the market price of the common stock was $35 per share and the option price was $40 per share. The average market price during 1981 was $36 per share and the price on December 31, 1981, was $38 per share. There are 250,000 common shares issued and outstanding.

g. $3,000,000, 4-percent cumulative preferred stock. The shares were issued for par in 1978. Each $100 share is convertible into one share of common stock. All required dividends have been paid each year. The bank prime interest rate during 1978 was 7 percent and during 1981 was 5 percent.

h. 40,000 stock purchase warrants were sold on April 1, 1981, for $10 each. One warrant plus $40 in cash can be exchanged for one common share. The market price of the common stock at the time of the grant was $35 per share. The average market prices during the remaining three quarters of the year were $38, $50, and $60 per share, respectively. The closing market prices during the three quarters were $42, $58, and $68 per share, respectively. The market price exceeded the option price for substantially all of the third quarter.

i. $2,000,000, 6-percent noncumulative and participating preferred stock. $4,000,000 par value of common stock outstanding. Net income for 1981 was $800,000, and dividends totaling $450,000 were paid during the year.

**22.28** (Adapted from CPA Examination.) The controller of Lafayette Corporation has requested assistance in calculating primary earnings per share and fully diluted earnings per share for presentation in the Company's income statement for the year ended September 30, 1981. The Company's net income is $540,000 for fiscal year 1980–1981.

Your working papers disclose the following opening balances and transactions in the Company's capital stock accounts during the year:

1. Common stock (stated value $10, authorized 600,000 shares):
   Balance, October 1, 1980—issued and outstanding 120,000 shares.
   December 1, 1980—280,000 shares (stated value $10) issued at $39 per share.

2. Treasury stock—common:
   March 1, 1981—purchased 40,000 shares at $38 per share.
   April 1, 1981—sold 40,000 shares at $40 per share.

3. Stock purchase warrants, Series A (each warrant is exchangeable for two common shares at $30 per share):
   October 1, 1980—25,000 warrants issued at $6 each.

4. Stock purchase warrants, Series B (each warrant is exchangeable with $40 for one common share):
   April 1, 1981—20,000 warrants authorized and issued at $10 each.

5. First mortgage bonds, $5\frac{1}{2}$ percent, due 1996 (nonconvertible; priced to yield 5 percent when issued):
   Balance October 1, 1980—authorized, issued, and outstanding—the face value of $1,400,000.

6. Convertible debentures, 7 percent, due 1990 (each $1,000 bond is convertible at any time until maturity into 25 common shares).
   October 1, 1980—authorized and issued at their face value (no premium or discount) of $2,400,000.

The following table shows market prices for the Company's securities and the assumed bank prime interest rate during 1980 through 1981:

| | Price (or Rate) at | | | Average for Year Ended September 30, 1981 |
|---|---|---|---|---|
| | **October 1, 1980** | **April 1, 1981** | **September 30, 1981** | |
| Common Stock ........... | 33 | 40 | $36\frac{1}{4}$ | $37\frac{1}{2}$ |
| First Mortgage Bonds ..... | $88\frac{1}{2}$ | 87 | 86 | 87 |
| Convertible Debentures .... | 100 | 120 | 119 | 115 |
| Series A Warrants ......... | 6 | 22 | $19\frac{1}{2}$ | 15 |
| Series B Warrants ......... | — | 10 | 9 | $9\frac{1}{2}$ |
| Bank Prime Interest Rate .. | 8% | $7\frac{3}{4}$% | $7\frac{1}{2}$% | $7\frac{3}{4}$% |

Prepare a schedule computing **(a)** the primary earnings per share and **(b)** the fully diluted earnings per share that should be presented in the Company's income statement for the year ended September 30, 1981. A supporting schedule computing the number of shares to be used in these computations should also be prepared. You may assume that the market price for its common shares was sufficiently stable during the year so that the annual average market price may be used where appropriate in your calculations. The income tax rate is 46 percent.

**22.29** (Adapted from CPA Examination.) The shareholders' equity section of Lowe Company's balance sheet as of December 31, 1981, contains the following:

| | |
|---|---:|
| $1.00 Cumulative Convertible Preferred Stock (par value $25 a share; authorized 1,600,000 shares, issued 1,400,000, converted to common 750,000, and outstanding 650,000 shares; involuntary liquidation value, $30 a share, aggregating $19,500,000) .......................................... | $16,250,000 |
| Common Stock (par value $.25 a share; authorized 15,000,000 shares, issued and outstanding 8,800,000 shares) ........................................... | 2,200,000 |
| Additional Paid-in Capital .................................................. | 32,750,000 |
| Retained Earnings ....................................................... | 40,595,000 |
| Total Shareholders' Equity ............................................ | $91,795,000 |

Included in the liabilities of Lowe Company are 5$\frac{1}{2}$-percent convertible subordinated debentures issued at their face value of $20,000,000 in 1980. The debentures are due in 1990 and until then are convertible into the common stock of Lowe Company at the rate of five shares of common stock for each $100 debenture. To date none of these has been converted.

On April 2, 1981, Lowe Company issued 1,400,000 shares of convertible preferred stock at $40 per share. Quarterly dividends have been paid on these shares on the last day of each quarter. The preferred stock is convertible into common stock at the rate of two shares of common for each share of preferred. On October 1, 1981, 150,000 shares and on November 1, 1981, 600,000 shares of the preferred stock were converted into common stock.

During July 1980, Lowe Company granted options to its officers and key employees to purchase 500,000 shares of the Company's common stock at a price of $20 a share. The options do not become exercisable until 1982.

During 1981, dividend payments and average market prices of the Lowe common stock have been as follows:

| | Dividend per Share | Average Market Price per Share | Ending Market Price per Share |
|---|---:|---:|---:|
| First Quarter ............................. | $.10 | $18 | $19 |
| Second Quarter .......................... | .15 | 25 | 28 |
| Third Quarter ............................ | .10 | 30 | 28 |
| Fourth Quarter .......................... | .15 | 25 | 25 |

Assume that the bank prime interest rate was 7 percent throughout 1980 and 1981. Lowe Company's consolidated net income for the year ended December 31, 1981, was $9,200,000. The provision for income taxes was computed at a rate of 46 percent.

**a.** Prepare a schedule that shows the evaluation of the common stock equivalency status of **(1)** the convertible debentures, **(2)** the convertible preferred stock, and **(3)** the employee stock options.

**b.** Prepare a schedule that shows for 1981 the computation of **(1)** the weighted average number of shares for computing primary earnings per share and **(2)** the weighted average number of shares for computing fully diluted earnings per share. Use quarterly market prices as appropriate in applying the treasury-stock method. The market price of the common shares throughout 1980 and the first quarter of 1981 was less than $20 per share. The market price throughout the second quarter of 1981 exceeded $20.

c. Prepare a schedule that shows for 1981 the computation to the nearest cent of (1) primary earnings per share, and (2) fully diluted earnings per share.

22.30   (Adapted from CPA Examination.) Exhibit 22.5 sets forth the short-term debt, long-term

---

*Exhibit 22.5*
**Darren Company**
**Explanation of Short-Term Debt, Long-Term Debt, and Shareholders' Equity Including Transactions during the Year Ended December 31, 1981**

| | |
|---|---:|
| Short-Term Debt: | |
| Notes Payable—Banks | $ 4,000,000 |
| Current Portion of Long-Term Debt | 10,000,000 |
| Total Short-Term Debt | $ 14,000,000 |
| | |
| Long-Term Debt: | |
| 4% Convertible Debentures Due April 15, 1989 | $ 30,000,000 |
| Other Long-Term Debt Less Current Portions | 20,000,000 |
| Total Long-Term Debt | $ 50,000,000 |
| | |
| Shareholders Equity: | |
| $4.00 Cumulative, Convertible Preferred Stock; Par Value $20 per Share; Authorized 2,000,000 Shares; Issued and Outstanding 1,200,000 Shares; Liquidation Preference $30 per Share Aggregating $39,000,000 | $ 24,000,000 |
| Common Stock; Par Value $1 per Share; Authorized 20,000,000 Shares; Issued 7,500,000 Shares Including 600,000 Shares Held in Treasury | 7,500,000 |
| Additional Paid-in Capital | 106,200,000 |
| Retained Earnings | 76,500,000 |
| Total | $214,200,000 |
| Less Cost of 600,000 Shares of Common Stock Held in Treasury (acquired prior to 1981) | 900,000 |
| Total Shareholders' Equity | $213,300,000 |
| Total Long-Term Debt and Shareholders' Equity | $263,300,000 |

---

debt, and shareholders' equity of Darren Company as of December 31, 1981. The president of Darren has requested that you assist the controller in preparing figures for earnings-per-share computations.

The "Other Long-Term Debt" and the related amounts due within 1 year are amounts due on unsecured promissory notes that require payments each year to maturity. The interest rates on these borrowings range from 6 to 7 percent. At the time that these monies were borrowed, the bank prime interest rate was 7 percent.

The 4-percent convertible debentures were issued at their face value of $30,000,000 in 1973 when the bank prime interest rate was 5 percent. The debentures are due in 1989 and until then are convertible into the common stock of Darren at the rate of 25 shares for each $1,000 debenture.

The $4.00 cumulative, convertible preferred stock was issued in 1980. The stock had a market value of $75 at the time of issuance, when the bank prime interest rate was 9 percent. On July 1, 1981, and on October 1, 1981, holders of the preferred stock converted 80,000 and

20,000 preferred shares, respectively, into common stock. Each share of preferred stock is convertible into 1.2 shares of common stock.

On April 1, 1981, Darren acquired plant and equipment by the issuance of 800,000 shares of Darren common stock.

On October 1, 1980, the company granted options to its officers and selected employees to purchase 100,000 shares of Darren's common stock at a price of $33 per share. The options are not exercisable until 1983.

*Additional information:*

The average and ending market prices during 1981 of Darren common stock are given below. The market price exceeded the option price for substantially all of the third quarter of the year.

| | Average Market Price | Ending Market Price |
|---|---|---|
| First Quarter | $31 | $29 |
| Second Quarter | 32 | 33 |
| Third Quarter | 35 | 33 |
| Fourth Quarter | 37 | 34 |
| Average for the Year | 34 | — |
| December 31, 1981 | — | 34 |

Quarterly dividends on the preferred stock have been paid through December 31, 1981. Dividends paid on the common stock were $.50 per share for each quarter.

The net income of Darren Company for the year ended December 31, 1981, was $8,600,000. There were no extraordinary items. The provision for income taxes was computed at a rate of 46 percent.

**a.** Prepare a schedule that shows the adjusted number of shares (denominator amount) for 1981 to compute **(1)** primary earnings per share and **(2)** fully diluted earnings per share. Use the market prices for each quarter in these calculations.

**b.** Prepare a schedule that shows the adjusted net income (numerator amount) for 1981 to compute **(1)** primary earnings per share and **(2)** fully diluted earnings per share.

**c.** Compute primary and fully diluted earnings per share for 1981.

**22.31** (Adapted from CPA Examination.) Howard Corporation is a publicly owned company whose shares are traded on a national stock exchange. At December 31, 1980, Howard had 25,000,000 shares of $10-par-value common stock authorized, of which 15,000,000 shares were issued and 14,000,000 shares were outstanding.

The shareholders' equity accounts at December 31, 1980, had the following balances:

| | |
|---|---|
| Common Stock | $150,000,000 |
| Additional Paid-in Capital | 80,000,000 |
| Retained Earnings | 50,000,000 |
| Treasury Stock | 18,000,000 |

During 1981, Howard had the following transactions:

1. On February 1, 1981, a secondary distribution of 2,000,000 shares of $10-par-value common stock was completed. The stock was sold to the public at $18 per share, net of offering costs.

2. On February 15, 1981, Howard issued at $110 per share, 100,000 shares of $100-par-value, 8-percent cumulative preferred stock with 100,000 detachable warrants. Each warrant contained one right that with $20 could be exchanged for one share of $10-par-value common stock. On February 15, 1981, the market price for one stock right was $1.

3. On March 1, 1981, Howard reacquired 20,000 shares of its common stock for $18.50 per share. Howard uses the cost method to account for treasury stock.

4. On March 15, 1981, when the common stock was trading for $21 per share, a major shareholder donated 10,000 shares, which are appropriately recorded as treasury stock.

5. On March 31, 1981, Howard declared a semiannual cash dividend on common stock of $0.10 per share, payable on April 30, 1981, to shareholders of record on April 10, 1981. The appropriate state law prohibits cash dividends on treasury stock.

6. On April 15, 1981, when the market price of the stock rights was $2 each and the market price of the common stock was $22 per share, 30,000 stock rights were exercised. Howard issued new shares to settle the transaction.

7. On April 30, 1981, employees exercised 100,000 options that were granted in 1979 under a noncompensatory stock option plan. When the options were granted, each option had a preemptive right and entitled the employee to purchase one share of common stock for $20 per share. On April 30, 1981, the market price of the common stock was $23 per share. Howard issued new shares to settle the transaction.

8. On June 30, 1981, Howard sold the 20,000 treasury shares reacquired on March 1, 1981, and an additional 280,000 treasury shares costing $5,600,000 that were on hand at the beginning of the year. The selling price was $25 per share.

9. On September 30, 1981, Howard declared a semiannual cash dividend on common stock of $0.10 per share and the yearly dividend on preferred stock, both payable on October 30, 1981, to shareholders of record on October 10, 1981. The appropriate state law prohibits cash dividends on treasury stock.

10. On December 31, 1981, the remaining outstanding rights expired.

11. Net income for 1981 was $25,000,000.

Prepare a work sheet to be used to summarize, for each transaction, the changes in Howard's shareholders' equity accounts for 1981. The columns on this work sheet should have the following headings:

Date of Transaction (or Beginning Date)
Common Stock—Number of Shares
Common Stock—Amount
Preferred Stock—Number of Shares
Preferred Stock—Amount
Common Stock Warrants—Number of Rights
Common Stock Warrants—Amount
Additional Paid-in Capital
Retained Earnings
Treasury Stock—Number of Shares
Treasury Stock—Amount

Show supporting computations in good form.

22.32 Webster Corporation is a publicly owned corporation whose shares are traded on a national stock exchange. At December 31, 1980, its shareholders' equity accounts included the information shown in Exhibit 22.6.

The following events or transactions occurred during 1981.

1. January 20. 3,000 shares of treasury stock are sold for $17 per share.

2. February 15. Rights to acquire 10,000 shares of common stock for $20 per share are issued to various shareholders. The rights expire on August 15, 1981.

3. March 10. Land with a market value of $50,000 is given to Webster Corporation as an inducement to locate in Hanover City.

*Exhibit 22.6*

**Webster Corporation**
**Shareholders' Equity**
**as of December 31, 1980**

| | |
|---|---:|
| 4% Convertible Preferred Stock, $100 par value, issued at $103, each share convertible into 5 shares of common stock, 20,000 authorized, 10,000 issued and outstanding | $1,000,000 |
| Common Stock, $10 par value, 200,000 shares authorized, 100,000 shares issued, 95,000 shares outstanding | 1,000,000 |
| Additional Paid-in Capital—Preferred Stock | 30,000 |
| Additional Paid-in Capital—Common Stock | 200,000 |
| Retained Earnings | 800,000 |
| Total | $3,030,000 |
| Less Cost of Treasury Stock—at cost (5,000 shares) | (75,000) |
| Total Shareholders' Equity | $2,955,000 |

4. March 30. The first quarter's dividend on the preferred stock is declared and paid. In addition, a dividend of $.20 per share is declared and paid on outstanding common stock.

5. April 15. Holders of rights to 4,000 shares of common stock exercise their rights.

6. May 20. 1,000 shares of convertible preferred stock are acquired on the open market for $190 per share and retired.

7. June 30. Stock options are granted to various employees to purchase 5,000 shares of common stock for $22 per share, the market price on June 30. The stock option plan is noncompensatory.

8. June 30. The preferred stock dividend is declared and paid. In addition, a common stock dividend of $.20 per outstanding share is declared and paid.

9. July 1. Convertible bonds with a face value of $1,000,000 are issued on the market to yield 10 percent. The issue price is $828,409. The bonds have a coupon rate of 8 percent, payable semiannually on January 1 and July 1 of each year, and mature in 20 years from the date of issue. Each $1,000 bond is convertible into 40 shares of common stock. The bank prime interest rate on July 1 is 12 percent.

10. August 15. Holders of rights to 3,000 shares of common stock exercise their rights. The remaining rights lapse.

11. September 15. Holders of 2,000 shares of preferred stock exercise their option to convert their shares into common stock. The transaction is recorded using book values.

12. September 30. The preferred stock dividend is declared and paid. In addition, a common stock dividend of $.20 per outstanding share is declared and paid.

13. October 15. 800 shares of common stock are acquired on the open market for $30 per share and held as treasury stock.

14. December 1. Employees holding options to 2,000 shares of common stock exercise their options.

15. December 31. The preferred stock dividend is declared and paid. A common stock dividend of $.20 per share is declared and paid on the outstanding common stock.

16. December 31. Interest expense on the convertible bonds is recognized.

17. December 31. Net income for the year of $300,000, after deducting interest computed in **16,** is closed to Retained Earnings.

a. Prepare journal entries for each of the transactions or events listed above.

b. Set up a work sheet with the following columns:

Date
Preferred Stock—Number of Shares
Preferred Stock—Par Value
Common Stock—Number of Shares
Common Stock—Par Value
Additional Paid-in Capital—Preferred Stock
Additional Paid-in Capital—Common Stock
Retained Earnings
Treasury Stock—Number of Shares
Treasury Stock—Cost

Complete the work sheet by entering data for each of the transactions or events during the year.

c. Calculate earnings per outstanding common share.

d. Determine if the convertible bonds and convertible preferred stock are common stock equivalents and if the stock options are dilutive. The average and ending market prices for Webster Corporation's common stock for each quarter of 1981 were as follows:

|  | Average | Ending |
|---|---|---|
| First Quarter | $15 | $17 |
| Second Quarter | 18 | 22 |
| Third Quarter | 25 | 31 |
| Fourth Quarter | 32 | 32 |

The market price of the common stock exceeded $22 for all of the third quarter of 1981. The market price was $32 per share throughout the fourth quarter. The bank prime interest rate when the convertible preferred stock was originally issued was 6 percent. The income tax rate is 46 percent.

e. Calculate primary earnings per share.
f. Calculate fully diluted earnings per share.

23.1 Retained earnings is a measure of the accumulated net income of a corporation since its inception, reduced by dividend distributions to shareholders, amounts transferred to paid-in capital accounts, and certain other charges and credits. For many firms, the retention of funds generated by earnings is the most important source of capital for expansion. This chapter discusses the accounting for retained earnings, with emphasis on dividend distributions and on adjustments for accounting changes, errors in previous financial statements, and quasi-reorganizations.

## Distributions to Shareholders

23.2 Chapter 21 pointed out that accounting distinguishes between capital contributed by owners and earnings generated from that capital. Likewise, accounting distinguishes between distributions to shareholders that represent a return of contributed capital and distributions "out of earnings." Distributions representing a return of capital are relatively infrequent. They occur primarily when a firm continues paying regular dividends despite operating losses and zero or negative retained earnings. Distributions "out of capital" (referred to as *liquidating dividends*) reduce corporate assets and re-

duce Additional Paid-in Capital. Most corporate distributions are "out of earnings." That is, they represent payments to owners of net assets generated by earnings from the use of their capital by the corporation. Distributions "out of earnings" reduce corporate assets and Retained Earnings.

### Dividend Policy

23.3 The board of directors of a corporation has the legal authority to declare dividends. In considering whether or not to declare a dividend, the directors must conclude both (1) that the declaration of a dividend is legal and (2) that it would be financially expedient.

23.4 **Statutory Restrictions on Dividends** State corporate laws impose certain restrictions on the directors' freedom to declare dividends. These restrictions are designed primarily to protect creditors, who otherwise might be in a precarious position because neither directors nor shareholders are liable for debts of a corporation. (The modern agency theory of economics suggests that creditors need no such protection. So long as creditors know the rules of the game, the interest rate they charge for loans will adequately reflect their risks.)

23.5 Generally, the laws provide that dividends "may not be paid out of capital" but must be "paid out of earnings." That is, the maximum amount of assets available for dividend distributions is as follows:

$$\begin{matrix} \text{Maximum Amount} \\ \text{of Assets Legally} \\ \text{Available for} \\ \text{Dividends} \end{matrix} = \begin{matrix} \text{Total} \\ \text{Assets} \end{matrix} - \begin{matrix} \text{Total} \\ \text{Liabilities} \end{matrix} - \begin{matrix} \text{Legal} \\ \text{Capital} \end{matrix}.$$

As Chapter 21 pointed out, the definition of "legal capital" varies among the states. In some jurisdictions, legal capital is defined as the total amount paid in by shareholders. In other jurisdictions, legal capital includes only the par or stated values of outstanding common shares. In these cases, assets equal in amount to Additional Paid-in Capital are available for dividends. In some jurisdictions, dividends may be declared out of earnings of the current period even if there is an accumulated deficit from previous periods. There are other specialized features and variations among the state statutes.

23.6    For most companies, the statutory restrictions on dividends are of little consequence in establishing dividend policy. Most profitable corporations retain a large portion of the net assets generated by earnings for growth and expansion. Thus the amount of assets *legally* available for dividends can be substantial. Dividends are most commonly restricted for contractual or financial reasons.

23.7    Legal restrictions on dividends also have little influence on accounting for shareholders' equity, net income, and dividends. The balance sheet does not spell out the amount of legal capital or the amount legally available for dividends. Disclosure should be made, however, of any important legal restrictions on dividends. For example, some state statutes provide that "treasury stock may be acquired only with [net assets generated by] retained earnings." By acquiring its own shares, a corporation reduces the amount of assets legally available for dividends. Under these circumstances, the amount of the restrictions on dividends should be disclosed in a note to the financial statements.*

---

*Accounting Principles Board, *Accounting Principles Board Opinion No. 6* (1965), par. 13.

**Contractual Restrictions on Dividends**  23.8
Contracts with bondholders, lessors, or preferred shareholders often place restrictions on dividend payments and, thereby, compel the retention of earnings. For example, a recent financial statement of the Caterpillar Tractor Company contained the following note:

There are varying restrictions on the payment of cash dividends under the indentures relating to long-term debt. . . . [U]nder the terms of the most restrictive indenture, approximately $695 million of "profit employed in the business" [retained earnings of $1.8 billion ] was not available for the payment of dividends.

A recent financial statement of the Northrop Corporation contained the following note:

The corporation's loan and credit agreements contain restrictions relating to the payment of dividends, acquisition of the corporation's outstanding common stock, maintenance of working capital, etc. . . . [U]nder the most restrictive covenant, $97,353,000 of retained earnings [retained earnings of $206.5 million] was restricted as to the payment of dividends.

Bond contracts often provide that the retire-  23.9
ment of the obligation shall be made "out of earnings." Such a provision involves curtailing dividends, so that sufficient assets will be built up from the generation of earnings over time to retire the debt. *Accounting Series Release No. 280* requires firms to disclose significant restrictions which limit the payment of dividends to shareholders and which limit the payment of dividends by subsidiaries to their parent companies.†

**Dividends and Corporate Financial Pol-**  23.10
**icy**  Dividends are seldom declared up to the limit of the amount legally available for distribution. Some of the reasons why the directors may decide to allow assets and retained earnings to increase as a matter of corporate financial policy are as follows:

**1.** Funds may be needed to finance expansion.

---

†*Accounting Series Release No. 280,* SEC (1980).

**2.** The earnings may not be reflected in a corresponding increase of available cash.

**3.** A restriction of dividends in prosperous years may permit the continued payment of dividends in poor years.

**4.** It may be considered desirable to reduce the amount of indebtedness rather than declare dividends in an amount equal to net income.

23.11   *Financing Expansion* Many corporations have financed substantial increases in their receivables, inventories, or plant and equipment without issuing bonds or additional shares of stock. Funds provided by operations that are not paid out as dividends may be used to acquire additional assets such as plant facilities. Increased retained earnings cannot be associated with any particular item or group of items in the balance sheet, but it can be correct to say that expansion is, as a matter of policy, financed through the retention of earnings. From the corporation's standpoint, the overall financial result is much the same as if a substantial amount of cash had been distributed as dividends and an equal amount of cash had been obtained through issuing additional shares of stock. It has, however, saved the trouble and cost of finding buyers and issuing the additional stock certificates. In addition, owners have been saved, or deferred, income taxes on the dividend receipts.

23.12   *Earnings Are Not Cash* In earlier chapters we emphasized that net assets generated by earnings do not represent a fund of available cash. Although there are ample earnings, the directors might decide that cash cannot be spared for dividends equal to the net income of the period. Such factors as a maturing bank loan, an increase in the replacement cost of merchandise, or the need for new machinery might easily consume all available cash in spite of substantial earnings. The statement of changes in financial position, discussed in Chapters 4 and 24, helps the reader understand how earnings, and other sources of funds, have been used during the year.

*Equalization of Dividends* Many shareholders of corporations want to receive a regular minimum cash return. In order to accommodate such shareholders and to create a general impression of corporate stability, directors commonly attempt to declare a regular dividend. They try to maintain the regular dividend through good years and bad. When earnings and financial policy permit, they may declare "extra" dividends.   23.13

The legal requirements for declaring regular dividends can be met by retaining part of the income over several periods to build up a balance in retained earnings. Such a policy, however, does not mean that a fund of cash will always be available for the regular dividends. Managing cash is a specialized problem of corporate finance; cash for dividends must be anticipated just as well as cash for the purchase of equipment, the retirement of debts, and so on. Borrowing from the bank to pay the regular dividend is not objectionable provided that the corporation's financial condition justifies the increase in liabilities that results.   23.14

*Voluntary Reduction of Indebtedness* Contractual arrangements for reducing long-term debt may impose legal restrictions on the directors' dividend-paying powers. Even when there is no contractual obligation to do so, the directors may decide to reduce the amount of the liabilities and use the funds provided by operations for this purpose, rather than paying dividends.   23.15

*Summary of Dividend Policy* Shareholders who want to maintain their proportion of ownership in a growing firm will prefer a policy that restricts dividends in order to finance expansion. If dividends are declared, such shareholders will use the funds received to acquire an equivalent amount of the new shares issued to finance the expansion. These shareholders will be saved transaction costs and will be able to defer individual income taxes. If the corporation pays dividends, the shareholders must pay income taxes on the receipts before they can be reinvested. If the funds are reinvested directly by the corporation, there is a deferral   23.16

of, and possibly a saving in, personal income taxes.

23.17    Other shareholders may want a steady flow of cash and are unable, for contractual or psychological reasons, to sell a portion of their shares to raise cash if regular dividends are not declared. Such shareholders will resent being forced to reinvest in the corporation when expansion is financed through the retention of earnings. They may attempt to force the board of directors to adopt a more liberal dividend policy or change their investment to corporations that have more liberal dividend policies.

23.18    The degree to which expansion should be financed through retention of earnings is basically a problem of managerial finance, not accounting. Research in finance suggests that, within wide limits, what a firm does makes little difference so long as it tends to follow the same policy over time. Shareholders who want assets generated by earnings reinvested can invest in shares of firms that finance expansion with earnings, whereas others who want a flow of cash can invest in shares of firms that pay out most of the assets generated by earnings as dividends.

## Form of Dividends

23.19    Dividends are most commonly paid in cash. Dividends may also be paid with other corporate assets. If a corporation distributes shares of its own preferred or common stock, it is described as a *stock dividend.* As discussed later in this chapter, stock dividends are entirely different in character from distributions to shareholders of cash or other assets.

23.20    **Cash Dividends** There are three dates of significance in accounting for dividends. On the *date of declaration,* or *declaration date,* a formal announcement is made by the board of directors of their intention to issue a dividend. A dividend, once declared, generally cannot be rescinded without shareholders' consent (exceptions include fraudulent or illegal dividends). Thus, a legal liability is created at the time of declaration.

A journal entry such as the following should be made to record the dividend declaration:

| | | |
|---|---|---|
| Retained Earnings ............... | 10,000 | |
|    Dividend Payable ............. | | 10,000 |

Note that the Retained Earnings account is debited, not an expense account. Expenses are a measure of the cost incurred in *generating* revenues. Dividends are a distribution of assets generated from the earnings process. Some firms debit a temporary Dividends Declared account at the time of declaration. At the end of the accounting period, the amount in the Dividends Declared account is closed to Retained Earnings. Because most dividends are paid within approximately 4 to 6 weeks after declaration, the Dividend Payable account is a current liability.

   The second date of significance is the *date of record,* or *record date*. On this date, usu- 23.21 ally 2 to 3 weeks after the date of declaration, the list of shareholders entitled to receive the dividend is compiled. The holder on the date of record, not the date of declaration, is entitled to receive the dividend. After the record date, the shares are said to trade "ex-dividend," which means that the holder as of the record date will receive the dividend when it is paid even though the shares may no longer be owned by that holder.

   The final date of significance is the *date of* 23.22 *payment,* or *payment date*. This date usually follows the record date by a few weeks and marks the actual distribution of cash or other assets.

**Noncash Dividends** Corporations occa- 23.23 sionally distribute inventories, land, securities of other firms, or other assets as dividends. Such dividends are referred to as *dividends in kind*. Dividends in kind are rare but are sometimes found among small, closely held corporations.

   Accounting Principles Board *Opinion No.* 23.24 *29* requires that dividends in kind be recorded at the market value of the assets distributed if that market value can be measured objectively and would be realizable if the distributing corporation sold the asset outright at the time of distribution.* The difference between the market value and book value of the asset distributed is recognized as a gain or loss to be included in the determination of net income for the period. For example, assume that the board of directors declare a dividend payable in merchandise inventory of the firm. Two dollars of merchandise inventory at retail prices is to be distributed to shareholders for each share of outstanding common stock. If there are 10,000 shares outstanding, the journal entry on the date of declaration is

Retained Earnings  ............... 20,000
    Dividend Payable  ............      20,000

Because the dividend is to be paid within one year with current assets, Dividend Payable is classified as a current liability. Even if the dividend were payable in land, equipment, or other noncurrent assets, the Dividend Payable account would be classified as a current liability. The land, equipment, or other asset to be distributed would be reclassified from a noncurrent to a current asset category.

23.25  When the dividend in kind is distributed, the liability is debited, the asset distributed is credited for its book value, and a gain or loss recognized. For example, if the cost of goods distributed is $1.60 per unit, then the following entry would be made at the time merchandise is distributed to shareholders:

Dividend Payable  ................. 20,000
    Merchandise Inventory  ........    16,000
    Gain on Distribution of
        Inventory  ................      4,000

The gain is included in net income for the period.

23.26  **Stock Dividends** Assume that a company retains a significant portion of the assets generated by earnings each period and invests them in land, buildings, equipment, and similar assets. The Retained Earnings account will increasingly reflect net assets that are more or less permanently committed to the business. To indicate such a permanent commitment, amounts may be transferred from the Retained Earnings account to the contributed capital accounts by way of a *stock dividend*. When a stock dividend is issued, shareholders receive additional shares in the corporation in proportion to their existing holdings without making any additional contributions. For example, if a 10-percent stock dividend is issued, each shareholder receives one additional share for each ten shares held.

23.27  Generally accepted accounting principles require that a stock dividend be recorded by transferring from Retained Earnings to the contributed capital accounts an amount equal to the market value of the stock on the date the stock dividend is declared.† For example, the directors of a corporation may decide to issue a stock dividend of 10,000 additional shares of common stock with a par value of $10 per share at a time when the market price is $38 per share. The journal entry on the date of declaration is

Retained Earnings  ............. 380,000
    Stock Dividend Distributable .    380,000

Unlike dividends payable in cash or other assets, the Stock Dividend Distributable account is not classified as a liability on the balance sheet. No corporate assets will be distributed in settlement of the stock dividend. In addition, stock dividends are not legal liabilities of the firm. Although not commonly done, stock dividends can be rescinded by the board of directors. The Stock Dividend Distributable account is classified among the contributed capital accounts in the shareholders' section of the balance sheet.

23.28  When the stock dividend is issued, the following entry is made:

Stock Dividend Distributable  ..... 380,000
    Common Stock  .............    100,000
    Additional Paid-in Capital  ....    280,000

---

*Accounting Principles Board, *Accounting Principles Board Opinion No. 29* (1973), par. 23.

†*Accounting Research Bulletin No. 43*, AICPA (1953), chap. 7B, par. 10.

23.29   Thus, the declaration and issuance of a stock dividend have no effect on total assets, total liabilities, or total shareholders' equity. The most important internal effect of a stock dividend is to relabel a portion of Retained Earnings that had legally been available for dividends as a more permanent form of owners' equity.

23.30   Shareholders should not celebrate upon receiving a stock dividend. If the shares are of the same type as those held before, each shareholder's proportionate interest in the owners' equity of the corporation and proportionate voting power will not have changed. The book value per share of common stock (total common shareholders' equity divided by the number of outstanding common shares) will have decreased, but the total book value of each shareholder's interest will remain unchanged, because a proportionally larger number of shares will be held. Likewise, the market value of each share of stock should decrease in inverse proportion to the stock dividend, but, all else being equal, the total market value of the shareholders' holdings will not change. Shareholders cannot dispose of the additional shares without affecting their proportionate interests in the corporation. To describe such a distribution of shares as a "dividend" is misleading but is, nevertheless, generally accepted terminology.

23.31   **Stock Splits** Stock splits (or, more technically, split-ups) are similar in nature to a stock dividend. Additional shares are issued in proportion to existing holdings. In a stock split, however, it is common for the par or stated value of stock to be reduced in proportion to the additional shares issued. A corporation may, for example, have 1,000 shares of $100-par-value stock outstanding, and, by a stock split, exchange those shares for 2,000 shares of $50-par-value stock (a two-for-one split) or 4,000 shares of $25-par-value stock (a four-for-one split). Some stock splits are carried out without changing the par or stated value. For example, a corporation may merely distribute one new $10-par-value share for each $10-par-value share owned. If the shares outstanding have no par or stated value, then the stock split simply results in the issuance of additional stock certificates.

23.32   The accounting for stock dividends and stock splits differs under generally accepted accounting principles. A stock dividend requires the transfer from Retained Earnings to the contributed capital accounts of an amount equal to the market value of the shares on the date the stock dividend is declared. On the other hand, no entry is required for a stock split if the par or stated value is proportionally reduced in relation to the stock split. In circumstances where the par or stated value is not changed, or the change is not in proportion to the additional shares issued, transfers from Additional Paid-in Capital to Capital Stock are necessary. Note, however, that market values are not used in recording stock splits as they are for stock dividends.*

23.33   The justification offered for this difference in accounting treatment relates to the underlying intentions of the corporation. A stock dividend is defined in *Accounting Research Bulletin No. 43,* Chapter 7B, as:

. . . an issuance by a corporation of its own common shares to its common shareholders without consideration and under conditions indicating that such action is prompted mainly by a desire to give the recipient shareholders some ostensibly separate evidence of a part of their respective interests in accumulated corporate earnings without distribution of cash or other property which the board of directors deems necessary or desirable to retain in the business.

*ARB No. 43* defines a stock split as:

. . . an issuance by a corporation of its own common shares to its own common shareholders without consideration and under conditions indicating that such action is prompted mainly by a desire to increase the number of outstanding shares for the purpose of effecting a reduction in their unit market price and, thereby, of obtaining wider distribution and improved marketability of the shares.

---

*Ibid., chap. 7B.

Thus, if a part of Retained Earnings is to be permanently capitalized, the transaction should be accounted for as a stock dividend. If the distribution is intended primarily to reduce the market price of the outstanding stock, the transaction should be accounted for as a stock split. To provide some objectivity to the process of determining whether a particular distribution is a stock dividend or a stock split, *ARB No. 43* specifies that increases of less than 20 to 25 percent in the number of outstanding shares are considered stock dividends, whereas increases of greater than 20 to 25 percent are stock splits.

23.34  Current accounting practice for stock distributions is subject to the following criticisms:

**1.** Stock market prices adjust downward for *both* stock dividends and stock splits in proportion to the additional shares issued, suggesting the lack of empirical support for different accounting treatments.

**2.** The dividing line between stock dividends and stock splits of 20 to 25 percent of the currently outstanding stock is arbitrary and lacks theoretical support.

**3.** The effect of the differing accounting treatments for stock dividends and stock splits on Retained Earnings can be misleading. The distribution of a small number of shares as a stock dividend can reduce Retained Earnings by a larger amount than the distribution of a much larger number of shares in a stock split.

23.35  **Reverse Stock Splits** A reverse stock split occurs whenever a split results in a reduction in the number of shares outstanding. For example, the par value of stock may be increased from $10 to $20 and one new $20-par-value share issued for each two $10-par-value shares outstanding. Reverse stock splits generally result in an increase in the market value of the stock in inverse proportion to the smaller number of shares outstanding. Increasing the market price per share appears to be the primary purpose of a reverse stock split. The accounting for reverse stock splits is similar to that for regular

stock splits. An entry is made only when the decrease in the number of shares outstanding is not in proportion to the change in par or stated value.

**Stock Dividends and Stock Splits: Treasury Stock** Practice varies as to whether treasury shares participate in a stock dividend or stock split. Technically, treasury stock is the same as authorized but unissued stock and, therefore, should not participate in the stock dividend or stock split. However, if all $100-par-value shares are being replaced with new $50-par-value shares, then the shares held in the treasury must also be replaced. Some state laws prohibit treasury shares from receiving a stock dividend.  23.36

**Stock Dividends and Stock Splits and Earnings-per-Share Calculations** When stock dividends, stock splits, or reverse stock splits occur during a period, retroactive recognition must be given to the increase or decrease in the number of shares outstanding for all periods being reported in calculating earnings per share.[*] If the stock dividend or split occurs after the period reported but before the financial statements are issued, retroactive recognition should also be given to the new number of shares outstanding for all periods presented.  23.37

## Restrictions on Retained Earnings

As discussed in previous sections, there may be legal, contractual, or financial restrictions that prevent a firm from paying dividends in an amount equal to the balance in the Retained Earnings account. One method of disclosing these restrictions is the use of a note to the financial statements. (See Caterpillar Tractor and Northrop Corporations' quotations earlier in the chapter.) A second approach is the declaration of a stock dividend. A third approach sometimes used is to appropriate Retained Earnings. Appropria-  23.38

[*]Accounting Principles Board, *Accounting Principles Board Opinion No. 15* (1969).

tions of Retained Earnings may be made as follows:

```
Retained Earnings  ...........  2,000,000
    Retained Earnings—
    Appropriated for Plant
    Expansion  ............             2,000,000
Retained Earnings  ..........  1,000,000
    Retained Earnings—
    Appropriated for Bond
    Retirement  ...........              1,000,000
```

The appropriation of Retained Earnings is merely a method of disclosing some of the reasons why dividends equal to Retained Earnings are not being paid.

23.39    The use of Retained Earnings appropriations is subject to the following criticisms:

1. Such appropriations may be confusing or misleading. The appropriation of Retained Earnings does not necessarily result in the setting aside, or segregation, of assets for the purpose indicated. For example, an appropriation of Retained Earnings for bond retirement does not ensure that cash will be available to redeem the bonds when they are due. It merely indicates the reason why some of the assets generated by earnings are not being paid in dividends. If a firm wished to ensure that sufficient cash would be available to redeem the bonds, then a bond sinking fund (discussed in Chapter 14) should be established. Each year, an entry such as the following would be made:

```
Bond Sinking Fund  .............  100,000
    Cash  .....................              100,000
```

An appropriation of Retained Earnings might also be made to indicate to shareholders the reason for the retention of a portion of the earnings of the year:

```
Retained Earnings  ..............  100,000
    Retained Earnings—
    Appropriated for Bond
    Retirement  ...............             100,000
```

If the bond issue had a maturity value of $1,000,000, the following entry would be made to redeem the bonds:

```
Bonds Payable  ..............  1,000,000
    Bond Sinking Fund  ......             1,000,000
```

Because the Retained Earnings appropriation is no longer needed, the following entry would also be made:

```
Retained Earnings—
    Appropriated for Bond
    Retirement  ...............  1,000,000
        Retained Earnings  .......             1,000,000
```

2. A second objection to retained earnings appropriations is that, taken to its logical conclusion, all Retained Earnings should be appropriated for some purpose. Retained Earnings in the balance sheet might appear as follows:

| Retained Earnings: | |
|---|---:|
| Appropriated for Plant Expansion  .. | $2,000,000 |
| Appropriated for Bond Retirement  .. | 1,000,000 |
| Appropriated for Preferred Stock Retirement  ..................... | 500,000 |
| Appropriated for Working Capital Purposes  ..................... | 700,000 |
| Appropriated for Contingencies  .... | 1,200,000 |
| Total Retained Earnings  ........ | $5,400,000 |

Not only might such disclosures be confusing to many statement readers, but the disclosures are of questionable informational value. Most users of financial statements are aware of the need for corporations to retain a portion of their earnings for growth and expansion, retirement of debt, and similar purposes without having a detailed list of the reasons for retention. Significant legal or statutory restrictions on the payment of dividends can be more effectively disclosed in the notes to the financial statements. Attempts to segregate equities also contradicts the principle, discussed in Chapter 17, that all the equities finance all the assets, except in rare cases of nonrecourse loans.

## Restatements of Retained Earnings

Retained earnings may be periodically re-    23.40
stated for **(1)** prior-period adjustments, **(2)** errors in previous financial statements, **(3)** accounting changes, and **(4)** quasi-reorganizations.

## Prior-Period Adjustments

23.41  Consider the following events that might have an impact on the financial position of a firm:

1. A customer has filed a lawsuit against a company, claiming damages for injuries sustained 3 years ago from using the company's products.

2. The Internal Revenue Service has disallowed certain deductions in a firm's income tax return of 4 years ago and assessed the firm for additional income taxes.

3. A new government has taken power in a particular foreign country and is threatening to expropriate all of a company's assets located in the country.

23.42  These items are examples of potential losses that may require recognition as a *loss contingency*. Recall from Chapter 15 that an estimated loss from a loss contingency should be accrued by a charge to income and a credit to an estimated liability only if both of the following conditions are met:*

1. Information available prior to the issuance of the financial statements indicates that it is probable that an asset has been impaired or that a liability has been incurred at the date of the financial statements. It is implicit in this condition that it must be probable that one or more future events will occur confirming the fact of the loss.

2. The amount of loss can be reasonably estimated.

23.43  For some lawsuits, income tax assessments, and similar loss contingencies, these conditions for the accrual of the estimated loss are satisfied in the year the asset impairment or liability incurrence takes place. In other cases, an asset may have been impaired or a liability may have been incurred, but the amount of the loss is difficult to estimate. For example, there may be numerous claims against a company for damages sustained in using a particular product of the company. Although the company expects to be found guilty, the range of possible damage awards may be wide and no one estimate in the range may be better than any other. In these cases, a loss contingency must be recognized and stated at the amount at the lower end of the range of possible losses. The notes to the financial statements should then indicate that the loss may turn out to be as large as the amount at the upper end of the range.† In many cases, however, significant uncertainty exists concerning whether an asset has actually been impaired or a liability incurred. For example, a firm may feel that it has an adequate legal defense against lawsuits, or it may feel that it has sufficient justification for the income tax deductions claimed. In these cases, the conditions for the recognition of the loss contingency are not satisfied until some confirming event occurs in the future (final judgment in a lawsuit, settlement of income tax dispute).

23.44  At the time of the confirming event, the loss must be recognized. An important question arises at this point, however. Should the loss be recognized as an adjustment of earnings of the prior year when the event causing the loss occurred, or should the loss be recognized as an element in determining net income of the current period when the confirming event occurred?

23.45  Advocates of treating the loss as a prior-period adjustment (charged to Retained Earnings at the beginning of the current period) offer the following arguments:

1. The time-series trend in reported earnings will be more meaningful if losses arising from events of a prior period are recognized as an element of net income of that period, instead of biasing the current period's earnings.

2. A better matching of the loss with the period when the loss occurred is achieved.

23.46  Advocates of recognizing the loss as an ele-

*Financial Accounting Standards Board, *Statement of Financial Accounting Standards No. 5* (1975), par. 8.

†Financial Accounting Standards Board, *Interpretation No. 14* (1976), par. 3.

ment in determining the current period's earnings offer the following arguments:

1. All revenues, gains, expenses, and losses relating to the earnings activity of a firm should be reported in the income statement. In this way, the income statements over a period of years will present a history of a firm's earnings performance. If the loss is treated as an adjustment of Retained Earnings at the beginning of the current period, it will not be included in the income statement originally issued for any period.

2. Financial statement users may overlook the fact that a loss has occurred if the loss is included in an analysis of changes in retained earnings instead of prominently disclosed in the income statement.

23.47 Financial Accounting Standards Board *Statement No. 16* requires (with a few minor exceptions) that "all items of profit and loss recognized during a period, including accruals of estimated losses from loss contingencies, shall be included in the determination of net income for that period."* This pronouncement requires that losses from lawsuits, income tax disputes, and similar events be included in the determination of income from continuing operations and not treated as prior-period adjustments. The only two items that qualify for treatment as an adjustment of a prior year's earnings under *Statement No. 16* are (1) corrections of errors in financial statements of prior periods (discussed in the next section) and (2) adjustments that result from realization of income tax benefits of preacquisition operating loss carryforwards of purchased subsidiaries (considered in advanced accounting principles texts).† Thus, prior-period adjustments are rare in financial reporting. Losses that relate to activities of a prior period, but

that are recognized during the current period, must be included in net income of the current period. If the amounts involved are material, then the nature of the loss and the amount should be disclosed separately in the income statement.

## Corrections of Errors in Prior Years' Financial Statements

The accounting systems of most large business firms contain internal checks and controls to ensure that transactions are recorded in the proper accounts and in the correct amounts. Errors that occur in the accounting and recording process are usually discovered and corrected soon after they occur. Errors that are discovered in subsequent periods tend to be immaterial and are often ignored.                                       23.48

Smaller firms tend to have less sophisticated accounting systems, with fewer internal controls. Hence, the likelihood that accounting and recording errors will be made is greater. Many of these errors are not discovered until a year or more after the errors occurred.                                       23.49

Accounting Principles Board *Opinion No. 20* defines errors in previously issued financial statements as "mathematical mistakes, mistakes in the application of accounting principles, or oversight or misuse of facts that existed at the time the financial statements were prepared." An error in a previously issued financial statement is treated as a prior-period adjustment. Retained earnings as of the beginning of the current period is charged or credited for the cumulative effect of the error on earnings of prior years.**                                       23.50

Errors tend to be of three general types: (1) intra-balance sheet errors, (2) intra-income statement errors, and (3) inter-balance sheet/income statement errors.                                       23.51

**Intra-Balance Sheet Errors** Intra-balance sheet errors result from debiting or crediting an incorrect balance sheet account to record                                       23.52

---

*Financial Accounting Standards Board, *Statement of Financial Accounting Standards No. 16* (1977), par. 10.
†There are also several adjustments of prior *interim* period's earnings of the current year permitted by *Statement No. 16*. Such adjustments are considered in advanced accounting texts where the topic of interim-period reporting is discussed in detail.

**Accounting Principles Board, *Accounting Principles Board Opinion No. 20* (1971), par. 36.

a transaction. For example, a short-term investment of $10,000 of excess cash in marketable securities might be debited to Investment in A Company instead of Marketable Securities and classified in the Investments section of the balance sheet. The payment of $1,000 owed to a supplier might be debited to Salaries Payable instead of Accounts Payable.

23.53    Intra-balance sheet errors are errors of classification. Individual asset, liability, or shareholders' equity accounts may be incorrectly stated. Total assets, total liabilities, and total shareholders' equity, however, will normally be properly stated. Intra-balance sheet errors are corrected by making reclassification entries, such as the following:

| | | |
|---|---|---|
| Marketable Securities | 10,000 | |
|     Investment in A Company | | 10,000 |
| | | |
| Accounts Payable | 1,000 | |
|     Salaries Payable | | 1,000 |

Individual balance sheet accounts will continue to be misstated until these reclassification entries are made. Although intra-balance sheet errors do not directly affect revenue or expense accounts, there may be indirect effects of such errors on net income. For instance, the misclassification of the investment in the above example may result in an error in the amount of the unrealized loss recognized for the period on marketable securities under the lower-of-cost-or-market method. This latter error is considered an inter-balance sheet/income statement error (discussed later in this section).

23.54    **Intra-Income Statement Errors** Intra-income statement errors result from debiting or crediting an incorrect revenue or expense account in recording a transaction. These errors are likewise classification errors. For example, salary costs of $2,000 might be debited in error to Insurance Expense. Interest earned of $500 might be credited in error to Sales Revenue, increasing it, or to Interest Expense, reducing it.

23.55    Intra-income statement errors affect the amounts in individual revenue and expense accounts. Net income, however, will be correctly stated. If these errors are discovered before the books are closed for a period and the financial statements are issued, then reclassification entries such as the following should be made:

| | | |
|---|---|---|
| Salary Expense | 2,000 | |
|     Insurance Expense | | 2,000 |
| | | |
| Sales Revenue (or Interest Expense) | 500 | |
|     Interest Revenue | | 500 |

If the error is discovered in a subsequent period, no formal correcting entry is necessary. The overstatement of an individual revenue or expense account is offset by an understatement of another individual revenue or expense account in an equal amount. Thus, *cumulative* net income and retained earnings are correctly stated. If an income statement for the year of the error is included for comparative purposes in subsequent years' financial statements, the misclassification should be corrected if the amounts are material, even though no formal entry is made.

**Inter-Balance Sheet/Income Statement Errors**    23.56
Inter-balance sheet/income statement errors affect accounts on both the balance sheet and the income statement. Adjustments for these types of errors in prior years' financial statements are charged or credited to the beginning balance in Retained Earnings. Two types of errors might be found: (1) counterbalancing, and (2) non-counterbalancing.

*Counterbalancing Errors* Counterbalancing    23.57
errors are those that occur in one period but that are offset, or counterbalanced, in the next period with an error in the opposite direction. Most counterbalancing errors occur as a result of a failure to make year-end accruals. For example, assume that a firm neglected to accrue wages payable of $10,000 at the end of 1980. Wages Expense will be understated and pretax income overstated for 1980 by $10,000. Wages Payable on December 31, 1980, will likewise be understated by $10,000. When wages are paid in the early part of January 1981, Wages Expense will be debited and Cash credited for the amount of the payroll. Wages Expense

for 1981 will be overstated and pretax income understated by $10,000 for 1981.

23.58    If the error is discovered during 1981, the following entry must be made:

```
Retained Earnings  ...............  10,000
    Wages Expense  ..............         10,000
```

The debit to Retained Earnings corrects for the overstatement of pretax income in 1980. The credit to Wages Expense corrects for the overstatement in 1981. If the error is considered material enough to warrant filing an amended income tax return for 1980 and the income tax rate is 40 percent, then the following entry must also be made:

```
Income Tax Refund Receivable  .......  4,000
    Retained Earnings  ..............        4,000
```

The debit to the receivable is for the excess taxes paid during 1980 arising from the overstatement of income. The credit to Retained Earnings is for the overstatement of Income Tax Expense during 1980.

23.59    If the error is not discovered until after the books have been closed for 1981, no correcting entry need be made. The overstatement of income during 1980 is offset by an understatement of equal amount during 1981. Thus, *cumulative* net income and Retained Earnings are correctly stated by the end of 1981. If the error is discovered after the books have been closed but before the financial statements for 1981 have been issued, the error should be corrected in the financial statements even though a formal journal entry need not be made.

23.60    *Noncounterbalancing Errors* Noncounterbalancing errors are those that occur in one period and are not automatically offset, or counterbalanced, in the next period. For example, a machine with a 5-year life might be acquired at the beginning of 1981 for $10,000 and charged to Cost of Goods Sold. Cost of Goods Sold for 1981 is overstated by $10,000 and, assuming that the straight-line depreciation method is used, Depreciation Expense for 1981 is understated by $2,000. Also, Depreciation Expense for the years 1982 through 1985 will be understated by

$2,000 each year. This error will not correct itself until the end of 1985, when the asset will have been fully depreciated. At that time, the amount charged to Cost of Goods Sold during 1981 is equal to the depreciation that would have been recognized during the years 1981 through 1985.

23.61    If the error is discovered during 1981 before depreciation for the year is recorded, then the following correcting entry must be made:

```
Equipment  ......................  10,000
    Cost of Goods Sold  ...........        10,000
```

If the error is discovered after depreciation has been calculated but before the books have been closed for 1981, the following entries must be made in addition to the one above:

```
Depreciation Expense  ..............  2,000
    Accumulated Depreciation  .......        2,000

Income Tax Expense  ..............  3,200
    Income Tax Payable  ...........        3,200
$3,200 = .40 × ($10,000 − $2,000).
```

23.62    Assume instead that the error is not discovered until the early part of 1982. The following correcting entry must be made:

```
Equipment  ......................  10,000
    Accumulated Depreciation  ......        2,000
    Retained Earnings  ..............        8,000
```

If an amended income tax return is filed for 1981, the following entry must also be made:

```
Retained Earnings  .................  3,200
    Income Tax Payable  ...........        3,200
```

23.63    If the error is not discovered until the early part of 1983, the following correcting entry must be made:

```
Equipment  ......................  10,000
    Accumulated Depreciation  ......        4,000
    Retained Earnings  ..............        6,000
```

The entry to reflect the amounts in an amended tax return is

```
Retained Earnings  .................  2,400
    Income Tax Payable  ...........        2,400
$2,400 = .40 × ($8,000 − $2,000).
```

23.64 **Comprehensive Illustration of Error Analysis** This section presents a comprehensive illustration of error analysis. It is unlikely that a single firm would have as many errors as are illustrated below.

23.65    The income statements of Roderick Corporation revealed the following amounts of net income for the years ending December 31, 1979, 1980, and 1981:

| | |
|---|---|
| 1979 | $25,600 |
| 1980 | 33,700 |
| 1981 | 28,700 |

23.66 An examination of the accounts revealed the following errors:

**1.** Wages earned by workers during the last few days of each year were consistently not accrued at each year end. The amounts omitted were as follows:

| | |
|---|---|
| December 31, 1978 | $3,000 |
| December 31, 1979 | 7,500 |
| December 31, 1980 | 4,200 |
| December 31, 1981 | 5,100 |

**2.** A 3-year insurance policy was acquired on July 1, 1980, with the 3-year premium of $3,600 paid on that date and charged to Insurance Expense.

**3.** As a result of an error in the taking of physical inventories, the inventory at the end of 1979 was understated by $2,000 and the inventory at the end of 1981 was overstated by $1,500.

**4.** Through a coding error in a computer program, commissions paid to salesclerks were charged to Maintenance Expense instead of Commission Expense each year as follows:

| | |
|---|---|
| 1979 | $ 8,600 |
| 1980 | 10,000 |
| 1981 | 11,500 |

**5.** An office machine costing $20,000 was acquired on July 1, 1979, and correctly debited to the Office Machinery and Equipment account. The machine has a 4-year life and a $4,000 salvage value. Depreciation is based on the straight-line method. The firm neglected to consider the salvage value in calculating the depreciation charge each year.

23.67    A useful approach to error analysis is to prepare a work sheet to recalculate net income for each year. We shall assume that amended tax returns will be filed, that the income tax rate is 40 percent, and that the books have not been closed for 1981. Exhibit 23.1 presents an analysis of these errors on net income.

23.68 *Wage Accrual Omission* The failure to accrue wages at the end of each year is a counterbalancing error affecting both the balance sheet and income statement. The failure to accrue wages at the end of *1978* means that, other things being equal, Wage Expense for 1979 is overstated and income is understated by $3,000. Hence, $3,000 is added to reported net income. The failure to accrue wages at the end of 1979 means that Wage Expense is understated and pretax income overstated by $7,500. Hence, $7,500 is subtracted from reported net income. Note the manner in which the errors counterbalance each other from year to year. The journal entry to correct the books as of the end of 1981 is

| | | |
|---|---|---|
| Wage Expense | 900 | |
| Retained Earnings | 4,200 | |
| Wages Payable | | 5,100 |

The debit to Wage Expense of $900 is the net of the $4,200 overstatement for 1980 wages and the $5,100 understatement for 1981 wages. The $4,200 debit to Retained Earnings is for the net *cumulative* error in Retained Earnings as of January 1, 1981. The errors from failing to accrue wages for all years prior to 1980 automatically corrected themselves. The only error not corrected as of January 1, 1981, is the accrual of $4,200 omitted on December 31, 1980. Note that these two debit entries are based on pretax amounts. It is usually easier to consider the tax consequences of these corrections separately after all errors have been analyzed. The credit to Wages Payable of $5,100 is for the accrual omitted on December 31, 1981.

*Exhibit 23.1*
**Work Sheet for Analysis of Errors of
Roderick Corporation**

| | Increases (Decreases) in Income for Year | | | Journal Entry to Make Correction Required at December 31, 1981 | | |
|---|---|---|---|---|---|---|
| | **1979** | **1980** | **1981** | | | |
| Net Income as Reported | $25,600 | $33,700 | $28,700 | | | |
| (1) Failure to Accrue Wages at End of: | | | | | | |
| 1978 | $ 3,000 | | | | | |
| 1979 | (7,500) | $ 7,500 | | Wage Expense | 900 | |
| 1980 | | (4,200) | 4,200 | Retained Earnings | 4,200 | |
| 1981 | | | (5,100) | Wages Payable | | 5,100 |
| (2) Three-Year Insurance Policy Charged to | | 3,600 | | Prepaid Insurance | 1,800 | |
| Expense | | (600) | (1,200) | Insurance Expense | 1,200 | |
| | | | | Retained Earnings | | 3,000 |
| (3) Error in Physical Inventory Count at End of: | | | | | | |
| 1979 | 2,000 | (2,000) | | Cost of Goods Sold | 1,500 | |
| 1981 | | | (1,500) | Merchandise Inventory | | 1,500 |
| (4) Commissions Charged in Error to Maintenance | | | | Commission Expense | 11,500 | |
| Expense | — | — | — | Maintenance Expense | | 11,500 |
| (5) Error in Calculating Straight-Line Depreciation | 500 | 1,000 | 1,000 | Accumulated Depreciation | 2,500 | |
| | | | | Depreciation Expense | | 1,000 |
| | | | | Retained Earnings | | 1,500 |
| Net Change in Pretax Income | $ (2,000) | $ 5,300 | $ (2,600) | Retained Earnings | 1,320 | |
| Tax Effect at 40% | 800 | (2,120) | 1,040 | Income Tax Expense | | 1,040 |
| Change in Net Income as Reported | $ (1,200) | $ 3,180 | $ (1,560) | Income Tax Payable | | 280 |
| Revised Net Income | $24,400 | $36,880 | $27,140 | | | |

23.69  *Prepaid Insurance Expense* The error in recording the insurance premium paid is an example of a noncounterbalancing error. Pretax income for 1980 is understated by $3,000 because the premium paid in advance on a 3-year insurance policy was treated as an expense of 1980. Only $600 should have been expensed that year. In addition, pretax income for 1981 is overstated by $1,200 because a portion of the insurance cost was not allocated to expenses of 1981. The journal entry to correct the books as of the end of 1981 is

| Prepaid Insurance | 1,800 | |
|---|---|---|
| Insurance Expense | 1,200 | |
| Retained Earnings | | 3,000 |

The debit of $1,800 to Prepaid Insurance represents the cost of coverage from January 1, 1982, to June 30, 1983. The debit of $1,200 to Insurance Expense is the cost of coverage expired during 1981 but not recorded. The cumulative error in Retained Earnings as of the beginning of 1981 is $3,000 (= $3,600 − $600) before taxes.

*Errors in Physical Inventories* The error in  23.70 the physical inventory count is another example of a counterbalancing error. The understatement of inventory on December 31, 1979, leads to an overstatement of cost of goods sold and an understatement of pretax income for 1979. The understatement of ending inventory on December 31, 1979, means that the beginning inventory on January 1, 1980, is also understated. Other things being equal, an understatement of beginning inventory leads to an understatement of cost of goods sold and an overstatement of pretax income. Thus, the inventory error caused pretax income for 1979 to be understated and that for 1980 to be overstated. By the end of 1980, this error has corrected itself.

There is also an error in the physical in-  23.71 ventory at the end of 1981. The ending inventory is overstated by $1,500, cost of goods sold is understated by $1,500, and pretax income is overstated by $1,500. This error will correct itself automatically in 1982. However, the error is discovered before the books are closed for 1981, so the error must be corrected. The entry is

```
Cost of Goods Sold  ................  1,500
     Merchandise Inventory  ..........        1,500
```

23.72 *Commission Costs Charged to Maintenance Expense* The improper charging of commission costs to Maintenance Expense is an intra-income statement error. At the end of each of the years 1979, 1980, and 1981, net income and retained earnings are stated correctly. Because the books are still open for 1981, the classification error should be corrected with the following entry:

```
Commission Expense  .............  11,500
     Maintenance Expense  ........       11,500
```

23.73 *Error in Calculation of Depreciation* The failure to consider salvage value in the calculation of depreciation under the straight-line method is an example of a noncounterbalancing error. The depreciation charge is overstated by $1,000 [= (.25 × $20,000) − (.25 × $16,000)] for each full year of depreciation taken. Because the machine was acquired on July 1, 1979, only one-half of a full year's depreciation was recognized in 1979. The entry to correct the depreciation error is

```
Accumulated Depreciation  ..........  2,500
     Depreciation Expense  ............       1,000
     Retained Earnings  ..............       1,500
```

The debit of $2,500 to Accumulated Depreciation is for the excess depreciation claimed during 1979, 1980, and 1981; $2,500 = $500 + $1,000 + $1,000. Because depreciation expense for 1981 is overstated, this account is credited for $1,000. The overstated depreciation expenses for 1979 and 1980 were closed to Retained Earnings in those years. Hence, Retained Earnings is credited for $1,500. Depreciation expense for 1982 will be based on $20,000 cost less $4,000 salvage value and a 4-year total life.

23.74 *Correction of Income Taxes* In virtually all cases, income taxes for the current and prior years will also have to be corrected. Because income taxes are based on *income* before taxes, not on individual revenues and expenses, the correcting entry for income taxes is made most easily after all individual errors have been corrected. The net change in pretax income is a $2,000 decrease for 1979, a $5,300 increase for 1980, and a $2,600 decrease for 1981. Assuming that none of these changes represents a permanent difference between book and taxable income, the income tax provision for each year must be adjusted by 40 percent of these amounts. The journal entry is as follows:

```
Retained Earnings  ...................  1,320
     Income Tax Expense  ...........       1,040
     Income Tax Payable  ............        280
```

For 1979 and 1980, income tax expense is increased by $1,320 (= $2,120 − $800). Retained Earnings is debited for this increase in income taxes on prior years' book incomes. Income tax expense for 1981 must be decreased by $1,040, because the pretax book income on which the income tax expense was originally computed for the year is overstated by $2,600. Assuming that amended income tax returns will be filed for prior years and that the return for 1981 will be corrected, there is an additional liability for the 3-year period of $280 (= $2,120 − $800 − $1,040). This amount is credited to Income Tax Payable. In some cases, the correction of errors from prior years will result in a refund receivable from the government for the overpayment of income taxes.

23.75 *Comprehensive Correction Entry* Once an error analysis, such as that shown in Exhibit 23.1, has been performed, the correction of the books can be made in one composite entry as follows:

```
Wage Expense  .................          900
Insurance Expense  ...............       1,200
Cost of Goods Sold  ..............       1,500
Commission Expense  .............      11,500
Prepaid Insurance  ...............       1,800
Accumulated Depreciation  .........      2,500
Retained Earnings  ...............       1,020
     Maintenance Expense  .........           11,500
     Depreciation Expense  .........           1,000
     Income Tax Expense  ..........           1,040
     Wages Payable  ..............           5,100
     Merchandise Inventory  ........          1,500
     Income Tax Payable  ..........            280
```

The amount debited to Retained Earnings is $1,020 (= $4,200 − $3,000 − $1,500 + $1,320).

23.76 *Disclosure of Error Correction* Because the errors are discovered before the financial statements for 1981 are issued, no disclosure of the errors for 1981 is necessary. Disclosure is required of the errors in the financial statements for 1979 and 1980. The amounts for various revenues, expenses, assets, and equities in the financial statements for 1979 and 1980 included for comparative purposes in the 1981 annual report must be restated for the errors discovered. In addition, the analysis of changes in retained earnings must disclose the cumulative effect of the errors on retained earnings as of January 1, 1981. Assuming that the balance in Retained Earnings on January 1, 1981, before the errors are discovered was $436,500 and that dividends of $10,500 were declared during 1981, the analysis of changes in retained earnings would appear as follows:

| | |
|---|---:|
| Retained Earnings, January 1, 1981 (as previously reported) ............... | $436,500 |
| Correction of Errors in Previous Financial Statements ................ | (1,020) |
| Retained Earnings, January 1, 1981 (as corrected) ........................ | $435,480 |
| Net Income for 1981 ................ | 27,140 |
| Less Dividends Declared ............ | (10,500) |
| Retained Earnings, December 31, 1981 ... | $452,120 |

## Adjustments for Accounting Changes

23.77 Firms sometimes make changes in their accounting and recording process. For example, a firm might switch from the completed-contract to the percentage-of-completion method of recognizing income from long-term contracts or from a FIFO to a LIFO cost-flow assumption for inventories and cost of goods sold. These are examples of *changes in accounting principles* or methods. Firms might also change the estimated useful lives or salvage values for depreciable assets, the percentage used for estimating uncollectible accounts, or the claim rate used for estimating warranty costs. These are examples of *changes in accounting estimates*. Finally, a firm may acquire new companies or dispose of companies previously owned. These are examples of *changes in the reporting entity*.

23.78 The amounts originally reported in the financial statements for prior years would have been different if these changes had been made in a prior period instead of in the current period. An important question arises as to when the income effects of accounting changes should be recognized. At least three possibilities can be suggested:

**1.** Recognize the cumulative effect of the change in prior years' earnings as a prior-period adjustment (that is, adjust the beginning balance in Retained Earnings for the current year and restate prior years' financial statements accordingly).

**2.** Recognize the entire cumulative effect of the change in prior years' earnings as an element in calculating net income in the year of the change.

**3.** Spread the cumulative effect of the change in prior years' earnings over the year of the change and some appropriate number of future years.

23.79 Advocates of the prior-period adjustment approach argue that the time-series trend in earnings can be most meaningfully analyzed if the net income amounts are based on the same methods of accounting and recording through time. When accounting changes occur, the past time series in earnings should be corrected to reflect the new accounting procedures.

23.80 Advocates of the current-period recognition approach offer three arguments. First, all items of income should flow through the income statement and not be charged or credited directly to Retained Earnings. Second, accounting changes occur frequently enough that the continual revision of previously reported amounts will lessen user confidence in the financial statements. Third, the likelihood that a user will overlook an accounting change is lessened if the effect of the change is prominently disclosed in the current period's income statement.

23.81    Advocates of the current and future, or prospective, approach to recognition argue that accounting changes are an inevitable part of the accounting process. In many cases the amounts involved are not material enough to warrant a separate "catch-up" entry. The changes should merely be permitted to work themselves out over the current and future periods.

23.82    APB *Opinion No. 20* specifies the required accounting treatment of changes in accounting principles, changes in accounting estimates, and changes in the reporting entity. As discussed below, some of these changes are treated as prior-period adjustments, some are treated as adjustments of the current period's net income, and some are adjusted prospectively.

23.83    **Change in Accounting Principle: General Rule** Firms sometimes change accounting principles because the Financial Accounting Standards Board creates a new accounting principle, expresses a preference for a particular accounting principle, or rejects a specific accounting principle. For example, many firms changed their method of accounting for long-term leases in 1977 as a result of the issuance of FASB *Statement No. 13*. In other cases, firms switch their accounting principles because they feel that the new accounting principle better reflects economic reality for their particular operations. For example, many firms in recent years have switched from a FIFO to a LIFO cost-flow assumption for inventories and from the deferral method to the flow-through method of accounting for investment tax credits. The burden of justifying changes in accounting principles that are not brought about by a pronouncement of an official rule-making body rests with the firm making the change.*

23.84    The general rule for recognizing changes in accounting principles might be summarized as follows:

1. Financial statements for prior periods included for comparative purposes in the financial statements for the year of the change should be presented as previously reported.
2. The cumulative effect of changing to a new accounting principle on the amount of retained earnings at the beginning of the period in which the change is made should be included in net income of the period of the change but segregated in a separate section after Extraordinary Items in the income statement.
3. The effect of adopting the new accounting principle on income before extraordinary items and on net income (and on the related per-share amounts) of the period of the change should be disclosed.
4. Income before extraordinary items and net income computed on a pro forma basis should be shown on the face of the income statement for all periods presented as if the newly adopted accounting principle had been applied during all periods affected.

Thus, the cumulative effect of the change on Retained Earnings at the beginning of the period is included in net income for the year of the change.† Recognizing that this approach tends to bias the time-series trend in earnings, however, APB *Opinion No. 20* requires a pro forma presentation of income before extraordinary items and net income assuming that the new accounting principle had been used in prior years. This treatment of changes in accounting principles is a compromise between the positions taken by advocates of the prior-period-adjustment and current-period-adjustment approaches.

*Illustration of the General Rule for Changes in Accounting Principles* Bower Corporation    23.85

---

*Ibid., par. 16. Note that a change from an accounting principle that is not generally acceptable (such as direct costing) to one that is generally acceptable (such as absorption costing) is considered an error in a prior years' financial statements, not a change in an accounting principle.

†In the case of a switch from a weighted-average or FIFO cost-flow assumption to a LIFO cost-flow assumption, determination of the cumulative effect of the change is often impossible. (LIFO layers would need to be reconstructed beginning with the firm's first year of operations.) In these cases, disclosure is limited to showing the effect of the change on the results of operations for the year of the change.

*Exhibit 23.2*
**Book Value of Plant and Equipment Based on Accelerated and Straight-Line Depreciation**

| | Based on the Accelerated Depreciation Actually Used | If Straight-Line Depreciation Had Been Used |
|---|---|---|
| Plant and Equipment .... | $10,000,000 | $10,000,000 |
| Accumulated Depreciation .. | (6,500,000) | (4,800,000) |
| Net Plant and Equipment .... | $ 3,500,000 | $ 5,200,000 |

has used an accelerated method of depreciation for both tax and book purposes for many years. Early in 1981, it decides to switch to the straight-line method for book purposes. It will continue to use the accelerated depreciation method for tax purposes. Its plant and equipment account as it appears on the books on January 1, 1981, before the accounting change and as it would appear if the straight-line depreciation method had been used in prior years is shown in Exhibit 23.2. Assuming that the firm is subject to an income tax rate of 40 percent, the following journal entry would be made to reflect the change in accounting principle:

| | | |
|---|---|---|
| Accumulated Depreciation ($6,500,000 − $4,800,000) ... | 1,700,000 | |
| Deferred Income Taxes (.40 × $1,700,000) ...... | | 680,000 |
| Cumulative Effect of Change in Accounting Principle (.60 × $1,700,000) ............ | | 1,020,000 |

The debit of $1,700,000 to Accumulated Depreciation is for the excess of the depreciation actually taken under the accelerated depreciation method in prior years over the amount that would have been taken under the straight-line method. Because the use of different depreciation methods for tax and

book purposes creates a timing difference, the Deferred Income Taxes account must be credited for 40 percent of the *cumulative* difference between tax and pretax book income. The cumulative difference of $1,700,000 is equal to the difference in accumulated depreciation under the two methods. The account, Cumulative Effect of Change in Accounting Principle, is credited with the cumulative effect of the change on all prior years' earnings. This account is included in the income statement for the current year.

23.86 Exhibit 23.3 illustrates the disclosures required for changes in accounting principles under the general rule. (The derivation of the amounts shown in Exhibit 23.3 is not discussed here.) Note in the top portion of Exhibit 23.3 that **(1)** income before extraordinary items for 1981, the year of the change, is based on the new accounting principle, **(2)** the cumulative effect of the change on all prior years' earnings is disclosed on a single line between extraordinary items and net income for 1981, and **(3)** the income amounts for prior years included for comparative purposes are the amounts originally reported in those prior years. The lower portion of Exhibit 23.3 shows the pro forma amounts that would have been reported for prior years had the new accounting principle been used in those years. Note that the pro forma amount of income before extraordinary items for 1981 of $1,200,000 is the same as the amount in the top portion of Exhibit 23.3. Income for the year of the change is to be based on the new accounting principle.

23.87 **Change in Accounting Principle: Exceptions to General Rule** APB *Opinion No. 20* provides for six exceptions to the general rule that the cumulative effects of accounting changes should be recognized in income of the period of the change. The exceptions apply to:

**1.** A change *from* LIFO to any other cost-flow assumption.

**2.** A change in the method of accounting for long-term construction-type contracts.

**3.** A change to or from the "full-cost"

*Exhibit 23.3*
**Bower Corporation Partial Income Statements Illustrating Change in Accounting Principle**

| Year Ended December 31: | 1981 | 1980 | 1979 | 1978 | 1977 |
|---|---|---|---|---|---|
| Income before Extraordinary Item and Cumulative Effect of a Change in Accounting Principle ................. | $1,200,000 | $1,100,000 | $1,300,000 | $1,000,000 | $800,000 |
| Extraordinary Item ...................... | (35,000) | 100,000 | | 40,000 | |
| Cumulative Effect on Prior Years (to December 31, 1980) of Changing to a Different Depreciation Method (Note A) .. | 1,020,000 | | | | |
| Net Income .......................... | $2,185,000 | $1,200,000 | $1,300,000 | $1,040,000 | $800,000 |
| Earnings per Common Share—Assuming No Dilution: | | | | | |
| Income before Extraordinary Item and Cumulative Effect of Change in Accounting Principle ............... | $1.20 | $1.10 | $1.30 | $1.00 | $0.80 |
| Extraordinary Item .................... | (0.04) | 0.10 | — | 0.04 | — |
| Cumulative Effect on Prior Years (to December 31, 1980) of Changing to a Different Depreciation Method ........ | 1.02 | — | — | — | — |
| Net Income ......................... | $2.18 | $1.20 | $1.30 | $1.04 | $0.80 |
| Earnings per Common Share—Assuming Full Dilution: | | | | | |
| Income before Extraordinary Item and Cumulative Effect of Change in Accounting Principle ............... | $1.11 | $1.02 | $1.20 | $0.93 | $0.75 |
| Extraordinary Item .................... | (0.03) | 0.09 | — | 0.04 | — |
| Cumulative Effect on Prior Years (to December 31, 1980) of Changing to a Different Depreciation Method ....... | 0.94 | — | — | — | — |
| Net Income ......................... | $2.02 | $1.11 | $1.20 | $0.97 | 0.75 |
| Pro Forma Amounts Assuming That the New Depreciation Method Is Applied Retroactively: | | | | | |
| Income before Extraordinary Item .... | $1,200,000 | $1,228,500 | $1,425,000 | $1,115,000 | $931,000 |
| Earnings per Common Share— Assuming No Dilution .......... | $1.20 | $1.23 | $1.43 | $1.12 | $0.93 |
| Earnings per Common Share— Assuming Full Dilution .......... | $1.11 | $1.15 | $1.33 | $1.04 | $0.87 |
| Net Income ...................... | $1,165,000 | $1,328,000 | $1,425,000 | $1,155,000 | $931,000 |
| Earnings per Common Share— Assuming No Dilution .......... | $1.17 | $1.32 | $1.43 | $1.16 | $0.93 |
| Earnings per Common Share— Assuming Full Dilution .......... | $1.08 | $1.24 | $1.33 | $1.10 | $0.87 |

**Note A:** The Bower Corporation switched from accelerated depreciation to the straight-line method of depreciation as of January 1, 1981. The change in accounting principle increased income before extraordinary items and changes in accounting principles for 1981 by $127,000 ($.13 per share assuming no dilution and $.11 per share assuming full dilution) over the amounts that would have been reported if the accelerated depreciation method had continued to be used.

method of accounting used in the extractive industries.

**4.** A change from the lower-of-cost-or-market method to the equity method of accounting for intercorporate investments because the ownership percentage increases from less than 20 percent to 20 percent or more.

**5.** Any change in accounting principles prior to a firm's initial public offering of capital stock.

**6.** Any accounting principle change required to be treated retroactively by a new pronouncement (for example, Financial Accounting Standards Board *Statement No. 11* on contingencies).

23.88 In each of these six cases, the change in accounting principles should be treated as a prior-period adjustment. The cumulative effect of the change on Retained Earnings as of the beginning of the period should be charged or credited to Retained Earnings. The amount should be disclosed in the analysis of changes in retained earnings as an addition or subtraction to the balance at the beginning of the period of change. In addition, all prior years' financial statements (not just income amounts) should be restated retroactively to reflect the new accounting method (no pro forma amounts are shown because the revised amounts are the only ones presented).

23.89 The Accounting Principles Board provided no rationale for the first four of these six situations in which the general rule is not followed. Perhaps the amounts involved were felt to be so material that current recognition of the cumulative effects of the change would seriously distort the current period's earnings. Retroactive application of the new accounting methods by firms initially going public is reasonable, because financial statements are being issued to the public for the first time.

23.90 **Change in Accounting Estimate** As a routine part of the accounting process, certain estimates about future events must be made. Examples include the rate of uncollectible accounts, service lives and salvage values of

depreciable assets, warranty costs, and the amount of recoverable mineral reserves. As more experience is acquired, or new information is obtained, these estimates are likely to be changed periodically. These changes are referred to as *changes in accounting estimates.*

23.91 Changes in accounting estimates differ from errors in prior years' financial statements. Changes in accounting estimates result from new information not available at the time the original estimates were made. Errors result from a misuse of information available at the time the original measurements were made. For example, the change in the estimated salvage value of a depreciable asset is a change in an accounting estimate. The failure to consider salvage value in the calculation of depreciation expense under the straight-line method is an error. Changes in accounting estimates also usually differ from changes in accounting principles. A reduction in the estimated useful life of a depreciable asset is a change in an accounting estimate, whereas a switch from the sum-of-the-years'-digits method to the straight-line method is a change in an accounting principle. In some cases, however, changes in accounting estimates and accounting principles are difficult to distinguish. A firm that had previously capitalized and then amortized certain costs may begin recording the costs as expenses as incurred because future benefits have become doubtful. Is this a change in an accounting estimate or a change in an accounting principle (capitalize/amortize to immediate expensing)? Accounting Principles Board *Opinion No. 20* requires that such changes be considered changes in accounting estimates, because the change is related to the continuing process of obtaining additional information and revising estimates.

23.92 The effects of changes in accounting estimates should be accounted for in **(1)** the period of change if the change affects that period only or **(2)** the period of change and future periods if the change affects both. A change in an accounting estimate cannot be accounted for by restating amounts reported in financial statements of prior periods or by reporting pro forma amounts for prior periods.* In requiring current and prospective adjustment for changes in accounting estimates, the Accounting Principles Board gave consideration to the frequency with which such changes occur and the possible damaging effects on user confidence in financial statements if retroactive changes were continually being made. The bias introduced in the times series of earnings by not adjusting retroactively was felt to be tolerable.

23.93   *Example 1* Wellwood Department Store has based its provision for uncollectible accounts on 3 percent of credit sales. The credit balance in Allowance for Uncollectible Accounts on December 31, 1981, before the provision for 1981 sales is made, is $160,000. Three percent of credit sales for 1981 is $240,000 (= .03 × $8,000,000). An aging of the accounts reveals that the 3-percent rate used has been too high. A rate of 2 percent would be more appropriate. The aging indicates that a balance of only $230,000 is needed in the allowance account on December 31, 1981. The entry to reflect this change in the accounting estimate is

Sales Contra, Estimated
    Uncollectibles  . . . . . . . . . . . . . . . . .  70,000
        Allowance for Uncollectible
            Accounts  . . . . . . . . . . . . . . . . .       70,000

This is a "catch-up" type of entry. As a result of providing for uncollectible accounts at 3 percent of credit sales in prior years, the balance in the allowance account has been permitted to build up. The provision for 1981 is correspondingly reduced ($70,000 versus $240,000) to reflect the new rate of estimated uncollectible accounts. The provision for uncollectible accounts in 1982 and future years will be based on the revised estimated rate of uncollectibles of 2 percent.

23.94   *Example 2* An office machine was acquired on January 1, 1976, for $9,200. The machine

had an estimated useful life of 10 years and an estimated salvage value of $200. It is depreciated by the straight-line method. On December 31, 1981, before the books are closed for the year, it is decided that, in light of evidence presently available, a total useful life of 15 years with the same salvage value estimate of $200 would be a more reasonable estimate. The depreciation recorded for each of the years 1976 through 1980 under the straight-line method would have been $900 [= ($9,200 − $200)/10]. Thus, the book value of the machine before depreciation is recognized for 1981 is $4,700 [= $9,200 − ($900 × 5)]. The depreciation charge for each of the 10 *remaining* years must be revised for this change in estimated useful life. Depreciation for 1981 and each of the next 9 years will be $450 [= ($4,700 − $200)/10] per year. Figure 23.1 presents graphically the original and revised depreciation pattern.

23.95   Material changes in accounting estimates should be disclosed in a note to the financial statements.

**Change in Reporting Entity**   A change in a   23.96
reporting entity occurs in cases such as the following:

**1.** Consolidated or combined statements are reported whereas statements of individual companies were presented previously.

**2.** The specific subsidiaries comprising the group of companies for which consolidated statements are prepared are changed (for example, an unconsolidated finance subsidiary previously accounted for using the equity method is now consolidated).

**3.** The specific companies included in combined financial statements are changed.

**4.** A business combination occurs and is accounted for using the pooling-of-interests method.

When a change in a reporting entity occurs,   23.97
all prior years' financial statements should be restated to reflect the new reporting entity. The financial statements for the period of the change should describe the nature of the change and the reasons for it. In addi-

---

*Accounting Principles Board, *Accounting Principles Board Opinion No. 20* (1971), par. 31.

### Figure 23.1
**Illustration of Revised Depreciation Schedule. Asset's Service Life Estimate Is Increased from 10 to 15 Years in 1981. The Straight-Line Method Is Used. Asset Cost $9,200 and Has Estimated Salvage Value of $200.**

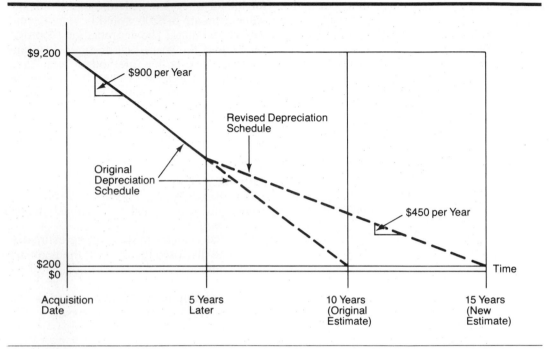

tion, the effect of the change on income before extraordinary items, net income, and related per-share amounts should be disclosed for all periods presented. Financial statements of subsequent periods need not repeat the disclosures.*

### Quasi-Reorganizations

23.98    A firm experiencing several years of net losses may find that it has a debit balance, or a deficit, in Retained Earnings. Most state laws prohibit firms from paying dividends in such cases. Such a firm might have valuable assets, superior managerial talents, or other

*Ibid., pars. 34–35.

attributes that indicate a potential for operating profitably. However, with an inability to pay dividends, it may be unable to obtain the equity capital needed to turn the losses into profits.

23.99    If such a firm is unable to obtain financing, it will probably eventually become insolvent or go bankrupt. Under supervision of a court, the assets of the firm will be sold and the cash distributed to creditors and owners.

23.100    Recognizing that some firms operating unprofitably may be worth saving, many state laws permit firms with deficits in Retained Earnings to execute a quasi-reorganization. A *quasi-reorganization* is a mechanism for eliminating a deficit in Retained Earnings and giving the entity a fresh start. The entity will then be legally able to pay dividends as soon as it is profitable, instead of waiting until accumulated profits are large enough to eliminate the deficit in Retained Earnings.

23.101   The quasi-reorganization process consists of the following steps:

**1.** The assets and liabilities of the firm are restated to their current market values.

**2.** The Additional Paid-in Capital account must be set at an amount large enough to eliminate the deficit in Retained Earnings. This might be done by reducing the par or stated value of the common stock or by having shareholders donate some of their capital stock to the corporation.

**3.** The debit balance in Retained Earnings is eliminated by crediting Retained Earnings and debiting Additional Paid-in Capital.

23.102   The following journal entries are typical of those made in a quasi-reorganization, when Retained Earnings has a $60,000 debit balance before the quasi-reorganization:

| | | |
|---|---|---|
| Retained Earnings | 80,000 | |
| Bonds Payable | 5,000 | |
| Merchandise Inventory | | 40,000 |
| Land | | 15,000 |
| Buildings and Equipment | | 30,000 |

To revalue assets and liabilities to their current market value. In this case, both assets and liabilities are reduced and the debit balance in Retained Earnings is increased from $60,000 to $140,000.

| | | |
|---|---|---|
| Common Stock | 200,000 | |
| Additional Paid-in Capital | | 200,000 |

To reduce the par value of 10,000 shares of outstanding common stock from $30 per share to $10 per share.

| | | |
|---|---|---|
| Additional Paid-in Capital | 140,000 | |
| Retained Earnings | | 140,000 |

To eliminate the deficit in Retained Earnings, decreasing Additional Paid-in Capital.

As a result of a quasi-reorganization, Re-   23.103 tained Earnings must have a zero balance. There may, however, be additional paid-in capital arising from the quasi-reorganization.

The financial statements for the year of   23.104 the quasi-reorganization should disclose the details of the amounts involved (asset and liability revaluations, additional paid-in capital created, deficit in Retained Earnings eliminated). In addition, the Retained Earnings account on the balance sheet should be dated for approximately 10 years after the reorganization to indicate when the reorganization took place.* Disclosure of dated Retained Earnings on December 31, 1981, might take the following form:

**Shareholders' Equity**

| | |
|---|---|
| Common Stock, $10 Par Value, 10,000 Shares Issued and Outstanding | $100,000 |
| Additional Paid-in Capital | 85,000 |
| Retained Earnings (since quasi-reorganization on January 2, 1977) | 28,600 |
| Total Shareholders' Equity | $213,600 |

*Accounting Research Bulletin No. 46, AICPA (1956).*

## Questions and Short Cases

**23.1**   Review the meaning of the following concepts or terms discussed in this chapter.

**a.** Distribution out of capital.

**b.** Distribution out of earnings.

**c.** Statutory restrictions on dividends.

**d.** Contractual restrictions on dividends.

**e.** Financial considerations in dividend policy decisions.

**f.** Date of declaration.

**g.** Date of record.

**h.** Date of payment.

**i.** Dividends in kind.

**j.** Stock dividend.

**k.** Stock split.

**l.** Reverse stock split.

**m.** Appropriation of retained earnings.

**n.** Loss contingency.

**o.** Prior-period adjustment.

**p.** Errors in prior years' financial statements.

**q.** Intra-balance sheet errors.

r. Intra-income statement errors.

s. Inter–balance sheet/income statement errors.

t. Counterbalancing errors.

u. Noncounterbalancing errors.

v. Change in accounting principle.

w. Change in accounting estimate.

x. Change in reporting entity.

y. Quasi-reorganization.

**23.2**    Distinguish between the amount of earnings retained in the business and the balance in the Retained Earnings account.

**23.3**    In what sense is the statement that dividends are paid "out of earnings" a misnomer?

**23.4**    As a bondholder of a corporation, would you be willing to give management wide latitude in decisions to distribute stock dividends or would you want restrictions placed in the bond contract regarding the extent of stock dividends? Explain.

**23.5**    Explain the distinction between a plant expansion fund and an appropriation of retained earnings for plant expansion.

**23.6**    Compare the position of a shareholder who receives a cash dividend with that of one who receives a stock dividend.

**23.7**    Distinguish between a stock dividend and a stock split, as to both their purposes and the accounting treatment followed.

**23.8**    Weinberg Corporation sent the following notice to its shareholders at the end of 1981: "Dividends of $4.50 were paid during 1981 for each share of common stock outstanding. Our records indicate that $1.20 of this amount represents a liquidating dividend." If there were 10,000 shares of common stock outstanding during 1981, how would Weinberg Corporation have recorded the $45,000 paid during the year?

**23.9**    At the annual shareholders' meeting, the president of the Santa Cris Corporation made the following statement: "The net income for the year, after taxes, was $1,096,000. The directors have decided that the corporation can only afford to distribute $500,000 as a cash dividend." Are the two sentences of this statement compatible?

**23.10**    A certain corporation retained almost all of its earnings, only rarely paying a cash dividend. When some of the shareholders objected, the reply of the president was: "Why do you want cash dividends? You would just have to go to the trouble of reinvesting them. Where can you possibly find a better investment than our own company?" Comment.

**23.11**    Describe three methods of disclosing restrictions on dividends. Which of the three methods of disclosure is most likely to be used for statutory restrictions on dividends?

**23.12**    An appropriation of retained earnings for the retirement of bonds used to be labeled "Reserve for Bond Retirement." Suggest reasons why this terminology is no longer considered acceptable.

**23.13**    Corporation A purchased 10,000 shares of its stock on the open market for $15 a share and treated the shares as treasury stock. When the market price of the stock increased to $20 per share, the shares were distributed as a stock dividend. Corporation B also purchased 10,000 shares of its common stock on the open market for $15 a share and held the shares as treasury stock. When the market price of the stock increased to $20 per share, Corporation B sold the shares on the open market for $200,000 and distributed the proceeds as a cash dividend. Discuss the effect of these transactions on net income and the various shareholders' equity accounts.

**23.14** Corporation C, Corporation D, and Corporation E each had 100,000 shares of common stock outstanding on January 1, 1981. On April 1, 1981, Corporation C issued a 10-percent stock dividend, Corporation D issued 10,000 new shares of stock on the open market, and Corporation E sold on the open market 10,000 shares previously held as treasury stock (held for 6 months). In calculating the weighted-average number of common shares outstanding, how would the transactions on April 1 be treated?

**23.15** A firm anticipated that a major strike at one of its principal suppliers early in 1982 would severely reduce available raw materials and cause the shut-down of production for several months. In anticipation of the losses from such a strike, the firm made a provision for estimated losses against its earnings for 1981. When the losses actually occurred in 1982, they were charged against the provision. Evaluate this accounting treatment.

**23.16** A corporation was sued by the federal government for illegal collusion with competitors in fixing prices in 1978. Although the corporation realized in 1978 that it would be found guilty of price fixing, it could not arrive at a reasonable estimate of the damage claim that it would be required to pay. The case was settled in 1981, with the corporation paying $6,000,000 in damages. Give the theoretical arguments to recognizing this $6,000,000 loss as **(a)** a prior-period adjustment during 1981, and **(b)** an element in determining net income for 1981.

**23.17** Adjustments for accounting changes and errors might be made retroactively, currently, or prospectively. Indicate the types of accounting changes and errors that are treated in each one of the three ways.

**23.18** A firm acquired a machine for $10,000 and charged the amount to Depreciation Expense. In what sense is the term "noncounterbalancing error" in relation to this error a misnomer?

**23.19** (Adapted from CPA Examination.) Accounting Principles Board *Opinion No. 20* is concerned with accounting changes.
   **a.** Define, discuss and illustrate each of the following in such a way that one can be distinguished from the other:
   **(1)** An accounting change.
   **(2)** A correction of an error in previously issued financial statements.
   **b.** Discuss the justification for a change in accounting principle.
   **c.** Discuss the reporting (as required by APB *Opinion No. 20)* of a change from the LIFO method to another method of inventory pricing.

**23.20** (Adapted from CPA Examination.) Sometimes a business entity may change its method of accounting for certain items. The change may be classified as a change in accounting principle, a change in accounting estimate, or a change in reporting entity.
   Listed below are three independent, unrelated sets of facts relating to accounting changes.

**Situation I.** A company determined that the depreciable lives of its fixed assets are presently too long to fairly match the cost of the fixed assets with the revenue produced. The company decided at the beginning of the current year to reduce the depreciable lives of all of its existing fixed assets by 5 years.

**Situation II.** On December 31, 1980, Gary Company owned 51 percent of Allen Company, at which time Gary reported its investment using the lower of cost or market method because of political uncertainties in the country in which Allen was located. On January 2, 1981, the management of Gary Company was satisfied that the political uncertainties were resolved and the assets of the company were in no danger of nationalization. Accordingly, Gary will prepare consolidated financial statements for Gary and Allen for the year ended December 31, 1981.

**Situation III.** A company decides in January 1981 to adopt the straight-line method of depreciation for plant equipment. The straight-line method will be used for new acquisitions as well as for previously acquired plant equipment for which depreciation had been provided on an accelerated basis.

For each of the situations described above, provide the information indicated below. Complete your discussion of each situation before going on to the next situation.
**a.** Type of accounting change.
**b.** Manner of reporting the change under current generally accepted accounting principles including a discussion, where applicable, of how amounts are computed.
**c.** Effect of the change on the statement of financial position and the income statement.
**d.** Footnote disclosures that would be necessary.

**23.21**   Set up a work sheet with eight columns labeled as follows:

| 1980 | | | | 1981 | | | |
|---|---|---|---|---|---|---|---|
| Net Income | Assets | Liabilities | Owners' Equity | Net Income | Assets | Liabilities | Owners' Equity |

Using O (overstated), U (understated), or N (no effect), indicate the effect of each of the independent errors below on net income for 1980 and 1981, and on assets, liabilities, and owners' equity at the end of 1980 and 1981 before any correcting entries for the errors are made. Ignore income taxes.
**a.** Ending inventory on December 31, 1980, is understated.
**b.** Ending inventory on December 31, 1981, is overstated.
**c.** Rentals received in advance for the period October 1, 1980, to September 30, 1981, are credited to Rental Revenue.
**d.** A machine having a 5-year useful life was acquired on July 1, 1980, and charged to Repairs Expense.
**e.** A 2-year insurance policy was acquired on January 1, 1980. The premium was paid in advance on this date and charged to Insurance Expense.
**f.** An unrealized loss from price declines in long-term securities held as investments was charged against earnings at the end of 1980. Market prices reversed themselves in 1981 so that an unrealized gain was included in earnings at the end of 1981.
**g.** Salaries earned by office employees during 1980 and 1981 were charged in error to Travel Expense.
**h.** Office supplies acquired on account on December 29, 1980, were included in the physical inventory on December 31, 1980, but not recorded on the books as purchases until January 3, 1981. Such supplies were used during 1981.
**i.** A stock dividend on June 5, 1980, was recorded at the par value of the shares issued.
**j.** A gain on sale of treasury stock on February 10, 1981, was included in net income for 1981.
**k.** A bonus earned by management during 1981 was not recorded until it was paid early in 1982.

l. Bonds were issued on July 1, 1980, at a discount. The discount was charged to Interest Expense during 1980. The bonds mature in 1991.

m. Shares of common stock were issued for a new automobile on September 1, 1980. The transaction was recorded using the par value of the shares issued, although the market value per share was higher.

**23.22**  A combined statement of income and retained earnings might include the following categories:

| | |
|---|---|
| Income from Continuing Operations | (1) |
| Income from Discontinued Operations | (2) |
| Extraordinary Gains and Losses | (3) |
| Cumulative Effect of Accounting Changes | (4) |
| Net Income | * |
| Less Dividends Declared | (5) |
| Increase in Retained Earnings for Year | * |
| Retained Earnings, Beginning of Year (as Previously Reported) | * |
| Adjustments to Beginning Balance in Retained Earnings | (6) |
| Retained Earnings, Beginning of Year (as Adjusted) | * |
| Retained Earnings, End of Year | * |

Using the numbers above, indicate the classification of each of the following independent items in a combined statement of income and retained earnings. If an item would not appear in one of the above categories, indicate this by using the number (7).

a. Loss from the settlement of a damage suit involving the sale of mislabeled meats 3 years ago. The company felt that it had an adequate defense and, therefore, had not previously made a provision for the loss.

b. A change from the straight-line method to the sum-of-the-years'-digits method of depreciation on computer equipment.

c. Costs during the last several days of the year incurred in relocating two major plants.

d. Overstatement of merchandise inventory at the end of the preceding year because several pages of the inventory summary were counted twice.

e. Gain from the sale of treasury stock acquired in a preceding year.

f. A change from a weighted-average to a first-in, first-out cost-flow assumption for inventories and cost of goods sold.

g. Federal income tax reduction during the current year arising from the carryforward of net operating losses of prior years.

h. A change from the completed-contract method to the percentage-of-completion method of income recognition on long-term contracts.

i. An adjustment in Allowance for Uncollectible Accounts after an aging revealed that prior years' provisions had been too large.

j. An increase in the annual depreciation rate for certain machinery due to a decrease in expected useful life.

k. A change from direct costing to absorption costing for inventories.

l. A switch from the declining-balance method to the straight-line method of depreciation when assets reach 60 percent of their estimated useful life.

m. Understatement of depreciation expense in prior years because salvage value was subtracted from the book value of assets in calculating depreciation under the declining-balance method.

n. A change from a first-in, first-out to a last-in, first-out cost-flow assumption for inventories and cost of goods sold.

o. A switch from the direct charge-off method to the allowance method of accounting for uncollectible accounts immediately prior to a firm's initial public offering of securities.

p. Reversal of an allowance for government contract claims, charged to earnings of prior years, after final settlement with authorities.

q. A change from the last-in, first-out to the first-in, first-out cost-flow assumption for inventories and cost of goods sold.

r. An unexpected increase in warranty costs relating to products sold in previous years.

s. A write-off of "goodwill" relating to an investment in an unconsolidated subsidiary due to the bankruptcy of the subsidiary.

t. Adjustment of utility rates of prior years by a rate board, requiring the refunding to customers of amounts previously reported as revenues.

u. Loss from the major devaluation of a foreign currency.

v. Adjustment relating to the understatement of ending inventory 2 years ago.

w. A switch from the lower of cost or market method to the equity method of accounting for intercorporate investments because the ownership percentage increased from 18 percent to 25 percent.

x. Declaration of a 10-percent stock dividend.

y. Elimination of a deficit in retained earnings as of the beginning of the current year through a quasi-reorganization.

z. A loss from the retirement of long-term debt.

## Problems and Exercises

23.23    On January 15, 1981, the board of directors of Jackson Corporation declared a 10-percent common stock dividend to common shareholders of record on January 25, 1981. The dividend was distributed on February 5, 1981. The market price of the stock was as follows: January 15, 1981: $12 per share; January 25, 1981: $15 per share; February 5, 1981: $13 per share. There were 20,000 shares of $5-par-value common stock issued and outstanding prior to the stock dividend. Give the journal entries to account for this stock dividend.

23.24    Rainey Corporation operates in a state in which legal capital is defined as the total amount in the Common Stock and Additional Paid-in Capital accounts. Stock dividends, once capitalized, are part of legal capital. The shareholders' equity of Rainey Corporation on January 1, 1977, is as follows:

| | |
|---|---:|
| Common Stock, $10 Par Value, 50,000 Shares Issued and Outstanding | $500,000 |
| Additional Paid-in Capital | 200,000 |
| Retained Earnings | 50,000 |
| Total | $750,000 |

Net income (loss) for 1977 through 1981 was as follows:

| | |
|---|---:|
| 1977 | $60,000 |
| 1978 | 20,000 |
| 1979 | 5,000 |
| 1980 | (10,000) |
| 1981 | (40,000) |

Dividends for the years 1977 through 1981 were as follows:

1. 1977: A cash dividend of $.50 per share was declared on November 30, 1977, to shareholders of record on December 15, 1977. The dividend was paid on December 31, 1977.

2. 1978: A dividend of $.50 per share payable in merchandise of Rainey Corporation was

declared on November 30, 1978, to shareholders of record on December 15, 1978. The dividend was paid on December 24, 1978. The gross profit percentage of Rainey Corporation is 20 percent.

3. 1979: A 10-percent stock dividend was declared on December 3, 1979, to shareholders of record on December 18, 1979. The stock dividend was distributed on December 29, 1979. The market price of the stock was $12 per share on December 3, 1979, $12.25 per share on December 18, 1979, and $11.75 per share on December 29, 1979.

4. 1980: A cash dividend of $.50 per share was declared on November 24, 1980, to shareholders of record on December 14, 1980. The dividend was paid on December 31, 1980.

5. 1981: A 30-percent stock dividend was declared on October 1, 1981, to shareholders of record on October 15, 1981. The stock dividend was distributed on October 25, 1981. The market price of the shares was $10.50 per share on October 1, 1981, $10.25 per share on October 15, 1981, and $9.00 per share on October 25, 1981.

a. Give the journal entries to record each of the dividends during the years 1977 through 1981.
b. Prepare an analysis of changes in Common Stock, Additional Paid-in Capital, and Retained Earnings for the years 1977 through 1981.

23.25   Record in journal entry form the following transactions or events of Campbell Corporation during 1981. You may assume that there are sufficient balances in the Additional Paid-in Capital and Retained Earnings accounts to record these transactions. The income tax rate is 45 percent.

1. A plant expansion fund is established on January 15, 1981. Securities costing $500,000 are acquired and placed in the fund. Retained earnings are appropriated for the same amount.

2. An error in recording Salaries Payable at the end of 1980 is discovered on March 6, 1981. The accrual of $10,000 on December 31, 1980, was credited to Deferred Income Taxes. When the salaries were paid on January 5, 1981, Salaries Payable was debited.

3. A 2-for-1 stock split is declared on April 1, 1981, on the 10,000 shares of outstanding $10-par-value common stock. The par value is to be reduced to $8.

4. A customer has sued Campbell Corporation for $1,000,000 for injuries sustained while shopping in one of Campbell Corporation's department stores. Campbell Corporation feels that it is possible, but not probable, that the customer will win the case.

5. Securities in the plant expansion fund costing $150,000 are sold for $175,000 on June 15, 1981.

6. An expenditure of $160,000 is made from the Plant Expansion Fund on September 5, 1981, to purchase equipment. A corresponding amount of appropriated retained earnings is reduced.

7. A machine acquired on January 2, 1978, for $20,000 and depreciated using the double-declining-balance method and zero estimated salvage value has a book value of $4,220 on January 2, 1981. A switch to the straight-line method is made on January 2, 1981, for this machine so that the machine will be fully depreciated by the end of its 5-year useful life. Campbell Corporation follows this same switchover procedure on all of its depreciable assets.

23.26   Record in journal entry form the following events of Stanley Corporation. You may assume that there are sufficient balances in the Additional Paid-in Capital and Retained Earnings accounts to record these events.

1. A bond sinking fund is established. A check for $1,000,000 is issued to State Street Bank, which is to serve as trustee and invest the funds. To inform financial statement users of the restrictions on dividends imposed by bondholders, an appropriation of retained earnings of $1,000,000 is made.

2. Stanley Corporation has been sued by several customers for defective products that it sold. It estimates that losses from these lawsuits will be $600,000. In addition, Stanley Corporation estimates that other customers will sue for damages relating to the same defective products. The estimated loss from these lawsuits, although not yet filed, is $1,500,000. Stanley Corporation appropriates $2,100,000 of retained earnings relating to these estimated losses.

3. A 50-percent stock dividend is declared on the 50,000 shares of outstanding $10-par-value common stock. The market price of the common stock on the date of declaration is $25 per share.

4. All court suits relating to the damage claims in (2) have been settled at a total cost of $2,250,000.

5. A dividend of $2.00 per share payable in merchandise of Stanley Corporation is declared. The gross profit rate on the merchandise is 25 percent.

6. The dividend in (5) is distributed.

23.27    The shareholders' equity of Hobson Corporation on January 1, 1981, is as follows:

| | |
|---|---:|
| Preferred Stock, $100 Par Value, 6% Cumulative Dividends, 10,000 Shares Issued and Outstanding | $1,000,000 |
| Common Stock, $10 Par Value, 200,000 Shares Issued and Outstanding | 2,000,000 |
| Additional Paid-in Capital | 500,000 |
| Retained Earnings | 1,300,000 |
| Total | $4,800,000 |
| Less Cost of Treasury Stock (10,000 shares) | (150,000) |
| Total Shareholders' Equity | $4,650,000 |

The following transactions and events occurred during 1981.

1. January 15, 1981: 2,000 shares of treasury stock were sold for $17 per share.

2. April 1, 1981: 10,000 shares of common stock were issued for $18 per share.

3. July 1, 1981: A 10-percent stock dividend was declared when the market price was $20 per share. Treasury shares do not participate in stock dividends.

4. July 15, 1981: The stock dividend declared on July 1, 1981, was distributed, when the market price was $22 per share.

5. September 1, 1981: 3,000 shares of common stock and 1,000 shares of preferred stock are acquired on the open market for $19 and $102 per share, respectively.

6. October 1, 1981: A 2-for-1 stock split of the common stock was declared and the par value of the stock was reduced from $10 to $5 per share. The market price was $21 per share. The stock split was executed immediately.

7. December 31, 1981: The preferred stock dividend for the year was declared and paid.

Hobson Corporation had net income of $500,000 during 1981. The firm has a simple capital structure for purposes of calculating earnings per share. The income tax rate is 46 percent.

a. Determine the weighted average number of common shares outstanding for 1981 for purposes of calculating earnings per common share.
b. Calculate earnings per common share for 1981.

**23.28** Rice Corporation reported net income of $3,000,000 for 1980, its first year of operations. On April 1, 1981, subsequent to the issuance of the 1980 financial statements, the firm changed its method of accounting for manufactured inventories. During 1980, manufacturing overhead costs were treated as period expenses. Such costs will now be considered product costs. Had the manufacturing overhead costs been treated as product costs during 1980, income before income taxes would have increased $500,000.

On September 1, 1981, Rice Corporation discovered a mathematical error in the calculation of depreciation on office facilities for 1980. The error resulted in an overstatement of income before taxes and taxable income for 1980 by $300,000.

The income tax rate is 40 percent during both years. An amended income tax return will be filed for 1980.

Prepare the journal entries to adjust the accounts for the change in the method of accounting and for the mathematical error.

**23.29** Watson Corporation began operations in 1977. It computed depreciation for both tax and book purposes in accordance with the ACRS system until January 1, 1981. On this date, the firm decided to switch to the straight-line method of depreciation for book purposes on all existing as well as new assets. Assume that this change in the method of depreciation can be justified. The ACRS method will continue to be used for tax purposes. The income tax rate is 40 percent.

Depreciation for 1977 through 1981 under the ACRS and straight-line methods is as follows:

|      | ACRS Method | Straight-Line Method |
|------|-------------|----------------------|
| 1977 | $9,000      | $5,200               |
| 1978 | 8,000       | 5,200                |
| 1979 | 8,000       | 5,000                |
| 1980 | 7,000       | 5,800                |
| 1981 | 8,000       | 6,000                |

a. Give the journal entries to record this change in the accounting method and any related tax effects during 1981.
b. Income before taxes and depreciation and before adjustments for the accounting change for 1981 is $50,000. Prepare a condensed income statement for 1981 indicating the disclosures required of the change in the accounting method. The difference in depreciation methods is the only timing difference between book and taxable income. There are no permanent differences.

**23.30** Fisk Corporation acquired a machine on July 1, 1979, for $150,000. At the date of acquisition, the machine had an estimated useful life of 10 years and a $10,000 estimated salvage value. The machine is depreciated using the straight-line method.

Early in 1981, the firm changed its maintenance policies. As a consequence, the machine was expected to have a total useful life of 12, instead of 10, years and an estimated salvage value of $15,000.

Compute the amount of depreciation expense for 1981.

**23.31** The following errors are discovered in the accounts of Drago Corporation at the end of 1981 before the books are closed for the year:

Accounts Payable for Utilities and Other Miscellaneous Services Received:

| | |
|---|---|
| December 31, 1979 ................................................... | $10,000 understated |
| December 31, 1980 ................................................... | $12,000 understated |
| December 31, 1981 ................................................... | $ 3,000 overstated |

Merchandise Inventory (due to mathematical errors in taking physical inventory):

| | |
|---|---|
| December 31, 1980 ................................................... | $15,000 overstated |
| December 31, 1981 ................................................... | $12,000 understated |

Prepaid Rent:

| | |
|---|---|
| December 31, 1979 ................................................... | $ 4,000 understated |
| December 31, 1980 ................................................... | $ 3,000 overstated |
| December 31, 1981 ................................................... | $ 6,000 understated |

Accumulated Depreciation on Office Equipment:

| | |
|---|---|
| December 31, 1978 ................................................... | $      0 |
| December 31, 1979 ................................................... | $ 2,000 understated |
| December 31, 1980 ................................................... | $ 5,000 understated |
| December 31, 1981 ................................................... | $ 9,000 understated |

Subscription Fees Received in Advance:

| | |
|---|---|
| December 31, 1980 ................................................... | $ 8,000 understated |
| December 31, 1981 ................................................... | $10,000 overstated |

**a.** Prepare an analysis to determine the under- or overstatement of net income for 1979, 1980, and 1981. The income tax rate is 40 percent. Assume that an amended income tax return will be filed for 1979 and 1980.

**b.** Prepare journal entries to correct the books on December 31, 1981.

**23.32**    Steele Corporation reported net income of $22,000 in 1979, and $25,000 in 1980. Its net income for 1981 has been determined to be $30,000. However, an examination of its accounts at the end of 1981 before the books have been closed reveals the following errors.

**1.** Wages earned by employees at year end but not accrued are as follows:

| | |
|---|---|
| December 31, 1978 ............................................................. | $4,000 |
| December 31, 1979 ............................................................. | $6,000 |
| December 31, 1980 ............................................................. | $3,000 |
| December 31, 1981 ............................................................. | $8,000 |

**2.** A 1-year insurance premium of $6,000 was paid in advance on July 1, 1980, and charged to Prepayments. No other entries relating to this policy have been made.

**3.** A machine costing $20,000 and with a 5-year useful life and zero estimated salvage value was acquired on April 1, 1975, and charged to Repair Expense. The straight-line method of depreciation should have been used on this machine.

**4.** Inventory items that were acquired during the last few days of the year and included in the physical inventory but not recorded as purchases until the first few days of the next year were as follows:

| | |
|---|---|
| December 31, 1978 ............................................................. | $ 5,000 |
| December 31, 1980 ............................................................. | $12,000 |

**5.** Salaries paid to corporate officers were charged to Selling Expenses instead of Administrative Expenses as follows:

| | |
|---|---|
| 1979 | $30,000 |
| 1981 | $40,000 |

a. Prepare an analysis to determine the effect of the errors above on net income for 1979, 1980, and 1981. The income tax rate is 45 percent for 1979, 42 percent for 1980, and 40 percent for 1981.

b. Give the journal entries on December 31, 1981, to correct the books for each of the errors.

**23.33**  Evans Corporation acquired machinery on January 1, 1979, at a cost of $100,000. At the time of acquisition, the machinery was expected to have a 5-year useful life and a $25,000 salvage value. During 1979 and 1980, the machinery was depreciated using the straight-line method.

Early in 1981, Evans Corporation discovered that it had neglected to consider the estimated salvage value in calculating depreciation for 1979 and 1980. In addition, a decision was made to change from the straight-line method to the sum-of-the-years'-digits method of depreciation for 1981. Recent information indicates that the machinery will have a total useful life of 6 years and an estimated salvage value of $5,000 at the end of its 6-year life.

Give all required journal entries during 1981 to reflect the above information. Be sure to record depreciation expense for 1981. Ignore income taxes in this problem.

**23.34**  (Adapted from CPA Examination.) Current conditions warrant that the Austin Company have a quasi-reorganization (corporate readjustment) at December 31, 1981. Selected balance sheet items prior to the quasi-reorganization (corporate readjustment) are as follows:

Inventory was recorded in the accounting records at December 31, 1981, at its market value of $3,000,000.

Property, plant, and equipment was recorded in the accounting records at December 31, 1981, at $6,000,000 net of accumulated depreciation.

Shareholders' equity consisted of:

| | |
|---|---|
| Common Stock, Par Value $10 per Share; Authorized, Issued, and Outstanding 350,000 Shares | $3,500,000 |
| Additional Paid-in Capital | 800,000 |
| Retained Earnings (deficit) | (450,000) |
| Total Shareholders' Equity | $3,850,000 |

Additional information is as follows:

Property, plant, and equipment had a fair value of $4,000,000.

The par value of the common stock is to be reduced from $10 per share to $5 per share.

Prepare the shareholders' equity section of the Austin Company's balance sheet at December 31, 1981, as it should appear after the quasi-reorganization (corporate readjustment) has been accomplished. Show supporting computations in good form. Ignore income tax and deferred tax considerations.

**23.35**  (Adapted from CPA Examination.) You have been engaged to examine the financial statements of Zurich Corporation for the year ended December 31, 1981. In the course of your examination you have ascertained the following information.

1. A check for $1,500 representing the repayment of an employee loan was received on December 29, 1981, but was not recorded until January 2, 1982.

2. Zurich uses the allowance method of accounting for uncollectible trade accounts receivable. The allowance is based on 3 percent of past-due accounts (over 120 days) and 1 percent of current accounts as of the close of each month. As a result of a changing economic climate, the amount of past-due accounts has increased significantly, and management has decided to increase the percentage based on past-due accounts to 5 percent. The following balances are available:

|  | As of November 30, 1981 | As of December 31, 1981 |
|---|---|---|
|  | Dr. (Cr.) | Dr. (Cr.) |
| Accounts Receivable ............................. | $390,000 | $430,000 |
| Past-Due Accounts (included in Accounts Receivable) .. | 12,000 | 30,000 |
| Allowance for Uncollectible Accounts ................ | (28,000) | 9,000 |

3. The merchandise inventory on December 31, 1980, did *not* include merchandise having a cost of $7,000, which had been included in Purchases for the year and was stored in a public warehouse. The merchandise was sold during 1981. Merchandise having a cost of $3,000 was erroneously counted twice and included twice in the merchandise inventory on December 31, 1981. Zurich uses a periodic inventory system.

4. On January 2, 1981, Zurich had a new machine delivered and installed in its main factory. The cost of this machine was $97,000, and the machine is being depreciated on the straight-line method over an estimated useful life of 10 years. When the new machine was installed, Zurich paid for the following items, which were not included in the cost of the machine but were charged to repairs and maintenance:

| | |
|---|---|
| Delivery Expense ..................................................... | $ 2,500 |
| Installation Costs ...................................................... | 8,000 |
| Rearrangement of Related Equipment ............................. | 4,000 |
| | $14,500 |

5. On January 1, 1980, Zurich leased a building for 10 years at a monthly rental of $12,000. On that date, Zurich paid the landlord the following amounts:

| | |
|---|---|
| Rent Deposit ........................................................ | $  6,000 |
| First Month's Rent .................................................. | 12,000 |
| Last Month's Rent ................................................... | 12,000 |
| Installation of New Walls and Offices ............................. | 80,000 |
| | $110,000 |

The entire amount was charged to rent expense in 1980.

6. In January 1980, Zurich issued $200,000 of 8-percent, 10-year bonds at 97. This discount was charged to interest expense in 1980. Interest on the bonds is payable on December 31 of each year. Zurich has recorded interest expense of $22,000 for 1980 and $16,000 for 1981. Zurich normally uses the straight-line method for amortizing bond premium and discount.

7. On May 3, 1981, Zurich exchanged 500 shares of treasury stock (its $50-par-value common stock) for a parcel of land to be used as a site for a new factory. The treasury stock had cost $70 per share when it was acquired and on May 3, 1981, it had a fair market value of $80 per share. The land was capitalized at $40,000, and Zurich recorded a gain of $5,000 on the sale of its treasury stock.

8. The account "advertising and promotion expense" for 1981 included an amount of $75,000 which represented the cost of printing sales catalogs for a special promotional campaign in January 1982.

9. Zurich was named as a defendant in a law suit by a former customer. Zurich's counsel has advised management that Zurich has a good defense and that counsel does *not* anticipate that there will be any impairment of Zurich's assets or that any significant liabilities will be incurred as a result of this litigation. Management, however, wishes to be conservative and, therefore, has established a loss contingency of $100,000 against earnings for 1981.

Prepare a schedule showing the effect of errors upon the financial statements for 1981. The items in the schedule should be presented in the same order as the facts are given with corresponding numbers 1 through 9. Use the following column headings for your schedule:

| No. | Explanation | Income Statement Dr. (Cr.) | Balance Sheet December 31, 1981 Dr.  (Cr.)  Account |
|-----|-------------|----------------------------|------------------------------------------------------|

23.36 (Adapted from CPA Examination.) You have been engaged by the Plentiful Heat Company to adjust its financial statements for the years ended June 30, 1981, and June 30, 1980. The company manufactures, sells, and services forced-air heating systems for the home. The company's financial statements for the year ended June 30, 1979, were audited by another CPA, who gave an unqualified opinion thereon.

   The company's financial statements as prepared by its controller for the years ended June 30, 1981, and June 30, 1980, are shown in Exhibits 23.4 and 23.5.

The following additional information regarding the company is available:

Your review of accounts receivable disclosed that the following items are included in the Accounts Receivable account balance at June 30, 1981:

| | |
|---|---:|
| Receivables from Officers (1981) | $11,800 |
| Customer Trade Accounts Receivable Known to Be Uncollectible from Sales Recorded in Fiscal Year 1980 | 80,000 |

Historical data indicate that 2 percent of heating system sales for the year ended June 30, 1981, will prove uncollectible. No accounts receivable have been written off during the year ended June 30, 1981.

On June 30, 1980, spare parts costing $17,280 were on hand, but had not been included in the physical inventory on that date although the liability for them had been recorded. In addition, the inventory on June 30, 1981 included spare parts sold during April 1981 for $5,000 and returned on June 17, 1981. *No* entry had been made to adjust the customer's account for the return, and the merchandise was included in the inventory at selling price, which was 125 percent of cost.

*Exhibit 23.4*
**Plentiful Heat Company**
**Balance Sheet**

| ASSETS | June 30, 1981 | June 30, 1980 |
|---|---|---|
| **Current Assets:** | | |
| Cash | $ 120,000 | $ 103,000 |
| Accounts Receivable (less allowance for doubtful accounts of $95,000 at both June 30, 1981, and June 30, 1980) | 824,000 | 602,000 |
| Inventory, Heating Systems | 1,801,000 | 1,604,000 |
| Inventory, Spare Parts | 198,000 | 137,000 |
| Prepayments | 144,000 | 144,000 |
| Total Current Assets | $3,087,000 | $2,590,000 |
| **Property and Equipment:** | | |
| Land | $ 113,000 | — |
| Machinery and Equipment (less accumulated depreciation of $923,000 at June 30, 1981, and $751,000 at June 30, 1980) | 1,561,150 | $1,522,000 |
| Leasehold Improvements (less accumulated amortization of $1,050). | 82,950 | — |
| Total Property and Equipment | $1,757,100 | $1,522,000 |
| Total Assets | $4,844,100 | $4,112,000 |
| **LIABILITIES AND SHAREHOLDERS' EQUITY** | | |
| **Current Liabilities:** | | |
| Accounts Payable | $ 449,000 | $ 462,000 |
| Other Liabilities | 82,000 | 46,000 |
| Total Current Liabilities | $ 531,000 | $ 508,000 |
| **Shareholders' Equity:** | | |
| Common Stock, Authorized 100,000 Shares, Par Value $10 per Share, Issued and Outstanding 53,300 Shares at June 30, 1981, and 53,000 Shares at June 30, 1980 | $ 533,000 | $ 530,000 |
| Retained Earnings | 3,780,100 | 3,074,000 |
| Total Shareholders' Equity | $4,313,100 | $3,604,000 |
| Total Liabilities and Shareholders' Equity | $4,844,100 | $4,112,000 |

Annual service contracts are sold to homeowners for $70, covering labor charges on all service or repair calls during the year as well as an annual inspection and cleaning of the heating system. All contracts commence on January 1 of each year. With few exceptions, almost all repair calls occur between September 1 and June 30, and during this period the number of calls remains stable from month to month. During the months of July and August, the company performs its annual inspection and cleaning service for contract holders. The charge for a similar inspection and cleaning service to customers who do not have contracts is $10. The company sold 400 contracts in the calendar year 1980 and 600 contracts in the calendar year 1981. The amounts received from customers during 1980 and 1981 on these contracts were credited to Revenue from Service and Repairs. The company had $10,200 of service contract fees received in advance on its June 30, 1979, balance sheet.

On June 2, 1981, the company paid $110,000 cash and issued 300 shares of its $10-par-value common stock having a fair market value of $27 per share at the date of transfer for a parcel of property consisting of land and an unused building. The property was acquired in order to secure a building site for a new warehouse. At the date of transfer, the company assumed

*Exhibit 23.5*
**Plentiful Heat Company**
**Statement of Income**

| | Year Ended June 30, | |
| --- | ---: | ---: |
| | **1981** | **1980** |
| Sales of Heating Systems | $4,907,000 | $4,265,000 |
| Revenues from Service and Repairs | 73,000 | 49,000 |
| Total Revenues | $4,980,000 | $4,314,000 |
| Cost of Sales | $3,121,000 | $2,650,000 |
| Cost of Service and Repairs | 41,000 | 27,000 |
| Total | $3,162,000 | $2,677,000 |
| Gross Margin | $1,818,000 | $1,637,000 |
| Selling, General, and Administrative Expenses | 1,111,900 | 1,004,000 |
| Income before Income Taxes | $ 706,100 | $ 633,000 |

and paid property taxes in arrears of $2,000. By June 18, the building was demolished at a cost of $20,000. Scrap materials recovered from the demolition yielded $16,000.

The payment of the property taxes and the net cost of demolishing the building were charged to selling, general, and administrative expenses. The issuance of the 300 shares of stock had *no* material effect on the market for the company's common stock.

On April 1, 1980, the company leased a building to be used as its corporate headquarters. The lease, which was appropriately not capitalized, was for 15 years at an annual rental of $96,000, payable in advance on each April 1. On that date, the company paid the landlord the sum of $144,000 and charged this amount to prepayments. This payment covered the first year's rent and a refundable security deposit to be held in escrow by the landlord. On April 1, 1981, the annual rental of $96,000 was paid.

On April 1, 1981, the company had an interoffice communications system installed in its offices at a cost of $84,000. This system has an estimated useful life of 20 years, but the system will have to be abandoned by the company if its lease is not renewed.

The company has an incentive commission plan for its salespeople entitling them to an additional commission when actual quarterly sales exceed budgeted estimates. An analysis of the account, Incentive Commission Expense, at June 30, 1981, follows:

| **Amount** | **For Quarter Ending** | **Date Paid** |
| :---: | :---: | :---: |
| $18,000 | June 30, 1980 | July 10, 1980 |
| 21,000 | September 30, 1980 | October 11, 1980 |
| 26,000 | December 31, 1980 | January 9, 1981 |
| 17,000 | June 30, 1981 | July 11, 1981 |
| $82,000 | | |

Note: *No* payment was made for the first quarter of the calendar year 1981, as quarterly sales did *not* meet the requirements of the plan.

Prepare a work sheet showing the adjustments required to correct the financial statements of the Plentiful Heat Company for the years ended June 30, 1981, and June 30, 1980. Though these entries may be used later to prepare entries to adjust the books, their purpose on this work sheet is to adjust the amounts shown in the financial statements. Show supporting computations in good form. Ignore income taxes and deferred tax considerations in your answer. The columns on this work sheet should have the following headings:

| | June 30, 1981 | | | | | June 30, 1980 | | | | |
| | Income Statement | | Balance Sheet | | | Income Statement | | Balance Sheet | | |
| Explanation | Dr. | (Cr.) | Dr. | (Cr.) | Account | Dr. | (Cr.) | Dr. | (Cr.) | Account |
|---|---|---|---|---|---|---|---|---|---|---|

**23.37** (Adapted from CPA Examination.) The Noble Corporation is in the process of negotiating a loan for expansion purposes. The books and records have never been audited, and the bank has requested that an audit be performed. Noble has prepared comparative financial statements for the years ended December 31, 1981 and 1980, as shown in Exhibits 23.6 and 23.7.

*Exhibit 23.6*
**Noble Corporation**
**Balance Sheet**
**as of December 31, 1981 and 1980**

| ASSETS | 1981 | 1980 |
|---|---|---|
| Current Assets | | |
| Cash | $163,000 | $ 82,000 |
| Accounts Receivable | 392,000 | 296,000 |
| Allowance for Uncollectible Accounts | (37,000) | (18,000) |
| Marketable Securities, at Cost | 78,000 | 78,000 |
| Merchandise Inventory | 207,000 | 202,000 |
| Total Current Assets | $803,000 | $640,000 |
| Fixed Assets | | |
| Property, Plant, and Equipment | $167,000 | $169,500 |
| Accumulated Depreciation | (121,600) | (106,400) |
| Total Fixed Assets | $ 45,400 | $ 63,100 |
| Total Assets | $848,400 | $703,100 |
| **LIABILITIES AND SHAREHOLDERS' EQUITY** | | |
| Liabilities | | |
| Accounts Payable | $121,400 | $196,100 |
| Shareholders' Equity | | |
| Common Stock, Par Value $10, Authorized 50,000 Shares, Issued and Outstanding 26,000 Shares | $260,000 | $260,000 |
| Retained Earnings | 467,000 | 247,000 |
| Total Shareholders' Equity | $727,000 | $507,000 |
| Total Liabilities and Shareholders' Equity | $848,400 | $703,100 |

During the course of the audit, the following additional facts were determined:

1. An analysis of collections and losses on accounts receivable during the past 2 years indicates a drop in anticipated losses due to bad debts. After consultation with management it was agreed that the loss experience rate on sales should be reduced from the recorded 2 percent to 1 percent, beginning with the year ended December 31, 1981. Estimated losses from uncollectible accounts are charged to Administrative Expenses.

2. An analysis of marketable securities revealed that this investment portfolio consisted entirely of short-term investments in marketable equity securities that were acquired in 1980. The total market valuation for these investments as of the end of each year was as follows:

| | |
|---|---|
| December 31, 1980 | $81,000 |
| December 31, 1981 | $62,000 |

*Exhibit 23.7*
**Noble Corporation**
**Statement of Income**
**for the Years Ended**
**December 31, 1981 and 1980**

|  | 1981 | 1980 |
|---|---|---|
| Sales | $1,000,000 | $900,000 |
| Cost of Sales | 430,000 | 395,000 |
| Gross Profit | $ 570,000 | $505,000 |
| Operating Expenses | $ 210,000 | $205,000 |
| Administrative Expenses | 140,000 | 105,000 |
| Total Expenses | $ 350,000 | $310,000 |
| Net Income | $ 220,000 | $195,000 |

3. The merchandise inventory at December 31, 1980, was overstated by $4,000 and the merchandise inventory at December 31, 1981, was overstated by $6,100.

4. On January 2, 1980, equipment costing $12,000 (estimated useful life of 10 years and residual value of $1,000) was incorrectly charged to operating expenses. Noble records depreciation on the straight-line method. In 1981, fully depreciated equipment (with no residual value) that originally cost $17,500 was sold as scrap for $2,500. Noble credited the proceeds of $2,500 to property and equipment.

5. An analysis of 1980 operating expenses revealed that Noble charged to expense a 3-year insurance premium of $2,700 on January 1, 1980.

a. Prepare a schedule showing the computation of corrected net income for the years ended December 31, 1981 and 1980, assuming that any adjustments are to be reported on comparative statements for the 2 years. The first items on your schedule should be the net income for each year. The income tax rate is 40 percent. An amended income tax return will be filed for 1980.

b. Prepare the journal entries to correct the books at December 31, 1981. The books for 1981 have not been closed.

23.38    (Adapted from CPA Examination.) The financial statements of the Quality Company showed income before income taxes of $4,030,000 for the year ended December 31, 1981, and $3,330,000 for the year ended December 31, 1980. Additional information is as follows:

Capital expenditures were $2,800,000 in 1981 and $4,000,000 in 1980. Included in the 1981 capital expenditures is equipment purchased for $1,000,000 on January 1, 1981, with no salvage value. Quality used straight-line depreciation based on a 10-year estimated life in its financial statements. As a result of additional information now available, it is estimated that this equipment should have only an 8-year life.

Quality made an error in its financial statements that should be regarded as material. A payment of $180,000 was made in January 1981 and charged to expense in 1981 for insurance premiums applicable to policies commencing and expiring in 1980. No liability had been recorded for this item at December 31, 1980.

The allowance for doubtful accounts reflected in Quality's financial statements was $7,000 at December 31, 1981, and $97,000 at December 31, 1980. During 1981, $90,000 of uncollectible receivables were written off against the allowance for doubtful accounts. In 1980, the provision for doubtful accounts was based on a percentage of net sales. The 1981 provision has not yet been recorded. Net sales were $58,500,000 for the year ended December 31, 1981, and $49,230,000 for the year ended December 31, 1980. Based on the latest available facts, the 1981 provision for doubtful accounts is estimated to be 0.2 percent of net sales.

A review of the estimated warranty liability at December 31, 1981, which is included in "Other Liabilities" in Quality's financial statements, has disclosed that this estimated liability should be increased $170,000 as a result of an unexpected increase in material and labor costs.

Quality has two large blast furnaces that it uses in its manufacturing process. These furnaces must be relined periodically. Furnace A was relined in January 1975 at a cost of $230,000 and in January 1980 at a cost of $280,000. Furnace B was relined for the first time in January 1981 at a cost of $300,000. In Quality's financial statements, these costs were expensed as incurred.

Because a relining will last for 5 years, a more appropriate matching of revenues and costs would have resulted if the cost of the relining had been capitalized and depreciated over the productive life of the relining. Quality has decided to make a change in accounting principle from expensing relining costs as incurred to capitalizing them and depreciating them over their productive life on a straight-line basis with a full year's depreciation in the year of relining. This change meets the requirements for a change in accounting principle under APB *Opinion No. 20*.

**a.** For the years ended December 31, 1981 and 1980, prepare a work sheet reconciling income before income taxes as given above with income before income taxes and cumulative effect of a change in accounting principle as adjusted for the above additional information. Show supporting computations in good form. Ignore income taxes and deferred tax considerations in your answer. The work sheet should have the following format:

| | Year Ended December 31 | |
|---|---|---|
| | **1981** | **1980** |
| Income before Income Taxes and before Adjustments ........ | $4,030,000 | $3,330,000 |
| | | |
| Adjustments .............................................. | _____ | _____ |
| Net Adjustments ........................................ | _____ | _____ |
| Income before Income Taxes and Cumulative Effect of a Change in Accounting Principle, after Adjustments ......... | $_____ | $_____ |

**b.** For the year ended December 31, 1981, compute the cumulative effect before income taxes of the change in accounting principle from expensing to capitalizing relining costs. Ignore income taxes and deferred tax considerations in your answer.

23.39    (Adapted from CPA Examination.) Ruwe Corporation has decided that in the preparation of its 1981 financial statements two changes will be made from the methods used in prior years:

**1.** *Depreciation*. Ruwe has always used the ACRS depreciation method for tax and financial reporting purposes but has decided to change during 1981 to the straight-line method for financial reporting only. The effect of this change is as follows:

| | Excess of ACRS Depreciation over Straight-Line Depreciation |
|---|---|
| Prior to 1980 .................................................................. | $1,300,000 |
| 1980 ......................................................................... | 101,000 |
| 1981 ......................................................................... | 99,000 |
| Total ..................................................................... | $1,500,000 |

Depreciation is charged to cost of sales and to selling, general, and administrative expenses on the basis of 75 percent and 25 percent, respectively.

2. *Estimated Uncollectible Accounts.* In the past, Ruwe has recognized estimated uncollectible accounts equal to 1.5 percent of net sales. After careful review it has been decided that a rate of 2 percent is more appropriate for 1981. The estimated uncollectible accounts provision is charged to selling, general, and administrative expenses.

The information in Exhibits 23.8 and 23.9 is taken from preliminary financial statements, prepared before giving effect to the two changes. There have been no timing differences between any book and tax items prior to the above changes. The effective tax rate is 48 percent.

*Exhibit 23.8*
**Ruwe Corporation**
**Condensed Balance Sheet**
**December 31, 1981**
**with Comparative Figures for 1980**

| ASSETS | 1981 | 1980 |
|---|---|---|
| Current Assets ............................................. | $43,561,000 | $43,900,000 |
| Fixed Assets, at Cost ..................................... | 45,792,000 | 43,974,000 |
| Less Accumulated Depreciation ........................... | (23,761,000) | (22,946,000) |
| Total ................................................. | $65,592,000 | $64,928,000 |
| **LIABILITIES AND SHAREHOLDERS' EQUITY** | | |
| Current Liabilities ........................................ | $21,124,000 | $23,650,000 |
| Long-Term Debt ........................................... | 15,154,000 | 14,097,000 |
| Capital Stock ............................................. | 11,620,000 | 11,620,000 |
| Retained Earnings ......................................... | 17,694,000 | 15,561,000 |
| Total ................................................. | $65,592,000 | $64,928,000 |

a. Assuming that the books have not been closed for 1981, give the journal entries for the two accounting changes. Be sure to consider any income tax effects.
b. Compute for the items listed below the amounts that would appear on the comparative (1981 and 1980) financial statements of Ruwe Corporation after adjustment for the two accounting changes. Show amounts for both 1981 and 1980, and prepare supporting schedules as necessary.

(1) Accumulated depreciation.
(2) Deferred tax liability.
(3) Selling, general, and administrative expenses.
(4) Current portion of federal income tax expense.

---

*Exhibit 23.9*
**Ruwe Corporation**
**Income Statement**
**for the Year Ended December 31, 1981**
**with Comparative Figures for 1980**

| | 1981 | 1980 |
|---|---|---|
| Net Sales .............................................. | $80,520,000 | $78,920,000 |
| Cost of Sales ......................................... | 54,847,000 | 53,074,000 |
| | $25,673,000 | $25,846,000 |
| Selling, General, and Administrative Expenses ................. | 19,540,000 | 18,411,000 |
| | $ 6,133,000 | $ 7,435,000 |
| Other Income (Expense), Net .............................. | (1,198,000) | (1,079,000) |
| Income before Federal Income Taxes ........................ | $ 4,935,000 | $ 6,356,000 |
| Federal Income Taxes .................................... | 2,368,800 | 3,050,880 |
| Net Income ............................................ | $ 2,566,200 | $ 3,305,120 |

---

**(5)** Deferred portion of federal income tax expense.
**(6)** Retained earnings.
**(7)** Pro forma net income.

**23.40** (Adapted from CPA Examination.) You have been engaged to examine the financial statements of Helen Corporation for the year 1981. The bookkeeper who maintains the financial records has prepared all of the unaudited financial statements for the corporation since its organization on January 2, 1979.

In the course of your examination you discover the following:

1. The corporation includes sales taxes collected from customers in the Sales account. When sales tax collections for a month are remitted to the taxing authority on the 15th of the following month, the Sales Tax Expense account is charged. All sales are subject to a 3-percent sales tax. Total sales plus sales taxes for 1979 through 1981 were $495,430, $762,200 and $924,940, respectively. The totals of the Sales Tax Expense account for the 3 years were $12,300, $21,780 and $26,640.

2. Furniture and fixtures were purchased on January 2, 1979, for $12,000 but no portion of the cost has been charged to depreciation. The corporation wishes to use the straight-line method for these assets, which have been estimated to have a life of 10 years and no salvage value.

3. In January 1979, installation costs of $5,700 on new machinery were charged to Repairs Expense. Other costs of this machinery of $30,000 were correctly recorded and have been depreciated using the straight-line method with an estimated life of 10 years and no salvage value. Current estimates are that the machinery has a total life of 14 years and a salvage value of $4,200.

4. An account payable of $8,000 for merchandise purchased on December 23, 1979, was recorded in January 1980. This merchandise was not included in either the physical or recorded inventory on December 31, 1979.

5. Merchandise having a cost of $6,550 was stored in a separate warehouse and was not included in the December 31, 1980, inventory, and merchandise having a cost of $2,180 was included twice in the December 31, 1981, inventory. The corporation uses a periodic inventory method.

6. The year-end salary accrual of $1,925 on December 31, 1981, has not been recorded.

7. A check for $1,895 from a customer to apply to his account was received on December 30, 1979, but was not recorded until January 2, 1980.

8. Quarterly dividends of $2,500 have been declared near the end of each calendar quarter since the corporation was organized. The bookkeeper has consistently followed the practice of recording all dividends at the date of payment, which is the 15th of the month following the month of declaration.

9. At December 31, 1979, sales catalogs advertising a special January 1980 white sale were on hand, but their cost of $1,360 was included in Advertising Expense for 1979.

10. At December 31, 1981, there was an unexplained cash shortage of $48.

11. When the 500 shares of outstanding stock having a par value of $100 were initially issued on January 2, 1979, the $55,000 cash received for them was credited to the Common Stock account.

12. The corporation has used the direct write-off method of accounting for bad debts. Accounts written off during each of the 3 years amount to $1,745, $2,200, and $5,625, respectively. The corporation has decided that the allowance method would be more appropriate. The estimated balances for the Allowance for Doubtful Accounts at the end of each of the 3 years are $6,100, $8,350, and $9,150.

13. On January 2, 1980, $100,000 of 6-percent 20-year bonds were issued for $98,000. The $2,000 discount was charged to Interest Expense. The bookkeeper records interest only on the interest payment dates of January 2 and July 1. Because premiums and discounts on bonds are seldom material, the straight-line method of amortization is normally used.

14. A pension plan adopted on January 2, 1981, includes a provision for a pension fund to be administered by a trustee. The employees who joined the corporation in 1979 and 1980 were given credit for their past service. A payment of $25,000 for the full amount of these past service costs was paid into the fund immediately. A second payment of $15,000 was made into the fund near the end of 1981. However, actuarial computations indicate that pension costs attributable to 1981 employee services are $16,600. The only entries applicable to the pension fund made during 1981 were debits to Pension Expense and credits to Cash. The maximum annual provision for past service cost under generally accepted accounting principles is 10 percent of the past service cost.

15. Property tax assessments of $15,600, $16,080, and $15,900 were made on January 1 of 1979, 1980, and 1981, respectively. The assessments are billed on July 1 of each year, the beginning of the fiscal year of the taxing authority, and taxes are paid in two equal installments on September 10 and December 10. The bookkeeper has always charged Property Tax Expense on the dates the cash payments are made. The corporation wishes to charge the tax expense against revenue during the fiscal year of the taxing authority.

a. Prepare a work sheet to indicate the changes in pretax income for 1979, 1980, and 1981. Your work sheet should have the following columns:

| | 1979 Income | | 1980 Income | | 1981 Income | |
|---|---|---|---|---|---|---|
| **Explanation** | **Debit** | **Credit** | **Debit** | **Credit** | **Debit** | **Credit** |

b. Give the journal entries to correct the books as of December 31, 1981, assuming that the books have not been closed for 1981.

c. Give the journal entries to correct income taxes for the 3 years, assuming that an amended tax return will be filed and that the income tax rate is 40 percent.

*Part Five*
**Financial Statement
Preparation and Analysis**

# Chapter 24
# Statement of Changes in Financial Position: A Closer Look

24.1 The statement of changes in financial position reports the flows of funds into and out of a business during a period of time. Chapter 4 discusses the various concepts of funds. It illustrates the procedures, using a simple example, for preparing the statement of changes in financial position. Subsequent chapters discuss the effects on the statement of changes in financial position of accounting for individual revenues, expenses, assets, liabilities, and shareholders' equities. This chapter presents a comprehensive illustration of the components of the statement of changes in financial position and the procedures for preparing it.

## Review of the Procedures for Preparing the Statement of Changes in Financial Position

24.2 The steps involved in preparing the statement of changes in financial position are as follows:

**1.** Obtain comparative balance sheets for the beginning and end of the period covered by the statement.

**2.** Prepare a T-account work sheet. The first T-account is a master account for all accounts included in the desired definition of funds. If funds are defined as working capital, as is usual, then the master T-account is labeled "Working Capital" and is merely an aggregation of the individual current asset and current liability accounts. If funds are defined as cash, then the master T-account is labeled "Cash." The master T-account should be separated into two sections, labeled "Operations" and "Other (Nonoperating)." Enter in the master T-account the beginning and ending balances in the appropriate funds accounts (for example, working capital). Next, prepare a T-account for each nonfunds balance sheet account and enter the beginning and ending balances in each account from the comparative balance sheets.

**3.** Explain the change in the master (funds) account between the beginning and end of the period by explaining or accounting for the change in each nonfunds account. This step is accomplished by reconstructing the entries recorded in the accounts during the period and entering them in the appropriate T-accounts on the work sheet. Once the changes in the nonfunds accounts have been explained, the change in the funds accounts in the master T-account will also have been explained. Note that the entries made in the T-account work sheet are memorandum entries only. They do not affect the accounts in

*Exhibit 24.1*
**Cole-Vatter Corporation**
**Statement of Changes in Financial**
**Position for the Year Ending**
**December 31, 1981**

**Part I: Sources and Uses of Working Capital**
**Sources of Working Capital**

A.　From Operations:

| | | | |
|---|---|---|---|
| (1) Income from Continuing Operations | | | $50,000 |
| Add Expenses and Losses Not Using Working Capital | | | |
| (2) Depreciation | $ 30,000 | | |
| (3) Goodwill Amortization Expense | 2,000 | | |
| (4) Losses from Company A (Accounted for on Equity Method) | 3,500 | | |
| (5) Loss on Sale of Land | 1,200 | | |
| (6) Deferred Income Tax Credits (Tax Expense Greater Than Tax Payable)[a] | 1,500 | | |
| (7) Bond Discount Amortization Expense (Interest Expense Greater Than Interest Payable) | 600 | | |
| (8) Minority Shareholders' Equity in Income of Consolidated Subsidiary | 400 | | |
| Total Additions | | 39,200 | |
| Subtract Revenues and Gains Not Providing Working Capital | | | |
| (9) Equity in Earnings of Company B in Excess of Dividends (Accounted for Using the Equity Method) | $ (800) | | |
| (10) Gain on Sale of Equipment | (200) | | |
| (11) Deferred Income Tax Debits (Tax Payable Greater Than Tax Expense)[a] | — | | |
| (12) Bond Premium Amortization (Interest Payable Greater Than Interest Expense) | (300) | | |
| Total Subtractions | | (1,300) | |
| (13) Working Capital Provided by Continuing Operations | | $87,900 | |
| (14) Income (Loss) from Discontinued Operations | $(13,500) | | |
| (15) Add: Depreciation Expense | 3,000 | | |
| (16) Loss on Disposal of Segment | 5,500 | | |
| (17) Subtract: Deferred Income Taxes | (1,000) | | |
| (18) Working Capital Provided (Used) by Discontinued Operations | | (6,000) | |
| (19) Extraordinary Gains and Losses | $ 1,500 | | |
| (20) Subtract: Gain on Bond Retirement Not Providing Working Capital | (2,500) | | |
| (21) Working Capital Provided (Used) by Extraordinary Items | | (1,000) | |
| (22) Cumulative Effect of Change in Accounting Principles | $ 6,000 | | |
| (23) Add: Deferred Income Taxes on Change in Depreciation Method | 4,400 | | |
| (24) Subtract: Cumulative Change in Depreciation Method Not Providing Working Capital | (9,200) | | |
| (25) Working Capital Provided by Accounting Principles Change | | 1,200 | |
| (26) Total Working Capital Provided by Operations | | $82,100 | |
| B.　Issuance of Long-Term Debt or Capital Stock: | | | |
| (27) Bonds Issued (10%) | $ 20,250 | | |
| (28) Mortgage Assumed (to Acquire Land) | 1,500 | | |
| (29) Lease Capitalized | 200 | | |
| (30) Common Stock Issued for Options Exercised by Employees | 50 | | |
| (31) Common Stock Issued on Open Market | 500 | | |
| (32) Treasury Stock Sold | 20 | | |
| (33) Total from Issuance of Long-Term Debt or Capital Stock | | 22,520 | |
| C.　Sale of Noncurrent Assets: | | | |
| (34) Sale of Land | $ 700 | | |
| (35) Sale of Equipment | 6,300 | | |
| (36) Sale of Segment | 10,000 | | |
| (37) Total from Sale of Noncurrent Assets | | 17,000 | |
| (38) Total Sources of Working Capital | | $121,620 | |

*Exhibit 24.1 (continued)*

**Uses of Working Capital**

A.   Distributions to Owners:

| | | |
|---|---:|---:|
| (39) Cash Dividends on Common Stock ($.50 per Share) | $ 7,000 | |
| (40) Cash Dividends on Preferred Stock | 400 | |
| (41) Total Uses for Distributions to Owners | | $ 7,400 |
| B.   Redemption of Long-Term Debt or Capital Stock: | | |
| (42) Bonds (8%, $12,000 Face Value, Maturing in 1991) | $ 10,000 | |
| (43) Preferred Stock (6%) | 3,000 | |
| (44) Acquisitions of Common Stock for Treasury | 5,000 | |
| (45) Total Uses from Redemption of Long-Term Debt or Capital Stock | | 18,000 |
| C.   Acquisition of Noncurrent Assets: | | |
| (46) Land | $ 1,500 | |
| (47) Equipment | 22,500 | |
| (48) Equipment Capitalized under Lease | 200 | |
| (49) Stock of Company C for Investment Purposes | 18,000 | |
| (50) Total Uses for Acquisition of Noncurrent Assets | | 42,200 |
| (51) Total Working Capital Used | | $ 67,600 |
| (52) Sources (Line 38) of Working Capital Minus Uses (Line 51) of Working Capital | | $ 54,020 |

**Part II: Analysis of Changes in Working Capital**

Current Asset Item Changes

| | | |
|---|---:|---:|
| (53)   Cash | $ 21,300 | |
| (54)   Marketable Securities | (2,300) | |
| (55)   Receivables | 29,200 | |
| (56)   Inventories | 23,500 | |
| (57) Increase (Decrease) in Current Asset Items | | $ 71,700 |
| Current Liability Item Changes | | |
| (58)   Payables | $ 14,880 | |
| (59)   Notes | 2,800 | |
| (60) Increase (Decrease) in Current Liability Items | | 17,680 |
| Increase (Decrease) in Working Capital for Year: | | |
| (61) Current Asset Changes (Line 57) Minus Current Liability Changes (Line 60) | | $ 54,020 |

ᵃAn amount will be shown for either Deferred Tax Credits or Deferred Tax Debits, but not both.

the general ledger. In the paragraphs that follow, these memorandum entries are designated with an **a** following the transaction number.

**4.** Prepare a formal statement of changes in financial position using information from the T-account work sheet and the comparative balance sheets.

You may find it useful to review the work sheet format at this time by referring to Exhibit 4.4. The goal is to prepare a statement that explains the three major sources and three major uses of funds illustrated in Figure 4.1.

# Components of a Comprehensive Statement of Changes in Financial Position

This section presents a detailed example of   24.3 a statement of changes in financial position, and an explanation of how some of the items are derived. Exhibit 24.1 presents a statement of changes in financial position for Cole-Vatter Corporation for 1981. Each entry in the exhibit is numbered for reference in later explanations. No published statement we know of contains all of the items included in Exhibit 24.1, but this much detail is shown to illustrate the various items that may appear in the statement. As the individual items are discussed, you may wish to review the accounting for them from previous chapters.

## Definition and Disclosure of Changes in Funds

24.4 The statement of changes in financial position of Cole-Vatter Corporation defines funds as "working capital." Part I of the statement shows the sources and uses of working capital that account for or explain the change in working capital for the period. The sources of working capital are classified into three categories: **(A)** operations, **(B)** issuance of long-term debt or capital stock, and **(C)** sale of noncurrent assets. The uses of working capital are also classified into three categories: **(A)** distributions to owners, **(B)** redemption of long-term debt or capital stock, and **(C)** acquisition of noncurrent assets. Part II of the statement shows the changes in the individual working capital accounts.

## Working Capital Provided by Operations

24.5 The first section of the statement shows the amount of working capital generated by operations. Note two features of this section of the statement. First, working capital provided by continuing operations, discontinued operations, extraordinary items, and changes in accounting principles are shown separately (lines 13, 18, 21, and 25). The rationale for this separate disclosure is similar to that for segregating sources of income in the income statement. A financial statement user wishing to predict the amount of working capital to be generated from operations in the future will likely want to distinguish between activities and events that are continuing and those that are expected to be nonrecurring. In preparing a T-account work sheet, the "Operations" section of the master T-account must be separated into subsections for each of these sources of income.

24.6 Second, note that working capital is seldom increased or decreased in an amount precisely equal to income or loss for the period. Some revenues and gains do not provide working capital, and some expenses and losses do not use working capital. Most published statements begin with income for the period (from continuing operations, discontinued operations, and so on). Then, amounts are added for expenses and losses that do not use working capital, and amounts are subtracted for revenues and gains that do not provide working capital from operations to derive working capital provided by operations. That is, working capital is initially assumed to increase by the amount of income for the period. Some expenses and losses have been subtracted in calculating income but do not use working capital. These are added back to income (lines 2 through 8). This addback has the effect of *eliminating* nonfunds expenses and losses from the computation of working capital from operations. Likewise, some revenues and gains have been added in calculating net income but do not provide working capital. These are subtracted from net income (lines 9 through 12). This subtraction has the effect of *eliminating* nonfunds revenues and gains from the computation of working capital from operations. This approach to calculating working capital from operations might be referred to as the "bottom-up method," because we begin with net income and work back up through the revenues, gains, expenses, and losses on the income statement.

24.7 As discussed in Chapter 4, we prefer a "top-down" approach to calculating working capital from operations. Under this approach, only revenues and gains that increase working capital from operations and expenses and losses that decrease working capital are included in the computations. This approach reduces the likelihood that users will be misled into thinking of depreciation and other nonfunds expenses as sources of funds. Few firms, however, use this reporting format.

## Working Capital Provided by Continuing Operations

24.8 The statement of changes in financial position begins with the computation of working capital from continuing operations. Working capital is assumed to increase provisionally by the amount of income from continuing operations for the period. The analytical entry on the work sheet to reflect this provisional increase is

(1a)

```
Working Capital (Operations—
    Continuing Operations) .......... 50,000
        Retained Earnings  ............      50,000
```

Note again that this entry is made only in the T-account work sheet. Exhibit 24.2, which appears at the end of this section, contains the work sheet with this entry. It does not affect the general ledger.

24.9    Expenses and losses not using working capital are then added and revenues and gains not providing working capital from operations are subtracted in deriving working capital from continuing operations. Some of the more common addbacks and subtractions are discussed in the following sections.

## Addbacks to Income from Continuing Operations

24.10   **Depreciation (Line 2)** The most common addback is for depreciation. The journal entry made during 1981 by Cole-Vatter Corporation to record depreciation is

(2)

```
Work-in Process Inventory  ........  20,000
Depreciation Expense  .............  10,000
    Accumulated Depreciation  .....      30,000
To record depreciation on manufac-
turing facilities as a product cost and
on selling and administrative facilities
as a period expense.
```

It is clear that depreciation on selling and administrative facilities is an expense that does not use working capital and must be added back to income from continuing operations. The rationale for adding back depreciation on manufacturing facilities is perhaps not as clear. Consider these two extreme cases. Suppose that all of the units of product worked on during the period were completed and sold by the end of the period. In this case, depreciation on manufacturing fa-

cilities is included in Cost of Goods Sold. Because a portion of Cost of Goods Sold is an expense that did not use working capital, the depreciation must be added back to income. Suppose instead that none of the units of product worked on during the period was sold by the end of the period. In this case, depreciation on manufacturing facilities increased the inventory accounts (Work-in-Process Inventory and Finished Goods Inventory). It results in a transfer from noncurrent assets to current assets and thus increases working capital. Because the units produced have not been sold, none of this depreciation is reflected yet as an expense in calculating income from continuing operations. The depreciation does represent a source of working capital from operations and must be added. Thus, in either case, the depreciation must be added to net income in calculating funds from continuing operations. The analytical entry on the T-account work sheet is

(2a)

```
Working Capital (Operations—
    Continuing Operations) .......... 30,000
        Accumulated Depreciation  .....      30,000
```

**Goodwill Amortization (Line 3)** The amor-   24.11
tization of goodwill and other intangibles is an expense that does not use working capital. The analytical entry is

(3a)

```
Working Capital (Operations—
    Continuing Operations) .......... 2,000
        Goodwill  ....................      2,000
```

**Equity in Losses from Company A (Line**   24.12
**4)** Recall from Chapter 14 that investments in 20-percent- to 50-percent-owned affiliated companies are accounted for using the equity method. During 1981, Company A operated at a loss. Cole-Vatter Corporation recorded its share of this loss by making the following journal entry:

(4)

```
Equity in Loss of Company A  ......... 3,500
    Investment in Company A  ........      3,500
```

This loss reduced income from continuing operations and a noncurrent asset account,

Investment in Company A. The loss must therefore be added back, as follows:

(4a)

Working Capital (Operations—
    Continuing Operations) . . . . . . . . . . . 3,500
        Investment in Company A . . . . . . . . .     3,500

24.13 **Loss on Sale of Land (Line 5)** The disposition of noncurrent assets presents a subtle problem in the preparation of the statement of changes in financial position: Should the proceeds of the sale be considered an operating or a nonoperating source of working capital? In most cases, the assets sold are an integral part of operating activities. On the other hand, these assets are normally purchased for use in operations rather than for resale. We prefer to treat all such sale proceeds as a nonoperating source of working capital.

24.14     During 1981, Cole-Vatter Corporation sold a tract of land for $700 (see line 34) and realized a loss of $1,200 (see line 5). The journal entry made during 1981 to record the sale is

(5)

Cash . . . . . . . . . . . . . . . . . . . . . . . . . . . . . 700
Loss on Sale of Land . . . . . . . . . . . . . . . 1,200
        Land . . . . . . . . . . . . . . . . . . . . . . . . .     1,900

The working capital generated by this sale is $700. This amount is shown on line (34) as a nonoperating source of working capital. Income from continuing operations includes the loss on the sale of $1,200. Because this loss reduced income from continuing operations but did not use working capital, it must be added back. The analytical entry to record the sale of land is

(5a)

Working Capital (Other Sources—Sale
    of Noncurrent Assets) . . . . . . . . . . . . . . 700
Working Capital (Operations—
    Continuing Operations) . . . . . . . . . . . 1,200
        Land . . . . . . . . . . . . . . . . . . . . . . . . .     1,900

24.15 **Deferred Income Tax Credits (Line 6)** As Chapter 20 discusses, income tax expense often differs from income taxes payable because of the use of different methods of ac-

counting for book and tax purposes. Deferred income taxes must be provided for timing differences between pretax book income and taxable income. When pretax book income exceeds taxable income, income tax expense exceeds income taxes payable and a deferred tax credit is recorded. Assume:

**(1)** That pretax book income is $92,600,

**(2)** There are no permanent differences,

**(3)** Timing differences of $3,260 result from the use of ACRS depreciation for tax and the straight-line method for book, and

**(4)** The income tax rate is 46 percent.

Then, the journal entry to record income taxes from continuing operations for Cole-Vatter Corporation for 1981 is

(6)

Income Tax Expense . . . . . . . . . . . . . . 42,600
    Income Taxes Payable—
        Current . . . . . . . . . . . . . . . . . . . .     41,100
    Deferred Income Taxes
        (noncurrent) . . . . . . . . . . . . . . . .     1,500
($42,600 = .46 × $92,600; $1,500 = .46 × $3,260.)

Working capital has decreased by $41,100, the amount of income taxes currently payable. Income from continuing operations, however, has been decreased by $42,600, the amount of income tax expense. Of this amount, $1,500 is an expense that does not use working capital and must be added back. The analytical entry is

(6a)

Working Capital (Operations—
    Continuing Operations . . . . . . . . . . . 1,500
        Deferred Income Taxes . . . . . . . .     1,500

24.16     A portion of the Deferred Income Taxes account can be classified as a current liability and, therefore, part of working capital (as would be the case if revenue were recognized at the time of sale for financial reporting and at the time of collection using the installment method for tax purposes). Then entry (6a) includes only the portion of the deferred tax provision that increases noncurrent deferred income taxes.

**24.17 Bond Discount Amortization (Line 7)** Recall from Chapter 17 that bonds are issued at a discount whenever the coupon rate is less than the market interest rate at the time of issue. This discount must be amortized over the life of the bonds and recognized as additional interest expense. Assume that the discount for Cole-Vatter Corporation relates to bonds that have a face value of $50,000 and have a coupon interest rate of 8 percent. The journal entry made during 1981 to recognize interest expense on these bonds is

(7)
Interest Expense ................. 4,600
   Interest Payable ............... 4,000
   Discount on Bonds Payable .... 600
The $600 discount amortization was indicated on line (7).

Working capital has decreased by $4,000, the amount of the coupon interest payment. Income from continuing operations has decreased by $4,600, the amount of interest expense. Of this amount, $600 is an expense that does not use working capital and must be added back. The analytical entry is

(7a)
Working Capital (Operations—
   Continuing Operations) .......... 600
    Discount on Bonds Payable .... 600

**24.18 Minority Interest in Income Retained (Line 8)** The appendix to Chapter 14 discusses briefly the preparation of consolidated financial statements. (This topic is discussed more fully in advanced accounting principles texts.) In calculating consolidated income from continuing operations, the minority interest's share of the earnings of a consolidated subsidiary is shown as a subtraction. The journal entry made on Cole-Vatter Corporation's books during 1981 to record the minority interest share of a consolidated subsidiary's earnings is

(8)
Minority Interest in Earnings of
   Consolidated Subsidiary ........ 400
    Minority Interest in Consolidated
     Subsidiary .................. 400
The account debited appears on the income statement. The account credited appears on the balance sheet.

The debit in the above entry is a subtraction from income from continuing operations that does not use working capital. (The Minority Interest in Consolidated Subsidiary account is a noncurrent equity account.) The amount of the debit must therefore be added back. The analytical entry is

(8a)
Working Capital (Operations—
   Continuing Operations) ........... 400
    Minority Interest in Consolidated
     Subsidiary ................... 400

If the consolidated subsidiary had declared a dividend during the year, working capital would have decreased. The dividend would probably be shown with other dividends on line (39) or (40), although some companies consider dividends paid to minority shareholders as an operating use of working capital.

## Subtractions from Income from Continuing Operations

**Equity in Earnings of Company B in Excess of Dividends (Line 9)** When an affiliated company, accounted for on the equity basis, generates a net income, the analytical entry is just the opposite to that made earlier on line (4) for a net loss. Assume that during 1981, Cole-Vatter Corporation's equity in the earnings of Company B is $1,200 and that $400 of dividends is received from Company B during the year. The combined journal entry made during 1981 to record these events is **24.19**

(9)
Cash .............................. 400
Investment in Company B ........... 800
   Equity in Earnings of Company B . 1,200

Working capital generated from this investment totaled $400 during 1981. Under the equity method, income from continuing operations included the $1,200 equity in earnings of Company B. A subtraction is required for that portion of revenues, or equity in earnings, that did not increase working capital. The analytical entry is

(9a)

Investment in Company B  ...........   800
  Working Capital (Operations—
    Continuing Operations)  .......        800

24.20  **Gain on Sale of Equipment (Line 10)** The journal entry made during 1981 to record the sale of equipment is

(10)

Cash (Line 35)  ....................  6,300
Accumulated Depreciation (assumed) . 3,900
  Equipment (assumed)  ..........      10,000
  Gain on Sale of Equipment (Line
    10)  .........................        200

The working capital generated by this sale is $6,300. As before, this amount is classified as a nonoperating source of working capital (line 35). Income from continuing operations includes the $200 gain on the sale. If the $200 is not subtracted from income from continuing operations, the working capital generated by the transaction will be overstated. The analytical entry is

(10a)

Working Capital (Other Sources—Sale
  of Noncurrent Assets)  .............  6,300
Accumulated Depreciation  .........  3,900
  Equipment  ...................      10,000
  Working Capital (Operations—
    Continuing Operations)  .......        200

Chapter 11 discusses and illustrates an alternative presentation of gain on sale of noncurrent assets. See paragraph 11.101.

24.21  **Deferred Income Tax Debits (Line 11)** In some instances, taxable income exceeds pretax book income. The most common cause seen in practice is for warranties, which are expenses in the period of sale for book but become deductions for tax only in a later period when repairs or replacements are made. In these cases, income taxes payable exceed income tax expense. Because more working capital is used than the expense subtracted in calculating income from continuing operations, a subtraction is required. For 1981, Cole-Vatter Corporation had an excess of income tax expense over income taxes payable, and the required adjustment was discussed previously. If income taxes payable—say, $100—exceed income tax expense—say, $80—then the following journal entry is made during the year:

(11)

Income Tax Expense  ................   80
Deferred Income Taxes or Prepaid
  Income Taxes  ....................   20
  Income Taxes Payable—
    Current  ......................        100

The analytical entry on the work sheet is

(11a)

Deferred Income Tax Debits  ..........   20
  Working Capital (Operations—
    Continuing Operations)  .........        20

If the Deferred Income Tax Debit account includes amounts classified in current and noncurrent asset or liability categories, only the noncurrent amounts are included in entry (11a).

**Bond Premium Amortization (Line 12)**  24.22
Bonds are issued at a premium whenever the coupon rate is greater than the market interest rate at the time of issue. This premium must be amortized over the life of the bonds. The amortization is treated as a reduction in interest expense. Assume that the premium for Cole-Vatter Corporation relates to a second bond issue having a face value of $20,000 and a coupon rate of 12 percent. The journal entry made during 1981 to recognize interest expense on these bonds is

(12)

Interest Expense  .....................  2,100
Premium on Bonds Payable  ..........   300
  Interest Payable  ................      2,400

The $300 premium amortization was indicated on line (12).

Interest expense is less than the amount of the coupon payments. Working Capital in excess of interest expense is used. The excess is technically a reduction in the amount initially borrowed. As such, it could be shown as a nonoperating use of funds to retire debt (such as on line 42 in Exhibit 24.1).

Because the amounts involved are usually small, the excess is generally included in the operating section of the T-account work sheet. The analytical entry is

(12a)

| | | |
|---|---|---|
| Premium on Bonds Payable | 300 | |
| Working Capital (Operations— | | |
| Continuing Operations) | | 300 |

**24.23 Summary of Adjustments for Income from Continuing Operations** The adjustments in lines (1) through (12) convert income from continuing operations, computed on the basis of accrual accounting, to the amount of working capital provided by continuing operations. Line (13) indicates that continuing operations provided $87,900 of working capital during 1981. Most financial analysts place considerable importance on the amount of working capital (or other definition of funds) generated by operations. If a firm is to sustain itself and grow over the long run, operations must provide the largest portion of funds.

## Working Capital Provided (Used) by Discontinued Operations

**24.24** A firm that disposes of a major segment of its business during a period must present in a separate section of the income statement for the period both the income of the segment prior to the measurement date and any gain or loss on disposal. The loss from discontinued operations incurred by Cole-Vatter Corporation during 1981 was composed of the following:

| | |
|---|---|
| Net Loss prior to Measurement Date (after Current Income Tax Savings of $6,000 and Deferred Income Taxes of $1,000) | $ 9,500 |
| Loss on Sale of Segment (after Current Income Tax Savings of $1,500) | 4,000 |
| Total Loss for 1981 | $13,500 |

Working capital is assumed to decrease provisionally by the amount of the loss. The analytical entry is

(14a)

| | | |
|---|---|---|
| Retained Earnings | 13,500 | |
| Working Capital (Operations— | | |
| Discontinued Operations) | | 13,500 |

To convert income from discontinued operations to a working capital basis requires some of the same types of adjustments as those in lines (2) through (12). The net loss prior to the measurement date includes depreciation expense of $3,000. Because this expense has been subtracted in calculating the net loss but did not use working capital, it must be added back. The analytical entry is  **24.25**

(15a)

| | | |
|---|---|---|
| Working Capital (Operations— | | |
| Discontinued Operations) | 3,000 | |
| Accumulated Depreciation | | 3,000 |

The loss is net of income tax savings of $7,000, of which $6,000 represents current taxes and $1,000 represents deferred taxes. The journal entry made during 1981 to record income taxes for the segment is  **24.26**

(17)

| | | |
|---|---|---|
| Income Taxes Payable—Current | 6,000 | |
| Deferred Income Taxes | 1,000 | |
| Income Tax Expense— | | |
| Discontinued Operations | | 7,000 |

Of the $7,000 shown as a reduction in income tax expense resulting from the loss, $1,000 did not reduce a current liability. That amount must be shown as a reduction in the working capital section of the T-account work sheet. The analytical entry is

(17a)

| | | |
|---|---|---|
| Deferred Income Taxes | 1,000 | |
| Working Capital (Operations— | | |
| Discontinued Operations) | | 1,000 |

The segment was disposed of for $10,000  **24.27**  (line 36). The disposal at this price resulted in a loss before income taxes of $5,500 (= $4,000 + $1,500). Thus, the book value of the net assets of the segment prior to disposal was $15,500 (= $10,000 + $5,500). Assume that this segment was involved in leasing. All cash held by the segment prior to disposal was used to discharge creditors' claims. Thus, the segment's only asset was equipment leased to others (assume cost of $50,000 and accumulated depreciation of $34,500). The journal entry made by Cole-Vatter Corporation at the time of disposal is

```
(16)
Cash .......................... 10,000
Accumulated Depreciation ......... 34,500
Loss on Sale of Segment ........... 5,500
    Equipment ...................        50,000
```

Working capital of $10,000 was generated by the disposal and this amount is shown on line (36) as a nonoperating source. The loss on disposal has been subtracted in calculating income from discontinued operations. Because the loss did not use working capital, it is added back. The analytical entry is

```
(16a)
Working Capital (Other Sources—
    Sale of Noncurrent Assets) ....... 10,000
Accumulated Depreciation ......... 34,500
Working Capital (Operations—
    Discontinued Operations) ........ 5,500
        Equipment .................        50,000
```

## Working Capital Provided by Extraordinary Items

24.28 Chapter 2 indicates that extraordinary gains and losses appear infrequently in corporate annual reports. The most common extraordinary item is a gain or loss on retirement of bonds prior to maturity. The income statement of Cole-Vatter Corporation for 1981 indicates the following:

**Extraordinary Gains and Losses**
Gain on Bond Retirement (Net of Current
   Income Taxes of $1,000) .............. $1,500

24.29 Working capital is assumed to increase provisionally by the amount of the extraordinary gain. The analytical entry is

```
(19a)
Working Capital (Operations—
    Extraordinary Gains and
    Losses) ...................... 1,500
        Retained Earnings ...........        1,500
```

The pretax gain on the sale was $2,500 (= $1,500 + $1,000). Line (42) indicates that $10,000 was used during the year to retire bonds having a $12,000 face value. The journal entry made during the year was    24.30

```
(20)
Bonds Payable .................... 12,000
Premium on Bonds Payable ........    500
    Cash ........................        10,000
    Gain on Retirement of Bonds ...         2,500
```

Working capital of $10,000 was used to redeem these bonds, and this amount is shown as a nonoperating use on line (42). The gain on retirement is included in extraordinary income but did not provide working capital. The analytical entry is

```
(20a)
Bonds Payable .................... 12,000
Premium on Bonds Payable ........    500
    Working Capital (Other Uses—
        Redemption of Long-Term
        Debt or Capital Stock) .......        10,000
    Working Capital (Operations—
        Extraordinary Gains and
        Losses) ...................         2,500
```

The $1,000 use of working capital shown on line (21) represents the current income taxes paid on the gain.

## Working Capital Provided by Accounting Changes

Chapter 23 discusses the accounting for    24.31 changes in accounting principles. In general, the cumulative effect on prior years' earnings of the change in accounting principles is included in net income for the period of the change but segregated in a separate section of the income statement. The income statement of Cole-Vatter Corporation for 1981 contains the following:

**Cumulative Effects of Changes in Accounting Principles**
Change in the Treatment of Certain
   Manufacturing Overhead Costs for
   Inventories (Net of Current Income
   Taxes of $600) ...................... $1,200

Change from the Sum-of-the-Years'-Digits to the Straight-Line Method of Depreciation (Net of Deferred Income Taxes of $4,400) ..................... 4,800

    Total ........................... $6,000

24.32 Working capital is assumed to increase provisionally by the amount of income from the accounting changes. The analytical entry is

(22a)
Working Capital (Operations—
    Accounting Changes) .......... 6,000
        Retained Earnings ............ 6,000

24.33 The journal entry made during 1981 to record the change in the treatment of manufacturing overhead costs is

(22)
Inventories .... ............... 1,800
    Cumulative Effect of Change
        in Treatment of Overhead
        Costs ................... 1,200
    Income Taxes Payable—
        Current ................... 600

Working capital increased by $1,200 (= $1,800 − $600). Because a provisional increase in working capital of $1,200 has already been included in the amount on line (22), no addback or subtraction is necessary for the inventory accounting change.

24.34    The journal entries made during 1981 to record the change in depreciation method are

(23)
Accumulated Depreciation ......... 9,200
    Cumulative Effect of Change in
        Depreciation Method ........ 9,200

(24)
Income Tax Expense—Accounting
    Changes ..................... 4,400
        Deferred Income Taxes ........ 4,400

This accounting change has no effect on working capital. The analytical entries for this accounting change are

(23a)
Accumulated Depreciation ......... 9,200
    Working Capital (Operations—
        Accounting Change) ........ 9,200

(24a)
Working Capital (Operations—
    Accounting Changes) ........... 4,400
        Deferred Income Taxes ........ 4,400

24.35 Working capital provided by operations during 1981 totaled $82,100 (line 26). This total was derived from four sources: $87,900 (line 13) provided by continuing operations, $6,000 (line 18) used by discontinued operations, $1,000 (line 21) used by extraordinary items, and $1,200 (line 25) provided by accounting changes.

## Other Sources of Working Capital

24.36 Working capital is normally derived from two sources other than operations: (1) financing activities (issuance of long-term debt or capital stock), and (2) sale of noncurrent assets.

24.37 **Issuance of Long-Term Debt or Capital Stock** In addition to funds generated by operations, an important source of working capital for many firms is new long-term financing.

24.38 *Issuance of Bonds* Line (27) indicates that bonds were issued during 1981 for $20,250. If it is assumed that the bonds had a face value of $20,000 and were issued at a premium, the journal entry made during 1981 was

(27)
Cash ........................... 20,250
    Bonds Payable ................ 20,000
    Premium on Bonds Payable .... 250

The analytical entry to record the bond issue is

(27a)
Working Capital (Other Sources—
    Issuance of Bonds or Capital
        Stock) ........................ 20,250
        Bonds Payable ................ 20,000
        Premium on Bonds Payable ..... 250

24.39 *Mortgage Assumed* During 1981, Cole-Vatter Corporation acquired land costing $1,500 and financed the acquisition by assuming a $1,500 mortgage. The entry made to record this transaction is

```
(28)
Land ..............................  1,500
      Mortgage Payable ..............          1,500
```

Working capital is not affected by this transaction. The transaction, however, affects the structure of the firm's assets and equities. Accounting Principles Board *Opinion No. 19* requires that transactions that affect the structure of assets or equities but that do not flow through working capital accounts be shown as though they did. That is, a dual transaction is assumed. First, a mortgage is assumed to be issued for cash. Second, the cash is assumed to be used for the acquisition of land. The disclosure of such transactions as both a source and use of working capital is said to follow the "all financial resources concept" of funds.

24.40    The transaction for Cole-Vatter Corporation is recorded as if two separate transactions had occurred:

```
(28)
Cash .............................  1,500
      Mortgage Payable ..............          1,500

(46)
Land .............................  1,500
      Cash .........................          1,500
```

The analytical entries entered on the T-account work sheet are

```
(28a)
Working Capital (Other Sources—
   Issuance of Bonds or Capital
   Stock ........................  1,500
      Mortgage Payable ..............          1,500

(46a)
Land .............................  1,500
      Working Capital (Other Uses—
      Acquisition of Noncurrent
      Assets) ......................          1,500
```

24.41    *Lease Capitalized* The capitalization of the lease also follows the dual transactions assumption. The journal entries are equivalent to

```
(29)
Cash .............................  200
      Capitalized Lease Obligation ......          200

(48)
Equipment .........................  200
      Cash .........................          200
```

The analytical entries are

```
(29a)
Working Capital (Other Sources—
   Issuance of Bonds or Capital Stock) .  200
      Capitalized Lease Obligation ......          200

(48a)
Equipment .........................  200
      Working Capital (Other Uses—
      Acquisition of Noncurrent
      Assets) ......................          200
```

*Common Stock Issued* The issuance of common stock, whether to employees or on the open market, provides working capital equal to the proceeds. If the common stock issued during 1981 (lines 30 and 31) had an aggregate par value of $450, then the analytical entry would be    24.42

```
(30a, 31a)
Working Capital (Other Sources—
   Issuance of Bonds or Capital Stock,
   $50 + $500) ......................  550
      Common Stock ..................          450
      Additional Paid-in Capital .........          100
```

*Treasury Stock Sold* During 1981, the accounting records of Cole-Vatter Corporation indicate that treasury stock costing $16 was sold for $20. The analytical entry is    24.43

```
(32a)
Working Capital (Other Sources—
   Issuance of Bonds or Capital Stock) .  20
      Treasury Stock .................          16
      Additional Paid-in Capital .........          4
```

Recall from Chapter 21 that "gains" from the sale of treasury stock are not included in net income. Sales of treasury stock are considered capital transactions, so the "gain" is credited to Additional Paid-in Capital.

**Sale of Noncurrent Assets** Firms generally do not derive a significant percentage of    24.44

their working capital from the sale of non-current assets. Most noncurrent assets are acquired for use rather than for resale. As a consequence, noncurrent assets are frequently sold near the end of their useful life for small salvage amounts. Cole-Vatter Corporation received $17,000 of working capital during 1981 from the sale of noncurrent assets. A large portion of this amount was derived from the disposal of the segment. The analytical entries to record the sources of working capital in lines (34), (35), and (36) were presented earlier when the effects of these sales on working capital from operations were discussed.

## Uses of Working Capital

24.45   Working capital is typically used for dividends, reductions in long-term debt or capital stock (financing), or acquisition of noncurrent assets (investments).

24.46   **Distributions to Owners** The analytical entries to record the cash dividends during 1981 are

(39a)

| | | |
|---|---|---|
| Retained Earnings | 7,000 | |
| Working Capital (Uses | | |
| Distributions to Owners) | | 7,000 |

(40a)

| | | |
|---|---|---|
| Retained Earnings | 400 | |
| Working Capital (Uses | | |
| Distributions to Owners) | | 400 |

Note that dividends use working capital at the time they are declared because Dividends Payable, a current liability, is credited. The payment of the dividend does not affect working capital. Dividends in kind may or may not affect working capital, depending on the type of asset distributed (compare distributions of inventory and land). Stock dividends do not affect working capital. Amounts are merely transferred within the shareholders' equity section of the balance sheet. Because a stock dividend does not change the relative equity interest of shareholders, the structure of the equities does not change. Stock dividends, therefore,

need not be disclosed in a statement of changes in financial position under the all financial resources concept.

**Redemption of Long-Term Debt or Capital Stock** During 1981, Cole-Vatter Corporation redeemed bonds and preferred stock and acquired shares of treasury stock.     24.47

*Redemption of Bonds* Firms tend to maintain a relatively constant level of debt in their capital structures. When one bond issue matures, it is often replaced with a new bond issue. It is therefore not uncommon to see the proceeds of a new bond issue shown among the sources of working capital in the same year that bonds of an approximately equal amount are redeemed and shown among the uses. For Cole-Vatter Corporation, new 10-percent bonds were issued (see line 27) for $20,250 and outstanding 8-percent bonds were redeemed for $10,000. Approximately half of the proceeds of the new bond issue was therefore used for other purposes (operations, acquisition of noncurrent assets). The analytical entry to record the redemption of the bonds was presented earlier when the gain on the redemption was discussed in the context of working capital provided by extraordinary items.     24.48

*Preferred Stock Redeemed* Some firms have agreements with preferred shareholders providing that the preferred shares must be systematically redeemed over some specified period of time. Other firms voluntarily redeem preferred shares and replace them with either debt or common stock equity. Unlike interest on debt, dividends on preferred stock are not deductible in calculating taxable income. Preferred shares have a senior claim on the assets and income of a firm relative to common shares, and their issuance increases the risk of the common shares.     24.49

During 1981, outstanding preferred stock was redeemed for $3,000. If we assume that the shares were originally issued for their par value of $2,500, the following entry would be made at the time of redemption:     24.50

(43)

| | | |
|---|---|---|
| Preferred Stock | 2,500 | |
| Retained Earnings | 500 | |
| Cash | | 3,000 |

The analytical entry to record this transaction is

(43a)

| | | |
|---|---|---|
| Preferred Stock | 2,500 | |
| Retained Earnings | 500 | |
| Working Capital (Uses— | | |
| Redemption of Long-Term | | |
| Debt or Capital Stock) | | 3,000 |

24.51 *Treasury Stock Acquired* Sales and purchases of treasury stock tend to be a minor source and use of working capital for most firms. Assuming that the cost method is used, the analytical entry to record the acquisition of treasury stock is

(44a)

| | | |
|---|---|---|
| Treasury Stock | 5,000 | |
| Working Capital (Uses— | | |
| Redemption of Long-Term | | |
| Debt or Capital Stock) | | 5,000 |

24.52 **Acquisition of Noncurrent Assets** The major use of working capital for most firms is the acquisition of noncurrent assets. Depreciable assets must be replaced as they wear out if productive capacity is to be maintained. Investments in depreciable and other noncurrent assets must increase if a firm is to grow. In predicting future earnings for a firm, financial analysts often study the recent pattern of acquisitions of noncurrent assets.

24.53 The analytical entries for the land and equipment capitalized under leases were presented earlier. The analytical entries for the equipment and stock of Company C acquired are as follows:

(47a)

| | | |
|---|---|---|
| Equipment | 22,500 | |
| Working Capital (Uses— | | |
| Acquisition of Noncurrent | | |
| Assets) | | 22,500 |

(49a)

| | | |
|---|---|---|
| Investment in Company C | 18,000 | |
| Working Capital (Uses— | | |
| Acquisition of Noncurrent | | |
| Assets) | | 18,000 |

## Summary of Analytical Entries

24.54 Exhibit 24.2 presents a work sheet for Cole-Vatter Corporation for 1981. The beginning and ending balances in each account are assumed for purposes of illustration. To aid in preparing the formal statement of changes in financial position, it is helpful to label each of the entries in the Working Capital T-account. The extent of labeling depends on the number and complexity of the transactions during the period.

## Defining Cash Flows from Operations

24.55 Earlier in this chapter, we pointed out that the proceeds from the sale of noncurrent assets could be considered either as an operating or as a nonoperating source of working capital. Given that most noncurrent assets (for example, buildings, equipment) are acquired for use in operations rather than as a means of generating income from resale, we prefer to treat the proceeds of sales as a nonoperating source of working capital. Any gains or losses on such sales are either subtracted from or added to net income to derive working capital provided by operations.

24.56 When funds are defined as cash, similar classification questions are encountered. Recall from Chapter 4 that the changes in current asset and current liability accounts are either added to or subtracted from net income to derive cash flow provided by operations. For example, if Accounts Receivable increases by $10,000 during a period, the analytical entry is

(1a)

| | | |
|---|---|---|
| Accounts Receivable | 10,000 | |
| Cash (Operations—Net | | |
| Income) | | 10,000 |

This entry is made to recognize the fact that cash did not increase by the full amount of sales revenue included in the calculation of net income.

24.57   Consider now the following entries involving cash and some other current asset account.

(2)

| Cash | 20,000 | |
| Marketable Securities | | 15,000 |
| Gain on Sale of Marketable Securities | | 5,000 |

Shares are sold for a price greater than cost.

(3)

| Cash | 50,000 | |
| Notes Payable to Banks— Current | | 50,000 |

Cash is borrowed at a bank using a short-term note.

(4)

| Current Portion of Long-Term Debt | 100,000 | |
| Cash | | 100,000 |

Debt is discharged at maturity with cash.

(5)

| Dividends Payable | 30,000 | |
| Cash | | 30,000 |

Cash is used to pay dividend.

The question arises as to whether these transactions imply operating or nonoperating sources and uses of cash. As was the case with the proceeds from the sale of noncurrent assets, cases could be made for classifying these transactions either as operating or as nonoperating.

24.58   Our preference is to treat these transactions as nonoperating sources and uses of cash. We think of cash flow provided by operations as the amount of inflows of cash from customers minus the outflows of cash to employees, suppliers, governmental units, and other factor inputs. Temporary investments of excess cash, temporary borrowing of needed cash, repayments of long-term debt, and payments of dividends are not integrally related to operations. Thus the

analytical entries for transactions (2) to (5) above are

(2a)

| Cash (Other Sources—Sale of Noncash Assets) | 20,000 | |
| Marketable Securities | | 15,000 |
| Cash (Operations—Net Income) | | 5,000 |

(3a)

| Cash (Other Sources—Issuance of Debt or Capital Stock) | 50,000 | |
| Notes Payable to Banks— Current | | 50,000 |

(4a)

| Current Portion of Long-Term Debt | 100,000 | |
| Cash (Other Uses— Redemption of Debt or Capital Stock) | | 100,000 |

(5a)

| Dividends Payable | 30,000 | |
| Cash (Other Uses— Distributions to Owners) | | 30,000 |

Most current asset and current liability accounts, other than those above, generally relate to operating activities of a firm (inventories, prepayments, accounts payable, and so on). Changes in these accounts are treated in the same way as accounts receivable, illustrated in analytical entry (1a).

## Work Sheet Preparation in a Net Changes Format

24.59   In preparing a T-account work sheet, the beginning and ending balances in various accounts are entered in the T-accounts. The transactions occurring during the period that account for the changes between the beginning and end of the period are then entered in the T-accounts.

24.60   In some cases, problems (for example, Problem 24.23 at the end of this chapter) provide only the net change in individual accounts during a period. The beginning and ending balances are not given. In such cases,

*Exhibit 24.2*
**Work Sheet for Statement of
Changes in Financial Position for
Cole-Vatter Corporation for 1981**

| | | | | Working Capital | | | |
|---|---|---|---|---|---|---|---|
| | | | ✓ | 100,000 | | | |
| | | | | From Operations— | | | |
| | | | | Continuing Operations | | | |
| Income from Continuing Operations | (1a) | 50,000 | | 800 | (9a) | Equity in Earnings of Company B |
| Depreciation | (2a) | 30,000 | | 200 | (10a) | Gain on Sale of Equipment |
| Goodwill Amortization | (3a) | 2,000 | | 300 | (12a) | Bond Premium Amortization Expense |
| Losses from Company A | (4a) | 3,500 | | | | |
| Loss on Sale of Land | (5a) | 1,200 | | | | |
| Deferred Income Taxes | (6a) | 1,500 | | | | |
| Bond Discount Amortization | (7a) | 600 | | | | |
| Minority Shareholders' Equity in Income | (8a) | 400 | | | | |

| | | | Discontinued Operations | | | |
|---|---|---|---|---|---|---|
| Depreciation Expense | (15a) | 3,000 | 13,500 | (14a) | Loss from Discontinued Operations |
| Loss on Disposal of Segment | (16a) | 5,500 | 1,000 | (17a) | Deferred Income Taxes |

| | | | Extraordinary Gains and Losses | | | |
|---|---|---|---|---|---|---|
| Extraordinary Gain | (19a) | 1,500 | 2,500 | (20a) | Gain on Bond Retirement |

| | | | Accounting Changes | | | |
|---|---|---|---|---|---|---|
| Cumulative Effect of Accounting | | | | | |
|   Changes | (22a) | 6,000 | 9,200 | (23a) | Change in Depreciation |
| Deferred Income Taxes | (24a) | 4,400 | | | Method |

| | | Other (Nonoperating) | | |
|---|---|---|---|---|
| | | Distributions to Owners | | |
| | | 7,000 | (39a) | Dividends on Common Stock |
| | | 400 | (40a) | Dividends on Preferred Stock |

| | | | Issuance or Redemption of Long-Term Debt or Capital Stock | | | |
|---|---|---|---|---|---|---|
| Bonds Issued | (27a) | 20,250 | 10,000 | (20a) | Bonds Retired |
| Mortgage Assumed | (28a) | 1,500 | 3,000 | (43a) | Preferred Stock Retired |
| Lease Capitalized | (29a) | 200 | 5,000 | (44a) | Treasury Stock Acquired |
| Common Stock Issued | (31a) | 550 | | | |
| Treasury Stock Sold | (32a) | 20 | | | |

| | | | Sale or Acquisition of Noncurrent Assets | | | |
|---|---|---|---|---|---|---|
| Land Sold | (5a) | 700 | 1,500 | (46a) | Land Acquired |
| Equipment Sold | (10a) | 6,300 | 22,500 | (47a) | Equipment Acquired |
| Segment Sold | (16a) | 10,000 | 200 | (48a) | Equipment Acquired under Lease |
| | | | 18,000 | (49a) | Capital Stock Acquired |
| | ✓ | 154,020 | | | |

| Investments | | | | | Land | | | | Building | | |
|---|---|---|---|---|---|---|---|---|---|---|---|
| ✓ | 40,000 | | | ✓ | 8,000 | | | ✓ | 80,000 | |
| (9a) | 800 | 3,500 | (4a) | (46a) | 1,500 | 1,900 | (5a) | | | |
| (49a) | 18,000 | | | | | | | | | |
| ✓ | 55,300 | | | ✓ | 7,600 | | | ✓ | 80,000 | |

*Exhibit 24.2 (continued)*

| Equipment | | | |
|---|---|---|---|
| √ | 178,000 | | |
| (48a) | 200 | 10,000 | (10a) |
| (47a) | 22,500 | 50,000 | (16a) |
| √ | 140,700 | | |

| Accumulated Depreciation | | | |
|---|---|---|---|
| | | 136,000 | √ |
| (10a) | 3,900 | 30,000 | (2a) |
| (16a) | 34,500 | 3,000 | (15a) |
| (23a) | 9,200 | | |
| | | 121,400 | √ |

| Goodwill | | | |
|---|---|---|---|
| √ | 30,000 | | |
| | | 2,000 | (3a) |
| √ | 28,000 | | |

| Bonds Payable | | | |
|---|---|---|---|
| | | 90,000 | √ |
| (20a) | 12,000 | 20,000 | (27a) |
| | | 98,000 | √ |

| Discount on Bonds Payable | | | |
|---|---|---|---|
| √ | 3,000 | | |
| | | 600 | (7a) |
| | 2,400 | | |

| Premium on Bonds Payable | | | |
|---|---|---|---|
| | | 2,500 | √ |
| (12a) | 300 | 250 | (27a) |
| (20a) | 500 | | |
| | | 1,950 | √ |

| Mortgage Payable | | | |
|---|---|---|---|
| | | 60,000 | √ |
| | | 1,500 | (28a) |
| | | 61,500 | √ |

| Capitalized Lease Obligation | | | |
|---|---|---|---|
| | | — | |
| | | 200 | (29a) |
| | | 200 | √ |

| Deferred Income Taxes | | | |
|---|---|---|---|
| | | 15,000 | √ |
| (17a) | 1,000 | 1,500 | (6a) |
| | | 4,400 | (24a) |
| | | 19,900 | √ |

| Minority Interest in Consolidated Subsidiary | | | |
|---|---|---|---|
| | | 5,500 | √ |
| | | 400 | (8a) |
| | | 5,000 | √ |

| Preferred Stock | | | |
|---|---|---|---|
| | | 20,000 | √ |
| (43a) | 2,500 | | |
| | | 17,500 | √ |

| Common Stock | | | |
|---|---|---|---|
| | | 30,000 | √ |
| | | 450 | (31a) |
| | | 30,450 | √ |

| Additional Paid-in Capital | | | |
|---|---|---|---|
| | | 50,000 | √ |
| | | 100 | (31a) |
| | | 4 | (32a) |
| | | 50,104 | √ |

| Retained Earnings | | | |
|---|---|---|---|
| | | 31,100 | √ |
| (14a) | 13,500 | 50,000 | (1a) |
| (39a) | 7,000 | 1,500 | (19a) |
| (40a) | 400 | 6,000 | (22a) |
| (43a) | 500 | | |
| | | 67,200 | √ |

| Treasury Stock | | | |
|---|---|---|---|
| √ | 1,100 | | |
| (44a) | 5,000 | 16 | (32a) |
| √ | 6,084 | | |

the T-account work sheet must be altered. Instead of using a single T-account, a double T-account is used. A double T-account resembles a single T-account except that a second horizontal line is drawn. In the space between the two horizontal lines is entered the net change in the account during the period to be explained.

**Example** The Land account of Cole-Vatter Corporation had a beginning balance of $8,000 and an ending balance of $7,600 for 1981 (see Exhibit 24.2). Land costing $1,500 was acquired and land costing $1,900 was sold for $700 during the year. Assume that the beginning and ending balances were not given. The only information provided is that

24.61

land decreased by $400 during the year. The work sheet using single and double T-accounts would include the following for the Land account:

| Land | | | | Land | | | |
|---|---|---|---|---|---|---|---|
| ✓ | 8,000 | | | | | 400 | |
| (46a) | 1,500 | 1,900 | (5a) | (46a) 1,500 | | 1,900 | (5a) |
| ✓ | 7,600 | | | | | | |

Single T-Account                Double T-Account

Single and double T-accounts serve the same function: They indicate the change in the account during the period to be explained and are used in reconstructing the journal entries made during the period that account for the change. When the problem data provide comparative balance sheets, we prefer the single T-account format because it is a direct extension of T-accounts as used in previous chapters and other accounting courses.

## Questions and Short Cases

**24.1** Review the meaning of the following concepts or terms discussed in this chapter.
  **a.** Separation of working capital from operations into amounts derived from continuing operations, discontinued operations, extraordinary gains and losses, and accounting changes.
  **b.** Depreciation on manufacturing equipment as an addback versus an addition to net income.
  **c.** Proceeds from the sale of noncurrent assets as an operating versus a nonoperating source of funds.
  **d.** All financial resources concept of funds.
  **e.** Dual transactions assumption.
  **f.** Single versus double T-account.

**24.2** "A short-term bank loan obtained in order to finance the acquisition of inventory should be considered an operating source of cash. After all, such a bank loan is, in substance, the same as financing through accounts payable." Comment.

**24.3** APB *Opinion No. 19* requires that funds be defined as all financial resources. Yet most published statements of changes in financial position report the sources and uses of working capital. What accounts for this difference in the definition of funds?

**24.4** Transactions required to be disclosed under the all financial resources concept affect non-funds accounts. Assume that funds are defined as working capital. Give two examples of transactions that fit each of the following categories:
  **a.** Increase in one noncurrent asset and decrease in another noncurrent asset.
  **b.** Increase in one noncurrent equity and decrease in another noncurrent equity.
  **c.** Increase in one noncurrent asset and increase in one noncurrent equity.
  **d.** Decrease in one noncurrent asset and decrease in one noncurrent equity.

**24.5** The following transactions need not be disclosed in a statement of changes in financial position employing the all financial resources concept. Indicate the likely rationale in each case.
  **a.** A fully depreciated machine used for the last year is finally retired from service and written off with a debit to Accumulated Depreciation and a credit to Property, Plant, and Equipment of equal amount.
  **b.** A 10-percent stock dividend is declared and distributed on outstanding common stock.

**24.6**   "Depreciation is never a source of working capital." Do you agree? Why or why not?

**24.7**   Refer to Exhibit 4.13 (Question **4.15**), where a simplified funds statement is presented. For each of the transactions below, indicate the number(s) of the line(s) in Exhibit 4.13 that would be affected assuming that funds are defined as working capital. If net income is affected, be sure to indicate if it increases or decreases net income. Ignore income tax effects.

   **a.** Long-term bonds are retired using funds in a bond sinking fund.
   **b.** A cash dividend is received from an unconsolidated subsidiary accounted for using the equity method.
   **c.** Accounts are written off as uncollectible when the allowance method is used.
   **d.** Marketable securities are purchased for cash.
   **e.** Land is sold for an amount greater than its acquisition cost.
   **f.** A firm's annual cash contribution to a bond sinking fund is made.
   **g.** A fully amortized patent is written off.
   **h.** Land is given in settlement of annual legal fees of the corporate attorney.
   **i.** Preferred stock is converted into common stock.
   **j.** Inventory items are written down to reflect a lower-of-cost-or-market valuation.
   **k.** The Deferred Income Tax (Credit) account is decreased for the year because of a reversal of timing differences originating in a previous period.
   **l.** The Premium on Bonds Payable account is amortized for the year.
   **m.** Acquisition of a majority interest in the common stock of a supplier by issuing long-term convertible bonds.
   **n.** Reduction in the account, Rental Fees Received in Advance, when the rental services are provided.
   **o.** Declaration and issuance of a 10-percent stock dividend.
   **p.** Reclassification as a current liability of long-term debt maturing within the next year.
   **q.** Provision is made for estimated uncollectible accounts when the allowance method is used.
   **r.** Income is recognized using the percentage-of-completion method for long-term contracts.
   **s.** Land is donated to a firm by a local government as an inducement to locate manufacturing facilities in the area.
   **t.** Write-down of long-term investments in securities to reflect a lower-of-cost-or-market valuation.
   **u.** Research and development costs are incurred during the period.
   **v.** Depreciation is recorded on selling and administrative facilities.
   **w.** Depreciation is recorded on manufacturing facilities.
   **x.** Treasury stock is sold for an amount less than its repurchase price.
   **y.** A 6-month loan is obtained from a local bank.

**24.8**   (Adapted from CPA Examination.) The statement of changes in financial position is normally a required basic financial statement for each period for which an earnings statement is presented. The reporting entity has flexibility in form, content, and terminology of this statement to meet the objectives of differing circumstances. For example, the concept of "funds" may be interpreted to mean, among other things, cash or working capital. However, the statement should be prepared based on the "all financial resources" concept.

   **a.** What is the "all financial resources" concept?
   **b.** What are two types of financial transactions that would be disclosed under the "all financial resources" concept that would not be disclosed without this concept?
   **c.** What effect, if any, would each of the following seven items have on the preparation of a statement of changes in financial position prepared in accordance with generally accepted accounting principles using the cash concept of funds?

        **(1)** Accounts receivable—trade.

        **(2)** Inventory.

        **(3)** Depreciation.

        **(4)** Deferred income tax credit from interperiod allocation.

        **(5)** Issuance of long-term debt in payment for a building.

        **(6)** Payoff of current portion of debt.

        **(7)** Sale of a fixed asset resulting in a loss.

**24.9**  (Adapted from CPA Examination.) Chen Engineering Company is a young and growing producer of electronic measuring instruments and technical equipment. You have been retained by Chen to advise it in the preparation of a statement of changes in financial position. For the fiscal year ended October 31, 1981, you have obtained the following information concerning certain events and transactions of Chen.

    **(1)** The amount of reported earnings for the fiscal year was $800,000, which included a deduction for an extraordinary loss of $93,000 (see item 5 below).

    **(2)** Depreciation expense of $240,000 was included in the earnings statement.

    **(3)** Uncollectible accounts receivable of $30,000 were written off against the allowance for uncollectible accounts. Also, $37,000 of bad debts expense was included in calculating earnings for the fiscal year, and the same amount was added to the allowance for uncollectible accounts.

    **(4)** A gain of $4,700 was realized on the sale of a machine; it originally cost $75,000, of which $25,000 was undepreciated on the date of sale.

    **(5)** On April 1, 1981, a freak lightning storm caused an uninsured inventory loss of $93,000 ($180,000 loss, less reduction in income taxes of $87,000). This extraordinary loss was included in calculating earnings as indicated in **(1)** above.

    **(6)** On July 3, 1981, building and land were purchased for $600,000; Chen gave in payment $100,000 cash, $200,000 market value of its unissued common stock, and a $300,000 purchase-money mortgage.

    **(7)** On August 3, 1981, $700,000 face value of Chen's 6-percent convertible debentures were converted into $140,000 par value of its common stock. The bonds were originally issued at face value.

    **(8)** The board of directors declared a $320,000 cash dividend on October 20, 1981, payable on November 15, 1981, to shareholders of record on November 5, 1981.

For each of the eight numbered items above, explain whether each item is a source or use of working capital and explain how it should be disclosed in Chen's statement of changes in financial position for the fiscal year ended October 31, 1981. If any item is neither a source nor a use of working capital, explain why it is not and indicate the disclosure, if any, that should be made of the item in Chen's statement of changes in financial position for the fiscal year ended October 31, 1981.

**24.10**  (Adapted from CPA Examination.) The statement of changes in financial position shown in Exhibit 24.3 was prepared by the controller of the Clovis Company. The controller indicated that this statement was prepared under the "all financial resources" concept of funds, which is the broadest concept of funds and includes all transactions providing or requiring funds.

Notes to Statement of Source and Application of Funds:

1. The City of Camden donated a plant site to Clovis Company valued by the board of directors at $115,000. The Company purchased adjoining property for $135,000.

2. Research and development expenditures of $25,000 incurred in 1981 were expensed. These expenses were considered abnormally large for 1 year.

3. Equipment with a book value of $5,000 was sold for $8,000.

*Exhibit 24.3*
**Clovis Company**
**Statement of Changes in Financial Position**
**December 31, 1981**

Funds were provided by:

| | |
|---|---|
| Contribution of plant site by the City of Camden (Note 1) | $115,000 |
| Net income (Note 2) | 75,000 |
| Issuance of note payable—due 1985 | 60,000 |
| Depreciation and amortization | 50,000 |
| Deferred income taxes relating to accelerated depreciation | 10,000 |
| Sale of equipment—book value (Note 3) | 5,000 |
| Total funds provided | $315,000 |

Funds were applied to:

| | |
|---|---|
| Acquisition of future plant site (Note 1) | $250,000 |
| Increase in working capital | 30,000 |
| Cash dividends declared but not paid | 20,000 |
| Acquisition of equipment | 15,000 |
| Total funds applied | $315,000 |

a. Why is it considered desirable to present a statement of changes in financial position in financial reports?

b. Define and discuss the relative merits of the following three concepts used in funds-flow analysis in terms of their measurement accuracy and freedom from manipulation (window dressing) in one accounting period:

(1) Cash concept of funds.

(2) Net quick monetary assets concept of funds.

(3) Working capital concept of funds

c. Identify and discuss the weaknesses in presentation and disclosure in the statement of changes in financial position for Clovis Company. Your discussion should explain why you consider them to be weaknesses and what you consider the proper treatment of the items to be. Do not prepare a revised statement.

# Problems and Exercises

24.11   (Adapted from CPA Examination.) The management of Hatfield Corporation, concerned over a decrease in working capital, has provided you with the comparative analysis of changes in account balances between December 31, 1980, and December 31, 1981, shown in Exhibit 24.4.

During 1981 the following transactions occurred:

(1) New machinery was purchased for $386,000. In addition, certain obsolete machinery, having a book value of $61,000, was sold for $48,000. No other entries were recorded in Machinery and Equipment or related accounts other than provisions for depreciation.

(2) Hatfield paid $2,000 legal costs in a successful defense of a new patent. Amortization of patents amounting to $4,200 was recorded.

(3) Preferred stock, par value $100, was purchased at 110 and subsequently canceled. The premium paid was charged to retained earnings.

(4) On December 10, 1981, the board of directors declared a cash dividend of $0.20 per share payable to holders of common stock on January 10, 1982.

*Exhibit 24.4*
**Hatfield Corporation**
**Changes in Account Balances**
**between December 31, 1980, and**
**December 31, 1981**

| | December 31 1981 | December 31 1980 | Increase (Decrease) |
|---|---|---|---|
| **Debit Balances** | | | |
| Cash | $ 145,000 | $ 186,000 | $ (41,000) |
| Accounts Receivable | 253,000 | 273,000 | (20,000) |
| Inventories | 483,000 | 538,000 | (55,000) |
| Securities Held for Plant Expansion Purposes | 150,000 | — | 150,000 |
| Machinery and Equipment | 927,000 | 647,000 | 280,000 |
| Leasehold Improvements | 87,000 | 87,000 | — |
| Patents | 27,800 | 30,000 | (2,200) |
| Totals | $2,072,800 | $1,761,000 | $311,800 |
| | | | |
| **Credit Balances** | | | |
| Allowance for Uncollectible Accounts Receivable | $ 14,000 | $ 17,000 | $ (3,000) |
| Accumulated Depreciation of Machinery and Equipment | 416,000 | 372,000 | 44,000 |
| Allowance for Amortization of Leasehold Improvements | 58,000 | 49,000 | 9,000 |
| Accounts Payable | 232,800 | 105,000 | 127,800 |
| Cash Dividends Payable | 40,000 | — | 40,000 |
| Current Portion of 6% Serial Bonds Payable | 50,000 | 50,000 | — |
| 6% Serial Bonds Payable | 250,000 | 300,000 | (50,000) |
| Preferred Stock | 90,000 | 100,000 | (10,000) |
| Common Stock | 500,000 | 500,000 | — |
| Retained Earnings | 422,000 | 268,000 | 154,000 |
| Totals | $2,072,800 | $1,761,000 | $311,800 |

(5) A comparative analysis of retained earnings as of December 31, 1981 and 1980, is presented below:

| | December 31 1981 | December 31 1980 |
|---|---|---|
| Balance, January 1 | $268,000 | $131,000 |
| Net Income | 195,000 | 172,000 |
| | $463,000 | $303,000 |
| Dividends Declared | (40,000) | (35,000) |
| Premium on Preferred Stock Repurchased | (1,000) | — |
| Balance, December 31 | $422,000 | $268,000 |

a. Prepare a T-account work sheet for the preparation of a statement of changes in financial position, defining funds as working capital but employing the all financial resources concept.

b. Prepare a formal statement of changes in financial position for Hatfield Corporation for the year ending December 31, 1981.

**24.12**   (Adapted from CPA Examination.) Exhibit 24.5 presents comparative statements of financial position of Area Corporation as of December 31, 1981, and December 31, 1980.

*Exhibit 24.5*
**Area Corporation**
**Comparative Statements**
**of Financial Position**

|  | December 31 1981 | December 31 1980 | Increase (Decrease) |
|---|---|---|---|
| **Assets** | | | |
| Current Assets: | | | |
| Cash | $ 450,000 | $ 287,000 | $163,000 |
| Notes Receivable | 45,000 | 50,000 | (5,000) |
| Accounts Receivable (Net of Allowance for Uncollectible Accounts of $17,100 and $24,700, Respectively) | 479,200 | 380,000 | 99,200 |
| Inventories | 460,000 | 298,000 | 162,000 |
| Total Current Assets | $1,434,200 | $1,015,000 | $419,200 |
| Investment in Common Stock of Reading Company | $ — | $ 39,000 | $ (39,000) |
| Investment in Common Stock of Zip Corporation | 246,300 | — | 246,300 |
| Total | $ 246,300 | $ 39,000 | $207,300 |
| Machinery and Equipment | $ 455,000 | $ 381,000 | $ 74,000 |
| Less: Accumulated Depreciation | (193,000) | (144,000) | 49,000 |
| Total | $ 262,000 | $ 237,000 | $ 25,000 |
| Patents (Less Accumulated Amortization) | $ 26,000 | $ 19,000 | $ 7,000 |
| Total Assets | $1,968,500 | $1,310,000 | $658,500 |
| | | | |
| **Liabilities and Shareholders' Equity** | | | |
| Current Liabilities: | | | |
| Dividends Payable | $ 181,000 | $ — | $181,000 |
| Accounts Payable | 156,000 | 40,800 | 115,200 |
| Accrued Liabilities | 92,000 | 84,000 | 8,000 |
| Total Current Liabilities | $ 429,000 | $ 124,800 | $304,200 |
| | | | |
| Shareholders' Equity: | | | |
| Preferred Stock, Par Value $2; Authorized 50,000 Shares; Issued and Outstanding, 30,000 Shares and 26,500 Shares, Respectively | $ 60,000 | $ 53,000 | $ 7,000 |
| Capital Contributed in Excess of Par—Preferred Stock | 6,000 | 2,500 | 3,500 |
| Common Stock, Par Value $10; Authorized 100,000 Shares; Issued and Outstanding, 75,200 Shares and 70,000 Shares, Respectively | 752,000 | 700,000 | 52,000 |
| Capital Contributed in Excess of Par—Common Stock | 20,000 | 9,600 | 10,400 |
| Earnings Appropriated for Contingencies | 85,000 | — | 85,000 |
| Retained Earnings | 616,500 | 420,100 | 196,400 |
| Total Shareholders' Equity | $1,539,500 | $1,185,200 | $354,300 |
| Total Liabilities and Shareholders' Equity | $1,968,500 | $1,310,000 | $658,500 |

The following additional information is given.

(1) For the year ended December 31, 1981, Area Corporation reported net income of $496,000.

(2) Uncollectible accounts receivable of $4,000 were written off against the allowance for uncollectible accounts receivable.

(3) Area's investment in the common stock of Reading Company was made in 1977 and represented a 3-percent interest in the outstanding common stock of Reading. During 1981, Area sold this investment for $26,000.

(4) Amortization of patents charged to operations during 1981 was $3,000.

(5) On January 1, 1981, Area acquired 90 percent of the outstanding common stock of Zip Corporation (45,000 shares, par value $10 per share). The transaction was accounted for as a purchase. To consummate this transaction, Area paid $72,000 cash and issued 3,500 shares of its preferred stock and 2,400 shares of its common stock. The consideration paid was equal to the underlying book value of the assets acquired. The fair market value of Area's stock on the date of the transaction was as follows:

| Preferred | ..................... | $ 3 |
| Common | ..................... | 12 |

Zip Corporation is considered to be an unrelated business and not compatible with the operations of Area Corporation; therefore, consolidation of the two companies is *not* required. For the year ended December 31, 1981, Zip Corporation reported net income of $150,000.

(6) During 1981, machinery and equipment that was acquired in 1975 at a cost of $22,000 was sold as scrap for $3,200. At the date of sale, this machinery had an undepreciated cost of $4,400.

In addition, Area acquired new machinery and equipment at a cost of $81,000. The remaining increase in machinery and equipment resulted from major repairs made to machinery that were accounted for as capital expenditures.

(7) On January 1, 1981, Area declared and issued a 4-percent stock dividend on its common stock. The market value of the shares on that date was $12 a share. The market value of the shares was not affected by the dividend distribution. On December 31, 1981, cash dividends were declared on both the common and preferred stock as follows:

| Common | ..................... | $145,000 |
| Preferred | ..................... | 36,000 |

(8) In December 1981, a reserve for a contingent loss of $85,000 arising from a law suit was established by a charge against retained earnings.

a. Prepare a T-account work sheet for the preparation of a statement of changes in financial position, defining funds as working capital but employing the all financial resources concept.

b. Prepare a formal statement of changes in financial position for Area Corporation for the year ending December 31, 1981.

24.13   Financial statement data for the Claire Corporation for the years ending December 31, 1980, and December 31, 1981, are presented in Exhibit 24.6.

You are also given the following additional information:

(1) Net income to shareholders for the year was $818,300. Dividends declared during the year were $97,900 for preferred stock and $121,190 for common stock.

*Exhibit 24.6*
**Claire Corporation**
**Comparative Balance Sheet**

| ASSETS | 12/31/1981 | 12/31/1980 |
|---|---:|---:|
| **Current Assets** | | |
| Cash | $    400,690 | $  423,600 |
| Accounts Receivable | 687,590 | 517,230 |
| Inventory | 2,434,020 | 2,370,370 |
| Total Current Assets | $ 3,522,300 | $3,311,200 |
| | | |
| **Noncurrent Assets** | | |
| Investments | $    350,000 | $  300,000 |
| Land | 1,050,000 | 1,140,000 |
| Buildings | 3,900,000 | 2,250,000 |
| Accumulated Depreciation, Buildings | (430,000) | (475,000) |
| Equipment | 2,800,000 | 2,400,000 |
| Accumulated Depreciation, Equipment | (1,375,000) | (1,289,000) |
| Delivery Equipment | 37,500 | 29,500 |
| Accumulated Depreciation, Delivery Equipment | (16,500) | (13,000) |
| Leasehold Improvements | 69,000 | 72,000 |
| Bond Sinking Fund | 300,000 | 250,000 |
| Goodwill | 50,000 | 60,000 |
| Total Noncurrent Assets | $ 6,735,000 | $4,724,500 |
| Total Assets | $10,257,300 | $8,035,700 |

| LIABILITIES AND SHAREHOLDERS' EQUITY | | |
|---|---:|---:|
| **Current Liabilities** | | |
| Accounts Payable | $    373,140 | $  291,080 |
| Short-Term Notes Payable | 815,090 | 730,520 |
| Total Current Liabilities | $ 1,188,230 | $1,021,600 |
| | | |
| **Long-Term Liabilities** | | |
| Bonds Payable | $ 1,900,000 | $1,000,000 |
| Discount on Bonds | (202,461) | (104,651) |
| Total Long-Term Liabilities | $ 1,697,539 | $  895,349 |
| Total Liabilities | $ 2,885,769 | $1,916,949 |
| | | |
| **Shareholders' Equity** | | |
| Preferred Stock | $    937,000 | $  302,000 |
| Premium on Preferred Stock | 18,570 | — |
| Common Stock | 2,000,000 | 2,000,000 |
| Retained Earnings | 4,415,961 | 3,816,751 |
| Total Shareholders' Equity | $ 7,371,531 | $6,118,751 |
| Total Liabilities and Shareholders' Equity | $10,257,300 | $8,035,700 |

(2) Land stated at $90,000 was sold during the year for $105,000.

(3) Buildings originally costing $414,000 were sold for $110,000. Depreciation expense for buildings for the year was $197,000.

(4) Equipment with a book value of $42,000 was sold for $39,000. Depreciation expense for equipment for the year was $214,000.

(5) The bonds outstanding on January 1, 1981, have an annual coupon rate of 4 percent and had been issued several years ago at a price to yield 5 percent per year. Discount is amortized with the effective-interest method. The bond indenture requires an annual payment of $50,000 to a sinking fund. On December 31, 1981, $900,000 5-percent bonds were issued at a price to yield 6 percent.

(6) No delivery equipment was sold during the year.

**a.** Prepare a T-account work sheet for the preparation of a statement of changes in financial position, defining funds as working capital but employing the all financial resources concept.

**b.** Prepare a formal statement of changes in financial position for Claire Corporation for the year ending December 31, 1981.

**24.14** The income statement for 1981 and the comparative balance sheets on December 31, 1980 and 1981, for Calmes Corporation are shown in Exhibits 24.7 and 24.8, respectively.

The following additional information is known:

(1) The intercorporate investments were acquired at the book value of the underlying net assets.

(2) Machinery and equipment costing $500,000 and with a book value of $100,000 were sold for cash during 1981.

(3) The bonds carry 6-percent annual coupons, payable on December 31 of each year. Calmes Corporation uses the effective-interest method of amortization.

(4) During 1981, Calmes Corporation paid $85,000 to the lessor of property represented on the balance sheet by "Property Rights Acquired under Lease."

(5) The only transaction affecting common and preferred stock during 1981 was the sale of treasury stock.

**a.** Prepare a T-account work sheet for the preparation of a statement of changes in financial position for Calmes Corporation for 1981, defining funds as working capital but employing an all financial resources concept.

**b.** Prepare a formal statement of changes in financial position.

**24.15** The balances in the accounts of Regal Corporation on December 31, 1980 and 1981, are shown in Exhibit 24.9.

The following additional information concerning transactions during 1981 is available.

(1) Net income for 1981 was $74,197.

(2) During the year 75 shares of common stock were purchased for $111 and are being held as treasury stock. The retirement method of accounting for treasury stock transactions is used. All "losses" on the acquisition of treasury stock are charged to Additional Paid-in Capital. Subsequent to the stock reacquisition, a cash dividend of $10 per share was declared and paid.

(3) The total premium paid on life insurance policies during 1981 was $1,673, of which $927 was charged to expense.

(4) Machinery costing $31,365 was acquired during the year. Machinery costing $32,625 and on which depreciation of $29,105 had been taken was sold for $1,000.

*Exhibit 24.7*
**Calmes Corporation (Problem 24.14)**
**Consolidated Statement of Income**
**and Retained Earnings**
**for the Year**
**Ended December 31, 1981**

**Revenues**

| | | |
|---|---|---|
| Sales | | $6,000,000 |
| Less Estimated Uncollectible Accounts | | 60,000 |
| Net Sales | | $5,940,000 |
| Gain on Sale of Machinery and Equipment | | 100,000 |
| Income from Completed Contracts | | 960,000 |
| Equity in Earnings of Unconsolidated Subsidiaries and Affiliates: | | |
| Calmes Finance Corporation | $900,000 | |
| Richardson Company | 50,000 | |
| Anthony Company | 50,000 | |
| | | 1,000,000 |
| Total Revenues | | $8,000,000 |

**Expenses**

| | |
|---|---|
| Cost of Goods Sold | $2,500,000 |
| Employee Payroll | 1,500,000 |
| Depreciation of Plant and Equipment and Amortization of Leased Property Rights | 500,000 |
| Amortization of Intangibles | 100,000 |
| Interest | 300,000 |
| General Corporate | 100,000 |
| Income Taxes—Current | 700,000 |
| Income Taxes—Deferred | 100,000 |
| Total Expenses | $5,800,000 |
| Net Income before Minority Interest | $2,200,000 |
| Minority Interest in Earnings | 200,000 |
| Net Income | $2,000,000 |
| Less: Dividends on Preferred Shares | 60,000 |
| Dividends on Common Shares | 840,000 |
| Increase in Retained Earnings | $1,100,000 |
| Retained Earnings, January 1, 1981 | 1,400,000 |
| Retained Earnings, December 31, 1981 | $2,500,000 |
| Primary Earnings per Common Share | $1.94 |
| Fully Diluted Earnings per Share (assuming conversion of preferred stock) | $1.25 |

(5) The serial bonds mature at the rate of $5,000 per year. In addition to the $5,000 of bonds retired during 1981, the company purchased and retired $8,500 of the bonds for $7,055. The bonds had a book value of $8,225 at the time of retirement.

(6) Accounts totaling $3,702 were written off as uncollectible during 1981.

(7) The estimated loss from the damage suit was established as a loss contingency in 1979.

*Exhibit 24.8*
**Calmes Corporation (Problem 24.14)**
**Consolidated Balance Sheets**

| | December 31 | |
| --- | --- | --- |
| | **1981** | **1980** |
| **ASSETS** | | |
| **Current Assets** | | |
| Cash ..................................................... | $ 50,000 | $ 100,000 |
| Marketable Securities at Lower of Cost or Market (Market Value, $160,000) ............................................. | 150,000 | — |
| Accounts Receivable (Net of Estimated Uncollectibles of $80,000 in 1981 and $50,000 in 1980) .................................. | 300,000 | 250,000 |
| Merchandise Inventory......................................... | 700,000 | 600,000 |
| Accumulated Costs under Contracts in Process in Excess of Progress Billings ........................................... | 200,000 | 150,000 |
| Prepayments ................................................ | 100,000 | 100,000 |
| Total Current Assets ..................................... | $ 1,500,000 | $1,200,000 |
| **Investments (at Equity)** | | |
| Calmes Finance Corporation (100% Owned) ..................... | $ 2,000,000 | $1,100,000 |
| Richardson Company (50% Owned) ............................ | 500,000 | 450,000 |
| Anthony Company (25% Owned) .............................. | 100,000 | 50,000 |
| Total Investments ....................................... | $ 2,600,000 | $1,600,000 |
| **Property, Plant, and Equipment** | | |
| Land ...................................................... | $ 250,000 | $ 200,000 |
| Building .................................................... | 2,000,000 | 2,000,000 |
| Machinery and Equipment ................................... | 4,000,000 | 3,650,000 |
| Property Rights Acquired under Lease ........................ | 750,000 | 750,000 |
| Total ................................................... | $ 7,000,000 | $6,600,000 |
| Less Accumulated Depreciation and Amortization ................ | (2,000,000) | (1,900,000) |
| Total Property, Plant, and Equipment ....................... | $ 5,000,000 | $4,700,000 |
| **Intangibles (at Net Book Value)** | | |
| Patent ..................................................... | $ 200,000 | $ 250,000 |
| Goodwill ................................................... | 700,000 | 750,000 |
| Total Intangibles ........................................ | $ 900,000 | $1,000,000 |
| Total Assets ............................................ | $10,000,000 | $8,500,000 |

The damage claim was unexpectedly settled out of court during 1981 at a cost to Regal Corporation of $39,000.

(8) Marketable securities costing $35,000 were sold during 1981 for $32,000. Marketable securities costing $10,000 were acquired during the year.

(9) All income is subject to an income tax rate of 40 percent.

a. Prepare a T-account work sheet for the preparation of a statement of changes in financial position, defining funds as working capital but employing the all financial resources concept.

*Exhibit 24.8 (continued)*

## LIABILITIES AND SHAREHOLDERS' EQUITY

**Current Liabilities**

| | | |
|---|---|---|
| Notes Payable | $ 250,000 | $ 200,000 |
| Accounts Payable | 350,000 | 330,000 |
| Salaries Payable | 150,000 | 120,000 |
| Income Taxes Payable | 200,000 | 150,000 |
| Rent Received in Advance | 50,000 | — |
| Other Current Liabilities | 200,000 | 100,000 |
| Total Current Liabilities | $ 1,200,000 | $ 900,000 |

**Long-Term Debt**

| | | |
|---|---|---|
| Bonds Payable (Net of Discount of $176,000 in 1981 and $200,000 in 1980) | $ 1,824,000 | $1,800,000 |
| Equipment Mortgage Indebtedness | 176,000 | 650,000 |
| Capitalized Lease Obligations | 500,000 | 550,000 |
| Total Long-Term Debt | $ 2,500,000 | $3,000,000 |

| | | |
|---|---|---|
| **Deferred Income Taxes** | $ 800,000 | $ 700,000 |

| | | |
|---|---|---|
| **Minority Interest in Subsidiary** | $ 500,000 | $ 300,000 |

**Shareholders' Equity**

| | | |
|---|---|---|
| Convertible Preferred Stock | $ 1,000,000 | $1,000,000 |
| Common Stock | 1,000,000 | 1,000,000 |
| Additional Paid-in Capital | 1,000,000 | 900,000 |
| Retained Earnings | 2,500,000 | 1,400,000 |
| Total | $ 5,500,000 | $4,300,000 |
| Less Cost of Treasury Shares | (500,000) | (700,000) |
| Total Shareholders' Equity | $ 5,000,000 | $3,600,000 |
| Total Liabilities and Shareholders' Equity | $10,000,000 | $8,500,000 |

**b.** Prepare a formal statement of changes in financial position for Regal Corporation for the year ending December 31, 1981.

**24.16**   Refer to the data for Regal Corporation in Problem **24.15**. Prepare a T-account work sheet for the preparation of a statement of changes in financial position, defining funds as cash but employing the all financial resources concept.

**24.17**   (Adapted from CPA Examination.) Bencivenga Company has prepared its financial statements for the year ended December 31, 1980, and for the 3 months ended March 31, 1981. You have been asked to prepare a statement of changes in financial position on a working capital basis for the 3 months ended March 31, 1981. The company's balance sheet data at December 31, 1980, and March 31, 1981, are shown in Exhibit 24.10, and its income statement data for the 3 months ended March 31, 1981, are shown in Exhibit 24.11. You have previously satisfied yourself as to the correctness of the amounts presented.

Your discussion with the company's controller and a review of the financial records have revealed the following information:

*Exhibit 24.9*
**Regal Corporation (Problems 24.15 and 24.16)**
**Trial Balance Amounts**

| | December 31 | |
| --- | --- | --- |
| | 1980 | 1981 |
| **DEBITS** | | |
| Cash ......................................................... | $ 40,409 | $ 30,337 |
| Marketable Securities (at Lower of Cost or Market)—Net .............. | 112,500 | 85,000 |
| Accounts Receivable ......................................... | 67,186 | 65,638 |
| Inventories ................................................. | 81,164 | 86,938 |
| Prepayments ............................................... | 710 | 755 |
| Cash Surrender Value of Life Insurance ........................... | 8,315 | 9,061 |
| Unamortized Bond Discount .................................. | 4,305 | 3,867 |
| Land, Building, and Equipment ................................. | 172,778 | 206,782 |
| Total Debits ............................................ | $487,367 | $488,378 |
| | | |
| **CREDITS** | | |
| Allowance for Uncollectible Accounts ............................. | $ 4,630 | $ 3,815 |
| Accumulated Depreciation .................................... | 96,618 | 81,633 |
| Notes Payable—Current ...................................... | 40,000 | 45,000 |
| Accounts Payable ........................................... | 34,081 | 31,314 |
| Accrued Liabilities .......................................... | 12,307 | 21,263 |
| Estimated Loss from Damage Suit .............................. | 37,500 | — |
| Serial Bonds Payable ........................................ | 82,000 | 68,500 |
| Common Stock, $100 Par Value ................................ | 100,000 | 92,500 |
| Additional Paid-in Capital .................................... | 11,000 | 10,175 |
| Retained Earnings .......................................... | 69,231 | 134,178 |
| Total Credits ........................................... | $487,367 | $488,378 |

(1) On January 8, 1981, the company sold marketable securities for cash. These securities had been held for more than 6 months. No marketable securities were purchased during 1981.

(2) The company's preferred stock is convertible into common stock at a rate of one share of preferred for two shares of common. The preferred stock and common stock have par values of $2 and $1, respectively.

(3) On January 17, 1981, three acres of land were condemned. An award of $32,000 in cash was received on March 22, 1981. Purchase of additional land as a replacement is not contemplated by the company. The gain is taxed at capital gain rates.

(4) On March 25, 1981, the company purchased equipment for cash.

(5) On March 29, 1981, bonds payable were issued by the company at par for cash.

(6) The investment in the 30-percent-owned company included an amount attributable to goodwill of $3,220 at December 31, 1980. Goodwill is being amortized at an annual rate of $480.

(7) The company's tax rate is 40 percent for regular income and 20 percent for capital gains.

a. Prepare a T-account work sheet for the preparation of a statement of changes in financial position, defining funds as working capital but employing the all financial resources concept.

b. Prepare a formal statement of changes in financial position for Bencivenga Company for the 3 months ending March 31, 1981.

*Exhibit 24.10*
**Bencivenga Company (Problems 24.17 and 24.18)**
**Balance Sheet**

|  | Dec. 31, 1980 | Mar. 31, 1981 |
|---|---|---|
| Cash | $ 25,300 | $ 87,400 |
| Marketable Securities | 16,500 | 7,300 |
| Accounts Receivable, Net | 24,320 | 49,320 |
| Inventory | 31,090 | 48,590 |
| Total Current Assets | $ 97,210 | $192,610 |
| Land | 40,000 | 18,700 |
| Building | 250,000 | 250,000 |
| Equipment | — | 81,500 |
| Accumulated Depreciation | (15,000) | (16,250) |
| Investment in 30%-Owned Company | 61,220 | 66,980 |
| Other Assets | 15,100 | 15,100 |
| Total Assets | $448,530 | $608,640 |
|  |  |  |
| Accounts Payable | $ 21,220 | $ 17,330 |
| Dividend Payable | — | 8,000 |
| Income Taxes Payable | — | 34,616 |
| Total Current Liabilities | $ 21,220 | $ 59,946 |
| Other Liabilities | 186,000 | 186,000 |
| Bonds Payable | 50,000 | 115,000 |
| Discount on Bonds Payable | (2,300) | (2,150) |
| Deferred Income Taxes | 510 | 846 |
| Preferred Stock | 30,000 | — |
| Common Stock | 80,000 | 110,000 |
| Dividends Declared | — | (8,000) |
| Retained Earnings | 83,100 | 146,998 |
| Total Equities | $448,530 | $608,640 |

*Exhibit 24.11*
**Bencivenga Company (Problems 24.17 and 24.18)**
**Income Statement Data**
**For the 3 Months**
**Ended March 31, 1981**

|  |  |
|---|---|
| Sales | $242,807 |
| Gain on Sale of Marketable Securities | 2,400 |
| Equity in Earnings of 30%-Owned Company | 5,880 |
| Gain on Condemnation of Land | 10,700 |
|  | $261,787 |
| Cost of Sales | $138,407 |
| General and Administrative Expenses | 22,130 |
| Depreciation | 1,250 |
| Interest Expense | 1,150 |
| Income Taxes | 34,952 |
|  | $197,889 |
| Net Income | $ 63,898 |

**24.18** Refer to the data for Bencivenga Company in Problem **24.17.** Prepare a T-account work sheet for the preparation of a statement of changes in financial position, defining funds as cash but employing the all financial resources concept.

**24.19** (Adapted from CPA Examination.) The comparative balance sheets for the Plainview Corporation are shown in Exhibit 24.12.

The following additional information relates to 1981 activities:

**(1)** The Retained Earnings account was analyzed as follows:

| | | |
|---|---:|---:|
| Retained Earnings, December 31, 1980 | | $758,200 |
| Add Net Income after Extraordinary Items | | 236,580 |
| Subtotal | | $994,780 |
| Deduct: | | |
| Cash Dividends | $130,000 | |
| Loss on Reissue of Treasury Stock | 3,000 | |
| 10% Stock Dividend | 100,200 | 233,200 |
| Retained Earnings, December 31, 1981 | | $761,580 |

*Exhibit 24.12*
**Plainview Corporation ( Problems 24.19 and 24.20)**
**Comparative Balance Sheets**
**December 31, 1981 and 1980**

| | 1981 | 1980 | Increase (Decrease) |
|---|---:|---:|---:|
| **ASSETS** | | | |
| Cash | $ 142,100 | $ 165,300 | $ (23,200) |
| Marketable Securities (at Cost) | 122,800 | 129,200 | (6,400) |
| Accounts Receivable (Net) | 312,000 | 371,200 | (59,200) |
| Inventories | 255,200 | 124,100 | 131,100 |
| Prepayments | 23,400 | 22,000 | 1,400 |
| Bond Sinking Fund | — | 63,000 | (63,000) |
| Investment in Subsidiary (at Equity) | 134,080 | 152,000 | (17,920) |
| Plant and Equipment (Net) | 1,443,700 | 1,534,600 | (90,900) |
| Total Assets | $2,433,280 | $2,561,400 | $(128,120) |
| **EQUITIES** | | | |
| Accounts Payable | $ 238,100 | $ 213,300 | $ 24,800 |
| Notes Payable—Current | — | 145,000 | (145,000) |
| Accrued Payables | 16,500 | 18,000 | (1,500) |
| Income Taxes Payable | 97,500 | 31,000 | 66,500 |
| Deferred Income Taxes (Noncurrent) | 127,900 | 128,400 | (500) |
| 6% Mortgage Bonds Payable (Due 1993) | — | 300,000 | (300,000) |
| Premium on Mortgage Bonds | — | 10,000 | (10,000) |
| 8% Debentures Payable (Due 2001) | 125,000 | — | 125,000 |
| Common Stock, $10 Par Value | 1,033,500 | 950,000 | 83,500 |
| Additional Paid-in Capital | 67,700 | 51,000 | 16,700 |
| Retained Earnings | 761,580 | 758,200 | 3,380 |
| Treasury Stock—at Cost of $3 per Share | (34,500) | (43,500) | 9,000 |
| Total Equities | $2,433,280 | $2,561,400 | $(128,120) |

(2) On January 2, 1981, marketable securities costing $110,000 were sold for $127,000. The proceeds from this sale, the funds in the bond sinking fund, and the amount received from the issuance of the 8-percent debentures were used to retire the 6-percent mortgage bonds. Any gain or loss on the retirement is taxed currently at 40 percent.

(3) The treasury stock was reissued on February 28, 1981. All "losses" on the reissue of treasury stock are charged to retained earnings.

(4) The stock dividend was declared on October 31, 1981, when the market price of Plainview Corporation's stock was $12 per share.

(5) On April 30, 1981, a fire destroyed a warehouse, which cost $100,000 and on which depreciation of $65,000 had accumulated. The loss was not insured.

(6) Plant and equipment transactions consisted of the sale of a building at its book value of $4,000 and the purchase of machinery for $28,000.

(7) Accounts receivable written off as uncollectible were $16,300 in 1980 and $18,500 in 1981. Expired insurance recorded in 1980 was $4,100 and $3,900 in 1981.

(8) The subsidiary, which is 80-percent owned, reported a loss of $22,400 for 1981.

a. Prepare a T-account work sheet for Plainview Corporation for 1981, defining funds as working capital but employing the all financial resources concept.

b. Prepare a formal statement of changes in financial position for the year ending December 31, 1981, applying the all financial resources concept.

24.20    Refer to the data in Problem **24.19** for Plainview Corporation for 1981. Prepare a T-account work sheet for the preparation of a statement of changes in financial position, defining funds as cash but employing the all financial resources concept.

24.21    (Adapted from CPA Examination.) Your firm has been engaged to examine the financial statements of Lanning Corporation for the year ending December 31, 1981. Under your supervision, your assistant has prepared the comparative balance sheet at December 31, 1981 and 1980, shown in Exhibit 24.13, and the income statement for the year ending December 31, 1981, shown in Exhibit 24.14.

The following additional information has been extracted from your audit work papers:

(1) During January 1981, Lanning decided to change its product mix. To accomplish this, new machinery and equipment costing $1,000,000 was purchased on February 15, 1981. The vendor supplying the machinery and equipment was paid as follows:

(a) Cash payment of $100,000.

(b) Issuance of 5,000 shares of $100 par value preferred stock with a fair value of $500,000.

(c) Issuance of a $400,000, 8-percent note secured by the machinery and equipment and payable in 20 equal annual installments plus interest on February 15 of each year until paid in full.

(2) The new machinery and equipment replaced dissimilar machinery and equipment that had an original cost of $720,000 and accumulated depreciation at February 15, 1981, of $504,000. The old machinery and equipment was sold for cash on February 15, 1981.

a. Prepare a T-account work sheet for Lanning Corporation for 1981, defining funds as working capital but employing the all financial resources concept.

b. Prepare a formal statement of changes in financial position for the year ending December 31, 1981.

24.22    Refer to the data in Problem **24.21** for Lanning Corporation for 1981. Prepare a T-account work sheet for the preparation of the statement of changes in financial position, defining funds as cash but employing the all financial resources concept.

*Exhibit 24.13*
**Lanning Corporation (Problems 24.21 and 24.22)**
**Balance Sheet**
**December 31, 1981**
**with Comparative Figures for 1980**

|  | 1981 | 1980 |
|---|---|---|
| **ASSETS** | | |
| Current Assets | | |
| Cash | $ 326,500 | $ 231,000 |
| Accounts Receivable, Net | 621,000 | 614,000 |
| Inventories | 1,373,000 | 1,293,000 |
| Prepaid Expenses | 160,000 | 175,000 |
| Total Current Assets | $2,480,500 | $2,313,000 |
| Investment in and Advances to 35%-Owned Corporation | $ 940,000 | $ 625,000 |
| Fixed Assets: | | |
| Land | $ 54,200 | $ 54,200 |
| Buildings | 758,000 | 758,000 |
| Machinery and Equipment | 1,584,000 | 1,304,000 |
| Accumulated Depreciation | (513,000) | (816,000) |
| Total Fixed Assets | $1,883,200 | $1,300,200 |
| Deferred Organizational Costs | — | $ 150,000 |
| Total | $5,303,700 | $4,388,200 |
| **LIABILITIES AND OWNERS' EQUITY** | | |
| Current Liabilities: | | |
| Notes Payable, Bank | $ 200,000 | $ 250,000 |
| Accounts Payable | 501,800 | 498,000 |
| Accrued Liabilities | 187,500 | 271,000 |
| Current Portion of Long-Term Debt | 70,000 | 50,000 |
| Income Taxes Payable | 10,000 | 26,000 |
| Total Current Liabilities | $ 969,300 | $1,095,000 |
| Long-Term Liabilities: | | |
| $6\frac{1}{2}$% Serial Debentures Payable | $ 900,000 | $ 950,000 |
| 8%-Secured Note Payable | 380,000 | — |
| Deferred Income Taxes | 119,000 | 167,000 |
| Total Long-Term Liabilities | $1,399,000 | $1,117,000 |
| Owners' Equity: | | |
| Preferred Stock | $ 500,000 | — |
| Common Stock | 1,621,000 | $1,621,000 |
| Retained Earnings | 949,400 | 555,200 |
| Treasury Stock Common, at Cost | (135,000) | — |
| Total Owners' Equity | $2,935,400 | $2,176,200 |
| Total | $5,303,700 | $4,388,200 |

**24.23**    (Adapted from CPA Examination.) The schedule of net changes in balance sheet accounts at December 31, 1981, compared to December 31, 1980, that is shown in Exhibit 24.15 was prepared from the records of the Sodium Company. The statement of changes in financial position for the year ending December 31, 1981, has not yet been prepared.

The following additional information is available:

*Exhibit 24.14*
**Lanning Corporation (Problems 24.21 and 24.22)**
**Income Statement**
**For the Year Ended December 31, 1981**

| | |
|---|---:|
| **Continuing Operations:** | |
| Sales | $5,300,000 |
| Cost of Goods Sold | (3,600,000) |
| Gross Margin on Sales | $1,700,000 |
| Selling, General, and Administrative Expenses | (563,000) |
| Operating Income | $1,137,000 |
| Other Income (Expense): | |
| Interest Expense | (112,000) |
| Gain on Sale of Equipment | 385,000 |
| Equity in the Earnings of 35%-Owned Corporation | 75,000 |
| Income from Continuing Operations before Income Taxes | $1,485,000 |
| Income Taxes: | |
| Current | $(688,800) |
| Deferred | (24,000) (712,800) |
| Income from Continuing Operations | $ 772,200 |
| **Accounting Changes:** | |
| Write-off of Deferred Organization Costs Less Applicable Deferred Income Tax of $72,000 | (78,000) |
| Net Income | $ 694,200 |

(1) The net income for the year ended December 31, 1981, was $172,300. There were no extraordinary items.

(2) During the year ended December 31, 1981, uncollectible accounts receivable of $26,400 were written off by a charge to allowance for doubtful accounts.

(3) A comparison of property, plant, and equipment as of the end of each year follows:

| | December 31 1981 | December 31 1980 | Net Increase (Decrease) |
|---|---:|---:|---:|
| Property, Plant, and Equipment | $570,500 | $510,000 | $60,500 |
| Less: Accumulated Depreciation | 224,500 | 228,000 | (3,500) |
| Property, Plant, and Equipment, Net | $346,000 | $282,000 | $64,000 |

During 1981, machinery was purchased at a cost of $45,000. In addition, machinery that was acquired in 1975 at a cost of $48,000 was sold for $3,600. At the date of sale, the machinery had an undepreciated cost of $4,200. The remaining increase in property, plant, and equipment resulted from the acquisition of a tract of land for a new plant site.

(4) The bonds payable mature at the rate of $28,000 every year.

(5) In January 1981, the company issued an additional 10,000 shares of its common stock at $14 per share upon the exercise of outstanding stock options held by key employees. In May 1981, the company declared and issued a 5-percent stock dividend on its outstanding stock. During the year, a cash dividend was paid on the common stock. On December 31, 1981, there were 840,000 shares of common stock outstanding.

(6) The appropriation of retained earnings for possible future inventory price decline was provided by a charge against retained earnings, in anticipation of an expected future drop in the market related to goods in inventory.

*Exhibit 24.15*
**Sodium Company (Problem 24.23)**
**Changes in Balance Sheet Accounts**
**For the Year Ended December 31, 1981**

| | Net Change Increase (Decrease) |
|---|---:|
| **Assets** | |
| Cash | $ 50,000 |
| Accounts Receivable, Net | 76,000 |
| Inventories | 37,000 |
| Prepayments | 1,000 |
| Property, Plant, and Equipment, Net | 64,000 |
| Total Assets | $228,000 |
| **Liabilities** | |
| Accounts Payable | $ (55,500) |
| Notes Payable—Current | (15,000) |
| Accrued Liabilities | 33,000 |
| Bonds Payable | (28,000) |
| Less:Unamortized Bond Discount | 1,200 |
| Total Liabilities | $(64,300) |
| **Shareholders' Equity** | |
| Common Stock $10 Par Value | 500,000 |
| Capital Contributed in Excess of Par Value | 200,000 |
| Retained Earnings | (437,700) |
| Appropriation of Retained Earnings for Possible Future Inventory Price Decline | 30,000 |
| Total Shareholders' Equity | $292,300 |
| Total Liabilities and Shareholders' Equity | $228,000 |

*Exhibit 24.16*
**Quinta Company (Problem 24.24)**
**Postclosing Trial Balance,**
**December 31, 1981**

| **Debit Balances** | |
|---|---:|
| Working Capital | $200,000 |
| Land | 40,000 |
| Building and Equipment | 500,000 |
| Investments | 100,000 |
| | $840,000 |
| **Credit Balances** | |
| Accumulated Depreciation | $200,000 |
| Bonds Payable | 100,000 |
| Common Stock | 200,000 |
| Retained Earnings | 340,000 |
| | $840,000 |

a. Prepare a T-account work sheet for the preparation of a statement of changes in financial position, defining funds as working capital. Instead of using the usual form of T-account, the work sheet should use a double T-account.

b. Prepare a formal statement of changes in financial position for the year ending December 31, 1981.

24.24  The Quinta Company presents the postclosing trial balance for the year 1981 shown in Exhibit 24.16, and the statement of changes in financial position for the year 1981 shown in Exhibit 24.17.

The accumulated depreciation of the equipment sold was $20,000. Current liabilities were $75,000 at the start of the year and $125,000 at the end of the year.

Prepare a balance sheet for the beginning of the year, January 1, 1981.

---

*Exhibit 24.17*
**Quinta Company (Problem 24.24)**
**Statement of Changes in Financial**
**Position for the Year 1981**
**(in Thousands of Dollars)**

### SOURCES OF WORKING CAPITAL

| | | |
|---|---:|---:|
| A. From Operations | | |
| Net Income | | $200 |
| Additions for Expenses and Losses Not Using Working Capital: | | |
| Depreciation | $ 60 | |
| Loss on Sale of Investments | 10 | |
| Total Additions | $ 70 | |
| Subtractions for Gains Not Producing Working Capital: | | |
| Gain on Sale of Buildings and Equipment | (5) | 65 |
| Working Capital Provided by Operations | | 265 |
| B. Proceeds of Issues of Securities and Debt | | |
| Common Stock Issue | $ 50 | |
| Bond Issue | 50 | |
| Total Proceeds | | 100 |
| C. Proceeds of Disposition of Noncurrent Assets | | |
| Sale of Investments | $ 40 | |
| Sale of Buildings and Equipment | 15 | |
| Sale of Land | 10 | |
| Total Proceeds | | 65 |
| Total Sources of Working Capital | | $430 |

### USES OF WORKING CAPITAL

| | | |
|---|---:|---:|
| A. Dividends | $200 | |
| B. Acquisition of Buildings and Equipment | 130 | |
| Total Uses of Working Capital | | $330 |
| Increase in Working Capital for Year | | |
| (sources minus uses) | | $100 |
| | | |
| Net Increase in Working Capital Items | | |
| (current asset increases minus current liability increases) | | $100 |

---

24.25  A balance sheet for the Quintus Company at January 1, 1981, is shown in Exhibit 24.18. A statement of changes in financial position and an analysis of changes in working capital for the year 1981 for the Quintus Company are shown in Exhibit 24.19.

The shareholders' equity account, Premium on Common Stock, was $5,784 on December 31, 1981. Plant and equipment sold had originally cost $12,974.

Prepare a balance sheet for the Quintus Company for December 31, 1981.

---

### Exhibit 24.18
### Quintus Company (Problems 24.25 and 24.26)
### Balance Sheet
### for January 1, 1981

#### ASSETS

**Current Assets**

| | |
|---|---:|
| Cash | $ 12,974 |
| Receivables | 27,045 |
| Inventories | 49,206 |
| Total Current Assets | $ 89,225 |

**Noncurrent Assets**

| | |
|---|---:|
| Land | $ 4,563 |
| Plant and Equipment | 157,594 |
| Less Accumulated Depreciation | (59,899) |
| Investment in Quintus Credit Corporation | 1,230 |
| Patents | 332 |
| Goodwill | 11,500 |
| Total Noncurrent Assets | $115,320 |
| Total Assets | $204,545 |

#### LIABILITIES AND SHAREHOLDERS' EQUITY

**Current Liabilities**

| | |
|---|---:|
| Accounts Payable | $ 45,331 |
| Income Taxes Payable | 9,752 |
| Total Current Liabilities | $ 55,083 |

**Noncurrent Liabilities**

| | |
|---|---:|
| Bonds Payable | $ 51,550 |
| Premium on Bonds Payable | 146 |
| Deferred Taxes | 7,194 |
| Total Noncurrent Liabilities | $ 58,890 |

**Shareholders' Equity**

| | |
|---|---:|
| Preferred Stock | $ 5,007 |
| Common Stock | 12,764 |
| Premium on Common Stock | 3,960 |
| Retained Earnings | 68,841 |
| Total Shareholders' Equity | $ 90,572 |
| Total Liabilities and Shareholders' Equity | $204,545 |

---

**24.26** A statement of changes in financial position including an analysis of changes in working capital for the Quintus Company for the year 1980 is presented in Exhibit 24.20.

Common stock outstanding on January 1, 1980, had a par value of $10,392. Accumulated depreciation on the plant and equipment sold was $807.

Prepare a balance sheet on January 1, 1980, using data from the statement of changes in financial position above and the balance sheet on January 1, 1981, in Problem **24.25**, as needed.

*Exhibit 24.19*
**Quintus Company (Problems 24.25 and 24.26)**
**Statement of Changes in Financial Position**
**for the Year 1981**

### SOURCES OF WORKING CAPITAL

From Operations:

| | | |
|---|---:|---:|
| Net Income | | $ 13,238 |
| Add Expenses and Losses Not Using Working Capital: | | |
| Depreciation | $ 11,085 | |
| Amortization of Patents | 27 | |
| Amortization of Goodwill | 2,300 | |
| Loss on Sale of Plant and Equipment | 472 | |
| Income Tax Timing Differences | 2,588 | |
| Total Addition to Working Capital for Expense and Loss Adjustments | | 16,472 |
| Subtract Revenues and Gains Not Providing Working Capital: | | |
| Gain: | | |
| Bond Premium Amortization | $     39 | |
| Gain on Sale of Land | 107 | |
| Share of Year's Earnings Retained by Quintus Credit Corporation | | |
| Accounted for on Equity Method | 208 | |
| Total Subtractions | | (354) |
| Working Capital Provided by Operations | | $ 29,356 |
| From Issue of Common Stock | | 9,863 |
| From Disposition of Long-Term Assets | | |
| Sale of Plant and Equipment | $  1,056 | |
| Sale of Land | 314 | |
| Proceeds from Disposition of Noncurrent Assets | | 1,370 |
| Total Sources of Working Capital | | $ 40,589 |

### USES OF WORKING CAPITAL

| | | |
|---|---:|---:|
| Distributions to Owners: | | |
| Dividends on Preferred Stock | $  4,719 | |
| Dividends on Common Stock | 5,094 | |
| Total Distributions to Owners | | $  9,813 |
| Retirement of Preferred Stock at Par Value | | 522 |
| Purchases of Plant and Equipment | | 13,983 |
| Total Uses of Working Capital | | $ 24,318 |
| Increase in Working Capital for Year | | $16,271 |

### ANALYSIS OF CHANGES IN WORKING CAPITAL

| | | |
|---|---:|---:|
| Current Asset Item Increases (Decreases): | | |
| Cash | $ (1,598) | |
| Receivables | 4,010 | |
| Inventories | (2,714) | |
| Decrease in Current Asset Items | | $   (302) |
| Current Liability Item (Increases) Decreases: | | |
| Accounts Payable | $ 13,718 | |
| Income Tax Payable | 2,855 | |
| Decrease in Current Liability Items | | 16,573 |
| Increase in Working Capital for Year | | $16,271 |

*Exhibit 24.20*
**Quintus Company (Problem 24.26)**
**Statement of Changes in Financial Position**
**for the Year 1980**

### SOURCES OF WORKING CAPITAL

| | | |
|---|---:|---:|
| From Operations: | | |
| Net Income | | $10,808 |
| Add Expenses and Losses Not Using Working Capital: | | |
| Depreciation | $11,987 | |
| Amortization of Patents | 25 | |
| Amortization of Goodwill | 2,300 | |
| Losses from Quintus Credit Corporation Accounted for on Equity | | |
| Method | 148 | |
| Income Tax Timing Differences | 2,283 | |
| Total Addition to Working Capital from Expense and Loss Adjustments | | 16,743 |
| Subtract Revenues and Gains Not Providing Working Capital: | | |
| Bond Premium Amortization | $   22 | |
| Gain on Sale of Plant and Equipment | 87 | |
| Total Subtractions | | (109) |
| Total Sources from Operations | | $27,442 |
| From Issue of Securities and Debt: | | |
| Bond Issue (Par Value $28,000) | $28,073 | |
| Common Stock Issued | 3,231 | |
| Proceeds from Securities and Debt Issues | | 31,304 |
| From Disposition of Plant and Equipment | | 326 |
| Total Sources of Working Capital | | $59,072 |

### USES OF WORKING CAPITAL

| | | |
|---|---:|---:|
| Distributions to Owners: | | |
| Dividends on Preferred Stock | $ 5,037 | |
| Dividends on Common Stock | 1,792 | |
| Total Distributions to Owners | | $ 6,829 |
| Retirement of Preferred Stock at Par Value | | 617 |
| For Acquisitions of Long-Term Assets: | | |
| Land | $   467 | |
| Plant and Equipment | 39,149 | |
| Patents | 58 | |
| Total Used for Acquisition of Long-Term Assets | | 39,674 |
| Total Uses of Working Capital | | $47,120 |
| Increase in Working Capital for Year | | $11,952 |

### ANALYSIS OF CHANGES IN WORKING CAPITAL

| | | |
|---|---:|---:|
| Current Asset Item Increases (Decreases): | | |
| Cash | $ 4,769 | |
| Receivables | 8,924 | |
| Inventories | 9,184 | |
| Increase in Current Asset Items | | $22,877 |
| Current Liability Item (Increases) Decreases: | | |
| Accounts Payable | $ (8,768) | |
| Income Tax Payable | (2,157) | |
| Increase in Current Liability Items | | 10,925 |
| Increase in Working Capital for Year | | $11,952 |

*Exhibit 24.21*
**Kenwood Corporation (Problems 24.27 and 24.28) Statement of Financial Position**

| | December 31 | | Increase |
| Assets | Year 2 | Year 1 | (Decrease) |
|---|---|---|---|
| Current Assets: | | | |
| Cash ......................................... | $ 100,000 | $ 90,000 | $ 10,000 |
| Accounts Receivable (Net of Allowance for Uncollectible | | | |
| Accounts of $10,000 and $8,000, Respectively) ............. | 210,000 | 140,000 | 70,000 |
| Inventories ...................................... | 260,000 | 220,000 | 40,000 |
| Total Current Assets ...................................... | $ 570,000 | $ 450,000 | $120,000 |
| Land ......................................... | 325,000 | 200,000 | 125,000 |
| Plant and Equipment ...................................... | 580,000 | 633,000 | (53,000) |
| Less: Accumulated Depreciation ............................ | (90,000) | (100,000) | 10,000 |
| Patents ......................................... | 30,000 | 33,000 | (3,000) |
| Total Assets ......................................... | $1,415,000 | $1,216,000 | $199,000 |
| | | | |
| **Liabilities and Shareholders' Equity** | | | |
| Liabilities: | | | |
| Current Liabilities: | | | |
| Accounts Payable ...................................... | $ 260,000 | $ 200,000 | $ 60,000 |
| Accrued Liabilities ...................................... | 200,000 | 210,000 | (10,000) |
| Total Current Liabilities ............................... | $ 460,000 | $ 410,000 | $ 50,000 |
| Deferred Income Taxes ...................................... | 140,000 | 100,000 | 40,000 |
| Long-term Bonds (Due December 15, Year 13) .............. | 130,000 | 180,000 | (50,000) |
| Total Liabilities ...................................... | $ 730,000 | $ 690,000 | $ 40,000 |
| | | | |
| **Shareholders' Equity:** | | | |
| Common Stock, Par Value $5, Authorized 100,000 Shares, | | | |
| Issued and Outstanding 50,000 and 42,000 Shares, | | | |
| Respectively ...................................... | $ 250,000 | $ 210,000 | $ 40,000 |
| Additional Paid-in Capital ...................................... | 233,000 | 170,000 | 63,000 |
| Retained Earnings ...................................... | 202,000 | 146,000 | 56,000 |
| Total Shareholders' Equity ............................... | $ 685,000 | $ 526,000 | $159,000 |
| Total Liabilities and Shareholders' Equity .................... | $1,415,000 | $1,216,000 | $199,000 |

**24.27**  (Adapted from CPA Examination.) Exhibit 24.21 presents a comparative statement of financial position for Kenwood Corporation as of December 31 of Year 1 and Year 2. Exhibit 24.22 presents an income statement for Year 2. The following additional information has been obtained.

1. On February 2, Year 2, Kenwood issued a 10 percent stock dividend to shareholders of record on January 15, Year 2. The market price per share of the common stock on February 2, Year 2, was $15.

2. On March 1, Year 2, Kenwood issued 3,800 shares of common stock for land. The common stock and land had current market values of approximately $40,000 on March 1, Year 2.

3. On April 15, Year 2, Kenwood repurchased long-term bonds with a face and book value of $50,000. The gain of $22,000 was reported as an extraordinary item on the income statement.

---

*Exhibit 24.22*
**Kenwood Corporation (Problems 24.27 and 24.28)**
**Income Statement**
**For the Year Ended December 31, 1979**

---

| | | |
|---|---:|---:|
| Sales | | $1,000,000 |
| Expenses: | | |
| Cost of Goods Sold | $ 560,000 | |
| Salary and Wages | 190,000 | |
| Depreciation | 20,000 | |
| Amortization | 3,000 | |
| Loss on Sale of Equipment | 4,000 | |
| Interest | 16,000 | |
| Miscellaneous | 8,000 | |
| Total Expenses | | $ 801,000 |
| Income before Income Taxes and Extraordinary Item | | $ 199,000 |
| Income Taxes | | |
| Current | $ 50,000 | |
| Deferred | 40,000 | |
| Provision for Income Taxes | | $ 90,000 |
| Income before Extraordinary Item | | $ 109,000 |
| Extraordinary Item—Gain on Repurchase of Long-term Bonds | | |
| (Net of $10,000 Income Tax) | | 12,000 |
| Net Income | | $ 121,000 |
| | | |
| Earnings per Share: | | |
| Income before Extraordinary Item | | $2.21 |
| Extraordinary Item | | .24 |
| Net Income | | $2.45 |

---

4. On June 30, Year 2, Kenwood sold equipment costing $53,000, with a book value of $23,000, for $19,000 cash.

5. On September 30, Year 2, Kenwood declared and paid a $0.04 per share cash dividend to shareholders of record August 1, Year 2.

6. On October 10, Year 2, Kenwood purchased land for $85,000 cash.

7. Deferred income taxes represent timing differences relating to the use of ACRS depreciation for income tax reporting and straight-line depreciation methods for financial statement reporting.

    a. Prepare a T-account work sheet for the preparation of a statement of changes in financial position, defining funds as working capital but employing the all financial resources concept.

    b. Prepare a formal statement of changes in financial position for Kenwood corporation for the year ended December 31, Year 2.

**24.28** Refer to the data for Kenwood Corporation in Problem **24.27**. Prepare a T-account work sheet for the preparation of a statement of changes in financial position, defining funds as cash but employing the all financial resources concept. Also prepare a formal statement of changes in financial position for Kenwood Corporation for the year ended December 31, Year 2.

# Chapter 25
# *Financial Statement Analysis*

25.1  Previous chapters presented the accounting concepts, principles, and procedures that underlie the preparation of financial statements. Little consideration was given to the interpretation or analysis of these statements. This chapter describes some of the more common tools of financial statement analysis and illustrates their use in the analysis of the financial statements of International Corporation presented in Appendix A. An understanding of the ways in which accounting information is used should permit you to evaluate more effectively alternative methods of measuring and disclosing accounting information.

## Objectives of Financial Statement Analysis

25.2  Financial statements report the results of past performance and the current financial position of a firm. An investor in a firm's bonds or stock is interested in the expected future performance and financial position of the firm. Data from the financial statements are useful to the extent that they aid the user in assessing or predicting variables of interest in the investment decision.

25.3  Modern investment theory teaches that investment decisions are made in terms of the expected return and risk associated with investment alternatives. For example, assume that you recently inherited $50,000 and must decide what to do with the bequest. You have narrowed the investment decision either to purchasing a certificate of deposit at a local bank or to purchasing shares of common stock of International Corporation, currently selling for $25 per share. Your decision will be based on the *return* anticipated from each investment and the *risk* associated with that return.

25.4  The bank is currently paying interest at the rate of 10 percent on certificates of deposit. Because it is unlikely that the bank will go out of business, you are virtually certain of earning 10 percent each year.

25.5  The return from investing in the shares of common stock of International Corporation has two components. First, the firm paid a cash dividend in 1981, the most recent year, of $.95 per share, and it is anticipated that this dividend will continue in the future. Second, the market price of the stock is likely to change between the date the shares are purchased and the date in the future when they are sold. The difference between the eventual selling price per share and the $25 purchase price, often called a *capital gain,* is a second component of the return from buying the stock.

25.6  Compared to interest on the certificate of deposit, the return from the common stock investment is more risky. Future dividends and market price changes are likely to be associated, at least partially, with the profitability of the firm. Future income might be less than is currently anticipated if competitors introduce new products that erode International Corporation's share of its sales market. Future income might be greater than currently anticipated if International Corporation makes important discoveries or introduces successful new products. The market price of International Corporation's shares will probably also be affected by economy-wide factors such as inflation and unemployment. Also, specific industry factors such as raw materials shortages or government antitrust actions may influence the market price of the stock. Because most individuals prefer less risk to more risk, you will probably demand a higher expected return from the purchase of International Corporation's shares than if you invest the inheritance in a certificate of deposit.

25.7    There are numerous sources of information that might be consulted in assessing the return and risk of investment alternatives. One such source is the financial statements prepared by firms and distributed periodically to shareholders and potential investors. These financial statements, based on the results of past activities, can be analyzed in order to obtain useful information for predicting future rates of return and for assessing risk.

25.8    The first question likely to be raised in analyzing a set of financial statements is "What do I look for?" Most financial statement analysis is directed at some aspect of either a firm's *profitability* or a firm's *risk*.

25.9    For example, assume that you are interested in acquiring a firm's common stock and wish to predict future dividends and market price changes for the stock. Dividends and market price changes are likely to be affected, at least partially, by the future profitability of the firm. The firm's past earnings performance can be analyzed as a basis for predicting its future profitability.

25.10    Suppose instead that you wish to acquire a firm's long-term bonds. Your return will be primarily in the form of periodic contractual interest receipts. Of particular concern here is the likelihood (risk) that the firm will have sufficient cash available to make the required periodic interest payments when due and to repay the principal at maturity. The focus of financial statement analysis in this case is the long-term solvency risk, or long-run cash-generating ability, of the firm.

25.11    Finally, assume that you plan to extend a loan to a firm, expecting repayment of the loan with interest in 6 months. The focus of financial statement analysis in this case is the short-term liquidity risk of the firm.

25.12    Before analyzing a set of financial statements, it is important that the objective of the analysis be clearly specified. The analytical techniques used will differ, as we show in this chapter, depending on the purpose of the analysis.

## Role of Financial Statement Analysis in an Efficient Capital Market

25.13    Theoretical and empirical work during the past decade has shown that the stock market is efficient in reacting to published information about a firm. That is, market participants react intelligently and quickly to information they receive, so that market prices continually reflect underlying economic values.

25.14    Two questions regarding the role of financial statement analysis in an efficient market might be raised:

**1.** Do market participants have the necessary technical knowledge of financial accounting and reporting to react intelligently to financial statement information?

**2.** If the market reacts quickly to information contained in the financial statements, what benefit is derived from analyzing such statements?

### Sophistication of Market Participants

25.15    There are two schools of thought regarding the level of accounting sophistication of market participants. One school argues that market participants are primarily small individual investors. Such participants have neither the time nor expertise to interpret and analyze financial statements and detect the subtleties of financial reports. They, therefore, make incorrect investment decisions on the basis of differences that are illusory. Extrapolating the behavior of these individuals, the market is believed to react naively to the release of new information and thus to be inefficient.

25.16    A second school of thought argues that market participants lacking the necessary accounting expertise use the services of information and decision intermediaries to aid in their investment decisions. Professional financial analysts are an example of the former, and mutual funds and pension funds are examples of the latter. These intermediaries possess the necessary accounting expertise to react intelligently to reported information. By following the advice or accepting the decisions of these intermediaries, individual investors effectively behave as if they had considerable accounting sophistication. Thus, the market reacts intelligently to new information.

25.17    Based on a comprehensive survey of theoretical and empirical work on efficient capital markets, Basu* concludes:

> . . . . our survey of previous research on the association between stock prices and accounting information reveals that the market's reaction to financial statement data is, indeed, quite sophisticated. Stock prices seem to adjust both rapidly and unbiasedly to the release of financial statement data. In addition to reported "face of the statement" accounting numbers, information in the notes to the financial statements, as well as that in other forms of disclosure, seems to be impounded in stock market prices. To the extent financial statement data *per se* are not timely, the market seems to have turned to alternate sources of information. More important, the market reaction to accounting numbers does not seem to be mechanistic or naive. On the contrary, the evidence is consistent with the view that the market does look behind financial statement numbers of the underlying economic phenomena. For exam-

---

*S. Basu, *Inflation Accounting, Capital Market Efficiency and Security Prices,* Society of Management Accountants of Canada, 1978, p. 25.

ple, the market does not seem to be tricked by accounting changes that increase reported earnings but have no economic consequences on the entity, nor does it seem fooled by an arbitrary choice of alternative accounting methods. In short, the reaction to financial statements and other data is consistent with what one would expect in an efficient capital market.

## Benefit of Financial Statement Analysis

One implication of an efficient capital market is that financial statements cannot be routinely analyzed to find "undervalued" or "overvalued" securities. Any new information reported in the financial statements is quickly impounded in security prices. What, then, is the value of financial statement analysis?    25.18

One response is that such analysis must be done by someone, presumably by sophisticated financial analysts, if the market is to react appropriately to new information. Such analysis, however, is done soon after the information is released and quickly impounded in market prices.    25.19

A second response is that much financial statement analysis must be done outside of a capital market setting. Banks grant credit to business firms and are interested in the liquidity of these enterprises. Investment bankers must set offering prices for the shares of firms initially going public. Government antitrust agencies must compare the relative profitability of various firms and industries in deciding antitrust actions.    25.20

As an accountant, you probably will not be heavily involved in financial statement analysis. However, you will often be faced with questions regarding the measurement and disclosure of information to be used by financial analysts. A knowledge of financial statement analysis should help you to make these statements more useful.    25.21

## Usefulness of Ratios

The various items in financial statements may be difficult to interpret in the form in which they are presented. For example, the    25.22

profitability of a firm may be difficult to assess by looking at the amount of net income alone. It is helpful to compare earnings with the assets or capital required to generate those earnings. This relationship, and other important ones between various items in the financial statements, can be expressed in the form of ratios. Some ratios compare items within the income statement; some use only balance sheet data; others relate items from more than one statement. Ratios are useful tools of financial statement analysis because they conveniently summarize data in a form that is more easily understood, interpreted, and compared.

25.23 Ratios are, by themselves, difficult to interpret. For example, does a rate of return on common stock of 8.6 percent reflect a good performance? Once calculated, the ratios must be compared with some standard. Several possible standards might be used:

**1.** The planned ratio for the period being analyzed.

**2.** The corresponding ratio during the preceding period for the same firm.

**3.** The corresponding ratio for a similar firm in the same industry.

**4.** The average ratio for others firms in the same industry.

Difficulties encountered in using these bases for comparison are discussed later.

25.24 In the sections that follow, several ratios and other tools for assessing profitability, short-term liquidity risk, and long-run solvency risk are discussed. The analysis compares amounts for International Corporation for 1981 with the corresponding amounts for 1979 and 1980. Such an analysis is referred to as *time-series analysis*. Comparison of a given firm's ratios with those of other firms for a particular period is referred to as *cross-section analysis*. Cross-section analysis is discussed more fully later in the chapter.

## Measures of Profitability

25.25 Usually the most important question asked about a business is "How profitable is it?" Most financial statement analysis is directed at various aspects of this question. Some measures of profitability relate earnings to resources or capital employed, other computations relate earnings and various expenses to sales, whereas a third group seeks to explain profitability by measuring the efficiency with which inventories, receivables, or other assets have been managed.

## Rate of Return on Assets

25.26 The most important profitability ratio for assessing management's performance in using assets to generate earnings is the *rate of return on assets*. This ratio is often called the *return on investment,* or *ROI,* or the *all-capital earnings rate.* It is calculated as follows:

$$\text{Rate of Return on Assets} = \frac{\begin{array}{c}\text{Net Income}\\+\\\text{Interest Expense Net}\\\text{of Income Tax Savings}\\+\\\text{Minority Interest in Earnings}\end{array}}{\text{Average Total Assets}}.$$

25.27 Management's performance in using assets is independent of how the acquisition of those assets has been financed. Thus, the earnings figure in the numerator of the rate of return on assets is income before deducting any payments or distributions to the providers of capital. Because interest is a payment to a furnisher of capital, interest expense should not be deducted in measuring the return on total assets. To derive income before interest charges, it is usually easier to start with net income and add to that figure. The amount added to net income is not, however, the interest expense shown on the income statement. Because interest expense is deductible in calculating taxable income, interest expense does not reduce *aftertax* net income by the full amount of interest expense. The amount added back to net income is interest expense reduced by income tax savings.

25.28 If a consolidated subsidiary is not wholly owned by the parent company, the minority interest's share of earnings must also be added back to net income. In a consolidated balance sheet, all of the assets of a subsidiary are combined with those of the parent company (that is, the parent's share plus the minority interest's share in the assets). Because the denominator includes all of the assets of the consolidated entity, the numerator should include all of the income, not just the parent's share. (Consolidated financial statements are discussed in Chapter 14 and in advanced accounting principles textbooks.)

25.29    Because the earnings rate *during the year* is being computed, the measure of investment should reflect the average amount of assets during the year. A crude, but usually satisfactory, figure for average total assets is one-half the sum of total assets at the beginning and at the end of the year.

25.30    The calculation of rate of return on assets for International Corporation for 1981 is as follows:

$$\frac{\begin{array}{c}\text{Net Income} \\ + \\ \text{Interest Expense Net of} \\ \text{Income Tax} \\ \text{Savings} \\ + \\ \text{Minority Interest} \\ \text{in Earnings}\end{array}}{\text{Average Total Assets}}$$

$$= \frac{\$165.2 + [\$76.4 - .46(\$76.4)] + \$2.5}{.5(\$4,813.6 + \$4,866.3)}$$

$$= 4.3\%.$$

The rate of return on assets was 1.8 percent for 1980 and 4.5 percent for 1979.* Thus, the overall return from using assets increased between 1980 and 1981, but the increase appears to be a return to the level experienced in 1979.

25.31    One might question, however, whether the income measure in the numerator should be net income or only income from continuing operations. If the objective is to assess changes in the ongoing profitability of the firm, perhaps only the amounts relating to continuing operations should be included in the calculation. The return on assets from continuing operations for 1981 is calculated as follows:

---

*The calculation of certain ratios for 1979 and 1980 requires balance sheet data from the preceding year. Because these data are not provided in Appendix A, the calculation of ratios for 1979 and 1980 is not shown.

$$\frac{\begin{array}{c}\text{Income from} \\ \text{Continuing Operations} \\ + \\ \text{Interest Expense Net of} \\ \text{Income Tax Savings} \\ + \\ \text{Minority Interest} \\ \text{in Earnings}\end{array}}{\begin{array}{c}\text{Average Total Assets} \\ \text{Relating to} \\ \text{Continuing Operations}\end{array}}$$

$$= \frac{\$178.6 + [\$76.4 - .46(\$76.4)] + \$2.5}{.5[(\$4,813.6 - \$202.4) + (\$4,866.3 - \$95.5)]}$$

$$= \frac{\$222.4}{\$4,691.0} = 4.7\%.$$

The corresponding amounts were 4.1 percent for 1980 and 5.0 percent for 1979. Thus, although both measures of return on assets increased between 1980 and 1981, the improvement is not as dramatic when only continuing operations and the three-year trend are considered.

## Disaggregating the Rate of Return on Assets

One means of studying changes in the rate    25.32 of return on assets is to disaggregate the ratio into two other ratios as follows:

$$\begin{array}{c}\text{Rate of} \\ \text{Return} \\ \text{on Assets}\end{array} = \begin{array}{c}\text{Profit Margin Ratio} \\ \text{(before interest expense} \\ \text{and related income tax} \\ \text{savings and minority} \\ \text{interest in earnings)}\end{array} \times \begin{array}{c}\text{Total Assets} \\ \text{Turnover} \\ \text{Ratio}\end{array}$$

or

$$\frac{\begin{array}{c}\text{Net Income} \\ + \\ \text{Interest Expense} \\ \text{Net of Income} \\ \text{Tax Savings} \\ + \\ \text{Minority Interest} \\ \text{in Earnings}\end{array}}{\begin{array}{c}\text{Average Total} \\ \text{Assets}\end{array}} = \frac{\begin{array}{c}\text{Net Income} \\ + \\ \text{Interest Expense} \\ \text{Net of Income} \\ \text{Tax Savings} \\ + \\ \text{Minority Interest} \\ \text{in Earnings}\end{array}}{\text{Revenue}} \times \frac{\text{Revenue}}{\begin{array}{c}\text{Average Total} \\ \text{Assets}\end{array}}$$

The profit margin ratio is a measure of a firm's ability to control the level of costs, or expenses, relative to revenues generated. By holding down costs, a firm will be able to increase the profits from a given amount of revenue and thereby improve its profit margin ratio. The total assets turnover ratio is a measure of a firm's ability to generate revenues from a particular level of investment in assets.

25.33     The disaggregation of the rate of return on assets from continuing operations for International Corporation for 1981 is as follows:

$$\frac{\$222.4}{\$4,691.0} = \frac{\$222.4}{\$5,928.6} \times \frac{\$5,928.6}{\$4,691.0}$$

$$4.7\% = 3.7\% \times 1.3.$$

The corresponding amounts are 4.2 percent (= 3.5 percent × 1.2) for 1980 and 5.0 percent (= 4.3 percent × 1.2) for 1979. Thus, there has been a small improvement in both the profit margin and the total assets turnover between 1980 and 1981, but performance is still not as favorable as that for 1979.

25.34     Improving the rate of return on assets can be accomplished by increasing the profit margin ratio, the rate of asset turnover, or both. Some firms, however, may have little flexibility in altering one of these components. For example, a firm committed under a 3-year labor union contract may have little control over wage rates paid. Or a firm operating under market- or government-imposed price controls may not be able to increase the prices of its products. In these cases, the opportunities for improving the profit margin ratio may be limited. In order to increase the rate of return on assets, the level of investment in assets such as inventory, plant, and equipment must be reduced or, to put it another way, revenues per dollar of assets must be increased.

## Analyzing Changes in the Profit Margin Ratio

25.35     Profit, or net income, is measured by subtracting various expenses from revenues. To identify the reasons for a change in the profit margin ratio, changes in a firm's expenses relative to sales must be examined. One approach is to express individual expenses and net income as a percentage of revenues. Such an analysis is presented in Exhibit 25.1 for International Corporation. Note that the conventional income statement format has been altered somewhat in this analysis by subtracting interest expense (net of its re-

lated income tax savings) and minority interest in earnings as the last expense items. The percentage on the line "Income from Continuing Operations before Interest and Related Income Tax Savings and before Minority Interest in Earnings" corresponds to the profit margin ratio (before interest and related tax savings and minority interest in earnings) presented in the preceding section.

The analysis in Exhibit 25.1 indicates that     25.36 the improvement in the profit margin ratio between 1980 and 1981 is due primarily to a decrease in the percentage of cost of goods sold to sales. This improvement was offset by an increase in selling, general, and administrative expenses and income tax expense. The amounts for 1981 are similar to those for 1979 and may merely represent a return of the percentages to their normal levels. The reasons for these changing percentages, although small, might be explored further with management. The amount or trend in a particular ratio cannot, by itself, be a basis for investing or not investing in a firm. Ratios merely indicate areas where additional analysis is required. For example, the decreasing percentage of cost of goods sold to sales might reflect the use of more efficient production techniques or the realization of economies of scale as fixed manufacturing costs are spread over a larger number of units (a phenomenon called *operating leverage*). On the other hand, the selling price might have been raised by a larger percentage amount than increases in the replacement costs of inventory. If competitors do not follow similar price increases, International Corporation might eventually lose customers and hurt its profitability.

## Analyzing Changes in the Total Assets Turnover Ratio

The total assets turnover ratio depends on     25.37 the turnover ratios for its individual asset components. Three turnover ratios are commonly calculated: accounts receivable turnover, inventory turnover, and fixed asset turnover.

**Accounts Receivable Turnover**  The rate at     25.38 which accounts receivable turn over gives an indication of their nearness to being con-

*Exhibit 25.1*
**Net Income, Income from Continuing and
Discontinued Operations, and Expenses as
a Percentage of Revenues for International
Corporation for 1979–1981**

|  | 1981 | 1980 | 1979 |
|---|---|---|---|
| Revenues | 100.0% | 100.0% | 100.0% |
| Expenses: |  |  |  |
| Cost of Goods Sold | (78.4)% | (80.0)% | (76.6)% |
| Selling, General, and Administrative | (13.5) | (12.4) | (13.5) |
| Depreciation | (2.2) | (2.1) | (2.1) |
| Income Taxes Excluding Amount Relating to Interest | (2.2) | (2.0) | (3.4) |
| Total | (96.3)% | (96.5)% | (95.6)% |
| Income from Continuing Operations before Interest and Related Tax Savings and before Minority Interest | 3.7 % | 3.5 % | 4.4 % |
| Interest (Net of Tax Savings) | (.6) | (1.0) | (.7) |
| Minority Interest | (.1) | (.1) | (.1) |
| Income from Continuing Operations | 3.0 % | 2.4 % | 3.6 % |
| Loss from Discontinued Operations | (.2) | (1.9) | (.4) |
| Net Income | 2.8 % | .5 % | 3.2 % |

verted into cash. The accounts receivable turnover is calculated by dividing net sales on account by average accounts receivable. For International Corporation, the accounts receivable turnover for 1981, assuming that all sales are on account (that is, none are for immediate cash), is calculated as follows:

$$\frac{\text{Net Sales on Account}}{\text{Average Accounts Receivable}} = \frac{\$5,862.7}{.5(\$1,247.1 + \$1,142.3)}$$

$$= 4.9 \text{ times per year.}$$

The concept of accounts receivable turnover is often expressed in terms of the average number of days receivables are outstanding before cash is collected. The calculation is to divide the accounts receivable turnover ratio into 365 days. The average number of days that accounts receivable are outstanding for International Corporation for 1981 is 74.5 days (= 365 days/4.9 times per year). Thus, on average, accounts receivable are collected 2$^1/_2$ months after the date of sale. The accounts receivable turnover for 1980 was 4.5 and for 1979 was 4.0. Thus, the average number of days receivables are outstanding was reduced over the three years.

25.39     The interpretation of the average collec-

tion period depends on the terms of sale. If the terms of sale for International Corporation are "net 30 days," the accounts receivable turnover indicates that collections are not being made in accordance with the stated terms. Such a ratio would warrant a review of the credit and collection activity for an explanation and for possible corrective action. If the firm offers terms of "net 90 days," then the results indicate that accounts receivable are being handled well.

**Inventory Turnover** The inventory turn-    25.40
over ratio is considered to be a significant indicator of the efficiency of operations for many businesses. It is calculated by dividing cost of goods sold by the average inventory during the period. The inventory turnover for International Corporation for 1981 is calculated as follows:

$$\frac{\text{Cost of Goods Sold}}{\text{Average Inventory}} = \frac{\$4,647.2}{.5(\$1,073.0 + \$1,040.6)}$$

$$= 4.4 \text{ times per year.}$$

Thus, inventory is typically on hand an average of 83.0 days (= 365/4.4) before it is sold. The inventory turnover for 1980 was 4.1 and for 1979 was 4.0.

25.41    The interpretation of the inventory turnover figure involves two opposing considerations. Management would like to sell as many goods as possible with a minimum of capital tied up in inventories. An increase in the rate of inventory turnover between periods would seem to indicate more profitable use of the investment in inventory. On the other hand, management does not want to have so little inventory on hand that shortages result and customers are turned away. An increase in the rate of inventory turnover in this case may mean a loss of customers and thereby offset any advantage gained by decreased investment in inventory. Some trade-offs are therefore required in deciding the optimum level of inventory for each firm and thus the desirable rate of inventory turnover.

25.42    The inventory turnover ratio is sometimes calculated by dividing sales, rather than cost of goods sold, by the average inventory. As long as there is a relatively constant relationship between selling prices and cost of goods sold, changes in the *trend* of the inventory turnover can usually be identified with either measure. It is inappropriate to use sales in the numerator if the inventory turnover ratio is to be used to calculate the average number of days inventory is on hand until sale.

25.43    **Plant Asset Turnover** The plant asset turnover ratio is a measure of the relationship between sales and the investment in plant assets such as property, plant, and equipment. It is calculated by dividing sales by average plant assets during the year. The plant assets turnover ratio for International Corporation for 1981 is

$$\frac{\text{Sales}}{\text{Average Plant Assets}} = \frac{\$5,862.7}{.5(\$1,298.6 + \$1,380.7)}$$
$$= 4.4 \text{ times per year.}$$

Thus, for each dollar invested in fixed assets during 1981, $4.40 was generated in sales. The plant asset turnover for 1980 was also 4.4 and for 1979 was 4.5.

25.44    Changes in the plant asset turnover ratio must be interpreted carefully. Investments in plant assets (for example, production facilities) are often made several periods before the time when sales are generated from products manufactured in the plant. Thus, a low or decreasing rate of plant asset turnover may be indicative of an expanding firm preparing for future growth. On the other hand, a firm may cut back its capital expenditures if the near-term outlook for its products is poor. Such action could lead to an increase in the plant asset turnover ratio.

25.45    We noted earlier that the total assets turnover of International Corporation increased from 1.2 to 1.3 between 1980 and 1981. Most of the increase is due to increases in the turnover of receivables and inventories.

25.46    **Summary of the Analysis of the Rate of Return on Assets** This section began by stating that the rate of return on assets is a useful measure for assessing management's performance. The rate of return on assets was then disaggregated into profit margin and total assets turnover components. The profit margin ratio was in turn disaggregated by relating various expenses and net income to sales. The total assets turnover was further analyzed by calculating turnover ratios for accounts receivable, inventory, and plant assets.

## Rate of Return on Common Shareholders' Equity

25.47    The investor in a firm's common stock is probably more interested in the *rate of return on common shareholders' equity* than the rate of return on assets. To compute the amount of earnings assignable to common stock equity, the earnings allocable to any preferred stock equity, usually the dividends on preferred stock declared during the period, must be deducted from net income. The capital provided during the period by common shareholders can be determined by averaging the aggregate par value of common stock, capital contributed in excess of par value on common stock, and retained earnings (or by deducting the equity of preferred shareholders from total shareholders' equity) at the beginning and end of the period.

25.48  The rate of return on common shareholders' equity of International Corporation for 1981 is calculated as

$$\frac{\text{Net Income} - \text{Dividends on Preferred Stock}}{\text{Average Common Shareholders' Equity}}$$

$$= \frac{\$165.2 - \$0}{.5[(\$1,924.1 - \$30.5) + (\$2,001.7 - \$16.6)]}$$

$$= \frac{\$165.2}{\$1,939.4}$$

$$= 8.5\%.$$

The rate of return on common shareholders' equity of International Corporation, 8.5 percent,* is larger in this case than the rate of return on assets (4.3 percent). The return to the common shareholders' equity is larger than the rate of return on assets because the aggregate payments to the other suppliers of capital (for example, creditors and bondholders) are less than the overall 4.3 percent rate of return generated from capital that they provided. Because common shareholders have a residual claim on the assets and earnings of a firm, they have a claim on all earnings in excess of the cost (including interest on borrowed funds) of generating those earnings.

25.49  The common shareholders earned a higher rate of return only because they undertook more risk in their investment. These shareholders were placed in a riskier position because International Corporation incurred debt obligations with fixed payment dates. Failure to make these fixed interest payments could result in the firm being declared insolvent. The phenomenon of common shareholders trading extra risk for a potentially higher return is called *financial leverage* and is discussed next.

### Financial Leverage: Trading on the Equity

25.50  Financing with debt and preferred stock to increase the potential return to the residual common shareholders' equity is referred to as *financial leverage* or *trading on the equity*. So long as a higher rate of return can be earned on assets than is paid for the capital used to acquire those assets, then the rate of return to owners can be increased. Exhibit 25.2 explores this phenomenon. Leveraged Company and No-Debt Company both have $100,000 of assets. Leveraged Company borrows $40,000 at a 10-percent annual rate. No-Debt Company raises all its capital from owners. Both companies pay income taxes at the rate of 40 percent.

25.51  Consider first a "good" earnings year. Both companies earn $10,000 before interest charges (but after taxes except for tax effects of interest charges).† This represents a rate of return on assets for both companies of 10 percent (= $10,000/$100,000). Leveraged Company's net income is $7,600 [= $10,000 − (1 − .40 tax rate) × (.10 interest rate × $40,000 borrowed)], representing a rate of return on common shareholders' equity of 12.7 percent (= $7,600/$60,000). Net income of No-Debt Company is $10,000, representing a rate of return on shareholders' equity of 10 percent. Leverage increased the rate of return to shareholders of Leveraged Company, because the capital contributed by the long-term debtors earned 10 percent but required an aftertax interest payment of only 6 percent [=(1 − .40 tax rate) × (.10 interest rate)]. This additional 4-percent return on each dollar of assets increases the return to the common shareholders.

25.52  Although leverage increased the return to the common stock equity during the "good" earnings year, the increase would be larger if a larger proportion of the assets were financed with long-term borrowing and the firm were made more risky. For example, assume that the assets of $100,000 were financed with $50,000 of long-term borrowing and $50,000 of shareholders' equity. Net income of Leveraged Company in this case would be $7,000 [= $10,000 − (1 − .40 tax rate) × (.10 × $50,000 borrowed)]. The rate

---

*As was the case with the rate of return on assets, the income measure in the numerator might be income from continuing operations only.

†That is, income before taxes and before interest charges is $16,667; $10,000 = (1 − .40) × $16,667.

*Exhibit 25.2*

**Effects of Leverage on Rate of Return on Shareholders' Equity (Income Tax Rate Is 40% of Pretax Income)**

| | Long-Term Equities | | Income after Taxes but before Interest Charges[a] | Aftertax Interest Charges[b] | Net Income | Rate of Return on Total Assets[c] (%) | Rate of Return on Common Shareholders' Equity[c] (%) |
|---|---|---|---|---|---|---|---|
| | Long-Term Borrowing at 10% per Year | Shareholders' Equity | | | | | |
| **Good Earnings Year** | | | | | | | |
| Leveraged Company .............. | $40,000 | $ 60,000 | $10,000 | $2,400 | $ 7,600 | 10.0% | 12.7% |
| No-Debt Company .............. | — | 100,000 | 10,000 | — | 10,000 | 10.0 | 10.0 |
| **Neutral Earnings Year** | | | | | | | |
| Leveraged Company .............. | 40,000 | 60,000 | 6,000 | 2,400 | 3,600 | 6.0 | 6.0 |
| No-Debt Company .............. | — | 100,000 | 6,000 | — | 6,000 | 6.0 | 6.0 |
| **Bad Earnings Year** | | | | | | | |
| Leveraged Company .............. | 40,000 | 60,000 | 4,000 | 2,400 | 1,600 | 4.0 | 2.7 |
| No-Debt Company .............. | — | 100,000 | 4,000 | — | 4,000 | 4.0 | 4.0 |

[a] But not including any income tax savings caused by interest charges. Income before taxes and interest for *good* year is $16,667; for *neutral* year is $10,000; for *bad* year is $6,667.

[b] $40,000 (borrowed) × .10 (interest rate) × [1 − .40 (income tax rate)]. The numbers shown in the preceding column for aftertax income do not include the effects of interest on taxes.

[c] In each year, the rate of return on assets is the same for both companies as the rate of return on common shareholders' equity for No-Debt Company, 10%, 6%, and 4% charges, respectively.

of return on common stock equity would be 14 percent (= \$7,000/\$50,000). This rate compares with a rate of return on common stock equity of 12.7 percent when long-term debt was only 40 percent of the total capital provided.

25.53   Financial leverage increases the rate of return on common stock equity when the rate of return on assets is larger than the aftertax cost of debt. The greater the proportion of debt in the capital structure, however, the greater the risk borne by the common shareholders. Debt cannot, of course, be increased without limit. As more debt is added to the capital structure, the risk of default or insolvency becomes greater. Lenders, including investors in a firm's bonds, will require a higher and higher return (interest rate) to compensate for this additional risk. A point will be reached when the aftertax cost of debt will exceed the rate of return that can be earned on assets. At this point, leverage can no longer increase the potential rate of return to common stock equity. For most large manufacturing firms, total liabilities represent between 30 percent and 60 percent of total capital.

25.54   Exhibit 25.2 also demonstrates the effect of leverage in a "neutral" earnings year and in a "bad" earnings year. In the "neutral" earnings year, the rate of return to common shareholders is neither increased nor decreased by leverage, because the return on assets is 6 percent and the aftertax cost of long-term debt is 6 percent. In the "bad" earnings year, the return on assets of 4 percent is less than the aftertax cost of debt of 6 percent. The return on common shareholders' equity therefore drops—to only 2.7 percent—below the rate of return on assets. Clearly, financial leverage can work in two ways. It can enhance owners' rate of return in good years, but owners run the risk that bad earnings years will be even worse than they would be without the borrowing.

## Disaggregating the Rate of Return on Common Shareholders' Equity

25.55   The rate of return on common shareholders' equity can be disaggregated into several components in a manner similar to the disaggregation of the rate of return on assets. The rate of return on common shareholders might be disaggregated as follows:

$$\begin{array}{l} \text{Rate of Return} \\ \text{on Common} \\ \text{Shareholders'} \\ \text{Equity} \end{array} = \begin{array}{l} \text{Profit Margin Ratio} \\ \text{(after interest and} \\ \text{minority interest in} \\ \text{earnings, and after} \\ \text{preferred dividends)} \end{array} \times \begin{array}{l} \text{Total} \\ \text{Assets} \\ \text{Turnover} \\ \text{Ratio} \end{array} \times \begin{array}{l} \text{Leverage} \\ \text{Ratio} \end{array}$$

or, in terms of items seen in the financial statements:

$$\frac{\begin{array}{l}\text{Net Income} \\ - \\ \text{Dividends on} \\ \text{Preferred Shares}\end{array}}{\begin{array}{l}\text{Average Common} \\ \text{Shareholders'} \\ \text{Equity}\end{array}}$$

$$= \frac{\begin{array}{l}\text{Net Income} \\ - \\ \text{Dividends on} \\ \text{Preferred Shares}\end{array}}{\text{Revenues}} \times \frac{\text{Revenues}}{\begin{array}{l}\text{Average} \\ \text{Total} \\ \text{Assets}\end{array}} \times \frac{\begin{array}{l}\text{Average} \\ \text{Total} \\ \text{Assets} \\ \text{or} \\ \text{Equities}\end{array}}{\begin{array}{l}\text{Average} \\ \text{Common} \\ \text{Shareholders'} \\ \text{Equity}\end{array}} .$$

25.56   The profit margin ratio indicates the portion of the revenue dollar left over for the common shareholders after all operating costs have been covered and all claims of creditors, minority shareholders, and preferred shareholders have been subtracted. The total assets turnover, as discussed earlier, indicates the revenues generated from each dollar of assets. The leverage ratio indicates the extent to which capital (assets or total equities) have been provided by common shareholders. The larger is the leverage ratio, the smaller the portion of capital provided by common shareholders and the larger the proportion provided by creditors and preferred shareholders. Thus, the larger the leverage ratio, the greater will be the extent of leverage.

25.57   The disaggregation of the rate of return on common shareholders' equity ratio for International Corporation for 1981 is as follows:

$$\frac{\$165.2 - \$0}{.5[(\$1,924.1 - \$30.5) + (\$2,001.7 - \$16.6)]}$$

$$= \frac{\$165.2 - \$0}{\$5,928.6} \times \frac{\$5,928.6}{.5(\$4,813.6 + \$4,866.3)} \times \frac{.5(\$4,813.6 + \$4,866.3)}{.5[(\$1,924.1 - \$30.5) + (\$2,001.7 - \$16.6)]}$$

$$8.5\% = 2.8\% \times 1.2 \text{ times} \times 2.5.$$

The return on common shareholders' equity can be increased by improving the profit margin ratio, the assets turnover ratio, or the extent of financial leverage.

## Earnings per Share of Common Stock

25.58 Another measure of profitability is earnings per share of common stock. Chapter 22 discusses the calculation of earnings per share, including both primary and fully diluted earnings per share.

25.59 Earnings per share has been criticized as a measure of profitability because it does not consider the amount of assets or capital required to generate that level of earnings. Two firms with the same earnings and earnings per share will not be equally profitable if one of the firms requires twice the amount of assets or capital to generate those earnings than does the other firm.

25.60 Earnings per share amounts are also difficult to interpret when comparing firms. For example, assume that two firms have identical earnings, common shareholders' equity, and rates of return on common shareholders' equity. One firm may have a lower earnings per share simply because it has a larger number of shares outstanding (due perhaps to the use of a lower par value for its shares).

25.61 Earnings-per-share amounts are often compared with the market price of the stock. This is usually expressed as a *price-earnings ratio* (= market price per share/earnings per share). For example, the common stock of International Corporation is selling for $25 per share at the end of 1981. The price-earnings ratio, often called the P/E ratio, is 13.2 to 1 (= $25/$1.89). This ratio is often presented in tables of stock market prices and in financial periodicals. The relationship is sometimes expressed by saying that "the stock is selling at 13.2 times earnings."

## Measures of Short-Term Liquidity Risk

25.62 Investors or creditors whose claims will become payable in the near future are interested in the short-term liquidity or "nearness to cash" of a firm's assets. One tool for predicting whether or not cash will be available when the claims become due is a budget of cash receipts and disbursements for several months or quarters in the future. Such budgets are often prepared for management and used internally for planning cash requirements. Budgets of cash receipts and disbursements are not generally available for use by persons outside a firm. Investors must therefore use other tools in assessing short-term liquidity.

## Funds Flow from Operations

25.63 The statement of changes in financial position is one published source of information for assessing liquidity. The amount of working capital provided by operations indicates the extent to which the operating activities have generated sufficient working capital for the payment of dividends and the acquisition of fixed assets. The statement also discloses the extent to which additional financing has been used for those purposes. Appendix Exhibit A.3 at the back of the book indicates that working capital provided by continuing operations for International Corporation was relatively steady between 1980 and 1981 but decreased significantly from its level in 1979.

25.64 In some instances, a more restrictive definition of funds than working capital may provide more useful information about the impact of operations on liquidity. For example, operations may be a net provider of working capital but most of the increase in funds might be associated with an increase in accounts receivable and inventory. In this case, operations could be a net user, rather than provider, of cash. Additional insights into the impact of operations on liquidity can be obtained by calculating the amount of cash flow provided by operations.

25.65    Most published statements of changes in financial position define funds as working capital. To convert working capital provided by operations to cash flow provided by operations involves the following steps:

**1.** Begin with the amount of working capital provided by operations.

**2.** Add the amount of the change in current operating accounts (other than cash) that experienced a net credit change during the period. These are decreases in receivables, inventories, and prepayments, and increases in current operating liability accounts.

**3.** Subtract the amount of the change in current operating accounts that experienced a net debit change during the period. These are increases in receivables, inventories,

and prepayments, and decreases in current operating liability accounts.

**4.** The result is cash flow provided by operations. Exhibit 25.3 presents the analysis for International Corporation. Cash flow provided by operations was substantially larger than working capital provided by operations in 1981 and 1980. In addition, whereas working capital from operations decreased slightly between the two years, cash flow from operations increased significantly between 1980 and 1981. The improved cash flow from operations was due primarily to increased collections from customers (decrease in accounts receivable and increase in billings on uncompleted contracts). Operations provided significantly more cash in 1981 and 1980 than in 1979.

When converting working capital from operations to cash flow from operations, a    25.66

---

*Exhibit 25.3*
**Conversion of Working Capital Provided by Operations to Cash Flow Provided by Operations for International Corporation for the Years 1979–1981**

|  | 1981 | 1980 | 1979 |
|---|---|---|---|
| Working Capital Provided by Continuing Operations | $315.6 | $319.2 | $355.3 |
| Plus: |  |  |  |
| Decrease in Customers' Receivables | 104.8 | 61.1 | — |
| Decrease in Inventories and Cost of Uncompleted Contracts | 57.1 | 69.8 | — |
| Decrease in Prepaid and Other Current Assets | 73.8 | 1.9 | — |
| Increase in Accounts Payable | — | — | 54.3 |
| Increase in Income Taxes | 25.5 | — | 13.7 |
| Increase in Billings on Uncompleted Contracts | 227.7 | 155.7 | — |
| Increase in Other Current Liabilities | 92.2 | 100.3 | 36.6 |
| Less: |  |  |  |
| Increase in Customers' Receivables | — | — | (292.0) |
| Increase in Inventories and Cost of Uncompleted Contracts | — | — | (41.8) |
| Increase in Prepaid and Other Current Assets | — | — | (36.2) |
| Decrease in Accounts Payable | (31.5) | (12.5) | — |
| Decrease in Income Taxes | — | (80.9) | — |
| Decrease in Billings on Uncompleted Contracts | — | — | (75.2) |
| Cash Flow Provided by Continuing Operations | $865.2 | $614.6 | $ 14.7 |
| Working Capital Absorbed by Discontinued Operations | $ (13.4) | $ (81.0) | $ (15.2) |
| Plus: Increase in Estimated Future Costs—Discontinued Businesses | — | 46.4 | 35.3 |
| Less: Decrease in Estimated Future Costs—Discontinued Businesses | (14.2) | — | — |
| Cash Flow Absorbed by Discontinued Operations | $ (27.6) | $ (34.6) | $ (20.1) |
| Cash Flow Provided (Used) by Operations | $837.6 | $580.0 | $ (5.4) |

question arises regarding the treatment of short-term bank loans. Should changes in this current liability account be considered an *operating* source or use of cash? One view holds that short-term borrowing from banks is similar to purchases on account from suppliers. Both represent forms of short-term financing for operations. According to this view, changes in short-term bank loans should be added to or subtracted from working capital from operations, as appropriate, in deriving cash flow from operations. Another view holds that cash flow from operations should measure only the amount of cash derived from customers net of amounts paid to suppliers, employees, and other providers of goods or services to operations. According to this view, changes in bank loans are not an operating source or use of cash and should be excluded from the conversion of working capital to cash flow from operations. This second approach was followed in Exhibit 25.3. Similar questions arise regarding the treatment of changes in the Marketable Securities, Dividends Payable, and Current Maturities of Long-Term Debt accounts.

25.67    Several ratios are also useful in assessing the short-term liquidity of a firm. The most popular ones are the current ratio, the quick ratio, and the accounts receivable and inventory turnover ratios.

## Current Ratio

25.68    The *current ratio* is calculated by dividing current assets by current liabilities. It is commonly expressed as a ratio such as "2 to 1" or "2:1," meaning that current assets are twice as large as current liabilities. The current ratio of International Corporation on December 31, 1980 and 1981, is

$$\text{Current Ratio} = \frac{\text{Current Assets}}{\text{Current Liabilities}}.$$

December 31, 1980:  $\dfrac{\$2,839.5}{\$1,828.0} = 1.6:1.$

December 31, 1981:  $\dfrac{\$2,840.6}{\$2,023.4} = 1.4:1.$

This ratio is presumed to indicate the ability of the concern to meet its current obliga-

tions, and is therefore of particular significance to short-term creditors. Although an excess of current assets over current liabilities is generally considered desirable from the creditor's viewpoint, changes in the trend of the ratio may be difficult to interpret. For example, when the current ratio is larger than 1 to 1, an increase of equal amount in both current assets and current liabilities results in a decline in the ratio, whereas equal decreases result in an increased current ratio.

If a corporation has a particularly profitable year, the large current liability for income taxes may cause a decline in the current ratio. In a recession period, business is contracting, current liabilities are paid, and even though the current assets may be at a low point, the ratio will often go to high levels. In a boom period, just the reverse effect might occur. In other words, a very high current ratio may accompany unsatisfactory business conditions, whereas a falling ratio may accompany profitable operations.    25.69

Furthermore, the current ratio is susceptible to "window dressing"; that is, management can take deliberate steps to produce a financial statement that presents a better current ratio at the balance sheet date than the average or normal current ratio. For example, toward the close of a fiscal year normal purchases on account may be delayed. Or loans to officers, classified as noncurrent assets, may be collected and the proceeds used to reduce current liabilities. These actions may be taken so that the current ratio will appear as favorable as possible in the annual financial statements at the balance sheet date.    25.70

Although the current ratio is probably the most common ratio presented in statement analysis, there are limitations in its use as discussed above. Its trends are difficult to interpret and, if overemphasized, it can easily lead to undesirable business practices as well as misinterpretation of financial condition.    25.71

## Quick Ratio

A variation of the current ratio, usually known as the *quick ratio* or *acid-test ratio*,    25.72

is computed by including in the numerator of the fraction only those current assets that could be converted quickly into cash. The items customarily included are cash, marketable securities, and receivables, but it would be better to make a study of the facts in each case before deciding whether or not to include receivables and to exclude inventories. In some businesses the inventory of merchandise might be converted into cash more quickly than the receivables of other businesses.

25.73    Assuming that the accounts receivable of International Corporation are included but that inventory is excluded, the quick ratio on December 31, 1980 and 1981, is

$$\text{Quick Ratio} = \frac{\text{Cash, Marketable Securities, Accounts Receivable}}{\text{Current Liabilities}} .$$

December 31, 1980:    $\dfrac{\$1,384.9}{\$1,828.0} = .76$ .

December 31, 1981:    $\dfrac{\$1,516.9}{\$2,023.4} = .75$ .

Both the current ratio and quick ratio decreased between the two balance sheet dates.

## Accounts Receivable and Inventory Turnover Ratios

25.74    The rates of turnover of accounts receivable and inventory, discussed in the section on profitability, also provide information for assessing short-term liquidity. Recall that dividing 365 days by the accounts receivable and inventory turnover ratios indicates the average days that receivables and inventories are outstanding. The average days receivables were outstanding for International Corporation during 1981 was shown earlier to be 74.5 days. Thus, approximately half of the accounts receivable on the December 31, 1981, balance sheet should be collected by the middle of March 1982. The average days inventory was on hand during 1981 was 83.0 days. If this turnover rate continues in 1982, then approximately half of this inventory should be sold by the last week in March of 1982 and turned into cash on average about

75 days later (that is, the average collection period on receivables).

## Other Short-Term Liquidity Ratios

25.75    Several other ratios are sometimes used to assess short-term liquidity. One ratio relates cash *inflow* from operations to the average amount of current liabilities during a period. This ratio is intended to provide information similar to the current ratio but is not as susceptible to year-end window dressing. Another ratio sometimes encountered is the *defensive interval*.* It is calculated by dividing the average daily cash expenditures for operating expenses into a firm's most liquid assets, generally cash, marketable securities, and accounts receivable. The defensive interval is the number of days the firm could theoretically remain in business without additional sales or new financing. In studies of bond default and bankruptcy, this ratio has been found to be a good predictor.

25.76    Summarizing the analysis of International Corporation's short-term liquidity, we have noted the following.

**1.** Working capital and cash flow provided by operations have been positive during the last 2 years. Cash flow provided by operations has been significantly larger than working capital from operations and has been growing. The growth is due primarily to an increase in the rate of collections from customers.

**2.** The average collection period on receivables and the average days inventories are on hand have both decreased during the last 3 years, indicating that both receivables and inventory are nearer to being turned into cash than before.

**3.** The current ratio and quick ratio both decreased slightly between December 31, 1980, and December 31, 1981. Because of the limitations of these ratios discussed earlier and the indications of increased liquidity

---

*George H. Sorter and George Benston, "Appraising the Defensive Position of a Firm: The Interval Measure," *The Accounting Review* 35 (October 1960), pp. 633–640.

from operations, receivables, and inventories, it would be unwise to place too much emphasis on these current and quick ratio readings.

## Measures of Long-Term Solvency Risk

25.77  Measures of long-term solvency are used in assessing the firm's ability to meet interest and principal payments on long-term debt and similar obligations as they become due. If the payments cannot be made on time, the firm becomes *insolvent* and may have to be reorganized or liquidated.

25.78  Perhaps the best indicator of long-term solvency is a firm's ability to generate profits over a period of years. If a firm is profitable, it will either generate sufficient capital from operations or be able to obtain needed capital from creditors and owners. The measures of profitability discussed previously are therefore applicable for this purpose as well. Two other commonly used measures of long-term solvency are debt ratios and the number of times that interest charges are earned.

### Debt Ratios

25.79  There are several variations of the debt ratio, but the one most commonly encountered in financial analysis is the *long-term debt ratio*. It reports the portion of the firm's long-term capital that is furnished by debt holders. To calculate this ratio, divide total noncurrent liabilities by the sum of total noncurrent liabilities, minority interest in consolidated subsidiaries, and total shareholders' equity.

25.80  Another form of the debt ratio is the *debt-equity ratio*. To calculate the debt-equity ratio, divide total liabilities (current and noncurrent) by total equities (liabilities plus shareholders' equity = total assets).

25.81  The two forms of the debt ratio for International Corporation on December 31, 1980 and 1981, are shown in Exhibit 25.4. In general, the higher these ratios, the higher the likelihood that the firm may be unable to meet fixed interest and principal payments in the future. The decision for most firms is how much financial leverage, with its attendant risk, they can afford to assume. Funds obtained from issuing bonds or borrowing from a bank have a relatively low interest cost but require fixed, periodic payments that increase the likelihood of bankruptcy. In assessing the debt ratios, analysts customarily vary the standard in direct relation to the stability of the firm's earnings. The more stable the earnings, the higher the debt ratio that is considered acceptable or safe. The debt ratios of public utilities are customarily high, on the order of 60 to 70 percent. The stability of public utility earnings makes these ratios acceptable to many investors who would be dissatisfied with such large leverage for firms with less stable earnings.

25.82  Because several variations of the debt ratio appear in corporate annual reports, care in making comparisons of debt ratios among firms is necessary.

---

*Exhibit 25.4*
***International Corporation***
***Debt Ratios***

$$\frac{\text{Long-Term}}{\text{Debt Ratio}} = \frac{\text{Total Noncurrent Liabilities}}{\text{Total Noncurrent Liabilities} + \text{Minority Interest} + \text{Shareholders' Equity}}$$

Dec. 31, 1980: $\dfrac{\$1,002.8}{\$2,985.6} = 33.6\%$

Dec. 31, 1981: $\dfrac{\$\ 780.0}{\$2,842.9} = 27.4\%$

$$\text{Debt-Equity Ratio} = \frac{\text{Total Liabilities}}{\text{Total Liabilities} + \text{Minority Interest} + \text{Shareholders' Equity}}$$

Dec. 31, 1980: $\dfrac{\$1,828.0 + \$1,002.8}{\$4,813.6} = 58.8\%$

Dec. 31, 1981: $\dfrac{\$2,023.4 + \$\ 780.0}{\$4,866.3} = 57.6\%$

## Interest Coverage: Times Interest Charges Earned

25.83 Another measure of long-term solvency is the *number of times that interest charges are earned,* or covered. This ratio is calculated by dividing net income before interest and income tax expenses by interest expense. For International Corporation, the times interest earned ratios for 1979, 1980, and 1981 based on income from continuing operations are

$$\text{Times Interest Charges Earned} = \frac{\text{Net Income (from continuing operations) before Interest and Income Taxes}}{\text{Interest Expense}}.$$

$$1979: \quad \frac{\$183.5 + \$69.3 + \$145.9}{\$69.3} = 5.8 \text{ times}.$$

$$1980: \quad \frac{\$138.9 + \$111.3 + \$64.0}{\$111.3} = 2.8 \text{ times}.$$

$$1981: \quad \frac{\$178.6 + \$ 76.4 + \$93.8}{\$76.4} = 4.6 \text{ times}.$$

Thus, the decrease in bonded indebtedness (see Exhibit 25.4) during the 2-year period coupled with the growth in net income before interest and income taxes provided increasing coverage of the fixed interest charges. The coverage ratio appears to be returning to its 1979 level, however.

25.84 The purpose of this ratio is to indicate the relative protection of bondholders and to assess the probability that the firm will be forced into bankruptcy by a failure to meet required interest payments. If periodic repayments of principal on long-term liabilities are also required, the repayments might be included in the denominator of the ratio. Fixed lease and pension payments might also be included in the calculations. If so, the ratio would be described as the *number of times that fixed charges were earned,* or covered.

25.85 The times interest or fixed charges earned ratios can be criticized as measures for assessing long-term solvency because the ratios use earnings rather than cash flows in the numerator. Interest and other fixed payment obligations are paid with cash, and not with earnings. When the value of the ratio is relatively low (for example, two to three times), some measure of cash flows, such as cash flows from operations, may be preferable in the numerator.

## Other Analytical Tools

25.86 In addition to ratios, several other tools might be used in analyzing financial statements. *Trend statements* show the changes over time in various components of the fi-

*Exhibit 25.5*
### International Corporation
### Trend Income Statement

|  | 1978 | 1979 | 1980 | 1981 |
| --- | --- | --- | --- | --- |
| Revenues: | | | | |
| Sales | 100.0 | 112.4 | 128.5 | 129.9 |
| Equity in Income | 100.0 | 105.6 | −97.1 | 43.6 |
| Other | 100.0 | 98.7 | 109.4 | 78.1 |
| Expenses: | | | | |
| Cost of Goods Sold | 100.0 | 110.5 | 125.6 | 125.0 |
| Selling, Administrative, and General | 100.0 | 115.2 | 132.8 | 146.3 |
| Depreciation | 100.0 | 107.9 | 115.7 | 120.7 |
| Interest | 100.0 | 125.6 | 120.3 | 82.6 |
| Income Taxes | 100.0 | 107.3 | 118.7 | 174.1 |
| Minority Interest | 100.0 | 105.6 | 112.8 | 84.8 |
| Income from Continuing Operations | 100.0 | 108.7 | 119.4 | 153.5 |

nancial statements relative to some base year. Exhibit 25.5 presents a trend income statement for International Corporation using the amounts for various revenues and expenses for 1978 (amounts not provided) as the base.

25.87 The trend income statement indicates that selling prices have been increased in line with the increases in cost of goods sold. Selling, general, and administrative expenses, however, have increased at a faster rate than the increases in selling prices. In the last 2 years, interest expense has decreased significantly and income taxes have increased significantly.

25.88 Trend statements must be interpreted cautiously. Relatively small *dollar changes* in certain items from one year to the next can result in significant changes in the trend index amount if the dollar base is small. For example, the minority interest in net income decreased from $3.3 million to $2.5 million between 1980 and 1981. The trend index decreased from 112.8 to 84.8. Given the insignificance of the minority interest amount relative to other revenues and expenses for International Corporation, this change would probably not be considered important.

25.89 Another analytical tool is *common-size statements*. In common-size statements, all amounts for a given period or point in time are stated as a proportion of some common amount. For example, a common-size income statement (such as that presented in Exhibit 25.1) might express all items as a percentage of sales. A common-size balance sheet might express all items as a percentage of total assets or total equities. A common-size statement of changes in financial position might state all items as a percentage of total sources or total uses of funds.

25.90 Exhibit 25.6 presents a common-size condensed balance sheet for International Corporation as of December 31, 1980, and December 31, 1981. Each balance sheet component is expressed as a percentage of total assets or equities. There are no major shifts in the asset mix between the two years. On the equities side, there is a shift out of long-term and into short-term debt.

25.91 Changes in the percentage amounts in the common-size statement from one period to the next must also be interpreted cautiously. The percentage amount can change even if there is no change in the dollar amount of an item. For example, cash may be $100,000 at the beginning and end of an accounting pe-

*Exhibit 25.6*
**International Corporation**
**Common-Size Balance Sheets**

| | December 31, 1980 | December 31, 1981 |
|---|---|---|
| **ASSETS** | | |
| Current Assets | 59.0% | 58.4% |
| Investments | 4.7 | 5.9 |
| Estimated Realizable Value—Discontinued Businesses | 4.2 | 2.0 |
| Plant and Equipment—Net | 27.0 | 28.4 |
| Other Assets | 5.1 | 5.3 |
| Total | 100.0% | 100.0% |
| **LIABILITIES AND SHAREHOLDERS' EQUITY** | | |
| Current Liabilities | 38.0% | 41.6% |
| Noncurrent Liabilities | 20.8 | 16.0 |
| Minority Interest | 1.2 | 1.3 |
| Shareholders' Equity | 40.0 | 41.1 |
| Total | 100.0% | 100.0% |

riod. If total assets increase during the period because equipment is acquired under a long-term mortgage arrangement, the proportion of total assets comprised of cash will go down. The decreased percentage does not necessarily imply that the firm is less liquid.

## Interpreting the Results of Financial Statement Analysis

25.92  The results of ratio, trend, and common-size statement analysis are difficult to interpret without some standard or base for comparison. Several common standards for comparison are discussed below.

### Time-Series Analysis

25.93  One approach is to compare various ratio amounts with the corresponding amounts for the same firm from earlier periods. This is the approach followed throughout this chapter in interpreting the ratios for International Corporation. The principal advantage of this approach is that it permits the analyst to focus on *changes* in the profitability, liquidity, and solvency of a firm, given its particular set of operating strategies and policies, product lines, production techniques, accounting methods, and so forth. The principal weakness of this approach is that economy-wide and industry factors are not explicitly taken into consideration in interpreting the ratios. For example, a decrease in the rate of return on assets from 8 percent to 6 percent for a particular firm might be viewed as an unhealthy sign. However, if it is recognized that the economy was in a recession during the period and most other firms found their rates of return cut in half, then the 25-percent decrease in rate of return would be interpreted differently.

25.94  The Securities and Exchange Commission requires that the annual report to shareholders and the 10–K report submitted to the SEC include a discussion by management of the reasons for important changes in a firm's profitability, liquidity, and capital structure.* These explanations are helpful in interpreting the results of a time-series analysis.

### Cross-Section Analysis

25.95  A second approach is to compare various ratio amounts with similar amounts for the same time period for other firms in the industry. There are several sources of standard, or average, industry ratios, including those published by Dun & Bradstreet, Robert Morris Associates, Prentice-Hall, and the Federal Trade Commission. The major strength of using standard industry ratios is that a firm is compared with its competitors operating in similar input and output markets. Thus, economy-wide and industry factors affecting all firms will impact the ratios of each of the firms. The concern in interpreting the performance of a particular firm is whether it did better, about the same, or worse than its competitors.

25.96  There are two major weaknesses of using standard industry ratios. First, firms seldom do business in only one industry. Most large firms are diversified. International Corporation, for example, does business in power systems, industry products, and broadcasting. (See Note 21 to International Corporation's financial statements, Exhibit A.4.) The rates of return and risk from these activities differ. The amount of capital required for these activities also differs. Yet International Corporation is classified in only one industry category in calculating average industry ratios. If other firms classified in that industry are also diversified but diversified into different product lines, then the average ratios lose meaning.

25.97  A second weakness of average industry ratios is that no adjustments are made for differences in accounting principles used by various firms. We have seen in earlier chapters that the choice of inventory cost-flow assumption (FIFO versus LIFO) and depreciation method and the treatment of pensions and deferred taxes can have a signifi-

*Accounting Series Release No. 279, SEC (September 1980).

cant impact on the financial statements. Unless these and other differences in accounting methods are filtered out, comparisons of financial statement ratios may be misleading. The next section discusses techniques for adjusting financial statements for differences in accounting principles.

## Adjustments for Accounting Principles

25.98 Published financial statements and notes in recent years have increasingly included information that permits the analyst to adjust the reported amounts for differences between firms in the accounting principles used. This section discusses adjustments for the cost-flow assumption (FIFO versus LIFO), the depreciation method, and the recognition of certain liabilities (pensions and deferred taxes).

### FIFO versus LIFO Cost-Flow Assumption

25.99 Chapter 9 points out that no accounting method for inventories based on historical cost can simultaneously report current data in both the income statement and the balance sheet. If a firm reports current prices in the income statement under LIFO, then its balance sheet amount for ending inventory contains *very* old data. The SEC is concerned that readers of financial statements not be misled by out-of-date information. It requires firms using LIFO to disclose in notes to the financial statements the amounts by which LIFO inventories would have increased if they had been recorded at current cost. From this disclosure and the inventory equation, we can compute what a LIFO firm's income would have been had it been using FIFO instead. In this way, the financial statements of firms using LIFO can be made more comparable with the financial statements of firms using FIFO.

25.100 Notes 1 and 9 to the financial statements of International Corporation in Appendix A state, in part:

The cost of the inventories of the consolidated companies is calculated principally by the LIFO method. . . . The replacement cost over the cost of inventories valued on the LIFO basis was approximately $370 million at December 31, 1981, and $340 million at December 31, 1980.

International Corporation's beginning inven-

---

*Exhibit 25.7*
**International Corporation Inventory Data from Financial Statements and Footnotes**

(Amounts shown in boldface are given in International Corporation's financial statements. Other amounts are computed as indicated.)

| | Dollar Amounts in Millions | | |
|---|---|---|---|
| | **LIFO Cost-Flow Assumption (Actually Used)** + | **Excess of FIFO over LIFO Amount** = | **FIFO Cost-Flow Assumption (Hypothetical)** |
| Beginning Inventory | **$1,073.0**[a] | **$340.0** | $1,413.0 |
| Purchases | 4,614.8[a] | 0 | 4,614.8 |
| Cost of Goods Available for Sale | $5,687.8 | **$340.0** | $6,027.8 |
| Less Ending Inventory | **1,040.6** | 370.0 | 1,410.6 |
| Cost of Goods Sold | **$4,647.2** | $ (30.0)[b] | $4,617.2 |

Order of computation of amounts not presented in International Corporation's financial statements:

[a]Purchases = Cost of Goods Sold + Ending Inventory − Beginning Inventory.
  $4,614.8  =  $4,647.2  +  $1,040.6  −  $1,073.0.
[b]$(30.0) = $340.0 − $370.0.

tories under LIFO (see Exhibit A.2) amounted to $1,073.0 million, its ending inventory amounted to $1,040.6 million, and its cost of goods sold totaled $4,647.2 million. Exhibit 25.7 demonstrates the calculation of cost of goods sold on a FIFO basis. Recall from the inventory equation,

$$\text{Beginning Inventory} + \text{Purchases} - \text{Ending Inventory} = \text{Cost of Goods Sold}.$$

FIFO's higher beginning inventory increases reported cost of goods available for sale and the cost of goods sold by $340 million, relative to LIFO. FIFO's higher ending inventory decreases cost of goods sold by $370 million, relative to LIFO. Hence, the cost of goods sold is $370 million minus $340 million, or $30 million less under FIFO than it was under LIFO. International Corporation's pretax income would be $30 million more under FIFO than under the LIFO flow assumption actually used.

25.101    To examine the impact of the restatement to a FIFO flow assumption on various profitability ratios, it is often helpful to begin by expressing the effect of the change on the financial statements in journal entry form. If FIFO had been used for both book and tax purposes rather than LIFO, the balance sheet at the beginning of the year, January 1, 1981, would have differed as follows:

| | | |
|---|---|---|
| Inventories | 340,000,000 | |
|   Retained Earnings (.54 × $340 million) | | 183,600,000 |
|   Cash and Other Assets (.46 × $340 million) | | 156,400,000 |

Beginning inventories would have been larger by $340 million. Cumulative net income for all years prior to 1981 would have been higher by $340 million times the complement of the income tax rate. If the income tax rate is 46 percent, then cumulative net income and retained earnings would have been $183.6 million (= .54 × $340 million) higher. By using FIFO, rather than LIFO, for income tax purposes, $156.4 million (= .46 × $340 million) additional taxes would have been paid. Because the cash saved has likely been invested in other assets, the credit for taxes paid cannot be made entirely to Cash.

25.102    The entries to recognize the increase in the excess of FIFO over LIFO inventory amounts and to record the income effects are as follows:

| | | |
|---|---|---|
| Inventories | 30,000,000 | |
|   Cost of Goods Sold | | 30,000,000 |

To restate ending inventories to a FIFO basis and restate the cost of goods sold for 1981.

---

Exhibit 25.8
**Rates of Return for International Corporation for 1981 Using LIFO and Using FIFO**

| | LIFO Cost-Flow Assumption (Actually Used) | FIFO Cost-Flow Assumption (Hypothetical) |
|---|---|---|
| Rate of Return on Assets | $= \dfrac{\$\ 222.4^a}{\$4,691.0}$ $= 4.7\%$ | $= \dfrac{\$222.4 + \$30.0 - \$13.8}{\$4,691.0 + .5(\$340.0 - \$370.0) - .5(\$156.4 + \$170.2)}$ $= 4.9\%$ |
| Rate of Return on Common Shareholders' Equity | $= \dfrac{\$\ 165.2^b}{\$1,939.4}$ $= 8.5\%$ | $= \dfrac{\$165.2 + \$30.0 - \$13.8}{\$1.934.4 + .5(\$183.6 + \$199.8)}$ $= 8.5\%$ |

ª See paragraph 25.31.
ᵇ See paragraph 25.48.

| | | |
|---|---|---|
| Income Tax Expense ....... | 13,800,000 | |
| Cash or Income Tax Payable ............. | | 13,800,000 |

To recognize additional income taxes on 1981 earnings; $13.8 million = .46 × $30 million.

| | | |
|---|---|---|
| Cost of Goods Sold ........ | 30,000,000 | |
| Income Tax Expense ... | | 13,800,000 |
| Retained Earnings ..... | | 16,200,000 |

To close the temporary income statement accounts to Retained Earnings.

25.103 Exhibit 25.8 presents the rate of return on assets and the rate of return on common shareholders' equity of International Corporation for 1981 based on the LIFO cost-flow assumption actually used and the hypothetical amounts if FIFO had been used. The rate of return on assets is slightly higher under FIFO than under LIFO. The return on common shareholders' equity is approximately the same under the two cost-flow assumptions. Although the ratios for International Corporation are not dramatically different when adjustments are made for the cost-flow assumptions used, the differences for some firms are often much larger.

## Depreciation Methods

25.104 Most firms calculate depreciation using the Accelerated Cost Recovery System (ACRS) for tax purposes in order to minimize the present value of income tax payments. For financial reporting, most firms use the straight-line depreciation method. However, some firms use the double declining balance or sum-of-the-year's-digits depreciation method for financial reporting. Thus, published financial statements are based on accelerated depreciation methods for some firms and the straight-line method for other firms. For capital-intensive firms with large investments in depreciable assets, these differences in depreciation methods can have a significant impact on the analysis of these firms' profitability.

25.105 Because most firms take the maximum depreciation deductions allowed by law on their returns, the analyst can achieve comparability of income statements across firms by converting the depreciation charges reported in the financial statements to the amounts claimed on the tax return. The resulting amounts of depreciation may not be "right" in some sense of measuring the disappearance of long-term assets' future benefits, but will be comparable from one firm to another.

25.106 Firms that use an ACRS depreciation method for tax and some other method for book are required to recognize deferred taxes for the timing difference between taxable income and pretax book income. The notes to the financial statements will usually indicate the amount of deferred taxes provided for timing differences relating to depreciation. For example, Note 5 to the financial statements of International Corporation indicates that deferred taxes of $21.3 million were provided during 1981 relating to depreciation timing differences. With this information, it is possible to estimate the amount of the excess of depreciation claimed on the tax return over the amount reported in the financial statements. The $21.3 million deferred tax amount is equal to the timing difference for depreciation multiplied by the marginal tax rate. Because the marginal tax rate for most corporations is 46 percent, the excess of tax over book depreciation is estimated to be $46.3 million (= $21.3 million/.46). Multiplying this amount by the complement of the tax rate indicates the decrease in net income from using ACRS depreciation rather than straight-line depreciation for financial reporting: $25.0 million = $46.3 million × (1.00 − .46). Net income for 1981 for International Corporation would have been $140.2 million (= $165.2 million − $25.0 million) if ACRS depreciation had been used for financial reporting, as compared to $165.2 million when the straight-line method is used.

25.107 Computing the effect of using ACRS depreciation on the balance sheet is more difficult. To do so requires knowing the proportion of the Deferred Income Taxes account on the balance sheet that relates to depreciation timing differences. Such information is seldom disclosed. As a consequence, the adjustments to reported amounts for differences between firms in the depreciation method used must generally focus on the income statement effect.

## Recognition of Supplemental Actuarial Value for Pension Plan

25.108    Chapter 19 points out that generally accepted accounting principles do not require the recognition as a liability of the supplemental actuarial value of a pension plan. Because the notes to the financial statements disclose the amount of the supplemental actuarial value, the analyst can treat the obligation as a liability.

25.109    Note 4 to the financial statements of International Corporation states, in part:

Unrecognized supplemental actuarial value at December 31, 1980, was estimated at $587 million. . . . Based on the latest actuarial valuation, which recognizes the increased pension liabilities resulting from wage and salary improvements and increases for retirees effective July 1, 1981, unrecognized supplemental actuarial value approximates $616 million . . . at December 31, 1981.

One entry to recognize the supplemental actuarial value on December 31, 1980, is

| | | |
|---|---|---|
| Retained Earnings (.54 × $587 million) | 316,980,000 | |
| Prepaid Income Taxes (.46 × $587 million) | 270,020,000 | |
| Pension Liability | | 587,000,000 |

The debit to Retained Earnings* for $316,980,000 reflects the additional pension expense, net of income taxes, that would have been recognized in years prior to 1981 if the supplemental actuarial value had been recognized as a liability. For income tax purposes, pension expense cannot be deducted in calculating taxable income until the supplemental actuarial value is funded. Thus, the recognition of pension expense for book purposes earlier than for tax purposes cre-

---

*Chapter 19 discusses the merit of debiting an asset account for this adjustment. See paragraph 19.36.

ates a timing difference. Because book income is less than taxable income, income taxes will be prepaid.†

25.110    The entry made to recognize the increase in the supplemental actuarial value during 1981 is

| | | |
|---|---|---|
| Pension Expense (.54 × $29 million) | 15,660,000 | |
| Prepaid Income Taxes (.46 × $29 million) | 13,340,000 | |
| Pension Liability | | 29,000,000 |

25.111    Exhibit 25.9 shows the calculation of the rates of return on assets and on common shareholders' equity, and the debt/equity ratio based on the reported amounts for International Corporation and the amounts that would have been reported if the supplemental actuarial value had been recognized as a liability. The rates of return are less and the debt/equity ratios have increased significantly.

## Treatment of Deferred Income Taxes

25.112    As Chapters 15 and 20 discuss, considerable controversy exists regarding whether deferred taxes should be provided for timing differences between book and taxable income, particularly when the likelihood of a reversal of the timing differences is low. In some cases, it may be considered desirable to eliminate the effects of deferred tax accounting on the financial statements.

25.113    The balance sheet of International Corporation in Exhibit A.2 discloses the following relating to deferred income taxes:

| | December 31, | |
|---|---|---|
| | **1981** | **1980** |
| Deferred Current Income Taxes | $ 53.6 | $ 31.1 |
| Deferred Noncurrent Income Taxes | 117.5 | 97.3 |
| Total | $171.1 | $128.4 |

---

†Most prepayments, such as for rent or insurance, are recognized as an expense as the rental or insurance services are consumed. Prepaid income taxes are recognized as an expense in future periods when the timing differences that gave rise to the prepaid taxes reverse.

*Exhibit 25.9*
**Rates of Return and Debt/Equity Ratios for International Corporation Assuming Supplemental Actuarial Value Was[a] and Was Not Recognized as a Liability**

| | | Supplemental Actuarial Value Not Recognized | | Supplemental Actuarial Value Recognized |
|---|---|---|---|---|
| Rate of Return on Assets | = | $\dfrac{\$\ 222.4}{\$4,691.0}$ | = | $\dfrac{\$222.4 - \$15.7}{\$4,691.0 + .5(\$270.0 + \$283.4)}$ |
| | = | 4.7% | | = 4.1% |
| Rate of Return on Common Shareholders' Equity | = | $\dfrac{\$\ 165.2}{\$1,939.4}$ | = | $\dfrac{\$165.2 - \$15.7}{\$1,939.4 - .5(\$317.0 + \$332.6)}$ |
| | = | 8.5% | | = 6.6% |
| Debt/Equity Ratio December 31, 1980 | = | $\dfrac{\$2,830.8}{\$4,813.6}$ | = | $\dfrac{\$2,830.8 + \$587.0}{\$4,813.6 - \$317.0}$ |
| | = | 58.8% | | = 76.0% |
| December 31, 1981 | = | $\dfrac{\$2,803.4}{\$4,866.3}$ | = | $\dfrac{\$2,803.4 + \$616.0}{\$4,866.3 - \$332.6}$ |
| | = | 57.6% | | = 75.4% |

[a]Corresponding debits made in part to Retained Earnings account.

Note 5 to the financial statements indicates that deferred income tax expense for 1981 was $43.8 million. The entry to eliminate the effects of deferred tax accounting as of December 31, 1980, is

Deferred Current Income Taxes ........ 31.1
Deferred Noncurrent Income Taxes .... 97.3
    Retained Earnings ............... 128.4

Because the deferred tax provision in years prior to 1981 reduced net income, the reversal of the effects of deferred tax accounting increases retained earnings.

25.114    The entries to eliminate the effects on the amounts for 1981 are

Deferred Current Income Taxes ........ 22.5
Deferred Noncurrent Income Taxes .... 20.2
Other Accounts ...................... 1.1
    Income Tax Expense ............. 43.8

The deferred tax provision of $43.8 million during 1981 does not reconcile precisely with the change in the current and noncurrent deferred tax liability accounts. Interna-

tional Corporation apparently has a minor amount of prepaid income taxes included among other assets. Based on the information provided, it is not possible to eliminate the effects of prepaid taxes from total assets. In any case, the amount involved is probably small.

25.115    Exhibit 25.10 shows the calculation of the rates of return on assets and on common shareholders' equity and the debt/equity ratio based on the reported amounts for International Corporation and the amounts that would have been reported if deferred taxes had not been recorded. The rates of return are larger and the debt/equity ratios are smaller.

## Summary of Adjustments

25.116    The adjustments discussed above for the cost-flow assumption and the treatment of pensions and deferred taxes are illustrative of the transformations that can be made to

*Exhibit 25.10*
**Rates of Return and Debt/Equity
Ratios for International Corporation
Assuming Deferred Taxes Were and
Were Not Recognized**

|  | Deferred Taxes Recognized | Deferred Taxes Not Recognized |
|---|---|---|
| Rate of Return on Assets | $= \dfrac{\$\ 222.4}{\$4,691.0}$ $= 4.7\%$ | $= \dfrac{\$222.4 + \$43.8}{\$4,691.0}$ $= 5.6\%$ |
| Rate of Return on Common Shareholders' Equity | $= \dfrac{\$\ 165.2}{\$1,939.4}$ $= 8.5\%$ | $= \dfrac{\$165.2 + \$43.8}{\$1,939.4 + .5(\$128.4 + \$172.2)}$ $= 9.96\%$ |
| Debt/Equity Ratio December 31, 1980 | $= \dfrac{\$2,830.8}{\$4,813.6}$ $= 58.8\%$ | $= \dfrac{\$2,830.8 - \$128.4}{\$4,813.6 + \$128.4}$ $= 54.7\%$ |
| December 31, 1981 | $= \dfrac{\$2,803.4}{\$4,866.3}$ $= 57.6\%$ | $= \dfrac{\$2,830.4 - \$171.1}{\$4,866.3 + \$172.2}$ $= 52.2\%$ |

reported data.* Similar adjustments might be made for the depreciation method used, the recognition of certain long-term leases, or other items. Empirical research on the efficiency of capital markets suggests that investors do filter out the effects of differences in accounting principles when using reported financial statement data.†

---

*More adjustments of this sort are illustrated for the thirty companies in the Dow-Jones Industrials in Daniel A. Lasman and Roman L. Weil, "Adjusting the Debt-Equity Ratio," *Financial Analysts Journal* 34 (Sept./Oct. 1978), pp. 49–58. An analysis of the effects of alternative accounting principles on various financial statement ratios is presented in James P. Dawson, Peter M. Neupert, and Clyde P. Stickney, "Restating Financial Statements for Alternative GAAP's: Is It Worth the Effort?" *Financial Analysts Journal* 36 (Nov./Dec. 1980), pp. 38–46.

†For a review of the theory of efficient markets and its implications for accounting, see Nicholas J. Gonedes and Nicholas Dopuch, "Capital Market Equilibrium, Information-Production, and Selected Accounting Techniques: Theoretical Framework and Review of Empirical Work," *Studies on Financial Accounting Objectives: 1974,* Supplement to Vol. 12, *Journal of Accounting Research,* pp. 48–129.

# Limitations of Financial Statement Analysis

The analytical computations discussed in this chapter have a number of limitations that should be kept in mind by anyone preparing or using them. Several of the more important limitations are the following:   25.117

**1.** The ratios and other analytical tools are based on financial statement data and are therefore subject to the same criticisms as the financial statements (for example, use of acquisition cost rather than current replacement cost or net realizable value; the latitude permitted firms in selecting from among various generally accepted accounting principles).

**2.** Changes in many ratios are highly associated, or correlated, with each other. For example, the changes in the current ratio and quick ratio between two different times are often in the same direction and approximately proportional. It is therefore not necessary to compute all the ratios to assess a particular factor.

**3.** When comparing the size of a ratio between periods for the same firm, one must recognize conditions that have changed between the periods being compared (for example, different product lines or geographical markets served, changes in economic conditions, changes in prices).

**4.** When comparing ratios of a particular firm with those of similar firms, one must recognize differences between the firms (for example, use of different methods of accounting, differences in the method of operations, type of financing, and so on).

*Exhibit 25.11*
**Summary of Financial Statement Ratios**

| Ratio | Numerator | Denominator |
|---|---|---|
| Rate of Return on Assets | Net Income[a] + Interest Expense[b] (net of tax savings) | Average Total Assets during the Period |
| Profit Margin Ratio (before interest effects) | Net Income[a] + Interest Expense[b] (net of tax savings) | Revenues |
| Various Expense Ratios | Various Expenses | Revenues |
| Total Assets Turnover Ratio | Revenues | Average Total Assets during the Period |
| Accounts Receivable Turnover Ratio | Net Sales on Accounts | Average Accounts Receivable during the Period |
| Inventory Turnover Ratio | Cost of Goods Sold | Average Inventory during the Period |
| Plant Asset Turnover Ratio | Sales | Average Plant Assets during the Period |
| Rate of Return on Common Stock Equity | Net Income[a] − Preferred Stock Dividends | Average Common Shareholders' Equity during the Period |
| Profit Margin (after interest, minority interest in earnings, and preferred dividends) | Net Income[a] − Preferred Stock Dividends | Revenues |
| Leverage Ratio | Average Total Assets or Equities during the Period | Average Common Shareholders' Equity during the Period |
| Earnings per Share of Stock[c] | Net Income − Preferred Stock Dividends | Weighted Average Number of Common Shares Outstanding during the Period |
| Current Ratio | Current Assets | Current Liabilities |
| Quick or Acid-Test Ratio | Highly Liquid Assets (ordinarily, cash, marketable securities, and receivables)[d] | Current Liabilities |
| Long-Term Debt Ratio | Total Noncurrent Liabilities | Total Noncurrent Liabilities Plus Shareholders' Equity |
| Debt-Equity Ratio | Total Liabilities | Total Equities (liabilities plus shareholders' equity) |
| Times Interest Charges Earned | Net Income before Interest and Income Taxes | Interest Expense |

[a]If a firm has income or loss from discontinued operations or extraordinary gains or losses, it may be desirable to use only income from continuing operations in the numerator.

[b]If a consolidated subsidiary is not owned entirely by the parent corporation, the minority interest share of earnings must also be added back to net income.

[c]This calculation can be more complicated when there are convertible securities, options, or warrants outstanding and where there is income from discontinued operations or extraordinary gains or losses.

[d]Receivables could conceivably be excluded for some firms and inventories included for others. Such refinements are seldom employed in practice.

25.118 Results of financial statement analyses cannot be used by themselves as direct indications of good or poor management. Such analyses merely indicate areas that might be investigated further. For example, a decrease in the turnover of raw materials inventory, ordinarily considered to be an undesirable trend, may reflect the accumulation of scarce materials that will keep the plant operating at full capacity during shortages when competitors have been forced to restrict operations or to close down. Ratios derived from financial statements must be combined with an investigation of other facts before valid conclusions can be drawn.

## Summary

25.119 Exhibit 25.11 summarizes the calculation of the ratios discussed in this chapter.

25.120 We began this chapter by raising the question: Should you invest your inheritance in a savings account or in the shares of common stock of International Corporation? Our analysis of International Corporation showed that it has been profitable in the last 2 years, has reduced its long-term debt, and has generated significant amounts of cash from operations. Additional analysis of information in the footnotes to the financial statements would reveal useful information about International Corporation's effective income tax rate, maturity structure of long-term debt, segment profitability, and other factors of interest. In addition to such analyses, at least three other inputs are necessary before making the investment decisions. First, you must consider other sources of information besides the financial statements to determine if relevant information for projecting rates of return or for assessing risk needs to be considered. Second, you must decide your attitude toward, or willingness to assume, risk. Third, you must decide if you think the stock market price of the shares makes them an attractive purchase.* It is at this stage in the investment decision that the analysis becomes particularly subjective.

---

*Other important factors cannot be discussed here; but are in finance texts. Perhaps the most important question of all is how a particular investment fits in with the investor's entire portfolio. Modern research suggests that the suitability of a potential investment depends more on the attributes of the other components of an investment portfolio and the risk attitude of the investor than it does on the attributes of the potential investment itself.

## Questions and Short Cases

**25.1** Review the meaning of the following concepts or terms discussed in this chapter.

a. Risk and return.
b. Profitability.
c. Short-term liquidity risk.
d. Long-term solvency risk.
e. Time-series analysis.
f. Cross-section analysis.
g. Rate of return on assets.
h. Profit margin and expense ratios.
i. Total assets turnover ratio.
j. Accounts receivable turnover ratio.
k. Inventory turnover ratio.
l. Plant asset turnover ratio.
m. Rate of return on common shareholders' equity.

n. Operating leverage.
o. Financial leverage.
p. Leverage ratio.
q. Earnings per share (primary and fully diluted).
r. Price-earnings ratio.
s. Working capital versus cash flow provided by operations.
t. Current ratio.
u. Quick ratio.
v. Long-term debt ratio.
w. Debt/equity ratio.
x. Times interest charges earned ratio.

**25.2** Modern financial theory suggests that investment alternatives should be assessed in terms of expected return and the uncertainty or risk associated with that return. For the following

personal investments, indicate how expected return might be measured, and suggest some of the factors affecting the risk or uncertainty of that return:
a. Rental of an apartment under a 3-year rental agreement.
b. Purchase of an automobile for cash.
c. Purchase of a house under a 20-year mortgage agreement.

25.3 Under what circumstances will the rate of return on the common stock equity be more than the rate of return on assets? Under what circumstances will it be less?

25.4 A company president recently stated: "The operations of our company are such that we can use effectively only a small amount of financial leverage." Explain.

25.5 In calculating the inventory turnover, when might the use of the average of the beginning and ending inventories lead to an inaccurate result?

25.6 It has been suggested that for any given firm at a particular time there is an optimal inventory turnover ratio. Explain.

25.7 A firm's working capital from operations has increased steadily with net income over the last 3 years. Cash flow from operations has decreased each year, however. What might account for this result?

25.8 Describe several factors that might limit the comparability of a firm's current ratio over several periods.

25.9 Describe several factors that might limit the comparability of one firm's current ratio with that of another firm in the same industry.

25.10 Illustrate with amounts how a decrease in working capital can accompany an increase in the current ratio.

25.11 In discussing objectivity, verifiability, and uncertainty of amounts reported on the balance sheet, a noted accountant—Robert K. Elliott—once remarked that there were only two numbers on the balance sheet about which there is absolutely no uncertainty. The two numbers Elliott had in mind are the date and the number of common shares outstanding. Elliott had in mind uncertainty about the current present value of the future benefits of assets and the current present value of payments to be made to discharge liabilities. Explain why there is uncertainty about the amounts recorded for each of the following accounts:
a. Cash.
b. Accounts Receivable.
c. Accounts Payable.
d. Taxes Payable.
e. Withheld Income Taxes Payable.

25.12 (Adapted from CMA Examination.) Thorpe Company is a wholesale distributor of professional equipment and supplies. The company's sales have averaged about $900,000 annually for the 3-year period 1979–1981. The firm's total assets at the end of 1981 amounted to $850,000.

The president of Thorpe Company has asked the controller to prepare a report that summarizes the financial aspects of the company's operations for the past 3 years. This report will be presented to the Board of Directors at their next meeting.

In addition to comparative financial statements, the controller has decided to present a number of relevant financial ratios that can assist in the identification and interpretation of trends. At the request of the controller, the accounting staff has calculated the following ratios for the 3-year period 1979–1981.

| | 1979 | 1980 | 1981 |
|---|---|---|---|
| Current Ratio .......................................... | 2.00 | 2.13 | 2.18 |
| Acid-Test (Quick) Ratio ................................. | 1.20 | 1.10 | 0.97 |
| Accounts Receivable Turnover .......................... | 9.72 | 8.57 | 7.13 |
| Inventory Turnover ..................................... | 5.25 | 4.80 | 3.80 |
| Sales to Fixed Assets (Fixed Asset Turnover) ............ | 1.75 | 1.88 | 1.99 |
| Sales as a Percent of 1978 Sales ...................... | 1.00 | 1.03 | 1.06 |
| Gross Margin Percentage ............................... | 40.0 | 38.6 | 38.5 |
| Net Income to Sales ................................... | 7.8% | 7.8% | 8.0% |
| Return on Total Assets ................................ | 8.5% | 8.6% | 8.7% |
| Return on Shareholders' Equity ........................ | 15.1% | 14.6% | 14.1% |
| Percent of Total Debt to Total Assets ................... | 44.0% | 41.0% | 38.0% |
| Percent of Long-Term Debt to Total Assets .............. | 25.0% | 22.0% | 19.0% |

In the preparation of the report, the controller has decided first to examine the financial ratios independently of any other data to determine if the ratios themselves reveal any significant trends over the 3-year period.

a. The current ratio is increasing while the acid-test (quick) ratio is decreasing. Using the ratios provided, identify and explain the contributing factor(s) for this apparently divergent trend.

b. In terms of the ratios provided, what conclusion(s) can be drawn regarding the company's use of financial leverage during the period 1979–1981?

c. Using the ratios provided, what conclusion(s) can be drawn regarding the company's net investment in plant and equipment?

25.13   (Adapted from CPA Examination.) As the CPA responsible for an "opinion" audit engagement, you are requested by the client to provide, at the earliest possible date, some key ratios based on the final figures appearing on the comparative financial statements. This information is to be used to convince creditors that the client business is solvent and to support the use of going-concern valuation procedures in the financial statements. The client wishes to save time by concentrating on only these key data.

The data requested and the computations taken from the financial statements follow:

| | Last Year | This Year |
|---|---|---|
| Current Ratio ........................................... | 2.0:1 | 2.5:1 |
| Quick (Acid-Test) Ratio ................................. | 1.2:1 | .7:1 |
| Property, Plant, and Equipment to Owners' Equity .............. | 2.3:1 | 2.6.1 |
| Sales to Owners' Equity ................................. | 2.8:1 | 2.5:1 |
| Net Income ............................................ | Down 10% | Up 30% |
| Earnings per Common Share ............................. | $2.40 | $3.12 |
| Book Value per Common Share ........................... | Up 8% | Up 5% |

a. The client asks that you prepare a list of brief comments stating how each of these items supports the solvency and going-concern potential of the business. The client wishes to use these comments to support a presentation of data to creditors. You are to prepare the comments as requested, giving the implications and the limitations of each item separately and then the collective inference one may draw from them about the client's solvency and going-concern potential.

b. Having done as the client requested in part **a**, prepare a brief listing of additional ratio analysis-type data for this client that you think creditors are going to ask for to supplement the data provided in part **a**. Explain why you think the additional data will be helpful to these creditors in evaluating this client's solvency.

c. What warnings should you offer these creditors about the limitations of ratio analysis for the purpose stated here?

**25.14**   Indicate the generally accepted accounting principle, or method, described in each of the following statements. Indicate your reasoning.

   **a.** This inventory cost-flow assumption results in reporting the largest net income during periods of rising prices.

   **b.** This method of accounting for uncollectible accounts recognizes the implied income reduction in the period of sale.

   **c.** This method of accounting for long-term investments in the securities of unconsolidated subsidiaries or other corporations usually requires an adjustment to net income to calculate working capital provided by operations in the statement of changes in financial position.

   **d.** This method of accounting for long-term leases by the lessee gives rise to a noncurrent liability.

   **e.** This inventory cost-flow assumption results in approximately the same balance sheet amount as the FIFO flow assumption.

   **f.** This method of amortizing bond premium or discount provides a uniform annual rate of interest revenue or expense over the life of the bond.

   **g.** During periods of rising prices, this inventory-valuation basis produces approximately the same results as the acquisition-cost valuation basis.

   **h.** When specific customers' accounts are deemed uncollectible and written off, this method of accounting results in a decrease in the current ratio.

   **i.** This method of depreciation generally provides the largest amounts of depreciation expense during the first several years of an asset's life.

   **j.** This method of accounting for intercorporate investments in securities can result in a decrease in the investor's total shareholders' equity without affecting retained earnings.

   **k.** The method of recognizing income from long-term contracts generally results in the least fluctuation in earnings over several periods.

   **l.** When specific customers' accounts are deemed uncollectible and are written off, this method of accounting has no effect on working capital.

   **m.** When used in calculating taxable income, this inventory cost-flow assumption must also be used in calculating net income reported to shareholders.

   **n.** Under this method of accounting for long-term leases of equipment by the lessor, an amount for depreciation expense on the leased equipment will appear on the income statement.

   **o.** This method of amortizing bond premium or discount provides a uniform annual amount of interest revenue or expense over the life of the bonds.

**25.15**   Indicate the accounting principle, or procedure, apparently being used to record each of the following independent transactions. Indicate your reasoning.

   **a.** Losses from Uncollectible Accounts . . . . . . . . . . . . . . . . . . . . . . . . . . . . . . . . . . . . . . . X
        Accounts Receivable . . . . . . . . . . . . . . . . . . . . . . . . . . . . . . . . . . . . . . . . . . . . . . . . . X

   **b.** Cash . . . . . . . . . . . . . . . . . . . . . . . . . . . . . . . . . . . . . . . . . . . . . . . . . . . . . . . . . . . . . . X
        Dividend Income . . . . . . . . . . . . . . . . . . . . . . . . . . . . . . . . . . . . . . . . . . . . . . . . . . . X

   **c.** Income Taxes Payable—Current . . . . . . . . . . . . . . . . . . . . . . . . . . . . . . . . . . . . . . . . X
        Deferred Investment Tax Credits . . . . . . . . . . . . . . . . . . . . . . . . . . . . . . . . . . . . . . . X

   **d.** Unrealized Loss from Price Declines in Marketable Securities . . . . . . . . . . . . . . . . . . . . X
        Allowance to Reduce Marketable Securities to Market . . . . . . . . . . . . . . . . . . . . . . . . X

**e.** Cash ........................................................................ X

Investment in Unconsolidated Subsidiary ......................................... X

Dividend declared and received from unconsolidated subsidiary.

**f.** Sales Contra, Estimated Uncollectibles .............................................. X

Allowance for Uncollectible Accounts .......................................... X

**25.16** Indicate the accounting principle, or procedure, apparently being used to record each of the following independent transactions. Give your reasoning.

**a.** Rent Expense (for Lease Contract) .................................................. X

Cash ....................................................................... X

**b.** Advertising Expense ................................................................ X

Deferred Advertising Costs ...................................................... X

**c.** Investment in Unconsolidated Subsidiary ............................................. X

Equity in Earnings of Unconsolidated Subsidiary .................................. X

**d.** Allowance for Uncollectible Accounts ................................................ X

Accounts Receivable .......................................................... X

**e.** Loss from Price Decline of Inventories .............................................. X

Merchandise Inventories ....................................................... X

**f.** Income Taxes Payable—Current .................................................... X

Income Tax Expense (from Investment Credit) .................................... X

**g.** Liability under Long-Term Lease .................................................... X

Interest Expense ............................................................... X

Cash ....................................................................... X

**25.17** Indicate the accounting principle that provides the most conservative measure of earnings in each of the following cases.

a. FIFO, LIFO, or weighted-average cost-flow assumption for inventories during periods of rising prices.

b. FIFO, LIFO, or weighted-average cost-flow assumption for inventories during periods of declining prices.

c. Lower of cost or market method or equity method of accounting for long-term investments in the securities of unconsolidated subsidiaries where dividends declared by the subsidiary are less than its earnings.

d. Sum-of-the-years'-digits or straight-line depreciation method during the first one-third of an asset's life.

e. Sum-of-the-years'-digits or straight-line depreciation method during the last one-third of an asset's life.

f. Deferral or flow-through method of accounting for the investment tax credit in the year qualifying assets are acquired.

g. The valuation of inventories at acquisition cost or lower of cost or market.

h. Lower of cost or market method or equity method of accounting for long-term investments in the securities of unconsolidated subsidiaries where the investee realizes net losses and does not pay dividends.

i. Effective-interest or straight-line method of amortizing bond premium in the first year that bonds are outstanding.

j. Effective-interest or straight-line method of amortizing bond discount in the first year that bonds are outstanding.

## Problems and Exercises

**25.18** The following data are taken from the 1981 annual reports of Alabama Company and Carolina Company:

|  | Alabama Co. | Carolina Co. |
|---|---|---|
| Sales | $2,000,000 | $2,400,000 |
| Expenses Other Than Interest and Income Taxes | 1,700,000 | 2,150,000 |
| Interest Expense | 100,000 | 50,000 |
| Income Tax Expense at 40% | 80,000 | 80,000 |
| Net Income | 120,000 | 120,000 |
| Average Total Assets during the Year | 1,500,000 | 1,000,000 |

a. Calculate the rate of return on assets for each company.

b. Disaggregate the rate of return in part **a** into profit margin and total assets turnover components.

c. Comment on the relative performance of the two companies.

**25.19** The following information is taken from the annual reports of two companies, one of which is a retailer of quality men's clothes and the other of which is a discount household goods store. Neither company had any interest-bearing debt during the year. Identify which of these companies is likely to be the clothing retailer and which is likely to be the discount store. Explain.

|  | Company A | Company B |
|---|---|---|
| Sales | $3,000,000 | $3,000,000 |
| Net Income | 60,000 | 300,000 |
| Average Total Assets | 600,000 | 3,000,000 |

**25.20** Net income attributable to common shareholders' equity of Florida Corporation during 1981 was $250,000. Earnings per share were $.50 during the period. The average common shareholders' equity during 1981 was $2,500,000. The market price at year-end was $6.00 per share.

a. Calculate the rate of return on common shareholders' equity for 1981.

b. Calculate the rate of return currently being earned on the market price of the stock (the ratio of earnings per common share to market price per common share).

c. Why is there a difference between the rates of return determined in parts **a** and **b**?

**25.21** The revenues of Lev Company were $1,000 for the year. A financial analyst computed the following ratios for Lev Company using the year-end balances for balance sheet amounts:

| | |
|---|---|
| Debt/Equity Ratio (all liabilities/all equities) | $73^{1}/_3$% |
| Income Tax Expense as a Percentage of Pretax Income | 40% |
| Net Income as a Percentage of Revenue | 12% |
| Rate of Return on Shareholders' Equity | 10% |
| Rate of Return on Assets | 6% |

From this information, compute each of the following items:

a. Interest expense.       d. Net income.
b. Income tax expense.   e. Total assets.
c. Total expenses.        f. Total liabilities.

**25.22**   Refer to the data below for the Adelsman Company.

|  | Year 1 | Year 2 | Year 3 |
|---|---|---|---|
| Rate of Return on Common Shareholders' Equity (end of year) .. | 8% | 10% | 11% |
| Earnings per Share ........................................ | $3.00 | $4.00 | $4.40 |
| Times Interest Charges Earned .............................. | 10 | 5 | 4 |
| Debt-Equity Ratio (liabilities/all equities) ...................... | 20% | 50% | 60% |

The income tax rate was 40 percent in each year and 100,000 common shares were outstanding throughout the period.

a. Did the company's profitability increase over the 3-year period? How can you tell? (Hint: Compute the rate of return on assets.)
b. Did risk increase? How can you tell?
c. Are shareholders better off in year 3 than in year 1?

**25.23**   Exhibit 25.12 shows five items from the financial statements for three companies for a recent year.

a. Compute the rate of return on assets for each company. Which company seems to be most successful according to this ratio?
b. Disaggregate the rate of return on assets into profit margin and total assets turnover ratios. Which company seems to be most successful according to the profit margin ratio?
c. Compute the rate of return on common shareholders' equity for each company. Which company seems to be the most successful according to this ratio?
d. The three companies are American Telephone & Telegraph, Safeway Stores, and Sears, Roebuck and Company. (Actual dollar amounts are disguised but relation between numbers are preserved.) Which of the companies corresponds to A, B, and C? What clues did you use in reaching your conclusion?

*Exhibit 25.12*
**Comparison of Operations
and Investment**

|  | Company A | Company B | Company C |
|---|---|---|---|
| **For Year** | | | |
| Operating Revenues ......................... | $28,947,200 | $13,639,900 | $9,716,900 |
| Net Income before Interest[a] ................... | 4,295,800 | 824,600 | 156,400 |
| Net Income to Common Shareholders[b] ......... | 2,915,800 | 522,600 | 148,600 |
| **Average during Year** | | | |
| Total Assets ............................... | 77,107,200 | 10,885,000 | 1,532,400 |
| Common Shareholders' Equity ............... | 29,769,200 | 5,118,800 | 743,830 |

[a]Net income + interest expense × (1 − tax rate).

[b]Net income − preferred stock dividends.

**25.24** The Borrowing Company has total assets of $100,000 during the year. It has borrowed $20,000 at a 10 percent annual rate and pays income taxes at a rate of 40 percent of pretax income. Shareholders' equity is $80,000.

a. What must net income be for the rate of return on shareholders' equity to equal the rate of return on assets (the all capital earnings rate)?

b. What is the rate of return on shareholders' equity for the net income calculated above in part **a**?

c. What must income before interest and income taxes be to achieve this net income?

d. Repeat parts **a, b,** and **c,** assuming borrowing of $80,000 and shareholders' equity of $20,000.

e. Compare the results from the two different debt-equity relations. What generalizations can be made?

**25.25** Company A and Company B both start the year 1980 with $1 million of shareholders' equity and 100,000 shares of common stock outstanding. During 1980 both companies earn net income of $100,000, a rate of return of 10 percent on shareholders' equity. Company A declares and pays $100,000 of dividends to common shareholders at the end of 1980, whereas Company B retains all its earnings, declaring no dividends. During 1981, both companies earn net income equal to 10 percent of shareholders' equity at the beginning of 1981.

a. Compute earnings per share for Company A and for Company B for 1980 and for 1981.

b. Compute the rate of growth in earnings per share for Company A and Company B, comparing earnings per share in 1981 with earnings per share in 1980.

c. Using the rate of growth in earnings per share as the criterion, which company's management appears to be doing a better job for its shareholders? Comment on this result.

**25.26** (Adapted from CMA Examination.) The Virgil Company is planning to invest $10 million in an expansion program that is expected to increase income before interest and taxes by $2.5 million. Currently, Virgil Company has total equities of $40 million, 25 percent of which is debt and 75 percent of which is shareholders' equity, represented by 1 million shares. The expansion can be financed with the issuance of 200,000 new shares at $50 each or by issuing long-term debt at an annual interest rate of 10 percent. The following is an excerpt from the most recent income statement:

| | |
|---|---:|
| Earnings before Interest and Taxes ......................................... | $10,500,000 |
| Less: Interest Expense ..................................................... | 500,000 |
| Earnings Before Income Taxes ............................................. | $10,000,000 |
| Income Taxes (at 40%) .................................................... | 4,000,000 |
| Net Income ................................................................. | $ 6,000,000 |

Assume that Virgil Company maintains its current earnings on its present assets, achieves the planned earnings from the new program, and that the tax rate remains at 40 percent.

a. What will be earnings per share if the expansion is financed with debt?

b. What will be earnings per share if the expansion is financed by issuing new shares?

c. At what level of earnings before interest and taxes will earnings per share be the same, whichever of the two financing programs is used?

d. At what level of earnings before interest and taxes will the rate of return on shareholders' equity be the same, whichever of the two financing plans is used?

**25.27**  **a.** Compute the ratio of return on common shareholders' equity in each of the independent cases below.

| Case | Total Assets | Interest-Bearing Debt | Common Share-holders' Equity | Rate of Return on Assets | Aftertax Cost of Interest-Bearing Debt |
|------|------|------|------|------|------|
| A ........................ | $200 | $100 | $100 | 6% | 6% |
| B ........................ | $200 | $100 | $100 | 8% | 6% |
| C ........................ | $200 | $120 | $ 80 | 8% | 6% |
| D ........................ | $200 | $100 | $100 | 4% | 6% |
| E ........................ | $200 | $ 50 | $100 | 6% | 6% |
| F ........................ | $200 | $ 50 | $100 | 5% | 6% |

**b.** In which of the cases is leverage working to the advantage of the common shareholders?

**25.28**  Merchandise inventory costing $30,000 is purchased on account. Indicate the effect (increase, decrease, no effect) of this transaction on **(1)** working capital and **(2)** the current ratio, assuming that current assets and current liabilities immediately prior to the transaction were as follows:

  **a.** Current assets, $120,000; current liabilities, $120,000.
  **b.** Current assets, $120,000; current liabilities, $150,000.
  **c.** Current assets, $120,000; current liabilities, $80,000.

**25.29**  Assuming an excess of current assets over current liabilities, indicate the effect of the following on the current ratio:

  **a.** The acquisition of government bonds for cash.
  **b.** The borrowing of funds from a bank on a 6-month, noninterest-bearing note.
  **c.** The issuance of bonds for cash.
  **d.** The payment of a short-term note at the bank.
  **e.** The recording of accrued interest on a note receivable.
  **f.** The receipt of a noninterest-bearing, 2-month note from a customer to apply to an account receivable.
  **g.** The sale of machinery and equipment at less than book value.

**25.30**  The following information relates to the activities of Tennessee Corporation and Kentucky Corporation for 1981:

| | Tennessee Corp. | Kentucky Corp. |
|------|------|------|
| Sales on Account, 1981 ........................................ | $4,050,000 | $2,560,000 |
| Accounts Receivable, December 31, 1980 ........................ | 960,000 | 500,000 |
| Accounts Receivable, December 31, 1981 ........................ | 840,000 | 780,000 |

  **a.** Compute the accounts receivable turnover of each company.
  **b.** Compute the average number of days that accounts receivable are outstanding for each company.
  **c.** Which company is managing its accounts receivable more efficiently?

**25.31**  Indicate the effects (increase, decrease, no effect) of the independent transactions below on **(1)** earnings per share, **(2)** working capital, and **(3)** quick ratio, where accounts receivable are *included* but merchandise inventory is *excluded* from "quick assets." State any necessary assumptions.

**a.** Merchandise inventory costing $240,000 is sold on account for $300,000.

**b.** Dividends of $160,000 are declared. The dividends will be paid during the next accounting period.

**c.** Merchandise inventory costing $410,000 is purchased on account.

**d.** A machine costing $80,000 and on which $60,000 depreciation had been taken is sold for $16,000.

**e.** Merchandise inventory purchased for cash in the amount of $7,000 is returned to the supplier because it is defective. A cash reimbursement is received.

**f.** 10,000 shares of $10 par value common stock were issued on the last day of the accounting period for $15 per share. The proceeds were used to acquire the assets of another firm composed of the following: accounts receivable, $30,000; merchandise inventory, $60,000; plant and equipment, $100,000. The acquiring firm also agreed to assume current liabilities of $40,000 of the acquired company.

**g.** Marketable securities costing $16,000 are sold for $20,000.

**25.32** The following data are taken from the financial statements of the Press Company:

|  | Dec. 31, 1981 | Dec. 31, 1980 |
|---|---|---|
| Current Assets | $210,000 | $180,000 |
| Noncurrent Assets | 275,000 | 255,000 |
| Current Liabilities | 78,000 | 85,000 |
| Long-Term Liabilities | 75,000 | 30,000 |
| Common Stock (10,000 shares) | 300,000 | 300,000 |
| Retained Earnings | 32,000 | 20,000 |

|  | 1981 Operations |
|---|---|
| Net Income | $72,000 |
| Interest Expense | 3,000 |
| Income Taxes (40% rate) | 48,000 |
| Dividends Declared | 60,000 |

Calculate the following ratios:

**a.** Rate of return on assets.

**b.** Rate of return on shareholders' equity.

**c.** Earnings per share of common stock.

**d.** Current ratio (both dates).

**e.** Times interest earned.

**f.** Debt-equity ratio (both dates).

**25.33** The income statements and balance sheets of Illinois Corporation and Ohio Corporation are presented in Exhibits 25.13 and 25.14, respectively. Assume that the balances in asset and equity accounts at year-end approximate the average balances during the period. The income tax rate is 40 percent. On the basis of this information, which company is

**a.** More profitable?

**b.** More liquid?

**c.** More secure in terms of long-term solvency?

Use financial ratios, as appropriate, in doing your analysis.

*Exhibit 25.13*
**Income Statements
for the Year 1981
(Problem P25.16)**

|  | Illinois Corp. | Ohio Corp. |
|---|---|---|
| Sales | $4,300,000 | $3,000,000 |
| *Less Expenses:* | | |
| Cost of Goods Sold | $2,800,000 | $1,400,000 |
| Selling and Administrative Expenses | 330,000 | 580,000 |
| Interest Expense | 100,000 | 200,000 |
| Income Tax Expense | 428,000 | 328,000 |
| Total Expenses | $3,658,000 | $2,508,000 |
| Net Income | $ 642,000 | $ 492,000 |

*Exhibit 25.14*
**Balance Sheets
December 31, 1981
(Problem P25.16)**

|  | Illinois Corp. | Ohio Corp. |
|---|---|---|
| **Assets** | | |
| Cash | $ 100,000 | $ 50,000 |
| Accounts Receivable (net) | 700,000 | 400,000 |
| Merchandise Inventory | 1,200,000 | 750,000 |
| Plant and Equipment (net) | 4,000,000 | 4,800,000 |
| Total Assets | $6,000,000 | $6,000,000 |
| **Equities** | | |
| Accounts Payable | $ 572,000 | $ 172,000 |
| Income Taxes Payable | 428,000 | 328,000 |
| Long-Term Bonds Payable (10%) | 1,000,000 | 2,000,000 |
| Capital Stock | 2,000,000 | 2,000,000 |
| Retained Earnings | 2,000,000 | 1,500,000 |
| Total Equities | $6,000,000 | $6,000,000 |

**25.34**   The information in Exhibits 25.15 and 25.16 is taken from the financial statements of the
Eastern Oil Company for the years ending December 31, 1980 and 1981. On the basis of this
information, assess the relative (**a**) profitability, (**b**) liquidity, (**c**) solvency of the firm as between 1980 and 1981. Assume that the balances in the asset and equity accounts at year-end
approximate the average balances during the period. Also assume an income tax rate of 48
percent.

**25.35**   Comparative balance sheets, an income statement, and a statement of changes in financial
position of Solinger Electric Corporation for 1981 are shown in Exhibits 25.17, 25.18, and
25.19, respectively. Income taxes are 40 percent of pretax income.
a. Calculate the following ratios for Solinger Electric Corporation for 1981:
(**1**)  Rate of return on assets.

*Exhibit 25.15*
**Eastern Oil Company**
**Statement of Income for the**
**Years 1981 and 1980**
**(Problem 25.34)**

|  | (Amounts in Millions) | |
| --- | --- | --- |
| **Assets** | **December 31, 1981** | **December 31, 1980** |
| Cash | $ 921.0 | $ 866.1 |
| Receivables (net) | 1,198.3 | 1,173.2 |
| Inventories | 1,676.0 | 1,566.0 |
| Plant and Equipment (net) | 11,930.4 | 11,305.3 |
| Other Noncurrent Assets | 4,589.5 | 4,331.2 |
| Total Assets | $20,315.2 | $19,241.8 |
|  |  |  |
| **Equities** |  |  |
| Current Liabilities | $ 3,329.7 | $ 3,240.1 |
| Long-Term Liabilities | 5,392.6 | 5,051.0 |
| Capital Stock (average shares outstanding in 1981: 224,100,000; in 1980: 221,000,000) | 2,640.5 | 2,608.4 |
| Retained Earnings | 8,952.4 | 8,342.3 |
| Total Equities | $20,315.2 | $19,241.8 |

*Exhibit 25.16*
**Eastern Oil Company**
**Consolidated Statement of**
**Financial Position**
**(Problem 25.34)**

|  | (Amounts in Millions) | |
| --- | --- | --- |
|  | **1981** | **1980** |
| **Revenues** |  |  |
| Sales | $20,361.7 | $18,143.3 |
| Other Revenue | 801.4 | 553.4 |
| Total Revenues | $21,163.1 | $18,696.7 |
|  |  |  |
| **Expenses** |  |  |
| Crude Oil and Product Costs | $ 6,283.8 | $ 5,520.7 |
| Selling and Administrative Expenses | 11,806.8 | 10,415.2 |
| Interest Expenses | 261.7 | 241.6 |
| Income Taxes Expense | 1,349.2 | 1,209.2 |
| Total Expenses | $19,701.5 | $17,386.7 |
|  |  |  |
| **Net Income to Shareholders** | $ 1,461.6 | $ 1,310.0 |

(2) Rate of return on common stock equity.
(3) Earnings per share.
(4) Accounts receivable turnover (assuming that all sales are made on account).

*Exhibit 25.17*
**Solinger Electric Corporation**
**Comparative Balance Sheets**
**for December 31, 1980 and 1981**
**(Problem 25.35)**

| ASSETS | December 31, 1980 | December 31, 1981 |
|---|---|---|
| **Current Assets** | | |
| Cash | $ 30,000 | $  3,000 |
| Accounts Receivable | 20,000 | 55,000 |
| Merchandise Inventory | 40,000 | 50,000 |
| Total Current Assets | $ 90,000 | $108,000 |
| **Noncurrent Assets** | | |
| Buildings and Equipment (cost) | $100,000 | $225,000 |
| Accumulated Depreciation | (30,000) | (40,000) |
| Total Noncurrent Assets | $ 70,000 | $185,000 |
| Total Assets | $160,000 | $293,000 |
| **EQUITIES** | | |
| **Current Liabilities** | | |
| Accounts Payable—Merchandise Suppliers | $ 30,000 | $ 50,000 |
| Accounts Payable—Other Suppliers | 10,000 | 12,000 |
| Salaries Payable | 5,000 | 6,000 |
| Total Current Liabilities | $ 45,000 | $ 68,000 |
| **Noncurrent Liabilities** | | |
| Bonds Payable | 0 | 100,000 |
| Total Liabilities | $ 45,000 | $168,000 |
| **Owners' Equity** | | |
| Capital Stock ($10 par value) | $100,000 | $100,000 |
| Retained Earnings | 15,000 | 25,000 |
| Total Owners' Equity | $115,000 | $125,000 |
| Total Equities | $160,000 | $293,000 |

(5) Inventory turnover.
(6) Plant asset turnover.
(7) Current ratio on December 31, 1980, and December 31, 1981.
(8) Quick ratio on December 31, 1980, and December 31, 1981 (assuming that merchandise inventories are excluded from quick assets).
(9) Debt-equity ratio on December 31, 1980, and December 31, 1981.
(10) Times interest charges earned ratio.
b. Was Solinger Electric Corporation successfully leveraged during 1981?
c. Assume that the bonds were issued on November 1, 1981. At what annual interest rate were the bonds apparently issued?
d. If Solinger Electric Corporation earns the same rate of return on assets in 1982 as it realized in 1981, and issues no more debt, will the firm be successfully leveraged in 1982?
e. Calculate the amount of cash flow provided by operations during 1981.

*Exhibit 25.18*
**Solinger Electric Corporation**
**Income Statement for the Year 1981 (Problem 25.35)**

| | |
|---|---:|
| Sales Revenue | $125,000 |
| | |
| *Less Expenses:* | |
| Cost of Goods Sold | $ 60,000 |
| Salaries | 19,667 |
| Depreciation | 10,000 |
| Interest | 2,000 |
| Income Taxes | 13,333 |
| Total Expenses | $105,000 |
| Net Income | $ 20,000 |

*Exhibit 25.19*
**Solinger Electric Corporation Statement of Changes in Financial Position for the Year 1981 (Problem 25.35)**

### SECTION I. SOURCES AND USES OF WORKING CAPITAL

**Sources of Working Capital**
*Operations*

| | | |
|---|---:|---:|
| Net Income | $ 20,000 | |
| *Add Back Expenses Not Using Working Capital:* | | |
| Depreciation | 10,000 | |
| Total Sources from Operations | | $ 30,000 |
| Proceeds from Long-Term Bonds Issued | | 100,000 |
| Total Sources of Working Capital | | $130,000 |

**Uses of Working Capital**

| | |
|---|---:|
| Dividends | $ 10,000 |
| Acquisition of Buildings and Equipment | 125,000 |
| Total Uses of Working Capital | $135,000 |
| Net Decrease in Working Capital during the Year (sources minus uses) | $ 5,000 |

### SECTION II. ANALYSIS OF CHANGES IN WORKING CAPITAL ACCOUNTS

**Current Asset Item Increases (Decreases)**

| | | |
|---|---:|---:|
| Cash | $(27,000) | |
| Accounts Receivable | 35,000 | |
| Merchandise Inventory | 10,000 | |
| Net Increase (Decrease) in Current Asset Items | | $ 18,000 |

**Current Liability Increases (Decreases)**

| | | |
|---|---:|---:|
| Accounts Payable—Merchandise Suppliers | $ 20,000 | |
| Accounts Payable—Other Suppliers | 2,000 | |
| Salaries Payable | 1,000 | |
| Net Increase (Decrease) in Current Liability Items | | 23,000 |
| Net Decrease in Working Capital during the Year (net increase In current liability items minus net increase in current asset items) | | $ 5,000 |

25.36   Exhibits 25.20, 25.21, and 25.22 show the comparative balance sheets, income statement, and statement of changes in financial position of Nykerk Electronics Corporation for 1981.

*Exhibit 25.20*
**Nykerk Electronics Corporation**
**Comparative Balance Sheets**
**(Problem 25.36)**

| | ($ in Thousands) | |
| | December 31 | |
| ASSETS | 1981 | 1980 |
| --- | --- | --- |
| **Current Assets** | | |
| Cash | $ 1,300 | $ 1,100 |
| Marketable Securities | 300 | 300 |
| Accounts Receivable (net) | 2,600 | 2,500 |
| Inventories | 7,300 | 6,900 |
| Total Current Assets | $11,500 | $10,800 |
| | | |
| **Noncurrent Assets** | | |
| Plant and Equipment | $ 5,200 | $ 4,500 |
| Less Accumulated Depreciation | (1,300) | (1,000) |
| Net Plant and Equipment | $ 3,900 | $ 3,500 |
| Land | 1,200 | 1,200 |
| Total Noncurrent Assets | $ 5,100 | $ 4,700 |
| **Total Assets** | $16,600 | $15,500 |

| LIABILITIES AND SHAREHOLDERS' EQUITY | | |
| --- | --- | --- |
| **Current Liabilities** | | |
| Accounts Payable | $ 1,600 | $ 1,700 |
| Accrued Payables | 800 | 900 |
| Income Taxes Payable | 300 | 200 |
| Notes Payable | 1,900 | 1,200 |
| Total Current Liabilities | $ 4,000 | $ 4,000 |
| | | |
| **Long-Term Liabilities** | | |
| Bonds Payable (8%) | $ 2,000 | $ 2,100 |
| Mortgage Payable | 200 | 200 |
| Total Long-Term Liabilities | $ 2,200 | $ 2,300 |
| | | |
| **Total Liabilities** | $ 6,800 | $ 6,300 |
| | | |
| **Shareholders' Equity** | | |
| Preferred Stock (6%, $100 par) | $ 2,000 | $ 2,000 |
| Common Stock ($1 par) | 500 | 500 |
| Additional Paid-in Capital | 2,500 | 2,500 |
| Total Contributed Capital | $ 5,000 | $ 5,000 |
| Retained Earnings | 4,800 | 4,200 |
| Total Shareholders' Equity | $ 9,800 | $ 9,200 |
| **Total Liabilities and Shareholders' Equity** | $16,600 | $15,500 |

---

*Exhibit 25.21*
**Nykerk Electronics Corporation**
**Statement of Income and Retained**
**Earnings for the Year 1981**
**(Problem 25.36)**

| | | ($ in Thousands) |
|---|---|---|
| **Revenues** | | |
| Sales ........ | | $26,500 |
| Less Sales Allowances, Returns, and Discounts ............ | | (600) |
| Net Sales ........ | | $25,900 |
| Interest and Other Revenues ........ | | 200 |
| Total Revenues ........ | | $26,100 |
| | | |
| **Expenses** | | |
| Cost of Goods Sold ........ | | $20,500 |
| Selling and Administrative Expenses: | | |
| Selling Expenses ........ | $2,120 | |
| Administrative Expenses ........ | 1,000 | |
| Depreciation ........ | 300 | |
| Total Selling and Administrative Expenses ........ | | 3,420 |
| Interest Expense ........ | | 180 |
| Income Tax Expense ........ | | 800 |
| Total Expenses ........ | | $24,900 |
| Net Income to Shareholders ........ | | $ 1,200 |
| | | |
| **Dividends** | | |
| Dividends on Preferred Shares ........ | $ 120 | |
| Dividends on Common Shares ........ | 480 | |
| Total Dividends ........ | | 600 |
| Addition to Retained Earnings for Year ........ | | $ 600 |
| Retained Earnings, January 1, 1981 ........ | | 4,200 |
| Retained Earnings, December 31, 1981 ........ | | $ 4,800 |

**a.** Calculate the following ratios for Nykerk Electronics Corporation for 1981:
**(1)** Rate of return on assets.
**(2)** Rate of return on common stock equity.
**(3)** Earnings per share.
**(4)** Accounts receivable turnover (assuming that all sales are made on account).
**(5)** Inventory turnover.
**(6)** Plant asset turnover.
**(7)** Current ratio on December 31, 1980, and December 31, 1981.
**(8)** Quick ratio on December 31, 1980, and December 31, 1981.
**(9)** Debt-equity ratio on December 31, 1980, and December 31, 1981.
**(10)** Times interest charges earned ratio.
**b.** Calculate the amount of cash flow provided by operations for 1981. For this purpose, do not include the change in Notes Payable in the analysis.
**c.** Was Nykerk Electronics Corporation successfully leveraged during 1981?

25.37 (Adapted from CPA Examination.) The December 31 balance sheet of Ratio, Inc., is presented below. These are the only accounts in Ratio's balance sheet. Amounts indicated by a question mark (?) can be calculated from the additional information given.

*Exhibit 25.22*
**Nykerk Electronics Corporation**
**Statement of Changes in Financial**
**Position for the Year 1981**
**(Problem 25.36)**

|  | | ($ in Thousands) |
|---|---|---|
| *Sources of Working Capital:* | | |
| Net Income | $1,200 | |
| Add Back Expenses Not Using Working Capital: | | |
| Depreciation Expense | 300 | |
| Working Capital Provided by Operations | | $1,500 |
| *Uses of Working Capital:* | | |
| Preferred Stock Dividend | $  120 | |
| Common Stock Dividend | 480 | |
| Purchase of Plant and Equipment | 700 | |
| Redemption of Bonds Payable | 100 | 1,400 |
| **Increase in Working Capital for the Year** | | $  100 |
| *Analysis of Increases (Decreases) in Working Capital Amounts* | | |
| Cash | | $  200 |
| Marketable Securities | | 0 |
| Accounts Receivable (net) | | 100 |
| Inventories | | 400 |
| Accounts Payable | | 100 |
| Accrued Payables | | 100 |
| Income Taxes Payable | | (100) |
| Notes Payable | | (700) |
| **Increase in Working Capital for the Year** | | $  100 |

*Additional Information.*
Current ratio (at year end): 1.5 to 1.
Total liabilities divided by total shareholders' equity: .8.
Inventory turnover based on sales and ending inventory: 15 times.

| **Assets** | |
|---|---|
| Cash | $ 25,000 |
| Accounts Receivable (net) | ? |
| Inventory | ? |
| Property, Plant, and Equipment (net) | 294,000 |
| Total | $432,000 |

| **Liabilities and Shareholders' Equity** | |
|---|---|
| Accounts Payable (trade) | $   ? |
| Income Taxes Payable (current) | 25,000 |
| Long-Term Debt | ? |
| Common Stock | 300,000 |
| Retained Earnings | ? |
| Total | $   ? |

Inventory turnover based on cost of goods sold and ending inventory: 10.5 times.
Gross margin: $315,000.

a. What was Ratio's December 31 balance in trade accounts payable?

b. What was Ratio's December 31 balance in retained earnings?

c. What was Ratio's December 31 balance in the inventory account?

25.38   (Adapted from CPA Examination.) This question concerns the various interrelationships among financial statements, accounts (or groups of accounts) among those statements, and accounts (or groups of accounts) within each statement. The following information is presented for Woods Company for the year ended December 31, 1981:

The statement of changes in financial position.

Selected information from the income statement.

Selected information regarding the January 1 and December 31 balance sheets.

Information regarding the correction of an error.

Partially completed balance sheets at January 1 (prior to restatement) and December 31. The omitted account and groups-of-account balances are numbered from (1) through (16) and can be calculated from the other information given.

## Woods Company
## Statement of Changes in Financial Position

| | | |
|---|---:|---:|
| Working Capital, January 1, 1981 | | $16,500 |
| Add Resources Provided: | | |
| Operations: | | |
| Net Loss for 1981 | $ (2,885) | |
| Adjustments Not Involving Working Capital: | | |
| Bond Premium Amortization | (500) | |
| Deferred Income Taxes | (200) | |
| Depreciation Expense | 3,000 | |
| Goodwill Amortization for 1981 | 2,000 | |
| Total from Operations | $ 1,415 | |
| Portion of Proceeds of Equipment Sold Representing Undepreciated Cost | 10,000 | |
| Proceeds from Reissue of Treasury Stock | 11,400 | |
| Par Value of Common Stock Issued to Reacquire Preferred Stock | 7,500 | |
| Total Resources Provided | $30,315 | |
| Subtract Resources Applied: | | |
| Purchase of Land | 14,715 | |
| Current Maturity of Long-Term Bond Debt | 7,200 | |
| Par Value of Preferred Stock Reacquired by Issuing Common Stock | 7,500 | |
| Total Resources Applied | $29,415 | |
| Increase in Working Capital | | 900 |
| Working Capital, December 31, 1981 | | $17,400 |

## Information from the Income Statement

| | |
|---|---:|
| Sales, Uncollectible Accounts Adjustment | $ 750 |
| Bond Interest Expense (net of amortization of bond premium) | $3,500 |

| | | |
|---|---|---|
| Loss before Tax Adjustment .............................................. | | $(3,900) |
| Less: | | |
|    Income Tax Adjustment (refund due) ................................ | $815 | |
|    Deferred Income Taxes ............................................ | 200 | 1,015 |
| Net Loss after Tax Adjustment ........................................... | | $(2,885) |

## Information Regarding January 1 and December 31 Balance Sheets

The book value of the equipment sold was two-thirds of the cost of that equipment.

| | Selected Ratios | |
|---|---|---|
| | **January 1, 1981 (Prior to Restatement)** | **December 31, 1981** |
| Current Ratio ......................... | ? | 3 to 1 |
| Total Shareholders' Equity Divided by Total Liabilities .......................... | 4 to 3 | ? |

## Information Regarding the Correction of an Error

Woods Company had neglected to amortize $2,000 of goodwill in 1980. The correction of this material error has been appropriately made in 1981.

## Balance Sheet

| | January 1, 1981 (Prior to Restatement) | December 31, 1981 |
|---|---|---|
| Current Assets ......................... | $22,000 | $ (5) |
| Building and Equipment .................. | 92,000 | (6) |
| Accumulated Depreciation ................ | (25,000) | (7) |
| Land ................................... | (1) | (8) |
| Goodwill ............................... | 12,000 | (9) |
| Total Assets ........................... | $ (?) | $ (?) |
| Current Liabilities ...................... | $ (2) | (10) |
| Bonds Payable (8%) .................... | (3) | (11) |
| Bond Premium ......................... | (?) | (12) |
| Deferred Income Taxes ................. | (4) | 1,700 |
| Common Stock ......................... | 66,000 | (13) |
| Paid-in Capital ......................... | 13,000 | (14) |
| Preferred Stock ....................... | 16,000 | (15) |
| Retained Earnings (deficit) ............... | (6,000) | (16) |
| Treasury Stock (at cost) ................. | (9,000) | 0 |
| Total Liabilities and Shareholders' Equity .. | $ (?) | $ (?) |

Calculate the amount for each of the 16 numbered items in the balance sheet. Provide supporting computations for your responses.

*Exhibit 25.23*
**Data for Ratio Detective Exercise**
**(Problem 25.39)**

| | **Company Numbers** | | | | | | |
|---|---|---|---|---|---|---|---|
| | (1) | (2) | (3) | (4) | (5) | (6) | (7) |
| **Balance Sheet at End of Year** | | | | | | | |
| Current Receivables .... | 0.31% | 29.11% | 6.81% | 25.25% | 3.45% | 38.78% | 17.64% |
| Inventories ............ | 7.80 | 0.00 | 3.14 | 0.00 | 6.45 | 14.94 | 20.57 |
| Net Plant and Equipment[a] . | 8.50 | 9.63 | 11.13 | 19.88 | 49.87 | 15.59 | 37.60 |
| All Other Assets ........ | 2.16 | 7.02 | 25.59 | 32.93 | 24.05 | 15.54 | 30.07 |
| Total Assets .......... | 18.78% | 45.76% | 46.67% | 78.06% | 83.83% | 84.85% | 105.88% |
| | | | | | | | |
| *Cost of Plant and | | | | | | | |
| Equipment (gross) ...... | 14.64% | 14.80% | 19.57% | 29.03% | 79.03% | 24.80% | 59.73% |
| | | | | | | | |
| Current Liabilities ...... | 6.08% | 9.82% | 6.41% | 17.49% | 14.83% | 35.28% | 27.68% |
| Long-Term Liabilities ... | 2.12 | 7.96 | 0.00 | 0.00 | 0.00 | 8.33 | 1.33 |
| Owners' Equity ........ | 10.58 | 27.98 | 40.25 | 60.57 | 69.00 | 41.24 | 76.86 |
| Total Equities ......... | 18.78% | 45.76% | 46.67% | 78.06% | 83.83% | 84.85% | 105.88% |
| **Income Statement for Year** | | | | | | | |
| Revenues ............. | 100.00% | 100.00% | 100.00% | 100.00% | 100.00% | 100.00% | 100.00% |
| Cost of Goods Sold | | | | | | | |
| (Excluding Depreciation) | | | | | | | |
| or Operating Expenses[a] | 78.97% | 53.77% | 48.21% | 59.07% | 68.62% | 60.88% | 33.29% |
| Depreciation ........... | 1.04 | 1.39 | 1.72 | 2.07 | 4.07 | 1.09 | 3.02 |
| Interest Expense ....... | 0.16 | .52 | 0.00 | 0.08 | 0.02 | 1.35 | 0.73 |
| Advertising Expense .... | 3.72 | 0.00 | 11.43 | 0.06 | 4.39 | 2.93 | 2.28 |
| Research and Develop- | | | | | | | |
| ment Expense ........ | 0.00 | 1.00 | 0.00 | 0.00 | 0.15 | 0.00 | 9.06 |
| Income Taxes .......... | 1.28 | .53 | 9.59 | 6.52 | 7.87 | 3.78 | 8.55 |
| All Other Items (net) .... | 13.33 | 18.88 | 18.58 | 24.52 | 6.40 | 24.39 | 27.66 |
| Total Expenses ......... | 98.50% | 76.08% | 89.53% | 92.32% | 91.51% | 94.41% | 84.59% |
| Net Income ............ | 1.50% | 23.92% | 10.47% | 7.68% | 8.49% | 5.59% | 15.41% |

**25.39** In this problem, you become a financial analyst/detective. The condensed financial statements in Exhibit 25.23 are constructed on a percentage basis. In all cases, total sales revenues are shown as 100.00 percent. All other numbers were divided by sales revenue for the year.

The 13 companies (all corporations except for the accounting firm) shown here represent the following industries:
(1) Advertising and public opinion survey firm.
(2) Beer brewery.
(3) Department store chain (which carries its own receivables).
(4) Distiller of hard liquor.
(5) Drug manufacturer.
(6) Finance company (lends money to consumers).
(7) Grocery store chain.

## Exhibit 25.23 (continued)

| | Company Numbers | | | | | |
|---|---|---|---|---|---|---|
| | **(8)** | **(9)** | **(10)** | **(11)** | **(12)** | **(13)** |
| **Balance Sheet at End of Year** | | | | | | |
| Current Receivables ...... | 12.94% | 9.16% | 25.18% | 27.07% | 13.10% | 653.94% |
| Inventories .............. | 15.47 | 56.89 | 79.53 | 0.00 | 1.62 | 0.00 |
| Net Plant and Equipment[a] . | 70.29 | 28.36 | 19.22 | 2.64 | 251.62 | 2.88 |
| All Other Assets ......... | 18.37 | 26.42 | 24.72 | 223.91 | 23.68 | 200.37 |
| Total Assets ............ | 117.08% | 120.82% | 148.65% | 253.63% | 290.01% | 857.18% |
| | | | | | | |
| *Cost of Plant and | | | | | | |
| Equipment (Gross) ..... | 167.16% | 42.40% | 35.08% | 4.45% | 320.90% | 3.81% |
| Current Liabilities ........ | 19.37% | 33.01% | 20.42% | 161.37% | 28.01% | 377.56% |
| Long-Term Liabilities ..... | 20.62 | 34.07 | 36.09 | 10.62 | 115.50 | 280.79 |
| Owners' Equity .......... | 77.09 | 53.74 | 92.13 | 81.63 | 146.51 | 198.83 |
| Total Equities ........ | 117.08% | 120.82% | 148.65% | 253.63% | 290.01% | 857.18% |
| | | | | | | |
| **Income Statement for Year** | | | | | | |
| Revenues .............. | 100.00% | 100.00% | 100.00% | 100.00% | 100.00% | 100.00% |
| Cost of Goods Sold (Excluding Depreciation) or Operating Expenses[a] .. | 81.92% | 57.35% | 42.92% | 82.61% | 45.23% | 47.69% |
| Depreciation ............ | 5.81 | 1.90 | 1.97 | 0.05 | 14.55 | 0.00 |
| Interest Expense ........ | 1.23 | 2.69 | 3.11 | 1.07 | 7.15 | 24.33 |
| Advertising Expense ...... | 0.00 | 6.93 | 13.04 | 0.00 | 0.00 | 0.00 |
| Research and Development Expense .... ........ | 0.76 | 0.00 | 0.00 | 0.00 | 0.71 | 0.00 |
| Income Taxes ........... | 2.15 | 7.47 | 10.63 | 3.92 | 8.73 | 12.89 |
| All Other Items (net) ....... | 3.81 | 14.82 | 17.99 | 2.97 | 11.51 | −5.57 |
| Total Expenses ....... | 95.68% | 91.16% | 89.66% | 90.62% | 87.89% | 79.35% |
| Net Income ............. | 4.32% | 8.84% | 10.34% | 9.38% | 12.11% | 20.65% |

[a]Represents operating expenses for the following companies: advertising/public opinion survey firm, insurance company, finance company, and the public accounting partnership.

(8)  Insurance company.
(9)  Manufacturer of tobacco products, mainly cigarettes.
(10) Public accounting (CPA) partnership.
(11) Soft drink bottler.
(12) Steel manufacturer.
(13) Utility company.

Use whatever clues you can to identify who is who. As an aid to identifying which company is which, you may find the data in the accompanying Exhibit 25.24 to be helpful. This exhibit

*Exhibit 25.24*
**Key Business Ratios
Median Ratios for Business
of the Types Indicated
(Problem 25.39)**

| Type of Business | Current Ratio (Times) (1) | Net Income as a Percentage of Sales (2) | Rate of Return in Shareholders' Equity (3) | Shareholders' Equity[a] as a Percentage of Sales (4) | Inventory as a Percentage of Sales (5) |
|---|---|---|---|---|---|
| Department Store ......... | 2.81 | 1.61% | 5.47% | 27.5% | 17.5% |
| Grocery Store ... | 1.63 | 0.94 | 12.78 | 7.8 | 6.2 |
| Beer, Wine, and Alcoholic Beverages ..... | 1.96 | 1.58 | 11.91 | 12.2 | 12.5 |
| Tobacco and Tobacco Products ...... | 2.25 | 0.93 | 11.85 | 8.3 | 6.3 |
| Blast Furnace, Steel Works, and Rolling Mills .......... | 2.46 | 4.45 | 10.31 | 38.6 | 21.3 |
| Drugs ........... | 2.46 | 6.15 | 14.37 | 45.7 | 22.7 |
| Soft Drink, Bottled and Canned ... | 2.10 | 6.46 | 19.05 | 27.7 | 5.1 |

Source: Dun & Bradstreet, Inc., *Key Business Ratios*. The document from which these data are developed lists 14 ratios for about 90 kinds of businesses. The entire document can be ordered at no cost from Public Relations Department, Dun & Bradstreet, Inc., 99 Church Street, New York, New York 10007.

[a]Dun & Bradstreet uses tangible shareholders' equity for this ratio. They subtract from owners' equity shown in the balance sheet the net book value of intangible assets.

is adapted from data published by Dun & Bradstreet, Inc., and is reproduced here with their permission. The ratios shown are median ratios for several individual firms of the business type listed. There is not a perfect relation between the ratios shown for a given type of business and that same ratio for the particular company shown in Exhibit 25.23.

25.40 The purpose of this problem is to help you understand how to compare income appearing in financial statements that use a given system of inventory accounting with income reported by a different system of inventory accounting. In comparing income under one set of conditions, denoted F (think FIFO), with another set, denoted L (think LIFO), the following two relations hold:

(I) $$\text{Income (System F)} - \text{Income (System L)} = \text{Increase in Ending Inventory (System F)} - \text{Increase in Ending Inventory (System L)}.$$

(II) $$\text{Income (System F)} - \text{Income (System L)} = \begin{bmatrix} \text{Ending Inventory (System F)} \\ - \text{Ending Inventory (System L)} \end{bmatrix} - \begin{bmatrix} \text{Beginning Inventory (System F)} \\ - \text{Beginning Inventory (System L)} \end{bmatrix}.$$

We use the symbols F and L to evoke the thoughts FIFO and LIFO as you read these equations, but keep in mind that the equations hold whatever comparisons are being made.

For example, condition F might represent a specific identification method of measuring cost of goods sold, whereas L might represent a weighted-average cost-flow assumption with a perpetual inventory method.

Some people are made nervous by algebra; others find it useful for understanding. The remainder of this section derives the above relations algebraically. There are several ways other than algebra to grasp these two relations. Do not be intimidated by the algebra; if you are uncomfortable with it, then study Exhibit 25.7 with these two relations in mind and skip down to the example below.

We use the following two equations:

$$\text{Margin} = \text{Revenue} - \text{Cost of Goods Sold}.$$

$$\text{Cost of Goods Sold} = \text{Beginning Inventory} + \text{Purchases} - \text{Ending Inventory}.$$

We abbreviate the components of these equations as follows:

$$M = R - COGS.$$

$$COGS = BI + P - EI.$$

A subscript on a symbol denotes the quantity under a particular set of inventory conditions, either F or L. Thus,

(1) $\qquad M_F = R_F - COGS_F \quad \text{and} \quad COGS_F = BI_F + P_F - EI_F.$

(2) $\qquad M_L = R_L - COGS_L \quad \text{and} \quad COGS_L = BI_L + P_L - EI_L.$

But note that both revenues and purchases are unaffected by the inventory conditions, so that

$$R_F = R_L \quad \text{and} \quad P_F = P_L.$$

Thus if we subtract equations (2) from (1), we get

(3) $\qquad\qquad\qquad\qquad M_F - M_L = - COGS_F + COGS_L.$

and

(4) $\qquad\qquad COGS_F - COGS_L = (BI_F - BI_L) - (EI_F - EI_L).$

Now, if we multiply both sides of equation (4) by $-1$, we get

(5) $\qquad\qquad - COGS_F + COGS_L = (EI_F - EI_L) - (BI_F - BI_L).$

Substituting equation (5)'s results into equation (3) yields

(6) $\qquad\qquad M_F - M_L = (EI_F - EI_L) - (BI_F - BI_L).$

Equation (6) is the second relation mentioned above (II) as being useful in comparing inventory conditions. The first term in parentheses on the right-hand side is the difference between ending inventories, and the second is the difference between beginning inventories. Exhibit 25.7 illustrates this relation. International Corporation's hypothetical FIFO income is derived from footnote information about the excess of FIFO beginning and ending inventories over their LIFO amounts.

If we rearrange the terms on the right-hand side of equation (6), we get

(7) $$M_F - M_L = (EI_F - BI_F) - (EI_L - BI_L).$$

The right-hand side of (7) is the increase in inventory during the year under conditions F minus the increase in inventory during the period under conditions L. Thus, equation (7) is the first relation (I) mentioned above as being useful in comparing incomes under two sets of inventory conditions.

Exhibit 9.8 illustrates this relation. For example, the difference between FIFO and LIFO income (or gross margins) is $5 (= $30 − $25). The difference between the FIFO and LIFO increases in inventory during the period is also $5 (= $34 − $29). This relation can also be seen in Exhibit 9.8 by comparing FIFO and weighted-average income differences ($3) or weighted-average and LIFO differences ($2).

The inventory relations can be used to analyze financial statements as illustrated here. Consider the data for the Skelton Company shown in Exhibit 25.25. The Skelton Company has ending inventory of zero at the end of 1979. The accompanying exhibit shows inventory at the end of each of the next 2 years under three different accounting methods. (The data could equally well represent ending inventory for three different companies at the end of the 3 years.)

---

*Exhibit 25.25*
**Skelton Company**
**Ending Inventory under**
**Various Accounting Methods**

| Date | FIFO Flow Cost Basis | FIFO Flow Lower-of-Cost-or-Market Basis | LIFO Flow Cost Basis |
|---|---|---|---|
| 12/31/1979 | $    0 | $    0 | $    0 |
| 12/31/1980 | 13,000 | 13,000 | 10,000 |
| 12/31/1981 | 15,000 | 14,500 | 16,000 |

a. Did prices go up or down in 1980?
b. Did prices go up or down in 1981?
c. Is income for 1980 larger under FIFO or LIFO and by how much?
d. Which inventory method shows the largest income for 1981?
e. Which inventory method would show the largest income for the 2 years combined?

**25.41** (Note: This problem should not be attempted until Problem **25.40** has been read.) The Burch Corporation began a merchandising business on January 1, 1979. It acquired merchandise costing $100,000 in 1979, $125,000 in 1980, and $135,000 in 1981. Information about Burch Corporation's inventory, as it would appear on the balance sheet under different inventory methods, is as follows:

In answering each of the following questions, indicate how the answer is deduced. You may assume that in any one year, prices moved only up or down, but not both in the same year.
a. Did prices go up or down in 1979?
b. Did prices go up or down in 1981?
c. Which inventory method would show the highest income for 1979?
d. Which inventory method would show the highest income for 1981?
e. Which inventory method would show the highest income for 1980?
f. Which inventory method would show the lowest income for all 3 years combined?

**Burch Corporation
Inventory Valuations for Balance
Sheet under Various
Assumptions**

| Date | LIFO Cost | FIFO Cost | Lower of FIFO Cost or Market |
|---|---|---|---|
| 12/31/1979 ..................................... | $40,800 | $40,000 | $37,000 |
| 12/31/1980 ..................................... | 36,400 | 36,000 | 34,000 |
| 12/31/1981 ..................................... | 41,200 | 44,000 | 44,000 |

g. For 1981, how much higher or lower would income be on the FIFO cost basis than it would be on the lower-of-cost-or-market basis?

25.42   Exhibit 25.7 illustrated the calculation of pretax income for the International Corporation using a LIFO and a FIFO cost-flow assumption. Shown in Exhibit 25.26 are General Electric Company's inventories for a period of years under the LIFO assumption actually used and under FIFO as they would have been if it had been used. Also shown is the firm's pretax income as a result of using LIFO.

a. Determine the pretax income for years 2 through 6, assuming that a FIFO cost-flow assumption had been used.

b. Calculate the percentage change in pretax income for each of the years 3 through 6 under both LIFO and FIFO (that is, the increase in pretax income in year 3 relative to year 2, the increase in pretax income in year 4 relative to year 3, and so on).

c. Calculate the percentage change in pretax income between year 2 and year 6 (that is, the 5-year period taken as a whole) under both LIFO and FIFO.

d. Did the quantity of items in inventory increase or decrease during each of the years 3 through 6? How can you tell?

e. Did the acquisition cost of items in inventory increase or decrease during each of the years 3 through 6? How can you tell?

*Exhibit 25.26*
**General Electric Company
(Problem 25.42)**

| | Amounts in Millions | |
|---|---|---|
| **End of Year** | **LIFO Ending Inventory** | **FIFO Ending Inventory** |
| 1 .......................................... | $1,611.7 | $1,884.5 |
| 2 .......................................... | 1,759.0 | 2,063.1 |
| 3 .......................................... | 1,986.2 | 2,415.9 |
| 4 .......................................... | 2,257.0 | 3,040.7 |
| 5 .......................................... | 2,202.9 | 3,166.6 |
| 6 .......................................... | 2,354.4 | 3,515.2 |
| **For the Year** | | **Pretax Income Using LIFO** |
| 2 .......................................... | | $  897.2 |
| 3 .......................................... | | 1,011.6 |
| 4 .......................................... | | 1,000.7 |
| 5 .......................................... | | 1,174.0 |
| 6 .......................................... | | 1,627.5 |

f. Assume for this part that the inventory value under LIFO at the end of year 1 of $1,611.7 is the initial LIFO layer. This layer may be viewed as the bottom layer on a cake. Construct a figure showing the addition or subtraction of LIFO layers for each of the years 2 through 6.

g. The current assets and current liabilities of the General Electric Company at the end of years 2 through 6 using a LIFO cost-flow assumption are shown below.

| End of Year | Amounts in Millions | |
|---|---|---|
| | Current Assets | Current Liabilities |
| 2 | $3,979.3 | $2,869.7 |
| 3 | 4,485.4 | 3,492.4 |
| 4 | 5,222.6 | 3,879.5 |
| 5 | 5,750.4 | 4,163.0 |
| 6 | 6,685.0 | 4,604.9 |

Compute General Electric's current ratio for each year using the above data.

h. Recompute General Electric's current ratio for each year using a FIFO cost-flow assumption for inventories. Although it is unrealistic to do so, assume for this part that there are no changes in income taxes payable or current liabilities. (To make the figures realistic after taxes, ending LIFO inventory should be increased by about *one-half* the difference between FIFO and LIFO ending inventory amounts. Why?)

25.43 The Strawcab Company owns one depreciable asset. The asset originally had a depreciable life of 6 years. It is 4 years old at the end of the current year. It had an estimated salvage value of $4,000 when new. This estimate has not changed. The company uses sum-of-the-years'-digits depreciation on its tax return and straight-line depreciation on its financial statements. The company's income tax rate is 40 percent of pretax taxable income. The footnotes to the financial statements indicate that the only cause of timing differences between the financial statements and tax returns is depreciation and that the income tax expense differs from income taxes payable by $1,200.

a. Which is larger this year, income taxes payable or income tax expense, and by how much?

b. What is the acquisition cost of the asset?

c. Assume the same general facts as above except the asset had an original depreciable life of 8 years, is 2 years old at the end of the current year, and has an estimated salvage value of $2,000. The difference between income tax expense and income taxes payable this year was reported to be $1,600. Repeat parts a and b.

25.44 The following selected data were taken from the financial statements of Sprouse Corporation for 1981:

| Balance Sheet | December 31, 1981 | December 31, 1980 |
|---|---|---|
| Current Assets | $400,000 | $350,000 |
| Noncurrent Assets | 600,000 | 550,000 |
| Current Liabilities | 300,000 | 250,000 |
| Noncurrent Liabilities | 300,000 | 300,000 |
| Common Shareholders' Equity | 400,000 | 350,000 |
| **Income Statement for 1981** | | |
| Net Income | | $140,000 |
| Interest Expense | | 20,000 |

Noncurrent liabilities include deferred income taxes of $80,000 on December 31, 1980, and $100,000 on December 31, 1981. All of the deferred taxes amount relates to depreciation timing differences. The income tax rate is 46 percent. The unrecognized supplemental actuarial value of the pension plan was $150,000 on December 31, 1980, and $180,000 on December 31, 1981.

a. Calculate the rate of return on assets and the rate of return on shareholders' equity for 1981 and the debt-equity ratio on December 31, 1980, and December 31, 1981, based on the amounts taken from the financial statements.

b. What would net income have been if depreciation for financial reporting was based on the depreciation method as used for tax purposes?

c. Give the entries that would be made to recognize the supplemental actuarial value as a liability.

d. Repeat part **a,** but use the restated amounts from part **c** in which supplemental actuarial value is recognized as a liability.

e. Referring to the original financial statement data, give the entries that would be made to eliminate deferred income tax accounting.

f. Repeat part **a,** but use the restated amounts from part **e** in which deferred tax accounting is eliminated.

25.45    On January 1, 1981, two corporations are formed to operate merchandising businesses. The firms are alike in all respects except for their methods of accounting. Ruzicka Company chooses the accounting principles that will minimize its reported net income. Murphy Company chooses the accounting principles that will maximize its reported net income but, where different procedures are permitted, will use accounting methods that minimize its taxable income. The following events occur during 1981.

(1) Both companies issue 500,000 shares of $1-par-value common shares for $6 per share on January 2, 1981.

(2) Both firms acquire equipment on January 2, 1981, for $1,650,000 cash. The equipment is estimated to have a 10-year life and zero salvage value. An investment tax credit of 10 percent is applicable to this equipment.

(3) Both firms engage in extensive sales promotion activities during 1981, incurring costs of $400,000.

(4) The two firms make the following purchases of merchandise inventory:

| Date | Units Purchased | Unit Price | Cost of Purchases |
|---|---|---|---|
| January 2 ....................... | 50,000 | $6.00 | $  300,000 |
| April 1 ......................... | 60,000 | 6.20 | 372,000 |
| August 15 ...................... | 40,000 | 6.25 | 250,000 |
| November 30 .................... | 50,000 | 6.50 | 325,000 |
| Total ...................... | 200,000 | | $1,247,000 |

(5) During the year both firms sell 140,000 units at an average price of $15 each.

(6) Selling, general, and administrative expenses during the year other than advertising total $100,000.

The Ruzicka Company uses the following accounting methods (for both book and tax purposes): LIFO inventory cost-flow assumption, sum-of-the-years'-digits depreciation method, immediate expensing of the cost of sales promotion, and the deferral method of accounting for the investment credit.

The Murphy Company uses the following accounting methods: FIFO inventory cost-flow assumption for both book and tax purposes, the straight-line depreciation method for book and the double-declining-balance method for tax purposes, capitalization and amortization of the costs of the sales promotion campaign over 4 years for book and immediate expensing for tax purposes, and the flow-through method of accounting for the investment credit.

**a.** Prepare comparative income statements for the two firms for the year 1981. Include separate computations of income tax expense. The income tax rate is 20 percent of the first $25,000 of taxable income, 22 percent of the next $25,000, and 48 percent of the remainder.

**b.** Prepare comparative balance sheets for the two firms as of December 31, 1981. Both firms have $1 million of outstanding accounts receivable on this date and a single current liability for income taxes payable for the year.

**c.** Prepare comparative statements of changes in financial position for the two firms for the year 1981.

**25.46** The Langston Corporation is formed on January 2, 1981, with the issuance at par of 100,000 shares of $10-par-value common stock for cash. During 1981, the following transactions occur:

(1) The assets of the Dee's Department Store are acquired on January 2, 1981, for $800,000 cash. The market values of the identifiable assets received are as follows: accounts receivable, $200,000; merchandise inventory, $400,000 (200,000 units); store equipment, $150,000. The acquisition is accounted for as a purchase.

(2) Merchandise inventory is purchased during 1981 as follows:

| Date | Units Purchased | Unit Price | Cost of Purchase |
|------|----------------|-----------|------------------|
| April 1 | 30,000 | $2.10 | $ 63,000 |
| August 1 | 20,000 | 2.20 | 44,000 |
| October 1 | 50,000 | 2.40 | 120,000 |
| Total | 100,000 | | $227,000 |

(3) During the year, 210,000 units are sold at an average price of $3.20.

(4) Extensive training programs are held during the year to acquaint previous employees of Dee's Department Store with the merchandising policies and procedures of Langston Corporation. The costs incurred in the training programs total $50,000.

(5) Selling, general, and administrative costs incurred and recognized as an expense during 1981 are $80,000.

(6) The store equipment is estimated to have a 5-year useful life and zero salvage value.

(7) The income tax rate is 20 percent of the first $25,000 of taxable income, 22 percent of the next $25,000, and 48 percent of the remainder. Goodwill arising from a corporate acquisition is not deductible in determining taxable income. Ignore investment tax credit provisions in this problem.

The management of Langston Corporation is uncertain about the accounting methods that should be used in preparing its financial statements. The choice has been narrowed to two sets of accounting methods, and you have been asked to determine net income for 1981 using each set.

**a.** Set A consists of the following accounting methods (for book and tax purposes): LIFO inventory cost-flow assumption, double-declining-balance depreciation method, immediate expensing of the costs of the training program, amortization of goodwill over 10 years.

**b.** Set B consists of the following accounting methods: FIFO inventory-costing assumption, straight-line depreciation for book and double-declining-balance for tax purposes, capitalization and amortization of the costs of the training program over 5 years for book and immediate expensing for tax purposes, amortization of goodwill over 40 years.

25.47 Net income of Miller Corporation for the year ending December 31, 1981, is $600,000 based on the accounting methods actually used by the firm. You have been asked to compute the amount of net income that would have been reported under several alternative accounting methods. The income tax rate is 40 percent, and the same accounting methods are used for financial reporting and income tax purposes unless otherwise indicated. Each of the following questions should be considered independently.

a. Miller Corporation acquired a machine costing $300,000 on January 1, 1981. The machine was depreciated during 1981 using the straight-line method based on a 5-year useful life and zero salvage value. What would net income have been if the sum-of-the-years'-digits depreciation method had been used? Ignore the investment tax credit.

b. Miller Corporation obtained an investment tax credit of $10,000 on the machine acquired in part a. It accounted for the investment credit using the flow-through method. What would net income have been if the deferral method had been used? In responding to this question, assume that the machine was depreciated using the straight-line method based on a 5-year life and zero salvage value. Also assume that this is the first year that investment tax credits have been realized by Miller Corporation.

c. Miller Corporation used the lower-of-cost-or-market method of accounting for its 18-percent investment in the common shares of General Tools Corporation. During 1981, General Tools Corporation earned $200,000 and paid dividends of $50,000. The market value of General Tools Corporation was the same at the end of 1981 as it was at the beginning of 1981. What would net income have been during 1981 if Miller Corporation continued to account for the investment under the lower-of-cost-or-market method for income tax purposes but used the equity method for financial reporting purposes?

d. Miller Corporation used the FIFO inventory cost flow assumption. Under FIFO, the January 1, 1981, inventory was $300,000 and the December 31, 1981, inventory was $320,000. Under LIFO, the January 1, 1981, inventory would have been $240,000 and the December 31, 1981, inventory would have been $230,000. What would net income have been if the LIFO inventory costing assumption had been used?

25.48 Two conventional calculations of the debt-equity ratio were discussed in this chapter. This problem focuses on the following definition:

$$\frac{\text{Debt-Equity}}{\text{Ratio}} = \frac{\text{Total Long-Term Financing}}{\text{Owners' Equity}}.$$

Many analysts use this ratio to assess the risk in the financial structure of a corporation. The higher the debt-equity ratio, other things being equal, the greater the risk. Some analysts construct ratios from conventional, historical-cost financial statements without adjustment. This problem illustrates how the assessment of the relative risk of companies can change as more sophisticated analysis of the financial statements is undertaken. In this problem, various adjustments to the conventional financial statements are made and new versions of the debt-equity ratio are compared.

Data for Eastman Kodak, General Motors, and Zenith for a recent year are shown below. All data are taken from the financial statements of the three companies for the same year. Dollar amounts are in millions. The income tax rate is 46 percent. Parts a through e should be considered independently, not cumulatively.

| Financial Statement Data | (Dollar Amounts in Millions) | | |
| --- | --- | --- | --- |
| | Eastman Kodak | General Motors | Zenith |
| 1. Long-Term Debt | $ 152.4 | $ 1,668.7 | $ 50.0 |
| 2. Deferred Tax Credits (balance sheet) | 144.0 | 472.5 | 18.3 |
| 3. Owners' Equity | 4,026.3 | 14,385.2 | 292.4 |
| 4. Excess of Current (FIFO) Cost over LIFO Cost of Ending Inventory | 330.3 | 299.5 | 9.2 |
| 5. Unrecognized Supplemental Actuarial Value of Pension Plan | 520.0 | 3,000.0 | None |
| 6. Long-Term Debt of Financing Subsidiary | None | 6,509.2 | None |

a. Compute the debt-equity ratio for each of the three companies. Include deferred income taxes with long-term debt in the numerator.

b. Compute the debt-equity ratio for each of the three companies assuming that a FIFO instead of a LIFO cost-flow assumption had been used.

c. Compute the debt-equity ratio for each of the three companies assuming that the supplemental actuarial value had been recognized as a liability.

d. Compute the debt-equity ratio for each of the three companies assuming that deferred taxes had not been recognized for timing differences.

e. Compute the debt-equity ratio for each of the three companies assuming that long-term debt of financing subsidiaries is included in liabilities.

f. Compute the debt-equity ratio for each of the three companies showing the cumulative effect of parts a through e.

g. What conclusions can be drawn about the relative risk of these three companies from the analysis above?

# Chapter 26
## *Accounting for Changing Prices*

26.1 The most persistent and significant criticism of the conventional accounting model based on historical, or acquisition, costs is that it ignores the economic facts of life. Throughout the world, a steady and rapid upward movement in prices has been occurring during the last decade. Yet, until recently, this important economic phenomenon largely went unrecognized under generally accepted accounting principles. FASB *Statement No. 33* (1979), however, now requires that the conventional financial statements be supplemented with certain information about the impact of changing prices on a firm. This chapter discusses the accounting problems associated with changing prices and illustrates techniques for dealing with them.

## Impact of Changing Prices on Conventional Financial Statements

26.2 The accounting problems associated with changing prices might be separated into those related to *changes in general price levels* and those associated with *changes in prices of specific goods and services*. This distinction might be grasped most easily by considering the manner in which a price index is constructed.

## Nature and Construction of Price Indices

26.3 A *price index* is a measure of the prices of a group, or "basket," of goods and services between two dates. For example, assume that we wish to construct a price index for food to measure the change in overall prices between January 1 and December 31 of a particular year. We begin by constructing a typical market basket for food items. To keep the illustration simple, suppose we specify that a typical market basket includes meat, starch, vegetable, beverage, and bread. We ascertain the price of a specific commodity in each of these food groupings at the beginning and end of a year. The prices of the individual commodities at each date are summed to obtain the aggregate market price of the basket of goods. The aggregate market price at one date is then compared to the aggregate price at the other date to obtain a price index. Exhibit 26.1 illustrates the construction of such a price index.

26.4 Prices for this group of commodities increased an average of 10 percent between the beginning and end of the year. The prices of the individual commodities, however, changed at different rates. The price of bread remained relatively stable, while the price of rice decreased. The prices of sirloin steak, frozen vegetables, and beer increased

*Exhibit 26.1*
**Illustration of the Construction
of a Price Index**

| Commodity | January 1 | December 31 | Percentage Change in Market Price of Individual Commodities |
|---|---|---|---|
| Sirloin steak (pound) | $3.00 | $3.30 | +10% |
| Rice (32 ounces) | 1.20 | 1.10 | − 8 |
| Frozen vegetables (package) | .60 | .69 | +15 |
| Beer (six-pack) | 1.90 | 2.32 | +22 |
| Bread (loaf) | .60 | .62 | + 3 |
| Total | $7.30 | $8.03 | |
| Price index, where January 1 prices equal 100. | 100 | 110 (= $8.03/$7.30) | |

significantly, but only that of the frozen vegetables and the beer increased more than the average 10 percent for the group.

26.5 Price indices are constructed by the federal government for many different groupings, or baskets, of commodities. Some of these indices are based on a wide assortment of goods and services and are intended as measures of price changes in general. The two most important *general price indices* are the Gross National Product Implicit Price Deflator Index (issued quarterly) and the Consumer Price Index (issued monthly). Indices are constructed for many specific groupings of goods and services, such as women's apparel, men's shoes, automobiles, and refrigerators. Even these more *specific price indices,* however, contain an assortment of goods of various qualities, dimensions, and styles within the particular product category.

## Accounting Problems Associated with General Price-Level Changes

26.6 The conventional accounting model rests on the assumption that a *constant* or *uniform measuring unit* is used in recording the results of transactions and events in the accounts. That is, the measuring unit (the dollar) used in recording the acquisition of a machine costing $10,000 five years ago is assumed to have the same economic signifi-

cance as the measuring unit used in recording the acquisition of merchandise inventory one week ago for $10,000.

26.7 As general price levels change, however, the purchasing power of the dollar, or its command over goods and services, changes. The general purchasing power sacrificed to acquire the machine five years ago is not equivalent to the purchasing power sacrificed last week to acquire the merchandise inventory. In terms of general purchasing power, therefore, the dollar does not represent a constant, or uniform, measuring unit through time. The amounts assigned to individual assets in the conventional financial statements cannot be meaningfully summed to obtain a measure of total assets. Likewise, the portion of the acquisition cost of various assets recognized as an expense of the current period (cost of goods sold, depreciation expense) cannot be meaningfully matched with revenues of the period.

## Accounting Problems Associated with Specific Price Changes

26.8 The conventional accounting model also rests on the *realization convention.* Changes in the market prices of individual assets and liabilities are generally not recognized as gains or losses in measuring net income until the assets are sold or the liabilities are paid (an exception is the recognition of unrealized losses on marketable securities and inventories using the lower-of-cost-or-market basis). The assets and liabilities continue to be reported in the balance sheet at historical cost.

26.9     Management, however, bases many decisions on information about changes in the costs and prices of individual assets and liabilities. In pricing decisions, management considers the current cost of replacing the good or service sold. In plant asset replacement decisions, management considers the current market values of individual assets held relative to the acquisition costs of assets with similar operating characteristics. In refinancing decisions, management considers the current market value of outstanding debt relative to the cost of issuing new debt. By using historical-cost valuations and the realization convention, the conventional financial statements fail to reflect accurately the results of management's decisions in the firm's current economic environment.

## Official Pronouncement on Accounting for Changing Prices

26.10     *Statement No. 33* of the Financial Accounting Standards Board requires firms with inventories and gross property, plant, and equipment exceeding $125 million or total assets exceeding $1 billion to publish certain supplementary information on the impact of changing prices.* Firms must report (1) income from continuing operations on a historical-cost basis but adjusted to reflect changes in the general purchasing power of the dollar (referred to as *historical-cost/constant-dollar accounting*) and (2) income from continuing operations based on the current cost of individual assets, liabilities, revenues, and expenses (referred to as either *current-cost/nominal-dollar accounting* or *current-cost/constant-dollar accounting*, de-

---

*The Securities and Exchange Commission, in *Accounting Series Release No. 279,* requires all publicly-held firms, even those that do not meet the size requirements of *Statement No. 33,* to include at least a narrative discussion of the effects of changing prices.

pending on the measuring unit used). Certain other supplementary information, discussed more fully later in this chapter, must also be disclosed. Subsequent *Statements* extend these disclosures to mining, oil, and gas companies *(Statement No. 39),* timber companies *(Statement No. 40),* income-producing real estate firms *(Statement No. 41),* and motion picture films *(Statement No. 46).*

    These *Statements* do not require the issue    26.11 of a comprehensive set of financial statements reflecting the effects of changing prices. Rather, only selected financial statement items need be disclosed. The FASB has indicated that it intends to study the usefulness of such supplementary information and will issue additional *Statements* in the future.

    This chapter describes and illustrates various approaches to accounting for changing    26.12 prices. The illustrations are somewhat more comprehensive than the disclosures currently required by the FASB. An understanding of the various approaches, however, will equip you to comprehend both the disclosures currently required and additional disclosures that may become required in the future.

## Constant-Dollar Accounting

### Objective of Constant-Dollar Accounting

    The attribute measured in conventional financial statements is the historical sacrifice    26.13 in general purchasing power made at the time assets were acquired or liabilities were incurred. The measuring unit is the nominal number of dollars either received or expended at the time of these transactions. Conventional financial statements are therefore based on *historical-cost valuations* and a *nominal-dollar measuring unit.*

    Because dollars received or paid over    26.14 time represent different amounts of purchasing power, conventional financial statements are not based on a common, or uniform, measuring unit. The objective of constant-dollar accounting is to state all financial statement amounts in dollars of uniform purchasing power, thereby obtaining a constant, or uniform, measuring unit. The attribute measured is still the historical sacrifice in general purchasing power made when assets were acquired or liabilities were incurred. That historical sacrifice, however, is measured in terms of a uniform measuring unit. The restatement of conventional financial statement amounts to reflect changes in the purchasing power of the measuring unit is referred to as *historical-cost/constant-dollar accounting*. The measuring unit used in the conventional financial statements is referred to as a *nominal dollar*. In constant-dollar statements, the unit is a *constant dollar*. To distinguish constant dollars from nominal dollars, the letter "C" precedes the dollar sign in constant-dollar financial statements (for example, C$10,000).

26.15    Selecting the date for the constant-dollar measuring unit is an arbitrary choice. Some have suggested that the date ought to be the base year of the price index used for restatement. Others have suggested using the end of the current year. Still others, including the FASB for certain supplementary disclosures, advocate using midyear of the most recent year being reported. The procedures are analogous, whatever date is used.

26.16    The general approach is to convert the number of dollars received or expended at various price levels (nominal dollars) to an equivalent number of dollars in the terms of the general price level on some common date (constant dollars). For example, assume that two parcels of land are held on December 31, 1981, at which time an index of the general price level is 155.* Tract A was acquired during 1973 for $100,000, when the general price index was 100. Tract B was acquired during 1976, when the general price index was 116. The acquisition cost of these parcels of land could be restated in terms of

the general price level during 1973 (price index = 100), the general price level during 1976 (price index = 116), or the general price level at the end of 1981 (price index = 155). Exhibit 26.2 demonstrates the restatement procedure. The year of the constant dollar is also indicated.

26.17    The sacrifice in general purchasing power made during 1973 when tract A was acquired for $100,000 is equivalent to sacrificing C$116,000 (= 116/100 × $100,000) of 1976 general purchasing power and to sacrificing C$155,000 (= 155/100 × $100,000) of December 31, 1981, general purchasing power. Likewise, the sacrifice in general purchasing power made during 1976 when tract B was acquired for $100,000 is equivalent to sacrificing C$86,207 (= 100/116 × $100,000) of 1973 general purchasing power and to sacrificing $133,621 (= 155/116 × $100,000) of December 31, 1981, general purchasing power. The restated amounts in Exhibit 26.2 use a measuring unit of constant, or uniform, general purchasing power. For the sake of simplicity, we use dollars of general purchasing power at the end of the most current year as the measuring unit in the illustrations and problems in this chapter.

26.18    Two important aspects of the constant-dollar restatement procedure should be noted in Exhibit 26.2. First, the procedure does not represent a departure from the use of historical cost as the valuation method. As is illustrated later, the restatements to a constant-dollar basis are based on the amounts reported in the conventional nominal-dollar financial statements. Second, the amounts shown for constant-dollar restated acquisition cost do not attempt to reflect the current market prices of these two parcels of land. The market prices of the land could have changed in an entirely different direction and pattern from that of the general price-level change. The focus of the constant-dollar restatement procedure is on making the measuring unit used in acquisition cost−based accounting systems more comparable over time and not on reflecting current market prices of individual assets and equities.

---

*The values given for price indices throughout this chapter are assumed for illustrative purposes; they are not the actual values of indices published by the federal government.

*Exhibit 26.2*
**Illustration of Constant-Dollar Restatement Procedure for Land**

| Item | Acquisition Cost Measured in Nominal Dollars | Acquisition Cost Measured in Constant Dollars | | |
| --- | --- | --- | --- | --- |
| | | General Price Index = 100 | General Price Index = 116 | General Price Index = 155 |
| Tract A ................. | $100,000 | | | |
| $100,000 × 100/100 ...... | | C$$_{1973}$100,000 | | |
| $100,000 × 116/100 ...... | | | C$$_{1976}$116,000 | |
| $100,000 × 155/100 ...... | | | | C$$_{1981}$155,000 |
| | | | | |
| Tract B ................. | $100,000 | | | |
| $100,000 × 100/116 ...... | | C$$_{1973}$86,207 | | |
| $100,000 × 116/116 ...... | | | C$$_{1976}$100,000 | |
| $100,000 × 155/116 ...... | | | | C$$_{1981}$133,621 |

## Restatement of Monetary and Nonmonetary Items

26.19 An important distinction is made in the constant-dollar restatement procedure between monetary items and nonmonetary items.

26.20 **Monetary Items** A *monetary item* is either cash or a claim receivable or payable in a specified number of dollars or other currency unit, without reference to future prices of goods or services. Examples of monetary items are cash, accounts, notes, and interest receivable; accounts, notes, and interest payable; income taxes payable, and bonds.

26.21 In preparing a constant-dollar restated balance sheet, the valuation of monetary items at the number of dollars due automatically states them in terms of the general purchasing power of the dollar at that time. No restatement is therefore necessary, and the conventionally reported and restated amounts are the same. For example, assume that a firm has $30,000 of cash on hand on December 31, 1981. On the conventionally prepared balance sheet, this item would be stated at $30,000, the amount of cash on hand. On the constant-dollar restated balance sheet, this item would also be reported at C$30,000, representing $30,000 of December 31, 1981, general purchasing power.

26.22 Because monetary items are receivable or payable in a specified number of dollars rather than in terms of a given amount of general purchasing power, holding monetary items over time while the general purchasing power of the dollar changes causes *purchasing power,* or *inflation, gains and losses.* During a period of inflation, a holder of monetary assets loses general purchasing power. For example, a firm with outstanding notes receivable incurs a purchasing-power loss, because the dollars loaned had more general purchasing power than the dollars to be received when the note is collected. Likewise, a debtor holding monetary liabilities gains in general purchasing power during periods of inflation, because the dollars required to repay the debt have less purchasing power than the dollars originally borrowed. The gain or loss from holding monetary items is an element of constant-dollar net income but is not included in net income as conventionally reported.

26.23 **Nonmonetary Items** A *nonmonetary item* is an asset or equity that does not represent a claim to or for a specified number of dollars or other currency unit. That is, if an item is not a monetary item, then it must be non-monetary. Examples of nonmonetary items are inventory, land, buildings, equipment, common stock, and retained earnings, including the temporary accounts for revenues and expenses. In conventionally prepared financial statements, nonmonetary items are stated in terms of varying amounts of general purchasing power. The amount depends on the date the nonmonetary asset was acquired or the nonmonetary equity arose. As illustrated in Exhibit 26.2 with the two parcels of land, the conventionally reported amounts of these items are restated to an equivalent number of dollars of constant purchasing power as of the date of the balance sheet. The restatement is for the *cumulative* inflation since the parcels of land were acquired. The amount of this restatement does not represent a gain or loss to be included in net income, but merely an adjustment to make the measuring unit comparable.

26.24     One way to understand that the increased number on the balance sheet does not represent a gain is to consider restating an amount shown on a British balance sheet in pounds sterling to U.S. dollars. Suppose that £100 of inventory is restated to $220 of inventory. No gain has occurred, only a translation from one measuring unit to the other. Similarly, plant assets acquired for $100 in an earlier year when the general price index was 100 can be restated as C$220 in a year when the price index is 220 without recognizing a gain. The change in amounts is merely a translation from one measuring unit to another, not a gain. Appendix 26.1 indicates the monetary versus nonmonetary classification of various accounts in the financial statements for purposes of constant-dollar accounting.

## Constant-Dollar Restatement Procedure

26.25     The procedure for restating the conventional financial statements to a constant-dollar basis is as follows:

**1.** The assets and equities on the most recent balance sheet are separated into mone-

tary and nonmonetary items. The monetary items are extended to the constant-dollar balance sheet using the same amounts as are reported in the conventional balance sheet. The nonmonetary items are restated from the purchasing power of the dollar when the nonmonetary assets were acquired or nonmonetary equities were incurred to the equivalent number of dollars of purchasing power on the date of the balance sheet. FASB *Statement No. 33* requires that the Consumer Price Index for all Urban Consumers be used for the restatement.* The restatement involves multiplying the historical amount by a restatement ratio. The numerator of the ratio is the Consumer Price Index for the date of the balance sheet and the denominator is the Consumer Price Index when the asset was acquired or the equity was incurred. Because the Consumer Price Index (CPI) is issued monthly, the index used is for the month that includes the date of the balance sheet and the index for the month that includes the date of acquisition. Restated Retained Earnings is the residual, or "plug," to equate constant-dollar assets and constant-dollar equities. The "plug" is checked by independent calculations in the next step.

**2.** Calculate the restated retained earnings amount at the end of the year by restating each of the amounts in the Retained Earnings account during the period. Reconcile the result to that from step **1**. This step generally involves three substeps.

**a.** Calculate the constant-dollar balance in Retained Earnings at the beginning of the period. If constant-dollar financial statements were prepared for the preceding period, the constant-dollar amount of Retained Earnings at the end of the preceding period is restated to end-of-the-current-period constant dollars. This restatement involves multiplying the constant-dollar beginning Retained Earnings amount by a ratio. The numerator of the ratio is the CPI at the end of the current

_____

*Financial Accounting Standards Board, *Statement of Financial Accounting Standards No. 33* (1979), par. 39.

period and the denominator is the CPI at the end of the preceding period. As discussed later, the calculation of the constant-dollar amount of retained earnings is more complex in the first year that constant-dollar statements are prepared.

**b.** Calculate the amount of constant-dollar net income for the current period. Each revenue and expense is restated from the purchasing power of the dollar when the measurements underlying the revenues and expenses were initially made to the purchasing power on the date of the balance sheet. In addition, the purchasing-power gain or loss for the period on net monetary items is calculated and included in constant-dollar net income.

**c.** Restate dividends and any other changes in the Retained Earnings account during the period.

26.26 If the restatement procedure has been performed correctly, then the amount of restated Retained Earnings at the end of the period as determined in step **2** should be equal to the residual, or "plug," in step **1**.

## Illustration of the Constant-Dollar Restatement Procedure

Exhibit 26.3 presents the 1981 income statement and Exhibit 26.4 presents the 1980–1981 comparative balance sheet of Sweeney Corporation used to illustrate the restatement procedure. These financial statements are based on historical-cost valuations and a nominal-dollar measuring unit. Exhibit 26.5 presents assumed amounts for an index of consumer prices for various dates. The amounts shown are based on the average prices for each month. When an index for the end of a month is needed, the average index for the month is generally considered a satisfactory approximation. 26.27

**Step 1: Restate the End-of-the-Period Balance Sheet** The accounts on the balance sheet on December 31, 1981, are classified into monetary and nonmonetary categories. Each item is then restated as appropriate. Exhibit 26.6 summarizes the restatements. 26.28

*Cash and Accounts Receivable* Cash and Accounts Receivable are monetary items. 26.29

---

*Exhibit 26.3*
**Income Statement for Sweeney Corporation in Nominal Dollars for the Year 1981**

| | |
|---|---:|
| Revenues and Gains: | |
|   Product Sales | $520,000 |
|   Gain on Sale of Equipment | 8,000 |
|     Total Revenues and Gains | $528,000 |
| | |
| Expenses and Losses: | |
|   Cost of Goods Sold | $396,000 |
|   Selling and Administrative | 59,000 |
|   Depreciation | 17,000 |
|   Interest | 10,000 |
|   Income Taxes | 20,000 |
|     Total Expenses and Losses | $502,000 |
| | |
| Net Income | $ 26,000 |
| Earnings per Common Share (based on 10,000 outstanding shares) | $ 2.60 |

*Exhibit 26.4*
**Comparative Balance Sheet for Sweeney
Corporation in Nominal Dollars**

| | December 31, 1981 | December 31, 1980 |
|---|---|---|
| **ASSETS** | | |
| Current Assets: | | |
| Cash ........................................ | $ 36,000 | $ 20,000 |
| Accounts Receivable (net) ...................... | 80,000 | 70,000 |
| Inventories (at first-in, first-out) .............. | 104,000 | 100,000 |
| Total Current Assets ...................... | $220,000 | $190,000 |
| Property, Plant, and Equipment: | | |
| Land ......................................... | $ 16,000 | $ 16,000 |
| Building (net of accumulated depreciation) ..................... | 42,000 | 44,000 |
| Equipment (net of accumulated depreciation) ................. | 122,000 | 130,000 |
| Total Property, Plant, and Equipment ...................... | $180,000 | $190,000 |
| Total Assets ........................................ | $400,000 | $380,000 |
| **LIABILITIES AND SHAREHOLDERS' EQUITY** | | |
| Current Liabilities: | | |
| Accounts Payable ............................ | $ 62,000 | $ 50,000 |
| Salaries Payable ............................ | 8,000 | 10,000 |
| Total Current Liabilities ..................... | $ 70,000 | $ 60,000 |
| Bonds Payable ................................ | 100,000 | 100,000 |
| Total Liabilities .......................... | $170,000 | $160,000 |
| Shareholders' Equity: | | |
| Common Stock ($1 par value, 10,000 shares issued and outstanding) ............................... | $ 10,000 | $ 10,000 |
| Additional Paid-in Capital ...................... | 15,000 | 15,000 |
| Retained Earnings ........................... | 205,000 | 195,000 |
| Total Shareholders' Equity .................... | $230,000 | $220,000 |
| Total Liabilities and Shareholders' Equity ........................... | $400,000 | $380,000 |

They are either a specified number of dollars or are claims to a specified number of dollars regardless of changes in the price level. They are therefore extended to the constant-dollar balance sheet at the same amounts as shown in the nominal-dollar balance sheet.

26.30   *Inventories* Inventories are nonmonetary items, because they are not claims to specific cash amounts. They are stated in the conventional balance sheet in terms of historical acquisition costs. These historical-cost amounts must be restated to an equivalent number of constant dollars. To do so requires knowing the dates of acquisition and the historical costs, which presents a special problem. Most firms do not use specific identification in the valuation of their inventories and cost of goods sold. Instead, a cost-flow assumption (FIFO, LIFO, weighted-average) is used. The constant-dollar restatement must be consistent with the assumption used.

26.31   Sweeney Corporation uses a FIFO cost-flow assumption. The inventory turnover ratio is 3.88 [= $396,000/.5($100,000 + $104,000)]. Thus, the inventory on hand at the end of the year represents about one-fourth of the year's purchases. If inventories are assumed to be acquired more or less

Exhibit 26.5
**Index of Consumer Prices for
Various Dates**

| Date | Index |
| --- | --- |
| January 1971 (when corporation was formed and land was acquired) | 104.3 |
| Average for the Year 1972 (when building was constructed) | 106.5 |
| April 1975 (when equipment was acquired) | 162.4 |
| November 1978 (when equipment was acquired) | 178.5 |
| October 1980 | 198.2 |
| November 1980 | 199.3 |
| December 1980 | 201.6 |
| January 1981 | 202.3 |
| February 1981 | 204.6 |
| March 1981 | 206.9 |
| April 1981 | 209.2 |
| May 1981 | 211.5 |
| June 1981 (when equipment was sold) | 214.1 |
| July 1981 (when equipment was acquired) | 216.6 |
| August 1981 | 218.4 |
| September 1981 | 220.6 |
| October 1981 | 222.3 |
| November 1981 | 223.9 |
| December 1981 | 225.0 |
| Average 1981 | 214.6 |

continuously throughout the year, then the ending inventory was acquired during the last quarter of the year. The average price index for the last quarter is 223.7 [= (222.3 + 223.9 + 225.0)/3]. The ending inventory on a constant-dollar basis is C$104,604 ( = $104,000 × 225.0/223.7)

26.32    If a LIFO or weighted-average cost-flow assumption had been used, the price index in the denominator of the restatement ratio would be changed to reflect the purchases from which the ending inventory was assumed to come (for example, each LIFO layer).

26.33    If the lower-of-cost-or-market valuation had been used and some inventory items had been stated in terms of market prices at the end of the year, no restatement would be required for these items. They would already be stated in terms of end-of-the-year dollars. Although the acquisition cost for an item may be less than market value in the conventional financial statements, its restated acquisition cost for the constant-dollar financial statements may exceed its market value. In this case, the lower market value is used. Thus, some items may be reported at market value in constant-dollar financial statements even though they are stated at acquisition cost in the conventional, nominal-dollar financial statements.

*Property, Plant, and Equipment* Constant-    26.34 dollar restatements of property, plant, and equipment are straightforward. But because large numbers of items and an equally large number of acquisition dates are involved, the initial restatement process can be tedious.

Sweeney Corporation acquired the land    26.35 when the corporation was formed in 1971. The price index at this time was 104.3. Land is therefore restated to C$34,516 (= $16,000 × 225.0/104.3). Note that the restatement is for the *cumulative* inflation since the land was acquired.

The building was constructed during 1972    26.36 at a cost of $80,000 when the average price index was 106.5. The book value of the building on December 31, 1981, is $42,000 in nominal dollars. The book value of the build-

*Exhibit 26.6*
**Restatement of Balance Sheet
from Nominal to Constant Dollars
for Sweeney Corporation, December 31, 1981**

|  | Nominal Dollars | Restatement Ratio | Constant December 31, 1981, Dollars |
|---|---|---|---|
| **Assets** | | | |
| Current Assets: | | | |
| Cash | $ 36,000 | 225.0/225.0 | C$ 36,000 |
| Accounts Receivable (net) | 80,000 | 225.0/225.0 | 80,000 |
| Inventories (at first-in, first-out) | 104,000 | 225.0/223.7 | 104,604 |
| Total Current Assets | $220,000 | | C$220,604 |
| Property, Plant, and Equipment: | | | |
| Land | $ 16,000 | 225.0/104.3 | C$ 34,516 |
| Building (net of accumulated depreciation) | 42,000 | 225.0/106.5 | 88,732 |
| Equipment (net of accumulated depreciation): | | | |
| 1975 Acquisitions | 36,000 | 225.0/162.4 | 49,877 |
| 1978 Acquisitions | 77,000 | 225.0/178.5 | 97,059 |
| 1981 Acquisitions | 9,000 | 225.0/216.6 | 9,349 |
| Total Property, Plant, and Equipment | $180,000 | | C$279,533 |
| Total Assets | $400,000 | | C$500,137 |
| **Liabilities and Shareholders' Equity** | | | |
| Current Liabilities: | | | |
| Accounts Payable | $ 62,000 | 225.0/225.0 | C$ 62,000 |
| Salaries Payable | 8,000 | 225.0/225.0 | 8,000 |
| Total Current Liabilities | 70,000 | | C$ 70,000 |
| Bonds Payable | 100,000 | 225.0/225.0 | 100,000 |
| Total Liabilities | $170,000 | | C$170,000 |
| Shareholders' Equity: | | | |
| Common Stock ($1 par value, 10,000 shares issued and outstanding) | 10,000 | 225.0/104.3 | C$ 21,572 |
| Additional Paid-in Capital | 15,000 | 225.0/104.3 | 32,359 |
| Retained Earnings | 205,000 | Plug | 276,206 |
| Total Shareholders' Equity | $230,000 | | C$330,137 |
| Total Liabilities and Shareholders' Equity | $400,000 | | C$500,137 |

ing is restated to C$88,732 (= $42,000 × 225.0/106.5).

26.37 The equipment held by Sweeney Corporation on December 31, 1981, consists of these items acquired over several years with net depreciated book value as follows:

| | |
|---|---|
| 1975 Acquisitions | $ 36,000 |
| 1978 Acquisitions | 77,000 |
| 1981 Acquisitions | 9,000 |
| Total Net Book Value of Equipment | $122,000 |

Each of these amounts is restated for the change in the purchasing power of the dollar between the date of acquisition and December 31, 1981, as follows:

1975 Acquisitions: $36,000 × 225.0/162.4 = C$49,877
1978 Acquisitions: $77,000 × 225.0/178.5 = C$97,059
1981 Acquisitions: $ 9,000 × 225.0/216.6 = C$9,349

*Current Liabilities* Accounts Payable and Salaries Payable are both monetary items and are extended to the constant-dollar statements at the same amount shown in the nominal-dollar balance sheet. 26.38

**26.39** *Bonds Payable* Bonds are stated in terms of the present value of the number of dollars payable on the bond. As such, bonds are monetary items and do not require restatement on December 31, 1981. A premium or discount account is also a monetary item because these accounts are adjunct or contra accounts to a monetary item.

**26.40** *Common Stock and Additional Paid-in Capital* These accounts are stated at the numbers of dollars received when the common stock was issued and are therefore nonmonetary items. The price index at the time of issue in 1971 was 104.3. The restated amounts are as follows:

Common Stock: $10,000 × 225.0/104.3 = C$21,572
Additional Paid-
  in Capital.   $15,000 × 225.0/104.3 = C$32,359

**26.41** *Retained Earnings* Restated Retained Earnings is the amount necessary to equate restated assets and restated equities. As indicated in Exhibit 26.6, the restated balance in Retained Earnings on December 31, 1981, is C$276,206.

**26.42** **Step 2: Reconcile to End-of-the-Period Retained Earnings** The second step is to trace the changes in the Retained Earnings account in order to reconcile them to the ending balance in restated Retained Earnings of C$276,206.

**26.43** *Restate Beginning Balance in Retained Earnings* We begin by calculating the restated beginning balance in Retained Earnings. In the first year constant-dollar financial statements are prepared, this step requires that the entire balance sheet at the beginning of the period be restated to the price level as of the beginning of the period; Retained Earnings must then be rolled forward to the price level at the end of the period. Exhibit 26.7 demonstrates this initial restatement. All balance sheet amounts are restated in terms of dollars of *December 31, 1980,* purchasing power. Restated Retained Earnings on December 31, 1980, is C$248,595. In terms of dollars of *December*

*31, 1981,* purchasing power this represents C$277,450 (= C$248,595 × 225.0/201.6).

**26.44** In subsequent years, restatement of the beginning-of-the-period balance sheet as illustrated in Exhibit 26.7 is not necessary. The restated beginning balance in Retained Earnings will simply be equal to the restated ending balance in Retained Earnings of the previous year. All that is required is that the restated beginning balance be rolled forward for one year of general price-level change.

**26.45** *Restate Income before Purchasing Power Gain or Loss* The next step is to restate the revenues and expenses in the income statement. Exhibit 26.8 summarizes the restatements.

**26.46** Product sales, selling and administrative expenses, interest, and income taxes occurred evenly over the year. Consequently, measurements of their nominal-dollar amounts were made evenly over the year. Their restatement is based on the average price index for 1981 of 214.6.

**26.47** Calculating the constant-dollar gain on the sale of equipment is made easier by reconstructing the journal entry made in nominal dollars. The equipment sold had been acquired for $16,000 in 1975. Accumulated depreciation up to the time of sale in June 1981 was $13,000. The equipment was sold for $11,000. The nominal-dollar journal entry to record the sale is

| | | |
|---|---|---|
| Cash | 11,000 | |
| Accumulated Depreciation | 13,000 | |
|   Equipment | | 16,000 |
|   Gain on Sale | | 8,000 |

The constant-dollar gain is calculated as follows:

| | |
|---|---|
| Selling Price: $11,000 × 225.0[a]/214.1[b] . | C$11,560 |
| Less Book Value: ($16,000 − $13,000) | |
|   × 225.0[a]/162.4[c] | 4,156 |
| Constant-Dollar Gain on Sale | C$ 7,404 |

[a]Index at balance sheet date.
[b]Index at time of sale.
[c]Index at time of acquisition.

Note that the selling price, book value, and gain are all stated in terms of constant December 31, 1981, dollars.

*Exhibit 26.7*
**Restatement of Balance Sheet
from Nominal Dollars to Constant Dollars
for Sweeney Corporation, December 31, 1980**

| | Nominal Dollars | Restatement Ratio | Constant December 31, 1980, Dollars |
|---|---|---|---|
| **Assets** | | | |
| Current Assets: | | | |
| Cash ............................... | $ 20,000 | 201.6/201.6 | C$ 20,000 |
| Accounts Receivable .................. | 70,000 | 201.6/201.6 | 70,000 |
| Inventories ......................... | 100,000 | 201.6/199.7[a] | 100,951 |
| Total Current Assets ................ | $190,000 | | C$190,951 |
| Property, Plant, and Equipment: | | | |
| Land ............................... | 16,000 | 201.6/104.3 | C$ 30,926 |
| Building (net of accumulated depreciation) .... | 44,000 | 201.6/106.5 | 83,290 |
| Equipment (net of accumulated depreciation) .. | | | |
| 1975 Acquisitions ..................... | 44,000 | 201.6/162.4 | 54,621 |
| 1978 Acquisitions ..................... | 86,000 | 201.6/178.5 | 97,129 |
| Total Property, Plant, and Equipment .. | $190,000 | | C$265,966 |
| Total Assets ...................... | $380,000 | | C$456,917 |
| **Liabilities and Shareholders' Equity** | | | |
| Current Liabilities: | | | |
| Accounts Payable ..................... | $ 50,000 | 201.6/201.6 | C$ 50,000 |
| Salaries Payable ..................... | 10,000 | 201.6/201.6 | 10,000 |
| Total Current Liabilities ............. | $ 60,000 | | C$ 60,000 |
| Bonds Payable ...................... | 100,000 | 201.6/201.6 | 100,000 |
| Total Liabilities .................... | $160,000 | | C$160,000 |
| Shareholders' Equity: | | | |
| Common Stock ....................... | $ 10,000 | 201.6/104.3 | C$ 19,329 |
| Additional Paid-in Capital ............. | 15,000 | 201.6/104.3 | 28,993 |
| Retained Earnings ................... | 195,000 | Plug | 248,595 |
| Total Shareholders' Equity ........... | $220,000 | | C$296,917 |
| Total Liabilities and Shareholders' Equity ....... | $380,000 | | C$456,917 |

[a]199.7 = (198.2 + 199.3 + 201.6)/3.

26.48    Exhibit 26.9 shows the calculation of constant-dollar cost of goods sold for 1981. Here, too, it is useful to begin with the nominal-dollar amounts. The inventory at the beginning and end of 1981 is obtained from Exhibit 26.4, and the cost of goods sold is obtained from Exhibit 26.3. Purchases for the period are then derived from the inventory equation:

$$\text{Purchases} = \frac{\text{Cost of}}{\text{Goods Sold}} + \frac{\text{Ending}}{\text{Inventory}} - \frac{\text{Beginning}}{\text{Inventory}}.$$

The restatement of both the beginning and ending inventories is based on a FIFO cost-flow assumption. Because the inventory turnover is approximately four times each year, the inventories were acquired during the last quarter of their respective years. Because purchases are assumed to occur evenly over each year, the average price index for 1981 is used in the denominator in restating purchases. Constant-dollar cost of goods sold on a FIFO basis is C$427,450.

26.49    Depreciation expense in the conventional financial statements is stated in terms of dollars of varying purchasing power. These

*Exhibit 26.8*
**Restatement of Income Statement
for Sweeney Corporation from Nominal
Dollars to Constant Dollars
for the Year 1981**

| | Nominal Dollars | Restatement Ratio | Constant December 31, 1981, Dollars |
|---|---|---|---|
| Revenues and Gains: | | | |
| Product Sales | $520,000 | 225.0/214.6 | C$545,200 |
| Gain on Sale of Equipment | 8,000 | Paragraph 26.47 | 7,404 |
| Total Revenues and Gains | $528,000 | | C$552,604 |
| | | | |
| Expenses: | | | |
| Cost of Goods Sold | 396,000 | Exhibit 26.9 | C$427,450 |
| Selling and Administrative | 59,000 | 225.0/214.6 | 61,859 |
| Depreciation: 1972 Acquisitions | 2,000 | 225.0/106.5 | 4,225 |
| 1975 Acquisitions | 5,000 | 225.0/162.4 | 6,927 |
| 1970 Acquisitions | 9,000 | 225.0/178.5 | 11,345 |
| 1981 Acquisitions | 1,000 | 225.0/216.6 | 1,039 |
| Interest | 10,000 | 225.0/214.6 | 10,485 |
| Income Taxes | 20,000 | 225.0/214.6 | 20,969 |
| Total Expenses | $502,000 | | C$544,299 |
| | | | |
| Income before Purchasing Power Gain or Loss | $ 26,000 | | C$ 8,305 |
| Purchasing Power Gain or Net Monetary Position | — | Exhibit 26.10 | 6,451 |
| Net Income | $ 26,000 | | C$ 14,756 |

amounts must be restated to dollars of constant December 31, 1981, purchasing power. Internal records of Sweeney Corporation indicate that depreciation expense of $17,000 is composed of the following:

| | |
|---|---|
| Building | $ 2,000 |
| Equipment: | |
| 1975 Acquisitions | 5,000 |
| 1978 Acquisitions | 9,000 |
| 1981 Acquisitions | 1,000 |
| Total Nominal-Dollar Depreciation | $17,000 |

The restatement of these amounts is as follows:

| | | |
|---|---|---|
| Building: | $2,000 × 225.0[a]/106.5[b] = | C$ 4,225 |
| Equipment: | | |
| 1975 Acquisitions: | $5,000 × 225.0[a]/162.4[b] = | 6,927 |
| 1978 Acquisitions: | $9,000 × 225.0[a]/178.5[b] = | 11,345 |
| 1981 Acquisitions: | $1,000 × 225.0[a]/216.6[b] = | 1,039 |
| Total Constant-Dollar Depreciation: | | C$23,536 |

[a]Index at balance sheet date.
[b]Index at time of acquisitions.

Exhibit 26.8 indicates that income before the purchasing power gain or loss on a constant-dollar basis is C$8,305, compared to $26,000 in nominal dollars.                              26.50

*Calculate the Purchasing Power Gain or Loss* Purchasing power gains and losses appear in income statements based on a constant-dollar measuring unit. The gain or loss arises from holding monetary assets and monetary equities over time while the general purchasing power of the dollar changes. Exhibit 26.10 presents the calculations for Sweeney Corporation for 1981. Two steps are involved in the calculations:          26.51

1. Prepare an analysis of the net changes in monetary accounts during the year in nominal dollars. That is, starting with the net monetary asset or net monetary equity position at the beginning of the year, add all transactions causing monetary assets to increase or monetary equities to decrease (net

---

*Exhibit 26.9*
**Calculation of Constant-Dollar**
**Cost of Goods Sold**
**for Sweeney Corporation for 1981**

| | Nominal Dollars | Restatement Ratio | Constant December 31, 1981, Dollars |
|---|---|---|---|
| Beginning Inventory | $100,000 | 225.0/199.7[a] | C$112,669 |
| Purchases | 400,000 | 225.0/214.6[b] | 419,385 |
| Available for Sale | 500,000 | | C$532,054 |
| Less Ending Inventory | 104,000 | 225.0/223.7[c] | 104,604 |
| Cost of Goods Sold | $396,000 | | C$427,450 |

[a]199.7 = (198.2 + 199.3 + 201.6)/3.
[b]214.6 is the average index for the year.
[c]223.7 = (222.3 + 223.9 + 225.0)/3.

debit changes in monetary accounts); subtract all transactions causing monetary assets to decrease or monetary equities to increase (net credit changes in monetary accounts). The result is the ending net monetary asset or net monetary equity position. This step is perhaps the most time-consuming in the constant-dollar restatement process, because an analysis of changes in monetary accounts is not routinely prepared as part of the accounting process each period. (The analysis is analogous to a statement of changes in financial position in which funds are defined as net monetary assets and equities.) If the beginning balance plus (or minus) the transactions identified as affecting

---

*Exhibit 26.10*
**Calculation of Purchasing Power Gain or Loss**
**for Sweeney Corporation for the Year 1981**

| | Nominal Dollars | Restatement Ratio | Constant December 31, 1981, Dollars |
|---|---|---|---|
| Net Monetary Asset (Equity) Position, January 1, 1981 | $( 70,000) | 225.0/201.6 | C$ ( 78,125) |
| Add Increases in Net Monetary Assets: | | | |
|     From Product Sales | 520,000 | 225.0/214.6 | 545,200 |
|     From Sale of Equipment | 11,000 | 225.0/214.1 | 11,560 |
| Less Decreases in Net Monetary Assets: | | | |
|     From Purchase of Inventories | (400,000) | 225.0/214.6 | (419,385) |
|     From Selling and Administrative Costs | ( 59,000) | 225.0/214.6 | ( 61,859) |
|     From Interest Cost | ( 10,000) | 225.0/214.6 | ( 10,485) |
|     From Income Taxes | ( 20,000) | 225.0/214.6 | ( 20,969) |
|     From Dividends | ( 16,000) | 225.0/225.0 | ( 16,000) |
|     From Equipment Purchased | ( 10,000) | 225.0/216.6 | ( 10,388) |
| Actual Net Monetary Asset (Equity) Position, December 31, 1981 | $( 54,000) | | |
| Constant-Dollar Net Monetary Asset (Equity) Position, December 31, 1981 | | | C$ ( 60,451) |
| Purchasing Power Gain: C$60,451 − C$54,000 | | | C$ 6,451 |

monetary accounts during the period does not reconcile to the actual ending balance in net monetary accounts as shown on the balance sheet, then some transactions have been overlooked.

**2.** Restate the beginning balance and each transaction affecting a monetary account from the nominal dollars when the measurements were made to the dollars of constant purchasing power at the end of the period. Note in this step that Sales Revenue, Interest Expense, Income Tax Expense, and so on are not the accounts being restated. These restatements were made in calculating constant-dollar income before the purchasing power gain or loss in Exhibit 26.8. The restatement in Exhibit 26.10 is for the other half of the journal entry (debit to Accounts Receivable, credit to Cash or Accounts Payable). The constant-dollar, net monetary liability position on December 31, 1981, is C$60,451. Because the actual net liability position is only $54,000, Sweeney Corporation had a purchasing power gain of C$6,451 (= C$60,451 − C$54,000) during the year. The major cause of this gain is the long-term debt outstanding. The debt will be paid at maturity with dollars of smaller purchasing power than the dollars initially received when the debt was issued. A portion of this total gain is recognized each period under constant-dollar accounting. The recognition of a purchasing power gain on long term debt is one of the most important reasons why constant-dollar net income (including the purchasing power gain) exceeds nominal-dollar net income for some firms in some years.

*Restate Other Transactions Affecting Retained Earnings* The final step is to restate any transactions affecting the Retained Earnings account other than net income for the period. For Sweeney Corporation, only dividends require restatement. Exhibit 26.11 shows the restatement of dividends which were declared and paid on December 31, 1981, as well as the reconciliation of constant-dollar Retained Earnings to an ending balance of C$276,206. Because this amount is the same as the amount treated as a plug to Retained Earnings in Exhibit 26.6, the restatement process has been carried out correctly. 26.52

**Constant-Dollar Date Other Than Current Year-End** Constant-dollar disclosures are not always based on the purchasing power of the dollar at the end of the current year. Some use the purchasing power for the base year of the price index. That is, the year when the price index was 100 is used— 1967 in the case of the CPI. The advantage of a base-year constant-dollar measure is that financial statement amounts for prior years included for comparative purposes in current annual reports remain the same each year. The 1975 numbers are the same in the 1981 or the 1980 report. The numbers in old annual reports are not "rolled forward" each year to be restated in end-of-current-year dollars. The FASB requires supplementary disclosure using as the measuring unit the purchasing power of mid-current-year dollars in some cases. The advantage of this otherwise-awkward date is that many in- 26.53

*Exhibit 26.11*
**Reconciliation of Retained Earnings in Nominal Dollars and Constant Dollars for Sweeney Corporation for the Year 1981**

|  | Nominal Dollars | Restatement Ratio | Constant December 31, 1981, Dollars |
|---|---|---|---|
| Balance, January 1, 1981 | $195,000 | Paragraph 26.43 | C$277,450 |
| Plus: Net Income | 26,000 | Exhibit 26.8 | 14,756 |
| Less: Dividends | (16,000) | 225.0/225.0 | (16,000) |
| Balance, December 31, 1981 | $205,000 |  | C$276,206 |

come statement accounts in nominal dollars are already stated in units of mid-year purchasing power. Any revenue or expense occurring evenly throughout the year is so stated. Typically, cost of goods sold and depreciation expense are the only major items not spread evenly throughout the current year. Thus restatement is usually required in the income statement for only those two items when a mid-current-year unit is used.

26.54   In this chapter, we restate all items to end-of-current-year purchasing power. Once all items are stated in end-of-current-year constant dollars, a further restatement to some other constant-dollar unit is mechanical. For example, assume that the price index for the base year is 100.0, for the middle of the current year is 214.6, and for the end of the current year is 225.0. To restate all items to base-year constant dollars, multiply end-of-current-year measurements by 100.0/225.0 = 0.444. To restate to middle-of-current-year constant dollars, multiply all end-of-current-year measurements by 214.6/225.0 = 0.954.

## Evaluation of Constant-Dollar Accounting

26.55   The procedures for restating financial statements to a constant-dollar basis can be traced back to before 1920.* Yet it was not until 1979 that disclosure of constant-dollar information became a part of generally accepted accounting principles. The usefulness of constant-dollar information has been, and continues to be, controversial.

26.56   **The Case for Constant-Dollar Accounting** Proponents of constant-dollar accounting offer the following arguments:

---

*See Livingston Middleditch, Jr., ''Should Accounts Reflect the Changing Value of the Dollar?'' *Journal of Accountancy* 25 (February 1918), pp. 114–120. This article was ''rediscovered'' and reprinted by Stephen A. Zeff (ed.) in *Asset Appreciation, Business Income and Price-Level Accounting: 1918–1935* (New York: Arno Press, 1976). Generally, however, the credit for developing constant-dollar accounting is given to Henry W. Sweeney for his *Stabilized Accounting* (New York: Harper & Bros., 1936).

**1.** Constant-dollar accounting makes the results of arithmetic operations more meaningful. If the measuring unit (the dollar) varies over time because of changes in the general purchasing power of the dollar, then additions and subtractions of recorded amounts cannot be made meaningfully.

**2.** Constant-dollar accounting makes inter-period comparisons more meaningful. Changes in the amount of an item (sales, cost of goods sold) are difficult to interpret if the measuring unit used is not the same over time.

**3.** Constant-dollar accounting provides useful information about the comparative impact of inflation across firms. Inflation affects firms differently, depending on the age and composition of their assets and equities. Heavily capital-intensive firms are likely to report significantly larger constant-dollar depreciation expense than nominal-dollar depreciation expense. Highly leveraged firms will report a larger purchasing-power gain during periods of increasing prices than firms that use relatively little debt. Constant-dollar accounting reports these differing effects of inflation across firms.

**4.** Constant-dollar accounting improves the meaning and measurement of net income. Revenues and expenses are matched in terms of a constant measuring unit. Also, a gain or loss is explicitly recognized for the change in the general purchasing power of monetary assets and equities held. Income before the purchasing power gain or loss must exceed any loss of purchasing power of monetary assets and equities if the purchasing power of the monetary, or financial, capital of the firm is to be maintained.†

**5.** Government policy-makers are accus-

---

†The nature of the purchasing power gain or loss is sometimes misunderstood. In conventional financial statements, interest expense is based on the interest rate negotiated between the borrower and lender at the time of the loan. That interest rate partly depends on both the lender's and borrower's expectations of the rate of inflation during the term of the loan. Lenders are aware that, when inflation occurs during the term

tomed to using real, not nominal, dollar measuring units. To report corporate accounting data in nominal, rather than real, terms may work to the disadvantage of corporations in government policy decisions.

26.57 **The Case against Constant-Dollar Accounting** Opponents of constant-dollar accounting argue that it fails to measure the economically significant effects of changing prices on a firm. They argue as follows:

**1.** With respect to nonmonetary items, the strategies that firms follow in coping with inflation focus on changes in the prices of the specific goods and services that the firm normally acquires and not on changes in the prices of a broad market basket of consumer goods and services. Raw materials are purchased early in anticipation of increased acquisition costs. A capital-intensive plant is

constructed in anticipation of increased labor costs. Yet, under constant-dollar accounting, the results of these decisions are judged against a standard based on changes in the general purchasing power of the dollar.

**2.** With respect to monetary items, the purchasing-power gain or loss is based on an inappropriate index of purchasing power. Users of financial statements are interested in a firm's ability to maintain the purchasing power of its monetary assets for the particular kinds of goods and services that it normally purchases.

Users must recognize that constant-dollar      26.58
financial statements are not designed to provide information about the effects of changes in specific prices on the performance and financial position of a firm. An educational effort is required to inform statement users as to the kinds of interpretations that should and should not be made from constant-dollar financial statements. FASB *Statement No. 33* requires that only certain constant-dollar information be disclosed (discussed later in this chapter). These limited disclosures provide an opportunity for studying the costs of preparing constant-dollar financial statements as well as for educating statement users as to the potential value of the information disclosed.

## Current-Value Accounting

### Objective of Current-Value Accounting

The objective of current-value accounting is      26.59
to report the effects of specific price changes on the operating performance and financial position of a firm. It provides measurements of current value, which is thought more relevant to decision making than historical acquisition cost. As Chapter 5 discusses, however, there are different approaches to calculating current values, each of which provides different information about the impact of changing prices. Three valuation methods are discussed below.

---

of a loan, they will be repaid with dollars that have less general purchasing power than the dollars loaned. Thus, for a given default risk, lenders will ask a higher interest rate, the more inflation they expect.

Borrowers, on the other hand, are willing to pay a higher interest rate in times of expected inflation because they expect to repay the loan with "cheaper" dollars; that is, they expect the real value of the debt to fall. Thus the interest expense on the borrower's conventional income statement reflects the inflation expected by both the borrower and the lender at the time the debt was issued. But the reported interest expense is partly offset by the reduction in the reported cost of borrowing caused by the general inflation that reduces the value of the dollars to be repaid.

Whether either the borrower or the lender benefits at the other's expense depends on the amount of unexpected inflation during the term of the loan. If the actual rate of inflation during the term of the loan is greater than that expected at the time the loan was made, then the borrower benefits at the expense of the lender. The dollars actually repaid have less general purchasing power than they were expected to have at the time the loan was made.

In any case, the purchasing power gain reported by a borrower (or loss reported by a lender) in times of general price increase is conceptually an offset to reported interest expense (or revenue). The net interest after purchasing-power gain (or loss) shows the cost of borrowing (or return to lender) in terms of general purchasing power sacrificed or earned.

For an expanded discussion of these issues, see Robert S. Kaplan, "Purchasing Power Gains on Debt: The Effect of Expected and Unexpected Inflation," *Accounting Review 52* (April 1977), pp. 369–378.

26.60 **1. Current Cost of Replacing the Service Potential Embodied in the Specific Assets of a Firm** This measure is equal to the amount a firm would have to pay currently to replace the service potential embodied in its specific assets. It takes into account the inherent technological capabilities and levels of obsolescence of the existing assets. For example, if a firm owned a 2-year-old automobile, it would base its current replacement-cost valuation on the prices of similar 2-year-old automobiles in the used car market. If replacement cost amounts for identical, used assets are not available, then the replacement cost of new assets with similar service potential would be used. The replacement cost of the new asset must be adjusted downward, however, for both the used condition of the existing asset and any technological changes that have occurred. The fact that the firm would probably not acquire a similar 2-year-old automobile if replacement were made is not considered important in this approach to measuring current replacement cost. Income each period is composed of two elements: **(a)** an operating margin equal to the difference between sales revenue and the current cost of replacing the service potential of the specific assets consumed in generating revenues, and **(b)** holding gains and losses equal to the changes in the current replacement costs of the firm's particular assets. FASB *Statement No. 33* uses this measure of current value and refers to it as *current cost*. It uses the term "increases in current cost amounts" to refer to holding gains.

26.61 **2. Current Price at Which Existing Assets Could Be Sold** This measure, often referred to as *net realizable value* or *exit value,* is equal to the net cash amount that a firm would receive if it sold its existing assets after subtracting any costs of disposal. Income each period is composed of two elements: **(a)** a purchasing margin equal to the difference between the net realizable, or exit, value of an asset at the time it is acquired and the acquisition cost of the asset, and **(b)** a holding gain or loss equal to changes in the net realizable value of assets while they are held. FASB *Statement No. 33* prescribes that assets expected to be sold (for example, inventories) should be stated at net realizable value if the amount is less than the current cost [measure **(1)** above] of the specific assets.

**3. Present Value of Future Cash Flows** 26.62 This measure is equal to the present, or discounted, value of the net cash flows expected to be generated from an asset. Income each period under this valuation method comprises three elements: **(a)** a purchasing margin equal to the difference between the present value of the net future cash flows from an asset at the time of acquisition and the acquisition cost of an asset, **(b)** interest revenue each period as cash flows become nearer realization, and **(c)** a holding gain or loss arising either from changes in the amounts of future cash flows (due to changing prices, competition, or other factors) or from changes in the discount rate used. The reserve recognition accounting method discussed in Chapter 13 uses present values of future cash flows as the valuation method for depletable resources. FASB *Statement No. 33* prescribes that assets expected to be used instead of sold (for example, depreciable assets) should be stated at the present value of the future cash flows if this amount is less than the current cost [measure **(1)** above] of the specific assets.

As a basis for providing information about 26.63 the effects of changes in specific prices on a firm, *Statement No. 33* requires that the current cost of existing assets [measure **(1)**] be used in most cases. This valuation basis reports the cost of replacing the specific productive capacity that the firm has chosen to use. These current costs are matched against sales revenue to provide information on a firm's ability to cope with the specific price changes it faces.

The use of net realizable values can be 26.64 criticized in that changes in the exit values of assets which firms intend to use instead of sell, such as depreciable assets, are usually not considered in management's actions to cope with specific price changes. The approach of using net present values can be criticized in that changes in the valuation of assets may be due to factors other than specific price changes (for example, change in the discount rate, change in the pattern of cash flows). Thus, although each of the three valuation methods has strengths and weaknesses with respect to asset valuation and income measurement (see summary in Exhibit 5.3), the approach of using the current cost of existing assets best captures the separate effects of changes in specific prices on a firm.

## Financial Statements Based on Current Costs

26.65   The accounting procedures for preparing financial statements that reflect changes in specific prices are similar, regardless of which of the three valuation methods is used. In this section and the next, the procedures for preparing financial statements based on the current cost of existing assets are discussed and illustrated. As with constant-dollar restatements, the restatements for changes in current costs can be most easily performed after the conventional financial statements have been prepared. Formal journal entries to restate historical-cost amounts for either general or specific price changes are not necessary.

26.66   FASB *Statement No. 33* requires restatement to current costs of selected asset and expense items only. In the discussion and illustration that follow, consideration is given to changing the valuation basis to current cost for all items in the financial statements. The more limited measurements and disclosures required by *Statement No. 33* are discussed later.

26.67   **Restatements of Assets**   Cash and accounts receivable are normally stated on the balance sheet at their current cash or cash-equivalent value, and therefore do not require restatement for specific price changes. Most other assets will be recorded at unadjusted or adjusted acquisition costs, which differ from current cost. The current costs of marketable securities and investments in se-

curities can usually be calculated from quoted market prices on organized securities exchanges. The current cost of inventories can be found in current invoices, in vendors' price lists, from standard manufacturing costs that reflect current costs, or by revising historical costs using price indices for the specific goods and services measured. The current cost of property, plant, and equipment can be found directly through current invoice prices or prices quoted in active markets for land and used plant and equipment. Alternatively, historical-cost amounts may be restated using price indices for the particular items of property, plant, and equipment.

**Restatement of Equities**   As with cash   26.68
and accounts receivable, most current liabilities are stated at their current cash-equivalent value and do not require restatement. On the other hand, the book value of long-term debt, based on the market rate of interest at the time of issue, will likely differ from the current market price of the debt based on current market rates of interest. The current cost of debt can be found by referring to quoted market prices for the outstanding debt obligation. The excess of the current cost of assets over the current cost of liabilities and preferred stock is the equity of the common shareholders. Any further breakdown of the common shareholders' equity into the current cost of the contributed capital and current cost of retained earnings is of questionable usefulness.

**Restatement of Revenues and Expenses**   26.69
Sales revenues and most operating expenses (except cost of goods sold and depreciation) are likely to be stated at amounts close to their current costs, and no restatement is usually necessary. Cost of goods sold must be restated to the current cost of goods at the time they were sold. As with inventories on the balance sheet, current invoice prices or vendors' price lists usually provide the basis for calculating the current cost of goods sold.

The calculation of depreciation expense is   26.70
more controversial. One view holds that the

net change in value of a depreciable asset each period is reported either as appreciation (net increase in value) or as depreciation (net decrease in value). By the time the asset has been retired, its historical cost will have been written off. The increases and decreases in value that occur will be reported each period.

26.71    Others argue that a change in value of a long-term asset consists of a "using up" of service potential and a value change or holding gain on what is left. The value change in the remaining service potential can exceed the value of the service used up, so the value at the end of the year is greater than at the beginning. Still, to separate the decline caused by the "using up" from the more-than-offsetting value change provides information useful to understanding the current operating performance of the business.

26.72    *Statement No. 33* requires that the decline in current value caused by "using up" service potential be separated from the increase in current value arising from holding gains (or holding losses contributing to further declines in value). In current-cost accounting, depreciation should attempt to measure as expense the current cost of the service potential used up, even when value changes in remaining service potential offset this expense.

26.73    The calculation of income tax expense on a current-cost basis is controversial. Some accountants argue that income tax expense should be based on pretax current-cost income. The total income from the acquisition and sale of any asset is the difference between the amount of cash received at the time of sale and the amount of cash expended at the time of acquisition. Current-cost accounting merely affects the period in which the income is recognized (through increased expenses and holding gains and losses). The differences between current-cost amounts and historical-cost amounts are therefore timing differences, for which deferred income taxes should be provided in the usual fashion. Other accountants argue that differences between current-cost and historical-cost amounts are permanent differences. Income tax expense in the current-

cost income statement should, according to their view, be based on pretax historical-cost income. FASB *Statement No. 33* requires that the latter treatment be followed.

## Illustration of Financial Statements Based on Current Costs

26.74    Exhibit 26.12 presents selected financial statement data for Sweeney Corporation, discussed earlier in the chapter, on both a historical-cost and a current-cost basis. For balance sheet and income statement amounts not shown, it is assumed that the historical-cost and current-cost amounts are the same.

26.75    **Current-Cost Income Statement** The current-cost income statement is divided into two main sections: (1) the operating margin, equal to the difference between revenues and expenses measured in terms of current costs, and (2) holding gains and losses. The holding gains and losses section is further divided into realized holding gains and losses and unrealized holding gains and losses. This classification scheme parallels that discussed in Chapter 9 with respect to inventories (see Exhibits 9.7 and 9.8). An illustration might cement understanding of the calculations involved.

27.76    *Example* A company acquired two items of inventory on November 1, 1980, for $10 each. On December 31, 1980, these items had a current cost of $12 each. On July 1, 1981, one of the two items was sold for $18 at a time when its current cost was $15. On December 31, 1981, the current cost of the item remaining in inventory was $17. A current-cost income statement appears in Exhibit 26.13. The operating margin is equal to the difference between the selling price of the item sold and its current cost at the time of sale on July 1, 1981, of $15. The operating margin indicates a firm's success in setting selling prices to cover the current costs of assets consumed. The realized holding gain is the difference between the current cost and the historical cost of the item sold ($5 =

*Exhibit 26.12*
**Historical- and Current-Cost Data
for Sweeney Corporation for 1981**

| | December 31, 1981 | | December 31, 1980 | |
|---|---|---|---|---|
| **Balance Sheet** | **Historical Cost** | **Current Cost** | **Historical Cost** | **Current Cost** |
| Inventories ........................................ | $104,000 | $106,000 | $100,000 | $101,500 |
| Land ............................................... | 16,000 | 31,000 | 16,000 | 30,000 |
| Building (net) .................................... | 42,000 | 62,500 | 44,000 | 63,000 |
| Equipment (net) ................................ | 122,000 | 187,000 | 130,000 | 192,000 |

| | For the Year Ended December 31, 1981 | |
|---|---|---|
| **Income Statement** | **Historical Cost** | **Current Cost** |
| Cost of Goods Sold ................................ | $396,000 | $403,000 |
| Depreciation ......................................... | 17,000 | 40,000 |
| Gain on Sale of Equipment ......................... | 8,000 | 2,000 |

$15 − $10). This holding gain represents the increase in the cost of the item from the time it was acquired until the time it was sold. The operating margin of $3 plus the realized holding gain of $5 is equal to net income as reported in the conventional financial statements based on historical costs. In the current-cost income statement, net income is segregated into the two components, operating margin and realized holding gain or loss. The unrealized holding gain for 1981 is the difference between the cumulative unrealized holding gain on inventory at the end of the year and the cumulative unrealized holding gain on inventory at the beginning of the year ($3 = $7 − $4). This unrealized holding gain will become realized when the inventory is sold. Until then, the cumulative unrealized holding gain is reflected in the valuation of inventory on the balance sheet.

*Exhibit 26.13*
**Current-Cost Income Statement
for a Company for the Year 1981**

| | | | |
|---|---|---|---|
| Sales ....................................................... | $18 | | |
| Current Cost of Goods Sold ................................... | (15) | | |
| Operating Margin ............................................. | | | $ 3 |
| Realized Holding Gain: | | | |
|     Current Cost of Goods Sold ............................. | $15 | | |
|     Historical Cost of Goods Sold ........................... | (10) | | 5 |
| Conventional Gross Margin ................................... | | | $ 8 |
| Unrealized Holding Gain for 1981: | | | |
|   Cumulative Unrealized Holding Gain, December 31, 1981: | | | |
|     Ending Inventory at Current Cost ....................... | $17 | | |
|     Ending Inventory at Historical Cost ..................... | (10) | $ 7 | |
|   Cumulative Unrealized Holding Gain, December 31, 1980: | | | |
|     Beginning Inventory at Current Cost .................... | $24 | | |
|     Beginning Inventory at Historical Cost ................. | (20) | (4) | 3 |
| Net Income on Current-Cost Basis ........................... | | | $11 |

26.77    The current-cost income statement for Sweeney Corporation for 1981, using the format described above, is shown in Exhibit 26.14.

26.78    *Revenues and Gains* Revenues from product sales are assumed to be the same under his-

torical-cost and current-cost systems. The $8,000 gain on sale of equipment under a historical-cost system is equal to the difference between the selling price of $11,000 and the book value of $3,000 (= $16,000 − $13,000). Under a current-cost system, the gain is equal to the difference between the selling

---

### Exhibit 26.14
### Income Statement Based on Historical and Current Cost for Sweeney Corporation for the Year 1981

|  | Historical Cost | Current Cost |
|---|---|---|
| Revenues and Gains: |  |  |
| Product Sales | $520,000 | $520,000 |
| Gain on Sale of Equipment | 8,000 | 2,000 |
| Total Revenues and Gains | $528,000 | $522,000 |
| Expenses: |  |  |
| Cost of Goods Sold | $396,000 | $403,000 |
| Selling and Administrative | 59,000 | 59,000 |
| Depreciation | 17,000 | 40,000 |
| Interest | 10,000 | 40,000 |
| Income Taxes | 20,000 | 10,000 |
| Total Expenses | $502,000 | 20,000 |
| | | $532,000 |
| Operating Margin | — | $ (10,000)[a] |
| Realized Holding Gains: |  |  |
| Inventory Sold ($403,000 − $396,000) | — | $  7,000 |
| Depreciable Assets Used ($40,000 − $17,000) | — | 23,000 |
| Equipment Sold ($8,000 − $2,000) | — | 6,000 |
| Total Realized Holding Gains | — | $ 36,000 |
| Conventional Net Income | $ 26,000 | — |
| Operation Margin Plus Realized Holding Gains | — | $ 26,000 |
| Unrealized Holding Gains and Losses (calculations show below): |  |  |
| Inventories | — | $    500 |
| Land | — | 1,000 |
| Building | — | 1,500 |
| Equipment | — | 3,000 |
| Total Unrealized Holding Gains and Losses | — | $  6,000 |
| Current-Cost Net Income | — | $ 32,000 |

**Calculation of Unrealized Holding Gain or Loss for 1981**

|  | Cumulative Unrealized Holding Gain (or Loss) | | Increase in Unrealized Gain (or Loss) for 1981 |
|---|---|---|---|
|  | **End of Period** | **Beginning of Period** |  |
| Inventories | $106,000 − $104,000 = $ 2,000 | $101,500 − $100,000 = $ 1,500 | $  500 |
| Land | $ 31,000 − $ 16,000 = $15,000 | $ 30,000 − $ 16,000 = $14,000 | 1,000 |
| Building | $ 62,500 − $ 42,000 = $20,500 | $ 63,000 − $ 44,000 = $19,000 | 1,500 |
| Equipment | $187,000 − $122,000 = $65,000 | $192,000 − $130,000 = $62,000 | 3,000 |

[a]*Statement No. 33* refers to this amount as income from continuing operations on a current-cost basis. See discussion on disclosure later in this chapter.

price of $11,000 and the current cost of replacing the asset—$9,000 in the example. In markets with no transaction costs, the selling price and current cost should be the same, and no gain or loss would be recognized. In real markets with transaction costs, there is a difference in the price at which Sweeney Corporation could sell the equipment and the price at which it could be purchased. The gain on sale is $2,000 (= $11,000 − $9,000).

26.79 *Expenses and Losses* Cost of Goods Sold and Depreciation Expense are stated at the current cost of the items sold or services used during the period. Selling and administrative, interest, and income tax expenses are assumed to be the same on a historical-cost and a current-cost basis. The operating margin is a negative $10,000, indicating that selling prices were inadequate to cover the current cost of assets consumed in operations.

26.80 *Realized Holding Gains and Losses* The realized holding gains are equal to the difference between the current-cost and historical-cost amounts for various expenses and gains. Note that virtually all of the gain on sale of the equipment is a holding gain. Under a current-cost system, this gain would have been recognized piecemeal over the life of the equipment as prices for the equipment increased. Under a historical-cost system, all of the gain is recognized in the period of sale.

26.81 Note also that the $26,000 conventional net income amount represents a $36,000 realized holding gain netted against a loss of $10,000 on operating margin. A firm that generates a large portion of its income from realized holding gains instead of from operating margins, but distributes dividends equal to net income in the conventional financial statements, is not likely to be able to replace its assets as they wear out and remain in business without significant inflows of new capital.

26.82 *Unrealized Holding Gains and Losses* The unrealized holding gain or loss for 1981 on various assets is the *incremental* unrealized

amount for the year. The incremental gain or loss is calculated by subtracting the *cumulative* unrealized gain or loss at the beginning of the year from the *cumulative* unrealized gain or loss at the end of the year. Incremental holding gains are recognized on the inventories, land, building, and equipment. There were no incremental losses during 1981.*

**Current-Cost Balance Sheet** The balance 26.83 sheet based on current costs is shown in Exhibit 26.15. Retained Earnings is the amount necessary to equate assets and equities.

## Evaluation of Current-Cost Accounting

As with constant-dollar accounting, current-cost accounting continues to be controversial. 26.84

**The Case for Current-Cost Accounting** 26.85 Advocates of current-cost accounting offer the following arguments.

1. Management's actions to cope with changing prices are based on expected changes in the prices of the particular goods and services normally acquired by a firm. Current-cost financial statements provide a consistent basis on which to evaluate management's actions and performance.

2. Current-cost income is separated into operating margins and holding gains and losses, permitting statement users to assess the impact of changing prices on the profitability of the firm.

3. Current-cost balance sheets provide a more realistic indication of the current economic value of assets and liabilities than do the balance sheets based on historical costs.

---

*Controversy exists as to whether holding gains and losses should be considered as elements of income. A firm that purchases assets early in anticipation of increasing prices (thereby realizing holding gains) may in fact be better off than a firm that purchases later at the higher price. The firm cannot pay dividends equal to the holding gain, however, without impairing its ability to replace the productive capacity, or service potential, of the assets.

*Exhibit 26.15*
**Comparative Balance Sheet
for Sweeney Corporation in Current Costs,
December 31, 1981 and 1980**

| | December 31, 1981 | December 31, 1980 |
|---|---|---|
| **ASSETS** | | |
| Current Assets: | | |
| Cash ......................................... | $ 36,000 | $ 20,000 |
| Accounts Receivable (net) ..................... | 80,000 | 70,000 |
| Inventories ................................... | 106,000 | 101,500 |
| Total Current Assets ...................... | $222,000 | $191,500 |
| Property, Plant, and Equipment: | | |
| Land ......................................... | $ 31,000 | $ 30,000 |
| Building (net of accumulated depreciation) ....... | 62,500 | 63,000 |
| Equipment (net of accumulated depreciation) .... | 187,000 | 192,000 |
| Total Property, Plant, and Equipment ........ | $280,500 | $285,000 |
| Total Assets ..................................... | $502,500 | $476,500 |
| **LIABILITIES AND SHAREHOLDERS' EQUITY** | | |
| Current Liabilities: | | |
| Accounts Payable ............................ | $ 62,000 | $ 50,000 |
| Salaries Payable ............................ | 8,000 | 10,000 |
| Total Current Liabilities .................... | $ 70,000 | $ 60,000 |
| Bonds Payable .............................. | $100,000 | $100,000 |
| Total Liabilities ............................ | $170,000 | $160,000 |
| Shareholders' Equity: | | |
| Common Stock ............................... | | |
| Additional Paid-in Capital ..................... | } $332,500[a] | } $316,500[a] |
| Retained Earnings ............................ | | |
| Total Shareholders' Equity ................. | $332,500 | $316,500 |
| Total Liabilities and Shareholders' Equity ............ | $502,500 | $476,500 |

[a]Common shareholders' equity on a current-cost basis is equal to the difference between assets at current cost and liabilities plus preferred shareholders' equity at current cost. It is not meaningful to separate common shareholders' equity into the portions attributable to contributed capital and retained earnings.

26.86 **The Case against Current-Cost Accounting** Opponents of current-cost accounting offer the following arguments:

**1.** Current-cost amounts are often difficult to calculate, particularly for specialized used assets, raising questions about the reliability and comparability of current-cost data among firms.

**2.** Current-cost accounting in nominal dollars fails to recognize that the measuring unit used to calculate current-cost amounts is not of the same dimension over time. Changes in the general purchasing power of the dollar make current-cost amounts on the balance sheet at the beginning and end of the period noncomparable. Likewise, net income amounts over time using current costs are not based on a constant measuring unit.

**3.** Changes in current costs relative to changes in the general price level are not considered in measuring holding gains and losses under nominal-dollar, current-cost accounting. An 8 percent holding gain on a tract of land, measured on a current-cost basis, has one meaning when the general price level increases 6 percent and another meaning when general prices increase by 10 percent.

**4.** Current-cost accounting fails to recognize purchasing power, or inflation, gains or losses on monetary items. As discussed earlier in this chapter, monetary items gain or lose purchasing power as they are held over time. These gains and losses are often equally as important as holding gains and losses on inventories, depreciable assets, and similar items.

### Constant-Dollar and Current-Cost Accounting

26.87 A careful study of the arguments for and against constant-dollar accounting and current-cost accounting reveals that most of the criticisms of these two approaches to accounting for changing prices could be overcome by combining the two methodologies. Because constant-dollar accounting deals with the measuring unit and current-cost accounting deals with the attribute measured, there are no theoretical obstacles to combining the two approaches.

26.88 **Example** Refer to the earlier example for Sweeney Corporation. The equipment sold during 1981 for $11,000 had been acquired during 1975 for $16,000 when an index of consumer prices was 162.4. The equipment was sold during 1981, when its book value was $3,000 (= $16,000 − $13,000), its current cost was $9,000, and an index of consumer prices was 214.1. The index at the end of 1981 was 225.0. Exhibit 26.16 shows the calculation of the gain on the sale of equipment under (1) historical costs in nominal dollars, (2) historical costs stated in constant dollars, (3) current costs in nominal dollars, and (4) current costs stated in constant dollars.

26.89 The gain in column (1) matches the selling price measured in nominal dollars at the time of sale with the book value of equipment measured in the nominal dollars expended

six years ago (adjusted for depreciation to date of sale). The gain in column (2) equalizes the measuring unit, relative to the amounts in column (1), by stating both the selling price and book value in terms of dollars of December 31, 1981, purchasing power. The total gain in column (3) of $8,000 is identical to the gain in column (1). In column (3), however, the gain is separated into a gain from the sale and a gain from holding the equipment while its current cost increased. [Note in column (3) that there would be a decrease of $6,000 (= $9,000 − $3,000) in the *unrealized* holding gain for the portion of the realized holding gain resulting from changes in current costs in prior years while the equipment was held.] The amounts in column (3) are not stated in dollars of constant purchasing power. The gain on sale is stated in terms of dollars of purchasing power at the time of sale, whereas the realized holding gain is stated in terms of dollars both at the time of sale (the $9,000 current cost) and at the time the equipment was acquired in 1975 (the $3,000 book value). In column (4), these differences in the measuring unit are removed. Both the gain on sale and the holding gain are stated in terms of dollars of December 31, 1981, purchasing power.

26.90 **Example** Refer again to the data for Sweeney Corporation. Exhibit 26.14 indicates that an unrealized holding gain of $1,000 was recognized on the land. The calculation of this unrealized holding gain is based on a mixture of dollars of varying purchasing powers. To restate the unrealized holding gain on a constant-dollar basis, the following adjustments are necessary:

| | |
|---|---|
| Current Cost at End of Year in December 31, 1981, Dollars | C$31,000 |
| Historical Cost at End of Year in December 31, 1981, Dollars, $16,000 × 225.0/104.3 | (34,516) |
| Unrealized Holding Gain (Loss) at End of Year | C$ (3,516) |
| Current Cost at Beginning of Year in December 31, 1981, Dollars, $30,000 × 225.0/201.6 | C$33,482 |

*Exhibit 26.16*
**Calculation of Gain on Sale of Equipment
for Sweeney Corporation**

| | (1) Historical Cost/ Nominal Dollars | (2) Historical Cost/ Constant Dollars | (3) Current Cost/ Nominal Dollars | (4) Current Cost/ Constant Dollars |
|---|---|---|---|---|
| Selling Price: | | | | |
| Nominal Price ... | $11,000 | | $11,000 | |
| Constant-Dollar Price $11,000 × 225.0/214.1 . | | C$11,560 | | C$11,560 |
| Less Adjusted Cost: | | | | |
| Historical/Nominal . | 3,000 | | | |
| Historical/Constant, $3,000 × 225.0/162.4 .... | | 4,156 | | |
| Current/Nominal . | | | 9,000 | |
| Current/Constant, $9,000 × 225.0/214.1 .... | | | | 9,458 |
| Gain on Sale ........ | $ 8,000 | C$ 7,404 | $ 2,000 | C$ 2,102 |
| Plus Realized Holding Gain: | | | | |
| Current/Nominal, $9,000– $3,000 ........ | | | $ 6,000 | |
| Current/Constant, ($9,000 × 225.0/214.1) – ($3,000 × 225.0/162.4) .... | | | | 5,302 |
| Total Gain .......... | $ 8,000 | C$ 7,404 | $ 8,000 | C$ 7,404 |

| | |
|---|---|
| Historical Cost at Beginning of Year in December 31, 1981, Dollars, $16,000 × 225.0/104.3 ...................... | 34,516 |
| Unrealized Holding Gain (Loss) at Beginning of Year ................. | C$ (1,034) |
| Incremental Holding Gain (Loss) for the Year ........................... | C$ (2,482) |

Each amount is stated in terms of constant December 31, 1981, dollars. The $1,000 unrealized holding gain on a current-cost basis measured in nominal dollars is restated to an unrealized holding loss on a constant-dollar, current-cost basis. Thus, it can be seen that

increases in the current cost of land have not kept pace with changes in the general price level. The incremental holding loss of C$2,482 is the holding loss net of general price inflation.

## Required Disclosures of the Effects of Changing Prices

FASB *Statement No. 33* requires the disclosure of certain supplementary information about the effects of changing prices. This *Statement* encourages, but does not require, the presentation of a full set of financial statements based on historical-cost/constant

26.91

dollars and on current cost. Rather, the following minimum disclosures must be made:

1. Income from continuing operations for the current fiscal year on a historical-cost/constant-dollar basis.

2. The purchasing-power gain or loss on net monetary items for the current fiscal year.

3. Income from continuing operations for the current fiscal year on a current-cost basis (referred to as *operating margin* throughout this chapter).

4. Current cost of inventory and property, plant, and equipment at the end of the current fiscal year.

5. Increases or decreases for the current fiscal year in the current-cost amounts of inventory and property, plant, and equipment (we have referred to these increases and decreases as *holding gains and losses*), net of inflation (that is, stated on a constant-dollar basis).

6. For the five most recent fiscal years, the following items must be disclosed:
   a. Net sales and other operating revenue.
   b. Historical-cost/constant-dollar information:
      • Income from continuing operations.
      • Income per common share from continuing operations.
      • Purchasing power gain or loss on monetary items.
      • Net assets at fiscal year-end.
   c. Current-cost information:
      • Income from continuing operations.
      • Income per common share from continuing operations.
      • Increases or decreases in current-cost amounts of inventory and property, plant, and equipment, net of inflation.
      • Net assets at fiscal year-end.
   d. Other information:
      • Cash dividends declared per common share.
      • Market price per common share at fiscal year-end.

26.92  *Accounting Series Release No. 279* requires firms to include a narrative discussion of the effects of changing prices on the firm. This narrative discussion is included either in the note containing the above disclosures or in management's discussion and analysis of financial condition and results of operations. Note 23 to the financial statements of International Corporation (see Appendix A, Exhibit A.4) illustrates the supplementary disclosures required by FASB *Statement No. 33* and *ASR No. 279*.

*Statement No. 33,* when originally issued,    26.93
excluded certain specialized assets from its current-cost disclosure requirements. The FASB wished to study these specialized assets more fully to assess the applicability of current-cost disclosures. Four recent pronouncements now extend, with some modification, the requirements of *Statement No. 33* to these assets.

1. *Statement No. 39* — Mining and Oil and Gas Assets. Current-cost information as prescribed by *Statement No. 33* must now be disclosed for mineral resource assets. Because of difficulties in measuring the current cost of finding mineral resource assets, *Statement No. 39* permits firms to measure current cost by restating historical cost amounts with specific price indices. Because some firms use successful-efforts costing while other firms use full costing, the resulting current cost amounts are not comparable among firms. *Statement No. 39* also requires the disclosure of information about the quantities of proved mineral reserves (see discussion in Chapter 13).

2. *Statement No. 40* — Timberlands and Growing Timber Assets. These assets and related expenses may be stated at either their historical-cost/constant-dollar amounts or at their current-cost amounts. Because of difficulties in measuring the current cost for growing timber, the FASB permits firms to use either approach to measuring the effect of changing prices. The FASB's position in this case seems questionable. Constant-dollar accounting and current-cost accounting are designed to solve different problems (that is, a measuring unit problem versus a valuation problem). Permitting either method to be used reduces comparability among firms and could confuse financial statement users.

**3.** *Statement No. 41*—Income-Producing Real Estate Assets. These assets and related expenses may also be stated either at their historical-cost/constant-dollar amounts or at their current-cost amounts. The FASB's requirements in this case, as with timberlands and growing timber, may be viewed as a compromise position. Respondents to an earlier Exposure Draft argued that current cost is largely irrelevant in the case of income-producing real estate. Future cash flows from rentals and current market (exit) values of real estate properties are the relevant items of information about changing prices. The FASB, however, felt that these two items of information were not measurable with sufficient reliability for inclusion in financial reports. Firms that feel that current-cost amounts are irrelevant in the case of income-producing real estate will likely report only historical-cost/constant-dollar information. Therefore, no information about the effects of changes in specific prices will be disclosed.

**4.** *Statement No. 46*—Motion Picture Films. As with timberlands and income-producing real estate, motion picture films may be stated at either their historical-cost/constant-dollar amounts or at their current cost amounts.

26.94 These four pronouncements reflect the political nature of the standard-setting process. Much of the criticism of the Exposure Draft of *Statement No. 33* came from firms with mineral resource, timber, income-producing real estate, and motion picture film assets. The FASB excluded these assets from the current-cost requirements of *Statement No. 33*. The positions finally taken on these assets in *Statements No. 39, 40, 41,* and *46* reflect the compromises required in order to obtain majority agreement on a position within the FASB.

## Changing Prices and the Statement of Changes in Financial Position

26.95 Of the three principal financial statements, the statement of changes in financial position

is the least affected by changing prices. Most transactions affecting the flow of funds and reported in the statement of changes in financial position occur during the period being reported. Any adjustment of these amounts for either general or specific price changes would reflect price changes for approximately one year or less.

26.96 As is the case in preparing the statement of changes in financial position in historical-cost/nominal dollars, the restated statement reflecting either general or specific price changes can be most easily prepared after the balance sheet and income statement have been restated for price changes. The amounts included in the restated statement of changes in financial position can usually be obtained from either the restated balance sheet or the restated income statement.

26.97 FASB *Statement No. 33* does not require the disclosure of information about the effects of inflation on the statement of changes in financial position.

## Summary

26.98 Accounting for changing prices is currently in a period of transition and experimentation. Financial statement preparers and users have recognized for many years that changing prices, either in general or for specific goods and services, bring to question the validity and meaningfulness of conventional financial statements based on historical cost and nominal dollars. The pronouncements by the Financial Accounting Standards Board provide firms considerable flexibility in the way changing prices are accounted for and disclosed. Whether constant-dollar accounting, current-cost accounting, or some other approach replaces or regularly supplements the historical-cost/nominal-dollar financial statements will depend on the benefits of the disclosures as perceived by users relative to the cost of generating the necessary data. It is as yet too early to evaluate effectively these benefits and costs.

*Appendix 26.1*
**Monetary and Nonmonetary Classification of**
**Balance Sheet Accounts**
**(Excerpts from FASB Statement No. 33, Appendix D)**

| | Monetary | Nonmonetary |
|---|---|---|
| **Assets** | | |
| Cash on Hand, Demand Deposits, Time Deposits ............. | X | |
| Marketable Securities: | | |
|    Common Stock ...................................... | | X |
|    Preferred Stock (nonconvertible, nonparticipating) ....... | | X |
|    Preferred Stock (convertible, participating) ............. | (See discussion at left) | |
|      If market values the security primarily as a fixed income | | |
|      security, then it is monetary; if it values the security | | |
|      primarily as a residual equity security, it is nonmonetary. | | |
|    Convertible Bonds ................................... | (See discussion for preferred stock) | |
|    Bonds (other than convertibles) ....................... | X | |
| Accounts and Notes Receivable ......................... | X | |
| Allowance for Uncollectible Accounts ...................... | X | |
| Inventories ......................................... | | X |
| Prepayments ........................................ | | X |
| Refundable Deposits .................................. | X | |
| Investments in Securities: | | |
|    Common Stocks ..................................... | | X |
|    Preferred Stocks .................................... | (See discussion for preferred stock above) | |
|    Bonds ............................................ | (See discussion for preferred stock above) | |
| Property, Plant, and Equipment ......................... | | X |
| Accumulated Depreciation ............................. | | X |
| Patents, Trademarks, Goodwill .......................... | | X |
| **Liabilities** | | |
| Accounts, Notes, and Other Current Payables .............. | X | |
| Advances from Customers for Future Goods or Services ...... | | X |
| Obligations under Warranties ........................... | | X |
| Bonds Payable ...................................... | X | |
| Unamortized Premium or Discount on Bonds Payable ........ | X | |
| Deferred Income Taxes ............................... | X | |
| **Shareholders' Equity** | | |
| Preferred Stock ...................................... | (See discussion at left) | |
|    Nonmonetary until constant-dollar amount equals the | | |
|    call price; preferred stock then becomes a monetary | | |
|    item. | | |
| Common Stock ....................................... | | X |
| Additional Paid-In Capital .............................. | | X |
| Treasury Stock ...................................... | | X |

# Questions and Short Cases*

**26.1**   Review the meaning of the following concepts or terms discussed in this chapter.
   **a.** Constant monetary measuring-unit assumption.
   **b.** Realization convention.

---

*The values given for price indices throughout the questions and problems are assumed for illustration
purposes and do not equal the actual values of these indices as published by the federal government.

    c. General versus specific price changes.
    d. General purchasing power of the dollar.
    e. Monetary versus nonmonetary items.
    f. Purchasing power gain or loss on monetary items.
    g. Restatement adjustment for nonmonetary items.
    h. Current cost of replacing the service potential of existing assets.
    i. Net realizable value.
    j. Present value of future cash flows.
    k. Operating margin.
    l. Realized holding gain or loss.
    m. Unrealized holding gain or loss.
    n. Realized holding gain or loss net of inflation.

**26.2** The accounting problems associated with changing prices have been described as *general* and *specific*. Explain.

**26.3** "Financial statements prepared under generally accepted accounting principles reflect dollars of mixed purchasing power." Explain the meaning of this statement in relation to the balance sheet, the income statement, and the statement of changes in financial position.

**26.4** The restatement of beginning-of-the-period monetary items from the general purchasing power of the dollar at the beginning of the period to the general purchasing power at the end of the period results in a purchasing power gain or loss. The restatement of nonmonetary items, however, does not give rise to a gain or loss in constant-dollar accounting. Explain the reason for this difference in treatment.

**26.5** Under what conditions will a firm report:
    a. A purchasing power gain on monetary items?
    b. A purchasing power loss on monetary items?

**26.6** For which types of asset and equity structures would you expect:
    a. Significant differences between earnings as conventionally reported in nominal dollars and as stated in constant dollars?
    b. Insignificant differences between the two earnings measures?

**26.7** For purposes of preparing constant-dollar financial statements, indicate whether each of the following accounts is **(1)** a monetary item, **(2)** a nonmonetary item, or **(3)** an item that could be either monetary or nonmonetary, depending on the circumstances.
    a. Notes Receivable.
    b. Allowance for Uncollectible Accounts.
    c. Prepaid Rent.
    d. Marketable Equity Securities.
    e. Property Rights Acquired under Capital Leases.
    f. Patents.
    g. Salaries Payable.
    h. Subscription Fees Received in Advance.
    i. Deferred Income Taxes.
    j. Premium on Bonds Payable.
    k. Preferred Stock.
    l. Additional Paid-in Capital.

m. Treasury Stock.
n. Interest Revenue.
o. Cost of Goods Sold.

26.8   Marketable equity securities may require a write-down to market value in the constant-dollar financial statements, even though no such write-down was required in the nominal-dollar financial statements. Explain.

26.9   "The distinction between monetary and nonmonetary items can be summarized as follows: All current assets and liabilities are monetary items, whereas all noncurrent assets and equities are nonmonetary items." Do you agree? Why or why not?

26.10   "Preferred stock may be either a monetary or a nonmonetary item, depending on the circumstances." Explain.

26.11   "To calculate the beginning balance in Retained Earnings stated in terms of dollars of end-of-the-period purchasing power, all that is necessary is to multiply the beginning nominal dollar balance by the following ratio: Consumer Price Index at the end of period/Consumer Price Index at the beginning of period." Do you agree? Why or why not?

26.12   Is the Gain on Sale of Equipment account a monetary item or a nonmonetary item? Explain.

26.13   During a period of rising prices, cost of goods sold under LIFO usually exceeds cost of goods sold under FIFO in the conventional financial statements. It is possible, however, for cost of goods sold under FIFO to exceed cost of goods sold under LIFO in the constant-dollar financial statements. How might this arise?

26.14   A student remarks: "I understand the meaning of the 'actual ending balance in monetary accounts' for a period. This is simply the amount of cash on hand plus the amounts receivable from others less the amounts payable to others. What I don't understand is the meaning of the 'constant-dollar ending balance in net monetary accounts' used in calculating the purchasing power gain or loss." Respond to this student's dilemma.

26.15   "Constant-dollar net income indicates the extent to which the purchasing power of a firm's capital has been maintained during a period." Do you agree? Why or why not?

26.16   A firm owns 500 electric adding machines acquired 10 years ago. These machines have capabilities for adding, subtracting, multiplying, and dividing. How might you determine the current replacement cost of these machines?

26.17   The current cost of an asset is considered an *entry value,* whereas its net realizable value is considered an *exit value.* In which of these two categories would you classify the present value of an asset's future cash flows?

26.18   With respect to reflecting the effects of changes in specific prices on a firm, discuss the strengths and weaknesses of each of the following 3 valuation methods:
a. Current replacement cost.
b. Net realizable value.
c. Present value of future cash flows.

26.19   "The operating margin in current-cost income statements indicates the extent to which the purchasing power of a firm's capital has been maintained during a period." Do you agree? Why or why not?

26.20   In what sense is the realized holding gain on depreciable assets used (= current-cost depreciation − historical cost depreciation) considered a "realized" gain? (Hint: Contrast the realized holding gain on inventory items sold with the realized holding gain on depreciable assets used.)

26.21   In calculating the unrealized holding gain or loss for a period, why is the cumulative holding gain or loss at the beginning of the period subtracted in the calculation?

26.22   "All realized holding gains or losses were once unrealized holding gains or losses." Do you agree? Why or why not?

26.23   A firm reports a realized holding gain on the sale of land in its current-cost/nominal-dollar income statement but a realized holding loss on land in its current-cost/constant-dollar income statement. What is the likely explanation for this difference?

26.24   "Current-cost/constant-dollar financial statements overcome most of the criticisms directed at current-cost/nominal-dollar financial statements or historical-cost/constant-dollar financial statements by themselves." Explain.

26.25   Why is there no holding gain or loss on nonmonetary assets and equities in constant-dollar financial statements?

26.26   Why is there no purchasing power gain or loss on monetary assets and equities in current-cost financial statements?

26.27   (Adapted from CPA Examination.)
    a. Constant-dollar financial statements are prepared in an effort to eliminate the effects of inflation or deflation. An integral part of determining restated amounts and applicable gain or loss from restatement is the segregation of all assets and liabilities into monetary and nonmonetary classifications. One reason for this classification is that purchasing power gains and losses for monetary items are calculated.
       What are the factors that determine whether an asset or liability is classified as monetary or nonmonetary? Include in your response the justification for recognizing gains and losses from monetary items and not for nonmonetary items.
    b. Proponents of constant-dollar financial statements state that a basic weakness of financial statements not adjusted for price-level changes is that they are made up of "mixed dollars."
    (1) What is meant by the term "mixed dollars" and why is this a weakness of nominal-dollar financial statements?
    (2) Explain how financial statements restated for price-level changes eliminate this weakness. Use property, plant, and equipment as your example in this discussion.

26.28   An index of consumer prices on various dates is assumed to be as follows:

| | | | |
|---|---|---|---|
| January 1980 | 222 | June 1980 | 232 |
| February 1980 | 224 | July 1980 | 234 |
| March 1980 | 226 | August 1980 | 236 |
| April 1980 | 228 | September 1980 | 238 |
| May 1980 | 230 | October 1980 | 240 |

A firm desires to prepare constant-dollar financial statements (comparative balance sheet and income statement) for 1981, stated in terms of dollars of December 31, 1981, general purchasing power. Indicate the restatement ratio (numerator and denominator amounts) for each of the following items:

a. Cash on December 31, 1981.
b. Bonds Payable on December 31, 1980.
c. Depreciation Expense for 1981 on equipment acquired during June 1980.
d. Allowance for Uncollectible Accounts on December 31, 1980.
e. Merchandise Inventory on December 31, 1981 (FIFO cost-flow assumption used; inventory turnover rate is two times per year).
f. Interest Revenue for 1981 on bonds acquired on November 15, 1980.
g. Deferred Income Tax Expense for 1981.
h. Accounts Payable on December 31, 1980.
i. Merchandise Inventory on December 31, 1980 (FIFO cost-flow assumption used; inventory turnover rate is four times a year).
j. Prepayments on December 31, 1981 (relates to rent prepaid on November 15, 1981).
k. Preferred Stock on December 31, 1981 (issued at par value of $100 on July 15, 1980; call price $106).
l. Discount on Bonds Payable on December 31, 1981 (bonds were issued on February 15, 1980).
m. Property Rights Acquired under Lease on December 31, 1981 (lease signed on February 10, 1981).
n. Investment in Common Stock on December 31, 1981 (stock acquired on April 20, 1980).
o. Capitalized Lease Obligation on December 31, 1981 (lease signed on February 10, 1981).
p. Deferred Income Taxes on December 31, 1980.
q. Gain on Sale of Equipment for 1981 (equipment acquired during January 1980 is sold on June 15, 1981)
r. Treasury Stock on December 31, 1980 (acquired on September 15, 1980).

26.29  (Written from materials prepared by Lawrence Revsine.) Economists define income, roughly, as what's left at the end of a period after capital has been maintained. That is, income is dividends for the period plus "capital" at the end of the period less "capital" at the beginning of the period. The definition of income then depends on the definition of capital. This case explores the kinds of "capital" maintained by various measures of "income."

All examples are based on the following assumptions:

(1) On January 1, the Lawrence Company acquires 2 units of inventory at a cost of $10 each, $20 total. Its balance sheet shows assets of $20 and contributed capital of $20.
(2) During the year, the general price level increases by 10 percent.
(3) On December 31, the current replacement cost of inventory is $13 per unit and the firm sells 1 unit of inventory for $18 cash. The firm distributes cash dividends equal to income, whatever it is for a given measure of income.

a. Construct an income statement and a balance sheet for year-end, using conventional accounting—nominal-dollar measuring unit and asset measurements based on historical costs. You should find income equal to $8 and total assets at year-end of $20. Explain the statement "conventional accounting maintains capital in terms of assets' historical cost in dollars."

b. Construct an income statement and a balance sheet for year-end where the measuring unit is nominal dollars and asset measurements are based on current costs. Income excludes holding gains. You should find income equal to $5 and total assets at year-end of $26. Explain the statement "current-cost, nominal-dollar income excluding holding gains maintains the physical capacity of the firm's capital."

c. Construct an income statement and a balance sheet for year-end where the measuring unit is nominal dollars and asset measurements are based on current costs. Income includes all holding gains. You should find income equal to $11 and total assets at year-end of $20. Explain the statement "current-cost, nominal-dollar income including all holding gains maintains the dollar amount of assets' current values."

d. Construct an income statement and a balance sheet for year-end where the measuring unit is constant dollars and asset measurements are based on historical costs. You should find income equal to C$7 and total assets at year-end of C$22. Explain the statement "constant-dollar, historical-cost income maintains the purchasing power of assets' historical cost."

e. Construct an income statement and a balance sheet for year-end where the measuring unit is constant dollars and asset measurements are based on current costs. Income excludes holding gains. You should find income equal to C$5 and total assets at year-end of C$26. Explain the statement that "constant-dollar, current-cost income excluding holding gains maintains the purchasing power invested in the firm's physical capacity."

f. Construct an income statement and a balance sheet for year-end where income is measured in constant dollars and asset measurements are based on current costs. Income includes holding gains. You should find income equal to C$9 and total assets at year-end of C$22. Explain the statement "constant-dollar, current-cost income including holding gains maintains the purchasing power of assets' current values."

26.30 A steel company owns a blast furnace built in the late 1940s for $6 million. The furnace can produce 3,000 tons of hot metal per day. The old furnace requires relatively large amounts of fossil fuels and labor.

The modern functional equivalent is a basic oxygen furnace. A basic oxygen furnace that produces 3,000 tons of hot metal per day costs $60 million. It uses relatively less labor and fuel, saving $6 million per year in operating costs. Both furnaces, with proper maintenance, can be used for the indefinite future. Assuming a discount rate of 15 percent, the present value of these operating costs savings is $40 million (= $6 million/.15).

What is the current cost of the blast furnace?

## Problems and Exercises*

26.31 Gordon Electronics Company had a net monetary asset position of $400,000 on January 1, 1981, at which time an index of consumer prices is 211.5. Transactions during 1981 and the associated amounts of the price index (PI) are listed below.

(1) Purchases, all on account, totaled $600,000 (PI = 217.1).
(2) Sales, all on account, totaled $1,000,000 (PI = 217.1).
(3) Collections from customers for sales on account, $700,000 (PI = 219.3).

_____

*The values given for price indices throughout the questions and problems are assumed for illustration purposes and do not equal the actual values of these indices as published by the federal government.

(4) Payments to suppliers for purchases on account, $400,000 (PI = 219.3).
(5) Declaration of a $200,000 dividend, payable during January 1982 (PI = 226.2).

The price index on December 31, 1981, is 226.2.
   a. Calculate the purchasing power gain or loss for 1981 in terms of constant December 31, 1981, dollars.
   b. Repeat part **a** but assume a net monetary liability position of $400,000 on January 1, 1981.

26.32   On January 1, 1981, the Robert Logue family had $1,500 in its checking account and $6,000 in a savings account. The unpaid balance on the mortgage on their home totaled $30,000, whereas unpaid bills relating to purchases during December 1980 amounted to $1,300. An index of consumer prices on January 1, 1981, is 180. During 1981, the following transactions occurred [price index (PI) is shown in parentheses]:
   (1) Robert Logue's take-home salary during 1981 was $25,000 (average PI = 190).
   (2) The unpaid bills of $1,300 on January 1, 1981, were paid (PI = 182).
   (3) Principal repayments of $2,500 were made during 1981 on the home mortgage loan (average PI = 190).
   (4) Food, clothing, interest, and other costs incurred by the family during 1981 totaled $24,400, of which $22,800 was paid in cash (average PI = 190).
   (5) Interest earned and added to the savings account totaled $360 (average PI = 190).
   (6) In addition to the interest earned in (5), $3,000 was transferred from the savings to the checking account during 1981 (PI = 188). The price index on December 31, 1981, is 200.

   Calculate the purchasing power gain or loss for the family during 1981 in terms of constant December 31, 1981, dollars.

26.33   An index of consumer prices at the end of each of the years 1977 through 1981 is as follows:

| | |
|---|---|
| 1977 | 163.2 |
| 1978 | 171.5 |
| 1979 | 189.7 |
| 1980 | 204.6 |
| 1981 | 221.7 |

   a. In December 1980, the Virgil Corporation purchased land for $300,000. The land was held until December 31, 1981, when it was sold for $400,000. Calculate the constant-dollar gain or loss on the sale of land for 1981 in terms of constant December 31, 1981, dollars.
   b. On January 1, 1978, the Davis Company purchased equipment for $300,000. The equipment was being depreciated over an estimated life of 10 years using the straight-line method and zero estimated salvage value. On December 31, 1981, the equipment was sold for $200,000. Calculate the constant-dollar gain or loss on the sale of equipment for 1981.
   c. An analysis of Solomon Corporation's Machinery and Equipment account as of December 31, 1981, is as follows:

**Machinery and Equipment**

| | |
|---|---|
| Acquired December 1978 | $400,000 |
| Acquired December 1980 | 100,000 |
| Total | $500,000 |

**Accumulated Depreciation**

| | |
|---|---|
| On equipment acquired in December 1978 | $160,000 |
| On equipment acquired in December 1980 | 20,000 |
| Total | $180,000 |

Calculate the constant-dollar amount for Machinery and Equipment Net of Accumulated Depreciation on December 31, 1981.

26.34 Sutter Manufacturing Corporation depreciates its machinery using the straight-line method over a 10-year life and zero estimated salvage value. A full year's depreciation is taken in the year of acquisition and none in the year of disposal. Acquisitions, which took place evenly over the appropriate years, were as follows: 1979, $1,000,000; 1980, $200,000; 1981, $400,000. An index of average consumer prices is 189.6 during 1979, 203.6 during 1980, and 217.5 during 1981. The price index on December 31, 1981, is 224.2.

a. Calculate the amount of depreciation expense for 1981 and the book value of the machinery on December 31, 1981, using historical costs and nominal dollars.

b. Repeat part a using historical costs and constant dollars of December 31, 1981, purchasing power.

26.35 Northside Development Corporation acquired a parcel of land on July 1, 1980, for $70,000. The tract was sold on July 1, 1981, for $146,000. An index of consumer prices and the current cost of the land on various dates are assumed to be as follows:

| | Price Index | Current Cost |
|---|---|---|
| July 1, 1980 | 203.6 | $ 70,000 |
| December 31, 1980 | 208.9 | 89,000 |
| July 1, 1981 | 214.6 | 146,000 |
| December 31, 1981 | 218.0 | 171,000 |

Calculate the amount of income or loss for 1981 relating to this land based on:
a. Historical-cost/nominal dollars.
b. Historical-cost/constant dollars of December 31, 1981, purchasing power.
c. Current-cost/nominal dollars.
d. Current-cost/constant dollars of December 31, 1981, purchasing power.

26.36 United Manufacturing Corporation purchased a new machine on January 1, 1981, for $500,000. The machine is to be depreciated using the straight-line method and a 10-year life. Estimated salvage value is zero. An index of consumer prices was 201.6 on January 1, 1981, and 225.0 on December 31, 1981. The average index for 1981 was 213.3.

a. Calculate the amount of depreciation expense for 1981 and the book value of the machine on December 31, 1981, using historical costs and nominal dollars.

b. Repeat part a using historical costs and constant dollars of December 31, 1981, purchasing power.

c. The current cost of this same machine on December 31, 1981, is $560,000 if acquired in new condition. Ignoring general price-level changes, determine depreciation expense based on the average current cost for 1981, the realized holding gain or loss for 1981, the unrealized holding gain or loss for 1981, and the book value of the machine on December 31, 1981, based on current costs.

d. Repeat part c but state all amounts in terms of dollars of constant December 31, 1981, purchasing power.

26.37 Skelton Corporation issued $100,000 face-value, 10-percent bonds on January 1, 1981. The bonds were issued at par value. Using information given below for each of the years 1981 through 1984, give the amount of the following:

(1) Interest expense on a current-cost, constant-dollar basis, using the general purchasing power of the dollar at the end of each year.

(2) Purchasing power gain or loss for each year.

(3) Holding gains or losses for each year reflecting changes in the price of the bonds but ignoring changes in the general price level.

(4) Holding gains or losses for each year reflecting both the changes in the price of the bonds and the changes in the general price level.

1981: The market rate of interest for these bonds remained at 10 percent and there was no general price inflation.

1982: The market rate of interest required for these bonds increased to 12 percent on January 2, 1982, and the market price decreased to $85,000. There was no general price inflation.

1983: The market rate of interest for these bonds remained at 12 percent and the rate of general price inflation for the year was 9 percent.

1984: The creditworthiness of Skelton Corporation improved so that the market required rate of return decreased from 12 percent to 8 percent on January 2, 1984, and the market price increased to $118,000. The rate of general price inflation for the year was 6 percent.

26.38   The financial statements of Roderick Corporation for 1981, its first year of operations, are shown in Exhibit 26.17. An index of consumer prices on various dates was as follows:

| | |
|---|---:|
| (1) On January 1, 1981, when common stock was issued | 160 |
| (2) When store equipment was acquired | 165 |
| (3) When merchandise inventory was acquired | 170 |
| (4) When sales were made | 180 |
| (5) When selling and administrative costs were incurred | 175 |
| (6) On December 31, 1981 | 200 |

a. Restate the balance sheet on December 31, 1981, to the general purchasing power of the dollar on December 31, 1981.

b. Restate the income statement for the year 1981 to the general purchasing power of the dollar on December 31, 1981. Include a separate calculation of the purchasing power gain or loss.

26.39   Refer to the data for Roderick Corporation for 1981 in Problem 26.38. Assume the following additional information about current cost for 1981:

| | December 31, 1981 |
|---|---:|
| Merchandise Inventory | $350,000 |
| Store Equipment (net) | 340,000 |

| | For the Year 1981 |
|---|---:|
| Cost of Goods Sold | $290,000 |
| Depreciation Expense | 42,000 |

Prepare an income statement for 1981, showing separately the operating margin, the realized holding gain or loss, and the unrealized holding gain or loss.

26.40   Refer to the data in Problems 26.38 and 26.39 for Roderick Corporation for 1981. Calculate the amount of realized and unrealized holding gains and losses for 1981 net of general price inflation. Depreciable assets were used evenly over the year. The average price index was 175 during 1981.

*Exhibit 26.17*
## Roderick Corporation
### Financial Statements for the Year 1981

**Balance Sheet at December 31, 1981**

### Assets

| | |
|---|---:|
| Cash | $ 50,000 |
| Accounts Receivable | 180,000 |
| Merchandise Inventory | 300,000 |
| Store Equipment | 300,000 |
| Less Accumulated Depreciation | (30,000) |
| Total Assets | $800,000 |

### Equities

| | |
|---|---:|
| Accounts Payable | $ 50,000 |
| Common Stock | 500,000 |
| Additional Paid-in Capital | 100,000 |
| Retained Earnings | 150,000 |
| Total Equities | $800,000 |

**Income Statement for the Year 1981**

| | |
|---|---:|
| Sales Revenue | $500,000 |
| *Less Expenses:* | |
| Cost of Goods Sold | $250,000 |
| Depreciation Expense | 30,000 |
| Selling and Administrative Expenses | 70,000 |
| Total Expenses | $350,000 |
| Net Income | $150,000 |

**Statement of Changes in Financial Position
for the Year 1981**

### Sources of Working Capital

| | |
|---|---:|
| Net Income | $150,000 |
| Add Back Depreciation Expense Not Using Working Capital | 30,000 |
| Working Capital Provided by Operations | $180,000 |
| Issuance of Common Stock | 600,000 |
| Total Sources of Working Capital | $780,000 |

### Uses of Working Capital

| | |
|---|---:|
| Purchase of Store Equipment | 300,000 |
| **Net Increase in Working Capital** | $480,000 |

### Analysis of Increases (Decreases) in Working Capital

| | |
|---|---:|
| Cash | $ 50,000 |
| Accounts Receivable | 180,000 |
| Merchandise Inventory | 300,000 |
| Accounts Payable | (50,000) |
| **Net Increase in Working Capital** | $480,000 |

26.41 The financial statements of the Roderick Corporation (see Problem 26.38) for 1982, its second year of operations, are shown in Exhibit 26.18. The following additional information is

*Exhibit 26.18*
**Roderick Corporation**
**Financial Statements**
**for the Year 1982**

### Balance Sheet at December 31, 1982

**Assets**

| | |
|---|---:|
| Cash | $ 90,000 |
| Accounts Receivable | 190,000 |
| Merchandise Inventory (based on FIFO) | 450,000 |
| Store Equipment | 400,000 |
| Accumulated Depreciation | (70,000) |
| Total Assets | $1,060,000 |

**Equities**

| | |
|---|---:|
| Accounts Payable | $ 70,000 |
| Mortgage Payable | 90,000 |
| Common Stock | 500,000 |
| Additional Paid-in Capital | 100,000 |
| Retained Earnings | 300,000 |
| Total Equities | $1,060,000 |

### Income Statement for the Year 1982

| | |
|---|---:|
| Sales Revenue | $ 750,000 |

*Less Expenses:*

| | |
|---|---:|
| Cost of Goods Sold | $ 400,000 |
| Depreciation Expense | 40,000 |
| Selling and Administrative Expenses | 110,000 |
| Total Expenses | $ 550,000 |
| Net Income | $ 200,000 |

### Statement of Changes in Financial Position
### for the Year 1982

**Sources of Working Capital**

| | | |
|---|---:|---:|
| Net Income | $200,000 | |
| Add Back Depreciation Expense Not Using Working Capital | 40,000 | |
| Working Capital Provided by Operations | $240,000 | |
| Mortgage Liability Assumed in Acquiring Store Equipment | 100,000 | |
| Total Sources of Working Capital | | $ 340,000 |

**Uses of Working Capital**

| | | |
|---|---:|---:|
| Dividends Paid | $ 50,000 | |
| Mortgage Liability Partial Payment | 10,000 | |
| Store Equipment Acquired | 100,000 | |
| Total Uses of Working Capital | | 160,000 |
| **Net Increase in Working Capital** | | $ 180,000 |

**Analysis of Increases (Decreases) in Working Capital**

| | |
|---|---:|
| Cash | $ 40,000 |
| Accounts Receivable | 10,000 |
| Merchandise Inventory | 150,000 |
| Accounts Payable | (20,000) |
| **Net Increase in Working Capital** | $180,000 |

available: Store equipment costing $100,000 was acquired during the year. The acquisition was financed by long-term borrowing, with the equipment serving as collateral. The equipment is depreciated using the straight-line method over a 10-year life with zero estimated salvage value. A full year's depreciation is taken in the year of acquisition.

An index of consumer prices on various dates was as follows:

**(1)** On January 1, 1982 ........................................................ 200
**(2)** When store equipment was acquired ............................................. 202
**(3)** When merchandise inventory was acquired ....................................... 204
**(4)** When sales were made ......................................................... 215
**(5)** When selling and administrative costs were incurred .............................. 212
**(6)** When mortgage payments were made ........................................... 225
**(7)** When dividend was declared and paid .......................................... 225
**(8)** On December 31, 1982 ........................................................ 225

**a.** Restate the balance sheet on December 31, 1982, to the general purchasing power of the dollar on December 31, 1982.
**b.** Restate the income statement for the year ending December 31, 1982, to the general purchasing power of the dollar on December 31, 1982. Include a separate calculation of the purchasing power gain or loss.

**26.42**  Refer to the data for Roderick Corporation for 1982 in Problem **26.41**. Assume the following additional information about current costs:

|  | December 31, 1982 |
|---|---|
| Merchandise Inventory ............................................. | $525,000 |
| Store Equipment (net) ............................................. | 390,000 |

|  | For the Year 1982 |
|---|---|
| Cost of Goods Sold ............................................... | $460,000 |
| Depreciation Expense ............................................. | 53,000 |

Prepare an income statement for 1982, showing separately the operating margin, the realized holding gain or loss, and the unrealized holding gain or loss.

**26.43**  Refer to the data in Problems **26.41** and **26.42** for Roderick Corporation for 1982. Calculate the amount of realized and unrealized holding gains and losses for 1982 net of general price inflation. Depreciable assets were used evenly over the year. The average price index was 212.

**26.44**  The Whitmyer Corporation was formed on January 1, 1981, to conduct an office rental business. Listed below are various transactions and other events of the firm during 1981. The values of an index of consumer prices (PI) at the time of each transaction are also shown.
(1) January 1, 1981 (PI = 100): Capital stock is issued for $1,000,000.
(2) January 2, 1981 (PI = 100): Land costing $100,000 and a building costing $1,500,000 are acquired. A cash payment of $900,000 is made, with a long-term, 10-percent mortgage assumed for the remainder of the purchase price.
(3) January 2, 1981, to December 1, 1981 (average PI = 106): Rentals of $300,000 are collected in cash.

(4) January 2, 1981, to December 31, 1981 (average PI = 106): Operating costs incurred evenly over the year total $60,000, of which $50,000 are paid in cash and the remainder are on account. All of these costs expired during 1981.

(5) January 2, 1981, to December 31, 1981 (average PI = 106): Interest costs are accrued monthly on the mortgage payable and were paid on December 31, 1981.

(6) December 31, 1981 (PI = 110): Depreciation on the building is calculated using the straight-line method, a 30-year life, and zero salvage value.

(7) December 31, 1981 (PI = 110): A cash dividend of $75,000 is declared and paid.

a. Set up T-accounts as needed and enter the transactions during the year based on the conventional accounting model.

b. Prepare a balance sheet as of December 31, 1981, and an income statement for 1981 using the conventional accounting model.

c. Repeat part b, but restate the conventional financial statements to a constant-dollar basis.

**26.45**  Refer to the data for Whitmyer Corporation in Problem **26.44**. Assume the following current-cost data for 1981:

|  | December 31, 1981 |
|---|---|
| Land | $  108,000 |
| Building (net) | 1,615,000 |

|  | For the Year 1981 |
|---|---|
| Depreciation Expense | $    57,000 |

The amounts reported for interest and other operating expenses in the historical-dollar income statement closely approximate the current cost of the services consumed.

a. Prepare an income statement for 1981, showing separately the operating margin, the realized holding gain or loss, and the unrealized holding gain or loss. Ignore changes in the general price index.

h. Repeat step a, but restate all amounts to a constant-dollar basis.

**26.46**  (Adapted from CPA Examination.) The Jones Corporation, a retailer, was organized during January 1979 with the issuance of 60,000 shares of $10-par-value common stock. The firm wishes to prepare constant-dollar financial statements for the first time during 1981. The postclosing trial balance taken from its accounts on December 31, 1981, is as follows:

|  | Debit | Credit |
|---|---|---|
| Cash and Receivables (net) | $530,000 | |
| Marketable Securities (common stock) | 125,000 | |
| Merchandise Inventory | 410,000 | |
| Equipment | 780,000 | |
| Accumulated Depreciation | | $172,000 |
| Accounts Payable | | 177,000 |
| Bonds Payable | | 500,000 |
| Common Stock | | 600,000 |
| Retained Earnings | | 396,000 |

The following additional information is obtained:

(1) Net monetary liabilities on January 1, 1981, were $197,000. Current liabilities on this date totaled $165,000.

(2) Net income for 1981 was $300,000, whereas dividends of $50,000 were declared and paid during December 1981. These were the only items affecting Retained Earnings during the period.

(3) Purchases of inventory items ($920,000) exceeded the cost of goods sold by $10,000. A LIFO cost-flow assumption is used. Purchases and sales occur evenly over each year. The inventory on December 31, 1981, consisted of the following layers, which were added evenly over their respective years:

| | |
|---|---:|
| 1979 Layer | $380,000 |
| 1980 Layer | 20,000 |
| 1981 Layer | 10,000 |
| Total | $410,000 |

(4) Depreciation is computed using the straight-line method, with a full year's depreciation taken in the year of acquisition and none in the year of sale. The depreciation rate is 10 percent, and no salvage value is anticipated. Acquisitions and sales have been made evenly for each year. The equipment sold during 1981 for a total of $35,000 was acquired during 1979. An analysis of the equipment account reveals the following:

| Year | Beginning Balance | Acquisitions | Disposals | Ending Balance |
|---|---:|---:|---:|---:|
| 1979 | — | $500,000 | — | $500,000 |
| 1980 | $500,000 | 20,000 | — | 520,000 |
| 1981 | 520,000 | 300,000 | $40,000 | 780,000 |

(5) The bonds were issued in December 1979 at par value. The marketable securities were acquired during December 1980 and are stated at acquisition cost, which is less than market value.

(6) An index of consumer prices on various dates is as follows:

| | |
|---|---:|
| January 1979 | 160 |
| December 1979 | 180 |
| December 1980 | 200 |
| December 1981 | 220 |
| Average 1979 | 170 |
| Average 1980 | 190 |
| Average 1981 | 210 |

a. Prepare a constant-dollar balance sheet on December 31, 1981, stated in terms of dollars of December 31, 1981, general purchasing power. Retained Earnings should be the amount necessary to equal restated total assets and restated total equities.

b. Reconcile to the restated Retained Earnings amount in part **a** by (1) calculating the restated beginning balance in Retained Earnings, (2) calculating restated net income including the purchasing power gain or loss on monetary items, and (3) calculating restated dividends.

26.47 Hanover Corporation was organized on July 1, 1975, with the issuance of 100,000 shares of $10-par-value common stock for $15 a share. Its comparative balance sheets on December 31, 1980, December 31, 1981, and December 31, 1982, and its comparative income statements and statements of changes in financial position for 1981 and 1982 are shown in Exhibits 26.19, 26.20, and 26.21.

*Exhibit 26.19*
**Hanover Corporation**
**Comparative Balance Sheets**

|  | December 31, 1980 | December 31, 1981 | December 31, 1982 |
|---|---|---|---|
| **ASSETS** | | | |
| Current Assets: | | | |
| Cash | $ 220,000 | $ 428,000 | $ 630,000 |
| Accounts Receivable | 430,000 | 610,000 | 680,000 |
| Inventories | 840,000 | 950,000 | 1,240,000 |
| Prepayments | 10,000 | 12,000 | 15,000 |
| Total Current Assets | $1,500,000 | $2,000,000 | $2,565,000 |
| Investment in Common Stock | $ 300,000 | $ 300,000 | $ 300,000 |
| Property, Plant, and Equipment: | | | |
| Land | $ 100,000 | $ 115,000 | $ 930,000 |
| Building | 1,200,000 | 1,150,000 | 1,100,000 |
| Equipment | 900,000 | 2,435,000 | 2,105,000 |
| Total Property, Plant, and Equipment | $2,200,000 | $3,700,000 | $4,135,000 |
| Total Assets | $4,000,000 | $6,000,000 | $7,000,000 |
| **LIABILITIES AND SHAREHOLDERS' EQUITY** | | | |
| Current Liabilities: | | | |
| Accounts Payable | $ 630,000 | $ 845,000 | $ 780,000 |
| Income Taxes Payable | 245,000 | 305,000 | 360,000 |
| Rental Fees Received in Advance | 25,000 | 40,000 | 60,000 |
| Total Current Liabilities | $ 900,000 | $1,190,000 | $1,200,000 |
| Long-Term Liabilities: | | | |
| Bonds Payable | $ 700,000 | $1,000,000 | $1,000,000 |
| Deferred Income Taxes | 100,000 | 130,000 | 170,000 |
| Total Long-Term Liabilities | $ 800,000 | $1,130,000 | $1,170,000 |
| Total Liabilities | $1,700,000 | $2,320,000 | $2,370,000 |
| Shareholders' Equity: | | | |
| Preferred Stock, $100 par value, $112 call price | — | $1,100,000 | $1,100,000 |
| Common Stock; $10 par value | $1,000,000 | 1,000,000 | 1,200,000 |
| Additional Paid-in Capital | 500,000 | 500,000 | 800,000 |
| Retained Earnings | 800,000 | 1,080,000 | 1,530,000 |
| Total Shareholders' Equity | $2,300,000 | $3,680,000 | $4,630,000 |
| Total Liabilities and Shareholders' Equity | $4,000,000 | $6,000,000 | $7,000,000 |

*Exhibit 26.20*
**Hanover Corporation**
**Comparative Income Statement**

| | 1981 | 1982 |
|---|---:|---:|
| **Revenues** | | |
| Sales Revenue | $7,000,000 | $7,600,000 |
| Rental Revenue | 25,000 | 40,000 |
| Dividend Revenue | 15,000 | 16,000 |
| Gain on Sale of Equipment | — | 7,000 |
| Total Revenues | $7,040,000 | $7,663,000 |
| **Expenses** | | |
| Cost of Goods Sold | $3,500,000 | $3,800,000 |
| Selling and Administrative | 2,375,000 | 2,421,000 |
| Depreciation | 315,000 | 352,000 |
| Income Taxes: Current | 420,000 | 450,000 |
| Deferred | 30,000 | 40,000 |
| Total Expenses | $6,640,000 | $7,063,000 |
| Net Income | $ 400,000 | $ 600,000 |

*Exhibit 26.21*
**Hanover Corporation**
**Comparative Statements of Changes**
**in Financial Position**

| | 1981 | 1982 |
|---|---:|---:|
| **Sources of Working Capital** | | |
| Operations: | | |
| Net Income | $ 400,000 | $ 600,000 |
| Plus: Depreciation Expense | 315,000 | 352,000 |
| Deferred Taxes | 30,000 | 40,000 |
| Less: Gain on Sale of Equipment | — | (7,000) |
| Working Capital Provided by Operations | $ 745,000 | $ 985,000 |
| Other Sources: | | |
| Issuance of Bonds | 300,000 | — |
| Issuance of Preferred Stock | 1,100,000 | — |
| Issuance of Common Stock | — | 500,000 |
| Sale of Equipment | — | 35,000 |
| Total Sources | $2,145,000 | $1,520,000 |
| **Uses of Working Capital** | | |
| Dividends | $ 120,000 | $ 150,000 |
| Acquisition of Land | 15,000 | 815,000 |
| Acquisition of Equipment | 1,800,000 | — |
| Total Uses | $1,935,000 | $ 965,000 |
| **Net Change in Working Capital** | $ 210,000 | $ 555,000 |

The following information is also available:

(1) Purchases and sales of inventory occur evenly over each year. A FIFO cost-flow assumption is used.

(2) Prepayments of insurance premiums are made on December 15 of each year for coverage during the next calendar year.

(3) The investment in common stock was made on March 15, 1979, and is carried at cost. The market value of the common stock at December 31, 1980, was $390,000; December 31, 1981, $420,000; December 31, 1982, $480,000. Dividends on the stock are received on December 31 of each year.

(4) Property, plant, and equipment is composed of the following:

| Type | Date Acquired | Acquisition Cost | Depreciable Life |
|------|---------------|------------------|------------------|
| Land | 7/01/75 | $ 100,000 | — |
| Land | 8/15/81 | $ 15,000 | — |
| Land | 3/20/82 | $ 815,000 | — |
| Building | 1/02/77 | $1,400,000 | 28 |
| Equipment | 7/01/75 | $ 400,000 | 10 |
| Equipment | 1/02/80 | $ 900,000 | 5 |
| Equipment | 7/01/81 | $1,800,000 | 20 |

The straight-line depreciation method is used for all depreciable assets. On January 2, 1982, equipment acquired on July 1, 1975, for $80,000 was sold for $35,000.

(5) Rental Fees Received in Advance represent rents received on November 15 of each year as advance payments on rent of storage space for the next calendar year.

(6) The Bonds Payable account consists of the following:

| Date of Issue | Principal Amount | Issue Price |
|---------------|------------------|-------------|
| 7/1/78 | $700,000 | Par |
| 7/1/81 | $300,000 | Par |

(7) The preferred stock was issued on October 15, 1981, at par value.

(8) On June 15, 1982, 20,000 shares of common stock were issued for $25 a share.

(9) Dividends are declared on December 15 and paid on December 31 of each year.

(10) An index of consumer prices for various months is as follows:

| | | | |
|---|---|---|---|
| July 1975 | 90 | October 1981 | 201 |
| December 1975 | 100 | November 1981 | 204 |
| January 1977 | 125 | December 1981 | 206 |
| March 1979 | 150 | Average 1981 | 194 |
| January 1980 | 160 | January 1982 | 207 |
| October 1980 | 176 | February 1982 | 209 |
| November 1980 | 178 | March 1982 | 210 |
| December 1980 | 180 | April 1982 | 212 |
| January 1981 | 182 | May 1982 | 214 |
| February 1981 | 184 | June 1982 | 215 |
| March 1981 | 186 | July 1982 | 217 |
| April 1981 | 188 | August 1982 | 218 |
| May 1981 | 190 | September 1982 | 220 |
| June 1981 | 192 | October 1982 | 222 |
| July 1981 | 195 | November 1982 | 223 |
| August 1981 | 197 | December 1982 | 225 |
| September 1981 | 199 | Average 1982 | 216 |

Because prices do not change materially during a month, the price index for any month is considered sufficiently accurate for restating any transactions during the month or at the end of the month to a constant-dollar basis.

a. Prepare a constant-dollar balance sheet for December 31, 1981, stated in terms of dollars of December 31, 1981, general purchasing power.

b. Prepare a constant-dollar balance sheet for December 31, 1980, and an income statement for the year 1981, both stated in dollars of December 31, 1981, general purchasing power.

c. Prepare an analysis of changes in retained earnings for 1981, stated in dollars of December 31, 1981, general purchasing power.

26.48 Refer to the data for Hanover Corporation in Problem **26.47.**

a. Prepare a constant-dollar balance sheet for December 31, 1982, stated in terms of dollars of December 31, 1982, general purchasing power.

b. Prepare a constant-dollar balance sheet for December 31, 1981, and an income statement for 1982, both stated in terms of dollars of December 31, 1982, general purchasing power.

c. Prepare an analysis of changes in retained earnings for 1982 stated in terms of dollars of December 31, 1982, general purchasing power.

26.49 Refer to the data in Problem **26.47** for Hanover Corporation. The following current-cost information is obtained:

| | December 31, 1980 | December 31, 1981 | December 31, 1982 |
|---|---|---|---|
| Inventories | $ 860,000 | $ 980,000 | $1,290,000 |
| Investment in Common Stock | 390,000 | 420,000 | 480,000 |
| Land | 225,000 | 250,000 | 1,200,000 |
| Buildings | 1,400,000 | 1,300,000 | 1,225,000 |
| Equipment | 1,050,000 | 2,765,000 | 2,245,000 |

| | Year Ended December 31 | |
|---|---|---|
| | 1981 | 1982 |
| Cost of Goods Sold | $3,625,000 | $3,975,000 |
| Depreciation Expense | 455,000 | 495,000 |

For other financial statement accounts, the historical-cost and current-cost amounts are approximately the same.

a. Prepare comparative balance sheets for December 31, 1981, and December 31, 1980, at current cost.

b. Prepare a combined statement of income and changes in retained earnings for 1981 based on current cost. The income statement should be separated into three sections: operating margin, realized holding gains and losses, and unrealized holding gains and losses. The change in retained earnings should reconcile with the change in retained earnings shown in the comparative balance sheets in part **a.**

26.50 Refer to the data in Problems **26.47** and **26.49** for Hanover Corporation.

a. Prepare a comparative balance sheet for December 31, 1982, and December 31, 1981, at current cost.

b. Prepare a combined statement of income and changes in retained earnings for 1982 based on current cost. The equipment sold had a current cost of $34,000 at the time of sale. The income statement should be separated into three sections: operating margin, realized holding gains and losses, and unrealized holding gains and losses. The change in retained earnings should reconcile with the change in retained earnings shown in the comparative balance sheets in part **a**.

26.51   Refer to the data in Problems **26.47** and **26.49** for Hanover Corporation. Calculate the amount of the realized and unrealized holding gains and losses for 1981 stated in terms of dollars of December 31, 1981, general purchasing power.

26.52   Refer to the data in Problems **26.47**, **26.48**, and **26.49** for Hanover Corporation. Calculate the amount of the realized and the unrealized holding gain or loss for 1982 net of inflation, stated in terms of dollars of December 31, 1982, general purchasing power.

26.53   The Pepper River Electric Company (PREC) produces electricity. Its current oil-burning plant is several years old and is capable of producing electricity for 20 more years. It can produce 1 million kilowatt-hours of electricity per month by burning 2,000 barrels of fuel oil. Fuel oil now costs $15 per barrel. If PREC were to rebuild a 20-year, oil-burning plant today, the cost would be $10 million. Because of the drastic increases in oil prices since the current plant was built, PREC would not build an oil-burning plant today. Instead, it would build a coal-burning plant. The coal-burning plant would cost $11 million to build. It would have the same life as the oil-burning plant and produce 1 million kilowatt-hours of electricity per month by burning 100 tons of coal at a cost of $80 per ton.

   Assume a cost of capital of 1 percent per month and that all costs are incurred at the end of the month.
   a. What is the present value of the cash savings from using a coal-burning rather than an oil-burning plant? The present value of an annuity for 240 periods at 2 percent per period is 90.82.
   b. What is the current replacement cost of the Company's current ability to produce 1 million kilowatt-hours of electricity per month?
   c. What are the appropriate replacement cost disclosures?

26.54   On January 1, 1981, ABC Company issues a 10-year semiannual bond with a face value of $1,000. The coupon rate is 8 percent, and the market rate is 9 percent. Over the next 3 years, interest rates fluctuate as follows:

| | |
|---|---|
| June 30, 1981 | 8 percent |
| January 1, 1981 | 7 percent |
| June 30, 1982 | 6 percent |
| January 1, 1983 | 7 percent |
| June 30, 1983 | 8 percent |
| January 1, 1984 | 9 percent |

ABC uses the effective-interest method to amortize the bond discount. Prepare journal entries under the historical-cost and current-cost accounting bases. For current-cost purposes, assume that interest expense for each semiannual period is calculated using the market interest rate and the market value of the debt prevailing at the beginning of the semiannual period.

# Part Six
## Appendices and Tables

# Appendix A
## Corporate Financial Statements Illustrated and Annotated

A.1 This appendix illustrates current financial reporting with a comprehensive set of corporate financial statements prepared in accordance with generally accepted accounting principles.

A.2 The financial statements are those of the International Corporation (IC), a fictitious company. These statements are, however, adapted from the actual statements of a well-known major company in the United States that has worldwide operations. We have omitted some materials from that company's annual report because of its specialized nature; we have added some material to illustrate significant financial reporting on matters not applicable to the actual company.

A.3 This appendix is organized into four exhibits, as follows:

Exhibit A.1. International Corporation Consolidated Statements of Income and Retained Earnings

Exhibit A.2. International Corporation Consolidated Balance Sheet

Exhibit A.3. International Corporation Consolidated Statement of Changes in Financial Position

Exhibit A.4. International Corporation Notes to Financial Statements.

A.4 First we have presented the exhibits that comprise the financial statements. Then we have included our own notes and comments related to the items in the financial statements. Our comments are numbered to correspond with the note numbers used by International Corporation in Exhibit A.4. The financial statements of International Corporation begin on the following page. Our commentary begins on page A-20.

*Exhibit A.1*
**International Corporation**
**Consolidated Statements of**
**Income and Retained Earnings**
**(Dollar Amounts in Millions)**

| Income Statement | Year Ended Dec. 31, 1981 | Year Ended Dec. 31, 1980 | Year Ended Dec. 31, 1979 |
|---|---|---|---|
| Revenues: | | | |
| Sales (Net of Estimated Uncollectibles—Note 8) | $5,862.7 | $5,798.5 | $5,101.1 |
| Equity in Income (Loss) from Nonconsolidated Subsidiaries and Affiliated Companies (Note 3) | 14.5 | (32.3) | 3.9 |
| Other Revenues | 51.4 | 71.9 | 63.0 |
| | $5,928.6 | $5,838.1 | $5,168.0 |
| Expenses: | | | |
| Cost of Goods Sold | $4,647.2 | $4,669.7 | $3,960.4 |
| Selling, Administration, and General | 801.3 | 727.4 | 698.8 |
| Depreciation | 128.8 | 123.5 | 107.6 |
| Interest | 76.4 | 111.3 | 69.3 |
| Income Taxes (Note 5) | 93.8 | 64.0 | 145.9 |
| Minority Interest in Net Income of Consolidated Subsidiaries | 2.5 | 3.3 | 2.5 |
| | $5,750.0 | $5,699.2 | $4,984.5 |
| Income from Continuing Operations | $ 178.6 | $ 138.9 | $ 183.5 |
| Discontinued Operations (Note 2): | | | |
| Loss from Operations of Discontinued Businesses (Net of Tax Savings of $35.3 in 1980 and $18.7 in 1979) | — | (39.8) | (21.6) |
| Loss on Disposal of Discontinued Businesses (Net of Tax Savings of $10.1 in 1981 and $42.0 in 1980) | (13.4) | (71.0) | — |
| Net Income | $ 165.2 | $ 28.1 | $ 161.9 |
| Earnings per Common Share: | | | |
| Continuing Operations | $2.04 | $1.57 | $2.06 |
| Discontinued Operations: | | | |
| Loss from Operations | — | (.45) | (.24) |
| Loss on Disposal | (.15) | (.80) | — |
| Net Income per Common Share | $1.89 | $ .32 | $1.82 |
| **Retained Earnings** | | | |
| Retained Earnings at Beginning of Year | $1,162.6 | $1,220.9 | $1,145.7 |
| Plus: | | | |
| Net Income | 165.2 | 28.1 | 161.9 |
| Less: | | | |
| Dividends Declared on Preferred Stock | (.9) | (1.2) | (1.2) |
| Dividends Declared on Common Stock | (84.6) | (85.2) | (85.5) |
| Retained Earnings at End of Year | $1,242.3 | $1,162.6 | $1,220.9 |

The financial information in the notes is an integral part of these financial statements.

*Exhibit A.2*
**International Corporation
Consolidated Balance Sheet
(Dollar Amounts in Millions)**

| | At Dec. 31 1981 | At Dec. 31 1980 |
|---|---|---|
| **Assets** | | |
| Current Assets: | | |
| Cash | $  118.0 | $  98.9 |
| Marketable Securities (Note 7) | 256.6 | 38.9 |
| Customer Receivables (Note 8) | 1,142.3 | 1,247.1 |
| Inventories (Note 9) | 1,040.6 | 1,073.0 |
| Costs and Income of Uncompleted Contracts in Excess of Related Billings (Note 10) | 172.5 | 197.2 |
| Prepaid and Other Current Assets | 110.6 | 184.4 |
| Total Current Assets | $2,840.6 | $2,839.5 |
| Investments (Note 11) | 289.2 | 226.2 |
| Estimated Realizable Value—Discontinued Businesses (Note 2) | 95.5 | 202.4 |
| Plant and Equipment, Net (Note 12) | 1,380.7 | 1,298.6 |
| Other Assets (Note 13) | 260.3 | 246.9 |
| Total Assets | $4,866.3 | $4,813.6 |
| | | |
| **Liabilities and Shareholders' Equity** | | |
| Current Liabilities: | | |
| Short-Term Loans and Current Portion of Long-Term Debt (Notes 14 and 15) | $  131.8 | $  236.1 |
| Accounts Payable—Trade | 361.3 | 392.8 |
| Accrued Payrolls and Payroll Deductions | 201.1 | 180.5 |
| Income Taxes Currently Payable | 50.2 | 47.2 |
| Deferred Current Income Taxes | 53.6 | 31.1 |
| Estimated Future Liabilities—Discontinued Businesses | 32.2 | 46.4 |
| Billings on Uncompleted Contracts in Excess of Related Costs and Income (Note 10) | 739.5 | 511.8 |
| Other Current Liabilities | 453.7 | 382.1 |
| Total Current Liabilities | $2,023.4 | $1,828.0 |
| Noncurrent Liabilities | $  52.3 | $  62.4 |
| Deferred Noncurrent Income Taxes | 117.5 | 97.3 |
| Debentures and Other Debt (Notes 18 and 19) | 610.2 | 843.1 |
| Total Noncurrent Liabilities | $  780.0 | $1,002.8 |
| Minority Interest | $  61.2 | $  58.7 |
| Shareholders' Equity (Notes 17 and 18): | | |
| Cumulative Preferred Stock | 16.6 | 30.5 |
| Common Stock | 277.1 | 277.1 |
| Capital in Excess of Par Value | 490.7 | 480.9 |
| Retained Earnings | 1,242.3 | 1,162.6 |
| | $2026.7 | $1951.1 |
| Less: Treasury Stock, at Cost | (25.0) | (27.0) |
| Total Shareholders' Equity | $2,001.7 | $1,924.1 |
| Total Liabilities and Shareholders' Equity | $4,866.3 | $4,813.6 |

The financial information in the notes is an integral part of these financial statements.

*Exhibit A.3*
**International Corporation**
**Consolidated Statement of Changes in**
**Financial Position**
**(Dollar Amounts in Millions)**

| | Year Ended Dec. 31, 1981 | Year Ended Dec. 31, 1980 | Year Ended Dec. 31, 1979 |
|---|---|---|---|
| **Changes in Financial Position** | | | |
| Working Capital Provided: | | | |
| Net Income from Continuing Operations | $ 178.6 | $ 138.9 | $ 183.5 |
| Add (Subtract) Income Charges (Credits) Not Affecting Working Capital: | | | |
| Depreciation | 128.8 | 123.5 | 107.6 |
| Deferred Income Taxes | 20.2 | 21.2 | 65.6 |
| Minority Interest in Net Income of Consolidated Subsidiaries | 2.5 | 3.3 | 2.5 |
| Equity in Losses (Income) of Nonconsolidated Subsidiaries and Affiliated Companies | (14.5) | 32.3 | (3.9) |
| Working Capital Provided by Continuing Operations | $ 315.6 | $ 319.2 | $ 355.3 |
| Losses Applicable to Discontinued Operations | $ (13.4) | $(110.8) | $ (21.6) |
| Add (Subtract) Income Charges (Credits) Not Affecting Working Capital: | | | |
| Depreciation | — | 10.1 | 7.6 |
| Deferred Income Taxes | — | (4.9) | (1.2) |
| Loss on Disposal (Less $46.4 Current Estimated Future Costs in 1980) | — | 24.6 | — |
| Working Capital Absorbed by Discontinued Operations | $ (13.4) | $ (81.0) | $ (15.2) |
| Other Sources: | | | |
| Realization of Estimated Value—Discontinued Businesses | $ 125.9 | — | — |
| Increase in Debentures and Other Debt | 45.0 | $ 219.7 | $ 69.2 |
| Issuance of Common Stock to Employees | 19.1 | 25.5 | 26.3 |
| Sale of Long-Term Investments | 17.0 | — | — |
| Total Other Sources | $ 207.0 | $ 245.2 | $ 95.5 |
| Total Resources Provided | $ 509.2 | $ 483.4 | $ 435.6 |
| Working Capital Applied: | | | |
| Expenditures for New and Improved Facilities | $ 187.5 | $ 356.7 | $ 202.4 |
| Dividend Declarations | 85.5 | 86.4 | 86.7 |
| Reduction in Debentures and Other Debt | 277.9 | 48.3 | 26.6 |
| Purchase of Long-Term Investments | 106.7 | 40.5 | 14.3 |
| Acquisition of Common Stock for Treasury | 14.2 | 39.4 | 36.3 |
| Purchase of Preferred Stock for Cancellation | 6.9 | — | — |
| Other—Net | 24.8 | 6.1 | 40.9 |
| Total Resources Applied | $ 703.1 | $ 577.5 | $ 407.2 |
| Net Change in Working Capital | $(194.3) | $ (94.1) | $ 28.4 |
| **Analysis of Changes in Working Capital** | | | |
| Increase (Decrease) in Working Capital: | | | |
| Cash and Marketable Securities | $ 236.8 | $ 8.5 | $ (9.9) |
| Customer Receivables | (104.8) | (61.1) | 292.0 |
| Inventories and Costs of Uncompleted Contracts in Excess of Related Billings | (57.1) | (69.8) | 41.8 |
| Prepaid and Other Current Assets | (73.8) | (1.9) | 36.2 |
| Short-Term Loans and Current Portion of Long-Term Debt | 104.3 | 239.2 | (267.0) |
| Accounts Payable—Trade | 31.5 | 12.5 | (54.3) |
| Income Taxes (Including Deferred Income Taxes) | (25.5) | 80.9 | (13.7) |
| Estimated Future Costs—Discontinued Businesses | 14.2 | (46.4) | (35.3) |
| Billings on Uncompleted Contracts in Excess of Related Costs | (227.7) | (155.7) | 75.2 |
| All Other Current Liabilities | (92.2) | (100.3) | (36.6) |
| Net Change in Working Capital | $(194.3) | $ (94.1) | $ 28.4 |

The financial information in the notes is an integral part of these financial statements.

*Exhibit A.4*
**International Corporation**
**Notes to Financial Statements**

### Note 1—Summary of Significant Accounting Policies

The major accounting principles and policies followed by International are presented to assist the reader in evaluating the consolidated financial statements and other data in this report.

**Principles of Consolidation:** The financial statements include the consolidation of all significant wholly and majority-owned subsidiaries except International Credit Company and Suburban Development Corporation. The equity method of accounting is followed for nonconsolidated subsidiaries and for investments in significant affiliates (20 to 50 percent owned).

The assets and liabilities of non-U.S. subsidiaries are translated at current exchange rates except that plant and equipment are translated at rates in effect at dates of acquisition. Income and expense amounts, except depreciation, are translated at rates prevailing during the year. Translation adjustments in the consolidated financial statements are not material.

**Sales** are recorded as products are shipped on substantially all contracts. All sales are made on account. The percentage-of-completion method is used only for certain orders with durations generally in excess of 5 years and for certain construction projects where this method of accounting is consistent with industry practices. In accordance with these practices, Long-Term Contracts in Process are stated at cost plus estimated profits recognized to date. In accordance with terms of the particular contracts, progress payments are obtained from customers. The amounts of long-term contracts do not exceed realizable value.

**Inventories:** The cost of the inventories of the consolidated companies is determined principally by the LIFO method. Inventories not on LIFO are valued at current standard costs, which approximate actual or average cost. The elements of cost included in inventories are direct labor, direct material, and factory overhead.

**Pension Plans** cover substantially all employees of the corporation. Funds to pay benefits under the plans are being held by a pension trust. It is the policy of the Corporation to fund each year the amount actuarially determined to be necessary to provide benefits earned during the year and to amortize liability for supplemental actuarial value over a period of 30 years.

**Depreciation** on plant and equipment acquired since January 1, 1968, is provided by the straight-line method based on guideline lives. Plant and equipment acquired prior to that date is depreciated using accelerated methods. Accelerated depreciation methods using guideline lives, giving effect to the class life system for assets acquired since 1970, are used for federal income tax purposes.

**Deferred Income Taxes** are provided for timing differences between financial and tax reporting, principally related to long-term contracts in process, depreciation, certain leasing transactions by International Credit Company, and loss on discontinued operations. Timing differences for long-term contracts result from the use of the percentage-of-completion method for financial reporting and the completed-contract method for income tax reporting.

Deferred federal income taxes are not provided on the undistributed earnings of certain subsidiaries when such earnings have been indefinitely reinvested.

**The Investment Credit** on all qualified assets is recorded under the flow-through method of accounting as a reduction of the current provision for federal income taxes except for investment credit on assets leased to others by the International Credit Company. Investment credit on such leased assets is deferred and amortized over the terms of the respective leases.

**Note 2**—Discontinued operations: During 1980, decisions were reached to dispose of two major business segments, the trade book publication business and the mail-order book club business.

The Corporation agreed to sell the publication business to East Consolidated Industries, Inc. (ECI), in exchange for cash and securities, resulting in provisions for losses on disposal in 1980 of $55 million (net of income tax savings of $30 million).

During 1980, the Corporation sold the member list and inventories of the International Book Club. The remaining portion of the mail-order book club business was to have been phased out during 1981. A provision for disposal costs of $16 million (net of income tax savings of $12 million) was charged against income in 1980. A comprehensive review and analysis of the progression of the phase-out resulted in an additional provision for losses on disposal of $13 million (net of income tax savings of $10 million) against income in 1981. This additional provision was required due to extended time needed to complete successive stages of the planned phase-out, higher than anticipated costs of inventory disposal, excessive returns of books, and lower than anticipated collection of outstanding receivables.

Estimated Realizable Value—Discontinued Businesses includes the assets and liabilities to be disposed.

**Note 3**—Equity in Income (Loss) from Nonconsolidated Subsidiaries and Affiliated Companies includes pretax losses of Suburban Development Corporation (SDC) amounting to $25.9 million, $40.8 million, and $26.2 million for the years ended December 31, 1981, 1980, and 1979, respectively. During 1980, the total SDC short-term debt guaranteed by International in the amount of $85 million was repaid with funds provided by the parent company.

**Note 4**—The corporation and its subsidiaries have several pension plans covering substantially all employees. Pension expense was $66.2 million in 1981, $68.7 million in 1980, and $65.3 million in 1979. These amounts include amortization of supplemental actuarial value, sometimes called actuarial accrued liability, over 30 years. No changes in actuarial assumptions were made in either year. Cash payments equal to the amount of pension expense are made to independent pension plan administrators.

Unrecognized supplemental actuarial value at December 31, 1980, was estimated at $587 million, of which $444 million represented unfunded vested benefits. Based on the latest actuarial valuation, which recognizes the increased pension obligations resulting from wage and salary improvements and increases for retirees effective July 1, 1981, unrecognized supplemental actuarial value approximates $616 million, of which $508 million represents unfunded vested benefits at December 31, 1981.

For purposes of computing unfunded supplemental actuarial value, securities were valued at market value. On December 31, 1981, certain defined-benefit plans had accumulated benefits in excess of net assets and others had net assets in excess of accumulated benefits. The benefit and asset information for those plans on an aggregate basis as of that date follows.

| **Pension Plan Assets and Accumulated Benefits**<br>**(Dollar Amounts in Millions)** | Year Ended<br>Dec. 31,<br>1981 |
|---|---|
| **Plans with Assets in Excess of Benefits** | |
| Actuarial Present Value of Accumulated Benefits: | |
|     Vested ................................................ | $308.5 |
|     Nonvested ........................................... | 318.9 |
|     Total ................................................. | $627.4 |
| Net Assets Available for Benefits ...................... | $643.7 |
| **Plans with Benefits in Excess of Assets** | |
| Actuarial Present Value of Accumulated Benefits: | |
|     Vested ................................................ | $252.1 |
|     Nonvested ........................................... | 38.3 |
|     Total ................................................. | $290.4 |
| Net Assets Available for Benefits ...................... | $277.1 |

The actuarial present value of accumulated benefits results from applying actuarial assumptions to reflect the time value of money and the probability of making those future payments that are attributable under the plans' provisions to the service employees have rendered. The significant actuarial assumptions used for the plans were as follows:

1. Life expectancy of participants according to the 1971 Group Annuity Mortality Table,

2. An average retirement age of 68, and

3. An investment return of 6.25 percent.

Net pension assets are measured at fair market value on December 31, 1981.

| **Statement of Changes in Net Pension Assets Available for Benefits**<br>**(Dollar Amounts in Millions)** | Year Ended<br>Dec. 31,<br>1981 | Year Ended<br>Dec. 31,<br>1980 | Year Ended<br>Dec. 31,<br>1979 |
|---|---|---|---|
| Book Value—Beginning of Year—At Market ..................... | $877.4 | $851.6 | $777.9 |
| Additions: | | | |
| Company Contributions ......................................... | $ 66.2 | $ 68.7 | $ 65.3 |
| Employee Contributions ........................................ | 11.7 | 10.7 | 9.8 |
| Income from Investments (Dividends, Interest, and Unrealized Gains<br>    and Losses from Changes in Market Value) .................... | 35.8 | 34.7 | 32.4 |
| Net Gain (Loss) from Disposal of Assets ......................... | 3.6 | (27.6) | 15.2 |
| | $117.3 | $ 86.5 | $122.7 |
| Deductions: | | | |
| Benefit Payments ............................................. | $ (71.6) | $ (59.9) | $ (47.7) |
| Fees, Asset Transfers, etc. ..................................... | ( 2.3) | ( .8) | ( 1.3) |
| Total Deductions ............................................. | $ (73.9) | $ (60.7) | $ (49.0) |
| Book Value—End of Year—at Market .......................... | $920.8 | $877.4 | $851.6 |

The divestment of the publication business provided for the assumption of the related pension liability by East Consolidated Industries, Inc., and the transfer of the proportionate share of pension fund assets.

Various pension arrangements, which are normally supplementary to required government plans, are in effect for most non-U.S. subsidiary companies.

**Note 5**—Income tax expense for financial reporting was reduced by investment tax credits of $12.9 million in 1981, $9.9 million in 1980, and $8.9 million in 1979. In addition, investment tax credit of $4.7 million has been deferred at the end of 1981 by International Credit Company and remains to be amortized.

Income before taxes is earned in the United States and in foreign countries. The sources of pretax earnings from continuing operations for the years 1981, 1980, and 1979 follow:

| Sources of Earnings from Continuing Operations before Income Taxes | Year Ended Dec. 31, 1981 | Year Ended Dec. 31, 1980 | Year Ended Dec. 31, 1979 |
|---|---|---|---|
| U.S. Earnings | $121.1 | $ 96.8 | $154.8 |
| Foreign Earnings | 151.3 | 106.1 | 174.6 |
| Total | $272.4 | $202.9 | $329.4 |

All discontinued operations are in the U.S.

| Income Taxes (Dollar Amounts in Millions) | Year Ended Dec. 31, 1981 | Year Ended Dec. 31, 1980 | Year Ended Dec. 31, 1979 |
|---|---|---|---|
| Continuing Operations: | | | |
| Currently Payable: | | | |
| Federal | $ 45.9 | $ 69.0 | $ 44.1 |
| State | 5.3 | 6.9 | 8.6 |
| Non-U.S. | 37.2 | 29.5 | 28.8 |
| | $ 88.4 | $105.4 | $ 81.5 |
| Deferred: | | | |
| Federal | $ 4.3 | $ (39.7) | $ 54.9 |
| State | .9 | (4.2) | 8.0 |
| Non-U.S. | .2 | 2.5 | 1.5 |
| | $ 5.4 | $ (41.4) | $ 64.4 |
| Total Income Tax Expense Caused by Continuing Operations | $ 93.8 | $ 64.0 | $145.9 |
| Discontinued Operations: | | | |
| Currently Payable | $(48.5) | $ (38.0) | $ (18.7) |
| Deferred | 38.4 | (39.3) | — |
| Total Income Tax Expense Caused by Discontinued Operations | $(10.1) | $ (77.3) | $ (18.7) |
| Total Income Tax Expense | $ 83.7 | $ (13.3) | $127.2 |

Deferred tax expense results from timing differences in the recognition of revenue and expense for tax and financial statement purposes. The source of these differences for the years 1981, 1980, and 1979 and the tax effect of each follows:

| Income Taxes Deferred (Dollar Amounts in Millions) | Year Ended Dec. 31, 1981 | Year Ended Dec. 31, 1980 | Year Ended Dec. 31, 1979 |
|---|---|---|---|
| Excess of Tax over Book Depreciation | $ 21.3 | $ 26.5 | $42.8 |
| Difference between Financial and Tax Reporting on Long-Term Contracts in Process | 13.2 | (41.0) | 33.9 |
| Provisions for Warranties | (29.1) | (26.9) | (12.3) |
| | $ 5.4 | $(41.4) | $64.4 |
| Losses Recorded in Prior Years on Discontinued Operations Currently Deductible for Tax Purposes | 38.4 | (39.3) | — |
| Total | $ 43.8 | $(80.7) | $64.4 |

Deferred federal income taxes have not been provided on cumulative undistributed earnings of $275 million from certain subsidiaries which have been reinvested for an indefinite period as of December 31, 1981.

The federal income tax returns of the Corporation and its wholly owned subsidiaries are settled through December 31, 1973, and it is believed that adequate provisions for taxes have been made through the current year, December 31, 1981.

The reconciliation between the federal statutory tax rate and the International effective consolidated tax rate for 1981, 1980, and 1979 is as follows:

| | Year Ended Dec. 31, 1981 | | Year Ended Dec. 31, 1980 | | Year Ended Dec. 31, 1979 | |
|---|---|---|---|---|---|---|
| **Effective Consolidated Tax Rate** (Dollar Amounts in Millions) | Amount | Effective Rate | Amount | Effective Rate | Amount | Effective Rate |
| Tax Expense if Based on Federal Statutory Tax Rate Applied to Income before Taxes of Continuing Operations ..................... | $126.5 | 46.0% | $94.9 | 46.0% | $152.7 | 46.0% |
| Increases (Reductions) in Taxes Resulting from: | | | | | | |
| Income of U.S. Subsidiaries Exempt from Tax or Subject to Tax at Reduced Rates ................. | (25.5) | (9.3) | (22.6) | (11.0) | (22.9) | (6.9) |
| Investment Tax Credit ............. | (12.9) | (4.7) | (9.9) | (4.8) | (8.9) | (2.7) |
| State and Local Income Taxes Less Reduction in Federal Income Tax .. | 3.2 | 1.2 | 1.4 | 0.7 | 8.6 | 2.6 |
| Miscellaneous Items .............. | 2.5 | 0.9 | 0.2 | 0.1 | 16.4 | 4.9 |
| Total—Continuing Operations ...... | $ 93.8 | 34.1% | $64.0 | 31.0% | $145.9 | 43.9% |
| Tax Applicable to Discontinued Operations ..................... | (10.1) | | (77.3) | | (18.7) | |
| Income Taxes (Reduction) .......... | $ 83.7 | | $(13.3) | | $127.2 | |

U.S. subsidiaries exempt from tax are U.S. possessions companies, and subsidiaries subject to reduced income tax rates include a Domestic International Sales Corporation (DISC) and a Western Hemisphere Trade Corporation.

**Note 6**—Research and development costs of $135, $132, and $125 million were incurred in each of the years 1981, 1980, and 1979, respectively. The costs were expensed during their respective years of incurrence in accord with *Statement of Financial Accounting Standards No. 2.*

**Note 7**—Marketable securities at December 31 of $256.6 million in 1981 and $38.9 million in 1980 are recorded at cost, which is less than market value of $260 million on December 31, 1981, and $40 million on December 31, 1980.

**Note 8**—Customer receivables are net of allowances for uncollectible accounts of $15 million for 1981 and $18 million for 1980. A provision for estimated uncollectibles of $60 million was made during 1981 and is subtracted from sales revenue in the income statement.

**Note 9—Inventories**
The replacement cost over the cost of inventories valued on the LIFO basis was approximately $370 million at December 31, 1981, and $340 million at December 31, 1980. During 1981, some inventory quantities valued on the LIFO basis were reduced. This reduction resulted in a liquidation of LIFO inventory quantities carried at lower costs prevailing in prior years as compared with the cost of these purchases had they been made in late 1981, the effect of which increased net income by approximately $10 million.

**Note 10**—Progress billings have increased due to the extension of progress payments to a wider range of products and work delayed at the request of customers. A contract-by-contract analysis of contracts with progress billing terms reflects an excess of contract costs and income over progress billings and an excess of progress billings over contract costs and income as shown in the table that follows.

| Costs and Income of Uncompleted Contracts in Excess of Related Billings (Dollar Amounts in Millions) | At Dec. 31, 1981 | At Dec. 31, 1980 |
|---|---|---|
| Costs and Income | $ 702.7 | $ 694.6 |
| Less Progress Billings on Contracts | (530.2) | (497.4) |
| Excess of Costs and Income | $ 172.5 | $ 197.2 |
| **Billings on Uncompleted Contracts In Excess of Related Costs (Dollar Amounts in Millions)** | | |
| Progress Billings on Contracts | $1,896.4 | $1,389.0 |
| Less Costs and Income | (1,156.9) | (877.2) |
| Excess of Progress Billings | $ 739.5 | $ 511.8 |

Contract costs do not include certain costs expended on behalf of customers which are charged to income currently.

**Note 11**—Investments include International Credit Company and other significant unconsolidated affiliates, valued at cost plus equity in undistributed earnings since acquisition. Condensed financial statements of the Credit Company are shown on the next page.

**Note 12—Plant and Equipment**

| Plant and Equipment, at Cost (Dollar Amounts in Millions) | At Dec. 31, 1981 | At Dec. 31, 1980 |
|---|---|---|
| Land and Buildings | $ 753.8 | $ 727.1 |
| Machinery and Equipment | 1,660.6 | 1,563.7 |
| Construction in Progress | 130.2 | 90.2 |
| | $2,544.6 | $2,381.0 |
| Less: Accumulated Depreciation | 1,163.9 | 1,082.4 |
| Total | $1,380.7 | $1,298.6 |

The Construction-in-Progress account was increased by $14.1 million in 1981 and $8.5 million in 1980 by capitalization of interest charges. The amount capitalized was based on current borrowing rates applied to the average balance in the account during the year.

**Note 13**—Other assets include goodwill of $80 million in 1981 and $88 million in 1980. Goodwill acquired prior to November 1, 1970, is not being amortized. Goodwill of $14.2 million at December 31, 1981, and $15.1 million at December 31, 1980, resulting from business combinations subsequent to November 1, 1970, remained to be amortized over the estimated period to be benefited, not to exceed 40 years. Because the original cost of the goodwill being amortized was $19.3 million, the amounts already amortized were $5.1 million and $4.2 million by the end of 1981 and 1980, respectively.

## International Credit Company
## Condensed Consolidated Financial Statements
## (Dollar Amounts in Millions)

| | Year Ended Dec. 31, 1981 | Year Ended Dec. 31, 1980 | Year Ended Dec. 31, 1979 |
|---|---|---|---|
| **Statement of Income** | | | |
| Total Earned Income | $141.7 | $147.9 | $129.2 |
| Less: | | | |
| Operating Expense | 34.3 | 31.7 | 32.3 |
| Provision for Losses on Receivables | 16.7 | 8.6 | 7.3 |
| Interest | 67.3 | 89.1 | 65.8 |
| Income Taxes | 12.0 | 10.0 | 12.1 |
| Net Income | $ 11.4 | $ 8.5 | $ 11.7 |
| | | | |
| **Statement of Changes in Financial Position** | | | |
| Financial Resources Provided by: | | | |
| Net Income | $ 11.4 | $ 8.5 | $ 11.7 |
| Sale of Investments | 26.5 | — | — |
| Increases in Accrued Interest, Accounts Payable, and Other Liabilities | 16.5 | 3.6 | 7.8 |
| Increase (Decrease) in Long-Term Debt | (23.4) | 111.6 | 60.5 |
| Other—Net | 6.0 | (1.7) | (2.2) |
| | $ 37.0 | $122.0 | $ 77.8 |
| | | | |
| Financial Resources Were Used for: | | | |
| Increase (Decrease) in Receivables, Net of Unearned Finance Charges and Provision for Losses | $ (26.3) | $ 95.6 | $ 37.9 |
| Receivables Written Off | 12.7 | 6.8 | 5.8 |
| Decrease in Short-Term Notes Payable | 48.7 | 8.3 | 23.3 |
| Increase in Investments | 1.9 | 11.3 | 10.8 |
| | $ 37.0 | $122.0 | $ 77.8 |

| | At Dec. 31, 1981 | At Dec. 31, 1980 |
|---|---|---|
| **Balance Sheet** | | |
| Cash | $ 20.8 | $ 11.5 |
| Receivables Less Unearned Finance Charges and Allowance for Losses | 1,110.1 | 1,123.8 |
| Investments and Other Assets | 13.0 | 38.6 |
| Total Assets | $1,143.9 | $1,173.9 |
| | | |
| Short-Term Notes Payable and Other Liabilities | $ 652.1 | $ 670.0 |
| Long-Term Senior Debt | 270.0 | 280.0 |
| Subordinated Debt | 70.0 | 83.4 |
| Total Liabilities | 992.1 | 1,033.4 |
| Capital | 59.5 | 59.5 |
| Retained Earnings | 92.3 | 81.0 |
| Total Liabilities and Shareholders' Equity | $1,143.9 | $1,173.9 |

**Note 14**—Short-term loans amounted to $99 million on December 31, 1981, and $187 million on December 31, 1980. The maximum amounts of borrowings outstanding were $239 million in 1981 and $566 million in 1980. The average aggregate short-term borrowings outstanding during 1981 totaled $203 million at a 10.7-percent approximate weighted-average interest rate.

Short-term credit arrangements include $65 million master notes under which the corporation may borrow at the 180-day commercial paper rate, domestic bank lines of credit totaling $100 million at the prime commercial rate, and $277 million of credit available to subsidiaries, principally outside the United States, at the most favorable local rates. Of these lines, $309 million was unused at December 31, 1981.

**Note 15**—Compensating balance arrangements without contractual withdrawal restrictions exist under the $100 million open bank lines of credit. Similar arrangements exist with banks that provide $55 million of credit lines for the International Credit Company. These arrangements provided for balances ranging from 10 to 25 percent of the line of credit to assure future credit availability and for loans outstanding. The average balance of corporate funds identified during the year for compensating balance purposes was not material.

### Note 16—Debentures and Other Debt

| Debentures and Other Debt (Dollar Amounts in Millions) | Interest Rates | Year of Maturity | Amount At Dec. 31, 1981 | At Dec. 31, 1980 |
|---|---|---|---|---|
| Debentures | $5^1/_2$% | 1987 | $ 75.0 | $ 90.0 |
| Debentures | $7^3/_8$% | 1991 | 145.2 | 160.0 |
| Debentures | $10^3/_4$% | 1993 | 71.4 | 100.0 |
| Other Debt | Various | Various | 318.6 | 493.1 |
| Total | | | $610.2 | $843.1 |

Total interest charges were $90.5 million in 1981, $119.8 million in 1980, and $77.0 million in 1979. Portions of these amounts—$14.1 million in 1981, $8.5 million in 1980, and $7.7 million in 1979—were capitalized into Construction in Progress; see Note 12. The remaining amounts are reported as interest expense on the income statement.

The $10^3/_4$ percent indenture requires sinking fund deposits of $10 million annually beginning in 1982. Sinking fund deposits of $15 million annually until maturity and $8 million annually until maturity are being provided under the terms of the $5^1/_2$ percent and the $7^3/_8$ percent indentures, respectively.

Other debt includes the present value of capitalized lease obligations. See Note 19. Other debt also includes $142 million of borrowings outside the United States with an average rate of 7.6 percent and $13 million in notes convertible into the corporation's common stock.

Long-term debt maturing in each of the following years is: 1982, $33 million; 1983, $54 million; 1984, $65 million; 1985, $42 million; and 1986, $42 million.

### Note 17—Stock Options

On April 24, 1980, the stockholders of the corporation approved the 1980 Stock Option Plan, which provides for granting of options to purchase 1.2 million shares of common stock at a minimum of 100 percent of market value at the date of grant. The 1980 plan authorizes qualified stock options, nonqualified stock options, or combinations of both. The terms of the options are substantially the same except that nonqualified options for terms up to 10 years may be granted. The plan provides for a limit on options granted to any one employee of 50,000 shares; the options may not be exercised for 1 year after the date of grant, and the period during which options may be granted expires on March 31, 1985.

| | 1981 | | 1980 | |
|---|---|---|---|---|
| | Shares | Average Price per Share | Shares | Average Price per Share |
| **Stock Options** | | | | |
| Outstanding at Beginning of Year | 743,200 | $22.37 | 593,806 | $31.30 |
| Granted | 223,400 | 17.73 | 402,700 | 12.96 |
| Exercised | (12,200) | 13.00 | — | — |
| Terminated | (359,800) | 32.40 | (253,306) | 28.35 |
| Outstanding at End of Year | 594,600 | 14.75 | 743,200 | 22.37 |
| Exercisable at End of Year | 371,200 | 12.95 | 340,500 | 33.50 |

## Note 18—International Corporation Consolidated Statement of Capital

| Consolidated Statement of Contributed Capital (Dollar Amounts in Millions) | Cumulative Preferred Stock | Common Stock | Capital in Excess of Par Value | Treasury Stock at Cost | Total |
|---|---|---|---|---|---|
| Balance at January 1, 1979 | $30.5 | $276.5 | $486.4 | $ (8.8) | $784.6 |
| 210,118 Shares of Common Stock Issued under Stock Option, Employee Stock, and Savings and Investment Plans | — | .6 | 6.9 | — | 7.5 |
| 1,047,537 Shares Acquired for Treasury | | | | (36.3) | (36.3) |
| 580,155 Treasury Shares Delivered under Employee Stock and Savings and Investment Plans | | | (1.6) | 20.3 | 18.7 |
| 15,238 Treasury Shares Issued for a Business Acquired | | | .1 | .2 | .3 |
| Other—Net | | | .1 | .1 | .5 |
| Balance at January 1, 1980 | $30.5 | $277.1 | $491.9 | $(24.2) | $775.3 |
| 3,106,300 Shares Acquired for Treasury | | | | (39.4) | (39.4) |
| 1,863,140 Treasury Shares Delivered under Employee Stock and Savings and Investment Plans | | | (10.8) | 36.3 | 25.5 |
| 18,500 Treasury Shares Issued for a Business Acquired | | | | .3 | .3 |
| Other—Net | | | (.2) | | (.2) |
| Balance at December 31, 1980 | $30.5 | $277.1 | $480.9 | $(27.0) | $761.5 |
| 138,892 Shares of Cumulative Preferred Stock Purchased for Cancellation | (13.9) | | 6.9 | | (7.0) |
| 1,029,100 Shares Acquired for Treasury | | | | (14.2) | (14.2) |
| 1,400,993 Treasury Shares Delivered under Stock Option, Employee Stock, and Savings and Investment Plans | | | 3.1 | 15.6 | 18.7 |
| Other—Net | | | (.2) | .6 | .4 |
| Balance at December 31, 1981 | $16.6 | $277.1 | $490.7 | $(25.0) | $759.4 |

Cumulative preferred stock, par value $100, authorized 235,954 shares at December 31, 1981, and 374,846 shares at both December 31, 1980, and December 31, 1979; 3.80-percent Series B, issued and outstanding 165,928 shares at December 31, 1981, and 304,820 shares at both December 31, 1980, and December 31, 1979.

Common stock, par value $3.125; authorized 120,000,000 shares at December 31, 1981, 1980, and 1979; issued (including treasury shares) 88,674,610 shares at December 31, 1981, 1980, and 1979.

Common stock held in treasury amounted to 1,596,722 shares at December 31, 1981; 2,008,717 shares at December 31, 1980; and 798,453 at December 31, 1979.

Treasury shares are used to supply stock for the various plans under which common stock is distributed to employees.

Although there are no restrictions on the retained earnings of the parent company, not all of the amounts shown for retained earnings represent amounts legally available for dividends. Part of the retained earnings—$102.3 million on December 31, 1981, and $96.7 million on December 31, 1980—represent retained earnings of unconsolidated subsidiaries and affiliates accounted for with the equity method.

**Note 19**—Lease payments for rentals under noncancelable capital leases amounted to $66 million in 1981, $60 million in 1980, and $58 million in 1979. The amounts for each of these major classes were as shown in the accompanying schedule.

| Classes of Property Held under Capital Leases (Dollar Amounts in Millions) | Dec. 31, 1981 | Dec. 31, 1980 |
|---|---|---|
| Land | $169.4 | $157.8 |
| Building | 103.6 | 101.9 |
| Computers and Peripheral Equipment | 83.3 | 74.1 |
| Other | 24.5 | 18.3 |
| | $380.8 | $352.1 |
| Less Accumulated Amortization | (117.1) | (103.6) |
| | $263.7 | $248.5 |

Minimum annual lease payments, primarily for rentals of land, buildings, and computers, under noncancelable leases total $250 million. Those having an original term of more than 1 year are $47 million in 1982, $37 million in 1983, $33 million in 1984, $29 million in 1985, and $16 million in 1986. The total rentals for years ending after 1986 are approximately $88 million. The amount representing interest is $110 million at December 31, 1981.

Capital leases have been recorded as long-term debt included with "Debentures and Other Debt" and the related property rights amortized under the straight-line method. The present value of these capital leases (10-percent weighted-average interest rate) on December 31, 1981, is $16 million and was $142 million on December 31, 1980.

**Note 20**—Contingent Liabilities: At December 31, 1981, the corporation was guarantor of customers' notes sold to bank and other liabilities aggregating $232 million.

There are various claims and pending actions against International Corporation and its subsidiaries in respect of commercial matters, including warranties and product liability, governmental regulations including environmental and safety matters, civil rights, patent matters, taxes, and other matters arising out of the conduct of the business. Certain of these actions purport to be class actions, seeking damages in very large amounts. The amounts of liability on these claims and actions at December 31, 1981, were not determinable but, in the opinion of the management, the ultimate liability resulting will not materially affect the consolidated financial position or results of operations of International Corporation and its consolidated subsidiaries.

**Note 21**—Presented below is selected financial information about the major segments of International Corporation. The segment amounts are reconciled to the amounts shown in the consolidated statements.

| (Dollar Amounts in Millions) | Power Systems | Industry Products | Broadcasting | Adjustments and Eliminations | Consolidated |
|---|---|---|---|---|---|
| **1979** | | | | | |
| Sales to Unaffiliated Customers ......... | $1,800.8 | $1,971.2 | $1,329.1 | — | $5,101.1 |
| Intersegment Sales ................... | 83.2 | 81.6 | — | $(164.8) | — |
| Total Segment Revenues ........... | $1,884.0 | $2,052.8 | $1,329.1 | $(164.8) | $5,101.1 |
| Operating Profit ..................... | $ 156.9 | $ 167.2 | $ 83.1 | $ (21.1) | $ 386.1 |
| Equity in Net Loss of Nonconsolidated Subsidiaries and Affiliated Companies ................................ | | | | | 3.3 |
| Central Corporate Revenues ............................ | | | | | 59.4 |
| Central Corporate Expenses ............................ | | | | | (50.1) |
| Interest Expense .......................................... | | | | | (69.3) |
| Income Tax Expense ...................................... | | | | | (145.9) |
| Loss from Discontinued Operations ................... | | | | | (21.0) |
| Net Income ................................................ | | | | | $ 161.9 |
| Identifiable Assets at Dec. 31, 1979 ....... | $1,358.4 | $1,250.2 | $ 905.0 | $ (63.0) | $3,450.6 |
| Investment in Net Assets of Unconsolidated and Affiliated Companies ................................ | | | | | 185.9 |
| Corporate Assets ......................................... | | | | | 771.2 |
| Total Assets ......................................... | | | | | $4,407.7 |
| **1980** | | | | | |
| Sales to Unaffiliated Customers .......... | $2,047.0 | $2,240.7 | $1,510.8 | — | $5,798.5 |
| Intersegment Sales ................... | 94.0 | 92.7 | | $(187.3) | — |
| Total Segment Revenues ........... | $2,141.6 | $2,333.4 | $1,510.8 | $(187.3) | $5,798.5 |
| Operating Profit ..................... | $ 131.3 | $ 140.0 | $ 69.6 | $ (17.7) | $ 323.2 |
| Equity in Net Loss of Nonconsolidated Subsidiaries and Affiliated Companies ................................ | | | | | (32.3) |
| Central Corporate Revenues ............................ | | | | | 72.0 |
| Central Corporate Expenses ............................ | | | | | (48.7) |
| Interest Expense .......................................... | | | | | (111.3) |
| Income Tax Expense ...................................... | | | | | (64.0) |
| Loss from Discontinued Operations ................... | | | | | (110.8) |
| Net Income ................................................ | | | | | $ 28.1 |
| Identifiable Assets at Dec. 31, 1980 ...... | $1,463.2 | $1,367.4 | $ 982.0 | $ (68.4) | $3,744.2 |
| Investment in Net Assets of Unconsolidated and Affiliated Companies ................................ | | | | | 226.2 |
| Corporate Assets ......................................... | | | | | 843.2 |
| Total Assets ......................................... | | | | | $4,813.6 |

| (Dollar Amounts in Millions) | Power Systems | Industry Products | Broadcasting | Adjustments and Eliminations | Consolidated |
|---|---|---|---|---|---|
| **1981** | | | | | |
| Sales to Unaffiliated Customers ......... | $2,194.2 | $2,286.9 | $1,381.6 | $ — | $5,862.7 |
| Intersegment Sales ................... | 98.5 | 97.8 | — | (196.3) | — |
| Total Segment Revenues .......... | $2,292.7 | $2,384.7 | $1,381.6 | $(196.3) | $5,862.7 |
| Operating Profit ...................... | $ 140.4 | $ 159.5 | $ 56.4 | $ (18.4) | $ 337.9 |
| Equity in Net Income of Nonconsolidated Subsidiaries and Affiliated Companies ...................................... | | | | | 14.5 |
| Central Corporate Revenues ...................................... | | | | | 51.3 |
| Central Corporate Expenses ...................................... | | | | | (54.9) |
| Interest Expense ...................................... | | | | | (76.4) |
| Income Tax Expense ...................................... | | | | | (93.8) |
| Loss from Discontinued Operations ...................................... | | | | | (13.4) |
| Net Income ...................................... | | | | | $ 165.2 |
| Identifiable Assets at Dec. 31, 1981 ...... | $1,469.9 | $1,369.4 | $ 947.8 | $ (66.4) | $3,720.7 |
| Investment in Net Assets of Unconsolidated and Affiliated Companies ...................................... | | | | | 289.2 |
| Corporate Assets ...................................... | | | | | 856.4 |
| Total Assets ...................................... | | | | | $4,866.3 |

The amounts shown for segment revenues, operating profit, and assets can be reclassified in terms of geographical location as follows:

| (Dollar Amounts in Millions) | Domestic | Foreign | Adjustments and Eliminations | Consolidated |
|---|---|---|---|---|
| **1979** | | | | |
| Sales to Unaffiliated Customers ........................ | $3,210.6 | $1,890.5 | — | $5,101.1 |
| Intersegment Sales .................................. | 64.5 | 46.7 | $(111.2) | — |
| Total Segment Revenues ......................... | $3,275.1 | $1,937.2 | $(111.2) | $5,101.1 |
| Operating Profit ..................................... | $ 193.5 | $ 213.7 | $ (21.1) | $ 386.1 |
| Identifiable Assets on Dec. 31, 1979 .................. | $1,935.7 | $1,552.8 | $ (37.9) | $3,450.6 |
| **1980** | | | | |
| Sales to Unaffiliated Customers ........................ | $3,644.0 | $2,154.5 | — | $5,798.5 |
| Intersegment Sales .................................. | 78.9 | 47.5 | $(126.4) | — |
| Total Segment Revenues ......................... | $3,722.9 | $2,202.0 | $(126.4) | $5,798.5 |
| Operating Profit ..................................... | $ 160.7 | $ 176.2 | $ (13.7) | $ 323.2 |
| Identifiable Assets on Dec. 31, 1980 .................. | $2,146.2 | $1,640.3 | $ (42.3) | $3,744.2 |
| **1981** | | | | |
| Sales to Unaffiliated Customers ........................ | $3,655.4 | $2,207.3 | — | $5,862.7 |
| Intersegment Sales .................................. | 84.9 | 53.6 | $(136.5) | — |
| Total Segment Revenues ......................... | $3,740.3 | $2,260.9 | $(138.5) | $5,862.7 |
| Operating Profit ..................................... | $ 156.2 | $ 195.3 | $ (13.6) | $ 337.9 |
| Identifiable Assets on Dec. 31, 1981 .................. | $2,076.3 | $1,685.1 | $ (40.7) | $3,720.7 |

Intersegment sales prices (called transfer prices) are based on external market prices for similar goods. Expenses deducted in determining segment operating profit include direct segment expenses plus indirect expenses that can be assigned, or allocated, on a reasonable basis. Central corporate expenses, interest expense, and income tax expense are not subtracted in determining segment operating profit.

**Note 22**—Presented below is selected quarterly financial information for 1980 and 1981.

| | Quarter | | | | |
| (Dollar Amounts in Millions) | First | Second | Third | Fourth | Total Year |
|---|---|---|---|---|---|
| **Sales:** | | | | | |
| 1980 | $1,320.1 | $1,433.2 | $1,470.6 | $1,574.6 | $5,798.5 |
| 1981 | 1,323.2 | 1,434.8 | 1,446.3 | 1,658.4 | 5,862.7 |
| **Earnings:** | | | | | |
| Continuing Operations, | | | | | |
| 1980 | 29.2 | 32.7 | 42.5 | 34.5 | 138.9 |
| 1981 | 33.0 | 41.6 | 50.0 | 54.0 | 178.6 |
| Discontinued Operations, | | | | | |
| 1980 | — | — | — | (110.8) | (110.8) |
| 1981 | — | — | (13.4) | — | (13.4) |
| Net Income, | | | | | |
| 1980 | 29.2 | 32.7 | 42.5 | (76.3) | 28.1 |
| 1981 | 33.0 | 41.6 | 36.6 | 54.0 | 165.2 |
| **Earnings per Common Share:** | | | | | |
| Continuing Operations, | | | | | |
| 1980 | $0.33 | $0.37 | $0.48 | $0.39 | $1.57 |
| 1981 | .38 | .47 | .57 | .62 | 2.04 |
| Discontinued Operations, | | | | | |
| 1980 | — | — | — | (1.25) | (1.25) |
| 1981 | — | — | (.15) | — | (.15) |
| Net Income, | | | | | |
| 1980 | .33 | .37 | .48 | (.86) | .32 |
| 1981 | .38 | .47 | .42 | .62 | 1.89 |
| **Dividends per Common Share:** | | | | | |
| 1980 | $0.243 | $0.243 | $0.243 | $0.243 | $0.972 |
| 1981 | .243 | .243 | .243 | .243 | .972 |
| **Common Stock Prices per Share:** | | | | | |
| 1980—High | $15 | $26 | $18$3/4$ | $13$5/8$ | $26 |
| Low | 11$1/2$ | 12$7/8$ | 9$7/8$ | 8 | 8 |
| 1981—High | 15$1/2$ | 19$1/4$ | 14$1/8$ | 20 | 20 |
| Low | 9$3/4$ | 13$1/4$ | 10$3/4$ | 12$7/8$ | 9$3/4$ |

## Note 23—Effects of Changing Prices

The two accompanying exhibits show the effects of changing general and specific prices on the operations and financial position of International. In these exhibits the amount for income tax expense, the depreciation method, and the assumptions for depreciation—salvage values and estimates of lives—are the same as those in income statements included in the primary financial statements. The constant-dollar calculations are based on the Consumer Price Index, Hypothetical* (CPI-H). The current cost of inventory is computed from vendors' invoices for purchased goods and from current standard costs for manufactured goods. Standard costs are updated at each year-end. For items of plant and equipment, current costs are obtained, where possible, from dealers' price quotations for similar used assets. Approximately 20 percent of the net book value of property, plant, and equipment is costed in this fashion. For the other items of property, plant, and equipment, current costs are estimated by first finding the replacement cost new of assets with the same productive capacity and then reducing that amount, where appropriate, by the present value of the operating cost savings that would result if those assets were being used, rather than the assets International actually uses. These methods were used for assets both in and outside of the United States.

## Report of Independent Accountants

To the Board of Directors and Shareholders of
International Corporation

We have examined the statement of financial position of International Corporation and consolidated subsidiaries as of December 31, 1981 and 1980, and the related statements of current and retained earnings and changes in financial position for the years ended December 31, 1981, 1980, and 1979. Our examination was made in accordance with generally accepted auditing standards and accordingly included such tests of the accounting records and such other auditing procedures as we considered necessary in the circumstances.

In our opinion, the aforementioned financial statements present fairly the financial position of International Corporation and consolidated subsidiaries at December 31, 1981 and 1980, and the results of their operations and the changes in their financial position for the years ended December 31, 1981, 1980, and 1979, in conformity with generally accepted accounting principles applied on a consistent basis.

*Stuckey Wells & Co.*

1101 E. 58th St.
Chicago, Illinois 60637

February 11, 1982

---

*Authors' note:* In reality, firms use the Consumers' Price Index for All Urban Consumers (CPI-U). We use the designation CPI-H to remind the reader that these data are hypothetical.

### Five-Year Comparison of Selected Supplementary Financial Data Adjusted for Effects of Changing Prices (Amounts Shown in Millions of Average 1981 Dollars, Except for per-Share Amounts Shown in Average 1981 Dollars and Price Index Shown in Index Form)

|  | 1977 | 1978 | 1979 | 1980 | 1981 |
|---|---|---|---|---|---|
| Net Sales (Millions) .................. | C$6,259.2 | C$6,338.1 | C$6,409.6 | C$6,499.7 | C$5,862.7 |
| **Historical Cost Information Adjusted for General Inflation** |  |  |  |  |  |
| Income (Loss) from Continuing |  |  |  |  |  |
|   Operations (Millions) ............... | 164.5 | 165.9 | 129.9 | 82.3 | 41.5 |
|     Per Share ....................... | 1.95 | 1.87 | 1.46 | 0.93 | 0.47 |
| Gain (Loss) from Declines in Purchasing Power of Net Amounts of Monetary Items Owed (Receivable) |  |  |  |  |  |
|   Debt of Parent (Millions) ........... | 48.7 | 37.1 | 46.4 | 73.9 | 96.6 |
|   Receivables of Nonconsolidated |  |  |  |  |  |
|     Subsidiaries (Millions) ........... | (17.8) | (17.7) | (18.34) | (18.0) | (16.6) |
| Net Assets at Year-End (Millions) ....... | 854.4 | 908.9 | 927.5 | 866.8 | 759.4 |
| **Current Cost Information** |  |  |  |  |  |
| Income (Loss) from Continuing |  |  |  |  |  |
|   Operations (Millions) ............... | 138.2 | 132.9 | 130.2 | 84.2 | 63.5 |
|     Per Share ....................... | 1.64 | 1.50 | 1.46 | 0.95 | 0.72 |
| Excess (Shortage) of Increase in Current Cost of Inventory and Plant over Increases in the General Price Level |  |  |  |  |  |
|   (Millions) ....................... | 14.6 | 23.7 | 10.9 | (53.3) | (322.7) |
| Net Assets at Year-End (Millions) ....... | 878.0 | 905.1 | 923.6 | 857.0 | 755.8 |
| **Other Information** |  |  |  |  |  |
| Cash Dividends Declared per Share ..... | 1.30 | 1.27 | 1.23 | 1.11 | .97 |
| Market Price per Share at Year-End ..... | 24.04 | 27.22 | 32.09 | 18.52 | 18.00 |
| Average Consumer Price Index (CPI-H[a]) | 101.5 | 105.4 | 219.1 | 245.6 | 275.3 |

[a]*Author's note:* In reality, firms use the Consumers' Price Index for All Urban Consumers (CPI-U). We use the designation CPI-H to remind the reader that these data are hypothetical.

*International Corporation Statement of*
*Income from Continuing Operations*
*Adjusted for Changing Prices*
*For the Year Ended December 31, 1981*
*(In Millions of Dollars)*

| | Historical Cost/ Nominal Dollars as Reported in the Primary Financial Statement | Adjusted for General Inflation Average 1981 Dollars | Adjusted for Changes in Specific Prices (Current Costs) |
|---|---|---|---|
| Sales and Other Revenues | $5,914.1 | C$5,914.1 | C$5,914.1 |
| Equity in Income from Nonconsolidated Affiliates | 14.5 | 14.5 | 14.5 |
| | $5,928.6 | C$5,928.6 | C$5,928.6 |
| Cost of Goods Sold (Excluding Depreciation) | 4,647.2 | C$4,654.3 | C$4,705.2 |
| Depreciation | 128.8 | 258.8 | 185.9 |
| Other Operating Expenses | 803.8 | 803.8 | 803.8 |
| Interest Expense | 76.4 | 76.4 | 76.4 |
| Income Taxes | 93.8 | 93.8 | 93.8 |
| | $5,750.0 | C$5,887.1 | C$5,865.1 |
| Income from Continuing Operations | $ 178.6 | C$ 41.5 | C$ 63.5 |
| Gain (Loss) from Declines in Purchasing Power of Net Amounts of Monetary Items Owed (Receivable): Debt of Parent Company | — | C$ 96.6 | C$ 96.6 |
| (Receivables) of Nonconsolidated Affiliates Accounted for on Equity Method | — | C$ (16.6) | C$ (16.6) |
| Unrealized Holding Gains on Inventory and Plant | — | — | C$ 30.6 |
| Realized Holding Gains on Inventory and Plant | — | — | 115.1 |
| Increase in Specific Prices (Current Costs) of Inventories and Property, Plant, and Equipment Held During Year[a]. | | | C$ 145.7 |
| Effect of Increase in General Price Level | | | (468.4) |
| Excess of Increase in Specific Prices over Increase in the General Price Level for Inventory and Property | | | C$ (322.7) |
| (Losses) from Discontinued Operations | $ (13.4) | | |

[a]At December 31, 1981, the current cost of inventory was $1,452.9, and the current cost of property, plant, and equipment, net of accumulated depreciation, was $1,989.2.

## Authors' Notes

### Note 1: Summary of Significant Accounting Policies

A.5 The first note to published financial statements is the "Summary of Significant Accounting Policies" as required by APB *Opinion No. 22* (1972).

**Consolidation Policies** The consolidation A.6 policy of International Corporation (IC), an industrial company, is fairly standard. All majority-owned subsidiaries are consolidated except for those engaged in financial operations and real estate development. The equity method is used for the nonconsolidated affiliates. The issues involved in deciding whether or not to consolidate are discussed in the Appendix to Chapter 14. Our own view is that financial statements are more useful if all majority-owned companies are consolidated, but the presentation in Note 11 of Exhibit A.4 allows us to make the required adjustment for the major subsidiary reported on the equity method.

A.7    **Revenue Recognition** IC uses the completed-sales method in recognizing revenue and the completed-contract method for long-term construction contracts, except for certain contracts extending over 5 years or more, where the percentage-of-completion method is used. See Chapter 8.

A.8    **Cost-Flow Assumption for Inventories** IC uses a LIFO cost-flow assumption for inventories, choosing to report lower income and to reduce current income taxes payable in times of rising prices. See Note 9 below.

A.9    **Pensions** See our Note 4 below.

A.10    **Depreciation** Most industrial companies use the straight-line depreciation method for financial statements and accelerated methods for tax reporting. This leads to the accounting for deferred income taxes, discussed below in Note 5.

A.11    **Deferred Income Taxes** APB *Opinion No. 11* (1967) requires an adjustment of income tax expense for differences between financial income and taxable income that are viewed as temporary. See Note 5 below. Income reported in the consolidated income statement earned by subsidiaries that do not plan to declare dividends in the indefinite future is not currently taxable to the parent, and this difference between financial and taxable income is treated as if permanent. Thus, no deferred taxes need be provided for this income.

A.12    **Investment Credit** The investment credit provides a reduction in income taxes otherwise payable when a company purchases qualifying long-term assets. The accounting possibilities of this benefit are discussed in Chapter 20. IC uses the flow-through method (increasing current income over what it would be if the deferral method were used) for its investment credits, whereas its nonconsolidated subsidiary uses the deferral method.

## Note 2: Discontinued Operations

APB *Opinion No. 30* (1973) requires that the    A.13 effects on income from segments that have been discontinued (or are expected to be discontinued) be reported separately in the financial statements.

## Note 3: Operations of Nonconsolidated Subsidiaries

IC uses the equity method for two noncon-    A.14 solidated subsidiaries. The effects on income for both of these subsidiaries are shown on one line in the income statement. The note provides more information on the operations of one subsidiary, Suburban Development Corporation, which engages in real estate development.

## Note 4: Pensions

The APB (*Opinion No. 8*, 1966), the FASB,    A.15 and the SEC require disclosures of current expense for pension plans and the present value of current commitments made to employees for retirement plans. The funds that IC has contributed to pay the pensions are in a separate pension trust. The changes in the amounts in that trust fund are shown in a separate schedule reported by IC. These pension assets are not included in the consolidated balance sheet totals.

## Note 5: Income Taxes

The first schedule in IC's Note 5 shows the    A.16 separation of pretax income between U.S. and foreign sources, as required by the SEC. The second schedule in IC's Note 5 starts with the amount of income taxes currently payable because of continuing operations. Next are the amounts of currently reported income tax expense for which no taxes are currently payable. These deferred taxes are caused by differences viewed as temporary between pretax income reported on the financial statements and pretax income reported on the tax return. Finally, as required by APB *Opinion No. 30,* the schedule shows separately the income tax effects of discontinued operations. The bottom line of this first schedule shows the total income tax expense reported in the income statement, Exhibit A.1. Notice that in 1980, IC showed a loss from discontinued operations on the financial statements and negative income tax expense. On the tax returns, however, the pretax income from both continuing and discontinued operations was positive, and there was $67.4 (= $105.4 − $38.0) million of income taxes payable that year.

A.17     The third schedule in IC's Note 5, showing the causes of the various deferred tax items, is required by the SEC. First, depreciation claimed on the tax return because of the use of accelerated methods exceeded the amount of depreciation charges on the income statement where the straight-line method is used. If the marginal tax rate is 46 percent, then the excess of tax over financial statement depreciation in 1981 must have been $46.3 (= $21.3/.46) million. Even though 1980 taxes payable were larger than tax expense because of reversals of total timing differences, the net effect of accelerated depreciation on the tax return was to reduce taxes currently payable by $26.5 million.

A.18     The next timing difference originates in the method of revenue recognition. IC uses the percentage-of-completion method for some contracts in its financial statements, but, attempting to minimize the present value of its tax burden, uses the completed-contract method on the tax return. In 1981, the financial statements report larger revenues on these long-term contracts than does the tax return. In 1980, the situation was just the opposite.

A.19     The expected costs of warranties is deducted from income on the financial statements in the year the product is sold, but for tax purposes the cost of warranties is a deduction only when actual repairs or replacements are made. Thus from warranties alone, financial statement income is less than taxable income. This is viewed as a timing difference leading to prepaid income taxes, an asset.

A.20     The fourth schedule in Note 5, like the third, is required by the SEC. This schedule helps us understand why it is that a company with a marginal tax rate of 46 percent (the legal rate) usually reports income tax expense different from 46 percent, between 30 and 44 percent in the case of IC. Most of the difference arises because of permanent differences—financial statement revenue never subject to tax, such as foreign income exempt from taxes, or taxed at lower rates, such as corporate dividends received. See the discussion in Chapter 20.

A.21     International Corporation is not unusual in having unsettled tax returns outstanding for almost a decade, since 1973. The Internal Revenue Service typically takes more than 10 years to settle with U.S. Steel about its annual tax return.

## Note 6: Research and Development

A.22   FASB *Statement of Financial Accounting Standards No. 2* (1974) requires the expensing of all costs for research and development except those that are contractually reimbursable. It is clear that companies would not engage in R & D projects year after year unless they expected some future benefits from the R & D. If there are future benefits, then we conclude that they should be reported as assets on the balance sheet. The FASB does not agree. See the discussion in Chapter 13.

## Note 7: Marketable Securities

A.23   FASB *Statement of Financial Accounting Standards No. 12* (1975) requires that marketable equity securities be shown at the lower of cost or market and that the portfolios of such securities classified as a current asset be accounted for separately, and in a different way, from the portfolio of such securities classified as a noncurrent asset.

Chapter 6 discusses some of the details. IC classifies all its securities as current assets and the market value at the two year-ends is immaterially different from cost, so the disclosure is relatively simple.

## Note 8: Customer Receivables

A.24  APB *Opinion No. 10* (1966) and FASB *Statement of Financial Accounting Standards No. 5* (1975) effectively require companies to use the allowance method, rather than the direct write-off method, of accounting for the effects of receivables that are expected to be uncollectible. This note discloses the estimated uncollectible amounts subtracted from gross customer receivables in arriving at the net balance sheet amount.

## Note 9: Inventories

A.25  The SEC requires that companies using a LIFO cost-flow assumption report in notes to the financial statements the current value of beginning and ending inventories. Under LIFO, earliest purchases, usually made at lower prices, remain in balance sheet inventory amounts. (Last-in, first-out for goods sold means the same thing as first-in, still-here for ending inventory; LIFO = FISH.) The discussion in Chapter 25 illustrates how to calculate the approximate effects on income of IC's using the LIFO cost-flow assumption rather than FIFO. Pretax income for 1981 would have been about $30 (= $370 − $340) million larger had IC used a FIFO flow assumption. The Internal Revenue Service will not allow taxpayers using LIFO to report the hypothetical effect on income of using FIFO, but the SEC requires disclosure sufficient for us to be able to calculate it.

## Note 10: Costs and Billings of Uncompleted Contracts

A.26  As Note 1 indicates, IC uses the completed-contract method of revenue recognition for many long-term contracts. (The indication comes from the statement that the percentage-of-completion method is used *only* for

certain contracts.) The information given here relates to contracts accounted for on the completed-contract method, discussed in Chapter 8.

A.27  As assets are put into production on a long-term contract and liabilities (such as for wages) are incurred, the following journal entry is made:

Temporary Account A (or Construction in
    Process) ............................... X
        Assets Used or Liabilities Incurred ....... X
To record work on contract.

As payments are due to be made to the company according to the terms of the contract, but before the contract is completed, the following entry is made:

Accounts Receivable ...................... Y
    Temporary Account A (or Progress
        Billings) ........................... Y
To record amount due from customers.

At the end of the period, Temporary Account A will have a debit balance if X is greater than Y or a credit balance if Y is greater than X. If there is a debit balance, then the balance $X - Y$ is reported as an asset, Excess of Costs (over progress billings for uncompleted contracts). If the progress billings exceed the costs incurred, then the credit balance in Temporary Account A is $Y - X$ and is reported as a current liability with the title Excess of Progress Billings (over related costs for uncompleted contracts).

A.28  The contracts with debit balances in Temporary Account A must be reported separately from those with credit balances in accordance with *Accounting Research Bulletin No. 45* (1955). Because IC has some contracts with billings in excess of costs and others with costs in excess of billings, both the liability and the asset are shown in the balance sheet. See Chapter 8.

## Note 11: Investments in Nonconsolidated Subsidiaries

A.29  The operations of the International Credit Company are sufficiently different in nature from those of IC that IC chooses not to con-

A.30     solidate but to use the equity method of accounting for this subsidiary. See the discussion in the Appendix to Chapter 14.

A.30     Condensed financial statements for the Credit Company are shown in IC's Note 11 (Exhibit A.4). If the Credit Company were consolidated, then all the assets, $1,143.9 million at the end of 1981, would be added in with IC's assets, and all of the liabilities, $992.1 million, would be added in with IC's liabilities. IC's consolidated balance sheet would be kept in balance by reducing the Investment account ($289.2 million shown in Exhibit A.2) by the current carrying amount of the investment in the Credit Company, $151.8 (= $1,143.9 − $992.1) million. Thus balance sheet asset and liability totals would both increase by $992.1 million. IC's consolidated net income would not be affected, but certain important ratios, such as the all-capital earnings rate and the debt-equity ratio, would be reduced.

A.31     For a discussion of the effects of the equity method on the statement of changes in financial position, Exhibit A.3, see Chapter 14.

## Note 12: Plant and Equipment

A.32     The schedule shown in IC's Note 12 gives details of plant and equipment accounts that might otherwise appear on the balance sheet. Construction in Progress is plant and equipment that is being added by IC, but that is not yet complete and functioning. In addition to labor and material costs, the amounts include capitalization of interest charges.

## Note 13: Goodwill from Business Combinations and Subsidiaries

A.33     APB *Opinion No. 17* (1970) requires that goodwill acquired (the excess of cost of a purchased subsidiary over the fair value of the net assets acquired) after October 31, 1970, must be amortized over a period not to exceed 40 years. See the discussion in Chapters 13 and 14. Goodwill acquired before November 1, 1970, need not be amortized.

A.34     IC does not own 100 percent of all of its consolidated subsidiaries. This we can determine from the existence of the account Minority Interest on IC's consolidated balance sheet and the deduction for minority interest in net income for consolidated subsidiaries on IC's income statement. See the Appendix to Chapter 14 for a discussion of the minority interest.

## Notes 14, 15, and 16: Debt Financing

A.35     The three notes on borrowings enable the reader to assess the maturity structure of the outstanding debt and the components of current interest expense. Note 14 presents short-term debt; Note 15, required by the SEC, presents information concerning compensating balances; Note 16 presents intermediate-term debt maturities and long-term debt obligations. Compensating balances are sometimes required by lending banks. The effect of a required compensating balance is to increase the effective interest rate. The SEC deems it important that financial statement readers be able to approximate the true interest rate on borrowings, not just the quoted rate, and thus requires this disclosure. The FASB requires disclosure of total interest charges and the portions of those amounts capitalized into Construction in Progress.

## Note 17: Stock Option Plans

A.36     *Accounting Research Bulletin No. 43* (1953) requires the disclosure of the details of stock option plans and of the currently outstanding options. At the end of 1981, the market price of a share of IC common stock was about $20.00. The average price of the 371,200 options exercisable at the end of 1982 was about $13.00. Thus, if all the options were exercised, the present owners' equity would be diluted approximately $2.6 million [= ($20 − $13) × 371,200 shares] in comparison to the issue of new shares at the current market price.

## Note 18: Owners' Capital Accounts

A.37     APB *Opinion No. 12* (1966) requires the disclosure of all changes in owners' equity accounts. IC shows the sources of the changes in the retained earnings account in a statement just below the income statement, Exhibit A.1. The schedule shown in Note 18 shows the sources of the changes in the other owners' equity accounts. The SEC requires disclosure of restrictions on dividend declarations and of amounts of retained earnings resulting from use of the equity method. IC discloses that approximately $100 million of retained earnings in each year are those of unconsolidated subsidiaries and affiliates accounted for with the equity method.

## Note 19: Leases

A.38 Chapter 18 explains the issues in accounting for long-term noncancelable leases. The first paragraph of IC's Note 19 includes the disclosure on payment commitments that is required by FASB *Statement of Financial Accounting Standards No. 13* (1976).

## Note 20: Contingent Liabilities

A.39 Contingent liabilities, in contrast with estimated liabilities, are not shown in the financial statements according to FASB *Statement of Financial Accounting Standards No. 5* (1975). The causes of uncertainty and the possibility of future losses should be disclosed in the notes, as IC does in Note 20.

## Note 21: Segment Report

A.40 FASB *Statement of Financial Accounting Standards No. 14* requires the disclosure of revenue, operating profit, and identifiable assets for major segments of a firm. International Corporation uses both industry and geographical location (domestic versus foreign) as the bases for identifying segments. Note the types of items that reconcile the sum of segment operating profit with consolidated net income.

## Note 22: Interim Reporting

A.41 These quarterly disclosures are required by SEC *Accounting Series Release No. 177.*

Note that sales do not show a particularly strong seasonal pattern but quarterly net income varies significantly during the year.

## Note 23: Effects of Changing Prices

A.42 FASB *Statement No. 33* (1979) requires these disclosures. Note that there is no such price index as the CPI-H (which stands for CPI-Hypothetical). The FASB requires use of the CPI-U (Consumer Price Index for all urban consumers). Because the price index for 1981 cannot be known until after the end of 1981 and this book goes to press before then, we have constructed a hypothetical price index for use in this sample disclosure.

A.43 The first column of the supplementary income statement shows the conventional financial statements based on nominal dollar measures of historical cost. The second column shows constant dollar measures of historical cost. The third column shows current costs. The measuring unit in the third column can be interpreted either as nominal dollars or as constant dollars of 1981 year-average purchasing power. One of the reasons that the FASB suggests using year-average dollars as the measuring unit is that the numbers that appear in the third column of this statement will be essentially the same whether the current costs are measured using constant average-year dollars or nominal dollars. The FASB requires supplementary data on income from continuing operations only.

### Constant-Dollar Accounting Disclosures

A.44 The numbers shown in the middle column of the Statement of Income from Continuing Operations are based on historical costs measured in constant dollars. The notation "C$" denotes constant dollars. The FASB allows use of the notation "$" and we suspect that many, maybe even most, companies will use the simpler, if less precise, "$" symbol.

A.45 The only feature shown here not explained in Chapter 26 is the accounting for the equity method income from nonconsolidated affiliates. The revenues and expenses of the finance subsidiary are spread evenly throughout the year, so the constant dollar amount stated in mid-year dollars is the same as the nominal dollar amount. The nonconsolidated subsidiary has, however, substantial amounts of net monetary assets because it is a finance company, which lends money. It has purchasing power losses on its net receivables. These losses are shown separately from the gains of the parent. FASB *Statement No. 33* allows several alternative treatments of equity method income in constant-dollar statements, but the one shown here is preferred. One allowed alternative merely reports the effect of restating the individual debits and credits to the investment account for changes in general prices, much the same as the debits and credits to the plant and accumulated depreciation are restated. Then, no purchasing power gain (or loss) from the nonconsolidated subsidiary's net monetary debt (or assets) appears.

A.46 **Current-Cost Accounting Disclosures** The items in the current-cost column are measured in constant dollars (of mid-year purchasing power), but because these appear the same as when they are measured in nominal dollars, FASB *Statement No. 33* allows the symbol "$" to be used in the third column, instead of "C$." The numbers in the bottom part of the third column, purchasing power gains (or losses) and holding gains net of inflation are measured in constant dollars. We think confusion is reduced if the same symbol is used throughout the entire third column. Because C$ is correct for all the numbers, whereas $ is not as precise, we prefer using C$ throughout. FASB *Statement No. 33* uses $ throughout the third column in its example disclosure. Firms that also use the $ symbol are following the highest authority, even though the usage is not as precise as is possible.

A.47    FASB *Statement No. 33* does not use the terms "holding gains" and "holding losses." Instead, it uses the term "increases in specific prices of inventory and plant." The FASB's explanation in paragraph 135 of this choice suggests that the term *gain* implies that the amounts can be distributed to owners without impairing operating capacity

of the firm. Holding gains cannot be distributed without impairing physical operating capacity, but the term *gain* does not imply distributability. Because the term "holding gain" is so evocative of what has happened (while correctly emphasizing the credit portion of the underlying journal entry), whereas the term "increase in specific prices" is more vague and sounds to us like the debit portion of the journal entry, we prefer to use the terms "holding gain" and "holding loss." The FASB does not forbid use of these terms.

A.48    Observe that whereas International had both realized and unrealized holding gains during 1981, general prices increased faster during the year than did the current costs of the specific assets held by the firm. Thus, by the end of the year, the current costs of the specific assets held had failed by more than $300 million to keep up with general inflation. Data in the 5-year summary show that also in 1980 current costs of specific assets held failed to increase as rapidly as the general price level. In earlier years, current costs of assets held did rise faster than the general price level.

A.49    The first (three-column) disclosure enables comparisons of income from continuing operations on both the constant-dollar and current-cost bases with dividends declared. In 1981, income conventionally reported was $178.6 million, or $2.04 per share. Dividends were $.97 per share or, seemingly, a payout of 48 percent of current earnings. Dividends of $.97 are more than one-and-a-third times as large as income from continuing operations restated to a current-cost basis of $.72 per share. If income from continuing operations is restated to a constant-dollar basis, dividends ($.97) are more than twice restated income (C$.47).

**Five-Year Summary** The 5-year summary A.50 shows data in a format useful for following the trend of items over time. Data for 5 years are shown in constant dollars. FASB *Statement No. 33* permits the use in this summary of either current 1981 dollars or dollars of some base period, such as 1967, which is the base period for the CPI. Using current dollars expresses the data in units that reflect current experience, but it requires the data of the 4 earlier years in the 5-year summary to be restated each year to reflect the change in the measuring unit. If the summary is stated in base-period dollars, there is no need for annual revision of those data.

A.51   Excerpts from the 5-year constant-dollar summary and from the nominal dollar amounts, not all shown in this Appendix, are instructive. See Exhibit A.5. Observe, for example, that the market price of a share of International common stock is shown as C$24.64 for 1977. Its actual market price at the end of 1977 was $17.00. (The amount shown is derived from C$25.79 = $17.00 × 275.3/181.5.) Whereas the nominal dollar amount of a share has increased slightly (from $17 to $18) over the 4-year period from the end of 1977 to the end of 1981, the general purchasing power represented by an investment in that share has declined by about 30 percent, from C$25.79 to C$18.00. Similarly, although nominal dollar sales have increased over the 5 years from $4 billion to nearly $6 billion, sales measured in constant dollars have actually declined.

A.52   One purpose of the constant-dollar restatement procedure is to do for conventionally reported net income what Exhibit A.5 does for conventionally reported sales, dividends, and market prices per share. Because the reported net income number is an aggregation of differently dated dollars (costs incurred at one time are subtracted from revenues recognized at another time), the final, reported net income figure cannot be simply restated. Instead, each of the items in the income statement must be restated to constant dollars before the aggregating additions and subtractions are carried out.

## Report of Independent Accountants

A.53   The auditor's report attached by the accounting firm of Stuckey Wells & Co. is an unqualified ("clean") opinion. A qualified opinion would be shown if, for example, the company changed accounting principles during the year, such as from FIFO to LIFO (an "except for" qualification to consistency).

---

### Exhibit A.5
**International Corporation**
**Comparison of Selected Nominal-Dollar and Constant-Dollar Amounts**

|  | 1977 | 1978 | 1979 | 1980 | 1981 |
|---|---|---|---|---|---|
| Sales (in Millions) |  |  |  |  |  |
| Nominal Dollars | $4,126.6 | $4,498.6 | $5,101.1 | $5,798.5 | $5,862.7 |
| Constant Dollars | C$6,259.2 | C$6,338.1 | C$6,409.6 | C$6,499.7 | C$5,862.7 |
| Dividends per Share |  |  |  |  |  |
| Nominal Dollars | $0.90 | $0.94 | $0.97 | $0.97 | $0.97 |
| Constant Dollars | C$1.37 | C$1.32 | C$1.22 | C$1.09 | C$0.97 |
| Year-End Market Price per Share |  |  |  |  |  |
| Nominal Dollars | $17.00 | $19.00 | $25.38 | $16.25 | $18.00 |
| Constant Dollars | C$25.79 | C$26.77 | C$31.89 | C$18.22 | C$18.00 |
| CPI-H | 181.5 | 195.4 | 219.1 | 245.6 | 275.3 |

Source: In each column, the constant dollar amount is derived as

$$\frac{\text{Nominal-Dollar}}{\text{Amount}} \times \frac{275.3}{\text{CPI-H in That Column}}.$$

## Questions

**A.1**  Review the meaning of the following concepts or terms discussed in Appendix A.
a. Consolidated financial statements.
b. Discontinued operations.
c. Deferred income tax debit.
d. LIFO = FISH.
e. Progress billings.
f. Excess of costs over progress billings for uncompleted contracts.
g. Excess of progress billings over related costs for uncompleted contracts.
h. Compensating balance.
i. Qualified opinion.

**A.2**  Assume that all sales of International Corporation for the year 1981 were made on account. How much cash was collected from customers?

**A.3**  What dividends were declared during 1981 by IC's nonconsolidated subsidiaries accounted for with the equity method?

**A.4**  Assuming a marginal tax rate of 46 percent, by what amount did the depreciation charge claimed on the tax return for 1980 differ from the depreciation expense reported on the financial statements for 1980?

**A.5**  Assuming a marginal tax rate of 46 percent, by what amount did revenues from long-term contracts in process reported on the income statement differ from the amount reported on the tax return for 1981?

**A.6**  IC's research and development costs have averaged $135 million per year for the past 10 years and have been expensed as incurred. How would the financial statements at December 31, 1981, differ if those costs had instead been capitalized and amortized over a 5-year period using the straight-line method? Ignore income tax effects.

**A.7**  What would be the effect on pretax income for 1981 if IC's marketable securities had a market value of $240 million on December 31, 1981?

**A.8**  Refer to IC's Note 9. Explain why the decline in inventory quantities during 1981 caused income to increase.

## Problem

**A.9**  Exhibits A.6, A.7, and A.8 present a set of financial statements for Kaplan Corporation, and include an income statement and statement of changes in financial position for 1981 and a comparative balance sheet on December 31, 1980 and 1981. Following the financial statements is a series of notes providing additional information on certain items in the financial statements. These financial statements and notes do not contain all required disclosures. Questions about the financial statements follow the notes. We suggest that you carefully study the statements and notes before attempting to respond to the questions.

*Exhibit A.6*
**Kaplan Corporation**
**Income Statement**
**for the Year 1981**
**(Amounts in Thousands)**

**Revenues:**

| | |
|---|---:|
| Sales | $12,000 |
| Less Sales Contra, Estimated Uncollectibles | 120 |
| Net Sales | $11,880 |
| Equity in Earnings of Unconsolidated Affiliates | 300 |
| Dividend Revenue | 20 |
| Gain on Sale of Marketable Securities | 30 |
| Total Revenues | $12,230 |

**Expenses:**

| | |
|---|---:|
| Cost of Goods Sold | $ 7,200 |
| Selling and Administrative | 2,569 |
| Loss on Sale of Equipment | 80 |
| Unrealized Loss from Price Decline of Marketable Equity Securities | 20 |
| Interest (Notes 7 and 8) | 561 |
| Total Expenses | $10,430 |
| Net Income before Income Taxes and Minority Interest | $ 1,800 |
| Income Tax Expense | 720 |
| Net Income before Minority Interest | $ 1,080 |
| Minority Interest in Earnings of Heimann Corporation | 40 |
| Net Income | $ 1,040 |

Note 1:  Summary of Accounting Policies

*Basis of Consolidation* The financial statements of Kaplan Corporation are consolidated with Heimann Corporation, an 80%-owned subsidiary acquired on January 2, 1980, in a transaction accounted for using the purchase method.

*Marketable Securities* Marketable securities are stated at the lower of acquisition cost or market.

*Accounts Receivable* Uncollectible accounts of customers are accounted for using the allowance method.

*Inventories* Inventories are determined using a last-in, first-out (LIFO) cost-flow assumption.

*Investments* Investments of less than 20% of the outstanding common stock of other companies are accounted for using the lower-of-cost-or-market method. Investments of greater than or equal to 20% of the outstanding common stock of unconsolidated affiliates and subsidiaries are accounted for using the equity method.

*Buildings and Equipment* Depreciation for financial reporting purposes is calculated using the straight-line method. For income tax purposes, the sum-of-the-years'-digits method is used.

*Goodwill* Goodwill arising from corporate acquisitions is amortized over a period of 10 years.

*Bond Discount and Premium* Discount and premium on bonds payable are amortized using the effective-interest method.

*Exhibit A.7*
**Kaplan Corporation**
**Balance Sheets**
**December 31, 1980 and 1981**
**(Amounts in Thousands)**

| | December 31, 1980 | December 31, 1981 |
|---|---|---|
| **ASSETS** | | |
| **Current Assets:** | | |
| Cash | $ 1,470 | $ 2,739 |
| Marketable Securities (Note 2) | 450 | 550 |
| Accounts Receivable (Net; Note 3) | 2,300 | 2,850 |
| Inventories (Note 4) | 2,590 | 3,110 |
| Prepayments | 800 | 970 |
| Total Current Assets | $ 7,610 | $10,219 |
| **Investments** (Note 5): | | |
| Investment in Maher Corporation (10%) | $ 200 | $ 185 |
| Investment in Johnson Corporation (30%) | 310 | 410 |
| Investment in Burton Credit Corporation (100%) | 800 | 930 |
| Total Investments | $ 1,310 | $ 1,525 |
| **Property, Plant, and Equipment:** | | |
| Land | $ 400 | $ 500 |
| Buildings | 800 | 940 |
| Equipment | 3,300 | 3,800 |
| Total Cost | $ 4,500 | $ 5,240 |
| Less Accumulated Depreciation | (1,200) | (930) |
| Net Property, Plant, and Equipment | $ 3,300 | $ 4,310 |
| Goodwill (Note 6) | 90 | 80 |
| Total Assets | $12,310 | $16,134 |

*Deferred Income Taxes* Deferred income taxes are provided for timing differences between book income and taxable income.

*Investment Tax Credit* The investment tax credit is accounted for using the flow-through method.

Note 2: Marketable securities are shown net of an allowance for market price declines below acquisition cost of $50,000 on December 31, 1980, and $70,000 on December 31, 1981.

Note 3: Accounts receivable are shown net of an allowance for uncollectible accounts of $200,000 on December 31, 1980, and $250,000 on December 31, 1981.

Note 4: Inventories consist of the following:

| | December 31, 1980 | December 31, 1981 |
|---|---|---|
| Raw Materials | $ 330,000 | $ 380,000 |
| Work in Process | 460,000 | 530,000 |
| Finished Goods | 1,800,000 | 2,200,000 |
| Total | $2,590,000 | $3,110,000 |

## Exhibit A.7 (continued)

|  | December 31, 1980 | December 31, 1981 |
|---|---|---|
| **LIABILITIES AND SHAREHOLDERS' EQUITY** | | |
| **Current Liabilities:** | | |
| Note Payable (Note 7) | $   — | $  1,000 |
| Accounts Payable | 1,070 | 2,425 |
| Salaries Payable | 800 | 600 |
| Interest Payable | 300 | 400 |
| Income Taxes Payable | 250 | 375 |
| Total Current Liabilities | $ 2,420 | $ 4,800 |
| **Long-Term Liabilities:** | | |
| Bonds Payable (Note 8) | $ 6,209 | $ 6,209 |
| Deferred Income Taxes | 820 | 940 |
| Total Long-Term Liabilities | $ 7,029 | $ 7,149 |
| Minority Interest | $   180 | $   214 |
| **Shareholders' Equity:** | | |
| Common Shares ($10 par value) | $   500 | $   600 |
| Additional Paid-in Capital | 800 | 1,205 |
| Unrealized Loss on Valuation of Investments | (25) | (40) |
| Retained Earnings | 1,436 | 2,226 |
| Total | $ 2,711 | $ 3,991 |
| Less Treasury Shares (at Cost) | (30) | (20) |
| Total Shareholders' Equity | $ 2,681 | $ 3,971 |
| Total Liabilities and Shareholders' Equity | $12,310 | $16,134 |

The current cost of inventories exceeded the amounts determined on a LIFO basis by $420,000 on December 31, 1980, and $730,000 on December 31, 1981.

Note 5: Condensed financial statements for Burton Credit Corporation, a wholly owned, unconsolidated subsidiary, are shown in Exhibit A 9

Note 6: On January 2, 1980, Kaplan Corporation acquired 80% of the outstanding common shares of Heimann Corporation by issuing 20,000 shares of Kaplan Corporation common stock. The Kaplan Corporation shares were selling on January 2, 1980, for $40 a share. Any difference between the acquisition price and the book value of the net assets acquired was considered goodwill and is being amortized over a period of 10 years from the date of acquisition.

Note 7: The note payable included under current liabilities is a 1-year note due on January 2, 1982. The note requires annual interest payments on December 31 of each year.

Note 8: Bonds payable are the following:

|  | December 31, 1980 | December 31, 1981 |
|---|---|---|
| 4%, $2,000,000 Bonds Due December 31, 1985, with Interest Payable Semiannually | $1,800,920 | $1,829,390 |
| 10%, $3,000,000 Bonds Due December 31, 1989, with Interest Payable Semiannually | 3,407,720 | 3,379,790 |
| 8%, $1,000,000 Bonds Due on December 31, 1995, with Interest Payable Semiannually | 1,000,000 | 1,000,000 |
| Total | $6,208,640 | $6,209,180 |

**a.** Marketable securities costing $180,000 were sold during 1981. Find the price at which these securities were sold.

**b.** Refer to part **a.** Find the cost of marketable securities purchased during 1981.

**c.** What was the amount of specific customers' accounts written off as uncollectible during 1981?

**d.** Assume that all sales are made on account. Find the amount of cash collected from customers during the year.

**e.** Compute the costs of units completed and transferred to the finished-goods storeroom during 1981.

**f.** Direct labor and overhead costs incurred in manufacturing during the year totaled $4,500,000. Compute the cost of raw materials purchased during 1981.

**g.** Assume that the amounts disclosed in Note 4 for the current cost of inventories represent the amounts that would be obtained from using a first-in, first-out (FIFO) cost-flow assumption. What would cost of goods sold have been if FIFO rather than LIFO had been used?

**h.** Prepare an analysis that explains the causes of the changes in each of the three intercorporate investment accounts.

**i.** Assume that Burton Credit Corporation had been consolidated with Kaplan Corporation instead of being treated as an unconsolidated subsidiary. Prepare a condensed consolidated balance sheet on December 31, 1981, and a condensed consolidated income statement for 1981 for Kaplan Corporation and Burton Credit Corporation.

**j.** Prepare an analysis that explains the change in each of the following four accounts during 1981: Land, Building, Equipment, and Accumulated Depreciation.

**k.** Give the journal entry made on Kaplan Corporation's books on January 2, 1980, when it acquired Heimann Corporation.

**l.** Compute the book value of the net assets of Heimann Corporation on January 2, 1980.

**m.** Compute the total amount of dividends declared by Heimann Corporation during 1981.

**n.** The 4-percent bonds payable were initially priced to yield 6 percent compounded semiannually. The 10-percent bonds were initially priced to yield 8 percent compounded semiannually. Using the appropriate present value tables at the back of the book, demonstrate that $1,800,920 and $3,407,720 (see Note 8) were the correct valuations of these two bond issues on December 31, 1980.

**o.** Calculate the amount of interest expense and any amortization of discount or premium for 1981 on each of the three long-term bond issues (see Note 8).

**p.** Compute the amount of interest actually paid in cash during 1981.

**q.** Compute the amount of income taxes actually paid during 1981.

**r.** On July 1, 1981, Kaplan Corporation sold 10,000 shares of its common stock on the open market for $50 a share. Prepare an analysis explaining the change during 1981 in each of the following accounts: Common Shares, Additional Paid-in Capital, Retained Earnings, Treasury Shares.

*Exhibit A.8*
**Kaplan Corporation**
**Statement of Changes**
**in Financial Position**
**For the Year 1981**
**(Amounts in Thousands)**

**Sources of Working Capital:**

*Operations:*

| | |
|---|---:|
| Net Income | $1,040 |
| Plus Expenses and Losses Not Using Working Capital: | |
|     Depreciation | 560 |
|     Deferred Taxes | 120 |
|     Loss on Sale of Equipment | 80 |
|     Minority Interest in Undistributed Earnings of Consolidated Subsidiaries | 34 |
|     Amortization of Discount on Bonds | 28 |
|     Amortization of Goodwill | 10 |
| Less Revenues and Gains Not Providing Working Capital: | |
|     Equity in Earnings of Affiliates and Subsidiaries in Excess of Dividends | |
|       Received | (180) |
|     Amortization of Premium on Bonds | (28) |

| | |
|---|---:|
| Working Capital Provided by Operations | $1,664 |
| Equipment Sold | 150 |
| Common Shares Issued | 500 |
| Treasury Shares Sold | 15 |
|     Total Sources | $2,329 |

**Uses of Working Capital:**

| | |
|---|---:|
| Dividends | $  250 |
| Investments in Securities (Johnson Corporation) | 50 |
| Acquisition of Land | 100 |
| Acquisition of Building | 300 |
| Acquisition of Equipment | 1,400 |
|     Total Uses | $2,100 |
| Net Change in Working Capital | $  229 |

**Increases in Working Capital:**

| | |
|---|---:|
| Cash | $1,269 |
| Marketable Securities | 100 |
| Accounts Receivable | 550 |
| Inventories | 520 |
| Prepayments | 170 |
| Salaries Payable | 200 |
|     Total Increases | $2,809 |

**Decreases in Working Capital:**

| | |
|---|---:|
| Notes Payable | $1,000 |
| Accounts Payable | 1,355 |
| Interest Payable | 100 |
| Income Taxes Payable | 125 |
|     Total Decreases | $2,580 |
| Net Change in Working Capital | $  229 |

*Exhibit A.9*
**Burton Credit Corporation**
**(Amounts in Thousands)**

| | December 31, 1980 | December 31, 1981 |
|---|---|---|
| **BALANCE SHEET** | | |
| Cash and Marketable Securities ........................ | $ 760 | $ 840 |
| Accounts Receivable (Net) ........................... | 6,590 | 7,400 |
| Other Assets ......................................... | 1,050 | 1,260 |
| Total Assets ..................................... | $8,400 | $9,500 |
| Notes Payable Due within 1 Year ...................... | $3,900 | $4,300 |
| Long-Term Note Payable ............................. | 2,620 | 3,100 |
| Other Liabilities ..................................... | 1,080 | 1,170 |
| Common Stock ....................................... | 100 | 100 |
| Additional Paid-in Capital ............................. | 300 | 300 |
| Retained Earnings ................................... | 400 | 530 |
| Total Equities .................................... | $8,400 | $9,500 |
| **STATEMENT OF INCOME AND RETAINED EARNINGS** | | |
| Revenues ............................................. | | $680 |
| Expenses ............................................. | | 520 |
| Net Income ............................................ | | $160 |
| Less Dividends ........................................ | | (30) |
| Increase in Retained Earnings for 1981 ................... | | 130 |
| Retained Earnings, December 31, 1980 ................... | | 400 |
| Retained Earnings, December 31, 1981 ................... | | $530 |

# Appendix B
# *Compound Interest Concepts and Applications*

B.1 Money is a scarce resource, which its owner can use to command other resources. Like owners of other scarce resources, owners of money can permit others (borrowers) to rent the use of their money for a period of time. Payment for the use of money differs little from other rental payments, such as those made to a landlord for the use of property or to a car rental agency for the use of a car. Payment for the use of money is called *interest*. Accounting is concerned with interest because it must record transactions in which the use of money is bought and sold.

B.2 Accountants and managers are concerned with interest calculations for another, equally important, reason. Expenditures for an asset most often do not occur at the same time as the receipts for services produced by that asset. Money received sooner is more valuable than money received later. The difference in timing can affect whether or not acquiring an asset is profitable. Amounts of money received at different times are different commodities. Managers use interest calculations to make amounts of money to be paid or received at different times comparable. For example, an analyst might compare two amounts to be received at two different times by using interest calculations to find the equivalent value of one amount at the time the other is due.

B.3 Contracts involving a series of money payments over time, such as bonds, mortgages, notes, and leases, are evaluated by finding the *present value* of the stream of payments. The present value of a stream of payments is a single amount of money at the present time that is the economic equivalent of the entire stream.

## Compound Interest Concepts

B.4 The quotation of interest "cost" is typically specified as a percentage of the amount borrowed per unit of time. Examples are 6 percent per year and 1 percent per month. Another example occurs in the context of discounts on purchases. The terms of sale "2/10, net/30" is equivalent to 2 percent for 20 days because if the discount is not taken, payment can be delayed and the money can be used for up to an extra 20 (= 30 − 10) days.

B.5 The amount borrowed or loaned is called the *principal*. To *compound* interest means that the amount of interest earned during a period is added to the principal and the principal for the next interest period is correspondingly larger.

B.6 For example, if you deposit $1,000 in a savings account that pays compound interest at the rate of 6 percent per year, you will earn $60 by the end of 1 year. If you do not withdraw the $60, then $1,060 will be earning interest during the second year. During the second year your principal of $1,060 will earn $63.60 interest, $60 on the initial deposit of $1,000 and $3.60 on the $60 earned during the first year. By the end of the second year, you will have $1,123.60.

B.7    When only the original principal earns interest during the entire life of the loan, the interest due at the time the loan is repaid is called *simple* interest. In simple interest calculations, interest on previously earned interest is ignored. The use of simple interest calculations in accounting arises in the following way. If you borrow $10,000 at a rate of 12 percent per year, but compute interest for any month as $100 (= $10,000 × .12 × $^1/_{12}$), then you are using a simple interest calculation.

B.8    The "force," or effect, of compound interest is more substantial than many people realize. For example, compounded annually at 6 percent, money "doubles itself" in less than 12 years. Put another way, if you invest $49.70 in a savings account that pays 6 percent compounded annually, you will have $100 in 12 years. If the Indians who sold Manhattan Island for $24 in May 1626 had been able to invest that principal at 8 percent compounded annually, the principal would have grown to $17.6 *trillion* by May 1981, 355 years later. The rate of interest affects the amount of accumulation more than you might expect. If the investment earned 6 percent rather than 8 percent, the $24 would have grown to $23 *billion* in 355 years; if the rate were 4 percent, the $24 would have grown to a mere $27 *million*.

B.9    At simple interest of 6 percent per year, the Indians' $24 would have grown to only $535 in 355 years, $24 of principal and $511 of simple interest (= $24 × .06 × 355). Nearly all economic calculations involve compound interest.

B.10    Problems involving compound interest generally fall into two groups with respect to time: First, there are the problems for which we want to know the future value of money invested or loaned today; second, there are the problems for which we want to know the

present value, or today's value, of money to be received or paid at later dates. In addition, the accountant must compute the rate of interest implied by certain payment streams.

## Future Value

When $1.00 is invested today at 6 percent   B.11 compounded annually, it will grow to $1.06000 at the end of 1 year, $1.12360 at the end of 2 years, $1.19102 at the end of 3 years, and so on according to the formula

$$F_n = P(1 + r)^n$$

where

$F_n$ represents the accumulation or future value,

$P$ represents the one-time investment today,

$r$ is the interest rate per period, and

$n$ is the number of periods from today.

The amount $F_n$ is the future value of the present payment, $P$, compounded at $r$ percent per period for $n$ periods. Table 1, at the end of Appendix B, shows the future values of $P = $1 for various numbers of periods and for various interest rates. Extracts from that table are shown here in Table B.1.

*Table B.1*
**(Excerpt from Table 1)**
**Future Value of $1 at 6%**
**and 8% per Period**
$F_n = (1 + r)^n$

| Number of Periods = n | Rate = r | |
|---|---|---|
| | 6% | 8% |
| 1 | 1.06000 | 1.08000 |
| 2 | 1.12360 | 1.16640 |
| 3 | 1.19102 | 1.25971 |
| 10 | 1.79085 | 2.15892 |
| 20 | 3.20714 | 4.66096 |

## Example Problems in Determining Future Value

B.12   **Example 1** How much will $1,000 deposited today at 6 percent compounded annually be worth 10 years from now?

B.13   One dollar deposited today at 6 percent will grow to $1.79085; therefore $1,000 will grow to $1,000 $(1.06)^{10}$ = $1,000 × 1.79085 = $1,790.85.

B.14   **Example 2** Macaulay Corporation deposits $10,000 in an expansion fund today. The fund will earn 8 percent per year. How much will the $10,000 grow to in 10 years if the entire fund and all interest earned on it is left on deposit in the fund?

B.15   One dollar deposited today at 8 percent will grow to $2.15892 in 10 years. Therefore, $10,000 will grow to $21,589 (= $10,000 × 2.15892) in 10 years.

## Present Value

B.16   The preceding section developed the tools for computing the future value, $F_n$, of a sum of money, $P$, deposited or invested today. $P$ is known; $F_n$ is calculated. This section deals with the problems of calculating how much principal, $P$, has to be invested today in order to have a specified amount, $F_n$, at the end of $n$ periods. The future amount, $F_n$, the interest rate, $r$, and the number of periods, $n$, are known; $P$ is to be found. In order to have $1 one year from today when interest is earned at 6 percent, $P$ of $.94340 must be invested today. That is, $F_1 = P(1.06)^1$ or $1 = $.94340 × 1.06. Because $F_n = P(1 + r)^n$, dividing both sides of the equation by $(1 + r)^n$ yields

$$\frac{F_n}{(1 + r)^n} = P$$

or

$$P = \frac{F_n}{(1 + r)^n} = F_n(1 + r)^{-n}.$$

## Present-Value Terminology

The number $(1 + r)^{-n}$ is the present value of   B.17
$1 to be received after $n$ periods when interest is earned at $r$ percent per period. The term *discount* is used in this context as follows: The *discounted* present value of $1 to be received $n$ periods in the future is $(1 + r)^{-n}$ when the *discount* rate is $r$ percent per period for $n$ periods. The number $r$ is the discount *rate* and the number $(1 + r)^{-n}$ is the discount *factor* for $n$ periods. A discount factor $(1 + r)^{-n}$ is merely the reciprocal, or inverse, of a number, $(1 + r)^n$, in Table B.1. Therefore, tables of discount factors are not necessary for present-value calculations if tables of future values are at hand. But present-value calculations are so frequently needed, and division is so onerous, that tables of discount factors are as widely available as tables of future values. Table 2 at the end of Appendix B shows discount factors or, equivalently, present values of $1 for various interest (or discount) rates for various numbers of periods. Table B.2 shows extracts from that table.

## Example Problems in Determining Present Values

**Example 3** What is the present value of $1   B.18
due 10 years from now if the interest rate (or equivalently, the discount rate) $r$ is 6 percent per year?

### Table B.2
**(Excerpt from Table 2)**
**Present Value of $1 at 6%**
**and 8% per Period**
$P = F_n(1 + r)^{-n}$

| Number of Periods = n | Rate = r | |
|---|---|---|
| | 6% | 8% |
| 1 | .94340 | .92593 |
| 2 | .89000 | .85734 |
| 3 | .83962 | .79383 |
| 10 | .55839 | .46319 |
| 20 | .31180 | .21455 |

B.19    From Table B.2, 6-percent column, 10-period row, the present value of $1 to be received 10 periods hence at 6 percent is $.55839.

B.20    **Example 4** (This example is used in Chapter 17.) You issue a noninterest-bearing note that promises to pay $13,500 three years from today in exchange for undeveloped land. How much is that promise worth today if the discount rate is 8 percent per period?

B.21    One dollar received 3 years hence discounted at 8 percent has a present value of $.79383. Thus, the promise is worth $13,500 × .79383 = $10,717.

## Changing the Compounding Period: Nominal and Effective Rates

B.22    "Twelve percent, compounded annually" is the price for a loan; this means that interest is added to or *converted* into principal once a year at the rate of 12 percent. Often, however, the price for a loan states that compounding is to take place more than once a year. A savings bank may advertise that it pays 6 percent, compounded quarterly. This means that at the end of each quarter the bank credits savings accounts with interest calculated at the rate 1.5 percent (= 6 percent/4). The interest payment can be withdrawn or left on deposit to earn more interest.

B.23    If $10,000 is invested today at 12 percent compounded annually, its future value 1 year later is $11,200. If the rate of interest is stated as 12 percent compounded semiannually, then 6 percent interest is added to the principal every 6 months. At the end of the first 6 months, $10,000 will have grown to $10,600, so that the accumulation will be $10,600 × 1.06 = $11,236 by the end of the year. Notice that 12 percent compounded *semiannually* is equivalent to 12.36 percent compounded *annually*.

B.24    Suppose that the price is quoted as 12 percent, compounded quarterly. Then an additional 3 percent of the principal will be added

to, or converted into, principal every 3 months. By the end of the year, $10,000 will grow to $10,000 × (1.03)$^4$ = $10,000 × 1.12551 = $11,255. Twelve percent compounded quarterly is equivalent to 12.55 percent compounded annually. If 12 percent is compounded monthly, then $1 will grow to $1 × (1.01)$^{12}$ = $1.12683 and $10,000 will grow to $11,268. Thus, 12 percent compounded monthly is equivalent to 12.68 percent compounded annually.

B.25    For a given *nominal* rate, such as the 12 percent in the examples above, the more often interest is compounded or converted into principal, the higher the *effective* rate of interest paid. If a nominal rate, $r$, is compounded $m$ times per year, then the effective rate is $(1 + r/m)^m - 1$.

B.26    In practice, to solve problems that require computation of interest quoted at a nominal rate of $r$ percent per period compounded $m$ times per period for $n$ periods, merely use the tables for rate $r/m$ and $m \times n$ periods. For example, 12 percent compounded quarterly for 7 years is equivalent to the rate found in the interest tables for $r = 12/4 = 3$ percent for $m \times n = 4 \times 7 = 28$ periods.

B.27    Some savings banks advertise that they compound interest daily or even continuously. The mathematics of calculus provides a mechanism for finding the effective rate when interest is compounded continuously. We shall not go into details but merely state that if interest is compounded continuously at nominal rate $r$ per year, then the effective annual rate is $e^r - 1$, where $e$ is the base of the natural logarithms. Tables of values of $e^r$ are widely available.* Six percent per year compounded continuously is equivalent to 6.1837 percent compounded annually; 12 percent per year compounded continuously is equivalent to 12.75 percent compounded annually. Do not confuse the compounding period with the payment period. Some banks, for example, compound interest daily but pay interest quarterly. You can be sure

---

*See, for example, Sidney Davidson and Roman L. Weil (eds.), *Handbook of Modern Accounting,* 2nd ed. (New York: McGraw-Hill Book Company, 1977), chap. 8, Exhibit 1.

that such banks do not employ clerks or even computers to calculate interest every day. They merely use tables to derive an equivalent effective rate to apply at the end of each quarter.

### Example Problems in Changing the Compounding Period

B.28 **Example 5** What is the future value 5 years hence of $600 invested at 8 percent compounded quarterly?

B.29    Eight percent compounded four times per year for 5 years is equivalent to 2 percent per period compounded for 20 periods. Table 1 shows the value of $F_{20} = (1.02)^{20}$ to be 1.48595. Six hundred dollars, then, would grow to $600 \times 1.48595 = $891.57.

B.30 **Example 6** How much money must be invested today at 6 percent compounded semiannually in order to have $1,000 four years from today?

B.31    Six percent compounded two times a year for 4 years is equivalent to 3 percent per period compounded for 8 periods. The *present* value, Table 2, of $1 received 8 periods hence at 3 percent per period is $.78941. That is, $.78941 invested today for 8 periods at an interest rate of 3 percent per period will grow to $1. To have $1,000 in 8 periods (4 years), $789.41 (= $1,000 × $.78941) must be invested today.

B.32 **Example 7** If prices increased at the rate of 6 percent during each of two consecutive 6-month periods, how much did prices increase during the entire year?

B.33    If a price index is 100.00 at the start of the year, it will be $100.00 \times (1.06)^2 = 112.36$ at the end of the year. The price change for the entire year is $(112.36/100.00) - 1 = 12.36$ percent.

### Annuities

B.34    An *annuity* is a series of equal payments made at the beginning or end of equal periods of time. Examples of annuities include monthly rental payments, semiannual corporate bond coupon (or interest) payments, and annual payments to a retired employee under a pension plan. Armed with an understanding of the tables for future and present values, you can solve any annuity problem. Annuities arise so often, however, and their solution is so tedious without special tables that annuity problems warrant special study and the use of special tables.

### Terminology for Annuities

B.35    The terminology used for annuities can be confusing because not all writers use the same terms. Definitions of the terms used in this text follow.

B.36    An annuity whose payments occur at the *end* of each period is called an *ordinary annuity* or an *annuity in arrears*. Semiannual corporate bond coupon payments are usually paid in arrears or, equivalently, the first payment does not occur until after the bond has been outstanding for 6 months.

B.37    An annuity whose payments occur at the *beginning* of each period is called an *annuity due* or an *annuity in advance*. Rent is usually paid in advance, so that a series of rental payments is an annuity due.

B.38    A *deferred* annuity is one whose first payment is at some time later than the end of the first period.

B.39    Annuities can be paid forever. Such annuities are called *perpetuities*. Bonds that promise payments forever are called *consols*. The British and Canadian governments have, from time to time, issued consols. A perpetuity can be in arrears or in advance. The only difference between the two is the timing of the first payment.

B.40    Annuities can be confusing. Their study is made easier with a *time line* such as the one shown below.

A time line marks the end of each period, numbers the period, shows the payments to be received or paid, and shows the time at which the annuity is valued. The time line just pictured represents an ordinary annuity (in arrears) for six periods of $30 to be valued at the end of period 6. The end of period 0 is "now." The first payment is to be received one period from now. Note that the general term "period" is used instead of "years." The period may be 1 month, 3 months, 6 months, 12 months, or some other length of time.

## Ordinary Annuities (Annuities in Arrears)

B.41 Table 3 at the end of this appendix shows the future values of ordinary annuities. Table B.3 reproduces extracts from that table.

---

*Table B.3*
**(Excerpt from Table 3)**
**Future Value of an Ordinary Annuity of $1 per Period at 6% and 8%**

| Number of Periods = n | Rate = r | |
| --- | --- | --- |
| | 6% | 8% |
| 1 | 1.00000 | 1.00000 |
| 2 | 2.06000 | 2.08000 |
| 3 | 3.18360 | 3.24640 |
| 5 | 5.63709 | 5.86660 |
| 10 | 13.18079 | 14.48656 |
| 20 | 36.78559 | 45.76196 |

---

B.42 Consider an ordinary annuity for three periods at 6 percent. The time line for the future value of such an annuity is

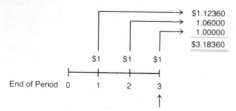

The $1 received at the end of the first period earns interest for two periods, so it is worth $1.12360 at the end of period 3. (See Table B.1.) The $1 received at the end of the second period grows to $1.06 by the end of period 3, and the $1 received at the end of period 3 is, of course, worth $1 at the end of

period 3. The entire annuity is worth $3.18360 at the end of period 3. This is the amount shown in Table B.3 for the future value of an ordinary annuity for three periods at 6 percent. Factors for the future value of an annuity for a particular number of periods are merely the sum of the factors for the future value of $1 for each of the periods. The future value of an ordinary annuity is calculated as follows:

$$\begin{matrix} \text{Future Value of} \\ \text{Ordinary Annuity} \end{matrix} = \begin{matrix} \text{Periodic} \\ \text{Payment} \end{matrix} \times \begin{matrix} \text{Factor for the Future} \\ \text{Value of an Ordinary} \\ \text{Annuity.} \end{matrix}$$

Thus,

$$\$3.18360 \quad = \quad \$1 \quad \times \quad 3.18360.$$

Table 4 at the end of Appendix B shows the present value of ordinary annuities. Table B.4 reproduces extracts from Table 4.

---

*Table B.4*
**(Excerpt from Table 4)**
**Present Value of an Ordinary Annuity of $1 per Period at 6% and 8%**

| Number of Periods = n | Rate = r | |
| --- | --- | --- |
| | 6% | 8% |
| 1 | .94340 | .92593 |
| 2 | 1.83339 | 1.78326 |
| 3 | 2.67301 | 2.57710 |
| 5 | 4.21236 | 3.99271 |
| 10 | 7.36009 | 6.71008 |
| 20 | 11.46992 | 9.81815 |

---

The time line for the present value of an ordinary annuity of $1 per period for three periods, discounted at 6 percent, is   B.43

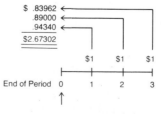

The $1 to be received at the end of period 1 has a present value of $.94340, the $1 to be received at the end of period 2 has a present value of $.89000, and the dollar to be received at the end of the third period has a present value of $.83962. Each of these numbers comes from Table B.2. The present value of the annuity is the sum of these individual present values, $2.67302, shown in Table B.4 as 2.67301 (our calculation differs because of roundings).

B.44    The present value of an ordinary annuity for $n$ periods is the sum of the present value of $1 received 1 period from now plus the present value of $1 received two periods from now, and so on until we add on the present value of $1 received $n$ periods from now. The present value of an ordinary annuity is calculated as follows:

$$\begin{matrix}\text{Present Value} \\ \text{of an} \\ \text{Ordinary Annuity}\end{matrix} = \begin{matrix}\text{Periodic} \\ \text{Payment}\end{matrix} \times \begin{matrix}\text{Factor for the} \\ \text{Present} \\ \text{Value of an Ordinary} \\ \text{Annuity.}\end{matrix}$$

Thus,

$$\$2.67301 \quad = \quad \$1 \quad \times \quad 2.67301.$$

## Example Problems Involving Ordinary Annuities

B.45    **Example 8** An individual plans to invest $1,000 at the end of each of the next 20 years in a savings account. The savings account accumulates interest of 8 percent compounded annually. What will be the balance in the savings account at the end of 20 years?
    The time line for this problem is

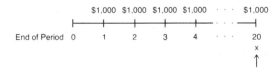

B.46    The symbol $x$ denotes the amount to be calculated. Table 3 indicates that the factor for the future value of an annuity at 8 percent for 20 periods is 45.76196. Thus,

$$\begin{matrix}\text{Future Value} \\ \text{of an} \\ \text{Ordinary Annuity}\end{matrix} = \begin{matrix}\text{Periodic} \\ \text{Payment}\end{matrix} \times \begin{matrix}\text{Factor for} \\ \text{the Future} \\ \text{Value of an} \\ \text{Ordinary Annuity.}\end{matrix}$$

$$x \quad = \$ \,1,000 \times \quad 45.76196.$$

$$x \quad = \$45,762.$$

B.47    **Example 9** Parents are accumulating a fund to send their child to college. The parents will invest a fixed amount at the end of each calendar quarter for the next 10 years. The funds will accumulate in a savings certificate that promises to pay 8 percent interest compounded quarterly. What amount must be invested to accumulate a fund of $12,000?
    The time line for this problem is

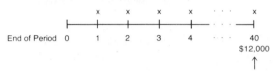

B.48

This problem is similar to Example 8 because both involve periodic investments of cash that accumulate interest over time until a specific time in the future. In Example 8, the periodic investment is given and the future value is computed. In Example 9, the future value is given and the periodic investment is computed. Table 3 indicates that the future value of an annuity at 2 percent (= 8 percent per year/4 quarters per year) per period for 40 (= 4 quarters per year × 10 years) periods is 60.40198. Thus,

$$\begin{matrix}\text{Future Value} \\ \text{of an} \\ \text{Ordinary Annuity}\end{matrix} = \begin{matrix}\text{Periodic} \\ \text{Payment}\end{matrix} \times \begin{matrix}\text{Factor for} \\ \text{the Future} \\ \text{Value of an} \\ \text{Ordinary Annuity.}\end{matrix}$$

$$\$12,000 \quad = \quad x \quad \times \quad 60.40198.$$

$$x \quad = \frac{\$12,000}{60.40198}.$$

$$x \quad = \$199.$$

B.49    Because the periodic payment is being calculated, the future value amount of $12,000 is divided by the future value factor.

B.50    **Example 10** An individual wishes to receive $40 every 6 months, starting 6 months hence, for the next 10 years. How much must be invested today in a savings account if the interest rate on the savings account is 8 percent compounded semiannually?
    The time line is

The factor from Table 4 for the present value of an annuity at 4 percent (= 8 percent per year/2 semiannual periods per year) for 20 (= 2 periods per year × 10 years) periods is 13.59033. Thus,

$$
\begin{array}{ccc}
\begin{array}{c}\text{Present Value}\\\text{of an}\\\text{Ordinary Annuity}\end{array} & = \begin{array}{c}\text{Periodic}\\\text{Payment}\end{array} \times & \begin{array}{c}\text{Factor for}\\\text{the Present}\\\text{Value of an}\\\text{Ordinary Annuity.}\end{array}\\
x & = \$40 \times & 13.59033.\\
x & = \$543.61.
\end{array}
$$

If \$543.61 is invested today, the principal plus interest compounded on the principal will provide sufficient funds so that \$40 can be withdrawn every 6 months for the next 10 years. (This example illustrates the calculations that would be made to find the present value at the time of issue of 8-percent semiannual coupon payments on bonds with a face value of \$1,000 maturing in 10 years and issued at par; see the discussion in Chapter 17.)

B.51 **Example 11** (Midwestern Products Company mortgage example, from Chapter 17) A company borrows \$30,000 from a savings-and-loan association. The interest rate on the loan is 8 percent compounded semiannually. The company agrees to repay the loan in equal semiannual installments over the next 5 years. The first payment is to be made 6 months from now. What is the amount of the required semiannual payment?

The time line is

End of Period 0 1 2 3 4 · · · 10
\$30,000

B.52 This problem is similar to Example 10 because both involve periodic payments in the future that are discounted to today. In Example 10, the periodic payments were given and the present value was computed. In Example 11, the present value is given and the periodic payment is computed. Table 4 indicates that the present value of annuity at 4 percent (= 8 percent per year/2 semiannual

periods per year) for 10 (= 2 periods per year × 5 years) periods is 8.11090. Thus,

$$
\begin{array}{ccc}
\begin{array}{c}\text{Present Value}\\\text{of an}\\\text{Ordinary Annuity}\end{array} & = \begin{array}{c}\text{Periodic}\\\text{Payment}\end{array} \times & \begin{array}{c}\text{Factor for}\\\text{the Present}\\\text{Value of an}\\\text{Ordinary Annuity.}\end{array}\\
\$30,000 & = x \times & 8.11090.\\
x & = \dfrac{\$30,000}{8.11090}.\\
x & = \$3,699.
\end{array}
$$

Because the periodic payment is being calculated, the present value amount of \$30,000 must be divided by the present value factor. (You may wish to turn to Exhibit 17.1 to study the amortization table for this loan. The amount of each semiannual payment shown there is \$3,700 rather than \$3,699, but the last payment is less than \$3,700.)

B.53 **Example 12** (User Company lease example, from Chapter 18) A company signs a lease acquiring the right to use property for 3 years. Lease payments of \$12,500 are to be made annually at the end of this and the next 2 years. The discount, or interest, rate is 12 percent per year. What is the present value of the lease payments?

B.54 The time line is

\$12,500 \$12,500 \$12,500

End of Period 0 1 2 3
x

The factor from Table 4 for the present value of an annuity at 12 percent for 3 periods is 2.40183. Thus,

$$
\begin{array}{ccc}
\begin{array}{c}\text{Present Value}\\\text{of an}\\\text{Ordinary Annuity}\end{array} & = \begin{array}{c}\text{Periodic}\\\text{Payment}\end{array} \times & \begin{array}{c}\text{Factor for}\\\text{the Present}\\\text{Value of an}\\\text{Ordinary Annuity.}\end{array}\\
x & = \$12,500 \times & 2.40183.\\
x & = \$30,000.
\end{array}
$$

In the User Company example in Chapter 18, the cost of the equipment is given at \$30,000 and the periodic rental payment is computed with an annuity factor of 2.40. Thus,

$$\begin{array}{ccc} \text{Present Value} \\ \text{of an} & = \begin{array}{c}\text{Periodic}\\\text{Payment}\end{array} \times & \begin{array}{c}\text{Factor for}\\\text{the Present}\\\text{Value of}\\\text{an Annuity.}\end{array} \\ \text{Ordinary Annuity} \end{array}$$

$$\$30,000 = x \times 2.40(183).$$

$$x = \frac{\$30,000}{2.40}$$

$$x = \$12,500.$$

**B.55**  **Example 13** (Pension funding example) A company is obligated to make annual payments to a pension fund at the end of the next 30 years. The present value of those payments is to be $100,000. What must the annual payment be if the fund is projected to earn interest at the rate of 8 percent per year?

**B.56**  The time line is

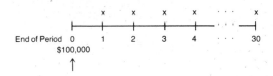

End of Period 0  1  2  3  4  · · ·  30
$100,000

Table 4 indicates that the factor for the present value of $1 paid at the end of the next 30 periods at 8 percent per period is 11.25778. Thus,

$$\begin{array}{ccc} \text{Present Value} \\ \text{of an} & = \begin{array}{c}\text{Periodic}\\\text{Payment}\end{array} \times & \begin{array}{c}\text{Factor for}\\\text{the Present}\\\text{Value of an}\\\text{Ordinary Annuity.}\end{array} \\ \text{Ordinary Annuity} \end{array}$$

$$\$100,000 = x \times 11.25778$$

$$x = \frac{\$100,000}{11.25778}$$

$$x = \$8,883.$$

**B.57**  **Example 14** Mr. Mason is 62 years old. He wishes to invest equal amounts on his sixty-third, sixty-fourth, and sixty-fifth birthdays so that starting on his sixty-sixth birthday he can withdraw $5,000 on each birthday for 10 years. His investments will earn 8 percent per year. How much should be invested on the sixty-third through sixty-fifth birthdays?

**B.58**  The time line for this problem is

x   x   x  −$5,000 −$5,000 · · · −$5,000

End of
Year  62  63  64  65  66  67   · · ·   75

On his sixty-fifth birthday, Mr. Mason needs to have accumulated a fund equal to the present value of an annuity of $5,000 per period for 10 periods, discounted at 8 percent per period. The factor from Table 4 for 8 percent and 10 periods is 6.71008. Thus,

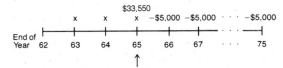

$$\begin{array}{ccc} \text{Present Value} \\ \text{of an} & = \begin{array}{c}\text{Period}\\\text{Payment}\end{array} \times & \begin{array}{c}\text{Factor for}\\\text{the Present}\\\text{Value of an}\\\text{Ordinary Annuity.}\end{array} \\ \text{Ordinary Annuity} \end{array}$$

$$x = \$5,000 \times 6.71008.$$

$$x = \$33,550.$$

The time line now appears as follows:

$33,550

x   x   x  −$5,000 −$5,000 · · · −$5,000

End of
Year  62  63  64  65  66  67   · · ·   75

The question now becomes: How much must be invested on Mr. Mason's sixty-third, sixty-fourth, and sixty-fifth birthdays to accumulate to a fund of $33,550 on his sixty-fifth birthday? The factor for the future value of an annuity for three periods at 8 percent is 3.24640. Thus,

$$\begin{array}{ccc} \text{Future Value} \\ \text{of an} & = \begin{array}{c}\text{Periodic}\\\text{Payment}\end{array} \times & \begin{array}{c}\text{Factor for}\\\text{the Future}\\\text{Value of an}\\\text{Ordinary Annuity.}\end{array} \\ \text{Ordinary Annuity} \end{array}$$

$$\$33,550 = x \times 3.24640.$$

$$x = \frac{\$33,550}{3.24640}.$$

$$x = \$10,335.$$

In the solution above, all calculations are expressed in terms of equivalent amounts on Mr. Mason's sixty-fifth birthday. That is, the present value of an annuity of $5,000 per period for 10 periods at 8 percent is equal to the future value of an annuity of $10,335 per period for 3 periods at 8 percent and both of these amounts are equal to $33,550. The problem could have been worked by selecting any common time period between Mr. Mason's sixty-second and seventy-fifth birthdays.

**B.59**  One possibility would be to express all calculations in terms of equivalent amounts on Mr. Mason's sixty-second birthday. To solve the problem in this way, first find the present value on Mr. Mason's *sixty-fifth* birthday of an annuity of $5,000 per period for 10 periods ($33,550 = $5,000 × 6.71008). Discount $33,550 back three periods using Table 2 for the present value of $1 ($26,633 = $33,550 × .79383). The result is the present value of the payments to be made to Mr. Mason *measured as of his sixty-second birthday*. Then find the amounts that must be invested by Mr. Mason on his sixty-third, sixty-fourth, and sixty-fifth birthdays that have a *present value* on his sixty-second birthday equal to $26,633. The calculation is as follows:

$$\begin{matrix} \text{Present Value} \\ \text{of an} \\ \text{Ordinary Annuity} \end{matrix} = \begin{matrix} \text{Periodic} \\ \text{Payment} \end{matrix} \times \begin{matrix} \text{Factor for} \\ \text{the Present} \\ \text{Value of an} \\ \text{Ordinary Annuity.} \end{matrix}$$

$$\$26,633 = x \times 2.57710.$$
$$x = \$10,335.$$

The amount $10,335 is the same as that found above.

## Annuities in Advance (Annuities Due)

B.60 The time line for the future value of a three-period annuity in advance is

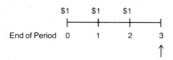

Notice that the future value is defined as of the *end* of the period at the start of which the last payment is made. When tables of ordinary annuities are available, tables for annuities due are unnecessary.

B.61 Compare the time line for the future value of an annuity in advance for three periods *with the time line relabeled to show start of period* and the time line for the future value of an ordinary annuity (in arrears) for four periods.

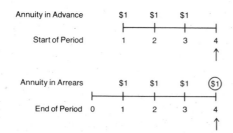

A $1 annuity in advance for *n* periods has a future value equal to the future value of a $1 annuity in arrears for *n* + 1 periods *minus* $1. The $1 circled in the time line for the annuity in arrears is the $1 that must be subtracted to calculate the future value of an annuity in advance because no annuity payment is made at the end of period 3. The "note" at the foot of Table 3 states: "To convert from this table to values of an annuity in advance, determine the annuity in arrears above for one more period and subtract 1.00000."

## Example Problem Involving Future Value of Annuity Due

**Example 15** An individual plans to invest $1,000 a year at the beginning of each of the next 10 years in a savings account paying interest of 6 percent per year. The first payment is to be made today. What will be the amount in the savings account at the end of the tenth year?    B.62

The time line is    B.63

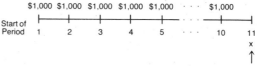

The factor for the future value of an annuity for 11 (= 10 + 1) periods is 14.97164. Because a $1,000 investment is not made at the end of the tenth year, 1.000 is subtracted from 14.97164 to obtain the factor for the annuity in advance of 13.97164. The future value of the annuity in advance is

$$\begin{matrix} \text{Future Value} \\ \text{of an} \\ \text{Annuity} \\ \text{in Advance} \end{matrix} = \begin{matrix} \text{Periodic} \\ \text{Payment} \end{matrix} \times \begin{matrix} \text{Factor for} \\ \text{the Future Value} \\ \text{of an} \\ \text{Annuity} \\ \text{in Advance.} \end{matrix}$$

$$x = \$1,000 \times 13.97164.$$
$$x = \$13,972.$$

## Example Problems Involving Present Value of Annuities Due

The time line for the present value of an annuity in advance for three periods is    B.64

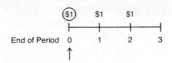

Notice that except for the first, circled payment, it looks just like the present value of an ordinary annuity for two periods. A $1 annuity in advance for *n* periods has a present value equal to the present value of a $1 annuity in arrears for *n* − 1 periods *plus* $1. The "note" at the foot of Table 4 states: "To convert from this table to values of an annuity in advance, determine the annuity in arrears above for one less period and add 1.00000."

B.65  **Example 16** What is the present value of rents of $350 to be paid monthly, in advance, for one year when the discount rate is 1 percent per month?

B.66  The time line is

The present value of $1 per period *in arrears* for 11 periods at 1 percent per period is $10.36763; the present value of $1 per period in advance for 12 periods is $10.36763 + $1.00 = $11.36763, and the present value of this year's rent is $350 × 11.36763 = $3,979.

B.67  **Example 17** Mr. Mason is 62 years old today. He wishes to invest an amount today and equal amounts on his sixty-third, sixty-fourth, and sixty-fifth birthdays so that starting on his sixty-sixth birthday he can withdraw $5,000 on each birthday for 11 years. His investments will earn 8 percent per year. How much should be invested on the sixty-second through sixty-fifth birthdays?

B.68  The time line for this problem is

On his sixty-sixth birthday Mr. Mason needs to have accumulated an amount large enough to fund an 11-year, $5,000 annuity in advance. An 11-year, $1 annuity in advance has a present value of $7.71008 = $6.71008 + $1 (Table 4, 10 periods, 8 percent). Mr. Mason then needs on his sixty-sixth birthday an accumulation of $5,000 × 7.71008 = $38,550. For each $4 that Mr. Mason invests, $1 each on his sixty-second, sixty-third, sixty-fourth, and sixty-fifth birthdays, he will have $4.86660 = $5.86660 − $1 (see Table 3 for five periods at 8 percent) on his sixty-sixth birthday. Because each $1 of annuity deposited on the sixty-second through sixty-fifth birthdays grows to $4.86660, Mr. Mason must deposit $38,550/4.86660 = $7,921 on each of the sixty-second through sixty-fifth birthdays to accumulate $38,550.

## Deferred Annuities

B.69  When the first payment of an annuity occurs some time after the end of the first period, the annuity is *deferred*. The time line for an ordinary annuity of $1 per period for four periods deferred for two periods is

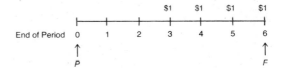

B.70  The arrow marked *P* shows the time for which the present value is calculated; the arrow marked *F* shows when the future value is calculated. The *future* value is not affected by the deferral and equals the future value of an ordinary annuity for four periods.

Notice that the time line for the present value looks like one for an ordinary annuity for six periods *minus* an ordinary annuity for two periods:

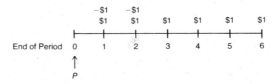

Calculate the present value of an annuity of *n* payments deferred for *d* periods by subtracting the present value of an annuity for

*d* periods from the present value of an annuity for *n* + *d* periods.

### Example Problem Involving Deferred Annuities

B.71 **Example 18** Refer to the data in Example 14. Recall that Mr. Mason wants to withdraw $5,000 per year on his sixty-sixth through his seventy-fifth birthdays. He wishes to invest a sufficient amount on his sixty-third, sixty-fourth, and sixty-fifth birthdays to provide a fund for the later withdrawals.

B.72 The time line is

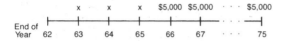

As of his sixty-second birthday, the $5,000 series of payments on Mr. Mason's sixty-sixth through seventy-fifth birthdays is a deferred annuity.

B.73 We demonstrated earlier that the present value of this deferred annuity on his sixty-second birthday could be calculated by finding the present value of an ordinary annuity for 10 periods (providing a present value of the annuity on his sixty-fifth birthday of $33,550) and then discounting this single sum back three periods using the factor for the present value of $1 (providing a present value of the deferred annuity on his sixty-second birthday of $26,633). This present value amount can also be calculated using the factor for the present value of an annuity for 13 periods (10 payments deferred for three periods) of 7.90378 and subtracting the factor for the present value of an annuity for three periods of 2.57710. The net amount is 5.32668 (= 7.90378 − 2.57710). Multiplying by the $5,000 payment amount, we find the present value of the deferred annuity on Mr. Mason's sixty-second birthday ($26,633 = $5,000 × 5.32668). The required investment can then be computed as shown previously.

## Perpetuities

B.74 A periodic payment to be received forever is called a *perpetuity*. Future values of perpetuities are undefined. If $1 is to be received at the end of every period and the discount rate is *r* percent, then the present value of the perpetuity is $1/*r*. This expression can be derived with algebra or by observing what happens in the expression for the present value of an ordinary annuity of $*A* per payment as *n*, the number of payments, approaches infinity:

$$P_A = \frac{A[1 - (1 + r)^{-n}]}{r}.$$

As *n* approaches infinity, $(1 + r)^{-n}$ approaches zero, so that $P_A$ approaches $A(1/r)$. If the first payment of the perpetuity occurs now, the present value is $A[1 + 1/r]$.

### Examples of Perpetuities

B.75 **Example 19** The Canadian government offers to pay $30 every 6 months forever in the form of a perpetual bond. What is that bond worth if the discount rate is 14 percent compounded semiannually?

B.76 Fourteen percent compounded semiannually is equivalent to 7 percent per 6-month period. If the first payment occurs 6 months from now, the present value is $30/.07 = $429. If the first payment occurs today, the present value is $30 + $429 = $459.

B.77 **Example 20** Every 2 years, Ms. Young has been giving $10,000 to the University to provide a scholarship for an entering student in a 2-year business administration course. If the University earns 8 percent per year on its investments, what single payment can Ms. Young give to the University to provide such a scholarship every 2 years forever, starting 2 years hence?

B.78 A perpetuity in arrears assumes one payment at the end of each period. Here, the period is 2 years; 8 percent compounded once a year over 2 years is equivalent to a rate of $(1.08)^2 − 1 = .16640$ or 16.64 percent compounded once per 2-year period. Consequently, the present value of the perpetuity paid in arrears every 2 years is $60,096 (= $10,000/.16640). A gift of $60,096 will be sufficient to provide a $10,000 scholarship forever. A gift of $70,096 (= $60,096 + $10,000) is required if the first scholarship is to be awarded now.

## Combinations of Cash Flows

B.79 Financial instruments may combine annuities and single payments. Bonds typically pay a specified sum every 6 months and a single, lump-sum payment along with the final periodic payment. Here is a simple example: The Macaulay Corporation promises to pay $40 every 6 months for 10 years, the first payment to occur 6 months from now, and an additional $1,000, ten years from now. If payments are discounted at 8 percent, compounded semiannually, then the $1,000 single payment has a present value of $1,000 × .45639 = $456.39 (Table 2, 20 periods, 4 percent) and the present value of the annuity is $40 × 13.59033 = $543.61 (Table 4, 20 periods, 4 percent). The sum of the two components is $1,000. (This is a $1,000-par-value, 10-year bond with 8 percent semiannual coupons issued at par to yield 8 percent compounded semiannually. See also the discussion in Chapter 17.)

## Life-Contingent Annuities

B.80 The annuities discussed above all last for a certain or specified number of payments. Such annuities are sometimes called *certain annuities* to distinguish them from *contingent annuities,* for which the number of payments depends on an event to occur at an uncertain date. For example, businesses often want to know the cost of an annuity (pension) that will be paid only so long as the annuitant (retired employee) lives. Such annuities are called *life-contingent* or *life annuities*. The details of life-annuity calculations are beyond the scope of this text, but

an unrealistic, hypothetical example is shown below to indicate the subtleties of life annuities.

B.81 Mr. Caplan is 65 years old today, and he has an unusual disease. He will die either 1½ years from today or 10½ years from today. Mr. Caplan has no family, and his employer wishes to purchase an ordinary life annuity for Mr. Caplan that will pay him $10,000 on his sixty-sixth birthday and $10,000 on every birthday thereafter on which Mr. Caplan is still alive. Funds invested in the annuity will earn 10 percent per year. How much should Mr. Caplan's life annuity cost?

**The Wrong Calculation** Mr. Caplan's life B.82 expectancy is 6 years: one-half chance of his living 1½ years plus one-half chance of his living 10½ years. The employer expects that six payments will be made to Mr. Caplan. The present value of an ordinary annuity of $1 for 6 years at 10 percent is $4.35526 (Table 4). Therefore the annuity will cost $43,553.

B.83 When a series of payments has uncertain length, the expected value of those payments is *not* the present value of an annuity for the expected life, but is the weighted average of the present values of the separate payments where the weights are the probabilities of the payment's being made.

**The Right Calculation** Mr. Caplan will re- B.84 ceive one payment for certain. The present value of that payment of $10,000 at 10 percent is $9,091 (Table 2). Mr. Caplan will receive nine further payments if he survives the critical second year. Those nine payments have a present value of $52,355, which is equal to the present value of a nine-year ordinary annuity that is deferred for 1 year, $61,446 − $9,091 (Table 4). The probability is one-half that Mr. Caplan will survive to receive those nine payments. Thus, their *expected* present value is $26,178 (= .5 × $52,355), and the *expected* present value of the entire life annuity is $9,091 + $26,178 = $35,269.

B.85 Mr. Caplan's life annuity, calculated correctly, costs only 81 percent as much as is found by the incorrect calculation. Actuaries for insurance companies use mortality tables to estimate probabilities of an annuitant's receiving each payment and, from those data, calculate the expected cost of a life annuity. Different mortality tables have been used for men and women because of the difference in life expectancies.

## Implicit Interest Rates: Finding Internal Rates of Return

B.86   In the preceding examples, we knew the interest rate and computed a future value or a present value given stated cash payments. Or we computed the required payments given their known future value or their known present value. In some calculations, we know the present or future value and the periodic payments; we must find the implicit interest rate. For example, Chapter 17 illustrates a case in which we know that the cash price of some equipment is $10,500 and that the asset was acquired using a note. The note is noninterest-bearing, has a face value of $13,500, and matures in 3 years. In order to compute interest expense over the 3-year period, the implicit interest rate must be known. The time line for this problem is

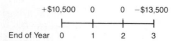

The implicit interest rate is $r$, such that

(I) $$\$10,550 = \frac{\$13,500}{(1 + r)^3}.$$

(II) $$0 = \$10,500 - \frac{\$13,500}{(1 + r)^3}.$$

That is, the present value of $13,500 discounted three periods at $r$ percent per period is $10,500. The present value of all current and future cash flows nets to zero when future flows are discounted at $r$ per period. In general, the only way to find such an $r$ is

a trial-and-error procedure.* The procedure is called "finding the internal rate of return" of a series of cash flows. The *internal rate of return* of a series of cash flows is the discount rate that equates the net present value of that series of cash flows to zero. The steps in finding the internal rate of return are as follows:

1. Make an educated guess, called the "trial rate," at the internal rate of return. If you have no idea what to guess, try zero.

2. Calculate the present value of all the cash flows (including the one at the end of year 0).

3. If the present value of the cash flows is zero, stop. The current trial rate is the internal rate of return.

4. If the amount found in step **2** is less than zero, try a larger interest rate as the trial rate and go back to step **2**.

5. If the amount found in step **2** is greater than zero, try a smaller interest rate as the new trial rate and go back to step **2**.

The iterations below illustrate the process for the example in equation (II).

| Iteration Number | Trial Rate = $r$ | Net Present Value: Right-Hand Side of (II) |
|---|---|---|
| 1 ............... | 0.00% | − $3,500 |
| 2 ............... | 10.00 | + 357 |
| 3 ............... | 5.00 | − 1,162 |
| 4 ............... | 7.50 | − 367 |
| 5 ............... | 8.75 | + 3 |

With a trial rate of 8.75 percent, the right-hand side is close enough to zero so that 8.75 percent can be used as the implicit interest rate. Continued iterations would find trial rates even closer to the true rate, which is about 8.7380 percent.

Finding the internal rate of return for a series of cash flows can be tedious and should not be attempted unless one has at least a desk calculator. An exponential feature, the   B.87

---

*In cases where $r$ appears only in one term, as here, $r$ can be found analytically. Here, $r = (\$13,500/\$10,500)^{1/3} - 1 = .087380$.

feature that allows the computation of $(1 + r)$ raised to various powers, helps.*

## Example Problems Involving Finding Implicit Interest Rates

B.88   **Example 21** The Alexis Company acquires a machine with a cash price of $10,500. It pays for the machine by giving a note promising to make payments equal to 7 percent of the face value, $840, at the end of each of the next 3 years and a single payment of $12,000 in 3 years. What is the implicit interest rate in the loan?

B.89   The time line for this problem is

$10,500  −$840  −$840  −$12,840

End of Period   0   1   2   3

The implicit interest rate is $r$, such that†

(III)   $$\$10{,}500 = \frac{\$840}{(1+r)} + \frac{\$840}{(1+r)^2} + \frac{\$12{,}840}{(1+r)^3}.$$

The internal rate of return is found to the nearest tenth of 1 percent to be 12.2 percent:

| Iteration Number | Trial Rate | Right-Hand Side of (III) |
|---|---|---|
| 1 | 7.0% | $12,000 |
| 2 | 15.0 | 9,808 |
| 3 | 11.0 | 10,827 |
| 4 | 13.0 | 10,300 |
| 5 | 12.0 | 10,559 |
| 6 | 12.5 | 10,428 |
| 7 | 12.3 | 10,480 |
| 8 | 12.2 | 10,506 |
| 9 | 12.1 | 10,532 |

*There are ways to guess the trial rate that will approximate the true rate in fewer iterations than the method described here. If you want to find internal rates of return efficiently with successive trial rates, then refer to a mathematical reference book to learn about the "Newton search" method, sometimes called the "method of false position."

†Compare this formulation to that in equation (II), above. Note that the left-hand side is zero in one case but not in the other. The left-hand side can be either a nonzero number or zero, depending on what seems convenient for the particular context.

B.90   **Example 22** (Equally spaced payments of equal amounts) In some contexts, such as mortgages or leases, one knows the amount of a series of future periodic payments, which are identical in all periods, and the present value of those future payments. For example, a firm may borrow $100,000 and agree to repay the loan in 20 payments of $11,746 each at the end of each of the next 20 years. In order to calculate interest expense each period, the interest rate implicit in the loan must be found.

B.91   The given information might be summarized as follows:

| Present Value of an Ordinary Annuity | | Periodic Payment | × | Factor for the Present Value of an Ordinary Annuity. |
|---|---|---|---|---|
| $100,000 | = | $11,746 | × | x. |

$$x = \frac{\$100{,}000}{\$11{,}746}.$$

$$x = 8.51353.$$

The factor that will discount 20 payments of $11,746 to a present value of $100,000 is 8.51353. To find the interest rate implicit in the discounting, scan the 20-payment row of Table 4 to find the *factor* 8.51353. The interest rate at the head of the column is the implicit interest rate, approximately 10 percent in the example.

B.92   **Example 23** (Finding internal rate of return for compound interest depreciation; see example in Chapter 12) An investment costing $11,400 today provides the following after-tax cash inflows at the ends of each of the next five periods: $5,000, $4,000, $3,000, $2,000, $1,000. What is the internal rate of return on these flows? That is, find $r$ such that

(IV)   $$0 = -\$11{,}400 + \frac{\$5{,}000}{(1+r)} + \frac{\$4{,}000}{(1+r)^2} + \frac{\$3{,}000}{(1+r)^3} + \frac{\$2{,}000}{(1+r)^4} + \frac{\$1{,}000}{(1+r)^5}.$$

The resulting rate is used in constructing a schedule of depreciation charges for the compound interest method of depreciation. Trial rates $r$ produced the following sequence of estimates of the internal rate of return:

| Iteration Number | Trial Rate | Right-Hand Side of (IV) |
|---|---|---|
| 1 .................... | 0.00% | + $3,600 |
| 2 .................... | 10.00 | + 692 |
| 3 .................... | 15.00 | − 414 |
| 4 .................... | 12.50 | + 115 |
| 5 .................... | 13.50 | − 102 |
| 6 .................... | 13.00 | + 6 |
| 7 .................... | 13.10 | − 16 |
| 8 .................... | 13.01 | + 4 |
| 9 .................... | 13.02 | + 2 |
| 10 .................... | 13.03 | − 1 |

The estimating process is carried several steps further than is necessary. To the nearest whole percent point, the internal rate of return is 13 percent. This figure is used in Chapter 12 in constructing the depreciation schedule in Exhibit 12.4. Because the exact rate is not used there, the depreciation figure for the last period shown requires a plug and implies a $10 rounding error.

B.93    To the nearest one-hundredth of a percent, the internal rate of return is 13.03 percent. Further trials find an even more accurate answer, $r = 13.027$ percent, which implies a plug for an error of only $0.09. Physical scientists learn early in their training not to use more significant digits in calculations than are warranted by the accuracy of the measuring devices. Accountants, too, should not carry calculations beyond the point of accuracy. Given the likely uncertainty in the estimates of cash flows, an estimate of the internal rate of return accurate to the nearest whole percentage point will lead to a depreciation schedule that serves its intended purpose.

B.94    **Example 24** (Internal rate of return calculation to find effective interest rate on a serial bond issue) Lexie's Fashionables raises funds through a serial bond issue. Each bond in the issue has $1,000 face amount and carries 10-percent *annual* coupons. Seven bonds are issued as a group: One matures 3 years after the issue date, one matures 4 years after the issue date, and five mature 5 years after the issue date. The market pays 8 percent interest for the 3-year bond, 10 percent interest for the 4-year bond, and 12 percent interest for the 5-year bonds. What are the initial issue proceeds? What single interest rate can be used in accounting for these bonds with the effective interest method?

The time line for this problem is                B.95

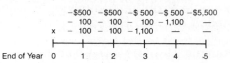

The bond maturing at the end of year 3 was issued to yield 8 percent:

| | | |
|---|---|---|
| (Table 4) | $ 100 × 2.57710 = | $ 257.71 |
| (Table 2) | 1,000 × .79383 = | 793.83 |
| Initial Proceeds .......... | | $1,051.54 |

The bond maturing at the end of year 4 was issued to yield 10 percent (par) ............. $1,000.00

The bonds maturing at the end of year 5 were issued to yield 12 percent:

| | | |
|---|---|---|
| (Table 4) | $ 500 × 3.60478 = | $1,802.39 |
| (Table 2) | 5,000 × .56743 = | 2,837.15 |
| Initial Proceeds ........ | | $4,639.54 |

The total proceeds are $6,691.08 = $1,051.54 + $1,000.00 + $4,639.54. The effective interest rate on the entire serial bond issue is $r$ such that

$$(V) \qquad \$6,691.08 = \frac{\$700}{(1 + r)} + \frac{\$700}{(1 + r)^2} + \frac{\$1,700}{(1 + r)^3}$$
$$+ \frac{\$1,600}{(1 + r)^4} + \frac{\$5,500}{(1 + r)^5}.$$

The rate appears to be between 10 and 12 percent per year. The trial rates used in finding the internal rate of return resulted in the following steps:

| Iteration Number | Trial Rate | Right-Hand Side of (V) |
|---|---|---|
| 1 ................ | 10.00% | $7,000.00 |
| 2 ................ | 12.00 | 6,530.74 |
| 3 ................ | 11.00 | 6,759.74 |
| 4 ................ | 11.50 | 6,643.88 |
| 5 ................ | 11.25 | 6,701.46 |
| 6 ................ | 11.40 | 6,666.83 |
| 7 ................ | 11.30 | 6,689.89 |

A rate of 11.3 percent is close enough, as the amortization schedule in Exhibit B.1 shows.

*Exhibit B.1*
**Amortization Schedule for Serial Bond
Issue of Annual 10% Coupon Bonds:
$1,000 Maturing in 3 Years Issued to Yield 8%;
$1,000 Maturing in 4 Years Issued to Yield 10%;
$5,000 Maturing in 5 Years Issued to Yield 12%
Proceeds of Initial Issue = $6,691
Effective Annual Interest on Entire
Issue = 11.3%**

**Annual Journal Entry**
Dr. Interest Expense ..................................... Amount in Column (3)
Dr. or Cr. Bond Liability  ..................................       Amount in Column (5)
    Cr. Cash  ..........................................       Amount in Column (4)

| Year (1) | Bond Liability Start of Period (2) | Effective Interest Expense at 11.3% (3) | Interest and Serial Bond Principal Payment (4) | Added to (Subtracted from) Bond Liability (5) | Bond Liability End of Period (6) |
|---|---|---|---|---|---|
| 0 | | | | | $6,691 |
| 1 | $6,691 | $756 | $ 700 | $ 56 | 6,747 |
| 2 | 6,747 | 762 | 700 | 62 | 6,809 |
| 3 | 6,809 | 769 | 1,700 | (931) | 5,878 |
| 4 | 5,878 | 664 | 1,600 | (936) | 4,942 |
| 5 | 4,942 | 558 | 5,500 | (4,942) | 0 |

## Summary

B.96  To compare or to compute with payments made at different times requires that the payments be made comparable. The methods of compound interest are used. Given a set of payments and an interest rate, either a future value or a present value can be computed.

Given future value or present value and an interest rate, the required payments can be computed. Given payments and either the present value or the future value, the interest rate can be computed, generally by a trial-and-error process. That interest rate is often called the "implicit interest rate" or the "internal rate of return."

## Questions and Short Cases

B.1  Review the following concepts or terms discussed in this appendix.
a. Compound interest.
b. Principal.
c. Simple interest.
d. Future value.
e. Present value.
f. Discounted value.
g. Discount factor.
h. Discount rate.
i. Ordinary annuity (annuity in arrears).
j. Annuity in advance (annuity due).
k. Contingent annuity.
l. Perpetuity.
m. Deferred annuity.
n. Implicit interest rate (internal rate of return).

B.2  What is interest?

**B.3** Distinguish between simple and compound interest.

**B.4** Distinguish between the discounted present value of a stream of future payments and their net present value. If there is no distinction, then so state.

**B.5** Distinguish between an annuity due and an ordinary annuity.

**B.6** The terms of sale "2/10, net/30" mean that a discount of 2 percent from gross invoice price can be taken if the invoice is paid within 10 days and that otherwise the full amount is due within 30 days.
   a. Write an expression for the implied annual rate of interest being offered, if the entire discount is viewed as being interest for funds received sooner rather than later. (Note that 98 percent of the gross invoice price is being borrowed for 20 days.)
   b. The tables at the back of the book do not permit the exact evaluation of the expression derived in part a. The rate of interest implied is 44.59 percent per year. Use the tables to convince yourself that this astounding (to some) answer must be close to correct.

**B.7** Describe the distortions, if any, caused by using simple interest computations for periods less than 1 year in a context where compound interest is required for yearly interest.

**B.8** Does the present value of a given amount to be paid in 10 years increase or decrease if the interest rate increases? Suppose that the amount were due in 5 years? 20 years? Does the present value of an annuity to be paid for 10 years increase or decrease if the discount rate decreases? Suppose that the annuity were for 5 years? 20 years?

**B.9** Rather than pay you $100 a month for the next 20 years, the person who injured you in an automobile accident is willing to pay a single amount now to settle your claim for injuries. Would you rather an interest rate of 6 percent or 12 percent be used in computing the present value of the lump-sum settlement? Comment or explain.

**B.10** Describe each of the arithmetic relations between numbers in compound interest tables described below.
   a. A number in Table 1 (future value of a single payment) and the corresponding number (same row and same column) in Table 2 (present value of a single payment).
   b. A number in Table 4 (present value of an ordinary annuity) and the numbers in Table 2 (present value of a single payment) for the same column as the number in Table 4.
   c. A number in Table 3 (future value of an ordinary annuity) and the corresponding number (same row and same column) in Table 4 (present value of an ordinary annuity).
   d. Note that no similarly simple statement can relate numbers in Table 3 to Table 1.

**B.11** Describe the "implicit interest rate" for a series of cash flows and a procedure for finding it.

**B.12** The Wisher Washer Company purchased a made-to-order machine tool for grinding washing machine parts. The machine cost $100,000 and was installed yesterday. Today, a salesperson offers to sell the company a machine tool that will do exactly the same work but costs only $50,000. Assume that the discount rate is 12 percent, that both machines will last for 5 years, that both machines will be depreciated on a straight-line basis with no salvage value, that the income tax rate is and will continue to be 40 percent, and that Wisher Washer Company earns sufficient income that any loss from disposing of or depreciating the "old" machine can be used to offset other taxable income.

How much, at a minimum, must the "old" machine fetch upon resale at this time to make the net present value of the cash flow from disposing the "old" machine and replacing it with the new, greater than or equal to zero?

**B.13**   Xenophon Company has undertaken an investment project that has a net present value of zero when cash flows are discounted at its cost of capital of 12 percent per year. The investment project has a 5-year life. The initial investment to undertake this project is $100,000. Suppose that Xenophon Company finances the project by borrowing $100,000 at a rate of 8 percent per year. It will make $8,000 interest payments at the end of each of the next 5 years and repay the $100,000 at the end of the fifth year.

a.   What is the present value at the start of the project of the benefits of financial leverage? That is, compute the net present value of the debt service payments, including principal repayment, using the 12-percent discount rate, and subtract that amount from the $100,000 borrowed.

b.   Repeat the requirements of part **a** assuming that the investment project has a 10-year life and that the $100,000 is borrowed for 10 years with interest paid annually and the principal repaid at maturity.

c.   How might the analysis done in parts **a** and **b** above mislead an accountant who confused the benefits of financial leverage with a specific investment project? (Hint: See the discussion in Question **18.27**.)

**B.14**   On January 1 of year 1, Outergarments, Inc., opened a new textile plant for the production of synthetic fabrics. The plant is on leased land; 20 years remain on the nonrenewable lease.

The cost of the plant was $2 million. Net cash flow to be derived from the project is estimated to be $300,000 per year. The company does not normally invest in such projects unless the anticipated yield is at least 12 percent.

On December 31, the company finds cash flows from the plant to be $280,000 for the year. On the same day, farm experts predict cotton production to be unusually low for the next 2 years. Outergarments estimates the resulting increase in demand for synthetic fabrics to boost cash flows to $350,000 for each of the next 2 years. Subsequent years' estimates remain unchanged. Ignore tax considerations.

a.   Calculate the present value of the future expected cash flows from the plant when it was opened.

b.   What is the present value of the plant 1 year later, immediately after the reestimation of future cash flows?

c.   On the day following the cotton production news release, Overalls Company announces plans to build a synthetic fabrics plant to be opened in 3 years. Outergarments, Inc., makes no further changes in estimates for years 2 through 4, but reduces the estimated annual cash flows for subsequent years to $200,000. What is the value of the Outergarments' present plant on January 1 of year 2, after the new projections?

d.   On January 2 of year 2, an investor contacts Outergarments about purchasing a 20-percent share of the plant. If the investor expects to earn at least a 12-percent annual return on the investment, what is the maximum amount that the investor can pay? Assume that the investor and Outergarments, Inc., use the same estimates of annual cash flows as found in part **c**.

## Problems and Exercises

**B.15** State the rate per period and the number of periods, in each of the following:
   **a.** 12 percent per annum, for 5 years, compounded annually.
   **b.** 12 percent per annum, for 5 years, compounded semiannually.
   **c.** 12 percent per annum, for 5 years, compounded quarterly.
   **d.** 12 percent per annum, for 5 years, compounded monthly.

**B.16** Compute the future value of:
   **a.** $100 invested for 5 years at 4 percent compounded annually.
   **b.** $500 invested for 15 periods at 2 percent compounded once per period.
   **c.** $200 invested for 8 years at 3 percent compounded semiannually.
   **d.** $2,500 invested for 14 years at 8 percent compounded quarterly.
   **e.** $600 invested for 3 years at 12 percent compounded monthly.

**B.17** Compute the present value of:
   **a.** $100 due in 33 years at 4 percent compounded annually.
   **b.** $50 due in 27 years at 6 percent compounded semiannually.
   **c.** $250 due in 8 years at 8 percent compounded quarterly.
   **d.** $1,000 due in 2 years at 12 percent compounded monthly.

**B.18** Compute the amount (future value) of an ordinary annuity (an annuity in arrears) of:
   **a.** 13 rents of $100 at $1^1/_2$ percent per period.
   **b.** 8 rents of $850 at 6 percent per period.
   **c.** 27 rents of $375 at 4 percent per period.
   **d.** 35 rents of $1,400 at 3 percent per period.

**B.19** What is the amount (future value) of an annuity due (in advance) of:
   **a.** 13 rents of $200 each at 6 percent per period?
   **b.** 9 rents of $75 each at 4 percent per period?
   **c.** 24 rents of $100 each at 2 percent per period?

**B.20** Compute the present value of an ordinary annuity (an annuity in arrears) of:
   **a.** $1,000 for 29 years at 4 percent per year.
   **b.** $1,500 for 31 years at 6 percent per year.
   **c.** $400 for 41 years at 8 percent per year.
   **d.** $750 for 75 years at 10 percent per year.

**B.21** What is the present value of an annuity due (in advance) of:
   **a.** 28 rents of $50 at 12 percent per period?
   **b.** 32 rents of $45 at 10 percent per period?

**B.22** Mr. Adams has $500 to invest. He wishes to know how much it will amount to if he invests it at:
   **a.** 6 percent per year for 21 years.
   **b.** 8 percent per year for 33 years.

**B.23** Ms. Black wishes to have $15,000 at the end of 8 years. How much must she invest today to accomplish this purpose if the interest rate is:
   **a.** 6 percent per year?
   **b.** 8 percent per year?

**B.24**   Mr. Case plans to set aside $4,000 each year, the first payment to be made on January 1, year 1, and the last on January 1, year 10. How much will he have accumulated by January 1, year 10, if the interest rate is:
a. 6 percent per year?
b. 8 percent per year?

**B.25**   Ms. David wants to have $450,000 on her sixty-fifth birthday. She asks you to tell her how much she must deposit on each birthday from her fifty-eighth to sixty-fifth, inclusive, in order to receive this amount. Assume an interest rate of:
a. 4 percent per year.
b. 6 percent per year.

**B.26**   Mr. Edwards invests $900 on June 1 of each year from year 1 to year 11, inclusive, 11 payments total. How much will he have accumulated on June 1, year 12 (note that 1 year elapses after last payment), if the interest rate is:
a. 5 percent per year?
b. 10 percent per year?

**B.27**   Ms. Frank has $145,000, which she deposits with an insurance company on February 1, year 1, to purchase an annuity. The annuity consists of six annual payments, the first to be made on February 1, year 2. How much will she receive in each payment? Assume an interest rate of:
a. 4 percent per year.
b. 6 percent per year.

**B.28**   In the preceding Problems **B.22–B.27**, you have been asked to compute a number. First you must decide what factor from the tables is appropriate and then you use that factor in the appropriate calculation. Notice that the last step could be omitted. You could write an arithmetic expression showing the factor you want to use without actually copying down the number and doing the arithmetic. For example, define the following notation: T($i$, $p$, $r$) means Table $i$ (1, 2, 3, or 4), row $p$ (periods 1 to 20, 22, 24, . . . , 40, 45, 50, 100), and column $r$ (interest rates from 1/2 percent up to 20 percent). Thus, T(3, 16, 12) would be the factor in Table 3 for 16 periods and an interest rate of 12 percent per period, which is 42.75328. Using this notation, you can write an expression for any compound interest problem. Any clerk can evaluate the expression.

You can check that you understand this notation by observing that the following are true statements:

T(1, 20, 8)  =   4.66096
T(2, 12, 5)  =    .55684
T(3, 16, 12) = 42.75328
T(4, 10, 20) =   4.19247

In the following questions, write an expression for the correct answer using the notation introduced here, but do not attempt to evaluate the expression.
a. Work the **a** parts of Problems **B.22** and **B.23**.
b. Work the **b** parts of Problems **B.24–B.27**.
c. How might the use of this notation make it easier for your instructor to write examination questions on compound interest?

**B.29** How much must Mr. Grady invest on July 1 of each of the years 1 through 7, inclusive, to have $300,000 on July 1, year 8? Assume an interest rate of:
**a.** 8 percent per year.
**b.** 10 percent per year.

**B.30** Ms. Howe wishes to provide her two sons with an income of $7,500 each for 5 years. How much must she invest on January 1, year 1, to provide for five such payments, the first to be made on January 1, year 3. Assume interest rates of:
**a.** 6 percent per year.
**b.** 10 percent per year.

**B.31** Mr. Irons borrowed money from a friend, and he agreed to repay $8,000 on March 1 of this year. On that date he was unable to pay his friend, so he made the following arrangement with the Regional Loan Company: the loan company paid the friend the $8,000 on March 1, and Mr. Irons agreed to repay the loan in a series of five equal annual payments. Assume an interest rate of 8 percent per year. How much must Mr. Irons pay each year if he makes the first payment on March 1 of
**a.** This year?
**b.** Next year?
**c.** Two years from now?

**B.32** Ms. Jones bought a car for $4,500, and agreed to pay for it in 12 equal monthly installments with interest at 12 percent per year, the first payment to be made immediately. What is the monthly payment?

**B.33** Mr. Karls agrees to lease a certain property for 10 years at the following annual rentals, payable in advance:
Years 1 and 2—$1,000 per year.
Years 3 to 6—$2,000 per year.
Years 7 to 10—$2,500 per year.

What single immediate sum will pay all of these rents if they are discounted at:
**a.** 6 percent per year?
**b.** 8 percent per year?
**c.** 10 percent per year?

**B.34** In order to establish a fund that will provide a scholarship of $3,000 a year indefinitely, with the first award to occur now, how much must be deposited if the fund earns:
**a.** 6 percent per period?
**b.** 8 percent per period?

**B.35** Consider the scholarship fund in the preceding problem. Suppose that the first scholarship is not to be awarded until 1 year from now. How much should be deposited if the fund earns:
**a.** 6 percent per period?
**b.** 8 percent per period?

Suppose that the first scholarship is not to be awarded until 5 years from now. How much should be deposited if the fund earns:
**c.** 6 percent per year?
**d.** 8 percent per year?

**B.36**   The state helps a rural county maintain a bridge and has agreed to pay $6,000 now and every 2 years thereafter forever toward the expenses. The state wishes to discharge its obligation by paying a single sum to the county now in lieu of the payment due and all future payments. How much should the state pay the county if the discount rate is
   **a.** 4 percent per year?
   **b.** 6 percent per year?

**B.37**   Mr. and Mrs. Clark want to establish a fund that will pay a $25,000 prize to an outstanding academic accountant. The first prize is to be awarded 4 years from now, and the prize is to be awarded every 10 years thereafter. How much should be deposited if the fund earns:
   **a.** 8 percent per year?
   **b.** 10 percent per year?

**B.38**   An oil-drilling company figures that $300 must be spent for an initial supply of drill bits and that $100 must be spent every month to replace the worn-out bits. What is the present value of the cost of the bits if the company plans to be in business indefinitely and discounts payments at 1 percent per month?

**B.39**   If you promise to leave $25,000 on deposit at the Quarter Savings Bank for 4 years, the bank will give you a new car now and your $25,000 back at the end of 4 years. How much are you, in effect, paying today for the car if the bank pays 8 percent interest compounded quarterly (2 percent paid four times per year)?

**B.40**   When the General Electric Company first introduced the Lucalox ceramic, screw-in light bulb, the bulb cost $3\frac{1}{2}$ times as much as an ordinary bulb but lasted 5 times as long. An ordinary bulb cost $.50 and lasted about 8 months. If a firm has a discount rate of 12 percent compounded three times a year, how much would it save in present-value dollars by using one Lucalox bulb?

**B.41**   The Roberts Dairy Company switched from delivery trucks with regular gasoline engines to ones with diesel engines. The diesel trucks cost $2,000 more than the ordinary gasoline trucks, but $600 per year less to operate. Assume that the operating costs are saved at the end of each month. If Roberts Dairy uses a discount rate of 1 percent per month, approximately how many months, at a minimum, must the diesel trucks remain in service for the switch to be worthwhile?

**B.42**   In the mid-1950s, International Business Machines Corporation (IBM) entered into a consent judgment with the U.S. Justice Department by agreeing to offer its business machines for sale. Prior to that time IBM would only rent its machines.
   **a.** Assume that the type 402 accounting machine had been renting for $5,220 per year, paid in advance, and the selling price of $27,950 was set so that it was equal to the present value of seven rental payments. What annual discount rate did IBM use in determining the selling price?
   **b.** If a type 82 card sorter had been rented for $55 a month, paid in advance, and the purchase price had been set at $3,400, what number of rental payments is equivalent to the purchase price? Assume that the rental payments were discounted at $\frac{1}{2}$ percent per month.
   **c.** If a type 24 keypunch machine had been rented for $40 per month, paid in advance, and if IBM wanted to set a purchase price so that the price would be equal to the discounted present value of 48 months' rent discounted at $\frac{1}{2}$ percent per month, what should the purchase price be?

**B.43** Find the implicit interest rate for the following loans, each of which is for $10,000 and requires payments as shown.

a. $5,530.67 at the end of years 1 and 2.
b. $1,627.45 at the end of years 1 through 10.
c. $1,556.66 at the end of years 1 through 13.
d. $2,053.39 at the end of years 1 through 20.

**B.44** Find the implicit interest rate for the following loans, each of which is for $10,000 and requires payments as shown.

a. $2,921.46 at the end of years 3 through 7.
b. $2,101.77 at the end of years 2 through 10.
c. $24,883.20 at the end of year 5 only.

**B.45** Compute the implicit interest rates for each of the following single-payment notes.

a. $10,000 is borrowed; a payment of $15,208.75 is due in 3 years.
b. $10,000 is borrowed; a payment of $15,036.30 is due in 3½ years. (Find a semiannual rate.)
c. $10,000 is borrowed; a payment of $21,068.50 is due in 4¾ years. (Find a quarterly rate.)

**B.46** The Garden Winery Company invests $10,000 at the end of year zero so that it may receive the following stream of payments (initial investment also shown):

| End of Year | Cash Payment |
|---|---|
| 0 | −$10,000 |
| 1 | 4,000 |
| 2 | 3,400 |
| 3 | 3,100 |
| 4 | 2,800 |

What is the present value at the end of year zero of that stream of payments if the discount rate is:

a. 0 percent per year?
b. 2 percent per year?
c. 6 percent per year?
d. 10 percent per year?
e. 14 percent per year? (Use these discount factors: 1.000, .877, .767, .675, and .592.)
f. Construct a graph that shows the discount rate on the horizontal axis and the net present value for the Garden Winery payment on the vertical axis. Plot the points derived in a–e.
g. Is the line connecting the plotted points a straight line?
h. What is the implicit interest rate for these flows?

**B.47** Two parents are accumulating a fund to send their child to college. The parents will invest a fixed amount in a savings certificate at the end of each calendar quarter starting on March 30, 1981. The savings certificate earns 6 percent compounded quarterly. Starting March 30, 1987, the parents will withdraw $1,000 at the end of each calendar quarter for 4 years to use to pay bills.

The parents expect to make payments through the end of 1990 (for a total of 10 years and 40 payments). How much must be paid into the fund quarterly for 10 years so that $1,000 can be withdrawn quarterly for the last 4 years?

**B.48** A group of investors has decided to purchase a large herd of beef cattle, to sell cattle as calves are born, and to sell the entire herd after 6 years. They have also agreed that no investment of the syndicate should return less than 10 percent per year. They purchase the cattle on January 1, 1980, for a price of $1,200,000, and they expect to sell the herd remaining on December 31, 1985, for the same price. The projected net cash flows from sale of beef during the 6 years is $200,000 per year.

On December 31, 1980, the syndicate finds that its cash flow from the herd is $210,000. But during December, the herd was stricken with a disease and 20 percent of the cattle died. The syndicate wants to restock the herd, and they decide to sell only enough beef to cover expenses until the herd grows to its original size. They anticipate that this process will result in zero cash flow for 1981, and $200,000 for each of the remaining 4 years.

Ignore tax considerations in your calculations.

a. Calculate the present value of the herd to the syndicate at time of purchase.
b. If there had been no disease, what would have been the value of the herd on January 1, 1981? Use only future cash flows for this and subsequent computations.
c. What was the value of the herd on January 1, 1981, after the disease and the decision to restock?
d. What was the cost to the syndicate of the disease?
e. On January 1, 1981, an investor who has a 25-percent interest in the herd decides to sell out. What is the least amount that the investor should be willing to accept for the 25-percent share? Assume that the investor is looking at alternative investments that would yield 10 percent per year.

**B.49** Shanks Company issued a series of 8-percent, semiannual coupon bonds: $100,000 mature in 1 year, $100,000 mature in 2 years, and $200,000 mature in 3 years. The 1-year bonds were issued for $100,950 to yield 7 percent, compounded semiannually. The 2-year bonds were issued at par for $100,000 to yield 8 percent compounded semiannually. The 3-year bonds were issued for $183,493 to yield about 11.3 percent, compounded semiannually. The total issue proceeds were $384,443 (= $100,950 + $100,000 + $183,493).

a. What is the implicit interest rate for the entire bond issue?
b. Construct an amortization schedule for this serial bond issue similar to the one in Exhibit B.1.

**B.50** September 1 of Year One, the partnership of Charles, Leslie, and Eli received $5,000 cash from Davis for a single payment note promising a single payment of principal and interest to Davis of $5,450 due August 31 of Year Two. The interest rate stated in the note was 9 percent per year. On January 1 of Year Two the holder of the note, Davis, needed cash and offered to return the note to the partnership for a single payment of $4,500.

What was the implicit annual interest rate in Davis' offer to sell the note back to the partnership for a single payment of $4,500?

**B.51** (Adapted from CPA Examination.) On January 1, Year 1, the Pitt Company sold a patent to Chatham, Inc., which had a net carrying value on Pitt's books of $10,000. Chatham gave Pitt an $80,000 noninterest bearing note payable in five equal annual installments of $16,000, with the first payment due and paid on January 1, Year 2. There was no established exchange price for the patent, and the note has no ready market. The prevailing rate of interest for a note of this type at January 1, Year 1, was 12 percent.

Prepare a schedule showing the income or loss before income taxes (rounded to the nearest dollar) that Pitt should record for the years ended December 31, Year 1 and Year 2, as a result of the above facts.

*(margin annotations)*
$m$ = times per period
$R/m$
$m \times n$

## TABLE 1
### Future Value of $1

$F_n = P(1 + r)^n$

$r$ = interest rate; $n$ = number of periods until valuation; $P = \$1$

| Periods $n$ | ¼% | ½% | ¾% | 1% | 1½% | 2% | 3% | 4% | 5% | 6% | 7% | 8% | 10% | 12% | 15% | 20% |
|---|---|---|---|---|---|---|---|---|---|---|---|---|---|---|---|---|
| 1 | 1.00250 | 1.00500 | 1.00750 | 1.01000 | 1.01500 | 1.02000 | 1.03000 | 1.04000 | 1.05000 | 1.06000 | 1.07000 | 1.08000 | 1.10000 | 1.12000 | 1.15000 | 1.20000 |
| 2 | 1.00501 | 1.01003 | 1.01506 | 1.02010 | 1.03023 | 1.04040 | 1.06090 | 1.08160 | 1.10250 | 1.12360 | 1.14490 | 1.16640 | 1.21000 | 1.25440 | 1.32250 | 1.44000 |
| 3 | 1.00752 | 1.01508 | 1.02267 | 1.03030 | 1.04568 | 1.06121 | 1.09273 | 1.12486 | 1.15763 | 1.19102 | 1.22504 | 1.25971 | 1.33100 | 1.40493 | 1.52088 | 1.72800 |
| 4 | 1.01004 | 1.02015 | 1.03034 | 1.04060 | 1.06136 | 1.08243 | 1.12551 | 1.16986 | 1.21551 | 1.26248 | 1.31080 | 1.36049 | 1.46410 | 1.57352 | 1.74901 | 2.07360 |
| 5 | 1.01256 | 1.02525 | 1.03807 | 1.05101 | 1.07728 | 1.10408 | 1.15927 | 1.21665 | 1.27628 | 1.33823 | 1.40255 | 1.46933 | 1.61051 | 1.76234 | 2.01136 | 2.48832 |
| 6 | 1.01509 | 1.03038 | 1.04585 | 1.06152 | 1.09344 | 1.12616 | 1.19405 | 1.26532 | 1.34010 | 1.41852 | 1.50073 | 1.58687 | 1.77156 | 1.97382 | 2.31306 | 2.98598 |
| 7 | 1.01763 | 1.03553 | 1.05370 | 1.07214 | 1.10984 | 1.14869 | 1.22987 | 1.31593 | 1.40710 | 1.50363 | 1.60578 | 1.71382 | 1.94872 | 2.21068 | 2.66002 | 3.58318 |
| 8 | 1.02018 | 1.04071 | 1.06160 | 1.08286 | 1.12649 | 1.17166 | 1.26677 | 1.36857 | 1.47746 | 1.59385 | 1.71819 | 1.85093 | 2.14359 | 2.47596 | 3.05902 | 4.29982 |
| 9 | 1.02273 | 1.04591 | 1.06956 | 1.09369 | 1.14339 | 1.19509 | 1.30477 | 1.42331 | 1.55133 | 1.68948 | 1.83846 | 1.99900 | 2.35795 | 2.77308 | 3.51788 | 5.15978 |
| 10 | 1.02528 | 1.05114 | 1.07758 | 1.10462 | 1.16054 | 1.21899 | 1.34392 | 1.48024 | 1.62889 | 1.79085 | 1.96715 | 2.15892 | 2.59374 | 3.10585 | 4.04556 | 6.19174 |
| 11 | 1.02785 | 1.05640 | 1.08566 | 1.11567 | 1.17795 | 1.24337 | 1.38423 | 1.53945 | 1.71034 | 1.89830 | 2.10485 | 2.33164 | 2.85312 | 3.47855 | 4.65239 | 7.43008 |
| 12 | 1.03042 | 1.06168 | 1.09381 | 1.12683 | 1.19562 | 1.26824 | 1.42576 | 1.60103 | 1.79586 | 2.01220 | 2.25219 | 2.51817 | 3.13843 | 3.89598 | 5.35025 | 8.91610 |
| 13 | 1.03299 | 1.06699 | 1.10201 | 1.13809 | 1.21355 | 1.29361 | 1.46853 | 1.66507 | 1.88565 | 2.13293 | 2.40985 | 2.71962 | 3.45227 | 4.36349 | 6.15279 | 10.69932 |
| 14 | 1.03557 | 1.07232 | 1.11028 | 1.14947 | 1.23176 | 1.31948 | 1.51259 | 1.73168 | 1.97993 | 2.26090 | 2.57853 | 2.93719 | 3.79750 | 4.88711 | 7.07571 | 12.83918 |
| 15 | 1.03816 | 1.07768 | 1.11860 | 1.16097 | 1.25023 | 1.34587 | 1.55797 | 1.80094 | 2.07893 | 2.39656 | 2.75903 | 3.17217 | 4.17725 | 5.47357 | 8.13706 | 15.40702 |
| 16 | 1.04076 | 1.08307 | 1.12699 | 1.17258 | 1.26899 | 1.37279 | 1.60471 | 1.87298 | 2.18287 | 2.54035 | 2.95216 | 3.42594 | 4.59497 | 6.13039 | 9.35762 | 18.48843 |
| 17 | 1.04336 | 1.08849 | 1.13544 | 1.18430 | 1.28802 | 1.40024 | 1.65285 | 1.94790 | 2.29202 | 2.69277 | 3.15882 | 3.70002 | 5.05447 | 6.86604 | 10.76126 | 22.18611 |
| 18 | 1.04597 | 1.09393 | 1.14396 | 1.19615 | 1.30734 | 1.42825 | 1.70243 | 2.02582 | 2.40662 | 2.85434 | 3.37993 | 3.99602 | 5.55992 | 7.68997 | 12.37545 | 26.62333 |
| 19 | 1.04858 | 1.09940 | 1.15254 | 1.20811 | 1.32695 | 1.45681 | 1.75351 | 2.10685 | 2.52695 | 3.02560 | 3.61653 | 4.31570 | 6.11591 | 8.61276 | 14.23177 | 31.94800 |
| 20 | 1.05121 | 1.10490 | 1.16118 | 1.22019 | 1.34686 | 1.48595 | 1.80611 | 2.19112 | 2.65330 | 3.20714 | 3.86968 | 4.66096 | 6.72750 | 9.64629 | 16.36654 | 38.33760 |
| 22 | 1.05647 | 1.11597 | 1.17867 | 1.24472 | 1.38756 | 1.54598 | 1.91610 | 2.36992 | 2.92526 | 3.60354 | 4.43040 | 5.43654 | 8.14027 | 12.10031 | 21.64475 | 55.20614 |
| 24 | 1.06176 | 1.12716 | 1.19641 | 1.26973 | 1.42950 | 1.60844 | 2.03279 | 2.56330 | 3.22510 | 4.04893 | 5.07237 | 6.34118 | 9.84973 | 15.17863 | 28.62518 | 79.49685 |
| 26 | 1.06707 | 1.13846 | 1.21443 | 1.29526 | 1.47271 | 1.67342 | 2.15659 | 2.77247 | 3.55567 | 4.54938 | 5.80735 | 7.39635 | 11.91818 | 19.04007 | 37.85680 | 114.4755 |
| 28 | 1.07241 | 1.14987 | 1.23271 | 1.32129 | 1.51722 | 1.74102 | 2.28793 | 2.99870 | 3.92013 | 5.11169 | 6.64884 | 8.62711 | 14.42099 | 23.88387 | 50.06561 | 164.8447 |
| 30 | 1.07778 | 1.16140 | 1.25127 | 1.34785 | 1.56308 | 1.81136 | 2.42726 | 3.24340 | 4.32194 | 5.74349 | 7.61226 | 10.06266 | 17.44940 | 29.95992 | 66.21177 | 237.3763 |
| 32 | 1.08318 | 1.17304 | 1.27011 | 1.37494 | 1.61032 | 1.88454 | 2.57508 | 3.50806 | 4.76494 | 6.45339 | 8.71527 | 11.73708 | 21.11378 | 37.58173 | 87.56507 | 341.8219 |
| 34 | 1.08860 | 1.18480 | 1.28923 | 1.40258 | 1.65900 | 1.96068 | 2.73191 | 3.79432 | 5.25335 | 7.25103 | 9.97811 | 13.69013 | 25.54767 | 47.14252 | 115.80480 | 492.2235 |
| 36 | 1.09405 | 1.19668 | 1.30865 | 1.43077 | 1.70914 | 2.03989 | 2.89828 | 4.10393 | 5.79182 | 8.14725 | 11.42394 | 15.96817 | 30.91268 | 59.13557 | 153.15185 | 708.8019 |
| 38 | 1.09953 | 1.20868 | 1.32835 | 1.45953 | 1.76080 | 2.12230 | 3.07478 | 4.43881 | 6.38548 | 9.15425 | 13.07927 | 18.62528 | 37.40434 | 74.17966 | 202.54332 | 1020.675 |
| 40 | 1.10503 | 1.22079 | 1.34835 | 1.48886 | 1.81402 | 2.20804 | 3.26204 | 4.80102 | 7.03999 | 10.28572 | 14.97446 | 21.72452 | 45.25926 | 93.05097 | 267.86355 | 1469.772 |
| 45 | 1.11892 | 1.25162 | 1.39968 | 1.56481 | 1.95421 | 2.43785 | 3.78160 | 5.84118 | 8.98501 | 13.76461 | 21.00245 | 31.92045 | 72.89048 | 163.9876 | 538.76927 | 3657.262 |
| 50 | 1.13297 | 1.28323 | 1.45296 | 1.64463 | 2.10524 | 2.69159 | 4.38391 | 7.10668 | 11.46740 | 18.42015 | 29.45703 | 46.90161 | 117.3909 | 289.0022 | 1083.65744 | 9100.438 |
| 100 | 1.28362 | 1.64667 | 2.11108 | 2.70481 | 4.43205 | 7.24465 | 19.21863 | 50.50495 | 131.5013 | 339.3021 | 867.7163 | 2199.761 | 13780.61 | 83522.27 | $117 \times 10^4$ | $828 \times 10^5$ |

## TABLE 2
### Present Value of $1

$$P = F_n(1 + r)^{-n}$$

$r$ = discount rate; $n$ = number of periods until payment; $P$ = $1

| Periods = n | 1/4% | 1/2% | 3/4% | 1% | 1 1/2% | 2% | 3% | 4% | 5% | 6% | 7% | 8% | 10% | 12% | 15% | 20% |
|---|---|---|---|---|---|---|---|---|---|---|---|---|---|---|---|---|
| 1 | .99751 | .99502 | .99256 | .99010 | .98522 | .98039 | .97087 | .96154 | .95238 | .94340 | .93458 | .92593 | .90909 | .89286 | .86957 | .83333 |
| 2 | .99502 | .99007 | .98517 | .98030 | .97066 | .96117 | .94260 | .92456 | .90703 | .89000 | .87344 | .85734 | .82645 | .79719 | .75614 | .69444 |
| 3 | .99254 | .98515 | .97783 | .97059 | .95632 | .94232 | .91514 | .88900 | .86384 | .83962 | .81630 | .79383 | .75131 | .71178 | .65752 | .57870 |
| 4 | .99006 | .98025 | .97055 | .96098 | .94218 | .92385 | .88849 | .85480 | .82270 | .79209 | .76290 | .73503 | .68301 | .63552 | .57175 | .48225 |
| 5 | .98759 | .97537 | .96333 | .95147 | .92826 | .90573 | .86261 | .82193 | .78353 | .74726 | .71299 | .68058 | .62092 | .56743 | .49718 | .40188 |
| 6 | .98513 | .97052 | .95616 | .94205 | .91454 | .88797 | .83748 | .79031 | .74622 | .70496 | .66634 | .63017 | .56447 | .50663 | .43233 | .33490 |
| 7 | .98267 | .96569 | .94904 | .93272 | .90103 | .87056 | .81309 | .75992 | .71068 | .66506 | .62275 | .58349 | .51316 | .45235 | .37594 | .27908 |
| 8 | .98022 | .96089 | .94198 | .92348 | .88771 | .85349 | .78941 | .73069 | .67684 | .62741 | .58201 | .54027 | .46651 | .40388 | .32690 | .23257 |
| 9 | .97778 | .95610 | .93496 | .91434 | .87459 | .83676 | .76642 | .70259 | .64461 | .59190 | .54393 | .50025 | .42410 | .36061 | .28426 | .19381 |
| 10 | .97534 | .95135 | .92800 | .90529 | .86167 | .82035 | .74409 | .67556 | .61391 | .55839 | .50835 | .46319 | .38554 | .32197 | .24718 | .16151 |
| 11 | .97291 | .94661 | .92109 | .89632 | .84893 | .80426 | .72242 | .64958 | .58468 | .52679 | .47509 | .42888 | .35049 | .28748 | .21494 | .13459 |
| 12 | .97048 | .94191 | .91424 | .88745 | .83639 | .78849 | .70138 | .62460 | .55684 | .49697 | .44401 | .39711 | .31863 | .25668 | .18691 | .11216 |
| 13 | .96806 | .93722 | .90743 | .87866 | .82403 | .77303 | .68095 | .60057 | .53032 | .46884 | .41496 | .36770 | .28966 | .22917 | .16253 | .09346 |
| 14 | .96565 | .93256 | .90068 | .86996 | .81185 | .75788 | .66112 | .57748 | .50507 | .44230 | .38782 | .34046 | .26333 | .20462 | .14133 | .07789 |
| 15 | .96324 | .92792 | .89397 | .86135 | .79985 | .74301 | .64186 | .55526 | .48102 | .41727 | .36245 | .31524 | .23939 | .18270 | .12289 | .06491 |
| 16 | .96084 | .92330 | .88732 | .85282 | .78803 | .72845 | .62317 | .53391 | .45811 | .39365 | .33873 | .29189 | .21763 | .16312 | .10686 | .05409 |
| 17 | .95844 | .91871 | .88071 | .84438 | .77639 | .71416 | .60502 | .51337 | .43630 | .37136 | .31657 | .27027 | .19784 | .14564 | .09293 | .04507 |
| 18 | .95605 | .91414 | .87416 | .83602 | .76491 | .70016 | .58739 | .49363 | .41552 | .35034 | .29586 | .25025 | .17986 | .13004 | .08081 | .03756 |
| 19 | .95367 | .90959 | .86765 | .82774 | .75361 | .68643 | .57029 | .47464 | .39573 | .33051 | .27651 | .23171 | .16351 | .11611 | .07027 | .03130 |
| 20 | .95129 | .90506 | .86119 | .81954 | .74247 | .67297 | .55368 | .45639 | .37689 | .31180 | .25842 | .21455 | .14864 | .10367 | .06110 | .02608 |
| 22 | .94655 | .89608 | .84842 | .80340 | .72069 | .64684 | .52189 | .42196 | .34185 | .27751 | .22571 | .18394 | .12285 | .08264 | .04620 | .01811 |
| 24 | .94184 | .88719 | .83583 | .78757 | .69954 | .62172 | .49193 | .39012 | .31007 | .24698 | .19715 | .15770 | .10153 | .06588 | .03493 | .01258 |
| 26 | .93714 | .87838 | .82343 | .77205 | .67902 | .59758 | .46369 | .36069 | .28124 | .21981 | .17220 | .13520 | .08391 | .05252 | .02642 | .00874 |
| 28 | .93248 | .86966 | .81122 | .75684 | .65910 | .57437 | .43708 | .33348 | .25509 | .19563 | .15040 | .11591 | .06934 | .04187 | .01997 | .00607 |
| 30 | .92783 | .86103 | .79919 | .74192 | .63976 | .55207 | .41199 | .30832 | .23138 | .17411 | .13137 | .09938 | .05731 | .03338 | .01510 | .00421 |
| 32 | .92321 | .85248 | .78733 | .72730 | .62099 | .53063 | .38834 | .28506 | .20987 | .15496 | .11474 | .08520 | .04736 | .02661 | .01142 | .00293 |
| 34 | .91861 | .84402 | .77565 | .71297 | .60277 | .51003 | .36604 | .26355 | .19035 | .13791 | .10022 | .07305 | .03914 | .02121 | .00864 | .00203 |
| 36 | .91403 | .83564 | .76415 | .69892 | .58509 | .49022 | .34503 | .24367 | .17266 | .12274 | .08754 | .06262 | .03235 | .01691 | .00653 | .00141 |
| 38 | .90948 | .82735 | .75281 | .68515 | .56792 | .47119 | .32523 | .22529 | .15661 | .10924 | .07646 | .05369 | .02673 | .01348 | .00494 | .00098 |
| 40 | .90495 | .81914 | .74165 | .67165 | .55126 | .45289 | .30656 | .20829 | .14205 | .09722 | .06678 | .04603 | .02209 | .01075 | .00373 | .00068 |
| 45 | .89372 | .79896 | .71445 | .63905 | .51171 | .41020 | .26444 | .17120 | .11130 | .07265 | .04761 | .03133 | .01372 | .00610 | .00186 | .00027 |
| 50 | .88263 | .77929 | .68825 | .60804 | .47500 | .37153 | .22811 | .14071 | .08720 | .05429 | .03395 | .02132 | .00852 | .00346 | .00092 | .00011 |
| 100 | .77904 | .60729 | .47369 | .36971 | .22563 | .13803 | .05203 | .01980 | .00760 | .00295 | .00115 | .00045 | .00007 | .00001 | .00000 | .00000 |

**TABLE 3**
**Future Value of Annuity of $1 in Arrears**

$$F = \frac{(1 + r)^n - 1}{r}$$

r = interest rate; n = number of payments

| No. of Payments = n | 1/4% | 1/2% | 3/4% | 1% | 1 1/2% | 2% | 3% | 4% | 5% | 6% | 7% | 8% | 10% | 12% | 15% | 20% |
|---|---|---|---|---|---|---|---|---|---|---|---|---|---|---|---|---|
| 1 | 1.00000 | 1.00000 | 1.00000 | 1.00000 | 1.00000 | 1.00000 | 1.00000 | 1.00000 | 1.00000 | 1.00000 | 1.00000 | 1.00000 | 1.00000 | 1.00000 | 1.00000 | 1.00000 |
| 2 | 2.00250 | 2.00500 | 2.00750 | 2.01000 | 2.01500 | 2.02000 | 2.03000 | 2.04000 | 2.05000 | 2.06000 | 2.07000 | 2.08000 | 2.10000 | 2.12000 | 2.15000 | 2.20000 |
| 3 | 3.00751 | 3.01503 | 3.02256 | 3.03010 | 3.04523 | 3.06040 | 3.09090 | 3.12160 | 3.15250 | 3.18360 | 3.21490 | 3.24640 | 3.31000 | 3.37440 | 3.47250 | 3.64000 |
| 4 | 4.01503 | 4.03010 | 4.04523 | 4.06040 | 4.09090 | 4.12161 | 4.18363 | 4.24646 | 4.31013 | 4.37462 | 4.43994 | 4.50611 | 4.64100 | 4.77933 | 4.99338 | 5.36800 |
| 5 | 5.02506 | 5.05025 | 5.07556 | 5.10101 | 5.15227 | 5.20404 | 5.30914 | 5.41632 | 5.52563 | 5.63709 | 5.75074 | 5.86660 | 6.10510 | 6.35285 | 6.74238 | 7.44160 |
| 6 | 6.03763 | 6.07550 | 6.11363 | 6.15202 | 6.22955 | 6.30812 | 6.46641 | 6.63298 | 6.80191 | 6.97532 | 7.15329 | 7.33593 | 7.71561 | 8.11519 | 8.75374 | 9.92992 |
| 7 | 7.05272 | 7.10588 | 7.15948 | 7.21354 | 7.32299 | 7.43428 | 7.66246 | 7.89829 | 8.14201 | 8.39384 | 8.65402 | 8.92280 | 9.48717 | 10.08901 | 11.06680 | 12.91590 |
| 8 | 8.07035 | 8.14141 | 8.21318 | 8.28567 | 8.43284 | 8.58297 | 8.89234 | 9.21423 | 9.54911 | 9.89747 | 10.25980 | 10.63663 | 11.43589 | 12.29969 | 13.72682 | 16.49908 |
| 9 | 9.09053 | 9.18212 | 9.27478 | 9.36853 | 9.55933 | 9.75463 | 10.15911 | 10.58280 | 11.02656 | 11.49132 | 11.97799 | 12.48756 | 13.57948 | 14.77566 | 16.78584 | 20.79890 |
| 10 | 10.11325 | 10.22803 | 10.34434 | 10.46221 | 10.70272 | 10.94972 | 11.46388 | 12.00611 | 12.57789 | 13.18079 | 13.81645 | 14.48656 | 15.93742 | 17.54874 | 20.30372 | 25.95868 |
| 11 | 11.13854 | 11.27917 | 11.42192 | 11.56683 | 11.86326 | 12.16872 | 12.80780 | 13.48635 | 14.20679 | 14.97164 | 15.78360 | 16.64549 | 18.53117 | 20.65458 | 24.34928 | 32.15042 |
| 12 | 12.16638 | 12.33556 | 12.50759 | 12.68250 | 13.04121 | 13.41209 | 14.19203 | 15.02581 | 15.91713 | 16.86994 | 17.88845 | 18.97713 | 21.38428 | 24.13313 | 29.00167 | 39.58050 |
| 13 | 13.19680 | 13.39724 | 13.60139 | 13.80933 | 14.23683 | 14.68033 | 15.61779 | 16.62684 | 17.71298 | 18.88214 | 20.14064 | 21.49530 | 24.52271 | 28.02911 | 34.35192 | 48.49660 |
| 14 | 14.22979 | 14.46423 | 14.70340 | 14.94742 | 15.45038 | 15.97394 | 17.08632 | 18.29191 | 19.59863 | 21.01507 | 22.55049 | 24.21492 | 27.97498 | 32.39260 | 40.50471 | 59.19592 |
| 15 | 15.26537 | 15.53655 | 15.81368 | 16.09690 | 16.68214 | 17.29342 | 18.59891 | 20.02359 | 21.57856 | 23.27597 | 25.12902 | 27.15211 | 31.77248 | 37.27971 | 47.58041 | 72.03511 |
| 16 | 16.30353 | 16.61423 | 16.93228 | 17.25786 | 17.93237 | 18.63929 | 20.15688 | 21.82453 | 23.65749 | 25.67253 | 27.88805 | 30.32428 | 35.94973 | 42.75328 | 55.71747 | 87.44213 |
| 17 | 17.34429 | 17.69730 | 18.05927 | 18.43044 | 19.20136 | 20.01207 | 21.76159 | 23.69751 | 25.84037 | 28.21288 | 30.84022 | 33.75023 | 40.54470 | 48.88367 | 65.07509 | 105.9306 |
| 18 | 18.38765 | 18.78579 | 19.19472 | 19.61475 | 20.48938 | 21.41231 | 23.41444 | 25.64541 | 28.13238 | 30.90565 | 33.99903 | 37.45024 | 45.59917 | 55.74971 | 75.83636 | 128.1167 |
| 19 | 19.43362 | 19.87972 | 20.33868 | 20.81090 | 21.79672 | 22.84056 | 25.11687 | 27.67123 | 30.53900 | 33.75999 | 37.37896 | 41.44626 | 51.15909 | 63.43968 | 88.21181 | 154.7400 |
| 20 | 20.48220 | 20.97912 | 21.49122 | 22.01900 | 23.12367 | 24.29737 | 26.87037 | 29.77808 | 33.06595 | 36.78559 | 40.99549 | 45.76196 | 57.27500 | 72.05244 | 102.44358 | 186.6880 |
| 22 | 22.58724 | 23.19443 | 23.82230 | 24.47159 | 25.83758 | 27.29898 | 30.53678 | 34.24797 | 38.50521 | 43.39229 | 49.00574 | 55.45676 | 71.40275 | 92.50258 | 137.63164 | 271.0307 |
| 24 | 24.70282 | 25.43196 | 26.18847 | 26.97346 | 28.63352 | 30.42186 | 34.42647 | 39.08260 | 44.50200 | 50.81558 | 58.17667 | 66.76476 | 88.49733 | 118.1552 | 184.16784 | 392.4842 |
| 26 | 26.82899 | 27.69191 | 28.59027 | 29.52563 | 31.51397 | 33.67091 | 38.55304 | 44.31174 | 51.11345 | 59.15638 | 68.67647 | 79.95442 | 109.1818 | 150.3339 | 245.71197 | 567.3773 |
| 28 | 28.96580 | 29.97452 | 31.02823 | 32.12910 | 34.48148 | 37.05121 | 42.93092 | 49.96758 | 58.40258 | 68.52811 | 80.69769 | 95.33883 | 134.2099 | 190.6989 | 327.10408 | 819.2233 |
| 30 | 31.11331 | 32.28002 | 33.50290 | 34.78489 | 37.53868 | 40.56808 | 47.57542 | 56.08494 | 66.43885 | 79.05819 | 94.46079 | 113.2832 | 164.4940 | 241.3327 | 434.74515 | 1181.881 |
| 32 | 33.27157 | 34.60862 | 36.01483 | 37.49407 | 40.68829 | 44.22703 | 52.50276 | 62.70147 | 75.29883 | 90.88978 | 110.2181 | 134.2135 | 201.1378 | 304.8477 | 577.10046 | 1704.109 |
| 34 | 35.44064 | 36.96058 | 38.56458 | 40.25770 | 43.93309 | 48.03380 | 57.73018 | 69.85791 | 85.06696 | 104.1838 | 128.2588 | 158.6267 | 245.4767 | 384.5210 | 765.36535 | 2456.118 |
| 36 | 37.62056 | 39.33610 | 41.15272 | 43.07688 | 47.27597 | 51.99437 | 63.27594 | 77.59831 | 95.83632 | 119.1209 | 148.9135 | 187.1022 | 299.1268 | 484.4631 | 1014.34568 | 3539.009 |
| 38 | 39.81140 | 41.73545 | 43.77982 | 45.95272 | 50.71989 | 56.11494 | 69.15945 | 85.97034 | 107.7095 | 135.9042 | 172.5610 | 220.3159 | 364.0434 | 609.8305 | 1343.62216 | 5098.373 |
| 40 | 42.01320 | 44.15885 | 46.44648 | 48.88637 | 54.26789 | 60.40198 | 75.40126 | 95.02552 | 120.7998 | 154.7620 | 199.6351 | 259.0565 | 442.5926 | 767.0914 | 1779.09031 | 7343.858 |
| 45 | 47.56606 | 50.32416 | 53.29011 | 56.48107 | 63.61420 | 71.89271 | 92.71986 | 121.0294 | 159.7002 | 212.7435 | 285.7493 | 386.5056 | 718.9048 | 1358.230 | 3585.12846 | 18281.31 |
| 50 | 53.18868 | 56.64516 | 60.39426 | 64.46318 | 73.68283 | 84.57940 | 112.7969 | 152.6671 | 209.3480 | 290.3359 | 406.5289 | 573.7702 | 1163.909 | 2400.018 | 7217.71628 | 45497.19 |
| 100 | 113.44996 | 129.33370 | 148.14451 | 170.4814 | 228.8030 | 312.2323 | 607.2877 | 1237.624 | 2610.025 | 5638.368 | 12381.66 | 27484.52 | 137796.1 | 696010.5 | 783 × 10⁴ | 414 × 10⁶ |

Note: To convert from this table to values of an annuity in advance, determine the annuity in arrears above for one more period and subtract 1.00000.

# TABLE 4
## Present Value of an Annuity of $1 in Arrears

$$P_A = \frac{1 - (1+r)^{-n}}{r}$$

r = discount rate; n = number of payments

| No. of Payments = n | 1/4% | 1/2% | 3/4% | 1% | 1½% | 2% | 3% | 4% | 5% | 6% | 7% | 8% | 10% | 12% | 15% | 20% |
|---|---|---|---|---|---|---|---|---|---|---|---|---|---|---|---|---|
| 1 | 0.99751 | 0.99502 | 0.99255 | .99010 | .98522 | .98039 | .97087 | .96154 | .95238 | .94340 | .93458 | .92593 | .90909 | .89286 | 0.86957 | .83333 |
| 2 | 1.99252 | 1.98510 | 1.97772 | 1.97040 | 1.95588 | 1.94156 | 1.91347 | 1.88609 | 1.85941 | 1.83339 | 1.80802 | 1.78326 | 1.73554 | 1.69005 | 1.62571 | 1.52778 |
| 3 | 2.98506 | 2.97025 | 2.95556 | 2.94099 | 2.91220 | 2.88388 | 2.82861 | 2.77509 | 2.72325 | 2.67301 | 2.62432 | 2.57710 | 2.48685 | 2.40183 | 2.28323 | 2.10648 |
| 4 | 3.97512 | 3.95050 | 3.92611 | 3.90197 | 3.85438 | 3.80773 | 3.71710 | 3.62990 | 3.54595 | 3.46511 | 3.38721 | 3.31213 | 3.16987 | 3.03735 | 2.85498 | 2.58873 |
| 5 | 4.96272 | 4.92587 | 4.88944 | 4.85343 | 4.78254 | 4.71346 | 4.57971 | 4.45182 | 4.32948 | 4.21236 | 4.10020 | 3.99271 | 3.79079 | 3.60478 | 3.35216 | 2.99061 |
| 6 | 5.94785 | 5.89638 | 5.84560 | 5.79548 | 5.69719 | 5.60143 | 5.41719 | 5.24214 | 5.07569 | 4.91732 | 4.76654 | 4.62288 | 4.35526 | 4.11141 | 3.78448 | 3.32551 |
| 7 | 6.93052 | 6.86207 | 6.79464 | 6.72819 | 6.59821 | 6.47199 | 6.23028 | 6.00205 | 5.78637 | 5.58238 | 5.38929 | 5.20637 | 4.86842 | 4.56376 | 4.16042 | 3.60459 |
| 8 | 7.91074 | 7.82296 | 7.73661 | 7.65168 | 7.48593 | 7.32548 | 7.01969 | 6.73274 | 6.46321 | 6.20979 | 5.97130 | 5.74664 | 5.33493 | 4.96764 | 4.48732 | 3.83716 |
| 9 | 8.88852 | 8.77906 | 8.67158 | 8.56602 | 8.36052 | 8.16224 | 7.78611 | 7.43533 | 7.10782 | 6.80169 | 6.51523 | 6.24689 | 5.75902 | 5.32825 | 4.77158 | 4.03097 |
| 10 | 9.86386 | 9.73041 | 9.59953 | 9.47130 | 9.22218 | 8.98259 | 8.53020 | 8.11090 | 7.72173 | 7.36009 | 7.02358 | 6.71008 | 6.14457 | 5.65022 | 5.01877 | 4.19247 |
| 11 | 10.83677 | 10.67703 | 10.52067 | 10.36763 | 10.07112 | 9.78685 | 9.25262 | 8.76048 | 8.30641 | 7.88687 | 7.49867 | 7.13896 | 6.49506 | 5.93770 | 5.23371 | 4.32706 |
| 12 | 11.80725 | 11.61893 | 11.43491 | 11.25508 | 10.90751 | 10.57534 | 9.95400 | 9.38507 | 8.86325 | 8.38384 | 7.94269 | 7.53608 | 6.81369 | 6.19437 | 5.42062 | 4.43922 |
| 13 | 12.77532 | 12.55615 | 12.34235 | 12.13374 | 11.73153 | 11.34837 | 10.63496 | 9.98565 | 9.39357 | 8.85268 | 8.35765 | 7.90378 | 7.10336 | 6.42355 | 5.58315 | 4.53268 |
| 14 | 13.74096 | 13.48871 | 13.24302 | 13.00370 | 12.54338 | 12.10625 | 11.29607 | 10.56312 | 9.89864 | 9.29498 | 8.74547 | 8.24424 | 7.36669 | 6.62817 | 5.72448 | 4.61057 |
| 15 | 14.70420 | 14.41662 | 14.13699 | 13.86505 | 13.34326 | 12.84926 | 11.93794 | 11.11839 | 10.37966 | 9.71225 | 9.10791 | 8.55948 | 7.60608 | 6.81086 | 5.84737 | 4.67547 |
| 16 | 15.66504 | 15.33993 | 15.02431 | 14.71787 | 14.13126 | 13.57771 | 12.56110 | 11.65230 | 10.83777 | 10.10590 | 9.44665 | 8.85137 | 7.82371 | 6.97399 | 5.95423 | 4.72956 |
| 17 | 16.62348 | 16.25863 | 15.90502 | 15.56225 | 14.90765 | 14.29187 | 13.16612 | 12.16567 | 11.27407 | 10.47726 | 9.76322 | 9.12164 | 8.02155 | 7.11963 | 6.04716 | 4.77463 |
| 18 | 17.57953 | 17.17277 | 16.77913 | 16.39827 | 15.67256 | 14.99203 | 13.75351 | 12.65930 | 11.68959 | 10.82760 | 10.05909 | 9.37189 | 8.20141 | 7.24967 | 6.12797 | 4.81219 |
| 19 | 18.53320 | 18.08236 | 17.64683 | 17.22601 | 16.42617 | 15.67846 | 14.32380 | 13.13394 | 12.08532 | 11.15812 | 10.33560 | 9.60360 | 8.36492 | 7.36578 | 6.19823 | 4.84350 |
| 20 | 19.48449 | 18.98742 | 18.50802 | 18.04555 | 17.16864 | 16.35143 | 14.87747 | 13.59033 | 12.46221 | 11.46992 | 10.59401 | 9.81815 | 8.51356 | 7.46944 | 6.25933 | 4.86958 |
| 22 | 21.37995 | 20.78406 | 20.21121 | 19.66038 | 18.62082 | 17.65805 | 15.93692 | 14.45112 | 13.16300 | 12.04158 | 11.06124 | 10.20074 | 8.77154 | 7.64465 | 6.35866 | 4.90943 |
| 24 | 23.26598 | 22.56287 | 21.88915 | 21.24339 | 20.03041 | 18.91393 | 16.93554 | 15.24696 | 13.79864 | 12.55036 | 11.46933 | 10.52876 | 8.98474 | 7.78432 | 6.43377 | 4.93710 |
| 26 | 25.14261 | 24.32402 | 23.54219 | 22.79520 | 21.39863 | 20.12104 | 17.87684 | 15.98277 | 14.37519 | 13.00317 | 11.82578 | 10.80998 | 9.16095 | 7.89566 | 6.49056 | 4.95632 |
| 28 | 27.00989 | 26.06769 | 25.17071 | 24.31644 | 22.72672 | 21.28127 | 18.76411 | 16.66306 | 14.89813 | 13.43616 | 12.13711 | 11.05108 | 9.30657 | 7.98442 | 6.53351 | 4.96967 |
| 30 | 28.86787 | 27.79405 | 26.77503 | 25.80771 | 24.01584 | 22.39646 | 19.60044 | 17.29203 | 15.37245 | 13.76483 | 12.40904 | 11.25778 | 9.42691 | 8.05518 | 6.56598 | 4.97894 |
| 32 | 30.71660 | 29.50328 | 28.35565 | 27.26959 | 25.26714 | 23.46833 | 20.38877 | 17.87355 | 15.80268 | 14.08404 | 12.64656 | 11.43500 | 9.52638 | 8.11159 | 6.59053 | 4.98537 |
| 34 | 32.55611 | 31.19555 | 29.91273 | 28.70267 | 26.48173 | 24.49859 | 21.13184 | 18.41120 | 16.19290 | 14.36814 | 12.85401 | 11.58693 | 9.60857 | 8.15656 | 6.60910 | 4.98984 |
| 36 | 34.38647 | 32.87102 | 31.44681 | 30.10751 | 27.66068 | 25.48884 | 21.83225 | 18.90828 | 16.54685 | 14.62099 | 13.03521 | 11.71719 | 9.67651 | 8.19241 | 6.62314 | 4.99295 |
| 38 | 36.20770 | 34.52985 | 32.95803 | 31.48466 | 28.80505 | 26.44064 | 22.49246 | 19.36786 | 16.86789 | 14.84602 | 13.19347 | 11.82887 | 9.73265 | 8.22099 | 6.63375 | 4.99510 |
| 40 | 38.01986 | 36.17223 | 34.44694 | 32.83469 | 29.91585 | 27.35548 | 23.11477 | 19.79277 | 17.15909 | 15.04630 | 13.33171 | 11.92461 | 9.77905 | 8.24378 | 6.64178 | 4.99660 |
| 45 | 42.51088 | 40.20720 | 38.07318 | 36.09451 | 32.55234 | 29.49016 | 24.51871 | 20.72004 | 17.77407 | 15.45583 | 13.60552 | 12.10840 | 9.86281 | 8.28252 | 6.65429 | 4.99863 |
| 50 | 46.94617 | 44.14279 | 41.56645 | 39.19612 | 34.99969 | 31.42361 | 25.72976 | 21.48218 | 18.25593 | 15.73186 | 13.80075 | 12.23348 | 9.91481 | 8.30450 | 6.66051 | 4.99945 |
| 100 | 88.38248 | 78.54264 | 70.17462 | 63.02888 | 51.62478 | 43.09835 | 31.59891 | 24.50500 | 19.84791 | 16.61755 | 14.26925 | 12.49432 | 9.99927 | 8.33323 | 6.66666 | 5.00000 |

Note: To convert from this table to values of an annuity in advance, determine the annuity in arrears above for one less period and add 1.00000.

## TABLE 5
### Bond Values in Percent of Par: 6% Semiannual Coupons

$$\text{Bond Value} = \frac{6}{r} + \left(100 - \frac{6}{r}\right)\left(1 + \frac{r}{2}\right)^{-2n}$$

$r$ = yield to maturity; $n$ = years to maturity

| Market Yield Percent per Year Compounded Semiannually | Years to Maturity | | | | | | | |
|---|---|---|---|---|---|---|---|---|
| | $1/2$ | 5 | 10 | 15 | $19^{1}/_{2}$ | 20 | 30 | 40 |
| 3.0 | 101.478 | 113.833 | 125.753 | 136.024 | 144.047 | 144.874 | 159.071 | 169.611 |
| 3.5 | 101.228 | 111.376 | 120.941 | 128.982 | 135.118 | 135.743 | 146.205 | 153.600 |
| 4.0 | 100.980 | 108.983 | 116.351 | 122.396 | 126.903 | 127.355 | 134.761 | 139.745 |
| 4.5 | 100.734 | 106.650 | 111.973 | 116.234 | 119.337 | 119.645 | 124.562 | 127.712 |
| 5.0 | 100.488 | 104.376 | 107.795 | 110.465 | 112.365 | 112.551 | 115.454 | 117.226 |
| 5.1 | 100.439 | 103.928 | 106.982 | 109.356 | 111.037 | 111.202 | 113.752 | 115.293 |
| 5.2 | 100.390 | 103.483 | 106.177 | 108.262 | 109.731 | 109.874 | 112.087 | 113.411 |
| 5.3 | 100.341 | 103.040 | 105.380 | 107.181 | 108.445 | 108.568 | 110.458 | 111.578 |
| 5.4 | 100.292 | 102.599 | 104.590 | 106.115 | 107.180 | 107.283 | 108.864 | 109.792 |
| 5.5 | 100.243 | 102.160 | 103.807 | 105.062 | 105.935 | 106.019 | 107.306 | 108.053 |
| 5.6 | 100.195 | 101.724 | 103.031 | 104.023 | 104.710 | 104.776 | 105.780 | 106.359 |
| 5.7 | 100.146 | 101.289 | 102.263 | 102.998 | 103.504 | 103.553 | 104.288 | 104.707 |
| 5.8 | 100.097 | 100.857 | 101.502 | 101.986 | 102.317 | 102.349 | 102.828 | 103.098 |
| 5.9 | 100.049 | 100.428 | 100.747 | 100.986 | 101.149 | 101.165 | 101.399 | 101.529 |
| 6.0 | 100 | 100 | 100 | 100 | 100 | 100 | 100 | 100 |
| 6.1 | 99.9515 | 99.5746 | 99.2595 | 99.0262 | 98.8685 | 98.8535 | 98.6309 | 98.5088 |
| 6.2 | 99.9030 | 99.1513 | 98.5259 | 98.0650 | 97.7549 | 97.7254 | 97.2907 | 97.0546 |
| 6.3 | 99.8546 | 98.7302 | 97.7990 | 97.1161 | 96.6587 | 96.6153 | 95.9787 | 95.6364 |
| 6.4 | 99.8062 | 98.3112 | 97.0787 | 96.1793 | 95.5796 | 95.5229 | 94.6942 | 94.2529 |
| 6.5 | 99.7579 | 97.8944 | 96.3651 | 95.2545 | 94.5174 | 94.4478 | 93.4365 | 92.9031 |
| 6.6 | 99.7096 | 97.4797 | 95.6580 | 94.3414 | 93.4717 | 93.3899 | 92.2050 | 91.5860 |
| 6.7 | 99.6613 | 97.0670 | 94.9574 | 93.4400 | 92.4423 | 92.3486 | 90.9989 | 90.3007 |
| 6.8 | 99.6132 | 96.6565 | 94.2632 | 92.5501 | 91.4288 | 91.3238 | 89.8178 | 89.0461 |
| 6.9 | 99.5650 | 96.2480 | 93.5753 | 91.6714 | 90.4310 | 90.3152 | 88.6608 | 87.8213 |
| 7.0 | 99.5169 | 95.8417 | 92.8938 | 90.8039 | 89.4487 | 89.3224 | 87.5276 | 86.6255 |
| 7.5 | 99.2771 | 93.8404 | 89.5779 | 86.6281 | 84.7588 | 84.5868 | 82.1966 | 81.0519 |
| 8.0 | 99.0385 | 91.8891 | 86.4097 | 82.7080 | 80.4155 | 80.2072 | 77.3765 | 76.0846 |
| 8.5 | 98.8010 | 89.9864 | 83.3820 | 79.0262 | 76.3899 | 76.1534 | 73.0090 | 71.6412 |
| 9.0 | 98.5646 | 88.1309 | 80.4881 | 75.5666 | 72.6555 | 72.3976 | 69.0430 | 67.6520 |

## TABLE 6
### Bond Values in Percent of Par:
### 8% Semiannual Coupons

$$\text{Bond Value} = 8/r + \left(100 - \frac{8}{r}\right)\left(1 + \frac{r}{2}\right)^{-2n}$$

$r$ = yield to maturity; $n$ = years to maturity

| Market Yield Percent per Year Compounded Semiannually | Years to Maturity | | | | | | | |
|---|---|---|---|---|---|---|---|---|
| | $1/2$ | 5 | 10 | 15 | $19\frac{1}{2}$ | 20 | 30 | 40 |
| 5.0 | 101.463 | 113.128 | 123.384 | 131.396 | 137.096 | 137.654 | 146.363 | 151.678 |
| 5.5 | 101.217 | 110.800 | 119.034 | 125.312 | 129.675 | 130.098 | 136.528 | 140.266 |
| 6.0 | 100.971 | 108.530 | 114.877 | 119.600 | 122.808 | 123.115 | 127.676 | 130.201 |
| 6.5 | 100.726 | 106.317 | 110.905 | 114.236 | 116.448 | 116.656 | 119.690 | 121.291 |
| 7.0 | 100.483 | 104.158 | 107.106 | 109.196 | 110.551 | 110.678 | 112.472 | 113.374 |
| 7.1 | 100.435 | 103.733 | 106.367 | 108.225 | 109.424 | 109.536 | 111.113 | 111.898 |
| 7.2 | 100.386 | 103.310 | 105.634 | 107.266 | 108.314 | 108.411 | 109.780 | 110.455 |
| 7.3 | 100.338 | 102.889 | 104.908 | 106.318 | 107.220 | 107.303 | 108.473 | 109.044 |
| 7.4 | 100.289 | 102.470 | 104.188 | 105.382 | 106.142 | 106.212 | 107.191 | 107.665 |
| 7.5 | 100.241 | 102.053 | 103.474 | 104.457 | 105.080 | 105.138 | 105.934 | 106.316 |
| 7.6 | 100.193 | 101.638 | 102.767 | 103.544 | 104.034 | 104.079 | 104.702 | 104.997 |
| 7.7 | 100.144 | 101.226 | 102.066 | 102.642 | 103.003 | 103.036 | 103.492 | 103.706 |
| 7.8 | 100.096 | 100.815 | 101.371 | 101.750 | 101.987 | 102.009 | 102.306 | 102.444 |
| 7.9 | 100.048 | 100.407 | 100.683 | 100.870 | 100.986 | 100.997 | 101.142. | 101.209 |
| 8.0 | 100 | 100 | 100 | 100 | 100 | 100 | 100 | 100 |
| 8.1 | 99.9519 | 99.5955 | 99.3235 | 99.1406 | 99.0279 | 99.0177 | 98.8794 | 98.8170 |
| 8.2 | 99.9039 | 99.1929 | 98.6529 | 98.2916 | 98.0699 | 98.0498 | 97.7798 | 97.6589 |
| 8.3 | 99.8560 | 98.7924 | 97.9882 | 97.4528 | 97.1257 | 97.0962 | 96.7006 | 96.5253 |
| 8.4 | 99.8081 | 98.3938 | 97.3294 | 96.6240 | 96.1951 | 96.1566 | 95.6414 | 95.4152 |
| 8.5 | 99.7602 | 97.9973 | 96.6764 | 95.8052 | 95.2780 | 95.2307 | 94.6018 | 94.3282 |
| 8.6 | 99.7124 | 97.6027 | 96.0291 | 94.9962 | 94.3709 | 94.3100 | 93.5812 | 93.2636 |
| 8.7 | 99.6646 | 97.2100 | 95.3875 | 94.1969 | 93.4829 | 93.4191 | 92.5792 | 92.2208 |
| 8.8 | 99.6169 | 96.8193 | 94.7514 | 93.4071 | 92.6045 | 92.5331 | 91.5955 | 91.1992 |
| 8.9 | 99.5692 | 96.4305 | 94.1210 | 92.6266 | 91.7387 | 91.6598 | 90.6295 | 90.1982 |
| 9.0 | 99.5215 | 96.0436 | 93.4960 | 91.8555 | 90.8851 | 90.7992 | 89.6810 | 89.2173 |
| 9.5 | 99.2840 | 94.1378 | 90.4520 | 88.1347 | 86.7949 | 86.6777 | 85.1858 | 84.5961 |
| 10.0 | 99.0476 | 92.2783 | 87.5378 | 84.6275 | 82.9830 | 82.8409 | 81.0707 | 80.4035 |
| 10.5 | 98.8123 | 90.4639 | 84.7472 | 81.3201 | 79.4271 | 79.2656 | 77.2956 | 76.5876 |
| 11.0 | 98.5782 | 88.6935 | 82.0744 | 78.1994 | 76.1070 | 75.9308 | 73.8252 | 73.1036 |

# Index

# EXCERPTS FROM THE TABLES APPEARING AFTER APPENDIX B

## TABLE 2
### Present Value of $1

$$P = F_n(1 + r)^{-n}$$

r = discount rate; n = number of periods until payment; P = $1

| Periods = n | ¼% | ½% | ¾% | 1% | 1½% | 2% | 3% | 4% | 5% | 6% | 7% | 8% | 10% | 12% | 15% | 20% |
|---|---|---|---|---|---|---|---|---|---|---|---|---|---|---|---|---|
| 1 | .99751 | .99502 | .99256 | .99010 | .98522 | .98039 | .97087 | .96154 | .95238 | .94340 | .93458 | .92593 | .90909 | .89286 | .86957 | .83333 |
| 2 | .99502 | .99007 | .98517 | .98030 | .97066 | .96117 | .94260 | .92456 | .90703 | .89000 | .87344 | .85734 | .82645 | .79719 | .75614 | .69444 |
| 3 | .99254 | .98515 | .97783 | .97059 | .95632 | .94232 | .91514 | .88900 | .86384 | .83962 | .81630 | .79383 | .75131 | .71178 | .65752 | .57870 |
| 4 | .99006 | .98025 | .97055 | .96098 | .94218 | .92385 | .88849 | .85480 | .82270 | .79209 | .76290 | .73503 | .68301 | .63552 | .57175 | .48225 |
| 5 | .98759 | .97537 | .96333 | .95147 | .92826 | .90573 | .86261 | .82193 | .78353 | .74726 | .71299 | .68058 | .62092 | .56743 | .49718 | .40188 |
| 6 | .98513 | .97052 | .95616 | .94205 | .91454 | .88797 | .83748 | .79031 | .74622 | .70496 | .66634 | .63017 | .56447 | .50663 | .43233 | .33490 |
| 7 | .98267 | .96569 | .94904 | .93272 | .90103 | .87056 | .81309 | .75992 | .71068 | .66506 | .62275 | .58349 | .51316 | .45235 | .37594 | .27908 |
| 8 | .98022 | .96089 | .94198 | .92348 | .88771 | .85349 | .78941 | .73069 | .67684 | .62741 | .58201 | .54027 | .46651 | .40388 | .32690 | .23257 |
| 9 | .97778 | .95610 | .93496 | .91434 | .87459 | .83676 | .76642 | .70259 | .64461 | .59190 | .54393 | .50025 | .42410 | .36061 | .28426 | .19381 |
| 10 | .97534 | .95135 | .92800 | .90529 | .86167 | .82035 | .74409 | .67556 | .61391 | .55839 | .50835 | .46319 | .38554 | .32197 | .24718 | .16151 |
| 11 | .97291 | .94661 | .92109 | .89632 | .84893 | .80426 | .72242 | .64958 | .58468 | .52679 | .47509 | .42888 | .35049 | .28748 | .21494 | .13459 |
| 12 | .97048 | .94191 | .91424 | .88745 | .83639 | .78849 | .70138 | .62460 | .55684 | .49697 | .44401 | .39711 | .31863 | .25668 | .18691 | .11216 |
| 13 | .96806 | .93722 | .90743 | .87866 | .82403 | .77303 | .68095 | .60057 | .53032 | .46884 | .41496 | .36770 | .28966 | .22917 | .16253 | .09346 |
| 14 | .96565 | .93256 | .90068 | .86996 | .81185 | .75788 | .66112 | .57748 | .50507 | .44230 | .38782 | .34046 | .26333 | .20462 | .14133 | .07789 |
| 15 | .96324 | .92792 | .89397 | .86135 | .79985 | .74301 | .64186 | .55526 | .48102 | .41727 | .36245 | .31524 | .23939 | .18270 | .12289 | .06491 |
| 16 | .96084 | .92330 | .88732 | .85282 | .78803 | .72845 | .62317 | .53391 | .45811 | .39365 | .33873 | .29189 | .21763 | .16312 | .10686 | .05409 |
| 17 | .95844 | .91871 | .88071 | .84438 | .77639 | .71416 | .60502 | .51337 | .43630 | .37136 | .31657 | .27027 | .19784 | .14564 | .09293 | .04507 |
| 18 | .95605 | .91414 | .87416 | .83602 | .76491 | .70016 | .58739 | .49363 | .41552 | .35034 | .29586 | .25025 | .17986 | .13004 | .08081 | .03756 |
| 19 | .95367 | .90959 | .86765 | .82774 | .75361 | .68643 | .57029 | .47464 | .39573 | .33051 | .27651 | .23171 | .16351 | .11611 | .07027 | .03130 |
| 20 | .95129 | .90506 | .86119 | .81954 | .74247 | .67297 | .55368 | .45639 | .37689 | .31180 | .25842 | .21455 | .14864 | .10367 | .06110 | .02608 |
| 22 | .94655 | .89608 | .84842 | .80340 | .72069 | .64684 | .52189 | .42196 | .34185 | .27751 | .22571 | .18394 | .12285 | .08264 | .04620 | .01811 |
| 24 | .94184 | .88719 | .83583 | .78757 | .69954 | .62172 | .49193 | .39012 | .31007 | .24698 | .19715 | .15770 | .10153 | .06588 | .03493 | .01258 |
| 26 | .93714 | .87838 | .82343 | .77205 | .67902 | .59758 | .46369 | .36069 | .28124 | .21981 | .17220 | .13520 | .08391 | .05252 | .02642 | .00874 |
| 28 | .93248 | .86966 | .81122 | .75684 | .65910 | .57437 | .43708 | .33348 | .25509 | .19563 | .15040 | .11591 | .06934 | .04187 | .01997 | .00607 |
| 30 | .92783 | .86103 | .79919 | .74192 | .63976 | .55207 | .41199 | .30832 | .23138 | .17411 | .13137 | .09938 | .05731 | .03338 | .01510 | .00421 |
| 32 | .92321 | .85248 | .78733 | .72730 | .62099 | .53063 | .38834 | .28506 | .20987 | .15496 | .11474 | .08520 | .04736 | .02661 | .01142 | .00293 |
| 34 | .91861 | .84402 | .77565 | .71297 | .60277 | .51003 | .36604 | .26355 | .19035 | .13791 | .10022 | .07305 | .03914 | .02121 | .00864 | .00203 |
| 36 | .91403 | .83564 | .76415 | .69892 | .58509 | .49022 | .34503 | .24367 | .17266 | .12274 | .08754 | .06262 | .03235 | .01691 | .00653 | .00141 |
| 38 | .90948 | .82735 | .75281 | .68515 | .56792 | .47119 | .32523 | .22529 | .15661 | .10924 | .07646 | .05369 | .02673 | .01348 | .00494 | .00098 |
| 40 | .90495 | .81914 | .74165 | .67165 | .55126 | .45289 | .30656 | .20829 | .14205 | .09722 | .06678 | .04603 | .02209 | .01075 | .00373 | .00068 |
| 45 | .89372 | .79896 | .71445 | .63905 | .51171 | .41020 | .26444 | .17120 | .11130 | .07265 | .04761 | .03133 | .01372 | .00610 | .00186 | .00027 |
| 50 | .88263 | .77929 | .68825 | .60804 | .47500 | .37153 | .22811 | .14071 | .08720 | .05429 | .03395 | .02132 | .00852 | .00346 | .00092 | .00011 |
| 100 | .77904 | .60729 | .47369 | .36971 | .22563 | .13803 | .05203 | .01980 | .00760 | .00295 | .00115 | .00045 | .00007 | .00001 | .00000 | .00000 |